Len Lewis
Plas y Coed
3 Smithy Meadow
Guilsfield, Welshpool SY21 9█  N⌐
01938 552023

INVOICE   25/8/01

TERENCE HILTON SECKER
CYPRESS LODGE, 1 GREEN LANE
CLOSE, GREEN LANE, FROME,
SOMERSET, BA11   4PA

BRITISH ATHLETICS £15

INCLUDES POSTAGE

MANY THANKS

Len Lewis

Published by: Umbra Software Limited,
Unit 1, Bredbury Business Park,
Bredbury Park Way, Bredbury, Stockport SK6 2SN
Tel: 0161 406 6320   Fax: 0161 406 6732

ISBN 1 898258 05 8

Front Cover: ROGER BLACK. 10 years after his last solo appearance on the cover Roger is back, complete with the British record and two Olympic Silver medals.

All photos by: All photographs provided by Mark Shearman,
22 Grovelands Road, Purley, Surrey CR8 4LA
Tel: 0181-660 0156   Fax: 0181-660 3437
His help is greatly appreciated.

Distributed by: Old Bakehouse Publications,
The Old Bakehouse, Church Street,
Abertillery, Gwent NP3 1EA
Tel: 01495 212600   Fax: 01495 216222

Printed in
Great Britain by: J.R. Davies (Printers) Limited,
The Old Bakehouse, Church Street, Abertillery, Gwent NP3 1EA
Tel: 01495 212600   Fax: 01495 216222

CONTENTS

NATIONAL UNION OF TRACK STATISTICIANS AND COMPILERS

Honorary President: Norris D McWhirter CBE

Vice Presidents: Peter E May   Leonard F Gebbett   Richard Hymans   Martin H James
Patrick E Brian Colin Young   Andrew Huxtable   Tim G Lynch-Staunton

Honorary Members: Roberto L Quercetani, John Bromhead, Jimmy Green, Ted O'Neill

Executive Committee: Les Crouch (Chairman)   Dr Shirley E Hitchcock (Hon Sec)
John M Powell (Treasurer)

Stanley Greenberg	Peter J Matthews	Melvyn F Watman	Lionel Peters
Elizabeth Sissons	Bob Sparks	Alfred P Wilkins	Stuart Mazdon
Sally Gandee	Dr. Tim Grose	Joe Barrass	

Members:

Glen Bishop	Cliff Gould	Bill Myers
Arnold Black	William Green	Anthony O'Neill
John Brant	Roger W H Gynn	D K R (Bob) Phillips
Ian Buchanan	Ian Hodge	Thomas Pollak
David Burton	Melvyn Jones	Martin Rix
Mark Butler	Alan Keys	Michael Sheridan
Mark Cawte	Alan Lindop	Richard A Simmons
Geoffrey Clarke (Hon.Aud.)	Peter Lovesey	Ian R Smith
Andrew Clatworthy	John Lunn	Sandy Sutherland
Justin Clouder	David Lynch	Ian Tempest
Dave Cocksedge	Peter V Martin	Dave Terry
Eric Cowe	Anthony G Miller	Dr Chris Thorne
Alan A Currie	Steve Mitchell	John L J Walsh
Brenda Currie	Keith Morbey	Malcolm Warburton
John T Glover	Wilf Morgan	Rob Whittingham

Compilation

General Editor - Rob Whittingham

Assistant Editors - Ian Hodge, Peter Matthews, Liz Sissons

Records - Bob Sparks All Time Lists and Index - Martin Rix, Tony Miller
Results - Rob Whittingham, Ian Hodge, Brian Webster

Men's Lists - Ian Hodge (HJ,PV and overall), Joe Barrass (sprints),
Tim Grose (800m to 10,000m), Steve Mitchell (5000m, 10,000m), John Walsh (Marathon),
Shirley Hitchcock (hurdles), Bill Myers (LJ,TJ),Tony O'Neill (throws).

Under 20 & Under 17 Men - Ian Hodge with above compilers and Melvyn Jones

Under 15 Men - Ian Hodge and Melvyn Jones   Under 13 Men - Roy Waters

Women's Lists - Liz Sissons, Tony Miller (Under 17),
John Brant (Under 15), Bill Green (Under 13)

Walks - John Powell   Relays - Keith Morbey   Multi-Events - Alan Lindop

Also acknowledgements for specific help to Arnold Black (Scotland) , John Glover and
Alan Keys (Northern Ireland) and various other NUTS members.

ABBREVIATIONS & NOTES

A - mark set at altitude over 1000m
a - automatic timing only known
      to one tenth of a second
D - performance made in a Decathlon
dh - downhill
e - estimated time
et - extra trial
ex - exhibition
h - heat
H - performance made in a Heptathlon
hc - handicap race
i - indoor
jo - jump off
m - position in race when intermediate
      time taken
mx- performance in mixed race
O - performance made in an Octathlon
o - over age
P - performance made in a Pentathlon

Q - qualifying round
q - quarter final
r - race number
s - semi final
t - track
u - unofficial time
un - unconfirmed performance
w - wind assisted (> 2.0 m/sec)
W - wind assisted (over 4m/sec in
                      decathlon/heptathlon)
x - relay team may include outside
      age-group members
+ - intermediate time
* - legal performance where best is
      wind assisted
" - photo electric cell time
- Unratified (may not be ratifiable)
& - as yet unratified
§ - now competes for another nation
¶ - drugs ban

AGE GROUP DESIGNATIONS

Men's events:

U13 - Under 13	(born 1.9.83 or later)
U15 - Under 15	(born 1.9.81 to 31.8.83)
U17 - Under 17	(born 1.9.79 to 31.8.81)
U20 - Under 20	(born 1.1.77 to 31.8.79)
V - Veteran	(age 40 or over)

Women's events:

U13 - Under 13	(born 1.9.83 or later)
U15 - Under 15	(born 1.9.81 to 31.8.83)
U17 - Under 17	(born 1.9.79 to 31.8.81)
U20 - Under 20	(born 1.1.77 to 31.8.79)
V - Veteran	(age 35 or over)

Care must be taken with very young age groups for athletes with an unknown date of birth from Northern Ireland since their age groups differ slightly.

Italics indicates the athlete competes for a British club but is not eligible to represent Britain.

MULTI - EVENTS

Pentathlon, Heptathlon and Decathlon lists show the complete breakdown of individual performances in the following order:

Pentathlon (women) - 100mH, SP, HJ, LJ, 800m; Junior: LJ, SP, 75mH, HJ, 800m
Heptathlon (women) - 100mH, HJ, SP, 200m (1st day); LJ, JT, 800m (2nd day) (80mH - Inters)
Decathlon (men)   - 100m, LJ, SP, HJ, 400m (1st day); 110mH, DT, PV, JT, 1500m (2nd day)

Totals which include performances made with following winds in excess of 4 m/s are denoted by W. The date shown is the second day of competition.

RANKING LISTS:

These show the best performances in each event recorded during the 1996 season.
For each performance the following details are shown:

Performance; wind reading (where appropriate); name (with, where appropriate, age-group category); date of birth (DDMMYY); position in competition; venue; date.

The following numbers are used, although strength of performance or lack of information may vary the guidelines -

50 perfomances   100 athletes for each standard event

Age Groups - 40 Under 20, 30 Under 17, 20 Under 15, 10 Under 13

In the junior men, athletes are shown in older age groups if their performances merit this, e.g. an U15 can appear in the U17 list etc. For junior women, athletes are shown in their age group as per womens rules. Although juniors of any age will be shown in the main list on merit.

INDEX

Club details and previous personal bests, where better than those recorded in 1996, are shown in the index for all athletes in the main lists.

VENUES

Major venues for athletics - the name by which the stadium is denoted is shown in capitals:

LONDON (xx)

B	Barn Elms, Barnes	Hu	Hurlingham
BP	Battersea Park	Nh	Terence McMillan, Newham, Plaistow
Col	Colindale (Metropolitan Police track)	PH	Parliament Hill Fields, Camden
CP	Crystal Palace, Nat. Sports Cen. Norwood	SP	Southwark Park
Elt	Sutcliffe Park, Eltham	TB	Tooting Bec
EL	East London, Mile End	WC	White City Stadium
Ha	New River Sports Centre, Haringey	WF	Waltham Forest, Walthamstow
He	Barnet Copthall Stadium, Hendon	WL	West London Stadium

ABERDEEN, Chris Anderson Stadium, Balgowrie
ALDERSHOT Military Stadium (Army)
ANDOVER, Charlton Sports Centre
ANTRIM Forum
BARKING, Mayesbrook Park
BARRY, Jenner Park
BASILDON, Gloucester Park
BASINGSTOKE, Down Grange
BEBINGTON, The Oval, Wirral
BEDFORD, Newnham Track, Barkers Lane
BELFAST, Mary Peters Track
BIRMINGHAM, Alexander Stadium, Perry Park
      (Un) University Track, Edgbaston
BLACKBURN, Witton Park
BLACKPOOL, Stanley Park
BOLTON
BOURNEMOUTH, Kings Park
BRACKNELL, John Nike Stadium, Bracknell SC
BRAUNTON, North Devon Athletic Track
BRIERLEY HILL, The Dell, Dudley
BRIGHTON Sports Arena, Withdean
BRISTOL, Whitchurch Stadium
BROMLEY, Norman Park
CAMBRIDGE, Wilberton Road
CANNOCK, Festival Stadium, Pye Green Road
CARLISLE, Sheepmount Stadium
CHELTENHAM, Prince of Wales Stadium
CLECKHEATON, Pr. Mary Pl. Fields, Spenbro
COATBRIDGE
COLWYN BAY, Eirias Park Arena
CORBY, Rockingham Triangle
COSFORD (RAF), Indoor and outdoor arenas
COVENTRY, Warwick Univ., Kirby Corner Rd
CRAWLEY Leisure Centre, Haslett Avenue
CREWE, Cumberland Road Sports Ground
CROYDON Arena
CUDWORTH, Dorothy Hyman Sports Centre
CWMBRAN Sports Centre
DARTFORD, Central Park
DERBY, Moorways Stadium
EDINBURGH, Meadowbank Sports Centre
ENFIELD, Q. Eliz. II Stadium, Carterhatch Lane
GATESHEAD International Stadium
GLASGOW, Crown Point
      Indoors: Kelvin Hall
GRANGEMOUTH Stadium, Falkirk
GRIMSBY, K George V Stadium, Weelsby Rd
HARLOW Sports Centre
HARROW, Bannister Sports Centre, Hatch End
HIGH WYCOMBE, Handy Cross Track
HOO, Deangate Stadium, Rochester
HORNCHURCH Stadium, Havering, Upminster
HORSHAM, Broadbridge Heath Sports Centre
HULL, Costello Stadium
ILFORD, Cricklefields Athletic Ground
IPSWICH, Northgate Sports Centre
ISLEWORTH, Borough Road College
JARROW, Monckton Stadium

JERSEY, Greve D'Azette, Jersey, CI
KINGSTON, K Meadow, Kingston-u-Thames
KIRKBY Sports Centre, Liverpool
LEAMINGTON, Edmonscote Track
LEEDS, Carnegie College
LEICESTER, Saffron Lane Sports Centre
LINCOLN, Yarborough Sports Centre
LIVERPOOL, Wavertree Track
LOUGHBOROUGH, Ashby Rd Stadium (Univ)
LUTON, Stockwood Park
MANCHESTER, Wythenshawe Park
MANSFIELD, Berry Hill Athletcs Track
MELKSHAM, Christie Miller Sports Centre
MIDDLESBROUGH, Clairville Stadium
MOTSPUR PARK
NORWICH, Norfolk Athletics Track, Earlham
NOTTINGHAM, Harvey Hadden Stadium
OXFORD, Iffley Road (University)
PERIVALE Park Tr, Ruislip Rd,Greenford, Mx
PETERBOROUGH, Embankment Track
PITREAVIE Playing Fields, Dunfermline
PLYMOUTH, Brickfields Stad,Devonport(R.N)
PORTSMOUTH, Mountbatten Cen, Alex. Park
      (RN) Stadium, Burnaby Road
READING, Palmer Park
REDDITCH, Abbey Stadium
ROTHERHAM, Herringthorpe Stadium
ST. IVES, St. Ivo Outdoor Centre
SHEFFIELD, Don Valley Stadium
      (W) Woodburn Road, Attercliffe
SOLIHULL, Tudor Grange Park
SOUTHAMPTON, Shirley Sports Centre
SOUTHEND, Southchurch Park Stadium
STOKE, Northwood C,Hanley, Stoke-on-Trent
STRETFORD, Longford Park
SUNDERLAND, Silksworth
SUTTON COLDFIELD,Wyndley Leisure Cent.
SWANSEA, Morfa Stadium, Landore
SWINDON, Thamesdown Tr., County Ground
THURROCK, Blackshots Stadium, Grays
WARLEY, Hadley Playing Fields, Smethwick
WARRINGTON, Victoria Park, Knutsford Rd
WATFORD, Woodside Stadium, Garston
WELWYN, Gosling Stad, Welwyn Garden City
WIGAN, Robin Park
WINDSOR, Vansittart Road Track
WISHAW Stadium
WOKING, Blackmore Crescent, Sheerwater
WOLVERHAMPTON Stadium, Aldersley Road
WOODFORD, Ashton P Fields,Woodford Br.
WORTHING, West Park, Shaftesbury Avenue
WREXHAM, Queensway Sports Complex
YATE, Broadlane Track, Gloucester
YEOVIL Recreation Centre, Chilton Grove

Note also, in Ireland
DUBLIN (B) Belfield
      (M) Morton Stad. (Santry)

INTRODUCTION - by Rob Whittingham

An Olympic year but no gold medals, however there are many areas of great promise in the performances detailed in this year's annual.

First I must thank the many people who make the book possible. Peter Matthews and Ian Hodge have, as usual, devoted large amounts of their time to ensure the accuracy of the annual. Also Tony Miller has helped a great deal with many areas. I have again received assistance from Geoff Blamire, Mike Kubiena and Julie Fletcher at Umbra Software and Marty has done a large amount of proof reading.

I have always tried each year to improve the annual and this year sees the culmination of a project I started some time ago. The all-time lists are now fifty deep in all the standard events and the junior all-time listings have been improved. This has only been possible by the help given by Martin Rix. I have assisted Martin in the production of a new all-time book which will become available soon. I hope most of the readers of this Annual will obtain a copy as it looks like becoming the definitive book in this area. Also for the first time Men's Under 13 lists have been added. I have never seen any previous lists of this nature and there is always the possibility or errors. Any reader with corrections is most welcome to write to me.

I have now further refined the treatment of resident foreign athletes with their performances being shown at the foot of the main lists. Again I have been tough on who is considered for these lists and apologize if any genuine residents have been omitted.

Much has been said in recent times about the poor performances of British athletes, but I tend to take a more pragmatic view. Whilst it is true that certain areas of athletics which used to be very strong for Britain are a little weak , equally there are areas where the level of performances have never been greater. The extended all-time lists give much scope to the reader for analysis.

I have included for the third year the top performers in the TSB Junior Rankings. The lists continue to raise a great deal of interest for the young athletes and TSB are to congratulated for their initiative.

For readers on the net, new junior rankings are posted daily from May 1st at
http://www.tsb.co.uk

My thanks to the B.A.F. and TSB for their financial assistance.

Any corrections are always welcome.

Rob Whittingham
April 1997   7 Birch Green   Glossop   SK13 8PR

BAF & OTHER ADDRESSES

British Athletic Federation
225A Bristol Road
Edgbaston
Birmingham
B5 7UB
Tel: 0121 440 5000

AAA of England
225A Bristol Road
Edgbaston
Birmingham
B5 7UB
Tel: 0121 440 5000

SCOTLAND
Scotland A.F.
Caledonia House
South Gyle
Edinburgh
Tel: 0131 317 7320

WALES
A.A. of Wales
Morfa Stadium Landore
Swansea
West Glamorgan SA1 7DF
Tel: 01792 456237

NORTHERN IRELAND
Northern Ireland A.A.F.
Honorary Secretary: J.Allen
House of Sport
Upper Malone Road
Belfast BT9 5LA
Tel: 01232 381222

Midland Counties A.A.
Edgebaston House
3 Duchess Place
Hagley Road
Birmingham
B16 8NM
Tel: 0121 452 1500

North of Engnd A.A.
Studio 106, EMCO House
5/7 New York Road
Leeds LS2 7PJ
Tel: 01532 461835

South of England A.A.
Suite 36 City of London Fruit Exchange
Brushfield St
London E1 6EU
Tel: 0171 247 2963

Commonwealth Games Councils:
England
General Secretary: Miss A.Hogbin
1 Wandsworth Plain
London SW18 1EH
Tel: 0181 871 2677

Northern Ireland
Honorary Secretary: R.J.McColgan MBE
22 Mountcoole Park, Cave Hill
Belfast BT14 8JR
Tel: 01232 716558

Scotland
Honorary Secretary: G.A.Hunter OBE
139 Old Dalkeith Road
Little France
Edinburgh EH16 4SZ
Tel: 0131 664 1070

Wales
Honorary Secretary: M.John MBE
Pennant
Blaenau, Ammanford
Dyfed SA18 3BZ
Tel: 0269 850390

British Athletics League
Honorary Secretary: M.Ison
7 Green Hill Avenue
Luton
Beds LU2 7DN
Tel: 01582 26283

National Young Athletes' League
Honorary Secretary: R.Sales
78 Orchard Road
South Ockendon
Essex RM15 6HH
Tel: 01708 852178

Supporters Club - British Athletics Club
Honorary Secretary: Mrs M.Pieri
11 Railway Road
Newbury, Berks RG14 7PE
Tel: 01635 33400

Sports Council
The Sports Council
16 Upper Woburn Place
London WC1H OQP
Tel: 0171 388 1277

Athletics Weekly
Editor: David Clarke
Bretton Court, Bretton
Peterborough PE3 8DZ
Tel: 01733 261144

National Union of Track Statisticians
Secretary: Dr. S. Hitchcock
2 Chudleigh Close
Bedford
MK40 3AW

MAJOR OUTDOOR FIXTURES IN 1997

APRIL

13	Flora London Marathon	London

MAY

10-11	County Championships	Various
10-11	District Championships (Scotland)	Various
25-26	Inter-Counties	Bedford
31	Welsh Games	Cardiff

JUNE

7	GB v GER (U20)	Manhein, GER
14	GB v FRA v GER (U23)	Hexham
21	Welsh Championships	Cwmbran
21-22	European Cup	Munich, GER
28	Scottish Championships	
28-29	European Cup Combined Events	Tallin, EST
29	British Grand Prix	Sheffield

JULY

5-6	AAA U20 Championships	Bedford
11-12	TSB English Schools Championships	Sheffield
11-13	BAF/BUPA World Championship Trials	Birmingham
11-13	European U23 Championships	Turku, FIN
24-27	European Junior Chamionships	Ljubljana, SLO

AUGUST

1-10	World Championships	Athens, GRE
2	NI Championships	Antrim
16-17	AAA U17/U15 Championships	Birmingham
27-31	World Student Games	Sicily, ITA
24-25	AAA Championships	Birmingham

SEPTEMBER

7	British Grand Prix II	Gateshead

BEST AUTHENTIC PERFORMANCES (MEN)

(as at 31 Dec 1996)

W = World, E = European, C = Commonwealth, A = UK All-Comers, N = UK, J = Junior

Event	Cat	Time		Athlete	Nat	Date		Venue
100 m	W,C	9.84		Donovan Bailey	CAN	27 Jul	96	Atlanta
	E,N	9.87		Linford Christie		15 Aug	93	Stuttgart
	A	10.03		Jon Drummond	USA	15 Jul	94	London (CP)
	WJ	10.05	#	Davidson Ezinwa	NGR	3 Jan	90	Bauchi
		10.08	A	Obadele Thompson	BAR	16 Apr	94	El Paso
	EJ	10.14		Sven Matthes	GER	13 Sep	88	Berlin
	NJ	10.21		Jamie Henderson		6 Aug	87	Birmingham
200 m	W,E	19.32		Michael Johnson	USA	1 Aug	96	Atlanta
	C	19.68		Frank Fredericks	NAM	1 Aug	96	Atlanta
	A	19.85		Michael Johnson	USA	6 Jul	90	Edinburgh
	N	19.87	A&	John Regis		31 Jul	94	Sestriere
		19.94		John Regis		20 Aug	93	Stuttgart
	WJ	20.07	#	Lorenzo Daniel	USA	18 May	85	Starkville
		20.13		Roy Martin	USA	16 Jun	85	Indianapolis
	EJ	20.37		Jürgen Evers	GER	28 Aug	83	Schwechat
	NJ	20.54		Ade Mafe		25 Aug	85	Cottbus
300 m	W	31.48		Danny Everett	USA	3 Sep	90	Jerez de la Frontera
		31.48		Roberto Hernández	CUB	3 Sep	90	Jerez de la Frontera
	E,C,A,N	31.67		John Regis	Eng	17 Jul	92	Gateshead
	WJ	32.08		Steve Lewis	USA	28 Sep	88	Seoul
	EJ,NJ	32.53		Mark Richardson		14 Jul	91	London (Ha)
400 m	W	43.29		Butch Reynolds	USA	17 Aug	88	Zürich
	E	44.33		Thomas Schönlebe	GER	3 Sep	87	Rome
	C	44.17		Innocent Egbunike	NGR	19 Aug	87	Zürich
	A	43.98		Michael Johnson	USA	10 Jul	92	London (CP)
	N	44.37		Roger Black		3 Jul	96	Lausanne
	WJ	43.87		Steve Lewis	USA	28 Sep	88	Seoul
	EJ	45.01		Thomas Schönlebe	GER	15 Jul	84	Berlin
	NJ	45.36		Roger Black		24 Aug	85	Cottbus
600 m	W	1:12.81		Johnny Gray	USA	24 May	86	Santa Monica
	E,C,A,N	1:14.95		Steve Heard	Eng	14 Jul	91	London (Ha)
	NJ	1:16.79		Andrew Lill		24 Jul	90	Mansfield
800 m	W,E,C,N	1:41.73	"	Sebastian Coe	Eng	10 Jun	81	Florence
	A	1:43.22		Steve Cram		31 Jul	86	Edinburgh
	WJ	1:44.9	y#	Jim Ryun	USA	10 Jun	66	Terre Haute
		1:44.3		Joaquim Cruz	BRA	27 Jun	81	Rio de Janeiro
	EJ	1:45.45		Andreas Busse	GER	7 Jun	78	Ostrava
	NJ	1:45.64		David Sharpe		5 Sep	86	Brussels
1000 m	W,E,C,N	2:12.18		Sebastian Coe	Eng	11 Jul	81	Oslo
	A	2:12.88		Steve Cram		9 Aug	85	Gateshead
	WJ	2:16.84		Ali Hakimi	TUN	28 Jul	95	Lindau
	EJ	2:18.31		Andreas Busse	GER	7 Aug	77	Dresden
	NJ	2:18.98		David Sharpe		19 Aug	86	Birmingham
1500 m	W	3:27.37		Noureddine Morceli	ALG	12 Jul	95	Nice
	E,C,N	3:29.67		Steve Cram	Eng	16 Jul	85	Nice
	A	3:30.72		Noureddine Morceli	ALG	15 Jul	94	London (CP)
	WJ	3:34.63	#	Daniel Komen	KEN	5 Jun	95	Moscow
		3:34.92		Kipkoech Cheruiyot	KEN	26 Jul	83	Munich
	EJ	3:35.51		Reyes Estévez	SPA	16 Aug	95	Zürich
	NJ	3:36.6		Graham Williamson		17 Jul	79	Oslo

1 Mile	W	3:44.39		Noureddine Morceli	ALG	5 Sep 93	Rieti
	E,C,N	3:46.32		Steve Cram	Eng	27 Jul 85	Oslo
	A	3:49.49		Steve Cram		12 Sep 86	London (CP)
	WJ	3:51.3		Jim Ryun	USA	17 Jul 66	Berkeley
	EJ,NJ	3:53.15		Graham Williamson		17 Jul 79	Oslo
2000 m	W	4:47.88		Noureddine Morceli	ALG	3 Jul 95	Paris
	E,C,N	4:51.39		Steve Cram	Eng	4 Aug 85	Budapest
	A	4:55.20		Steve Cram		28 Aug 88	London (CP)
	WJ	5:00.6	+e	Daniel Komen	KEN	25 Jul 95	Monaco
	EJ	5:04.4		Harald Hudak	GER	30 Jun 76	Oslo
	NJ	5:06.56		Jon Richards		7 Jul 82	Oslo
3000 m	W,C	7:20.67		Daniel Komen	KEN	1 Sep 96	Rieti
	E,A,N	7:32.79		Dave Moorcroft		17 Jul 82	London (CP)
	WJ	7:35.52		Philip Mosima	KEN	12 Jul 96	London (CP)
	EJ	7:43.20		Ari Paunonen	FIN	22 Jun 77	Cologne
	NJ	7:48.28		Jon Richards		9 Jul 83	Oslo
2 Miles	W,C	8:03.54		Daniel Komen	KEN	14 Jul 96	Lappeenranta
	E	8:13.2	i	Emiel Puttemans	BEL	18 Feb 73	Berlin
	E,A,N	8:13.51		Steve Ovett		15 Sep 78	London (CP)
	WJ	8:25.2		Jim Ryun	USA	13 May 66	Los Angeles
	EJ,NJ	8:28.31		Steve Binns		31 Aug 79	London (CP)
5000 m	W	12:44.39		Haile Gebrselassie	ETH	16 Aug 95	Zürich
	C	12:45.09		Daniel Komen	KEN	14 Aug 96	Zürich
	E,N	13:00.41		Dave Moorcroft		7 Jul 82	Oslo
	A	13:06.72		William Sigei	KEN	15 Jul 94	London (CP)
	WJ	12:53.72		Philip Mosima	KEN	5 Jun 96	Rome
	EJ,NJ	13:27.04		Steve Binns		14 Sep 79	London (CP)
10 km	W	26:38.08		Salah Hissou	MAR	23 Aug 96	Brussels
	C	26:52.23		William Sigei	KEN	22 Jul 94	Stockholm
	E	27:13.81		Fernando Mamede	POR	2 Jul 84	Stockholm
	A	27:20.38		Aloÿs Nizigama	BUR	7 Jul 95	London (CP)
	N	27:23.06		Eamonn Martin		2 Jul 88	Oslo
	WJ	27:11.18		Richard Chelimo	KEN	25 Jun 91	Hengelo
	EJ	28:22.48		Christian Leuprecht	ITA	4 Sep 90	Koblenz
	NJ	29:21.9		Jon Brown		21 Apr 90	Walnut
20 km	W	56:55.6		Arturo Barrios	MEX	30 Mar 91	La Flèche
	E	57:18.4		Dionisio Castro	POR	31 Mar 90	La Flèche
	C,N	57:28.7		Carl Thackery	Eng	31 Mar 90	La Flèche
	A	58:39.0		Ron Hill		9 Nov 68	Leicester
1 Hour	W	21,101 m		Arturo Barrios	MEX	30 Mar 91	La Flèche
	E	20,944 m		Jos Hermens	HOL	1 May 76	Papendal
	C,N	20,855 m		Carl Thackery	Eng	31 Mar 90	La Flèche
	A	20,472 m		Ron Hill		9 Nov 68	Leicester
	NJ	18,221 m		Eddie Twohig		16 Jun 81	Leamington
25 km	W	1:13:55.8		Toshihiko Seko	JAP	22 Mar 81	Christchurch, NZ
	E	1:14:16.8		Pekka Päivärintä	FIN	15 May 75	Oulu
	C,A,N	1:15:22.6		Ron Hill	Eng	21 Jul 65	Bolton
30 km	W	1:29:18.78		Toshihiko Seko	JAP	22 Mar 81	Christchurch, NZ
	E,C,A,N	1:31:30.4		Jim Alder	Sco	5 Sep 70	London (CP)
Half Marathon	W,C	59:47		Moses Tanui	KEN	3 Apr 93	Milan
	A	60:02		Benson Masya	KEN	18 Sep 94	Tyneside
	E,N	60:09		Paul Evans		15 Jan 95	Marrakesh
	WJ	62:11		Meck Mothuli	RSA	3 Oct 93	Brussels
	NJ	66:48		Alan Wilson		29 May 83	Kirkintilloch

Event		Time/Mark		Athlete	Nat		Date		Venue
Maratho		2:06:5		Belayneh Dinsam	E T	1	Ap	8	Rotterda
		2:07:1		Carlos Lope	P O	2	Ap	8	Rotterda
		2:07:0		Sammy Lele	K E	2	Se	9	Berli
		2:07:1		Steve Jone		2	Oc	8	Chicag
		2:08:1		Steve Jone		2	Ap	8	Londo
	W	2:12:4		Negash Dub	E T	1	Oc	8	Beijin
		2:12:4		Tesfayi Dad	E T		Oc	8	Berli
	N	2:23:2		Eddie Twohi		2	Ma	8	Wolverhampto
2km S	W,	5:14.4		Julius Kariuk	K E	2	Au	9	Roveret
		5:18.3		Alessandro Lambruschin	I T	1	Se	8	Veron
		5:19.6		Samson Obwoch	K E	1	Ju	8	Birmingha
		5:19.8		Mark Rowlan		2	Au	8	London (CP
	WJ,E	5:25.0		Arsenios Tsimino	G R		Oc	8	Athen
	N	5:29.6		Colin Reit		1	Au	7	Bydgoszc
3km S	W,	7:59.1		Moses Kiptanu	K E	1	Au	9	Züric
		8:07.6		Joseph Mahmou	F R	2	Au	8	Brussel
		8:08.1		Patrick San	K E		Ju	9	London (CP
		8:07.9		Mark Rowlan		3	Se	8	Seou
	W	8:19.2		Daniel Njeng	K E	1	Ju	9	Toky
	E	8:29.5		Ralf Pönitzsc	G E	1	Au	7	Warsa
	N	8:29.8		Paul Davies-Hal		3	Au	8	London (CP
110m	W,E,C,	12.9		Colin Jackso	Wa	2	Au	9	Stuttgar
		13.0		Colin Jackso			Se	9	Sheffiel
	W	13.2		Renaldo Nehemia	U S	1	Au	7	Züric
	EJ,N	13.4		Colin Jackso		1	Ju	8	Athen
200m	WECA	22.6		Colin Jackso	Wa		Ju	9	Cardif
	N	23.		Jon Ridgeo		1	Se	8	Thurroc
		24.0		Paul Gra		1	Se	8	London (CP
400m		46.7		Kevin Youn	U S		Au	9	Barcelon
		47.3		Stéphane Diagan	F R		Ju	9	Lausann
		47.1		Samuel Matet	Z A		Au	9	Züric
		47.6		Kevin Youn	U S	1	Au	9	Sheffiel
		47.8		Kriss Akabus			Au	9	Barcelon
	W	48.0		Danny Harri	U S	1	Ju	8	Los Angele
	E	48.7		Vladimir Budk	R U	1	Au	8	Mosco
	N	50.2		Martin Brigg		2	Au	8	Schwecha
Hig		2.4		Javier Sotomayo	C U	2	Ju	9	Salamanc
Jum		2.4		Patrik Sjöber	S W	3	Ju	8	Stockhol
		2.4	i	Carlo Thränhard	G E	2	Fe	8	Berli
	(C,N	2.3	i	Steve Smit	E n		Fe	9	Wupperta
		2.3		Troy Kem	B H	1	Ju	9	Nic
	N,WJ,EJ,N	2.3		Steve Smit		2	Se	9	Seou
		2.3		Steve Smit		2	Au	9	Stuttgar
		2.4		Javier Sotomayo	C U	1	Ju	9	London (CP
	WJ,E	2.3		Dragutin Topi	C R	1	Au	9	Plovdi
Pol	W,	6.1	i	Sergey Bubk	U K	2	Fe	9	Donets
Vaul		6.1		Sergey Bubk	U K	3	Ju	9	Sestrier
		6.0		Okkert Brit	R S	1	Au	9	Cologn
		6.0		Sergey Bubk	U K	1	Se	9	London (CP
		5.7		Nick Buckfiel		1	Ju	9	Birmingha
	WJ,E	5.8		Maksim Taraso	R U	1	Ju	8	Bryans
	N	5.5		Neil Winte			Au	9	San Giulian

12

Event		Mark		Athlete	Country	Date	Place
Long	W	8.95		Mike Powell	USA	30 Aug 91	Tokyo
Jump	E	8.86	A	Robert Emmiyan	ARM	22 May 87	Tsakhkadzor
	C	8.52		James Beckford	JAM	29 May 96	Innsbruck
	A	8.54		Mike Powell	USA	10 Sep 93	London (CP)
	N	8.23		Lynn Davies		30 Jun 68	Berne
	WJ	8.34		Randy Williams	USA	8 Sep 72	Munich
	EJ	8.24		Volodymyr Ochkan	UKR	21 Jun 87	St. Petersburg
	NJ	7.98		Stewart Faulkner		6 Aug 88	Birmingham
Triple	W,E,C,N	18.29		Jonathan Edwards	Eng	7 Aug 95	Gothenburg
Jump	A	18.00		Jonathan Edwards		27 Aug 95	London (CP)
	WJ,EJ	17.50		Volker Mai	GER	23 Jun 85	Erfurt
	NJ	16.58		Tosi Fasinro		15 Jun 91	Espoo
Shot	W	23.12		Randy Barnes	USA	20 May 90	Los Angeles
	E	23.06		Ulf Timmermann	GER	22 May 88	Khaniá
	C,N	21.68		Geoff Capes	Eng	18 May 80	Cwmbrân
	A	22.28	#	Brian Oldfield	USA	18 Jun 75	Edinburgh
		21.72		Ulf Timmermann	GER	5 Aug 89	Gateshead
	WJ	21.05	i#	Terry Albritton	USA	22 Feb 74	New York
		20.65	#	Mike Carter	USA	5 Jul 79	Boston
		20.38		Terry Albritton	USA	27 Apr 74	Walnut
	EJ	20.20		Udo Beyer	GER	6 Jul 74	Leipzig
	NJ	18.21	i#	Matt Simson		3 Feb 89	Cosford
		18.11		Matt Simson		27 Aug 89	Varazdin
Discus	W,E	74.08		Jürgen Schult	GER	6 Jun 86	Neubrandenburg
	C	67.80		Adewale Olukoju	NGR	11 May 91	Los Angeles
	A	68.32		John Powell	USA	30 Aug 82	London (CP)
	N	65.16	#	Richard Slaney		1 Jul 85	Eugene
		64.32		Bill Tancred		10 Aug 74	Woodford
	WJ	65.62	#	Werner Reiterer	AUS	15 Dec 87	Melbourne
	(WJ),EJ	63.64		Werner Hartmann	GER	25 Jun 78	Strasbourg
	NJ	55.10		Glen Smith		31 Aug 91	Brierley Hill
Hammer	W,E	86.74		Yuriy Sedykh	UKR/RUS	30 Aug 86	Stuttgart
	C	77.58		Sean Carlin	AUS	11 Feb 94	Adelaide
	A	85.60		Yuriy Sedykh	UKR/RUS	13 Jul 84	London (CP)
	N	77.54		Martin Girvan		12 May 84	Wolverhampton
	WJ,EJ	78.14		Roland Steuk	GER	30 Jun 78	Leipzig
	NJ	67.48		Paul Head		16 Sep 84	Karlovac
Javelin	W,E	98.48		Jan Zelezny	CZE	25 May 96	Jena
	C,N	91.46		Steve Backley	Eng	25 Jan 92	Auckland
	A	95.66		Jan Zelezny	CZE	29 Aug 93	Sheffield
	WJ,EJ	82.52		Harri Haatainen	FIN	25 May 96	Leppävirta
	NJ	79.50		Steve Backley		5 Jun 88	Derby
Pent.	W,A	4123		Bill Toomey	USA	16 Aug 69	London (CP)
	E	4079		Rein Aun	EST	17 Jul 68	Tartu
	C,N	3841		Barry King	Eng	20 May 70	Santa Barbara
Dec.	W,	8891		Dan O'Brien	USA	5 Sep 92	Talence
	E,C,N	8847		Daley Thompson	Eng	9 Aug 84	Los Angeles
	A	8663		Daley Thompson		28 Jul 86	Edinburgh
	WJ,EJ	8397		Torsten Voss	GER	7 Jul 82	Erfurt
	NJ	8082		Daley Thompson		31 Jul 77	Sittard
(1986 Javelin)							
	E,C,N	8811	#	Daley Thompson	Eng	28 Aug 86	Stuttgart
	WJ,EJ	8114	#	Michael Kohnle	GER	25 Aug 89	Varazdin
	NJ	7488	#	David Bigham		9 Aug 90	Plovdiv

13

4x100m	W	37.40		United States		8 Aug 92	Barcelona
		37.40		United States		21 Aug 93	Stuttgart
	E,N	37.77		UK National Team		22 Aug 93	Stuttgart
	C	37.69		Canada		3 Aug 96	Atlanta
	A	38.39		UK National Team		5 Aug 89	Gateshead
	WJ	39.00	A	United States		18 Jul 83	Colorado Springs
	EJ	39.21	#	UK National Team		20 Sep 92	Seoul
	(EJ)	39.25		West Germany		28 Aug 83	Schwechat
	NJ	39.21		UK National Team		20 Sep 92	Seoul

4x200m	W	1:18.68		Santa Monica T.C.	USA	17 Apr 94	Walnut
	E	1:21.10		Italy		29 Sep 83	Cagliari
	C	1:20.79		Jamaica		24 Apr 88	Walnut
	A,N	1:21.29		UK National Team		23 Jun 89	Birmingham
	NJ	1:27.46	i	UK National Team		28 Jan 89	Glasgow
		1:27.6		Borough of Enfield		13 Jun 82	London (He)

4x400m	W	2:54.29		United States		22 Aug 93	Stuttgart
	E,N	2:56.60		UK National Team		3 Aug 96	Atlanta
	C	2:57.53		UK National Team	Eng	1 Sep 91	Tokyo
	A	2:59.85		UK National Team		19 Aug 96	Gateshead
	WJ	3:01.90		United States		20 Jul 86	Athens
	EJ,NJ	3:03.80	#	UK National Team		12 Aug 90	Plovdiv
	(EJ)	3:04.58		East Germany		23 Aug 81	Utrecht

4x800m	WECAN	7:03.89		UK National Team	Eng	30 Aug 82	London (CP)
	NJ	7:35.3		Liverpool Harriers		14 Aug 90	Leeds

4x1500m	W,E	14:38.8		West Germany		17 Aug 77	Cologne
	C	14:40.4		New Zealand		22 Aug 73	Oslo
	A	15:04.7		Italy		5 Jun 92	Sheffield
	N	14:56.8	a#	UK National Team		23 Jun 79	Bourges
		15:04.6		UK National Team		5 May 76	Athens
	NJ	16:03.2		BMC Junior Squad		30 Apr 96	Stretford

4x1mile	W,E	15:49.08		Ireland		17 Aug 85	Dublin (B)
	C	15:59.57		New Zealand		1 Mar 83	Auckland
	A	16:21.1		BMC National Squad		10 Jul 93	Oxford
	N	16:17.4		Bristol A.C.		24 Apr 75	Des Moines
	WJ,EJ,NJ	16:56.8		BMC Junior Squad		10 Jul 93	Oxford

Track Walking

1500 m	W,E	5:12.0		Algis Grigaliunas	LIT	12 May 90	Vilnius
	C	5:19.1		Dave Smith	AUS	7 Feb 83	Melbourne
	N	5:19.22	i	Tim Berrett §		9 Feb 90	East Rutherford

1 mile	W,E	5:36.9		Algis Grigaliunas	LIT	12 May 90	Vilnius
	C	5:54.6	i	Marcel Jobin	CAN	16 Feb 80	Houston
	N	5:56.39	i	Tim Berrett §		2 Feb 90	New York
	(C),A,(N)	5:59.1		Darrell Stone	Eng	2 Jul 89	Portsmouth
	NJ	6:09.2		Phil Vesty		23 Jun 82	Leicester

3000 m	W,E	10:47.11		Giovanni DeBenedictis	ITA	19 May 90	S. G. Valdarno
	C	10:56.22		Andrew Jachno	AUS	7 Feb 91	Melbourne
	A	11:19.00	i	Axel Noack	GER	23 Feb 90	Glasgow
		11:19.9		Tim Berrett	CAN	20 Apr 92	Tonbridge
	N	11:24.4		Mark Easton		10 May 89	Tonbridge
	WJ,EJ	11:13.2		Jozef Pribilinec	SVK	28 Mar 79	Banská Bystrica
	NJ	11:54.23		Tim Berrett §		23 Jun 84	London (CP)

Event	Cat	Time		Athlete	Country	Date			Location
5000 m	W,E	18:07.08	i	Mikhail Shchennikov	RUS	14	Feb	95	Moscow
		18:17.22		Robert Korzeniowski	POL	3	Jul	92	Reims
	C	18:52.20	i	Dave Smith	AUS	7	Mar	87	Indianapolis
		18:52.87		Dave Smith	AUS	21	Feb	86	Canberra
	A	18:56.27	i	Axel Noack	GER	23	Feb	90	Glasgow
	(A),N	19:35.0		Darrell Stone		16	May	89	Brighton
	WJ,EJ	19:19.3		Mikhail Shchennikov	RUS	9	Aug	86	Chemnitz
	NJ	20:16.40		Philip King		26	Jun	93	Lübeck
10 km	W,E	38:02.60		Jozef Pribilinec	SVK	30	Aug	85	Banská Bystrica
	C	38:06.6		Dave Smith	AUS	25	Sep	86	Sydney
	A	39:26.02		Guillaume Leblanc	CAN	29	Jun	90	Gateshead
	N	40:06.65		Ian McCombie		4	Jun	89	Jarrow
	WJ,EJ	38:54.75		Ralf Kowalsky	GER	24	Jun	81	Cottbus
	NJ	41:52.13		Darrell Stone		7	Aug	87	Birmingham
(Road)	NJ	41:46		Darrell Stone		26	Sep	87	Paris
1 Hour	W	15,577 m		Bernardo Segura	MEX	7	May	94	Fana
	E	15,447 m		Jozef Pribilinec	SVK	6	Sep	86	Hildesheim
	C	15,300 m		Dave Smith	AUS	6	Sep	86	Hildesheim
	A	14,383 m		Anatoliy Solomin	UKR	26	Aug	77	Edinburgh
	N	14,324 m	#	Ian McCombie		7	Jul	85	London (SP)
		14,158 m		Mark Easton		12	Sep	87	Woodford
	NJ	13,487 m		Darrell Stone		12	Sep	87	Woodford
20 km	W	1:17:25.6		Bernardo Segura	MEX	7	May	94	Fana
	E	1:18:35.2		Stefan Johansson	SWE	15	May	92	Fana
	C	1:20:12.3		Nick A'Hern	AUS	8	May	93	Fana
	A	1:24:07.6	#	Phil Vesty		1	Dec	84	Leicester
		1:24:22.0		José Marín	SPA	28	Jun	81	Brighton
	N	1:23:26.5		Ian McCombie		26	May	90	Fana
	WJ,EJ	1:22:42		Andrey Perlov	RUS	6	Sep	80	Donetsk
	NJ	1:31:34.4		Gordon Vale		28	Jun	81	Brighton
2 Hours	W,E	29,572 m		Maurizio Damilano	ITA	4	Oct	92	Cuneo
	C	28,800 m	#	Guillaume Leblanc	CAN	16	Jun	90	Sept Iles
		27,123 m		Willi Sawall	AUS	24	May	80	Melbourne
	A,N	27,262 m	#	Chris Maddocks		31	Dec	89	Plymouth
	(A)	26,265 m		Jordi Llopart	SPA	28	Jun	81	Brighton
	(N)	26,037 m		Ron Wallwork		31	Jul	71	Blackburn
30 km	W,E	2:01:44.1		Maurizio Damilano	ITA	4	Oct	92	Cuneo
	C	2:04:55.7		Guillaume Leblanc	CAN	16	Jun	90	Sept Iles
	A,N	2:11:54	#	Chris Maddocks		31	Dec	89	Plymouth
	(A)	2:17:26.4		Jordi Llopart	SPA	28	Jun	81	Brighton
	(N)	2:19:18		Chris Maddocks		22	Sep	84	Birmingham
50 km	W,E	3:40:57.9		Thierry Toutain	FRA	29	Sep	96	Héricourt
	C	3:43:50.0		Simon Baker	AUS	9	Sep	90	Melbourne
	A	4:03:52		Gerhard Weidner	GER	1	Jun	75	Woodford
	N	4:05:44.6		Paul Blagg		26	May	90	Fana

Race Walking - Fastest Recorded Times

Event	Cat	Time		Athlete	Country	Date			Location
20 km	W	1:17:25.6	t	Bernardo Segura	MEX	7	May	94	Fana
	E	1:18:13		Pavol Blazek	SVK	16	Sep	90	Hildesheim
	C	1:19:22		Dave Smith	AUS	19	Jul	87	Hobart
	A	1:21:42		José Marin	SPA	29	Sep	85	St. John's, IoM
	N	1:22:03		Ian McCombie		23	Sep	88	Seoul
	WJ	1:19:38		Yu Guohui	CHN	8	Mar	96	Zhuhai
	EJ	1:21:40		Ralf Kowalsky	GER	7	Aug	81	Jena
	NJ	1:26:13		Tim Berrett §		25	Feb	84	Dartford

15

30 km	W,E	2:01:44.1 t	Maurizio Damilano	ITA	4	Oct	92	Cuneo
	C	2:04:55.7 t	Guillaume Leblanc	CAN	16	Jun	90	Sept Iles
	A	2:07:47	Simon Baker	AUS	31	Jul	86	Edinburgh
	N	2:07:56	Ian McCombie		27	Apr	86	Edinburgh
	NJ	2:30:46	Phil Vesty		31	Jul	82	London (VP)
50 km	W,E	3:37:41	Andrey Perlov	RUS	5	Aug	89	St. Petersburg
	C	3:43:13	Simon Baker	AUS	28	May	89	L'Hospitalet
	A	3:47:31	Hartwig Gauder	GER	28	Sep	85	St. John's IoM
	N	3:51:37	Chris Maddocks		28	Oct	90	Burrator
	WJ,EJ	4:07:23	Aleksandr Volgin	RUS	27	Sep	86	Zhytomyr
	NJ	4:18:18	Gordon Vale		24	Oct	81	Lassing

RECORDS set in 1996

100m	C	9.87	Frank Fredericks	NAM	25	Jun	96	Helsinki
	C	9.86	Frank Fredericks	NAM	3	Jul	96	Lausanne
	W,C	9.84	Donovan Bailey	CAN	27	Jul	96	Atlanta
200m	W	19.66	Michael Johnson	USA	23	Jun	96	Atlanta
	C	19.85	Ato Boldon	TRI	3	Jul	96	Lausanne
	C	19.82	Frank Fredericks	NAM	5	Jul	96	Oslo
	W	19.32	Michael Johnson	USA	1	Aug	96	Atlanta
	C	19.68	Frank Fredericks	NAM	1	Aug	96	Atlanta
400m	N	44.39	Roger Black		16	Jun	96	Birmingham
	N	44.37	Roger Black		3	Jul	96	Lausanne
3000m	WJ	7:37.35	Philip Mosima	KEN	3	Jul	96	Lausanne
	WJ	7:35.52	Philip Mosima	KEN	12	Jul	96	London (CP)
	C	7:25.16	Daniel Komen	KEN	10	Aug	96	Monte Carlo
	W,C	7:20.67	Daniel Komen	KEN	1	Sep	96	Rieti
2 miles	W,C	8:03.54	Daniel Komen	KEN	14	Jul	96	Lappeenranta
5000m	C,WJ	12:53.72	Philip Mosima	KEN	5	Jun	96	Rome
	C	12:51.60	Daniel Komen	KEN	8	Jul	96	Stockholm
	C	12:45.09	Daniel Komen	KEN	14	Aug	96	Zürich
10km	W	26:38.08	Salah Hissou	MAR	23	Aug	96	Brussels
PV	N	5.71	Nick Buckfield		16	Jun	96	Birmingham
LJ	C	8.52	James Beckford	JAM	26	May	96	Innsbruck
JT	W,E	98.48	Jan Zelezny	CZE	25	May	96	Jena
	WJ,EJ	82.52	Harri Haatainen	FIN	25	May	96	Leppävirta

Relays

4x100m	C	37.69	Canada		3	Aug	96	Atlanta
4x400m	E,N	2:56.60	UK National Team		3	Aug	96	Atlanta
	A	2:59.85	UK National Team		19	Aug	96	Gateshead

Track Walking

50km	W,E	3:40:57.9	Thierry Toutain	FRA	29	Sep	96	Héricourt

Race Walking

20km	WJ	1:19:38	Yu Guohui	CHN	8	Mar	96	Zhuhai

WOMEN'S EVENTS

100 m	W	10.49		Florence Griffith Joyner	USA	16	Jul	88	Indianapolis
	E	10.77		Irina Privalova	RUS	6	Jul	94	Lausanne
	C	10.74		Merlene Ottey	JAM	7	Sep	96	Milan
	A	11.02		Merlene Ottey	JAM	14	Jul	89	London (CP)
	N	11.10		Kathy Smallwood/Cook		5	Sep	81	Rome
	WJ,EJ	10.88	#	Marlies Oelsner/Göhr	GER	1	Jul	77	Dresden
		10.89		Kathrin Krabbe	GER	20	Jul	88	Berlin
	NJ	11.27	A	Kathy Smallwood/Cook		9	Sep	79	Mexico City
200 m	W	21.34		Florence Griffith Joyner	USA	29	Sep	88	Seoul
	E	21.71		Marita Koch	GER	10	Jun	79	Chemnitz
		21.71	#	Marita Koch	GER	21	Jul	84	Potsdam
		21.71		Heike Drechsler	GER	29	Jun	86	Jena
		21.71	#	Heike Drechsler	GER	29	Aug	86	Stuttgart
	C	21.64		Merlene Ottey	JAM	13	Sep	91	Brussels
	A	22.23		Merlene Ottey	JAM	9	Sep	94	London (CP)
	N	22.10		Kathy Cook		9	Aug	84	Los Angeles
	WJ,EJ	22.19		Natalya Bochina	RUS	30	Jul	80	Moscow
	NJ	22.70	A	Kathy Smallwood/Cook		12	Sep	79	Mexico City
300 m	W,E	34.1	#	Marita Koch	GER	6	Oct	85	Canberra
		35.00	+	Marie-José Pérec	FRA	27	Aug	91	Tokyo
	C,A,N	35.46		Kathy Cook		18	Aug	84	London (CP)
	(A)	35.46		Chandra Cheeseborough	USA	18	Aug	84	London (CP)
	WJ,EJ,NJ	36.2		Donna Murray/Hartley		7	Aug	74	London (CP)
	WJ,EJ	36.24		Grit Breuer	GER	29	Aug	90	Split
	NJ	36.46		Linsey Macdonald		13	Jul	80	London (CP)
400 m	W,E	47.60		Marita Koch	GER	6	Oct	85	Canberra
	C	48.63		Cathy Freeman	AUS	29	Jul	96	Atlanta
	N	49.43		Kathy Cook		6	Aug	84	Los Angeles
	A	49.33		Tatjána Kocembová	CS	20	Aug	83	London (CP)
	WJ,EJ	49.42		Grit Breuer	GER	27	Aug	91	Tokyo
	NJ	51.16		Linsey Macdonald		15	Jun	80	London (CP)
600 m	W,E	1:23.5		Doina Melinte	ROM	27	Jul	86	Poiana Brasov
	C	1:26.0		Charlene Rendina	AUS	12	Mar	79	Adelaide
	A	1:25.90		Delisa Walton-Floyd	USA	28	Aug	88	London (CP)
	N	1:26.18		Diane Edwards/Modahl		22	Aug	87	London (CP)
	NJ	1:27.33		Lorraine Baker		13	Jul	80	London (CP)
800 m	W,E	1:53.28		Jarmila Kratochvílová	CZE	26	Jul	83	Munich
	C,N	1:56.21		Kelly Holmes	Eng	9	Sep	95	Monaco
	A	1:57.14		Jarmila Kratochvílová	CZE	24	Jun	85	Belfast
	WJ	1:57.18		Wang Yuan	CHN	8	Sep	93	Beijing
	EJ	1:57.45	#	Hildegard Ullrich	GER	31	Aug	78	Prague
	(EJ)	1:59.17		Birte Bruns	GER	20	Jul	88	Berlin
	NJ	2:01.11		Lynne MacDougall/McIntyre		18	Aug	84	London (CP)
1000 m	W,E	2:28.98		Svetlana Masterkova	RUS	23	Aug	96	Brussels
	C	2:29.66		Maria Lurdes Mutola	MOZ	23	Aug	96	Brussels
	A,N	2:32.82		Kelly Holmes	Eng	23	Jul	95	Sheffield
	WJ,EJ	2:35.4	a	Irina Nikitina	RUS	5	Aug	79	Podolsk
	NJ	2:38.58		Jo White		9	Sep	77	London (CP)
1500 m	W	3:50.46		Qu Yunxia	CHN	11	Sep	93	Beijing
	E	3:52.47		Tatyana Kazankina	RUS	13	Aug	80	Zürich
	C,N,(EJ),NJ	3:59.96		Zola Budd/Pieterse	Eng	30	Aug	85	Brussels
	A	3:59.31		Ravilya Agletdinova	BLR	5	Jun	83	Birmingham
	WJ	3:59.81		Wang Yuan	CHN	11	Sep	93	Beijing
	EJ	4:03.45		Anita Weyerman	SWZ	3	Jul	96	Lausanne

Event	Cat	Time	Name	Nat	Date	Place
1 Mile	W,E	4:12.56	Svetlana Masterkova	RUS	14 Aug 96	Zürich
	C,N,WJ,EJ,NJ	4:17.57	Zola Budd/Pieterse	Eng	21 Aug 85	Zürich
	A	4:19.59	Mary Slaney	USA	2 Aug 85	London (CP)
2000 m	W,E,A	5:25.36	Sonia O'Sullivan	IRE	8 Jul 94	Edinburgh
	C,N	5:26.93	Yvonne Murray	Sco	8 Jul 94	Edinburgh
	WJ,EJ,NJ	5:33.15	Zola Budd/Pieterse		13 Jul 84	London (CP)
3000 m	W	8:06.11	Wang Junxia	CHN	13 Sep 93	Beijing
	E,A	8:21.64	Sonia O'Sullivan	IRE	15 Jul 94	London (CP)
	C,N,NJ	8:28.83	Zola Budd/Pieterse	Eng	7 Sep 85	Rome
	WJ,EJ	8:28.83 #	Zola Budd/Pieterse		7 Sep 85	Rome
	(WJ)	8:36.45	Ma Ningning	CHN	6 Jun 93	Jinan
	(EJ)	8:40.08	Gabriela Szabo	ROM	10 Aug 94	Helsinki
5000 m	W,E	14:36.45	Fernanda Ribeiro	POR	22 Jul 95	Hechtel
	C	14:46.41	Rose Cheruiyot	KEN	16 Aug 96	Cologne
	A	14:47.64	Sonia O'Sullivan	IRE	7 Jul 95	London (CP)
	N	14:46.76	Paula Radcliffe		16 Aug 96	Cologne
	WJ	14:45.90	Jiang Bo	CHN	24 Oct 95	Nanjing
	EJ,NJ	14:48.07	Zola Budd/Pieterse		26 Aug 85	London (CP)
	(EJ)	14:56.22	Annemari Sandell	FIN	8 Jul 96	Stockholm
10 km	W	29:31.78	Wang Junxia	CHN	8 Sep 93	Beijing
	E	30:13.74	Ingrid Kristiansen	NOR	5 Jul 86	Oslo
	C,A	30:52.51	Elana Meyer	RSA	10 Sep 94	London (CP)
	N	30:57.07	Liz McColgan		25 Jun 91	Hengelo
	WJ	31:15.38 #	Sally Barsosio	KEN	21 Aug 93	Stuttgart
		31:40.56	Delillah Asiago	KEN	16 Jun 91	Tokyo
	(WJ,EJ)	31:40.42 &	Annemari Sandell	FIN	27 Jul 96	Atlanta
	EJ	31:54.29	Annemari Sandell	FIN	9 Aug 95	Gothenburg
1 Hour	W,E	18,084 m	Silvana Cruciata	ITA	4 May 81	Rome
	C,A,N	16,460 m i	Bronwen Cardy-Wise	Wal	8 Mar 92	Birmingham
		16,272 m	Zina Marchant	Eng	30 Mar 88	London (TB)
20 km	W	1:06:48.8	Izumi Maki	JAP	19 Sep 93	Amagasaki
	E	1:06:55.5 #	Rosa Mota	POR	14 May 83	Lisbon
	C,A,N	1:21:43.0 #	Eleanor Adams/Robinson	Eng	16 Oct 82	London (He)
25 km	W,E	1:29:29.2	Karolina Szabó	HUN	22 Apr 88	Budapest
	C,A,N	1:42:36.9 #	Eleanor Adams/Robinson	Eng	16 Oct 82	London (He)
30 km	W,E	1:47:05.6	Karolina Szabó	HUN	22 Apr 88	Budapest
	C,A,N	2:03:53.0 #	Eleanor Adams/Robinson	Eng	16 Oct 82	London (He)
Half Marathon	W,C	67:12	Tegla Loroupe	KEN	10 Mar 96	Lisbon
	E	67:58	Uta Pippig	GER	19 Mar 95	Kyoto
	A,N	68:42	Liz McColgan		11 Oct 92	Dundee
Distance unverified		66:40	Ingrid Kristiansen	NOR	5 Apr 87	Sandnes
Downhill (.16%)		67:11	Liz McColgan	Sco	26 Jan 92	Tokyo
	WJ	69:05	Delillah Asiago	KEN	5 May 91	Exeter
	NJ	77:52 #	Kathy Williams		28 Mar 82	Barry
		78:00	Karen Whapshott/Downer		4 Apr 82	Fleet
Marathon	W,E,A	2:21:06	Ingrid Kristiansen	NOR	21 Apr 85	London
	C	2:23:51	Lisa Martin/Ondieki	AUS	31 Jan 88	Osaka
	N	2:25:56	Véronique Marot		23 Apr 89	London
	WJ	2:30:15	Gu Dongmei	CHN	4 Apr 93	Tianjin
	NJ	2:58:58	Tracy Howard		9 May 82	London
2km St	W,E	6:11.84	Marina Pluzhnikova	RUS	25 Jul 94	St. Petersburg
	C,A,N	7:04.7mx&	Sally Young	Eng	14 Jul 93	Sutton
		7:13.3 (2'6")	Sally Young		11 Aug 93	Watford
	NJ	7:52.8 (2'6")	Victoria Wilkinson		25 Sep 93	Leeds
100mH	W,E	12.21	Yordanka Donkova	BUL	20 Aug 88	Stara Zagora
	C	12.57	Michelle Freeman	JAM	29 Jul 96	Atlanta
	A	12.51	Ginka Zagorcheva	BUL	12 Sep 86	London (CP)

Event		Mark		Athlete	Nat	Date			Place
100mH	N	12.80		Angie Thorp		31	Jul	96	Atlanta
	WJ	12.84		Aliuska López	CUB	16	Jul	87	Zagreb
	EJ	12.88		Yelena Ovcharova	UKR	25	Jun	95	Lille
	NJ	13.25		Diane Allahgreen		21	Jul	94	Lisbon
400mH	W	52.61		Kim Batten	USA	11	Aug	95	Gothenburg
	E,C,N	52.74		Sally Gunnell	Eng	19	Aug	93	Stuttgart
	A	53.69		Sandra Farmer-Patrick	USA	10	Sep	93	London (CP)
	WJ	55.20		Leslie Maxie	USA	9	Jun	84	San Jose
	EJ	55.46		Ionela Tirlea	ROM	11	Aug	95	Gothenburg
	NJ	57.27		Vicki Jamison		28	Jul	96	Bedford
High Jump	W,E	2.09		Stefka Kostadinova	BUL	30	Aug	87	Rome
	C	1.99	i	Debbie Brill	CAN	23	Jan	82	Edmonton
		1.98		Debbie Brill	CAN	2	Sep	84	Rieti
		1.98		Vanessa Ward	AUS	12	Feb	89	Perth
		1.98		Alison Inverarity	AUS	17	Jul	94	Ingolstadt
	A	2.03		Ulrike Meyfarth	GER	21	Aug	83	London (CP)
		2.03		Tamara Bykova	RUS	21	Aug	83	London (CP)
	N	1.95		Diana Elliott/Davies		26	Jun	82	Oslo
	WJ,EJ	2.01	#	Olga Turchak	KAZ	7	Jul	86	Moscow
		2.01		Heike Balck	GER	18	Jun	89	Chemnitz
	NJ	1.91		Lea Haggett		2	Jun	91	Khaniá
Pole Vault	W,C	4.45		Emma George	AUS	14	Jul	96	Sapporo
	E	4.27	&	Daniela Bártová	CZE	18	Sep	96	Oristano
	(E)	4.23		Daniela Bártová	CZE	31	Aug	96	Jablonec
	A	4.14		Daniela Bártová	CZE	2	Jul	95	Gateshead
	N	4.00		Janine Whitlock		14	Sep	96	Telford
	WJ,EJ	4.17		Vasa Flosadóttir	ISL	28	Sep	96	Bordeaux
	NJ	3.70		Rhian Clarke		10	Aug	96	London (He)
		3.70	&	Rhian Clarke		26	Aug	96	Peterborough
Long Jump	W,E	7.52		Galina Chistyakova	RUS	11	Jun	88	St. Petersburg
	C	7.12		Chioma Ajunwa	NGR	1	Aug	96	Atlanta
	N,NJ	6.90		Beverly Kinch		14	Aug	83	Helsinki
	A	7.14		Galina Chistyakova	RUS	24	Jun	89	Birmingham
	WJ,EJ	7.14	#	Heike Daute/Drechsler	GER	4	Jun	83	Bratislava
		6.98		Heike Daute/Drechsler	GER	18	Aug	82	Potsdam
Triple Jump	W,E	15.50		Inessa Kravets	UKR	10	Aug	95	Gothenburg
	C,N	14.78		Ashia Hansen	Eng	25	Aug	96	Sheffield
	A	14.84		Sárka Kaspárková	CZE	25	Aug	96	Sheffield
	WJ,EJ	14.62		Tereza Marinova	BUL	25	Aug	96	Sydney
	NJ	13.05		Michelle Griffith		16	Jun	90	London (CP)
Shot	W,E	22.63		Natalya Lisovskaya	RUS	6	Jun	87	Moscow
	C	19.74		Gael Mulhall/Martin	AUS	14	Jul	84	Berkeley
	A	21.95		Natalya Lisovskaya	RUS	29	Jul	88	Edinburgh
	N	19.36		Judy Oakes		14	Aug	88	Gateshead
	WJ,EJ	20.54		Astrid Kumbernuss	GER	1	Jul	89	Orimattila
	NJ	17.10		Myrtle Augee		16	Jun	84	London (CP)
Discus	W,E	76.80		Gabriele Reinsch	GER	9	Jul	88	Neubrandenburg
	C	68.72		Daniele Costian	AUS	22	Jan	94	Auckland
	A	73.04		Ilke Wyludda	GER	5	Aug	89	Gateshead
	N	67.48		Meg Ritchie		26	Apr	81	Walnut
	WJ,EJ	74.40		Ilke Wyludda	GER	13	Sep	88	Berlin
	NJ	54.78		Lynda Whiteley		4	Oct	82	Brisbane
Hammer	W,E	69.46	#	Olga Kuzenkova	RUS	17	Feb	96	Sydney
		69.42	&	Mihaela Melinte	ROM	12	May	96	Cluj-Napoca
	(W,E)	68.16		Olga Kuzenkova	RUS	18	Jun	95	Moscow
	C,A	65.24		Debbie Sosimenko	AUS	15	Jul	95	Birmingham

Event		Mark		Athlete	Nat	Date	Venue
Hammer	N	64.90		Lorraine Shaw		10 Jun 95	Bedford
	WJ,EJ	65.48		Mihaela Melinte	ROM	25 Feb 94	Bucharest
	NJ	55.44	#	Lyn Sprules		19 Jul 94	Haslemere
		54.48		Lyn Sprules		2 Jul 94	Bedford
Javelin	W,E	80.00		Petra Felke	GER	8 Sep 88	Potsdam
	C,N	77.44		Fatima Whitbread	Eng	28 Aug 86	Stuttgart
	A	75.62		Fatima Whitbread		25 May 87	Derby
	WJ,EJ	71.88		Antoaneta Todorova	BUL	15 Aug 81	Zagreb
	NJ	60.14		Fatima Whitbread		7 May 80	Grays
Hept.	W	7291		Jackie Joyner-Kersee	USA	24 Sep 88	Seoul
	E	7007		Larisa Nikitina	RUS	11 Jun 89	Bryansk
	C	6695		Jane Flemming	AUS	28 Jan 90	Auckland
	A	6419		Birgit Clarius	GER	21 Jul 91	Sheffield
	N	6645		Denise Lewis		26 May 96	Götzis
	WJ,EJ	6465		Sybille Thiele	GER	28 Aug 83	Schwechat
	NJ	5833		Joanne Mulliner		11 Aug 85	Lons-le-Saunier
4x100m	W,E	41.37		East Germany		6 Oct 85	Canberra
	C	41.94		Jamaica		1 Sep 91	Tokyo
		41.94		Jamaica		22 Aug 93	Stuttgart
	A	41.87		East Germany		5 Aug 89	Gateshead
	N	42.43		UK National Team		1 Aug 80	Moscow
	WJ,EJ	43.33	#	East Germany		20 Jul 88	Berlin
		43.48		East Germany		31 Jul 88	Sudbury
	NJ	44.16		UK National Team		12 Aug 90	Plovdiv
4x200m	W,E	1:28.15		East Germany		9 Aug 80	Jena
	C,N	1:31.57		UK National Team	Eng	20 Aug 77	London (CP)
	A	1:31.49		Russia		5 Jun 93	Portsmouth
	NJ	1:42.2		London Olympiades AC		19 Aug 72	Bracknell
4x400m	W,E	3:15.17		U.S.S.R.		1 Oct 88	Seoul
	C	3:21.04		Nigeria		3 Aug 96	Atlanta
	A	3:20.79		Czechoslovakia		21 Aug 83	London (CP)
	N	3:22.01		UK National Team		1 Sep 91	Tokyo
	WJ,EJ	3:28.39		East Germany		31 Jul 88	Sudbury
	NJ	3:35.10		UK National Team		25 Aug 85	Cottbus
4x800m	W,E	7:50.17		U.S.S.R.		5 Aug 84	Moscow
	C	8:20.73		UK National Team	Eng	5 Jun 93	Portsmouth
	A	7:57.08		Russia		5 Jun 93	Portsmouth
	N	8:19.9	m	UK National Team		5 Jun 92	Sheffield
	NJ	8:53.1		Havering AC		24 May 80	Birmingham
4x1500m	W	17:18.10	#	Villanova Univ	USA/IRE	27 Apr 90	Philadelphia
	(W),E	17:22.30		Providence Univ	IRE	26 Apr 91	Philadelphia
	C,N	18:12.1		BMC National Squad	Eng	30 Apr 96	Stretford
	NJ	19:06.7		BMC Junior Squad		30 Apr 96	Stretford
4x1mile	WECAN	19:17.3		BMC National Squad	Eng	10 Jul 93	Oxford

Track Walking

Event		Mark		Athlete	Nat	Date	Venue
1500 m	W,C	5:50.51		Kerry Saxby-Junna	AUS	20 Jun 91	Sydney
	E	5:53.0		Sada Eidikyte	LIT	12 May 90	Vilnius
	A	6:04.5	i	Beate Anders/Gummelt	GER	4 Mar 90	Glasgow
1 Mile	W, E	6:16.72	i	Sada Eidikyte	LIT	12 May 90	Vilnius
		6:19.39		Ileana Salvador	ITA	15 Jun 91	Siderno
	C	6:47.9		Sue Cook	AUS	14 Mar 81	Canberra
	A	6:30.7	i	Beate Anders/Gummelt	GER	4 Mar 90	Glasgow
	(A),N	7:14.3		Carol Tyson		17 Sep 77	London (PH)
	NJ	7:31.6		Kate Horwill		22 Aug 93	Solihull

Event	Cat	Time		Name	Country	Date	Place
3000 m	W,E	11:44.00	i	Alina Ivanova	RUS	7 Feb 92	Moscow
		11:48.24		Ileana Salvador	ITA	29 Aug 93	Padua
	C	11:51.26		Kerry Saxby-Junna	AUS	7 Feb 91	Melbourne
	A	12:32.37	+	Yelena Nikolayeva	RUS	19 Jun 88	Portsmouth
	N	12:49.16		Betty Sworowski		28 Jul 90	Wrexham
	WJ,EJ	12:29.98	i	Susana Feitór	POR	6 Mar 93	Braga
	WJ	12:39.1		Wang Yan	CHN	30 Mar 86	Beijing
	EJ	12:53.61	+	Oksana Shchastnaya	RUS	7 Aug 87	Birmingham
	NJ	13:03.4		Vicky Lupton		18 May 91	Sheffield
5000 m	W,C	20:03.0	#	Kerry Saxby-Junna	AUS	11 Feb 96	Sydney
	W,C	20:13.26		Kerry Saxby-Junna	AUS	25 Feb 96	Hobart
	E	20:07.52	#	Beate Anders/Gummelt	GER	23 Jun 90	Rostock
		20:21.69		Anna-Rita Sidoti	ITA	1 Jul 95	Cesenatico
	A	21:08.65		Yelena Nikolayeva	RUS	19 Jun 88	Portsmouth
	N	21:52.38	&	Vicky Lupton		9 Aug 95	Sheffield
		22:02.06		Betty Sworowski		28 Aug 89	Gateshead
(Road)	N	21:36		Vicky Lupton		18 Jul 92	Sheffield
	WJ,EJ	20:31.4		Irina Stankina	RUS	10 Feb 96	Adler
	NJ	22:36.81		Vicky Lupton		15 Jun 91	Espoo
10 km	W,E	41:56.23		Nadezhda Ryashkina	UKR	24 Jul 90	Seattle
	C	41:57.22		Kerry Saxby-Junna	AUS	24 Jul 90	Seattle
	A,N	45:18.8		Vicky Lupton		2 Sep 95	Watford
	WJ	42:49.7		Gao Hongmiao	CHN	15 Mar 92	Jinan
	EJ	44:51.67		Claudia Iovan	ROM	14 Jun 96	Bucharest
	NJ	47:04		Vicky Lupton		30 Mar 91	Sheffield
1 Hour	W	12,771 m		Victoria Herazo	USA	20 Oct 91	Cambridge, Mass
	E	12,644 m		Giuliana Salce	ITA	25 Apr 86	Ostia
	C	12,555 m		Sue Cook	AUS	29 Jun 85	Canberra
	A,N,NJ	11,590 m		Lisa Langford		13 Sep 86	Woodford
20 km	W,E	1:35:29.5		Madelein Svensson	SWE	10 Jul 91	Borås
	C,N	1:58:37.8		Margaret Lewis	Eng	15 Sep 71	Sotteville
	WJ	1:48:18.6		Sue Liers/Westerfield	USA	20 Mar 77	Kings Point
50 km	W,E	5:13:49.8		Zofia Turosz	POL	13 Oct 85	Warsaw
	C,N	5:26:59		Sandra Brown	Eng	27 Oct 90	Etrechy

Road Walking - Fastest Recorded Times

Event	Cat	Time		Name	Country	Date	Place
10 km	W,E	41:04		Yelena Nikolayeva	RUS	20 Apr 96	Sochi
	C	41:30		Kerry Saxby-Junna	AUS	27 Aug 88	Canberra
	A	43:27		Graciella Mendoza	MEX	8 Oct 89	Hull
	N	45:18.8 t		Vicky Lupton		2 Sep 95	Watford
	WJ,EJ	41:55		Irina Stankina	RUS	11 Feb 95	Adler
	NJ	47:30		Vicky Lupton		17 Mar 91	Sheffield
20 km	W,C	1:29:40		Kerry Saxby-Junna	AUS	13 May 88	Värnamo
	E	1:30:42		Olga Kardopoltseva	BLR	29 Apr 90	Kaliningrad
	A,N	1:40:45		Irene Bateman		9 Apr 83	Basildon
	WJ,EJ	1:34:31		Tatyana Titova	RUS	4 Oct 87	Alushta
	NJ	1:52:03		Vicky Lupton		13 Oct 91	Sheffield
50 km	WECAN	4:50:51		Sandra Brown	Eng	13 Jul 91	Basildon

RECORDS set in 1996

Event	Cat	Time	Name	Country	Date	Place
100m	C	10.74	Merlene Ottey	JAM	7 Sep 96	Milan
400m	C	48.63	Cathy Freeman	AUS	29 Jul 96	Atlanta
1000m	W,E	2:28.98	Svetlana Masterkova	RUS	23 Aug 96	Brussels
	C	2:29.66	Maria Lurdes Mutola	MOZ	23 Aug 96	Brussels
1500m	EJ	4:03.45	Anita Weyermann	SWZ	3 Jul 96	Lausanne
1 Mile	W,E	4:12.56	Svetlana Masterkova	RUS	14 Aug 96	Zürich
5000m	EJ	14:59.28	Anita Weyermann	SWZ	5 Jun 96	Rome
	EJ	14:56.22	Annemari Sandell	FIN	8 Jul 96	Stockholm

21

5000	C	14:46.41		Rose Cheruiyot	KEN	16 Aug 96	Cologne
	N	14:46.76		Paula Radcliffe		16 Aug 96	Cologne
10km	WJ	31:40.42	&	Annemari Sandell	FIN	27 Jul 96	Atlanta
HMar	W,C	67:12		Tegla Loroupe	KEN	10 Mar 96	Lisbon
100mh	C	12.57		Michelle Freeman	JAM	29 Jul 96	Atlanta
	N	12.80		Angie Thorp		31 Jul 96	Atlanta
400mh	NJ	57.87		Vicki Jamison		22 Jun 96	Belfast
	NJ	57.27		Vicki Jamison		28 Jul 96	Bedford
PV	W,C	4.30		Emma George	AUS	28 Jan 96	Perth
	W,C	4.41		Emma George	AUS	28 Jan 96	Perth
	WJ	4.10	#	Melissa Price	USA	13 Apr 96	Fresno
	EJ	4.00	&	Amandine Homo	FRA	26 Apr 96	Thonon
	EJ	4.01		Amandine Homo	FRA	1 May 96	St-Brieuc
	NJ	3.50		Clare Ridgley		6 May 96	Luton
	WJ	4.10	#	Melissa Price	USA	11 May 96	Modesto
	EJ	4.02		Julie Vigourt	FRA	12 May 96	Châlon/Saune
	NJ	3.50		Rhian Clarke		19 May 96	Loughborough
	WJ,EJ	4.11		Nasta Ryshich	GER	26 May 96	Schwechat
	N	3.81		Kate Staples		26 May 96	Ljubljana
	N	3.90		Kate Staples		26 May 96	Ljubljana
	NJ	3.50	&	Clare Ridgley		26 May 96	Bedford
	WJ,EJ	4.12		Nastja Ryshich	GER	29 May 96	Bratislava
	NJ	3.55		Rhian Clarke		1 Jun 96	Newport
	NJ	3.60		Rhian Clarke		1 Jun 96	Newport
	NJ	3.65		Rhian Clarke		1 Jun 96	Newport
	WJ,EJ	4.13		Nastja Ryshich	GER	15 Jun 96	Mannheim
	WJ,EJ	4.15		Nastja Ryshich	GER	21 Jun 96	Cologne
	W,C	4.42		Emma George	AUS	29 Jun 96	Reims
	W,C	4.45		Emma George	AUS	14 Jul 96	Sapporo
	NJ	3.65	&	Rhian Clarke		20 Jul 96	Birmingham
	N	3.91	#	Janine Whitlock		28 Jul 96	Lincoln
	NJ	3.70		Rhian Clarke		10 Aug 96	London (He)
	NJ	3.70	&	Rhian Clarke		26 Aug 96	Peterborough
	E	4.23		Daniela Bártová	CZE	31 Aug 96	Jablonec
	E	4.25	&	Daniela Bártová	CZE	4 Sep 96	Pula
	N	3.91	&	Janine Whitlock		11 Sep 96	Salgótarján
	N	3.92		Janine Whitlock		14 Sep 96	Telford
	N	4.00		Janine Whitlock		14 Sep 96	Telford
	E	4.27	&	Daniela Bártová	CZE	18 Sep 96	Oristano
	WJ,EJ	4.17		Vasa Flosadóttir	ISL	28 Sep 96	Bordeaux
LJ	C	7.12		Chioma Ajunwa		1 Aug 96	Atlanta
TJ	WJ,EJ	14.41	&	Tereza Marinova	BUL	6 Jul 96	Bucharest
	C, N	14.67		Ashia Hansen	Eng	11 Aug 96	London (CP)
	C, N	14.78		Ashia Hansen	Eng	25 Aug 96	Sheffield
	A	14.84		Sárka Kaspárková	CZE	25 Aug 96	Sheffield
	WJ,EJ	14.62		Tereza Marinova	BUL	25 Aug 96	Sydney
HT	C	69.46	#	Olga Kuzenkova	RUS	17 Feb 96	Sydney
	W, E	69.42		Mihaela Melinte	ROM	12 May 96	Cluj-Napoca
Hept.	N	6645		Denise Lewis		26 May 96	Götzis

Relay

4x400m	C	3:21.04		Nigeria		3 Aug 96	Atlanta

Track Walking

5km	W,C	20:03.0	#	Kerry-Saxby-Junna	AUS	11 Feb 96	Sydney
	W,C	20:13.26		Kerry-Saxby-Junna	AUS	25 Feb 96	Hobart
	WJ,EJ	20:31.4		Irina Stankina	RUS	10 Feb 96	Adler
10km	EJ	44:51.67		Claudia Iovan	ROM	14 Jun 96	Bucharest

Road Walking

10km	W,E	41:04		Yelena Nikolayeva	RUS	20 Apr 96	Sochi

NATIONAL RECORDS OF THE UNITED KINGDOM (MEN)

(as at 31 Dec 96)

These are the best authentic performances for the four countries of the U.K.
E = England S = Scotland W = Wales NI = Northern Ireland

100 m	E	9.87	Linford Christie	15 Aug 93	Stuttgart, GER
	S	10.11	Allan Wells	24 Jul 80	Moscow, RUS
	W	10.29	Colin Jackson	28 Jul 90	Wrexham
	NI	10.46	Mark Forsythe	17 Jun 89	Tel Aviv, ISR
200 m	E	19.87 A&	John Regis	31 Jul 94	Sestriere, ITA
		19.94	John Regis	20 Aug 93	Stuttgart, GER
	S	20.21	Allan Wells	28 Jul 80	Moscow, RUS
	W	20.43	Doug Turner	9 Jun 96	Tallinn, EST
	NI	20.81	Paul McBurney	24 Aug 94	Victoria, CAN
300 m	E	31.67	John Regis	17 Jul 92	Gateshead
	W	32.25	Jamie Baulch	11 Aug 96	London (CP)
	S	32.44	David Jenkins	4 Jul 75	London (CP)
	NI	33.77	Simon Baird	24 Jun 85	Belfast
400 m	E	44.37	Roger Black	3 Jul 96	Lausanne, SWZ
	W	44.57	Jamie Baulch	3 Jul 96	Lausanne, SWZ
	S	44.93	David Jenkins	21 Jun 75	Eugene, USA
	NI	46.49	Paul McBurney	22 Aug 94	Victoria, CAN
600 m	E	1:14.95	Steve Heard	14 Jul 91	London (Ha)
	S	1:15.4	Tom McKean	21 Jul 91	Grangemouth
	W	1:18.02	Glen Grant	2 Aug 78	Edmonton, CAN
	NI	1:18.3 i	Joe Chivers	14 Dec 74	Cosford
		1:20.1	Kenneth Thompson	24 May 80	Belfast
800 m	E	1:41.73 "	Sebastian Coe	10 Jun 81	Florence, ITA
	S	1:43.88	Tom McKean	28 Jul 89	London (CP)
	W	1:45.44	Neil Horsfield	28 Jul 90	Wrexham
	NI	1:46.94	Mark Kirk	20 Jul 87	Belfast
1000 m	E	2:12.18	Sebastian Coe	11 Jul 81	Oslo, NOR
	S	2:16.82	Graham Williamson	17 Jul 84	Edinburgh
	W	2:17.36	Neil Horsfield	9 Aug 91	Gateshead
	NI	2:19.05	Mark Kirk	5 Aug 87	Oslo, NOR
1500 m	E	3:29.67	Steve Cram	16 Jul 85	Nice, FRA
	S	3:33.83	John Robson	4 Sep 79	Brussels, BEL
	NI	3:34.76	Gary Lough	9 Sep 95	Monaco, MON
	W	3:35.08	Neil Horsfield	10 Aug 90	Brussels, BEL
1 Mile	E	3:46.32	Steve Cram	27 Jul 85	Oslo, NOR
	S	3:50.64	Graham Williamson	13 Jul 82	Cork, IRE
	W	3:54.29	Neil Horsfield	8 Jul 86	Cork, IRE
	NI	3:55.0	Jim McGuinness	11 Jul 77	Dublin (B), IRE
2000 m	E	4:51.39	Steve Cram	4 Aug 85	Budapest, HUN
	S	4:58.38	Graham Williamson	29 Aug 83	London (CP)
	NI	5:02.61	Steve Martin	19 Jun 84	Belfast
	W	5:05.32	Tony Simmons	4 Jul 75	London (CP)
3000 m	E	7:32.79	Dave Moorcroft	17 Jul 82	London (CP)
	S	7:45.81	John Robson	13 Jul 84	London (CP)
	·W	7:46.40	Ian Hamer	20 Jan 90	Auckland, NZ
	NI	7:49.1	Paul Lawther	27 Jun 78	Oslo, NOR

2 Miles	E	8:13.51	Steve Ovett	15 Sep 78	London (CP)
	S	8:19.37	Nat Muir	27 Jun 80	London (CP)
	W	8:20.28	David James	27 Jun 80	London (CP)
	NI	8:30.6	Paul Lawther	28 May 77	Belfast
5000 m	E	13:00.41	Dave Moorcroft	7 Jul 82	Oslo, NOR
	W	13:09.80	Ian Hamer	9 Jun 92	Rome, ITA
	S	13:17.9	Nat Muir	15 Jul 80	Oslo, NOR
	NI	13:39.11	Terry Greene	31 Jul 86	Edinburgh
10 km	E	27:23.06	Eamonn Martin	2 Jul 88	Oslo, NOR
	W	27:39.14	Steve Jones	9 Jul 83	Oslo, NOR
	S	27:43.03	Ian Stewart	9 Sep 77	London (CP)
	NI	28:40.03	John McLaughlin	29 May 83	Edinburgh
20 km	E	57:28.7	Carl Thackery	31 Mar 90	La Flèche, FRA
	S	59:24.0	Jim Alder	9 Nov 68	Leicester
1 Hour	E	20,855 m	Carl Thackery	31 Mar 90	La Flèche, FRA
	S	20,201 m	Jim Alder	9 Nov 68	Leicester
	W	18,587 m	Malcolm Edwards	15 Sep 89	Westhofen, GER
25 km	E	1:15:22.6	Ron Hill	21 Jul 65	Bolton
	S	1:15:34.3	Jim Alder	5 Sep 70	London (CP)
30 km	S	1:31:30.4	Jim Alder	5 Sep 70	London (CP)
	E	1:31:56.4	Tim Johnston	5 Sep 70	London (CP)
	W	1:33:49.0	Bernie Plain	1 Dec 73	Bristol
Half Marathon	E	60:09	Paul Evans	15 Jan 95	Marrakesh, MAR
	W	60:59	Steve Jones	8 Jun 86	Tyneside
	NI	62:16	Jim Haughey	20 Sep 87	Philadelphia, USA
	S	62:19 #	Mike Carroll	3 Jun 90	Irvine, USA
		62:28	Allister Hutton	21 Jun 87	Tyneside
Marathon	W	2:07:13	Steve Jones	20 Oct 85	Chicago, USA
	E	2:08:33	Charlie Spedding	21 Apr 85	London
	S	2:09:18	Allister Hutton	21 Apr 85	London
	NI	2:13:06	Greg Hannon	13 May 79	Coventry
2km St	E	5:19.86	Mark Rowland	28 Aug 88	London (CP)
	S	5:21.77	Tom Hanlon	11 Jun 92	Caserta, ITA
	W	5:23.6	Roger Hackney	10 Jun 82	Birmingham
	NI	5:31.09	Peter McColgan	5 Aug 86	Gateshead
3km St	E	8:07.96	Mark Rowland	30 Sep 88	Seoul, SKO
	S	8:12.58	Tom Hanlon	3 Aug 91	Monaco, MON
	W	8:18.91	Roger Hackney	31 Jul 88	Hechtel, BEL
	NI	8:27.93	Peter McColgan	25 Jun 91	Hengelo, HOL
110m H	W	12.91	Colin Jackson	20 Aug 93	Stuttgart, GER
	E	13.00	Tony Jarrett	20 Aug 93	Stuttgart, GER
	S	13.86	Kenneth Campbell	23 Aug 94	Victoria, CAN
	NI	14.19	C.J. Kirkpatrick	16 Jun 73	Edinburgh
200m H	W	22.63	Colin Jackson	1 Jun 91	Cardiff
	E	22.79	John Regis	1 Jun 91	Cardiff
	S	23.76	Angus McKenzie	22 Aug 81	Edinburgh
	NI	24.81	Terry Price	31 Aug 92	Belfast
400m H	E	47.82	Kriss Akabusi	6 Aug 92	Barcelona, SPA
	NI	49.60	Phil Beattie	28 Jul 86	Edinburgh
	W	50.01	Phil Harries	5 Jun 88	Derby
	S	50.79	Mark Davidson	18 Jun 89	Sittard, HOL

Event		Mark		Athlete	Date			Venue
High	E	2.38	i	Steve Smith	4	Feb	94	Wuppertal, GER
Jump		2.37		Steve Smith	20	Sep	92	Seoul, SKO
		2.37		Steve Smith	22	Aug	93	Stuttgart, GER
	S	2.31		Geoff Parsons	26	Aug	94	Victoria, CAN
	W	2.24		John Hill	23	Aug	85	Cottbus, GER
	NI	2.20		Floyd Manderson	14	Jul	85	London (CP)
		2.20		Floyd Manderson	21	Jun	86	London (CP)
		2.20		Floyd Manderson	16	Aug	86	Leiden, HOL
Pole	E	5.71		Nick Buckfield	16	Jun	96	Birmingham
Vault	W	5.60		Neil Winter	19	Aug	95	Enfield
	NI	5.25		Mike Bull	22	Sep	73	London (CP)
	S	5.21		Graham Eggleton	10	Jul	82	Grangemouth
Long	W	8.23		Lynn Davies	30	Jun	68	Berne, SWZ
Jump	E	8.15		Stewart Faulkner	16	Jul	90	Belfast
	NI	8.14		Mark Forsythe	7	Jul	91	Rhede, GER
	S	7.86		Darren Ritchie	15	Jun	96	Birmingham
Triple	E	18.29		Jonathan Edwards	7	Aug	95	Gothenburg, SWE
Jump	S	16.17		John Mackenzie	17	Sep	94	Bedford
	W	15.90		David Wood	16	Sep	84	Karlovac, CRO
	NI	15.78		Micky McDonald	31	Jul	94	Corby
Shot	E	21.68		Geoff Capes	18	May	80	Cwmbrân
	W	19.85		Paul Edwards ¶	2	Jul	89	Walton
	S	18.93		Paul Buxton	13	May	77	Los Angeles, USA
	NI	16.35		Michael Atkinson	18	Jul	81	Dublin (B), IRE
		16.35		John Reynolds	16	Aug	86	Leiden, HOL
Discus	E	65.16	#	Richard Slaney	1	Jul	85	Eugene, USA
		64.32		Bill Tancred	10	Aug	74	Woodford
	S	59.84	#	Colin Sutherland ¶	10	Jun	78	San Jose, USA
		58.58		Darrin Morris	22	Jun	91	Enfield
	W	57.12		Paul Edwards ¶	10	Aug	88	London (Col)
	NI	51.76		John Moreland	1	Jul	95	Antrim
Hammer	NI	77.54		Martin Girvan	12	May	84	Wolverhampton
	E	77.30		David Smith	13	Jul	85	London (CP)
	S	75.40		Chris Black	23	Jul	83	London (CP)
	W	68.64		Shaun Pickering	7	Apr	84	Stanford, USA
Javelin	E	91.46		Steve Backley	25	Jan	92	Auckland, NZ
	W	81.70		Nigel Bevan	28	Jun	92	Birmingham
	NI	70.34		Damien Crawford	20	Jul	91	Hayes
	S	69.20		Roddy James	28	Apr	89	Des Moines, USA
Decathlon	E	8847		Daley Thompson	9	Aug	84	Los Angeles, USA
	S	7885	h	Brad McStravick	6	May	84	Birmingham
		7856		Brad McStravick	28	May	84	Cwmbrân
	NI	7874		Colin Boreham	23	May	82	Götzis, AUT
	W	7308	h	Clive Longe	29	Jun	69	Kassel, GER
		7268		Paul Edwards	14	Aug	83	Bonn, GER
4x100m	E	37.98		D. Braithwaite, J. Regis, M. Adam, L. Christie (UK)	1	Sep	90	Split, CRO
	S	39.24		D. Jenkins, A. Wells, C. Sharp, A. McMaster	12	Aug	78	Edmonton, CAN
	W	40.0	ay	T. Davies, L. Davies, K. Jones, R. Jones	13	Aug	66	Kingston, JAM
	NI	40.71		J. McAdorey, I. Craig, P. Brizzell, M. Allen	22	Jun	96	Belfast

4x400m	E	2:57.53	R. Black, D. Redmond, J. Regis, K. Akabusi (UK)	1 Sep 91	Tokyo, JAP
	W	3:03.68	P. Maitland, J. Baulch, P.Gray, I.Thomas	27 Aug 94	Victoria, CAN
	S	3:04.68	M. Davison, T. McKean, D. Strang, B. Whittle	3 Feb 90	Auckland, NZ
	NI	3:11.81	??, ??, ??, ??	1 Sep 85	Tel Aviv, ISR

Track Walking

3000 m	E	11:24.4	Mark Easton	10 May 89	Tonbridge
	W	11:45.77	Steve Johnson	28 Jun 87	Cwmbrân
	S	11:53.3	Martin Bell	9 Aug 95	Birmingham
	NI	13:35.6	Arthur Agnew	18 Jun 77	Belfast
5000 m	E	19:22.29 i	Martin Rush	8 Feb 92	Birmingham
		19:35.0	Darrell Stone	16 May 89	Brighton
	W	20:08.04 i	Steve Barry	5 Mar 83	Budapest, HUN
		20:22.0	Steve Barry	20 Mar 82	London (WL)
	S	20:13.0	Martin Bell	2 May 92	Enfield
	NI	25:06.2	G. Smyth	13 Jul 80	London (He)
10 km	E	40:06.65	Ian McCombie	4 Jun 89	Jarrow
	W	41:13.62	Steve Barry	19 Jun 82	London (CP)
	S	41:13.65	Martin Bell	22 Jul 95	Cardiff
	NI	48:42.41	Stephen Murphy	31 Jul 83	Edinburgh
20 km	E	1:23:26.5	Ian McCombie	26 May 90	Fana, NOR
	W	1:26:22.0	Steve Barry	28 Jun 81	Brighton
	S	1:44:37.0	Derek Howie	19 Aug 78	Brighton
30 km	E	2:11:54 #	Chris Maddocks	31 Dec 89	Plymouth
		2:19:18	Chris Maddocks	22 Sep 84	Birmingham
50 km	E	4:05:44.6	Paul Blagg	26 May 90	Fana, NOR
1 Hour	E	14,324 m #	Ian McCombie	7 Jul 85	London (SP)
		14,158 m	Mark Easton	12 Sep 87	Woodford
	W	13,987 m	Steve Barry	28 Jun 81	Brighton
	S	13,393 m	Bill Sutherland	27 Sep 69	London (He)
2 Hours	E	27,262 m #	Chris Maddocks	31 Dec 89	Plymouth
		26,037 m	Ron Wallwork	31 Jul 71	Blackburn

Road Walking

10 km	E	40:17	Chris Maddocks	30 Apr 89	Burrator
	W	40:35	Steve Barry	14 May 83	Southport
	S	42:08	Martin Bell	4 Mar 89	Kenilworth
	NI	51:53	Arthur Agnew	6 Aug 80	Helsinki, FIN
		51:53	G. Smyth	6 Aug 80	Helsinki, FIN
20 km	E	1:22:03	Ian McCombie	23 Sep 88	Seoul, SKO
	W	1:22:51	Steve Barry	26 Feb 83	Douglas
	S	1:25:42	Martin Bell	9 May 92	Lancaster
	NI	1:47:49	Arthur Agnew	4 Nov 78	Ashbourne, IRE
30 km	E	2:07:56	Ian McCombie	27 Apr 86	Edinburgh
	W	2:10:16	Steve Barry	7 Oct 82	Brisbane, AUS
	S	2:22:21	Martin Bell	8 May 94	Cardiff
50 km	E	3:51:37	Chris Maddocks	28 Oct 90	Burrator
	W	4:11:59	Bob Dobson	22 Oct 81	Lassing, AUT
	S	4:14:59	Graham White	5 Mar 95	Burrator

NATIONAL RECORDS OF THE UNITED KINGDOM (WOMEN)

100 m	E	11.10	Kathy Smallwood/Cook	5 Sep 81	Rome, ITA
	W	11.39	Sallyanne Short	12 Jul 92	Cwmbrân
	S	11.40	Helen Golden/Hogarth	20 Jul 74	London (CP)
	NI	11.91	Joan Atkinson	1 Sep 61	Sofia, BUL
200 m	E	22.10	Kathy Cook	9 Aug 84	Los Angeles, USA
	W	22.80	Michelle Scutt	12 Jun 82	Antrim
	S	22.98	Sandra Whittaker	8 Aug 84	Los Angeles, USA
	NI	23.62	Linda McCurry	8 Aug 78	Edmonton, CAN
300 m	E	35.46	Kathy Cook	18 Aug 84	London (CP)
	W	36.01	Michelle Probert/Scutt	13 Jul 80	London (CP)
	S	36.46	Linsey Macdonald	13 Jul 80	London (CP)
	NI	38.20	Linda McCurry	2 Aug 78	Edmonton, CAN
400 m	E	49.43	Kathy Cook	6 Aug 84	Los Angeles, USA
	W	50.63	Michelle Scutt	31 May 82	Cwmbrân
	S	51.16	Linsey Macdonald	15 Jun 80	London (CP)
	NI	52.4	Stephanie Llewellyn	1 Jul 95	London (He)
		52.54	Stephanie Llewellyn	9 Jul 95	Cwmbrân
600 m	E	1:26.18	Diane Edwards/Modahl	22 Aug 87	London (CP)
	W	1:26.5	Kirsty McDermott/Wade	21 Aug 85	Zürich, SWZ
	S	1:27.4 i	Linsey Macdonald	12 Dec 81	Cosford
		1:29.88	Anne Clarkson/Purvis	25 Sep 82	Brisbane, AUS
	NI	1:29.46	Joanna Latimer	19 May 93	Birmingham
800 m	E	1:56.21	Kelly Holmes	9 Sep 95	Monaco, MON
	W	1:57.42	Kirsty McDermott/Wade	24 Jun 85	Belfast
	S	2:00.15	Rosemary Stirling/Wright	3 Sep 72	Munich, GER
	NI	2:03.27	Joanna Latimer	29 Jun 94	Helsinki, FIN
1000 m	E	2:32.82	Kelly Holmes	23 Jul 95	Sheffield
	W	2:33.70	Kirsty McDermott/Wade	9 Aug 85	Gateshead
	S	2:37.05	Chris Whittingham	27 Jun 86	Gateshead
	NI	2:48.59	Jane Ewing	26 Jun 90	Antrim
1500 m	E	3:59.96	Zola Budd	30 Aug 85	Brussels, BEL
	W	4:00.73	Kirsty Wade	26 Jul 87	Gateshead
	S	4:01.20	Yvonne Murray	4 Jul 87	Oslo, NOR
	NI	4:11.46	Ursula McKee/McGloin	20 Jan 90	Auckland, NZ
1 Mile	E	4:17.57	Zola Budd	21 Aug 85	Zürich, SWZ
	W	4:19.41	Kirsty McDermott/Wade	27 Jul 85	Oslo, NOR
	S	4:22.64	Yvonne Murray	22 Jul 94	Oslo, NOR
	NI	4:38.86	Ursula McKee/McGloin	7 Jan 90	Sydney, AUS
2000 m	S	5:26.93	Yvonne Murray	8 Jul 94	Edinburgh
	E	5:30.19	Zola Budd	11 Jul 86	London (CP)
	W	5:45.81 i	Kirsty Wade	13 Mar 87	Cosford
		5:50.17	Susan Tooby/Wightman	13 Jul 84	London (CP)
	NI	5:57.24	Ursula McKee/McGloin	25 Jun 90	Antrim
3000 m	E	8:28.83	Zola Budd	7 Sep 85	Rome, ITA
	S	8:29.02	Yvonne Murray	25 Sep 88	Seoul, SKO
	W	8:47.59	Angela Tooby	5 Jul 88	Stockholm, SWE
	NI	9:16.25	Ursula McKee/McGloin	7 Jun 90	Helsinki, FIN
5000 m	E	14:46.76	Paula Radcliffe	16 Aug 96	Cologne, GER
	S	14:56.94	Yvonne Murray	7 Jul 95	London (CP)
	W	15:13.22	Angela Tooby	5 Aug 87	Oslo, NOR
	NI	17:27.15	Angela McCullagh		

10 km	S	30:57.07	Liz McColgan	25 Jun 91	Hengelo, HOL
	E	31:07.88	Jill Hunter	30 Jun 91	Frankfurt, GER
	W	31:55.30	Angela Tooby	4 Sep 87	Rome, ITA
	NI	41:16.4	Wendy Dyer	Jun 89	Antrim
Half	S	1:07:11	Liz McColgan	26 Jan 92	Tokyo, JAP
Marathon	E	1:09:39	Andrea Wallace	21 Mar 93	Bath
	W	1:09:56	Susan Tooby/Wightman	24 Jul 88	Tyneside
	NI	1:15:57 #	Moira O'Boyle/O'Neill	23 Mar 86	Cavan, IRE
		1:16:23	Moira O'Neill	24 Sep 88	Londonderry
Marathon	E	2:25:56	Véronique Marot	23 Apr 89	London
	S	2:27:32	Liz McColgan	3 Nov 91	New York, USA
	W	2:31:33	Susan Tooby/Wightman	23 Sep 88	Seoul, SKO
	NI	2:37:06	Moira O'Neill	31 Oct 88	Dublin, IRE
100m H	E	12.80	Angie Thorp	31 Jul 96	Atlanta, USA
	W	12.91	Kay Morley-Brown	2 Feb 90	Auckland, NZ
	NI	13.29	Mary Peters	2 Sep 72	Munich, GER
	S	13.35	Pat Rollo	30 Jul 83	London (CP)
400m H	E	52.74	Sally Gunnell	19 Aug 93	Stuttgart, GER
	NI	55.91	Elaine McLaughlin	26 Sep 88	Seoul, SKO
	S	57.43	Liz Sutherland	6 Jul 78	Düsseldorf, GER
	W	56.43	Alyson Layzell	16 Jun 96	Birmingham
High	E	1.95	Diana Elliott/Davies	26 Jun 82	Oslo, NOR
Jump	NI	1.92	Janet Boyle	29 Sep 88	Seoul, SKO
	S	1.91	Jayne Barnetson	7 Jul 89	Edinburgh
	W	1.84	Sarah Rowe	22 Aug 81	Utrecht, HOL
		1.84	Sarah Rowe	31 May 82	Cwmbrân
Pole	E	4.00	Janine Whitlock	14 Sep 96	Telford
Vault	W	3.70	Rhian Clarke	10 Aug 96	London (He)
		3.70	Rhian Clarke	26 Aug 96	Peterborough
	S	3.60 ?	Alison Murray/Jessee	1 Jun 96	Las Cruces, USA
Long	E	6.90	Beverly Kinch	14 Aug 83	Helsinki, FIN
Jump	W	6.52	Gillian Regan	29 Aug 82	Swansea
	S	6.43	Myra Nimmo/McAskill	27 May 73	Edinburgh
	NI	6.11	Thelma Hopkins	29 Sep 56	Budapest, HUN
		6.11	Michelle Rea	11 Aug 90	Oporto, POR
Triple	E	14.78	Ashia Hansen	25 Aug 96	Sheffield
Jump	S	12.89	Karen Hambrook/Skeggs	17 May 92	London (CP)
	W	12.40	Katie Evans	20 Jul 96	Birmingham
	NI	11.79	Michelle Rea	16 Jun 91	Grangemouth
Shot	E	19.36	Judy Oakes	14 Aug 88	Gateshead
	S	18.99	Meg Ritchie	7 May 83	Tucson, USA
	W	19.06 i	Venissa Head	7 Apr 84	St. Athan
		18.93	Venissa Head	13 May 84	Haverfordwest
	NI	16.40 i	Mary Peters	28 Feb 70	Bucharest, ROM
		16.31	Mary Peters	1 Jun 66	Belfast
Discus	S	67.48	Meg Ritchie	26 Apr 81	Walnut, USA
	W	64.68	Venissa Head	18 Jul 83	Athens, GRE
	NI	60.72	Jacqui McKernan	18 Jul 93	Buffalo, USA
	E	58.56	Debbie Callaway	19 May 96	Loughborough
Hammer	E	64.90	Lorraine Shaw	10 Jun 95	Bedford
	W	53.26	Sarah Moore	25 May 96	Cardiff
	S	50.12	Jean Clark	28 Aug 95	Welwyn Garden City
	NI	48.90	Julie Kirkpatrick	15 Jun 96	Dublin

Javelin	E	77.44	Fatima Whitbread	28 Aug 86	Stuttgart, GER
	S	62.22	Diane Royle	18 May 85	Stretford
	W	59.40	Karen Hough	28 Aug 86	Stuttgart, GER
	NI	49.10	Alison Moffitt	16 Jun 96	Dublin
Hept.	E	6645	Denise Lewis	26 May 96	Götzis, AUT
	S	5803	Jayne Barnetson	20 Aug 89	Kiyev, UKR
	W	5642	Sarah Rowe	23 Aug 81	Utrecht, HOL
	NI	5065 h	Catherine Scott	13 Sep 87	Tullamore, IRE
		4564	Wendy Phillips	18 Jul 82	Birmingham

4x100m	E	42.43	H. Oakes, K. Cook, (UK)		
			B. Callender, S. Lannaman	1 Aug 80	Moscow, RUS
	S	45.2	A. Robb, S. Pringle, (ESH)		
			H. Hogarth, E. Sutherland	27 Jun 70	London (CP)
		45.37	J. Booth, K. Hogg,		
			J. Neilson, S. Whittaker	8 Jun 86	Lloret de Mar, SPA
	W	45.37	H. Miles, S. Lewis,		
			S. Short, C. Smart	2 Aug 86	Edinburgh
	NI	46.36	K. Graham, H. Gourlay,		
			J. Robinson, R. Gaylor	31 Aug 85	Tel Aviv, ISR
4x400m	E	3:22.01	L. Hanson, P. Smith, (UK)		
			S. Gunnell, L. Keough	1 Sep 91	Tokyo, JAP
	S	3:32.92	S. Whittaker, A. Purvis,		
			A. Baxter, L. Macdonald	9 Oct 82	Brisbane, AUS
	W	3:35.60	C. Smart, K. Wade,		
			D. Fryar, M. Scutt	4 Jul 82	Dublin (M), IRE
	NI	3:40.12	Z. Arnold, V. Jamison,		
			J. Latimer, S. Llewellyn	22 Jun 96	Belfast

Track Walking

3000 m	E	12:49.16	Betty Sworowski	28 Jul 90	Wrexham
	S	13:16.23	Verity Snook	27 May 96	Bedford
	W	14:28.2	Karen Dunster	18 May 91	Portsmouth
5000 m	E	21:52.38 *	Vicky Lupton	9 Aug 95	Sheffield
	S	23:22.52	Verity Larby/Snook	18 Jun 94	Horsham
	W	24:32.92	Karen Nipper	21 Jul 84	Lyngby, DEN
10 km	E	45:18.8	Vicky Lupton	2 Sep 95	Watford
	S	47:10.07	Verity Larby/Snook	20 Jun 93	Horsham
	W	50:25.0	Lisa Simpson	1 Apr 87	Hornchurch
1 Hour	E	11,590 m	Lisa Langford	13 Sep 86	Woodford

Road Walking

5 km	E	21:36	Vicky Lupton	18 Jul 92	Sheffield
	W	23:35	Lisa Simpson	31 Oct 87	Cardiff
	S	23:36	Verity Snook	3 Feb 96	London (CP)
10 km	E	45:18.8 t	Vicky Lupton	2 Sep 95	Watford
	S	46:06	Verity Larby/Snook	25 Aug 94	Victoria, CAN
	W	49:33	Lisa Simpson	14 Mar 87	Ham
20 km	E	1:40:45	Irene Bateman	9 Apr 83	Basildon
50 km	E	4:50:51	Sandra Brown	13 Jul 91	Basildon

BRITISH INDOOR RECORDS
as at March 1997

MEN

Event	Time/Mark	Athlete	Date	Venue
50 m	5.76	Selwyn Clarke	19 Feb 83	Dortmund, GER
60 m	6.47	Linford Christie	19 Feb 95	Lieven, FRA
200 m	20.25	Linford Christie	19 Feb 95	Lieven, FRA
300 m	32.90	Ade Mafe	31 Jan 92	Karlsruhe, GER
400 m	45.39	Jamie Baulch	8 Feb 97	Birmingham
800 m	1:44.91	Sebastian Coe	12 Mar 83	Cosford
1000 m	2:17.86	Matthew Yates	22 Feb 92	Birmingham
1500 m	3:34.20	Peter Elliott	27 Feb 90	Seville, SPA
1 mile	3:52.02	Peter Elliott	9 Feb 90	East Rutherford, USA
2000 m	5:05.20	John Gladwin	15 Mar 87	Cosford
3000 m	7:43.31	John Mayock	23 Feb 97	Birmingham
5000 m	13:21.27	Nick Rose	12 Feb 82	New York, USA
50 m Hurdles	6.48	Colin Jackson	14 Mar 92	Birmingham
60 m Hurdles	7.30	Colin Jackson	6 Mar 94	Sindelfingen, GER
High Jump	2.38	Steve Smith	4 Feb 94	Wuppertal, GER
Pole Vault	5.61	Nick Buckfield	4 Feb 96	Birmingham
Long Jump	8.05	Barrington Williams	11 Feb 89	Cosford
	8.05 #	Stewart Faulkner	27 Feb 90	Seville, SPA
Triple Jump	17.31	Keith Connor	13 Mar 81	Detroit, USA
Shot	20.98	Geoff Capes	16 Jan 76	Los Angeles, USA
	20.98 #	Geoff Capes	14 Feb 76	Winnipeg, CAN
Heptathlon	5978	Alex Kruger	12 Mar 95	Barcelona, SPA

(7.16, 7.23, 14.79, 2.16, 8.36, 4.90, 2:48.66)

5000m Walk	19:22.29	Martin Rush	8 Feb 92	Birmingham
4 x 200m Relay	1:22.11	UK National Team	3 Mar 91	Glasgow

(Linford Christie, Darren Braithwaite, Ade Mafe, John Regis)

4 x 400m Relay	3:07.04	England	13 Mar 87	Cosford

(Kermit Bentham, John Regis, Steve Heard, Paul Harmsworth)

WOMEN

Event	Time/Mark	Athlete	Date	Venue
50 m	6.21	Wendy Hoyte	22 Feb 81	Grenoble, FRA
60 m	7.13	Beverly Kinch	23 Feb 86	Madrid, SPA
200 m	22.96	Donna Fraser	23 Feb 97	Birmingham
400 m	51.69	Phylis Smith	23 Feb 97	Birmingham
800 m	2:01.12	Jane Colebrook/Finch	13 Mar 77	San Sebastian, SPA
1000 m	2:38.95	Kirsty Wade	1 Feb 87	Stuttgart, GER
1500 m	4:06.87	Zola Budd	25 Jan 86	Cosford
1 mile	4:23.86	Kirsty Wade	5 Feb 88	New York, USA
2000 m	5:40.86	Yvonne Murray	20 Feb 93	Birmingham
3000 m	8:34.80	Liz McColgan	4 Mar 89	Budapest, HUN
5000 m	15:03.17	Liz McColgan	22 Feb 92	Birmingham
50 m Hurdles	7.03	Yvette Wray/Luker	21 Feb 81	Grenoble, FRA
60 m Hurdles	8.01	Jacqui Agyepong	12 Mar 95	Barcelona, SPA
High Jump	1.95	Debbie Marti	23 Feb 97	Birmingham
Pole Vault	3.90	Janine Whitlock	23 Feb 97	Birmingham
	3.90	Rhian Clarke	8 Mar 97	Paris, FRA
Long Jump	6.70	Susan Hearnshaw/Telfer	3 Mar 84	Göteborg, SWE
	6.70	Jo Wise	9 Mar 97	Paris, FRA
Triple Jump	14.70	Ashia Hansen	8 Mar 97	Paris, FRA
Shot	19.06	Venissa Head	7 Apr 84	St. Athan
Pentathlon	4363	Kim Hagger	4 Feb 84	Vittel, FRA

(8.44, 1.82, 11.89, 6.31, 2:27.08)

3000m Walk	13:12.01	Julie Drake	12 Mar 93	Toronto, CAN
4 x 200m Relay	1:33.96	UK National Team	23 Feb 90	Glasgow

(Paula Dunn, Jennifer Stoute, Linda Keough, Sally Gunnell)

4 x 400m Relay	3:32.25	UK National Team	9 Mar 97	Paris, FRA

(Phylis Smith, Sally Gunnell, Michelle Thomas, Donna Fraser)

two oN/

UK ALL TIME LISTS - MEN
as at 31 December 1996

100 METRES

9.87	Linford Christie	15 Aug 93	
10.09	Jason Livingston ¶	13 Jun 92	
10.11	Allan Wells	24 Jul 80	
10.12	Darren Braithwaite	15 Jul 95	
10.15	Michael Rosswess	15 Sep 91	
10.15	John Regis	29 May 93	
10.17	Darren Campbell	29 May 96	
10.17	Ian Mackie	25 Aug 96	
10.20	Cameron Sharp	24 Aug 83	
10.20	Elliot Bunney	14 Jun 86	10
10.21 A	Ainsley Bennett	8 Sep 79	
10.21	Jamie Henderson	6 Aug 87	
10.22	Mike McFarlane	20 Jun 86	
10.23	Marcus Adam	26 Jul 91	
10.23	Jason John	15 Jul 94	
10.23	Terry Williams	22 Aug 94	
10.25	Jason Gardener	21 Jul 94	
10.26	Daley Thompson	27 Aug 86	
10.26	Ernest Obeng	1 Aug 87	
	10.21 for Ghana	11 Aug 80	
10.29	Peter Radford (10.31?)	13 Sep 58	20
10.29	Colin Jackson	28 Jul 90	
10.30	Clarence Callender	26 Jul 91	
10.30	Julian Golding	28 Jun 95	
10.32	Buster Watson	1 Jul 83	
10.32	Donovan Reid	4 Aug 84	
10.32	Lincoln Asquith	11 Aug 86	
10.32	Lenny Paul	29 May 93	
10.32	Toby Box	28 Jun 95	
10.33	Brian Green	15 Jul 72	
10.33	Solomon Wariso	19 Jun 94	30
10.34	Drew McMaster	9 Jul 83	
10.34	Barrington Williams	5 Aug 88	
10.35 A	Barrie Kelly	13 Oct 68	
10.35	Brian Taylor	29 May 93	
10.35	Kevin Williams	26 May 96	
10.35	Owusu Dako	8 Jul 96	
10.36	David Jenkins	24 Jun 72	
10.36	Allyn Condon	15 Jun 96	
10.37	Micky Morris	23 Aug 87	
10.37	Steve Gookey	20 Jul 91	40
10.38	Adrian Patrick	11 Aug 96	
10.39	Ray Burke	13 Jun 92	
10.40	Trevor Hoyte	11 Aug 79	
10.40	Jim Evans	24 Jul 82	
10.40	Paul White	31 Aug 95	

hand timing

10.1	David Jenkins	20 May 72
10.1	Brian Green	3 Jun 72
10.1	Ernest Obeng (for GHA)	2 Aug 79
10.2	McDonald Bailey	25 Aug 51
10.2	Menzies Campbell	20 May 67
10.2	Drew McMaster	29 Jun 80
10.2	Ed Cutting	19 May 84
10.2	Derek Redmond	2 May 87

wind assisted

10.02	Allan Wells	4 Oct 82	
10.07	Cameron Sharp	4 Oct 82	
10.07	John Regis	28 Aug 90	
10.07	Toby Box	11 Jun 94	
10.07	Michael Rosswess	11 Jun 94	
10.08	Mike McFarlane	27 May 84	
10.08	Jason John	11 Jun 94	
10.10	Donovan Reid	26 Jun 83	
10.11	Drew McMaster	26 Jun 83	
10.12	Buster Watson	27 May 84	10
10.14	Ernest Obeng	20 Jun 87	
10.14	Marcus Adam	28 Jan 90	
10.17	Terry Williams	23 Aug 94	
10.20	Lincoln Asquith	6 Jul 85	
10.25	Lenny Paul	14 Jul 91	
10.26	Peter Little	21 May 80	
10.26	Doug Turner	13 Jul 96	
10.27	Barrington Williams	2 Jul 88	
10.27	Clarence Callender	22 Jun 91	
10.29	Trevor Cameron	11 Jun 94	20
10.30	Owusu Dako	1 Jun 96	
10.31	Jim Evans	22 Aug 81	
10.32	Brian Green	16 Jun 72	
10.32	Harry King	22 Aug 81	
10.33	Steve Gookey	20 Jul 91	
10.33	Danny Joyce	10 Jun 95	
10.33	Allyn Condon	13 Apr 96	
10.34	Phil Davies	13 Jul 86	
10.34	Jason Fergus	5 Jun 94	
10.35	Nigel Walker	26 Aug 89	30
10.36	Les Piggot	15 Jul 72	
10.37	Earl Tulloch	22 Aug 81	
10.37	Courtney Rumbolt	25 Jun 88	
10.38	Don Halliday	17 Jul 70	
10.38	Ian Green	17 Jul 70	
10.38	Kevin Mark	3 Jul 93	
10.38	Ejike Wodu	3 Jul 93	
10.38	Jamie Henthorn	25 May 96	
10.39	Trevor McKenzie	21 Jul 84	
10.39	David Kirton	4 Jun 87	40
10.39	Dave Clark	3 Jun 90	
10.39	Andrew Mensah	15 Jun 94	

hand timing - wind assisted

10.0	Allan Wells	16 Jun 79
10.0	Drew McMaster	1 Jun 80
10.1	David Roberts	17 Jul 82
10.2	Ian Green	20 May 70
10.2	Les Piggot	19 Aug 72
10.2	Eugene Gilkes	7 Jul 84
10.2	Andy Carrott	5 Jul 88
10.2	Dave Clark	25 Jun 89

200 METRES (* 220 yards time less 0.12)

19.87 A	John Regis	31 Jul 94
19.94		20 Aug 93
20.09	Linford Christie	28 Sep 88
20.21	Allan Wells	28 Jul 80
20.36	Todd Bennett	28 May 84
20.41	Marcus Adam	13 Jun 92
20.42 A	Ainsley Bennett	12 Sep 79
20.84		31 Aug 80
20.43	Mike McFarlane	7 Oct 82
20.43	Doug Turner	9 Jun 96
20.47	Cameron Sharp	9 Sep 82
20.47	Darren Braithwaite	13 May 95
20.50	Terry Williams	24 Aug 94
20.50	Tony Jarrett	16 Jul 95
20.50	Solomon Wariso	16 Jul 95
20.51	Michael Rosswess	28 Sep 88
20.54	Ade Mafe	25 Aug 85
20.56	Roger Black	4 May 96
20.57	Owusu Dako	16 Jul 95
20.62	Buster Watson	5 Jun 83
20.62	Donovan Reid	28 May 84
20.66 A	Dick Steane	15 Oct 68
20.66	David Jenkins	27 Aug 73
20.67	Doug Walker	29 Jun 96
20.70	Chris Monk	20 Aug 73
20.72	Toby Box	24 Aug 94
20.73 A	Ralph Banthorpe	15 Oct 68
20.75	Dave Clark	20 Jan 90
20.75	Julian Golding	7 Jul 95
20.76	Andy Carrott	5 Jul 88
20.76	Clarence Callender	24 Jun 91
20.77	Drew McMaster	9 Jul 83
20.79	Phil Goedluck	6 Aug 94
20.79	Paul White	27 May 96
20.81	Mike St. Louis	21 Jun 86
20.81	Paul McBurney	24 Aug 94
20.83	Martin Reynolds	22 Jul 70
20.83	Claude Moseley	23 Aug 81
20.84	Brian Green	4 Sep 71
20.84	Earl Tulloch	25 May 81
20.84	Jamie Baulch	24 Aug 94
20.84	Allyn Condon	15 Jun 96
20.85	Richard Ashby	25 Aug 85
20.85	Mark Richardson	4 May 96
20.86	Lincoln Asquith	28 Aug 83
20.86	Roger Hunter	5 May 84
20.86	Gus McCuaig	28 May 84
20.86	Darren Campbell	4 Aug 93
20.86	Jason John	1 Jul 95
20.86	Marlon Devonish	7 Sep 96
20.87	Mark Smith	28 Jul 90
20.88	Daley Thompson	18 Aug 79
20.88	Phil Brown	28 May 84
20.89	Mark Forsythe	12 Aug 90
20.90 *	Menzies Campbell	23 Jun 67
20.90	Glen Cohen	14 Aug 76
20.90	Mark Allen	27 May 96
20.91	Trevor Hoyte	11 Jul 80
20.91	Nigel Will	27 Aug 89
20.91	Ian Mackie	23 Jul 94

wind assisted (* 220 yards time less 0.12)

20.10	Marcus Adam	1 Feb 90
20.11	Allan Wells	20 Jun 80
20.26	Ade Mafe	1 Feb 90
20.48	Michael Rosswess	9 Sep 90
20.51	Jason John	2 Jul 93
20.53	Doug Walker	8 May 95
20.55	Buster Watson	10 Aug 85
20.55	Darren Campbell	2 Jul 93
20.61	Martin Reynolds	22 Jul 70
20.62	Adrian Patrick	10 Jun 95
20.64	Drew McMaster	23 Aug 80
20.64	Allyn Condon	6 Jul 96
20.69	Julian Golding	2 Jul 95
20.70 *	David Jones	20 May 61
20.70	Trevor Hoyte	14 Sep 79
20.73	Phil Goedluck	23 Apr 95
20.84	Nigel Stickings	9 Jul 93
20.85	Phil Brown	28 May 84
20.85	Mark Smith	1 Jul 90
20.88	Trevor Cameron	12 Jun 94
20.89	Tim Bonsor	10 Aug 78
20.89	David Grindley	13 Jun 93
20.91	Peter Little	21 May 80

hand timing (* 220 yards time less 0.1)

20.3	David Jenkins	19 Aug 72
20.4 *	Peter Radford	28 May 60
20.6	Donovan Reid	1 Jul 84
20.7 *	Menzies Campbell	10 Jun 67
20.7	Martin Reynolds	2 Aug 70
20.7	Brian Green	3 Jun 72
20.7	Drew McMaster	16 Aug 80
20.7	Claude Moseley	28 Aug 81
20.7	Julian Golding	13 May 95

wind assisted

20.4	Buster Watson	11 Aug 85
20.5	Roger Black	6 Jul 96
20.6	Ainsley Bennett	22 Jun 74
20.6	Mark Richardson	6 Jul 96

300 METRES

31.67	John Regis	17 Jul 92
32.08	Roger Black	8 Aug 86
32.14	Todd Bennett	18 Aug 84
32.14	Mark Richardson	11 Aug 96
32.25	Jamie Baulch	11 Aug 96
32.32	Derek Redmond	16 Jul 88
32.44	David Jenkins	4 Jul 75
32.45	David Grindley	19 Jun 93
32.52	Iwan Thomas	11 Aug 96
32.59	Kriss Akabusi	14 Jul 91
32.61	Brian Whittle	16 Jul 88
32.73	Du'aine Ladejo	4 Sep 94
32.73	Paul Slythe	12 Jul 96
32.73	Guy Bullock	12 Jul 96
32.75	Ade Mafe	16 Jul 88
32.76	Mark Hylton	11 Aug 96

during 400m

32.06 +	Roger Black	29 Aug 91
32.26 +	Derek Redmond	1 Sep 87
32.35 +	David Grindley	26 Jun 93

32

400 METRES

	44.37	Roger Black	3 Jul 96
	44.47	David Grindley	3 Aug 92
	44.50	Derek Redmond	1 Sep 87
	44.52	Mark Richardson	3 Jul 96
	44.57	Jamie Baulch	3 Jul 96
	44.66 A	Iwan Thomas	14 Apr 96
	44.69		16 Jun 96
	44.66	Du'aine Ladejo	16 Jun 96
	44.93	David Jenkins	21 Jun 75
	44.93	Kriss Akabusi	7 Aug 88
10	45.22	Brian Whittle	25 Sep 88
	45.26	Phil Brown	26 May 85
	45.27	Todd Bennett	7 Aug 88
	45.30	Ade Mafe	23 Jul 93
	45.33	Paul Sanders	15 Jun 91
	45.47	David McKenzie	12 Jun 94
	45.48	John Regis	17 Apr 93
	45.49	Glen Cohen	21 May 78
	45.57	Mark Hylton	16 Jun 96
	45.63	Adrian Patrick	5 Jul 95
20	45.64	Paul Harmsworth	7 Aug 88
	45.65	Alan Bell	14 Jun 80
	45.67	Roger Hunter	19 May 85
	45.74	Steve Heard	26 May 85
	45.75	Robbie Brightwell	19 Oct 64
	45.76	Guy Bullock	16 Jun 96
	45.81	Terry Whitehead	14 Jun 80
	45.88	Wayne McDonald	17 Aug 91
	45.91 A	Martin Winbolt-Lewis	17 Oct 68
	45.92	Mark Thomas	27 Jun 87
30	45.97	Steve Scutt	14 Sep 79
	46.02	Jared Deacon	31 Aug 96
	46.03	Peter Crampton	8 Aug 87
	46.04	Alan Slack	27 Jun 85
	46.08	Tim Graham	19 Oct 64
	46.08	Rod Milne	15 Jun 80
	46.10	Peter Gabbett	7 Sep 72
	46.11	Martin Reynolds	4 Sep 72
	46.15	Ainsley Bennett	29 Aug 75
	46.16	Gary Armstrong	15 Jul 72
40	46.16	Claude Moseley	1 Jul 83
	46.18	Garry Cook	14 Jun 80
	46.19	Roy Dickens	28 May 84
	46.20	David Nolan	9 Jun 96
	46.24	Mel Fowell	15 Jun 80
	46.27	Richard Ashton	6 Aug 78
	46.31	Neil Jackson	14 Jun 80
	46.31	Kent Ulyatt	10 Sep 95
	46.34	Tim O'Dell	19 Aug 95
	46.34	Nick Budden	15 Jun 96
50	46.35 A	Colin Campbell	17 Oct 68
	46.37	Gary Cadogan	27 Jun 87
	46.39	Danny Laing	25 Sep 78
	46.39	Alex Fugallo	12 Jun 94

hand timing (* 440 yards time less 0.3)

45.6 *	Robbie Brightwell	14 Jul 62
45.7	Adrian Metcalfe	2 Sep 61
45.9	Colin Campbell	2 Jul 68
46.0	Garry Cook	20 May 81

600 METRES

1:14.95	Steve Heard	14 Jul 91
1:15.0 +	Sebastian Coe	10 Jun 81
1:15.4	Garry Cook	30 Jul 84
1:15.4	Tom McKean	21 Jul 91
1:15.6	David Jenkins	3 Aug 74
1:15.94	Brian Whittle	28 Jul 92

800 METRES (* 880 yards time less 0.70)

1:41.73"	Sebastian Coe	10 Jun 81	
1:42.88	Steve Cram	21 Aug 85	
1:42.97	Peter Elliott	30 May 90	
1:43.84	Martin Steele	10 Jul 93	
1:43.88	Tom McKean	28 Jul 89	
1:43.98	David Sharpe	19 Aug 92	
1:44.09	Steve Ovett	31 Aug 78	
1:44.55	Garry Cook	29 Aug 84	
1:44.59	Tony Morrell	2 Jul 88	
1:44.65	Ikem Billy	21 Jul 84	10
1:44.65	Steve Heard	26 Aug 92	
1:44.92	Curtis Robb	15 Aug 93	
1:45.05	Matthew Yates	26 Aug 92	
1:45.12	Andy Carter	14 Jul 73	
1:45.14	Chris McGeorge	28 Jun 83	
1:45.14	John Gladwin	22 Jul 86	
1:45.31	Robert Harrison	21 Jul 84	
1:45.35	Kevin McKay	16 Aug 92	
1:45.44	Neil Horsfield	28 Jul 90	
1:45.47	Brian Whittle	20 Jul 90	20
1:45.6	Graham Williamson	12 Jun 83	
1:45.64	Paul Herbert	5 Jun 88	
1:45.66	Paul Forbes	8 Jun 83	
1:45.69	Steve Crabb	17 Aug 88	
1:45.69	Craig Winrow	21 Jun 96	
1:45.76	Frank Clement	10 Jul 76	
1:45.81	David Strang	12 Jul 96	
1:46.10	Gary Marlow	10 Jul 87	
1:46.1	Colin Campbell	26 Jul 72	
1:46.16	Gareth Brown	2 Jul 84	30
1:46.20	David Warren	29 Jun 80	
1:46.21	Peter Browne	14 Jul 73	
1:46.26	Phil Lewis	27 Jan 74	
1:46.3 a	Chris Carter	4 Sep 66	
1:46.37	Andrew Lill	28 Jun 92	
1:46.51	John Boulter	18 Jun 66	
1:46.57	Andy Hart	12 Jul 96	
1:46.6	Derek Johnson	9 Aug 57	
1:46.63	Peter Hoffman	11 Jun 78	
1:46.64	David Moorcroft	25 Jul 82	40
1:46.65	Steve Caldwell	31 May 82	
1:46.70 *	John Davies I	3 Jun 68	
1:46.70	Atle Douglas	9 Jun 88	
1:46.72	Mal Edwards	13 Sep 87	
1:46.8	Bob Adams	9 Aug 69	
1:46.8	Dave Cropper	1 Jul 73	
1:46.8	David McMeekin	6 Jun 74	
1:46.92	Colin Szwed	7 Aug 82	
1:46.94	Mark Kirk	20 Jul 87	
1:47.0	Brian Hewson	13 Sep 58	50
1:47.0	Mike Rawson	13 Sep 58	

1000 METRES

2:12.18	Sebastian Coe	11 Jul 81
2:12.88	Steve Cram	9 Aug 85
2:15.91	Steve Ovett	6 Sep 79
2:16.30	Peter Elliott	17 Jan 90
2:16.34	Matthew Yates	6 Jul 90
2:16.82	Graham Williamson	17 Jul 84
2:16.99	Tony Morrell	28 Aug 88
2:17.14	John Gladwin	6 Jul 90
2:17.20	Robert Harrison	18 Aug 84
10 2:17.36	Neil Horsfield	9 Aug 91
2:17.43	Gareth Brown	18 Aug 84
2:17.45	Chris McGeorge	20 Aug 84
2:17.63	Kevin McKay	14 Jul 89
2:17.75	Steve Crabb	5 Aug 87

1500 METRES (+ during 1 mile)

3:29.67	Steve Cram	16 Jul 85
3:29.77	Sebastian Coe	7 Sep 86
3:30.77	Steve Ovett	4 Sep 83
3:32.69	Peter Elliott	16 Sep 90
3:33.34	Steve Crabb	4 Jul 87
3:33.38	John Mayock	1 Sep 96
3:33.79	Dave Moorcroft	27 Jul 82
3:33.83	John Robson	4 Sep 79
3:34.00	Matthew Yates	13 Sep 91
10 3:34.01	Graham Williamson	28 Jun 83
3:34.1 +	Tony Morrell	14 Jul 90
3:34.47	Anthony Whiteman	28 Jun 96
3:34.50	Adrian Passey	4 Jul 87
3:34.53	Mark Rowland	27 Jul 88
3:34.76	Gary Lough	9 Sep 95
3:35.08	Neil Horsfield	10 Aug 90
3:35.26	John Gladwin	5 Sep 86
3:35.28	Jack Buckner	1 Jul 86
3:35.66	Frank Clement	12 Aug 78
20 3:35.74	Rob Harrison	26 May 86
3:35.94	Paul Larkins	10 Jul 87
3:35.94	Kevin McKay	19 Jun 92
3:36.53	David Strang	15 Jul 94
3:36.81	Mike Kearns	26 Jul 77
3:37.55	Colin Reitz	27 Jun 85
3:37.64	Brendan Foster	2 Feb 74
3:37.88	Jason Dullforce	17 Jul 92
3:37.97	Rod Finch	30 Jul 93
3:37.99	Rob Denmark	5 Jun 95
30 3:38.05	Glen Grant	12 Aug 78
3:38.06	Tim Hutchings	31 Aug 84
3:38.08	Tom Hanlon	28 Jun 92
3:38.1	Jim McGuinness	1 Aug 77
3:38.2 a	James Espir	11 Jul 80
3:38.22	Peter Stewart	15 Jul 72
3:38.31	Matt Barnes	23 Jul 93
3:38.52	Ray Smedley	15 Jul 72
3:38.56	Curtis Robb	26 Jun 93
3:38.64	Simon Fairbrother	17 Jun 92
3:38.65	Ian Stewart II	8 Aug 81
40 3:38.66	Glen Stewart	26 May 96
3:38.68	John Kirkbride	15 Jul 72
3:38.7	Jim Douglas	27 Jun 72
3:38.78	Mark Scruton	17 Jun 84

3:38.8	Paul Lawther	12 Jun 77
3:38.9	Ian Hamer	5 Aug 89
3:38.93	Brian Treacy	28 Aug 94
3:39.0	David Lewis	9 Aug 83
3:39.06	Andy Keith	5 Jun 93
3:39.10	Alan Simpson	15 Aug 64
3:39.1	Neil Caddy	14 Aug 96 50
3:39.12	Ian Stewart I	1 Sep 69

ONE MILE

3:46.32	Steve Cram	27 Jul 85
3:47.33	Sebastian Coe	28 Aug 81
3:48.40	Steve Ovett	26 Aug 81
3:49.20	Peter Elliott	2 Jul 88
3:49.34	Dave Moorcroft	26 Jun 82
3:50.32	John Mayock	5 Jul 96
3:50.64	Graham Williamson	13 Jul 82
3:51.02	John Gladwin	19 Aug 87
3:51.31	Tony Morrell	14 Jul 90
3:51.57	Jack Buckner	29 Aug 84 10
3:51.76hc	Steve Crabb	14 Aug 87
3:52.20		1 Jul 89
3:52.44	John Robson	11 Jul 81
3:52.75	Matthew Yates	10 Jul 93
3:52.99	Mark Rowland	10 Sep 86
3:53.20	Ian Stewart II	25 Aug 82
3:53.64	Kevin McKay	22 Jul 94
3:53.82	Gary Staines	12 Aug 90
3:53.85	Robert Harrison	15 Jul 86
3:54.2	Frank Clement	27 Jun 78
3:54.30	David Strang	22 Jul 94 20
3:54.39	Neil Horsfield	8 Jul 86
3:54.53	Tim Hutchings	31 Jul 82
3:54.87	Anthony Whiteman	25 Aug 96
3:54.9	Adrian Passey	20 Aug 89
3:55.0	Jim McGuinness	11 Jul 77
3:55.3	Peter Stewart	10 Jun 72
3:55.38	Rob Denmark	12 Aug 90
3:55.41	Colin Reitz	31 Jul 82
3:55.68	Alan Simpson	30 Aug 65
3:55.8	Geoff Smith	15 Aug 81 30
3:55.84	Neil Caddy	25 Aug 96
3:55.9	Brendan Foster	10 Jun 72
3:55.91	Gary Lough	27 Aug 95
3:55.96	David Lewis	23 Aug 83
3:56.0	Jim Douglas	10 Jun 72
3:56.04	Mike Downes	25 Aug 82
3:56.1	Neill Duggan	11 Jun 66
3:56.19	Ian Hamer	5 Jul 91
3:56.29 i	Andy Keith	22 Jan 94
3:56.36	Steve Martin	5 Aug 86 40
3:56.38	Mike McLeod	31 Aug 79
3:56.5	John Kirkbride	10 Jun 72
3:56.5	Paul Davies-Hale	20 Aug 89
3:56.6	Walter Wilkinson	31 May 71
3:56.65	Paul Larkins	17 Jul 87
3:56.7	James Espir	15 Aug 81
3:56.71	Chris McGeorge	5 Jul 88
3:56.8	Ian McCafferty	11 Jun 69
3:56.83	Simon Fairbrother	17 Aug 90
3:56.9 a	Ron Speirs	30 Apr 77 50

2000 METRES

4:51.39	Steve Cram	4 Aug 85
4:52.82	Peter Elliott	15 Sep 87
4:53.06	Jack Buckner	15 Sep 87
4:53.69	Gary Staines	15 Sep 87
4:57.71	Steve Ovett	7 Jul 82
4:58.38	Graham Williamson	29 Aug 83
4:58.84	Sebastian Coe	5 Jun 82
4:59.57	Nick Rose	3 Jun 78
5:00.37	Tim Hutchings	29 Aug 83
10 5:00.91	John Mayock	9 Sep 96
5:01.09	Eamonn Martin	19 Jun 84
5:01.48	Paul Larkins	5 Jun 88
5:02.35	Sean Cahill	4 Aug 85
5:02.61	Steve Martin	19 Jun 84
5:02.8 a	Frank Clement	10 Sep 78
5:02.86	David Moorcroft	19 Jul 86
5:02.93	Brendan Foster	4 Jul 75
5:02.98	Ian Stewart I	4 Jul 75
5:02.98	Gary Lough	11 Aug 96
20 5:02.99	Neil Caddy	11 Aug 96
5:03.16	David Bedford	8 Jul 72
5:03.8	Lawrie Spence	26 May 78
5:04.11	Rob Denmark	11 Aug 96
5:04.16	Eddie Wedderburn	15 Jul 83
5:04.51	Steve Harris	29 Aug 83
5:04.53	David Lewis	26 Jun 83
5:04.56	Geoff Smith	26 Jun 83

3000 METRES (+ during 2 Miles)

7:32.79	Dave Moorcroft	17 Jul 82
7:35.1	Brendan Foster	3 Aug 74
7:36.40	John Nuttall	10 Jul 96
7:39.55	Rob Denmark	1 Aug 93
7:40.4	Nick Rose	27 Jun 78
7:40.43	Jack Buckner	5 Jul 86
7:40.94	Eamonn Martin	9 Jul 83
7:41.3	Steve Ovett	23 Sep 77
7:41.79	Gary Staines	14 Jul 90
10 7:42.26	Graeme Fell	9 Jul 83
7:42.47	David Lewis	9 Jul 83
7:42.77	Billy Dee	18 Jul 92
7:43.03	Tim Hutchings	14 Jul 89
7:43.1 +	Steve Cram	29 Aug 83
7:43.90	Ian Stewart II	26 Jun 82
7:44.40	Colin Reitz	9 Jul 83
7:44.76	Paul Davies-Hale	20 Jul 85
7:45.2 +	Geoff Turnbull	12 Sep 86
7:45.29	Dennis Coates	9 Sep 77
20 7:45.81	John Robson	13 Jul 84
7:46.22 i	Mark Rowland	27 Feb 90
7:49.82		28 Jul 89
7:46.39	Adrian Royle	28 Jun 83
7:46.40	Ian Hamer	20 Jan 90
7:46.4	David Bedford	21 Jun 72
7:46.6 +	Dave Black	14 Sep 73
7:46.80 i	John Mayock	25 Feb 95
7:47.28		23 Jul 95
7:46.83	Ian Stewart I	26 May 76
7:46.85 i	Ricky Wilde	15 Mar 70

7:46.95	David James	26 May 80
30 7:47.12	Simon Mugglestone	27 Jun 88
7:47.54	Paul Larkins	14 Jul 89
7:47.56	Richard Callan	15 Jul 83
7:47.6	Dick Taylor	6 Sep 69
7:48.00	Richard Nerurkar	15 Jul 92
7:48.09	Adrian Passey	28 Jul 89
7:48.18	Mike McLeod	9 Jul 78
7:48.28	Jon Richards	9 Jul 83
7:48.6 +	Nat Muir	27 Jun 80
7:48.66	Julian Goater	26 May 80
40 7:48.81	Tim Redman	18 Aug 84
7:49.1	Paul Lawther	27 Jun 78
7:49.45	Gary Lough	30 May 95
7:49.47	Roger Hackney	13 Jul 84
7:49.64	Barry Smith	26 Jul 81
7:49.72	Ray Smedley	9 Jul 78
7:49.80	Steve Jones	13 Jul 84
7:49.83 i	Andy Keith	6 Feb 94
7:50.20	Jon Solly	8 Aug 86
7:50.38	Mark Scrutton	15 Jul 83
50 7:50.69	Sean Cahill	23 May 85
7:50.8	Ken Newton	3 Jun 82
7:50.82 i	Matthew Yates	4 Mar 93
7:50.90	Tom Buckner	10 Jul 92
7:51.0 +	Eddie Wedderburn	16 Jul 88
7:51.31	Tom Hanlon	10 Jul 92
7:51.53	Tony Simmons	23 Aug 78
7:51.53	Malcolm Prince	16 May 79
7:51.53	John Hartigan	14 Jul 89
7:51.72	Jon Brown	1 Aug 93

2 MILES

8:13.51	Steve Ovett	15 Sep 78
8:13.68	Brendan Foster	27 Aug 73
8:14.93	Steve Cram	29 Aug 83
8:15.53	Tim Hutchings	12 Sep 86
8:15.98	Geoff Turnbull	12 Sep 86
8:16.75	Dave Moorcroft	20 Aug 82
8:17.12	Jack Buckner	12 Sep 86
8:18.4 i	Nick Rose	17 Feb 78
8:22.41		15 Sep 78
8:18.98	Eamonn Martin	16 Jul 88
10 8:19.37	Nat Muir	27 Jun 80
8:20.28	David James	27 Jun 80
8:20.66	David Lewis	7 Sep 84
8:21.09	Barry Smith	27 Jun 80
8:21.86	David Black	14 Sep 73
8:21.97	Rob Denmark	9 Aug 91
8:22.0	Ian Stewart I	14 Aug 72
8:22.65	Ian Hamer	17 Jul 92
8:22.98	Geoff Smith	27 Jun 80
8:23.16	Gary Staines	9 Aug 91
20 8:23.80	Billy Dee	9 Aug 91
8:23.92	Ray Smedley	6 Aug 76
8:24.58	Adrian Royle	16 May 82
8:24.82	Eddie Wedderburn	16 Jul 88
8:25.02	Tony Simmons	6 Aug 76
8:25.52	Colin Reitz	19 Aug 86
8:25.6 a	Mike McLeod	26 Jan 80

5000 METRES

	Time	Name	Date
	13:00.41	Dave Moorcroft	7 Jul 82
	13:09.80	Ian Hamer	9 Jun 92
	13:10.15	Jack Buckner	31 Aug 86
	13:10.24	Rob Denmark	9 Jun 92
	13:11.50	Tim Hutchings	11 Jul 84
	13:14.28	Gary Staines	15 Aug 90
	13:14.6 a	Brendan Foster	29 Jan 74
	13:15.59	Julian Goater	11 Sep 81
	13:16.70	John Nuttall	8 Jun 95
10	13:17.21	David Bedford	14 Jul 72
	13:17.84	Eamonn Martin	14 Jul 89
	13:17.9	Nat Muir	15 Jul 80
	13:18.6	Steve Jones	10 Jun 82
	13:18.91	Nick Rose	28 Jun 84
	13:19.66	Ian McCafferty	14 Jul 72
	13:19.78	Jon Brown	2 Jul 93
	13:20.06	Steve Ovett	30 Jun 86
	13:21.13	David Lewis	4 Jul 85
	13:21.14	Barry Smith	7 Jun 81
20	13:21.2	Tony Simmons	23 May 76
	13:21.60	Paul Davies-Hale	8 Jul 88
	13:21.73	Geoff Turnbull	5 Sep 86
	13:21.83	Mark Rowland	1 Jun 88
	13:22.17 i	Geoff Smith	12 Feb 82
	13:26.33		8 Aug 81
	13:22.39	Jon Solly	7 Jul 86
	13:22.54	Dave Clarke	28 Jun 83
	13:22.73	Adrian Passey	2 Jul 95
	13:22.8 a	Ian Stewart I	25 Jul 70
	13:23.26	Mike McLeod	24 Jun 80
30	13:23.36	Richard Nerurkar	10 Aug 90
	13:23.48	John Doherty	1 Jun 85
	13:23.52	Dave Black	29 Jan 74
	13:23.71	Steve Binns	1 Jun 88
	13:25.38	Paul Evans	28 Jun 95
	13:26.0	Bernie Ford	30 Jul 77
	13:26.19	Adrian Royle	4 Jul 83
	13:26.2	Dick Taylor	13 Jun 70
	13:26.74	Craig Mochrie	25 Aug 89
	13:26.97	John Mayock	9 Jun 92
40	13:27.00	Keith Cullen	17 May 96
	13:27.14	Richard Callan	25 Aug 82
	13:27.41	Billy Dee	10 Jul 92
	13:28.15	Malcolm Prince	14 Sep 79
	13:28.29	Simon Mugglestone	8 Jul 88
	13:28.58	Steve Cram	3 Jun 89
	13:28.7 a	Charlie Spedding	13 Aug 78
	13:28.99	Steve Emson	4 Sep 79
	13:29.8 a	Allan Rushmer	25 Jul 70
	13:29.91	John Downes	4 Jul 94
50	13:29.93	Mark Roberts	10 Jun 84
	13:30.79	Steve Harris	18 Jun 83
	13:30.8	Ricky Wilde	5 Jul 72
	13:30.88	Tony Milovsorov	10 Jun 84
	13:31.3 a	Neil Coupland	21 Jun 77
	13:31.38	Jon Richards	13 Aug 87
	13:32.20	Mark Scrutton	9 Jun 82
	13:32.71	Mike Chorlton	10 Jun 84
	13:33.0	Mike Wiggs	30 Jun 65

10000 METRES

	Time	Name	Date	
	27:23.06	Eamonn Martin	2 Jul 88	
	27:30.3	Brendan Foster	23 Jun 78	
	27:30.80	David Bedford	13 Jul 73	
	27:31.19	Nick Rose	9 Jul 83	
	27:34.58	Julian Goater	26 Jun 82	
	27:36.27	David Black	29 Aug 78	
	27:39.14	Steve Jones	9 Jul 83	
	27:39.76	Mike McLeod	4 Sep 79	
	27:40.03	Richard Nerurkar	10 Jul 93	
	27:43.03	Ian Stewart I	9 Sep 77	10
	27:43.59	Tony Simmons	30 Jun 77	
	27:43.74	Bernie Ford	9 Sep 77	
	27:43.76	Geoff Smith	13 Jun 81	
	27:47.16	Adrian Royle	10 Apr 82	
	27:47.79	Paul Evans	5 Jul 93	
	27:48.73	Gary Staines	6 Jul 91	
	27:51.76	Jon Solly	20 Jun 86	
	27:55.66	Steve Binns	9 Jul 83	
	27:55.77	Dave Clarke	25 May 82	
	27:57.77	Ian Hamer	13 Sep 91	20
	27:59.12	Allister Hutton	30 May 86	
	27:59.24	Carl Thackery	16 Jul 87	
	27:59.33	Steve Harris	22 Jul 86	
	27:59.72	Jon Brown	29 Jul 96	
	28:00.62	Jim Brown	1 Aug 75	
	28:00.64	Billy Dee	13 Sep 91	
	28:03.34	Rob Denmark	11 Jun 94	
	28:04.04	Andy Bristow	17 Aug 90	
	28:04.2	Ian Robinson	20 Apr 96	
	28:05.2	Dave Murphy	10 Apr 81	30
	28:06.13	Barry Smith	7 Aug 81	
	28:06.6	Dick Taylor	22 Jun 69	
	28:07.43	John Nuttall	25 Aug 95	
	28:07.57	Tim Hutchings	7 Jul 90	
	28:08.12	Charlie Spedding	23 Jul 83	
	28:08.44	David Lewis	5 Jun 88	
	28:09.39	Mark Dalloway	5 Jun 88	
	28:11.07	Karl Harrison	20 Jun 86	
	28:11.71	Lachie Stewart	18 Jul 70	
	28:11.85	Lawrie Spence	29 May 83	40
	28:13.04	Gerry Helme	29 May 83	
	28:13.13	Colin Moore	29 Jun 90	
	28:13.36	Jack Buckner	13 Sep 91	
	28:14.08	Jon Richards	20 Jun 86	
	28:14.65	Mike Tagg	10 Aug 71	
	28:14.89	Bernie Plain	1 Aug 75	
	28:15.58	Martin McLoughlin	20 Jun 86	
	28:16.0	Mike Baxter	23 May 74	
	28:16.73	Neil Coupland	11 Jun 77	
	28:17.00	Justin Hobbs	29 Jun 94	50
	28:18.6	John Davies II	11 Apr 79	
	28:18.68	Terry Thornton	17 Aug 90	
	28:18.8	Nick Lees	7 May 79	
	28:19.97	Kevin Forster	29 May 83	
	28:20.29	Steve Kenyon	7 Aug 81	
	28:21.48	Roger Matthews	18 Jul 70	
	28:22.48	Paul Dugdale	10 Jul 93	
	28:22.53	Tony Staynings	11 Apr 80	
	28:23.02	Dave Long II	7 Jun 90	

10 KILOMETRES ROAD

Time	Name	Date
27:34	Nick Rose	1 Apr 84
27:53	Mike O'Reilly	19 Oct 86
27:55	Mark Scrutton	5 Mar 84
27:56	John Doherty	4 Jul 86
27:58	Steve Harris	5 Apr 86
27:59	Steve Jones	28 Apr 84
28:02	Steve Binns	15 Apr 89
28:03	Jon Solly	5 Apr 86
28:03	Jack Buckner	28 Feb 87
28:05	Jon Brown	17 Oct 93
28:06	Geoff Smith	2 Mar 85
28:07	Colin Reitz	28 Apr 84
28:07	Peter Whitehead	4 Jul 96
28:09	Dave Moorcroft	16 May 82
28:10	Adrian Leek	10 Mar 84
28:10	Dave Clarke	5 May 85
28:11	Jon Richards	5 May 85
28:12	Dave Murphy	19 May 85
28:13	Allister Hutton	28 Apr 84
28:13	Paul Evans	8 Jan 95
28:14	Karl Harrison	5 May 85
28:14	David Lewis	5 Apr 86
28:14	Eamonn Martin	30 Apr 89
28:17	Paul Davies-Hale	21 Apr 85
28:17	Colin Moore	5 May 85
28:18	Steve Kenyon	15 Sep 85
28:19	Peter Tootell	28 Apr 84
28:19	Nigel Gates	5 May 85
28:19	Terry Greene	4 Apr 87
28:21	Bod Westwood	28 Apr 84
28:21	Andrew Pearson	5 Nov 95

course measurement uncertain

Time	Name	Date
27:56	Steve Harris	4 Dec 83
28:00	Dave Lewis	5 Nov 83
28:00	Roger Hackney	4 Dec 83
28:01	Barry Smith	4 Dec 83
28:01	Steve Kenyon	21 Sep 86
28:04	Dave Bedford	27 Mar 77

downhill

Time	Name	Date
27:20	Jon Brown	23 Sep 95
27:57	Malcolm East	25 Sep 82

10 MILES ROAD

Time	Name	Date
46:02	Richard Nerurkar	17 Oct 93
46:11	Gary Staines	10 Oct 93
46:26	Carl Thackery	7 Apr 91
46:36	Paul Evans	22 Sep 96
46:41	Roger Hackney	6 Apr 86
46:42	Dave Murphy	28 Apr 84
46:43	Steve Kenyon	28 Aug 82
46:43	Nick Rose	25 Apr 87
46:48	Geoff Smith	2 May 82
46:49	Steve Jones	2 Apr 89
47:00	Paul Davies-Hale	10 Oct 93

intermediate times

Time	Name	Date
46:21 +	Nigel Adams	15 Sep 91
46:21 +	Carl Thackery	15 Sep 91
46:23 +	Allister Hutton	1 Jan 85
46:31 +	Nick Rose	15 Sep 85

course measurement uncertain

Time	Name	Date
45:13	Ian Stewart	8 May 77
45:37	Barry Smith	22 Mar 81
45:44	Mike McLeod	9 Apr 78
46:03	Colin Moore	29 Aug 83
46:08	Nick Rose	26 Apr 81
46:11	Steve Kenyon	20 Jun 81
46:14	Charlie Spedding	12 Oct 86
46:17	Brendan Foster	9 Apr 78

downhill

Time	Name	Date
46:05	Allister Hutton	3 Apr 82

HALF MARATHON

Time	Name	Date
1:00:59	Steve Jones	8 Jun 86
1:01:03	Nick Rose	15 Sep 85
1:01:04	Carl Thackery	12 Apr 87
1:01:06	Richard Nerurkar	14 Apr 96
1:01:17	David Lewis	20 Sep 92
1:01:30	Paul Evans	18 Sep 94
1:01:31	Steve Kenyon	8 Jun 86
1:01:39	Geoff Smith	25 Sep 83
1:01:39	Paul Davies-Hale	15 Sep 91
1:01:53	Nigel Adams	15 Sep 91
1:01:56	Mark Flint	22 Aug 93
1:02:07	Kevin Forster	5 Apr 87
1:02:07	Martyn Brewer	20 Sep 87
1:02:08	Steve Harris	20 Oct 85
1:02:11	Dave Clarke	5 Apr 92
1:02:15	Dave Murphy	16 Sep 84
1:02:16	Jim Haughey	20 Sep 87
1:02:16	Dave Long II	15 Mar 92
1:02:19	Dave Long I	11 Dec 81
1:02:22	Colin Moore	26 May 85
1:02:24	Jimmy Ashworth	8 Jun 86
1:02:25	Barry Royden	18 Sep 94
1:02:28	Terry Greene	12 Apr 86
1:02:28	Allister Hutton	21 Jun 87
1:02:30	Tony Milovsorov	21 Jun 87
1:02:33	Steve Brace	15 Sep 91
1:02:33	Billy Dee	4 Apr 93
1:02:33	Peter Whitehead	5 May 95
1:02:36	Roger Hackney	10 Sep 89
1:02:37	Rob Denmark	18 Sep 94
1:02:38	Gary Staines	17 Sep 95
1:02:39	Neil Tennant	8 May 88
1:02:39	Mike McLeod	18 Jun 89
1:02:40	Dave Swanston	20 Sep 92

intermediate time

Time	Name	Date
1:02:36 +	Ron Hill	23 Jul 70

course measurement uncertain

Time	Name	Date
1:00:09	Paul Evans	15 Jan 95
1:01:47	Dave Long II	17 Mar 91
1:02:08	Ray Smedly	28 Mar 82
1:02:09	Steve Anders	25 Sep 88
1:02:19	Mike Carroll	3 Jun 90
1:02:23	Charlie Spedding	15 Mar 87
1:02:40	Chris Bunyan	8 Dec 84

MARATHON

2:07:13	Steve Jones	20 Oct 85
2:08:33	Charlie Spedding	21 Apr 85
2:08:52	Paul Evans	20 Oct 96
2:09:08	Geoff Smith	23 Oct 83
2:09:12	Ian Thompson	31 Jan 74
2:09:16	Allister Hutton	21 Apr 85
2:09:24	Hugh Jones	9 May 82
2:09:28	Ron Hill	23 Jul 70
2:09:28	John Graham	23 May 81
2:09:43	Mike Gratton	17 Apr 83
2:09:54	Tony Milovsorov	23 Apr 89
2:10:03	Richard Nerurkar	31 Oct 93
2:10:12	Gerry Helme	17 Apr 83
2:10:30	Dave Long II	21 Apr 91
2:10:35	Steve Brace	21 Jan 96
2:10:39	Mike O'Reilly	5 Dec 93
2:10:48	Bill Adcocks	8 Dec 68
2:10:50	Eamonn Martin	18 Apr 93
2:10:51	Bernie Ford	2 Dec 79
2:10:52	Kevin Forster	17 Apr 88
2:10:55	Chris Bunyan	18 Apr 83
2:11:06	Dave Buzza	31 Oct 93
2:11:18	Dave Murphy	12 Jun 83
2:11:22	Dave Cannon	6 Sep 80
2:11:25	Paul Davies-Hale	29 Oct 89
2:11:25	Gary Staines	20 Oct 96
2:11:35	Malcolm East	20 Apr 81
2:11:36	Kenny Stuart	15 Jan 89
2:11:40	Steve Kenyon	13 Jun 82
2:11:43	Jimmy Ashworth	29 Sep 85
2:11:44	Jim Dingwall	17 Apr 83
2:11:50	Fraser Clyne	2 Dec 84
2:11:54	Martin McCarthy	17 Apr 83
2:11:58	Mark Hudspith	2 Apr 95
2:12:04	Jim Alder	23 Jul 70
2:12:07	Jon Solly	14 Oct 90
2:12:07	Mark Flint	17 Apr 94
2:12:12	Dennis Fowles	13 May 84
2:12:12	Andy Green	25 Apr 93
2:12:13	John Wheway	17 Apr 88
2:12:17	Dave Long I	16 Jan 82
2:12:19	Don Faircloth	23 Jul 70
2:12:23	Peter Whitehead	2 Apr 95
2:12:32	Trevor Wright	3 Dec 78
2:12:33	Tony Simmons	7 May 78
2:12:37	Carl Thackery	25 Oct 92
2:12:41	Derek Stevens	16 Jun 84
2:12:50	Jeff Norman	7 May 78
2:13:06	Greg Hannon	13 May 79
2:13:12	Chris Stewart	8 Dec 74

2000 METRES STEEPLECHASE

5:19.86	Mark Rowland	28 Aug 88
5:21.77	Tom Hanlon	11 Jun 92
5:23.56	Tom Buckner	17 Jul 92
5:23.6	Roger Hackney	10 Jun 82
5:23.71	Colin Walker	28 Aug 88
5:23.87	Colin Reitz	28 Jun 84
5:24.91	Eddie Wedderburn	19 Aug 86
5:26.24	Paul Davies-Hale	26 Aug 85
5:26.64	Nick Peach	19 Aug 86
5:26.82"	David Lewis	12 Jun 83
5:30.6	Dennis Coates	23 Apr 78
5:30.86	Tony Staynings	26 May 76
5:31.04	John Hartigan	17 Aug 90
5:31.09	Peter McColgan	5 Aug 86
5:31.43	John Bicourt	26 May 76

3000 METRES STEEPLECHASE

8:07.96	Mark Rowland	30 Sep 88
8:12.11	Colin Reitz	5 Sep 86
8:12.58	Tom Hanlon	3 Aug 91
8:15.16	Graeme Fell	17 Aug 83
8:18.32	Eddie Wedderburn	5 Jul 88
8:18.91	Roger Hackney	30 Jul 88
8:18.95	Dennis Coates	25 Jul 76
8:20.83	Paul Davies-Hale	10 Jun 84
8:22.48	John Davies II	13 Sep 74
8:22.82	John Bicourt	8 Jun 76
8:23.90	Justin Chaston	18 Jul 94
8:24.64	Spencer Duval	16 Jul 95
8:25.15	Colin Walker	28 Jun 92
8:25.50	Tom Buckner	28 Aug 92
8:26.05	Keith Cullen	21 Aug 95
8:26.33	Rob Hough	6 Jul 96
8:26.4	Andy Holden	15 Sep 72
8:26.6	Gordon Rimmer	4 Jun 80
8:27.21	Tony Staynings	15 Jun 80
8:27.8	Steve Hollings	5 Aug 73
8:27.93	Peter McColgan	25 Jun 91
8:28.6	David Bedford	10 Sep 71
8:29.46	Julian Marsay	14 Jul 79
8:29.72	David Lewis	29 May 83
8:30.6 a	Peter Griffiths	17 Jul 77
8:30.8	Gerry Stevens	1 Sep 69
8:31.09	Ian Gilmour	16 Jul 78
8:31.22	David Lee	19 Jun 92
8:32.00	Steve Jones	8 Aug 80
8:32.06	David Camp	10 Aug 74
8:32.13	Barry Knight	25 Jul 82
8:32.4 a	Maurice Herriott	17 Oct 64
8:33.0	John Jackson	13 Aug 69
8:33.8 a	Gareth Bryan-Jones	23 Jul 70
8:33.8	Peter Morris	4 Aug 73
8:33.83	Richard Charleston	24 May 80
8:33.89	Nick Peach	21 Jun 86
8:33.97	John Hartigan	20 Jul 90
8:34.77	Kevin Capper	18 Aug 85
8:34.83	Ken Baker	1 Jul 84
8:35.49	Micky Morris	14 Aug 76
8:35.52	Neil Smart	28 Aug 89
8:35.6	Ron McAndrew	9 Jul 71
8:35.8	John Wild	3 Aug 77
8:36.2 a	Bernie Hayward	26 Jan 74
8:36.55	Mick Hawkins	16 Jul 95
8:37.0	Ernie Pomfret	15 Jul 67
8:37.59	Dave Baptiste	28 Aug 89
8:37.68	Darren Mead	26 Jun 93
8:37.70	Ken Penney	19 Jul 91

110 METRES HURDLES

	Time	Name	Date
	12.91	Colin Jackson	20 Aug 93
	13.00	Tony Jarrett	20 Aug 93
	13.29	Jon Ridgeon	15 Jul 87
	13.42	David Nelson	27 Aug 91
	13.43	Mark Holtom	4 Oct 82
	13.44	Hugh Teape	14 Aug 92
	13.51	Nigel Walker	3 Aug 90
	13.52	Andy Tulloch	11 Aug 94
	13.53	Paul Gray	22 Aug 94
10	13.60	Wilbert Greaves	21 Aug 85
	13.60	Neil Owen	28 Jun 95
	13.69	Berwyn Price	18 Aug 73
	13.72	David Hemery	1 Aug 70
	13.75	Lloyd Cowan	17 Jul 94
	13.79	Alan Pascoe	17 Jun 72
	13.86	Ken Campbell	23 Aug 94
	13.96	Steve Buckeridge	31 May 86
	14.01	Ross Baillie	25 Aug 96
	14.02	Mark Lambeth	9 Jul 95
20	14.03	Brett St Louis	27 Jun 87
	14.03	Brian Taylor	19 May 96
	14.04	Daley Thompson	28 Aug 86
	14.04	Damien Greaves	25 Aug 96
	14.08	Paul Brice	26 Aug 83
	14.09	Colin Hamplett	11 Aug 90
	14.10	Graham Gower	15 Jul 72
	14.10	Bob Danville	4 Jul 76
	14.10	Jamie Quarry	25 Jun 94
	14.11	Neil Fraser	11 Jul 87
30	14.11	Ererton Harrison	31 Jul 91
	14.13	Mark Stern	22 Jun 96
	14.14	Mike Hogan	5 Sep 63
	14.14	Max Robertson	7 Jun 86
	14.14	Martin Nicholson	12 Jun 94
	14.16 A	Mike Parker	16 Oct 68
	14.26		17 Oct 64
	14.17	Colin Bovell	23 Jul 94
	14.18	Chris Breen	13 Jul 75
	14.18	James Archampong	21 Jul 94
	14.19	C. J. Kirkpatrick	16 Jun 73
40	14.20 A	Stuart Storey	16 Oct 68
	14.20	Kevin Lumsden	16 Jul 94
	14.21	David Wilson	15 Jul 72
	14.21	Alan Cronin	13 Jul 75
	14.21	Mark Whitby	14 Jun 85
	14.23	Alan Tapp	14 Jun 86
	14.24	Kieran Moore	7 Jun 86
	14.26	Peter Hildreth	14 Sep 58
	14.26	Phil Barthropp	24 Jun 84
	14.28	Gus McKenzie	25 May 80
50	14.28	Glenn MacDonald	22 Aug 82
	14.28	Nick Dakin	12 Jun 93
	14.29	Greg Dunson	28 Jun 86
	14.29	John Wallace	17 Sep 89
	14.29	Rhys Davies	25 Jun 90
	14.29	Jon Hazel	4 Jul 92
	14.32	Tony James	27 Jun 81
	14.34	Gary Oakes	5 Jul 80
	14.34	Norman Ashman	26 Jul 91

wind assisted

	Time	Name	Date
	13.49	Nigel Walker	3 Jun 89
	13.65	Berwyn Price	25 Aug 75
	13.66	David Hemery	18 Jul 70
	13.97	Brett St Louis	30 Jul 88
	13.99	Bob Danville	14 Aug 76
	14.06	Tony James	22 Aug 81
	14.08	David Wilson	15 Jul 72
	14.11	Mark Stern	20 Jun 93
	14.14	James Archampong	25 May 96
10	14.16	Mark Hatton	14 Jul 79
	14.17	C. J. Kirkpatrick	13 Jul 74
	14.19	Alan Cronin	25 Aug 75
	14.19	Norman Ashman	15 Aug 92
	14.22	Phil Barthropp	1 Jul 84
	14.23	Gus McKenzie	21 May 80
	14.23	John Wallace	26 Jul 86
	14.23	Greg Dunson	10 Jun 89
	14.25	Stuart Storey	18 Jul 70
	14.25	Glenn MacDonald	13 Jun 82
20	14.25	Anthony Brannen	30 Apr 95
	14.27	Richard Harbour	1 Jul 90
	14.30	David Humphreys	15 Jul 89
	14.33	Mark Johnson	10 Aug 85

hand timing

	Time	Name	Date
	13.5	Berwyn Price	1 Jul 73
	13.6	David Hemery	5 Jul 69
	13.7	Alan Pascoe	5 Jul 69
	13.7	C. J. Kirkpatrick	29 Jun 74
	13.8	Martin Nicholson	25 Jun 94
	13.9	Mike Parker	2 Oct 63
	13.9	David Wilson	29 Jun 74
	13.9	Brian Taylor	8 May 93
	14.1	Mike Hogan	5 Sep 63
10	14.1	Stuart Storey	2 Aug 67
	14.1	Colin Bovell	17 Jul 94
	14.1 y	Laurie Taitt	5 Sep 63
	14.2		2 Oct 63
	14.2	Bob Birrell	6 Sep 61
	14.2	Andy Todd	27 Oct 67
	14.2	Mark Whitby	12 May 84
	14.2	James Hughes	2 Jul 94
	14.2	Anthony Brannen	6 May 95
	14.2 y	Rodney Morrod	13 Jun 64

wind assisted

	Time	Name	Date
	12.8	Colin Jackson	10 Jan 90
	13.4	Berwyn Price	7 Jul 76
	13.5	Neil Owen	2 Jun 96
	13.5	Andy Tulloch	2 Jun 96
	13.7	Lloyd Cowan	27 Apr 95
	14.0	Laurie Taitt	13 Sep 62
	14.0 y	Bob Birrell	9 Sep 61
	14.1	Donald Finlay	8 Sep 37
	14.1	Neil Fraser	30 May 87
10	14.2	Jack Morgan	24 Apr 82
	14.2	Kieran Moore	1 Jun 85
	14.2	Mark Bishop	22 Jun 91
	14.2 y	Peter Hildreth	18 Aug 59
	14.2 y	Desmond Price	18 Aug 59
	14.2 y	Tony Hogarth	20 Jul 68
	14.2 y	Rupert Legge	20 Jul 68

400 METRES HURDLES

	47.82	Kriss Akabusi	6 Aug 92
	48.12 A	David Hemery	15 Oct 68
	48.52		2 Sep 72
	48.59	Alan Pascoe	30 Jun 75
	48.73	Jon Ridgeon	6 Sep 92
	49.03 A	John Sherwood	15 Oct 68
	49.88		13 Aug 69
	49.07	Gary Cadogan	22 Jul 94
	49.11	Gary Oakes	26 Jul 80
	49.25	Max Robertson	28 Aug 90
	49.26	Peter Crampton	8 Aug 94
10	49.49	Mark Holtom	20 Jul 85
	49.60	Phil Beattie	28 Jul 86
	49.65	Bill Hartley	2 Aug 75
	49.82	Martin Gillingham	14 Aug 87
	49.82	Gary Jennings	27 Jun 95
	49.86	Martin Briggs	6 Jun 84
	49.95	Steve Sole	24 Jul 83
	50.01	Philip Harries	5 Jun 88
	50.05	Lawrence Lynch	15 Jun 96
	50.1 a	John Cooper	16 Oct 64
20	50.16	Paul Thompson	17 May 96
	50.19	Steve Coupland	12 Jun 94
	50.31	Tony Williams	27 Jun 95
	50.36	Chris Rawlinson	9 Jun 96
	50.37	Bob Danville	27 Jul 82
	50.38	Andy Todd	18 Sep 69
	50.52	Paul Hibbert	30 Jun 96
	50.58	Colin O'Neill	29 Jan 74
	50.58	Mike Whittingham	7 Aug 82
	50.68	Peter Warden	18 Jun 66
30	50.70	Noel Levy	8 Jul 94
	50.71	Steve Hawkins	4 Jun 89
	50.79	Mark Davidson	17 Jun 89
	50.79	Lloyd Cowan	3 Jun 95
	50.82 "	Paul Atherton	12 Jun 83
	50.84	Mark Whitby	6 Jun 84
	50.86	Wilbert Greaves	18 May 80
	50.88	Greg Dunson	7 Jun 92
	50.91	Brian Whittle	5 Jun 93
	50.94	Trevor Burton	17 Jul 87
40	50.97	Dave Savage	15 Jun 96
	50.98	Tom Farrell	15 Jun 60
	50.98	Stan Devine	14 Jul 82
	51.04	Peter Kelly	12 Jun 76
	51.08	Tim Gwynne	30 May 94
	51.09	Steve Black	14 Jul 73
	51.15	Eddie Betts	26 Jun 94
	51.16	Keith van Vollenhoven	8 Aug 81
	51.17	Dave Scharer	21 Jul 70
	51.18	Barry Middleton	15 Jun 96
50	51.21	Steve James	23 Jun 78
	51.22	Roger Bell	13 Jul 79

hand timing

49.9	Andy Todd	9 Oct 69
50.5	Wilbert Greaves	12 Feb 80
50.7	Steve Black	20 Aug 74
50.7	Stewart McCallum	21 Mar 76
50.8	Dave Schärer	26 Jun 71

HIGH JUMP

	2.38 i	Steve Smith	4 Feb 94
	2.37		20 Sep 92
	2.37 i	Dalton Grant	13 Mar 94
	2.36		1 Sep 91
	2.32 i	Brendan Reilly	24 Feb 94
	2.31		17 Jul 92
	2.31	Geoff Parsons	26 Aug 94
	2.28 i	John Holman	28 Jan 89
	2.24		27 May 89
	2.26	James Brierley	3 Aug 96
	2.25	Floyd Manderson	20 Aug 88
	2.24	Mark Naylor	28 Jun 80
	2.24	John Hill	23 Aug 85
10	2.24	Phil McDonnell	26 Aug 85
	2.23	Mark Lakey	29 Aug 82
	2.23 i	David Abrahams	12 Mar 83
	2.19		7 Oct 82
	2.21	Fayyaz Ahmed	29 Jun 86
	2.21	Steve Chapman	30 Jul 89
	2.21	Ben Challenger	24 Aug 96
	2.20	Brian Burgess	11 Jun 78
	2.20	Trevor Llewelyn	15 Jul 83
	2.20	Byron Morrison	14 Jul 84
	2.20 i	Henderson Pierre	10 Jan 87
	2.18		16 Aug 86
20	2.20	Alex Kruger	18 Jun 88
	2.20	Ossie Cham	21 May 89
	2.20 i	Warren Caswell	10 Mar 90
	2.18		2 Sep 90
	2.20	Colin Bent	16 Jun 96
	2.19	David Barnetson	4 Jul 92
	2.19 i	Mike Robbins	3 Feb 96
	2.17		5 Aug 95
	2.18	Tim Foulger	23 Sep 79
	2.18	Rupert Charles	25 Jul 82
	2.18	Steve Ritchie	15 Jul 89
	2.18	Hopeton Lindo	23 Jul 89
	2.18	Andrew Lynch	9 Jul 95
30	2.17	Stuart Ohrland	27 Aug 94
	2.16 i	Mike Butterfield	23 Jan 76
	2.16 i	Claude Moseley	13 Apr 80
	2.16		19 Jul 81
	2.16 i	David Watson	13 Mar 82
	2.15		19 Aug 84
	2.16	Andy Hutchinson	2 Sep 84
	2.16	Mike Powell	3 Sep 88
	2.16	John Wallace	29 Jul 90
	2.16	Richard Aspden	7 Jul 95
	2.16	Rob Brocklebank	7 Jul 95
40	2.15 i	Andrew McIver	26 Jan 80
	2.15	Femi Abejide	6 Jun 82
	2.15	Leroy Lucas	19 Aug 84
	2.15	Paul Jeffs	14 Jun 85
	2.15	Canisus Alcindor	14 Jul 85
	2.15 i	John Hopper	25 Feb 90
	2.15	Stanley Osuide	1 Sep 91
	2.15	Darran Baker	19 Jul 92
	2.15 i	Darren Joseph	18 Feb 96
	2.15	Ian Holliday	2 Jun 96
50	2.15	Danny Graham	22 Jun 96

POLE VAULT

	Mark	Name	Date
	5.71	Nick Buckfield	16 Jun 96
	5.65	Keith Stock	7 Jul 81
	5.60	Neil Winter	19 Aug 95
	5.59	Brian Hooper	6 Sep 80
	5.52	Michael Edwards	13 May 93
	5.50	Paul Williamson	6 Jul 96
	5.45 i	Andy Ashurst	16 Feb 92
	5.40		19 Jun 88
	5.42	Mike Barber	26 Aug 95
	5.40 A	Jeff Gutteridge ¶	23 Apr 80
	5.40		5 Jun 83
10	5.40 i	Matthew Belsham	10 Feb 96
	5.35		26 Jun 93
	5.30 i	Ian Tullett	14 Mar 92
	5.30		7 Jun 92
	5.30 i	Kevin Hughes	25 Feb 95
	5.30		28 Aug 95
	5.30	Dean Mellor	17 Jun 95
	5.26	Mark Johnson	31 Aug 91
	5.25	Mike Bull	22 Sep 73
	5.25	Allan Williams	29 Aug 77
	5.25	Daley Thompson	15 Jun 86
	5.21	Graham Eggleton	10 Jul 82
	5.20	Billy Davey	5 Jun 83
20	5.20	Warren Siley	4 Aug 90
	5.20 ns	Tim Thomas	16 Jul 94
	5.10		23 Jul 94
	5.20	Mark Hodgkinson	25 Aug 96
	5.18	Steve Chappell	15 Jun 78
	5.15	Christian Linskey	23 Aug 96
	5.11	Andrew Gayle	10 Aug 91
	5.10	Darren Wright	12 Jun 88
	5.10	Paul Phelps	9 Jul 89
	5.10	Mark Grant	20 May 95
	5.10	Mark Davis	9 Jun 96
30	5.02	Bob Kingman	29 Aug 94
	5.01	Paul Hoad	16 Aug 86
	5.00	Richard Gammage	19 Aug 84
	5.00	Brian Taylor	5 May 91
	5.00	Dan Gilby	20 Jul 91
	5.00	Paul Wray	26 Jul 91
	5.00	Alex Greig	31 May 92
	5.00	Barry Thomas	23 Aug 92
	5.00	Neil Young	18 May 96
	5.00	Ian Wilding	1 Jun 96
40	5.00	Ben Flint	6 Jul 96
	4.98 A	Richard Williamson	17 Apr 78
	4.90	15 athletes	

LONG JUMP

	Mark	Name	Date
	8.23	Lynn Davies	30 Jun 68
	8.15	Stewart Faulkner	16 Jul 90
	8.14	Mark Forsythe	7 Jul 91
	8.10	Fred Salle	9 Sep 94
	8.08	Roy Mitchell	27 Sep 80
	8.05 i	Barrington Williams	11 Feb 89
	8.01		17 Jun 89
	8.01	Daley Thompson	8 Aug 84
	8.00	Derrick Brown	7 Aug 85
	7.98	Alan Lerwill	29 Jun 74
	7.94 i	Paul Johnson	10 Mar 89	10
	7.85		3 Jun 89
	7.91	John King	26 Sep 87
	7.91	Steve Phillips	10 Aug 91
	7.90	Ian Simpson	3 Jun 89
	7.89	John Morbey	8 Aug 66
	7.87	Keith Fleming	7 Jun 87
	7.86	Darren Ritchie	15 Jun 96
	7.84	Wayne Griffith	25 Aug 89
	7.79	Geoff Hignett	31 May 71
	7.79	Don Porter	13 Jul 75
20	7.77	Len Tyson	25 Jul 82
	7.76	Carl Howard	31 Jul 93
	7.75	Ken Cocks	2 Jul 78
	7.75	Trevor Hoyte	6 May 84
	7.75	Michael Morgan	30 Jul 94
	7.74	Fred Alsop	6 Jun 64
	7.74 i	Phil Scott	17 Feb 73
	7.68		27 May 73
	7.74 i	Aston Moore	10 Jan 81
	7.74	John Herbert	14 Jul 85
	7.74	David Burgess	4 Jul 87
30	7.74	Nathan Morgan	22 Aug 96
	7.73	Jason Canning	20 Apr 88
	7.72	Femi Abejide	20 Jun 86
	7.71	Billy Kirkpatrick	2 Jun 78
	7.71 i	Keith Connor	20 Feb 81
	7.70	Kevin Liddington	27 Aug 88
	7.68	Garry Slade	1 Aug 92
	7.67	Dave Walker	14 Sep 68
	7.67	Oni Onourah	15 Jun 96
	7.66	Tony Henry	12 Jun 77
40	7.66	Barry Nevison	7 Jul 85
	7.66	John Shepherd	18 Jun 88
	7.65 i	John Munroe	11 Feb 95
	7.64		24 Jun 95
	7.64	Gus Udo	6 Sep 80
	7.64	Eddie Starrs	11 Jul 81
	7.64 i	Enyinna Chukukere	6 Mar 94
	7.63	Henry Walters	15 Aug 81
	7.62	Peter Reed	18 May 68
	7.62	Colin Mitchell	11 Jul 78
	7.62	Dennis Costello	5 May 85
50	7.62	Duncan Mathieson	30 Jul 95

wind assisted

Mark	Name	Date
8.17	Mark Forsythe	11 Jun 89
8.16	Roy Mitchell	26 Jun 76
8.15	Alan Lerwill	29 May 72
8.12	Derrick Brown	14 Jun 86
8.11	Daley Thompson	7 Aug 78
8.04	Ian Simpson	3 Jun 89
7.97	Nathan Morgan	13 Jul 96
7.96	Colin Jackson	17 May 86
7.94	John Herbert	25 Jul 82
7.94	John King	20 Jun 86
7.93	David Burgess	15 Jun 86
7.91	Steve Ingram	18 Jun 94
7.89	John Shepherd	20 Jun 86
7.87	Paul Johnson	15 May 88

TRIPLE JUMP

Mark	Name	Date
18.29	Jonathan Edwards	7 Aug 95
17.57 A	Keith Connor	5 Jun 82
17.30		9 Jun 82
17.41	John Herbert	2 Sep 85
17.21	Tosi Fasinro	27 Jul 93
17.18	Francis Agyepong	7 Jul 95
17.06	Julian Golley	10 Sep 94
17.01	Eric McCalla	3 Aug 84
16.87	Mike Makin	2 Aug 86
16.86	Aston Moore	16 Aug 81
16.75	Vernon Samuels	7 Aug 88
16.58	Femi Akinsanya	15 Jun 96
16.53	Onochie Achike	24 Jul 94
16.46	Fred Alsop	16 Oct 64
16.32	Tayo Erogbogbo	21 Aug 95
16.30	Femi Abejide	27 Jun 85
16.29 i	David Johnson	1 Mar 78
16.18		22 Jun 75
16.26	Joe Sweeney	3 Aug 91
16.22	Derek Boosey	15 Jun 68
16.20	Rez Cameron	5 Jun 88
16.18	Tony Wadhams	6 Jul 69
16.17	John Mackenzie	17 Sep 94
16.16	Conroy Brown	19 Sep 81
16.15	Wayne Green	10 Jul 88
16.15	Michael Brown	23 Jul 89
16.13	Steven Anderson	11 Jun 83
16.10	Alan Lerwill	28 Aug 71
16.09	Courtney Charles	17 Jun 90
16.08	Craig Duncan	21 Jun 86
16.02	Peter Akwaboah	15 Jun 89
15.98	Frank Attoh	5 Sep 80
15.97	Mike Ralph	23 Jul 64
15.97	Carl Howard	6 May 95
15.95	Derek Browne	12 Jun 93
15.92	John Slaney	15 Oct 77
15.92	Lawrence Lynch	13 Jul 85
15.91 i	Akin Oyediran	3 Mar 84
15.91	Dave Emmanuel	31 Aug 91
15.90	David Wood	16 Sep 84
15.88	John Phillips	14 May 78
15.87	Chris Colman	15 Jul 78
15.87	Stewart Faulkner	22 Aug 87

wind assisted

Mark	Name	Date
18.43	Jonathan Edwards	25 Jun 95
17.81	Keith Connor	9 Oct 82
17.30	Tosi Fasinro	12 Jun 93
17.29 A	Francis Agyepong	29 Jul 95
17.24		2 Jul 95
17.02	Aston Moore	14 Jun 81
16.82	Vernon Samuels	24 Jun 89
16.67	Larry Achike	24 Jul 94
16.65	Fred Alsop	13 Aug 65
16.49	Tony Wadhams	16 Sep 69
16.38	Femi Abejide	10 Jun 89
16.38	Courtney Charles	22 Jul 90
16.33	David Johnson	28 May 78
16.32	Craig Duncan	20 Jun 87
16.32	Rez Cameron	21 May 89

SHOT

Mark	Name	Date
21.68	Geoff Capes	18 May 80
20.43	Mike Winch	22 May 74
20.33	Paul Edwards ¶	9 Jul 91
19.67	Mark Proctor	2 Jun 96
19.62	Shaun Pickering	10 May 96
19.56	Arthur Rowe	7 Aug 61
19.49	Matt Simson	28 Aug 94
19.44 i	Simon Williams	28 Jan 89
19.17		18 May 91
19.43	Bill Tancred	18 May 74
19.18	Jeff Teale ¶	7 Aug 68
19.01	Billy Cole	21 Jun 86
18.94	Bob Dale	12 Jun 76
18.93	Paul Buxton	13 May 77
18.85	Lee Newman	2 Jun 96
18.62	Martyn Lucking	2 Oct 62
18.59 i	Alan Carter	11 Apr 65
18.26		1 May 65
18.50	Mike Lindsay	2 Jul 63
18.46	Roger Kennedy	22 May 77
18.46 i	Simon Rodhouse	20 Feb 82
18.20		25 Jul 82
18.40	Stephan Hayward	9 Jun 96
18.35	Peter Tancred	9 Jul 74
18.34	Richard Slaney	3 Jul 83
18.14 i	Neal Brunning ¶	26 Jan 92
17.45		17 Aug 91
18.05	John Watts	19 Aug 72
18.04	Andy Vince	30 Apr 83
17.96	Nigel Spratley	28 Aug 94
17.95	Graham Savory	4 Jun 88
17.92	Nick Tabor	9 Apr 83
17.87	Bill Fuller	15 Jul 72
17.87 i	Ian Lindley	15 Mar 81
17.58		25 May 81
17.87 i	Antony Zaidman	22 Jan 83
17.22		4 Jul 81
17.79	John Alderson	31 Jul 74
17.78	Steve Whyte	11 Feb 89
17.62	Neil Gray	7 Jun 89
17.55	David Callaway	1 Aug 93
17.54	Eric Irvine	16 Aug 86
17.47	Carl Jennings	13 Sep 87
17.46	Mark Edwards	7 Sep 96
17.45	Abi Ekoku	3 Feb 90
17.44	Hamish Davidson	3 Jun 78
17.41	Lee Wiltshire	1 May 94
17.41	Jamie Cockburn	12 May 96
17.40	Barry King	11 Apr 70
17.40	Allan Seatory	27 Apr 75
17.36 i	Chris Ellis	8 Dec 84
17.26		10 Sep 86
17.30	Mark Aldridge	19 Sep 82
17.30	Carl Myerscough	3 Aug 96
17.25	Tony Satchwell	2 Jun 84
17.13	John Turton	29 Apr 77
17.04	Paul Reed	14 May 88
17.02	Gary Sollitt	18 May 96
16.95	Nick Morgan	23 Sep 61

DISCUS

	Mark	Name	Date
	65.16	Richard Slaney	1 Jul 85
	64.94	Bill Tancred	21 Jul 74
	63.56	Bob Weir	10 Jun 95
	62.36	Peter Tancred	8 May 80
	62.32	Glen Smith	1 Jun 96
	61.86	Paul Mardle	13 Jun 84
	61.62	Peter Gordon	15 Jun 91
	61.14	Simon Williams	18 Apr 92
	61.00	Allan Seatory	6 Oct 74
10	60.92	Graham Savory	10 May 86
	60.42	Mike Cushion	16 Aug 75
	60.08	Abi Ekoku	16 May 90
	59.84	Colin Sutherland ¶	10 Jun 78
	59.76	John Hillier	27 Jul 74
	59.70	John Watts	14 Jul 72
	59.50	Kevin Brown	9 Sep 95
	58.64	Steve Casey	19 May 91
	58.58	Darrin Morris	22 Jun 91
	58.34	Geoff Capes	29 Sep 73
20	58.34	Lee Newman	9 Jun 94
	58.08	Mike Winch	7 Sep 75
	57.58	Arthur McKenzie	17 Aug 69
	57.12	Paul Edwards ¶	10 Aug 88
	57.10	Dennis Roscoe	3 May 80
	57.00	Gerry Carr	17 Jul 65
	56.70	Roy Hollingsworth	14 Sep 63
	56.66	Gary Herrington	15 Jun 96
	56.46	Paul Reed	24 Apr 96
	56.42	Paul Buxton	6 Aug 76
30	56.40	Guy Dirkin	1 Aug 75
	56.10	Perris Wilkins	23 Jun 96
	55.68	Neville Thompson	12 Jun 93
	55.68	Leith Marar	24 Jul 96
	55.60	Jeff Clare	25 Jul 88
	55.52	Jamie Murphy	29 Jul 95
	55.42	Geoff Tyler	3 May 80
	55.34	Nick Woolcott	27 Jul 88
	55.32	Mike Lindsay	4 May 60
	55.04	Denzil McDonald	28 Aug 95
40	54.78	Colin Bastien	29 Mar 87
	54.38	Shaun Pickering	26 Aug 89
	54.36	Matt Symonds	24 Jun 95
	54.28	Mark Proctor	7 Aug 93
	54.26	Mark Pharoah	27 Nov 56
	54.00	Eric Cleaver	21 Oct 62
	53.80	Perris Wilkins	23 Jul 94
	53.76	John Turton	18 May 79
	53.76	Robert Russell	8 Sep 96
	53.64 A	Barry King	7 May 66
50	53.54	Tony Satchwell	30 Sep 73
	53.48	George Patience	11 Jul 87
	53.46	Neal Brunning ¶	1 May 91
	53.24	Andy Drzewiecki	8 Aug 76
	53.06	Mark Davies	20 Jun 92
	53.02	Nick Tabor	3 May 80
	52.80	Peter Nimmo	3 Apr 65
	52.38	Michael Jemi-Alade	30 Jun 87
	52.34	Ted Kelland	30 Jun 73
	52.26	Scott Hayes	24 Jun 95

HAMMER

	Mark	Name	Date
	77.54	Martin Girvan	12 May 84
	77.30	Dave Smith I	13 Jul 85
	77.02	Matt Mileham	11 May 84
	75.40	Chris Black	23 Jul 83
	75.10	Dave Smith II	27 May 96
	75.08	Bob Weir	3 Oct 82
	74.02	Paul Head	30 Aug 90
	73.86	Barry Williams	1 Jul 76
	73.80	Jason Byrne	19 Sep 92
10	73.20	Paul Dickenson	22 May 76
	72.48	Mick Jones	26 Jun 96
	71.60	Shane Peacock	24 Jun 90
	71.28	Peter Vivian	25 Jun 95
	71.00	Ian Chipchase	17 Aug 74
	70.88	Howard Payne	29 Jun 74
	70.30	Stewart Rogerson	14 Aug 88
	70.28	Paul Buxton	19 May 79
	69.52	Jim Whitehead	23 Sep 79
	68.64	Shaun Pickering	7 Apr 84
20	68.18	Ron James	2 Jun 82
	67.82	Steve Whyte	15 Apr 89
	67.34	John Pearson	25 Aug 96
	67.32	Gareth Cook	1 Jun 91
	65.36	Russell Devine	23 Apr 94
	65.30	Karl Andrews	2 Jul 94
	65.24	Steve Pearson	19 Jul 94
	64.96	Mike Ellis	4 Jun 59
	64.80	Bruce Fraser	30 Sep 73
	64.54	Michael Petra	30 May 79
30	64.36	Andrew Tolputt	27 Jun 87
	63.90	Bill Beauchamp	17 Jul 96
	63.74	Mark Sterling	18 Jul 84
	63.74	Chris Howe	15 Aug 90
	63.20	Peter Gordon	17 Sep 82
	63.16	Graham Callow	29 May 89
	62.70	Paul Barnard	19 Jul 95
	62.68	Iain Park	6 Jul 96
	62.60	Peter Weir	2 Aug 87
	62.60	Rob Earle	1 Aug 95
40	62.56	Adrian Palmer	6 Aug 94
	62.54	Tony Elvin	25 May 70
	62.42	Malcolm Fenton	16 May 82
	62.40	Lawrie Nisbet	5 Jul 86
	62.32	Peter Aston	6 Sep 75
	62.28	Lawrie Bryce	13 Oct 73
	62.24	Phil Scott	16 Jun 76
	62.24	Tony Kenneally	18 May 85
	62.20	Steve Minnikin	11 May 96
	62.16	Geoff Whaley	30 Apr 80
50	62.10	Chris Melluish	7 Sep 74
	62.00	Eric Berry	26 Aug 74
	61.72	Peter Seddon	10 May 67
	61.38	Russell Tolputt	7 Aug 85
	61.22	Malcolm Croad	25 Aug 92
	61.10	Vaughan Cooper	5 May 84
	60.96	Stuart Spratley	19 Jul 92
	60.92	Craig Ellams	28 Jul 96
	60.54	Niall McDonald	6 Jun 70
	60.42	Tom Campbell	31 May 75

JAVELIN (1986 model)

	91.46	Steve Backley	25 Jan 92
	86.94	Mike Hill	13 Jun 93
	83.84	Roald Bradstock	2 May 87
	83.06	Nick Nieland	15 Jun 96
	82.38	Colin Mackenzie	7 Aug 93
	81.70	Nigel Bevan	28 Jun 92
	80.98	Dave Ottley	24 Sep 88
	80.92	Mark Roberson	12 Jun 88
	78.54	Gary Jenson	17 Sep 89
10	77.84	Peter Yates	21 Feb 87
	76.66 i	Stuart Faben	3 Mar 96
	74.24		29 Jul 95
	75.52	Marcus Humphries	25 Jul 87
	75.32	Steve Harrison	9 Jul 95
	75.28	Nigel Stainton	5 Aug 89
	74.90	Darryl Brand	27 Jun 86
	74.72	Chris Crutchley	13 Jul 86
	74.70	Myles Cottrell	16 May 92
	73.88	Keith Beard	12 May 90
	73.26	David Messom	25 Apr 87
20	72.92	Stefan Baldwin	8 May 93
	71.86	Tony Hatton	3 May 93
	70.30	Tim Newenham	11 Jun 89
	70.12	Paul Morgan	12 Sep 87
	70.10	Richard Hooper	21 May 89
	70.00	Paul Bushnell	22 Jul 90
	70.00	Phil Parry	2 Jul 94
	69.90	Ken Hayford	5 Jul 87
	69.90	Tony Smith	6 Jul 96
	69.68	Shane Lewis	23 Apr 94
30	69.20	Roddy James	28 Apr 89
	69.02	Kevin Murch	3 Sep 89
	68.84	James Hurrion	12 Jul 91
	68.74	Jon Clarke	14 Jun 86
	68.74	Tony Norman	23 May 87
	68.70	Robert Mullen	2 Jul 96
	68.38	James Drennen	12 Jul 91
	68.30	Mark Lawrence	31 Jul 88
	68.10	Paul Edgington	12 Oct 86
	68.26	David Parker	19 May 96
40	67.62	Allan Holloway	25 Jun 89
	67.60	Dean Smahon	9 Jul 94
	67.48	Rob Laing	31 May 87
	67.44	John Guthrie	17 May 89
	67.22	Richard Atkinson	14 Aug 93
	67.16	Damien Crawford	12 Jul 92
	66.92	Demetrio Barros	7 Aug 93
	66.78	Trevor Ratcliffe	2 Jun 96
	66.62	Mark Francis	13 Jul 96
	66.60	Kevin Hill	23 Aug 94
50	66.48	Duncan MacDonald	19 May 96

rough tailed model

82.60	Colin Mackenzie	1 Jun 91
79.54	Gary Jenson	19 Jun 91
76.10	Keith Beard	18 May 91
70.34	Damien Crawford	20 Jul 91
70.16	James Hurrion	19 Jul 91
69.94	Tony Smith	22 Jun 91
67.92	Bruce Craven	7 Sep 91

DECATHLON (1985 Tables)

8847	Daley Thompson	9 Aug 84	
8131	Alex Kruger	2 Jul 95	
7980	Simon Shirley	24 Aug 94	
	8036 for AUS	29 Sep 88	
7922 w	Brad McStravick	28 May 84	
	7885 h	6 May 84	
7904	David Bigham	28 Jun 92	
7901 h	Peter Gabbett	22 May 72	
7889	Eugene Gilkes	18 May 86	
7874	Colin Boreham	23 May 82	
7861	Anthony Brannen	30 Apr 95	
7787	Brian Taylor	30 May 93	10
7766	Barry Thomas	2 Sep 95	
7748	Eric Hollingsworth	30 May 93	
7740	Greg Richards	7 Jun 87	
7713	James Stevenson	5 Jun 93	
7708	Fidelis Obikwu	28 May 84	
7663	Rafer Joseph	24 Aug 94	
7643 w	Tom Leeson	8 Sep 85	
	7565	11 Aug 85	
7610	Jamie Quarry	24 Aug 94	
7596 h	Mike Corden	27 Jun 76	
7594	Mark Bishop	3 Sep 89	20
7579 h	Mark Luscombe	8 May 88	
7535	Duncan Mathieson	24 Jun 90	
7515	Ken Hayford	9 Jun 85	
7500 h	Barry King	22 May 72	
7500	Pan Zeniou	2 Aug 81	
7480	Dean Macey	22 Aug 96	
7439	Kevan Lobb	19 Aug 84	
7431	Alan Drayton	8 Aug 78	
7425	Tony Southward	16 Jun 95	
7425 w	Paul Field	21 May 95	
	7295	2 Jul 95	30
7367 h	John Garner	8 May 88	
7363	Mike Bull	27 Jan 74	
7363 h	Nick Phipps	27 Jun 76	
7335	Stewart McCallum	19 Aug 73	
7308 h	Clive Longe	29 Jun 69	
7295	Stephen Rogers	4 Jun 95	
7275	Buster Watson	18 Jun 78	
7268	Paul Edwards ¶	14 Aug 83	
7240	Paul Allan	25 Aug 91	
7221	Andy Lewis	19 Jun 94	40
7198	Robert Betts	7 Aug 83	
7172 h	Dave Kidner	20 Aug 72	
7147 h	Justin Whitfield	12 May 85	
7136	Billy Jewers	3 Sep 89	
7112	Gavin Sunshine	30 Jul 93	
7094	Paul Howard	31 May 92	
7089 w	John Howell	18 Jun 78	
	7062 h	2 Jul 78	
7078	Steve Leader	19 Jun 94	
7076	Rob Laing	30 Jul 89	
7076 w	Trevor Sloman	22 Aug 93	
	6905	2 Jun 91	50
7061	Graham Flood	12 Jun 83	
7061	Gary James	20 Aug 89	
7053	George Robertson	18 May 86	

44

3000 METRES TRACK WALK

11:24.4	Mark Easton	10 May 89	
11:28.4	Phil Vesty	9 May 84	
11:29.6 i	Tim Berrett	21 Jan 90	
11:54.23		23 Jun 84	
11:31.0	Andi Drake	22 Jul 90	
11:32.2	Ian McCombie	20 Jul 88	
11:33.4	Steve Partington	12 Jul 95	
11:39.0 i+	Martin Rush	8 Feb 92	
11:49.48		1 Jul 84	
11:39.54	Andy Penn	22 May 91	
11:44.68	Roger Mills	7 Aug 81	
10 11:45.1	Chris Maddocks	9 Aug 87	
11:45.77	Steve Johnston	20 Jun 87	
11:47.12 i	Philip King	26 Feb 95	
11:49.64		29 May 95	
11:49.0	Darrell Stone	10 Jul 90	
11:51.1	Paul Nihill	5 Jun 71	
11:52.51	Sean Martindale	28 Jul 90	
11:53.3	Martin Bell	9 Aug 95	
11:53.46	Steve Barry	21 Aug 82	
11:54.7	Mike Parker	20 Apr 82	
11:55.0	Phil Embleton	24 May 71	

10000 METRES TRACK WALK

40:06.65	Ian McCombie	4 Jun 89	
40:53.60	Phil Vesty	28 May 84	
40:55.6	Martin Rush	14 Sep 91	
41:06.57	Chris Maddocks	20 Jun 87	
41:10.11	Darrell Stone	16 Jul 95	
41:13.62	Steve Barry	19 Jun 82	
41:13.65	Martin Bell	22 Jul 95	
41:14.3	Mark Easton	5 Feb 89	
41:14.61	Steve Partington	16 Jul 95	
10 41:18.64	Andi Drake	5 Jun 88	
41:49.06	Sean Martindale	26 Jun 90	
41:55.5	Phil Embleton	14 Apr 71	
41:59.10	Andy Penn	27 Jul 91	
42:06.35	Gordon Vale	2 Aug 81	
42:08.57	Paul Blagg	28 Aug 89	
42:23.0	Mike Parker	2 Feb 86	
42:28.0	Kieron Butler	22 Jun 93	
42:28.0	Philip King	17 May 95	
42:34.6	Paul Nihill	28 May 72	
20 42:35.6	Ken Matthews	1 Aug 60	

track short

40:54.7	Steve Barry	19 Mar 83

20 KILOMETRES ROAD WALK

1:22:03	Ian McCombie	23 Sep 88	
1:22:12	Chris Maddocks	3 May 92	
1:22:51	Steve Barry	26 Feb 83	
1:23:34	Andy Penn	29 Feb 92	
1:23:34	Martin Rush	29 Feb 92	
1:23:58	Darrell Stone	24 Feb 96	
1:24:04	Mark Easton	25 Feb 89	
1:24:04.0t	Andi Drake	26 May 90	
1:24:07.6t	Phil Vesty	1 Dec 84	
10 1:24:18	Steve Partington	12 Dec 90	
1:24:25	Tim Berrett	21 Apr 90	
1:24:50	Paul Nihill	30 Jul 72	
1:25:42	Martin Bell	9 May 92	
1:25:53.6t	Sean Martindale	28 Apr 89	
1:27:00	Roger Mills	30 Jun 80	
1:27:16	Les Morton	25 Feb 89	
1:27:35	Olly Flynn	3 Oct 76	
1:27:46	Brian Adams	11 Oct 75	
1:27:59	Phil Embleton	3 Apr 71	
1:28:02	Paul Blagg	27 Feb 82	20
1:28:15	Ken Matthews	23 Jul 60	
1:28:26	Chris Harvey	29 Sep 79	
1:28:30	Allan King	11 May 85	
1:28:34	Chris Smith	11 May 85	
1:28:37	Dave Jarman	30 Jun 80	
1:28:46	Jimmy Ball	4 Apr 87	
1:28:46	Steve Taylor	20 Dec 92	
1:28:50	Amos Seddon	3 Aug 74	
1:29:07	Philip King	20 Aug 95	
1:29:11	Chris Cheeseman	21 May 94	30
1:29:19	Stuart Phillips	31 May 92	
1:29:24	George Nibre	6 Apr 80	
1:29:29 +	Steve Johnson	16 Apr 89	
1:29:37	John Warhurst	28 Jul 73	
1:29:42	Dennis Jackson	10 May 86	
1:29:48	Mike Parker	8 May 82	
1:29:48	Martin Young	31 Mar 96	
1:29:49	Peter Marlow	3 Aug 74	
1:30:00	John Webb	18 May 68	

50 KILOMETRES ROAD WALK

3:51:37	Chris Maddocks	28 Oct 90	
3:57:48	Les Morton	30 Apr 89	
3:59:55	Paul Blagg	5 Sep 87	
4:03:08	Dennis Jackson	16 Mar 86	
4:06:01	Mark Easton	30 Apr 95	
4:06:14	Barry Graham	20 Apr 85	
4:07:23	Bob Dobson	21 Oct 79	
4:07:57	Ian Richards	20 Apr 80	
4:08:41	Adrian James	12 Apr 80	
4:09:15	Don Thompson	10 Oct 65	10
4:09:22	Mike Smith	27 Mar 89	
4:10:23	Darrell Stone	6 May 90	
4:10:42	Amos Seddon	9 Mar 80	
4:11:31	Paul Nihill	18 Oct 64	
4:12:00	Sean Martindale	16 Oct 93	
4:12:02	Martin Rush	28 Jul 91	
4:12:37	John Warhurst	27 May 72	
4:12:50	Darren Thorn	6 May 90	
4:13:25	Allan King	16 Apr 83	
4:14:03	Tom Misson	20 Jun 59	20
4:14:25	Dave Cotton	15 Jul 78	
4:14:59	Graham White	5 Mar 95	
4:15:14	Shaun Lightman	13 Oct 73	
4:15:22	Brian Adams	17 Sep 78	
4:15:52	Ray Middleton	27 May 72	
4:16:47	George Nibre	9 Mar 80	
4:17:24	Andi Drake	18 Oct 87	
4:17:34	Gordon Vale	9 Oct 83	
4:17:52	Stuart Elms	17 Apr 76	
4:18:30	Peter Ryan	10 Apr 82	

4 x 100 METRES RELAY

37.77	UK	22 Aug 93
Jackson, Jarrett, Regis, Christie		
37.98	UK	1 Sep 90
Braithwaite, Regis, Adam, Christie		
38.05	UK	21 Aug 93
John, Jarrett, Braithwaite, Christie		
38.08	UK	8 Aug 92
Adam, Jarrett, Regis, Christie		
38.09	UK	1 Sep 91
Jarrett, Regis, Braithwaite, Christie		
38.28	UK	1 Oct 88
Bunney, Regis, McFarlane, Christie		
38.34	UK	9 Sep 89
Callender, Regis, Adam, Christie		
38.36	UK	31 Aug 91
Jarrett, Regis, Braithwaite, Christie		
38.39	UK	5 Aug 89
Jarrett, Regis, Adam, Christie		
38.46	UK	10 Sep 94
Braithwaite, Jarrett, Regis, Christie		
38.52	UK	1 Oct 88
Bunney, Regis, McFarlane, Christie		
38.53	UK	26 Jun 93
John, Jarrett, Regis, Christie		
38.62	UK	1 Aug 80
McFarlane, Wells, Sharp, McMaster		
38.64	UK	7 Aug 91
Livingston ¶, Regis, Callender, Rosswess		
38.64	UK	7 Aug 92
Jarrett, Regis, Adam, Christie		
38.64	UK	15 Jul 94
John, Braithwaite, Regis, Christie		
38.67	England	3 Feb 90
Callender, Regis, Adam, Christie		
38.67	UK	1 Jun 96
K. Williams, Braithwaite, John, Campbell		
38.68	UK	11 Aug 84
Thompson, Reid, McFarlane, Wells		
38.71	UK	31 Aug 86
Bunney, Thompson, McFarlane, Christie		
38.72	UK	25 Jun 94
John, Wariso, Regis, Christie		
38.73	UK	24 Jun 95
Gardener, Jarrett, Braithwaite, Christie		
38.75	UK	12 Aug 95
Gardener, Braithwaite, Regis, Wariso		
38.76	UK	26 May 96
K. Williams, Braithwaite, Campbell, White		
38.80	UK	21 Aug 93
John, Jarrett, Braithwaite, Christie		
38.84	G. B. All Stars	17 Jul 92
Livingston ¶, John, Adam, Christie		
38.86	UK	19 Jun 88
Jackson, Christie, Regis, Obeng		
38.86	UK	16 Jul 88
McFarlane, Christie, Regis, Callender		
38.86	UK	5 Jun 93
Adam, Jarrett, Regis, John		

4 x 400 METRES RELAY

2:56.60	UK	3 Aug 96
Thomas, Baulch, Richardson, Black		
2:57.53	UK	1 Sep 91
Black, Redmond, Regis, Akabusi		
2:58.22	UK	1 Sep 90
Sanders, Akabusi, Regis, Black		
2:58.86	UK	6 Sep 87
Redmond, Akabusi, Black, Brown		
2:59.13	UK	11 Aug 84
Akabusi, Cook, Bennett, Brown		
2:59.13	UK	14 Aug 94
McKenzie, Whittle, Black, Ladejo		
2:59.49	UK	31 Aug 91
Mafe, Redmond, Richardson, Akabusi		
2:59.73	UK	8 Aug 92
Black, Grindley, Akabusi, Regis		
2:59.84	UK	31 Aug 86
Redmond, Akabusi, Whittle, Black		
2:59.85	UK	19 Aug 96
Baulch, Hylton, Richardson, Black		
3:00.25	UK	27 Jun 93
Ladejo, Akabusi, Regis, Grindley		
3:00.34	UK	25 Jun 95
Thomas, Patrick, Richardson, Black		
3:00.46	UK	10 Sep 72
Reynolds, Pascoe, Hemery, Jenkins		
3:00.58	UK	30 Jun 91
Sanders, Akabusi, Whittle, Black		
3:00.68	UK	11 Sep 82
Jenkins, Cook, Bennett, Brown		
3:00.93	UK	19 Jun 92
Redmond, Akabusi, Ladejo, Black		
3:01.03	UK - Under 23	19 Jul 92
McKenzie, Grindley, Richardson, Ladejo		
3:01.12	UK	28 Jun 87
Harmsworth, Whittle, Bennett, Black		
3:01.20	UK	7 Aug 92
Richardson, Akabusi, Black, Ladejo		
3:01.21 A	UK	20 Oct 68
Winbolt-Lewis, Campbell, Hemery, Sherwood		
3:01.22	UK	12 Aug 95
McKenzie, Patrick, Hylton, Richardson		
3:01.26	UK	9 Sep 72
Reynolds, Pascoe, Hemery, Jenkins		
3:01.26	UK	5 Aug 86
Akabusi, Black, Bennett, Brown		
3:01.34	UK	11 Sep 94
McKenzie, Ladejo, Baulch, Black		
3:01.36	UK	2 Aug 96
Thomas, Baulch, Ladejo, Richardson		
3:01.47	UK	5 Sep 87
Thomas, Akabusi, Bennett, Brown		
3:01.6 a	UK	21 Oct 64
Graham, Metcalfe, Cooper, Brightwell		
3:01.65	UK	7 Jul 85
Redmond, Akabusi, Slack, Bennett		
3:01.79	UK	2 Aug 96
Ladejo, Baulch, Hylton, Richardson		

UNDER 20

100 METRES

10.21	Jamie Henderson	6 Aug 87
10.25	Jason Livingston ¶	9 Aug 90
10.25	Jason Gardener	21 Jul 94
10.29	Peter Radford (10.31?)	13 Sep 58
10.32	Mike McFarlane	6 Aug 78
10.34	Lincoln Asquith	25 Aug 83
10.37	Darren Campbell	26 Jul 91
10.38	Elliot Bunney	22 Aug 85
10.39	Jason John	28 Jul 90
10.41	Dwain Chambers	28 Jul 95
10.41	Jamie Henthorn	28 Jul 95
10.43	Julian Golding	20 Jul 94
10.44	Steve Gookey	3 Aug 90
10.44	Jason Fergus	16 Sep 92
10.45	Darren Braithwaite	19 Jun 88
10.46	Marcus Adam	6 Aug 87
10.47	Danny Joyce	29 Jul 93
10.48	David Kirton	17 Jul 86

wind assisted

10.22	Lincoln Asquith	26 Jun 83
10.28	Darren Campbell	26 Jul 91
10.29	Mike McFarlane	7 Aug 78
10.29	Elliot Bunney	27 May 84
10.29	Trevor Cameron	11 Jun 94
10.34	Darren Braithwaite	25 Jun 88
10.34	Julian Golding	17 Sep 94
10.37	Courtney Rumbolt	25 Jun 88
10.37	Allyn Condon	3 Jul 93
10.38	Jason John	9 Aug 90
10.38	Kevin Mark	3 Jul 93
10.38	Ejike Wodu	3 Jul 93
10.38	Jamie Henthorn	25 May 96

hand timing

10.3	Martin Reynolds	29 Jun 68

200 METRES

20.54	Ade Mafe	25 Aug 85
20.67	David Jenkins	4 Sep 71
20.73 A	Ralph Banthorpe	15 Oct 68
20.78	John Regis	29 Sep 85
20.80	Mike McFarlane	1 Jul 79
20.85	Richard Ashby	25 Aug 85
20.86	Lincoln Asquith	28 Aug 83
20.86	Roger Hunter	5 May 84
20.87	Donovan Reid	7 Oct 82
20.87	Mark Smith	28 Jul 90
20.87	Darren Campbell	19 Sep 92
20.91	Jamie Baulch	18 Sep 92
20.91	Ian Mackie	23 Jul 94

wind assisted

20.61	Darren Campbell	11 Aug 91
20.73	Julian Golding	17 Sep 94
20.85	Mark Smith	1 Jul 90

hand timing

20.6	David Jenkins	19 Sep 71

wind assisted

20.7	Lincoln Asquith	2 Jul 83

400 METRES

45.36	Roger Black	24 Aug 85
45.41	David Grindley	10 Aug 91
45.45	David Jenkins	13 Aug 71
45.53	Mark Richardson	10 Aug 91
45.83	Mark Hylton	16 Jul 95
46.03	Peter Crampton	8 Aug 87
46.13	Guy Bullock	31 Jul 93
46.22	Wayne McDonald	17 Jun 89
46.32	Derek Redmond	9 Sep 84
46.46	Adrian Metcalfe	19 Sep 61
46.48	Roger Hunter	20 May 84
46.53	Mark Thomas	15 Sep 84
46.56	Roy Dickens	6 Sep 80
46.59	Carl Southam	17 Sep 92
46.63	Melvin Fowell	18 Aug 79
46.65	Darren Bernard	20 May 88
46.66	Du'aine Ladejo	9 Aug 90
46.77	Paul Dunn	31 May 82
46.78	Roger Jenkins	2 Sep 74
46.82	Phil Brown	31 Aug 80

hand timing

45.7	Adrian Metcalfe	2 Sep 61
46.6	Todd Bennett	1 Aug 81
46.7	Roger Jenkins	20 Aug 74

800 METRES (* 880 yards time less 0.70)

1:45.64	David Sharpe	5 Sep 86
1:45.77	Steve Ovett	4 Sep 74
1:46.46	John Gladwin	7 Jul 82
1:46.63	Curtis Robb	6 Jul 91
1:46.70*	John Davies I	3 Jun 68
1:47.0	Ikem Billy	12 Jun 83
1:47.02	Chris McGeorge	8 Aug 81
1:47.08	Atle Douglas	22 Aug 87
1:47.22	Kevin McKay	5 Jun 88
1:47.27	Tom Lerwill	22 Aug 96
1:47.35	Peter Elliott	23 Aug 81
1:47.53	Graham Williamson	1 Aug 79
1:47.56	Julian Spooner	24 Apr 79
1:47.70	Darryl Taylor	13 Jul 84
1:47.71	Dane Joseph	15 Sep 78
1:47.73	Colin Szwed	9 Sep 77
1:47.75	Garry Cook	3 Jul 77
1:47.79	Craig Winrow	20 Jul 90

1000 METRES

2:18.98	David Sharpe	19 Aug 86
2:19.92	Graham Williamson	8 Jul 79
2:20.0	Steve Ovett	17 Aug 73
2:20.02	Darryl Taylor	18 Aug 84
2:20.37	Johan Boakes	17 Jun 84
2:21.17	Curtis Robb	16 Sep 90
2:21.41	Stuart Paton	17 Sep 82
2:21.7 A	David Strang	26 Jan 87
2:21.71	Kevin Glastonbury	18 Jun 77
2:22.3	Chris McGeorge	19 Jul 81
2:22.69	Gary Staines	17 Sep 82

1500 METRES

3:36.6 +	Graham Williamson	17 Jul	79
3:40.09	Steve Cram	27 Aug	78
3:40.68	Brian Treacy	24 Jul	90
3:40.72	Gary Taylor	8 Jul	81
3:40.90	David Robertson	28 Jul	92
3:41.59	Chris Sly	22 Jul	77
3:42.2	Paul Wynn	9 Aug	83
3:42.5	Colin Reitz	8 Aug	79
3:42.67	Matthew Hibberd	28 Jul	92
3:42.7	David Sharpe	17 Oct	85
3:42.86	Stuart Paton	29 Aug	82
3:42.89	Alistair Currie	17 Jul	84
3:43.1 a	Paul Lawther	31 Jan	74
3:43.24	Nick Hopkins	15 Jun	85
3:43.37	Davey Wilson	4 Jul	87
3:43.39	Johan Boakes	30 May	87

ONE MILE

3:53.15	Graham Williamson	17 Jul	79
3:57.03	Steve Cram	14 Sep	79
3:58.68	Steve Flint	26 May	80
3:59.4	Steve Ovett	17 Jul	74
4:00.31	Johan Boakes	5 Aug	86
4:00.6	Simon Mugglestone	16 Sep	87
4:00.67	Brian Treacy	22 Aug	90
4:01.0	David Sharpe	3 May	86
4:01.5	Tony Leonard	12 Sep	77
4:01.5	Gary Staines	19 Sep	82

2000 METRES

5:06.56	Jon Richards	7 Jul	82

3000 METRES

7:48.28	Jon Richards	9 Jul	83
7:51.84	Steve Binns	8 Sep	79
7:56.28	John Doherty	13 Jul	80
7:59.55	Paul Davies-Hale	8 Aug	81
8:00.1 a	Micky Morton	11 Jul	78
8:00.7	Graham Williamson	29 Jul	78
8:00.73	David Black	24 Jul	71
8:00.8	Steve Anders	1 Aug	78
8:00.88	Paul Taylor	12 Jun	85
8:01.2	Ian Stewart I	7 Sep	68
8:01.26	Darius Burrows	21 Aug	94
8:01.43	Nat Muir	28 Aug	77
8:01.44	Colin Reitz	16 May	79

5000 METRES

13:27.04	Steve Binns	14 Sep	79
13:35.95	Paul Davies-Hale	11 Sep	81
13:37.4	David Black	10 Sep	71
13:43.82	Simon Mugglestone	24 May	87
13:44.64	Julian Goater	14 Jul	72
13:48.74	Jon Richards	28 May	83
13:48.84	John Doherty	8 Aug	80
13:49.1 a	Nat Muir	21 Aug	77
13:53.30	Ian Stewart I	3 Aug	68
13:53.3 a	Nick Lees	21 Aug	77
13:54.2	Mick Morton	1 Jul	78
13:54.52	Keith Cullen	8 Jun	91

10000 METRES

29:21.9	Jon Brown	21 Apr	90
29:38.6	Ray Crabb	18 Apr	73

2000 METRES STEEPLECHASE

5:29.61	Colin Reitz	18 Aug	79
5:31.12	Paul Davies-Hale	22 Aug	81
5:32.84	Tom Hanlon	20 Jul	86
5:34.8 a	Micky Morris	24 Aug	75
5:38.01	Ken Baker	1 Aug	82
5:38.2	Spencer Duval	8 Jul	89
5:39.3 a	Graeme Fell	11 Jul	78
5:39.93	Eddie Wedderburn	9 Sep	79
5:40.2	Paul Campbell	31 Jul	77
5:40.2	John Hartigan	27 Jun	84
5:40.87	Andrew Rodgers	25 Aug	83
5:40.9	Alastair O'Connor	25 Aug	90

3000 METRES STEEPLECHASE

8:29.85	Paul Davies-Hale	31 Aug	81
8:42.75	Colin Reitz	6 Jun	79
8:43.21	Kevin Nash	2 Jun	96
8:44.68	Alastair O'Connor	12 Aug	90
8:44.91	Ken Baker	30 May	82
8:45.65	Spencer Duval	17 Jun	89
8:47.1	Tom Conlon	6 Jul	80
8:47.49	Tom Hanlon	8 Jun	86
8:48.43	Graeme Fell	16 Jul	78
8:50.14	Dave Long I	13 Jul	73
8:51.02	Tony Staynings	14 Jul	72
8:54.15	Stuart Kefford	18 Sep	92
8:54.6	Micky Morris	7 Sep	75

110 METRES HURDLES (3'3")

13.77	Kevin Lumsdon	8 Aug	92
13.8	Jon Ridgeon	13 Jul	84
13.8	Paul Gray	16 Jul	88
14.0	Paul Brice	25 Jun	83
14.0	Colin Jackson	27 Aug	84
14.0	Neil Owen	2 Aug	92
14.06		4 Jul	92
14.0	James Hughes	11 May	93
14.14		30 May	93
14.0	Damien Greaves	8 Jul	95
14.01	Jamie Quarry	13 Jul	91
14.1	Mark Holtom	19 Jun	77
14.1	Brett St Louis	3 Aug	86
14.13	Derek Wilson	25 Jun	83
14.15	Mark Purser	13 Jul	91
14.18	Mark Whitby	25 Jun	83

wind assisted

13.6	Mark Holtom	9 Jul	77
13.8	Paul Brice	9 Jul	83
13.8	Colin Jackson	15 Jul	84
13.8	Brett St Louis	11 Jul	87
13.9	Tony Jarrett	12 Jul	86
13.92	Matthew Clements	27 Aug	94
14.10	Simon McAree	9 Jul	94
14.1	Derek Wilson	9 Jul	83
14.1	Jon Kell	26 May	84
14.1	Mark Stern	14 Jul	90

110 METRES HURDLES (3'6")

13.44	Colin Jackson	19 Jul 86
13.46	Jon Ridgeon	23 Aug 85
13.72	Tony Jarrett	24 May 87
13.91	David Nelson	21 Jun 86
13.97	Paul Gray	30 Jul 88
14.01	Ross Baillie	25 Aug 96
14.03	Brett St Louis	27 Jun 87
14.04	Damien Greaves	25 Aug 96
14.06	Mark Holtom	7 Aug 77
14.08	Paul Brice	26 Aug 83
14.14	Neil Owen	17 Sep 92
14.18	James Archampong	21 Jul 94
14.2	Andy Todd	27 Oct 67
14.2	Berwyn Price	8 Aug 70
	14.21	12 Sep 70
14.24	Nigel Walker	17 Sep 82

wind assisted

13.42	Colin Jackson	27 Jul 86
13.82	David Nelson	5 Jul 86
14.1	Peter Kelly	24 May 72

400 METRES HURDLES

50.22	Martin Briggs	28 Aug 83
50.70	Noel Levy	8 Jul 94
51.07	Philip Beattie	20 Aug 82
51.15 A	Andy Todd	18 Oct 67
51.31	Gary Oakes	9 Sep 77
51.48	Bob Brown	19 Jun 88
51.5	Max Robertson	10 Jul 82
	51.51	24 Jul 82
51.55	Mark Whitby	26 Aug 83
51.66	Paul Goacher	2 Aug 80
51.73	Matt Douglas	29 Jul 95
51.91	Peter Campbell	19 Jun 88
51.97	Bel Blik	17 Aug 85
52.1	Michael Bryars	30 Apr 83
52.2	Phil Harries	20 Jul 85
52.24	Andrew Abrahams	11 Aug 84
52.26	Gary Jennings	30 Jun 91
52.26	Charles Robertson-Adams	15 Jun 96

HIGH JUMP

2.37	Steve Smith	20 Sep 92
2.27	Brendan Reilly	27 May 90
2.26	James Brierley	3 Aug 96
2.25	Geoff Parsons	9 Jul 83
2.24	John Hill	23 Aug 85
2.23	Mark Lakey	29 Aug 82
2.22	Dalton Grant	3 Jul 85
2.21	Ben Challenger	24 Aug 96
2.20	Byron Morrison	14 Jul 84
2.18	Ossie Cham	14 Jun 80
2.18	Alex Kruger	26 Jun 82
2.18	Steve Ritchie	15 Jul 89
2.18	Hopeton Lindo	23 Jul 89
2.17	Stuart Ohrland	27 Aug 94
2.17	Mike Robbins	5 Aug 95

POLE VAULT

5.50	Neil Winter	9 Aug 92
5.30	Matthew Belsham	15 Sep 90
5.21	Andy Ashurst	2 Sep 84
5.20	Billy Davey	5 Jun 83
5.20	Warren Siley	4 Aug 90
5.20	Nick Buckfield	31 May 92
5.15	Christian Linskey	23 Aug 96
5.10	Brian Hooper	1 Oct 72
5.10	Michael Edwards	20 Jun 87
5.10	Mark Davis	9 Jun 96
5.05	Ian Tullett	22 Aug 87
5.05	Dean Mellor	7 Jul 90
5.02	Paul Williamson	29 May 93
5.00	Keith Stock	3 Jul 76
5.00	Bob Kingman	2 May 92
5.00	Tim Thomas	17 Jun 92
5.00	Mike Barber	1 Jul 92
5.00 ns	Ian Wilding	16 Jul 94
5.00	Neil Young	18 May 96
5.00	Ben Flint	6 Jul 96

LONG JUMP

7.98	Stewart Faulkner	6 Aug 88
7.91	Steve Phillips	10 Aug 91
7.84	Wayne Griffith	25 Aug 89
7.76	Carl Howard	31 Jul 93
7.74	Nathan Morgan	22 Aug 96
7.73	Jason Canning	20 Apr 88
7.72	Daley Thompson	21 May 77
7.70	Kevin Liddington	27 Aug 88
7.66	Barry Nevison	7 Jul 85
7.62	Colin Mitchell	11 Jul 78
7.61	Darren Gomersall	19 Jul 87

wind assisted

8.04	Stewart Faulkner	20 Aug 88
7.97	Nathan Morgan	13 Jul 96
7.96	Colin Jackson	17 May 86
7.82	Kevin Liddington	25 Jun 89
7.72	John Herbert	15 Jun 80

TRIPLE JUMP

16.58	Tosi Fasinro	15 Jun 91
16.53	Onochie Achike	24 Jul 94
16.24	Aston Moore	11 Jun 75
16.22	Mike Makin	17 May 81
16.13	Steven Anderson	11 Jun 83
16.03	John Herbert	23 Jun 81
15.95	Keith Connor	30 Aug 76
15.94	Vernon Samuels	27 Jun 82
15.93	Tayo Erogbogbo	17 Sep 94
15.92	Lawrence Lynch	13 Jul 85
15.88	Julian Golley	28 Jul 90
15.87	Stewart Faulkner	22 Aug 87

wind assisted

16.81	Tosi Fasinro	15 Jun 91
16.67	Onochie Achike	24 Jul 94
16.43	Mike Makin	14 Jun 81
16.31	Aston Moore	9 Aug 75
16.07	Vernon Samuels	14 Aug 82
16.01	Julian Golley	22 Jul 90

SHOT (7.26kg)
18.21 i	Matt Simson	3 Feb 89
18.11		27 Aug 89
17.78 i	Billy Cole	10 Mar 84
17.72		2 Jun 84
17.36 i	Chris Ellis	8 Dec 84
17.10		7 Jul 85
17.30	Carl Myerscough	3 Aug 96
17.26 i	Geoff Capes	16 Nov 68
16.80		30 Jul 68
17.22	Anthony Zaidman	4 Jul 81
16.61	Simon Williams	10 Aug 86
16.60	Alan Carter	11 May 63
16.48	Martyn Lucking	24 Aug 57
16.47	Paul Buxton	25 May 75
16.29 i	Emeka Udechuku	2 Mar 96
16.20		19 Aug 96
16.21	Mike Lindsay	29 Jul 57
16.20 i	Nigel Spratley	19 Mar 89
16.04		20 May 89
16.18	Tony Satchwell	23 Apr 72
16.10	Martin Fletcher	19 Jun 88
16.03	Jon Wood	26 Sep 70
15.94	Andy Vince	5 May 78
15.94	Mitchell Smith	23 Mar 85

SHOT (6.25kg)
19.47	Matt Simson	20 May 89
19.15	Billy Cole	19 May 84
18.66 i	Simon Williams	15 Nov 86
18.52		11 Jul 86
18.20 i	Chris Ellis	16 Feb 85
18.13		14 Jul 84
17.81	Anthony Zaidman	16 May 81
17.58	Nigel Spratley	28 May 89
17.32	Andy Vince	15 May 77
17.31	Mitchell Smith	11 Jun 85
17.30	Jamie Cockburn	20 Sep 92
17.30	Emeka Udechuku	25 Aug 96
17.26	Neil Gray	19 May 84
17.26 i	Neal Brunning ¶	9 Dec 89
17.08		21 Aug 88
17.22	Richard Slaney	20 Jul 75

DISCUS (2kg)
55.10	Glen Smith	31 Aug 91
53.42	Paul Mardle	25 Jul 81
53.40	Bob Weir	10 Aug 80
53.32	Paul Buxton	9 Aug 75
53.02	Simon Williams	16 Aug 86
52.94	Lee Newman	29 Aug 92
52.84	Jamie Murphy	14 Jun 92
52.14	Robert Russell	4 Jul 93
51.70	Richard Slaney	27 Jul 75
51.66	Neal Brunning ¶	30 Jul 88
51.10	Mike Lindsay	29 May 57
51.08	Peter Weir	1 Aug 82
51.04	Emeka Udechuku	3 Aug 96
50.74	Tony Satchwell	21 Aug 72
50.64	Colin Bastien	9 Jun 85

DISCUS (1.75kg)
60.76	Glen Smith	26 May 91
56.64	Jamie Murphy	19 May 90
56.10	Lee Newman	4 Jul 92
56.00	Simon Williams	17 May 86
55.94	Mark Davies	19 Aug 90
55.44	Neal Brunning ¶	8 Jul 89
55.00	Robert Russell	16 May 93
54.92	Emeka Udechuku	25 Aug 96
54.50	Paul Mardle	27 Jun 81
53.84	Bob Weir	14 Sep 80
53.50	Colin Bastien	8 Jun 85
53.24	Matt Symonds	21 Jun 87
53.22	Kevin Horne	18 Jul 82

HAMMER (7.26kg)
67.48	Paul Head	16 Sep 84
67.10	Jason Byrne	6 Aug 89
66.14	Martin Girvan	21 Jul 79
65.86	Bob Weir	6 Sep 80
65.30	Karl Andrews	2 Jul 94
64.14	Ian Chipchase	25 Sep 71
63.84	Andrew Tolputt	7 Sep 86
63.72	Gareth Cook	10 Jul 88
62.82	Mike Jones	29 Aug 82
62.02	Peter Vivian	1 Jul 89
61.34	Ron James	22 Apr 78
61.22	Malcolm Croad	25 Aug 92
61.10	Vaughan Cooper	5 May 84

HAMMER (6.25kg)
74.92	Jason Byrne	17 Dec 89
73.28	Bob Weir	14 Sep 80
72.66	Paul Head	2 Sep 84
71.84	Gareth Cook	28 May 88
70.36	Andrew Tolputt	21 Sep 86
69.10	Karl Andrews	1 Aug 94
68.84	Eric Berry	Jul 73
67.80	Martin Girvan	7 Jul 79
67.52	Vaughan Cooper	19 May 84
67.48	Mike Jones	2 Jun 82
66.38	Tony Kenneally	10 Jul 82
65.82	Dave Smith I	4 Jul 81

JAVELIN
79.50	Steve Backley	5 Jun 88
74.54	Gary Jenson	19 Sep 86
74.24	Mark Roberson	18 Jul 86
73.76	Nigel Bevan	29 Aug 87
71.74	Myles Cottrell	29 Jul 89
70.16 r	James Hurrion	19 Jul 91
69.62	Stefan Baldwin	8 Jul 89
68.74	Jon Clarke	14 Jun 86
68.38	James Drennen	12 Jul 91
68.30	Mark Lawrence	31 Jul 88
68.26	David Parker	19 May 96
67.92 r	Bruce Craven	7 Sep 91
67.22	Richard Atkinson	14 Aug 93
66.74	Stuart Faben	22 Jul 94
66.62	Mark Francis	13 Jul 96

DECATHLON (1985 Tables)

8082	Daley Thompson	31 Jul 77
7488	David Bigham	9 Aug 90
7480	Dean Macey	22 Aug 96
7299	Eugene Gilkes	24 May 81
7274	James Stevenson	24 Jun 90
7247 h	Brian Taylor	7 May 89
7169	Barry Thomas	5 Aug 90
7126	Fidelis Obikwu	16 Sep 79
7112	Gavin Sunshine	30 Jul 93
7018	Jamie Quarry	30 Jun 91
6958 h	Roy Mitchell	29 Sep 74
6936	Anthony Brannen	24 May 87
6925	Roger Hunter	4 Jun 95
6839	Mark Bushell	30 Apr 95
6812	Nigel Skinner	19 Aug 84
6809	Rafer Joseph	26 Jul 87
6801 w	Kevan Lobb	18 Jun 78

Junior implements

7134	Dean Macey	17 Sep 95
6958 w	Roger Hunter	18 Sep 94

3000 METRES TRACK WALK

11:54.23	Tim Berrett	23 Jun 84
12:01.89 i	Philip King	21 Feb 93
12:02.0		12 May 92
12:02.04	Phil Vesty	24 Jul 82
12:16.5	David Hucks	5 Aug 84
12:19.8	Gordon Vale	11 Mar 81
12:23.2	Martin Rush	18 Sep 83
12:23.53	Darrell Stone	19 Sep 87
12:24.45	Richard Dorman	5 Sep 80
12:25.8	Gareth Holloway	17 Jun 89
12:29.3	Ian Ashforth	19 May 85

5000 METRES TRACK WALK

20:16.40	Philip King	26 Jun 93
20:33.4 +	Darrell Stone	7 Aug 87
20:55.4	Tim Berrett	9 Jun 84
21:00.5 +	Phil Vesty	19 Jun 82
21:10.5 +	Gordon Vale	2 Aug 81

10000 METRES TRACK WALK

41:52.13	Darrell Stone	7 Aug 87
42:06.35	Gordon Vale	2 Aug 81
42:46.3	Phil Vesty	20 Mar 82
42:47.7	Philip King	2 May 92
43:04.09	Tim Berrett	25 Aug 83
43:42.75	Martin Rush	29 May 83
43:54.25	Gareth Brown	7 Aug 87
44:22.12	Gareth Holloway	5 Jun 88
44:22.38	Jon Vincent	1 Apr 89
44:30.0	Andy Penn	15 Mar 86

Road

41:46	Darrell Stone	26 Sep 87
42:29	Steve Hollier	10 Dec 95
42:39	Martin Rush	7 May 83
42:40	Tim Berrett	18 Feb 84

UNDER 17

100 METRES

10.67	Michael Nartey	28 Sep 91
10.69	Mike McFarlane	13 Aug 76
10.70	Steve Green	15 Jul 72
10.71	Luke Davis	12 Jul 96
10.72	Peter Little	6 Aug 77
10.72	Trevor Cameron	7 Aug 93
10.73	Danny Joyce	17 Aug 91
10.75	Elliot Bunney	28 May 83
10.75	Dwain Chambers	28 May 94
10.76	Paul Ashen	1 Aug 81
10.76	Kevin Mark	15 Aug 92
10.77	Mike Williams	26 Jul 87
10.78	Scott Fraser	13 Aug 94
10.79	Gary Thomas	31 Jul 82

overage

10.51	Lincoln Asquith	4 Oct 80

wind assisted

10.38	Kevin Mark	3 Jul 93
10.44	Luke Davis	13 Jul 96
10.56	Dwain Chambers	9 Jul 94
10.57	Trevor Cameron	3 Jul 93
10.62	Elliot Bunney	25 Jun 83
10.62	Jamie Nixon	7 Jul 85
10.65	Michael Williams	20 Jun 87
10.66	David Jackson	1 Jul 89
10.67	Daniel Plummer	13 Jul 96

hand timing

10.5	Michael Powell	17 Sep 78

200 METRES

20.92	Ade Mafe	27 Aug 83
21.24	Peter Little	21 Aug 77
21.25	Mark Richardson	24 Jul 88
21.44	Roger Hunter	2 Aug 81
21.51	Darren Campbell	15 Sep 90
21.53	Steven Eden	2 Aug 81
21.56	Trevor Cameron	8 Aug 93
21.58	Christian Malcolm	9 Jul 95
21.63	Richard Ashby	7 Aug 83
21.64	Elliot Bunney	7 Aug 83
21.65	Uvie Ugono	7 Aug 94
21.66	Marcus Adam	12 Aug 84
21.66	Ben Lewis	28 Sep 96
21.69	Michael Nartey	28 Sep 91
21.69	Philip Perigo	8 Jul 95

wind assisted

21.17	Mark Richardson	20 Aug 88
21.25	Trevor Cameron	25 Sep 93
21.32	Graham Beasley	9 Jul 94
21.38	Elliot Bunney	13 Aug 83

hand timing

21.5	Steve Green	6 Aug 72
21.5	Phil Brown	20 May 78
21.5	Lincoln Asquith	23 Aug 80
21.5	Jamie Nixon	12 May 85
21.5	Philip Perigo	12 Aug 95

wind assisted

21.0	Peter Little	30 Jul 77

400 METRES

46.43	Mark Richardson	28 Jul 88
46.74	Guy Bullock	17 Sep 92
47.81	Mark Hylton	17 Jul 93
47.86	Kris Stewart	13 Jul 96
48.05	David Naismith	10 Aug 96
48.11	Gary Thomas	18 Sep 82
48.25	Adrian Patrick	2 Sep 89
48.34	Richard McNabb	27 Aug 95
48.35	James Hilston	6 Aug 95
48.36	David Simpson	29 May 89
48.41	Mark Tyler	11 Aug 84
48.46	Philip Harvey	24 Jun 79
48.63	Wayne McDonald	19 Jul 86

hand timing

47.6	Kris Stewart	3 Aug 96
48.2	David Simpson	8 Jul 89
48.3	David McKenzie	21 Sep 86
48.4	Steve Ovett	20 Aug 72
48.4	Chris Thompson	1 Aug 81

800 METRES

1:49.9	Mark Sesay	18 Jul 89
1:50.7	Peter Elliott	16 Sep 79
1:50.90	Craig Winrow	21 Aug 88
1:51.0	Chris McGeorge	1 Jul 78
1:51.05	Malcolm Edwards	20 Sep 74
1:51.3	Julian Spooner	3 Aug 77
1:51.4	Kevin McKay	19 Aug 85
1:51.6	Neil Horsfield	31 Aug 83
1:51.6	David Gerard	21 Jul 84
1:51.8	Paul Burgess	14 Jul 87
1:51.9 +	Johan Boakes	17 Jun 84
1:52.0	Paul Causey	21 Jul 84

1000 METRES

2:20.37	Johan Boakes	17 Jun 84

1500 METRES

3:47.7	Steve Cram	14 May 77
3:48.49	Johan Boakes	28 Jun 84
3:49.9	Kelvin Newton	20 Jun 79
3:51.1	Jason Lobo	30 Aug 86
3:51.4	Darren Mead	26 Jul 85
3:51.7	Martin Forder	19 Sep 86
3:51.8	Mark Sesay	22 Aug 89
3:52.0	Stuart Poore	6 Sep 89
3:52.47	Simon Young	4 Aug 90
3:52.6	Glen Stewart	19 Sep 87
3:52.78	Clifton Bradley	2 Aug 81
3:52.9	Steve Johnson	8 Jul 89
3:53.0	Mark Bateman	31 Aug 74

ONE MILE

4:06.7	Barrie Williams	22 Apr 72
4:09.5	Colin Clarkson	29 Aug 77
4:09.6	Alistair Currie	9 Jun 81

2000 METRES

5:28.2 +	Kevin Steere	10 Jul 71

3000 METRES

8:13.42	Barrie Moss	15 Jul 72
8:15.34	Kevin Steere	30 Aug 71
8:19.08	Darren Mead	26 Aug 85
8:19.38	Johan Boakes	24 Jun 84
8:24.2	Simon Goodwin	16 Jul 80
8:24.2	Jason Lobo	13 Aug 86
8:25.2	Colin Clarkson	3 Aug 77
8:26.3	Paul Williams	10 Aug 83
8:26.6	Jon Dennis	23 Apr 86
8:26.92	Jon Richards	5 Sep 80
8:29.09	Steve Fury	18 Aug 84
8:29.4	Darrell Smith	16 Jul 83

overage

8:23.6	Ian Stewart II	14 Dec 77

5000 METRES

14:41.8	Nick Lees	24 Aug 74
14:46.8	Paul Williams	15 Dec 71

overage

14:30.6	Nick Lees	11 Dec 74
14:45.4	Ray Crabb	15 Dec 71

1500 METRES STEEPLECHASE

4:11.2	Steve Evans	15 Jul 74
4:12.3	Chris Sly	15 Jul 74
4:13.1	John Crowley	15 Jul 74
4:13.2	David Lewis	1 Jul 78
4:13.7	Danny Fleming	31 Jul 77
4:13.9	Eddie Wedderburn	31 Jul 77
4:14.0	David Robertson	8 Jul 89
4:14.4	Steven Arnold	7 Sep 85
4:15.0	David Caton	9 Jun 84
4:15.0	Spencer Duval	12 Jul 86
4:15.2	Garrie Richardson	8 Jul 89
4:15.3	John Wilson	26 Jul 75

overage

4:13.2	Darren Mead	16 Oct 85

2000 METRES STEEPLECHASE

5:55.0	David Lewis	20 Aug 78
5:59.2	Danny Fleming	6 Aug 77

3000 METRES STEEPLECHASE

9:16.6	Colin Reitz	19 Sep 76

100 METRES HURDLES

12.68	Matthew Clements	8 Aug 93
12.90	Stephen Markham	17 Aug 91
12.97	Jon Snade	8 Aug 93
13.01	Hugh Teape	3 Aug 80
13.05	Brett St Louis	4 Aug 85
13.07	Jon Ridgeon	7 Aug 83
13.07	David O'Leary	3 Aug 96
13.09	Damien Greaves	8 Jul 94
13.10	Ricky Glover	17 Aug 91
13.12	Ross Baillie	13 Aug 94
13.15	Perry Batchelor	4 Jul 92
13.16	Grant Adams	16 Aug 92
13.18	Richard Dunn	1 Jun 91
13.19	Colin Jackson	7 Aug 83
13.20	Nick Csemiczky	20 Jul 91

wind assisted

12.47	Matthew Clements	9 Jul 94
12.70	Damien Greaves	9 Jul 94
12.88	Nick Csemiczky	13 Jul 91
12.90	Ricky Glover	13 Jul 91
12.90	Ben Warmington	8 Jul 95
12.99	Neil Owen	1 Jul 90
13.01	Berian Davies	30 Jul 89
13.06	Dominic Lewis	29 May 89
13.11	Henrik Hartman	30 Jul 89

hand timing

12.8	Brett St Louis	28 Jul 85
12.8	Richard Dunn	29 Jun 91
12.9	Hugh Teape	31 Aug 80
13.0	Jon Ridgeon	11 Jun 83
13.0	Damien Greaves	30 Jul 94

wind assisted

12.6	Brett St Louis	20 Jul 85
12.9	Jon Ridgeon	9 Jul 83

110 METRES HURDLES (3'0")

13.71	Matthew Clements	19 May 94
14.16	Ben Warmington	12 Jul 95
14.19	Ross Baillie	19 May 94

hand timing

13.6	Jon Ridgeon	16 Jul 83

110 METRES HURDLES (3'3")

15.44	Ian Cawley	6 Aug 95

wind assisted

13.92	Matthew Clements	27 Aug 94
14.61	Damien Greaves	27 Aug 94
15.42	Ian Cawley	6 Aug 95

hand timing

14.5	Kieran Moore	30 Aug 80
14.7	Max Robertson	20 Sep 80

110 METRES HURDLES (3'6")

15.39	Jon Kell	7 Aug 82

400 METRES HURDLES (2'9")

52.81	Richard McDonald	10 Aug 96
53.14	Martin Briggs	2 Aug 80
53.30	Mark Rowlands	31 Jul 94
53.55	Charles Robertson-Adams	31 Jul 94
53.58	Noel Levy	13 Jul 91
53.64	Dean Park	17 May 94
53.69	Max Robertson	2 Aug 80
53.69	Bob Brown	9 Aug 86
53.71	Andrew Bargh	11 Jul 92
53.82	Robert Taylor	9 Aug 86
53.98	Paul Martin	11 Jul 92
54.01	Richard Warburton	20 Jul 91

hand timing

53.2	Philip Beattie	24 May 80

400 METRES HURDLES (3'0")

53.06	Philip Beattie	2 Aug 80
53.31	Richard McDonald	28 Jul 96
54.20	Noel Levy	28 Sep 91

hand timing

54.0	Bob Brown	1 Jul 86

HIGH JUMP

2.23	Mark Lakey	29 Aug 82
2.15	Ossie Cham	14 Jul 79
2.15	Brendan Reilly	7 May 89
2.15	Stanley Osuide	1 Sep 91
2.12	Femi Abejide	11 Jul 81
2.11	Leroy Lucas	6 Aug 83
2.10	Dalton Grant	18 Sep 82
2.10	Tim Blakeway	29 Aug 87
2.10	James Brierley	16 May 93
2.10	Martin Lloyd	28 Sep 96
2.09	Steve Smith	10 Sep 89
2.08	Ross Hepburn	29 Jul 78
2.08	Nick Hay	19 Aug 84
2.08	Sean McLean	14 Jul 91

overage

2.13 i	Colin McMaster	1 Dec 96

POLE VAULT

5.20	Neil Winter	2 Sep 90
5.15	Christian Linskey	23 Aug 96
4.90	Warren Siley	8 Sep 89
4.80	Billy Davey	14 Sep 80
4.76	Nick Buckfield	11 Jun 89
4.72	Ian Lewis	24 Aug 85
4.66	Michael Edwards	24 Aug 85
4.60	Ben Flint	10 Jun 95
4.53	Keith Stock	5 Sep 73
4.50	Christian North	26 Aug 90
4.50	Michael Barber	15 Sep 90
4.50	Neil Young	5 Jun 93
4.48	Mark Hodgkinson	17 Sep 88
4.45	Richard Hooper	21 Sep 80
4.45	Mark Davis	14 Sep 93
4.45	Rufus Cooper	3 Sep 95
4.45	Richard Smith	18 Aug 96

LONG JUMP

7.32	Kevin Liddington	16 May 87
7.25	Alan Slack	12 Jun 76
7.21	Hugh Teape	17 May 80
7.20	Hugh Davidson	21 Jun 80
7.19	Onochie Onuorah	8 Jul 89
7.18	Barry Nevison	1 May 83
7.17	Hugh Whyte	15 Jul 79
7.15	Matthew John	29 Jun 86
7.14	Stewart Faulkner	17 Aug 85
7.13	Mark Findlay	24 Sep 94
7.12	Peter Little	16 Jul 77
7.12	Winston Walker	13 Jul 79
7.12	John King	22 Sep 79
7.12	Zac Kerin	14 May 88

wind assisted

7.40	Matthew John	10 May 86
7.25	Nathan Morgan	27 Aug 94
7.23	Onochie Onuorah	26 May 90
7.22	Paul Hanson	7 Jul 78
7.18	Nicki Gordon	12 Sep 93
7.18	Kevin Hibbins	21 Jul 96
7.16	Marcellas Peters	18 Jun 94

53

TRIPLE JUMP

15.65	Vernon Samuels	18 Jul 81
15.50	Junior Campbell	18 May 86
15.45	Steven Anderson	2 Aug 81
15.28	Onochie Achike	22 Jun 91
15.14	Marvin Bramble	8 Aug 93
14.94	Hugh Teape	17 May 80
14.93	Mark Whitehead	26 Aug 85
14.90	Lawrence Lynch	21 Jul 84
14.84	Peter Vaughan	2 May 83
14.77	Carl Howard	13 Jul 90
14.76	Delroy Ricketts	13 Jul 90
14.76	Jonathan Wallace	3 Sep 95
14.75	Megarry Effiong	18 Jul 76
overage		
14.88	Ian Timbers	5 Oct 80
wind assisted		
15.25	Marvin Bramble	3 Jul 93
15.08	Lawrence Lynch	29 Apr 84
15.06	Craig Duncan	7 Aug 82
14.88	Carl Howard	13 Jul 90
14.87	Darren Gomersall	3 Aug 85
14.84	Nick Leech	8 Jul 78
14.79	Darren Parke	13 Jul 84
14.76	Eric McCalla	21 Aug 76

SHOT (7.26kg)

17.30	Carl Myerscough	3 Aug 96
16.03	Chris Ellis	11 Sep 82
15.81	Matt Simson	16 Aug 86

SHOT (6.25kg)

16.80	Chris Ellis	13 Sep 81
16.36	Neal Brunning ¶	31 Aug 87
16.26	Emeka Udechuku	23 Apr 95
overage		
16.62 i	Emeka Udechuku	16 Dec 95

SHOT (5kg)

21.20	Carl Myerscough	22 Sep 96
19.22	Chris Ellis	4 Jun 82
18.90	Neal Brunning ¶	6 Sep 87
18.44	Matt Simson	27 Jul 86
18.43	Emeka Udechuku	28 May 95
18.25	Billy Cole	1 Aug 81
17.91	Anthony Zaidman	28 May 78
17.76	George Brocklebank	22 Jul 79
17.36	Piers Selby	10 Jul 92
17.30	Jason Mulcahy	7 Jul 89
17.24	Mark Edwards	20 Aug 91
17.14	Bill Fuller	9 Jul 91
17.04	Jeff Clare	18 Jul 81
17.01	James Muirhead	7 Sep 87
overage		
18.73	Matt Simson	Nov 86
17.37 i	Guy Litherland	15 Dec 85
17.30 i	Simon Williams	1 Dec 84
downhill		
18.90	Matt Simson	23 Aug 86

DISCUS (2kg)

50.60	Carl Myerscough	28 Jul 96
48.96	Emeka Udechuku	19 Aug 95
46.64	Guy Litherland	29 Jun 85
46.52	Chris Symonds	19 Sep 87

DISCUS (1.75kg)

54.70	Emeka Udechuku	18 Jun 95
52.50	Paul Mardle	7 Jul 79
51.16	Chris Symonds	6 Sep 87

DISCUS (1.5kg)

62.22	Emeka Udechuku	10 Jul 95
58.14	Carl Myerscough	12 May 96
56.14	Chris Symonds	6 Sep 87
55.94	Simon Williams	9 Sep 84
55.90	Guy Litherland	14 Sep 85
55.72	Keith Homer	27 Jun 82
55.52	Glen Smith	14 May 88
55.36	Neal Brunning ¶	7 Jun 87
54.18	Matthew Symonds	21 Jul 84
53.80	Paul Mardle	19 May 79
52.76	Julian Willett	17 Jun 89
52.76	James South	1 Sep 91
52.62	Ashley Knott	22 Sep 91
52.40	Guy Dirkin	28 Jun 69
52.20	Lee Newman	4 Jun 89
52.04	Francis Bacon	20 May 78
downhill		
56.98	Neal Brunning ¶	11 Jul 87

HAMMER (7.26kg)

59.94	Andrew Tolputt	30 Sep 84
57.04	Peter Vivian	27 Jun 87
56.66	Paul Head	5 Sep 81

HAMMER (6.25kg)

66.70	Andrew Tolputt	2 Sep 84
62.52	Paul Head	16 May 81
61.72	Nick Steinmetz	30 Aug 93

HAMMER (5kg)

76.28	Andrew Tolputt	11 Aug 84
73.90	Paul Head	29 Aug 81
73.00	Nick Steinmetz	17 Jul 93
71.34	Tony Kenneally	7 Sep 80
70.82	Jason Byrne	20 Jun 87
68.62	Peter Vivian	16 May 87
67.64	Gareth Cook	22 Sep 85
67.48	Christopher Howe	24 Jun 84
66.92	Paul Murden	8 May 85
66.30	Malcolm Croad	21 Jul 90
64.82	Vaughan Cooper	13 May 82
64.40	Jonathan Bond	14 May 89
64.32	Neil Homer	18 Aug 84
64.18	Charles Beresford	1 May 89
63.54	Matt Spicer	16 May 87
63.40	Ian McLaughlin	8 Aug 92
downhill		
64.30	Wayne Clarke	23 Aug 92

JAVELIN (800g -1986 model)
68.26	David Parker	19 May 96
59.04	James Hurrion	27 Jun 90
59.04	Dan Carter	26 Aug 96

JAVELIN (800g Original model)
72.78	Gary Jenson	10 Sep 83
69.84	Colin Mackenzie	12 May 79
66.14	David Messom	14 May 81
65.32	Marcus Humphries	26 Aug 78

JAVELIN (700g)
73.56	David Parker	20 Jul 96
72.48	Gary Jenson	3 Jul 83
70.30	Colin Mackenzie	6 Jul 79
68.26	Ian Marsh	30 Jul 77
68.18	James Hurrion	3 Jun 90
66.88	David Messom	4 Jul 81
66.86	Michael Williams	16 Jul 79
66.52	Marcus Humphries	17 Sep 78
66.00	Dan Carter	1 Sep 96
65.92	Tim Kitney	10 Aug 96
65.68	Tim Eldridge	18 Aug 91
65.16	Mark Wells	31 May 77
64.92	Jason Beaumont	11 Jun 83
64.92	Paul Bushnell	20 Sep 85
64.80	Justin Rubio	1 Sep 85
64.68	Paul Godwin	20 May 90

DECATHLON (Senior Implements)
6484	David Bigham	27 Sep 87
6299	Tom Leesom	21 Sep 80
overage		
5943	John Ball	8 Oct 78

DECATHLON (Junior Implements)
6554	Jim Stevenson	25 Sep 88
6093	Robert Hughes	28 May 89

DECATHLON (U17 Implements)
6706	David Bigham	28 Jun 87
6047	Jeremy Lay	30 Jun 85

OCTATHLON
5423	Leo Barker	17 Sep 95
5378	Matthew Lewis	20 Sep 92
5311	Dean Macey	18 Sep 94
5208	Fyn Corcoran	18 Sep 94
5158	Edward Coats	25 Aug 96
5149	Paul Hourihan	19 Sep 93
5144	Marc Newton	17 Sep 95
5121	Chris Hindley	20 Sep 92
5102	Matt Douglas	22 Aug 93
5059	Mark Bushell	19 Sep 93
5051	Scott Walker	18 Sep 94
with 100m		
5531	Jim Stevenson	18 Sep 88
5304	Tom Leeson	28 Sep 80
5194	Bryan Long	26 Sep 76
5106	Jeremy Lay	29 Sep 85
5096	Onochie Onuorah	17 Sep 89

3000 METRES TRACK WALK
12:04.9	Philip King	18 May 91
12:35.94	David Hucks	30 Aug 82
12:50.9	Jon Vincent	8 Jul 87
12:50.67 i	Stuart Monk	18 Feb 95
12:52.9		12 Jul 95
13:03.5	Ian Ashforth	16 Sep 84
13:05.8	Sean Maxwell	8 Aug 76
13:08.4	Ian McCombie	8 Aug 76
13:09.74	Kirk Taylor	2 Jun 84
13:10.6	Niall Troy	23 Jul 78
13:12.7	Tim Berrett	16 Aug 81
overage		
12:44.8	Gordon Vale	11 Oct 78

5000 METRES TRACK WALK
20:46.5	Philip King	29 Sep 91
21:52.7	Stuart Monk	22 Jul 95
22:17.5	Russell Hutchings	27 Sep 86
22:32.5	Gareth Holloway	27 Sep 86
22:35.0	Ian Ashforth	6 Jun 84
22:37.0	Jonathan Bott	27 Sep 86
22:42.0	Martin Young	20 Aug 88
22:42.19	Jon Vincent	6 Jun 86
22:48.0	Matthew Hales	13 Nov 96
22:53.7	Tim Berrett	28 Jun 81
22:53.8	David Hucks	10 Mar 82
22:57.7	Michael Kemp	31 Aug 96
23:01.0	Karl Atton	19 Apr 88
23:16.5	Nathan Kavanagh	10 Jul 83
overage		
22:42.2	Michael Kemp	13 Oct 96
23:16.4	Gareth Brown	16 Dec 84
23:19.0	Mark Easton	12 Dec 79
Road		
21:33	Jon Vincent	1 Nov 86
22:04	Gareth Holloway	14 Sep 86
22:05	Karl Atton	19 Mar 88
22:16	Stuart Monk	11 Feb 95
22:25	Russell Hutchings	1 Nov 86
22:30	Gordon Vale	15 Oct 77
overage		
21:31	Gareth Holloway	1 Nov 86
21:35	Jon Bott	1 Nov 86
22:11	Gordon Vale	21 Oct 78
22:12	Nathan Kavanagh	22 Oct 83

10000 METRES TRACK WALK
43:56.5	Philip King	2 Feb 91
45:47.0	Ian Ashforth	12 Sep 84
46:11.0	Jon Vincent	20 May 87
47:36.60	Stuart Monk	2 Jul 95
overage		
46:34.0	Karl Atton	3 Dec 88
46:36.0	Gordon Vale	26 Nov 78
Road		
43:49	Philip King	29 Jun 91
45:43	Jon Vincent	7 Mar 87
overage		
44:50	Michael Kemp	16 Nov 96

UNDER 15

100 METRES

11.0	Norman Ellis	23 Jul 89
11.05	Jamie Nixon	21 Jul 84
11.10	Courage Edo	15 Aug 92
11.1	Michael Hitchen	24 Apr 77
11.1	Malcolm James	77
11.1	Ray Burke	25 Aug 84
11.1	Duncan Game	11 May 86
11.1	Michael Williams	31 Aug 86
11.1	Jeffrey Anderson	3 Jul 89
11.1	Matthew Clements	23 Aug 92
11.2	D. Smith	12 Jul 80
11.2	Martin Waldron	30 Aug 81
11.2	Chris Jagoe	26 Jun 83
11.2	Stephen Butler	2 Jul 88
11.2	Mark Walcott	2 Jul 88
11.2	Kevin Mark	24 Jul 91
11.2	Jermaine Williams	11 Apr 92
11.2	Chris Blake	27 Jun 93

wind assisted

11.00	Steve Wiggans	9 Jul 94
11.0	Malcolm James	24 Jun 77
11.0	Ian Strange	24 Jun 77
11.0	John Burt	6 Sep 80
11.0	Milton Thompson	6 Aug 89
11.0	Jeffrey Anderson	6 Aug 89
11.0	Matthew Clements	15 Sep 91
11.04	Joe Brown	13 Jul 96
11.05	Ray Burke	11 Aug 84
11.06	Duncan Game	5 Jul 86
11.06	Paul Chantler	9 Jul 94
11.1	Paul Ashen	6 Jul 79
11.1	Tony Cairns	21 Jun 86
11.1	Curtis Browne	14 Jul 90

200 METRES

22.2	Michael Williams	12 Jul 86
22.31		10 Aug 86
22.30	Jamie Nixon	29 Sep 84
22.3	Anthony Cairns	12 Jul 86
22.40	Ben Lewis	8 Jul 95
22.4	Duncan Game	29 Jun 86
22.54	Matthew Clements	16 Aug 92
22.6	Stuart Lawrenson	27 Jun 76
22.65	Daniel Angus	12 Jul 96
22.69	Chris Blake	8 Aug 93
22.7 *	Edward Osborn	18 Jul 59
22.7	Richard Ashby	13 Jun 81
22.7	Ade Mafe	5 Jul 81
22.7	Charles Gordon	14 Jul 90
22.7	Stephen Daly	11 Jun 94
22.7	Andre Duffus	30 Jul 94

overage

22.4	Ade Mafe	11 Nov 81

wind assisted

21.9	Anthony Cairns	21 Jun 86
22.26	Stephen Daly	9 Jul 94
22.39	André Duffus	9 Jul 94
22.46	Robert Allenby	9 Jul 94

400 METRES

49.8	Mark Tyler	25 Aug 82
49.9	David McKenzie	11 Aug 85
49.97		23 Jun 85
50.0	Simon Heaton	7 Jul 79
50.1	Ade Mafe	6 Sep 81
50.3	Malcolm James	29 Aug 77
50.65	Ian Lowthian	29 Jul 95
50.7	Cephas Howard	19 May 91
50.99		13 Jul 91
50.88	Aaron Evans	17 Aug 96
50.9	Alan Leonard	30 Aug 78
50.9	Noel Goode	7 Jul 79
51.00	Paul Roberts	22 Jul 84
51.0	Marc Newton	30 Jul 94
51.1	Jamie Brown	9 Jul 88
51.11	Leon Connike	29 Jul 95
51.2	Wayne Tarquini	28 Jul 71
51.2	Nicholas Bee	13 Jul 85
51.2	Guy Bullock	29 Jul 90

overage

50.5 i	Cephas Howard	14 Dec 91

800 METRES

1:56.1	Craig Winrow	12 Jul 86
1:56.6	Paul Burgess	13 Jul 85
1:57.1	Delroy Smith	12 Jul 86
1:57.12	Michael Combe	14 Aug 93
1:57.2 a	Tony Jarman	15 Sep 78
1:57.5	Noel Goode	11 Jul 79
1:57.7	Eric Kimani	15 Sep 81
1:57.7	Mark Sesay	11 Aug 87
1:57.87	Austin Finn	7 Jul 91
1:58.1	Piers Counsell	12 Jul 86
1:58.3 *	Dave Dutton	6 Aug 66
1:58.4	Graham Green	9 Sep 79

overage

1:53.6	David Gerrard	9 Nov 83
1:57.7	Stephen Gilbey	17 Oct 73

1000 METRES

2:38.2	Eric Kimani	11 Sep 81

1500 METRES

4:03.0	Glen Stewart	28 Aug 85
4:03.0	Scott West	28 Aug 90
4:03.52	Mike Isherwood	17 Sep 82
4:03.56	Richard Youngs	17 Sep 82
4:03.6	Douglas Stones	7 Jul 79
4:03.7	David Gerard	31 Jul 83
4:05.7	Ben Mabon	1 Sep 85
4:05.8	Graham Green	19 Jun 79
4:06.0	Eric Kimani	29 Jul 81
4:06.5	Paul Hemmings	18 Jul 82
4:06.8	Richard Green	7 Jun 70
4:07.18	Johan Boakes	17 Sep 82

ONE MILE

4:21.9	Glen Stewart	11 Sep 85

2000 METRES

5:45.8	Richard Slater	16 Jun 74

3000 METRES

8:47.0	Ben Mabon	16 Jul 85
8:48.8	Dale Smith	14 Aug 85
8:51.1	Mark Slowikowski	4 Jun 80
8:54.6	Gary Taylor	14 Sep 77
8:54.6	David Bean	22 Jul 79
8:56.0	Paul Ryder	29 Aug 79
8:56.4	Stuart Bond	10 Sep 91
8:57.0	Philip Hennessy	28 Jul 82
8:57.6	Chris Taylor	16 Jul 69
8:58.4	James Clarke	30 Sep 81
8:58.6	Robert Farish	22 Jul 79

overage

8:56.9	David Gerard	12 Oct 83

80 METRES HURDLES

10.71	Matthew Clements	15 Aug 92
11.0	Austin Drysdale	22 Jun 75
11.04	Leon McRae	8 Jul 95
11.07	Robert Hollinger	8 Jul 95
11.10	Seb Bastow	13 Jul 96
11.1	Ricky Glover	8 Jul 89
11.1	Tom Bradwell	13 Jul 90
11.20	Tony Lashley	13 Jul 91
11.2	David Colford	13 May 84
11.2	Dominic Lewis	26 Sep 87
11.2	Nick Dowsett	18 Sep 93

wind assisted

11.00	Tom Benn	9 Jul 94
11.02	Nick Dowsett	10 Jul 93
11.12	Sam Allen	10 Jul 93
11.17	Tony Lashley	18 Aug 91

100 METRES HURDLES (3'0")

13.3	Matthew Clements	23 Aug 92

HIGH JUMP

2.04	Ross Hepburn	22 Aug 76
2.01	Ken McKeown	10 Aug 96
1.97	Andrew Lynch	29 Aug 88
1.97	Wayne Gray	3 Sep 95
1.95	Mark Lakey	14 Sep 80
1.93	Ewan Gittins	21 Jul 84
1.91	Mark Smith	15 Jul 89
1.91	Edward Willers	9 Jul 94
1.91	Matthew Brereton	9 Jul 94
1.91	Jamie Russell	22 Sep 96

overage

1.94 i	Paul Byrne	10 Dec 77
1.91 i	Lee Broomfield	19 Dec 92

POLE VAULT

4.31	Richard Smith	28 Aug 95
4.30	Neil Winter	8 Jul 88
4.30	Christian Linskey	18 Jun 94
4.18	Ian Lewis	24 May 83
4.00	Jimmy Lewis	9 Sep 79
3.90	Peter Eyre	2 Jul 89
3.90	Martin Parley	6 Jun 92
3.90	Steve Francis	11 Sep 93
3.90	Andrew Correy	17 Aug 96
3.85	Steven Brown	2 Jun 96

overage

4.40	Neil Winter	1 Oct 88

LONG JUMP

6.79	Onochie Onuorah	17 Sep 88
6.77	Barry Nevison	30 Aug 81
6.74	Kevin Hibbins	17 Jun 95
6.63	Ian Strange	77
6.62	Martin Giraud	25 May 92
6.60	Courage Edo	8 Aug 92
6.59	Danny Smith	29 Aug 87
6.58	Tony Allen	8 Aug 82
6.52	Julian Danquah	7 Jul 67
6.51	Karl Hunter	22 May 77
6.51	Marcellas Peters	18 Sep 93

overage

6.59 i	David Gilkes	19 Dec 92
6.59 i	Marcellas Peters	11 Dec 93

wind assisted

7.12	Onochie Onuorah	17 Sep 88
6.72	David Gilkes	6 Apr 92
6.61	Kirk King	7 Jul 95
6.54	David Conway	7 Jul 78

downhill

6.77	Eric Wood	25 Aug 58

TRIPLE JUMP

13.86	Jamie Quarry	10 Jul 87
13.79	Paul Dundas	11 Jun 88
13.77	Eugene Hechevarria	16 Sep 78
13.71	Larry Achike	10 Jun 89
13.69	Vernon Samuels	25 Aug 79
13.60	Steven Anderson	9 Jun 79
13.60	Steve Folkard	11 Jul 80
13.57	Errol Burrows	11 Jul 80
13.56	Delroy Ricketts	18 Jun 88
13.55	Darren Yeo	15 Jul 89
13.55	Michael Duberry	14 Jul 90

wind uncertain

13.83	Vernon Samuels	30 Jun 79

wind assisted

13.92	Eugene Hechevarria	7 Jul 78
13.87	Vernon Samuels	20 Sep 79
13.83	Chris Tomlinson	12 Jul 96
13.73	Donovan Fraser	6 Jul 79
13.69	Kevin O'Shaughnessy	7 Jul 78
13.60	Dean Taylor	12 Jul 96

SHOT (4kg)

18.71	Chris Ellis	14 Jun 80
16.54	Geoff Hodgson	7 Jul 72
16.39	Peter Waterman	2 Jul 94
16.29	Neal Brunning ¶	11 Sep 85
16.14	Andrew Monaghan	19 Sep 70
16.11	Billy Cole	6 Jul 79
16.05	John Nicholls	29 Jun 80
16.01	Ian McLaughlin	18 Sep 91
15.96	James Muirhead	14 Sep 85
15.95	Spencer English	3 Aug 86
15.90	Antony Zaidman	12 Sep 76
15.90	Jason Mulcahy	6 Sep 87

overage

16.36 i	Billy Cole	1 Nov 79
15.94 i	Phil Adams	14 Dec 86

SHOT (5kg)

15.62	Chris Ellis	80

overage

15.93	Chris Ellis	7 Dec 80

DISCUS (1.25kg)

53.08	Emeka Udechuku	5 Sep 93
50.80	Paul Mardle	3 Sep 77
50.32	Chris Symonds	23 Jul 85
50.04	Keith Homer	11 Jul 80
49.36	James Muirhead	12 May 85
49.32	Julian Douglas	16 Sep 79
49.22	Spencer English	1 Jun 86
48.84	Witold Leonowicz	23 Aug 80
48.78	Neville Lynch	7 Sep 80
48.76	Ben Walker	15 Aug 92
48.30	Alan Rudkin	22 Aug 93
48.02	Matt Symonds	26 Jun 82

DISCUS (1.5kg)

44.20	Matt Symonds	18 Sep 82
44.10	Keith Homer	30 Aug 80

HAMMER (4kg)

70.78	Andrew Tolputt	9 Jul 82
67.24	Peter Vivian	22 Sep 85
65.42	Matthew Sutton	29 Sep 96
64.28	Jason Byrne	22 Sep 85
63.68	Paul Binley	29 Sep 85
63.30	Richard Fedder	26 Aug 79
63.16	Tony Kenneally	29 May 78
62.06	Nick Steinmetz	4 Aug 91
61.32	John Barnes	8 Jun 96
61.08	Neil Curtis	11 Sep 88
60.52	Ian McLaughlin	21 Aug 91
59.94	Mike Rowlatt	2 Sep 90
59.92	Adrian Johnson	21 Sep 86

HAMMER (5kg)

60.10	Andrew Tolputt	5 Sep 82
58.00	Peter Vivian	22 Sep 85

overage

58.06	Jason Byrne	27 Oct 85

HAMMER (6.25kg)

48.86	Peter Vivian	22 Sep 85

JAVELIN (600g)

62.70	Paul Godwin	20 May 89
60.56	David Messom	6 Jul 79
60.56	Clifton Green	3 Jul 94
60.34	Richard Lainson	18 Aug 96
59.88	James Hurrion	17 Sep 88
59.52	Paul Price	19 Aug 79
58.94	Dan Carter	7 Aug 94
58.74	Philips Olwenu	6 Aug 95
58.58	Justin Rubio	11 Jun 83
58.58	Rhys Williams	10 Aug 96
58.48	Andrew Ravenscroft	9 Aug 80

JAVELIN (700g)

58.76	Dan Carter	29 Aug 94
55.10	Michael Williams	24 Jul 77

PENTATHLON (80H,SP,LJ,HJ,800)

3187	Mark Newton	27 Aug 94
3163	Kevin Drury	27 Aug 94
3024	Tom Benn	17 Sep 94
3014	Chris Jenkins	21 Sep 96
2995	Marcellas Peters	18 Sep 93
2993	Sam Allen	18 Sep 93
2989	Ian Leaman	18 Sep 93
2964	Jamie Russell	21 Sep 96
2925	Scott Walker	19 Sep 92
2920	James Hodson	18 Sep 93
2898	Peter Watson	16 Sep 95

(100,SP,LJ,HJ,800)

3199	Onochie Onuorah	17 Sep 88
3085 w	Cephas Howard	21 Sep 91
3035	Ricky Glover	16 Sep 89

OCTATHLON (Under 15 implements)

3933	Aidan Turnbull	1 Oct 95

DECATHLON (Under 15 implements)

5341	Jamie Quarry	28 Jun 87

3000 METRES TRACK WALK

13:19.57	Philip King	29 May 89
13:35.0	Russell Hutchings	7 Sep 85
13:45.0	John Murphy	14 May 95
13:51.0	Robert Mecham	12 May 92
13:58.0	Jon Vincent	7 Sep 85
14:03.0	Neil Simpson	1 Apr 89
14:03.5	Nathan Kavanagh	20 Sep 81
14:13.0	Karl Atton	15 Mar 86
14:15.3	Matthew Hales	14 May 94
14:21.0	Sean Maxwell	21 May 74

overage

12:59.7	Philip King	10 Oct 89

Road

13:20	Jonathan Deakin	18 Sep 88
13:29	Robert Mecham	20 Apr 92
13:32	Russell Hutchings	10 Nov 84
13:38	Philip King	1 Apr 89
13:39	Neil Simpson	6 May 89
13:43	Nathan Kavanagh	21 Feb 81
13:52	Ben Allkins	2 Dec 89
13:54	John Jones	18 Sep 88

overage

13:30	Ben Allkins	1 Dec 90

5000 METRES TRACK WALK

23:53.9	Philip King	27 Jun 89
24:22.0	Robert Mecham	14 Jul 92

overage

23:17.0	Philip King	17 Dec 89
24:03.6	John Murphy	15 Oct 95

Road

23:56	Philip King	24 Sep 89

overage

23:15	Philip King	9 Dec 89

UNDER 13

100 METRES
11.6	Tristan Anthony	28 Aug 95
11.8	Cephas Howard	2 Jul 89
11.9	Stephen Buttler	26 Sep 87

200 METRES
24.0	Stephen Buttler	26 Jul 87
24.1	Tristan Anthony	30 Jul 95
24.4	Cephas Howard	3 Sep 89

400 METRES
55.1	Cephas Howard	2 Jul 89
56.1	Andrew French	4 Jul 92
56.5	Tony Gill	7 Apr 96
56.5	Craig Erskine	22 Sep 96

800 METRES
2:04.1	Ben Mabon	8 Jul 83
2:05.2	Eric Kimani	79

1500 METRES
4:20.5	Eric Kimani	4 May 79
4:20.5	Ben Mabon	18 Jun 83
4:22.3	David Geraud	12 Aug 81
4:23.9	Mark Slowikowski	12 Jul 78

3000 METRES
9:31.4	Ben Mabon	19 Jul 83
9:41.4	Mark Slowikowski	21 May 78
9:49.5	John Tilley	9 Jul 86
overage		
9:41.2	Graham Green	26 Oct 77

75 METRES HURDLES (2'6")
11.7	Stephen Cotterill	16 Jul 78

80 METRES HURDLES (2'6")
11.9	Richardson	1 Sep 73
11.9	Matthew Clements	27 Aug 90
12.1	Daniel Borrett	13 Aug 95

80 METRES HURDLES (2'9")
12.92	Sam Allen	18 Aug 91

HIGH JUMP
1.68	Sam Allen	22 Sep 91
1.67	Glen Carpenter	83
1.67	Jamie Dalton	28 Jun 92

POLE VAULT
3.40	Neil Winter	27 Jul 86
3.20	Ian Lewis	8 Sep 81
2.80	Philip Wade	11 Sep 94

LONG JUMP
5.65	Sam Allen	14 Sep 91
5.64	Kevin Hibbins	18 Jul 93
5.61	Robert Creese	23 Jun 90

TRIPLE JUMP
12.57	Rigsby Agoreyo	9 Aug 69
11.52	Daniel Hutchinson	2 Jul 92

SHOT (3.25kg)
13.36	Chris Hughes	21 Aug 91
12.61	A. Magan	2 Jul 94
12.60	Carl Saggers	26 Aug 96

SHOT (4kg)
11.99	Mark Griffiths	78

DISCUS (1kg)
42.38	Ben Barnes	1 Sep 91
38.92	Chris Hughes	28 Jul 91
38.50	Carl Saggers	15 Sep 96

DISCUS (1.25kg)
33.88	Chris Symonds	83

HAMMER (3.25kg)
44.38	Ross Thompson	4 Sep 94
38.10	Adam Brogan	88
38.02	S. Henderson	22 Sep 91

HAMMER (4kg)
38.64	Ross Thompson	14 Aug 94
32.92	P. Watson	9 Aug 80

JAVELIN (400g)
43.02	Max Shale	8 Aug 93
41.32	A. Westergren	5 Jul 80
41.20	S. Ahma	2 Jul 92

JAVELIN (600g)
39.62	P. Shearing	23 May 76

PENTATHLON (100,SP,LJ,HJ,800 - U15)
2390	Sam Allen	22 Sep 91
(75H,SP,LJ,HJ,800 - U13)		
2065	Richard Piper	10 Sep 95

2000 METRES TRACK WALK
9:40.3	Thomas Taylor	19 Jun 93

2500 METRES ROAD WALK
12:01	Grant Ringshaw	14 Sep 80
12:11	Gareth Brown	14 Sep 80

3000 METRES TRACK WALK
15:02.62	Lloyd Finch	21 Sep 96
15:15.5	Robert Mecham	25 Jul 89
overage		
14:47.0	Gareth Brown	11 Nov 80
14:51.0	Grant Ringshaw	10 Dec 80
Road		
14:44	Martin Young	22 Sep 84
14:48	John Griffiths	22 Oct 83
14:57	Jamie Nunn	7 Nov 87
overage		
14:31	Martin Young	16 Dec 84
14:35	Lloyd Finch	10 Nov 96
14:43	Grant Ringshaw	29 Nov 80
14:43	Gareth Brown	29 Nov 80

UK ALL TIME LISTS - WOMEN

100 METRES

11.10		Kathy Cook	5 Sep 81
11.15		Paula Thomas	23 Aug 94
11.16		Andrea Lynch	11 Jun 75
11.20		Sonia Lannaman	25 Jul 80
11.20		Heather Oakes	26 Sep 80
11.22	A	Beverley Callender	8 Sep 79
11.35			22 Jul 81
11.27		Stephanie Douglas	26 Jul 91
11.29		Beverly Kinch	6 Jul 90
11.31		Wendy Hoyte	4 Oct 82
11.31		Shirley Thomas	3 Jul 83
11.31		Simmone Jacobs	24 Sep 88
11.32		Joan Baptiste	24 Aug 83
11.34		Katharine Merry	25 Jun 94
11.35		Sharon Danville	20 Aug 77
11.36	A	Della Pascoe	14 Oct 68
11.39	A	Val Peat	14 Oct 68
11.39		Sallyanne Short	12 Jul 92
11.40		Helen Golden	20 Jul 74
11.41		Jayne Christian	27 May 84
11.42		Marcia Richardson	26 Jul 96
11.45		Helen Burkart	26 Aug 83
11.46	A	Donna Hartley	22 Mar 75
11.46		Eleanor Cohen	30 Jul 82
11.47		Mary Berkeley	20 Jun 87
11.48		Carmen Smart	26 Aug 89
11.48		Geraldine McLeod	26 May 96
11.49		Sophia Smith	25 Aug 96
11.50		Sandra Whittaker	14 Jun 86
11.50		Helen Miles	5 Aug 88
11.51		Kaye Jeffrey	28 May 83
11.52		Pippa Windle	6 Jun 86
11.53		Sharon Williams	31 Aug 95
11.54		Dorothy Hyman	15 Oct 64
11.54		Janis Neilson	24 May 87
11.54		Aileen McGillivary	27 Jun 92
11.55		Anita Neil	1 Sep 72
11.57		Michelle Scutt	2 Sep 84
11.5	a	Daphne Slater	15 Oct 64
11.59		Chris Bloomfield	28 Aug 93
11.59		Rebecca Drummond	8 Jul 95
11.60		Phylis Smith	24 May 87
11.60		Danaa Myhill	22 Aug 94
11.60		Shani Anderson	30 Jun 96
11.61		Diane Smith	9 Aug 90
11.61		Donna Hoggarth	16 Sep 92
11.63		Jane Parry	29 May 82
11.63		Paula Cohen	12 Jun 93
11.64		Georgina Oladapo	22 Aug 85
11.64		Jenni Stoute	3 Aug 90

hand timing

10.9	Andrea Lynch	28 May 77
11.1	Sonia Lannaman	29 Jun 80
11.1	Heather Oakes	29 Jun 80
11.1	Joan Baptiste	16 Jul 85
11.2	Helen Golden	29 Jun 74
11.2	Sharon Danville	25 Jun 77
11.2	Beverly Kinch	14 Jul 84
11.2	Geraldine McLeod	21 May 94

wind assisted

10.93	Sonia Lannaman	17 Jul 77
11.01	Heather Oakes	21 May 80
11.08	Kathy Cook	24 Aug 83
11.13	Beverly Kinch	6 Jul 83
11.13	Shirley Thomas	27 May 84
11.13	Paula Thomas	20 Aug 88
11.18	Wendy Hoyte	4 Oct 82
11.19	Beverley Callender	21 May 80
11.23	Joan Baptiste	24 Aug 83
11.23	Jayne Christian	17 Jul 84
11.26	Simmone Jacobs	27 May 84
11.27	Katharine Merry	11 Jun 94
11.34	Sandra Whittaker	22 May 83
11.36	Sallyanne Short	26 Aug 89
11.37	Val Peat	17 Jul 70
11.37	Kaye Jeffrey	22 May 83
11.37	Helen Burkart	11 Sep 83
11.39	Pippa Windle	24 Jul 87
11.39	Marcia Richardson	11 Jun 94
11.40	Phylis Smith	3 Jun 90
11.41	Helen Miles	20 Aug 88
11.43	Dorothy Hyman	2 Sep 60
11.43	Aileen McGillivary	10 Jul 93
11.45	Michelle Scutt	12 Jun 82
11.46	Geraldine McLeod	9 Jul 93
11.48	Jakki Harman	7 Jul 96
11.48	Angela Thorp	23 Jul 88
11.50	Margot Wells	15 Jul 78
11.50	Rebecca Drummond	9 Jul 94
11.50	Sophie Smith	23 Jul 95
11.51	Anita Neil	17 Jul 70
11.53	Sharon Dolby	16 Aug 86
11.55	Daphne Slater	15 Oct 64
11.55	Liz Sutherland	18 Jul 70
11.55	Maxine Ascroft	30 Jun 79
11.55	Ena Waldo	30 Jul 88
11.55	Donna Hoggarth	29 Aug 92
11.55	Clova Court	9 Sep 95
11.56	Sue Telfer	23 Jun 84
11.57	Rosalee Wilson	21 May 80
11.58	Liz Johns	17 Jul 71
11.58	Janine MacGregor	13 Sep 81
11.58	Danaa Myhill	11 Jun 94
11.59	Lynne Draper	20 Aug 88
11.61	Linsey Macdonald	16 Jun 79
11.61	Jane Parry	10 Sep 83
11.61	Georgina Oladapo	22 Aug 85
11.61	Louise Fraser	17 Jun 95
11.62	Kathleen Lithglow	25 Jun 88
11.63	Jenni Stoute	3 Aug 90
11.63	Catherine Murphy	27 Aug 94
11.64	Diane Glazebrook	3 Jun 89

hand timing - wind assisted

10.8	Sonia Lannaman	22 May 76
11.1	Sharon Danville	22 May 76
11.1	Beverly Kinch	9 May 87
11.2	Margaret Williams	15 May 76
11.2	Joan Baptiste	24 Apr 82

200 METRES

22.10	Kathy Cook	9 Aug 84		23.36	Lorna Boothe	30 Mar 80
22.58	Sonia Lannaman	18 May 80		23.39 A	Angela Bridgeman	12 Apr 86
22.69	Paula Thomas	26 Aug 94		23.41	Louise Fraser	16 Jun 91
22.72	Beverley Callender	30 Jul 80		23.44	Donna Fraser	23 Apr 95
22.73	Jennifer Stoute	3 Aug 92		23.46	Maureen Tranter	21 Jul 70
22.75	Donna Hartley	17 Jun 78		23.51	Carmen Smart	10 Jul 83
22.80	Michelle Scutt	12 Jun 82		23.52	Pippa Windle	25 Jul 87
22.85	Katharine Merry	12 Jun 94		**hand timing**		
22.86	Joan Baptiste	9 Aug 84		22.9	Heather Oakes	3 May 80
10 22.92	Heather Oakes	28 Aug 86		22.9	Helen Burkart	6 Aug 83
22.95	Simmone Jacobs	25 Apr 96		23.0	Helen Golden	30 Jun 74
22.98	Sandra Whittaker	8 Aug 84		23.1	Andrea Lynch	21 May 77
23.10	Diane Smith	11 Aug 90		23.1	Linda Keough	5 Jul 89
23.14	Helen Golden	7 Sep 73		23.2	Dorothy Hyman	3 Oct 63
23.14	Helen Burkart	17 Jul 82		23.2	Margaret Critchley	2 Aug 70
23.15	Andrea Lynch	25 Aug 75		23.3	Sharon Danville	30 Jun 74
23.17	Stephanie Douglas	12 Jun 94		23.3	Linsey Macdonald	8 May 82
23.18	Joslyn Hoyte-Smith	9 Jun 82		23.3	Louise Stuart	25 Aug 91
23.24	Sallyanne Short	28 Jun 92		23.4 A	Lillian Board	5 Oct 68
20 23.29	Verona Elder	17 Jun 78		23.4	Pippa Windle	2 Aug 87
23.29	Aileen McGillivary	25 Jul 93		23.4	Marcia Richardson	1 Aug 93
23.30	Sally Gunnell	13 Jun 93		23.4	Geraldine McLeod	1 Aug 93
23.33	Linsey Macdonald	9 Jun 82		23.4	Louise Fraser	1 Jul 95
23.34	Val Peat	19 Sep 69		**wind assisted**		
23.35	Melanie Neef	2 Jul 95		23.1	Margaret Critchley	14 Jul 74
23.36	Shirley Thomas	10 Jun 84		23.1	Sharon Danville	17 Sep 77
23.36	Louise Stuart	4 Aug 90		23.1	Linda McCurry	2 Jul 78
23.40	Dorothy Hyman	18 Aug 62		23.2	Debbie Bunn	2 Jul 78
23.40	Sharon Danville	9 Sep 77		23.2	Sybil Joseph	1 Jun 85
30 23.40	Phylis Smith	6 Jun 92		23.3	Angela Bridgeman	15 Aug 82
23.40	Catherine Murphy	16 Jul 95		23.3	Janis Nelson	1 Jun 86
23.42 A	Lillian Board	17 Oct 68		23.4	Wendy Hoyte	22 May 77
23.52		3 Aug 68		23.4	Hayley Clements	10 Aug 85
23.42	Debbie Bunn	17 Jun 78				
23.43	Sue Telfer	16 Jun 84		**300 METRES**		
23.46	Janine MacGregor	22 Aug 81		35.46	Kathy Cook	18 Aug 84
23.47 A	Angela Bridgeman	10 May 86		36.01	Michelle Scutt	13 Jul 80
23.47	Geraldine McLeod	24 Aug 94		36.44	Sally Gunnell	30 Jul 93
23.47	Donna Fraser	9 Jul 95		36.45	Joslyn Hoyte-Smith	5 Jul 80
23.48	Wendy Hoyte	7 Jun 75		36.46	Linsey Macdonald	13 Jul 80
23.48	Denise Ramsden	21 Aug 76		36.65	Joan Baptiste	18 Aug 84
40 23.48	Margaret Williams	21 Aug 76		36.69	Helen Burkart	9 Sep 83
23.49	Wendy Addison	16 Jun 84		36.92	Phylis Smith	11 Aug 96
23.51	Eleanor Thomas	16 Jul 78		36.95	Jennifer Stoute	21 Jul 91
23.51	Linda Keough	8 Jul 89		36.97	Donna Hartley	4 Jul 75
23.53	Marcia Richardson	9 Sep 95		37.30	Verona Elder	26 May 76
23.54	Jane Parry	30 Jul 83		37.31	Donna Fraser	12 Jul 96
23.55	Kaye Jeffrey	29 May 83		37.33	Melanie Neef	8 Jul 94
wind assisted				37.40	Tracy Lawton	18 Aug 84
22.48	Michelle Scutt	4 Jul 82		37.42	Angela Bridgeman	25 Sep 82
22.69	Beverley Callender	24 Jun 81		37.45	Jane Parry	18 Aug 84
22.90	Andrea Lynch	11 Jun 75		37.46	Linda Forsyth	30 Aug 82
22.97	Helen Golden	26 Jul 74		37.46 iA	Sharon Danville	14 Mar 81
23.00	Joslyn Hoyte-Smith	13 Jun 82		37.47	Allison Curbishley	11 Aug 96
23.11	Linsey Macdonald	5 Jul 80		**hand timing**		
23.14	Shirley Thomas	28 May 84		36.2	Donna Hartley	7 Aug 74
23.15	Margaret Critchley	22 Jul 70		37.0	Linda Keough	22 Jul 89
23.19	Sallyanne Short	29 Jan 90		**during 400**		
10 23.32	Louise Stuart	4 Jun 89		37.4 +	Georgina Oladapo	18 Jun 95

400 METRES

	49.43	Kathy Cook	6 Aug 84
	50.40	Phylis Smith	3 Aug 92
	50.63	Michelle Scutt	31 May 82
	50.75	Joslyn Hoyte-Smith	18 Jun 82
	50.93	Lorraine Hanson	26 Aug 91
	50.98	Linda Keough	26 Aug 91
	51.04	Sally Gunnell	20 Jul 94
	51.16	Linsey Macdonald	15 Jun 80
	51.18	Melanie Neef	6 Aug 95
10	51.28	Donna Hartley	12 Jul 75
	51.41	Sandra Douglas	2 Aug 92
	51.53	Jennifer Stoute	12 Aug 89
	51.58	Donna Fraser	26 Jul 96
	51.70	Verona Elder	10 Jun 78
	51.93	Janine MacGregor	28 Aug 81
	51.97	Linda Forsyth	31 May 82
	52.12 A	Lillian Board	16 Oct 68
	53.00		2 Sep 68
	52.13	Helen Burkart	28 Jun 84
	52.20	Ann Packer	17 Oct 64
20	52.26	Pat Beckford	14 Aug 88
	52.43	Gladys Taylor	2 Sep 84
	52.48	Georgina Oladapo	16 Jun 96
	52.52	Sybil Joseph	14 Sep 85
	52.54	Stephanie Llewellyn	9 Jul 95
	52.57 A	Janet Simpson	16 Oct 68
	52.65	Jane Parry	11 Jun 83
	52.67	Tracy Lawton	8 Jul 84
	52.71	Loreen Hall	18 Jun 88
	52.75	Sandra Leigh	12 Jul 91
	52.76	Allison Curbishley	16 Jun 96
30	52.79	Angela Piggford	2 Jul 89
	52.80	Sian Morris	18 Jun 83
	52.83	Ruth Kennedy	10 Jul 79
	52.85	Jannette Roscoe	3 Sep 74
	52.89	Janet Smith	6 Aug 88
	52.98	Karen Williams	6 Aug 78
	52.98	Dyanna Clarke	28 Jul 79
	52.99	Angela Bridgeman	24 Jul 82
	53.01 i	Marilyn Neufville	14 Mar 70
	53.08	Bev Goddard	21 Aug 76
40	53.12	Joy Grieveson	14 Sep 63
	53.22	Michelle Pierre	16 Jun 96
	53.23	Tracy Goddard	15 Jun 91
	53.24	Rosemary Wright	28 Aug 71
	53.25	Dawn Kitchen	16 Jun 90
	53.28 A	Diane Modahl	2 May 92
	53.38		13 Jun 93
	53.31	Liz Barnes	21 Jun 75
	53.32	Alison Reid	18 Jun 83
	53.32	Ann Middle	6 Aug 86
	53.34	Fiona Hargreaves	25 May 86

hand timing

51.2	Donna Hartley	28 Jul 78
51.4	Verona Elder	22 May 76
52.2	Liz Barnes	22 May 76
52.4	Stephanie Llewellyn	1 Jul 95
52.6	Marilyn Neufville	20 Jun 70
52.8	Lillian Board	9 Jul 67

600 METRES

1:26.0 +	Kelly Holmes	13 Aug 95
1:26.18	Diane Modahl	22 Aug 87
1:26.5 +	Kirsty Wade	21 Aug 85
1:26.7	Ann Griffiths	22 Jan 90
1:26.8	Shireen Baily	16 Jun 85

800 METRES

1:56.21	Kelly Holmes	9 Sep 95	
1:57.42	Kirsty Wade	24 Jun 85	
1:58.65	Diane Modahl	14 Jul 90	
1:58.97	Shireen Bailey	15 Sep 87	
1:59.05	Christina Cahill	4 Aug 79	
1:59.67	Lorraine Baker	15 Aug 86	
1:59.76	Paula Fryer	17 Jul 91	
1:59.81	Ann Griffiths	10 Aug 94	
2:00.15	Rosemary Wright	3 Sep 72	
2:00.20	Anne Purvis	7 Jul 82	10
2:00.30	Cherry Hanson	25 Jul 81	
2:00.39	Bev Nicholson	28 Aug 88	
2:00.55mx	Zola Budd	21 Jun 86	
2:00.6 a	Jane Finch	9 Jul 77	
2:00.80	Yvonne Murray	10 Jul 87	
2:01.1 a	Ann Packer	20 Oct 64	
2:01.11	Lynne MacIntyre	18 Aug 84	
2:01.2	Joan Allison	1 Jul 73	
2:01.2	Christine Whittingham	26 Aug 78	
2:01.24	Christine Benning	28 Jul 79	20
2:01.35	Liz Barnes	10 Jul 76	
2:01.36	Gillian Dainty	31 Aug 83	
2:01.40	Janet Bell	10 Jul 87	
2:01.48	Lesley Kiernan	11 Jun 77	
2:01.50	Lillian Board	18 Sep 69	
2:01.65	Teena Colebrook	21 Jul 84	
2:01.66	Pat Lowe	12 Aug 71	
2:01.67	Sonya Bowyer	24 Jun 95	
2:01.7	Ann Middle	28 Aug 91	
2:01.82	Linda Keough	1 Aug 93	30
2:01.86	Helen Thorpe	10 Jul 87	
2:01.87	Dawn Gandy	19 Jun 88	
2:01.93	Sue Bevan	19 Jul 91	
2:02.0	Margaret Coomber	1 Jul 73	
2:02.0	Jo White	13 Aug 77	
2:02.0	Lynne Robinson	26 Jul 89	
2:02.34	Lynn Gibson	14 Aug 92	
2:02.47	Abigail Hunte	16 Jul 95	
2:02.6	Evelyn McMeekin	20 Aug 78	
2:02.69	Natalie Tait	16 Jul 95	40
2:02.7 a	Janet Marlow	23 Jul 79	
2:02.79	Sue Morley	27 Jul 85	
2:02.83	Mary Kitson	21 Jul 91	
2:02.89	Wendy Sly	30 Jul 83	
2:02.9	Sheila Carey	10 Sep 71	
2:02.91	Carol Lightfoot	7 Jul 82	
2:02.92	Debbie Russell	2 Aug 85	
2:03.11	Mary Stewart	11 Jun 77	
2:03.17	Cathy Dawson	26 Aug 94	
2:03.18	Paula Newnham	17 Jun 78	50
2:03.18	Verona Elder	10 Jun 79	
2:03.2 +	Anne Smith	2 Jul 66	

1000 METRES

2:32.83	Kelly Holmes	23 Jul 95
2:33.70	Kirsty Wade	9 Aug 85
2:34.92	Christina Cahill	9 Aug 85
2:35.32	Shireen Bailey	19 Jul 86
2:35.51	Lorraine Baker	19 Jul 86
2:35.86	Diane Modahl	29 Aug 93
2:37.05	Christine Whittingham	27 Jun 86
2:37.29	Yvonne Murray	14 Jul 89
2:37.61	Bev Nicholson	14 Jul 89
10 2:37.82	Gillian Dainty	11 Sep 81
2:38.44	Evelyn McMeekin	23 Aug 78
2:38.58	Jo White	9 Sep 77
2:38.67	Lynne MacIntyre	19 Jul 86
2:38.83	Lynn Gibson	29 Aug 93
2:39.23	Teena Colebrook	24 Jul 90
2:39.29	Ann Williams	16 Sep 90
2:39.42	Mary Cotton	26 May 76

1500 METRES

3:59.96	Zola Budd	30 Aug 85
4:00.57	Christina Cahill	6 Jul 84
4:00.73	Kirsty Wade	26 Jul 87
4:01.13	Kelly Holmes	5 Jul 96
4:01.20	Yvonne Murray	4 Jul 87
4:01.38	Liz McColgan	4 Jul 87
4:01.53	Christine Benning	15 Aug 79
4:02.32	Shireen Bailey	1 Oct 88
4:03.17	Alison Wyeth	7 Aug 93
10 4:04.14	Wendy Sly	14 Aug 83
4:04.81	Sheila Carey	9 Sep 72
4:05.66	Bev Nicholson	20 Jul 90
4:05.75	Lynn Gibson	20 Jul 94
4:05.96	Lynne MacIntyre	20 Aug 84
4:06.0	Mary Cotton	24 Jun 78
4:06.24	Christine Whittingham	5 Jul 86
4:06.84	Paula Radcliffe	2 Jul 95
4:07.11	Janet Marlow	18 Aug 82
4:07.59	Ann Williams	9 Jun 92
20 4:07.69	Teena Colebrook	19 Aug 90
4:07.90	Gillian Dainty	16 Jun 84
4:09.26	Lisa York	13 Jun 92
4:09.29	Angela Davies	20 Jul 94
4:09.37	Joyce Smith	7 Sep 72
4:09.46	Karen Hutcheson	4 Sep 89
4:09.5	Penny Forse	6 Aug 80
4:10.07	Maxine Newman	28 Jun 92
4:10.10	Cherry Hanson	30 Aug 81
4:10.21	Kathy Carter	31 Jul 82
30 4:10.32	Lynne Robinson	30 Jul 94
4:10.41	Jo White	10 Jun 84
4:10.66	Joan Allison	2 Feb 74
4:10.7 mx	Sonia Bowyer	16 Jul 96
4:10.75	Sonia McGeorge	20 Jul 90
4:10.76	Ruth Partridge	16 Jun 84
4:11.00	Sue Morley	6 Jul 85
4:11.12	Bridget Smyth	26 May 85
4:11.23	Paula Fudge	31 Jul 81
4:11.24 i	Nicky Morris	7 Jan 89
40 4:11.46	Ursula McKee	20 Jan 90

4:11.51	Jane Shields	4 Sep 83
4:11.57	Sue Parker	18 Jun 96
4:11.75	Debbie Peel	31 Jul 82
4:11.82	Una English	28 Jun 82
4:11.85	Jo Dering	28 Jul 90
4:11.94	Lorraine Baker	5 Jul 90
4:12.19	Gill Settle	26 May 85
4:12.3	Diane Modahl	29 Apr 89
4:12.45	Glynis Penny	19 Aug 78
4:12.58	Carole Bradford	10 Aug 84 50

ONE MILE

4:17.57	Zola Budd	21 Aug 85
4:19.41	Kirsty Wade	27 Jul 85
4:22.64	Christina Cahill	7 Sep 84
4:22.64	Yvonne Murray	22 Jul 94
4:24.57	Christine Benning	7 Sep 84
4:24.87	Alison Wyeth	6 Jul 91
4:24.94	Paula Radcliffe	14 Aug 96
4:26.11	Liz McColgan	10 Jul 87
4:26.16	Teena Colebrook	14 Jul 90
4:26.52	Bev Hartigan	14 Aug 92 10
4:27.80	Lisa York	14 Aug 92
4:28.07	Wendy Sly	18 Aug 84
4:28.8	Karen Hutcheson	20 Aug 89
4:29.15	Suzanne Morley	18 Aug 84
4:30.08	Lynne MacIntyre	7 Sep 84
4:30.29	Jane Shields	9 Sep 83
4:30.89	Ruth Partridge	18 Aug 84
4:31.17	Lynn Gibson	1 Jul 94
4:31.24 i	Jo White	5 Feb 83
4:31.45	Shireen Bailey	17 Sep 89 20
4:31.65	Gillian Dainty	26 Jun 82
4:31.83	Angela Davies	1 Jul 94
4:32.00	Carole Bradford	18 Aug 84
4:32.32	Debbie Gunning	5 Jul 91
4:32.82	Monica Joyce	10 May 81
4:32.91	Lynne Robinson	14 Aug 92
4:33.01	Una English	14 Aug 92
4:33.12	Ann Griffiths	24 May 92
4:33.12	Sonia McGeorge	1 Jul 94
4:33.2	Janet Marlow	14 Sep 79 30

2000 METRES

5:26.93	Yvonne Murray	8 Jul 94
5:30.19	Zola Budd	11 Jul 86
5:33.85	Christina Cahill	13 Jul 84
5:37.00	Christine Benning	13 Jul 84
5:38.50	Alison Wyeth	29 Aug 93
5:39.20	Paula Radcliffe	29 Aug 93
5:40.24	Liz McColgan	22 Aug 87
5:42.15	Wendy Sly	17 Sep 82
5:43.24	Suzanne Morley	13 Jul 84
5:45.0 i	Bev Hartigan	20 Feb 93 10
5:45.15	Debbie Gunning	29 Aug 93
5:45.34	Lisa York	10 Jul 92
5:45.45	Ruth Partridge	13 Jul 84
5:45.81 i	Kirsty Wade	13 Mar 87
5:46.40	Sonia McGeorge	29 Aug 93
5:46.54	Una English	10 Jul 92

3000 METRES

	8:28.83	Zola Budd	7 Sep 85
	8:29.02	Yvonne Murray	25 Sep 88
	8:34.80 i	Liz McColgan	4 Mar 89
	8:38.23		15 Jul 91
	8:37.06	Wendy Sly	10 Aug 83
	8:37.07	Paula Radcliffe	10 Aug 96
	8:38.42	Alison Wyeth	16 Aug 93
	8:44.46	Christine Benning	22 Aug 84
	8:45.69	Jane Shields	10 Aug 83
	8:47.36	Jill Hunter	17 Aug 88
10	8:47.59	Angela Tooby	5 Jul 88
	8:47.7	Kirsty Wade	5 Aug 87
	8:47.71	Lisa York	31 Jul 92
	8:48.72	Karen Hutcheson	28 Jan 90
	8:48.74	Paula Fudge	29 Aug 78
	8:49.89	Christina Cahill	20 Jul 85
	8:50.52	Debbie Peel	7 Aug 82
	8:51.33	Sonia McGeorge	29 Aug 90
	8:51.40	Ruth Partridge	7 Aug 82
	8:52.79	Ann Ford	28 Aug 77
20	8:53.52 i	Nicola Morris	4 Mar 89
	8:59.46		24 Jun 89
	8:55.53	Joyce Smith	19 Jul 74
	8:56.09	Andrea Wallace	10 Jul 92
	8:56.39	Suzanne Morley	21 Jul 84
	8:57.17	Susan Tooby	6 Jun 84
	8:57.2	Kathy Carter	7 Apr 84
	8:58.44	Kathryn Binns	26 May 80
	8:58.59	Andrea Whitcombe	26 Jul 91
	8:59.39	Regina Joyce	8 May 81
	8:59.45	Jo Dering	11 Aug 90
30	8:59.65	Gillian Dainty	20 Jul 83
	9:00.21	Carole Bradford	9 Jul 85
	9:00.3	Bridget Smyth	20 Apr 91
	9:00.68	Alison Wright	23 Jun 81
	9:01.67	Melissa Watson	27 Jun 88
	9:02.25	Julie Holland	11 Aug 90
	9:02.47	Laura Adam	4 Jun 94
	9:03.35	Philippa Mason	19 Jul 86
	9:03.51	Rhona Makepeace	25 Feb 92
	9:03.88 i	Bev Hartigan	17 Feb 90
40	9:04.4	Sarah Bentley	22 Jun 96
	9:04.98	Lynne Harvey	25 Aug 82
	9:05.02	Sue Crehan	19 Aug 87
	9:05.03	Hilary Hollick	25 May 81
	9:05.14	Jill Clarke	15 Jul 85
	9:05.4	Mary Cotton	29 Jul 84
	9:05.49	Zahara Hyde	29 Jul 91
	9:05.65	Kerry Robinson	18 Apr 82
	9:05.80	Teena Colebrook	21 Apr 90
	9:05.98	Val Rowe	22 Sep 81
50	9:06.16	Helen Titterington	19 Jun 88

5000 METRES

14:46.76	Paula Radcliffe	16 Aug 96
14:48.07	Zola Budd	26 Aug 85
14:56.94	Yvonne Murray	7 Jul 95
14:59.56	Liz McColgan	22 Jul 95
15:00.37	Alison Wyeth	7 Jul 95
15:09.98	Jill Hunter	18 Jul 92
15:13.22	Angela Tooby	5 Aug 87
15:14.51	Paula Fudge	13 Sep 81
15:21.45	Wendy Sly	5 Aug 87
15:28.63	Andrea Wallace	2 Jul 92	10
15:29.04	Sonia McGeorge	27 May 96
15:31.78	Julie Holland	18 Jul 90
15:32.19	Susan Tooby	26 May 85
15:32.34	Jane Shields	5 Jun 88
15:34.16	Jill Clarke	26 May 85
15:38.84	Ann Ford	5 Jun 82
15:40.14	Helen Titterington	17 Jul 89
15:41.11	Angela Hulley	18 Jul 90
15:41.68	Debbie Peel	27 Jun 85
15:49.6	Kathryn Binns	5 Apr 80	20
15:51.62	Carol Haigh	26 May 85
15:52.2	Ruth Partridge	23 Aug 89
15:53.84	Heather Heasman	6 Jul 96
15:53.86	Sarah Bentley	22 Jul 95
15:56.0	Lucy Martin	15 May 90
15:56.15	Lucy Elliott	12 Jul 96
15:56.4 +	Sue Crehan	4 Jul 87
15:56.83	Suzanne Rigg	30 Jul 94
15:57.06	Louise Watson	24 Jun 95
15:58.8	Teresa Dyer	21 Jul 93	30
15:59.72	Teena Colebrook	3 Mar 90

10,000 METRES

30:57.07	Liz McColgan	25 Jun 91	
31:07.88	Jill Hunter	30 Jun 91	
31:53.36	Wendy Sly	8 Oct 88	
31:55.30	Angela Tooby	4 Sep 87	
31:56.97	Yvonne Murray	24 Aug 94	
32:20.95	Susan Tooby	2 Jul 88	
32:21.61	Andrea Wallace	6 Jun 92	
32:24.63	Sue Crehan	4 Jul 87	
32:32.42	Vikki McPherson	15 Jul 93	
32:36.09	Helen Titterington	29 Aug 89	10
32:41.29	Jenny Clague	20 Jun 93	
32:42.0	Jane Shields	24 Aug 88	
32:42.84	Angela Hulley	6 Aug 89	
32:44.06	Suzanne Rigg	27 Jun 93	
32:47.78	Julie Holland	31 Aug 90	
32:57.17	Kathy Binns	15 Aug 80	
32:58.2	Claire Lavers	20 Apr 91	
33:05.43	Elspeth Turner	1 Jun 88	
33:10.25	Shireen Samy	5 Jul 86	
33:10.94	Marina Samy	28 Jul 86	20
33:17.88	Karen Macleod	1 Jul 89	
33:19.19	Bernadette Madigan	27 Apr 85	
33:19.48	Heather Heasman	6 Jun 92	
33:21.46	Louise Watson	14 Jun 96	
33:23.25	Zahara Hyde	12 Jun 94	
33:26.79	Amanda Wright	6 Jun 92	
33:27.69	Jill Clarke	22 Jun 86	
33:30.0	Annette Bell	10 Aug 91	
33:34.03	Lynn Everington	26 May 86	
33:34.7	Priscilla Welch	2 Jun 84	30
33:34.77	Debbie Peel	22 Jun 86	
33:34.96	Carol Greenwood	12 Jun 94	

10 KILOMETRES ROAD

30:39	Liz McColgan	11 Mar 89
31:29	Wendy Sly	27 Mar 83
31:42	Jill Hunter	21 Jan 89
31:56	Andrea Wallace	4 Aug 91
32:14	Angela Tooby	31 Mar 84
32:15	Priscilla Welch	23 Mar 85
32:20	Zola Budd	2 Mar 85
32:27	Ruth Partridge	11 Mar 89
32:31	Heather Heasman	6 Nov 94
32:35	Suzanne Rigg	15 Aug 92
32:38	Jane Shields	23 Mar 85
32:41	Susan Tooby	4 Mar 84
32:41	Jill Clarke	21 Feb 87
32:42	Véronique Marot	30 Sep 84
32:43	Teresa Dyer	1 Jan 93
32:44	Carole Bradford	14 Oct 85
32:44	Paula Fudge	13 Mar 88
32:46	Kirsty Wade	28 Feb 87
32:46	Amanda Wright	25 Feb 96
32:47	Debbie Peel	15 Apr 84
32:47	Chris Benning	15 Mar 87

course measurement uncertain

31:43	Zola Budd	6 May 84
32:03	Paula Fudge	29 Aug 82
32:29	Yvonne Danson	13 Nov 94
32:36	Mary Cotton	5 Aug 84

10 MILES ROAD

51:41	Jill Hunter	20 Apr 91
51:51	Angela Hulley	18 Nov 89
52:14	Liz McColgan	6 Sep 92
52:53	Marian Sutton	6 Oct 96
53:42	Suzanne Rigg	10 Oct 93
53:44	Paula Fudge	21 Sep 85
53:44	Andrea Wallace	7 Mar 93
53:49	Véronique Marot	26 Aug 85
53:50	Yvonne Murray	6 Oct 96
53:51	Priscilla Welch	5 Apr 87

intermediate time

53:00 +	Andrea Wallace	5 May 91

course measurement uncertain

53:17	Joyce Smith	12 Oct 80
53:44	Sarah Rowell	10 Mar 84

HALF MARATHON

1:07:11	Liz McColgan	26 Jan 92
1:09:39	Andrea Wallace	21 Mar 93
1:09:56	Susan Tooby	24 Jul 88
1:11:17	Véronique Marot	21 Jun 87
1:11:36	Ann Ford	30 Jun 85
1:11:37	Paula Fudge	24 Jul 88
1:11:38	Sally Ellis	20 Mar 88
1:11:42	Maria Sutton	11 Jul 93
1:11:44	Jill Clarke	29 Mar 87
1:11:44	Lorna Irving	6 Sep 87
1:11:45	Karen Macleod	15 Mar 92

intermediate time

1:11:44 +	Sally-Ann Hales	21 Apr 85

course measurement uncertain

1:11:44	Karen Macleod	15 Jan 95

MARATHON

2:25:56	Véronique Marot	23 Apr 89
2:26:51	Priscilla Welch	10 May 87
2:27:32	Liz McColgan	3 Nov 91
2:28:06	Sarah Rowell	21 Apr 85
2:28:38	Sally-Ann Hales	21 Apr 85
2:29:29	Sally Eastall	8 Dec 91
2:29:43	Joyce Smith	9 May 82
2:29:47	Paula Fudge	30 Oct 88
2:30:38	Ann Ford	17 Apr 88
2:30:41	Marian Sutton	20 Oct 96
2:30:51	Angela Hulley	23 Sep 88
2:30:53	Yvonne Danson	17 Apr 95
2:31:33	Susan Tooby	23 Sep 88
2:31:33	Andrea Wallace	12 Apr 92
2:31:45	Lynn Harding	23 Apr 89
2:32:53	Gillian Burley	2 Dec 84
2:33:04	Sheila Catford	23 Apr 89
2:33:07	Nicola McCracken	22 Apr 90
2:33:16	Karen Macleod	27 Aug 94
2:33:22	Carolyn Naisby	6 Dec 87
2:33:24	Sally Ellis	23 Apr 89
2:33:38	Lynda Bain	21 Apr 85
2:34:11	Sally Goldsmith	3 Mar 96
2:34:19	Jill Clarke	23 Apr 89
2:34:21	Suzanne Rigg	24 Sep 95
2:34:26	Heather MacDuff	16 Oct 88
2:35:03	Sandra Branney	23 Apr 89
2:35:05	Carol Gould	26 Oct 80
2:35:10	Sue Crehan	17 Apr 88
2:35:18	Karen Holdsworth	29 Sep 85
2:35:18	Debbie Noy	13 Oct 91
2:35:32	Rose Ellis	23 Apr 89
2:35:39	Hayley Nash	27 Aug 94
2:35:53	Julie Barleycorn	13 May 84
2:36:06	Margaret Lockley	13 May 84
2:36:12	Kathryn Binns	12 Jun 82
2:36:21	Glynis Penny	17 Apr 83
2:36:29	Danielle Sanderson	7 Aug 94
2:36:31	Julia Gates	20 Apr 86
2:36:32	Marina Samy	23 Apr 89
2:36:34	Lorna Irving	1 Aug 86
2:36:40	Teresa Dyer	17 Apr 94
2:36:52	Gillian Horovitz	20 Jun 92
2:37:06	Moira O'Neill	31 Oct 88
2:37:14	Cath Mijovic	22 Oct 95
2:37:26	Caroline Horne	21 Apr 85
2:37:36	Sandra Mewett	17 Jan 88
2:37:37	Anne Roden	20 Apr 92
2:37:49	Alison Gooderham	17 Apr 88
2:38:17	Inez McLean	3 Feb 85

2000 METRES STEEPLECHASE (2'6")

6:53.7	Sharon Dixon	8 May 94
7:00.7	Sally Young	8 May 94

(3'0" barriers)

7:04.7mx	Sally Young	14 Jul 93
7:05.76	Veronica Boden	17 Jul 94

3000 METRES STEEPLECHASE (2'6")

10:52.6	Tanya Blake	22 Aug 93

100 METRES HURDLES

12.80	Angela Thorp	31 Jul 96
12.82	Sally Gunnell	17 Aug 88
12.87	Shirley Strong	24 Aug 83
12.90	Jacqui Agyepong	25 Jun 95
12.91	Kay Morley-Brown	2 Feb 90
13.03	Lesley-Ann Skeete	3 Aug 90
13.04	Clova Court	9 Aug 94
13.05	Judy Simpson	29 Aug 86
13.07	Lorna Boothe	7 Oct 82
13.08	Samantha Farquharson	4 Jul 94
13.11	Sharon Danville	22 Jun 76
13.16	Wendy Jeal	27 Aug 86
13.18	Denise Lewis	25 May 96
13.24	Kim Hagger	31 Aug 87
13.24	Keri Maddox	12 Jun 93
13.25	Diane Allahgreen	21 Jul 94
13.26	Michelle Edwards	3 Aug 90
13.29	Mary Peters	2 Sep 72
13.32	Sam Baker	29 Aug 93
13.34	Judy Vernon	7 Sep 73
13.34	Melanie Wilkins	15 Jul 95
13.35	Pat Rollo	30 Jul 83
13.36	Louise Fraser	17 Aug 91
13.44	Judith Robinson	1 Jul 89
13.45	Lorna Drysdale	20 Jul 74
13.45	Natasha Danvers	6 Aug 95
13.46	Tessa Sanderson	25 Jul 81
13.46	Natalie Byer	26 Aug 83
13.47	Heather Ross	16 Jun 84
13.49	Blondelle Caines	17 Jul 77
13.50 A	Yvette Wray	8 Sep 79
13.57		15 Jul 79
13.53	Ann Wilson	4 Sep 72
13.53	Lynne Green	27 Jun 88
13.54	Debbie Baker	7 Aug 88
13.57	Bethan Edwards	29 Aug 92
13.58	Lauraine Cameron	19 Jun 90

wind assisted

12.78	Shirley Strong	8 Oct 82
12.80	Sally Gunnell	29 Jul 88
12.84 A	Kay Morley-Brown	8 Aug 90
12.90	Lorna Boothe	8 Oct 82
13.01	Lesley-Ann Skeete	1 Feb 90
13.06	Sharon Danville	14 Jul 84
13.08	Michelle Campbell	26 May 95
13.12	Pat Rollo	27 May 84
13.13	Diane Allahgreen	30 Jun 96
13.20	Keri Maddox	2 Jul 93
13.22	Heather Ross	27 May 84
13.23	Melanie Wilkins	30 Jun 96
13.36	Judith Robinson	11 Jul 87

hand timing

13.0	Judy Vernon	29 Jun 74
13.0	Blondelle Caines	29 Jun 74
13.1	Melanie Wilkins	2 Jul 95
13.2	Pat Rollo	11 Jun 83

wind assisted

12.7	Kay Morley-Brown	10 Jan 90
12.9	Judy Vernon	18 May 74
13.1	Mary Peters	19 Aug 72

400 METRES HURDLES

52.74	Sally Gunnell	19 Aug 93
54.63	Gowry Retchakan	3 Aug 92
55.91	Elaine McLaughlin	26 Sep 88
56.04	Sue Morley	10 Aug 83
56.05	Wendy Cearns	13 Aug 89
56.06	Christine Warden	28 Jul 79
56.15	Jacqui Parker	27 Jul 91
56.26	Louise Fraser	7 Jun 92
56.43	Alyson Layzell	16 Jun 96
56.46	Yvette Wray	11 Jul 81
56.61	Louise Brunning	16 Jun 96
56.70	Lorraine Hanson	13 Aug 89
56.72	Gladys Taylor	6 Aug 84
57.00	Simone Laidlow	6 Aug 88
57.07	Verona Elder	15 Jul 83
57.27	Vicki Jamison	28 Jul 96
57.38	Sarah Dean	27 Jul 91
57.41	Jennifer Pearson	6 Aug 88
57.43	Liz Sutherland	6 Jul 78
57.49	Maureen Prendergast	16 Jun 84
57.52	Clare Sugden	3 Jun 90
57.55	Sharon Danville	8 May 81
57.76	Aileen Mills	5 Aug 86
57.79	Susan Dalgoutte	15 Jun 80
57.81	Margaret Southerden	10 Jul 82
57.86	Teresa Hoyle	29 Jul 83
58.02	Vyvyan Rhodes	28 Jun 92
58.04	Clare Bleasdale	16 Jul 94
58.09	Stephanie McCann	12 Jun 94
58.16	Diane Fryar	9 Jul 83
58.19	Sara Elson	4 Jul 92
58.28	Carol Dawkins	14 Sep 85
58.31	Jannette Roscoe	19 Jul 75
58.31	Fiona Laing	18 Sep 81
58.31	Alyson Evans	28 Jul 86
58.35	Debbie Skerritt	11 Jul 81
58.41	Lynn Parry	19 Jun 88
58.43	Jane Low	24 Aug 94
58.44	Maggie Still	19 Jun 88
58.51	Julie Vine	17 Jun 90
58.55	Jackie Stokoe	19 Jul 75
58.68	Kay Simpson	15 Jul 83
58.68	Vicky Lee	5 Aug 86
58.79	Sheila Peak	25 Jul 87
58.80	Sinead Dudgeon	15 Jun 96
58.83	Sue Smith	23 Jun 79
59.00	Debbie Church	12 Jun 86
59.04	Allison Curbishley	31 Jul 93
59.11	Janet Levermore	26 Jul 91
59.12	Tracy Allen	29 Jul 89

hand timing

57.5	Vicky Lee	28 Jun 86
57.8	Teresa Hoyle	26 Jul 86
58.0	Fiona Laing	28 Aug 81
58.2	Debbie Skerritt	6 Jun 81
58.6	Jane Finch	21 Sep 80
58.8	Veronica Boden	28 Jun 87
58.8	Allison Curbishley	5 May 96
59.0	Kim Wells	11 Jul 82
59.0	Caroline Whitehurst	8 Sep 85
59.0	Tracy Allen	9 Jul 88

HIGH JUMP

1.95	Diana Davies	26 Jun 82
1.94	Louise Gittens	25 May 80
1.94 i	Debbie Marti	3 Feb 91
1.94		9 Jun 96
1.94 i	Jo Jennings	13 Mar 93
1.90		29 Sep 88
1.92	Barbara Simmonds	31 Jul 82
1.92	Judy Simpson	8 Aug 83
1.92	Janet Boyle	29 Sep 88
1.92 i	Julia Bennett	10 Mar 90
1.89		11 Jun 94
1.92	Lea Haggett	16 Jun 96
1.91 [10]	Ann-Marie Cording	19 Sep 81
1.91	Gillian Evans	30 Apr 83
1.91	Jayne Barnetson	7 Jul 89
1.90	Kim Hagger	17 May 86
1.90	Sharon Hutchings	1 Aug 86
1.88 i	Debbie McDowell	17 Jan 88
1.82		7 May 88
1.88 i	Kerry Roberts	16 Feb 92
1.86		6 Jun 92
1.88 i	Kelly Mason	16 Feb 92
1.85		10 Aug 91
1.87	Barbara Lawton	22 Sep 73
1.87	Moira Maguire	11 May 80
1.87 [20]	Louise Manning	6 May 84
1.87	Michelle Dunkley	7 Jul 95
1.87	Rachael Forrest	7 Jul 95
1.87	Susan Jones	12 Jul 96
1.86	Claire Summerfield	7 Aug 82
1.86	Jennifer Little	11 May 86
1.86	Catherine Scott	8 May 87
1.85	Brenda Gibbs	20 Aug 77
1.85	Gillian Hitchen	3 Jun 78
1.85	Julie Major	8 Jul 94
1.84 [30]	Sarah Rowe	22 Aug 81
1.84	Ursula Fay	6 Aug 83
1.84	Tonia Phillpots	20 Aug 83
1.84	Denise Lewis	19 May 96
1.83	Linda Hedmark	4 Jul 71
1.83	Val Harrison	19 Jun 74
1.83 i	Ros Few	25 Feb 75
1.81		3 Jun 79
1.83	Denise Brown	8 Aug 80
1.83	Joanne Hilliard	4 Jun 83
1.83	Rhona Pinkerton	4 Aug 85
1.83 [40]	Marion Hughes	19 Jul 86
1.83	Tracey Clarke	2 Aug 87
1.83	Kay Fletcher	17 Jun 89
1.83	Hazel Melvin	2 Jun 96
1.82	Mary Peters	2 Sep 72
1.82	Wendy Phillips	19 Jul 80
1.82	Elaine Hickey	9 Aug 80
1.81	Anne Gilson	1 Aug 76
1.81	Joy Crouchley	30 Jun 79
1.81	Janet Heaney	10 Aug 80
1.81 [50]	Jackie Gilchrist	24 Jul 82
1.81	Tina Reeson	1 May 83
1.81	Jackie Kinsella	17 May 86
1.81	Caris Henderson	14 Jun 87
1.81	Claire Poulson	16 Sep 90
1.81 i	Gill Howard	3 Jan 92
1.81	Julie Crane	8 Jul 94
1.81	Lisa Brown	24 Jun 95

POLE VAULT

4.00	Janine Whitlock	14 Sep 96
3.90	Kate Staples	26 May 96
3.72	Linda Stanton	11 Jun 95
3.70	Rhian Clarke	10 Aug 96
3.70	Paula Wilson	26 Aug 96
3.55	Louise Schramm	22 Jun 96
3.55	Emma Hornby	3 Aug 96
3.51 i	Clare Ridgley	17 Feb 96
3.50		6 May 96
3.50	Fiona Harrison	25 Aug 96
3.40 i	Claire Morrison	26 Feb 95 [10]
3.30		18 Jun 95
3.30	Katie Alexander	20 Jul 96
3.30	Stacey Dicker	7 Sep 96
3.20	Samantha Stapleton	3 Aug 94
3.20	Larissa Lowe	26 May 96
3.20	Kimberley Rothman	26 Aug 96
3.20	Rebecca Roles	31 Aug 96
3.15	Maria Newton	20 Jul 96
3.10	Dawn-Alice Wright	10 Jul 94
3.10	Leanne Mellor	21 Aug 94
3.10 i	Sue Drummie	4 Feb 95 [20]
3.00		14 Jun 95
3.10	Fiona Peake	27 Apr 96
3.10 ex	Katherine Horner	4 Jun 96
3.00		25 Mar 95
3.00	Claudia Filce	20 May 95
3.00	Becky Ridgley	11 May 96
3.00	Kirsty Armstrong	27 Jul 96
3.00	Danielle Codd	17 Aug 96
3.00	Tracey Bloomfield	18 Aug 96
3.00	Elizabeth Hughes	1 Sep 96
3.00 i	Alison Davies	22 Dec 96

LONG JUMP

6.90	Beverly Kinch	14 Aug 83
6.88	Fiona May	18 Jul 90
6.83	Sue Telfer	6 May 84
6.76	Mary Rand	14 Oct 64
6.75	Joyce Oladapo	14 Sep 85
6.73	Sheila Sherwood	23 Jul 70
6.73	Yinka Idowu	7 Aug 93
6.70	Kim Hagger	30 Aug 86
6.69	Sue Reeve	10 Jun 79
6.67	Denise Lewis	28 May 95 [10]
6.63	Mary Berkeley	17 Jun 89
6.57	Joanne Wise	25 May 92
6.55	Ann Simmonds	22 Jul 70
6.52	Gillian Regan	29 Aug 82
6.52	Georgina Oladapo	16 Jun 84
6.51 i	Ruth Howell	23 Feb 74
6.49		16 Jun 72
6.47 A	Ashia Hansen	26 Jan 96
6.27		26 Jun 94

		Long Jump	
	6.45	Carol Zeniou	12 May 82
	6.45	Margaret Cheetham	18 Aug 84
20	6.44	Sharon Danville	15 Jun 77
	6.44	Barbara Clarke	13 Sep 81
	6.43	Moira Walls	18 Sep 70
	6.43	Myra Nimmo	27 May 73
	6.40	Judy Simpson	26 Aug 84
	6.40	Sharon Bowie	28 Jun 86
	6.39	Maureen Chitty	28 Jun 72
	6.39	Sue Longden	12 Sep 76
	6.37	Kelly Wenlock	24 Apr 82
	6.34 i	Barabara-Anne Barrett	20 Feb 71
	6.31		14 Aug 71
30	6.33 i	Barabara Lawton	21 Nov 70
	6.33	Glenys Morton	19 Jul 81
	6.33	Joanne Mulliner	13 Sep 86
	6.33	Joanne Dear	19 May 93
	6.32	Helen Cushen	7 Jun 87
	6.32	Jo Willoughby	28 May 89
	6.31	Lorraine Campbell	19 May 85
	6.28	Janet Peacock	4 May 77
	6.28	Vikki Schofield	16 Jul 95
	6.27	Alix Stevenson	13 Jun 70
40	6.27	Anita Neil	29 Aug 70
	6.27	Sandra Green	14 Jun 80
	6.27	Allison Manley	16 Aug 80
	6.27	Liz Ghojefa	23 Jul 95
	6.26	Maria Smallwood	14 Jun 80
	6.25 i	Evette Finikin	3 Feb 89
	6.25	Mandy Bell	16 May 92
	6.25	Lisa Armstrong	15 Jul 92
	6.24	Karen Murray	16 Jul 77
	6.24	Gladys Taylor	28 Jul 79
50	6.24	Sarah Claxton	15 Jun 96

wind assisted

7.00	Sue Telfer	27 May 84
6.98	Fiona May	4 Jun 89
6.93	Beverly Kinch	14 Aug 83
6.84	Sue Reeve	25 Jun 77
6.80	Joyce Oladapo	22 Jun 85
6.69	Joanne Wise	30 Jul 88
6.65	Mary Berkeley	4 Jun 89
6.57	Ann Simmonds	22 Aug 70
6.56	Judy Simpson	30 Aug 86
6.54	Ruth Howell	16 Jun 72
6.54	Myra Nimmo	19 Jun 76
6.49	Margaret Cheetham	4 Sep 83
6.48	Moira Walls	17 May 70
6.41	Allison Manley	28 Jul 79
6.40	Barabara-Anne Barrett	17 Jul 71
6.39	Alix Stevenson	6 Jun 70
6.39	Carolyn Ross	19 Apr 87
6.38	Joanne Mulliner	1 Jun 85
6.38	Jo Willoughby	6 Aug 89
6.38	Ann Brooks	7 Aug 94
6.36	Karen Murray	9 Jul 77
6.34	Janet Frank-Lynch	8 Jul 78
6.34	Jill Davies	12 Jul 96
6.34	Sarah Claxton	8 Jul 78
6.32	Diana Davies	22 May 88
6.32	Liz Ghojefa	16 Jul 94

TRIPLE JUMP

14.78	Ashia Hansen	25 Aug 96	
14.08	Michelle Griffith	11 Jun 94	
13.64	Rachel Kirby	7 Aug 94	
13.56	Mary Agyepong	5 Jun 92	
13.55	Connie Henry	11 Aug 96	
13.46	Evette Finikin	26 Jul 91	
13.03	Shani Anderson	4 May 96	
12.94	Lorna Turner	9 Jul 94	
12.89	Karen Skeggs	17 May 92	
12.67	Caroline Stead	1 Jun 96	10
12.64	Liz Ghojefa	4 Sep 93	
12.55	Pamela Anderson	29 Jun 96	
12.51	Kerensa Denham	11 May 96	
12.46	Debbie Rowe	1 Jun 96	
12.42	Elizabeth Gibbens	2 Jul 95	
12.40	Katie Evans	20 Jul 96	
12.31	Caroline Warden	23 Jul 94	
12.22	Mary Rand	18 Jun 59	
12.22	Allison Forbes	9 Sep 89	
12.22	Nicola Barr	16 Aug 92	20
12.20	Jodie Hurst	8 Jun 96	
12.18	Justina Cruickshank	26 May 96	
12.15 i	Fiona Watt	22 Jan 95	
11.91		29 Jun 96	
12.14	Jayne Ludlow	21 May 94	
12.13 i	Margaret Still	21 Jan 96	
12.03		2 Jun 96	
12.10	Jane Falconer	29 Aug 93	
12.04	Lea Haggett	4 Feb 96	
11.98	Ruth Irving	25 Feb 95	
11.91	Lisa Brown	30 Jul 95	
11.85	Lauraine Cameron	16 Jul 94	30
11.85	Jo Morris	30 Jun 96	
11.84	Jayne McCoy	7 Sep 91	
11.83	Marcia Richardson	4 Sep 93	
11.82	Rachel Atkinson	31 Jul 94	
11.82	Julia Johnson	30 Jun 96	
11.81	Linda Davidson	18 Apr 93	
11.79	Michelle Rea	16 Jun 91	
11.79	Michelle Dunkley	8 Sep 96	
11.76	Stephanie Dobson	10 Sep 94	
11.76	Lucy Clements	9 Jun 96	40
11.75	Liz Patrick	20 Jul 96	
11.74	Mandy Bell	16 May 92	
11.74	Stephanie Aneto	20 Jul 96	

wind assisted

12.93	Karen Skeggs	13 Jun 92
12.58	Katie Evans	31 Aug 96
12.55	Lauraine Cameron	29 Aug 93
12.37	Jane Falconer	29 Aug 93
12.34	Nicola Barr	10 Jun 92
12.21	Justina Cruickshank	19 May 96
12.20	Rachel Atkinson	28 Jul 96
12.18	Michelle Rea	29 Jun 91
12.07	Jo Morris	13 Jul 96
12.06	Fiona Watt	2 Jun 96
11.96	Lisa Brown	24 Jun 95
11.93	Jessie Aru	15 May 93
11.80	Kathryn Blackwood	4 Jul 93

SHOT

	Mark	Name	Date
	19.36	Judy Oakes	14 Aug 88
	19.06 i	Venissa Head	7 Apr 84
	18.93		13 May 84
	19.03	Myrtle Augee	2 Jun 90
	18.99	Meg Ritchie	7 May 83
	17.53	Angela Littlewood	24 Jul 80
	17.45	Yvonne Hanson-Nortey	28 Jul 89
	16.57	Maggie Lynes	20 Jul 94
	16.40 i	Mary Peters	28 Feb 70
	16.31		1 Jun 66
	16.29	Brenda Bedford	26 May 76
10	16.05	Janis Kerr	15 May 76
	15.85 i	Alison Grey	12 Feb 94
	15.69		11 Jun 94
	15.80	Sharon Andrews	30 Jul 93
	15.75 i	Caroline Savory	23 Feb 83
	15.50		19 Jun 83
	15.60 i	Justine Buttle	27 Feb 88
	15.45		25 Aug 88
	15.48	Mary Anderson	8 Sep 85
	15.46	Vanessa Redford	14 Jun 80
	15.45	Susan King	27 Mar 83
	15.41	Fatima Whitbread	29 Apr 84
	15.32 i	Helen Hounsell	13 Feb 82
	14.91		22 May 82
20	15.23	Judy Simpson	18 Jun 88
	15.21	Uju Efobi	18 Jun 88
	15.18	Suzanne Allday	18 May 64
	15.18 i	Helen Hounsell	Jan 79
	15.09		6 Sep 78
	15.09	Jayne Berry	22 Jul 93
	15.08	Janet Thompson	3 Jun 79
	15.08	Susan Tudor	30 May 82
	14.98 i	Sandra Smith	21 Dec 85
	14.95		18 Aug 85
	14.90	Tracy Axten	10 Sep 95
	14.88 i	Jenny Kelly	10 Mar 90
	14.73		18 May 91
30	14.88	Debbie Callaway	15 May 93
	14.77	Gay Porter	11 Apr 70
	14.76 i	Carol Cooksley	14 Dec 91
	14.71		1 Sep 90
	14.75 i	Cynthia Gregory	12 Dec 81
	14.70		29 Aug 81
	14.67	Rosemary Payne	23 Apr 74
	14.67	Jo Duncan	7 Sep 96
	14.66 i	Terri Salt	7 Jan 84
	14.62	Kathryn Farr	7 Jun 92
	14.60	Philippa Roles	4 Sep 96
	14.59	Dawn Grazette	19 May 91
	14.53	Emma Beales	12 Sep 92
40	14.46 i	Heather Stuart	3 Feb 73
	14.44	Irene Duffin	2 Jun 90
	14.42	Vickie Foster	18 Aug 96
	14.36	Denise Lewis	25 May 96
	14.29	Charmaine Johnson	10 Jul 93
	14.24	Helen Cowe	23 May 93
	14.23	Janet Beese	14 Jun 78
	14.23	Clova Court	10 Jul 93
	14.21	Lorraine Shaw	16 Jul 94

DISCUS

Mark	Name	Date	
67.48	Meg Ritchie	26 Apr 81	
64.68	Venissa Head	18 Jul 83	
60.72	Jacqui McKernan	18 Jul 93	
58.56	Debbie Callaway	19 May 96	
58.02	Rosemary Payne	3 Jun 72	
57.34	Shelley Drew	5 Jun 96	
57.32	Lynda Whiteley	16 Jun 84	
56.24	Sharon Andrews	12 Jun 94	
56.06	Kathryn Farr	27 Jun 87	
55.88	Tracy Axten	19 May 96	10
55.52	Jane Aucott	17 Jan 90	
55.42	Lesley Bryant	12 Sep 80	
55.06	Janet Kane	17 Jun 78	
55.04	Lorraine Shaw	14 May 94	
54.72	Karen Pugh	27 Jul 86	
54.68	Emma Beales	10 Jun 95	
54.46	Ellen Mulvihill	14 May 86	
54.46	Janette Picton	17 Aug 90	
54.24	Nicola Talbot	15 May 93	
53.96	Julia Avis	27 Apr 86	20
53.66	Rosanne Lister	22 Jun 91	
53.44	Judy Oakes	20 Aug 88	
53.16	Sarah Winckless	18 Jun 94	
52.58	Emma Merry	22 Aug 93	
52.52	Alison Grey	18 Jun 94	
52.46	Vanessa Redford	4 Jul 82	
51.82	Catherine Bradley	20 Jul 85	
51.60	Dorothy Chipchase	20 Jul 73	
51.38	Philippa Roles	22 Jun 96	
51.18	Angella Sellars	12 Aug 90	30
51.12	Joanne Hilliard	26 May 86	
50.58	Brenda Bedford	24 Aug 68	
50.06	Joanne Essex	7 May 89	
50.04	Morag Bremner	27 Apr 86	
49.92	Fiona Condon	10 Apr 82	
49.84	Janis Kerr	15 May 77	
49.84	Denise Sturman	12 Apr 81	
49.74	Sarah Henton	31 Aug 96	
49.66	Gay Porter	19 Aug 70	
49.58	Jackie Elsmore	2 Aug 75	40
49.48	Gwen Bird	20 Jul 91	
49.44	Myrtle Augee	14 May 95	
49.30	Amanda Barnes	18 Jun 88	
49.20	Jane Tabor	5 Apr 86	
49.12	Jean Fielding	14 Jul 74	
49.00	Tracey Whincup	26 Jun 84	
48.98	Angela Littlewood	6 Jun 82	
48.84	Uju Efobi	14 May 95	
48.76	Rachel Hopgood	27 May 96	
48.64	Helen Cowe	17 Sep 94	50
48.62	Vickie Foster	8 Jun 93	
48.54	Sandra Browne	3 Jul 88	
48.24	Lauren Keightley	28 Jul 96	
48.08	Donna Williams	12 Jul 96	
48.06	Yvonne Hanson-Nortey	13 Aug 89	
48.02	Natalie Hart	19 May 90	
48.00	Hilda Atkins	20 Feb 66	

downhill

Mark	Name	Date
51.04	Fiona Condon	7 Jul 79

HAMMER

64.90	Lorraine Shaw	10 Jun 95
59.54	Lyn Sprules	26 Aug 96
56.76	Esther Augee	15 May 93
55.00	Ann Gardner	26 Aug 96
54.42	Diana Holden	2 Sep 95
53.26	Sarah Moore	25 May 96
52.84	Fiona Whitehead	29 Jun 93
51.62	Julie Lavender	15 May 94
50.62	Helen Arnold	27 Jul 96
10 50.32	Irene Duffin	1 Jun 96
50.12	Jean Clark	28 Aug 95
49.80	Samantha Burns-Salmond	11 May 96
49.52	Rachael Beverley	28 Apr 96
48.98	Liz Pidgeon	21 Sep 96
48.90	Julie Kirkpatrick	15 Jun 96
48.78	Suzanne Last	5 May 96
48.32	Helen McCreadie	9 Jun 96
47.70	Angela Bonner	14 Apr 96
47.68	Catherine Garden	13 Jul 96
20 47.10	Karen Brown	11 Sep 93
47.08	Lesley Brannan	23 May 96
47.06	Caroline Manning	22 Jul 95
46.88	Janet Smith	25 Jun 94
46.84	Sarah Harrison	20 Jul 96
46.64	Myrtle Augee	5 Jul 95
46.00	Diane Smith	24 Aug 96
45.22	Lindsey Jones	1 Sep 96
45.00	Andrea Jenkins	7 Sep 96
44.90	Joanne Eley	3 Aug 96
30 44.64	Debbie Callaway	10 Aug 96
44.46	Kim Thompson	18 Jun 94
43.90	Vickie Foster	7 Sep 96
43.78	Suzanne Roberts	27 Jul 96
43.52	Helen Cowe	6 Jul 93
43.52	Cheryl Cunnane	7 May 95
43.52	Christine Bennett	10 Aug 96
43.34	Leanne Jones	15 May 96
43.02	Claire Burnett	25 May 96
42.86	Louise Kay	27 Jul 96
40 42.66	Sheena Parry	1 Jul 95
42.66	Zoe Derham	25 Aug 96
42.66	Philippa Roles	31 Aug 96
42.48	Imogen Martin	20 May 95
42.46	Lucy Mills	3 Aug 91
42.42	Tracy Shorts	9 Jun 96
42.38	Sally Giles	22 Jun 96
42.32	Annette O'Conor	10 Mar 90
42.32	Louise Campbell	9 Jun 96
42.12	Emma Jones	25 Jun 95
50 41.94	Sharon Nash	3 Sep 94
41.90	Jenny Cunnane	9 Apr 95
41.48	Tracy Oldfield	3 Aug 91
41.32	Linda Low	14 May 94
41.32	Allison Wood	19 Jul 94
41.30	Marcelle Edwards	16 Jun 96
41.04	Carys Parry	24 Aug 96
40.84	Pat McNab	14 Apr 91
40.74	Helen Wilding	23 Jun 96
40.66	Samantha Smith	21 May 94

JAVELIN

77.44	Fatima Whitbread	28 Aug 86
73.58	Tessa Sanderson	26 Jun 83
62.32	Sharon Gibson	16 May 87
62.22	Diane Royle	18 May 85
60.12	Shelley Holroyd	16 Jun 96
60.00	Julie Abel	24 May 87
59.40	Karen Hough	28 Aug 86
59.36	Kirsty Morrison	4 Sep 93
58.60	Jeanette Rose	30 May 82
58.20	Lorna Jackson	16 Jun 96 10
57.90	Anna Lockton	1 Jul 87
57.84	Amanda Liverton	3 Jun 90
56.96	Nicola Emblem	1 Feb 90
56.50	Caroline White	8 Jun 91
56.50	Denise Lewis	11 Aug 96
55.72	Karen Martin	25 Jul 92
55.70	Lynn Hayhoe	31 May 92
55.60	Susan Platt	15 Jun 68
55.38	Catherine Garside	19 May 84
55.36	Jackie Zaslona	30 Aug 80 20
55.30	Clova Court	27 Aug 91
55.04	Joanne Harding	24 May 87
54.50	Karen Costello	11 Jun 94
54.18	Rosemary Morgan	25 Apr 64
54.02	Janeen Williams	29 Mar 80
53.88	Sharon Corbett	21 Jul 73
53.32	Maxine Jervis	27 Jul 78
52.58	Shona Urquhart	17 Jun 83
52.48	Gail Hornby	22 Jun 90
52.40	Noelle Bradshaw	30 Jun 93 30
52.16	Sandra O'Toole	5 Apr 78
52.14	Amanda Caine	25 May 87
52.14	Jo Burton	25 Jun 94
52.10	Anne Goodlad	19 Aug 73
52.00	Lucy Stevenson	16 Aug 92
51.76	Lucy Burrell	11 Jun 94
51.56	Jean Randall	6 Aug 72
51.50	Pru French	9 Jul 72
51.48	Claire Faragher	14 Apr 91
51.32	Yvonne Fountain	22 Sep 74 40
51.08	Karen Slaughter	7 Jul 91
50.84	Shara Spragg	17 Jun 78
50.82	Anne Farquhar	25 Jul 70
50.80	Maxine Bennett	15 Jun 86
50.80	Janine King	4 May 96
50.58	Tina Fletcher	14 Aug 88
50.48	Caroline Hatton	11 Jun 89
50.48	Michelle Fields	15 May 93
50.38	Jacqui Barclay	13 May 84
50.32	Katie Granger	12 Sep 93 50
50.12	Karen Miller	25 Jul 87
50.04	Kim Lisbon	19 Feb 84
50.02	Angelique Pullen	31 Aug 85
49.84	Janette McClean	26 Aug 90
49.78	Mary Bloomfield	7 Aug 83
49.72	Michelle Poole	2 Mar 86
49.50	Averil Williams	16 Jul 60
49.38	Tracey Averies	20 May 84
49.28	Gina D'Arcy	15 Aug 82

HEPTATHLON (1985 Tables)

	6645	Denise Lewis	26 May 96
	6623	Judy Simpson	30 Aug 86
	6259	Kim Hagger	18 May 86
	6125	Tessa Sanderson	12 Jul 81
	6094 h	Joanne Mulliner	7 Jun 87
	6022	Clova Court	27 Aug 91
	5826	Jenny Kelly	3 Jul 94
	5803	Jayne Barnetson	20 Aug 89
	5776	Kathy Warren	12 Jul 81
10	5747 w	Julia Bennett	5 May 96
	5496		21 May 95
	5703	Kerry Jury	26 May 96
	5702	Yinka Idowu	21 May 95
	5700	Vikki Schofield	5 May 96
	5642	Sarah Rowe	23 Aug 81
	5633	Marcia Marriott	18 May 86
	5632	Emma Beales	1 Aug 93
	5618 w	Sarah Damn	5 May 96
	5392		30 Apr 95
	5594 h	Gillian Evans	22 May 83
	5548	Val Walsh	18 May 86
20	5517	Shona Urquhart	21 Aug 88
	5495	Charmaine Johnson	24 May 92
	5493	Sally Gunnell	28 May 84
	5455	Claire Phythian	19 May 95
	5446	Manndy Laing	7 Aug 83
	5434 w	Debbie Woolgar	8 Jul 90
	5380		18 Jun 89
	5424	Lisa Gibbs	1 Aug 93
	5420	Pauline Richards	19 Jun 94
	5409	Uju Efobi	19 Jun 94
	5391 w	Jackie Kinsella	22 Jun 86
	5331		19 Jul 86
30	5389	Sarah Owen	15 Aug 82
	5384 h	Sue Longden	8 May 82
	5353	Emma Lindsay	23 Aug 94
	5351	Wendy Laing	1 Aug 93
	5339	Tracy Joseph	4 Aug 96
	5332	Diana Bennett	26 May 96
	5297	Kim Price	24 Aug 86
	5273 w	Debbie Marti	11 Aug 85
	5216		7 Jul 85
	5258	Anne Hollman	26 May 96
	5244 h	Val Lemoignan	19 Apr 84
40	5242	Allison Manley	28 Mar 81
	5213	Nicola Gautier	28 Jul 96
	5208 h	Michelle Stone	30 Sep 84
	5208	Mary Anderson	24 Aug 86
	5190	Wendy Jeal	2 Jun 91
	5165	Rebecca Foster	1 Aug 93
	5143 h	Clover Wynter-Pink	25 Jun 95
	5140	Ese Oshevire	25 Jun 89
	5116 w	Julie Frampton	21 Jul 85
	5055		19 Aug 84
	5114	Louise Batho	22 Sep 96
50	5065 h	Catherine Scott	13 Sep 87
	5050	Teresa Springate	26 Aug 90
	5047	Rebecca Lewis	28 Jul 96
	5039	Sarah Booth	24 Aug 86

3000 METRES TRACK WALK

12:49.16	Betty Sworowski	28 Jul 90	
12:59.3	Vicky Lupton	14 May 95	
13:11.0	Lisa Langford	6 Jul 90	
13:12.01 i	Julie Drake	12 Mar 93	
13:16.0		11 Dec 90	
13:13.3	Carolyn Partington	12 Jul 95	
13:16.23	Verity Snook	27 May 96	
13:25.2	Carol Tyson	6 Jul 79	
13:28.0	Helen Elleker	22 Jul 90	
13:37.1	Beverley Allen	16 May 87	
13:42.10	Sylvia Black	23 May 90	10
13:43.0	Melanie Wright	5 Jul 94	
13:44.0	Virginia Birch	19 Jun 84	
13:46.3 +	Marion Fawkes	30 Jun 79	
13:48.0	Sarah Brown	16 May 87	
13:52.0	Lillian Millen	7 May 83	
13:56.0	Irene Bateman	20 Sep 80	
13:57.8	Jill Barrett	2 Jun 84	
14:02.29	Karen Smith	19 May 93	
14:02.8 +	Nicky Jackson	25 May 87	
14:04.1	Susan Ashforth	19 May 85	20

5000 METRES TRACK WALK

21:52.38	Vicky Lupton	9 Aug 95	
21:57.68	Lisa Langford	25 Jun 90	
22:02.06	Betty Sworowski	28 Aug 89	
22:37.47	Julie Drake	17 Jul 93	
22:40.19	Carolyn Partington	16 Jul 95	
22:51.23	Helen Elleker	25 Jun 90	
23:11.2	Carol Tyson	30 Jun 79	
23:15.04	Beverley Allen	25 May 87	
23:19.2	Marion Fawkes	30 Jun 79	
23:20.00	Virginia Birch	25 May 85	10
23:22.52	Verity Snook	19 Jun 94	
23:34.43	Sylvia Black	5 Jul 92	
23:35.54	Nicola Jackson	25 May 87	
23:38.3	Irene Bateman	28 Jun 81	
23:46.7	Lillian Millen	28 Jun 81	
23:47.0	Melanie Wright	29 May 94	
23:51.1	Jill Barrett	5 May 84	
23:55.27	Susan Ashforth	25 May 85	
24:00.0	Sarah Brown	21 May 91	
24:09.66	Elaine Callanin	16 Jul 95	20

5k Road - *where superior to track time*

21:36	Vicky Lupton	18 Jul 92
21:50	Betty Sworowski	6 May 90
22:45 +	Verity Snook	25 Aug 94
22:51	Marion Fawkes	29 Sep 79
22:59	Carol Tyson	29 Sep 79
23:00 +	Beverley Allen	1 Sep 87
23:13	Sylvia Black	13 Feb 93
23:24	Melanie Wright	9 Apr 95
23:25	Irene Bateman	29 Sep 79
23:35	Lisa Simpson	31 Oct 87
23:38	Jill Barrett	12 May 84
23:42	Lillian Millen	23 Apr 83
23:45 hc	Elaine Callanin	28 Jan 95
23:54	Vicky Lawrence	26 Sep 87
23:57	Sarah Brown	6 Dec 80

10000 METRES TRACK WALK

45:18.8	Vicky Lupton	2 Sep 95	
45:53.9	Julie Drake	26 May 90	
46:23.08	Betty Sworowski	4 Aug 91	
46:25.2	Helen Elleker	26 May 90	
47:10.07	Verity Snook	19 Jun 93	
47:56.3	Virginia Birch	15 Jun 85	
47:58.3	Beverley Allen	21 Jun 86	
48:11.4	Marion Fawkes	8 Jul 79	
48:20.0	Carolyn Partington	7 May 94	
48:34.0	Lisa Langford	15 Mar 86	10
48:34.5	Carol Tyson	22 Aug 81	
48:35.8	Melanie Wright	2 Sep 95	
48:56.5	Sarah Brown	18 Apr 91	
48:57.6	Irene Bateman	20 Mar 82	
49:27.0	Sylvia Black	22 Apr 95	
49:39.0	Karen Smith	22 May 91	
49:41.0	Elaine Callanin	22 Apr 95	
50:10.2	Brenda Lupton	17 Mar 84	
50:25.0mx	Lisa Simpson	1 Apr 87	
50:28.0	Andrea Crofts	21 Jul 92	20
50:46.0	Judy Farr	25 Mar 78	
50:50.0	Nicola Jackson	21 Jun 86	
50:52.3	Kim Braznell	31 Aug 96	
51:00.0	Karen Nipper	21 Feb 81	
51:03.0	Liz Corran	22 Apr 95	
51:03.0	Karen Kneale	22 Apr 95	

track short

48:52.5	Irene Bateman	19 Mar 83
50:11.2	Jill Barrett	19 Mar 83

Road - *where superior to track time*

45:42	Lisa Langford	3 May 87
45:59	Betty Sworowski	24 Aug 91
46:06	Verity Snook	25 Aug 94
46:26	Carolyn Partington	1 Jul 95
47:19	Melanie Wright	23 Sep 95
47:58	Nicola Jackson	27 Jun 87
47:59	Sylvia Black	29 Mar 92
48:18	Melanie Wright	9 May 92
48:30	Karen Smith	16 Apr 94
48:47	Irene Bateman	20 Jun 81
49:10	Vicky Lawrence	14 Mar 87
49:12	Elaine Callanin	20 Jun 81
49:14	Carolyn Brown	29 Mar 92
49:33	Lisa Simpson	14 Mar 87
49:37	Karen Kneale	26 May 96

20 KILOMETRES ROAD WALK

1:40:45	Irene Bateman	9 Apr 83
1:42:47	Vicky Lupton	1 Jul 95
1:43:50	Betty Sworowski	22 Feb 88
1:44:42	Lillian Millen	2 Apr 83
1:45:11	Elaine Callanin	16 Oct 95

50 KILOMETRES ROAD WALK

4:50:51	Sandra Brown	13 Jul 91
5:01:52	Lillian Millen	16 Apr 83
5:13:03 +	Irene Corlett	29 Apr 84
5:22:04	Cath Reader	2 May 93

4 x 100 METRES RELAY

42.43	UK	1 Aug 80	
	Oakes, Cook, Callender, Lannaman		
42.66	UK	11 Sep 82	
	Hoyte, Cook, Callender, S.Thomas		
42.71	UK	10 Aug 83	
	Baptiste, Cook, Callender, S.Thomas		
42.72	UK	3 Sep 78	
	Callender, Cook, Danville, Lannaman		
43.02	UK	26 Sep 80	
	Oakes, Cook, Callender, Scutt		
43.03	UK	15 Aug 81	
	Hoyte, Cook, Callender, S.Thomas		
43.06	UK	10 Aug 83	
	Baptiste, Cook, Callender, S.Thomas		
43.11	UK	11 Aug 84	
	Jacobs, Cook, Callender, Oakes		
43.15	England	9 Oct 82	
	Hoyte, Cook, Callender, Lannaman		
43.18	UK	4 Aug 79	10
	Barnett, Hoyte, Cook, Oakes		
43.18	UK	20 Aug 83	
	Baptiste, Cook, Callender, S.Thomas		
43.19	UK	20 Sep 80	
	Oakes, Cook, Callender, Scutt		
43.21	UK	18 Aug 82	
	Hoyte, Cook, Callender, S.Thomas		
43.26 A	UK Students	13 Sep 79	
	Luker, Cook, Patten, Callender		
43.30	UK	30 Aug 86	
	P. Thomas, Cook, Baptiste, Hoyte		
43.3	UK	1 Jul 80	
	Oakes, Cook, Callender, Lannaman		
43.32	UK	5 Jun 80	
	Oakes, Cook, Callender, Lannaman		
43.32	UK	1 Sep 90	
	Douglas, Kinch, Jacobs, P.Thomas		
43.35	UK	17 Aug 85	
	Christian, Baptiste, Joseph, Oakes		
43.36	UK	13 Jul 80	20
	Oakes, Cook, Callender, Lannaman		
43.36	UK	23 Jun 81	
	Hoyte, Cook, Callender, S.Thomas		
43.37	UK	30 Aug 82	
	Hoyte, Cook, Callender, S.Thomas		
43.38	UK	8 Aug 86	
	P. Thomas, Cook, Baptiste, Oakes		
43.39	England	2 Aug 86	
	P. Thomas, Cook, Baptiste, Oakes		
43.43	UK	31 Aug 91	
	Douglas, Kinch, Jacobs, P.Thomas		
43.44	UK	30 Jul 76	
	Hoyte, Ramsden, Danville, Lynch		
43.44	UK	31 Aug 86	
	P. Thomas, Cook, Baptiste, Hoyte		
43.46	UK	19 Jun 88	
	Miles, Baptiste, Jacobs, P.Thomas		
43.46	UK	25 Jun 94	
	Douglas, Merry, Jacobs, P.Thomas		
43.46	UK	28 Aug 94	30
	Douglas, McLeod, Jacobs, P.Thomas		

4 x 400 METRES RELAY

3:22.01　UK　　　　　　　　1 Sep 91
　Hanson, Smith, Gunnell, Keough
3:23.41　UK　　　　　　　　22 Aug 93
　Keough, Smith, Goddard, Gunnell
3:23.89　UK　　　　　　　　31 Aug 91
　Hanson, Smith, Gunnell, Keough
3:24.14　UK　　　　　　　　14 Aug 94
　Neef, Keough, Smith, Gunnell
3:24.23　UK　　　　　　　　8 Aug 92
　Smith, Douglas, Stoute, Gunnell
3:24.25　UK　　　　　　　　30 Jun 91
　Gunnell, Hanson, Stoute, Keough
3:24.36　UK　　　　　　　　5 Jun 93
　Smith, Goddard, Stoute, Gunnell
3:24.78　UK　　　　　　　　1 Sep 90
　Gunnell, Stoute, Beckford, Keough
3:25.20　UK　　　　　　　　7 Aug 92
　Douglas, Smith, Stoute, Gunnell
10　3:25.50　UK　　　　　　　12 Aug 95
　Neef, Llewellyn, Hanson, Oladapo
3:25.51　UK　　　　　　　　11 Aug 84
　Scutt, Barnett, Taylor, Hoyte-Smith
3:25.82　UK　　　　　　　　11 Sep 82
　Cook, Macdonald, Taylor, Hoyte-Smith
3:25.87　UK　　　　　　　　19 Jun 82
　Forsyth, Hoyte-Smith, Elder, Scutt
3:26.54　UK　　　　　　　　6 Aug 89
　Keough, Stoute, Piggford, Gunnell
3:26.6 a　UK　　　　　　　17 Aug 75
　Roscoe, Taylor, Elder, Hartley
3:26.89　UK　　　　　　　　1 Oct 88
　Keough, Stoute, Piggford, Gunnell
3:26.89　UK　　　　　　　　13 Aug 95
　Neef, Llewellyn, Hanson, Oladapo
3:27.04　UK　　　　　　　　21 Aug 93
　Keough, Smith, Goddard, Gunnell
3:27.06　England　　　　　28 Aug 94
　Smith, Goddard, Keough, Gunnell
20　3:27.09　UK　　　　　　　30 Jul 76
　Barnes, Taylor, Elder, Hartley
3:27.17　UK　　　　　　　　3 Sep 78
　Williams, Hoyte-Smith, Elder, Hartley
3:27.19　England　　　　　12 Aug 78
　Patten, Hoyte-Smith, Elder, Hartley
3:27.25　UK　　　　　　　　13 Aug 94
　Neef, Keough, Smith, Gunnell
3:27.27　UK　　　　　　　　16 Aug 81
　Forsyth, Scutt, Elder, Hoyte-Smith
3:27.29　UK　　　　　　　　21 Aug 83
　Scutt, Baxter, Hoyte-Smith, Cook
3:27.33　UK　　　　　　　　26 Jun 94
　Neef, Goddard, Smith, Gunnell
3:27.36　UK　　　　　　　　9 Sep 94
　Smith, Keough, Neef, Gunnell
3:27.5 a　UK　　　　　　　1 Aug 80
　Macdonald, Scutt, Hoyte-Smith, Hartley
3:27.68　UK　　　　　　　　10 Aug 84
　Scutt, Barnett, Taylor, Hoyte-Smith
30　3:27.8 a　UK　　　　　　5 Aug 79
　Barnes, Taylor, Elder, Hartley

UNDER 20

100 METRES

11.27 A	Kathy Smallwood	9 Sep 79
11.42		11 Aug 79
11.30	Bev Kinch	5 Jul 83
11.36 A	Della James	14 Oct 68
11.43	Shirley Thomas	7 Aug 82
11.45	Sonia Lannaman	1 Sep 72
11.45	Simmone Jacobs	6 Jul 84
11.52	Katharine Merry	16 Sep 92
11.53	Marcia Richardson	21 Jul 91
11.54	Wendy Clarke	8 Jun 75
11.59	Heather Hunte	9 Sep 77
11.59	Stephanie Douglas	23 Jul 88
11.59	Rebecca Drummond	8 Jul 95
11.61	Diane Smith	9 Aug 90
11.61	Donna Hoggarth	16 Sep 92

wind assisted

11.13	Bev Kinch	6 Jul 83
11.25	Shirley Thomas	20 Aug 81
11.26	Simmone Jacobs	27 May 84
11.40	Katharine Merry	3 Jul 93
11.43	Dorothy Hyman	2 Sep 60
11.45	Stephanie Douglas	25 Jun 88
11.47	Helen Golden	17 Jul 70
11.50	Rebecca Drummond	9 Jul 94
11.53	Wendy Clarke	22 Aug 75
11.53	Sharon Dolby	16 Aug 86
11.55	Donna Hoggarth	29 Aug 92
11.56	Sophia Smith	3 Jul 93
11.60	Sallyanne Short	27 Jul 86

hand timing

11.3	Sonia Lannaman	9 Jun 74
11.3	Heather Hunte	15 Jul 78
11.5	Jennifer Smart	1 Sep 61
11.5	Anita Neil	19 Jul 68
11.5	Vicky Shipman	3 Aug 96

wind assisted

11.2	Wendy Clarke	22 May 76
11.3	Helen Golden	30 May 70
11.3	Linsey Macdonald	3 May 80
11.4	Anita Neil	30 Jun 68
11.4	Helen Barnett	16 May 76
11.4	Jane Parry	5 Jul 80

200 METRES

22.70 A	Kathy Smallwood	12 Sep 79
22.84		5 Aug 79
23.10	Diane Smith	11 Aug 90
23.20	Katharine Merry	13 Jun 93
23.23	Sonia Lannaman	25 Aug 75
23.24	Sandra Whittaker	12 Jun 82
23.28	Simmone Jacobs	28 Aug 83
23.33	Linsey Macdonald	9 Jun 82
23.35	Donna Murray	26 May 74
23.42	Deborah Bunn	17 Jun 78
23.46	Shirley Thomas	31 May 82
23.48	Wendy Clarke	7 Jun 75
23.51	Sharon Colyear	26 May 74
23.54	Jane Parry	30 Jul 83
23.57	Sophia Smith	30 Jul 93

wind assisted

23.01	Simmone Jacobs	28 May 84
23.11	Linsey Macdonald	5 Jul 80
23.16	Donna Murray	27 Jul 74
23.42	Helen Golden	22 Jul 70
23.54	Janine MacGregor	17 Jun 78
23.55	Sallyanne Short	25 Jul 87

hand timing

23.1	Sonia Lannaman	7 Jun 75
23.3	Donna Murray	9 Jun 74
23.3	Sharon Colyear	30 Jun 74
23.3	Linsey Macdonald	8 May 82
23.4	Helen Barnett	17 Jul 76

wind assisted

22.9	Donna Murray	14 Jul 74
23.2	Deborah Bunn	2 Jul 78
23.3	Angela Bridgeman	15 Aug 82
23.4	Michelle Probert	9 Jul 77
23.4	Hayley Clements	10 Aug 85

400 METRES

51.16	Linsey Macdonald	15 Jun 80
51.77	Donna Murray	30 Jul 74
52.54	Donna Fraser	10 Aug 91
52.65	Jane Parry	11 Jun 83
52.80	Sian Morris	18 Jun 83
52.98	Karen Williams	6 Aug 78
52.99	Angela Bridgeman	24 Jul 82
53.01 i	Marilyn Neufville	14 Mar 70
53.08	Loreen Hall	29 Jul 84
53.14	Michelle Probert	28 Jul 79
53.20	Verona Bernard	8 Jul 72
53.48	Lillian Board	22 Sep 67
53.52	Ruth Kennedy	25 Sep 74
53.59	Janine MacGregor	11 Jul 78

hand timing

52.6	Marilyn Neufville	20 Jun 70
52.8	Lillian Board	9 Jul 67
52.9	Verona Bernard	15 Sep 72
53.3	Tracy Burges	5 Sep 81
53.5	Ruth Kennedy	30 Jun 74

600 METRES

1:27.33	Lorraine Baker	13 Jul 80

800 METRES

2:01.11	Lynne MacDougall	18 Aug 84
2:01.66	Lorraine Baker	26 Jun 82
2:02.00	Diane Edwards	14 Sep 85
2:02.0	Jo White	13 Aug 77
2:02.18	Lynne Robinson	18 Jul 86
2:02.8 a	Lesley Kiernan	2 Sep 74
2:02.88 i	Kirsty McDermott	22 Feb 81
2:04.01		29 Jul 81
2:03.11	Janet Prictoe	19 Aug 78
2:03.18	Paula Newnham	17 Jun 78
2:03.53	Christine McMeekin	25 Aug 75
2:04.30	Bridget Smyth	19 Aug 86
2:04.6	Janet Lawrence	26 Jul 77
2:04.7*	Rosemary Stirling	13 Aug 66
2:04.85	Louise Parker	28 Jul 79

1000 METRES

2:38.58	Jo White	9 Sep 77

1500 METRES

3:59.96	Zola Budd	30 Aug 85
4:05.96	Lynne MacDougall	20 Aug 84
4:11.12	Bridget Smyth	26 May 85
4:13.40	Wendy Smith	19 Aug 78
4:14.40	Janet Lawrence	20 Aug 77
4:14.50	Wendy Wright	20 Jun 87
4:14.56	Andrea Whitcombe	22 Aug 90
4:14.58	Ruth Smeeth	16 Jul 78
4:14.73	Mary Stewart	2 Feb 74
4:15.1	Yvonne Murray	18 Jul 82
4:15.39	Lisa York	26 Aug 89
4:15.55	Sandra Arthurton	29 Jul 78
4:16.10	Katie Fairbrass	29 May 83

ONE MILE

4:17.57	Zola Budd	21 Aug 85

2000 METRES

5:33.15	Zola Budd	13 Jul 84

3000 METRES

8:28.83	Zola Budd	7 Sep 85
8:51.78	Paula Radcliffe	20 Sep 92
9:03.35	Philippa Mason	19 Jul 86
9:04.14	Yvonne Murray	28 May 83
9:06.16	Helen Titterington	19 Jun 88
9:07.02	Carol Haigh	24 Jun 85
9:09.14	Lisa York	19 Jul 89
9:10.9	Julie Holland	7 Apr 84
9:12.28	Hayley Haining	20 Jul 91
9:12.97	Bernadette Madigan	30 Jun 79
9:13.81	Andrea Whitcombe	12 Aug 90
9:14.10	Maxine Newman	19 Jul 89

5000 METRES

14:48.07	Zola Budd	26 Aug 85

100 METRES HURDLES

13.25	Diane Allahgreen	21 Jul 94
13.30	Sally Gunnell	16 Jun 84
13.32	Keri Maddox	21 Jul 91
13.45	Natasha Danvers	6 Aug 95
13.46	Nathalie Byer	26 Aug 83
13.47	Sam Baker	30 Jun 91
13.49	Angela Thorp	30 Jun 91
13.50	Lesley-Ann Skeete	6 Jun 86
13.56	Wendy McDonnell	3 Jun 79
13.57	Bethan Edwards	29 Aug 92
13.58	Lauraine Cameron	19 Jun 90
13.68	Jacqui Agyepong	7 Aug 87

wind assisted

13.24	Lesley-Ann Skeete	7 Jun 86
13.39	Lauraine Cameron	1 Jul 90
13.45	Louise Fraser	30 Jul 89
13.45	Samantha Baker	30 Jun 91
13.46	Wendy McDonnell	30 Jun 79
13.55	Shirley Strong	10 Jul 77
13.56	Ann Girvan	15 Jul 84

hand timing

13.5	Christine Perera	19 Jul 68

wind assisted

13.1	Sally Gunnell	7 Jul 84
13.3	Keri Maddox	14 Jul 90
13.4	Judy Livermore	27 May 79
13.4	Sam Baker	14 Jul 90

400 METRES HURDLES

57.27	Vicki Jamison	28 Jul 96
58.02	Vyvyan Rhodes	28 Jun 92
58.37	Alyson Evans	1 Sep 85
58.68	Kay Simpson	15 Jul 83
58.76	Simone Gandy	28 May 84
59.00	Diane Heath	19 Jul 75
59.01	Sara Elson	24 Aug 89
59.04	Allison Curbishley	31 Jul 93
59.12	Tracy Allen	29 Jul 89
59.13	Sue Morley	12 Aug 79
59.52	Deborah Church	25 Jul 81
59.56	Lucy Elliott	26 Jul 86

hand timing

58.3	Simone Gandy	14 Jul 84
58.7	Sara Elson	18 Jun 89
59.0	Tracy Allen	9 Jul 88
59.3	Michelle Cooney	13 Jul 85
59.4	Diane Wade	21 Jul 79

HIGH JUMP

1.91	Lea Haggett	2 Jun 91
1.90	Jo Jennings	29 Sep 88
1.89	Debbie Marti	2 Jun 84
1.88	Jayne Barnetson	3 Aug 85
1.87	Louise Manning	6 May 84
1.87	Michelle Dunkley	7 Jul 95
1.87	Rachael Forrest	7 Jul 95
1.87	Susan Jones	12 Jul 96
1.86	Barbara Simmonds	9 Sep 79
1.86	Claire Summerfield	7 Aug 82
1.86	Michele Wheeler	31 May 87
1.85	Gillian Hitchen	3 Jun 78
1.85	Sharon McPeake	22 Sep 81
1.85	Julia Bennett	15 Apr 89

POLE VAULT

3.70	Rhian Clarke	10 Aug 96
3.51 i	Clare Ridgley	17 Feb 96
3.50		6 May 96
3.50	Fiona Harrison	25 Aug 96
3.20	Rebacca Roles	31 Aug 96
3.10	Dawn-Alice Wright	10 Jul 94
3.10	Leanne Mellor	21 Aug 94
3.10	Fiona Peake	27 Apr 96
3.10 ex	Katherine Horner	4 Jun 96
3.00		25 Mar 95
3.00	Becky Ridgley	11 May 96
3.00	Kirsty Armstrong	27 Jul 96
3.00	Danielle Codd	17 Aug 96
3.00	Tracey Bloomfield	18 Aug 96
3.00	Elizabeth Hughes	1 Sep 96

LONG JUMP

6.90	Bev Kinch	14 Aug 83
6.82	Fiona May	30 Jul 88
6.68	Sue Hearnshaw	22 Sep 79
6.63	Yinka Idowu	21 May 89
6.55	Joyce Oladapo	30 Jul 83
6.52	Georgina Oladapo	16 Jun 84
6.47	Joanne Wise	30 Jul 88
6.45	Margaret Cheetham	18 Aug 84
6.43	Moira Walls	18 Sep 70
6.43	Myra Nimmo	27 May 73
6.35	Sharon Bowie	1 Jun 85
6.34	Ann Wilson	3 Aug 68
6.33	Joanne Dear	19 May 93

wind assisted

6.93	Bev Kinch	14 Aug 83
6.88	Fiona May	30 Jul 88
6.71	Yinka Idowu	15 Jun 91
6.69	Joanne Wise	30 Jul 88
6.49	Margaret Cheetham	4 Sep 83
6.48	Moira Walls	17 May 70
6.41	Ann Wilson	30 Jun 68

TRIPLE JUMP

13.05	Michelle Griffith	16 Jun 90
12.43	Shani Anderson	26 Jun 93
12.42	Elizabeth Gibbens	2 Jul 95
12.27	Lorna Turner	25 May 91
12.22	Mary Bignal	18 Jun 59
12.20	Jodie Hurst	8 Jun 96
12.18	Justina Cruickshank	26 May 96
12.14	Jayne Ludlow	21 May 94
12.10	Jane Falconer	29 Aug 93
12.10	Pamela Anderson	2 Jul 95
11.91	Lisa Brown	30 Jul 95

wind assisted

12.48	Lorna Turner	30 Jun 91
12.44	Shani Anderson	9 Jul 94
12.37	Jane Falconer	29 Aug 93
12.21	Justina Cruickshank	19 May 96
12.07	Jo Morris	13 Jul 96
11.96	Lisa Brown	24 Jun 95
11.93	Jessie Aru	15 May 93

SHOT

17.10	Myrtle Augee	16 Jun 84
16.24 i	Judith Oakes	26 Feb 77
16.05		26 Aug 77
15.72 i	Alison Grey	29 Feb 92
15.26		13 Jul 91
15.60 i	Justine Buttle	27 Feb 88
15.45		25 Aug 88
15.48	Mary Anderson	8 Sep 85
15.45	Susan King	27 Mar 83
14.75 i	Cynthia Gregory	12 Dec 81
14.70		29 Aug 81
14.66 i	Terri Salt	7 Jan 84
14.60	Philippa Roles	4 Sep 96
14.59	Dawn Grazette	19 May 91
14.54	Carol Cooksley	9 Jul 88
14.54 i	Jayne Berry	18 Mar 89

DISCUS

54.78	Lynda Whiteley	4 Oct 82
53.10	Kathryn Farr	19 Jul 86
52.58	Emma Merry	22 Aug 93
51.82	Catherine Bradley	20 Jul 85
51.38	Philippa Roles	22 Jun 96
51.24	Jane Aucott	11 Jun 86
51.12	Janette Picton	6 Jun 82
50.44	Karen Pugh	8 Jul 83
50.34	Angela Sellers	27 Jul 86
50.30	Julia Avis	19 Sep 82
49.74	Shelley Drew	10 May 92
49.60	Fiona Condon	3 Jun 79

downhill

51.04	Fiona Condon	7 Jul 79

HAMMER

55.44	Lyn Sprules	19 Jul 94
53.34	Diana Holden	13 Aug 94
51.62	Julia Lavender	15 May 94
50.62	Helen Arnold	27 Jul 96
49.52	Rachael Beverley	28 Apr 96
49.48	Sam Burns-Salmond	13 Aug 95
48.98	Liz Pidgeon	21 Sep 96
47.68	Catherine Garden	13 Jul 96
46.84	Sarah Harrison	20 Jul 96
45.36	Sarah Moore	16 Sep 92

JAVELIN

60.14	Fatima Whitbread	7 May 80
59.40	Karen Hough	28 Aug 86
59.36	Kirsty Morrison	4 Sep 93
57.84	Amanda Liverton	3 Jun 90
57.82	Shelley Holroyd	9 Aug 92
57.80	Julie Abel	5 Jun 83
56.96	Nicola Emblem	1 Feb 90
55.72	Karen Martin	25 Jul 92
55.38	Catherine Garside	19 May 84
55.04	Tessa Sanderson	26 Sep 74
53.32	Maxine Jervis	27 Aug 78
52.52	Lorna Jackson	27 Aug 78
52.48	Gail Hornby	22 Jun 90
52.14	Jo Burton	25 Jun 94

HEPTATHLON (1985 Tables)

5833	Joanne Mulliner	11 Aug 85
5642	Sarah Rowe	23 Aug 81
5496	Yinka Idowu	3 Sep 89
5493	Sally Gunnell	28 May 84
5484	Denise Lewis	30 Jun 91
5459	Jennifer Kelly	30 Jul 88
5391 w	Jackie Kinsella	22 Jun 86
5331		19 Jul 86
5377	Uju Efobi	18 Jul 93
5299	Emma Beales	26 Aug 90
5273 w	Debbie Marti	11 Aug 85
5216		7 Jul 85
5246	Val Walsh	7 Aug 83
5213	Nicola Gautier	28 Jul 96
5208	Michelle Stone	30 Sep 84
5208	Mary Anderson	24 Aug 86

3000 METRES TRACK WALK

13:03.4	Vicky Lupton	18 May 91
13:47.0	Julie Drake	5 Jul 88
13:53.0 e+	Lisa Langford	23 Aug 85
14:04.1	Susan Ashforth	19 May 85
14:10.2	Carol Tyson	5 Sep 76
14:11.8	Carolyn Brown	18 Sep 92
14:12.0	Jill Barrett	11 Jun 83
14:12.8	Nicola Jackson	5 May 84
14:18.0	Gill Edgar	28 May 81
14:23.3	Joanne Pope	25 Jul 89

5000 METRES TRACK WALK

22:36.81	Vicky Lupton	15 Jun 91
23:31.67	Lisa Langford	23 Aug 85
23:55.27	Susan Ashforth	25 May 85
23:56.9	Julie Drake	24 May 88
24:02.15	Nicola Jackson	27 May 84
24:08.4	Jill Barrett	28 May 83
24:19.0	Victoria Lawrence	13 Jun 87
24:24.31	Andrea Crofts	4 Jun 89
24:27.73	Carolyn Brown	29 Aug 92
24:34.6	Tracey Devlin	17 Sep 89
24:35.0	Joanne Pope	16 Dec 90
24:35.16	Angela Hodd	25 May 87

Road - *where superior to track time*

23:05	Lisa Langford	2 Nov 85
23:18	Julie Drake	27 Feb 88
23:35	Lisa Simpson	31 Oct 87
23:44	Nicola Jackson	12 May 84
23:46	Jill Barrett	14 May 83
23:54	Victoria Lawrence	26 Sep 87
23:57	Sarah Brown	6 Dec 80
24:13	Gill Edgar	3 May 81
24:15	Carol Tyson	31 Jul 76

10,000 METRES TRACK WALK

47:04.0	Vicky Lupton	30 Mar 91
48:34.0	Lisa Langford	15 Mar 86
49:48.7	Julie Drake	7 Feb 88
50:25.0mx	Lisa Simpson	1 Apr 87
51:00.0	Karen Nipper	21 Feb 81
51:31.2	Helen Ringshaw	17 Mar 84
52:09.0	Elaine Cox	8 Apr 78
52:10.4	Sarah Brown	20 Mar 82
52:48.5	Kate Horwill	22 Aug 92

short

50:11.2	Jill Barrett	19 Mar 83

Road - *where superior to track time*

49:10	Victoria Lawrence	14 Mar 87
49:14	Carolyn Brown	29 Mar 92
49:26	Julie Drake	21 May 88
49:33	Lisa Simpson	14 Mar 87
49:47	Jill Barrett	24 Sep 83
51:15	Nicola Jackson	18 Nov 84

Note: LJ, Hep. Although Idowu competed for UK Juniors, she was a Nigerian citizen at the time.

UNDER 17

100 METRES

11.45	Sonia Lannaman	1 Sep 72
11.59	Simmone Jacobs	25 Aug 83
11.60	Katharine Merry	28 Jul 90
11.61	Diane Smith	9 Aug 90
11.65	Linsey Macdonald	22 May 79
11.69	Jane Parry	6 Jun 81
11.73	Etta Kessebeh	20 Aug 81
11.77	Hayley Clements	26 Jul 85
11.78	Tatum Nelson	16 May 94
11.79	Janet Smith	26 Jul 85
11.80	Sharon Dolby	26 Jul 85
11.81	Lisa Goreeph	6 Jun 82

wind assisted

11.50	Rebecca Drummond	9 Jul 94
11.61	Linsey Macdonald	16 Jun 79
11.62	Kathleen Lithgow	25 Jun 88
11.63	Sharon Dolby	10 Aug 85
11.72	Etta Kessebeh	19 Jul 81

hand timing

11.6	Denise Ramsden	19 Jul 68
11.6	Linsey Macdonald	25 May 80
11.6	Jane Parry	2 Aug 80
11.7	Michelle Probert	8 Aug 76

wind assisted

11.3	Linsey Macdonald	3 May 80
11.4	Sonia Lannaman	3 Jun 72
11.4	Jane Parry	5 Jul 80
11.5	Sharon Dolby	20 Jul 85

200 METRES

23.10	Diane Smith	11 Aug 90
23.28	Simmone Jacobs	28 Aug 83
23.42	Deborah Bunn	17 Jun 78
23.43	Linsey Macdonald	20 Aug 80
23.50	Katharine Merry	20 Jul 91
23.60	Michelle Probert	12 Sep 76
23.66	Jane Parry	15 Jun 80
23.69	Donna Fraser	1 Jul 89
23.79	Sharon Colyear	5 Sep 71
23.90	Angela Bridgeman	20 Aug 80
23.95	Helen Golden	30 Aug 69
23.97	Lisa Goreeph	31 Jul 82

wind assisted

23.11	Linsey Macdonald	5 Jul 80
23.41	Katharine Merry	15 Jun 91
23.64	Jane Parry	5 Jul 80
23.70	Sonia Lannaman	16 Jun 72
23.85	Helen Golden	1 Sep 69

hand timing (* 220 yards less 0.1)

23.8 *	Marilyn Neufville	27 Jul 78
23.8	Janet Smith	1 Jun 85
23.9	Fay Nixon	24 Jul 76
23.9	Hayley Clements	1 Jun 85

wind assisted

23.2	Deborah Bunn	2 Jul 78
23.4	Hayley Clements	10 Aug 85
23.6	Janet Smith	10 Aug 85

300 METRES

36.46	Linsey Macdonald	13 Jul 80
38.21	Lesley Owusu	27 Aug 95
38.95	Maria Bolsover	8 Jul 95
39.25	Rebecca White	17 Aug 96
39.34	Ruth Watson	12 Jul 96
39.40	Sophie Cocker	15 Aug 92
39.42	Alison Shingler	26 May 91
39.43	Lucy Chaffe	16 Jul 94
39.48	Suzanne McGowan	27 Jun 93
39.49	Lee McConnell	10 Sep 95
39.61	Helen Roscoe	8 Sep 96
39.66	Lindsay Impett	12 Jul 96

hand timing

38.2	Marilyn Neufville	6 Sep 69
38.6	Fay Nixon	10 Sep 77
38.7	Katharine Merry	1 Sep 91
39.2	Allison Curbishley	30 Aug 92
39.3	Sinead Dudgeon	13 Sep 92
39.5	Jo Sloane	5 Sep 93
39.6	Linda Keough	22 Jun 80

400 METRES

51.16	Linsey Macdonald	15 Jun 80
53.08	Loreen Hall	29 Jul 84
53.75	Linda Keough	8 Aug 80
54.01	Angela Bridgeman	16 Aug 80
54.25	Emma Langston	19 Jun 88
54.57	Lesley Owusu	9 Sep 95
54.84	Carol Candlish	25 Jul 81
54.86	Ruth Kennedy	20 Jul 73
55.03	Donna Fraser	6 Aug 88
55.13	Carolyn Wells	23 Aug 80

hand timing

53.7	Linda Keough	2 Aug 80
54.4	Marilyn Neufville	23 Aug 69
54.6	Evelyn McMeekin	15 Sep 73
54.6	Ruth Kennedy	19 Sep 73
54.8	Liz Beton	28 Aug 76

overage

54.2	Marilyn Neufville	9 Oct 69

600 METRES

1:27.33	Lorraine Baker	13 Jul 80

800 METRES

2:02.0	Jo White	13 Aug 77
2:03.66	Lesley Kiernan	26 Aug 73
2:03.72	Lorraine Baker	15 Jun 80
2:04.85	Louise Parker	28 Jul 79
2:06.5	Emma Langston	10 Aug 88
2:06.53	Lynne Robinson	6 Jul 85
2:06.8	Jayne Heathcote	31 May 87
2:07.0	Bridget Smyth	27 Jun 84
2:07.3	Amanda Alford	7 May 80
2:07.32	Amanda Pritchard	22 Jun 96
2:07.53	Sandra Arthurton	17 Sep 78
2:07.57	Mary Sonner	13 Sep 70
2:07.6	Natalie Tait	9 Jul 88
2:07.7	Karen Hughes	7 May 80
2:07.7	Michelle Wilkinson	31 Aug 88

1000 METRES

2:38.58	Jo White	9 Sep 77

1500 METRES

4:15.20	Bridget Smyth	29 Jul 84
4:15.55	Sandra Arthurton	29 Jul 78
4:16.8	Jo White	30 Jul 77
4:21.88	Jeina Mitchell	20 Jul 91
4:22.25	Karen Hughes	24 May 81
4:22.25	Clare Keller	7 Jul 85
4:22.51	Elise Lyon	31 Jul 82
4:23.11	Gillian Stacey	2 Sep 89
4:23.25	Denise Kiernan	20 Aug 77
4:23.37	Dawn Hargan	14 Jun 87
4:23.6	Janette Howes	5 Sep 81
4:23.75	Lynne MacDougall	24 May 81

3000 METRES

9:28.9	Bridget Smyth	21 Apr 84
9:30.0	Yvonne Murray	4 Jul 81
9:32.20	Nicola Slater	28 Aug 93
9:33.1	Alison Hollington	6 Jun 81
9:34.5	Louise Watson	28 Aug 88
9:34.79	Helen Titterington	28 Jun 86
9:36.8	Karen Hughes	4 Jun 80
9:38.1	Elise Lyon	12 Sep 81
9:38.2	Amanda Alford	7 Mar 79
9:39.9	Sharon Willicombe	8 Jul 88
9:40.0	Julie Adkin	12 Sep 87

overage

9:26.4	Jo White	7 Dec 77
9:38.8	Christine Brace	6 Oct 76

80 METRES HURDLES

11.07	Amanda Parker	7 Jun 86
11.12	Samantha Farquharson	7 Jun 86
11.13	Claire St John	2 Jun 79
11.16	Ann Girvan	4 Jul 81
11.16	Stephanie Douglas	27 Jul 85
11.20	Ann Wilson	11 Aug 66
11.20	Louise Brunning	25 Jul 87
11.23	Rachel Rigby	25 Jul 87
11.25	Louise Fraser	25 Jul 87
11.26	Liz Fairs	17 Jul 93
11.29	Nina Thompson	7 Aug 88

overage

11.10 A	Sue Scott	15 Oct 68

wind assisted

11.03	Wendy McDonnell	20 Aug 77
11.11	Liz Fairs	9 Jul 94
11.25	Sarina Mantle	13 Jul 96

hand timing

11.0	Wendy McDonnell	2 Jul 77
11.1	Ann Wilson	18 Sep 66
11.1	Angela Thorp	7 Jul 89
11.1	Liz Fairs	29 May 93
11.2	Linda Stephen	16 Jul 79
11.2	Lesley Scott	4 Aug 79
11.2	Nina Thompson	15 May 88
11.2	Jane Hale	27 May 89
11.2	Julie McAughtrie	27 May 93

wind assisted

10.9	Ann Wilson	16 Jul 66
10.9	Wendy McDonnell	9 Jul 77
10.9	Samantha Farquharson	20 Jul 85
11.0	Stephanie Douglas	20 Jul 85
11.1	Claire St John	16 Jul 79

100 METRES HURDLES (2'9")

13.73	Ann Girvan	7 Aug 82
13.88	Natasha Danvers	28 Aug 93
13.98	Claire St John	11 Aug 79
14.04	Lauraine Cameron	7 Aug 88
14.24	Pamela St Ange	2 Oct 82
14.24	Angela Thorp	9 Jul 89
14.39	Michelle Stone	18 Aug 84
14.40	Vicki Jamison	22 Jun 93
14.51	Susan Jones	29 May 94
14.52	Louise Brunning	26 Jun 88

wind assisted

13.67	Ann Girvan	4 Jul 82
13.76	Natasha Danvers	27 Aug 94
14.10	Sue Mapstone	25 Aug 73
14.27	Heather Ross	27 Aug 78

hand timing

13.7	Ann Girvan	29 Aug 81
14.1	Pamela St Ange	7 Aug 83
14.2	Nnenna Njoku	26 Jun 71

wind assisted

13.7	Nathalie Byer	4 Sep 82
13.9	Angela Thorp	9 Sep 89
14.1	Heather Ross	2 Jul 78

300 METRES HURDLES

41.99	Natasha Danvers	10 Jul 93
42.67	Vicki Jamison	17 Jul 93
42.91	Allison Curbishley	18 Aug 91
43.03	Valerie Theobalds	13 Aug 89
43.06	Claire Griffiths	18 Aug 91
43.08	Yewande Ige	13 Jul 96
43.12	Keri Maddox	6 Aug 88
43.28	Denise Bolton	5 Sep 93
43.38	Dextene McIntosh	31 Jul 94
43.44	Joanne Mersh	13 Jul 91
43.53	Catherine Murphy	21 Jul 90
43.75	Cicely Hall	28 May 95
43.80	Syreeta Williams	8 Sep 96
43.83	Vyvyan Rhodes	13 Aug 89
43.83	Gael Davies	8 Jul 95
43.88	Tracey Duncan	8 Jul 95

hand timing

42.4	Keri Maddox	8 May 88
42.5	Louise Brunning	8 May 88
42.8	Rachel Stafford	8 Jul 89
42.8	Vyvyan Rhodes	8 Jul 89
42.9	Valerie Theobalds	17 Jun 89
43.1	Patricia Byford	17 Jun 89
43.1	Charlotte Knowles	8 Jul 89
43.2	Rachael Kay	8 Jun 96
43.4	Joanne Mersh	15 Jun 91
43.5	Georgina Lee	7 Jul 89
43.6	Anne Hollman	16 Jun 90

400 METRES HURDLES

60.87	Karin Hendrickse	31 Jul 82
61.02	Claire Edwards	8 Sep 91
61.04	Allison Curbishley	26 Jul 92
61.10	Vicki Jamison	26 Jun 93
61.27	Kay Simpson	25 Jul 81
61.32	Debra Duncan	27 Jul 85
61.33	Denise Kiernan	17 Jul 77
61.59	Donna Pert	31 Jul 82
61.81	Joanna Douglas	27 Jul 85
61.87	Clare Bleasdale	19 Jul 86

hand timing

59.7	Keri Maddox	9 Jul 88
60.8	Jayne Puckeridge	9 Jul 88
61.5	Julie Lindsey	1 Sep 79

HIGH JUMP

1.89	Debbie Marti	2 Jun 84
1.85	Louise Manning	11 Sep 82
1.85	Jayne Barnetson	21 Jul 84
1.84	Ursula Fay	6 Aug 83
1.83	Jo Jennings	26 Jul 85
1.83	Tracey Clarke	2 Aug 87
1.82	Elaine Hickey	9 Aug 80
1.82	Kerry Roberts	16 Jul 83
1.82	Susan Jones	20 May 94
1.81	Barbara Simmonds	22 Jul 78
1.80	Carol Mathers	10 Jun 73
1.80	Susan Brown	28 Jul 79
1.80	Lea Haggett	3 Sep 88

POLE VAULT

3.44	Clare Ridgley	10 Sep 94
3.30 mx	Rhian Clarke	4 Jul 93
3.25		11 Sep 93
3.20	Rebecca Roles	31 Aug 96
3.00	Becky Ridgley	11 May 96
3.00	Kirsty Armstrong	27 Jul 96
3.00	Tracey Bloomfield	17 Aug 96
2.95	Dawn-Alice Wright	5 Jul 92
2.95	Sarah Hartley	24 Aug 96
2.80	Elizabeth Beckingsale	8 Jun 96
2.70	Katherine Horner	27 Apr 94
2.70	Bonny Elms	10 Mar 96

LONG JUMP

6.45	Margaret Cheetham	18 Aug 84
6.32	Georgina Oladapo	23 Jul 83
6.27	Fiona May	14 Jun 86
6.26	Joanne Wise	31 May 87
6.25	Sue Hearnshaw	9 Jul 77
6.24	Sarah Claxton	15 Jun 96
6.23	Sue Scott	27 Jul 68
6.22	Ann Wilson	18 Sep 66
6.22	Michelle Stone	28 Apr 84
6.18	Sheila Parkin	4 Aug 62

wind assisted

6.49	Margaret Cheetham	23 Sep 84
6.47	Fiona May	28 Jun 86
6.41	Sue Hearnshaw	9 Jul 77
6.34	Sarah Claxton	12 Jul 96
6.33	Sue Scott	27 Aug 68

TRIPLE JUMP

12.14	Jayne Ludlow	21 May 94
11.82	Julia Johnson	30 Jun 96
11.71	Hayley Warrilow	30 Jun 96
11.59	Tolu Jegede	30 Jun 96
11.48	Emma Hughes	10 Aug 96
11.44	Donna Quirie	8 Aug 93
11.44	Syreeta Williams	4 Aug 96
11.41	Shani Anderson	8 Sep 91
11.36	Rebecca White	10 May 95
11.35	Kathryn MacKenzie	24 Jul 93
11.32	Joyce Adams	15 Sep 96
11.25 i	Jessica Aru	24 Mar 91

wind assisted

11.50	Pamela Anderson	8 Aug 93
11.45	Nicky Ladrowski	13 Aug 95
11.36	Becky Ridgley	12 May 96

doubtful measurement

11.81	Fiona Hunter	24 Jun 95

SHOT

15.08	Justine Buttle	16 Aug 86
14.40	Susan King	17 May 81
14.04	Mary Anderson	6 May 84
13.94	Jennifer Bloss	13 May 67
13.89 i	Alison Grey	11 Feb 89
13.83		20 May 89
13.77	Terri Salt	17 Sep 83
13.68 i	Philippa Roles	26 Feb 94
13.65		6 Aug 94
13.64	Cynthia Gregory	20 Aug 80
13.58 i	Natalie Hart	19 Mar 88
13.49	Lana Newton	11 Jul 75
13.46	Julie Dunkley	22 Jun 96

overage

14.20 i	Terri Salt	10 Dec 83

DISCUS

51.60	Emma Merry	27 Jun 90
49.56	Jane Aucott	3 Aug 85
48.88	Philippa Roles	13 Aug 94
48.84	Karen Pugh	7 Aug 82
47.58	Catherine Bradley	14 Jul 84
47.54	Lauren Keightley	12 Jul 95
47.50	Sarah Symonds	16 May 90
47.24	Amanda Barnes	3 Aug 85
46.76	Fiona Condon	6 Aug 77
46.34	Janette Picton	26 Mar 79
45.72	Sarah Winckless	1 Jul 90
45.52	Jayne Thornton	12 May 86
45.50	Val Watson	3 May 75

HAMMER

47.68	Diana Holden	31 Jul 91
46.98	Helen Arnold	29 Jul 95
45.58	Julie Lavender	13 Sep 92
44.70	Rachel Beverley	15 Jul 95
43.64	Catherine Garden	30 Apr 95
42.66	Zoe Derham	25 Aug 96
42.14	Louise Kay	22 Jul 94
41.26	Sarah Harrison	5 Jul 95
41.04	Carys Parry	24 Aug 96

JAVELIN

56.02	Mandy Liverton	11 Jun 89
53.42	Karen Hough	15 Jul 84
53.22	Kirsty Morrison	15 Aug 92
51.50	Shelley Holroyd	22 Jul 89
50.82	Nicola Emblem	19 Jun 87
50.04	Kim Lisbon	19 Feb 84
50.02	Angelique Pullen	31 Aug 85
49.24	Jacqui Barclay	7 Aug 82
49.00	Kelly Morgan	27 Apr 96
48.34	Fatima Whitbread	29 Aug 77
48.00	Claire Taylor	17 Jun 92
·47.70	Sara Fry	7 Jul 78
47.50	Diane Williams	8 May 76

HEPTATHLON (1985 Tables) with 80mH

5037	Michelle Stone	1 Jul 84
5031	Yinka Idowu	18 Sep 88
4915	Denise Lewis	24 Jul 88
4861	Clover Wynter-Pink	26 Jun 94
4841	Rebecca Lewis	18 Sep 94
4839	Jackie Kinsella	21 Jul 85
4830 w	Katherine Livesey	22 Sep 96
4790		28 Jul 96
4794	Claire Phythian	22 May 88
4780	Danielle Freeman	23 Jun 96
4746	Chloe Cozens	22 Sep 96
4742	Julie Hollman	26 Sep 93
4673	Denise Bolton	19 Sep 93

with 100mH

5071	Debbie Marti	5 Jun 83

HEPTATHLON (1985 Tables) Senior

5208	Michelle Stone	30 Sep 84
5184	Claire Phythian	20 Aug 89
4815 w	Julie Hollman	2 May 93
4807		30 May 93
4784	Jackie Kinsella	12 May 85
4631	Ursula Fay	7 Sep 84

3000 METRES TRACK WALK

14:04.1	Susan Ashforth	19 May 85
14:21.0	Julie Drake	25 Jun 85
14:26.4	Sarah Brown	29 Oct 80

5000 METRES TRACK WALK

23:55.27	Susan Ashforth	25 May 85
24:22.3	Victoria Lawrence	21 Jun 86
24:34.6	Tracey Devlin	17 Sep 89
24:45.4	Karen Eden	9 Jul 78
24:57.5	Angela Hodd	24 Jun 86
25:13.8	Carla Jarvis	2 Jun 91
25:15.3	Vicky Lupton	3 Sep 88
25:18.5	Jill Barrett	16 Aug 80

overage

25:08.0	Julie Drake	22 Dec 85

Road - *where superior to track time*

23:57	Sarah Brown	6 Dec 80
24:20	Karen Eden	9 Dec 78

10000 METRES TRACK WALK

51:00.0	Karen Nipper	21 Feb 81

UNDER 15

100 METRES

11.67	Katharine Merry	13 May 89
11.86	Hayley Clements	2 Jul 83
11.89	Joanne Gardner	20 Aug 77
11.92	Jane Parry	20 Aug 77
11.95	Tatum Nelson	7 Aug 93
12.00	Diane Smith	15 Sep 89
12.02	Renate Chinyou	28 Aug 88
12.02	Sarah Wilhelmy	28 May 94
12.07	Margaret Cheetham	29 Jul 83
12.09	Libby Alder	8 Jul 95
12.10 A	Helen Seery	25 Jul 96
12.10	Lesley Owusu	7 Aug 93

wind assisted

11.47	Katharine Merry	17 Jun 89
11.67	Tatum Nelson	10 Jul 93
11.78	Jane Parry	8 Aug 78
11.84	Janis Walsh	26 May 74
11.88	Sarah Claxton	9 Jul 94
11.97	Yvonne Anderson	16 Jun 79
11.97	Renate Chinyou	20 Aug 88
12.06	Rachel Redmond	12 Jul 96

hand timing

11.8	Janis Walsh	7 Jul 74
11.8	Joanne Gardner	2 Jul 77
11.9	Sonia Lannaman	9 Aug 69
11.9	Linsey Macdonald	26 Aug 78
11.9	Jane Perry	22 Apr 79
11.9	Etta Kessebeh	11 Jul 80

wind assisted

11.7	Diane Smith	30 Jul 89
11.8	Sonia Lannaman	30 May 70
11.8	Deborah Bunn	28 Jun 75
11.8	Delmena Doyle	6 Jul 79

200 METRES

23.72	Katharine Merry	17 Jun 89
23.90	Diane Smith	3 Sep 89
24.05	Jane Parry	16 Jul 78
24.39	Hayley Clements	3 Jul 83
24.44	Rachel Kay	8 Jul 95
24.51	Tatum Nelson	8 Aug 93
24.54	Sarah Wilhelmy	31 Jul 94
24.58	Simmone Jacobs	25 Jul 81
24.58	Donna Fraser	22 Aug 87
24.59	Janet Smith	30 Jul 83
24.63	Dawn Flockhart	4 Jul 81

wind assisted

23.54	Katharine Merry	30 Jul 89
23.99	Sarah Wilhelmy	9 Jul 94
24.35	Tatum Nelson	27 Jun 93
24.41	Lesley Owusu	9 Jul 93

hand timing

23.8	Janis Walsh	23 Jun 74
24.1	Sonia Lannaman	29 Aug 70

wind assisted

23.6	Jane Parry	9 Jul 77
23.8	Diane Smith	9 Sep 89

300 METRES
| 41.1 | Maria Bolsover | 10 Apr 94 |

400 METRES
| 56.7 | Jane Colebrook | 25 Jun 72 |

600 METRES
| 1:36.47 | Sarah Willicombe | 12 Aug 90 |

800 METRES
2:06.5	Rachel Hughes	19 Jul 82
2:08.7	Emma Langston	12 Jul 86
2:09.58	Sally Ludlam	8 Jun 75
2:09.6	Isabel Linaker	1 Aug 90
2:09.77	Lorraine Baker	19 Aug 78
2:09.80	Hannah Curnock	15 Aug 92
2:10.1	Lesley Kiernan	9 Jul 71
2:10.3	Carol Pannell	9 Jul 71
2:10.6	Christina Boxer	10 Jul 71
2:10.6	Natalie Tait	12 Jul 86
2:10.66	Amanda Pritchard	15 Jul 94
2:10.76	Carolyn Wells	19 Aug 78
2:10.9	Emma Ward	30 Jun 96
2:10.96	Hayley Haining	7 Jun 86

1000 METRES
| 2:51.4 | Hayley Haining | 20 Aug 86 |

1500 METRES
4:23.45	Isabel Linaker	7 Jul 90
4:27.9	Joanne Davis	9 Jul 88
4:29.0	Claire Allen	8 Jul 89
4:29.1	Valerie Bothams	16 Jul 89
4:29.6	Lynne MacDougall	16 Jul 79
4:29.9	Heidi Hosking	9 Jul 88
4:30.4	Claire Nicholson	18 Jun 87
4:31.12	Karen Hughes	31 Aug 79
4:31.45	Amanda Alford	22 Jul 78
4:31.6	Michelle Lavercombe	13 Jun 81
4:31.70	Jenny Mockler	3 Aug 96
4:32.0	Elise Lyon	2 Apr 80
4:32.0	Jojo Tulloch	13 Jul 85
4:32.0	Julie Adkin	13 Aug 86

ONE MILE
| 4:54.7 | Hannah Curnock | 9 Sep 92 |

3000 METRES
| 10:00.6 | Louise Silva | 7 Mar 79 |

75 METRES HURDLES
10.93	Rachel Halstead-Peel	27 Jul 85
11.00	Louise Fraser	27 Jul 85
11.01	Nathalie Byer	16 Aug 80
11.08	Nicola Hall	29 May 94
11.09	Catherine Murphy	6 Aug 88
11.09	Orla Bermingham	25 Aug 90
11.13	Lydia Chadwick	7 Jun 86
11.13	Naomi Hodge-Dallaway	30 Jul 95
11.14	Serena Bailey	30 Jul 95
11.15	Rachel Rigby	27 Jul 85
11.16	Diane Allahgreen	12 Aug 89
11.18	Sarah Claxton	18 Sep 94

wind assisted
11.01	Naomi Hodge-Dallaway	8 Jul 95
11.05	Helen Worsey	13 Jul 96
11.06	Kate Forsyth	10 Jul 93
11.09	Luisa Giles	13 Jul 96

hand timing
11.0	Wendy McDonnell	31 Aug 75
11.0	Lydia Chadwick	12 Jul 86
11.0	Nina Thompson	4 Jul 87

wind assisted
10.7	Orla Bermingham	14 Jul 90
10.8	Nathalie Byer	12 Jul 80
10.8	Ann Girvan	12 Jul 80
10.9	Lauraine Cameron	16 Aug 86
10.9	Nina Thompson	7 Jun 87

HIGH JUMP
1.83	Ursula Fay	5 Jun 82
1.81	Debbie Marti	18 Sep 82
1.81	Lea Haggett	6 Jun 86
1.80	Jo Jennings	19 Aug 84
1.79 i	Julia Charlton	24 Feb 80
1.78		13 Jul 80
1.78	Claire Summerfield	28 Jul 79
1.75	Anne Gilson	2 Jun 73
1.75	Claire Smith (Nun)	8 Aug 82
1.75	Jane Falconer	10 Jun 89
1.74	Lorinda Matthews	19 Aug 77
1.74	Janice Anderson	27 Jun 87
1.74	Katharine Merry	18 Sep 88

overage
| 1.75 i | Alison Purton | 12 Dec 87 |

POLE VAULT
3.50	Fiona Harrison	25 Aug 96
2.65	Rhian Clarke	10 Aug 91
2.50	Tracey Bloomfield	31 Jul 94

overage - unconfirmed
| 2.80 | Rhian Clarke | 2 Oct 91 |

LONG JUMP
6.34	Margaret Cheetham	14 Aug 83
6.30	Fiona May	7 Jul 84
6.07	Georgina Oladapo	21 Jun 81
5.98	Sandy French	22 Jul 78
5.93	Jackie Harris	10 Jul 87
5.88	Sue Scott	11 Aug 66
5.86	Tammy McCammon	18 Aug 91
5.85	Kim Hagger	20 Aug 76
5.81	Yvonne Hallett	24 Aug 86
5.78	Pamela St Ange	15 Aug 81
5.76	Debbie Marti	31 Jul 82

overage
| 5.93 i | Sue Scott | 19 Nov 66 |

wind assisted
6.49	Margaret Cheetham	4 Sep 83
6.05	Katharine Merry	18 Sep 88
6.02	Michelle Stone	10 Jul 82
5.99	Sandy French	8 Jul 78
5.86	Donna Naylor	13 Jul 96
5.85	Karen Glen	8 Jul 78

SHOT (3.25kg)

14.27	Susan King	19 May 79
13.69	Gloria Achille	21 Jun 80
13.61	Justine Buttle	6 Aug 84
13.22	Emily Steele	23 Jul 89
13.11	Amy Wilson	2 Sep 95
13.08	Ashley Morris	11 Aug 84
13.05	Tracy Page	21 Jun 86
13.04	Navdeep Dhaliwal	16 May 92
12.97	Alison Grey	23 Aug 87
12.96	April Kalu	22 Jun 96
12.95	Cynthia Gregory	7 Jul 78
12.91	Terri Salt	24 Jul 81
12.86	Lucy Rann	28 May 95
12.85	Philippa Roles	19 Aug 92

overage

13.50 i	Philippa Roles	19 Dec 92
13.45 i	Susan Coyne	28 Oct 82
13.43 i	Navdeep Dhaliwal	19 Dec 92

SHOT (4kg)

12.16	Susan King	9 Sep 79

DISCUS

44.12	Philippa Roles	30 Aug 92
41.92	Catherine Garden	12 Sep 93
40.92	Sandra McDonald	24 Jun 78
40.84	Natalie Kerr	24 Jul 94
40.44	Catherine MacIntyre	12 Sep 82
40.34	Natalie Hart	23 Mar 86
40.22	Emma Merry	27 Aug 88
40.18	Kelly Mellis	17 Sep 94
40.14	Clare Tank	29 Aug 88
39.76	Alix Gallagher	6 Jun 87
39.38	Charladee Clarke	12 Aug 85
39.38	Alex Hajipavlis	13 Aug 95
39.36	Emma Carpenter	25 Aug 96
39.24	Coleen Edwards	28 Aug 83
39.20	Linda Higman	16 Sep 79
39.20	Mandy Hampton	19 Jul 81

HAMMER

38.00	Catherine Garden	14 Mar 93
34.18	Carys Parry	17 May 95

JAVELIN

48.40	Mandy Liverton	31 Aug 87
46.98	Kirsty Morrison	30 Jun 90
43.16	Shelley Holroyd	27 Jun 87
43.08	Karen Hough	4 Sep 82
42.70	Emily Steele	23 Sep 89
41.56	Goldie Sayers	12 Jul 96
41.50	Kelly Morgan	9 Jul 94
41.22	Maxine Worsfold	12 Jul 80
41.06	Heather Derbyshire	15 Aug 93
40.86	Julie Hawkins	28 Aug 77
40.80	Jenny Foster	16 Aug 92
40.74	Anna Bloxsome	16 Aug 87
40.72	Val Price	11 Aug 76
40.56	Julie Abel	3 Aug 80
40.54	Clover Wynter-Pink	10 Jul 92

PENTATHLON (with 800m & 75m hdls)

3518	Katharine Merry	18 Sep 88
3333	Jackie Harris	27 Jun 87
3296	Claire Everett	19 Sep 93
3225	Amy Nuttall	26 Jun 94
3216	Sally Gunnell	23 Aug 80
3213	Julie Hollman	22 Sep 91
3195	Julia Charlton	10 May 80
3193	Samantha Foster	26 Jun 94
3186	Lauraine Cameron	16 Aug 86
3175	Linda Wong	14 Sep 80
3167	Sandy French	5 Aug 78
3162	Claire Phythian	20 Sep 87
3153	Katie Budd	16 Sep 90
3150	Hazel Clarke	19 Sep 93

with 80mH

3441	Jane Shepherd	14 May 83
3350	Claire Smith	3 Jul 82
3295	Paula Khouri	16 Jul 83
3283	Jackie Kinsella	16 Jul 83

2500 METRES TRACK WALK

11:50.0	Susan Ashforth	12 Sep 84
12:17.0	Karen Eden	3 Sep 77
12:21.94	Tracey Devlin	30 Mar 87
12:22.5	Kim Macadam	21 Aug 83
12:24.6	Sarah Bennett	24 Apr 94

Road - *where superior to track time*

12:03	Nikola Ellis	5 May 84
12:04	Vicky Lawrence	5 May 84

3000 METRES TRACK WALK

14:56.4	Sarah Bennett	26 Sep 93
15:00.0	Susan Ashforth	19 Jun 84
15:00.6	Sally Wish	16 Jul 72
15:14.6	Amy Hales	31 Aug 96
15:16.4	Natalie Watson	31 Aug 96
15:18.3	Victoria Lawrence	17 Jul 83
15:19.0	Tracey Devlin	28 Mar 87
15:28.0	Kim Macadam	3 Sep 83
15:30.0	Nikola Ellis	1 Sep 84
15:31.0	Philippa Savage	3 Sep 88

overage

15:16.0	Helen Ringshaw	11 Nov 80

short track

15:18.7	Sharon Tonks	19 Mar 83

Road - *where superior to track time*

14:48	Nikola Ellis	16 Sep 84
14:55	Lisa Langford	6 Dec 80
14:58	Carol Brown	19 Aug 87
14:59	Julie Snead	16 Sep 84

overage

14:19	Susan Ashforth	20 Oct 84
14:41	Ruth Sugg	7 Nov 81
14:41	Lisa Langford	7 Nov 81

5000 METRES TRACK WALK

26:52.0	Nina Howley	14 Sep 92

Road - *where superior to track time*

26:20	Tracey Devlin	14 Feb 87
26:59	Joanne Clarke	9 Jun 83

UNDER 13

75 METRES
9.9	Sherie Pierre	21 Jul 96
10.0	Kelly Rea	30 Apr 95
10.0	Monique Parris	12 May 96
wind assisted		
9.96	Joanne Wainwright	8 Sep 96

80 METRES
10.2	Jane Riley	1 Jun 85
10.2	Helen Seery	20 May 89
10.3	Katharine Merry	6 Jun 87
10.3	Emma Ania	7 Sep 91
10.4	Susan Briggs	9 Sep 79
10.4	Tatum Nelson	1 Sep 91
10.5	Claire Ransome	1 Jun 85
10.5	Lynsey Scammens	18 Jun 89
10.5	Sarah Wilhelmy	12 Sep 92
10.5	Ayeesha Charles	12 Sep 92

100 METRES (y = 100 yards)
11.92	Jane Parry	20 Aug 77
12.1	Katharine Merry	26 Sep 87
11.1y	Sonia Lannaman	10 Aug 68
12.3	Joanne Gardner	24 Jun 75
12.3	Deborah Bunn	30 Aug 75
12.4	Lorraine Broxup	13 Jun 76
12.4	Sarah Claxton	31 Aug 92
12.5	Rachel Kay	26 Sep 93
wind assisted		
11.8	Deborah Bunn	28 Jun 75
12.3	Barbara Parham	7 Jul 73
12.3	Susan Croker	17 Jun 78
12.3	Gail Hayes	7 Jul 78
12.4	Janis Walsh	15 Jun 72

150 METRES
19.1	Emma Ania	7 Sep 91
19.2	Helen Seery	19 Feb 89
19.2	Kelly Rea	30 Apr 95
19.2	Rebecca Smith	30 Apr 95
19.4	Vernicha James	31 Aug 96
19.5	Karlene Palmer	1 Aug 93
19.5	Sherie Pierre	2 Jun 96
19.6	Sarah Wilhelmy	13 Sep 92
19.6	Laverne Slater	24 Jul 94
19.6	Stacy Hilling	27 Jul 94
19.6	Sarah Zawada	11 Sep 94

200 METRES
24.2	Jane Parry	28 May 77
25.4	Katharine Merry	21 Jun 87
25.4	Myra McShannon	8 May 88
25.6	Debbie Bunn	5 Jul 75
25.6	Joanne Gardner	24 Aug 75
25.6	Jane Riley	30 Jun 85
25.7	Jane Bradbeer	1 Aug 81
25.7	Donna Fraser	28 Sep 85
25.95	Sandy French	20 Aug 76
wind assisted		
23.6	Jane Parry	9 Jul 77

600 METRES
1:37.5	Hannah Wood	17 Jul 94
1:38.5	Jennifer Meadows	4 Apr 93
1:38.9	Emma Ward	17 Jul 94
1:40.9	Amanda O'Shea	25 Jul 92
1:41.3	Holly O'Connor	21 Jul 96
1:41.5	Adele Bevan	12 May 96
1:42.1	Alison Kerboas	26 Sep 93
1:42.26	Ellie Childs	14 May 95
1:42.4	Jemma Simpson	7 Apr 96
1:42.5	Francesca Green	26 Jul 92
1:42.5	Catherine Roberts	16 Jul 95

800 METRES
2:14.8	Janet Lawrence	10 Jul 71
2:15.05	Rachel Hughes	11 Sep 81
2:16.8	Angela Davies	25 Jul 83
2:17.20	Emma Langston	7 Sep 84
2:17.6	Michelle Wilkinson	22 Jun 85
2:17.9	Melissa Rooney	20 Jun 81
2:18.1	Lileath Rose	19 Jun 76
2:18.50	Jennifer Meadows	3 Jul 93
2:18.6	Jayne Heathcote	11 Jun 83
2:19.0	Michelle Cherry	6 Aug 83
2:19.0	Dawn Simpson	21 Jun 86

1500 METRES
4:36.9	Rachel Hughes	20 Jul 81
4:42.1	Stacy Washington	18 Jul 84
4:43.0	Julie Adkin	18 Jul 84
4:44.0	Paula Matheson	20 Jul 76
4:44.2	Clare Keller	13 Jun 81
4:44.7	Deborah Russell	18 Jul 76
4:44.9	Susan Jordan	20 Sep 81
4:46.8	Amanda Alford	11 Sep 76
4:47.1	Susan Byrom	29 Jun 85
4:47.6	Janet Lawrence	4 Sep 71
overage		
4:35.5	Rachel Hughes	2 Dec 81

70 METRES HURDLES
11.0	Katharine Merry	20 Sep 87
11.1	Sarah Claxton	14 Jun 92
11.17	Ann-Marie Massey	3 Sep 95
11.2	Claire Stuart	19 Jun 88
11.24	Alana Watson	8 Sep 96
11.3	Katie Challinor	22 Sep 91
11.3	Nicola Hall	23 Aug 92
11.3	Caroline Pearce	1 Aug 93
11.3	Naomi Hodge-Dallaway	30 Aug 93
11.3	Jennifer Molloy	25 Aug 96
wind assisted		
11.21	Sandra Gunn	4 Sep 88
11.26	Catriona Burr	4 Sep 88

75 METRES HURDLES
11.3	Katharine Merry	26 Sep 87
11.6	Jenny Vanes	26 Sep 87
11.78	Caroline Pearce	7 Aug 93
11.9	Cheryl Cox	4 Sep 71
11.9	Sharon McKinley	8 Aug 81
11.9	Adele Mesney	30 Jul 88

wind assisted

| 11.6 | Sarah Claxton | 5 Jul 92 |

HIGH JUMP

1.69	Katharine Merry	26 Sep 87
1.68	Julia Charlton	6 Aug 78
1.65	Debbie Marti	20 Sep 80
1.65	Jane Falconer	20 Sep 87
1.63	Lindsey Marriott	11 Aug 79
1.63	Paula Davidge	13 Sep 81
1.60	Denise Wilkinson	17 Jul 76
1.59	Julie O'Dell	28 Jul 74
1.59	Julia Cockram	18 May 80
1.59	Beverley Green	30 Aug 86

overage

| 1.62 i | Claire Summerfield | 20 Nov 77 |

POLE VAULT

| 2.30 | Lauren Stoney | 5 Aug 96 |

LONG JUMP

5.71	Sandy French	20 Aug 76
5.45	Sarah Wilhelmy	31 Aug 92
5.43	Margaret Cheetham	19 Sep 81
5.42	Katharine Merry	7 Jun 87
5.40	Kerrie Gray	1 Sep 84
5.38	Toyin Campbell	6 Aug 77
5.35	Deborah Bunn	7 Sep 75
5.34	Fiona May	12 Jun 82
5.33	Kathryn Dowsett	7 Sep 91
5.32	Ann Flannery	18 Sep 82

wind assisted

| 5.55 | Katharine Merry | 10 Jul 87 |

SHOT (2.72kg)

11.04	Amy Wilson	12 Sep 93
10.91	Catherine Garden	8 Sep 91
10.60	Lucy Rann	29 Aug 93
10.52	Faye Brennan	18 Aug 96
10.48	Julie Robin	1 Jul 89
10.48	Natalie Kerr	9 Aug 92
10.47	Navdeep Dhaliwal	1 Sep 90
10.46	Sandra Biddlecombe	4 Jul 90
10.41	Eleanor Garden	3 Sep 89
10.40	Fiona Hunter	18 Aug 91
10.40	Lisa Thompson	17 Aug 95

overage

| 11.57 i | Navdeep Dhaliwal | 12 Dec 90 |

SHOT (3.25kg)

12.20	Susan King	3 Sep 77
10.77	Michele Morgan	19 Jun 82
10.54	Claire Burnett	1 Sep 85
10.49	Alison Grey	3 Aug 85

overage

| 10.68 i | Rebecca Hyams | 21 Dec 85 |
| 10.64 i | Roxanne Blackwood | 10 Nov 86 |

DISCUS (0.75kg)

39.44	Catherine Garden	8 Sep 91
37.64	Sandra Biddlecombe	4 Jul 90
32.70	Claire Smithson	26 Aug 95
31.46	Sian Howe	21 Sep 96

30.54	Eleanor Garden	10 Sep 89
29.76	Navdeep Dhaliwal	19 Aug 90
29.62	Helen Gates	3 Jul 93
29.48	Rebecca Roles	16 May 92
29.18	Lucille Shaw	10 Jul 94
29.00	Elizabeth Hay	12 Sep 92

DISCUS (1kg)

34.22	Catherine Garden	25 Aug 91
31.34	Sandra Biddlecombe	9 Sep 90
30.54	Fiona Condon	15 Sep 73
30.02	Alison Moffitt	6 Jul 82
29.88	Iona Doyley	2 Sep 78
29.42	Eleanor Garden	27 Aug 89
29.12	Natalie Kerr	26 Jul 92
28.88	Jane Chapman	13 Sep 81
28.56	Amanda Franks	25 Aug 74
28.38	Sarah Hughes	9 Sep 84

overage

| 33.86 | Fiona Condon | 13 Oct 73 |

JAVELIN (400gm)

36.06	Samantha Redd	31 Aug 96
33.46	Emma Claydon	26 Jul 92
33.32	Melanie Vaggers	27 Sep 94
32.38	Eve Russell	30 Jul 95
31.58	Louise Telford	20 Aug 94
31.50	Sarah Ashdown	29 Sep 96
30.16	Tanya Hunt	27 Aug 95
30.82	Gillian Stewart	13 Sep 92
30.54	Lesley Richardson	16 Aug 92
30.46	Lucy Rann	8 Aug 93
30.40	Sarah Moss	8 Sep 96
30.24	Colette Doran	24 Aug 96

JAVELIN (600gm)

32.02	Claire Lacey	20 Sep 87
31.60	Emma Langston	2 Sep 84
31.44	Alison Moffitt	6 Jul 82
31.28	Eve Russell	2 Sep 95
31.04	Shelley Holroyd	Jun 85
30.82	Diane Williams	10 Jun 72
30.44	Heather Derbyshire	12 Sep 91
30.32	Debra Smith	83
30.28	Emily Steele	1 Aug 87
30.20	Samantha Redd	7 Sep 96
29.84	Lucy Rann	12 Jun 93

2500 METRES TRACK WALK

12:48.9	Claire Walker	20 Jul 85
12:50.5	Victoria Lawrence	4 Jul 82
12:55.3	Kelly Mann	11 May 96
12:59.0	Jo Pickett	22 Jun 92
13:08.2	Joanne Ashforth	20 Jul 85
13:10.2	Stephanie Cooper	9 May 82
13:18.0	Alison Warren	4 Jun 78
13:18.0	Karen Bowers	14 Apr 79
13:18.8	Janette McKenzie	20 May 79
13:00.0	Sarah Bennett	22 Jun 92

overage

| 12:49.0 | Karen Eden | 11 Oct 75 |

UK CLUB RELAY RECORDS

MEN

Seniors

4 x 100m	39.49	Haringey	1 Jun 91
4 x 200m	1:23.5	Team Solent	19 Jul 87
4 x 400m	3:04.48	Team Solent	29 Jun 90
1600m Medley	3:20.8	Wolverhampton & Bilston	1 Jun 75
4 x 800m	7:24.4*	North Staffs and Stone	27 Jun 65
4 x 1500m	15:12.6	Bristol	5 Aug 75

* = 4 x 880y time less 2.8sec

Under 20

4 x 100m	41.30	Victoria Park	14 Aug 76
4 x 200m	1:27.6	Enfield	13 Jun 82
4 x 400m	3:15.3	Enfield	5 Sep 82
1600m Medley	3:31.6	Cardiff	14 Aug 71
4 x 800m	7:35.3	Liverpool H	14 Aug 90
4 x 1500m	16:04.3	Blackburn	15 Sep 79
4 x 110H	1:04.8	Oundle Sch	19 May 79

Under 17

4 x 100m	42.22	Thames V H	24 Jun 89
4 x 200m	1:31.2	Hercules-W.	12 Jul 78
4 x 400m	3:23.1	Enfield	1 Oct 80
1600m Medley	3:36.1	Thurrock	13 Jun 84
4 x 800m	7:52.1	Clydebank	29 Aug 87
4 x 1500m	16:27.0	Liverpool H	14 Sep 88

Under 15

4 x 100m	44.62	Sale	29 Aug 93
4 x 200m	1:36.9	Belgrave	19 Sep 93
4 x 400m	3:31.5	Ayr Seaforth	5 Sep 82
1600m Medley	3:48.4	Blackheath	29 Sep 86
4 x 800m	8:13.28	Clydebank	2 Sep 89
4 x 1500m	17:52.4	Stretford	22 Oct 85

Under 13

4 x 100m	50.5	Blackheath	12 Sep 93
4 x 200m	1:49.7	Braintree	29 Aug 94
4 x 400m	4:04.5	Blackheath	12 Sep 93
1600m Medley	4:13.7	Blackheath	28 Sep 86
4 x 800m	9:29.8	Sale	28 Jun 88

WOMEN

Seniors

4 x 100m	43.79	Hounslow	18 Sep 82
4 x 200m	1:35.15	Stretford	14 Jul 91
4 x 400m	3:31.62	Essex Ladies	31 May 92
1600m Medley	3:50.6	Coventry Godiva	5 May 84
3 x 800m	6:32.4	Cambridge H	29 Jun 74
4 x 800m	8:41.0	Cambridge H	26 May 75

Under 20

4 x 100m	48.07	Sale	14 Sep 91
4 x 200m	1:47.3	Millfield School	11 May 96
4 x 400m	3:51.67	Sale	23 Sep 89
3 x 800m	7:33.2	Essex Ladies	12 Jun 94

Under 17

4 x 100m	47.52	Hounslow	2 Oct 82
4 x 200m	1:42.2	London Oly.	19 Aug 72
4 x 400m	3:52.1	City of Hull	3 Jul 82
1600m Medley	4:07.8	Warrington	14 Aug 75
3 x 800m	6:46.5	Haslemere	15 Sep 79
	6:46.5	Bromley L	1 Jul 84
4 x 800m	8:53.1	Havering	24 May 80

Under 15

4 x 100m	48.5	Haringey	15 Sep 79
4 x 200m	1:44.0	Bristol	15 Sep 79
3 x 800m	6:39.8	Havering	13 Sep 78
4 x 800m	9:21.4	Sale	5 Aug 78

Under 13

4 x 100m	53.16	Wigan	5 Sep 93
4 x 200m	1:52.5	Mitcham	24 Jul 82
3 x 800m	7:18.0	Mid Hants	14 Sep 83
4 x 800m	10:02.4	Warrington	16 Sep 75

GB & NI v RUS (indoors)   Birmingham   27 January 1996

MEN

60 Metres
1.	JASON GARDENER		6.55
2.	Pavel Galkin	RUS	6.66
3.	KEVIN WILLIAMS		6.72
4.	Andrey Grigoryev	RUS	7.02

200 Metres
1.	SOLOMON WARISO		21.03
2.	Andrey Fedoriv	RUS	21.16
3.	DOUG TURNER		21.19
4.	Konstantin Dyomin	RUS	21.58

400 Metres
1.	MARK HYLTON		46.96
2.	GUY BULLOCK		47.05
3.	Dmitriy Golovastov	RUS	47.08
	Mikhail Vdovin	RUS	Dnf

800 Metres
1.	Andrey Loginov	RUS	1:50.54
2.	Sergey Kozhevnikov	RUS	1:50.99
3.	EDDIE KING		1:51.25
4.	ANDY HART		1:51.43

1500 Metres
1.	ANTHONY WHITEMAN		3:39.47
2.	Andrey Zadorozhniy	RUS	3:44.27
3.	Andrey Ryazanov	RUS	3:44.28
4.	IAN GILLESPIE		3:44.48

3000 Metres
1.	Vener Kashayev	RUS	7:57.79
2.	NEIL CADDY		7:58.14
3.	Sergey Drygin	RUS	7:58.60
4.	ROD FINCH		7:58.63

60 Metres Hurdles
1.	Sergey Vetrov	RUS	7.85
2.	NEIL OWEN		7.87
3.	Aleksandr Markin	RUS	7.88
4.	ANDY TULLOCH		7.90

High Jump
1.	DALTON GRANT		2.34
2.	STEVE SMITH		2.30
3.	Aleksandr Kurelyuk	RUS	2.20
4.	Vyacheslav Voronin	RUS	2.15

Match Result Men
1.	GREAT BRITAIN & NI	69
2.	Russia	68

Pole Vault
1.	Yevgeniy Smiryagin	RUS	5.55
2.	NICK BUCKFIELD		5.50
3.	Vadim Strogalyov	RUS	5.50
4.	MATT BELSHAM		Nhc

Long Jump
1.	Kiril Sosunov	RUS	8.06
2.	Vyacheslav Taranov	RUS	7.67
3.	STEVE PHILLIPS		7.56
4.	CARL HOWARD		7.44

Triple Jump
1.	Andrey Kurennoy	RUS	16.49
2.	Viktor Sotnikov	RUS	16.24
3.	FRANCIS AGYEPONG		16.15
4.	TOSI FASINRO		15.79

Shot
1.	SHAUN PICKERING		19.10
2.	MARK PROCTOR		18.92
3.	Viktor Kapustin	RUS	18.88
4.	Aleksey Shidlovskiy	RUS	17.26

4 x 400 Metres Relay
1.	GREAT BRITAIN	3:08.47
	(PATRICK,BULLOCK,SLYTHE,HYLTON)	
2.	Russia	3:08.81
	(Voronin,Bey,Golovastov,Kosov)	

WOMEN

60 Metres
1.	Natalya Anisimova	gst/RUS	7.37
2.	Natalya Merzlyakova	RUS	7.42
3.	STEPHANIE DOUGLAS		7.43
4.	MARCIA RICHARDSON		7.44
5.	Galina Malchugina	RUS	7.48

200 Metres
1.	Svetlana Goncharenko	RUS	23.28
2.	Yekaterina Leshcheva	RUS	23.42
3.	CATHERINE MURPHY		23.46
4.	MELANIE NEEF		23.62

400 Metres
1.	Yelena Andreyeva	RUS	53.49
2.	Yulia Sotnikova	RUS	53.58
3.	STEPHANIE LLEWELLYN		54.12
4.	LESLEY OWUSU		55.20

800 Metres
1.	Irina Korzh	RUS	2:05.32
2.	Irina Platonova	RUS	2:05.33
3.	ANGELA DAVIES		2:06.27
4.	VICKY LAWRENCE		2:10.01

1500 Metres
1.	Irina Biryukova	RUS	4:13.05
2.	DEBBIE GUNNING		4:13.40
3.	ANN GRIFFITHS		4:16.25
	Yelena Mikhaolova	RUS	Dnf

3000 Metres
1.	SONIA McGEORGE		9:28.04
2.	Lidiya Vasilevskaya	RUS	9:30.35
3.	Yelena Kaledina	RUS	9:32.05
4.	SARAH BENTLEY		9:38.38

60 Metres Hurdles
1.	CLOVA COURT		8.35
2.	DIANA ALLAHGREEN		8.38
3.	Tatyana Lebedyeva	RUS	9.24
	Natalya Shekhodanova	RUS	Dnf

High Jump
1.	Natalya Golodnova	RUS	1.95
2.	Yekaterina Aleksandrova	RUS	1.92
3.	MICHELLE DUNKLEY		1.86
4.	DEBBIE MARTI		1.83

Pole Vault
1.	Svetlana Abramova	RUS	4.00
2.	Galina Yenvarenko	RUS	3.90
3.	KATE STAPLES		3.70
4.	LINDA STANTON		3.50

Match Result Women
1.	Russia	80
2.	GREAT BRITAIN & NI	57

Long Jump
1.	DENISE LEWIS		6.45
2.	Anna Mironova	RUS	6.33
3.	Tatyana Lebedyeva	RUS	6.05
4.	ANNE BROOKS		5.98

Triple Jump
1.	Natalya Kayukova	RUS	13.90
2.	MICHELLE GRIFFITH		13.46
3.	Irina Melnikova	RUS	13.33
4.	SHANI ANDERSON		12.96

Shot
1.	JUDY OAKES		18.63
2.	Irina Khudorozhkina	RUS	18.26
3.	Irina Korzhanenko	RUS	17.99
4.	MAGGIE LYNES		15.80

4 x 400 Metres Relay
1.	Russia	3:31.88
	(Goncharenko,Kotlyarova,Andreyeva,Chebykina)	
2.	GREAT BRITAIN	3:37.47
	(NEEF,FRASER,OWUSU,CURBISHLEY)	

Combined Match Result
1.	Russia	148
2.	GREAT BRITAIN & NI	126

AAA INDOOR CHAMPIONSHIPS Birmingham   3 - 4 February 1996

MEN

60 Metres (3 Feb)
1. MICHAEL ROSSWESS   6.68
2. KEVIN WILLIAMS   6.68
3. ADRIAN PATRICK   6.72
4. Josephus Thomas   SLE   6.77
5. DWAIN CHAMBERS   6.77
6. JASON FERGUS   6.79

200 Metres (4 Feb)
1. DOUGLAS TURNER   21.06
2. ALLYN CONDON   21.07
3. MARLON DEVONISH   21.42
4. PETER MAITLAND   21.60
5. JASON FERGUS   21.91
6. SCOTT DORSET   22.45

400 Metres (4 Feb)
1. MARK HYLTON   46.45
2. KENT ULYATT   47.04
3. GRAHAM HEALY   48.12
4. GARY CADOGAN   48.19
5. DAVID NOLAN   48.75
6. NOEL LEVY   48.93

800 Metres (4 Feb)
1. MARTIN STEELE   1:51.21
2. NOEL EDWARDS   1:51.69
3. ANDREW LILL   1:52.10
4. ANDY STUCKEY   1:52.76

WOMEN

60 Metres (3 Feb)
1. MARCIA RICHARDSON   7.34
2. GERALDINE McLEOD   7.36
3. BEV KINCH   7.41
4. SHARON WILLIAMS   7.42
5. DANAA CALLOW   7.42
6. Evadne McKenzie   JAM   7.54

200 Metres (4 Feb)
1. CATHERINE MURPHY   23.69
2. LOUISE FRASER   23.73
3. Elona Reinalda   AUS   24.22
4. CLOVA COURT   24.50
5. TRACY JOSEPH   24.86

400 Metres (4 Feb)
1. MELANIE NEEF   52.50
2. SALLY GUNNELL   53.07
3. ALLISON CURBISHLEY   53.52
4. ALANNA ROWBOTHAM   55.18
5. Marisa Smith   IRL   55.40
6. ELAINE SUTCLIFFE   56.05

800 Metres (4 Feb)
1. VICTORIA STERNE   2:06.41
2. MICHELLE FAHERTY   2:07.19
3. HAYLEY PARRY   2:07.54
4. ALICE BEECROFT   2:12.07
5. MARY MCCLUNG   2:17.60

1500 Metres (3 Feb)
1. TERENCE WEST   3:49.90
2. MATTHEW HIBBERD   3:51.22
3. ADAM DUKE   3:51.25
4. ROBERT SCANLON   3:51.68
5. GARTH WATSON   3:53.92
6. JOSEPH MILLS   3:55.96

3000 Metres (4 Feb)
1. MATTHEW SKELTON   8:00.48
2. IAN GILLESPIE   8:00.65
3. BRIAN TREACY   8:03.60
4. STEPHEN GREEN   8:09.36
5. NICHOLAS HOPKINS   8:10.99
6. DARIUS BURROWS   8:12.52

60 Metres Hurdles (3 Feb)
1. NEIL OWEN   7.81
2. Thomas Kearns   IRL   7.86
3. ANDREW TULLOCH   7.88
4. Sean Cahill   IRL   8.09
5. HUGH TEAPE   8.19
6. SIMON McAREE   8.26

High Jump (3 Feb)
1. MICHAEL ROBBINS   2.19
2. BEN CHALLENGER   2.16
3. Tyron Peacock   RSA   2.16
4. STUART OHRLAND   2.08
5. DARREN JOSEPH   2.08
6= ROBERT BROCKLEBANK   2.03
6= IAN MASSEY   2.03

1500 Metres (4 Feb)
1. ANGELA DAVIES   4:16.24
2. SHIRLEY GRIFFTHS   4:19.11
3. LYNNE ROBINSON   4:21.39
4. SARAH BENTLEY   4:22.85
5. CAROLINE SLIMIN   4:24.37

3000 Metres (18 Feb Birmingham)
1. SONIA McGEORGE   9:04.69
2. Teresa Duffy   IRL   9:12.20
3. LYNNE ROBINSON   9:37.68
4. LUCY FIELD   10:03.14
5. Nelma DeSilva   10:12.54

60 Metres Hurdles (4 Feb)
1. JACQUELINE AGYEPONG   8.17
2. Monica Grefstad   NOR   8.35
3. MELANIE WILKINS   8.37
4. CLOVA COURT   8.44
5. KERI MADDOX   8.57
6. JANE HALE   8.58

High Jump (3 Feb)
1. MICHELLE DUNKLEY   1.85
2. DEBORA MARTI   1.85
3= RACHAEL FORREST   1.80
3= JULIA BENNETT   1.80
3= Dalia Mikneviciute   LIT   1.80

Pole Vault (3 Feb)
1. NICK BUCKFIELD   5.61
2. MATT BELSHAM   5.30
3= ANDREW ASHURST   5.00
3= DEAN MELLOR   5.00
5. IAN TULLETT   4.90

Long Jump (3 Feb)
1. CHRIS DAVIDSON   7.60
2. Jonathan Kron   IRL   7.47
3. JOHN KING   7.46
4. NATHAN MORGAN   7.34
5. DARREN RITCHIE   7.33

Triple Jump (3 Feb)
1. FRANCIS AGYEPONG   16.55
2. FEMI AKINSANYA   15.73
3. TAYO EROGBOGBO   15.71
4. JOSEPH SWEENEY   15.67
5. JOHN HERBERT   15.61

Shot (4 Feb)
1. SHAUN PICKERING   17.88
2. DAVID CALLAWAY   17.04
3. STEPHAN HAYWARD   16.71
4. NIGEL SPRATLEY   16.21
5. LEE NEWMAN   16.05

Heptathlon
1. STEPHEN ROGERS   5252
2. J Hallisey   4865
3. ADRIAN FERRAND   4851
4. BRETT HEATH   4830

Pole Vault (4 Feb)
1. KATE STAPLES   3.70
2. JANINE WHITLOCK   3.70
3. LINDA STANTON   3.70
4. RHIAN CLARKE   3.50

Long Jump (3 Feb)
1. ANN BROOKS   6.01
2. VIKKI SCHOFIELD   5.95
3. Jacqui Stokes   IRL   5.84
4. JACKIE WHITE   5.64

Triple Jump (4 Feb)
1. MICHELLE GRIFFITH   13.18
2. SHANI ANDERSON   12.81
3. PAMELA ANDERSON   12.29
4. KATHERINE EVANS   12.04

Shot (3 Feb)
1. JUDY OAKES   18.57
2. MARGARET LYNES   15.58
3. ALISON GREY   14.51
4. DEBORAH CALLAWAY   14.21

Pentathlon (4 Feb)
1. SARAH DAMM   4058
2. KERRY JURY   3955
3. DIANA BENNETT   3851
4. CHARMAINE JOHNSON   3816

ESP v GB & NI v HOL v ITA v CZE Combined (indoors) Valencia, Spain 27 - 28 January 1996

MEN
Heptathlon
1.	Kamil Damasek	CZE	5981
2.	Gianni Iapichno	ITA	5866
3.	Roman Sebrle	CZE	5825
4.	BARRY THOMAS		5604
5.	Marzio Viti	ITA	5404
6.	Ferry Zijl	HOL	5398
7.	Remco V Veldhuizen	HOL	5391
8.	Jose Urena Vano	ESP	5384
9.	Jaime Penas Bermejo	ESP	5326
10.	Jiri Ryba	CZE	5211
11.	STEPHEN ROGERS		5089
12.	G. Hidalgo Corbalan	ESP	5326
dnf	RAFER JOSEPH		4083

WOMEN
Pentathlon
1.	Helena Vinarova	CZE	4366
2.	Gertrud Bacher	ITA	4226
3.	JULIA BENNETT		4223
4.	Immaculada Clopes	ESP	4211
5.	VIKKO SCHOFIELD		4186
6.	Karin Periginelli	ITA	4168
7.	Anoek Van Diessen	HOL	4167
8.	Katerina Nekolna	CZE	4075
9.	Elana Milan	ITA	4027
10.	Maniko Olsthoorn	HOL	3862
11.	M. Vegas Saiz	ESP	3778
12.	Hana Dolezelova	CZE	3576
13.	SARAH DAMM		3248

MEN Match Result
1.	Czech Republic	11806
2.	Italy	11270
3.	Holland	10789
4.	Spain	10710
5.	GREAT BRITAIN	10693

WOMEN Match Result
1.	Czech Republic	8441
2.	GREAT BRITAIN	8409
3.	Italy	8394
4.	Holland	8029
5.	Spain	7989

AUT v Eng v CRO v HUN v RUS v CZE (indoors) Vienna, Austria 17 February 1996

MEN
60 Metres
1. JASON FERGUS

200 Metres
1.	Christoph Postinger	AUT	21.00
2.	ALLYN CONDON		21.39

400 Metres
1.	H Devorak	AUT	49.05
3.	ANDY HART		50.52

800 Metres
1.	ANDY HART		1:49.01

1500 Metres
1.	L Vydra	CZE	3.43.07
3.	TERRY WEST		3:46.54

60 Metres Hurdles
1.	Herwig Röttl	AUT	7.68
3.	NEIL OWEN		7.79

High Jump
1.	Jan Janku	CZE	2.22
2.	MIKE ROBBINS		2.05

Pole Vault
1.	K Semyonov	RUS	5.35
2.	MATT BELSHAM		5.35

Long Jump
1.	Milan Gombala	CZE	7.88
5.	CHRIS DAVIDSON		7.57

Triple Jump
1.	FRANCIS AGYEPONG		16.47

Shot
1.	Jenö Kóczián	HUN	18.71

AUT v Eng v SLO v ROM v RUS v CZE (indoors) Vienna, Austria 17 February 1996

WOMEN
60 Metres
1.	J Perc	SLO	7.29
3.	BEV KINCH		7.40

200 Metres
1.	Erika Suchovská	CZE	23.34
3.	LOUISE FRASER		23.95

400 Metres
1.	B Petrahn	HUN	54.86
2.	ALLANA ROWBOTHAM		55.16

800 Metres
1.	Ludmila Formanová	CZE	2:03.35
5.	VICTORIA STERNE		2:08.26

1500 Metres
1.	Simona Ionescu	ROM	4:14.32
3.	DEBBIE GUNNING		4:19.20

60 Metres Hurdles
1.	DENISE LEWIS		8.32
4.	MELANIE WILKINS		8.44

High Jump
1.	Monika Gollner	AUT	1.89
6.	MICHELLE DUNKLEY		1.79

Pole Vault
1.	Ezster Szemeredi	HUN	4.00
4.	KATE STAPLES		3.40

Long Jump
1.	Ludmila Ninova	AUT	6.72
4.	DENISE LEWIS		6.34

Triple Jump
1.	Sárka Kasparková	CZE	13.75
3.	KATE EVANS		12.15

Shot
1.	JUDITH OAKES		18.40

AAA INDOOR JUNIOR CHAMPIONSHIPS Birmingham 17 - 18 February 1996

MEN

	Under 20			Under 17			Under 15	
60	Dwain Chambers	6.7		James Davis	7.2		Tristan Anthony	7.38
200	Dwain Chambers	21.47		Luke Davis	22.45		Tristan Anthony	23.64
400	Neil Jennings	48.9		Kris Stewart	49.2			
800	James Nolan (IRL)	1:54.03		Matthew Crompton	2:01.89		David Moulton	2:06.69
1500	Andrew Walker (IRL)	3:52.43		Ross Fittall	4:06.12			
3000	Mark Miles	8:40.73		Matthew Watson	9:03.77			
60H	Ross Baillie	8.19		Chris Baillie	8.33		Jonathon Crawshaw	8.85
HJ	Darren Joseph	2.15		Colin McMaster	2.00		Kenneth McKeown	1.85
PV	Craig Guite	4.60		Christian Linskey	4.70		Steven Brown	3.71
LJ	David Clerihew	7.24		James Morris	6.54		Richard Phelan (IRL)	5.87
TJ	Marvin Bramble	15.04		Richard McDonald	13.66			
SP	Carl Myerscough	15.13		Carl Myerscough	18.40		Liam Walsh	13.84
3kW	Stuart Monk	12:43.33						
Hept	Dean Macey	5026						

WOMEN

	Under 20			Under 17			Under 15	
60	Malgorzata Rostek	7.55		Sarah Wilhelmy	7.59		Fiona Harrison	7.82
200	Victoria Shipman	24.39		Sarah Wilhelmy	24.69		Sarah Zawada	25.4
400	Vicki Jamison	56.13	300	Lindsay Impett	40.77			
800	Emma Davies	2:13.08		Simone Hardy	2:15.58		Jennifer Mockler	2:20.49
1500	Juliette Oldfield	4:27.71		Emma Alberts	4:40.74			
3000	Paula Gowing	10:23.71						
60H	Natasha Danvers	8.39		Rachael Kay	8.71		Helen Worsey	9.26
HJ	Rachael Forrest	1.80		Hayley Young	1.75		Rachel Morris	1.70
PV	Clare Ridgley	3.51		Becky Ridgley	2.90			
LJ	Grainnie O'Malley (IRL)	5.66		Sarah Claxton	5.75		Fiona Harrison	5.52
TJ	Elizabeth Gibbens	12.20		Julia Johnson	11.40			
SP	Natasha Smith	14.09		Julie Dunkley	12.02		Elizabeth Bowyer	10.90
3kW	Sarah Bennett	15:22.20						
Pent	Nicola Gautier	3624						

GB & NI v FRA (indoors) Glasgow 24 February 1996

MEN

60 Metres
1. JASON JOHN   6.62
2. MICHAEL ROSSWESS   6.70
3. Stephane Cali   FRA 6.72
4. David Patros   FRA 6.84

200 Metres
1. JOHN REGIS   20.88
2. DOUG TURNER   21.19
3. Christophe Cheval FRA 21.27
4. Marc Foucan   FRA 21.78

400 Metres
1. DU'AINE LADEJO   46.39
2. Bruno Wavelet   FRA   47.20
3. Pierre Hilaire   FRA   47.42
4. MARK HYLTON   48.52

800 Metres
1. Jean Vialettes   FRA 1:50.35
2. ANTHONY WHITEMAN   1:50.62
3. EDDIE KING   1:50.69
4. Christophe Charrier FRA 1:51.30

1500 Metres
1. Kader Chekhemani FRA 3.46.35
2. TERRY WEST   3.46.88
3. ADAM DUKE   3:48.44
4. Pascal Blanc   FRA 3:48.60

3000 Metres
1. Eric Dubus   FRA 7:58.47
2. Atiq Naaji   FRA 7:58.84
3. MATTHEW SKELTON   7:59.14
4. IAN GILLESPIE   8:02.60

60 Metres Hurdles
1. Dan Philibert   FRA 7.71
2. NEIL OWEN   7.72
3. Vincent Clarico   FRA 7.83
4. ANDY TULLOCH   7.90

High Jump
1. DALTON GRANT   2.26
2. STEVE SMITH   2.26
3. Joel Vincent   FRA   2.26
4. Didier Detchenique FRA   2.23

Pole Vault
1. Alain Andji   FRA 5.60
2. Jean-Mrac Tailhardat FRA 5.60
3. NICK BUCKFIELD   5.30
4. MATT BELSHAM   5.30

Long Jump
1. Ronuald Ducros   FRA 7.69
2. Emmanuel Bangué   FRA 7.57
3. STEVEN PHILLIPS   7.47
4. CHRIS DAVIDSON   7.32

Triple Jump
1. FRANCIS AGYEPONG   16.92
2. Kenny Boudine   FRA   16.23
3. Colomba Fofana   FRA   16.17
4. FEMI AKINSANYA   16.05

Shot
1. MARK PROCTOR   18.09
2. STEPHAN HAYWARD   17.92
3. Jean Louis Lebon FRA   17.70
4. Marc Baloin   FRA   16.93

4 x 400 Metres Relay
1. GREAT BRITAIN   3:07.72
   (BULLOCK,NOLAN,ULYATT,LADEJO)
2. France   3:07.96
   (Foucan,Perle,July,Wavelet)

Match Result
1. GREAT BRITAIN   72
2. France   68

WOMEN

60 Metres
1.	BEV KINCH	7.33
2.	MARCIA RICHARDSON	7.39
3.	Marie-Joelle Dogbo FRA	7.43
4.	Laurence Droual FRA	7.50

200 Metres
1.	Fabe Dia FRA	23.77
2.	Christine Arron FRA	23.88
3.	DONNA FRASER	24.37
4.	VICTORIA SHIPMAN	24.90

400 Metres
1.	SALLY GUNNELL	53.28
2.	Marie Louis Bevis FRA	53.65
3.	ALLISON CURBISHLEY	54.05
4.	Evelyne Elien FRA	54.76

800 Metres
1.	Patricia Djaté FRA	2:03.43
2.	VICKIE LAWRENCE	2:06.66
3.	Virginie Fouquet FRA	2:07.46
4.	ANGELA DAVIES	2:08.57

1500 Metres
1.	DEBBIE GUNNING	4:17.02
2.	Frederique Quentin FRA	4:17.28
3.	SHIRLEY GRIFFITHS	4:21.72

3000 Metres
1.	Laurence Duquenoy FRA	9:05.44
2.	ALISON WYETH	9:05.45
3.	Blandine Ducret FRA	9:09.19
4.	SARAH BENTLEY	9:23.27

60 Metres Hurdles
1.	Monique Tourret FRA	8.09
2.	Anne Piquerau FRA	8.14
3.	CLOVA COURT	8.20
4.	MELANIE WILKINS	8.45

High Jump
1.	DEBBIE MARTI	1.89
2.	Maryse Maury FRA	1.89
3.	Isabelle Jeanne FRA	1.89
4.	MICHELLE DUNKLEY	1.86

Pole Vault
1.	KATE STAPLES	3.85
2.	Caroline Ammel FRA	3.85
3.	Julie Vigourt FRA	3.75
4.	LINDA STANTON	3.70

Long Jump
1.	DENISE LEWIS	6.48
2.	Linda Ferga FRA	6.33
3.	Marie Noelle Faulon FRA	6.25
4.	ANN BROOKS	6.05

Triple Jump
1.	MICHELLE GRIFFITH	13.51
2.	Sylvie Borda FRA	13.49
3.	Caroline Honore FRA	13.29
4.	SHANI ANDERSON	12.95

Shot
1.	JUDY OAKES	18.59
2.	Laurence Manfredi FRA	16.66
3.	MAGGIE LYNES	15.43
4.	Marie Brouzet FRA	15.19

4 x 400 Metres Relay
1.	France	3:36.25
	(Bevis,Opheltes,Nivet,Elien)	
2.	GREAT BRITAIN	3:38.09
	(FRASER,OWUSU,SUTCLIFFE,ROWBOTHAM)	

Match Result
1.	France	70
2.	GREAT BRITAIN	70

Overall Match Result
1.	GREAT BRITAIN	142
2.	France	138

FRA v GB & NI v GER v ITA (U20) (indoors) Lieven, France 2 March 1996

MEN

60 Metres
1r1	DWAIN CHAMBERS	6.68
4r2	MARTIN GIRAUD	6.94

200 Metres
1.	André Volkmann GER	21.29
3r1	IAN HORSBURGH	21.80
1r2	JAMIE HENTHORN	21.43

400 Metres
1r1	GEOFF DEARMAN	47.98
1r2	NEIL JENNINGS	48.96

800 Metres
1.	Mickael Hotyat FRA	1:52.93
4.	ALISTAIR DONALDSON	1:53.53
5.	ANDREW YOUNG	1:53.79

WOMEN

60 Metres
1.	Esther Moller GER	7.42
2.	MALGORZATA ROSTEK	7.52
4.	TATUM NELSON	7.60

200 Metres
1.	Febé Dia FRA	23.85
4r1	VICTORIA SHIPMAN	24.63
3r2	SARAH WILHELMY	24.37

400 Metres
1.	Ulrike Urbansky GER	53.82
2r1	LESLEY OWUSU	54.76
3r2	VICKI JAMISON	55.33

800 Metres
1.	Ivonne Teichmann GER	2:07.95
2.	ELLEN O'HARE	2:08.95
7.	EMMA DAVIES	2:13.51

60 Metres Hurdles Race 1
1.	Ivo Burkhardt GER	7.94
2.	ROSS BAILLIE	8.08

High Jump
1.	JAMES BRIERLEY	2.14
5.	DARREN JOSEPH	2.05

Pole Vault
1.	Danny Ecker GER	5.40
6.	CHRISTIAN LINSKEY	4.75
7.	CRAIG GUITE	4.50

Long Jump
1.	DAVID CLERIHEW	7.38
2.	NATHAN MORGAN	7.34

60 Metres Hurdles
1r1	NATASHA DANVERS	8.41
1r2	DENISE BOLTON	8.66

High Jump
1.	Christin Putzhofen GER	1.82
2.	MICHELLE DUNKLEY	1.78
3.	RACHAEL FORREST	1.74

Pole Vault
1.	Marie Poissonnier FRA	3.85
4.	RHIAN CLARKE	3.65
6.	CLARE RIDGLEY	3.35

Long Jump
1.	Sandra Stube GER	6.22
2.	SARAH CLAXTON	6.01
6.	DENISE BOLTON	3.62

Triple Jump
1.	Chrystele Legouguec FRA	12.58
5.	LIZ GIBBENS	12.26
8.	JODIE HURST	11.15

Triple Jump
1.	Colomba Fofana FRA	15.85
5.	MARVIN BRAMBLE	15.00
8.	ADAM SMITH	14.55

Shot
1.	Matthias Wiese GER	17.25
3.	EMEKA UDECHUKU	16.29
5.	CARL MYERSCOUGH	15.03

5kWalk
1.	Sven Albrecht GER	21:38.52
7.	SCOTT TAYLOR	24:16.01
	STUART MONK	disq

4 x 200 Metres Relay
1.	Germany	1:25.36
2.	GREAT BRITIAN	1:25.40

Shot
1.	Assunta Legnante ITA	15.42
6.	NATASHA SMITH	13.41
7.	PHILLIPA ROLES	13.37

3kWalk
1.	Melanie Seeger GER	13:25.11
7.	SARAH BENNETT	14:39.24
8.	DEBBIE WALLEN	15:30.16

4 x 200 Metres Relay
1.	France	1:36.46
3.	GREAT BRITIAN	1:38.34

Match Result
1.	Germany	276
2.	France	215.5
3.	GREAT BRITAIN & NI	204
4.	Italy	154.5

BAF CROSS COUNTRY CHAMPIONSHIPS Stakeford 3 March 1996

MEN

1.	KEITH CULLEN	31.26
2.	ANDREW PEARSON	31.28
3.	CHRIS SWEENEY	31.40
4.	ADRIAN PASSEY	31.56
5.	JOHN NUTTALL	32.05
6.	DARRIUS BURROWS	32.12
7.	STEVE HARRIS	32.13
8.	NICK COMERFORD	32.16
9.	ROBERT QUINN	32.17
10.	ROB DENMARK	32.26
11.	DAVE PAYNE	32.27
12.	JON SOLLY	32.28

WOMEN

1.	ALISON WYETH	18.22
2.	LIZ TALBOT	18.27
3.	ANGIE HULLEY	18.32
4.	VICKI MCPHERSON	18.33
5.	HELEN TITTERINGHAM	18.38
6.	ANDREA WHITCOMBE	18.43
7.	SARAH BENTLEY	18.48
8.	LOUISE WATSON	18.49
9.	HEATHER HEASMAN	18.53
10.	AMANDA PARKINSON	18.57
11.	WENDY ORE	19.07
12.	AUDREY SYM	19.09

JUNIOR MEN

1.	ALEX OLDFIELD	21.08
2.	KEVIN NASH	21.14
3.	SIMON WILKINSON	21.16
4.	ALLEN GRAFFIN	21.18
5.	SAM HAUGHIAN	21.34

JUNIOR WOMEN

1.	MICHELLE MANN	13.32
2.	SHEILA FAIRWEATHER	13.46
3.	TANYA POVEY	13.51
4.	JANE GROVES	13.57
5.	JULIETTE OLDFIELD	14.03

ENGLISH CROSS COUNTRY CHAMPIONSHIPS Newark 9 March 1996

MEN

1.	JOHN NUTTALL	40.35
2.	JOHN SHERBAN	40.55
3.	DOMINIC BANNISTER	41.04
4.	John Downes IRL	41.14
5.	MICHAEL HAWKINS	41.18
6.	STEFFAN WHITE	41.21
7.	BARRY ROYDEN	41.26
8.	MARTIN JONES	41.30
9.	ANDY BRISTOW	41.35
10.	IAN CORNFORD	41.36

MEN Under 20

1.	MATTHEW O'DOWD	31.45
2.	HUW LOBB	31.51
3.	KEVIN HOLLAND	31.56
4.	CHARLES SYKES	32.09
5.	IAN PIERCE	32.13
6.	MARK BEERLING	32.17

MEN Under 17

1.	PAUL MORBY	20.37
2.	MARK BROWN	20.42
3.	JONATHAN STEWART	20.49
4.	RYAN FALKNER	20.57
5.	P. RILEY	21.06
6.	NICK MAPP	21.10

WOMEN

1.	ALISON WYETH	21.59
2.	ANGIE HULLEY	22.03
3.	ANDREA WHITCOMBE	22.11
4.	RHONA MAKEPEACE	22.21
5.	ALISON BARNES	22.24
6.	HELEN TITTERINGHAM	22.36
7.	ANGELA JOINER	22.40
8.	LOUISE WATSON	22.42
9.	SARAH BRADBURY	22.47
10.	LUCY WRIGHT	22.51
dq	Nnenna Lynch USA	21.54

WOMEN Under 20

1.	Berhane Dagne	ETH	19.19
2.	AMANDA TREMBLE		19.25
3.	GETENESH TAMIRAT		19.33
4.	JOSIE GRAY		20.03

WOMEN Under 17

1.	AMBER GASCOIGNE	20.23
2.	CAROLINE WALSH	20.26
3.	SONIA THOMAS	20.26
4.	EMMA DEAKIN	20.38

WOMEN Under 15

1.	JODIE SWALLOW	15.15
2.	JENNY MOCKLER	15.27
3.	EMMA WARD	15.32
4.	NICOLA COATES	15.38

WOMEN Under 13

1.	SARAH RAVEN	13.51
2.	LUCY MICHAELSON	14.08
3.	LEONA WIDDICKS	14.15
4.	GEMMA VINEY	14.17

WORLD CROSS COUNTRY CHAMPIONSHIPS Stellenbosch, South Africa 23 March 1996

SENIOR MEN (12,150m)

1.	Paul Tergat	KEN	33:34
2.	Salah Hissou	MAR	33:56
3.	Ismael Kirui	KEN	33:57
4.	Paul Koech	KEN	34:10
5.	Haile Gebrselassie	ETH	34:28
6.	Joseph Kimani	KEN	34:30
7.	Khalid Skah	MAR	34:34
8.	Ismail Sghir	MAR	34:34
9.	William Kiptum	KEN	34:35
10.	Josephat Machuka	KEN	34:37
12.	JON BROWN		34.55
28.	JOHN NUTTALL		35:38
45.	ROB DENMARK		36:01
51.	ANDREW PEARSON		36:07
57.	KEITH CULLEN		36:17
59.	DARIUS BURROWS		36:19
87.	CHRIS SWEENEY		36:52
129.	ADRIAN PASSEY		37:36
151.	STEVE HARRIS		38:06

Men's Teams

1.	Kenya	33
2.	Morocco	99
3.	Ethiopia	107
5.	GREAT BRITAIN & NI	252

SENIOR WOMEN (6,300m)

1.	Gete Wami	ETH	20:12
2.	Rose Cheruiyot	KEN	20:18
3.	Naomi Mugo	KEN	20:21
4.	Derartu Tulu	ETH	20:21
5.	Colleen de Reuck	RSA	20:21
6.	Fernanda Ribeiro	POR	20:23
7.	Julia Vaquero	ESP	20:28
8.	Jane Ngotho	KEN	20:31
9.	Gabriela Szabo	ROM	20:37
10.	Birhane Adere	ETH	20:37
11.	Sally Barsosio	KEN	20:43
12.	Iulia Negura	ROM	20:55
19.	PAULA RADCLIFFE		21:13
49.	VIKKI McPHERSON		21:49
58.	ANGIE HULLEY		21:58
63.	ALISON WYETH		22:10
64.	ANDREA WHITCOMBE		22:14
96.	LIZ TALBOT		23:14

Women's Teams

1.	Kenya	24
2.	Ethiopia	44
3.	Romania	70
11.	GREAT BRITAIN & NI	189

JUNIOR MEN (8,350m)

1.	David Chelule	KEN	24:06
2.	Assefa Mezegebu	ETH	24:19
37.	ALLEN GRAFFIN		26:41
65.	KEVIN NASH		27:21
70.	SIMON WILKINSON		27:20
89.	SAM HAUGHIAN		28:04
110.	ALEX OLDFIELD		28:52
dnf	TOM MAYO		

Junior Men's Teams

1.	Kenya	13
12.	GREAT BRITAIN & NI	261

JUNIOR WOMEN (4,220m)

1.	Kutre Dulecha	ETH	13:27
2.	Annemarie Sandell	FIN	13:32
51.	TANYA POVEY		15:05
53.	MICHELLE MANN		15:12
75.	JULIETTE OLDFIELD		15:35
82.	JANE GROVES		15:42
dnf	SHEILA FAIRWEATHER		

Junior Women's Teams

1.	Kenya	21
12.	GREAT BRITAIN & NI	261

EUROPEAN INDOOR CHAMPIONSHIPS Stockholm, Sweden 8 - 10 March 1996

MEN

60 Metres (9 Mar)
1. Marc Blume   GER   6.62
2. JASON JOHN   6.64
3. Peter Karlsson   SWE   6.64
4. Charalambos Papadias GRE   6.65
5. Patrik Strenius   SWE   6.67
6. KEVIN WILLIAMS   6.72

3h1 JASON GARDENER   6.79

200 Metres (10 Mar)
1. Erik Wijmeersch   BEL   21.04
2. Alexios Alexopoulos GRE   21.05
3. Torbjorn Eriksson   SWE   21.07
4. Thomas Sbokos   GRE   21.74

4s1 MARLON DEVONISH   21.86
3s2 ALLYN CONDON   21.34
h4 DOUG TURNER   dq

400 Metres (10 Mar)
1. DU'AINE LADEJO   46.12
2. Pierre-Marie Hilaire FRA   46.82
3. Ashraf Saber   ITA   46.86
4. Julian Voelkel   GER   47.05

3s2 KENT ULYATT   52.05

800 Metres (10 Mar)
1. Roberto Parra   ESP   1:47.74
2. Giuseppe D'Urso   ITA   1:48.04
3. Wojciech Kaldowski   POL   1:48.40
4. Andres Diaz   ESP   1:48.63
5. Michael Wildner   AUT   1:48.64
6. Andrea Longo   ITA   1:49.19

WOMEN

60 Metres (9 Mar)
1. Ekaterini Thanou   GRE   7.15
2. Odiah Sidibe   FRA   7.25
3. Jerneja Perc   SLO   7.28
4. Natalya Merzlyakova RUS   7.29
5. Alenka Bikar   SLO   7.32
6. Eva Barati   HUN   7.44

5s2 BEV KINCH   7.36

200 Metres (10 Mar)
1. Sandra Myers   ESP   23.15
2. Erika Suchovska   CZE   23.16
3. Zlatka Georgieva   BUL   23.40
4. Alenka Bikar   SLO   23.68

400 Metres (10 Mar)
1. Grit Breuer   GER   50.81
2. Olga Kotlyarova   RUS   51.70
3. Tatyana Chebykina   RUS   51.71
4. Ionela Tirlea   ROM   52.90

800 Metres (10 Mar)
1. Patricia Djate   FRA   2:01.71
2. Stella Jongmans   NED   2:01.88
3. Svetlana Masterkova RUS   2:02.86
4. Ludmila Formanova   CZE   2:03.47
5. Steffi Graf   AUT   2:04.76
6. Ella Kovacs   ROM   2:05.39

1500 Metres (10 Mar)
1. Mateo Canellas   ESP   3:44.50
2. ANTHONY WHITEMAN   3:44.78
3. Kader Chekhemani   FRA   3:45.96
4. Lukos Vydra   CZE   3:46.20
5. Branko Zorko   CRO   3:46.82
6. Peter Philipp   SUI   3:47.55
9. TERRY WEST   3:49.83

3000 Metres (10 Mar)
1. Anacleto Jimenez   ESP   7:50.06
2. Christoph Impens   BEL   7:50.19
3. Panagiotis Papoulias GRE   7:50.80
4. Ovidiu Olteanu   ROM   7:50.94
5. Eric Dubus   FRA   7:53.53
6. Alberto Garcia   ESP   7:54.57

60 Metres Hurdles   (9 Mar)
1. Igor Kazanov   LAT   7.59
2. Guntis Peders   LAT   7.65
3. Jonathan N'senga   BEL   7.66
4. Falk Balzer   GER   7.67
5. Andrey Kislykh   RUS   7.72
6. Johan Lisabeth   BEL   7.78

High Jump (10 Mar)
1. Dragutin Topic   YUG   2.35
2. Leonid Pumalaynen   RUS   2.33
3. Steinar Hoen   NOR   2.31
4. Konstantin Matusevich ISR 2.31
5. Jaroslaw Kotewicz   POL   2.29
6. Arturo Ortiz   ESP   2.27

24Q DALTON GRANT   2.15

1500 Metres (10 Mar)
1. Carla Sacremento   POR   4:08.95
2. Yekaterina Podkopayeva RUS 4:09.65
3. Malgorzata Rydz   POL   4:10.50
4. Catalina Ghiorghiu   ROM   4:10.50
5. Theresia Kiesl   AUT   4:12.61
6. Sylvia Kühnemund   GER   4:13.34

6h2 DEBBIE GUNNING   4:18.32

3000 Metres (9 Mar)
1. Fernanda Ribeiro   POR   8:39.49
2. Sara Wedlund   SWE   8:50.32
3. Marta Dominguez   ESP   8:53.34
4. Blandine Bitzner-Ducret FRA 8:54.86
5. Maria Pantyukhova   RUS   8:55.40
6. Luminita Gogirlea   ROM   8:56.29

60 Metres Hurdles   (10 Mar)
1. Patricia Girard Leno FRA   7.89
2. Brigita Bukovec   SLO   7.90
3. Monique Tourret   FRA   8.09
4. Maria J Mardomingo   ESP   8.15
5. Anne Piquereau   FRA   8.25
6. Caren Jung   GER   9.87

Pole Vault (9 Mar)
1. Dmitriy Markov   BLR   5.85
2. Viktor Chistyakov   RUS   5.80
3. Pyotr Bochkaryov   RUS   5.80
4. Peter Widen   SWE   5.70
5. Martin Eriksson   SWE   5.70

7. NICK BUCKFIELD   5.55

Long Jump (8 Mar)
1. Mattias Sunneborn   SWE   8.06
2. Bogdan Tarus   ROM   8.03
3. Spyros Vasdekis   GRE   8.03
4. Gregor Cankar   SLO   8.01
5. Aleksandr Glovatskiy BLR   7.97

Triple Jump (10 Mar)
1. Maris Bruziks   LAT   16.97
2. FRANCIS AGYEPONG   16.93
3. Armen Martirosyan   ARM   16.74
4. Aleks'dr Aseledchenko RUS 16.70
5. Arne Holm   SWE   16.60

Shot (8 Mar)
1. Paolo Dal Soglio   ITA   20.50
2. Dirk Urban   GER   20.04
3. Oliver-Sven Buder   GER   19.91
4. Corrado Fantini   ITA   19.79
5. Markkus Koistinen   FIN   19.72

12. MARK PROCTOR   18.53
19Q SHAUN PICKERING   17.57

Heptathlon (10 Mar)
1. Erki Nool   EST   6188
2. Tomas Dvorak   CZE   6114
3. Jon Arnar Magnusson ISL   6069
4. Sebastian Chmara   POL   6016
5. Dezso Szabo   HUN   5957

dnf ALEX KRUGER   5049

High Jump (10 Mar)
1. Alina Astafei   GER   1.98
2. Niki Bakogianni   GRE   1.96
3. Olga Bolshova   MOL   1.94
4. Nele Zilinskiene   LIT   1.94
5. Monica Iagar   ROM   1.94
6. Kajsa Bergqvist   SWE   1.92

18=Q DEBBIE MARTI   1.80

High Jump (10 Mar)
1. Vala Flosadottir   ISL   4.16
2. Christine Adams   GER   4.05
3. Gabriela Mihalcea   ROM   4.05

11. KATE STAPLES   3.85

Long Jump (10 Mar)
1. Renata Neilsen   DEN   6.76
2. Yelena Sinchukova   RUS   6.75
3. Claudia Gerhardt   GER   6.74
4. Iva Prandzheva   BUL   6.73
5. Ludmila Ninova   AUT   6.65
6. Heli Koivula   CZE   6.55

8. DENISE LEWIS   6.42

Triple Jump (9 Mar)

1.	Iva Prandzheva	BUL	14.54
2.	Sárka Kaspárková	CZE	14.50
3.	Olga Vasdeki	GRE	14.30
4.	Natalya Kayukova	RUS	14.22
5.	Virge Naeris	EST	14.05
6.	Yelena Govorova	UKR	13.81

ASHIA HANSEN	3nj
22Q MICHELLE GRIFFITH	12.36

Shot (9 Mar)

1.	Astrid Kumbernuss	GER	19.79
2.	Irina Khudoroshkina	RUS	19.07
3.	Valentina Fedyushina	UKR	18.90
4.	JUDY OAKES		18.72
5.	Nadine Kleinert	GER	18.10
6.	Martina de le Puente	ESP	17.04

Pentathlon (8 Mar)

1.	Yelena Lebedyenko	RUS	4685
2.	Urszula Wlodarczyk	POL	4597
3.	Irina Vostrikova	RIS	4545
4.	Mona Steigauf	GER	4540
5.	Tiia Hautala	FIN	4450
6.	Karin Specht	GER	4403
11.	JULIA BENNETT		4225

LONDON MARATHON
21 April 1996

MEN

1.	Dionicio Ceron	MEX	2:10:00
2.	Vincent Rousseau	BEL	2:10:26
3.	PAUL EVANS		2:10:40
4.	Jackson Kabiga	KEN	2:10:43
5.	Antonio Serrano	ESP	2:10:55
6.	Domingos Castro	POR	2:11:12
7.	Eddy Hellebuyck	BEL	2:11:53
8.	Benson Maysa	KEN	2:12:43
9.	GARY STAINES		2:12:54
10.	Tesfaye Bekele	NOR	2:14:37
18.	MARK HUDSPITH		2:19:25
29.	GARY BISHOP		2:23:59
30.	GARY MCILROY		2:24:11
31.	TONY DUFFY		2:24:14
34.	TONY BARDEN		2:25:33
35.	PAUL FROUD		2:25:39
38.	PETER PLEASANTS		2:27:40
39.	DAVE HILL		2:28:02
42.	RICHARD SALES		2:29:26

WOMEN

1.	LIZ MCCOLGAN		2:27:54
2.	Joyce Chepchumba	KEN	2:30:09
3.	Malgorzata Sobanska	POL	3:30:17
4.	Angelina Kanana	KEN	2:30:25
5.	Anita Hakenstad	NOR	2:31:07
6.	Alina Ivanova	RUS	2:32:09
7.	Renata Kokowska	POL	2:32:46
8.	Firia Sultanova	RUS	2:32:50
9.	Jane Salumae	EST	2:33:18
10.	Yelena Mazovka	BLR	2:33:58
14.	SALLY EASTALL		2:38:59
15.	DANIELLE SANDERSON		2:39:46
18.	TRACY SWINDELL		2:44:49
19.	ZINA MARCHANT		2:45:42
20.	SANDRA BRANNEY		2:46:19
21.	DEBBIE PERCIVAL		2:48:49
24.	JANETTE PICTON		2:51:26
25.	JACKIE NEWTON		2:51:59
27.	LISA HOLLICK		2:54:16
29.	LIBBY JONES		2:55:01
32.	MEREDITH BLAKE		2:55:56
33.	JOANNA LODGE		2:56:57
35.	ZOE LOWE		2:57:08

IAAF ROAD RELAY
Copenhagen, Denmark 13 - 14 April 1996
(5000,10000,5000,10000,5000,7195)

MEN (14 Apr)

1. Kenya — 2:00:40
Simon Rono 13:45, Joseph Kimani 28:33, Mark Yatich 14:33,
Stephen Kirwa 29:00, David Kipruto 14:09, William Kiptum 20:40

2. Brasil — 2:01:24
Wanda Moura 13:49, Vanderlei de Lima 29:10, Edgar de Oliveira 14:26,
Delmir dos Santos 28:31, Tomix da Costa 14:26, Ronaldo da Costa 21:02

3. Ethiopia — 2:01:50
Erpassa Lemi 13:58, Kidane Gebremichael 29:20, Sisay Bezabih 14:23,
Abraham Assefa 29:13, Tegenu Abebe 14:42, Worku Bikila 20:14

4. Denmark — 2:02:38
Dennis Jensen 14:12, Jan B. Ikov 29:18, Rene Carlsen 14:21,
Klaus P. Hansen 29:24, Kare Sørensen 14:23, Carsten Jørensen 21:00

5. Russia — 2:03:37
Aleksandr Vasilyev 14:11, Sergey Fedotov 29:08, Aleksandr Boikhovitin 14:27,
Gennadiy Panin 29:41, Vladimir Gusukin 14:49, Yuriy Punda 21:21

6. Mexico — 2:03:48
David Galindo 14:07, Victor Rodríguez 30:15, Jesús Primo 14:55
Benjamin Paredes 29:35, Ruben Garcia 14:24, Martín Rodríguez 20:32

8. GREAT BRITAIN & NI — 2:03:55
Neil Caddy 14:20, Jon Solly 29:10, Ian Gillespie 14:30,
Chris Sweeney 29:35, Christian Stephenson 14:55, Robert Quinn 21:25

WOMEN (13 Apr)

1. Ethiopia — 2:16:04
Genet Gebregiorgios 15:53, Birhane Adere 32:21, Ayelech Worku 16:15,
Gete Wami 32:25, Getenesh Urge 16:00, Luchia Yishak 23:10

2. Romania — 2:18:41
Iulia Ionescu 15:59, Mariana Chirila 33:21, Lelia Deseinicu 16:16,
Iulia Negura 32:53, Luminita Gogirlea 16:33, Elena Fidatov 23:39

3. Japan — 2:18:58
Yukiko Okamoto 15:56, Naomi Sakashita 32:56, Ai Fukuchi 16:11,
Ikuyo Goto 33:38, Noriko Ura 16:08, Eri Yamaguchi 24:09

4. Italy — 2:20:02
Patrizio Di Napoli 16:00, Simona Viola 33:49, Silvia Sommaggio 16:04,
Maura Viceeconte 33:37, Sara Ferrari 16:36, Roberta Brunet 23:56

5. Norway — 2:20:56
Hilde Stavik 16:23, Gunhild Halle 32:53, Maiken Sorum 16:36,
Grete Kirkenberg 34:15, Stine Larsen 16:56, Anita Håkenstad 23:53

6. Russia — 2:21:30
Nina Belikova 16:11, Nadezhda Tatarenkova 33:52, Nadezhda Izadyorova 16:55
Natalya Solominskaya 34:27, Nadezhda Gallyamova 16:41, Lyudmila Petrova 23:24

7. GREAT BRITAIN & NI — 2:21:41
Rhona Makepeace 16:32, Suzanne Rigg 33:57, Amanda Wright 16:38
Angie Hulley 33:59, Sarah Bentley 16:37, Vikki McPherson 23:58

Welsh Games Wales v Ireland Cardiff 25 May 1996

MEN

100 Metres wind 5.1
1. DOUG TURNER   WAL   10.29w
2. JAMIE HENTHORN   gstWAL   10.38w
3. TREM. RUTHERFORD   WAL   10.47w

200 Metres wind -0.7
1. Ramon Clay   gst/USA   20.86
2. DOUG TURNER   WAL   20.98
3. TREM. RUTHERFORD   WAL   21.97

400 Metres
1. JAMIE BALUCH   WAL   46.08
2. GUY BULLOCK   gst   46.68

800 Metres
1. Laban Rotich   gst/KEN 1:45.82
8. DARRELL MAYNARD   WAL 1:50.85

1500 Metres
1. Lukas Moroga   gst/KEN 3:47.52
4. NICK COMERFORD   WAL 3:49.85

3000 Metres Steeplechase
1. Jonathan Kandie gst/KEN 8:31.80
6. ANDY EYNON   WAL 9:09.06

110 Metres Hurdles wind 4.3
1. COLIN JACKSON   WAL   13.26w
2. PAUL GRAY   WAL   13.62w

WOMEN

100 Metres wind 4.0
1. STEPHANIE DOUGLAS   gst   11.60w
2. CATHERINE MURPHY   WAL   11.66w
5. HELEN MILES   WAL   12.10w

200 Metres wind 2.1
1. CATHERINE MURPHY   WAL   24.10w
2. Jacqui Stokes   IRL   24.63w
4. ANGHARAD JAMES   WAL   25.86w

400 Metres
1. MICHELLE PIERRE   gst   54.94
2. GILLIAN CASHELL   WAL   55.75
3. KATHRYN BRIGHT   WAL   56.17

800 Metres
1. SONYA BOWYER   gst   2:02.12
2. Naomi Mugo   gst/KEN 2:02.15
3. HAYLEY PARRY   WAL   2:04.15
4. AMANDA PRITCHARD   WAL   2:10.66

1500 Metres
1. Pauline Konga   gst/KEN 4:18.75
2. LYNN GIBSON   gst   4:19.05
8. CLAIRE MARTIN   WAL   4:34.98

400 Metres Hurdles
1. Darko Juricic   CRO   53.16
2. MARK ROWLANDS   WAL   53.47
4. PHIL HARRIES   WAL   55.03

High Jump
1. Mark Mandy   IRL   2.24
3. DAVID NOLAN   WAL   2.05
4. MATTHEW PERRY   WAL   2.00

Pole Vault
1. KEVIN HUGHES   gst   5.15
2. IAN TULLETT   gst   5.15
3. TIM THOMAS   WAL   4.80

Long Jump
1. Sinisa Ergotic   CRO   7.71
6. ANTHONY MALCOLM   WAL   6.93

Triple Jump
1. EZRA CLARKE   gst   15.46
2. CHARLES COLE   WAL   13.95

Shot
1. John Farreley   IRL   14.88
2. ANDY TURNER   WAL   14.72
4. EWART HULSE   WAL   13.91

100 Metres Hurdles wind -0.3
1. DIANE ALLAHGREEN   gst   13.69
2. BETHAN EDWARDS   WAL   14.21
3. RACHEL KING   WAL   14.40

400 Metres Hurdles
1. ALYSON LAYZELL   WAL   59.72
4. KATHRYN WILLIAMS   WAL   63.17

High Jump
1. Breda Browne   IRL   1.70
2. TERESA ANDREWS   WAL   1.65

Pole Vault
1. JANINE WHITLOCK   gst   3.73
2. CLAUDIA FILCE   WAL   2.80
3. REBECCA ROLES   WAL   2.80

Long Jump
1. Jacqui Stokes   IRL   6.04
2. JAQUELINE WHITE   gst   5.82
4. NICOLA SHORT   WAL   5.48

Triple Jump
1. Cathrione Hannafin IRL   11.97
2. JAYNE LUDLOW   WAL   11.37w

Discus
1. John Menton   IRL   51.24
3. GARETH GILBERT   WAL   46.24
4. ANDY TURNER   WAL   46.02

Hammer
1. Edward Healy   IRL   57.86
3. ADRIAN PALMER   WAL   57.38
4. GRAHAM HOLDER   WAL   56.18

Javelin
1. NIGEL BEVAN   WAL   72.96
3. STUART LOUGHRAN   WAL   59.34

4 x 100 Metres Relay
1. WALES   40.74
(RUTHERFORD, TURNER, HENTHORN, JACKSON)
2. Ireland   41.62

4 x 400 Metres Relay
1. WALES   3:12.17
(D WILLIAMS, HARRIES, BAULCH, LLOYD)
2. Ireland   3:16.77

Match Result
1. WALES   110
2. Ireland   85

Shot
1. JAYNE BERRY   WAL   13.88
4. LESLEY BRANNAN   WAL   11.83

Discus
1. PHILIPPA ROLES   WAL   45.76
2. JAYNE FISHER   WAL   45.52

Hammer
1. SARAH MOORE   WAL   53.26
3. ANGELA BONNER   WAL   43.06

Javelin
1. TESSA SANDERSON   gst   60.60
3. ONYEMA AMADI   WAL   48.22
4. SIAN LAX   WAL   45.40

4 x 100 Metres Relay
1. WALES   47.17
(MILES, MURPHY, JAMES, PAINES)

4 x 400 Metres Relay
1. WALES   3:45.29
(CASHELL, TURNER, PARRY, LAYZELL)

Match Result
1. WALES   91.5
2: Ireland   69.5

EUROPEAN CUP Madrid, Spain 1 - 2 June 1996

MEN

100 Metres wind 0.8 (1 Jun)
1. LINFORD CHRISTIE   10.04
2. Marc Blume   GER   10.25
3. Vladislav Dologodin UKR   10.26
4. Pascal Theophile   FRA   10.34
5. Peter Karlsson   SWE   10.35
6. Venarcio Jose Murcia ESP   10.39
7. Giovanni Puggioni   ITA   10.40
8. Alexsandr Sokolov   RUS   10.57
9. Sami Lansivuori   FIN   10.66

200 Metres wind 2.5 (2 Jun)
1. LINFORD CHRISTIE   20.25w
2. Vladislav Dologodin UKR   20.39w
3. Torbjorn Eriksson   SWE   20.45w
4. Marc Blume   GER   20.50w
5. Christophe Cheval   FRA   20.66w
6. Angelo Cipolloni   ITA   20.69w
7. Jav. Navarro Sanchez ESP   20.79w
8. Ari Pakarinen   FIN   20.91w
9 Alek. Porkhomovskiy RUS   21.13w

400 Metres (1 Jun)
1. Uwe Jahn   GER   45.64
2. DU'AINE LADEJO   45.72
3. Jean Louis Rapnouil FRA   45.96
4. Valentin Kulbatskiy UKR   46.60
5. Andrea Nuti   ITA   46.66
6. Sergey Voronin   RUS   47.25
7. Niklas Wallenlind   SWE   47.32
8. Karl Louramo   FIN   47.39
9. Miguel Cuesta   ESP   47.52

800 Metres (2 Jun)
1. Roberto Parra ESP 1:44.97
2. Giuseppe D'Urso ITA 1:45.27
3. Nico Motchebon GER 1:45.98
4 DAVID STRANG 1:46.38
5. Bruno Konczylo FRA 1:46.63
6. Anatoliy Yakimovich UKR 1:46.80
7. Martin Enholm SWE 1:47.05
8. Tomi Kankare FIN 1:47.78
9. Sergey Kozhevnikov RUS 1:49.80

1500 Metres (1 Jun)
1. Fermin Cacho ESP 3:40.24
2. Rudiger Stenzel GER 3:40.53
3 ANTHONY WHITEMAN 3:41.21
4. Mickael Damian FRA 3:42.06
5. Jorgen Zaki SWE 3:42.10
6. Gennaro Di Napoli ITA 3:42.26
7. Andrey Zadorodzny RUS 3:45.96
8. Dmitry Lisitin UKR 3:48.95
9. Sami Valtonen FIN 3:50.65

3000 Metres (1 Jun)
1. Dieter Baumann GER 7:57.19
2. Isaac Vicosa ESP 7:57.80
3. Aless. Lambruschini ITA 7:58.44
4. Eric Dubus FRA 8:05.84
5. Kent Claesson SWE 8:07.81
6. Sergey Drygin RUS 8:08.25
7. Jukka Savonheimo FIN 8:08.42
8 GARY LOUGH 8:11.44
9. Igor Lishchinsky UKR 8.25.24

5000 Metres (2 Jun)
1. Gennaro Di Napoli ITA 13:52.34
2. Manuelo Pancorba ESP 13:55.18
3. Abdellah Behar FRA 13:57.15
4. KEITH CULLEN 14:00.61
5. Vener Kashayev RUS 14:06.33
6. Sergey Lebed UKR 14:08.24
7. Jonny Danielson SWE 14:24.99
8. Jirka Arndt GER 14:32.70
9. Pasi Mattila FIN 14:46.30

3000 Metres Steeplechase (2 Jun)
1. Steffan Brand GER 8:30.09
2. Angelo Carosi ITA 8:32.50
3. JUSTIN CHASTON 8:33.59
4. Vladimir Pronin RUS 8:36.38
5. Nadir Bosch FRA 8:37.20
6. Antonia Peula ESP 8:41.42
7. Ville Hautala FIN 8:45.33
8. Aleksey Patserin UKR 8:48.78
9. Patrick Flink SWE 9:02.14

110 Metres Hurdles -0.3 (2 Jun)
1. Florian Schwarthoff GER 13.20
2. COLIN JACKSON 13.63
3. Yevgeniy Pechenkin RUS 13.64
4. Dmitriy Kolesnichenko UKR 13.75
5. Dan Philibert FRA 13.77
6. Claes Albihn SWE 13.84
7. Antti Haapakoski FIN 13.96
8. Mauro Rossi ITA 14.18
9. Miguel De L Santos ESP 16.11

400 Metres Hurdles (1 Jun)
1. Fabrizo Mori ITA 49.45
2. JON RIDGEON 49.84
3. Sven Nylander SWE 50.18
4. Jimmy Coco FRA 50.27
5. Ruslan Mashchenko RUS 50.54
6. Steffen Kolb GER 51.08
7 Inigo Monreal ESP 51.48
8. Petteri Pulkkinen FIN 52.44
9. Vladimir Dobrydnev UKR 52.88

High Jump (1 Jun)
1. Arturo Ortiz ESP 2.27
2. Leonid Pumalaynen RUS 2.27
3 DALTON GRANT 2.27
4. Wolfgang Kreissig GER 2.27
5. Alessandro Canale ITA 2.24
6. Joel Vincent FRA 2.24
7. Stefan Holm SWE 2.21
8. Yuriy Sergiyenko UKR 2.21
9. Vesa Piira FIN 2.18

Pole Vault (2 Jun)
1. Pyotr Bochkaryev RUS 5.70
2. Tim Lobinger GER 5.60
3. Jose Arcos ESP 5.50
4 NICK BUCKFIELD 5.50
5= Jean Galfione FRA 5.40
5= Peter Widen SWE 5.40
7. Heikki Vaaraniemi FIN 5.30
8. Claudio Avogaro ITA 5.30
Dmitriy Kalinichenko UKR nh

Long Jump (1 Jun)
1. Simone Bianchi ITA 8.25
2. Jesus Olivan ESP 7.97
3. Bakri Daroueche FRA 7.96
4. Kiril Sosunov RUS 7.92
5. Mattias Sunneborn SWE 7.87
6. Volker Ehmann GER 7.69
7. Mika Kahma FIN 7.56
8. Sergey Glotov UKR 7.52
9. FRED SALLE 7.43

Triple Jump (2 Jun)
1. JONATHAN EDWARDS 17.79w
2. Vladimir Kravchenko UKR 17.29w
3. Gennadiy Markov RUS 17.12w
4. Charles Friedek GER 17.03w
5. Raul Chapado ESP 16.70w
6. Claes Rahm SWE 16.59w
7. Daniele Buttiglione ITA 16.40w
8. Janne Kinnunen FIN 16.31w
Kenny Boudine FRA nm

Shot (1 Jun)
1. Paulo Dal Soglio ITA 20.72
2. Oliver-Sven Buder GER 20.08
3. Yuriy Bilonoh UKR 19.86
4. Manuel Martinez ESP 19.54
5. Markus Koistinen FIN 19.40
6. SHAUN PICKERING 19.23
7. Aleksey Shidlovskiy RUS 18.59
8. Thomas Hammarsten SWE 18.43
9. Jean-Louis Lebon FRA 17.76

Discus (2 Jun)
1. David Martinez ESP 62.38
2. Sergey Lyakhov RUS 62.20
3. Jurgen Schult GER 61.96
4. Vitaliy Sidorov UKR 61.78
5. ROBERT WEIR 61.02
6. Diego Fortuna ITA 60.62
7. Timo Sinervo FIN 58.88
8. Jean Pons FRA 58.32
9. Stefan Fernholm SWE 56.84

Hammer (2 Jun)
1. Karsten Kobs GER 78.18
2. Marko Wahlman FIN 77.72
3. Enrico Sgrulletti ITA 77.44
4. Christophe Epalle FRA 77.16
5. Aleksandr Seleznev RUS 76.92
6. Thomas Sjostrom SWE 72.42
7. Artur Rubanko UKR 72.30
8. MICHAEL JONES 71.74
9. Jose Perez ESP 67.30

Javelin (1 Jun)
1. Raymond Hecht GER 88.86
2. Sergey Makarov RUS 84.96
3. Harri Hakkarainen FIN 81.44
4. Patrik Boden SWE 80.78
5 COLIN MacKENZIE 74.10
6. Gaetan Siakinuu FRA 72.32
7. Carlos Perez Auyanet ESP 72.06
8. Fabio De Gaspari ITA 71.56
9. Sergey Volochay UKR 65.14

4 x 100 Metres Relay (1 Jun)
1. Ukraine 38.53
2. Italy 38.66
3 GREAT BRITAIN 38.67
(WILLIAMS, BRAITHWAITE, JOHN, CAMPBELL)
4. Germany 38.78
5. Russia 38.94
6. Sweden 39.06
7. Spain 39.13
Finland & France dsq

4 x 400 Metres Relay (2 Jun)
1 GREAT BRITIAN 3:03.38
(RICHARDSON, BAULCH, HYLTON, LADEJO)
2. Germany 3:03.53
3. France 3:05.05
4. Russia 3:05.80
5. Ukraine 3:09.46
6. Spain 3:09.86
7. Sweden 3:09.91
8. Italy 3:10.69
9. Finland 3:14.15

Match Result
1. Germany 142
2. GREAT BRITAIN & NI 125
3. Italy 110
4. Spain 106
5. Russia 103
6. France 93.5
7. Ukraine 84
8. Sweden 75.5
9. Finland 53

WOMEN

100 Metres wind 0.3 (1 Jun)
1.	Marina Trandenkova	RUS	11.14
2.	Melanie Paschke	GER	11.19
3.	Irina Pukha	UKR	11.25
4.	Odiah Sidibe	FRA	11.39
5.	Nora Ivanova	BUL	11.39
6.	Natalya Safronnikova	BLR	11.44
7.	SIMMONE JACOBS		11.51
8.	Cristina Castro	ESP	11.95

200 Metres wind 1.6 (2 Jun)
1.	Marie-Jose Perec	FRA	22.34
2.	Melanie Paschke	GER	22.55
3.	KATHARINE MERRY		22.88
4.	Monika Gatchevska	BUL	22.99
5.	Natalya Safronnikova	BLR	23.04
6.	Sandra Myers	ESP	23.17
7.	Oksana Dyachenko	RUS	23.43
8.	Oksara Guskova	UKR	24.11

400 Metres (1 Jun)
1.	Grit Breuer	GER	50.22
2.	Anna Kozak	BLR	50.94
3.	Sandra Myers	ESP	51.10
4.	Olga Kotlyarova	RUS	51.67
5.	Tatyana Movchan	UKR	52.03
6.	Marie-louise Bevis	GER	52.07
7.	DONNA FRASER		52.37
8.	Rosita Milenova	BUL	55.22

800 Metres (1 Jun)
1.	Svetlana Masterkova	RUS	1:57.87
2.	KELLY HOLMES		1:58.20
3.	Natalya Dukhnova	BLR	1:59.70
4.	Yelena Buzhenko	UKR	2:00.03
5.	Patricia Djate	FRA	2:00.34
6.	Linda Kisabaka	GER	2:00.42
7.	Anna Menendez	ESP	2:01.71
8.	Petya Strashilova	BUL	2:04.63

1500 Metres (2 Jun)
1.	Olga Churbanova	RUS	4:09.57
2.	Sylvia Kuhnemund	GER	4:10.22
3.	Frederique Quentin	FRA	4:10.49
4.	Yelena Bychkovskaya	BLR	4:12.67
5.	Olga Zheleva	BUL	4:12.99
6.	Natalya Chernychova	UKR	4:14.54
7	ANGELA DAVIES		4:14.66
8.	Mayte Zuniga	ESP	4:17.26

3000 Metres (2 Jun)
1.	Blandine Bitzner	FRA	8:59.82
2.	Petra Wassiluk	GER	9:02.91
3.	Marta Dominguez	ESP	9:06.27
4.	Svetlana Miroshink	UKR	9:08.33
5.	SONIA McGEORGE		9:09.53
6.	Tatyana Nefedieva	BLR	9:20.33
7.	Lidia Vasilevskaya	RUS	9:23.35
8.	Evelina Danailova	BUL	9:26.54

5000 Metres (1 Jun)
1.	Kathrin Wesel	GER	15:40.36
2.	Julia Vaquero	ESP	15:41.99
3.	Farida Fates	FRA	15:47.72
4.	Yelena Vyazova	UKR	15:52.45
5.	Lyudmila Petrova	RUS	16:11.08
6.	Natalya Galaushko	BLR	16:18.05
7.	ANDREA WHITCOMBE		16:41.66
8.	Radka Naplatanova	BUL	16:42.09

100 Metres Hurdles 2.7 (2 Jun)
1.	Nadezhda Bodrova	UKR	12.89w
2.	Lidia Yurkova	BLR	12.99w
3.	ANGELA THORP		13.09w
4.	Gaby Roth	GER	13.09w
5.	Cecile Cinelu	FRA	13.12w
6.	Marina Azyabina	RUS	13.23w
7.	Maria-J Mardomingo	ESP	13.40w
8.	Yurka Christova	BUL	13.66w

400 Metres Hurdles (1 Jun)
1.	SALLY GUNNELL		56.84
2.	Silvia Rieger	GER	57.07
3.	Nelli Voronkova	BLR	57.39
4.	Tatyana Tereshchuk	UKR	57.47
5.	Maria Alonso	ESP	58.94
6.	Svetlana Starkova	RUS	59.56
7.	Carole Nelson	FRA	59.85
8.	Eliza Todorova	BUL	63.47

High Jump (2 Jun)
1.	Alina Astafei	GER	1.98
2.	Stefka Kostadinova	BUL	1.94
3.	Yelena Topchina	RUS	1.90
4=	Irina Mikhalchenko	UKR	1.87
4=	Tatyana Krahmova	BLR	1.87
4=	Isabelle Jeanne	FRA	1.87
7.	LEA HAGGETT		1.84
8.	Carlota Castrejana	ESP	1.81

Long Jump (2 Jun)
1.	Iva Prandjeva	BUL	6.84
2.	Yelena Sinchukova	RUS	6.81
3.	Claudia Gerhardt	GER	6.76
4.	DENISE LEWIS		6.66
5.	Yelena Khlopotnova	UKR	6.64
6.	Larisa Kuchinskaya	BLS	6.44
7.	Nadine Caster	FRA	6.36
8.	Imma Clopes	ESP	6.00

Triple Jump (1 Jun)
1.	ASHIA HANSEN		14.57
2.	Yelena Govorova	UKR	14.42
3.	Lyudmila Dubkova	RUS	14.14
4.	Petra Lobinger	GER	14.13
5.	Zhanna Gureyeva	BLR	13.74
6.	Concepcion Paredes	ESP	13.74
7.	Iva Prandjeva	BUL	13.60
8.	Sylvie Borda	FRA	13.49

Shot (2 Jun)
1.	Astrid Kumbernuss	GER	20.05
2	JUDY OAKES		19.00
3.	Svetlana Krivelyova	RUS	17.70
4.	Margarita Ramos	ESP	17.30
5.	Tatyana Khorkhulyova	BLR	17.02
6.	Valentina Fedyushina	UKR	16.90
7.	Laurence Manfredi	FRA	16.53
8.	Atanaska Angelova	BUL	15.64

Discus (1 Jun)
1.	Ilke Wyludda	GER	65.66
2.	Olga Chernyavskaya	RUS	65.06
3.	Irina Yatchenko	BLR	60.68
4.	Isabelle Devaluez	FRA	57.80
5.	Atanaska Angelova	BUL	57.16
6.	Viktoria Boyko	UKR	55.36
7.	Amgeles Barreiro	ESP	51.10
8.	DEBBIE CALLAWAY		50.86

Javelin (2 Jun)
1.	Oksana Ovchinnikova	RUS	65.72
2.	Natalya Shikolenko	BLR	62.52
3.	Tanja Damaske	GER	58.80
4.	TESSA SANDERSON		58.18
5.	Nadine Auzell	FRA	57.28
6.	Olga Ivankova	UKR	57.18
7.	Marta Miguez	ESP	50.52
8.	Ywka Christova	BUL	36.52

4 x 100 Metres Relay (1 Jun)
1.	Russia	42.55
2.	Germany	42.59
3.	France	43.13
4.	Ukraine	43.34
5.	Belarus	43.62
6.	Bulgaria	43.76
7.	GREAT BRITAIN	44.07
	(SMITH, THOMAS, JACOBS, MURPHY)	
8.	Spain	44.48

4 x 400 Metres Relay (2 Jun)
1.	Germany	3:26.19
2.	Ukraine	3:27.74
3.	Russia	3:28.54
4.	France	3:28.97
5.	GREAT BRITAIN	3:31.80
	(FRASER, CURBISHLEY, JOSEPH, GUNNELL)	
6.	Belarus	3:36.24
7.	Spain	3:39.51
8.	Bulgaria	3:50.45

Match Result
1.	Germany	115
2.	Russia	97
3.	Belarus	79
4.	Ukraine	78
5.	France	75
6.	GREAT BRITAIN & NI	73
7.	Spain	49
8.	Bulgaria	46

EST v Eng v POL v LAT v FIN v FLA Tallinn, Estonia 9 June 1996

MEN

100 Metres wind 0.0
1. Erik Wymeersch FLA 10.23
2. DARREN BRAITHWAITE 10.31

200 Metres wind 0.6
1. E Wymeersch FLA 20.42
2. DOUGLAS TURNER gst 20.43
3. SOLOMON WARISO 20.64

400 Metres
1. IWAN THOMAS gst 45.35
2. DAVID NOLAN 46.20
4. TIMOTHY O'DELL gst 46.81

800 Metres
1. CURTIS ROBB 1:45.73
2. Hezekiel Sepeng gst/RSA 1:45.86
3. DAVID STRANG gst 1:46.36
4. TERRY WEST gst 1:47.72

WOMEN

100 Metres wind 1.2
1. PAULA THOMAS 11.51
2. Anna Leszczynska POL 11.74
3. CATHERINE MURPHY gst 11.81

200 Metres wind 0.1
1. PAULA THOMAS 23.41
2. CATHERINE MURPHY gst 23.57

400 Metres
1. Tatyana Chebykina RUS 52.05
2. LINDA STAINES 53.41

Match Result

1500 Metres
1. Shane Healy IRL 3:40.85
2. Luc Bernaert FLA 3:47.23
4. DAVID ROBERTSON 3:47.68

110 Metres Hurdles wind 0.6
1. Krzysztof Mehlich POL 13.40
2. Yevgeniy Pechonkin RUS 13.47
4. NEIL OWEN 13.62

400 Metres Hurdles
1. Herbert Llewellyn gst/RSA 49.54
2. Pavel Januszewski POL 49.74
3. CHRIS RAWLINSON 50.36

High Jump
1. Ramon Kaju EST 2.13
2. Steiner Grini NOR 2.10

800 Metres
1. JEINA MITCHELL 2:05.12
5. VICKY STERNE gst 2:05.71

100 Metres Hurdles wind -0.1
1. Svetlana Laukhova RUS 13.09
2. Aneta Sosnowska POL 13.29
3. DIANE ALLAHGREEN 13.43

400 Metres Hurdles
1. Lana Jekabsone LAT 55.46
2. LOUISE FRASER 56.67

1. ENGLAND 98
2. Poland 88
3. Latvia 60

Pole Vault
1. Aleksandrs Obizhajevs LAT 5.50
2. PAUL WILLIAMSON 5.40

Long Jump
1. Dariusz Bontruk POL 7.60
2. NATHAN MORGAN 7.58

Shot
1. Ants Kiisa EST 18.43
2. A Lukasenko LAT 18.11

Javelin
1. Jari Hartikainen FIN 78.30
2. Heiko Väät EST 72.30

High Jump
1. DEBBI MARTI 1.94
2. Donata Wawrzyniak POL 1.89

Triple Jump
1. Heli koivula FIN 13.74
2. CONNIE HENRY 12.95
7. RACHEL KIRBY 12.92

Discus
1. Ellina Zvereva gst/BLR 66.00
4. TRACY AXTEN 52.64

4. Finland 56
5. Estonia 56
6. Flanders 52

FRA v GB v GER v RUS Multi Events Narbonne, France 27 - 28 July 1996

MEN DECATHLON

Under 20
1. Aleksandr Chtepa RUS 7075
2. Pierre Friteyre FRA 7021
6. LEO BARKER 6617
10. DAVID RALSON 5503
dnf DEAN MACEY 2110

Under 23
1. Aleksandr Averbukh RUS 7548
2. Axel Sacharowitz GER 7499
8. MARK BUSHELL 6798
10. BRETT HEATH 6498
dnf PAUL HOURIHAN 2412

Senior
1. Gerald Bayer GER 7688
2. Stefan Diebler GER 7558
3. Wilfrid Boulineau FRA 7497
7. WILLIAM GILLES 6749
8. ROGER HUNTER 6546
9. TONY SOUTHWARD 6386

WOMEN HEPTATHLON

Under 20
1. Yelizaveta Shalygina RUS 5778
2. Natalya Rashchupkina RUS 5767
6. NICOLA GAUTIER 5213
9. REBECCA LEWIS 5047
dnf ANGELA NYHAM

Under 23
1. Karin Specht GER 5705
2. Sophie Mépoint FRA 5502
9. LOUISE BATHO 5072
11. ANNE HOLLMAN 4948
dnf DIANA BENNETT 4136

Senior
1. Marie Collonvillé FRA 5939
2. Anne-Sophie Devillier FRA 5916
3. Astrid Retzke GER 5879
6. KERRY JURY 5642
9. JULIA BENNETT 5251
10. PAULINE RICHARDS 5217

Match Result MEN
1. Germany 43514
2. Russia 43480
3. France 42727
4. GREAT BRITAIN 38761

Match Result WOMEN
1. Russia 33281
2. France 33115
3. Germany 31173
4. GREAT BRITAIN 31173

Match Result Overall
1. Russia 76761
2. Germany 76259
3. France 75842
4. GREAT BRITAIN 69934

Olympic Trials/AAA CHAMPIONSHIPS Birmingham 14 - 16 June 1996

MEN

100 Metres wind 0.1 (15 Jun)
1.	LINFORD CHRISTIE	10.04
2.	DARREN BRAITHWAITE	10.25
3.	IAN MACKIE	10.26
4=	DARREN CAMPBELL	10.30
4=	JASON JOHN	10.30
6.	MICHAEL ROSSWESS	10.38
7.	ALLYN CONDON	10.43
8.	DWAIN CHAMBERS	10.49

200 Metres wind -0.5 (16 Jun)
1.	JOHN REGIS	20.54
2.	LINFORD CHRISTIE	20.54
3.	OWUSU DAKO	20.72
4.	DOUG TURNER	20.77
5.	DOUG WALKER	20.90
6.	JASON JOHN	21.00
7.	SOLOMON WARISO	21.04
8.	JULIAN GOLDING	21.20

400 Metres (16 Jun)
1.	ROGER BLACK	44.39
2.	DU'AINE LADEJO	44.66
3.	IWAN THOMAS	44.69
4.	JAMIE BAULCH	44.72
5.	MARK RICHARDSON	45.33
6.	MARK HYLTON	45.57
7.	GUY BULLOCK	45.76
8.	ADRIAN PATRICK	46.06

800 Metres (16 Jun)
1.	CURTIS ROBB	1:47.61
2.	DAVID STRANG	1:47.74
3.	TONY MORRELL	1:47.94
4.	ANDY HART	1:48.13
5.	CRAIG WINROW	1:48.67
6.	LEE CADWALLADER	1:49.15
7.	BRADLEY DONKIN	1:49.43
8.	GRANT GRAHAM	1:49.45

1500 Metres (16 Jun)
1.	JOHN MAYOCK	3:37.03
2.	ANTHONY WHITEMAN	3:37.19
3.	KEVIN MCKAY	3:37.90
4.	GARY LOUGH	3:39.18
5.	GLEN STEWART	3:41.12
6.	IAN GRIME	3:41.32
7.	STEPHEN GREEN	3:42.01
8.	NICK COMERFORD	3:42.20
9.	STUART MARGIOTTA	3:43.27
10.	RICHARD ASHE	3:43.54

5000 Metres (16 Jun)
1.	JOHN NUTTALL	13:48.35
2.	ROB DENMARK	13:51.72
3.	DARRIUS BURROWS	13:54.42
4.	KRIS BOWDITCH	13:55.32
5.	SPENCER BARDEN	13:56.20
6.	IAN GILLESPIE	14:00.06
7.	IAN HUDSPITH	14:00.98
8.	ROBERT WHALLEY	14:11.58
9.	ADRIAN PASSEY	14:16.92
10.	DAVID MILES	14:17.63

10000 Metres (14 Jun)
1.	ROB DENMARK	28:20.80
2.	JONATHON BROWN	28:21.40
3.	PAUL EVANS	28:28.31
4.	CHRIS SWEENEY	28:44.09
5.	IAN ROBINSON	28:46.06
6.	DERMOT DONNELLY	28:47.90
7.	STEVEN BROOKS	28:55.38
8.	ANDREW PEARSON	29:01.05
9.	IAN CORNFORD	29:08.66

3000 Metres Steeplechase (16 Jun)
1.	JUSTIN CHASTON	8:29.19
2.	KEITH CULLEN	8:30.80
3.	SPENCER DUVAL	8:36.71
4.	MICHAEL HAWKINS	8:41.54
5.	ROB HOUGH	8:43.30
6.	MATTHEW O'DOWD	8:44.26
7.	SPENCER NEWPORT	8:46.51
8.	ADRIAN GREEN	8:50.57
9.	LEE HURST	8:52.99

110 Metres Hurdles -0.1 (15 Jun)
1.	COLIN JACKSON	13.13
2.	TONY JARRETT	13.41
3.	ANDY TULLOCH	13.70
4.	PAUL GRAY	13.70
5.	NEIL OWEN	13.72
6.	KEN CAMPBELL	14.01
7.	MARK STERN	14.33
8.	MARTIN NICHOLSON	14.60

400 Metres Hurdles (16 Jun)
1.	JON RIDGEON	49.16
2.	PETER CRAMPTON	49.79
3.	GARY JENNINGS	50.46
4.	PAUL HIBBERT	50.67
5.	LAWRENCE LYNCH	50.75
6.	CHRIS RAWLINSON	51.43
7.	DAVID SAVAGE	51.89
	NOEL LEVY	dnf

High Jump (16 Jun)
1.	STEPHEN SMITH	2.31
2.	DALTON GRANT	2.27
3.	COLIN BENT	2.20
4.	GEOFF PARSONS	2.15
5.	ROB BROCKLEBANK	2.15
6.	IAN HOLLIDAY	2.10
7.	DARREN JOSEPH	2.10
8=	RICHARD ASPDEN	2.05
8=	TONY GILHOOLY	2.05
8=	MARK LATHAM	2.05

Pole Vault (16 Jun)
1.	NICK BUCKFIELD	5.71
2.	NEIL WINTER	5.40
3.	MIKE EDWARDS	5.30
4.	IAN TULLETT	5.30
5.	KEVIN HUGHES	5.30
6=	MIKE BARBER	5.30
6=	PAUL WILLIAMSON	5.30
8.	MATT BELSHAM	5.30

Long Jump (15 Jun)
1.	DARREN RITCHIE	7.86
2.	ONOCHIE ONUORAH	7.67
3.	STEWART FAULKNER	7.47
4.	JULIAN FLYNN	7.31
5.	STEVE PHILLIPS	7.31
6.	NATHAN MORGAN	7.25
7.	CARL HOWARD	7.23
8.	BARRINGTON WILLIAMS	7.19

Triple Jump (15 Jun)
1.	FRANCIS AGYEPONG	17.12
2.	FEMI AKINSANYA	16.58
3.	JULIAN GOLLEY	16.39
4.	TOSI FASINRO	16.38
5.	ONOCHIE ACHIKE	16.36
6.	JOHN HERBERT	15.86
7.	PAUL RALPH	15.55
8.	TAYO EROGBOGBO	15.45

Shot (15 Jun)
1.	MATTHEW SIMSON	18.82
2.	SEAN PICKERING	18.63
3.	MARK PROCTOR	17.91
4.	LEE NEWMAN	17.51
5.	STEPHAN HAYWARD	17.46
6.	JAMIE COCKBURN	16.83
7.	DAVID CALLAWAY	16.20
8.	ROBERT RUSSELL	16.10
9.	STEVE WHYTE	15.72

Discus (15 Jun)
1.	ROB WEIR	60.02
2.	SIMON WILLIAMS	57.54
3.	KEVIN BROWN	56.76
4.	GARY HERRINGTON	56.66
5.	GLEN SMITH	54.58
6.	LEITH MARAR	53.96
7.	NEVILLE THOMPSON	51.92
8.	ROBERT RUSSELL	51.64
9.	PAUL REED	49.68

Hammer (16 Jun)
1.	DAVE SMITH	72.58
2.	PAUL HEAD	71.48
3.	MICHAEL JONES	71.22
4.	PETER VIVIAN	67.56
5.	JOHN PEARSON	63.56
6.	STEPHEN PEARSON	62.86
7.	SHANE PEACOCK	61.86
8.	IAIN PARK	60.78

Javelin (15 Jun)
1.	NICK NIELAND	83.06
2.	MICK HILL	81.42
3.	COLIN MACKENZIE	78.74
4.	NIGEL BEVAN	73.54
5.	MARK ROBERTSON	73.46
6.	PETER YATES	65.62
7.	DAVID PARKER	64.90
8.	STEWART MCMILLAN	64.02
9.	RICHARD HOOPER	63.64

10000 Metres Walk (15Jun)
1. STEVE PARTINGTON   42:29.73
2. CHRIS CHEESEMAN   44:07.95
3. RICHARD OLDALE   44:15.75
4. MARTIN YOUNG   44:59.98
5. JAMIE O'RANE   45:09.42
6. ANDY O'RAWE   46:41.43
7. KARL ATTON   47:23.29
8. ALLAN KING   47:23.42

WOMEN
100 Metres wind -1.1 (15 Jun)
1. STEPHANIE DOUGLAS   11.55
2. SIMMONE JACOBS   11.57
3. MARCIA RICHARDSON   11.66
4. PAULA THOMAS   11.69
5. BEV KINCH   11.72
6. SOPHIA SMITH   11.86
7. CHRISTINE BLOOMFIELD 11.97
8. SHANI ANDERSON   11.99

200 Metres wind -0.2 (16 Jun)
1. SIMMONE JACOBS   23.11
2. KATHARINE MERRY   23.30
3. PAULA THOMAS   23.46
4. CATHERINE MURPHY   23.52
5. TRACY JOSEPH   23.72
6. JENNIFER STOUTE   23.75
7. JOICE MADUAKA   23.90
8. ALISON DAVIES   24.15

400 Metres (16 Jun)
1. PHYLIS SMITH   51.74
2. GEORGINA OLADAPO   52.48
3. ALLISON CURBISHLEY 52.76
4. DONNA FRASER   52.88
5. LINDA STAINES   52.92
6. MICHELLE PIERRE   53.22
7. MELANIE NEEF   53.23
8. SHARON TUNALEY   54.00

800 Metres (15 Jun)
1. KELLY HOLMES   1:57.84
2. DIANE MODAHL   1:59.87
3. NATALIE TAIT   2:02.76
4. SONYA BOWYER   2:02.85
5. VICKIE LAWRENCE   2:03.52
6. HAYLEY PARRY   2:04.17
7. JEINA MITCHELL   2:05.76
8. CLAIRE RAVEN   2:11.15

1500 Metres (16 Jun)
1. KELLY HOLMES   4:08.14
2. SUE PARKER   4:13.02
3. MICHELLE FAHERTY   4:14.19
4. ANGELA DAVIES   4:14.67
5. SHIRLEY GRIFFITHS   4:15.68
6. LYNN GIBSON   4:16.31
7. HELEN PATTINSON   4:16.84
8. LYNNE MACDOUGALL   4:17.10

5000 Metres (16 Jun)
1. PAULA RADCLIFFE   15:28.46
2. SONIA MCGEORGE   15:48.33
3. ALISON WYETH   15:48.91
4. ANDREA WHITCOMBE   16:03.40
5. SARAH BENTLEY   16:23.86

6. WENDY ORE   16:25.79
7. HAYLEY YELLING   16:41.55
8. ZAHARA HYDE   16:43.89

10000 Metres (14 Jun)
1. LOUISE WATSON   33:21.46
2. ANGIE HULLEY   33:33.37
3. VIKKI MCPHERSON   33:53.17
4. ANGHARAD MAIR   34:11.76
5. J THOMPSON   34:30.52
6. ALISON ROSE   34:44.89
7. JULIE COLEBY   35:18.43
8. SALLY LYNCH   35:54.43

100 Metres Hurdles -2.3 (16 Jun)
1. ANGELA THORP   13.26
2. DIANE ALLAHGREEN   13.27
3. DENISE LEWIS   13.41
4. MELANIE WILKINS   13.51
5. KERI MADDOX   13.60
6. JANE HALE   13.86
7. NATASHA DANVERS   14.00
8. KATY SKETCHLEY   14.16

400 Metres Hurdles (16 Jun)
1. SALLY GUNNELL   54.65
2. ALYSON LAYZELL   56.43
3. LOUISE FRASER   56.45
4. LOUISE BRUNNING   56.61
5. LORRAINE HANSON   57.13
6. GOWRY RETCHAKAN   57.85
7. VICKI JAMISON   59.15
8. SINEAD DUDGEON   60.48

High Jump (15 Jun)
1. DEBBI MARTI   1.94
2. LEA HAGGETT   1.92
3. JO JENNINGS   1.89
4= SUSAN JONES   1.80
4= HAZEL MELVIN   1.80
6= ALISON EVANS   1.75
6= KELLY THIRKLE   1.75
8. JULIE MAJOR   1.75

Pole Vault (15 Jun)
1. KATE STAPLES   3.80
2. JANINE WHITLOCK   3.70
3. LINDA STANTON   3.50
4. LOUISE SCHRAMM   3.50
5. RHIAN CLARKE   3.40
6= CLAIRE ADAMS   3.30
6= EMMA HORNBY   3.30
8. KATE ALEXANDER   3.10

Bedford 25 - 26 May
MEN

Decathlon
1. BARRY THOMAS   7701
2. BRIAN TAYLOR   7573
3. ANTHONY SOUTHWARD   7400
4. RAFER JOSEPH   7174
5. STEPHEN ROGERS   7150
6. WILLIAM GILLES   6800
7. MARK BUSHELL   6455
8. ADRIAN FERRAND   6437

Long Jump (16 Jun)
1. DENISE LEWIS   6.55
2. JOANNE WISE   6.42
3. ASHIA HANSEN   6.09
4. ANN BROOKS   6.08
5. ANDREA CORRE   6.03
6. RUTH IRVING   6.00
7. JADE JOHNSON   5.98

Triple Jump (16 Jun)
1. ASHIA HANSEN   14.25
2. MICHELLE GRIFFITH   13.78
3. CONNIE HENRY   13.18
4. RACHEL KIRBY   12.89
5. SHANI ANDERSON   12.84
6. MARY AGYEPONG   12.72

Shot (16 Jun)
1. JUDY OAKES   18.65
2. MYRTLE AUGEE   16.81
3. SHARON ANDREWS   14.83
4. ALISON GREY   14.66
5. CHARMAINE JOHNSON   13.79
6. JOANNE DUNCAN   13.72

Discus (15 Jun)
1. JACQUELINE MCKERNAN 54.12
2. SHELLEY DREW   53.68
3. DEBORAH CALLAWAY   52.52
4. TRACY AXTEN   51.42
5. SHARON ANDREWS   49.70
6. NICOLA TALBOT   49.10

Hammer (15 Jun)
1. LYN SPRULES   54.16
2. ANN GARDNER   51.58
3. DIANA HOLDEN   51.52
4. SARAH MOORE   50.34
5. HELEN MCCREADIE   47.92
6. IRENE DUFFIN   47.18

Javelin (16 Jul)
1. TESSA SANDERSON   62.88
2. SHELLEY HOLROYD   60.12
3. LORNA JACKSON   58.20
4. SHARON GIBSON   56.10
5. NOELLE BRADSHAW   46.56
6. ONYEMA AMADI   46.18

5000 Metres Walk (15 Jun)
1. VICTORIA LUPTON   23:04.57
2. MELANIE WRIGHT   24:36.65
3. CATHERINE CHARNOCK 25:00.22
4. BRENDA LUPTON   25:28.26
5. ELIZABETH CORRAN   25:52.99

WOMEN

Heptathlon
1. KERRY JURY   5703
2. PAULINE RICHARDS   5386
3. JULIA BENNETT   5356
4. DIANNA BENNETT   5332
5. TRACY JOSEPH   5280
6. ANNE HOLLMAN   5258
7. KIM CROWTHER   5025
8. KELLY SOTHERTON   4930

GB v GER v RUS U23 Hexham 14 July 1996

MEN

100 Metres wind -2.3
1. Demin Konstantin RUS 10.85
2. Christian Schacht GER 10.91
3. ALLYN CONDON 10.93
4. DANNY JOYCE 10.93

200 Metres wind -1.0
1. JULIAN GOLDING 21.20
2. ALLYN CONDON 21.21

400 Metres
1. GUY BULLOCK 46.07
2. JARED DEACON 46.78

800 Metres
1. EDDIE KING 1:53.62
2. Thomas Bobbert GER 1:53.92
4. JUSTIN SWIFT-SMITH 1:54.88

1500 Metres
1. NEIL CADDY 3:45.29
2. RICHARD ASHE 3:46.35

3000 Metres
1. DARIUS BURROWS 8:06.93
2. KRISTEN BOWDITCH 8:09.29

3000 Metres Steeplechase
1. Konstantin Tomskiy RUS 8:55.19
2. Aleksey Rudenko RUS 8:59.55
3. MATTHEW O'DOWD 9:00.41
5. DARREN PRESTON 9:20.16

110 Metres Hurdles wind 0.0
1. Sven Gohler GER 14.18
2. Andrey Kislykh RUS 14.26
3. JAMES ARCHAMPONG 14.54
5. SIMON McAREE 14.79

400 Metres Hurdles
1. Sven Timmerman GER 51.38
2. Diemand Markus GER 51.51
3. NOEL LEVY 51.55
4. BARRY MIDDLETON 51.77

High Jump
1. Vyacheslav Voronin RUS 2.29
2. Martin Buss GER 2.26
5. RICHARD ASPDEN 2.10
6. ROBERT BROCKLEBANK 2.10

Pole Vault
1. Vevgeniy Smiryagin RUS 5.60
2. Pavel Burlachenko RUS 5.40
3. IAN WILDING 4.80

Long Jump
1. Vyacheslav Taranov RUS 7.67
2. Michael Hesser GER 7.52
3. CHRIS DAVIDSON 7.50
5. DARREN RITCHIE 7.30

Triple Jump
1. Igor Gavrilenko RUS 16.26
2. Vyacheslav Taranov RUS 16.08
3. CARL HOWARD 15.67
4. EZRA CLARKE 15.52

Shot
1. Andy Dittmar GER 18.62
2. René Sack GER 18.27
3. STEPHAN HAYWARD 18.07
6. ROBERT RUSSELL 16.77

Discus
1. Tolga Köseoglu GER 63.36
2. Marko Jacobs GER 58.98
4. ROBERT RUSSELL 49.38
6. JAMES SOUTH 48.04

Hammer
1. DAVID SMITH 73.22
2. Konstantin Balandin RUS 69.28
4. IAIN PARK 61.12

Javelin
1. Christian Nicolay GER 71.64
2. Vladimir Tshizhov RUS 70.28
5. DUNCAN MACDONALD 58.44

5000 Metres Walk
1. Vladimir Stankin RUS 19:49.71
2. Dimitriy Yesipchuk RUS 19:59.07
5. PHILIP KING 21:58.57
6. DAVID KEOWN 22:47.37

4 x 100 Metres Relay
1. Germany 40.71
2. GREAT BRITAIN 40.75
3. Russia 40.99

4 x 400 Metres Relay
1. GREAT BRITAIN 3:06.66
2. Germany 3:11.23
3. Russia 3:14.76

Match Result
1. Russia 136
2. GREAT BRITAIN 133
3. Germany 127

WOMEN

100 Metres wind -1.8
1. SOPHIA SMITH 11.84
2. Oksana Dyachenko RUS 11.89
4. ELLENA RUDDOCK 12.03

200 Metres wind -1.0
1. CATHERINE MURPHY 24.20
2. Shanta Gosh GER 24.33
5. LOUISE WHITEHEAD 24.95

400 Metres
1. Natalya Chevtsova RUS 53.83
2. Sonya Wilmsmeyer GER 53.97
5. LISA VANNET 54.54
6. HELEN FROST 55.22

800 Metres
1. Simone Buetelsbache GER 2:06.04
2. JEINA MITCHELL 2:06.06
5. SARAH BULL 2:09.82

1500 Metres
1. Oksana Jelezniak RUS 4:23.31
2. Tatyana Tomachova RUS 4:23.48
4. HELEN PATTINSON 4:27.25
6. RHONDA MACPHEE 4:31.73

3000 Metres
1. Ludmila Biktasheva RUS 9:28.46
2. SARAH SALMON 9:40.87
4. HAYLEY YELLING 9:53.71

100 Metres Hurdles wind 0.0
1. DIANE ALLAHGREEN 13.66
2. Regina Ahlke GER 13.88
4. JANE HALE 14.30

400 Metres Hurdles
1. Anja Hocke GER 57.44
2. Anastassia Lemekhov RUS 59.34
4. SINEAD DUDGEON 60.33
5. KATHY THURSTON 60.60

High Jump
1. Svetlana Lapina RUS 1.89
2. Olga Kuznetsenkova RUS 1.86
4. DIANA BENNETT 1.70
6. SARA VEEVERS 1.70

Pole vault
1. Andrea Müller GER 4.00
2. Nastja Ryshich GER 4.00
4= KATIE ALEXANDER 3.10
6. DAWN ALICE WRIGHT 2.90

Long Jump
1. Stephane Hort GER 6.41
2. Anna Mironoya RUS 6.30
4. RUTH IRVING 5.92
6. ANNE HOLLMAN 5.42

Triple Jump
1. Marina Goryatcheva RUS 13.61
2. Nicole Herschmann GER 13.19
5. KATIE EVANS 12.36
6. KERENSA DENHAM 11.99

Shot
1. Claudia Mues GER 18.08
2. Nadine Kleinert GER 17.78
5. ELEANOR GATRELL 13.05
6. EMMA MERRY 12.53

Discus
1. Sabine Sievers GER 56.90
2. Kathleen Hering GER 54.48
4. EMMA MERRY 47.74
6. KAREN SMITH 40.86

Hammer
1. Simone Mathes GER 59.46
2. LYN SPRULES 59.18
6. DIANA HOLDEN 50.84

Javelin
1. Oksana Dudlina RUS 53.22
2. KAREN MARTIN 51.48
3. LORNA JACKSON 48.78

3000 Metres Walk
1. Natalia Trofimova RUS 12:33.58
2. Yelena Belyakova RUS 13:02.65
5. CATHERINE CHARNOCK 14:22.51
6. KATHERINE HORWILL 14:52.78

4 x 100 Metres Relay
1. GREAT BRITAIN 44.99
(ALLAHGREEN, MURPHY, SMITH, WHITEHEAD)
2. Germany 45.05
3. Russia 45.68

4 x 400 Metres Relay
1. Germany 3:36.99
2. Russia 3:38.59
3. GREAT BRITAIN 3:44.84

Match Result
1. Germany 160
2. Russia 134.5
3. GREAT BRITAIN 103.5

Overall Match Result
1. Germany 287
2. Russia 270.5
3. GREAT BRITAIN 236.5

OLYMPIC GAMES Atlanta, USA 16 July - 4 August 1996

MEN
100 Metres wind 0.7 (27 Jul)
1. Donovan Bailey CAN 9.84
2. Frank Fredericks NAM 9.89
3. Ato Boldon TRI 9.90
4. Dennis Mitchell USA 9.99
5. Michael Marsh USA 10.00
6. Davidson Ezinwa NGR 10.14
7. Michael Green JAM 10.16
dq LINFORD CHRISTIE

s2 IAN MACKIE dns
6q3 DARREN BRAITHWAITE 10.27

200 Metres wind 0.4 (1 Aug)
1. Michael Johnson USA 19.32
2. Frank Fredericks NAM 19.68
3. Ato Boldon TRI 19.80
4. Obadele Thompson BAR 20.14
5. Jeff Williams USA 20.17
6. Ivan Garcia CUB 20.21
7. Patrick Stevens BEL 20.27
8. Michael Marsh USA 20.48

6s1 JOHN REGIS 20.58
4q5 LINFORD CHRISTIE 20.59
4h2 OWUSU DAKO 20.83

400 Metres (29 Jul)
1. Michael Johnson USA 43.49
2. ROGER BLACK 44.41
3. Davis Kamoga UGA 44.53
4. Alvin Harrison USA 44.62
5. IWAN THOMAS 44.70
6. Roxbert Martin JAM 44.83
7. Davian Clarke JAM 44.99
dnf Ibrahim Ismail QAT

6q3 DU'AINE LADEJO 45.62

800 Metres (31 Jul)
1. Vebjorn Rodal NOR 1:42.58
2. Hezekiel Sepeng RSA 1:42.74
3. Fred Onyancha KEN 1:42.79
4. Norberto Tellez CUB 1:42.85
5. Nico Motchebon GER 1:43.91
6. David Kiptoo KEN 1:44.19
7. Johnny Gray USA 1:44.21
8. Benyounes Lahlou MAR 1:45.52

6s2 CURTIS ROBB 1:47.48
8s1 CRAIG WINROW 1:48.57
4h6 DAVID STRANG 1:47.96

1500 Metres (3 Aug)
1. Noureddine Morceli ALG 3:35.78
2. Fermin Cacho ESP 3:36.40
3. Stephen Kipkorir KEN 3:36.72
4. Laban Rotich KEN 3:37.39
5. William Tanui KEN 3:37.42
6. Abdi Bile SOM 3:38.03
7. Marko Koers NED 3:38.18
8. Ali Hakimi TUN 3:38.19
9. Mohamed Suleiman QAT 3:38.26
10. Driss Maazouzi MAR 3:39.65
11. JOHN MAYOCK 3:40.18
12. Hicham El Guerrouj MAR 3:40.78

7s2 ANTHONY WHITEMAN 3:36.11
12s2 KEVIN MCKAY 3:43.61

5000 Metres (3 Aug)
1. Venuste Niyongabo BUR 13:07.96
2. Paul Bitok KEN 13:08.16
3. Khalid Boulami MAR 13:08.37
4. Dieter Baumann GER 13:08.81
5. Thomas Nyariki KEN 13:12.29
6. Bob Kennedy USA 13:12.35
7. Enrique Molina ESP 13:12.91
8. Brahim Lahlafi MAR 13:13.26
9. Shem Kororia KEN 13:14.63
10. Fita Bayissa ETH 13:18.30
11. Smail Sghir MAR 13:22.89
12. Gennaro Di Napoli ITA 13:28.26

9s2 JOHN NUTTALL 14:08.39

10000 Metres (29 Jul)
1. Haile Gebrselassie ETH 27:07.34
2. Paul Tergat KEN 27:08.17
3. Salah Hissou MAR 27:24.67
4. Aloys Nizigama BUR 27:33.79
5. Josephat Machuka KEN 27:35.08
6. Paul Koech KEN 27:35.19
7. Khalid Skah MAR 27:46.98
8. Mathias Ntawalikura RWA 27:50.73
9. Stephane Franke GER 27:59.08
10. JON BROWN 27:59.72
11. Armando Quintanilla MEX 28:09.46
12. Marko Hhawu TAN 28:20.58
dnf PAUL EVANS

Marathon (4 Aug)
1. Josiah Thugwane RSA 2:12:36
2. Lee Bong-ju KOR 2:12:39
3. Eric Wainaina KEN 2:12:44
4. Martin Fiz ESP 2:13:20
5. RICHARD NERURKAR 2:13:39
6. German Silva MEX 2:14:29
7. Steve Moneghetti AUS 2:14:35
8. Benjamin Paredes MEX 2:14:55
9. Danilo Goffi ITA 2:15:08
10. Luiz dos Santos BRA 2:15:55
11. Carlos Grisales COL 2:15:56
12. Kim Yi-yong KOR 2:16:17
55. PETER WHITEHEAD 2:22:37
60. STEVE BRACE 2:23:28

3000 Metres Steeplechase (2 Aug)
1. Joseph Keter KEN 8:07.12
2. Moses Kiptanui KEN 8:08.33
3. Aless. Lambruschini ITA 8:11.28
4. Matthew Birir KEN 8:17.18
5. Mark Croghan USA 8:17.84
6. Steffan Brand GER 8:18.52
7. Brahim Boulami MAR 8:23.13
8. Jim Svenoy NOR 8:23.39
9. Angelo Carosi ITA 8:29.67
10. Martin Strege GER 8:30.31
11. Hicham Bouaouiche MAR 8:46.22
12. Marc Davis USA 9:51.96
9s2 JUSTIN CHASTON 8:28.50
11s1 KEITH CULLEN 8:46.74
10h1 SPENCER DUVAL 8:42.75

110 Metres Hurdles 0.6 (29 Jul)
1. Allen Johnson USA 12.95
2. Mark Crear USA 13.09
3. Florian Schwarthoff GER 13.17
4. COLIN JACKSON 13.19
5. Emillio Valle CUB 13.20
6. Eugene Swift USA 13.23
7. Kyle Vander-Kuyp AUS 13.40
8. Erik Batte CUB 13.43

6q4 ANDY TULLOCH 13.68
q1 TONY JARRETT dsq

400 Metres Hurdles (1 Aug)
1. Derrick Adkins USA 47.54
2. Samuel Matete ZAM 47.78
3. Calvin Davis USA 47.96
4. Sven Nylander SWE 47.98
5. Rohan Robinson AUS 48.30
6. Fabrizio Mori ITA 48.41
7. Everson Teixeira BRA 48.57
8. Eronilde Araujo BRA 48.78

7s1 JON RIDGEON 49.43
6h1 PETER CRAMPTON 49.76
6h7 GARY JENNINGS 50.41

High Jump (28 Jul)

1.	Charles Austin	USA	2.39
2.	Artur Partyka	POL	2.37
3.	STEVE SMITH		2.35
4.	Dragutin Topic	YUG	2.32
5.	Steinar Hoen	NOR	2.32
6.	Lambros Papakostas	GRE	2.32
7.	Tim Forsyth	AUS	2.32
8.	Lee Jin-taek	KOR	2.29
9.	Wolfgang Kreissig	GER	2.29
10.	Przemyslaw Radkiewicz	POL	2.29
11=	Jaroslaw Kotewicz	POL	2.25
11=	Javier Sotomayor	CUB	2.25

19Q DALTON GRANT   2.26

Pole Vault (2 Aug)

1.	Jean Galfione	FRA	5.92
2.	Igor Trandenkov	RUS	5.92
3.	Andrei Tivontchik	GER	5.92
4.	Igor Potapovich	KZK	5.86
5.	Pyotr Bochkaryov	RUS	5.86
6.	Dmitriy Markov	BLR	5.86
7.	Tim Lobinger	GER	5.80
8.	Lawrence Johnson	USA	5.70
9=	Alain Andji	FRA	5.70
9=	Michael Stolle	GER	5.70
11=	Jeff Hartwig	USA	5.60
11=	Danny Krasnov	ISR	5.60

20=Q NICK BUCKFIELD   5.40
24=Q NEIL WINTER   5.40

Long Jump (29 Jul)

1.	Carl Lewis	USA	8.50
2.	James Beckford	JAM	8.29
3.	Joe Greene	USA	8.24
4.	Emmanuel Bangue	FRA	8.19
5.	Mike Powell	USA	8.17
6.	Gregor Cankar	SLO	8.11
7.	Aleksandr Glovatskiy	BLR	8.07
8.	Mattias Sunneborn	SWE	8.06
9.	Huang Geng	CHN	7.99
10.	Yuriy Naumkin	RUS	7.96
11.	Andrey Ignatov	RUS	7.83
12.	Ivan Pedroso	CUB	7.75

Triple Jump (27 Jul)

1.	Kenny Harrison	USA	18.09
2.	JONATHAN EDWARDS		17.88
3.	Yoelvis Quesada	CUB	17.44
4.	Mike Conley	USA	17.40
5.	Armen Martirosyan	ARM	16.97
6.	Brian Wellman	BER	16.95
7.	Galin Georgiev	BUL	16.92
8.	Robert Howard	USA	16.90
9.	Viktor Sotnikov	RUS	16.84
10.	Volodomyr Kravchenko	UKR	16.62
11.	Frank Rutherford	BAH	16.38

13Q FRANCIS AGYEPONG   16.71

Shot (26 Jul)

1.	Randy Barnes	USA	21.62
2.	John Godina	USA	20.79
3.	Aleksandr Bagach	UKR	20.75
4.	Paolo Dal Soglio	ITA	20.74
5.	Oliver-Sven Buder	GER	20.51

6.	Roman Virastyuk	UKR	20.45
7.	C J Hunter	USA	20.39
8.	Dragan Peric	YUG	20.07
9.	Dmitriy Goncharuk	BLR	19.79
10.	Bilal Saad Mubarak	QAT	19.33
11.	Corrado Fantini	ITA	19.30

27Q SHAUN PICKERING   18.29

Discus (31 Jul)

1.	Lars Riedel	GER	69.40
2.	Vladimir Dubrovshchik	BLR	66.60
3.	Vasiliy Kaptyukh	BLR	65.80
4.	Anthony Washington	USA	65.42
5.	Virgilijus Alekna	LIT	65.30
6.	Jurgen Schult	GER	64.62
7.	Vitaliy Sidorov	UKR	63.78
8.	Vaclovas Kidykas	LIT	62.78
9.	Alexis Elizalde	CUB	62.70
10.	Attila Horvath	HUN	62.28
11.	Sergey Lyakhov	RUS	60.62
12.	Adam Setliff	USA	56.30

15Q BOB WEIR   61.64
36Q GLEN SMITH   54.88

Hammer (28 Jul)

1.	Balazs Kiss	HUN	81.24
2.	Lance Deal	USA	81.12
3.	Aleksiy Krykun	UKR	80.02
4.	Andrey Skvaruk	UKR	79.92
5.	Heinz Weis	GER	79.78
6.	Ilya Konovalov	RUS	78.72
7.	Igor Astapkovich	BLR	78.20
8.	Sergey Alay	BLR	77.38
9.	Enrico Sgrulletti	ITA	76.98
10.	Szymon Ziolkowski	POL	76.64
11.	Raphael Piolanti	FRA	75.24
12.	Vasiliy Sidorenko	RUS	74.68

32Q DAVID SMITH   69.32

Javelin (3 Aug)

1.	Jan Zelezny	CZE	88.16
2.	STEVE BACKLEY		87.44
3.	Seppo Raty	FIN	86.98
4.	Raymond Hecht	GER	86.88
5.	Boris Henry	GER	85.68
6.	Sergey Makarov	RUS	85.30
7.	Kimmo Kinnunen	FIN	84.02
8.	TomPukstys	USA	83.58
9.	Peter Blank	GER	81.82
10.	Kostas Gatsioudis	GRE	81.46
11.	Zhang Lianbiao	CHN	80.96
12.	MICK HILL		78.58

25Q NICK NIELAND   75.74

Decathlon (31 Jul/1 Aug)

1.	Dan O'Brien	USA	8824
2.	Frank Busemann	GER	8706
3.	Tomas Dvorak	CZE	8664
4.	Steve Fritz	USA	8644
5.	Eduard Hamalaninen	BLR	8613
6.	Erki Nool	EST	8543
7.	Robert Zmelik	CZE	8422
8.	Ramil Ganiyev	UZB	8318
9.	Antonio Penalver	ESP	8307

10.	Chris Huffins	USA	8300
11.	Christian Plaziat	FRA	8282
12.	Jon Arnar Magnusson	ISL	8274

dnf ALEX KRUGER

20 Kilometres Walk (26 Jul)

1.	Jefferson Perez	ECU	1:20:07
2.	Ilya Markov	RUS	1:20:16
3.	Bernado Segura	MEX	1:20:23
4.	Nick A'Hern	AUS	1:20:31
5.	Rishat Shafikov	RUS	1:20:41
6.	Aigars Fadejevs	LAT	1:20:47
7.	Mikhail Shchennikov	RUS	1:21:09
8.	Robert Korzeniowski	POL	1:21:13
9.	Yevgeniy Misyulya	BLR	1:21:16
10.	Thierry Toutain	FRA	1:21:56
11.	Daniel Plaza	ESP	1:22:05
12.	Mikhail Khmelnitskiy	BLR	1:22:17

50 Kilometres Walk (2 Aug)

1.	Robert Korzeniowski	POL	3:43:30
2.	Mikhail Shchennikov	RUS	3:43:46
3.	Valentin Massana	ESP	3:44:19
4.	Arturo Di Mezza	ITA	3:44:52
5.	Viktor Ginko	BLR	3:45:27
6.	Ignacio Zamudio	MEX	3:46:07
7.	Valentin Kononen	FIN	3:47:40
8.	Sergey Korepanov	KZK	3:48:42
9.	Daniel Garcia	MEX	3:50:05
10.	Tim Barrett	CAN	3:51:28
11.	Aleksandar Rakovic	YUG	3:51:31
12.	Axel Noack	GER	3:51:55

34 CHRIS MADDOCKS   4:18:41

4 x 100 Metres Relay (3 Aug)

1. Canada   37.69
(Esmie, Gilbert, Surin, Bailey)
2. USA   38.05
(Drummond, Harden, Marsh, Mitchell)
3. Brazil   38.41
(Arn Silva, R da Silva, Ribeiro, And Silva)
4. Ukraine   38.55
(Rurak, Osovych, Kramarenko, Dologodin)
5. Sweden   38.67
(P Karisson, Martensson, Hedner, Strenis)
6. Cuba   39.39
(Simon, Lamela, Isasi, Perez)
h GREAT BRITAIN   dnf
(JARRETT, BRAITHWAITE, CAMPBELL, DAKO)

4 x 400 Metres Relay (3 Aug)

1. USA   2:55.99
(Smith, Harrison, Mills, Maybank)
2. GREAT BRITAIN   2:56.60
(THOMAS, BAULCH, RICHARDSON, BLACK)
3. Jamaica   2:59.42
(McDonald, Martin, Haughton, D Clarke)
4. Senegal   3:00.64
(Diarra, Dia, Ndiaye, Faye)
5. Japan   3:00.76
(Karube, Ito, Osakada, Omori)
6. Poland   3:00.96
(Rysiukiewicz, Jedrusik, Haczek, Mackowiak)
7. Bahamas   3:02.71
(Oliver, McIntosh, Darling, Munnings)

WOMEN

100 Metres wind -0.7 (27 Jul)
1. Gail Devers   USA   10.94
2. Merlene Ottley   JAM   10.94
3. Gwen Torrence   USA   10.96
4. Chandra Sturrup   BAH   11.00
5. Marina Trandenhova RUS   11.06
6. Natalya Voronova   RUS   11.10
7. Mary Onyali   NGR   11.13
8. Zhanna Pintusevich UKR   11.14

5q3 SIMMONE JACOBS   11.47
7q2 MARCIA RICHARDSON   11.55
8q1 STEPHANIE DOUGLAS   11.75

200 Metres wind 0.3 (1 Aug)
1. Marie-Jose Perec   FRA   22.12
2. Merlene Ottley   JAM   22.24
3. Mary Onyali   NGR   22.38
4. Inger Miller   USA   22.41
5. Galina Malchugina   RUS   22.45
6. Chandra Sturrup   BAH   22.54
7. Juliet Cuthbert   JAM   22.60
8. Carlette Guidry   USA   22.61

6q3 SIMMONE JACOBS   22.96
5q2 KATHARINE MERRY   23.17

400 Metres (29 Jul)
1. Marie-Jose Perec   FRA   48.25
2. Cathy Freeman   AUS   48.63
3. Falilat Ogunkoya   NGR   49.10
4. Pauline Davis   BAH   49.28
5. Jearl Miles   USA   49.55
6. Fatima Yusuf   NGR   49.77
7. Sandie Richards   JAM   50.45
8. Grit Breuer   GER   50.71

7q1 DONNA FRASER   51.58
6q4 PHYLIS SMITH   52.16

800 Metres (29 Jul)
1. Svetlana Masterkova RUS   1:57.73
2. Ana Quirot   CUB   1:58.11
3. Maria Mutola   MOZ   1:58.71
4. KELLY HOLMES   1:58.81
5. Yelena Afansayeva   RUS   1:59.57
6. Patricia Djate   FRA   1:59.61
7. Natalya Duknova   BLR   2:00.32
8. Toni Hodgkinson   NZL   2:00.54

h   DIANE MODAHL   dnf

1500 Metres (3 Aug)
1. Svetlana Masterkova RUS   4:00.83
2. Gabriela Szabo   ROM   4:01.54
3. Theresia Kiesl   AUT   4:03.02
4. Leah Pells   CAN   4:03.56
5. Margaret Crowley   AUS   4:03.79
6. Carla Sacramento   POR   4:03.91
7. Lyudmila Borisova   RUS   4:05.90
8. Malgorzata Rydz   POL   4:05.92
9. Gwen Griffiths   RSA   4:06.33
10. Regina Jacobs   USA   4:07.21
11. KELLY HOLMES   4:07.46
12. Anna Brzezinska   POL   4:08.27

5000 Metres (28 Jul)
1. Wang Junxia   CHN 14:59.88
2. Pauline Konga   KEN 15:03.49
3. Roberta Brunet   ITA 15:07.52
4. Michiko Shimizu   JPN 15:09.05
5. PAULA RADCLIFFE   15:13.11
6. Yelena Romanova   RUS 15:14.09
7. Elena Fidatov   ROM 15:16.71
8. Rose Cheruiyot   KEN 15:17.33
9. Lynn Jennings   USA 15:17.50
10. Amy Rudolph   USA 15:19.77
11. Sara Wedlund   SWE 15:22.98
12. Ayelech Worku   ETH 15:28.81
15h1 ALISON WYETH   16:24.74
13h3 SONIA MCGEORGE   16:01.92

10000 Metres (2 Aug)
1. Fernanda Ribeiro   POR 31:01.63
2. Wang Junxia   CHN 31:02.58
3. Gete Wami   ETH 31:06.65
4. Deratu Tulu   ETH 31:10.46
5. Masako Chiba   JPN 31:20.62
6. Tegla Loroupe   KEN 31:23.22
7. Yuko Kawakami   JPN 31:23.23
8. Iulia Negura   ROM 31:26.46
9. Julia Vaquero   ESP 31:27.07
10. Sally Barsosio   KEN 31:53.38
11. Catherine McKiernan IRL 32.00.38
12. Annemari Sandell FIN 32:14.66

Marathon (28 Jul)
1. Fatuma Roba   ETH   2:26:05
2. Valentina Yegorova   RUS   2:28.05
3. Yuko Arimori   JPN   2:28:39
4. Katrin Dorre-Heining GER   2:28:45
5. Rocio Rios   ESP   2:30:50
6. Lidia Simon   ROM   2:31:04
7. Manuela Machado   POR   2:31:11
8. Sonja Krolik   GER   2:31:16
9. Ren Xiujuan   CHN   2:31:21
10. Anne Marie Lauck   USA   2:31:30
11. Malgorzata Sobanska POL   2:31:52
12. Izumi Maki   JPN   2:32:35

16. LIZ MCCOLGAN   2:34:30
45. KAREN MACLEOD   2:42:08
58. SUZANNE RIGG   2:52:09

100 Metres Hurdles 0.2 (31 Jul)
1. Ludmila Engquist   SWE   12.58
2. Brigita Bukovec   SLO   12.59
3. Patricia Girard-Leno   FRA   12.65
4. Gail Devers   USA   12.66
5. Dionne Rose   JAM   12.74
6. Michelle Freeman   JAM   12.76
7. Lynda Goode   USA   13.11
dq Natalya Skekhodanova   RUS   12.80

5s1 ANGELA THORP   12.80
7h1 JACQUI AGYEPONG   13.24

400 Metres Hurdles (31 Jul)
1. Deon Hemmings   JAM   52.82
2. Kim Batten   USA   53.08
3. Tonja Buford-Bailey   USA   53.22
4. Debbie Parris   JAM   53.97

5. Heike Meissner   GER   54.03
6. Rosey Edeh   CAN   54.39
7. Ionela Tirlea   ROM   54.40
8. Silvia Rieger   GER   54.57

s2 SALLY GUNNELL   dnf

High Jump (3 Aug)
1. Stefka Kostadinova BUL   2.05
2. Niki Bakogianni   GRE   2.03
3. Inga Babakova   UKR   2.01
4. Yelena Gulyayeva   RUS   1.99
5= Alina Astafei   GER   1.96
5= Tatyana Motkova   RUS   1.96
5= Nele Zilinskiene   LIT   1.96
8. Hanne Haugland   NOR   1.96
9= Britta Bilac   SLO   1.93
9= Tisha Waller   USA   1.93
dq Antonella Bevilacqua ITA 1.99

17Q LEA HAGGETT   1.90
20=Q DEBBIE MARTI   1.85

Long Jump (2 Aug)
1. Chioma Ajunwa   NGR   7.12
2. Fiona May   ITA   7.02
3. Jackie Joyner-Kersee USA 7.00
4. Niki Xanthou   GRE   6.97
5. Iryna Chekhovtsova UKR   6.97
6. Agata Karczmarek   POL   6.90
7. Nicole Boegman   AUS   6.73
8. Tunde Vaszi   HUN   6.60
9. Chantal Brunner   NZL   6.49w
10. Voula Patoulidou   GRE   6.37
dq Iva Prandzheva   BUL   6.82

24Q DENISE LEWIS   6.33

Triple Jump (31 Jul)
1. Inessa Kravets   UKR   15.33
2. Inna Lasovskaya   RUS   14.98
3. Sarka Kasparkova   CZE   14.98
4. ASHIA HANSEN   14.49
5. Olga Vasdeki   GRE   14.44
6. Ren Ruipeng   CHN   14.30
7. Rodica Mateescu   ROM   14.21
8. Jelena Blazevica   LAT   14.12
9. Yelena Govorova   UKR   14.09
10. Sheila Hudson   USA   14.02
11. Yelena Khlusovych UKR   13.81
dq Iva Prandzheva   BUL   14.92

18Q MICHELLE GRIFFITH   13.70

Shot (2 Aug)
1. Astrid Kumbernuss   GER   20.56
2. Sui Xinmei   CHN   19.88
3. Irina Khudorozhkina RUS   19.35
4. Vita Pavlysh   UKR   19.30
5. Connie Price-Smith USA   19.22
6. Stephanie Storp   GER   19.06
7. Kathrin Neimke   GER   18.92
8. Irina Korzhanenko   RUS   18.65
9. Ramona Pagel   USA   18.48
10. Belsis Laza   CUB   18.40
11. JUDY OAKES   18.34
12. Valentina Fedyushina UKR 17.99

103

Discus (29 Jul)

1.	Ilke Wyludda	GER	69.66
2.	Natalya Sadova	RUS	66.48
3.	Ellina Zvereva	BLR	65.64
4.	Franka Dietzsch	GER	65.48
5.	Xiao Yanling	CHN	64.72
6.	Olga Chernyavskaya	RUS	64.70
7.	Nicoleta Grasu	ROM	63.28
8.	Lisa-Marie Vizaniari	AUS	62.48
9.	Metta Bergmann	NOR	62.28
10.	Teresa Machado	POR	61.38
11.	Anja Gundler	GER	61.16
12.	Irina Yatchenko	BLR	60.46
20Q	JACQUI MCKERNAN		58.88

Javelin (27 Jul)

1.	Heli Rantanen	FIN	67.94
2.	Louise McPaul	AUS	65.54
3.	Trine Hattestad	NOR	64.98
4.	Isel Lopez	CUB	64.68
5.	Xiomara Rivero	CUB	64.48
6.	Karen Forkel	GER	64.18
7.	Mikaela Ingberg	FIN	61.52
8.	Li Lei	CHN	60.74
9.	Steffi Nerius	GER	60.20
10.	Felicea Tilea	ROM	59.94
11.	Odeyme Palma	CUB	59.70
12.	Natalya Shikolenko	BLR	58.56
14Q	TESSA SANDERSON		58.86
27Q	SHELLEY HOLROYD		54.72

Heptathlon (27/28 Jul)

1.	Ghada Shouaa	SYR	6780
2.	Natalya Sazanovich	BLR	6563
3.	DENISE LEWIS		6489
4.	Urszula Wlodarczyk	POL	6484
5.	Eunice Barber	SLE	6342
6.	Rita Inancsi	HUN	6336
7.	Sabine Braun	GER	6317
8.	Kelly Blair	USA	6307
9.	Sharon Hanson	USA	6292
10.	Remigia Nazaroviene	LIT	6254
11.	Mona Steigauf	GER	6246
12.	Regia Cardenas	CUB	6246

10 Kilometres Walk (29 Jul)

1.	Yelena Nikolayeva	RUS	41:49
2.	Elisabetta Perrone	ITA	42:12
3.	Wang Yan	CHN	42:19
4.	Gu Yan	CHN	42:34
5.	Rossella Giordano	ITA	42:43
6.	Olga Kardapoltseva	BLR	43:02
7.	Katarzyna Radtke	POL	43:05
8.	Valentina Tsybulskaya	BLR	43:21
9.	Maria Ubanik	HUN	43:32
10.	Yelena Gruzinova	RUS	43:50
11.	Annarita Sidoti	ITA	43:57
12.	Kerry Saxby-Junna	AUS	43:59
32.	VICKY LUPTON		47:05

4 x 100 Metres Relay (3 Aug)

1.	USA	41.95
	(Gaines, Devers, Miller, Torrence)	
2.	Bahamas	42.14
	(Clarke, Sturrup, Fynes, Davis)	
3.	Jamaica	42.24
	(Freeman, Cuthbert, Mitchell, Ottey)	
4.	Russia	42.27
	(Leshchova, Malchugina, N Voronova, Privalova)	
5.	Nigeria	42.56
	(Ajunwa, T-Shirey, O-Thompson, Onyali)	
6.	France	42.76
	(Citte, Sidibe, Girard-Leno, Perec)	
7.	Australia	43.70
	(Cripps, Hanigan, Hewitt, Lambert)	
8.	GREAT BRITAIN	43.93
	(THORP, RICHARDSON, JACOBS, MERRY)	

4 x 400 Metres Relay (3 Aug)

1.	USA	3:20.91
	(Stevens, Malone, Graham, Miles)	
2.	Nigeria	3:21.04
	(Afolabi, Yusuf, Opara, Ogunkoya)	
3.	Germany	3:21.14
	(Rohlander, Kisabaka, Rucker, Breuer)	
4.	Jamaica	3:21.69
	(Frazer, Richards, Cambell, Hemmings)	
5.	Russia	3:22.22
	(Chebykina, Goncharenko, Kulikova, Kotlyarova)	
6.	Cuba	3:25.85
	(Bonne, Duporty, Morales, Quirot)	
7.	CZE	3:26.99
	(Kostovalova, Formanova, Fushsova, Benesova)	
8.	France	3:28.46
	(Landre, Dorsile, Elien, Devassoigne)	
4h1	GREAT BRITAIN	3:28.13
	(SMITH, CURBISHLEY, FRASER, OLADAPO)	

ITA v GB & NI v FRA v ESP (U20) Nembro, Italy 3 August 1996

MEN

100 Metres Race 1 wind 1.6

1.	Alessandro Attene	ITA	10.4
3.	CHRISTIAN MALCOLM		10.5

100 Metres Race 2 wind 2.3

1.	Francesco Scuderi	ITA	10.1w
4.	UVIE UGONO		10.5w

200 Metres Race 1 wind -0.8

1.	UVIE UGONO	21.3

200 Metres Race 2 wind -1.3

1.	Ruddy Zami	FRA	21.0
3.	MARK FINDLAY		21.3

400 Metres Race 1

1.	KRIS STEWART		47.6
2.	IAN HORSBURGH	gst	47.8

400 Metres Race 2

1.	Edoardo Vallett	ITA	46.8
2.	GEOFF DEARMAN		47.0

800 Metres

1.	ANDY YOUNG	1:50.25
3.	CHRIS MOSS	1:50.62

1500 Metres

1.	Fouad Chouky	FRA	3:57.95
5.	GRANT CUDDY		3:59.95
7.	MIKE EAST		4:00.95

5000 Metres

1.	Davida Posada	ESP	14:35.5
5.	ALLEN GRAFFIN		15:01.2
7.	SAM HAUGHIAN		15:04.6

3000 Metres Steeplechase

1.	Antonio Alvarez	ESP	8:59.7
5.	BEN WHITBY		9:13.3
9.	SIMON WURR		9:46.6

110 Metres Hurdles Race 1 2.5

1.	Francois Ferrari	FRA	14.3w
4.	BEN WARMINGTON		16.2w

110 Metres Hurdles Race 2 2.0

1.	David Janin	FRA	14.1
3.	ROSS BAILLIE		14.2

400 Metres Hurdles Race 1

1.	CHARLES ROBERTSON-ADAMS	52.9

400 Metres Hurdles Race 2

1.	Francesco Filisetti	ITA	51.8
3.	MARK ROWLANDS		53.1

High Jump

1.	JAMES BRIERLEY	2.26
2.	BEN CHALLENGER	2.11

Pole Vault

1.	Romain Mesnil	FRA	5.10
3=	MARK DAVIS		4.80
5.	CHRISTIAN LINSKEY		4.60

Long Jump

1.	Raul Frenandez	ESP	7.88w
3.	NATHAN MORGAN		7.66w
5.	DAVID CLERIHEW		7.27w

Triple Jump

1.	Colomba Fofana	FRA	16.13
4.	JAMES PEACOCK		15.24
7.	MARVIN BRAMBLE		14.85

Shot
1. Iker Sukia   ESP   17.48
2. CARL MYERSCOUGH   17.30
4. EMEKA UDECHUKU   15.34

Discus
1. Yves Niare   FRA   51.56
2. EMEKA UDECHUKU   51.04
5. CARL MYERSCOUGH   48.22

Hammer
1. Anscari Saldago   ESP   63.56
6. JOHN URQUHART   55.92
8. MATTHEW BELL   53.42

Javelin
1. Didier Richard   FRA   71.32
4. DAVID PARKER   66.44
5. MARK FRANCIS   65.64

10000 Metres Walk
1. Francisco Fernandez   ESP   41:16.0
8. MATTHEW HALES   48:06.0
9. SCOTT TAYLOR   51:39.2

4 x 100 Metres Relay
1. France   40.1
3. GREAT BRITAIN   40.5
(MALCOLM, FINDLAY, UGONO, BAILLIE)

4 x 400 Metres Relay
1. Spain   3:10.0
2. GREAT BRITAIN   3:11.1
(HORSBURGH, ROWLANDS, STEWART, DEARMAN)

Match Result
1. Spain   194
2. France   193
3. GREAT BRITAIN   170
4. Italy   146

WOMEN
100 Metres Race 1 wind 1.6
1. Doris Deuel   FRA   11.5
2. VICTORIA SHIPMAN   11.5

100 Metres Race 2 wind 0.9
1. Manuela Levorato   ITA   11.5
5. MALGORZATA ROSTEK   12.0

200 Metres Race 1 wind -1.1
1. Sylviane Felix   FRA   23.86
2. SARAH WILHELMY   24.42

200 Metres Race 2 wind -2.3
1. Manuela Levorato   ITA   23.92
3. VICTORIA SHIPMAN   24.49
5. SUSAN WILLIAMS   gst   25.13

400 Metres Race 1
1. LESLEY OWUSU   54.9

400 Metres Race 2
1. Cindy Ega   FRA   54.3
2. EMMA SYMONDS   54.6

800 Metres
1. Natlia Rodriguez   ESP   2:06.23
2. ELLEN O'HARE   2:06.59
7. AMANDA PRITCHARD   2:11.89

1500 Metres
1. JULIETTE OLDFIELD   4:27.3
5. MICHELLE MANN   4:32.1

3000 Metres
1. Sara Ferrari   ITA   9:24.6
3. KATIE SKORUPSKA   9:46.6
6. SHEILA FAIRWEATHER   9:52.5

100 Metres Hurdles Race 1 2.3
1. Lydic Potin   FRA   13.8w
3. JULIE PRATT   14.1w

100 Metres Hurdles Race 2 2.3
1. Sandra Ingelmo   ESP   13.6w
2. DENISE BOLTON   13.7w

400 Metres Hurdles Race 1
1. KATHY WILLIAMS   60.7

400 Metres Hurdles Race 2
1. VICKI JAMISON   58.0

High Jump
1. Stefania Cadamuro   ITA   1.85
5. MICHELLE DUNKLEY   1.79
6. SUSAN JONES   1.79

Pole Vault
1. Amandine Homo   FRA   3.80
3. RHIAN CLARKE   3.60
8. CLAIRE RIDGLEY   3.00

Long Jump
1. Karine Gregoire   FRA   5.93w
5. DANIELLE FREEMAN   5.73w
8. LOUISE EDEN   5.62w

Triple Jump
1. Chrystele Le Gouguec FRA   13.21
7. ELIZABETH GIBBENS   11.86
8. JODIE HURST   11.58

Shot
1. Assunta Legnante   ITA   15.08
4. CHRISTINA BENNETT   13.70
5. PHILIPPA ROLES   13.68

Discus
1. Catherine Gery   FRA   49.08
2. PHILIPPA ROLES   47.62
3. LAUREN KEIGHTLEY   46.68

Hammer
1. Florence Ezeh   FRA   54.92
3. HELEN ARNOLD   48.52
6. RACHEL BEVERLEY   45.56

Javelin
1. Sarah Walter   FRA   52.38
3. TAMMIE FRANCIS   42.34
8. LOUISE SMITH   37.36

5000 Metres Walk
1. Laura Ferreiro   ESP   23:18.6
7. NICOLA HUCKERBY   26:32.2
8. SARAH BENNETT   26:53.9

4 x 100 Metres Relay
1. France   45.6
3. GREAT BRITAIN   46.4
(ROSTEK, WILHELMY, S WILLIAMS, SHIPMAN)

4 x 400 Metres Relay
1. France   3:40.3
2. GREAT BRITAIN   3:44.8
(SYMONDS, PRITCHARD, JAMISON, OWUSU)

Match Result
1. France   224.5
2. Italy   157.5
3. GREAT BRITAIN   155
4. Spain   130

Overall Match Result
1. France   417
2. GREAT BRITAIN   325
3. Spain   324

GB & NI v International Select   Gateshead 19 August 1996

MEN

100 Metres wind -0.3
1. Donovan Bailey   IS/CAN   10.19
2. IAN MACKIE   10.25
3. DARREN BRAITHWAITE   10.34
4. Glenroy Gilbert   IS/CAN   10.39

200 Metres wind -1.6
1. JOHN REGIS   20.62
2. LINFORD CHRISTIE   20.64
3. Jeff Williams   IS/USA   20.70
4. Rohsaan Griffin   IS/USA   20.95

400 Metres
1. ROGER BLACK   44.64
2. Derek Mills   IS/USA   45.11
3. MARK RICHARDSON   45.15
4. Jason Rouser   IS/USA   45.45

1500 Metres
1. JOHN MAYOCK   3:37.75
2. Rich Kenah   IS/USA   3:38.13
3. TONY WHITEMAN   3:39.04
4. Paul McMullen   IS/USA   3:39.85

3000 Metres
1. NEIL CADDY   8:03.59
2. Ron Harris   IS/USA   8:03.90
3. JOHN NUTTALL   8:05.14
4. Tom Nohily   IS/USA   8:05.56

110 Metres Hurdles wind 0.5
1. Allen Johnson   IS/USA   13.25
2. TONY JARRETT   13.33
3. COLIN JACKSON   13.43
4. Steve Brown   IS/USA   13.67

400 Metres Hurdles
1. Calvin Davis   IS/USA   48.99
2. JON RIDGEON   49.54
3. Eric Thomas   IS/USA   49.75
4. GARY CADOGAN   50.46

High Jump
1. Charles Austin   IS/USA   2.30
2. DALTON GRANT   2.30
3. Cameron Wright   IS/USA   2.20
4. COLIN BENT   2.15

Pole Vault
1. Pat Manson   IS/USA   5.60
2. Kory Tarpenning   IS/USA   5.60
3. NICK BUCKFIELD   5.50
4. NEIL WINTER   nh

Triple Jump
1. JONATHAN EDWARDS   17.38
2. FRANCIS AGYEPONG   16.62
3. Kenny Harrison   IS/USA   16.60
4. Desmond Hunt   IS/USA   16.56

Javelin
1. Tom Pukstys   IS/USA   85.38
2. STEVE BACKLEY   85.06
3. Todd Riech   IS/USA   82.12
4. MICK HILL   80.14

4 x 400 Metres Relay
1. GREAT BRITAIN   2:59.85
   (BAULCH, HYLTON, RICHARDSON, BLACK)
2. International Select   3:01.02

WOMEN

200 Metres wind -1.0
1. Juliet Cuthbert   IS/JAM   23.04
2. Treshell Mayo   IS/USA   23.20
3. CATHERINE MURPHY   23.95
4. TRACY JOSPEH   24.14

400 Metres
1. Kim Graham   IS/USA   51.24
2. PHYLIS SMITH   51.56
3. Merlene Frazer   IS/JAM   52.65
4. GEORGINA OLADAPO   53.61

800 Metres
1. Inez Turner   IS/JAM   2:06.54
2. SONYA BOWYER   2:07.79
3. VICKY LAWRENCE   2:08.24
4. Nekita Beasley   IS/USA   2:11.42

1500 Metres
1. Leah Pells   IS/CAN   4:09.24
2. Amy Rudolph   IS/USA   4:14.28
3. LYNN GIBSON   4:15.23
4. SUE PARKER   4:19.39

3000 Metres
1. PAULA RADCLIFFE   8:56.25
2. Cheri Goddard   IS/USA   9:12.03
3. ALISON WYETH   9:25.71
4. Kathy Franey   IS/USA   dnf

100 Metres Hurdles wind -0.4
1. Dionne Rose   IS/JAM   12.99
2. ANGELA THORP   13.04
3. Gillian Russell   IS/JAM   13.30
4. JACKIE AGYEPONG   13.30

High Jump
1. DEBBIE MARTI   1.90
2. LEA HAGGETT   1.85
3. Chis Livingston   IS/CAN   1.80
4. Wanita Dykstra   IS/CAN   1.75

Triple Jump
1. ASHIA HANSEN   14.51
2. Cynthea Rhodes   IS/USA   13.87
3. MICHELLE GRIFFITH   13.73
4. Diana Orrange   IS/USA   13.31

Javelin
1. Xiomara Rivero   IS/CUB   63.34
2. Isel Lopez   IS/CUB   62.90
3. TESSA SANDERSON   60.78
4. DENISE LEWIS   43.28

4 x 200 Metres Relay - Mixed
1. International Select   88.68
2. GREAT BRITIAN   88.73
   (MURPHY, JOSEPH, PATRICK, GOLDING)

Match Result
1. International Select 121
2. GREAT BRITAIN   113

Jumps International Salgotoran, Hungary 11 September 1996

MEN

High Jump
1. Charles Austin   USA   2.30
2. Sergey KIYugin   RUS   2.28
3. Istvan Kovacs   HUN   2.26
7. BEN CHALLENGER   2.10

Pole Vault
1. Maksim Tarasov   RUS   5.80
2. Vadim Strogalyov   RUS   5.52
3. PAUL WILLIAMSON   5.22

WOMEN

High Jump
1. Stefka Kostadinova   BUL   2.01
2. Natalya Golodnova   RUS   1.87
3. Dora Gyorffy   HUN   1.87
4. DEBBIE MARTI   1.84
5. JO JENNINGS   1.84

Pole Vault
1. JANINE WHITLOCK   3.91
2. Zsuzsa Szabo   HUN   3.81
3. Eszter Szemeredi   HUN   3.61

WORLD JUNIOR CHAMPIONSHIPS Sydney, Australia 21 - 25 August 1996

MEN

100 Metres wind 1.0 (22 Aug)
1.	Francis Obikwelu	NGR	10.21
2.	Segun Ogunkoya	NGR	10.25
3.	Francesco Scuderi	ITA	10.43
4.	JAMIE HENTHORN		10.45
5.	DWAIN CHAMBERS		10.47

200 Metres wind -1.6 (24 Aug)
1.	Francis Obikwelu	NGR	20.47
2.	Riaan Dempers	RSA	20.96
3.	Bryan Harrison	USA	21.10
8s2	CHRISTIAN MALCOLM		21.52
8s1	UVIE UGONO		21.70

400 Metres (23 Aug)
1.	Obea Moore	USA	45.27
2.	Jerome Davis	USA	45.86
3.	Shane Niemi	CAN	45.94
3s3	GEOFF DEARMAN		47.40
5h6	KRISS STEWART		48.05

800 Metres (23 Aug)
1.	Mwengi Mutua	KEN	1:48.21
2.	TOM LERWILL		1:48.40
3.	Grant Cremer	AUS	1:48.46

1500 Metres (25 Aug)
1.	Shadrack Langat	KEN	3:38.96
2.	Mohamed Yagoub	SUD	3:39.17
3.	Miloud Abaoub	ALG	3:39.37
7h3	GRANT CUDDY		3:52.81
8h1	TOM MAYO		4:01.35

5000 Metres (25 Aug)
1.	Assefa Mezegebu	ETH	13:35.30
2.	David Chelule	KEN	13:36.27
3.	Aaron Gabonewe	RSA	13:46.19

10000 Metres (21 Aug)
1.	Assefa Mezegebu	ETH	28:27.78
2.	David Chelule	KEN	28:29.14
3.	Tetsuhiro Furuta	JPN	28:31.61

3000 Metres Steeplechase (24 Aug)
1.	Julius Chelule	KEN	8:33.09
2.	Kipkurui Misoi	KEN	8:33.31
3.	Ali Ezzine	MAR	8:35.60
11.	KEVIN NASH		9:01.14
8h3	BEN WHITBY		9:04.40

110 Metres Hurdles 1.8 (25 Aug)
1.	Yoel Hernandez	CUB	13.83
2.	Tomasz Scigaczweski	POL	13.88
3.	Jovesa Naivalu	FIJ	13.91
4.	ROSS BAILLIE		14.01
5.	DAMIEN GREAVES		14.04

400 Metres Hurdles (23 Aug)
1.	Mubarak Al-Nubi Faraj	QAT	49.07
2.	Llewellyn Herbert	RSA	49.15
3.	Angelo Taylor	USA	50.18
4h2	CHARLES ROBERTSON-ADAMS		52.91
5h3	MARK ROWLANDS		53.63

High Jump (24 Aug)
1.	Mark Boswell	CAN	2.24
2=	Svatoslav Ton	CZE	2.21
2=	BEN CHALLENGER		2.21
7=	JAMES BRIERLEY		2.15

Pole Vault (25 Aug)
1.	Paul Burgess	AUS	5.35
2.	Patrik Kristiansson	SWE	5.30
3.	Danny Ecker	GER	5.30
11.	CHRISTIAN LINSKEY		5.00
22Q	MARK DAVIS		4.60

Long Jump (22 Aug)
1.	Aleksey Lukasevich	UKR	7.91
2.	Raul Fernandez	ESP	7.75
3.	NATHAN MORGAN		7.74

Triple Jump (25 Aug)
1.	Rene Luis Hernandez	CUB	16.50
2.	Michel Calvo	CUB	16.17
3.	Ionut Punga	ROM	16.15w

Shot (25 Aug)
1.	Ralf Bartels	GER	18.71
2.	Justin Anlezark	AUS	18.21
3.	Clay Cross	AUS	17.69
22Q	CARL MYERSCOUGH		14.57

Discus (22 Aug)
1.	Casey Malone	USA	56.22
2.	Roland Varga	HUN	55.20
3.	Frank Casanas	CUB	54.86

Hammer (24 Aug)
1.	Marciej Palyszko	POL	71.24
2.	Vadim Devyatosvskiy	BLR	70.88
3.	Roman Konevtsov	RUS	70.32

Javelin (25 Aug)
1.	Sergey Voynov	UZB	79.78
2.	Harri Haatainen	FIN	76.12
3.	Steven Madeo	AUS	73.88
17Q	DAVID PARKER		64.08

Decathlon (21/22 Aug)
1.	Attila Zsivotzky	HUN	7582
2.	DEAN MACEY		7480
3.	Chiel Warners	HOL	7368

10 Kilometres Walk (22 Aug)
1.	Francisco Fernandez	ESP	40:38.25
2.	David Marquez	ESP	41:03.73
3.	Nathan Deakes	AUS	41:11.44

4 x 100 Metres Relay (25 Aug)
1.	USA		39.66
	(Williams, Davis, Moore, Armstrong)		
2.	France		39.47
	(Cavre, Hery, Zami, Patros)		
3.	Australia		39.62
	(Missingham, Baxter, Pearce, Snell)		
7.	GREAT BRITAIN		40.32
	(MALCOLM, HENTHORN, UGONO, CHAMBERS)		

4 x 400 Metres Relay (25 Aug)
1.	USA		3:03.65
	(Johnson, Davis, Martin, Moore)		
2.	Japan		3:06.01
	(Takahashi, Tamesue, Okusako, Morita)		
3.	GREAT BRITAIN		3:06.76
	(STEWART, LERWILL, ROWLANDS, DEARMAN)		

WOMEN

100 Metres wind 0.6 (22 Aug)
1.	Nora Ivanova	BUL	11.32
2.	Andrea Anderson	USA	11.43
3.	Esther Moller	GER	11.46
8q3	MALGORZATA ROSTEK		12.11
8q2	REBECCA DRUMMOND		12.24

200 Metres wind -2.2 (24 Aug)
1.	Sylvianne Felix	FRA	23.16
2.	Lauren Hewitt	AUS	23.32
3.	Nora Ivanova	BUL	23.59
5q1	SARAH WILHELMY		24.29
5q4	VICTORIA SHIPMAN		24.48

400 Metres (23 Aug)
1.	Andreea Burlacu	ROM	52.32
2.	Suzianne Reid	USA	53.17
3.	Rosemary Hayward	AUS	53.28

800 Metres (23 Aug)
1.	Claudia Gesell	GER	2:02.67
2.	Kathleen Friedrich	GER	2:02.70
3.	Jebel Langat	KEN	2:03.21

1500 Metres (25 Aug)
1.	Kutre Dulecha	ETH	4:08.65
2.	Jackline Maranga	KEN	4:08.98
3.	Shura Hutesa	ETH	4:09.49

3000 Metres (22 Aug)
1.	Anita Weyermann	SUI	8:50.73
2.	Edna Kiplagat	KEN	8:53.06
3.	Etaferahu Tarekegne	ETH	8:53.77

5000 Metres (25 Aug)
1.	Ayelech Worku	ETH	15:40.03
2.	Olivera Jevtic	YUG	15:40.59
3.	Christina Iloc	ROM	15:41.44

100 Metres Hurdles 0.7 (25 Aug)
1.	Joyce Bates	USA	13.27
2.	Glory Alozie	NGR	13.30
3.	Tan Yali	CHN	13.37
6.	NATASHA DANVERS		14.00
5s2	DENISE BOLTON		14.07

400 Metres Hurdles (23 Aug)
1. Ulrike Urbansky   GER   56.65
2. VIKKI JAMISON   57.57
3. Tanya Jarrett   JAM   57.91

High Jump (25 Aug)
1. Yulia Lyakhova   RUS   1.93
2. Dora Gyorffy   HUN   1.91
3. Svetlana Lapina   RUS   1.91
9. MICHELLE DUNKLEY   1.80
19Q RACHAEL FORREST   1.70

Long Jump (23 Aug)
1. Guan Yingnan   CHN   6.53
2. Cristina Nicolau   ROM   6.47
3. Johanna Halkoaho   FIN   6.38
17Q SARAH CLAXTON   5.71

Triple Jump (25 Aug)
1. Tereza Marinova   BUL   14.62
2. Cristina Nicolau   ROM   13.64
3. Adelina Gavrila   ROM   13.50

Shot (24 Aug)
1. Song Ferma   CHN   16.58
2. Nadine Beckel   GER   16.39
3. Yelena Ivanenko   BLR   16.22

Discus (25 Aug)
1. Ma Shuli   CHN   56.32
2. Sua Seilala   USA   56.32
3. Zhang Yaqing   CHN   55.70
16Q PHILIPPA ROLES   46.48

Javelin (23 Aug)
1. Osleidis Menendes CUB   60.96
2. Nikolett Szabo   HUN   58.34
3. Bina Ramesh   FRA   57.70

Heptathlon (23/24 Aug)
1. Yelizaveta Shalygina RUS 5711
2. Johanna Halkoaho   FIN 5656
3. Hana Dolezelova   CZE 5504
10. NICOLA GAUTIER   5079

5 Kilometres Walk (24 Aug)
1. Irina Stankina   RUS   21:31.85
2. Olga Panferova   RUS   21:52.27
3. Claudia Iovan   ROM   21:57.11
21. NINA HOWLEY   25:12.23

4 x 100 Metres Relay (25 Aug)
1. USA   43.79
   (Anderson, White, Wright, Perry)
2. Jamaica   44.26
   (Robinson, Dowdie, Patterson, Bailey)
3. Germany   44.57
   (Abel, Moller, Kette, Wagner)
dnf GREAT BRITAIN
(ROSTEK, WILHELMY, SHIPMAN, DRUMMOND)

4 x 400 Metres Relay (25 Aug)
1. Germany   3:31.12
   (Muller, Gessell, Harstick, Urbansky)
2. Romania   3:32.16
   (Tudor, Safta, Ruicu, Burlacu)
3. Australia   3:32.47
   (Marshall, Lewis, Fowley, Hayward)

BAF HALF MARATHON CHAMPIONSHIPS
South Shields 15 September 1996

MEN
1. Benson Masya   KEN   61:43
2. PAUL EVANS   61:55
3. Antonio Serrano   ESP   61:58
4. GARY STAINES   63:28
5. EAMONN MARTIN   64:00
6. PETER WHITEHEAD   64:04
7. Kassa Tadesse   ETH   64:33
8. IAN HUDSPITH   64:34
9. BRIAN RUSHWORTH   64:47
10. MARK CROASDALE   64:54
11. DARREN HISCOX   64.56
12. STEPHEN GREEN   65:24

WOMEN
1. LIZ MCCOLGAN   70.28
2. Esther Kiplagat   KEN   70.36
3. Jane Salumae   EST   71.54
4. YVONNE MURRAY   72.25
5. MARIAN SUTTON   73.41
6. Rosanna Munerotto ITA   74.34
7. Cathy Shum   IRL   74.43
8. HAYLEY NASH   77.16
9. JACKIE NEWTON   77.41
10. TRACEY SWINDELL   77.56
11. TRUDI THOMSON   78.11
12. CLARE PAUZERS   79.42

IAAF WORLD HALF MARATHON CHAMPIONSHIPS
Palma, Spain 29 September 1996

MEN

1.	Stefano Baldini	ITA	61:17
2.	Josphat Kiprono	KEN	61:30
3.	Tendai Chimusasa	ZIM	62:00
4.	Carlos de la Torre	ESP	62:03
5.	Toshiyuki Hayata	JPN	62:05
6.	Niima Tuluway	TAN	62:30
7.	Delmir Dos Santos	BRA	62:44
8.	Alejandro Gomez	ESP	62:47
9.	Giacomo Leone	ITA	62:48
10.	Stephane Schweickhart	SUI	62:49
11.	Kebede Gemechu	ETH	62:52
12.	Masatoshi Ibata	JPN	63:07
22.	DAVE SWANSTON		63:44
41.	CHRIS ROBISON		65:10
62.	PHIL MAKEPEACE		66:36
88.	DAVE TUNE		69:26

WOMEN

1.	Ren Xiujuan	CHN	70:39
2.	Lidia Simon	ROM	70:57
3.	Aurica Buia	ROM	71:01
4.	Nuta Olaru	ROM	71:07
5.	Kanako Haginaga	JPN	71:18
6.	Christine Mallo	FRA	72:24
7.	Firiya Sultanova	RUS	72:34
8.	Heather Turland	AUS	72:46
9.	Zaiha Dahmani	FRA	72:46
10.	Lucilla Andreucci	ITA	72:50
11.	Cristina Pomacu	ROM	73:05
12.	Zola Pieterse	RSA	73:19
dq	Cristina Burca	ROM	72:37
28.	SALLY GOLDSMITH		75:33
44.	DANIELLE SANDERSON		76:56
47.	HAYLEY NASH		77:45
dnf	LIZ MCCOLGAN		

Team Result

1.	Italy	3:07:42
2.	Spain	3:08:36
3.	Japan	3:08.43
11.	GREAT BRITAIN	3:15:30

Team Result

1.	Romania	3:33.05
2.	France	3:38:44
3.	Italy	3:41:28
9.	GREAT BRITAIN	3:50:14

EUROPEAN CROSS COUNTRY CHAMPIONSHIPS
Charleroi, Belgium 1 December 1996

MEN

1.	JON BROWN		32:37
2.	Paulo Guerra	POR	33:12
3.	Mustapha Essaid	FRA	33:19
4.	Carsten Jørgensen	DEN	33:20
5.	Eduardo Henriques	POR	33:28
6.	Umberto Pusteria	ITA	33:36
7.	Vincent Rousseau	BEL	33:42
8.	Yann Millon	FRA	33:42
9.	Victor Almeida	POR	33:43
10.	A Arlati	ITA	33:44
11.	Jose Regalo	POR	33:54
12.	Alejandro Gomez	ESP	33:59
16.	ANDREW PEARSON		34:12
27.	SPENCER BARDEN		34:52
32.	DARRIUS BURROWS		35:01
49.	CHRISTIAN STEPHENSON		35:43

Team Result

1.	Portugal	27
2.	France	47
3.	Belgium	59
5.	GREAT BRITAIN	76

WOMEN

1.	Sara Wedlund	SWE	17:04
2.	Julia Vaquero	ESP	17:14
3.	Annemari Sandell	FIN	17:19
4.	Elena Fidatov	ROM	17:24
5.	Albertina Dias	POR	17:29
6.	Claudia Lokar	GER	17:35
7.	Yanna Oubouhou	FRA	17:36
8.	HAYLEY HAINING		17:37
9.	Laurence Vivier	FRA	17:39
10.	Anja Smolders	BEL	17:41
11.	Chyssie Girard	FRA	17:42
12.	Laurence Duqueroy	FRA	17:46
dq	Iulia Negura	ROM	16:58
15.	ANDREA WHITCOMBE		17:48
18.	SUZANNE RIGG		17:51
25.	LUCY ELLIOTT		18:03
34.	HAYLEY YELLING		18:12

Team Result

1.	France	27
2.	GREAT BRITAIN	39
3.	Belgium	43

JUNIOR MEN (INVITATION)

1.	Gert-Jan Liefers	HOL	22:01
2.	B Tamri	FRA	22:06
3.	Juan Carlos Higuero	ESP	22:17
6.	SAM HAUGHIAN		22:31
8.	MICHAEL EAST		22:33
11.	PAUL MORBY		22:49
18.	DAVE MITCHINSON		23:14

Team Result

1.	GREAT BRITAIN	25
2.	Belgium	29
3.	Germany	35

JUNIOR WOMEN (INVITATION)

1.	Alejandra Aguilar	ESP	11:10
2.	Sonja Knöpfli	SUI	11:14
3.	K Obronek	SLO	11:16
4.	AMBER GASCOIGNE		11:17
9.	AMY WATERLOW		11:34
10.	VICTORIA WILKINSON		11:35
15.	TANYA BRAZIER		11:44

Team Result

1.	GREAT BRITAIN	23
2.	Germany	24
3.	Belgium	47

REGIONAL CHAMPIONSHIPS

SCOTLAND
Glasgow, 29 June

MEN

100	Ken Campbell	10.88
200	Douglas Walker	20.67
400	Anders Lustgarten	47.97
800	Paul Walker	1:51.83
1500	Tony Johnston	3:59.83
5000	Philip Mowbray	14:16.42
10000	Bobby Quinn	29:47.77
3kSt	Graeme Croll	9:04.4
110H	Ken Campbell	14.16
400H	Barry Middleton	51.83
HJ	David Barnetson	2.10
PV	Iain Black	4.40
LJ	Darren Richie	7.63
TJ	Neil McMenemy	14.96
SP	Stephan Hayward	18.16
DT	Simon Williams	58.04
HT	Paul Head	68.74
JT	Phil Parry	63.76
Dec	Piere Faber (RSA)	6632
10kW		

WOMEN

100	Aileen McGillivary	12.17
200	Sinead Dudgeon	24.37
400	Vicki Jamison	55.03
800	Susan Hendry	2:11.67
1500	Lynne MacDougall	4:30.05
5000	Ann McPhail	17:02.17
100H	Katy Sketchley	13.99
400H	Jane Low	61.58
HJ	Hazel Melvin	1.70
PV	Janine Whitlock	3.20
LJ	Ruth Irving	5.95
TJ	Pamela Anderson	12.55
SP	Alison Grey	14.19
DT	Alison Grey	45.30
HT	Helen McCreadie	46.68
JT	Karen Costello	46.32
Hep	Emma Lindsay	4979
5kW		

WALES
Newport, 1 June

MEN

Tremayne Rutherford	10.96
Doug Turner	21.99
Joseph Lloyd	48.29
Darrell Maynard	1:54.75
James Ellis-Smith	3:50.71
Steven Brace	14:33.17
Dale Rixon	29:54.12
Phil Cook	9:33.21
James Archampong	14.3
Marvin Gray	52.8
Matthew Perry	2.06
Neil Winter	5.25
Anthony Malcolm	7.32
Charles Madiera Cole	14.04
Andy Turner	14.11
Andy Turner	44.78
Adrian Palmer	57.26
Stuart Loughran	58.02
Colin Bradley	48:21.67

WOMEN

Gael Davies	12.99
Gael Davies	26.79
Kathryn Bright	56.60
Hayley Parry	2:06.51
Hayley Parry	4:29.40
Angharad Mair	17:32.8
Bethan Edwards	14.0
Alyson Layzell	58.92
Teresa Andrews	1.65
Rhian Clarke	3.65
Nicola Short	5.74
Lesley Brannan	11.46
Philippa Roles	45.14
Sarah Moore	52.90
Onyema Amadi	48.34
Sian Woodcock	28:39

NORTHERN IRELAND
Antrim, 7 July

MEN

Ian Craig	10.57
Paul Brizzell	21.20
Paul McBurney	48.13
Richard Girvan	1:53.88
Eugene O'Neill (IRL)	3:54.38
Dermot Donnolly	14:04.72
Mark McDowell	9:15.82
Peter Coghlan (IRL)	14.03
Douglas Thom	52.37
Raymond Swan (IRL)	1.91
Gareth Devlin	6.73
Neil Stephenson	13.25
John Farrelly (IRL)	14.64
John Moreland	48.70
Ed Healy (IRL)	57.82
Damien Crawford	64.62
3kW Paul O'Callaghan (IRL)	12:51.92

WOMEN

Vicki Jamison	12.02
Vicki Jamison	24.34
Zoe Arnold	56.87
Aisling Molloy	2:08.80
Ann Terek	4:22.27
3000 Jill Bruce	9:40.01
Joanne Murphy	18.05
Gail Doyle	67.22
Jackie Vyschaft	1.70
Sarah Good	5.62
Liz Orr	10.47
Alison Moffitt	11.96
Jackie McKernan	57.24
Nicola Coffey (IRL)	47.12
Alison Moffitt	45.20

AREA CHAMPIONSHIPS

	SOUTH London (CP), 1-2 June		MIDLANDS Birmingham, 1-2 June		NORTH Sheffield, 1-2 June	
MEN						
100	Dwain Chambers	10.57	Paul White	10.48	Allyn Condon	10.66
200	Cypren Edmunds	21.32	Andrew Walcott	21.54	Allyn Condon	20.97
400	Adrian Patrick	46.29	Nick Budden	47.34	David Nolan	47.03
800	Justin Swift-Smith	1:53.5	James Mayo	1:49.82	Tony Morrell	1:52.30
1500	Adam Duke	3:50.23	Stefan White	3:47.27	Darren Spawforth	3:49.65
5000	Ian Hamilton	14:20.19	Simon Cotton	14:21.78	Paul Freary	14:05.90
10000	James Jackson	30:44.93	Simon Cotton	30:31.64	Terry Wall	30:49.48
3kSt	Kevin Nash	8:43.21	Raymond Plant	9:03.89	Mike Jubb	8:54.53
110H	Mark Stern	14.45	Greg Dunson	14.77	Martin Nicholson	14.53
400H	Lawrence Lynch	50.40	Paul Hibbert	51.89	Chris Rawlinson	50.88
HJ	Richard Aspden	2.10	Ben Challenger	2.05	Ian Holliday	2.15
PV	Kevin Hughes	5.20	Michael Barber	5.20	Andy Ashurst	5.10
LJ	Onochie Onuorah	7.41	Steve Phillips	7.60	Paul Johnson	7.25
TJ	Tosi Fasinro	15.97	Kori Stennett	14.84	Jon Hilton	14.92
SP	Matt Simson	18.99	Morris Fox	14.78	James Muirhead	16.22
DT	Simon Williams	55.14	Glen Smith	60.14	Robert Russell	52.80
HT	Paul Head	66.02	John Pearson	63.70	David Smith	65.26
JT	Trevor Ratcliffe	66.78	David Wilson	61.28	Steve Harrison	64.36
3kW	Gary Witton	12:42.76				
10kW	Nick Barrable	52:04.05				
Dec	Steve Leader	6829				

WOMEN						
100	Marcia Richardson	11.94	Victoria Shipman	11.88	Stephanie Douglas	11.65
200	Elona Reinalda	23.69	Sharon Tunaley	24.11	Susan Rawlinson	24.10
400	Linda Staines	53.44	Lorraine Hanson	53.48	Susan Rawlinson	54.59
800	Jeina Mitchell	2:04.87	Claire Raven	2:08.02	Michelle Faherty	2:07.13
1500	Michelle Wannell	4:35.49	Rhona Makepeace	4:26.34	Vickie Lawrence	4:22.72
3000	Mara Myers	9:26.10				
5000	Mara Myers	17:10.83	Anna Kostilek	18:29.04	Heather Heasman	16:00.85
100H	Melanie Wilkins	13.59	Kerri Maddox	13.58	Diane Allahgreen	13.48
400H	Louise Brunning	57.34	Josephine Peet	63.51	Louise Fraser	57.85
HJ	Debbie Marti	1.88	Kerry Jury	1.78	Susan Jones	1.80
PV	Louise Schramm	3.40	Emma Hornby	3.40	Rachel Foster	2.50
LJ	Liz Ghojefa	5.84	Jackie White	6.03	Ann Brooks	6.06
TJ	Michelle Griffith	14.04	Debbie Rowe	12.46	Margaret Still	12.03
SP	Myrtle Augee	16.17	Angela Lambourne	12.60	Carol Bennett	12.52
DT	Shelley Drew	54.22	Nicola Talbot	51.24	Rachel Hopgood	48.76
HT	Lyn Sprules	56.82	Ann Gardner	50.38	Samantha Burns Salmond	46.80
JT	Noelle Bradshaw	46.22	Sharon Gibson	53.08	Janine King	49.56
3kW	Cressida Van Doorn	16:17.61				
5kW	Catherine Charnock	25:01.01				
Hept	Tracy Joseph	5339				

AGE CHAMPIONSHIPS

Under 20 MEN
Bedford, 27-28 July

Event	Athlete	Mark
100	Dwain Chambers	10.42
200	Christian Malcolm	21.32
400	Geoff Dearman	47.55
800	James Nolan (IRL)	1:49.95
	2. Thomas Lerwill	1:50.21
1500	Andrew Walker (IRL)	3:47.21
	2. Grant Cuddy	3:49.36
5000	Andres Jones	14:39.57
3kSt	Benedict Whitby	8:59.09
110H	Damien Greaves	14.20
400H	Mark Rowlands	52.38
HJ	James Brierley	2.21
PV	Christian Linskey	5.10
LJ	Nathan Morgan	7.65
TJ	James Peacock	15.04
SP	Carl Myerscough	15.82
DT	Carl Myerscough	50.60
HT	John Thompson (IRL)	57.54
	2. John Urquhart	56.32
JT	David Parker	66.94
10kW	Jamie Costin (IRL)	44:55.20
	3. Matthew Hales	50:17.25

Bimingham, 17-18 July

Event	Athlete	Mark
3000	James Thie	8:34.17

Bimingham, 1-2 June

Event	Athlete	Mark
Dec	David Ralson	6199

Under 17
Birmingham, 17-18 August

Event	Athlete	Mark
	Steven Daly	11.01
	Ben Lewis	21.85
	David Naismith	48.60
	Ross Fittall	1:56.74
	Sam Boden	3:59.84
1500St	David Mitchinson	4:22.81
100H	David O'Leary	13.30
	Richard McDonald	52.81
	Martin Lloyd	2.00
	Richard Smith	4.45
	Alistair Gudgeon	6.57
	Peter Francis	13.78
	David Readle	16.89
	Luke Rosenberg	48.56
	Andrew Grierson	59.66
	Timothy Kitney	62.22
5kW	Matthew Hales	23:49.89

Bedford, 27 July

Event	Athlete	Mark
	Graham Ferguson	8:48.68

Under 15
Birmingham, 17-18 August

Event	Athlete	Mark
	Joe Brown	11.38
	Tristan Anthony	23.03
	Aaron Evans	50.88
	Colin Joyce	2:03.23
	Richard King	4:15.13
80H	Sebastian Bastow	11.38
	Kenneth McKeown	1.91
	Andrew Corey	3.90
	Richard Phelan (IRL)	6.21
	2. Mark Awanah	6.13
	Leon Burnett	13.31
	Paul Archer	14.96
	Liam Walsh	45.88
	Matthew Sutton	62.58
	Richard Lainson	60.34
3kW	Lloyd Finch	15:02.70

Bedford, 27 July

Event	Athlete	Mark
	Richard Ward	9:13.60

Under 20 WOMEN
Bedford, 27-28 July

Event	Athlete	Mark
100	Rebecca Drummond	11.69
200	Victoria Shipman	24.20
400	Emma Symonds	54.86
800	Amanda Pritchard	2:07.59
1500	Juliette Oldfield	4:30.1
3000	Michelle Mann	9:43.23
5000	Berhane Dagne (ETH)	16:40.00
100H	Natasha Danvers	13.78
400H	Vicki Jamison	57.27
HJ	Rachael Forrest	1.85
PV	Rhian Clarke	3.50
LJ	Sarah Claxton	6.23
TJ	Elizabeth Gibbens	12.17
SP	Philippa Roles	13.76
DT	Lauren Keightley	48.24
HT	Helen Arnold	50.62
JT	Tammie Francis	45.74
5kW	Rosaleigh Comerford (IRL)	24:40.2
	2. Nina Howley	24:48.1

Bimingham, 1-2 June

Event	Athlete	Mark
Hept	Nicola Gautier	5080

Under 17
Birmingham, 17-18 August

Event	Athlete	Mark
	Abiodun Oyepitan	12.06
	Helen Roscoe	25.2
300	Rebecca White	39.25
	Simone Hardy	2:15.19
	Camilla Waite	4:36.61
	*Kate Grimshaw	10:04.48
	* Bedford 28 July	
80H	Sarina Mantle	11.62
300H	Yawande Ige	43.79
	Antonia Bemrose	1.73
	Fiona Harrison	3.45
	Emma Hughes	5.67
	Julia Johnson	11.65
	Julie Dunkley	12.59
	Natalie Kerr	44.44
	Clara Thompson (IRL))	42.52
	2. Zoe Derham	42.10
	Lucy Rann	40.86
	Sarah Bennett	27:53.40

Under 15
Birmingham, 17-18 August

Event	Athlete	Mark
	Fiona Harrison	12.25
	Kimberley Canning	25.07
	Nikki Daniels	2:15.59
	Jennifer Mockler	4:39.47
75H	Helen Worsley	11.48
	Deirdre Ryan (IRL)	1.70
	2. Sophie McQueen	1.69
	Fiona Harrison	5.78
	Rachel Harley	11.37
	Emma Carpenter	35.96
	Melanie Vaggers	35.72
3kW	Katie Ford	16:07.95

UK MERIT RANKINGS 1996 Compiled by Peter Matthews

This is the 29th successive year that I have compiled annual merit rankings of British athletes. As usual they are based on an assessment of form during the outdoor season. The major factors by which the rankings are determined are win-loss record, performances in the major meetings, and sequence of marks.

I endeavour to be as objective as possible, but form can often provide conflicting evidence, or perhaps an athlete may not have shown good enough results against leading rivals, or in very important competition, to justify a ranking which his or her ability might otherwise warrant.

I can only rank athletes on what they have actually achieved. Much depends on having appropriate opportunities. It is obviously harder for an athlete living in a remote part of the UK than one who is close to the major centres of competition, and it may be hard to break into the élite who get the invitations for the prestige meetings. Difficulties also arise when athletes reach peak form at different parts of the season or through injury miss significant competition.

Once again it should be pointed out that the rankings are by no means necessarily the order in which I think the athletes would have finished in an idealised contest, but simply my attempt to assess what has actually happened in 1996.

I hope that I have not missed many performances, but I would be very pleased to receive any missing results at 10 Madgeways Close, Great Amwell, Herts SG12 9RU.

For each event the top 12 are ranked. On the first line is shown the athletes name, then their date of birth followed, in brackets, by the number of years ranked in the top 12 (including 1996) and their ranking last year (1995), and finally, their best mark prior to 1996. The following lines include their best six performances of the year (followed, for completeness, by significant indoor marks indicated by 'i', although indoor form, the subject of a separate assessment, is not considered in the rankings). Then follow placings at major meetings, providing a summary of the athlete's year at the event.

Abbreviations include

AAA v LC	AAA v Loughborough Students
BL	British League
CAU	Inter-Counties at Bedford
Cork	Cork City Sports
CP-GP	Securicor Games at Crystal Palace
Cup	Guardian Cup Final at Hendon
E.Clubs	European Clubs Cup
ECp	European Cup
E.Sch	English Schools
GhG	BUPA Gateshead Games
GPF	Grand Prix Final at Milan
HCl	Home Countries International
IR	Inter-regional at Birmingham
IS	Inter-Services
JInt	Junior international v France, Italy, Spain at Nembro
McD	McDonald Games at Sheffield
NvST	North v South of Thames v West at Luton
OG	Olympic Games
P-CP	Performance Games at Crystal Palace
SN4	Northern Ireland v Scotland, Wales, Turkey at Belfast
U23I	Under 23 international v Germany, Russia at Hexham
v IS	UK v International Select at Gateshead
WG	Welsh Games at Cardiff
WJ	World Junior Championships

BRITISH MERIT RANKINGS 1996 - MEN

100 METRES
1. **Linford Christie** 2.4.60 (14y, 1) 9.87 '93   10.00w, 10.03, 10.04, 10.04, 10.04, 10.04, 10.05, 10.06, 10.06, 10.10, 10.13, 10.14;   1 CAU, 1 ECp, 2 Rome, 1 AAA, 3 Paris, 1 GhG, 5 Lausanne, 2 Nice, 2 CP-GP, dq OG, 2 Sestriere, 3 Zürich, 5 Brussels, 3 McD, 1 Cup, BL1: -,-,-,1
2. **Ian Mackie** 27.2.75 (1y, -) 10.50 '94   10.17, 10.21w, 10.24, 10.25, 10.25, 10.26; 5 Athens, 1B Bedford, 3 CAU, 1 Dublin, 3 AAA, 1 SN4, 2 GhG, 4B Stockholm, 4 CP-GP, sf OG, 6h Zürich, 2 v IS, 2 McD
3. **Darren Braithwaite** 20.1.69 (8y, 2) 10.12 '95   10.13, 10.14, 10.19A, 10.22, 10.22A, 10.23; 1 Jo'burg, 1A Ljubljana, 4 Bratislava, 2 AAA, 2 Helsinki, 5 GhG, 4 Oslo, 5 Sestriere, qf OG, 3 v IS, 7 McD
4. **Darren Campbell** 12.9.73 (5y, 4) 10.34 '95, 10.28w '91   10.17, 10.21, 10.24, 10.24w, 10.25, 10.25; 1B Ljubljana, 1 Bratislava, 4= AAA, 6 Helsinki, 3 GhG, 5B Stockholm, 3 Nice, 3 CP-GP, 4 Linz, 6 McD, 7 GPF, BL1: -,-,1,-
5. **Jason John** 17.10.71 (7y, 3) 10.23/10.08w '94   10.25w, 10.30, 10.33, 10.36, 10.42, 10.50; 2 CAU, 1 Madrid, 4= AAA, 3 Lisbon, 5 La Laguna
6. **Michael Rosswess** 11.6.65 (8y, 7) 10.15 '91, 10.07w '94   10.32w, 10.38, 10.39, 10.44, 10.47, 10.49; 1 Bedford, 2A Ljubljana, 1 Riga, 6 AAA
7. **Allyn Condon** 24.8.74 (1y, -) 10.48 '95, 10.37w '93   10.33w, 10.36, 10.42, 10.42w, 10.43, 10.43; 1 North, 7 AAA, 1 Cork, 7 CP-CP, 3 U23I, BL1: 2B,2,1B,-
8. **Doug Turner** 2.12.66 (1y, -) 10.58 '95   10.26w, 10.29w;   1 WG, 2 La Laguna
9. **Owusu Dako** 23.5.73 (2y, 10) 10.42 '95   10.30w, 10.35, 10.42, 10.43;   2r3 Madrid, 4 Cottbus, 1C Stockholm
10. **Jamie Henthorn** 20.2.77 (1y,) 10.41 '95   10.38w, 10.45, 10.47, 10.48, 10.54, 10.54; 6 WG, 2 Welsh, 3 Dublin, 4sf AAA, 2 SN4, 1 Welsh-J, 2 AAA-J, 4 WJ
11. **Dwain Chambers** 5.4.78 (1y,) 10.41 '95   10.42, 10.47, 10.48, 10.48, 10.49, 10.51; 3 AAA v LC, 1 South, 8 AAA, 1 South-J, 2 IR, 1 AAA-J, 5 WJ, BL1: 3B,3,3,3
12. **Jason Livingston** 17.3.71 (3y, -) 10.09 '92   10.42, 10.48w, 10.50, 10.61; 10.6, 10.6;   2 BL1 (4), 3 Cup

Not ranked
    Kevin Williams 15.12.71 (0y, -) 10.50 '95   10.35, 10.50, 10.56, 10.57, 10.61, 10.73
    2B Ljubljana, 5sf AAA, BL1: 5,-,5,4
    Adrian Patrick 15.6.73 (0y, -) 10.7 '91   10.38, 10.47, 10.59; 10.3, 10.5 1 IR, 2 BEL Ch, BL3: -,-,1,1
    Paul White 1.9.74 (0y, -) 10.40 '95   10.42, 10.44w, 10.46w, 10.48; 10.4, 10.4w
    4 Athens, 2 AAA v LC, 3B Ljubljana, 1 Mid, BL3: 3,-,-,-
    Josephus Thomas SLE 11.7.71 10.45 '95, 10.43w '92   10.33w, 10.43, 10.49; 10.2;   2 Riga, 2 Dublin, 2 Cup

Christie completed 11 successive years as the British number one, a record for any event (previous best 10 by Geoff Capes). Perhaps a sign of the changing succession was when he suffered his first defeat at 100m by a British athlete since 1986 (Allan Wells). The man to do this was Mackie, who burst into international class, and ranks 2nd, with a 3-1 record over Braithwaite. He was one of five newcomers to 100 ranking. Campbell also had a good season and was 3-2 up on Braithwaite, but the former's series of times was a little better and crucially he was ahead at the AAAs. The two top juniors were closely matched, but Henthorn gets the nod over Chambers on the World Juniors placing. Livingston returns to the rankings after his drugs ban, and would probably have been higher if he had had a complete season.

200 METRES
1. **Linford Christie** 2.4.60 (12y, 1) 20.09 '88   20.25w, 20.29, 20.40, 20.54, 20.59, 20.64; 1 ECp, 3 Rome, 2 AAA, 2 Lausanne, 4qf OG, 2 v IS, 1 BL1 (4)
2. **John Regis** 13.10.66 (12y, 1) 19.87A '94, 19.94 '93   20.33A, 20.39A, 20.44A, 20.47, 20.51A, 20.52; 1 Roodepoort, 1 Pietersburg, 2 Pretoria, 5 Rome, 1 Moscow, 1 AAA, 4 Paris, 2 GhG, 4 CP-GP, 6sf OG, 1 v IS, 3 McD
3. **Doug Turner** 2.12.66 (2y, 8=) 20.75/20.68w '95   20.43, 20.48, 20.57w, 20.63w, 20.66, 20.71w; 1 IR, 1 WG, 1 Welsh, 2 Tallinn, 4 AAA, 1 La Laguna, 5 CP-GP, 1B v IS, 2 McD, BL1: 4,-,1,2
4. **Owusu Dako** 23.5.73 (3y, 7) 20.57 '95   20.58, 20.60, 20.72, 20.74, 20.76, 20.83; 1 BL1 (1), 3 AAA, 2 Lucerne, 3 GhG, 3 CP-GP, 4h OG
5. **Doug Walker** 28.7.73 (3y, 8=) 20.71 '94, 20.53w '95   20.67, 20.78, 20.85, 20.87, 20.87, 20.90; 1 B.Univs, 1 Bedford, 1 AAA v LC, 1 Dublin, 5 AAA, 1 Scot, 2 Gävle, 1B CP-GP, 1 Cup
6. **Solomon Wariso** 11.11.66 (5y, 3) 20.50 '95   20.64, 20.85, 20.91, 20.95, 21.04, 21.19; 21.1; 21.03i; 2 BL1 (1), 1 Middx, 4 Ljubljana, 2 Riga, 3 Tallinn, 7 AAA, 5 Helsinki, 3 La Laguna
7. **Julian Golding** 17.2.75 (3y, 6) 20.75/20.69w '95   20.69w, 20.76, 20.77, 20.79, 20.81, 20.82; 20.8; 3 Pretoria, 2 Middx, 2 Dublin, 8 AAA, 2B CP-GP, 1 U23I, 1 IR, 3 BEL Ch, 2 Crawley sf, 2B v IS, 5 McD, 1 BL2 (4)
8. **Roger Black** 31.3.66 (6y, -) 20.60 '90   20.56, 20.90, 20.99w; 20.5w;   1 Irvine, 9 BL3 (3), 4 GhG
9. **Jason John** 17.10.71 (5y, 11) 20.86 '95, 20.51w '93   20.87, 20.91, 20.95, 21.00, 21.43w, 21.51; 21.4; 1 BL1 (2), 6 AAA, 4 La Laguna
10. **Allyn Condon** 24.8.74 (2y, -) 20.95 '93   20.64w, 20.84, 20.94, 20.97, 21.21; 21.1; 21.07i; 3 AAA v LC, 1 North, 5sf AAA, 4B CP-GP, 2 U23I, BL1: 1B,2,2,3
11. **Darren Braithwaite** 20.1.69 (5y, 4) 20.47 '95   20.60A, 20.80A, 20.89A, 20.95A, 21.02, 21.08; 3 Roodepoort, 4 Pietersburg, 5 Pretoria, 1 Ljubljana, dns sf AAA
12. **Adrian Patrick** 15.6.73 (1y, -) 21.17/21.0/20.62w '95   20.93w, 21.02, 21.04; 20.9, 21.1, 21.2; 2 IR, 1 Crawley sf, 3B v IS, BL3: 2,1,-,1

114

Regis progressed a round further at the Olympics and beat Christie 2-1, winning when both ran 20.54 at the AAAs and 20.62 to 20.64 at the August Gateshead meeting. However, Christie was well ahead, 20.29 to 20.60 in Rome, won the European Cup race and beat several world top 10 men in Lausanne, so he just retains his top ranking. Regis got stuck in the 20.5-20.6 range in Europe after faster times at altitude in South Africa early in the year. Those following the big two made progress. Turner had the better marks, but was beaten by Dako on all three occasions they met, and Walker, 5th behind these two at the AAAs, lost only one other 200m race. Patrick was only newcomer to the 200m rankings. The 10th best standard was a record 20.86 in 1995 and is even better this year at 20.79.

400 METRES
1. **Roger Black** 31.3.66 (11y, 2) 44.59 '86   44.37, 44.39, 44.41, 44.64, 44.69, 44.72, 44.77, 44.81, 44.83, 44.88;
    3 Atlanta, 2 Eugene, 1 AAA, 2 Lausanne, 2 CP-GP, 2 OG, 4 Zürich, 1 v IS, 1 McD, 5 GPF, 1 Tokyo
2. **Iwan Thomas** 5.1.74 (3y, 6) 45.58 '95   44.66A, 44.69, 44.70, 44.71, 44.94, 44.98A;
    6 wins in S.Africa, 6 Atlanta, 1 Tallinn, 3 AAA, 1 Helsinki, 1 GhG, 6 Lausanne, 3 CP-GP, 5 OG, 5 McD, 3 Rieti, 6 GPF
3. **Jamie Baulch** 3.5.73 (3y, 3) 45.14 '95   44.57, 44.72, 44.97, 45.06, 45.08, 45.13;
    1 AUS Ch, 1 BL1 (1), 1 WG, 4 Bratislava, 4 Rome, 1 Nürnberg, 4 AAA, 2 Lucerne, 3 GhG,
    3B Lausanne, 6 CP-GP, 1B Zürich, 5 Brussels, 4 McD
4. **Mark Richardson** 26.7.72 (7y, 1) 44.81 '96   44.52, 44.97, 45.15, 45.31, 45.33, 45.34;
    4A Dijon, 1 Watford, 5 AAA, 4 GhG, 2B Lausanne, 5 CP-GP, 5 Zürich, 3 v IS, 8 Brussels, 2 McD
5. **Du'aine Ladejo** 14.2.71 (6y, 7) 44.94 '94   44.66, 45.19, 45.29, 45.50, 45.57, 45.62;
    3 Pretoria, 1 E.Clubs, 1 Ljubljana, 2 Bratislava, 2 ECp, 2 AAA, 2 Helsinki, 5 GhG, 6qf OG
6. **Mark Hylton** 24.9.76 (3y, 4) 45.83 '95   45.57, 45.76, 46.24, 46.39, 46.52, 46.77; 46.45i, 46.49i;
    3B Dijon, 2 Watford, 6 AAA, 8 GhG, 7 CP-GP, 6 McD, 1 BL3 (4)
7. **David Grindley** 29.10.72 (6y, 10) 44.47 '92   45.66, 45.85, 46.35, 46.39, 46.48, 46.82;
    1 Blackburn, 1A Dijon, 7 Lucerne, BL4: 1,1,-,-
8. **Guy Bullock** 15.10.75 (2y, -) 46.13 '93   45.76, 45.90, 46.07, 46.14, 46.20, 46.38;
    2 Blackburn, 2 WG, 2B Dijon, 7 AAA, 1 U23I, 2 IR
9. **Jared Deacon** 15.10.75 (2y, 11) 46.45 '95   46.02, 46.08, 46.21, 46.38, 46.54, 46.78;
    1 Bedford, 1B AAA v LC, 2 North, 5sf AAA, 1 Cork, 2 U23I, 3 Linz
10. **Adrian Patrick** 15.6.73 (4y, 5) 45.63 '95   46.06, 46.29, 46.39, 46.51, 46.73, 46.89;
    1 CAU, 1 South, 8 AAA, 3B GhG, BL3: 1,-,1,-
11. **David Nolan** 25.7.69 (2y, 12) 46.61 '95   46.20, 46.25, 46.32, 46.41, 46.48. 46.68;
    1 North, 2 Tallinn, 7sf AAA, 2 Cork, 1 IS, BL1: 2,-,2,1
12. **David McKenzie** 3.9.70 (5y, 8) 45.47 '95   46.28, 46.60, 46.67, 46.73, 46.74A;
    6 Pretoria, 2B Jo'burg, 6 Ljubljana, 6sf AAA, 1 BL1 (3), 1 IR, 1 BEL Ch
Not ranked
    Tim O'dell 29.5.70 (1y, 9) 46.34 '95   46.40, 46.57, 46.70, 46.73, 46.78, 46.79;
    5B Pretoria, 2 AAA v LC, 2 South, 5 Tallinn, 5sf AAA, 3 IR, 4 Linz, 3 Abingdon, 1 Cup, BL2: 1,-,2,1
    Nick Budden 17.11.75 (0y, -) 46.89 '93   46.34, 46.49, 46.71, 46.85, 47.26, 47.34;
    1 B.Univs, 1 Mid, 6sf AAA, 5B GhG, 6 IR
    Cori Henry 9.12.76 (0y, -) 0?   46.50, 46.55, 46.88, 47.20, 47.39, 47.59
    2 Mid, 7sf AAA, 1 E.Sch, 1 Königs W
    Paul Slythe 5.9.74 (0y, -) 47.03 '95   46.52, 46.68, 46.80, 47.00, 47.14, 47.21;
    1 Athens, 3 CAU, 3 South, 8sf AAA, 2B GhG, 3 Königs W, 1 Abingdon
Richardson, no. 1 in 1995 when he was ranked 6th in the world, drops to 4th yet he improved his pb by 0.34 , an indication of just how great a year this was for British 400m running. Black improved the British record twice and took the Olympic silver medal, and is top for the 4th time (also 1986, 1990-1). Thomas stormed into world-class, running 18 times under his 1995 best of 45.58, and Baulch ran three sub-45 second times and still did not make the Olympic trio. Ladejo smashed his pb by 0.28 at the AAAs and yet is only 5th on the season's rankings. Baulch was 3-3 with Richardson but had slightly better times and was well ahead at the AAAs. They rank ahead of Ladejo who was unable to follow-up his brilliant AAA 2nd place. There was a tough fight for all the remaining rankings. For the final spot McKenzie and O'dell were 1-1. All 12 had been ranked before. The 10th best of 46.06 smashed the previous record of 46.31 in 1995.

800 METRES
1. **Curtis Robb** 7.6.72 (6y, 1) 1:44.92 '93   1:45.73, 1:45.85, 1:46.42, 1:47.48, 1:47.61, 1:47.75;
    1 Riga, 1 Tallinn, 1 AAA, 3 Helsinki, 6 GhG, 11 CP-GP, 6sf OG
2. **Craig Winrow** 22.12.71 (5y, 3) 1:46.54 '94   1:45.69, 1:45.77, 1:45.85, 1:45.91, 1:46.66, 1:47.03;
    1 BL4 (1), 1 Wyth-May, 4 WG, 10 Rome, 5 Nürnberg, 5 AAA, 3 GhG, 8 CP-GP, 8sf OG, 7 McD, 8 Berlin
3. **David Strang** 13.12.68 (4y, 2) 1:45.85 '92   1:45.81, 1:46.06, 1:46.38, 1:46.41, 1:46.56, 1:47.70;
    2 Cape Town, 4 ECp, 3 Tallinn, 2 AAA, 4 Helsinki, 5 GhG, 7 CP-GP, 4h OG
4. **Andy Hart** 13.9.69 (2y, 10) 1:48.06 '92   1:46.57, 1:47.44, 1:48.0, 1:48.13, 1:48.55, 1:48.7;
    6 Wyth-May, 3 Zofingen, 1 BMC Lough, 3 AAA v LC, 1 Watford, 4 AAA, 1 Stretford, 4 GhG, 10 CP-GP, 10 McD
5. **Tom Lerwill** 17.5.77 (1y, -) 1:47.27, 1:48.40, 1:49.18, 1:49.2, 1:49.22, 1:49.98;
    1 Watford, 3B GhG, 2 AAA-J, 2 WJ; BL1: 2,-,1,-
6. **Tony Morrell** 3.5.62 (9y, 12=) 1:44.59 '88   1:47.94, 1:48.44, 1:49.04, 1:49.41, 1:49.97, 1:49.?;
    2 BL4 (1), 1 North, 3 AAA, 8 Lisbon, 8 GhG

7.   **Lee Cadwallader** 17.1.69 (2y, 4) 1:47.43 '93   1:48.37, 1:48.5, 1:49.09, 1:49.1, 1:49.15, 1:49.2;
     3 BL1 (1), 2 Wyth-May, 2 BMC Lough, 5 Ljubljana, 6 AAA, 2 Stretford, 7B GhG
8.   **Bradley Donkin** 6.12.71 (1y, -) 1:51.93 '95   1:48.25, 1:48.4, 1:48.63, 1:49.18, 1:49.43, 1:50.08;
     1 CAU, 2 North, 7 AAA, 6 Cork, 4B GhG, 4 Wyth-Jul, 1 Gh Dev, 9 McD, 1 Nth IC
9.   **Terry West** 19.11.68 (2y, -) 1:48.2 '92   1:47.70, 1:47.72, 1:50.31, 1:51.2;
     1B BL4 (1), 2 Ljubljana, 4 Tallinn, dnf h AAA, 6 Gh Dev
10. **Rupert Waters** 3.1.72 (1y, -) 1:50.3 '95   1:47.9, 1:48.7, 1:49.00, 1:49.0, 1:49.6, 1:50.27;
     2 B.Univs, 2B Wyth-May, 6 AAA v LC, 2 South, 4 Watford, 4h AAA, 6B GhG, 1 Batt.Pk,
     1 IR, 2 Wyth-Jul, 2 Gh Dev, 1 Cup, BL1: -,-,1B,2
11. **Robin Hooton** 5.5.73 (1y, -) 1:49.14 '95   1:47.7, 1:49.0, 1:49.99, 1:49.99, 1:50.59, 1:51.29;
     3 B.Univs, 7 AAA v LC, 3 Watford, 5sf AAA, 4 Scot, 1 Wyth-Jul, 7 Gh Dev, 1B BL3 (3)
12. **Grant Graham** 27.12.72 (1y, -) 1:49.55 '95   1:49.2, 1:49.45, 1:49.98, 1:50.04, 1:50.79, 1:51.00;
     3 BMC Lough, 3 CAU, 8 AAA, dnf-B GhG
Not ranked
     Anthony Whiteman 13.11.71 (1y, -) 1:48.45 '94   1:47.8, 1:50.4, 1:52.0; 1:50.62i;   BL3: 1,-,1,1

Robb is no.1 for the third time with Winrow and Strang swapping places from 1995. Again there was no one anywhere near world ranking, but at least the 10th best standard at 1:47.9 was a little better than in 1994 and 1995. Thanks notably to BMC races the depth of 1:48-1:49 level runs was good and one hopes that some can jump into international class from there. Hart made good progress and most encouraging was the marvellous World Junior silver by Lerwill, after taking nearly two seconds off his pb in the semi-final. There were five newcomers to the rankings. Whiteman was unbeaten but in his three League races did not meet any ranking contenders.

1500 METRES - 1 MILE

1.   **John Mayock** 26.10.70 (6y, 1) 3:34.05/3:51.89M '95   3:33.38, 3:50.32M (3:34.82), 3:33.94, 3:34.55, 3:36.23,
     3:36.40, 3:36.82, 3:37.03, 3:54.60M;
     1 CAU, 8 Moscow, 1 AAA, 2 Cork, 3 GhG, 3 CP-GP, 11 OG, 8 Zürich, 1 v IS, 6 Brussels, 2 E.Carr, 7 Berlin, 8 Rieti, 9 GPF
2.   **Anthony Whiteman** 13.11.71 (2y, -) 3:41.92 '94, 3:59.44M '95   3:34.47, 3:34.92, 3:36.11, 3:36.37, 3:36.68,
     3:37.00, 3:37.18, 3:37.19, 3:54.87M;
     3 Lille, 3 ECp, 3 Nürnberg, 2 AAA, 5 Paris, 4 Nice, 5 CP-GP, 7sf OG, 15 Monaco, 3 v IS, 3 E.Carr, 1 Hendon
3.   **Gary Lough** 6.7.70 (4y, 2) 3:34.76/3:55.91M '95   3:37.35, 3:38.13, 3:39.18, 3:40.98, 3:41.33, 3:41.37;
     7 Melbourne, 8h AUS Ch, 2 CAU, 11 Nürnberg, 4 AAA, 1 SN4, 2 GhG, 11 Stockholm, 11 GP-CP,
     2 Ch'ham, 11 Köln, dnf, Brussels, 13 Berlin
4.   **Kevin McKay** 9.2.69 (8y, 3) 3:35.94 '92, 3:53.64M '94   3:37.90, 3:38.02, 3:39.40, 3:41.21, 3:41.38, 3:43.61;
     4 Hengelo, 13 St Denis, 6 Seville, 3 AAA, 12 GhG, 1 BL1 (3), 16 CP-GP, 12sf OG
5.   **Neil Caddy** 18.3.75 (2y, 8) 3:39.67/3:59.6M '95   3:55.84M (c.3:40.7), 3:39.1, 3:39.58, 3:58.59M, 3:59.3M,
     3:41.94;   2 AAA v LC, 6 Rhede, 4h3 AAA, 8 Bath, 4 GhG, 12 CP-GP, 1 U23I, 10 Wyth-Jul,
     1 Ch'ham, 1 Cardiff, 1 Swindon, 7 E.Carr, 2 Hendon.
6.   **Glen Stewart** 7.12.70 (1y, -) 3:40.17 '94, 4:06.0M '91   3:38.66, 3:41.12, 3:59.56M, 3:42.67, 3:43.03, 3:43.11;
     1 BL3 (1), 1 Wyth-May, 1 BMC Lough, 1 Ljubljana, 5 AAA, 2 Helsinki, 8 GhG, 10 E.Carr
7.   **Ian Grime** 29.9.70 (1y, -) 3:40.35'94, 4:03.7M '90   3:40.1, 3:41.2, 3:41.32, 3:43.81, 3:44.37, 3:45.49;
     1 B.Univs, 1 AAA v LC, 6 AAA, 4 Århus, 9 GhG, 1 IR, 2 Swindon, 3 Cup, BL2: -,-,2,1
8.   **Rob Denmark** 23.11.68 (6y, 9) 3:37.99 '95, 3:55.38M '90   3:55.39M (c.3:40.9); 6 E.Carr
9.   **Curtis Robb** 7.6.72 (2y, -) 3:38.56 '93   3:38.95, 3:50.57; 1 BL1 (1), 2 Ljubljana
10. **Brian Treacy** 29.7.71 (3y, 5) 3:38.93 '94, 4:00.67M '90   3:40.47, 3:41.78, 3:42.72, 3:43.93, 3:46.46;
     8 Granada, 8 Seville, 4h AAA, 7 La Laguna, 2 Andujár
11. **Philip Healy** 1.10.70 (1y, -) 3:43.8/4:02.01M '93   3:40.95, 3:40.96, 3:41.17, 3:43.03, 3:43.10, 4:01.2M,
     4 Irish Ch, 11 Cork, 1 Antrim, 1 So'ton, 2 Hexham
12. **Jon Wild** 30.8.73 (1y, -) 3:41.40/3:59.79M '95   3:41.48, 3:42.00, 3:42.54, 3:42.63, 3:44.41, 3:47.26;   10 NCAA
Not ranked
     Steve Green 18.2.71 (1y, 11) 3:39.19/3:59.6iM '94, 4:06.5M '90   3:42.01, 3:43.76, 3:45.11, 3:46.3, 3:50.66';
     2 BL1 (1), 3 Wyth-May, 7 AAA, 15 Cork
     Richard Ashe 5.10.74 (0y, -) 3:42.9 '95   3:41.2, 3:59.98M, 3:42.5, 4:00.30M, 3:43.54, 3:46.35;
     5 Wyth-May, 10 AAA, 1 Wyth-Jul, 2 U23I, 11 E.Carr, 3 Hendon
     Robert Hough 3.6.72 (0y, -) 3:46.0 '92, 4:01.4M '95   3:41.3, 3:41.5, 4:00.42M, 3:47.5;
     1B Wyth-Jul, 4 Hendon, BL4: 1,1,-,1B

M = 1 mile time. Equivalents: 3:35.0m = 3:52.0M, 3:38.0m = 3:55.3M, 3:41.0m = 3:58.6M, 3:44.0m = 4:01.8M
     (Times in brackets are 1500m times en route to 1 mile)

Mayock retained his no.1 ranking and won the Emsley Carr Mile for the second time. Whiteman, whose only previous ranking was 9th in 1994, started with European indoor silver, and made impressive progress. Lough, who started slowly, just shades McKay, who beat him conclusively at the AAAs, for 3rd. Caddy moved up and is followed by the best of four newcomers, Stewart and Grime, but after them ranking gets tricky. Denmark had just one race, but that fast as he beat good runners in the Emsley Carr mile and Robb had just one fast time, but none of the others had much depth of performance. Treacy and Healy have now declared for Ireland, but I kept them in as British for this year.

3000 METRES (Not ranked this year)

John Nuttall 11.1.67 7:48.59 '95 7:36.40, 7:44.66, 7:48.44, 7:49.57, 8:05.14:
6 Hengelo, 7 Nice, 6 CP-GP, 2 Köln, 3 v IS
Rob Denmark 23.11.68 7:39.55 '93, 8:21.97M '91 7:45.45, 8:13.88; 12 CP-GP, 12 Brussels
Robert Whalley 11.2.68 8:09.72i '94 7:52.6, 8:00.13, 8:04.0; 1 Watford, 1 P-CP, 1 Stretford
Robert Hough 3.6.72 8:10.2i '93 7:52.9; 2 Stretford
Ian Gillespie 18.5.70 8:00.9 '95 7:53.49, 8:05.79; 7:57.87i, 8:00.65i, 8:02.60i, 8:06.71i; 8 CP-GP, 3 P-CP
Keith Cullen 13.6.72 7:58.25 '95 7:53.97; 9 CP-GP
Gary Lough 6.7.70 7:49.45 '95 7:54.12, 8:11.44; 3 Hobart, 8 ECp
Jon Wild 30.8.73 7:55.16 '95 8:07.4; 7:53.10i, 8:02.14i, 8:07.26i

5000 METRES

1. **John Nuttall** 11.1.67 (8y, 2) 13:16.70 '95 13:17.48, 13:48.35, 13:52.16, 14:08.39; 5 St Denis, 1 AAA, 9sf OG
2. **Jon Brown** 27.2.71 (6y, 4) 13:19.78 '93 13:20.11, 13:22.11, c13:57+; 8 Nürnberg, 12 Stockholm
3. **Rob Denmark** 23.11.68 (6y, 1) 13:10.24 '92 13:31.36, 13:41.87, 13:51.72; 15 Nürnberg, 2 AAA, 13 Berlin
4. **Keith Cullen** 13.6.72 (1y, -) 13:54.52 '91 13:27.00, 14:00.61; 4 Kerkrade, 4 ECp
5. **Paul Evans** 13.4.61 (6y, 5) 13:25.38 '95 13:47.40, 13:49.31, 13:53.23, c13:5++ (OG), 14:16.24;
    17 Nürnberg, 1 GhG, 1 BL1 (4), 1 Cup
6. **Ian Gillespie** 18.5.70 (1y, -) 0 13:40.68, 13:56.6, 13:56.67, 14:00.06, 14:06.57;
    1 Street, 19 St Denis, 6 AAA, 5 GhG, 14 Linz
7. **Chris Sweeney** 3.3.66 (1y, -) 13:57.80 '90 13:43.49, 14:05.81; 7 Cork, 6 GhG
8. **Kris Bowditch** 14.1.75 (1y, -) 14:07.86 '95 13:55.32, 14:06.55, 14:10.92, 14:11.77, 14:22.1; 4 AAA, 8 GhG
9. **Spencer Barden** 31.3.73 (1y, -) 13:57.63 '95 13:52.34, 13:56.20, 14:09.8, 14:09.97, 14:12.94;
    1 AAA v LC, 5 AAA, 9 GhG, 10 Linz, BL3: 1,-,-,1
10. **Darius Burrows** 8.8.75 (1y, -) 14:11.27 '94 13:54.42, 13:55.81, 14:14.43, 14:17.78, 14:22.85;
    3 Zofingen, 3 AAA, 15 GhG, 2 Cup
11. **Spencer Newport** 5.10.66 (1y, -) 13:56.82 '92 13:49.74, 14:06.79, 14:12.01, 14:22.7; 2 AAA v LC, 2 CAU, 8 Cork
12. **Ian Hudspith** 23.9.70 (1y, -) 14:15.43 '95 13:54.6, 14:00.3, 14:00.98; 14:19.40; 7 AAA, 14 GhG, 1 BL4 (1)
    Jon Wild 30.8.73 (0y, -) 13:49.15 '95 13:45.1, 14:10.67, 14:31.70; 16 Walnut, 12 AAA, 19 Hechtel

After five years at the top Denmark is displaced by Nuttall, runner-up in 1994 and 1995. With an amazing turnover, none of those in 5th to 12th places have been ranked before at 5000m. British distance running standards in depth continue to decline drastically. Last year I said that the 10th best of 13:49.15 was the worst since 1970 (record 13:28.44 in 1984). The 1996 10th was 13:50.04!

10,000 METRES

1. **Jon Brown** 27.2.71 (4y, 3) 28:08.31 '95 27:59.72, 28:19.85, 28:21.40; 2 AAA, 10 OG
2. **Rob Denmark** 23.11.68 (2y, -) 28:03.34 '94 28:20.80; 1 AAA
3. **Paul Evans** 13.4.61 (5y, 1) 27:47.79 '93 28:24.39, 28:28.31; 3 AAA, dnf OG
4. **Ian Robinson** 21.4.69 (2y, 5) 28:34.84 '95 28:04.2, 28:46.06; 2 Walnut, 5 AAA
5. **Chris Sweeney** 3.3.66 (1y, -) 29:15.64 '90 28:44.09; 4 AAA
6. **Dermot Donnelly** 23.9.70 (1y. -) 29:33.8 '95 28:47.90, 29:45.83; 1 CAU, 6 AAA
7. **Andrew Pearson** 14.9.71 (3y, -) 28:40.49 '93 28:32.0, 29:01.05; 17 Walnut, 8 AAA
8. **Martin Jones** 21.4.67 (3y, -) 28:33.18 '94 28:37.87; 4 Koblenz, dnf AAA
9. **Steve Brooks** 8.6.70 (2y, 8) 29:04.63 '95 28:55.38; 7 AAA
10. **Ian Cornford** 1.2.66 (1y, -) 30:07.61 '91 29:08.66; 9 AAA
11. **Mark Hudspith** 19.1.69 (1y, -) 29:02.38 '92 29:09.31, 29:50.80; 2 CAU, 10 AAA
12. **Karl Keska** 7.5.72 (1y, -) 30:27.19 '95 29:10.40, 29:28.84; 1 Westwood, 8 NCAA

Brown takes his first top ranking and both he and Evans made the Olympic final. The 10th best of 29:08.66 is the worst since 1965 (allowing for 6 miles conversions in the 1960s). The only other years above 29 minutes were 1985 and 1995.

MARATHON

1. **Paul Evans** 13.4.61 (5y, 1) 2:10:31 '95 1 Chicago 2:08:52, 3 London 2:10:40
2. **Richard Nerurkar** 6.1.64 (4y, 3) 2:10:03 '93 5 OG 2:13:39
3. **Eamonn Martin** 9.10.58 (4y, 4) 2:10:50 '93 4 Chicago 2:11:21
4. **Gary Staines** 3.7.63 (2y, 9) 2:16:04 '95 5 Chicago 2:11:25, 9 London 2:12:54
5. **Steve Brace** 7.7.61 ((8y, -) 2:10:57 '91 2 Houston 2:10:35, 8 Belgrade 2:15:47, 60 OG 2:23:28
6. **Jon Solly** 28.6.63 (3y, -) 2:12:07 '90 2 Turin 2:12:25, dnf London
7. **Dale Rixon** 8.7.66 (2y,-) 2:15:41 '94 4 Puteaux 2:13:41
8. **Mike O'Reilly** 23.4.58 (5y, -) 2:10:39 '93 21 Tokyo 2:16:19
9. **Peter Fleming** 5.1.61 (5y, 6) 2:13:33 '93 3 Duluth 2:16:58, 2 Columbus 2:20:00
10. **Bill Foster** 9.8.58 (3y, 7) 2:15:49 '95 19 Beijing 2:18:55, 25 London 2:22:13
11. **Peter Whitehead** 3.12.64 (3y, 2) 2:12:23 '95 55 OG 2:22:37
12. **Mark Hudspith** 19.1.69 (3y, 5) 2:11:58 '95 18 London 2:19:25
    Mark Flint 19.2.63 (1y, -) 2:12:07 '94 32 Berlin 2:18:55, 37 London 2:27:11, dnf Houston

The splendid Chicago result featured three of the top four, with Nerurkar's fine Olympic performace ranking him 2nd. Brace, the most experienced marathoner in the list, also ran a fast time, but there was a big gulf between the top men and the rest. Most unusually for this event there were no newcomers to the rankings. The 10th best time was a record 2:12:51 in 1983 and it was under 2:15 each year 1981-9 and 1991-2, but declined to 2:18:40 in 1995 and now 2:18:55 this year, the worst since 1970.

3000 METRES STEEPLECHASE
1. **Justin Chaston** 4.11.68 (7y, 2) 8:23.90 '94   8:28.32, 8:28.50, 8:29.19, 8:29.64, 8:30.33, 8:33.59;
    5 Walnut, 2 E.Clubs, 3 ECp, 1 AAA, 9sf OG, 1 BL1 (4), 15 Brussels, 1 Cup
2. **Keith Cullen** 13.6.72 (5y, 3) 8:26.05 '95   8:28.93, 8:30.69, 8:30.80, 8:31.26, 8:46.74, 8:47.88;
    6 Bratislava, 2 AAA, 12 Stockholm, 11sf OG
3. **Robert Hough** 3.6.72 (4y, 5) 8:36.18 '95   8:26.33, 8:29.83, 8:43.30, 8:49.49, 8:53.21;
    1 AAA v LC, 5 AAA, 2 Århus, 4 Hechtel
4. **Spencer Duval** 5.1.70 (6y, 1) 8:24.64 '95   8:36.71, 8:46.76, 8:49.67; 3 AAA, 10h OG
5. **Michael Hawkins** 24.10.61 (10y, 8) 8:36.55 '95   8:41.54, 8:45.12, 8:54.45, 9:01.78;   2 AAA v LC, 4 AAA
6. **Spencer Newport** 5.10.66 (5y, 10) 8:40.87 '92   8:46.51, 8:46.56, 8:50.43, 8:51.8, 8:53.91, 8:54.78;
    2 South, 7 AAA, 2 IR, BL2: 1,-,1,1
7. **Matt O'Dowd** 13.4.76 (1y, -) 9:10.83 '94   8:44.26, 8:49.34, 8:57.11, 9:00.41, 9:04.1, 9:08.22;
    4 B.Univs, 1 CAU, 6 AAA, 3 U23I
8. **Kevin Nash** 6.2.77 (1y, -) 9:07.22 '95   8:43.21, 8:50.37. 8:51.36, 8:53.72, 9:01.14, 9:01.42;
    3 AAA v LC, 1 South, 11 AAA, 2 AAA-J, 11 WJ
9. **Adrian Green** 30.5.68 (1y, -) 8:51.1 '89   8:50.14, 8:50.57, 8:53.99, 8:56.3, 8:57.83, 9:04.2;
    8 AAA, 1 IR, 2 McD, 2 Cup, BL2: -,1,2,2
10. **Lee Hurst** 29.7.72 (1y, -) 8:54.01 '95   8:48.34, 8:52.99, 8:54.63, 8:58.67, 9:05.3, 9:06.4;
    3 CAU, 2 North, 9 AAA, 3 McD
11. **Raymond Plant** 13.5.68 (1y, -) 9:09.1 '94   8:52.64, 8:53.30, 8:55.22, 8:58.79, 9:03.89, 9:04.39;
    1 Mid, 14 AAA, 3 IR,1 McD
12. **David Lee** 16.9.65 (6y, 9) 8:31.22 '92   8:48.60, 8:50.20, 8:55.81, 9:21.0;   2 Zofingen, 12 AAA, 4 BL2 (4)
Not ranked
    Jason Humm 11.1.71 (1y, -) 9:07.60 '94   8:49.03, 8:56.31, 9:04.64, 9:05.5, 9:08.60;   2 CAU, 3 South, 8h AAA
Chaston makes it to no.1 after ranking 12-8-7-4-3-2 in the years 1990-5. Although he did not run times as fast as in previous years he had a solid season and made the Olympic semi-final. Cullen was unlucky there with injury and Duval was fortunate to make the team as Hough ran poorly at the AAAs. Sadly we have nobody in top world class at the event. There was quite a gap after the top three (or four) and the 10th best declined again so that 8:48.60 has only twice been bettered (8:50.2 in 1976 and 8:48.84 in 1984) since 1970.

110 METRES HURDLES
1. **Colin Jackson** 18.2.67 (13y, 1) 12.91 '93, 12.8w '90   13.13, 13.13, 13.14w, 13.17, 13.19, 13.22;
    4 wins in AUS, 1 Cape Town, 1 Jo'burg, 1 WG, 2 Bratislava, 2 ECp, 4 Rome, 3 Nürnberg, 1 AAA, 1 GhG,
    2 Lausanne, 2 Stockholm, 4 OG, 3 Sestriere, 3 P-CP, 6 Zürich, 3 v IS, 2 Brussels, 3= McD
2. **Anthony Jarrett** 13.8.68 (11y, 2) 13.00 '93   13.24, 13.25, 13.25w, 13.27, 13.32, 13.32; 13.0w;
    1/2 Pretoria, 2 Cape Town, dq Atlanta, 1 Ljubljana, CAU, 1 Bratislava, 1 Riga, 2 AAA, 1 Helsinki, 2 GhG,
    dq Stockholm, 4 CP-GP, fell dq OG, 5 Sestriere, 1 P-CP, 1B Zürich, 2 v IS, 2 McD, 2 Berlin
3. **Andrew Tulloch** 1.4.67 (10y, 3) 13.52 '94   13.56, 13.57, 13.64, 13.64, 13.68; 13.5w;
    4 E.Clubs, 3 Ljubljana, 5 Bratislava, 4 Riga, 4 Helsinki, 3 AAA, 6 GhG, 1B Stockholm, 6 CP-GP, 6qf OG, 6 P-CP, 5 McD
4. **Paul Gray** 25.5.69 (7y, 5) 13.53 '94   13.61A, 13.62w, 13.63w, 13.63w, 13.70, 13.72;
    3 Melbourne, 2 AUS Ch, 3 Cape Town, 5 Jo'burg, 1 Bedford, 2 WG, 6 Bratislava, 6 Nürnberg,
    2 Lucerne, 4 AAA, 4 GhG, 7 Lausanne, 2B Stockholm, 8 CP-GP, 7 P-CP, 7 McD, 2 BL1 (1)
5. **Neil Owen** 18.10.73 (5y, 4) 13.60 '95   13.62, 13.65w, 13.68, 13.72, 13.73w, 13.75; 13.5w;
    6 Ljubljana, 3 Riga, 4 Tallinn, 5 AAA, 5 GhG, 7 CP-GP, 8 P-CP, 8 McD, 1 Cup, BL1: 1,-,1,1
6. **Kenneth Campbell** 30.9.72 (4y, 7) 13.86 '94   13.90, 13.93, 14.01, 14.01, 14.01, 14.04;
    1 B.Univs, 1 Scot, 3 Dublin, 6 AAA, 1 SN4, BL1: -,-,2,3
7. **Mark Stern** 22.5.72 (2y, -) 14.24/14.11w '93   14.13, 14.19, 14.19, 14.22, 14.28, 14.30;
    2 AAA v LC, 2 CAU, 1 South, 7 AAA, 3 Cork, 1 IR, 5 BEL Ch, BL1: 3,-,3,2
8. **James Archampong** 14.3.76 (1y, -) 14.18 '94   14.14w, 14.19, 14.33, 14.39, 14.40, 14.42; 14.1w, 14.3;
    2 B.Univs, 3 AAA v LC, 3 WG, 1 CAU, 1 Welsh, 3h AAA, 2 SN4, 3 U23I, 1 Stoke sf, BL2: 1,2,1,1
9. **Damien Greaves** 19.9.77 (2y, 10) 14.34 '95   14.04, 14.17, 14.20, 14.21, 14.22, 14.3; 14.2w;
    4 AAA v LC, 3 CAU, 4h AAA, 4 Cork, 1 AAA-J, 5 WJ, BL2: -,1,2,-
10. **Ross Baillie** 26.9.77 (1y, -) 14.54/14.4w '95   14.01, 14.12, 14.30, 14.43, 14.61, 14.74; 14.2;
    6 CAU, 2 Scot, 2 AAA-J, 4 WJ
11. **Brian Taylor** 13.8.70 (3y, -) 14.08 '91, 13.9 '93   14.03, 14.13, 14.38; 14.3, 14.6; 1 AAA v LC
12 **Martin Nicholson** 9.12.70 (4y, 12) 14.14/13.8 '94   14.44, 14.51, 14.53, 14.54, 14.56, 14.60;
    1B AAA v LC, 4 CAU, 1 North, 8 AAA, 4 IR, 2 Stoke sf, 1 Nth IC, BL1: 4,1,4,4
Jackson is UK No. 1 for the 9th time, the record for the event. He was 5-4 up on Jarrett, ranked in the UK top two for the 9th successive year. Baillie and Greaves excelled for 4th and 5th at the World Juniors, but Archampong beat Greaves 4-1 to rate higher. The 10th best of 14.13 is only 0.03 off the record.

400 METRES HURDLES

1. **Jon Ridgeon** 14.2.67 (3y, -) 48.73 '92   48.79, 49.04, 49.16, 49.25, 49.31, 49.43;
   2 E.Clubs, 1 WG, 5 Bratislava, 2 ECp, 1 AAA, 5 Helsinki, 3 GhG, 6 Stockholm,
   4 CP-GP, 7sf OG, 3 P-CP, 2B Zürich, 2 v IS, 2 McD, 3 Rieti
2. **Peter Crampton** 4.6.69 (4y, 2) 49.26 '94   49.78, 49.79, 49.93, 50.14, 50.16, 50.35;
   1 Yorks, 1 AAA v LC, 2 WG, 1 CAU, 2 AAA, 6 GhG, 8 CP-GP, 6h OG
3. **Gary Cadogan** 8.10.66 (4y, 3) 49.25 '93   50.00, 50.01, 50.14, 50.17, 50.20, 50.32;
   2 Ljubljana, 2 Riga, 4 Budapest, 6 Helsinki, 5 GhG, 7 CP-GP, 4 P-CP, 4 v IS, 8 McD
4. **Gary Jennings** 21.2.72 (4y, 1) 49.82 '95   50.18, 50.41, 50.46, 50.54, 50.63, 50.98;
   1 BL2 (2), 3 AAA, 8 GhG, 6 CP-GP, 6h OG, 6 P-CP, 6 McD, 1 Cup
5. **Paul Hibbert** 31.3.65 (4y, 11) 51.33 '95   50.52, 50.61, 50.67, 50.86, 51.09, 51.15;
   1B AAA v LC, 3 WG, 1 Mid, 4 AAA, 7 GhG, 1 IR, 1 Stoke sf, 7 P-CP, 2 Cup, BL1: 1,1,1,1
6. **Lawrence Lynch** 1.11.67 (8y, 5) 50.19 '91   50.05, 50.39, 50.40, 50.75, 51.07, 51.2;
   1 Middx, 1 Bedford, 2 CAU, 1 South, dq AAA, 2 Stoke sf, BL1: 2,2,4,-
7. **Chris Rawlinson** 19.5.72 (2y, 6) 50.90 '95   50.36, 50.88, 50.97, 51.33, 51.43, 52.21;
   2 Yorks, 1 North, 3 Tallinn, 5 AAA, 3 IR, 4 BL1 (1)
8. **Paul Thompson** 22.3.72 (1y, -) 52.39 '94   50.16, 51.00, 51.11, 51.13, 51.20, 51.28;   3h NCAA, 5sf AAA, 1B BL1 (3)
9. **Noel Levy** 22.6.75 (4y, -) 50.70 '94   50.85, 51.26, 51.32, 51.40, 51.55, 51.55;
   2 Bedford, 4 WG, 5 South, 4 Dublin, fell AAA, 3 U23
10. **David Savage** 13.11.72 (2y, 10) 51.39 '95   50.97, 51.32, 51.62, 51.89, 51.89, 52.28;
    6 Bedford, 2 North, 6 AAA, 3 Cup, BL1: 7,3,3,2
11. **Barry Middleton** 10.3.75 (1y, -) 52.46 '95   51.18, 51.30, 51.77, 51.83, 51.95, 52.08;
    4 Bedford, 3 Dublin, 6sf AAA, 1 SN4, 1 Scot, 4 U23
12. **Matthew Douglas** 26.11.76 (2y, 12) 51.73 '95   51.47, 52.00, 52.21, 52.26, 52.60. 52.61;
    3 Middx, 5 Bedford, 5 WG, 2 South, 6 Dublin, 6sf AAA

The return of Ridgeon was one of the happiest aspects of the 1996 season. Having last completed a race in May 1993, he returned to the 400mh in Australia in January with a 51.3 race. He then ran eight races in the 50.02-50.98, before breaking 50 seconds for the first time on 25 May. In all he ran 29 races at 400mh, 17 times under 50.0. A case of continuing improvement with a racing programme to put many to shame. Crampton is 2nd for the third successive year. Although Lynch had the faster times he was beaten 5-0 by Hibbert. Very close for the final place, which just went to Douglas who beat Eddie Betts 2-1. The 10th best of 50.97 is a new record (previous best 51.15 in 1994).

HIGH JUMP

1. **Steve Smith** 29.3.73 (7y, 1) 2.37 '92, 2.38i '94   2.35, 2.31, 2.30, 2.28, 2.28, 2.28; 2.36i, 2.30i, 2.30i;
   1 BL1 (1), 1 Hengelo, 4= Seville, 1 AAA, 1 GhG, 2 Lausanne, 5 Oslo, 5 Stockholm,
   4 CP-GP, 3 OG, 5 P-CP, 4= McD, nh GPF
2. **Dalton Grant** 8.4.66 (13y, 2) 2.36 '91, 2.37i '94   2.33, 2.31, 2.30, 2.30, 2.28, 2.28; 2.34i. 2.33i, 2.30i;
   3 Rio, 2 Bedford, 6 Rhede, 3 ECp, 3 Rome, 2 AAA, 4 Paris, 3 GhG, 10 Lausanne, 4 Nice, 2= CP-GP,
   dnq 19 OG, 2 P-CP. 9 Zürich, 4 Eberstadt, 2 v IS, 4= McD, 1 Cup, 7 GPF
3. **James Brierley** 31.7.77 (3y, 4) 2.17/2.18i '95   2.26, 2.21, 2.15, 2.15, 2.14, 2.10; 2.20i, 2.15i;
   2 Mannheim, 6 GhG, 8= CP-GP, 1 AAA-J, 1 JInt, 7= WJ, 1 BL4 (3)
4. **Ben Challenger** 7.3.78 (1y, -) 2.11 '95   2.21, 2.20, 2.15, 2.15, 2.15, 2.14; 2.18i, 2.16i;
   2 AAA v LC, 1 Mid, 3 Mannheim, 1 Mid-J, 1 E.Sch, 1 IR, 2 AAA-J, 2= WJ, 5 JumpsI
5. **Colin Bent** 12.4.70 (2y, -) 2.14 '95   2.20, 2.20, 2.15, 2.15, 2.15, 2.10; 2.11i;
   4 Bedford, 2 Mid, 1 CAU, 3 AAA, 7 Cork, 7 GhG, 2 IR, 7= P-CP, 1 IS, 4 v IS, 7 McD, 2 Cup, nh JumpsI, BL1: 4,2,-,-
6. **Geoff Parsons** 14.8.64 (15y, 5) 2.31 '94   2.15, 2.15, 2.14, 2.10, 2.05A; 2.15i;   4 AAA, 1 SN4
7. **Robert Brocklebank** 12.10.76 (3y, 10) 2.16 '95   2.15, 2.13, 2.10, 2.10, 2.10, 2.10; 2.15i. 2.14i;
   1 AAA v LC, 2 North, 5 AAA, 8 Cork, 6 U23I, 4 IR
8. **Ian Holliday** 9.12.73 (1y, -) 2.13 '95   2.15, 2.14, 2.10, 2.10, 2.05, 2.05;
   5 AAA v LC, 1 North, 6 AAA, 5 Cork, 2 Scot, 2 Nth IC, 3 IR; BL1: 3,3,2,2
9. **Richard Aspden** 15.10.76 (2y, 8) 2.16 '95   2.15, 2.10, 2.10, 2.10, 2.10, 2.10;
   7 E.Clubs, 1 South, 8= AAA, 2 Zoetemeer, 5 U23I, 2 Liverpool sf, 1 BEL Ch, 2 Abingdon, 3 Cup, BL1: 5,nh,-,1
10. **Danny Graham** 3.8.79 (1y, -) 2.05 '95   2.15, 2.12, 2.11, 2.10, 2.09, 2.08;
    4 North, 1 Nth-J, 2 E.Sch, 1 Jnr IA
11. **Stuart Ohrland** 6.9.75 (3y, 9) 2.17 '94   2.14, 2.13, 2.12, 2.11, 2.07, 2.05; 2.10i, 2.08i;
    6 AAA v LC, 2= South, 2= CAU, 11 AAA, 5 IR, 1 Abingdon
12. **Damon Rutland** 10.7.75 (1y, -) 2.13 '95   2.11, 2.10, 2.05, 2.05, 2.05, 2.05;   2= South, 1 Zoetemeer
Not ranked
   Brendan Reilly (23.12.72 (7y, -) 2.31 '92, 2.32i '94   2.23i
   Mark Mandy (Ireland) 19.11.72 2.25 '95   2.25, 2.24, 2.24, 2.23, 2.23, 2.22; 2.23i;
   1 Bedford, 1 WG, 1 Riga, 1 Dublin, 1 Irish Ch, 4 Cork, 8= CP-GP, dnq 23 OG, 6 P-CP, 4= McD
   Tyron Peacock (S.Africa) 16.12.76 2.10 '95   2.15, 2.11, 2.10, 2.10, 2.10, 2.10; 2.16i;
   3 Bedford, 2= CAU, 6 Cork, 1 Liverpool sf, BL1: 2,1,1,-

Smith 1st and Grant 2nd for the fourth successive year, but the 3rd ranked man for the previous three years, Brendan Reilly, drops out as he lost the year through injury after one competition, at 2.23 indoors. Smith excelled in Atlanta, but otherwise had a modest year by his high standards. Grant has now been in the top three for 11 successive years. Brierley moves up a place to 3rd although he was outjumped at the World Juniors by Challenger, who took a splendid silver medal. Parsons dropped out of the top-five, after 14 years, but still hangs on in sixth place ahead of improving youngsters.

POLE VAULT

1. **Nick Buckfield** 5.6.73 (6y, 1) 5.70 '95 5.71, 5.65, 5.60, 5.60, 5.60, 5.50 x 7; 5.61i, 5.55i, 5.55i;
   1 AAA v LC, 3 Dijon, 4 ECp, 2 Nürnberg, 1 AAA, 3 GhG, 8 CP-GP. dnq 20= OG, 3 v IS, 6 McD, BL2: 1,-,-,1
2. **Paul Williamson** 16.6.74 (3y, 3) 5.40 '95 5.50, 5.45, 5.45, 5.40, 5.40, 5.40; 1 B.Univs, 1 Blackburn, 2 AAA v LC,
   1 CAU, 2 North, 2 Tallinn, 6= AAA, 1 Cork, 1 Woking, 1= Stoke 28/6, 1 IR, 1 Nth IC, 4= McD, 3 JumpsI, 1 BL1 (4)
3. **Neil Winter** 21.3.74 (6y, 2) 5.60 '95 5.50, 5.40, 5.40, 5.40, 5.30, 5.25;
   1 Welsh, 2 AAA, 7= GhG, 9 CP-GP, dnq 24= OG, nh v IS, nh McD, BL1: -,3,2,3
4. **Michael Edwards** 19.10.68 (11y, 8) 5.52 '93 5.45, 5.41, 5.40, 5.40, 5.40, 5.36;
   6 AAA v LC, nh E.Clubs, 3 AAA, 7= GhG, BL1: 1,1,-,8
5= **Kevin Hughes** 30.4.73 (4y, 9) 5.30 '95 5.30, 5.30, 5.30, 5.25, 5.20, 5.20; 6 Dormagen, 1 WG,
   4 CAU, 1 South, 5 AAA, 4 Cork, 3 Woking, 6 GhG, 3 IR, 1 Wrexham, 3 BEL Ch, 2 P'bor, BL1: nh,2,1,4
5= **Michael Barber** 19.10.73 (5y, 4) 5.42 '95 5.30, 5.30, 5.30, 5.20, 5.20, 5.20, 5.20;
   2 Blackburn, 1 Mid, 6= AAA, 2 Cork, 1= Stoke 28/6, 2 IR, BL1: 2,6,3=,-
5= **Ian Tullett** 15.8.69 (10y, 5) 5.30 '92 5.30, 5.30, 5.20, 5.20, 5.20, 5.20;
   8 Dormagen, 2 WG, 2 CAU, 2g Mid, 4 AAA, 3 Cork, 2 Woking, 5 GhG, BL1: -,4,5,-
8. **Matt Belsham** 11.10.71 (7y, 10) 5.35 '93 5.35, 5.30, 5.30, 5.30, 5.25, 4.90; 5.40i, 5.35i;
   1 Dormagen, 8 AAA, nh Woking, nh IR, 1 P'bor, BL1: -,-,7,2
9 **Dean Mellor** 25.11.71 (7y, 7) 5.30 '95 5.21, 5.20, 5.20, 5.10, 5.00, 5.00; 5.10i, 5.01i;
   1 Yorks, 3 AAA v LC, 3 CAU, 9 AAA, BL4: 1,1,1,1
10. **Andrew Ashurst** 2.1.65 (13y, 6) 5.40 '88, 5.45i '92 5.20, 5.20, 5.20, 5.10, 5.10, 5.10; 5.20i;
    3 Blackburn, 2g Yorks, 1 North, 10 AAA, 5 Cork, 4 Woking, 3 Stoke 28/6, 2 Wrexham, BL1: 3,5,nh,5=?
11. **Christian Linskey** 14.6.80 (1y, -) 4.81 '95
    5.15, 5.11, 5.10, 5.10, 5.00, 5.00;
    4 AAA v LC, 4 North, 13= AAA, 1 Nth U17, 1 E.Sch-I, 1 Sch. Int, 1 AAA-J, 5 JInt, 11 WJ
12. **Mark Davis** 1.3.77 (1y, -) 5.00 '95 5.10, 5.10, 5.00, 5.00, 5.00. 4.95;
    6 AAA v LC, 5 CAU, 3 Mid, 11 AAA, 5 IR, 2 AAA-J, 4 JInt, dnq 22 WJ

Not ranked

Mark Hogkinson 20.7.72 (2y, -) 5.10 '95 5.20, 5.00, 5.00, 5.00, 5.00, 4.90;
nh AAA, 4 Wrexham, 3 P'Bor, BL1: nh, 11, 6,5=?

The top ten are the same as in 1995, although the order changes a little. Buckfield retained his top ranking, improving his British record at the AAAs, and Williamson moves up ahead of Winter. Barber and Tullett had an identical set of best marks, with Barber having a narrow 3-2 edge on win-loss; while Hughes had one more 5.30 clearance and was 3-3 v Barber, but although 4-6 down to Tullett, outjumped him 4-3! Belsham had better marks than those three, but a worse competitive record. Linskey, 16 in June, is the top newcomer, but is not the youngest ever, as Winter was 11th= at 15 in 1989. The 10th best standard matches the record set in 1995.

LONG JUMP

1. **Darren Ritchie** 14.2.75 (2y, 12) 7.46 '95 7.86, 7.68w, 7.63w, 7.51, 7.33, 7.33w; 7.48i, 7.40i;
   1 CAU, 4 Dublin, 1 AAA, 1 Scot, 2 SN4, 5 U23I, 8 Hechtel, BL1: 5,-,-,3
2. **Nathan Morgan** 30.6.78 (2y, 9) 7.39/7.43w '95 7.97w, 7.74, 7.66w, 7.65, 7.58, 7.56;
   1 AAA v LC, 9 Ljubljana, 2 Tallinn, 6 AAA, 1 E.Sch, 1 AAA-J, 3 JInt, 3 WJ
3. **Steve Phillips** 17.3.72 (6y, 3) 7.91 '91 7.79w (7.65), 7.75, 7.65w, 7.64w, 7.63, 7.61; 7.69i; 1 Warwicks,
   3 AAA v LC, 2 CAU, 3 WG, 1 Mid, 2 Lough 5/6, 5 AAA, 1 Fin.Pk, 1 IR, 1 Wrexham, 2 Welwyn, BL1: 2,1,1,1
4. **Fred Salle** 10.9.64 (10y, 1) 8.10 '94 7.79, 7.68w, 7.60, 7.43; 4 E.Clubs, 5 Ljubljana, 9 ECp, BL1: 1,nj,-,-
5. **Onochie Onuorah** 16.10.73 (3y, 2) 7.58/7.81w '95 7.67, 7.62, 7.44, 7.44w, 7.43, 7.41; 7.52i;
   1 B.Univs, 4 AAA v LC, 4 CAU, 1 South, 2 AAA, 3 Scot, BL1: 9,3,4,7
6. **Stewart Faulkner** 19.2.69 (9y, 4) 8.15 '90 7.54, 7.50, 7.50w, 7.48, 7.47, 7.38w;
   6 AAA v LC, 3 AAA, 3 Fin.Pk, 12 BEL Ch, BL1: 4,2,-,-
7. **Julian Flynn** 3.7.72 (1y, -) 7.52 '92 7.57, 7.49, 7.49, 7.48w, 7.44, 7.35
   2 Warwicks, 5 WG, 3 Mid, 4 AAA, 2 Fin.Pk, 2 IR, 2 Wrexham, 1 Welwyn, 2 BL1 (4)
8. **Chris Davidson** 4.12.75 (1y, -) 7.33 '95, 7.46w '94 7.54, 7.50, 7.41w (7.15), 7.37, 7.02; 7.60i, 7.57i;
   3 U23I, 1 Cup, BL2: 2,1,2,-
9. **Barrington Williams** 11.9.55 (10y, 6) 8.05i/8.01 '89 7.54w (7.42), 7.38, 7.26, 7.19, 7.03; 7.52i, 7.36i;
   2 Mid, 8 AAA, 3 Cork, 2 BL1 (3)
10. **John Shepherd** 23.12.61 (9y, 10=) 7.66 '88, 7.89w '86 7.46, 7.39, 7.31w, 7.29w, 7.27, 7.24;
    5 CAU, 7 South, BL3: -,-,1,4
11. **Carl Howard** 27.1.74 (5y, 7) 7.76 '93 7.31, 7.23, 7.23, 7.21; 7.44i, 7.43i; 2 BL2 (2), 7 AAA, 1 Crawley sf
12. **Paul Johnson** 8.3.68 (8y, -) 7.94i/7.85 '89. 7.87w '88 7.48, 7.25, 7.12, 7.06;
    2 Yorks, 1 North, 9 AAA, 5 Cork, 1 Nth IC

There was no clear-cut claimant to top ranking. Morgan produced the year's longest (wind-aided) jump to win the English Schools and took World Junior bronze. Ritchie won the AAAs with the longest 'legal' jump, Phillips had the best series of marks and Salle (who has an event record 13-year span in the rankings) some good competitions before his season ended prematurely. Ritchie and Phillips met four times, but while Phillips won the League clashes, Ritchie won CAU and AAA, and that just gives him the edge. Morgan was only 6th at the AAAs, the only time he met Ritchie, but beat Phillips 2-1. Quite a struggle to find 12 to rank, but note 4 Birchfield men in top 9!

TRIPLE JUMP

1. **Jonathan Edwards** 10.5.66 (11y, 1) 18.29/18.43w '95   17.88, 17.82, 17.79, 17.79w, 17.69, 17.68, 17.67A, 17.59, 17.59w, 17.55, 17.52, 17.50;   1 Atlanta, 1 ECp, 1 Rome, 1 Helsinki, 1 GhG, 1 Oslo, 1 Stockholm, 1 CP-GP, 2 OG, 1 Sestriere, 1 P-CP, 1 Zürich, 1 v IS, 1 Brussels, 1 McD, 1 Berlin, 1 GPF, 2 Tokyo; won 16/18.
2. **Francis Agyepong** 16.6.65 (14y, 2) 17.18/17.29Aw/17.24w '95   17.22w, 17.19w (16.89), 17.18, 17.12, 16.77, 16.71; 16.97i, 16.93i, 16.92i; 2 AAA v LC, 1 Florø, 2 Riga, 6 Rome, 1 AAA, 4 Helsinki, 2 GhG, 2 Oslo, 3 Stockholm, 2 CP-GP, dnq 13 OG, 3 P-CP, 13 Zürich, 2 v IS, 6 Brussels, 2 McD, 11 Berlin, 5 GPF
3. **Julian Golley** 12.9.71 (7y, 5) 17.06 '94   16.53, 16.45, 16.44, 16.39, 16.25w, 16.18;   4 AAA v LC, 1 CAU, 5 Riga, 3 AAA, 4 GhG, 6 CP-GP, 5 Sestriere, 7 P-CP, 6 McD; BL1: 2,-,2,-
4. **Femi Akinsanya** 29.11.69 (4y, 6) 16.03 '95   16.58, 16.23, 16.23w, 16.19, 16.17w (16.15), 15.99; 16.05i; 1 AAA v LC, 1 Lidingö, 2 AAA, 7 GhG, 7 CP-GP, 8 P-CP, 7 McD; BL3: 1,-,1,1
5. **Tosi Fasinro** 28.3.72 (7y, 4) 17.21/17.30w '93   16.38, 16.05, 15.97, 15.88, 15.70, 15.62; 15.79i; 1 Bedford, 5 Granada, 1 South, 4 AAA, 6 Århus, 8 GhG, BL1: 1,-,-,4
6. **Tayo Erogbogbo** 8.3.75 (3y, 3) 16.32 '95   16.25w, 16.12w, 15.91, 15.83, 15.79, 15.71;   1 B.Univs, 3 AAA v LC, 2 Lidingö, 2 CAU, 8 AAA, 1 BL1 (2). UK citizen from October.
7. **Onochie Achike** 31.1.75 (5y, 8) 16.53/16.67w '94   16.36, 16.04, 14.29; 5 AAA, 6 Luton
8. **John Herbert** 20.4.62 (16y, 9) 17.41 '85   15.90, 15.89, 15.86; 15.63i, 15.61i; 5 Florø, 6 AAA
9. **Joe Sweeney** 17.7.65 (9y, 7) 16.26 '91   15.75, 15.66, 15.37, 15.22, 14.65; 15.67i, 15.53i, 15.29i; 3 CAU, 2 South, BL3: 3,-,-,3
10. **Paul Ralph** 16.12.67 (2y, 10) 15.67/15.72w '95   15.67w, 15.65, 15.62, 15.55, 15.51w, 15.49;   4 CAU, 3 South, 7 AAA, BL3: 5,1,2,2
11. **Ezra Clarke** 9.12.74 (1y, -) 15.46 '94   15.63, 15.52, 15.46, 15.45w, 15.44, 15.24;   3 Bedford, 1 WG, 9 AAA, 4 U23I, 1 Cup, BL1: -,9,-,1
12. **James Peacock** 29.9.77 (1y, -) 15.04 '95   15.74w, 15.34w, 15.24, 15.12, 15.08, 15.04;   5 CAU, 1 Sth-J, 1 E.Sch, 1 AAA-J, 4 JInt

Not ranked
    Carl Howard 27.1.74 (2y, 12) 15.97 '95   15.67, 15.18, 15.16, 14.36; 2 Bedford, 3 U23I, 1 Crawley sf, 2 BL2 (2)

If not quite in his 1995 form, the superb Edwards remained Britain's top athlete at any event in world terms; he is UK no.1 for the 7th time. Agyepong was again on the edge of the world top ten. Akinsanya was ahead in the first half of the year, Golley in the second, but they ended 4-4, with Golley edging ahead on a better series of marks. Herbert is ranked for a triple jump record 16th time in 18 seasons. The standard declines after the top group so that the 10th best of 15.63 was the worst since 1983.

SHOT

1. **Shaun Pickering** 14.11.61 (14y, 3) 18.94 '95   19.62, 19.32, 19.23, 19.23, 19.10, 19.07; 19.10i; 4 Walnut, 6 E.Cup, 2 AAA, dnq 27 OG, 1 G'head 19/8, BL1: -,1,-,1
2. **Matthew Simson** 28.5.70 (10y, 2) 19.49 '94   19.22, 18.99, 18.95, 18.93, 18.84, 18.82;   1 WG, 1 South, 1 AAA, 3 GhG, 4 CP-GP, 1 Abingdon
3. **Mark Proctor** 15.1.63 (6y, 1) 19.37 '95   19.67, 19.15, 19.13, 18.70, 18.64, 18.18; 19.12i, 18.92i;   1 Tooting, 3 AAA, 6 GhG, 1 IS, 5 CP-GP, 2 Cup, BL2: 6,1,-,-
4. **Stephan Hayward** 30.7.74 (2y, 4) 18.62 '95   18.40, 18.20, 18.16, 18.07, 17.90, 17.83; 17.92i;   6 Halle, 1 Bedford, 1 CAU, 1 Dublin, 5 AAA, 1 SN4, 1 Scot, 3 U23I, 1 Liverpool sf, 1 Cup, BL1: 2,-,1,2
5. **Lee Newman** 1.5.73 (4y, 4) 18.46 '95   18.85, 18.56, 18.12, 18.11, 18.06, 17.79; 17.81i; 1 Luton, 5 E.Clubs, 2 South, 2 Tooting, 4 AAA, 7 GhG, 6 CP-GP, 2 Liverpool sf, 1 London, 3 Cup, BL1: 1,3,3,3
6. **James Cockburn** 30.1.73 (1y, -) 16.18 '94   17.41, 16.90, 16.83, 16.63; 3 CAU, 4 South, 4 Abingdon
7. **David Callaway** 4.9.63 (9y, 6) 17.55 '93   16.72, 16.70, 16.68, 16.68, 16.65, 16.54; 17.21i, 17.04i; 2 Luton, 1 Hants, 1 AAA v LC, 4 CAU, 6 South, 7 AAA, 1 IR, 3 BEL Ch, 2 London. 2 Abingdon, 4 Cup, BL1: 5,2,2,4
8. **Robert Russell** 5.8.74 (1y, -) 14.24 '94   16.77, 16.60, 16.59, 16.31, 16.30, 16.21; 16.37i, 16.32i;   5 CAU, 2 North, 8 AAA, 1 Cork, 2 IR, 6 U23I, 1 Nth IC, 2 Gateshead 19/8; BL1: 4,5,4,6
9. **Gary Sollitt** 13.1.72 (3y, 7) 16.94 '95   17.02, 16.57, 16.46, 16.26, 16.00, 15.92;   4 Luton, 2 Hants, 2 Bedford, 2 AAA v LC, 7 South, 6 Abingdon, BL3: -,-,1,2
10. **Mark Edwards** 2.12.74 (1y, -) 15.75 '94   17.46, 16.56, 16.35, 16.27, 15.73; 3 Gateshead 19/8, 1 Künzelsau
11. **James Muirhead** 26.1.71 (2y, 11) 16.60 '95   16.74, 16.52, 16.46, 16.45, 16.23, 16.21;   4 AAA v LC, 6 CAU, 1 North, 10 AAA, 2 Scot, 2 Nth IC, 3 Liverpool sf, BL1: 3,6,5,5
12. **Nigel Spratley** 1.4.70 (7y, 5) 17.96 '94   16.44, 16.42, 16.31, 16.02, 15.96, 15.93; 16.21i, 16.21i; 3 Luton, 5 South

Not ranked
    Simon Williams 17.10.67 (7y, -) 19.44i '89, 19.17 '91   15.78, 15.49; 17.68i, 16.77i; BL3: -,3,2,-
    Felix Hyde (Ghana) 7.8.76 17.38 '95   16.99, 16.93, 16.81, 16.49, 16.37, 16.35;   1 B.Univs, 3 AAA v LC, 2 CAU, 3 South, 2 BL2 (2)

Pickering achieved his ambition of competing at the Olympic Games and, although disappointing there, had a solid season to take top ranking for the first time. In their only clash Simson beat Pickering at the AAAs and had a splendidly consistent series of marks, exceeding 18.50 in 9 of his 11 competitions. Proctor was held back by injury, and did not recapture his indoor form outdoors in major meetings, in which his best was 18.02. Hayward made another big improvement – 15.74 in 1994, 16.88 in 1995 and up to 18.40 in 1996; he lost his first two clashes with Newman, but won the remaining four. Carl Myerscough (21.20 with the 5kg shot) offers enormous hope for the future. He produced a mighty 17.30 with the senior shot in the junior international, but, as his next best was 15.82, did not do enough to make his rankings debut. The 10th best of 17.21 (including indoors) has only once been bettered (17.29 in 1994).

DISCUS

1. **Robert Weir** 4.2.61 (9y, 1) 63.56 '95   62.40, 62.02, 61.64, 61.52, 61.02, 60.96;
   7 Modesto, 4 ECp, 1 AAA, dnq 5 OG, 1 Cup, 1 Braintree, BL1: -,1,1,1
2. **Glen Smith** 21.5.72 (6y, 4) 59.78 '94   62.32, 60.14, 60.08, 59.92, 59.72, 59.66; 7 Halle, 1 Lough 15/5,
   1 AAA v LC, 1 CAU, 1 Lough 1/6,1 Mid, 5 AAA, 1 GhG, 1 Hechtel, dnq 36 OG, 2 Künzelsau, ML2: 1,1,-,-
3. **Kevin Brown** 10.9.64 (12y, 2) 59.50 '95   58.66, 58.26, 57.64, 57.42, 57.00, 56.86;
   13 Halle, 2 Lough 15/5, 4 E.Clubs, 2 Lough 1/6, 2 Mid, 3 AAA, 2 GhG, 1 IR, 1 Liverpool sf, BL1: 1,2,2,4
4. **Simon Williams** 17.10.67 (10y, 3) 61.14 '92   58.04, 57.54, 57.20, 56.54, 55.94, 55.76;
   1 South, 2 AAA, 3 GhG, 1 Scot, 1 Enfield, 1 Hendon sf, BL3: -,1,1,-
5. **Gary Herrington** 31.3.61 (8y, 5) 56.32 '95   56.66, 55.74, 54.36, 54.34, 53.66, 52.78;
   6 Lough 15/5, 2 CAU, 3 Mid, 4 AAA, 1 Police, 2 IR, ML2: 2,2,1,-
6. **Leith Marar** 7.11.68 (4y, 6) 55.38 '95   55.68, 55.58, 55.24, 54.78, 54.66, 54.48;
   6 AAA, 4 GhG, 2 Enfield, 1 London, 2 Cup, BL1: 2,-,-,2
7. **Neville Thompson** 28.3.55 (17y, 8) 55.68 '93   54.74, 54.48, 53.62, 52.84, 52.76, 52.38;
   3 CAU, 2 South, 7 AAA, 3 IR, 2 Hendon sf, 4 BEL Ch, 1 Abingdon, 3 Cup, BL1: 3,3,3,3
8. **Paul Reed** 2.6.62 (7y, 10) 54.50 '94   56.46, 53.38, 53.18, 53.16, 52.52, 51.78;
   2 AAA v LC, 6 CAU, 2 North, 9 AAA, ? Police, 3 Leeds, BL4: 1,1,1,-
9. **Matt Symonds** 31.7.68 (2y, 12) 54.36 '95   53.22, 52.12, 51.44, 51.22, 51.10, 51.02;
   2 Luton, 4 CAU, 3 South, 10 AAA, 3 Hendon sf, 3 Abingdon, 5 Cup, BL1: 6,5,4,6
10. **Robert Russell** 5.8.74 (1y, -) 52.14 '93   53.76, 52.80, 51.98, 51.88, 51.64, 51.10;
    9 CAU, 1 North, 8 AAA, 4 U23I, 4 IR, 2 Liverpool sf, 6 Cup, 1 Leeds, BL1: 5,10,5,5
11. **Perris Wilkins** 12.11.68 (1y, -) 53.80 '94   56.10, 54.96, 52.54, 52.02, 51.90, 49.28;
    8 South, 12 AAA, 2 Abingdon
12. **Lee Newman** 1.5.73 (4y, 9) 58.34 '94   54.42, 53.16, 52.00, 51.24, 50.88, 47.38; 1 Luton, 6 BL1 (3)

Weir is top for the fourth successive year and sixth in all, with Smith overtaking Brown and Williams. Thompson's 17 years in the rankings is a record for the event, as is his 18-year span (1978-96). Symonds 4-3 v Russell.

HAMMER

1. **David Smith** 2.11.74 (3y, 2) 71.52 '95   75.10, 73.22, 72.58, 71.44, 71.30, 71.26;
   1 Luton, 8 Halle, 5 E.Clubs, 1 CAU, 1 AAA, 1 U23I, dnq 32 OG, 2 McD, 2 Cup, BL1: 2,2,1,1
2. **Paul Head** 1.7.65 (14y, 5) 74.02 '90   73.66, 72.90, 72.72, 72.60, 72.44, 71.86;
   nt Halle, 2 CAU, 1 South, 2 AAA, 1 Scot, 1 IR, 1 BEL Ch, 1 McD, 1 Cup, BL2: 1,1,1,1
3. **Michael Jones** 23.7.63 (15y, 3) 72.10 '88   72.48, 71.74, 71.66, 71.22, 70.90, 69.98;
   1 Colindale, 2 Luton, 5 Halle, 1 AAA v LC, 3 CAU, 8 ECp, 3 AAA, 1 Crawley, 3 Cup, BL1: 1,1,-,2
4. **Peter Vivian** 5.11.70 (6y, 1) 71.28 '95   68.62, 68.50, 68.00, 67.94, 67.56, 66.48;
   3 AUS Ch, 2 Colindale, 1 Middx, 4 AAA, 5 Cup, BL1: -,-,2,4
5. **John Pearson** 30.4.66 (8y, 7) 66.54 '94   67.34, 65.96, 65.64, 65.46, 65.26, 65.16;
   4 Colindale, 2 AAA v LC, 4 CAU, 1 Mid, 5 AAA, 3 IR, 3 McD
6. **Shane Peacock** 5.3.63 (11y, 6) 71.60 '90   66.88, 65.72, 65.72, 65.46, 64.90, 64.62;
   3 AAA v LC, 2 North, 7 AAA, 2 IR, 4 McD, 4 Cup, BL1: 3,-,3,3
7. **David Smith** 21.6.62 (12y, -) 77.30 '85   66.08, 65.26; 1 North
8. **Steve Pearson** 13.9.59 (6y, -) 65.24 '94   63.54, 63.12, 62.86, 62.80, 62.64, 62.40;
   6 AAA, 4 IR, 2 Liverpool sf, 6 Cup, BL1: 4,5,4,6
9. **Iain Park** 16.7.74 (1y, -) 56.56 '95   62.68, 62.62, 62.32, 62.32, 62.04, 62.00;
   1 Colindale U23, nt CAU, 3 South, 8 AAA, 2 SN4, 2 Scot, 4 U23I, 3 London, 5 McD, BL3: 1,1,1,1
10. **Bill Beauchamp** 9.9.70 (2y, 9) 62.92 '95   63.90, 63.72, 63.32, 62.40, 62.30, 62.28;
    3 Luton, 3 Colindale, 2 Middx, 5 CAU, 12 AAA, 5 IR, BL1: 9,4,8,-
11. **Gareth Cook** 20.2.69 (9y, 10) 67.32 '91   63.08, 62.64, 60.28, 60.06, 59.24, 59.16;   5 Colindale, 1 Surrey
12. **Paul Barnard** 27.7.72 (2y, 11) 62.70 '95   62.24, 60.82, 60.76, 60.34, 60.18, 60.08;
    1 B.Univs, 6 Colindale, 4 AAA v LC, 3 North, 10 AAA, 3 Scot, 6 IR, 6 McD, BL1: 5,10,6,7
nr **Phil Spivey** (Australia) 15.5.61 70.94 '86   65.30, 63.74, 63.64, 63.46, 63.08, 62.66;
    2 South, 2 Crawley, 1 Liverpool sf, BL1: 6,3,5,5

As well as his exciting 75.10 at the Inter-Counties Smith established a base in 71m+ territory and ranks number one for the first time. Head came through well, returning from injury, and having lost his first three clashes of the year with Smith beat him in the last two. Jones, as ever, contested fiercely but was 1-3 down to Head and 3-5 to Smith. Park is the one newcomer to the rankings.

JAVELIN

1. **Steve Backley** 12.2.69 (10y, 1) 91.46 '92 87.44, 85.58, 85.06, 84.46, 84.14, 82.70;
   2 GhG, 2 CP-GP, 2 OG, 1 P-CP, 6 Zürich, 2 v IS, 2 McD, 3 Tokyo
2. **Michael Hill** 22.10.64 (13y, 2) 86.94 '93 81.42, 80.60, 80.48, 80.26, 80.14, 79.24;
   2 Ljubljana, 2 Riga, 2 AAA, 5 GhG, 5 CP-GP, 12 OG, 3 P-CP, 4 v IS, 4 McD, 1 BL4 (2)
3. **Nick Nieland** 31.1.72 (5y, 6) 76.30 '95 83.06, 81.92, 80.30, 79.94, 79.70, 77.22;
   3 Halle, 4 Innsbruck, 1 AAA, 3 GhG, 6 Oslo, 8 CP-GP, dnq 25 OG, 4 P-CP, 3 McD, 1 Cup, BL1: 1,1,-,2
4. **Colin Mackenzie** 30.6.63 (15y, 3) 82.60 rough tail '91, 82.38 '93 81.06, 78.74, 77.42, 77.26, 75.40, 75.20;
   4 Halle, 1 AAA v LC, 1 Ljubljana, 5 ECp, 3 AAA, 6 GhG, 6 CP-GP, 7 P-CP, 8 McD, 3 Cup, 1 BL2 (1)
5. **Mark Roberson** 13.3.67 (11y, 5) 80.92 '88 78.54, 77.80, 77.60, 77.04, 76.76, 76.26;
   2 AAA v LC, 1 CAU, 6 Innsbruck, 4 AAA, 1 East, 1 IR, 6 P-CP, 1 P'bor, 2 Cup, BL1: 2,3,-,1
6. **Nigel Bevan** 3.1.68 (10y, 4) 81.70 '92 74.60, 74.36, 73.54, 72.96, 71.14, 70.88;
   1 E.Clubs, 1 WG, 4 AAA, 1 SN4, 4 Cup, BL1: -,2,1,3
7. **Stuart Faben** 28.2.75 (2y, 8) 74.24 '95 73.70; 76.66i
8. **Stefan Baldwin** 26.4.70 (4y, -) 72.92 '93 70.38, 67.90, 67.84, 65.56; 3 P'bor, BL3: -,1,1,1
9. **David Parker** 28.2.80 (1y, -) 62.60 '95 68.26, 67.36, 67.10, 66.94, 66.44, 64.90;
   3 AAA v LC, 2 CAU, 7 AAA, 1 AAA-J, 4 JInt, dnq 17 WJ
10. **Keith Beard** 8.11.61 (7y, -) 76.10 '91 72.76, 67.22, 63.80, 63.80, 61.64; 6 Dutch Ch
11. **Peter Yates** 15.6.57 (20y, -) 77.84 '87 67.14, 66.38, 65.96, 65.62, 65.48, 63.88; 6 AAA
12. **Mark Francis** 23.9.77 (1y, -) 64.44 '95 66.62, 66.50, 65.64, 65.26, 64.58, 64.58;
    1 Luton, 5 AAA v LC, 1 Sth-J, 1 E.Sch, 2 AAA-J, 5 JInt
nr **Tony Smith** 17.5.58 (4y, -) 69.94 '91 69.90, 66.20, 64.92, 64.18; BL1: -,4,2,-

Backley is number one for the 7th time and as in 1995 was over 81m in every competition. This time, however, he made a marvellous recovery from injury, just in time to gain the Olympic silver medal with his best throw of the year. Hill struggled for his usual form, but still made the Olympic final, a British record 12th time in major championships. That was just sufficient to rank him 2nd (for the 9th time) over Nieland, the vastly improved AAA champion, 3-3 v Hill overall. Mackenzie drops a place to 4th and Roberson is 5th for the third year running. After the top seven the standard drops alarmingly, but Parker is the youngest ever to be ranked at this event. Yates has ranked for an event record 20 seasons.

DECATHLON

1. **Simon Shirley** 3.8.66 (4y, 4) 8036 '88 7857, 7614; 19 Götzis, 11 ECp, dnf FRA Ch
2. **Barry Thomas** 28.4.72 (7y, 2) 7766 '95 7765, 7701, 7618; 1 POR Ch, 1 AAA, 15 ECp, dnf FRA Ch
3. **Brian Taylor** 13.8.70 (5y, -) 7787 '93 7573, 5972; 5 Bonn, 2 AAA, dnf ECp
4. **Anthony Southward** 31.1.71 (2y, 9) 7075 '95 7425, 7400w/7335, 6815; 2 North, 3 AAA, 25 ECp, dnf v 3N
5. **Dean Macey** 12.12.77 (1y, -) 6662 '95 7480, 7134; 1 Bonn, dnf v3N-J, 2 WJ
6. **Eric Hollingsworth** 6.12.62 (7y, -) 7748 '93 7204; 1 Sydney
7. **Rafer Joseph** 21.7.68 (7y, -) 7663 '94 7174, 6610; dnf POR Ch, 4 AAA, 1 HC
8. **Stephen Rogers** 1.9.71 (4y, 6) 7295 '95 7150; 5 AAA
9. **William Gilles** 15.2.73 (1y, -) 6601 '95 6800w (6790), 6757; 6 AAA, 7 v 3N
10. **Billy Jewers** 27.9.62 (2y, -) 7136 '89 6910; 1g Army
11. **Mark Bushell** 22.10.76 (2y, 11) 6839 '95 6798, 6455; 7 AAA, 8 v3N-U23 (nb Jnr imp: 7111, 6796; 1 E.Sch)
12. **Steve Leader** 24.11.66 (2y, -) 7078 '94 6829; 1 South, dnf HC
nr **Pierre Faber** (South Africa) 9.1.72 7555 '95 7581, 7132, 7020, 6631; 1 North, 20 Götzis, 1 M'bor, 1 Scot

Shirley achieved the best UK score of the year in beating AAA champion Thomas in the European Cup Super League and ranks no. 1 for the first time. Having qualified in 1995, Alex Kruger represented Britain at the Olympics, but he was not fit and did not complete a decathlon during 1996, so is not ranked. Taylor and Hollingsworth return after two years out. Excellent progress made by Southward and Macey. Standards slipped this year with only seven men over 7000 points.

20 KILOMETRES WALK

1. **Darrell Stone** 2.2.68 (8y, 1) 1:24:49 '95 1:23:27 sh '93 1:23:58, 1:24:30, 1:25:38, 1:26:44;
   1 Manx, 1 UK, 41 Eis, 15 Moscow
2. **Steve Partington** 17.9.65 (11y, 3) 1:24:09 '94 1:25:40, 1:27:12, 1:28:16, 1:29:00;
   3 Manx, 2 UK, 42 Eis, 19 Moscow
3. **Chris Maddocks** 28.3.57 (14y, 2) 1:22:12 '92 1:26:15, 1:28:27, 1:33:38; 4 Manx, 2 Irish, 1 South
4. **Andy Penn** 31.3.67 (7y, 5) 1:23:34 '92 1:28:39, 1:32:37; 3 UK, 21 Moscow
5. **Chris Cheeseman** 11.12.58 (3y, 6) 1:29:11 '94 1:29:50, 1:31:23, 1:32:26, 1:34:44, 1:35:07;
   6 Manx, 7 UK, 1 Essex, 1 Sutton Pk, 2 Dublin
6. **Martin Young** 11.7.72 (2y, 8) 1:30:28.6t '95 1:29:48, 1:32:46; 8 Irish, dnf UK, 2 Sutton Pk
7. **Richard Oldale** 26.1.66 (1y, -) 1:34:21.6t '95 1:33:17, 1:33:40, 1:33:52, 1:36:57;
   4 UK, 1 North, 25 Moscow, 1 Sheffield
8. **Kevin Walmsley** 6.9.67 (1y, -) 0 1:33:28, 1:33:30, 1:35:33; 10 Manx, 5 UK, 3 Dublin
9. **Steve Taylor** 19.3.66 (4y, -) 1:28:46 '92 1:34:27; 6 UK
10. **Andy O'Rawe** 8.9.63 (1y, -) 1:35:24 '94 1:34:05, 1:37:07; 4 Dublin, 3 Essex

Stone is top for the third successive year. (Eis = Eisenhüttenstadt, Moscow - 6 nations international.)

50 KILOMETRES WALK

1. **Chris Maddocks** 28.3.57 (10y, 1) 3:51:37 '90   34 OG 4:18:41, dnf Podebrady
2. **Chris Cheeseman** 11.12.58 (1y, -) 0   1 RWA 4:22:42
3. **Graham White** 28.3.59 (3y, 5) 4:14:59 '95   2 RWA 4:24:01
4. **Dennis Jackson** 29.6.45 (11y,) 4:03:08 '86   3 RWA 4:27:04
5. **Gareth Brown** 10.5.68 (2y, 6) 4:28:44 '95   12 Podebrady 4:27:22, dnf? RWA
6. **Steve Partington** 17.9.65 (2y, -) 4:48:51 '93   4 RWA 4:32:25
7. **Karl Atton** 14.9.71 (1y, -) 0   5 RWA 4:35:48
8. **Allan King** 3.12.56 (5y, -) 4:13:25 '83   6 RWA 4:39:01
9. **Chris Berwick** 1.5.46 (13y, 8=) 4:23:22 '86   7 RWA 4:48:01
10. **Jonathan Cocker** 26.9.71 (2y, 7) 4:33:01 '95   8 RWA 4:49:01, 19 Podebrady 4:58:08

Maddocks has an 18-year span in the rankings at this event and is top for the fifth time. Les Morton, disqualified at the Spanish Championships, is unranked for the first time since 1983.

BRITISH MERIT RANKINGS 1996 - WOMEN

100 METRES

1. **Simmone Jacobs** 5.9.66 (14y, 2) 11.31 '88, 11.26w '84   11.39, 11.43w, 11.47, 11.47, 11.51, 11.51; 11.5w;
    1 AAA v LC, 7 ECp, 2 AAA, 6 CP-GP, 5qf OG, 1 BL1 (2)
2. **Marcia Richardson** 10.2.72 (6y, 4) 11.45 '93, 11.39w '94   11.42, 11.44, 11.45w, 11.47, 11.48w, 11.55;
    3 Bratislava,1 South, 1 Dublin, 3 AAA, 2 Budapest, 2 Helsinki, 1 GhG, 4 CP-GP, 7qf OG, 3 McD, BL2: 2,1,1
3. **Stephanie Douglas** 22.1.69 (8y, 3) 11.27 '91   11.52, 11.55, 11.55w, 11.58, 11.60w, 11.61;
    2 Bedford, 1 WG, 5 Bratislava, 1 North, 4 Seville, 1 AAA, 7 CP-GP, 8qf OG
4. **Paula Thomas** 3.12.64 (11y, 1) 11.15 '94, 11.13w '88   11.46, 11.51, 11.53, 11.62, 11.63A, 11.68;
    1 Bedford, 1r2 Ljubljana, 1 Tallinn, 4 AAA, 3 Budapest, 1 BL1 (1)
5. **Bev Kinch** 14.1.64 (9y, -) 11.29 '90, 11.13w '83, 11.2 '84, 11.1w '87   11.50, 11.52, 11.57, 11.59, 11.63, 11.65;
    5 Nürnburg, 5 AAA, 2 GhG, 1 IR, 2 BEL Ch, BL3: 1,-,1
6. **Sophia Smith** 8.12.74 (4y, 8) 11.69/11.50w '95   11.49, 11.57, 11.62, 11.65, 11.69, 11.72; 11.6w;
    1B AAA v LC, 1r1 Ljubljana, 6 AAA, 5 GhG, 1 U23 I, 1 Nth IC, 1 McD, BL2: 3,-,2
7. **Geraldine McLeod** 24.9.71 (5y, -) 11.58/11.46w '93   11.2 '94   11.48, 11.57, 11.57A, 11.59, 11.61A, 11.62;
    2 Pretoria, 2r2 E.Clubs, 2r2 Ljubljana, 6 Bratislava, 8h AAA, 3 GhG, 8 Nice, 2 McD, 1 Cup, 3 BL2 (3)
8. **Katharine Merry** 21.9.74 (8y, 5) 11.34/11.27w '94   11.54, 11.70, 11.73; 11.5w; 1 BL2 (1), 1 CAU
9. **Shani Anderson** 7.8.75 (1y, -) 12.14 '94, 12.0/12.09w '95   11.60, 11.72, 11.74, 11.76, 11.77, 11.79;
    1 B.Univs, 2 AAA v LC, 2 South, 8 AAA, 4 GhG, 2B BL1 (3)
10. **Catherine Murphy** 21.9.75 (2y, 7) 11.78 '95, 11.63w '94   11.66w, 11.69A, 11.72w, 11.77, 11.81, 11.96;
    11.6, 11.8; 3 Pretoria, 2 WG, 3 Tallinn, 4 McD, 3 Cup; BL1: 3,-,1
11. **Aileen McGillivary** 13.8.70 (5y, -) 11.54 '92, 11.43w '93   11.64w, 11.68, 11.70w, 11.73, 11.74w, 11.77; 11.7w;
    2 CAU, 2 Dublin, 5sf AAA, 1 Scot, 2 SN4, 6 GhG, BL1: 5,2,-
12. **Christine Bloomfield** 12.2.68 (1y, -) 11.59 '93   11.69w, 11.71, 11.85, 11.85, 11.90, 11.97; 11.8;
    3 South, 7 AAA, 8 GhG, 3 IR, 6 McD, 2 Cup, BL1: 1B,4,2
nr **Angela Thorp** 7.12.72 (0y, -) 12.02 '94   11.48w; 11.7w; BL2: 4,2,-

The first three all made the Olympic quarter-finals, and Jacobs's faster times in Atlanta just give her top ranking over Richardson; they were 1-1 on win-loss. Jacobs has ranked each year from 1983, but this is her first top ranking at 100m, having been 2nd in 1988 and 3rd in 1992-3 and 1995. Merry was unbeaten, with a win over Richardson, but once again her season was cut short by injury, as was that of Thomas.

200 METRES

1. **Simmone Jacobs** 5.9.66 (13y, 4) 23.12 '91, 23.01w '84   22.95, 22.96, 23.11, 23.22, 23.29, 23.34;
    1 AAA v LC, 1 Ljubljana, 1 AAA, 3 GhG, 6qf OG, 8 McD
2. **Katharine Merry** 21.9.74 (6y, -) 22.85 '94   22.88, 23.14, 23.17, 23.29, 23.30, 23.50; 23.4;
    1r2 E.Clubs, 3 ECp, 2 AAA, 2 Cork, 5qf OG
3. **Paula Thomas** 3.12.64 (9y, 1) 22.69 '94   23.41, 23.46, 23.71, 23.75A, 23.84, 23.92A; 1 Tallinn, 3 AAA, 1 BL1 (1)
4. **Catherine Murphy** 21.9.75 (3y, 13) 23.40 '95   23.47A, 23.52, 23.52A, 23.57, 23.58w, 23.60w; 23.46i;
    1 Pretoria, 1 Bedford, 1 WG, 2 Tallinn, 4 AAA, 4 GhG, 1 U23I, 3 v IS, 1 Cup, BL1: 3,1,-
5. **Tracy Joseph** 29.11.69 (1y, -) 24.16i '94, 24.26 '91, 24.1 '89, 23.64w '92   23.9w '92
    23.57w, 23.72, 23.77, 23.82, 23.85, 23.86;   5 AAA, 2 BEL Ch, 4 v IS
6. **Jenny Stoute** 16.4.65 (9y, -) 22.73 '92   23.75, 23.76, 23.82, 23.82, 24.14, 24.26;
    4 Bedford, 2 WG, 2 South, 1 Dublin, 6 AAA
7. **Marcia Richardson** 10.2.72 (5y, 5) 23.53 '95, 23.4 '93   23.80, 24.05, 24.18; 23.7w, 23.9; 24.10i;
    3 South, BL2: 1,1,2
8. **Donna Fraser** 7.11.72 (5y, 6) 23.47/23.44w '95   23.62, 23.81, 24.05, 24.11, 24.34; 24.2;
    5 Fort-de-France, 1 Luton, 2 Basel, BL2: 2,2,-
9. **Sophia Smith** 8.12.74 (3y, -) 23.57 '93   23.80, 24.11, 24.15; 23.6w, 23.8; 1 Yorks, 1 Nth IC, 1 BL2 (3)
10. **Joice Maduaka** 30.9.73 (2y, 8) 23.81 '95   23.90, 24.17, 24.21, 24.30w, 24.31, 24.32;
    2 Luton, 2B AAA v LC, 3 CAU, 5 South, 7 AAA, 5 GhG, 4 IR

11.   **Geraldine McLeod** 24.9.71 (4y, -) 23.47 '94,23.4 '93   23.64A, 24.07, 24.07A; 23.82i; 2 Pretoria
12.   **Clova Court** 10.2.60 (3y, 10) 23.57 '90   23.94w; 23.8w; 24.22i, 24.50i; 3 BL2 (3), 2 Cup
nr   **Janine Whitlock** 11.8.73 (1y, -) 24.7 '95   23.99, 24.13, 24.18, 24.31, 24.48; 24.2;
      3 Luton, 2 Yorks, 3 AAA v LC, 2 CAU, 4 Cork, 2 Nth IC
      Elona Reinalda AUS 31.3.76 23.86 '95   23.69, 24.00, 24.12, 24.12, 24.14; 23.7, 23.9; 23.88i;
      2 Bedford, 1 CAU, 1 South, 2 BL1 (1)
Jacobs at last improved her fastest ever 200m time, which has been a wind aided 23.01w from 1984 with two sub-23 sec times and regains the no.1 ranking she held in 1991. Merry returned for second place, but her injury problems meant that she could not run quicker than when she achieved her fine European Cup 3rd.

400 METRES
1.   **Phylis Smith** 29.9.65 (7y, 5) 50.40 '92   51.29, 51.56, 51.74, 51.74, 52.0, 52.05, 52.09;
      1 AAA, 3 GhG, 5 CP-GP, 6qf OG, 2 v IS, 3 McD, 6 Berlin, BL1: 1,-,1
2.   **Sally Gunnell** 29.7.66 (8y, 9) 51.04 '94   51.45, 52.96; 53.07i, 53.28i, 53.87i, 54.21i; 1 Bedford, 2 GhG
3.   **Donna Fraser** 7.11.72 (4y, 6) 52.04 '95   51.58, 52.05, 52.37, 52.78, 52.88, 53.27;
      7 Fort-de-France, 3 Bedford, 1B AAA v LC, 4 Rhede, 2 Basel, 4 AAA, 5 Lucerne, 5 GhG, 7qf OG
4.   **Georgina Oladapo** 15.5.67 (2y, 4) 52.71 '95   52.48, 53.22, 53.61, 54.41; 3 Basel, 2 AAA, 4 v IS
5.   **Allison Curbishley** 3.6.76 (1y, -) 54.28 '95   52.76, 53.08, 53.12, 53.19, 53.40, 53.43;
      2 Bedford, 3 AAA, 7 GhG, 7 CP-GP
6.   **Linda Staines** 26.12.63 (13y, 7) 50.98 '91   52.71, 52.92, 53.07, 53.41, 53.44, 53.44;
      1 CAU, 1 South, 2 Tallinn, 5 AAA, 3 Lisbon, 4B GhG, 1 IR
7.   **Lorraine Hanson** 22.4.65 (7y, 2) 50.93 '91   52.83, 52.99, 53.3, 53.48, 53.7;
      1 Mid, 2 Cork, 2B GhG, 1 Cup, 1 BL2 (3)
8.   **Michelle Pierre** 30.9.73 (2y, 12) 54.05 '95   53.22, 53.44, 53.9, 54.17, 54.19, 54.2;
      4 Bedford, 1 WG, 2 South, 6 AAA, 5B GhG, BL2: -,1,2
9.   **Melanie Neef** 26.5.70 (3y, 1) 51.18 '95
      53.23, 53.51, 53.65, 53.90, 53.9, 54.25; 52.50i, 53.81i; 7 AAA, 6 Lucerne, 6B GhG
10.   **Stephanie Llewellyn** 31.12.68 (2y, 3) 52.4/52.54 '95   53.52, 53.64, 53.8, 53.8, 54.0, 54.46; 54.12i;
      3 AAA v LC, 2 CAU, 2h AAA, 2 SN4, 2 Cup, BL1: -,1,2
11.   **Susan Rawlinson** 13.10.70 (2y, 8) 53.4/53.69 '95   53.86, 54.26, 54.59, 54.80, 54.92, 55.11;
      2B AAA v LC, 3 CAU, 1 North, 3h AAA, 1 Nth IC, BL3: 1,-,1
12   **Sharon Tunaley** 2.9.68 (2y, 10) 53.58 '95   53.78, 54.00, 54.28, 54.39, 54.45, 54.6;
      2 AAA v LC, 4 CAU, 2 Mid, 8 AAA, 7B GhG, 1 BL4 (1)
With Neef sidelined by injury, Smith returns to the top spot she held in 1992-3 over Gunnell, top in 1994. Although only 4th at the AAAs Fraser set a pb in Atlanta and had many more good times than the AAA 2-3, Oladapo and Curbishley. Staines's 16-year span of ranking, 1980-96, is a record for the event and her 13 years in the top 12 ties the 400m record set by Verona Elder. The 10th best of 53.52 is the best since 1984 (record 53.0 in 1982).

800 METRES
1.   **Kelly Holmes** 19.4.70 (5y, 1) 1:56.21 '95   1:57.84, 1:58.20, 1:58.53, 1:58.80, 1:58.81, 1:58.87,
      1:59.82; 1 Ljubljana, 2 ECp, 1 AAA, 1 Helsinki, 1 GhG, 4 OG
2.   **Diane Modahl** 17.6.66 (12y, -) 1:58.65 '90   1:59.87, 2:00.69, 2:00.80, 2:00.95, 2:00.97, 2:02.03;
      4 Bratislava, 9 Hengelo, 6 St Denis, 2 Zagreb, 3 GhG, 8 Lausanne, 4 Nice, dnf ht OG, 1 BL1 (1)
3.   **Sonya Bowyer** 18.9.72 (3y, 2=) 2:01.67 '95   2:02.12, 2:02.5, 2:02.85, 2:03.79, 2:04.02, 2:04.1mx;
      1 Wyth-May, 2 AAA v LC, 1 WG, 4 Riga, 4 AAA, 4 Lucerne, 2 v IS, 7 McD
4.   **Lynn Gibson** 6.7.69 (4y, -) 2:02.34 '92   2:02.83, 2:03.66, 2:04.3mx, 2:04.5, 2:06.5, 2:07.61;
      1B AAA v LC, 4 CP-GP, 6 McD
5.   **Hayley Parry** 17.2.73 (1y, -) 2:09.07 '95   2:03.77, 2:03.86, 2:03.95, 2:04.15, 2:04.17, 2:04.51;
      1 B.Univs, 1 AAA v LC, 3 WG, 6 AAA, 2 Århus, 1 SN4, 4 GhG, 7 CP-GP
6.   **Natalie Tait** 24.8.72 (2y, 4) 2:02.69 '95   2:02.76, 2:05.26, 2:05.53, 2:05.76, 2:06.57, 2:06.7mx;
      1 BMC Lough, 2 South, 3 AAA, 4 Helsinki, 6 GhG, 2 Crawley sf
7.   **Vicki Lawrence** 9.6.73 (3y, 6) 2:04.42 '95   2:03.52, 2:04.8mx, 2:04.9mx, 2:05.18, 2:05.9, 2:06.02;
      2 Stretford, 3 Wyth-May, 1 Basel, 5 AAA, dnf GhG, 3 v IS, 2 North IC
8.   **Jeina Mitchell** 21.1.75 (1y, -) 2:05.85 '94   2:04.87, 2:05.12, 2:05.76, 2:06.06, 2:06.73, 2:07.53;
      3 B.Univs, 1 South, 1 Tallinn, 7 AAA, 2 Bath, 2 U23I, 1 BL2 (3)
9.   **Michelle Faherty** 10.8.68 (2y, 11) 2:05.3 '95   2:04.4mx, 2:05.97, 2:06.9, 2:07.13, 2:07.32, 2:08.4; 2:07.19i;
      4 Wyth-May, 3 AAA v LC, 1 North, 1 IR, 2 Wyth-Jul, 8 McD
10.   **Sue Parker** 24.3.70 (1y, -) 2:05.50 '93   2:04.9mx, 2:06.5, 2:07.2, 2:07.36, 2:07.72, 2:09.0;
      3 Stretford, 5 Wyth-May, 2 North, 3 IR, 1 Wyth-Jul
11.   **Angela Davies** 21.10.70 (2y, -) 2:03.67 '94   2:06.92, 2:07.5mx, 2:07.58, 2:07.6, 2:08.0, 2:08.37 2:06.27i;
      2 Wyth-May, 5 Basel, 2 IR, 1 Crawley sf, 3 BEL Ch
12.   **Vicky Sterne** 12.10.68 (2y, 12) 2:06.1 '95   2:04.63, 2:05.71, 2:07.1mx, 2:07.18, 2:08.35, 2:08.79; 2:06.41i;
      11 E.Clubs, 2 Ljubljana, 5 Tallinn, 2ht AAA, 6 IR
Holmes was clear at the top with Modahl jumping straight back in after her two-year enforced absence to rank second. Her reinstatement also means that she regained her 2nd ranking for 1994, with those who are published in BA 1995 from 2nd onwards moving down a place. Bowyer was a clear third as Tait, who beat her at the AAAs did not have enough to support that.

1500 METRES

1. **Kelly Holmes** 19.4.70 (3y, 1) 4:01.41 '94   4:01.13, 4:04.56, 4:05.88, 4:07.36, 4:07.46, 4:08.14;
    7 Atlanta, 1 Rome, 1 AAA, 2 Oslo, 1 IS, 11 OG
2. **Paula Radcliffe** 17.12.73 (3y, 3) 4:06.84/4:28.93M '95   4:24.94M (4:08.42), 4:19.48; 4 AAA v LC, 7 Zürich
3. **Susan Parker** 24.3.70 (4y, 8) 4:12.3 '93, 4:37.52M '95   4:11.57, 4:11.96, 4:12.75, 4:13.02, 4:16.21,
    4:17.4mx; 2 AAA v LC, 2 Funchal, 2 AAA, 1 Stockholm, 3 Cork, 4 GhG, 4 v IS, 1 BL1 (3)
4. **Alison Wyeth** 26.5.64 (10y, 4) 4:03.17 '93, 4:24.87M '91   4:11.00, 4:16.63; 12 Paris, 5 GhG
5. **Lynn Gibson** 6.7.69 (3y, -) 4:05.75/4:31.17M '94   4:12.32, 4:15.23, 4:15.8, 4:16.31, 4:16.4, 4:38.93M;
    2 Wyth-May, 2 WG, 6 AAA, 2 Cork, 8 GhG, 1 Wyth-Jul, 3 v IS, 1 Hendon
6. **Michelle Faherty** 10.8.68 (4y, 12) 4:15.37 '93, 4:38.64M '95   4:14.19, 4:15.66, 4:18.38, 4:39.44M, 4:18.90,
    4:19.54; 3 WG, 3 North, 3 AAA, 5 Cork, 6 GhG, 2 Hendon
7. **Angela Davies** 21.10.70 (4y, 5) 4:09.29/4:31.83M '94   4:13.52, 4:14.66, 4:14.67, 4:17.1, 4:18.91, 4:21.12;
    4:16.24i; 1 AAA v LC, 7 ECp, 4 AAA, 4 Cork, 11 GhG, 2 Wyth-Jul
8. **Sonya Bowyer** 18.9.72 (1y, -) 4:22.1mx '95, 4:22.3 '94   4:10.7mx, 4:17.4, 4:39.90M, 4:21.0mx, 4:23.7,
    4:27.7; 1 BL1 (2), 3 Wyth-Jul, 3 Hendon
9. **Shirley Griffiths** 23.6.72 (1y, -) 4:20.84i '95, 4:26.7 '93   4:15.68, 4:16.06, 4:19.57, 4:19.86, 4:44.60M,
    4:24.58; 1 Hong Kong, 2 North, 5 AAA, 6 Cork, 1 North IC, 1 McD
10. **Lynne MacDougall** 18.2.65 (7y, -) 4:05.96/4:30.08M '84   4:17.10, 4:18.81, 4:21.85, 4:23.7, 4:27.82,
    4:30.05; 1 CAU, 8 AAA, 1 SN4, 1 Scot,
11. **Debbie Gunning** 31.8.65 (6y, 5) 4:12.69 '90, 4:32.32M '91   4:17.4, 4:19.02, 4:19.16, 4:19.62, 4:21.28,
    4:22.89; 4:13.40i, 4:17.02i, 4:18.32i; 5 AAA v LC, 3 Florø, 9 AAA, 1 IR, 4 Wyth-Jul
12. **Hayley Parry** 17.2.73 (1y, -) 4:25.51/4:48.88M '95   4:16.9, 4:17.9, 4:22.0mx, 4:29.40, 4:36.2;
    3 Wyth-May, 1 Welsh, 5 Wyth-Jul, BL3: -,1,1

M = 1 mile time. Equivalents: 4:05.0m = 4:24.6M, 4:10.0m = 4:30.1M, 4:15.0m = 4:35.5M, 4:20.0m = 4:41.0M
Holmes, so plucky and unlucky to be injured for the Olympics, ranks first at both 800m and 1500m for the third successive year. Radcliffe ran only two races, but her fast time in Zürich was much better than those following. Parker had her best ever year to take 3rd. MacDougall was last ranked in 1990. The 10th best of 4:15.8 was the worst since 1980 (record 4:10.77 in 1990).

3000 METRES

1. **Paula Radcliffe** 17.12.73 (4y, 1) 8:40.40 '93   8:37.07, 8:51.3+, 8:53.0+, 8:56.25; 3 Monaco, 1 v IS
2. **Sarah Bentley** 21.5.67 (3y, 7) 9:10.9mx/9:12.72 '95   9:04.4, 9:21.0mx, 9:23.4mx; 9:23.27i, 9:38.38i; 4 Cork
3. **Alison Wyeth** 26.5.64 (8y, 3) 8:38.42 '93   9:09.25, 9:19.0mx, 9:25.71; 9:05.45i; 10 Nice, 3 v IS
4. **Sonia McGeorge** 2.11.64 (8y, -) 8:51.33 '90   9:09.53; 9:04.69i, 9:28.04i; 5 ECp
5. **Rhona Makepeace** 7.8.62 (3y, -) 9:03.51 '92   9:11.2mx, 9:15.1, 9:24.5mx, 9:32.97; 7 Cork, 3 AAA
6. **Susan Parker** 24.3.70 (3y, 12) 9:06.2 '92   9:11.68; 1 BL1 (1)
7. **Lucy Elliott** 9.3.66 (1y, -) 0   9:19.4, 9:21.20, 9:22.0, 9:32.39, 9:39.0; 6 McD, BL1: 4,2,1
8. **Debbie Gunning** 31.8.65 (3y, 11) 9:12.12 '94   9:26.46; 1 AAA

Not ranked
  Amanda Parkinson 21.7.71 (0y, -) 9:17.4mx '94, 9:29.9 '93   9:19.6, 9:36.11, 9:38.1, 9:42.38;
    8 Cork, 3 IR, 1 Nth IC
  Berhane Dagne (Eth) 7.10.77 9:22.4 '95   9:21.0, 9:21.6, 9:30.50, 9:38.25, 9:43.1; 1 Sth J, BL1: 3,1,3
No longer a championship event, but still raced at some major meetings.

5000 METRES (Previously ranked 1982-90, 1992 and 1995)

1. **Paula Radcliffe** 17.12.73 (2y, 1) 14:49.27 '95   14:46.76, 14:51.71, 14:56.36, 14:59.70, 15:09.50, 15:13.11;
    1 AAA, 2 CP-GP, 5 OG, 5 Köln, 4 Brussels, 4 GPF, 2 Tokyo
2. **Sonia McGeorge** 2.11.64 (2y, 10) 16:17.32 '95   15:29.04, 15:48.33, 16:01.92; 13 Hengelo, 2 AAA, 13h OG
3. **Alison Wyeth** 26.5.64 (4y, 4) 15:00.37 '95   15:48.91, 16:09.36, 16:18.96, 16:24.74;
    19 Hengelo, 3 AAA, 9 CP-GP, 15h OG
4. **Jill Hunter** 14.10.66 (5y, 5) 15:09.98 '92   15:51.55, 15:55.80; 9 Melbourne, 8 AUS Ch
5. **Andrea Whitcombe** 8.6.71 (2y, 9) 16:12.96 '95   16:00.0, 16:03.40, 16:05.36, 16:41.66;
    1 AAA v LC, 7 ECp, 4 AAA, 11 Helsinki
6. **Heather Heasman** 27.9.63 (2y, 11) 16:14 '95   15:53.84, 16:00.85, 16:16.9; 4 AAA v LC, 1 North, 8 Hechtel
7. **Lucy Elliott** 9.3.66 (1y, -) 0   15:56.15, 16:42.35?; dnf AAA, 8 CP-GP, 2 Cup
8. **Zahara Hyde** 12.1.63 (1y, -)   16:36.0 '94   16:04.12, 16:07.09, 16:43.89; 10 Portland, 5 Seattle, 8 AAA, dnf CP-GP
9. **Vikki McPherson** 1.6.71 (1y, -) 16:19.46 '94   16:06.2mx, 16:11.6mx
10. **Sarah Bentley** 21.5.67 (2y, 7) 15:53.86 '95   16:23.86, 16:25.82, 16:42.35; 5 AAA, 10 CP-GP, 3 Cup
11. **Wendy Ore** 23.5.66 (1y, -) 16:33.50 '93   16:25.79; 6 AAA
12. **Amanda Wright** 14.7.68 (2y, -) 16:04.51 '92   16:29.69; 1 CAU
nr   **Berhane Dagne** (Eth) 7.10.77 16:17.5mx '95   16:22.32, 16:40.72, 16:45.2; 1 AAA-J, 1 Stoke sf, 1 Cup
Another splendid season for Radcliffe, who retained her top ranking and beat Zola Budd's British record. After her –
a gulf, exacerbated by Wyeth's difficulties in coming back after her severe injury in Gothenburg 1995, although
McGeorge did well to make the Olympic team.

10000 METRES
1. **Louise Watson** 13.12.71 (2y, 4) 33:33.71 '95   33:21.46, 33:28.08, 33:53.0; 10 Koblenz, 1 AAA, 1 Loughbro
2. **Vikki McPherson** 1.6.71 (4y, -) 32:32.42 '93   33:17.74, 33:53.17; 8 Koblenz, 3 AAA
3. **Angela Hulley** 8.2.62 (6y, 6) 32:42.84 '89   33:33.37; 2 AAA
4. **Amanda Wright** 14.7.68 (2y, -) 33:26.79 '92   34:06.25; 12 Koblenz
5. **Angharad Mair** 30.3.61 (1y, -) 0   34:11.76; 4 AAA
6. **Sharon Dixon** 22.4.68 (1y, -) 35:08.23 '94   34:26.43; 1 B.Univs
7. **Sally Goldsmith** 18.1.61 (1y, -) 35:17.12 '94   34:28.13; 7 ITA Ch
8. **Joanne Thompson** 30.10.58 (2y, -) 33:56.04 '94   34:30.52; 5 AAA
9. **Zara Hyde** 12.1.63 (3y, 8) 33:23.25 '94   34:37.5; 2 Loughborough
10. **Mara Myers** 13.8.73 (1y, -) 0   34:41.28; 2 B.Univs
11. **Alison Rose** 27.9.67 (3y, -) 33:57.86 '94   34:44.89; 6 AAA
None of our top women distance runners ran a 10,000 metres on the track in 1996. McPherson ran the fastest time – well short of world standards – but Watson won the AAAs to take top ranking.

MARATHON
1. **Liz McColgan** 24.5.64 (5y, 1) 2:27:32 '91   1 London 2:27:54, 3 Tokyo 2:30:50, 16 OG 2:34:30
2. **Marian Sutton** 7.10.63 (5y, 2=) 2:32:26 '95   1 Chicago 2:30:41
3. **Karen Macleod** 24.4.58 (6y, 4=) 2:33:16 '94   6 Houston 2:33:50, 44 OG 2:42:08
4. **Sally Goldsmith** 18.1.61 (2y, 10) 2:38:39 '94   1 Vigarano 2:34:11
5. **Sally Eastall** 5.1.63 (5y, -) 2:29:29 '91   12 Houston 2:38:52, 14 London 2:38:59
6. **Danielle Sanderson** 26.10.62 (3y, -) 2:36:29 '94   15 London 2:39:46, 2 Dublin 2:41:12
7. **Angharad Mair** 30.3.61 (1y, -) 2:46:02 '95   1 Reykjavik 2:38:47
8. **Tracy Swindell** 8.11.66 (1y, -) 2:48:09 '94   4 Dublin 2:44:48, 18 London 2:44:49
9. **Trudi Thomson** 18.1.59 (2y, 6) 2:38:23 '95   5 Las Vegas 2:44:39, 1 Belfast 2:44:57, 5 Dublin 2:46:16
10. **Gillian Horovitz** 7.6.55 (10y, -) 2:36:52 '92   14 N. York 2:45:12, 11 Duluth 2:45:53, 13 Twin Cit 2:47:37, 2 Barb
11. **Zina Marchant** 30.9.50 (4y, -) 2:39:26 '91   19 London 2:45:42, 6 Dublin 2:47:07
12. **Debbie Noy** 31.10.64 (5y, -) 2:35:18 '91   1 Gosport 2:45:50
nr **Wendy Llewellyn** (NZ) 30.5.63 2:40:35 '95   8 Rotterdam 2:37:00, 3 Dublin 2:42:06, 4 Las Vegas 2:42:41
McColgan, London Marathon winner, ranks top for the fifth time ahead of Sutton, the winner in Chicago. Horovitz returns to the rankings for the first time since 1992; she was 2nd in the first year I ranked this event in 1979. The 10th best of 2:45:12 is the worst since 1982.

100 METRES HURDLES
1. **Angela Thorp** 7.12.72 (6y, 10) 13.28 '93   12.80, 12.93, 12.95w, 12.99, 13.02, 13.04;
    1 Yorks, 1 AAA v LC, 3 ECp, 1 AAA, 1 GhG, 5 CP-GP, 5sf OG, 3 P-CP, 7h Zürich, 2 v IS, 6 McD, 1 BL2 (1)
2. **Diane Allahgreen** 21.2.75 (4y, 6) 13.25 '94   13.13w, 13.27, 13.28, 13.38, 13.43, 13.44;
    1 Bedford, 3 AAA v LC, 1 WG, 1 North, 3 Tallinn, 2 AAA, 2 GhG, 8 CP-GP, 1 U23I, 1 Nth IC, 1 BL3 (2)
3. **Jackie Agyepong** 5.1.69 (9y, 1) 12.90 '95   13.18, 13.24, 13.30, 13.35, 13.36w, 13.47; 13.3w;
    2B Lausanne, 6 GhG, 6 CP-GP, 7h OG, 4 v IS, 7 McD, 2 Cup, 1 BL1 (3)
4. **Denise Lewis** 27.8.72 (5y, 7) 13.47 '94   13.18, 13.41, 13.45, 13.45, 13.52, 13.57;
    3 AAA, 6 P-CP, 8 McD, 1B BL2 (1)
5. **Melanie Wilkins** 18.1.73 (3y, 5) 13.34/13.1 '95   13.23w, 13.40w, 13.41, 13.50w, 13.51, 13.54; 13.5w;
    4 Bedford, 4 AAA v LC, 2 Basel, 1 South, 4 AAA, 5 GhG, 1 IR, 1 BEL Ch, BL1: 1,1,-
6. **Keri Maddox** 4.7.72 (7y, 3=) 13.24/13.20w '93   13.39w, 13.51w, 13.53, 13.57, 13.58, 13.60; 13.5;
    3 Bedford, 5 AAA v LC, 1 Basel, 1 Mid, 5 AAA, 7 GhG, 3 IR, 1 Künzelsau, BL4: 1,1,1
7. **Clova Court** 10.2.60 (6y, 3=) 13.04 '94   13.65, 13.71w, 13.9, 13.6, 13.7, 13.7, 13.7;
    2 IR, 1 Cup, BL2: 2,1,1
8. **Jane Hale** 4.1.74 (1y, -) 13.85 '93   13.59, 13.69, 13.79, 13.82, 13.86, 13.97; 13.7w;
    1 B.Univs, 2 Yorks, 2 Bedford, 2 AAA v LC, 1 CAU, 2 North, 6 AAA, 1 SN4, 4 U23I, BL1: -,3,2
9. **Samantha Farquharson** 15.12.69 (7y, 12) 13.08 '94   13.38w, 13.40, 13.43, 13.66, 13.68, 13.74; 13.6;
    1 AUS Ch, 5 Chemnitz, 6 Rhede, BL2: 3,-,2
10. **Natasha Danvers** 19.9.77 (3y, 8) 13.45 '95   13.74, 13.78, 13.80, 13.88, 13.99w, 14.00;
    7 AAA, 1 Sth-J, 1 AAA-J, 6 WJ, 2 BL2 (2)
11. **Michelle Campbell** 24.2.69 (7y, -) 13.26 '90, 13.08w '95   13.61w, 13.80; 13.3; 5r2 Walnut
12. **Katy Sketchley** 9.7.73 (1y, -) 14.15 '92   13.72w, 13.86, 13.93, 13.94, 13.99, 14.09; 13.8w, 13.9;
    1B Bedford, 6 AAA v LC, 2 CAU, 2 South, 8 AAA, 2 SN4, 1 Scot, 1 Abingdon, 1 Plate
Thorp, whose previous best ranking was 5th in 1993 and 1994, made a superb breakthrough to run a British record in narrowly failing to make the Olympic final. Allahgreen was 1-1 with Agyepong, who just came back in time from injury to take her Olympic place. Wilkins beat Maddox 4-2. The 10th best of 13:74 is the worst since 1982.

400 METRES HURDLES
1. **Sally Gunnell** 29.7.66 (8y, -) 52.74 '93   54.65, 55.29, 55.35, 55.64, 55.84, 56.03;
    3r2 Jena, 1 ECp, 3 Nürnberg, 1 AAA, 1 Zagreb, dnf Lausanne, dnf sf OG

2. **Louise Fraser** 10.10.70 (4y, 3) 56.26 '92 56.45, 56.67, 56.87, 57.50, 57.53, 57.77;
 1 Luton, 1 AAA v LC, 1= CAU, 1 North, 2 Tallinn, 3 AAA, 2 Liverpool sf, BL1: 1,1,-
3. **Alyson Layzell** 16.12.66 (3y, -) 58.31 '86 56.43, 57.39, 57.71, 57.79, 58.92, 59.72;
 1 WG, 1 Welsh, 3 Dublin, 2 AAA, 5 Lucerne
4. **Louise Brunning** 6.3.72 (3y, 4) 57.30 '95 56.61, 57.34, 57.67, 57.83, 58.57, 58.99;
 2 AAA v LC, 5 Basel, 1 South, 2 Dublin, 4 AAA
5. **Lorraine Hanson** 22.4.65 (6y, -) 56.70 '89 57.03, 57.13, 58.24, 58.24, 58.92, 59.0;
 1r2 E.Clubs, 4 Dublin, 5 AAA, 1 BL2 (1)
6. **Vicki Jamison** 19.5.77 (2y, -) 59.81 '95 57.27, 57.49, 57.57, 57.87, 58.0, 58.10;
 2 B.Univs, 4 AAA v LC, 1= CAU, 7 AAA, 1 SN4, 1 AAA-J, 1 JInt, 2 WJ
7. **Gowry Retchakan** 21.6.60 (8y, 2) 54.63 '92 57.78, 57.85, 58.07, 58.09, 58.34, 58.40;
 1B AAA v LC, 2 South, 6 AAA, BL3: 1,1,-
8. **Allison Curbishley** 3.6.76 (3y, -) 59.04 '93 58.8, 59.47, 59.8, 60.2; 1 B.Univs, 3 AAA v LC
9. **Sinead Dudgeon** 9.7.76 (1y, -) 61.34 '95 58.80, 59.39, 59.60, 60.1, 60.33, 60.48;
 3 B.Univs, 3 Bedford, 5 Dublin, 8 AAA, 2 SN4, 4 U23I, 1 Liverpool sf, 1 Cup, 1 BL1 (3)
10. **Vyvyan Rhodes** 5.5.73 (6y, 6) 58.02 '92 58.85, 59.40, 59.44, 59.72, 59.8, 59.82;
 1 Bedford, 3 CAU, 2 North, 6 Dublin, 3h AAA, 1 IR, 2 BL2 (1)
11. **Keri Maddox** 4.7.72 (1y, -) 59.49 '94 59.39, 59.6, 60.3, 60.8; 1 Künzelsau, BL4: -,1,1
12. **Sharon Allen** 23.10.68 (1y, -) 58.98 '90 59.54, 60.20, 61.27; 3h AAA

Even though her season was again marred by injury, Gunnell was top for a record eighth time at this event. 1995 no. 1 Jacqui Parker did not contest the 400mh. After ten years, Layzell made a remarkable return to hurdling, setting three Welsh records; she had ranked 8th in 1985 and 5th in 1986! Although Layzell narrowly beat Fraser at the AAAs, the latter had much the greater depth of performances, and ranks 2nd. Hanson returned to hurdling after four years concentrating on the flat.

HIGH JUMP
1. **Debbie Marti** 14.5.68 (12y, 3) 1.93 '92, 1.94i '91 1.94, 1.94, 1.92, 1.90, 1.90, 1.90; 2 Surrey, 1= Bedford,
 1 Ljubljana, 1 South, 1 Tallinn, 1 AAA, 1 Helsinki, nh Oslo, dnq 19= OG, 1 v IS, 1 McD, 4 JumpsI
2. **Lea Haggett** 9.5.72 (6y, 1) 1.91 '91 1.92, 1.90, 1.90, 1.89, 1.89, 1.88;
 1 AUS Ch, 1 Surrey, 1= Bedford, 7 ECp, 2 AAA, dnq 16 OG, 2 v IS, 2 McD
3. **Jo Jennings** 20.9.69 (8y, -) 1.94i '93, 1.90 '88 1.89, 1.86, 1.84, 1.84, 1.84, 1.83; 5 Bedford, 4 AAA v LC,
 2= CAU, 4 North, 3 AAA, 3 Helsinki, 1 IR, 1 Nth IC, 2 Jona, 7 Linz, 3 McD, 1 Cup, 5 JumpsI, BL1: 1,2,1
4. **Michelle Dunkley** 26.1.78 (2y, 4) 1.87 '95 1.85, 1.85, 1.85, 1.85, 1.84, 1.80; 1.86i, 1.86i. 1.86i;
 3 Bedford, 1 AAA v LC, 2= CAU, 2 ESch, 2 AAA-J, 5= JInt, 8= WJ
5. **Julia Bennett** 26.3.70 (9y, 5) 1.89 '94, 1.92i '90 1.88, 1.84, 1.84, 1.83, 1.83, 1.80; 1.88i, 1.85i;
 4 Surrey, 2 AAA v LC, 2 BEL Ch
6. **Hazel Melvin** 19.11.73 (4y, -) 1.81 '94 1.84, 1.83, 1.80, 1.80, 1.80, 1.78; 1.82i, 1.80i;
 6 Bedford, 4= AAA, 1 SN4, 1 Scot, 4 McD, 2 Cup, BL1: 3,3,2
7. **Susan Jones** 8.6.78 (3y, 11) 1.82 '94 1.87, 1.83, 1.83, 1.80, 1.80, 1.80; 3 AAA v LC, 1 CAU, 1 North,
 4= AAA, 2 Cork, 1 Nth-J, 1 E.Sch, 3 IR, 3 AAA-J, 5= JInt, 1 Jnr IA, 5 McD, 2 EJ Clubs, BL2: 1,2=,2
8. **Denise Lewis** 27.8.72 (4y, 7=) 1.87 '94 1.84, 1.84, 1.83, 1.78, 1.77, 1.75; 1B E.Clubs, 3 Cup, BL2: 3,1,1
9. **Rachael Forrest** 25.12.77 (2y, 6) 1.87 '95 1.85, 1.81, 1.78, 1.75, 1.75, 1.75; 1.80i, 1.80i, 1.80i;
 1 Mid J, 2 Mid, 3 E.Sch, 1 AAA-J, dnq 21= WJ, BL2: 4,2=,-
10. **Kerry Jury** 19.11.68 (1y, -) 1.74 '95 1.80, 1.80, 1.78, 1.77, 1,75, 1.75, 1.76i; 1 Mid, 4 IR
11. **Alison Evans** 13.12.73 (1y, -) 1.75 '94 1.80, 1.76, 1.75, 1.71, 1.70, 1.70; 3= Mid, 6= AAA, 5 IR
12. **Chloe Cozens** 9.4.80 (1y, -) 1.75i/1.69 '95 1.79, 1.76, 1.76, 1.74, 1.73, 1.72;
 1 Sth U17, 1 E,Sch-I, 1 Sch Int, 2 AAA U17
nr **Kelly Thirkle** 29.3.71 (6y, 12=) 1.88i '92, 1.85 '91 1.75, 1.75, 1.75, 1.75, 1.70, 1.70; 1.80i, 1.75i;
 7= Bedford, 2= North, 6= AAA, 5 Cork, BL1: 2,4,4
 Dalia Mikneviciute (Lit) 5.9.70 ?1.87 '90 1.85, 1.85, 1.84, 1.84, 1.83, 1.83; 1.85i;
 3 Surrey, 4 Bedford, 2 South, 2 IR, 1 BL1 (2)

Marti regained the top ranking with her fifth year at the top, from Haggett whom she beat 3-2, although Haggett fared better at the Olympics.

POLE VAULT
1. **Kate Staples** 2.11.65 (4y, 1) 3.80/3.90ex '95 3.90, 3.80, 3.80, 3.75, 3.75, 3.70; 3.85i, 3.85i;
 1 Bedford, 1 AAA v LC, 2 Ljubljana, 2 Riga, 1 AAA, 1 Woking,
2. **Janine Whitlock** 11.8.73 (2y, 7) 3.41/3.60i '95 4.00, 3.91, 3.91, 3.85, 3.80 7 times; 3.86i;
 2 Bedford, 3 AAA v LC, 1 WG, 3 CAU, 4 Riga, 2 AAA, 1 Scot, 8 Hechtel, 1 IR, 1 Wrexham, 1 Nth IC, 1
 London, 1 P'bor, 1 Hendon, 1 JumpsI
3. **Rhian Clarke** 19.4.77 (4y, 3=) 3.50 '95 3.70, 3.70, 3.65, 3.65, 3.60, 3.60; 3.65i;
 4 AAA v LC, 4 CAU, 1 Welsh, 5 AAA, 1 Sth-J, 2 IR, 1 AAA-J, 3 JInt, 1 Jnr IA, 4 Hendon, 3 P'Bor, BL1: -, 1, 1
4. **Linda Stanton** 22.6.73 (4y, 2) 3.72 '95 3.60, 3.60, 3.60, 3.50, 3.40; 3.70i, 3.70i, 3.70i, 3.70i;
 1 BL3 (1), 2 AAA v LC, 3 Riga, 3 AAA, 6 Stockholm, nh IR, 2 Nth IC
5. **Paula Wilson** 20.11.69 (3y, 9) 3.45 '94,3.50i '95 3.70, 3.56, 3.40, 3.40, 3.40, 3.40;
 2 Mid, 4 IR, 3 Stoke, 2 P'Bor, 1 BL2 (2)

6. **Louise Schramm** 18.12.71 (3y, 6) 3.30 '95   3.55, 3.50, 3.50, 3.50, 3.50, 3.45; 1 Ewell, 1 So'ton, 1 B.Univs,
   2 Luton, 3 Bedford, 6 AAA v LC, 2 CAU, 1 South, 4 AAA, 2 Woking, 3 BEL Ch, 2= Hendon, 2 London, 4 P'bor
7. **Clare Ridgley** 11.9.77 (4y, 3=) 3.45 '95   3.50, 3.50, 3.40, 3.40, 3.40, 3.30; 3.51i, 3.50i;
   2 Ewell, 2 So'ton, 1 Luton, 5 AAA v LC, 1 CAU, 2 AAA-J, 8 JInt
8. **Emma Hornby** 12.12.73 (1y, -) 3.10i/2.90 '95   3.55, 3.50, 3.45, 3.45, 3.40, 3.40;
   5 CAU, 1 Mid, 6= AAA, 3 IR, 3 Wrexham, 3 Stoke, 6 P'bor, BL2: 1, 2,1
9. **Fiona Harrison** 30.11.81 (1y, -) 3.05 '95   3.50, 3.45, 3.40, 3.21, 3.10, 3.00; 3.20i;
   1 AAA U17, 2= Hendon, 1 Stoke
10. **Claire Adams** 30.5.69 (4y, 5) 3.30/3.40i '95   3.30, 3.20, 3.20, 2.80; 3.30i, 3.20i; 3 Mid, 6= AAA, BL4: -,1,1
11. **Katie Alexander** 28.4.74 (3y, 8) 3.10 '95   3.30, 3.20, 3.20, 3.20, 3.20, 3.10;
   3 B.Univs, 4 Luton, 8 AAA, 4= U23I, 4 AAA-J, 5 Hendon, 2 BL1 (2)
12? **Alison Jessee** 13.1.67 (1y, -) 3.32? '95   3.60, 3.35, 3.30, 3.20, 3.20, 3.17; doubtful marks in USA

Whitlock became Britain's first 4m-vaulter, but she lost 4-0 to Staples before the latter was seriously injured in 'Gladiators' action. Staples had added two more British records and her competitive record, including the AAA title was enough to hold Whitlock off the top ranking - for now! Stanton lost much of the year through injury and, although she beat her twice, drops behind Clarke, who steadily improved the British junior record. 14 year-old Fiona Harrison makes the top ten – the youngest ever. The 10th best (3.10 in 1994 and 1995) rose to 3.30 (or 3.50 if Jessee is included) in 1996.

LONG JUMP
1. **Denise Lewis** 27.8.72 (5y, 1) 6.67 '95   6.66, 6.60, 6.55, 6.54, 6.39, 6.35; 6.49i, 6.48i;
   4 E.Clubs, 4 ECp, 1 AAA, 7 Linz, 2 Cup, BL2: 1,-,1
2. **Joanne Wise** 15.3.71 (7y, -) 6.57 '92, 6.69w '88   6.47, 6.42, 6.40, 6.39, 6.38w, 6.35;
   2 AAA, 1 IR, 1 Cup, 1 BL2 (2)
3. **Sarah Claxton** 23.9.79 (1y, -) 6.01 '95   6.34w, 6.27w (6.24), 6.23, 6.22, 6.22, 6.20;
   1 Luton, 1 AAA v LC, 1 CAU, 4 Mannheim, 1 Sth U17, 1 E.Sch-I, 1 Sch Int, 1 AAA-J, dnq 17 WJ
4. **Ashia Hansen** 5.12.71 (3y, -) 6.27 '94   6.47A, 6.11, 6.09, 5.94; 1 Roodepoort,1 Alfaz, 1 Middlesex, 3 AAA
5. **Ann Brooks** 4.5.71 (3y, 5) 6.16 '95, 6.38w '94   6.10, 6.08, 6.08, 6.08w, 6.06, 5.99; 6.05i;
   4 AAA v LC, 2 CAU, 1 North, 4 AAA, 3 IR, 1 Nth IC, BL2: 2,2,2
6. **Vikki Schofield** 29.12.72 (3y, 3) 6.28 '95   6.14, 6.11w, 6.01w, 5.98, 5.97, 5.94; 6.00i;
   3 AAA v LC, 2 North, 2 IR
7. **Jackie White** 12.1.71 (4y, 7) 5.98 '94, 6.11w '95   6.08w, 6.05w, 6.03, 6.03, 5.96, 5.95;
   2 AAA v LC, 2 WG, 1 Mid, 4 IR
8. **Jade Johnson** 7.6.80 (2y, 6) 6.13/6.24w '95   6.08, 6.03, 6.01, 5.98, 5.93, 5.90;
   7 AAA, 1 Sth U17, 3 E.Sch-I, 1 London
9. **Ruth Irving** 20.7.74 (4y, 9) 6.28 '94   6.00, 5.95, 5.92, 5.86, 5.79, 5.78;
   5 AAA v LC, 4 CAU, 3 North, 3 Dublin, 6 AAA, 1 Scot, 4 U23I, 2 Nth IC, 1 BL4 (1)
10. **Caroline Black** 19.5.72 (1y, -) 6.00 '92, 6.03w '91   6.00, 6.00w, 6.00w, 5.97, 5.96, 5.95;
   3 CAU, 8 AAA, 2 SN4, 2 Scot, 3 Cup; BL1: 1,3,2
11. **Liz Ghojefa** 24.2.69 (4y, 4) 6.27 '95   6.13, 6.04, 6.04, 6.02, 6.02, 5.92; ?6.10;
   2 Luton, 2 Surrey, 6 CAU, 1 South, 11 AAA, 6 BEL Ch, 2 London
12. **Debbie Marti** 14.5.68 (2y, 10) 6.19 '92, 6.22w '85   6.22, 6.00w (5.77), 5.93; 1 Plate
Not ranked
   Tracy Joseph 29.11.69 (1y, -) 5.62/5.74w '95   6.13, 6.04, 5.94, 5.90, 5.88, 5.82
   Julia Bennett 26.3.70 (1y, 12) 6.12 '94   6.05w, 5.96, 5.91; 6.01i, 5.89i; 1 Surrey

Lewis maintained her top ranking, and the best news was the return of Joanne Wise after missing two seasons. At 16 Claxton had a splendid season to gain third ranking. The standard in depth is again weak.

TRIPLE JUMP
1. **Ashia Hansen** 5.12.71 (6y, 1) 14.66 '95   14.78, 14.67, 14.64A, 14.57, 14.55, 14.51, 14.49; 14.58i, 14.57i;
   2 Bratislava, 1 ECp, 1 AAA, 1 GhG, 5 Lausanne, 2 CP-GP, 4 OG, 1 P-CP, 1 v IS, 2 McD, 1 BL1 (2)
2. **Michelle Griffith** 6.10.71 (7y, 2) 14.08 '94   14.04, 13.78, 13.73, 13.73, 13.70, 13.67; 1 Middx, 1 Bedford,
   1 Ljub, 7 Bratis, 1 South, 2 AAA, 4 GhG, 4 Stockholm, 4 CP-GP, dnq 18 OG, 5 P-CP, 3 v IS, 6 McD, 1 BL2 (1)
3. **Connie Henry** 15.4.72 (4y, -) 13.31 '94   13.55, 13.18, 13.07, 13.06, 12.95, 12.66;
   2 Middx, 3 Bedford, 1 CAU, 6 Tallinn, 3 AAA, 6 GhG, 1 IR, 6 P-CP
4. **Rachel Kirby** 18.5.69 (6y, 3) 13.64 '94   13.28, 13.03w (12.82), 12.92, 12.89w (12.72), 12.82;
   2 Bedford, 1 Basel, 7 Tallinn, 4 AAA, 4 Jona
5. **Shani Anderson** 7.8.75 (4y, -) 12.43 '93, 12.44 '94   13.03, 12.84, 12.52, 12.35, 11.86; 12.96i, 12.95i, 12.81i;
   1 B.Univs, 3 Middx, 2 Hendon, 2 AAA v LC, 5 AAA
6. **Mary Agyepong** 3.10.65 (3y, -) 13.56 '92   12.72, 12.65, 12.42, 12.31, 12.07, 12.00;
   3 Luton, 3 Hendon, 7 AAA v LC, 6 AAA, 1 BL1 (1)
7. **Caroline Stead** 14.9.71 (3y, 11) 12.17 '94   12.67, 12.50, 12.49, 12.46, 12.30, 12.23;
   2 Luton, 4 Middx, 1 Hendon, 2 South, 7 AAA, 1 Cork, 4 IR, 7 Jona, 1 London
8. **Pamela Anderson** 16.10.76 (2y, 12) 12.10 '95
   12.55, 12.44w, 12.37w, 12.27, 12.20, 12.13; 12.52i, 12.29i; 4 B.Univs, 3 CAU, 1 Dublin, 8 AAA, 1 Scot

9. **Karen Skeggs** 26.10.69 (7y, 4) 12.89/12.93w '92   12.61w, 12.47w, 12.42, 12.38, 12.34, 12.33; 12.49i;
   2 Kent, 4 Bedford, 4 CAU, 3 South, 10 AAA, 2 Scot, 1 Abingdon, BL4: -,1,1
10. **Katie Evans** 4.2.74 (2y, 10) 12.20 '95   12.58w, 12.40, 12.39w, 12.38, 12.37w, 12.36;
   1 Warwicks, 6 E.Clubs, 2 CAU, 2 Mid, nj AAA, 2 Cork, 5 U23I, 2 IR, 1 Cup, BL2: 2,2,1
11. **Debbie Rowe** 8.9.72 (3y, 8) 12.44 '95   12.46, 12.45w, 12.44, 12.32, 12.30, 12.22;
   2 B.Univs, 2 Warwicks, 1 AAA v LC, 6 CAU, 1 Lough 5/6, 1 Mid, 9 AAA, 3 IR, 3 Cup, BL2: 3,1,-
12. **Kerensa Denham** 8.3.74 (1y, -) 11.97 '94   12.51, 12.50, 12.42, 12.40, 12.08, 12.04;
   1 Luton, 1 Kent, 5 AAA v LC, 4 South, 11 AAA, 6 U23I, 2 London
nr **Elizabeth Gibbens** 5.4.77 (1y, 7) 12.42 '95   12.36w (12.20), 12.32w, 12.22, 12.20w, 12.17, 12.12; 12.26i,
   12.20i; 3 B.Univs, 3 Kent, 4 AAA v LC, 2 Lough 5/6, 1 South-J, 7 JInt, 1 AAA-J, 1 Jnr IA

Hansen added two more British records outdoors and one indoors, won the European Cup as in 1995, and consolidated her position in the world top ten. Griffith was again 2nd and exceeded 14m at the Southern, but otherwise got stuck in the 13.70 region. Henry had her best season for 3rd and there were a record five women over 13m. 6th to 11th were very close; Anderson beat Skeggs 3-0, Evans beat Rowe 5-3. The 10th best of 12.49 is a new record.

SHOT

1. **Judy Oakes** 14.2.58 (20y, 1) 19.36 '88   19.01, 19.00, 18.76, 18.70, 18.65, 18.65; 18.72i;
   1 Luton, 3 Halle, 2 Hengelo, 2 ECp, 1 AAA, 11 OG, 4 Köln, 1 London
2. **Myrtle Augee** 4.2.65 (15y, 3) 19.03 '90   16.81, 16.53, 16.46, 16.22, 16.17, 16.02;
   1 CAU, 1 South, 2 AAA, 1 Hendon sf, 1 Plate
3. **Sharon Andrews** 4.7.67 (12y, 7) 15.80 '93   15.24, 14.87, 14.83, 14.43, 14.24, 14.00;
   1 Essex, 3 Dublin, 3 AAA, 1 Cup, BL1: -,1,3
4. **Alison Grey** 12.5.73 (7y, 6) 15.85i/15.69 '94   14.66, 14.56, 14.55, 14.34, 14.19, 14.13; 14.51i, 14.35i;
   2 Dublin, 4 AAA, 2 SN4, 1 Scot, BL1: 2,2,1
5. **Tracy Axten** 20.7.63 (2y, 4) 14.90 '95   14.76, 14.47, 14.37, 14.32, 14.11, 13.97;
   2 Luton, 1 AAA v LC, 3 South, 1 Police, 1 Abingdon, BL3: 1,1,1
6. **Joanne Duncan** 27.12.66 (3y, 12) 14.29 '95   14.67, 14.51, 14.19, 14.13, 13,72, 13.70;
   2 Essex, 4 South, 6 AAA, 2 Abingdon, BL1: 4,3,2
7. **Debbie Callaway** 15.7.64 (5y, 5) 14.88 '93   14.48, 14.23, 14.04, 13.87, 13.86, 13.74; 14.25i, 14.21i;
   3 Luton, 2 AAA v LC, 3 CAU, 3 IR, 1 Crawley sf, 3 Abingdon, 3 London, 2 Cup, BL1: 1,9,5
8. **Vickie Foster** 1.4.71 (1y, -) 13.61 '93   14.42, 13.73, 13.65, 13.61, 13.59, 13.53;
   4 Luton, 2 South, 1 IR, 2 London
9. **Philippa Roles** 1.3.78 (2y, 10) 14.11 '95   14.60, 13.76, 13.68, 13.46, 13.48, 13.10; 13.68i;
   1 Welsh Sch, 1 Welsh J, 1 AAA-J, 5 Jnr Int, 2 BL3 (2)
10. **Emma Beales** 7.12.71 (4y, -) 14.53 '92   14.43, 13.67, 13.64, 13.41, 13.39, 13.37; 2 Hendon sf, 3 Plate
11. **Denise Lewis** 27.8.72 (1y, -) 13.58 '95   14.36, 13.92, 13.47, 13.40, 13.33; 1 Staffs, BL2: -,1,1
12. **Charmaine Johnson** 4.6.63 (1y, -) 14.29 '93   14.09, 13.79, 13.38, 13.22, 13.21, 12.93; 13.23i;
   5 AAA, 2 Crawley sf, 6 BEL Ch, BL2: 1,2,2
nr **Maggie Lynes** 19.2.63 (11y, 2) 16.57 '94   13.89; 15.80i, 15.58i, 15.53i, 15.50i, 15.43i, 15.32i

Judy Oakes achieves a record 14th number one ranking and, over 18m in all her 11 outdoor competitions as well as 8 times indoors, was a long way ahead of Augee. Oakes excelled for her best ever European Cup result and in making the Olympic final. Maggie Lynes drops out after 11 years in the top seven as she only had one outdoor competition at 13.89; on her indoor form she would have ranked 3rd. There was little between those in the second half of the rankings.

DISCUS

1. **Jacqueline McKernan** 1.7.65 (12y, 1) 60.72 '93   60.04, 58.88, 58.08, 57.24, 56.30, 55.66;
   nt Halle, 1 Lough 1/6, 2 Dublin, 1 AAA, 1 SN4, 4 GhG, 1 NI, dnq 20 OG, 10 Linz
2. **Shelley Drew** 8.8.73 (5y, 3) 55.70 '95   57.34, 55.02, 54.86, 54.70, 54.22, 53.92;
   1 B.Univs, 13 Halle, 3 AAA v LC, 1 South, 2 AAA, 6 GhG, 1 IR, 2 BEL Ch, 3 Abingdon
3. **Debbie Callaway** 15.7.64 (13y, 2) 57.00 '95   58.56, 54.58, 53.54, 53.38, 53.10, 52.98; 1 Luton, 2 Lough 15/5,
   16 Halle, 1 AAA v LC, 2 CAU, 8 ECp, 3 AAA, 5 GhG, 2 IR, 2 London, 2 Abingdon, 1 Cup, BL1: 1,1,1
4. **Tracy Axten** 20.7.63 (8y, 5) 54.40 '93   55.88, 55.38, 55.02, 54.20, 54.14, 53.90; 2 Luton, 1 Lough 15/5,
   2 AAA v LC, 1 CAU, 2 South, 4 AAA, 7 GhG, 1 Police, 1 London, 1 Abingdon, BL3: 1,1,1
5. **Sharon Andrews** 4.7.67 (10y, 6) 56.24 '94   52.10, 50.50, 50.00, 49.84, 49.70, 48.48;
   3 South, 4 Dublin, 5 AAA, 3 Cup, BL1: -,2,3
6. **Lorraine Shaw** 2.4.68 (4y, 8) 55.04 '94   52.34, 52.00, 47.02; 1 Künzelsau, BL1: 2,-,4
7. **Nicola Talbot** 17.2.72 (4y, -) 54.24 '93   51.24, 50.38, 49.68, 49.16, 49.10, 48.72;
   3 CAU, 1 Mid, 2 Lough 5/6, 6 AAA, 3 IR
8. **Philippa Roles** 1.3.78 (2y, 12) 49.12 '95   51.32, 48.90, 48.70, 48.22, 47.96, 47.82; 1 WG, 5 AAA v LC,
   1 Welsh, 6 Dublin, 6 Mannheim, 1 Welsh-J, 1 Welsh Sch, 2 AAA-J, 2 JInt, dnq 16 WJ; BL3: 3,2,-
9. **Alison Grey** 12.5.73 (4y, -) 52.52 '94   48.82, 48.64, 48.58, 48.06, 47.96, 47.92;
   5 Dublin, 7 AAA, 4 SN4, 1 Scot, BL1: 3,3,2
10. **Sarah Henton** 4.5.73 (1y, -) 48.18 '95   49.74, 49.52, 47.68, 47.12, 46.54, 46.14;
   3 B.Univs, 6B E.Clubs, 4 CAU, 4 South, 8 AAA, 2 Cup, BL2: -,1,1
11. **Emma Merry** 2.7.74 (7y, 9) 52.58 '93   49.64, 48.52, 47.76, 47.76, 47.74, 47.36;
   2 B.Univs, 3 Lough 15/5, 4 AAA v LC, 3 Lough 5/6, 4 U23I, 4 IR; BL2: -,2,2

12. **Emma Beales** 7.12.71 (6y, 4) 54.68 '95   50.70, 49.60, 48.36, 46.08, 45.52, 44.62; 1 Plate
nr   **Rachel Hopgood** 2.6.78 (0y, -) 48.04 '95   48.76, 48.12, 47.06, 45.96, 44.53, 43.54;
     5 CAU, 1 North, 9 AAA, 6 IR, 2 E.Sch, 1 BL2 (1)

McKernan was number one for the 8th time. Close for 2nd to 4th – Drew beat Callaway 3-2 and was 3-3 with Axten, who lost 3-4 to Callaway. The AAA order of Drew, Callaway, Axten is maintained.

HAMMER
1.   **Lorraine Shaw** 2.4.68 (4y, 1) 64.90 '95   61.34, 60.58, 59.84, 56.18, 53.20; 1 Colindale, 3 Halle, BL1: 1,-,1
2.   **Lyn Sprules** 11.9.75 (4y, 2) 55.44 '94   59.54, 59.18, 58.74, 58.08, 57.96, 57.88;
     2 Colindale, 9 Halle, 1 South, 1 AAA, 2 U23I, 1 IR, 1 BEL Ch, 1 Braintree, BL3: 1,1,-
3.   **Ann Gardner** 11.10.68 (5y, 5) 54.02 '93   55.00, 54.66, 54.30, 53.06, 51.58, 51.56;
     2 CAU, 1 Mid, 2 AAA, 2 IR
4.   **Sarah Moore** 15.3.73 (5y, 4) 53.00 '95   53.26, 52.90, 52.36, 52.02, 51.96, 51.84;
     3 Colindale, 2 Bedford, 1 WG, 1 Welsh, 4 AAA, 1 SN4, 1 P'Bor, BL4: 1,1,1
5.   **Diana Holden** 12.2.75 (6y, 3) 54.42 '95   52.06, 51.52, 51.32, 50.84, 50.42, 50.34;
     4 Colindale, 1 B.Univs, 1 Bedford, nt CAU, 2 South, 3 AAA, 6 U23I, 2 BL3 (2)
6.   **Irene Duffin** 10.8.60 (3y, 10) 47.74 '95   50.32, 50.10, 49.04, 49.04, 48.96, 48.62;
     5 Colindale, 2 Kent, 3 Bedford, 3 South, 6 AAA, 3 Cup, BL1: 3,1,5
7.   **Helen Arnold** 5.10.78 (2y,1 2) 46.98 '95   50.62, 50.22, 50.06, 49.08, 48.96, 48.72;
     3 CAU, 4 South, 7 AAA, 1 AAA-J, 4 JInt, 3 Braintree
8.   **Esther Augee** 1.1.64 (4y, -) 56.76 '93   50.72, 49.48, 49.36, 48.22, 48.10, 48.04;
     6 Colindale, 1 Kent, 1 CAU, 5 South, 8 AAA, 2 Stoke sf, 4 Cup, BL1: 2,6,-
9.   **Samantha Burns-Salmon** 13.4.76 (3y, 7) 49.48 '95   49.80, 49.24, 48.82, 48.64, 48.00, 46.92;
     2 B.Univs, 8 Colindale, 4 Bedford, 4 CAU, 1 North, 1 Nth IC, 2 P'bor, BL1: -,5,2
10. **Helen McCreadie** 10.5.75 (1y, -) 46.48 '95   48.32, 47.92, 47.66, 47.44, 47.34, 47.08;
     5 CAU, 5 AAA, 1 Scot, 2 Cup, BL1: 5,3,3
11. **Rachael Beverley** 23.7.79 (1y, -) 44.70 '95   49.52, 48.40, 48.14, 46.64, 46.36, 46.22;
     1B Colindale, 1 Nth-J, 9 AAA, 2 Scot-J, 3 Scot, 3 IR, 2 AAA-J, 6 JInt, 2 Jnr IA, 3 P'bor
12. **Marina Semenova** 12.7.64 (1y, -) 46.72 '95   48.20, 48.12, 48.02, 47.90, 47.02, 46.58;
     2 North, 4 IR, 1 Stoke sf, 1 Cup, BL2: 3,1,1
nr   **Elizabeth Pidgeon** 27.4.77 (0y, -) 0   48.98, 47.78, 47.30, 46.88, 46.08, 45.96;
     9 South, 2 Sth-J, 15 AAA, 3 AAA-J, 1 Jnr IA, BL1: -,7,6
     Julie Kirkpatrick 14.7.72 (2y, 9) 48.56 '95   48.90, 47.98, 46.24, 45.66, 45.26, 44.40;
     3 Dublin, 1 Irish Ch, 5 SN4, 1 NI, BL2: 1,-,2

Although restricted to five competitions, Shaw was top for the fourth successive year ahead of the fast improving Sprules. Holden is the only athlete to have been included in all six editions of women's hammer rankings. The 10th best of 49.52 is the best yet, nearly 2m better than 1995.

JAVELIN
1.   **Tessa Sanderson** 14.3.56 (22y, -) 73.58 '83   64.06, 62.88, 61.24, 60.78, 60.76, 60.64, 60.60;
     1 Bedford, 1 WG, 4 ECp, 1 AAA, 6 Stockholm, 1 CP-GP, dnq 14 OG, 2 P-CP, 3 v IS, 5 McD
2.   **Shelley Holroyd** 17.5.73 (8y, 2) 60.10 '93   60.12, 57.60, 57.58, 57.26, 56.72, 55.76;
     1 Luton, 2 Bedford, 2 WG, 2 AAA, 5 CP-GP, dnq 27 OG, 1 Cup, 1 BL1 (2)
3.   **Sharon Gibson** 31.12.61 (17y, 1) 62.32 '87   56.16, 56.10, 54.60, 53.30, 53.08, 52.22;
     6 Halle, 1 CAU, 1 Mid, 4 AAA, 1 IR, 1 Stoke sf, BL4: 1,1,1
4.   **Lorna Jackson** 9.1.74 (4y, 3) 55.48 '95   58.20, 55.68, 52.10, 51.64, 51.52, 50.80;   7 Halle, 3 Bedford,
     3 Ljubljana, 1 Dublin, 3 AAA, 2 SN4, 3 U23I, 7 P-CP, 2 Liverpool sf, 6 McD, 3 Cup, BL1: 1,3,1
5.   **Karen Martin** 24.11.74 (5y, 4) 55.72 '92   53.74, 53.56, 51.52, 51.48, 50.82, 48.74;
     10 AAA, 1 IS, 2 U23I, 6 P-CP, 2 Stoke sf, BL3: 1,-,1
6.   **Denise Lewis** 27.8.72 (2y, 6) 53.68 '94   56.50, 54.82, 48.30, 47.86, 47.00, 44.46;
     3 P-CP, 4 v IS, 7 McD, 4 Cup, 1 BL2 (2)
7.   **Amanda Liverton** 1.9.72 (9y, 7) 57.84 '90   54.44, 50.56, 50.06, 49.70, 47.08; 1 Exeter
8.   **Karen Costello** 21.10.68 (3y, 10) 54.50 '94   50.96, 49.92, 48.02, 47.76, 46.60, 46.32;
     1 Scot, 1 Liverpool sf, 2 Cup, BL1: -,2,2
9.   **Noelle Bradshaw** 18.12.63 (5y, 8) 52.40 '93   47.86, 47.68, 47.46, 46.84, 46.56, 46.22;
     2 Luton, 7 CAU, 1 South, 5 AAA, 2 IR, 1 BEL Ch
10. **Onyema Amadi** 28.6.73 (2y, 12) 49.04 '94   48.34, 48.22, 48.16, 44.24, 41.58;
     3 WG, 1 Welsh, 6 AAA, 3 SN4, BL3: -,2,2
11. **Lucy Stevenson** 30.1.73 (3y, -) 52.00 '92   48.18, 47.38, 47.16, 46.84, 46.18, 46.14;
     1 B.Univs, 2 CAU, 2 North, 7 AAA, 3 IR, 3 Liverpool sf, 1 Nth IC, BL1: -, 4,3
12. **Alison Moffitt** 6.10.69 (1y, -) 47.54 '93   49.10, 47.58, 47.14, 46.68, 46.34, 45.20;
     3 CAU, 3 Dublin, 1 Irish Ch, 4 SN4, 2 Scot
nr   **Janine King** 18.2.73 (1y, 9) 49.50 '94   50.80, 49.56, 47.10, 45.98, 45.96, 45.48;
     4 Bedford, 4 CAU, 1 North, 9 AAA, 5 IR, 4 Liverpool sf, BL1: 2,5,4

It was a wonderful return by Sanderson, who had missed the previous three seasons, for her 14th top ranking and 21 years in the top two. Nine women over 50 metres was at least an improvement on five in 1995. Northern Ireland record setter Moffitt is the only newcomer to the rankings.

HEPTATHLON

1. **Denise Lewis** 27.8.72 (8y, 1) 6325 '94   6645, 6489; 2 Götzis, 3 OG
2. **Kerry Jury** 19.11.68 (7y, 10) 5368 '95   5703, 5642, 5434, 5421, 5329; 1 North, 1 AAA, 24 ECp, 6 v 3N, 1 HC
3. **Julia Bennett** 26.3.70 (5y, 5) 5496 '95   5747w, 5356, 5251;   3 Alhama, 3 AAA, dnf ECp, 9 v 3N
4. **Vikki Schofield** 29.12.72 (6y, 4) 5671 '94   5700, 5362; 5 Alhama, dnf AAA, 28 ECp
5. **Sarah Damm** 12.9.70 (2y, 8) 5392 '95   5618w; 6 Alhama, dnf AAA, dnf ECp
6. **Pauline Richards** 30.6.68 (3y, 7) 5420 '94   5386, 5217, 5155w;   9 Alhama, 2 AAA, 10 v 3N
7. **Tracy Joseph** 29.11.69 (1y, -) 4790 '95   5339, 5280, 5238, 5195   2 POR Ch, 5 AAA, 1 South, 2 HC
8. **Diana Bennett** 14.6.74 (3y, 11) 5220 '95   5332, 5076, (4948); 1 Bonn, 4 AAA, dnf v 3N-U23
9. **Nicola Gautier** 21.3.78 (1y, -) 4543 '95   5213, 5208, 5111, 5080, 5079, 4941
   1 North-J, 1 AAA-J, 1 York, 6 v 3N-J, 10 WJ, 1 E.Sch
10. **Anne Hollman** 18.2.74 (3y, -) 5187w/5141 '93   5258, 4948; 6 AAA, 11 v 3N-23
11. **Louise Batho** 27.11.76 (1, -) 4635w/4626 '95   5114, 5102, 5072, 5020, 4923, 4839;
    2 North, 9 AAA, 1 Norwich, 9 v 3N-U23, 3 HC, 2 E.Sch
12. **Rebecca Lewis** 31.12.77 (1y, -) 4818 '95   5047, 5030, 5011, 5007; 2 AAA-J, 1 Telford, 9 v 3N-J, 4 HC (1 U20)
nr **Kim Crowther** 19.1.66 (4y, -) 5297 '86   5065, 5025; 7 AAA, 1 M'bor

To win the Olympic bronze medal after a moderate performance in her best event showed how Lewis has developed into a world-class performer. That, with her national record at Götzis, made her a clear choice for Britain's woman athlete of the year. This was her third year at the top in this event. After several years operating at 5200-5300 level Jury made a splendid leap in class; her previous best ranking was 6th in 1992. Batho improved her pb in each of her six heptathlons of 1996.

WALKS

3000m to 10,000m performances are on the track, unless indicated by R for road marks. All longer distances are on the road. Previous bests are shown for track 5000m and road or track 10km.

Priority is given in these rankings to form at the standard international distance of 10 kilometres, although performances at 3000m, 5000m and 20km are also taken into account.

1. **Victoria Lupton** 17.4.72 (8y, 1) 21:52.38 '95, 45:18.8t '95, 1:42:47 '95
   3km: 13:06.27, 13:16.53; 1 CAU
   5km: 23:04.57, 23:19, 24:33,8; 22:30R, 23:05R, 23:09+R, 23:43R; 1 North, 1 C'field, 1 AAA, 1 NAT
   10km: 47:05, 47:19, 47:35, 47:48, 49:15.0t; 1 Coventry, 1 UK, 12 Podebrady, dq Moscow, 33 OG, 1 AAA
   10M: 1:16:45, 1:22:11; 1 RWA   20km: 1:43:57. 1:46:43; 1 North, 1 RWA
2. **Verity Snook** 13.11.70 (8y, 4) 23:22.52 '94, 46:06 '94
   3km: 13:16:23; 2 CAU   5km: 24:16.1; 23:36R; 1 South
   10km: 47:12, 47:54, 48:13, 48:18, 51:03; 3 Manx, dq UK, 13 Podebrady, 27 Moscow, dq AAA
   20km: 1:54:15; 3 RWA
3. **Lisa Langford** 15.3.67 (12y, 1) 21:57.68 '90, 45:42 '87, 48:34.0t '86
   5km: 23:13R; 1 Mid   10km: 48:27; 2 UK
4. **Melanie Wright** 5.4.64 (7y, 5) 23:47.0 '94, 48:18 '92, 47:40sh '93
   3km: 14:04.72; 3 CAU   5km: 24:14.7, 24:36.65; 23:58R, 24:13R; 2 C'field, 2 AAA, 2 NAT, 1 Mid
   10km: 48:47, 49:15, 49:51, 50:24; 2 Coventry, dq Spanish, 3 UK, 17 Podebrady, 31 Moscow
5. **Carolyn Partington** 27.6.66 (4y, 3) 22:41.19 '95, 46:26 '95   10km: 48:00; 2 Manx
6. **Kim Braznell** (née Baird) 28.2.56 (4y, 6) 24:16.4 '95, 49:39 '95
   10km: 50:45, 50:52.3t, 51:28; 4 UK, 32 Moscow, 2 AAA   10M: 1:25:21; 1 Sutton Pk
7. **Karen Kneale** 23.4.69 (3y, 9) 51:03.0t '95
   3km: 14:06.0, 14:10.9, 14:23.55; 2 IR   5km: 24:40.69; 24:22R; 3 NAT, 1 Nth IC
   10km: 49:37, 50:37, 50:41, 50:50, 51:54; 6 Manx, 5 UK, 51 Eis, 2 Dublin
8. **Liz Corran** 23.9.55 (2y, 10) 25:13.03 '95, 51:03.0t '95, 1:55:10 '95
   3km: 14:15.0, 14:18.6; 1 IOM   5km: 24:40.91; 2 Nth IC
   10km: 51:17.1, 51:37, 52:00, 52:01, 52:03; 7 Manx, 1 IOM, 3 IA   20km: 1:47:10; 2 World Vets
9. **Sandra Brown** 1.4.49 (3y, -) 52:15 '93, 1:48:29 '91   20km: 1:48:46; 2 RWA
10. **Sylvia Black** 16.4.58 (13y, 8) 23:34.43 '92, 47:59 '92   3km: 14:23.50; 1 IR   5km: 24:26R; 4 NAT

Lupton achieved a clean sweep of national walks titles and regains the top ranking she held 1992-4, but lost in 1995 to Langford. Black squeezes in to achieve a 22-year span in the rankings, though she lost that record for any woman to Tessa Sanderson. There were no newcomers in the top ten.

With thanks to Tony Miller, Alan Lindop, Ian Hodge, Tony O'Neill, Martin Rix, Matthew Fraser-Moat and John Powell for their comments.

1996 LISTS - MEN

60 METRES - Indoors

6.55	Jason Gardener	U23	18.09.75	1	Birmingham	27	Jan
6.62				1	Birmingham	10	Feb
6.59	Linford Christie		2.04.60	1s1	Birmingham	3	Feb
6.74				1h2	Birmingham	3	Feb
6.59	Jason John		17.10.71	1r2	Glasgow	24	Feb
6.62				1	Glasgow	24	Feb
6.64				2s1	Birmingham	3	Feb
6.64				2	Stockholm, SWE	9	Mar
6.65				1	Birmingham	28	Jan
6.66				1rB	Birmingham	10	Feb
6.69				3s2	Stockholm, SWE	8	Mar
6.72				1h5	Stockholm, SWE	8	Mar
6.63	Darren Braithwaite		20.01.69	6	Lievin, FRA	18	Feb
6.64				4h2	Lievin, FRA	18	Feb
6.66				6	Stuttgart, GER	4	Feb
6.67				2h3	Stuttgart, GER	4	Feb
6.67				2	Tampere, FIN	12	Feb
6.69				4	Stockholm, SWE	25	Feb
6.70				5	Birmingham	10	Feb
6.67	Kevin Williams		15.12.71	1s3	Birmingham	3	Feb
6.68				2	Birmingham	3	Feb
6.69				3s1	Stockholm, SWE	8	Mar
6.72				1	Birmingham	6	Jan
6.72				1	Birmingham	27	Jan
6.72				2rB	Birmingham	10	Feb
6.72				2h2	Stockholm, SWE	8	Mar
6.72				6	Stockholm, SWE	9	Mar
6.67	Michael Rosswess		11.06.65	4	Birmingham	10	Feb
6.68				1	Birmingham	3	Feb
6.70				1s2	Birmingham	3	Feb
6.70				2	Glasgow	24	Feb
6.68	Dwain Chambers	U20	5.04.78	1	Lievin, FRA	2	Mar
6.73				1s1	Birmingham	17	Feb
6.70	Adrian Patrick		15.06.73	1ro	Birmingham	3	Feb
6.72				3	Birmingham	3	Feb
6.70	Jason Fergus		11.10.73	2ro	Birmingham	3	Feb
6.74				4	Birmingham	6	Jan
6.74	Doug Turner		2.12.66	3	Birmingham	6	Jan
	(10)						
6.74	Ian Mackie	U23	27.02.75	2rB	Glasgow	24	Feb

39 performances to 6.74 by 11 athletes

6.76	Paul White	U23	1.09.74	5	Birmingham	6	Jan
6.76	Terence Stamp		18.02.70	3rB	Birmingham	10	Feb
6.77	Curtis Browne	U23	11.09.75	4s1	Birmingham	3	Feb
6.78	Peter Maitland		21.01.73	1rB	Birmingham	27	Jan
6.78	John Regis		13.10.66	5h2	Lievin, FRA	18	Feb
6.79	Tremayne Rutherford		19.06.72	5s1	Birmingham	3	Feb
6.83	Owusu Dako		23.05.73	3s3	Birmingham	6	Jan
6.83	Courtney Rumbolt		26.07.69	2h6	Birmingham	3	Feb
6.84	Marlon Devonish	U23	1.06.76	2s1	Birmingham	6	Jan
	(20)						
6.84	Danny Joyce	U23	9.09.74	2h1	Birmingham	3	Feb
6.84	Ray Salami	U23	11.04.75	1rB	Birmingham	3	Feb
6.85	Oni Onuorah		16.10.73	3s1	Birmingham	6	Jan
6.85	Ray Burke		11.11.69	1h8	Birmingham	3	Feb
6.86	Daniel Money	U23	7.10.76	3s2	Birmingham	3	Feb
6.87	Martin Giraud	U20	16.11.77	2h2	Lievin, FRA	2	Mar
6.88	Michael Afilaka		16.11.71	4s3	Birmingham	6	Jan

6.88	Ken Campbell		30.09.72	2	Glasgow	13	Jan
6.88	Solomon Wariso		11.11.66	3h1	Birmingham	3	Feb
6.89	Cypren Edmunds		20.06.70	2	Glasgow	21	Jan
	(30)						
6.90	Mclean Okotie		31.07.69	5s3	Birmingham	6	Jan
6.90	Richard Rubenis		10.11.73	1rB	Birmingham	28	Jan
6.90	Sam Omonua	U23	16.06.76	7s1	Birmingham	3	Feb
6.90	Mark Phills		26.07.64	1	Birmingham	11	Feb
6.90	Mark Findlay	U20	20.03.78	2rB	Lievin, FRA	2	Mar
6.91	Scott Herbert	U23	12.02.74	4s1	Birmingham	6	Jan
6.91	Brian Taylor		13.08.70	5s1	Birmingham	6	Jan
6.91	Jamie Henderson		28.03.69	1s1	Glasgow	13	Jan
6.91	Seni Edu	U23	4.03.74	2	Glasgow	17	Mar
6.91	Mark Woodhouse	U23	1.11.75	3	Glasgow	17	Mar
	(40)						
6.92	Barrington Williams	V40	11.09.55	5s2	Birmingham	6	Jan
6.93	Brendon Ghent	U23	7.09.76	2h8	Birmingham	3	Feb
6.93	Ross Baillie	U20	26.09.77	1	Glasgow	3	Feb

Hand Timing

6.7	Chambers	U20	(6.68)	1	Birmingham	17	Feb
6.8	Courtney Rumbolt		(6.83)	1h2	Birmingham	6	Jan
6.8	Danny Joyce	U23	(6.84)	3s1	London (CP)	20	Jan
6.9	Mark Antoine		20.10.69	s	London (CP)	20	Jan
6.9	Damien Greaves	U20	19.09.77	3	Birmingham	17	Feb
6.9	Christian Malcolm	U20	3.06.79	4	Birmingham	17	Feb
6.9	Uvie Ugono	U20	8.03.78	2	Birmingham	24	Feb
6.9	Akinola Lashore		28.03.73	3	London (CP)	18	Dec
6.9	Bola Ojex		26.08.72	4	London (CP)	18	Dec
6.9	Nigel Vodal		19.11.72	5	London (CP)	18	Dec

Foreign

6.74	*Josephus Thomas*		*11.07.71*	*2*	*Birmingham*	*6*	*Jan*
6.87	*John McAdorey*	*U23*	*16.09.74*	*1*	*Glasgow*	*21*	*Jan*

100 METRES

10.03	0.1	Linford Christie	2.04.60	1q2	Atlanta, USA	26	Jul
10.04	0.8			1	Madrid, SPA	1	Jun
10.04	0.1			1	Birmingham	15	Jun
10.04	-0.4			5	Lausanne, SWZ	3	Jul
10.04	-0.6			3s2	Atlanta, USA	27	Jul
10.05	0.7			3	Paris, FRA	28	Jun
10.06	0.0			1	Nuremberg, GER	7	Jun
10.06	-1.4			3	Zurich, SWZ	14	Aug
10.10	0.4			2	Rome, ITA	5	Jun
10.13	2.0			1h1	Perth, AUS	28	Jan
10.14	0.4			5	Brussels, BEL	23	Aug
10.17	-0.4			2	Nice, FRA	10	Jul
10.17	-0.9			2h2	Zurich, SWZ	14	Aug
10.19	0.9			3	Sheffield	25	Aug
10.20	0.6			1	Arnsberg, GER	12	May
10.20	-1.0			1s1	Birmingham	15	Jun
10.26	-1.7			2	London (CP)	12	Jul
10.26	0.1			2h9	Atlanta, USA	26	Jul
10.28	0.5			1	Bedford	26	May
10.28	1.3			1	London (He)	31	Aug
10.29 A	-1.5			2	Sestriere, ITA	7	Aug
10.31	-0.1			1	Kingston	17	Aug
10.32				1h	Arnsberg, GER	12	May
10.32	1.0			1h1	Birmingham	14	Jun
10.37	0.1			1h1	Nuremberg, GER	7	Jun
10.50	-0.4			1	Lausanne, SWZ	3	Jul

Time	Wind	Name		DOB	Pos	Venue	Date
10.13	1.9	Darren Braithwaite		20.01.69	2	Helsinki, FIN	25 Jun
10.14	0.0				1	Ljubljana, SLO	26 May
10.19 A	-1.9				1	Pretoria, RSA	3 Feb
10.22 A	0.4				1	Johannesburg, RSA	14 Apr
10.22	1.2				2h2	Helsinki, FIN	25 Jun
10.23	-0.2				1s2	Birmingham	15 Jun
10.25	0.1				2	Birmingham	15 Jun
10.27	1.1				4	Bratislava, SVK	29 May
10.27	-0.3				4	Oslo, NOR	5 Jul
10.27	1.1				6q3	Atlanta, USA	26 Jul
10.29	-1.3				1h2	Birmingham	14 Jun
10.29	2.0				2h8	Atlanta, USA	26 Jul
10.31	0.0				2	Tallinn, EST	9 Jun
10.34	-0.3				3	Gateshead	19 Aug
10.37	0.9				7	Sheffield	25 Aug
10.39	-0.3				1	Cape Town, RSA	12 Apr
10.40 i					5	Tampere, FIN	12 Feb
10.48 A	-1.5				5	Sestriere, ITA	7 Aug
10.17	1.1	Darren Campbell		12.09.73	1	Bratislava, SVK	29 May
10.21	0.6				4	Linz, AUT	21 Aug
10.24	1.2				3h2	Helsinki, FIN	25 Jun
10.25	1.8				1rB	Ljubljana, SLO	26 May
10.25	1.5				7	Milan, ITA	7 Sep
10.26	1.9				6	Helsinki, FIN	25 Jun
10.29	1.8				5rB	Stockholm, SWE	8 Jul
10.30	-1.0				2s1	Birmingham	15 Jun
10.30	0.1				4=	Birmingham	15 Jun
10.32	-0.4				3	Nice, FRA	10 Jul
10.37	0.9				6	Sheffield	25 Aug
10.38	1.3				1s1a	Birmingham	15 Jun
		faulty start race rerun					
10.39	-0.2				3rB	Berlin, GER	30 Aug
10.41	0.3				1	Birmingham	6 Jul
10.41	-1.7				3	London (CP)	12 Jul
10.42	-0.3				1	Lahti, FIN	18 Aug
10.17	0.9	Ian Mackie	U23	27.02.75	2	Sheffield	25 Aug
10.24	1.8				4rB	Stockholm, SWE	8 Jul
10.25	-1.2				3q5	Atlanta, USA	26 Jul
10.25	-0.3				2	Gateshead	19 Aug
10.26	0.1				3	Birmingham	15 Jun
10.27	0.3				2h6	Atlanta, USA	26 Jul
10.33	0.1				6h1	Zurich, SWZ	14 Aug
10.34	0.0				1	Dublin, IRE	9 Jun
10.38	-0.3				1s3	Birmingham	15 Jun
10.42	-1.7				4	London (CP)	12 Jul
10.44	0.5				3	Bedford	26 May
10.45	-0.4				1h7	Birmingham	14 Jun
10.30	0.1	Jason John		17.10.71	4=	Birmingham	15 Jun
10.33	-0.2				2s2	Birmingham	15 Jun
10.36	0.5				2	Bedford	26 May
10.42	1.0				3	Lisbon, POR	21 Jun
10.50	-0.3				1h1	Bedford	26 May
10.35	1.8	Kevin Williams		15.12.71	2rB	Ljubljana, SLO	26 May
10.35	0.4	Owusu Dako		23.05.73	1rC	Stockholm, SWE	8 Jul
10.42	0.6				2rB	Chemnitz, GER	19 May
10.43	2.0				4	Cottbus, GER	9 Jun
10.36	-0.2	Allyn Condon	U23	24.08.74	3s2	Birmingham	15 Jun
10.42	0.9				1	Cork, IRE	22 Jun
10.43	-0.3				2h4	Birmingham	14 Jun
10.43	0.1				7	Birmingham	15 Jun
10.46	1.0				3	Gavle, SWE	2 Jul

Time	Wind	Name		Birthdate	Pos	City	Date	
10.38	0.1	Michael Rosswess		11.06.65	6	Birmingham	15	Jun
10.39	-0.3				1h4	Birmingham	14	Jun
10.44	-0.3				2s3	Birmingham	15	Jun
10.47	0.0				2	Ljubljana, SLO	26	May
10.49	0.5				4h1	Helsinki, FIN	25	Jun
10.38	0.2	Adrian Patrick		15.06.73	2	Oordegem, BEL	11	Aug
10.47	1.7				1h2	Oordegem, BEL	11	Aug
(10)								
10.39 A	0.7	John Regis		13.10.66	2	Pietersburg, RSA	3	Apr
10.45 A	0.1				2	Pretoria, RSA	8	Apr
10.41 A	0.7	Tony Jarrett		13.08.68	3	Pietersburg, RSA	3	Apr
10.48 A	0.1				3	Pretoria, RSA	8	Apr
10.49 A	0.4				5	Johannesburg, RSA	14	Apr
10.41	2.0	Marlon Devonish	U23	1.06.76	1	Kunzelsau, GER	7	Sep
10.42	1.8	Paul White	U23	1.09.74	3rB	Ljubljana, SLO	26	May
10.48					1	Birmingham	1	Jun
10.42	0.7	Dwain Chambers	U20	5.04.78	1	Bedford	27	Jul
10.47	1.0				5	Sydney, AUS	22	Aug
10.48	-0.2				1s2	Bedford	27	Jul
10.48	-0.5				2s1	Sydney, AUS	22	Aug
10.49	0.1				8	Birmingham	15	Jun
10.42	-0.1	Jason Livingston ¶		17.03.71	2	Kingston	17	Aug
10.50	1.3				3	London (He)	31	Aug
10.45		Terry Williams		15.11.68		Long Beach, USA	20	Apr
10.45	1.0	Jamie Henthorn	U20	20.02.77	4	Sydney, AUS	22	Aug
10.47	0.7				2	Bedford	27	Jul
10.48	1.6				2s2	Sydney, AUS	22	Aug
10.47 A	-1.9	Julian Golding	U23	17.02.75	2	Pretoria, RSA	3	Feb
10.53	-1.0				3s1	Birmingham	15	Jun
10.47	1.0	Danny Joyce	U23	9.09.74	2h1	Birmingham	14	Jun
(20)								
10.48 A	-1.9	Toby Box		9.09.72	3	Pretoria, RSA	3	Feb
10.80	1.1				6	Bedford	18	May
10.48	0.4	Roger Black		31.03.66	3	Irvine, USA	4	May
10.48	1.2	Jonathan Edwards		10.05.66	2	Tallahassee, USA	11	May

118 performances to 10.50 by 23 athletes including 1 indoors

Time	Wind	Name		Birthdate	Pos	City	Date	
10.51		Raymond Coker		28.07.73		Tallahassee, USA	5	May
10.51	0.9				3	Cork, IRE	22	Jun
10.51	0.3	Oni Onuorah		16.10.73	2	Birmingham	6	Jul
10.52	0.1	Jason Fergus		11.10.73	2h3	Birmingham	14	Jun
10.55	-1.0	Marcus Adam		28.02.68	4s1	Birmingham	15	Jun
10.55	0.7	Uvie Ugono	U20	8.03.78	3	Bedford	27	Jul
10.57	-0.7	Daniel Money	U23	7.10.76	1rB	Kingston	17	Aug
10.57	0.4	Michael Tietz	U20	14.09.77	1	Ljubljana, SLO	28	Sep
(30)								
10.59	0.9	Sam Omonua	U23	16.06.76	5	Cork, IRE	22	Jun
10.60	0.3	Mclean Okotie		31.07.69	4	Birmingham	6	Jul
10.60	0.7	Phillip Perigo	U20	25.09.78	4	Bedford	27	Jul
10.60	0.7	Christian Malcolm	U20	3.06.79	5	Bedford	27	Jul
10.62	0.7	Ross Baillie	U20	26.09.77	6	Bedford	27	Jul
10.62	1.3	Douglas Bignall	U23	20.10.74	5	London (He)	31	Aug
10.63	2.0	Brendon Ghent	U23	7.09.76	2	Kunzelsau, GER	7	Sep
10.64	1.6	Terence Stamp		18.02.70		Fullerton, USA	25	Apr
10.65	0.5	Michael Afilaka		16.11.71	1	Sheffield	4	May
10.65	-0.5	Marlon Dickson	U20	17.11.78	2rB	Birmingham	6	Jul
(40)								
10.66	-0.4	Ayo Falola		29.07.68	3h7	Birmingham	14	Jun
10.66	-0.5	Tremayne Rutherford		19.06.72	3rB	Birmingham	6	Jul
10.67	1.6	Phil Goedluck		10.09.67		Fullerton, USA	25	Apr
10.68	1.8	Brian Taylor		13.08.70	1D	Bedford	25	May
10.69	1.0	Mark Phills		26.07.64	4h1	Birmingham	14	Jun

10.69	-0.3	Mark Findlay	U20	20.03.78	3h4	Birmingham	14	Jun
10.70	0.6	Ian Craig		20.08.69	7	Bedford	26	May
10.70		Mark Woodhouse	U23	1.11.75	3	Birmingham	1	Jun
10.71	1.1	Paul Sampson	U20	12.07.77	2h2	Sheffield	12	Jul
10.71	1.4	Luke Davis	U17	1.01.80	1s1	Sheffield	12	Jul
	(50)							
10.73	1.1	Paul Slythe	U23	5.09.74	1	London (CP)	11	May
10.74	0.9	James Egan	U23	12.11.75	1	Sheffield	11	May
10.74	0.7	Cypren Edmunds		20.06.70	3rB	Bedford	18	May
10.75	1.1	Akinola Lashore		28.03.73	2	London (CP)	11	May
10.75	2.0	Tim O'Dell		29.05.70	1	Portsmouth	12	May
10.76	1.1	Mark McIntyre		14.10.70	3	London (CP)	11	May
10.78	-1.3	Ray Salami	U23	11.04.75	1s2	London (CP)	1	Jun
10.78	1.0	Sean Huxtable		27.10.70	5h1	Birmingham	14	Jun
10.78	1.1	Martin Giraud	U20	16.11.77	4h2	Sheffield	12	Jul
10.79	1.1	Chris Davidson	U23	4.12.75	4	London (CP)	11	May
	(60)							
10.79	0.5	Solomon Wariso		11.11.66	6h1	Helsinki, FIN	25	Jun
10.79	-0.6	Damien Greaves	U20	19.09.77	1h3	Sheffield	12	Jul
10.80	-0.5	Perry Kelly		1.10.69	5rB	Birmingham	6	Jul
10.81	0.4	Richard Davis	U20	3.05.78	2rB	Bedford	27	Jul
10.84	1.9	Mark Hylton	U23	24.09.76	1r2	Edinburgh	8	Jun
10.85	0.5	Seni Edu	U23	4.03.74	3	Sheffield	4	May
10.87		Dalton Powell		20.08.63	5	Birmingham	1	Jun
10.88		Andrew Walcott	U23	11.01.75	6	Birmingham	1	Jun
10.88	0.1	Ian Lonsdale		8.09.71	4h3	Birmingham	14	Jun
10.88	-1.5	Ken Campbell		30.09.72	1	Glasgow	29	Jun
	(70)							
10.89	2.0	Lee Fairclough		23.06.70	2	Portsmouth	11	May
10.89	-1.8	Scott Herbert	U23	12.02.74	3s3	London (CP)	1	Jun
10.89	1.9	Daniel Bonich	U20	22.11.78	1	London (He)	7	Jul
10.89	0.9	Steven Daly	U17	29.12.79	1	Cudworth	3	Aug
10.89	0.3	David McKenzie		3.09.70	5	London (CP)	18	Aug
10.90	0.9	Stephen Topliss	U20	17.07.78	2	Cudworth	3	Aug
10.90	0.9	Mark Stern		22.05.72	3h3	Oordegem, BEL	11	Aug
10.90		Martin Critchley	U23	9.11.74	1	Gateshead	31	Aug
10.91	-1.2	Mike Rey		19.07.68	1h2	London (CP)	1	Jun
10.91	1.9	Nigel Stickings		1.04.71	2rB	Edinburgh	8	Jun
	(80)							
10.91	1.0	Jamie Henderson		28.03.69	7h1	Birmingham	14	Jun
10.91	0.1	Trevor Cameron	U23	25.11.76	5h3	Birmingham	14	Jun
10.92	0.9	Tony Leigh		27.12.65	3	Cudworth	3	Aug
10.92		Evans Danso		29.11.72	1	Wrexham	4	Aug
10.93	0.9	Jared Deacon	U23	15.10.75	4	Cudworth	3	Aug
10.95	-0.6	Mark Walcott		24.11.73	2rC	Bedford	18	May
10.95		Leon Daniels	U23	1.11.75	7	Birmingham	1	Jun
10.95	-0.9	Ray Burke		11.11.69	5rB	London (He)	9	Jun
10.95	-0.4	Tim Barton		3.10.70	6h7	Birmingham	14	Jun
10.96		Jon Davis	U20	5.03.78	1	Antrim	25	May
	(90)							
10.97	2.0	Mark Avis		22.10.71	3	Portsmouth	12	May
10.97	2.0	Ben Green	U23	30.03.76	4	Portsmouth	12	May
10.98	1.9	Graeme Wilson	U20	11.06.78	3rB	Edinburgh	8	Jun
10.98	1.4	Aaron Harris	U17	19.07.80	3s1	Sheffield	12	Jul
10.98	1.2	Richard David	U20	15.08.77	4h1	Bedford	27	Jul
10.98	0.6	Kevin Farrell	U20	31.10.77	4	London (He)	1	Sep
10.99	-1.3	Akeem Ogunyemi	U23	4.06.74	5s2	London (CP)	1	Jun
10.99	1.9	Elliot Bunney		11.12.66	4rB	Edinburgh	8	Jun
10.99	-0.3	Rohan Samuel		30.01.66	5h4	Birmingham	14	Jun
10.99	-1.3	Ben Lewis	U17	6.03.81	1s1	Birmingham	18	Aug
	(100)							

Wind Assisted

10.00	2.5	Linford Christie		(10.03)	1	Perth, AUS	28	Jan
	10.16	2.4			1	Gateshead	30	Jun
10.21	2.4	Mackie	U23	(10.17)	2	Gateshead	30	Jun
	10.26	3.5			1	Edinburgh	5	Jun
10.24	2.4	Campbell		(10.17)	3	Gateshead	30	Jun
10.25	2.9	Jason John		(10.30)	1r2	Madrid, SPA	1	Jun
10.26	7.0	Doug Turner		2.12.66	2	La Laguna, SPA	13	Jul
	10.29	5.1			1	Cardiff	25	May
10.28	2.4	Braithwaite		(10.13)	5	Gateshead	30	Jun
10.30	3.5	Owusu Dako		(10.35)	2r4	Madrid, SPA	1	Jun
10.32	2.2	Michael Rosswess		(10.38)	1	Riga, LAT	2	Jun
10.33	2.9	Allyn Condon	U23	(10.36)	1	Azusa, USA	13	Apr
	10.42	2.7			1h2	Gavle, SWE	2	Jul
	10.48				2rB	Liverpool	4	May
10.38	5.1	Jamie Henthorn	U20	(10.45)	2	Cardiff	25	May
10.41	2.9	Jason Gardener	U23	18.09.75	1	Loughborough	19	May
10.44	2.9	White	U23	(10.42)	2	Loughborough	19	May
10.44	2.3	Luke Davis	U17	(10.71)	1	Sheffield	13	Jul
10.46	2.2	Uvie Ugono	U20	(10.55)	1s1	Bedford	27	Jul
10.47		Tremayne Rutherford		(10.66)	1rB	Liverpool	4	May
	10.47	5.1			3	Cardiff	25	May
10.48	2.5	Paul Sampson	U20	(10.71)	1	Sheffield	13	Jul
10.48	5.2	Livingston ¶		(10.42)	5	Pule, ITA	4	Sep
10.49	3.4	Ian Craig		(10.70)	1h2	Dublin, IRE	15	Jun
	24 performances to 10.50 by 18 athletes							
10.51	3.5	Doug Walker		28.07.73	2	Edinburgh	5	Jun
10.54	2.2	Ross Baillie	U20	(10.62)	2s1	Bedford	27	Jul
10.55	2.2	Phillip Perigo	U20	(10.60)	3s1	Bedford	27	Jul
10.56	2.5	Damien Greaves	U20	(10.79)	2	Sheffield	13	Jul
10.58	2.4	Paul Slythe	U23	(10.73)	2	Edinburgh	8	Jun
10.60	2.9	Michael Afilaka		(10.65)	4	Loughborough	19	May
10.60	2.2	Mark Findlay	U20	(10.69)	5s1	Bedford	27	Jul
10.62	2.5	Marlon Dickson	U20	(10.65)	4	Sheffield	13	Jul
10.64	2.3	Brian Taylor		(10.68)	1D	Lage, GER	15	Jun
10.65	2.7	Solomon Wariso		(10.79)	1	Liverpool	4	May
10.65		Cypren Edmunds		(10.74)	4rB	Liverpool	4	May
10.66		Toby Box		(10.80)	2	Liverpool	4	May
10.67	2.9	Mark Woodhouse	U23	(10.70)	5	Loughborough	19	May
10.67	2.3	Daniel Plummer	U17	4.01.81	2	Sheffield	13	Jul
10.68		Ray Burke		(10.95)	5rB	Liverpool	4	May
10.69		Barrington Williams	V40	11.09.55	6rB	Liverpool	4	May
10.75	2.5	Martin Giraud	U20	(10.78)	5	Sheffield	13	Jul
10.75	2.2	Richard Davis	U20	(10.81)	6s1	Bedford	27	Jul
10.75	2.2	Ben Lewis	U17	(10.99)	1	Birmingham	8	Sep
10.76	3.2	Seni Edu	U23	(10.85)	6rB	Loughborough	19	May
10.79	2.4	Ian Lonsdale		(10.88)	3	Edinburgh	8	Jun
10.82	3.2	Tim Barton		(10.95)	7rB	Loughborough	19	May
10.83		Nick Long	U20	1.02.79	7rB	Liverpool	4	May
10.84	2.4	Lee Fairclough		(10.89)	4	Edinburgh	8	Jun
10.84	2.5	Lance Iroche	U20	22.06.78	7	Sheffield	13	Jul
10.85	2.4	Jamie Henderson		(10.91)	5	Edinburgh	8	Jun
10.85	2.2	Tony Leigh		(10.92)	1h1	Cudworth	3	Aug
10.86	2.4	Mike Rey		(10.91)	6	Edinburgh	8	Jun
10.86	2.3	Aaron Harris	U17	(10.98)	3	Sheffield	13	Jul
10.88	2.3	Wayne Gray	U17	7.11.80	4	Sheffield	13	Jul
10.90	3.5	Ian Horsburgh	U20	10.01.78	4	Edinburgh	5	Jun

10.91	2.2	Barry Middleton	U23	10.03.75	1r2	Edinburgh	5	Jun
10.93	2.3	Tom Willetts	U17	26.09.79	5	Sheffield	13	Jul
10.97	2.2	Jim Watson		4.10.67	2rB	Edinburgh	5	Jun
10.97	4.8	Jonathan Farmer	U17	23.09.80	3	Stoke	22	Jun
10.98	3.5	Matt Henshaw	U20	16.05.78	2	Stoke	22	Jun
10.98	2.3	Solomon Povey	U17	8.02.80	6	Sheffield	13	Jul
10.99	3.5	M. Pusey	U20		3	Stoke	22	Jun
10.99	2.9	Gareth Gettinby	U20		4	Antrim	6	Jul

Hand Timing

10.0	-0.7	Linford Christie		(10.03)	1	Adelaide, AUS	26	Jan
10.3		Adrian Patrick		(10.38)	1	Watford	17	Aug
10.4		Paul White	U23	(10.42)	4	Athens, GRE	6	Apr
10.4 w					1	Loughborough	27	Apr
10.5		Tremayne Rutherford		(10.66)	1	Burcht, BEL	28	Apr
10.5		Oni Onuorah		(10.51)	2s2	Enfield	12	May
10.5		Gardener	U23	(10.41w)	1	Bath	15	May
10.5	1.8	Mclean Okotie		(10.60)	1	Loughborough	5	Jun
10.5		Terence Stamp		(10.64)	1	London (WL)	21	Jul
10.5	1.5	Christian Malcolm	U20	(10.60)	3r1	Nembro, ITA	3	Aug
10.5		Julian Golding	U23	(10.53)	1	Stoke	17	Aug
10.5		Sam Omonua	U23	(10.59)	1	Abingdon	24	Aug
10.5 w		Corri Henry	U23	9.12.76	1	Brierley Hill	11	Aug
		10.8	2.0		2	Nottingham	11	May
10.5 w	4.6	Daniel Money	U23	(10.57)	1	Leeds	8	Sep

14 performances to 10.5 by 13 athletes including 3 wind assisted

10.6		Andrew Bull		26.06.69	1	Jarrow	4	May
10.6		Brendon Ghent	U23	(10.63)	1	Cannock	4	May
10.6		Douglas Bignall	U23	(10.62)	1	London (WF)	13	Jul
10.6		Ray Salami	U23	(10.78)	1	Portsmouth	13	Jul
10.6		Mike Rey		(10.91)	2	London (WL)	21	Jul
10.6		Mark Woodhouse	U23	(10.70)	1	Abingdon	17	Aug
10.6 w		Courtney Rumbolt		26.07.69	2	Loughborough	27	Apr
10.6 w	2.7	Cypren Edmunds		(10.74)	2	Croydon	12	May
10.6 w		Akinola Lashore		(10.75)	2	Abingdon	25	Aug
10.6 w	4.6	Darren Scott		7.03.69	2	Leeds	8	Sep
10.7		Ian Lonsdale		(10.88)	1	St. Ives	1	May
10.7		Dave Deacon		19.03.65	2	Jarrow	4	May
10.7		Tim Barton		(10.95)	2	Cannock	4	May
10.7		Derek Morgan		4.04.69	1	Bath	11	May
10.7	2.0	Dalton Powell		(10.87)	1	Nottingham	11	May
10.7		Akeem Ogunyemi	U23	(10.99)	5s2	Enfield	12	May
10.7		Ejike Wodu	U23	15.12.74	5	Enfield	12	May
10.7		Alex Francis	U23	15.07.74	1	Loughborough	1	Jun
10.7		Kevin Mark	U23	15.09.76	1	Bournemouth	13	Jul
10.7	-1.6	Luke Davis	U17	(10.71)	1	Stoke	20	Jul
10.7		Paul Slythe	U23	(10.73)	3	Watford	17	Aug
10.7		Ian McGoay		13.10.69	1	Barking	17	Aug
10.7		Tim O'Dell		(10.75)	1	Southampton	8	Sep
10.7		Mark Avis		(10.97)	2	Southampton	8	Sep
10.7 w	2.1	Mark Walcott		(10.95)	2	Stoke	11	May
10.7 w		David McKenzie		(10.89)	1s1	Croydon	12	May
10.7 w		Graham Beasley	U20	24.10.77	1	Luton	16	Jun
10.7 w	3.5	Stephen Tucker		30.12.62	1	Coatbridge	23	Jun
		10.8			1	Glasgow	3	Jul
10.7 w		Marc Jones		7.07.66	1	London (Elt)	3	Aug
10.7 w		Sean Huxtable		(10.78)	3	Brierley Hill	11	Aug

10.7 w	4.6	Guy Bullock	U23	15.10.75	3	Leeds	8 Sep
10.8		Andy Hughes		10.07.67	1	Woodford	21 Apr
10.8		Richard Rubenis		10.11.73	3	Jarrow	4 May
10.8		Scott Herbert	U23	(10.89)	1	Milton Keynes	4 May
10.8		Evans Danso		(10.92)	1	London (Elt)	4 May
10.8		Lenny Paul		25.05.58	6s2	Enfield	12 May
10.8		Graeme Welsh	U23	8.10.75	1	Carlisle	25 May
10.8	1.9	Craig Hurst		30.12.70	1rB	Loughborough	5 Jun
10.8	1.8	Seni Edu	U23	(10.85)	3	Loughborough	5 Jun
10.8		Arif Shah	U20	29.11.78	1	Leicester	8 Jun
10.8		Mark Francis	U20	23.09.77	1	Sutton	22 Jun
10.8		Wayne Mitchell	U23	25.12.74	1	Bebington	6 Jul
10.8		Andrew Clegg		8.09.73	1	Lancaster	6 Jul
10.8	1.3	Lee Fairclough		(10.89)	2	Southampton	7 Jul
10.8		Daniel Bonich	U20	(10.89)	2	Bournemouth	13 Jul
10.8		Rohan Samuel		(10.99)	1	Harrow	17 Jul
10.8	-1.6	Kris Stewart	U17	11.04.80	2	Stoke	20 Jul
10.8	-1.7	David Nolan		25.07.69	2	Portsmouth (RN)	21 Jul
10.8		Mark Smith		18.11.71	4	London (WL)	21 Jul
10.8		Tony Waddington	U23	30.06.75	1	Basingstoke	3 Aug
10.8		Keith Fleming		26.06.65	1r2	Feltham	3 Aug
10.8		Bola Ojex		14.06.71	2	Sheffield	4 Aug
10.8		Gareth Gettinby	U20	(10.99w)	1	Belfast	10 Aug
10.8		Paul McBurney		14.03.72	2	Belfast	10 Aug
10.8		Stephen Topliss	U20	(10.90)	1	Lincoln	17 Aug
10.8		Graham Healy		27.04.70	2	Barking	17 Aug
10.8		Rob Lewis		2.10.67	1	Luton	17 Aug
10.8		Andi Knight		11.11.73	1	London (B Elms)	8 Sep
10.8 w	2.7	Darren Ritchie	U23	14.02.75	1	Aberdeen	28 Apr
10.8 w	2.5	Chris Carson	U17	16.10.79	2	Pitreavie	15 Jun
10.8 w	3.5	Jim Watson		(10.97w)	2	Coatbridge	23 Jun
10.8 w		Matthew Russell	U17	20.01.81	1	Basildon	23 Jun
10.8 w		Nizamul Hoque	U20	19.09.78	2rB	Blackpool	25 Aug

doubtful

10.6 w		Andre Silva	U17	18.11.80	1	Cardiff	8 May
10.7		Darren Burley	U17	13.01.80	1	Enfield	2 Jul

Foreign

10.2	1.1	*Josephus Thomas*		11.07.71	2	*LaGrange, USA*	13 Jul
		10.33 w 2.2			2	*Riga, LAT*	2 Jun
		10.43 1.3			2	*London (He)*	31 Aug
10.3	1.1	*Haroun Korjie*		17.02.72	3	*LaGrange, USA*	13 Jul
		10.70 -0.9			1rB	*London (He)*	9 Jun
10.5		*Carl Afilaka*		13.07.68	1	*Abingdon*	12 May
10.59 w 5.1		*Joslyn Thomas*		11.07.71	4	*Cardiff*	25 May
10.7		*Aiah Yambasu*		10.11.73	3	*London (WL)*	21 Jul
10.71 w 2.9		*John McAdorey*	U23	16.09.74	3	*Antrim*	6 Jul
		10.8			2	*Antrim*	11 May
		10.89 0.2			2s1	*Antrim*	6 Jul
10.77 w 2.5		*Bode Oluwa*	U23	15.11.76	6	*Sheffield*	13 Jul
		10.8			1	*Croydon*	8 Jun
		10.86 -0.2			1h1	*Sheffield*	12 Jul

Additional Under 20 (1 - 40 above)

10.9		Luke Grinnell		21.03.79	1	Bath	11 May
10.9		Plummer	U17	(10.67w)	1	Basildon	8 Jun
		11.02 0.3			1h1	Sheffield	12 Jul
10.9 w	2.5	Allan McBride	U17	31.12.79	1	Pitreavie	15 Jun
10.9 w		James Chatt	U17	11.02.80	2	Basildon	23 Jun
		11.08 1.2			1	London (CP)	11 May

Additional Under 17 (1 - 14 above)

11.0		Darren Burley	13.01.80	1	Enfield	12	May
	11.04	-0.4		1	London (CP)	29	Jun
11.0		James Burt		1	Southampton	15	Jun
11.0	-1.6	Carson	(10.8w)	3	Stoke	20	Jul
	11.04	-2.9		4	Birmingham	18	Aug
11.04	-0.4	Russell	(10.8w)	2	London (CP)	29	Jun
11.04	1.9	Povey	(10.98w)	3=	London (He)	7	Jul
11.04	-2.5	Stewart	(10.8)	1	Wishaw	13	Jul
11.05	-1.0	Willetts	(10.93w)	2s2	Birmingham	18	Aug
11.07	0.3	Gray	(10.88w)	2h1	Sheffield	12	Jul
11.1		Andrew Roberts	8.03.80	1	Jarrow	11	May
11.1		Leon McRae	3.11.80	1	Bath	15	May
11.1		Kevin Hibbins	7.11.80	1	Rugby	15	Jun
11.1		Henry Richards	15.05.81	2	Rugby	15	Jun
	(20)						
11.12 w	3.2	Darren Chin	20.06.81	4s2	Sheffield	12	Jul
11.14 w	4.8	Stuart Hock	5.05.80	4	Stoke	22	Jun
11.15 w	3.2	Robert Allenby	15.10.79	5s2	Sheffield	12	Jul
11.15 w	2.2	Christopher Lambert	6.04.81	3	Birmingham	8	Sep
11.16 w	4.8	Dominic Gordon	7.01.81	5	Stoke	22	Jun
11.18	1.4	Myrone Levy	12.02.81	1rB	Birmingham	8	Sep
11.20		Ben Harland	2.09.79	1	Swansea	6	Jul

doubtful

11.1 w	Robert Walsh		2	Cardiff	8	May

Under 15

11.04 w	3.6	Joe Brown	18.03.82	1	Sheffield	13	Jul
	11.28			1s1	Sheffield	12	Jul
11.11 w	3.6	Andrew Rose	17.08.82	2	Sheffield	13	Jul
	11.33	1.9		1h2	Sheffield	12	Jul
11.3		Daniel Angus	15.07.82	1	Middlesbrough	15	Jun
	11.31 w	2.3		2	Birmingham	8	Sep
11.3 w		Graham Crothers		1rB	Antrim	17	Jun
11.3 w		Gabriel Aboyo-Dana	20.11.81	1	London (BP)	14	Jul
	11.56	1.7		1h1	Sheffield	12	Jul
11.31 w	3.6	Mark Lewis-Francis	4.09.82	3	Sheffield	13	Jul
	11.37	1.7		2s2	Sheffield	12	Jul
11.33		Tim Benjamin	2.05.82	1	Swansea	6	Jul
11.47 w	2.3	Andrew Williams	9.03.82	3	Birmingham	8	Sep
	11.60	-2.1		3h1	Birmingham	18	Aug
11.48	1.5	Tyrone Keating	25.02.82	2	London (He)	7	Jul
11.48 w	3.6	Steve Foster	30.12.81	4	Sheffield	13	Jul
	11.62	1.7		2h1	Sheffield	12	Jul
	(10)						
11.5		Tristan Anthony	16.12.82	1	Bedford	2	Jun
	11.59	-0.6		1	London (CP)	29	Jun
11.5		Lee Bryan	24.11.81	1	Rugby	15	Jun
11.5		Chris Irving	30.09.81	1	York	18	Aug
11.5 w		Joel Semple	19.09.81	1r1	Antrim	17	Jun
11.5 w	2.3	Alex Golding	3.12.81	2	Cudworth	29	Jun
	11.52	1.8		1h2	Cudworth	29	Jun
11.5 w		John Bell	2.04.82	1	Grangemouth	14	Sep
11.51	1.9	Luke Bowling	4.11.81	2h2	Sheffield	12	Jul
11.53 w	3.6	Alastair Mark	8.12.81	5	Sheffield	13	Jul
	11.62			4s1	Sheffield	12	Jul
11.56 w	3.6	Grant Murdoch	30.09.82	6	Sheffield	13	Jul
	11.57			2s1	Sheffield	12	Jul
11.58	1.9	Chris Irwin	3.11.82	3h2	Sheffield	12	Jul
11.61		Jonathan Thomas		2	Swansea	6	Jul

Under 13

12.25 w 2.8	Leon Cameron			1	Birmingham	8	Sep
12.3	P. Wise			1	Southampton	9	Sep
12.5	Shuan Eaton			1	London (CP)	24	Jun

150 METRES

15.08	0.3	Linford Christie		2.04.60	1	London (CP)	11	Aug
	15.50	1.0			1	Cardiff	25	May
15.23	0.3	Ian Mackie	U23	27.02.75	2	London (CP)	11	Aug
15.24	0.3	Darren Braithwaite		20.01.69	3	London (CP)	11	Aug
15.34	0.3	Doug Turner		2.12.66	4	London (CP)	11	Aug
15.44	0.3	Darren Campbell		12.09.73	6	London (CP)	11	Aug
15.50	1.0	Owusu Dako		23.05.73	2	Cardiff	25	May
15.83	1.0	Julian Golding	U23	17.02.75	3	Cardiff	25	May
15.86	1.0	Allyn Condon	U23	24.08.74	4	Cardiff	25	May
16.31	1.0	Cypren Edmunds		20.06.70	6	Cardiff	25	May
16.35	1.0	Steve McCourt		6.05.71	7	Cardiff	25	May

very doubtful

15.9	Chris Carson	U17	26.10.79	1	Dundee	7	Jul

200 METRES

20.29	0.7	Linford Christie		2.04.60	3	Rome, ITA	5	Jun
	20.40	-0.9			2	Lausanne, SWZ	3	Jul
	20.54	-0.5			2	Birmingham	16	Jun
	20.59	1.9			4q5	Atlanta, USA	31	Jul
	20.64	-0.3			1h7	Atlanta, USA	31	Jul
	20.64	-1.6			2	Gateshead	19	Aug
	20.79	-0.6			2s2	Birmingham	16	Jun
	20.84	-0.7			1h1	Birmingham	15	Jun
	20.87	1.5			1	Kingston	17	Aug
20.33 A 0.1	John Regis		13.10.66	3	Pretoria, RSA	8	Apr
	20.39 A 1.1			1	Pietersburg, RSA	3	Apr
	20.44 A -0.3			1	Roodepoort, RSA	26	Jan
	20.47	-1.2			1	Moscow,RUS	7	Jun
	20.51 A 1.5			1	Pretoria, RSA	3	Feb
	20.52	-0.2			4	Paris, FRA	28	Jun
	20.54	-0.5			1	Birmingham	16	Jun
	20.56	0.3			3q4	Atlanta, USA	31	Jul
	20.58	0.3			6s1	Atlanta, USA	1	Aug
	20.60	0.7			5	Rome, ITA	5	Jun
	20.60	-0.6			1s2	Birmingham	16	Jun
	20.61	1.1			1	Cape Town, RSA	12	Apr
	20.62	-1.6			1	Gateshead	19	Aug
	20.63	1.9			3	Sheffield	25	Aug
	20.75	0.2			2h2	Birmingham	15	Jun
	20.77 i				1r4	Stuttgart, GER	4	Feb
	20.77	-0.8			4	London (CP)	12	Jul
	20.78	-0.5			3h5	Atlanta, USA	31	Jul
	20.86 i				2	Birmingham	10	Feb
	20.88 i				1	Glasgow	24	Feb
20.43	0.6	Doug Turner		2.12.66	2	Tallinn, EST	9	Jun
	20.48	1.9			2	Sheffield	25	Aug
	20.66	0.4			1rB	Gateshead	19	Aug
	20.74	-0.7			1s1	Birmingham	16	Jun
	20.77	-0.5			4	Birmingham	16	Jun
	20.87	-0.3			1	Stockholm, SWE	18	Jun
	20.89	-0.8			5	London (CP)	12	Jul
	20.91 i				1rB	Birmingham	10	Feb
	20.98	-0.7			2	Cardiff	25	May

Time	Wind	Name		DOB	Pos	Venue	Date	
20.56	1.4	Roger Black		31.03.66	1	Irvine, USA	4	May
20.90	-0.1				1	Reduit, MAU	21	Sep
20.58	-0.5	Owusu Dako		23.05.73	2	Lucerne, SWZ	25	Jun
20.60	0.2				1h2	Birmingham	15	Jun
20.72	-0.5				3	Birmingham	16	Jun
20.74	-0.8				3	London (CP)	12	Jul
20.76	-0.7				2s1	Birmingham	16	Jun
20.83	1.4				4h2	Atlanta, USA	31	Jul
20.60 A	-2.7	Darren Braithwaite		20.01.69	2	Johannesburg, RSA	14	Apr
20.80 A	1.1				4	Pietersburg, RSA	3	Apr
20.89 A	0.1				5	Pretoria, RSA	8	Apr
20.95 A	-0.3				3	Roodepoort, RSA	26	Jan
21.02	0.4				1	Ljubljana	26	May
20.64	0.6	Solomon Wariso		11.11.66	3	Tallinn, EST	9	Jun
20.85	1.3				2	Riga, LAT	2	Jun
20.91	0.5				5	Helsinki, FIN	25	Jun
20.95	-0.7				3s1	Birmingham	16	Jun
20.67	-0.9	Doug Walker		28.07.73	1	Glasgow	29	Jun
20.78	1.7				1	Bedford	18	May
20.85	-0.6				3s2	Birmingham	16	Jun
20.87	-0.6				1h4	Birmingham	15	Jun
20.87	1.9				2	Gavle, SWE	2	Jul
20.90	-0.5				5	Birmingham	16	Jun
20.93	-0.8				1rB	London (CP)	12	Jul
20.76		Julian Golding	U23	17.02.75	1	Zoetermeer, HOL	7	Jul
20.77	1.9				5	Sheffield	25	Aug
20.79	0.4				2rB	Gateshead	19	Aug
20.81	-0.3				1	Birmingham	20	Jul
20.82	0.0				2h1	Oordegem, BEL	10	Aug
20.91	-0.8				1h3	Birmingham	15	Jun
20.94 A	1.5				3	Pretoria, RSA	3	Feb
20.95	0.5				6	Helsinki, FIN	25	Jun
20.96	-0.8				2rB	London (CP)	12	Jul
20.96	-0.3				3	Konigs Wusterhausen, GER	27	Aug
20.98	-0.7				4s1	Birmingham	16	Jun
20.79	0.3	Paul White	U23	1.09.74	1	Bedford	27	May
(10)								
20.84	0.2	Allyn Condon	U23	24.08.74	3h2	Birmingham	15	Jun
20.94	-0.6				5s2	Birmingham	16	Jun
20.97	0.4				1	Sheffield	2	Jun
20.85	1.4	Mark Richardson		26.07.72	3	Irvine, USA	4	May
20.86	0.6	Marlon Devonish	U23	1.06.76	1	Kunzelsau, GER	7	Sep
20.87	0.2	Jason John		17.10.71	3rB	Granada, SPA	29	May
20.91	-0.6				4s2	Birmingham	16	Jun
20.95	-0.6				2h4	Birmingham	15	Jun
21.00	-0.5				6	Birmingham	16	Jun
20.90	0.3	Mark Allen		23.09.66	2	Bedford	27	May
20.98	-0.9				2	Glasgow	29	Jun
20.97	1.7	Jamie Baulch		3.05.73	2	Bedford	18	May
20.98	-0.8	Darren Campbell		12.09.73	3	Chemnitz, GER	19	May
21.00	0.3	Cypren Edmunds		20.06.70	3	Bedford	27	May

87 performances to 21.00 by 18 athletes including 4 indoors

Time	Wind	Name		DOB	Pos	Venue	Date	
21.02	0.4	Adrian Patrick		15.06.73	3rB	Gateshead	19	Aug
21.10	0.3	Nick Budden	U23	17.11.75	4	Bedford	27	May
(20)								
21.12	1.7	Terry Williams		15.11.68	5	Bedford	18	May
21.13 A	-0.3	Toby Box		9.09.72	4	Roodepoort, RSA	26	Jan
21.14	-0.9	Jared Deacon	U23	15.10.75	3	Glasgow	29	Jun
21.15	-0.7	Andrew Walcott	U23	11.01.75	2h1	Birmingham	15	Jun
21.19	0.4	Raymond Coker		28.07.73	2	Sheffield	2	Jun
21.20	0.3	Scott Herbert	U23	12.02.74	5	Bedford	27	May

Time	Wind	Name	Cat	Date	Pos	Venue	Date
21.22		Paul Slythe	U23	5.09.74	1	London (CP)	12 May
21.23 A	0.1	David McKenzie		3.09.70	3rB	Pretoria, RSA	8 Apr
21.25	0.5	Michael Rosswess		11.06.65	7	Helsinki, FIN	25 Jun
21.27	1.2	Christian Malcolm	U20	3.06.79	1s2	Bedford	28 Jul
		(30)					
21.28	0.6	Daniel Money	U23	7.10.76	3	London (He)	31 Aug
21.28	0.6	Brendon Ghent	U23	7.09.76	2	Kunzelsau, GER	7 Sep
21.29	-1.1	Uvie Ugono	U20	8.03.78	1	London (CP)	29 Jun
21.29	-1.1	Mark Findlay	U20	20.03.78	2	London (CP)	29 Jun
21.30 +		Iwan Thomas	U23	5.01.74	2m	Atlanta, USA	29 Jul
21.41 A	0.1				1	Pretoria, RSA	8 Apr
21.31	-0.6	Ayo Falola		29.07.68	7s2	Birmingham	16 Jun
21.34	0.4	Lewis Samuel		12.02.66	3	Sheffield	2 Jun
21.34	-0.3	Corri Henry	U23	9.12.76	3	Birmingham	20 Jul
21.37	-0.8	Marcus Adam		28.02.68	3h3	Birmingham	15 Jun
21.38	-1.1	Dwain Chambers	U20	5.04.78	3	London (CP)	29 Jun
		(40)					
21.39	0.0	David Grindley		29.10.72	4	Port Elizabeth, RSA	8 Mar
21.40	1.4	Mike Rey		19.07.68	1h5	London (CP)	2 Jun
21.41 i+		Du'aine Ladejo		14.02.71	1m	Birmingham	10 Feb
21.41 i		Jamie Henthorn	U20	20.02.77	1	Lievin, FRA	2 Mar
21.46					1	Carmarthen	30 Jun
21.45 i		Peter Maitland		21.01.73	3rB	Birmingham	27 Jan
21.49 i		Jason Fergus		11.10.73	3s3	Birmingham	7 Jan
21.49	0.6	Danny Joyce	U23	9.09.74	4	London (He)	31 Aug
21.50	-0.6	Tremayne Rutherford		19.06.72	1rB	Bedford	18 May
21.51	0.8	Phillip Perigo	U20	25.09.78	1h2	Sheffield	12 Jul
21.52	1.6	Sunny Adepegba		6.06.71	1h2	London (CP)	2 Jun
		(50)					
21.53	1.1	Nick Buckfield		5.06.73	1	Crawley	11 May
21.53	0.2	Seni Edu	U23	4.03.74	4h2	Birmingham	15 Jun
21.57	1.2	Daniel Caines	U20	15.05.79	3s2	Bedford	28 Jul
21.58	-1.3	Ian Mackie	U23	27.02.75	1	Edinburgh	12 May
21.58		Tim O'Dell		29.05.70	4	London (CP)	11 Aug
21.58	-0.7	Akinola Lashore		28.03.73	1	London (CP)	18 Aug
21.59 i		Darren Scott		7.03.69	3	Birmingham	7 Jan
21.59	1.6	Mark Phills		26.07.64	2h2	London (CP)	2 Jun
21.59	0.2	Mark Woodhouse	U23	1.11.75	5h2	Birmingham	15 Jun
21.60	1.4	Alex Fugallo		28.01.70	3h5	London (CP)	2 Jun
		(60)					
21.60	0.6	Douglas Bignall	U23	20.10.74	5	London (He)	31 Aug
21.62	1.2	Graham Beasley	U20	24.10.77	4s2	Bedford	28 Jul
21.63	1.5	Kevin Farrell	U20	31.10.77	1h1	Sheffield	12 Jul
21.63	-0.7	Ed White		16.11.73	2	London (CP)	18 Aug
21.66	0.0	Ben Lewis	U17	6.03.81	1	Ljubljana, SLO	28 Sep
21.67		Chris Davidson	U23	4.12.75	3	London (CP)	11 May
21.67		Sean Baldock	U23	3.12.76	5rB	London (CP)	11 Aug
21.70	0.4	Graeme Welsh	U23	8.10.75	3h2	Bedford	27 May
21.70	0.2	Steve McCourt		6.05.71	6h2	Birmingham	15 Jun
21.70	-1.1	Marlon Dickson	U20	17.11.78	5	London (CP)	29 Jun
		(70)					
21.71 i		Ross Baillie	U20	26.09.77	3	Birmingham	18 Feb
21.80	-0.7				1	Wishaw	13 Jul
21.72	-1.6	Kris Stewart	U17	11.04.80	1	Edinburgh	12 May
21.74	-0.6	Mark Walcott		24.11.73	4rB	Bedford	18 May
21.75	1.1	Michael Tietz	U20	14.09.77	3s1	Bedford	28 Jul
21.76	-1.3	Chris Carson	U17	26.10.79	1h2	Wishaw	13 Jul
21.76	0.6	Jason Livingston ¶		17.03.71	6	London (He)	31 Aug
21.80 i		Ian Horsburgh	U20	10.01.78	4rB	Lievin, FRA	2 Mar
21.90	-1.5				1	Edinburgh	12 May
21.85	0.3	Lee Fairclough		23.06.70	2	Portsmouth	11 May

21.86	-2.7	Michael Afilaka		16.11.71	1	Newport	8	Jun
21.88 i+		Mark Hylton	U23	24.09.76	1m	Birmingham	4	Feb
	(80)							
21.88	-0.6	Dalton Powell		20.08.63	6rB	Bedford	18	May
21.89 i		Scott Dorset		10.04.69	2h1	Birmingham	4	Feb
21.90	0.4	Paul Jamieson		21.06.73	4	Sheffield	2	Jun
21.94	1.6	Darren Burley	U17	13.01.80	1s1	Sheffield	13	Jul
21.94	1.1	Philip Robson	U20	7.02.77	4s1	Bedford	28	Jul
21.96	-0.4	Tony Leigh		27.12.65	2h1	Sheffield	2	Jun
21.98 i		Clive Morrison		19.09.65	1r3	Birmingham	28	Jan
21.98 i		Kevin Williams		15.12.71	1h6	Birmingham	4	Feb
21.98	1.7	Paul Sampson	U20	12.07.77	2	Cudworth	30	Jun
22.01	1.5	Matthew Ball	U20	7.09.78	2h1	Sheffield	12	Jul
	(90)							
22.02	0.4	Ben Green	U23	30.03.76	4h2	Bedford	27	May
22.02	-1.3	Sam Kabiswa		28.10.66	3	Birmingham	2	Jun
22.02	1.2	Nicholas Dawson	U20	11.05.78	6s2	Bedford	28	Jul
22.06 i		Mark Davidson		15.11.68	1	Glasgow	13	Jan
22.06	1.1	Justin Bird		3.05.71	5h1	Bedford	27	May
22.09	-1.6	Phil Goedluck		10.09.67	6h5	Birmingham	15	Jun
22.10	0.3	Ricky Alfred	U20	20.12.77	3h1	London (CP)	29	Jun
22.10	1.5	Ian Leaman	U20	14.10.78	3h3	Sheffield	12	Jul
22.13	0.4	Graeme Wilson	U20	11.06.78	5h2	Bedford	27	May
22.13	-0.3	Stephen Topliss	U20	17.07.78	2	Cudworth	3	Aug
	(100)							
22.13	-1.6	Luke Davis	U17	1.01.80	3	Birmingham	17	Aug
22.15	1.1	Steven Daly	U17	29.12.79	6h1	Bedford	27	May
22.18	0.8	Jonathan Moss	U20	24.09.78	4h2	Sheffield	12	Jul
22.20	1.6	Matthew Russell	U17	20.01.81	2s1	Sheffield	13	Jul

Wind Assisted

20.25	2.5	Linford Christie		(20.29)	1	Madrid, SPA	2	Jun
20.57	2.6	Turner		(20.43)	1	Zofingen, SWZ	27	May
		20.63	2.1		1	Birmingham	6	Jul
		20.71	2.7		1	La Laguna, SPA	13	Jul
20.64	2.1	Allyn Condon	U23	(20.84)	2	Birmingham	6	Jul
20.69	2.1	Julian Golding	U23	(20.76)	3	Oordegem, BEL	10	Aug
20.87	2.9	Regis		(20.33A)	2	Gateshead	30	Jun
20.87	2.9	Dako		(20.58)	3	Gateshead	30	Jun
20.93	4.4	Adrian Patrick		(21.02)	1	Edinburgh	8	Jun
20.99	2.9	Black		(20.56)	4	Gateshead	30	Jun
		10 performances to 21.00 by 8 athletes						
21.17	5.1	Mark Findlay	U20	(21.29)	1	Sheffield	13	Jul
21.20	5.1	Graham Beasley	U20	(21.62)	2	Sheffield	13	Jul
21.22	4.3	Ian Craig		20.08.69	1rB	Edinburgh	8	Jun
21.23	5.1	Phillip Perigo	U20	(21.51)	3	Sheffield	13	Jul
21.31	5.1	Du'aine Ladejo		(21.41i)	3	Liverpool	4	May
21.50	4.7	Darren Burley	U17	(21.94)	1	Sheffield	13	Jul
21.51	3.0	Mark Woodhouse	U23	(21.59)	2	Sheffield	6	May
21.51	5.1	Kevin Farrell	U20	(21.63)	5	Sheffield	13	Jul
21.55	4.7	Ben Lewis	U17	(21.66)	2	Sheffield	13	Jul
21.64	4.2	Philip Robson	U20	(21.94)	2	London (He)	7	Jul
21.71	2.1	Darren Scott		(21.59i)	6	Birmingham	6	Jul
21.77	5.1	Matthew Ball	U20	(22.01)	6	Sheffield	13	Jul
21.79	5.1	Nicholas Dawson	U20	(22.02)	7	Sheffield	13	Jul
21.81	3.8	Michael Champion	U23	3.01.75	5rB	Loughborough	19	May
21.86	4.3	David Gurr		20.06.70	3rB	Edinburgh	8	Jun
21.87	5.1	Ian Leaman	U20	(22.10)	8	Sheffield	13	Jul
21.89	4.7	Matthew Russell	U17	(22.20)	3	Sheffield	13	Jul
21.90	4.4	Ian Lonsdale		8.09.71	3	Edinburgh	8	Jun

22.02	3.0	Darren Walker	U23	21.03.75	4	Sheffield	6	May
22.04	4.2	Ben Watkins	U20	12.11.78	4	London (He)	7	Jul
22.05	3.8	Andi Knight		11.11.73	6rB	Loughborough	19	May
22.08	4.7	James Chatt	U17	11.02.80	4	Sheffield	13	Jul
22.14		Adam Tibbets	U20	14.12.78	1rB	Stoke	22	Jun
22.20	4.7	Kieron Downie	U17	19.11.79	5	Sheffield	13	Jul
22.20	2.4	Chris Bennett	U17	18.10.80	3	Street	24	Jul

Hand Timing

20.5 w	3.0	Roger Black		(20.56)	1	Enfield	6	Jul
20.6 w	3.0	Mark Richardson		(20.85)	2	Enfield	6	Jul
20.8		Golding	U23	(20.76)	1	Stoke	17	Aug
20.8 w		Corri Henry	U23	(21.34)	1	Brierley Hill	10	Aug
20.9	0.7	Adrian Patrick		(21.02)	1	Watford	17	Aug
20.9 w		White	U23	(20.79)	1	Loughborough	27	Apr
21.0 w	4.6	Daniel Money	U23	(21.28)	1	Leeds	8	Sep

7 performances to 21.0 by 7 athletes incuding 5 wind assisted

21.2	0.6	Iwan Thomas	U23	(21.41A)	1	Enfield	4	May
21.2	2.0	Mark Hylton	U23	(21.88i)	1rB	Enfield	6	Jul
21.2 w		Brendon Ghent	U23	(21.28)	2	Brierley Hill	10	Aug
21.3		Kent Ulyatt		10.04.72	1	Norwich	4	May
21.3		Guy Bullock	U23	15.10.75	2	Sheffield	8	Jun
21.3		Nigel Stickings		1.04.71	1	Bracknell	23	Jun
21.3 w	3.9	Mark Woodhouse	U23	(21.59)	1	Cannock	7	Sep
21.3 w	4.6	Darren Scott		(21.59i)	2	Leeds	8	Sep
21.5					2	Sheffield	4	Aug
21.4 w	4.2	Jason Fergus		(21.49i)	1	Thurrock	12	May
21.4 w	3.9	Graham Healy		27.04.70	2	Cannock	7	Sep
21.6					1	Barking	17	Aug
21.5		David Nolan		25.07.69	1	Woodford	27	Apr
21.5		Clayton Archer	U23	29.05.76	3h1	Enfield	11	May
21.5		Ray Salami	U23	11.04.75	3	Bracknell	23	Jun
21.5		Paul McBurney		14.03.72	1	Belfast	10	Aug
21.5 w	2.1	Tim O'Dell		(21.58)	1	Southampton	7	Jul
21.6		Alex Francis	U23	15.07.74	1rB	Loughborough	27	Apr
21.6	0.6	Onochie Achike	U23	31.01.75	3	Enfield	4	May
21.6	0.0	Phil Goedluck		(22.09)	4	Croydon	11	May
21.6		Marlon Dickson	U20	(21.70)	1	London (TB)	31	Jul
21.6 w	2.3	Michael Afilaka		(21.86)	1h	Stoke	11	May
21.8					1	Telford	27	Apr
21.6 w	2.1	Lee Fairclough		(21.85)	2	Southampton	7	Jul
21.7	1.6	Ian Craig		(21.22w)	1rB	Peterborough	4	May
21.7		Andrew Bull		26.06.69	1	Jarrow	4	May
21.7		Mark Stern		22.05.72	1	Peterborough	11	May
21.7		Luke Davis	U17	(22.13)	1	Birmingham	8	Jun
21.7		Anders Lustgarten	U23	9.02.74	1	Cheltenham	4	Aug
21.7		Michael Tietz	U20	(21.75)	1	Blackpool	25	Aug
21.7 w		Matthew Ball	U20	(22.01)	1	Pendle	9	Jun
21.7 w	3.2	Mark Avis		22.10.71	2rB	Abingdon	25	Aug
21.8	2.0				2rB	Enfield	6	Jul
21.7 w	3.2	Ian McGoay		13.10.69	3rB	Abingdon	25	Aug
21.8					1	Bournemouth	13	Jul
21.8		Lloyd Cowan		8.07.62		Pomona, USA	19	Apr
21.8		Oladipo Scott-Boyle	U23	17.06.74	1	Bedford	4	May
21.8		Livio Salvador-Aylott		18.07.73	1	Carn Brea	18	May
21.8		Mark Thomas		1.06.72	3	Sheffield	8	Jun
21.8		Richard Knowles	U23	12.11.75	1	Solihull	6	Jul
21.8		Barry Middleton	U23	10.03.75	1	Aberdeen	28	Jul

21.8		Tony Leigh		(21.96)	4	Stoke	17 Aug
21.8		Stephen Topliss	U20	(22.13)	1	Lincoln	17 Aug
21.8 w		Rob Lewis		2.10.67	1	Luton	17 Aug
21.8 w	4.2	Phil Lewis		12.01.70	1rB	Abingdon	25 Aug
21.9		Dave Deacon		19.03.65	2	Jarrow	4 May
21.9	-0.5	Mark Smith		18.11.71	1rB	Enfield	4 May
21.9		Tim Barton		3.10.70	2	Cannock	4 May
21.9		James Archampong	U23	14.03.76	1	Carmarthen	11 May
21.9		Scott Dorset		(21.89i)	3	Bracknell	11 May
21.9	1.0	Craig Hurst		30.12.70	1rB	Loughborough	5 Jun
21.9	1.8	Justin Bird		(22.06)	1	Coatbridge	23 Jun
21.9	1.8	Jim Watson		4.10.67	2	Coatbridge	23 Jun
21.9		Paul Sampson	U20	(21.98)	1	Middlesbrough	6 Jul
21.9	-0.5	Tendai Huntley	U23	12.09.76	1	Luton	7 Jul
21.9	-0.5	Tony Waddington	U23	30.06.75	2	Luton	7 Jul
21.9		Kieran Gajjar	U23	25.09.76	2	Wakefield	11 Aug
21.9	0.7	Dan Donovan		8.10.70	4	Watford	17 Aug
21.9		Chris Millard		19.07.66	1	Exeter	25 Aug
21.9	-1.4	Jon Ridgeon		14.02.67	1	Southampton	11 Sep
21.9 w	4.4	Mclean Okotie		31.07.69	2rB	Abingdon	25 Aug
22.0	1.1	Nizamul Hoque	U20	19.09.78	1	Enfield	11 May
22.0		Nigel Will		18.10.67	2	Peterborough	11 May
22.0		James Ward	U20	28.07.77	1	Sheffield	12 Jun
22.0		David Hutchison		18.08.70	1	Coatbridge	16 Jun
22.0		Simon Ciaravella		24.11.73	1	Watford	26 Jun
22.0	0.9	John Skeete	U20	8.09.78	2	Watford	6 Jul
22.0	2.0	Darren Jackson	U20	21.10.78	3rB	Enfield	6 Jul
22.0		Stephen Tucker		30.12.62	2	Aberdeen	28 Jul
22.0	1.6	Robert Collin		27.07.61	3rB	Watford	17 Aug
22.0		Julian Love	U20	21.06.78	1	Annan	25 Aug
22.0		Shane King	U23	8.02.74	1	Southampton	1 Sep
22.0		Richard Rubenis		10.11.73	1	Blackpool	8 Sep
22.0 w	3.9	Ian Craggs	U23	6.10.76	4	Cannock	7 Sep
22.0 w	3.9	James Douglas		4.04.71	3	Cannock	7 Sep

Foreign

20.6	0.0	Josephus Thomas		11.07.71	1	LaGrange, USA	13 Jul
21.13	1.3				5	Riga, LAT	2 Jun
21.1	0.0	Haroun Korjie		17.02.72	5	LaGrange, USA	13 Jul
21.57	1.5				4	Istanbul, TUR	19 May
21.20 w	2.8	Paul Brizzell	U23	3.10.76	1	Antrim	6 Jul
21.56					1	Dublin, IRE	6 Jul
21.6	1.6	Joslyn Thomas		11.07.71	1rB	Watford	6 Jul
22.15	-2.7				2	Newport	8 Jun
21.93	-0.1	John McAdorey	U23	16.09.74	1	Tullamore, IRE	23 Jun

Additional Under 17 (1 - 10 above)

22.1		Chatt		(22.08w)	1	Basildon	23 Jun
			22.26	-0.6	2	London (CP)	30 Jun
22.3		Richard McNabb		22.02.80	1	Hull	19 May
22.34	0.2	Allan McBride		31.12.79	3s1	Birmingham	17 Aug
22.4		Sinclair McLeod		12.12.80	1	London (Elt)	21 Jul
22.42 w	4.7	Darren Wall		6.04.80	6	Sheffield	13 Jul
			22.51	1.6	3s1	Sheffield	13 Jul
22.44 w		Anthony Gardner		19.09.80	2	Stoke	22 Jun
22.44 w	4.7	Graeme Read		24.10.79	7	Sheffield	13 Jul
22.47	1.0	Myrone Levy		12.02.81	1rB	Birmingham	8 Sep
22.48 w	3.3	Daniel Angus	U15	15.07.82	1	Sheffield	13 Jul
			22.65	1.7	1h3	Sheffield	12 Jul

22.49	0.2	Downie		(22.20w)	4s1	Birmingham	17	Aug
22.54 w	2.2	Steve Flaherty		16.10.79	3h4	Sheffield	12	Jul
22.68	1.6				5s1	Sheffield	13	Jul
22.55	0.3	Bennett		(22.20w)	1h1	Street	24	Jul
22.60	-0.6	Ben Harland		2.09.79	4s2	Birmingham	17	Aug
	(20)							
22.6		Jay Kilshaw		19.10.79	1	Crawley	7	Apr
22.6		Henry Richards		15.05.81	1	Derby	21	Jul
22.6 w	4.0	Steve Surety		18.02.80	2	Southend	28	Apr
22.61	-0.7	Daniel Plummer		4.01.81	2h2	London (CP)	30	Jun
22.63 w	2.5	Tristan Anthony	U15	16.12.82	1s1	Sheffield	13	Jul
23.03	-0.5				1	Birmingham	17	Aug
22.67	1.0	Christopher Lambert		6.04.81	2rB	Birmingham	8	Sep
22.70 w	3.6	Matthew Hough		1.06.80	2h2	Sheffield	12	Jul
22.7		Stuart Hock		5.05.80	1	Derby	21	Apr
22.7		Matthew Still		1.12.79	1	Southampton	21	Apr
22.7		Michael Strain		11.09.79	1	Glasgow	15	Sep
	(30)							
22.73	1.6	Neil Jones		22.10.79	6s1	Sheffield	13	Jul
22.75 w	2.5	Aaron Evans	U15	15.02.82	3s1	Sheffield	13	Jul
23.07	1.7				2h3	Sheffield	12	Jul
22.76 w	3.7	Paul Campbell		26.03.80	4h1	Sheffield	12	Jul
22.76 w	3.3	Lee Bryan	U15	24.11.81	3	Sheffield	13	Jul
22.90	2.0				1h4	Sheffield	12	Jul

Additional Under 15 (1 - 4 above)

22.80	0.3	Joe Brown		18.03.82	1rB	Birmingham	8	Sep
22.91	2.0	Tyrone Keating		25.02.82	2h4	Sheffield	12	Jul
23.04 w	3.3	David Smith		5.10.81	5	Sheffield	13	Jul
23.16	0.4				1	Birmingham	7	Sep
23.07 w	3.7	Alex Golding		3.12.81	2s2	Sheffield	13	Jul
23.20	0.9				2h1	Sheffield	12	Jul
23.2		Tim Benjamin		2.05.82	1	Cardiff	24	Jun
23.21					1	Swansea	6	Jul
23.27 w	3.0	Andrew Irving		30.09.81	2h2	Sheffield	12	Jul
23.3					1	York	18	Aug
	(10)							
23.41	1.0	Andrew Williams		9.03.82	3	Birmingham	8	Sep
23.42 w	3.7	Andrew Norman		27.01.82	5s2	Sheffield	13	Jul
23.46 w		Gary Hunter		10.09.81	1	Stoke	22	Jun
23.68					1h3	Birmingham	17	Aug
23.50	1.0	Gabriel Aboyo-Dana		20.11.81	4	Birmingham	8	Sep
23.51 w	3.0	Michael Farrugia		19.07.82	3h2	Sheffield	12	Jul
23.6					1	London (Nh)	21	Jul
23.68					1=	Birmingham	17	Aug
23.55		Bruce Gibb		10.10.81	2h1	Birmingham	17	Aug
23.6		Andrew Rose		17.08.82	1rB	Peterborough	21	Jul
23.62 w		Sean Harrison		25.01.82	1rB	Stoke	22	Jun
23.70	2.0	Simon Wright		27.09.81	3h4	Sheffield	12	Jul

Under 13

24.7		Richard Bolton		1.10.83	1	Solihull	21	Jul
24.79	0.1	Leon Cameron			1	Birmingham	8	Sep

300 METRES

32.14	Mark Richardson		26.07.72	1	London (CP)	11	Aug
32.25	Jamie Baulch		3.05.73	2	London (CP)	11	Aug
32.26	Roger Black		31.03.66	3	London (CP)	11	Aug
32.51	John Regis		13.10.66	4	London (CP)	11	Aug
32.52	Iwan Thomas	U23	5.01.74	5	London (CP)	11	Aug

32.73	Paul Slythe	U23	5.09.74	1	London (CP)	12	Jul
32.73	Guy Bullock	U23	15.10.75	2	London (CP)	12	Jul
32.75 A	Du'aine Ladejo		14.02.71	1	Roodepoort, RSA	26	Jan
32.76	Mark Hylton	U23	24.09.76	6	London (CP)	11	Aug
32.78	Jared Deacon	U23	15.10.75	3	London (CP)	12	Jul
(10)							
32.89	David McKenzie		3.09.70	4	London (CP)	12	Jul
32.89	Adrian Patrick		15.06.73	5	London (CP)	12	Jul
32.90	David Nolan		25.07.69	6	London (CP)	12	Jul
33.15	Doug Walker		28.07.73	1	Edinburgh	5	Jun
33.50	Tim O'Dell		29.05.70	7	London (CP)	12	Jul
33.79	David Grindley		29.10.72	8	London (CP)	11	Aug

400 METRES

44.37	Roger Black	31.03.66	2	Lausanne, SWZ	3	Jul
44.39			1	Birmingham	16	Jun
44.41			2	Atlanta, USA	29	Jul
44.64			1	Gateshead	19	Aug
44.69			1s1	Atlanta, USA	28	Jul
44.72			1q2	Atlanta, USA	27	Jul
44.77			2	Eugene, USA	26	May
44.81			3	Atlanta, USA	18	May
44.83			4	Zurich, SWZ	14	Aug
44.88			2	London (CP)	12	Jul
45.02			1s1	Birmingham	15	Jun
45.05			1	Sheffield	25	Aug
45.28			1h1	Atlanta, USA	26	Jul
45.33			1	Tokyo, JAP	16	Sep
45.42			5	Milan, ITA	7	Sep
46.05			1h1	Birmingham	14	Jun
44.52	Mark Richardson	26.07.72	2rB	Lausanne, SWZ	3	Jul
44.97			5	Zurich, SWZ	14	Aug
45.15			3	Gateshead	19	Aug
45.31			3s1	Birmingham	15	Jun
45.33			5	Birmingham	16	Jun
45.34			5	London (CP)	12	Jul
45.38			2	Sheffield	25	Aug
45.42			1	Rhede, GER	24	May
45.44			4	Gateshead	30	Jun
45.67			8	Brussels, BEL	23	Aug
46.10			4	Dijon, FRA	26	May
46.15			2	Modesto, USA	11	May
46.3			1	Watford	29	May
46.58			2h3	Birmingham	14	Jun
44.57	Jamie Baulch	3.05.73	3rB	Lausanne, SWZ	3	Jul
44.72			4	Birmingham	16	Jun
44.97			1	Nuremberg, GER	7	Jun
45.06			3	Gateshead	30	Jun
45.08			5	Brussels, BEL	23	Aug
45.13			1rB	Zurich, SWZ	14	Aug
45.22			1s2	Birmingham	15	Jun
45.29			2	Lucerne, SWZ	25	Jun
45.37			4	Rome, ITA	5	Jun
45.50			6	London (CP)	12	Jul
45.50			4	Sheffield	25	Aug
45.66			1	Brisbane, AUS	14	Mar
45.71			1	Melbourne, AUS	8	Mar
45.97			1h2	Melbourne, AUS	7	Mar
46.08			1	Cardiff	25	May
46.12			4	Salamanca, SPA	5	Jul

(Baulch)	46.15			4	Bratislava, SVK	29	May
	46.21			1h5	Birmingham	14	Jun
	46.32			3	Melbourne, AUS	29	Feb
	46.46			2	Perth, AUS	28	Jan
44.66 A	Iwan Thomas	U23	5.01.74	1	Johannesburg, RSA	14	Apr
	44.69			3	Birmingham	16	Jun
	44.70			5	Atlanta, USA	29	Jul
	44.71			6	Lausanne, SWZ	3	Jul
	44.94			1	Gateshead	30	Jun
	44.98 A			1	Pretoria, RSA	8	Apr
	45.01			4s2	Atlanta, USA	28	Jul
	45.04			2q4	Atlanta, USA	27	Jul
	45.08			3	London (CP)	12	Jul
	45.14 A			1	Pietersburg, RSA	3	Apr
	45.14			1	Helsinki, FIN	25	Jun
	45.22 A			1	Pretoria, RSA	3	Feb
	45.22			2h8	Atlanta, USA	26	Jul
	45.23			3	Rieti, ITA	1	Sep
	45.27			2s2	Birmingham	15	Jun
	45.35			1	Tallinn, EST	9	Jun
	45.37			6	Atlanta, USA	18	May
	45.45			6	Milan, ITA	7	Sep
	45.56			1	Cape Town, RSA	12	Apr
	45.58 A			1	Roodepoort, RSA	26	Jan
	45.77			5	Sheffield	25	Aug
	46.14			1h2	Birmingham	14	Jun
44.66	Du'aine Ladejo		14.02.71	2	Birmingham	16	Jun
	45.19			2	Helsinki, FIN	25	Jun
	45.29			2s1	Birmingham	15	Jun
	45.50			5	Gateshead	30	Jun
	45.57			2	Bratislava, SVK	29	May
	45.62			6q3	Atlanta, USA	27	Jul
	45.65 A			3	Pretoria, RSA	3	Feb
	45.67			1	Istanbul, TUR	18	May
	45.72			2	Madrid, SPA	1	Jun
	45.74			1	Ljubljana, SLO	26	May
	46.12 i			1	Stockholm, SWE	10	Mar
	46.27			3h4	Atlanta, USA	26	Jul
	46.39 i			1	Glasgow	24	Feb
	46.48 i			3	Birmingham	10	Feb
45.57	Mark Hylton	U23	24.09.76	6	Birmingham	16	Jun
	45.76			4s1	Birmingham	15	Jun
	46.24			6	Sheffield	25	Aug
	46.39			3rB	Dijon, FRA	26	May
	46.45 i			1	Birmingham	4	Feb
	46.49 i			4	Birmingham	10	Feb
45.66	David Grindley		29.10.72	1	Dijon, FRA	26	May
	45.85			1	Port Elizabeth, RSA	8	Mar
	46.35			2	Stellenbosch, RSA	1	Mar
	46.39			1	Blackburn	15	May
	46.48			5	Bratislava, SVK	29	May
45.76	Guy Bullock	U23	15.10.75	7	Birmingham	16	Jun
	45.90			3s2	Birmingham	15	Jun
	46.07			1	Hexham	14	Jul
	46.14			2	Zagreb, CRO	21	Jun
	46.20			2rB	Dijon, FRA	26	May
	46.38			2h5	Birmingham	14	Jun
46.02	Jared Deacon	U23	15.10.75	1	Gateshead	31	Aug
	46.08			5s1	Birmingham	15	Jun
	46.21			1	Cork, IRE	22	Jun
	46.38			3	Linz, AUT	21	Aug

46.06	Adrian Patrick		15.06.73	8	Birmingham	16	Jun
46.29				1	London (CP)	2	Jun
46.39				4s2	Birmingham	15	Jun
(10)							
46.20	David Nolan		25.07.69	2	Tallinn, EST	9	Jun
46.25				1rB	Gateshead	30	Jun
46.32				2	Cork, IRE	22	Jun
46.41				1	Aldershot	5	Jun
46.48				2h1	Birmingham	14	Jun
46.28	David McKenzie		3.09.70	1	Birmingham	20	Jul
46.34	Nick Budden	U23	17.11.75	6s1	Birmingham	15	Jun
46.49				1	Sheffield	6	May
46.40	Tim O'Dell		29.05.70	5s2	Birmingham	15	Jun
46.50	Corri Henry	U23	9.12.76	1	Sheffield	13	Jul
120 performances to 46.5 by 15 athletes including 5 indoors							
46.52	Paul Slythe	U23	5.09.74	1	Zoetermeer, HOL	7	Jul
46.80	Sean Baldock	U23	3.12.76	4h1	Birmingham	14	Jun
46.83	Richard Knowles	U23	12.11.75	2	Sheffield	6	May
46.83	Clayton Archer	U23	29.05.76	4rB	Gateshead	30	Jun
46.93	Anders Lustgarten	U23	9.02.74	3	Sheffield	6	May
(20)							
46.95	Doug Walker		28.07.73	1	Edinburgh	11	May
47.0	Geoff Dearman	U20	4.08.77	2	Nembro, ITA	3	Aug
47.40				3s3	Sydney, AUS	22	Aug
47.04 i	Kent Ulyatt		10.04.72	2	Birmingham	4	Feb
47.4				1	Kings Lynn	12	May
47.12	Dave Savage		13.11.72	4	Birmingham	20	Jul
47.15	Alex Francis	U23	15.07.74	1	Loughborough	19	May
47.19 A	Wayne/Ali McDonald		5.10.70	4rB	Johannesburg, RSA	19	Apr
47.83				4	Cardiff	25	May
47.2	Lee Fairclough		23.06.70	1	Portsmouth	21	Jul
47.61				8	London (CP)	2	Jun
47.38	Paul Hibbert		31.03.65	6	Cork, IRE	22	Jun
47.39	Martin Blade		30.05.68	6	London (CP)	2	Jun
47.4	Nick Buckfield		5.06.73	2	Stoke	17	Aug
(30)							
47.43	Steve McHardy	U23	8.01.76	4h2	Birmingham	14	Jun
47.49	Simon Ciaravella		24.11.73	5h1	Birmingham	14	Jun
47.6	Kris Stewart	U17	11.04.80	1rB	Nembro, ITA	3	Aug
47.86				1	Wishaw	13	Jul
47.65	Iain McGurk		17.10.71	6h1	Birmingham	14	Jun
47.7	Gary Jennings		21.02.72	1	Watford	6	Jul
48.61				5	Birmingham	1	Jun
47.7	Jon Ridgeon		14.02.67	1	London (B Elms)	8	Sep
47.76	Joe Lloyd		9.04.73	5	Sheffield	6	May
47.79	Matt Douglas	U23	26.11.76	1D	Worcester	24	Aug
47.8	Mark Smith		18.11.71	1	Thurrock	11	May
47.8	Ian Horsburgh	U20	10.01.78	2rB	Nembro, ITA	3	Aug
48.24				1	Wishaw	13	Jul
(40)							
47.86	George Sandy		22.04.71		LaGrange, USA	28	Jun
47.86	Eddie Williams		1.10.70	3	London (He)	31	Aug
47.90	Simon Heggie	U23	12.01.76	5h2	Birmingham	14	Jun
47.9	Graham Healy		27.04.70	2	Thurrock	11	May
47.94 i				2rB	Glasgow	24	Feb
48.36				2h5	London (CP)	1	Jun
47.9	Tom Lerwill	U20	17.05.77	1	London (BP)	14	Jul
47.97	Brian Darby		14.10.72	5h4	Birmingham	14	Jun
48.00	Noel Levy	U23	22.06.75	2	Luton	6	May
48.0	Paul McBurney		14.03.72	1	Belfast	18	May
48.08				1	Belfast	22	Jun

48.05	David Naismith	U17	15.12.79	2	London (He)	10 Aug
48.08	Lawrence Baird	U20	14.12.77	3	London (He)	10 Aug
(50)						
48.1	Mark Huggins		20.12.68	2	Sheffield	8 Jun
48.1	Mark Sesay		13.12.72	1	Leeds	8 Sep
48.17	Vince Rose		21.08.71	1	London (CP)	18 Aug
48.19 i	Gary Cadogan		8.10.66	4	Birmingham	4 Feb
48.2	Darrell Maynard		21.08.61	1	Cwmbran	11 May
48.2	Adam Mole	U23	31.08.75	1	Corby	12 May
48.2	Paul Walker		2.12.73	1	Glasgow	4 Aug
48.21				3	Kingston	17 Aug
48.27	Eddie King	U23	26.11.75	2	Antrim	6 Jul
48.29	Lewis Samuel		12.02.66	3rB	Birmingham	6 Jul
48.3	Sam Kabiswa		28.10.66	3	Crawley	28 Jul
48.59				1	Edinburgh	8 Jun
(60)						
48.3	Barry Middleton	U23	10.03.75	2	Glasgow	4 Aug
48.89				3	Edinburgh	11 May
48.31	Kermitt Bentham		16.04.60	2	London (CP)	18 Aug
48.40	Neil Jennings	U20	18.09.77	4	Sheffield	13 Jul
48.4	Brian Forbes	U23	6.09.74	2	Belfast	18 May
48.49				2	Dublin (M), IRE	16 Jun
48.4	Jason Levy		30.05.70	2	Stoke	28 Jul
48.43	David Williams	U23	22.12.75	2	Newport	1 Jun
48.5	Brian Holliman		12.08.72	1	Dumfries	18 Aug
48.52	Graham Hedman	U20	6.02.79	1rB	Bedford	28 Jul
48.53	Nizamul Hoque	U20	19.09.78	5	Bedford	28 Jul
48.54	Michael Parper	U20	20.05.78	2h4	Bedford	27 Jul
(70)						
48.55	Martyn Bucknall		2.11.70	1rB	Birmingham	20 Jul
48.59	Justin Bird		3.05.71	5h5	Birmingham	14 Jun
48.60	James Hilston	U20	25.02.79	2rB	Bedford	28 Jul
48.6	Philip Octave	U20	12.06.78	1	Aldershot	4 Aug
48.6	Matthew Aldwinkle	U23	23.08.74	1	Dudley	10 Aug
48.64				2	London (He)	1 Sep
48.6	Richard Rubenis		10.11.73	1rB	Telford	17 Aug
48.61	Douglas Thom		13.04.68	2	Edinburgh	11 May
48.62	Ayo Falola		29.07.68	3	Luton	6 May
48.63	Marvin Gray		18.12.71	2	London (He)	9 Jun
48.63	Lee Murphy	U20	11.03.77	2	London (He)	7 Jul
(80)						
48.68	Bryan McCoy	U23	31.12.75	3	Antrim	6 Jul
48.70	Trevor Painter		10.08.71	2	Cudworth	3 Aug
48.7	Richard McNabb	U17	22.02.80	2	Stoke	20 Jul
48.71				2	Sheffield	13 Jul
48.7	Jim Beattie		22.07.73	2	Greenock	4 Aug
48.7	Richard David	U20	15.08.77	1	London (TB)	21 Aug
48.85				5	London (He)	31 Aug
48.71	Alloy Wilson	U17	25.01.80	1	Birmingham	8 Sep
48.75	Mark Rowlands	U20	18.04.78	3rB	Belfast	22 Jun
48.80	Michael Bell	U20	23.11.77	7	Sheffield	13 Jul
48.80	Shane King	U23	8.02.74	4	Cudworth	3 Aug
48.8	Rowland Ifill	U23	11.11.75	1	Harrow	7 Jul
(90)						
48.8	Peter Brend	U20	2.02.77	1rB	Watford	17 Aug
49.34				7s1	Bedford	27 Jul
48.8	David Barnetson		1.07.71	2rB	Watford	17 Aug
48.8	Chris Harris			1	Woking	17 Aug
48.8	Dan Donovan		8.10.70	2	London (TB)	31 Aug
48.82	Alan Murray		2.05.67	3	Edinburgh	8 Jun
48.84	Mark Ponting	U20	28.04.77	2rB	London (He)	9 Jun

48.85	Chris Rawlinson		19.05.72	1h2	Bedford	26	May
48.9	James Shipp	U20	10.11.77	1	Barking	23	Jun
48.96				4	London (CP)	30	Jun
48.9	Tony Draper	U23	23.04.74	1	Bromley	17	Jul
48.9	Andrew Mitchell	U23	30.07.76	3	Watford	17	Aug
	(100)						
48.91	Hugh Kerr	U23	4.01.76	2h5	Sheffield	4	May
48.99	Ahmed Al-Kowarri	U20	30.11.78	1	Carmarthen	16	Jul
49.00 i	Lawrence Lynch		1.11.67	1	Birmingham	3	Feb
49.0	Nigel Hamer	U23	1.01.76	1	Loughborough	27	Apr
49.0	Craig Winrow		22.12.71	1rB	Jarrow	4	May
49.0	Ben Harper	U20	9.11.78	1	Thurrock	12	May
49.12				3	London (He)	7	Jul
49.0	Martin Steele		30.09.62	1	Wakefield	6	Jul
49.0	Lee Black	U20	26.11.78	2	Coventry	6	Jul
49.48				4h2	Sheffield	12	Jul
49.0	Jason Thompson		16.11.71	1	Dartford	13	Jul
49.0	Christopher Lawton		6.01.73	1	High Wycombe	3	Aug
	(110)						
49.0	Kieran Gajjar	U23	25.09.76	2	Wakefield	17	Aug
49.0	Otis Griffiths		4.02.70	1rB	Barking	17	Aug
49.0	Phil Lewis		12.01.70	1	Luton	17	Aug
49.04	Joe Gowan		18.11.67	2rB	Kingston	17	Aug

unconfirmed

| 47.5 | Mark Sesay | | 13.12.72 | | Atlanta, USA | | Apr |

disqualified

| 48.38 | Marvin Gray | | 18.12.71 | (5) | Cardiff | 25 | May |
| 48.99 | Oladipo Scott-Boyle | U23 | 17.06.74 | | London (TB) | 29 | May |

Foreign

| *47.76* | *Remi Edu* | *U20* | *14.12.78* | *2* | *London (He)* | *31* | *Aug* |
| *48.9* | *Tony Arro* | | *31.10.72* | *2* | *London (WL)* | | |

Additional Under 20 (1 - 24 above)

49.1	Simon Mathieson		20.01.79	4	Sheffield	8	Jun
49.2	Chris Moss		17.06.79	3rB	Enfield	4	May
49.25	Matthew Still	U17	1.12.79	3	Sheffield	13	Jul
49.3	Richard McDonald	U17	11.01.80	1h2	Pitreavie	19	Jun
49.59				2	Wishaw	13	Jul
49.3	Stephen Payne		30.01.78	1	Crawley	22	Jun
49.50				1	Portsmouth	12	May
49.4	Alasdair Donaldson		21.06.77	1	Pitreavie	18	Jun
	(30)						
49.4	Neil Kentish		30.09.77	2	Solihull	29	Jun
49.56				4h5	Bedford	27	Jul
49.4	Christian Creaby		11.10.78	2	Leeds	30	Jul
49.42	Chris Bennett	U17	18.10.80	1	Street	25	Jul
49.45	Matthew Richards		11.10.77	5	London (He)	10	Aug
49.48	Hugh Bannister		26.08.78	4h1	Bedford	27	Jul
49.50	Simon Plaskett		9.04.79	4	London (He)	7	Jul
49.5	Andrew Smith		26.03.78	1	Carlisle	21	Apr
49.58				3h1	Sheffield	1	Jun
49.5	Paul Curtis	U17	29.05.80	1	Crawley	10	Aug
50.06				3	London (CP)	30	Jun
49.60	Matthew Hill		15.12.77	1	Sheffield	12	May

Additional Under 17 (1 - 8 above)

49.67	Jay Kilshaw		19.10.79	4	Sheffield	13	Jul
49.7	Chris Carson		26.10.79	2	Coatbridge	16	Jun
	(10)						

49.8	Carl McMullen		9.11.79	3	Derby	15	Sep
	50.42			1	Stoke	22	Jun
49.84	Chris Page		13.11.80	2s3	Sheffield	12	Jul
50.0	James Chatt		11.02.80	1	Basildon	16	Jun
50.0	Colin Young		11.12.79	1	Solihull	29	Jun
50.42	Paul Campbell		26.03.80	2	Birmingham	8	Sep
50.5	M. Menlove			1	Thurrock	11	May
50.5	Lea Farmer		22.01.80	3	Stoke	20	Jul
	50.60			1	Swansea	6	Jul
50.60	Robert Nixon		20.09.79	2h1	London (CP)	29	Jun
50.6	Eshref Hassan		7.12.79	3	Southampton	15	Jun
	50.81			4s3	Sheffield	12	Jul
50.69	Ian Lowthian		10.10.80	2h5	Sheffield	12	Jul
	(20)						
50.70	Scott Burgin		2.04.80	2h4	Sheffield	12	Jul
50.7	Gary Stevenson		12.09.79	1	Pitreavie	17	Aug
50.73	Julian Packer		2.09.79	3h5	Sheffield	12	Jul
50.76	Simon Bullock		22.11.80	3h1	Birmingham	17	Aug
50.80	Marc Newton		15.03.80	2h1	Sheffield	12	Jul
50.8	Andrew Bilby		20.02.80	1	Croydon	11	May
	51.05			3s1	Sheffield	12	Jul
50.8	John Shenava		5.02.81	4	Stoke	20	Jul
50.88	Aaron Evans	U15	15.02.82	1	Birmingham	17	Aug
50.9	Elliott Cox		7.01.80	4	Southampton	15	Jun
	51.08			3h1	London (CP)	29	Jun
51.0	Neil Hewson		4.09.80	2	Bolton	16	Jun
	(30)						
51.01	David Singleton		21.10.79	3h2	Sheffield	12	Jul
51.02	Steve Flaherty		16.10.79	2h2	London (CP)	29	Jun

Additional Under 15 (1 above)

51.84	Paul Rawlinson		17.10.81	1h1	Sheffield	12	Jul
51.9	David Moulton		7.09.81	1	Kingston	8	Jun
	51.92			2	London (CP)	30	Jun
52.2	Emmanuel Farrugia		19.07.82	1	Walton	2	Jun
	52.45			2h3	Sheffield	12	Jul
52.3	Ben Caldwell		3.03.82	1	Stretford	8	Jun
	52.52			4h3	Sheffield	12	Jul
52.4	Adam Martin		12.10.81	1	Manchester (BV)	5	May
	53.27			3h1	Sheffield	12	Jul
52.5	Matthew Peleszok		17.10.81	1	Solihull	29	Jun
52.5	Geoffrey Djan		21.07.82	1	Mansfield	13	Sep
	52.64			2h1	Sheffield	12	Jul
52.52	James Derham		8.02.82	3h3	Sheffield	12	Jul
52.53	Mike Charville		7.05.82	1h2	Sheffield	12	Jul
	(10)						
52.56	Robert Atwell		17.10.81	2h2	Sheffield	12	Jul
52.6	Gary Hunter		10.09.81	1	Bebington	1	Sep
52.77	James Crump		8.09.81	2h2	Birmingham	17	Aug
52.8	Peter Arnold		29.06.82	1	Jarrow	5	May
52.8	Andrew Fulford		23.06.82	1	Swindon	14	Aug
52.8	Colin Joyce		21.10.81	1	Cambridge	15	Sep
53.1	Sean Harrison		25.01.82	1	St. Helens	30	Jun
53.29	Neil Smith			2	Birmingham	8	Sep
53.41	Richard Castillo		3.12.81	5h3	Sheffield	12	Jul
53.5	Jonathan Simpson		27.05.82	1	Pitreavie	23	Jun
	(20)						
53.6	Marlon Nunes		7.12.81	2	Yeovil	21	Jul
	53.96			4h2	Sheffield	12	Jul
53.61	John Oxley		7.03.82	3h2	Birmingham	17	Aug
53.69	Ryan Wilde		25.12.81	3h2	Sheffield	12	Jul

53.8	Brian McIlroy			2	Bebington	21	Jul
	53.94			4	Birmingham	8	Sep
53.9	Raymond Todd		7.03.82	1	Pitreavie	15	Jun
53.95	Robert Dobbs		19.04.82	4h1	Sheffield	12	Jul

Under 13

56.5	Tony Gill			1	Middlesbrough	7	Apr
56.5	Craig Erskine		26.09.83	1	Grangemouth	22	Sep

600 METRES

1:18.5	Andi Knight		26.10.68	1	London (PH)	7	Aug
1:19.4	Jason Dupuy		31.01.71	2	London (Elt)	20	Apr
1:19.8	Jason Thompson		16.11.71	3	London (Elt)	20	Apr
1:20.3	Martin Airey		28.10.70	4	London (Elt)	20	Apr

800 METRES

1:45.69	Craig Winrow		22.12.71	2	Zagreb, CRO	21	Jun
	1:45.77			5	Nuremberg, GER	7	Jun
	1:45.85			10	Rome, ITA	5	Jun
	1:45.91			8	London (CP)	12	Jul
	1:46.66			8	Berlin, GER	30	Aug
	1:47.03			2rB	Lausanne, SWZ	3	Jul
	1:47.05			3	Gateshead	30	Jun
	1:47.41			2h3	Atlanta, USA	28	Jul
	1:48.10			2	Arnsberg, GER	12	May
	1:48.3			1	Manchester	15	May
	1:48.40			1rB	Konigs Wusterhausen, GER	27	Aug
	1:48.57			8s1	Atlanta, USA	29	Jul
	1:48.64			4	Cardiff	25	May
	1:48.67			5	Birmingham	16	Jun
	1:48.79			7	Sheffield	25	Aug
1:45.73	Curtis Robb		7.06.72	1	Tallinn, EST	9	Jun
	1:45.85			2h1	Atlanta, USA	28	Jul
	1:46.42			3	Helsinki, FIN	25	Jun
	1:47.48			6s2	Atlanta, USA	29	Jul
	1:47.61			1	Birmingham	16	Jun
	1:47.75			1	Riga, LAT	2	Jun
	1:47.97			6	Gateshead	30	Jun
1:45.81	David Strang		13.12.68	7	London (CP)	12	Jul
	1:46.36			3	Tallinn, EST	9	Jun
	1:46.38			4	Madrid, SPA	2	Jun
	1:46.41			2	Cape Town, RSA	12	Apr
	1:46.56			4	Helsinki, FIN	25	Jun
	1:47.70			5	Gateshead	30	Jun
	1:47.74			2	Birmingham	16	Jun
	1:47.96			4h6	Atlanta, USA	28	Jul
1:46.57	Andy Hart		13.09.69	10	London (CP)	12	Jul
	1:47.44			4	Gateshead	30	Jun
	1:48.0			1	Watford	5	Jun
	1:48.13			4	Birmingham	16	Jun
	1:48.55			3	Zofingen, SWZ	27	May
	1:48.7			1	Stretford	25	Jun
1:47.27	Tom Lerwill	U20	17.05.77	2s1	Sydney, AUS	22	Aug
	1:48.40			2	Sydney, AUS	23	Aug
1:47.70	Terry West		19.11.68	2	Ljubljana, SLO	26	May
	1:47.72			4	Tallinn, EST	9	Jun
1:47.7	Robin Hooton		5.05.73	1	Manchester	30	Jul
1:47.8	Anthony Whiteman		13.11.71	1	Peterborough	4	May
1:47.83	Andrew Lill		9.08.71	11	Rhede, GER	24	May

155

1:47.9	Rupert Waters			3.01.72	2	Manchester	30	Jul
	1:48.7				1	London (BP)	14	Jul
(10)								
1:47.94	Tony Morrell			3.05.62	3	Birmingham	16	Jun
	1:48.44				8	Lisbon, POR	21	Jun
1:48.2	James Mayo	U23	24.02.75		3	Manchester	30	Jul
	1:48.7				1	Stretford	3	Sep
1:48.25	Bradley Donkin			6.12.71	6	Cork, IRE	22	Jun
	1:48.4				4r1	Manchester	30	Jul
	1:48.63				1	Gateshead	19	Aug
1:48.3	Gary Lough			6.07.70	1	Milton Keynes	24	Jul
	1:48.7				7	Manchester	30	Jul
1:48.37	Lee Cadwallader			17.01.69	5	Ljubljana, SLO	26	May
	1:48.5				2r1	Manchester	15	May
1:48.4	Tony Johnston			23.08.68	1	Stretford	16	Jul
1:48.5	Kevin McKay			9.02.69	2	Stretford	16	Jul
1:48.5	Eddie King	U23	26.11.75		5	Manchester	30	Jul
	1:48.9				4	Manchester	15	May
1:48.7	Andi Knight			26.10.68	6	Manchester	30	Jul
1:48.8	Jason Lobo			18.09.69	3	Manchester	15	May
(20)								
1:48.9	Justin Swift-Smith	U23	28.08.74		2	Watford	5	Jun
1:48.94	Paul Walker			2.12.73	1	Athens, USA	4	May
	64 performances to 1:49.0 by 22 athletes							
1:49.09	Clive Gilby			24.02.66	6	Riga, LAT	2	Jun
1:49.2	Grant Graham			27.12.72	3	Loughborough	18	May
1:49.2	Glen Stewart			7.12.70	8	Manchester	30	Jul
1:49.3	Adam Duke			5.10.73	3	London (BP)	14	Jul
1:49.3	Ian Grime			29.09.70	10	Manchester	30	Jul
1:49.32	Mark Griffin	U23	16.02.75		1	Zoetermeer, HOL	6	Jul
1:49.34 i	Mark Sesay			13.12.72	3	Gainesville, USA	2	Feb
	1:49.4				2	Stretford	3	Sep
1:49.38	Richard Ashe	U23	5.10.74		4	Gateshead	19	Aug
(30)								
1:49.4	Stuart Margiotta			19.11.69	2	Milton Keynes	24	Jul
1:49.41	Eddie Williams			1.10.70	3h1	Oordegem, BEL	10	Aug
1:49.5	Neil Caddy	U23	18.03.75		5	Loughborough	18	May
1:49.65	Ewan Calvert			28.11.73	2h5	Birmingham	14	Jun
1:49.7	Tony Mate	U23	15.12.74		2	Watford	28	Aug
1:49.72 i	Dave Locker	U23	28.03.75		7	Ames, USA	1	Mar
	1:51.1				2	Stretford	6	Aug
1:49.8	Robert Hough			3.06.72	1	Sheffield (W)	8	Jun
1:49.9	Alasdair Donaldson	U20	21.06.77		4	London (BP)	14	Jul
1:49.9	Matthew Davies			23.07.71	3	Milton Keynes	24	Jul
1:50.0	Grant Cuddy	U20	6.01.77		1rB	Stretford	25	Jun
(40)								
1:50.0	Phillip Tulba-Morrison			20.09.73	2rB	Watford	28	Aug
1:50.0	Matthew Yates			4.02.69	3	Watford	28	Aug
1:50.1	Jason Thompson			16.11.71	5	London (BP)	14	Jul
1:50.2	Nick Bentham			7.12.70	6	London (BP)	14	Jul
1:50.2	Martin Airey			28.10.70	4	Milton Keynes	24	Jul
1:50.22	Jon Wild			30.08.73	1	Emporia, USA	11	May
1:50.25	Andy Young	U20	20.06.77		1	Nembro, ITA	3	Aug
1:50.26	Mike Guegan			19.09.66	1	Edinburgh	8	Jun
1:50.3	Luke Veness			5.12.73	3rB	Watford	28	Aug
1:50.38	Gary Brown			21.07.67	10	Tallinn, EST	9	Jun
(50)								
1:50.4	Des Roache	U23	5.01.76		8	Loughborough	18	May
1:50.4	Darren Spawforth			1.08.69	2rB	Stretford	25	Jun
1:50.4	Vince Wilson			1.04.73	1	Jarrow	8	Jul
1:50.42	Philip Healy			1.10.70	3	Athens, USA	4	May

1:50.5	Grant Purves		6.04.73	1	Coatbridge	23	Jun
1:50.6	Dean Clark		20.12.73	5	Milton Keynes	24	Jul
1:50.61	Andrew Thomas	U20	15.05.79	3h5	Birmingham	14	Jun
1:50.62	Chris Moss	U20	17.06.79	3	Nembro, ITA	3	Aug
1:50.70	Dominic Hall		21.02.71	2rB	London (CP)	2	Jun
1:50.70	Mike Shevyn		12.12.71	4	Birmingham	6	Jul
(60)							
1:50.71	Steve Rees-Jones	U23	24.12.74	4h5	Birmingham	14	Jun
1:50.8	Rod Finch		5.08.67	2	Watford	17	Aug
1:50.85	Darrell Maynard		21.08.61	8	Cardiff	25	May
1:50.86	Noel Edwards		16.12.72	2	Birmingham	2	Jun
1:50.9	David Bullock	U23	18.12.74	2	Watford	29	May
1:50.9	Andrew Walling		3.04.73	3rB	Stretford	25	Jun
1:50.91	Jason Dupuy		31.01.71	2rB	London (CP)	2	Jun
1:51.14	Simon Fairbrother		28.03.68	4	London (He)	8	Jun
1:51.2	David Pamah		27.11.64	2rB	London (BP)	14	Jul
1:51.21 i	Martin Steele		30.09.62	1	Birmingham	4	Feb
(70)							
1:51.25	Matt Kloiber		22.11.71	5h4	Birmingham	14	Jun
1:51.32	Garth Watson		20.04.73	6h4	Birmingham	14	Jun
1:51.35	Ian Campbell		6.09.71	5	Birmingham	6	Jul
1:51.4	Martin Forder		7.08.70	3	Watford	26	Jun
1:51.4	Richard Girvan	U23	26.07.76	2rB	Manchester	30	Jul
1:51.4	Rob Scanlon	U23	13.04.74	6	Watford	28	Aug
1:51.43	Adam Mole	U23	31.08.75	3	Birmingham	2	Jun
1:51.5	Alex Rosen		30.09.71	3rB	London (BP)	14	Jul
1:51.5	Tony Draper	U23	23.04.74	2	Stoke	17	Aug
1:51.6	Paul Burgess		10.11.70	2rB	Jarrow	4	May
(80)							
1:51.6	Richard Lynch		14.07.64	3rB	Watford	5	Jun
1:51.6	Steve Mosley		10.01.66	7	Watford	28	Aug
1:51.7	Andy Renfree	U23	18.05.75		Watford	28	Aug
1:51.7	Steffan White		21.12.72		Watford	28	Aug
1:51.73	Andy Stuckey		24.04.72	4	Birmingham	2	Jun
1:51.8	Brett Mate	U23	15.12.74	1rB	Stretford	4	Jun
1:51.8	Brendan Smith	U20	20.07.77	4rB	Stretford	25	Jun
1:51.9	David Thornton		27.07.73	1rC	Manchester	30	Jul
1:51.96	John MacFadyen		1.08.72	1rB	Edinburgh	8	Jun
1:52.0	Sean Price		4.01.63	3rC	Manchester	15	May
(90)							
1:52.0	Patrick Davoren		13.03.72	6	Milton Keynes	24	Jul
1:52.04	Neil Kirk	U20	14.09.78	1	London (CP)	12	May
1:52.08	Dave Robertson		4.08.73	1	London (CP)	12	May
1:52.1	James Ellis-Smith		11.09.72	1	Crawley	28	May
1:52.1	Toby Gosnall		21.04.71	2rC	Watford	28	Aug
1:52.15	David Stanley	U20	16.01.79	2	London (CP)	30	Jun
1:52.2	Sean Kelly		8.11.72	1	Leeds	22	May
1:52.2	Chas McCaw		21.01.72	4	Watford	29	May
1:52.26	Paul Bennett		9.08.71	5	Birmingham	2	Jun
1:52.34	James Tonner	U23	3.06.75	4	Edinburgh	3	Jul
(100)							
1:52.4	James Guest	U23	29.07.74	1	Thurrock	11	May
1:52.4	Joe Mills		9.07.72	2rB	Watford	31	Jul
1:52.5	Mick Morris	U23	16.07.74	7	Stretford	16	Jul
1:52.5	Guy Amos		15.06.63	2	London (TB)	3	Aug
1:52.57	Louis Wells	U20	6.02.78	4	Edinburgh	8	Jun
1:52.57	Michael East	U20	20.01.78	2	Sheffield	13	Jul
1:52.6	Matt Hibberd		23.06.73	3rB	Loughborough	18	May
1:52.6	Dale Canning	U20	12.06.78	5	Watford	29	May
1:52.6	John Rodgers			1	Antrim	29	May
1:52.6	Russell Cartwright	U20	13.10.77	1	Milton Keynes	23	Jun
(110)							

1:52.6	Andrew Graffin	U20	20.12.77	1	Tonbridge	13	Aug
1:52.62	Tony Balogun		7.02.66	2	Luton	6	May
1:52.7	Adam Zawadski	U23	19.12.74	1	Cardiff	7	Aug
1:52.7	Michael Osbourn			5rC	Watford	28	Aug
1:52.7	Steve Sharp	U23	31.12.75	4rC	Watford	28	Aug

Foreign

1:48.8	*Des English*		*6.06.67*	*1*	*Watford*	*28*	*Aug*
1:51.2	*Shane Daly*		*21.03.73*	*1rC*	*Manchester*	*15*	*May*

Additional Under 20 (1 - 14 above)

1:52.89	Daniel Stevens		1.08.77	2rB	Bedford	28	Jul
1:53.1	Matthew Dixon		26.12.78	3	Stretford	21	May
1:53.1	Greg Taylor		1.08.77	1rB	Stretford	6	Aug
1:53.25	Ryan Davoile		29.09.78	2h2	Bedford	27	Jul
1:53.30	Tom Cartwright		22.06.79	3h4	Bedford	27	Jul
1:53.33	Yacin Yusuf		20.12.77	1	London (He)	7	Jul
(20)							
1:53.4	Simon Lees	U17	19.11.79	1	Wolverhampton	2	Jun
1:53.47	Tom Ranger		20.11.77	4rB	Bedford	28	Jul
1:53.5	Stuart Bailey		6.08.78	1rD	Stretford	25	Jun
1:53.60	Michael Combe		24.12.78	6	Bedford	28	Jul
1:53.6	Andrew Hennessy		24.08.77	1	Exeter	1	Sep
1:54.1	Tom Mayo		2.05.77	3	Corby	9	Jun
1:54.1	Sam Illidge		4.02.77	1rB	Stretford	16	Jul
1:54.36	Scott Poole		31.03.78	1	Antrim	8	Jun
1:54.39	Edward Matthews		17.09.77	2h5	Bedford	27	Jul
1:54.41	Sion Owen		6.03.79	5h4	Bedford	27	Jul
(30)							
1:54.5	Paul Morby		15.01.79	2	Leamington	12	May
1:54.5	Jason Beeraje		10.05.77	3	Sutton	22	Sep
1:54.6	Allen Graffin		20.12.77	2	Hoo	8	Jun
1:54.7	Clayton Bannon		15.03.77	7	Jarrow	8	Jul
1:54.73	Neil Speaight		9.09.78	4	London (CP)	30	Jun
1:54.9	Tom Adams		22.08.77	1	Watford	9	Jun
1:54.97	Stephen Briffett		22.10.78	4h3	Sheffield	12	Jul
1:54.98	Carl Tipton		4.02.77	5h2	Sheffield	12	Jul
1:55.0	Kevin Corr		17.04.79	1r7	Manchester	15	May
1:55.0	Roger Morley		20.09.77	4rB	Stretford	16	Jul

Additional Under 17 (1 above)

1:55.1	Paul Laslett		12.05.80	1rD	Watford	17	Jul
1:55.9	Simon Eyre		30.10.80	2	Stoke	20	Jul
1:56.1	Dominic St.George		12.10.79	3	Stoke	20	Jul
1:56.13	Brian Stopher		8.04.80	7h4	Bedford	27	Jul
1:56.23	Richard McDonald		11.01.80	1.	Sheffield	25	Aug
1:56.3	Sam Boden		16.02.80	3	Watford	28	Aug
1:56.37	Colin McLean		7.06.80	3	Street	25	Jul
1:56.5	Will Barry		4.09.79	2rC	Stretford	16	Jul
1:56.5	James Richardson		14.12.79	1	Watford	25	Sep
(10)							
1:56.55	Colin Young		11.12.79	3	London (He)	10	Aug
1:56.7	Tom Payn		18.10.79	1rC	Watford	29	May
1:56.7	Jim Hand		11.06.80	4	Stoke	20	Jul
1:56.74	Ross Fittall		4.09.79	1	Birmingham	17	Aug
1:56.8	Rob Jefferies		4.10.79	1	Rugby	15	Jun
1:56.8	Geoff Baxter		9.12.79	2	Bromley	21	Jul
1:56.9	Alex MacDonald		12.04.80	5	Glasgow	20	Aug
1:57.4	Jonathan Salt		14.12.79	2	Rugby	15	Jun
1:57.41	Glenn Antinori		5.04.80	3	Sheffield	25	Aug
1:57.49	Matthew Bailey		16.02.81	2	Cudworth	3	Aug

1:57.60	James Parker		28.10.79	4	Sheffield	13	Jul
1:57.6	Iain Murdoch		10.07.80	1	Wishaw	24	Aug
1:57.73	Tim Alexander		6.09.79	1h2	Birmingham	17	Aug
1:57.8	Tiernan Isles		7.01.80	2	Watford	25	Sep
1:57.9	Robert Nixon		20.09.79	1	Ilford	17	Sep
1:58.0	John Heanley		25.09.80	2	Windsor	21	Jul

Under 15

1:59.3	Andrew Fulford		23.06.82	1	Swindon	9	Jun
1:59.64	Colin Joyce		21.10.81	2	London (CP)	30	Jun
2:01.2	Matthew Peleszok		17.10.81	5	Rugby	26	Jun
2:01.8	Aaron McIndoe		19.05.82	1	Glasgow	20	Aug
	2:00.51 i	U17		1	Glasgow	1	Dec
2:02.5	David Moulton		7.09.81	1	Kingston	17	Mar
2:02.7	Conor Sweeney		28.12.81	1	Antrim	25	May
2:03.5	Glen Coppin		16.01.83	1	Watford	13	Jul
2:03.59	Richard Rohleder		28.02.82	3	London (CP)	30	Jun
2:03.79	Denis Murphy		22.09.81	2h1	Sheffield	12	Jul
2:04.27	Jamie Russell		1.10.81	4h1	Sheffield	12	Jul
2:04.30	(10) Ketan Desai		1.12.82	4	Sheffield	13	Jul
2:04.3	Matt Thomson		20.09.81	1	Cardiff	7	Aug
2:04.6	Ian Bateman		6.02.82	2r6	Stretford	16	Jul
2:04.64	Ben Caldwell		3.03.82	1	Cudworth	3	Aug
2:04.7	Gary Hunter		10.09.81	1	Douglas, IOM	7	Aug
2:04.78	Peter Bridger		6.09.81	1h2	Sheffield	12	Jul
2:04.84	Oliver Holme		10.11.81	2h2	Sheffield	12	Jul
2:04.9	Neil Gardener		7.09.81	1	Nottingham	23	Jun
2:05.04	Imran Hamblin		26.06.82	3h2	Sheffield	12	Jul
2:05.26	William Rohleder		28.02.82	3	Birmingham	18	Aug
2:05.27	(20) Warren McKinlay		4.10.81	4h2	Sheffield	12	Jul
2:05.3	Tim Brierley		3.12.81	2	Southampton	15	Jun
2:05.5	Thomas Duke		16.10.81	1	York	15	Jun

Under 13

2:13.4	Alex Spencer			5	Liverpool	8	Jun
2:14.3	Paul Brown		8.10.83	1	Solihull	15	Sep
2:15.5	David Kent		15.12.83	1	Watford	29	May
2:16.6	Thomas Bolton		24.11.83	1	Guildford	8	Sep
2:17.0	Kevin Scanlan		24.03.84	1	Newham	11	Aug

1000 METRES

2:18.48	John Mayock		26.10.70	5	London (CP)	11	Aug
2:18.78	Andy Hart		13.09.69	6	London (CP)	11	Aug
2:18.8 i	Anthony Whiteman		13.11.71	1	Birmingham	29	Feb
2:19.61	Robin Hooton		5.05.73	8	London (CP)	11	Aug
2:20.64	Craig Winrow		22.12.71	9	London (CP)	11	Aug
2:20.97 i	Matthew Yates		4.02.69	6	Birmingham	10	Feb
2:21.04	Kevin McKay		9.02.69	10	London (CP)	11	Aug
2:22.18	James Mayo	U23	24.02.75	11	London (CP)	11	Aug
2:23.3	Matt Hibberd		23.06.73	3	Stretford	30	Apr
2:23.4	Robert Hough		3.06.72	4	Stretford	30	Apr
2:23.66	(10) Rupert Waters		3.01.72	12	London (CP)	11	Aug
2:23.7	Steve Green		18.02.71	6	Stretford	30	Apr
2:24.71 i	Jon Wild		30.08.73	1	Manhattan Ka, USA	2	Feb
2:24.73 A	David Strang		13.12.68	2	Roodepoort, RSA	26	Jan
2:25.3 i	Bruno Witchalls	U23	22.03.75	2	Birmingham	29	Feb
2:25.3	Garth Watson		20.04.73	7	Stretford	30	Apr
2:25.4	Brendan Smith	U20	20.07.77	8	Stretford	30	Apr

1500 METRES

3:33.38	John Mayock	26.10.70	7	Rieti, ITA	1	Sep
3:33.94			6	Brussels, BEL	23	Aug
3:34.55			7s1	Atlanta, USA	1	Aug
3:34.82 +			4m	Oslo, NOR	5	Jul
3:36.23			8	Zurich, SWZ	14	Aug
3:36.40			3	London (CP)	12	Jul
3:36.82			2	Cork, IRE	22	Jun
3:37.03			1	Birmingham	16	Jun
3:37.48			8	Moscow, RUS	7	Jun
3:37.75			1	Gateshead	19	Aug
3:40.18			11	Atlanta, USA	3	Aug
3:40.2 +			2m	Sheffield	25	Aug
3:41.52			9	Milan, ITA	7	Sep
3:41.82			3	Gateshead	30	Jun
3:42.01			1h2	Birmingham	15	Jun
3:42.31			2h2	Atlanta, USA	29	Jul
3:34.47	Anthony Whiteman	13.11.71	5	Paris, FRA	28	Jun
3:34.92			4	Nice, FRA	10	Jul
3:36.11			7s2	Atlanta, USA	1	Aug
3:36.37			3	Nuremberg, GER	7	Jun
3:36.68			3rB	Villeneuve d'Ascq, FRA	25	May
3:37.00			5	London (CP)	12	Jul
3:37.18			15	Monaco, MON	10	Aug
3:37.19			2	Birmingham	16	Jun
3:39.04			3	Gateshead	19	Aug
3:39.47 i			1	Birmingham	27	Jan
3:40.5 +			4=m	Sheffield	25	Aug
3:40.74			4h5	Atlanta, USA	29	Jul
3:41.21			3	Madrid, SPA	1	Jun
3:41.25 i			1h1	Stockholm, SWE	9	Mar
3:37.35	Gary Lough	6.07.70	11	Cologne, GER	16	Aug
3:38.13			11	Stockholm, SWE	8	Jul
3:39.18			4	Birmingham	16	Jun
3:40.98			2	Gateshead	30	Jun
3:41.33			11	London (CP)	12	Jul
3:41.37			7	Melbourne, AUS	29	Feb
3:42.60			3h2	Birmingham	15	Jun
3:37.90	Kevin McKay	9.02.69	3	Birmingham	16	Jun
3:38.02			4h1	Atlanta, USA	29	Jul
3:39.40			6	Seville, SPA	6	Jun
3:41.21			13	St. Denis, FRA	3	Jun
3:41.38			4	Hengelo, HOL	27	May
3:38.66	Glen Stewart	7.12.70	1	Ljubljana, SLO	26	May
3:41.12			5	Birmingham	16	Jun
3:42.67			8	Gateshead	30	Jun
3:38.95	Curtis Robb	7.06.72	2	Ljubljana, SLO	26	May
3:39.1	Neil Caddy	U23 18.03.75	1	Swindon	14	Aug
3:39.58			6	Rhede, GER	24	May
3:40.7 +			6m	Sheffield	25	Aug
3:41.94			4	Gateshead	30	Jun
3:42.3			1	Cardiff	7	Aug
3:42.92			12	London (CP)	12	Jul
3:40.1	Ian Grime	29.09.70	2	Swindon	14	Aug
3:41.2			2	Loughborough	5	Jun
3:41.32			6	Birmingham	16	Jun
3:40.47	Brian Treacy	29.07.71	8	Seville, SPA	6	Jun
3:41.78			2	Andujar, SPA	5	Sep
3:42.72			7	La Laguna, SPA	13	Jul
3:40.7	Rob Whalley	11.02.68	3	Swindon	14	Aug

3:40.82	Darren Spawforth		1.08.69	9	Cork, IRE	22	Jun
3:40.9 +e	Rob Denmark		23.11.68	7	Sheffield	25	Aug
3:40.95	Philip Healy		1.10.70	11	Cork, IRE	22	Jun
	3:40.96			3	Chapel Hill, USA	11	May
	3:41.17			5rB	Santa Monica, USA	17	May
3:41.1	Steffan White		21.12.72	1	Loughborough	5	Jun
3:41.1	Ian Gillespie		18.05.70	4	Swindon	14	Aug
	3:42.4			2	Stretford	16	Jul
	3:42.7			5	Manchester	30	Jul
3:41.2	Richard Ashe	U23	5.10.74	1	Manchester	30	Jul
	3:42.5			1r1	Watford	10	Jul
3:41.3	Robert Hough		3.06.72	1	Sheffield	4	Aug
	3:41.5			1rB	Manchester	30	Jul
3:41.3	Rob Scanlon	U23	13.04.74	5	Swindon	14	Aug
3:41.4	Andy Keith		25.12.71	4	Dedham, USA	1	Jun
	3:42.90			1	Dedham, USA	25	May
3:41.48	Jon Wild		30.08.73	1h1	Eugene, USA	30	May
	3:42.00			10	Eugene, USA	31	May
	3:42.54			2	Fayetteville, USA	13	Apr
	3:42.63			1	Madison, USA	4	May
(20)							
3:41.8	Matt Skelton		8.11.72	3	Loughborough	5	Jun
3:42.0	Andy Hart		13.09.69	1	Stretford	16	Jul
3:42.0	Rod Finch		5.08.67	2	Manchester	30	Jul
3:42.01	Steve Green		18.02.71	7	Birmingham	16	Jun
3:42.1	Martin Forder		7.08.70	3r1	Manchester	30	Jul
3:42.20	Nick Comerford		23.04.66	8	Birmingham	16	Jun
3:42.37	Stuart Margiotta		19.11.69	2h2	Birmingham	15	Jun
	3:42.4			4	Manchester	30	Jul
3:42.5	Adam Duke		5.10.73	6	Swindon	14	Aug
3:42.55	John Nuttall		11.01.67	7	Gateshead	30	Jun
3:42.56	Dave Heath		22.05.65	11	Cape Town, RSA	12	Apr
(30)							
3:42.60	Matthew Yates		4.02.69	10	Hengelo, HOL	27	May
3:42.71	Karl Keska		7.05.72	2	Tucson, USA	30	Mar
3:42.86	Simon Fairbrother		28.03.68	4h2	Birmingham	15	Jun
3:43.0	Stuart Poore		30.12.72	8	Swindon	14	Aug

94 performances to 3:43.0 by 34 athletes including 2 indoors

3:43.13 i	Ian Campbell		6.09.71	1	Glasgow	4	Dec
	3:50.52			9h3	Birmingham	15	Jun
3:43.38	Vince Wilson		1.04.73	13	Cork, IRE	22	Jun
3:43.4	Tom Mayo	U20	2.05.77	5	Loughborough	5	Jun
3:43.5	Mark Griffin	U23	16.02.75	2	Watford	10	Jul
3:43.51 i	Terry West		19.11.68	1	Birmingham	10	Feb
	3:49.75			4	Loughborough	19	May
3:43.8	Spencer Barden		31.03.73	8	Manchester	30	Jul
(40)							
3:43.9	Dave Robertson		4.08.73	6	Loughborough	5	Jun
3:44.0	James Mayo	U23	24.02.75	3	Watford	10	Jul
3:44.2	Matthew Davies		23.07.71	9	Manchester	30	Jul
3:44.79	Tony Mate	U23	15.12.74	11h2	Birmingham	15	Jun
3:44.9	Paul Gardner		5.08.69	9	Swindon	14	Aug
3:45.17	Kim Critchley		15.07.73	2	Madison, USA	4	May
3:45.2	Des Roache	U23	5.01.76	2	Manchester	15	May
3:45.4	Julian Moorhouse		13.11.71	6	Watford	10	Jul
3:45.50	James Guest	U23	29.07.74	2	Sheffield	6	May
3:45.6	Tony Johnston		23.08.68	2	Southampton	7	Jul
(50)							
3:45.6	Brendan Smith	U20	20.07.77	4	Stretford	16	Jul
3:45.7	Phil Mowbray		19.03.73	3rB	Manchester	30	Jul
3:45.7	Adam Zawadski	U23	19.12.74	10	Swindon	14	Aug

3:45.73	Jason Boothroyd		26.11.69	3	Tuscaloosa, USA	23	Mar
3:45.9	Paul Larkins		19.05.63	1rB	Manchester	15	May
3:46.0	Phillip Tulba-Morrison		20.09.73	11	Swindon	14	Aug
3:46.1	Darius Burrows	U23	8.08.75	5rB	Manchester	30	Jul
3:46.1	Joe Mills		9.07.72	4rB	Manchester	30	Jul
3:46.14	James Ellis-Smith		11.09.72	3h1	Birmingham	15	Jun
3:46.3	Andy Renfree	U23	18.05.75	12	Swindon	14	Aug
(60)							
3:46.5	Kris Bowditch	U23	14.01.75	1rB	Stretford	16	Jul
3:46.6	Luke Veness		5.12.73	7	Watford	10	Jul
3:46.7	Paul Freary		3.04.68	5r1	Stretford	16	Jul
3:46.8	Rupert Waters		3.01.72	8	Watford	10	Jul
3:47.2	Ciaran Murphy		2.09.71	4	Manchester	15	May
3:47.22	Carl Leonard		19.01.73	5	Bloomington, USA	5	May
3:47.4 a	Ben Reese	U23	29.03.76		Tuscaloosa, USA	23	Apr
3:47.4	Grant Cuddy	U20	6.01.77	7r1	Stretford	16	Jul
3:47.4	Steve Mosley		10.01.66	14	Swindon	14	Aug
3:47.6	Martin Yelling		7.02.72	9	Watford	10	Jul
(70)							
3:47.6	Matt O'Dowd	U23	13.04.76	6	Stretford	20	Aug
3:47.7	Justin Swift-Smith	U23	28.08.74	15	Swindon	14	Aug
3:47.8	Dave Locker	U23	28.03.75	2rB	Stretford	16	Jul
3:47.8	Andrew Graffin	U20	20.12.77	1	Crawley	17	Jul
3:48.0	Carl Warren		28.09.69	4rB	Manchester	15	May
3:48.0	Patrick Davoren		13.03.72	1	Watford	5	Jun
3:48.0	Martin Airey		28.10.70	3	Bedford	7	Aug
3:48.1	Mike Proudlove		26.01.70	2	Stretford	4	Jun
3:48.1	Steve O'Gara		3.12.69	3rB	Stretford	16	Jul
3:48.3	Mark Miles	U20	24.03.77	10	Stretford	16	Jul
(80)							
3:48.32	Ivan Hollingsworth	U23	20.05.75	3	Sheffield	6	May
3:48.4	Russell Cartwright	U20	13.10.77	8	Southampton	7	Jul
3:48.44	Kevin Farrow	U23	8.09.75	8	Lincoln, USA	21	May
3:48.7	Steve Sharp	U23	31.12.75	6	Cardiff	2	May
3:48.9	Michael Wassell			4rB	Stretford	16	Jul
3:48.95	Kevin Hayes		10.11.70	7h3	Birmingham	15	Jun
3:49.09 A	David Strang		13.12.68	4	Pretoria, RSA	3	Feb
3:49.2	Matthew Smith	U23	26.12.74	17	Swindon	14	Aug
3:49.2	Jason Lobo		18.09.69	9	Stretford	20	Aug
3:49.30	Lee Cadwallader		17.01.69	1	London (He)	8	Jun
(90)							
3:49.3	Grant Graham		27.12.72	6	Manchester	15	May
3:49.3	Peter Steel		11.12.73	5rB	Stretford	16	Jul
3:49.32	Nick Bentham		7.12.70	4	London (CP)	5	May
3:49.40	Brad Glenton		2.11.69	1	Portsmouth	12	May
3:49.4	Gary Brown		21.07.67	3	Enfield	6	Jul
3:49.4	Jason Dullforce		6.08.70	2	Enfield	6	Jul
3:49.5	Paul Burgess		10.11.70	3rC	Manchester	15	May
3:49.5	Larry Mangleshot		28.05.63	2	London (PH)	7	Aug
3:49.8	Alex Rosen		30.09.71	3	London (PH)	7	Aug
3:50.0	Davey Wilson		7.09.68	1	Antrim	25	Jun
(100)							
3:50.06	Ed Bowen	U23	3.02.76	7	Birmingham	20	Jul
3:50.38	Kairn Stone	U23	21.10.76	3	Cardiff	25	May
3:50.4	Andrew Walling		3.04.73	4	Stretford	4	Jun
3:50.4	Danny McCormack	U23	22.03.75	6	Bedford	7	Aug
3:50.48	Michael East	U20	20.01.78	4	Bedford	28	Jul
3:50.5	Paul Morby	U20	15.01.79	1rD	Manchester	15	May
3:50.6	James Tonner	U23	3.06.75	1	Ayr	24	Jul
3:50.6	Simon Beardsall		16.06.70	4	London (PH)	7	Aug
3:50.7	Ian Mitchell	U23	10.03.76	6rB	Stretford	16	Jul

3:50.84	Peter Baker		6.02.73	2	Portsmouth	12 May
(110)						
3:50.86	James Starling		13.08.67	10h3	Birmingham	15 Jun
3:50.89 i	Garth Watson		20.04.73	6	Birmingham	10 Feb
3:50.95	Justin Chaston		4.11.68	7	Cardiff	25 May
3:51.0	Mark Steinle	U23	22.11.74	5	London (PH)	7 Aug

Foreign

3:41.13	*Des English*		6.06.67	5	*Ljubljana, SLO*	26 May
3:51.7	*Per Synnermann*		13.12.71	1	*Loughborough*	1 Jun

Additional Under 20 (1 - 8 above)

3:51.30	Alistair Moses		5.07.78	1	London (CP)	30 Jun
3:51.38	Matthew Dixon		26.12.78	1	Sheffield	13 Jul
(10)						
3:51.6	Allen Graffin		20.12.77	1	Luton	17 Aug
3:52.0	Chris Old		3.12.77	3	Jarrow	24 Jul
3:52.1	Andrew Hennessy		24.08.77	2	Street	12 May
3:53.01 i	Alasdair Donaldson		21.06.77	2	Birmingham	17 Feb
3:53.39	Yacin Yusuf		20.12.77	2	London (He)	10 Aug
3:53.93	Ben Whitby		6.01.77	4	London (CP)	30 Jun
3:54.3	Lee Garrett		2.09.78	4rB	Stretford	20 Aug
3:54.57	Michael Combe		24.12.78	2	Edinburgh	11 May
3:54.94	James Thie		27.06.78	9	Bedford	28 Jul

Under 17

3:58.6	Simon Lees		19.11.79	1	Birmingham	9 Jun
3:58.6	Colin McLean		7.06.80	15	Southampton	7 Jul
3:59.31	Ross Fittall		4.09.79	8h1	Birmingham	1 Jun
3:59.84	Sam Boden		16.02.80	1	Birmingham	18 Aug
3:59.9	Alex MacDonald		12.04.80	6	Glasgow	27 Aug
3:59.9	Iain Murdoch		10.07.80	7	Glasgow	27 Aug
4:02.3	Jonathan Stewart		15.06.80	2rB	Stretford	4 Jun
4:02.37	Gavin Thompson		9.04.80	2	Birmingham	18 Aug
4:03.21	Matthew Jones		15.09.79	2h2	Sheffield	12 Jul
4:03.38	Alan Old		1.12.79	1h1	Sheffield	12 Jul
(10)						
4:03.55	John Mooney		23.10.79	2h1	Sheffield	12 Jul
4:03.64	Michael Skinner		21.11.79	4h2	Sheffield	12 Jul
4:03.75	Geoff Baxter		9.12.79	4h1	Sheffield	12 Jul
4:03.9	William Goudie		16.12.80	5rB	Stretford	4 Jun
4:04.52	Brian Stopher		8.04.80	4	Sheffield	13 Jul
4:04.6	Oliver Laws		18.03.80	1rB	Wolverhampton	2 Jun
4:05.3	Paul Laslett		12.05.80	2	Watford	5 Jun
4:05.42	Ross Houston		5.12.79	2	Wishaw	13 Jul
4:06.1	Andrew Murphy		14.09.79	1	Watford	15 May
4:06.2	Daniel Rowen		30.12.79	1	Wolverhampton	2 Jun
(20)						
4:06.49	Richard Gilbert		29.06.80	5h2	Sheffield	12 Jul
4:06.81	Simon Firth		20.10.79	1	Sheffield	12 May
4:06.9	Mark Best		9.09.79	1	Portsmouth	8 Jun
4:06.9	Nicholas Dunne		12.02.80	2	Birmingham	9 Jun
4:07.3	Graham Ferguson		18.01.80	3	Pitreavie	11 Sep
4:07.36	Carl Morris		5.05.80	7h1	Sheffield	12 Jul
4:07.5	Joel Ellis		2.09.79	2	Wolverhampton	2 Jun

Under 15

4:11.40	Conor Sweeney		28.12.81	1	Tullamore, IRE	1 Jun
4:12.2	Richard Ward		5.05.82	1	London (TB)	31 Jul
4:13.59	Richard King		5.04.82	1	Sheffield	13 Jul
4:14.0	Robert Laming		26.06.82	1	Hoo	8 Jun

4:14.12	Neil Gardener		7.09.81	2	Sheffield	13	Jul
4:14.5	Antony Ford		26.05.83	1	Stretford	3	Jul
4:15.5	Mark Griffith		25.11.81	1	Hoo	2	Jun
4:15.69	Matt Thomson		20.09.81	5=	Sheffield	13	Jul
4:16.49	Thomas Carter		20.08.82	7	Sheffield	13	Jul
4:17.6	Glen Coppin		16.01.83	1	Peterborough	14	Jul
	(10)						
4:18.0	Mark Pollard		25.02.82	1	Pitreavie	15	Jun
4:18.1	Andrew Baddeley		20.06.82	1	Bebington	21	Jul
4:18.2	Chris Iddon		8.10.82	1	Bebington	21	Jul
4:18.53	Darren Bradley		7.01.82	3h2	Sheffield	12	Jul
4:19.10	Stephen Bates		5.11.81	1	Sheffield	11	May
4:19.1	Warren McKinlay		4.10.81	2	Cambridge	15	Sep
4:19.4	Aaron McIndoe		19.05.82	1	Glasgow	23	Jun
4:19.72	Daniel Beynon		23.01.82	1	Swansea	6	Jul
4:20.1	Andrew Mallows		18.01.82	1	Solihull	29	Jun
4:20.13	Gary Hodgson		21.03.82	9	Sheffield	13	Jul
	(20)						
4:20.40	Matt Flanagan		10.07.82	2	London (CP)	30	Jun
4:20.79	Steven Frost		12.12.81	3	London (CP)	30	Jun
4:21.0	Tony Read		14.10.81	1	Crawley	8	Jun
4:21.6	Robin Douglas		20.12.81	2	Kingston	8	Jun
4:21.9	Andrew Rayner		16.01.82	2	Hoo	2	Jun
4:21.9	Thomas Ganley		6.04.82	2	Hoo	8	Jun
4:21.9	Abdi Madar		25.11.81	3	Hoo	8	Jun
4:21.9	Kevin McKenna		3.01.82	2	Pitreavie	15	Jun

Under 13

4:34.8	David Kent		15.12.83		Watford	10	Jul
4:38.1	P. Hogbin			1	Southampton	9	Sep
4:39.7	Paul Brown		8.10.83	1	Loughborough	11	May

1 MILE

3:50.32	John Mayock		26.10.70	3	Oslo, NOR	5	Jul
	3:54.60			2	Sheffield	25	Aug
	3:54.67			7	Berlin, GER	30	Aug
3:54.87	Anthony Whiteman		13.11.71	3	Sheffield	25	Aug
	3:56.35			1	London (He)	31	Aug
3:55.39	Rob Denmark		23.11.68	6	Sheffield	25	Aug
3:55.84	Neil Caddy	U23	18.03.75	7	Sheffield	25	Aug
	3:58.59			2	London (He)	31	Aug
	3:59.3			1	Cheltenham	4	Aug
3:59.56	Glen Stewart		7.12.70	10	Sheffield	25	Aug
3:59.98	Richard Ashe	U23	5.10.74	3	London (He)	31	Aug
	4:00.30			11	Sheffield	25	Aug
4:00.0	Gary Lough		6.07.70	2	Cheltenham	4	Aug
	4:01.17			13	Berlin, GER	30	Aug
4:00.42	Robert Hough		3.06.72	4	London (He)	31	Aug
4:01.1	Ian Gillespie		18.05.70	3	Cheltenham	4	Aug
4:01.2	Philip Healy		1.10.70	1	Antrim	25	Jun
	(10)						
4:01.53	Steffan White		21.12.72	5	London (He)	31	Aug
	18 performances to 4:02.00 by 11 athletes						
4:02.1	Spencer Barden		31.03.73	4	Cheltenham	4	Aug
4:02.3	Andy Hart		13.09.69	1	Bath	19	Jun
4:03.12	Stuart Poore		30.12.72	6	London (He)	31	Aug
4:03.2	Stuart Margiotta		19.11.69	5	Cheltenham	4	Aug
4:03.3	Lee Cadwallader		17.01.69	4	Bath	19	Jun
4:03.6	Tony Johnston		23.08.68	5	Bath	19	Jun
4:04.50	Adam Zawadski	U23	19.12.74	1rB	London (He)	31	Aug

4:04.5	Vince Wilson		1.04.73	6	Bath	19	Jun
4:04.83 i	Ben Reese	U23	29.03.76	3	Notre Dame, USA	3	Feb
(20)							
4:04.9	Chris Stephenson	U23	22.07.74	7	Bath	19	Jun
4:05.0	Matt Skelton		8.11.72	7	Cheltenham	4	Aug
4:05.4	James Mayo	U23	24.02.75	1	Hexham	1	Aug
4:05.87	Des Roache	U23	5.01.76	2	Loughborough	19	May
4:05.9	Andy Renfree	U23	18.05.75	10	Bath	19	Jun
4:06.0	Tony Mate	U23	15.12.74	3	Hexham	1	Aug
4:06.0	Paul Gardner		5.08.69	8	Cheltenham	4	Aug
4:06.14 i	Kim Critchley		15.07.73	6	Fayetteville, USA	26	Jan
4:06.9	Steve O'Gara		3.12.69	4	Hexham	1	Aug
4:06.9	Rob Whalley		11.02.68	9	Cheltenham	4	Aug
(30)							
4:07.41 i	Jason Boothroyd		26.11.69	2	Lafayette, USA	10	Feb
4:07.48	Nick Comerford		23.04.66	3	Loughborough	19	May
4:07.76 i	Dave Locker	U23	28.03.75	4	Indianapolis, USA	9	Mar
4:08.4	Chris Nicolson		19.09.73	12	Bath	19	Jun
4:08.51	Robin Hooton		5.05.73	9	London (He)	31	Aug
4:08.56	Darius Burrows	U23	8.08.75	4	Loughborough	19	May
4:08.59	Patrick Davoren		13.03.72	3rB	London (He)	31	Aug
4:08.7	Steve Mosley		10.01.66	13	Bath	19	Jun
4:08.74	Ciaran Murphy		2.09.71	5	Loughborough	19	May
4:09.4	Phil Cook		7.05.69	14	Bath	19	Jun
(40)							
4:09.65	Grant Graham		27.12.72	7	Loughborough	19	May
4:09.78 i	Kevin Farrow	U23	8.09.75	5	Ames, USA	10	Feb
4:09.8	Justin Swift-Smith	U23	28.08.74	15	Bath	19	Jun
4:10.0	Ian Campbell		6.09.71	7	Hexham	1	Aug

2000 METRES

5:00.91	John Mayock		26.10.70	1	Sarajevo, BOS	9	Sep
5:02.98	Gary Lough		6.07.70	3	London (CP)	11	Aug
5:02.99	Neil Caddy	U23	18.03.75	4	London (CP)	11	Aug
5:04.11	Rob Denmark		23.11.68	7	London (CP)	11	Aug
5:05.3 +	John Nuttall		11.01.67	10m	Nice, FRA	10	Jul
	5:06.3 +			7m	London (CP)	12	Jul
	5:06.33			10	London (CP)	11	Aug
5:05.97	Glen Stewart		7.12.70	9	London (CP)	11	Aug
5:06.95	Rod Finch		5.08.67	11	London (CP)	11	Aug

3000 METRES

7:36.40	John Nuttall		11.01.67	7	Nice, FRA	10	Jul
	7:44.66			6	London (CP)	12	Jul
	7:48.44			6	Hengelo, HOL	27	May
	7:49.57			12	Cologne, GER	16	Aug
7:45.45	Rob Denmark		23.11.68	12	Brussels, BEL	23	Aug
7:52.6	Rob Whalley		11.02.68	1	Stretford	16	Jul
7:52.9	Robert Hough		3.06.72	2	Stretford	16	Jul
7:53.10 i	Jon Wild		30.08.73	3	Indianapolis, USA	9	Mar
	8:07.4			8	Stretford	16	Jul
7:53.49	Ian Gillespie		18.05.70	8	London (CP)	12	Jul
	7:57.87 i			7	Birmingham	10	Feb
7:53.97	Keith Cullen		13.06.72	9	London (CP)	12	Jul
7:54.12	Gary Lough		6.07.70	3	Hobart, AUS	25	Feb
7:55.29	Paul Evans		13.04.61	10	London (CP)	12	Jul
7:55.4	Ian Grime		29.09.70	3	Stretford	16	Jul
(10)							
7:55.83	Brian Treacy		29.07.71	1	Maia, POR	21	Aug
7:55.9 +e	Jon Brown		27.02.71	8m	Nuremberg, GER	7	Jun
	7:57.09 +			10m	Stockholm, SWE	8	Jul

7:57.59 i	Anthony Whiteman		13.11.71	6	Birmingham	10	Feb
7:58.14 i	Neil Caddy	U23	18.03.75	2	Birmingham	27	Jan
8:03.59				1	Gateshead	19	Aug
7:58.4	Spencer Barden		31.03.73	4	Stretford	16	Jul
7:58.63 i	Rod Finch		5.08.67	4	Birmingham	27	Jan
8:15.04				1	Aldershot	26	Jun
7:58.7	Darius Burrows	U23	8.08.75	5	Stretford	16	Jul
7:58.82 i	Matt Skelton		8.11.72	8	Birmingham	10	Feb
7:59.14 i				3	Glasgow	24	Feb

24 performances to 8:00.00 by 18 athletes including 7 indoors

8:00.3	Spencer Newport		5.10.66	6	Stretford	16	Jul
8:01.8	Andy Keith		25.12.71	1	Dedham, USA	18	May
(20)							
8:03.20	Steffan White		21.12.72	2	London (CP)	11	Aug
8:03.94	Karl Keska		7.05.72	2	Eugene, USA	23	Mar
8:05.72 i	Andrew Wedlake		30.11.71	4	Boston, USA	20	Jan
8:06.09 i	Tom Hanlon		20.05.67	11	Birmingham	10	Feb
8:06.9	Steve Green		18.02.71	7	Stretford	16	Jul
8:07.00 i	Nick Hopkins		28.08.66	2	Vienna, AUT	17	Feb
8:15.79				1	Luton	6	May
8:07.0	Martin Yelling		7.02.72	2	Watford	5	Jun
8:08.4	Ian Robinson		21.04.69	1	Stretford	25	Jun
8:08.6	Rob Scanlon	U23	13.04.74	9	Stretford	16	Jul
8:09.0	Martin Jones		21.04.67	10	Stretford	16	Jul
(30)							
8:09.29	Kris Bowditch	U23	14.01.75	2	Hexham	14	Jul
8:10.0	Paul Green		7.04.72	11	Stretford	16	Jul
8:10.1	Julian Moorhouse		13.11.71	1	Watford	31	Jul
8:11.59	Richard Findlow		4.12.66	2	Birmingham	20	Jul
8:12.8	Paul Roden		18.04.65	1	Stretford	21	May
8:12.81	Stuart Poore		30.12.72	7	Birmingham	4	Feb
8:12.88 i	Jason Lobo		18.09.69	8	Birmingham	4	Feb
8:12.9	Paul Wilson		12.11.69	1	Bellville, RSA	19	Jan
8:13.21	Gary Staines		3.07.63	4	Birmingham	20	Jul
8:13.5	Darrell Smith		10.04.67	2	Watford	31	Jul
(40)							
8:13.6	Clive Bonelle		2.04.71	2	Stretford	21	May
8:14.4	Dave Lee		16.09.65	12	Stretford	16	Jul
8:14.7	Stuart Margiotta		19.11.69	2	Loughborough	27	Apr
8:15.2	David Miles		16.11.65	13	Stretford	16	Jul
8:15.5	Matt O'Dowd	U23	13.04.76	1	Loughborough	5	Jun
8:16.5	Steve O'Gara		3.12.69	1	Jarrow	17	Jul
8:16.90	Malcolm Campbell		3.01.71	2	Aldershot	26	Jun
8:17.3 i	Des Roache	U23	5.01.76	1	Glasgow	14	Feb
8:17.5	Mark Steinle	U23	22.11.74	3	Watford	31	Jul
8:18.7	Dermot Donnelly		23.09.70	1	Belfast	28	Aug
(50)							
8:19.4	Terry Wall		12.06.70	2	Jarrow	17	Jul
8:19.7	Brendan Smith	U20	20.07.77	1	Stretford	3	Sep
8:20.6	Darren Spawforth		1.08.69	1	Stretford	6	Aug
8:21.37 i	Kevin Farrow	U23	8.09.75	2	Ames, USA	1	Mar
8:21.40	Andrew Morgan-Lee		1.03.69	2	Luton	6	May
8:21.43	Stuart Rankin		26.06.70	3	Aldershot	26	Jun
8:21.9	Alaister Russell		17.06.68	1	Pitreavie	21	Apr
8:21.93 i	Larry Matthews		11.08.65	12	Birmingham	4	Feb
8:22.07	Matthew Vaux-Harvey	U23	30.03.76	6	Birmingham	20	Jul
8:22.2	Aidan Walpole			2	Stretford	25	Jun
(60)							
8:22.34 i	Mark Benson		21.12.63	1	Glasgow	17	Mar
8:22.4	Martin Rush		25.12.64	1	Bath	19	Jun
8:22.46 i	Alan Tatham	U23	29.04.76	2	Glasgow	17	Mar

8:22.52 i	Matthew Smith	U23	26.12.74	2	Birmingham	29	Feb
8:22.7	Rob Berry		29.07.69	3	Stretford	25	Jun
8:23.0	Nick McCaffrey		26.06.68	3	Loughborough	5	Jun
8:23.18 i	Chris Nicolson		19.09.73	1	Glasgow	20	Jan
8:23.4	Ray Plant		13.05.68	4	Stretford	25	Jun
8:23.5	Danny McCormack	U23	22.03.75	5	Watford	31	Jul
8:23.6	Ken Chapman		13.04.67	5	Stretford	25	Jun
	(70)						
8:23.8	Tim Hyde		22.02.72	6	Watford	31	Jul
8:23.9	Simon Cotton		26.07.67	7	Watford	31	Jul
8:24.0	Mark Shaw			1	Cardiff	7	Aug
8:24.22	Allen Graffin	U20	20.12.77	1	Sheffield	13	Jul
8:24.5	David O'Donovan		26.10.72	2	Watford	28	Aug
8:24.7	Neil Wilkinson		12.03.69	6	Stretford	25	Jun

Foreign

8:15.7	*Ian Harpur*		*24.04.67*	*3*	*Watford*	*5*	*Jun*
8:22.0	*John Burke*		*18.05.70*	*2*	*Watford*	*10*	*Jul*

Additional Under 20 (1 - 2 above)

8:26.4	Daniel Hyde		5.10.77	4	Bath	19	Jun
8:26.66	Andres Jones		3.02.77	1	Carmarthen	16	Jul
8:26.8	Chris Old		3.12.77	3	Jarrow	17	Jul
8:27.32 i	Mark Miles		24.03.77	1	Birmingham	24	Feb
8:29.7	Sam Haughian		9.07.79	1rB	Watford	31	Jul
8:33.07	Andrew Graffin		20.12.77	2	London (He)	10	Aug
8:34.17	James Thie		27.06.78	1	Birmingham	17	Aug
8:34.74	Tim Boyle		4.07.78	2	Birmingham	17	Aug
	(10)						
8:37.1	Simon Wurr		7.01.77	4	Stretford	4	Jun
8:37.8	David Rose		26.06.78	1	Carlisle	12	May
8:37.82	Iain Reid		20.07.77	3	Birmingham	18	Aug
8:39.39	Abdusalam Mohammed		20.03.79	4	London (He)	10	Aug

Under 17

8:40.1	Oliver Laws		18.03.80	8	Stretford	25	Jun
8:41.4	Sam Boden		16.02.80	4	Watford	11	Sep
8:42.4	Graham Ferguson		18.01.80	14	Stretford	3	Sep
8:43.9	Jonathan Stewart		15.06.80	2	Stoke	20	Jul
8:51.6	Paul Gronow		14.09.79	4	Stoke	20	Jul
8:52.7	Gavin Thompson		9.04.80	1	Crawley	28	May
8:54.11	Neil Heppel		17.09.79	2	Enfield	4	Aug
8:55.0	Ryan Falkner		20.11.79	1	Loughborough	12	May
8:55.13	Alan Old		1.12.79	3	Bedford	27	Jul
8:55.9	Christopher Livesey		8.08.80	1	Blackpool	8	Jun
	(10)						
8:58.79	Chris Thompson		17.04.81	4	Bedford	27	Jul

Under 15

9:13.60	Richard Ward		5.05.82	1	Bedford	27	Jul
9:17.77	Matt Thomson		20.09.81	2	Bedford	27	Jul
9:18.33	Mark Griffith		25.11.81	3	Bedford	27	Jul
9:18.7	Glen Coppin		16.01.83	1	Watford	28	Aug
9:22.38	Matt Flanagan		10.07.82	4	Bedford	27	Jul
9:26.89	Stephen Thompson		5.12.82	5	Bedford	27	Jul
9:30.65	Thomas Ganley		6.04.82	2	Enfield	4	Aug
9:32.68	Jonathon Parker		27.02.82	1	Worcester	25	Aug
9:35.63	Kevin McKenna		3.01.82	6	Bedford	27	Jul
9:35.9	Daniel Moore		8.11.81	1	Ipswich	23	Jun
	(10)						
9:36.6	Andrew Mallows		18.01.82	1	Coventry	2	Jun

9:36.80	Adam Swanwick		4.01.82	1	Birmingham	8 Sep
9:36.90	James Walsh		22.09.81	2	Worcester	25 Aug
9:37.3	Richard Williams		22.10.81	2	Ipswich	23 Jun
9:37.5	S. James			1	Cheltenham	23 Jun
9:37.8	Kevin Broom		20.11.81	1	Wakefield	2 Jun
9:38.3	Daniel Ledgerwood		24.03.83	1	Windsor	21 Jul
9:39.5	Duncan Scott		5.02.82	1	Jarrow	12 May
9:39.6	N. Cartwright			1	Coventry	2 Jun
9:39.65	Alex Flynn		2.08.82	3	Enfield	4 Aug
(20)						
9:39.9	Carl Prior		20.01.82	1	Bolton	23 Jun

Under 13

10:03.3	Rob Skornia		19.03.84	1	Exeter	18 Apr
10:08.9	David Kent		15.12.83	1	Watford	15 Aug
10:15.0	Gary Fairbank		7.03.84	2	Kingston	28 Jul
10:20.9	Kevin Scanlan		24.03.84	1	Watford	31 Jul
10:23.5	Ross Penney		28.06.85	1rB	Kingston	28 Jul

2 MILES

8:49.79	Adrian Passey		2.09.64	4	Canberra, AUS	1 Dec
8:58.0	Andrew Pearson		14.09.71	1	Hexham	2 Aug
8:59.0	Chris Robison		16.03.61	2	Hexham	2 Aug
8:59.0	Paul Davies-Hale		21.06.62	3	Hexham	2 Aug

5000 METRES

13:17.48	John Nuttall		11.01.67	5	St. Denis, FRA	3 Jun
13:48.35				1	Birmingham	16 Jun
13:52.16				7h2	Atlanta, USA	31 Jul
13:20.10	Jon Brown		27.02.71	12	Stockholm, SWE	8 Jul
13:22.11				8	Nuremberg, GER	7 Jun
13:57.0 +e				11m	Atlanta, USA	29 Jul
13:27.00	Keith Cullen		13.06.72	4	Kerkrade, HOL	17 May
13:31.36	Rob Denmark		23.11.68	13	Berlin, GER	30 Aug
13:41.87				15	Nuremberg, GER	7 Jun
13:51.72				2	Birmingham	16 Jun
13:40.68	Ian Gillespie		18.05.70	19	St. Denis, FRA	3 Jun
13:56.6				1	Street	6 May
13:56.67				5	Gateshead	30 Jun
13:43.49	Chris Sweeney		3.03.66	7	Cork, IRE	22 Jun
13:45.1	Jon Wild		30.08.73	16	Walnut, USA	20 Apr
13:47.40	Paul Evans		13.04.61	1	Gateshead	30 Jun
13:49.31				17	Nuremberg, GER	7 Jun
13:53.23				1	London (He)	31 Aug
13:5? +e				m	Atlanta, USA	26 Jul
13:49.74	Spencer Newport		5.10.66	8	Cork, IRE	22 Jun
13:50.04	Chris Stephenson	U23	22.07.74	1	Chiba, JAP	22 Nov
(10)						
13:51.99	Rob Whalley		11.02.68	8	Linz, AUT	21 Aug
13:52.34	Spencer Barden		31.03.73	10	Linz, AUT	21 Aug
13:56.20				5	Birmingham	16 Jun
13:53.44	Adrian Passey		2.09.64	11	Cape Town, RSA	12 Apr
13:54.42	Darius Burrows	U23	8.08.75	3	Birmingham	16 Jun
13:55.81				2	London (He)	31 Aug
13:54.6	Ian Hudspith		23.09.70	1	Jarrow	4 May
13:55.32	Kris Bowditch	U23	14.01.75	4	Birmingham	16 Jun
13:55.34	Paul Freary		3.04.68	10	Cork, IRE	22 Jun
13:55.86	Justin Chaston		4.11.68	2	Austin, USA	4 Apr
13:56.04	Paul Wilson		12.11.69	5	Bellville, RSA	26 Mar

13:56.06	Karl Keska		7.05.72	1	Eugene, USA	6	Apr
13:56.85				2	Eugene, USA	20	Apr
(20)							
13:58.50	John Sherban		30.07.64	1	Seattle, USA	2	Mar

35 performances to 14:00.00 by 21 athletes

14:00.58	Andy Keith		25.12.71	7	Philadelphia, USA	25	Apr
14:04 +e	Martin Jones		21.04.67	m	Koblenz, GER	18	May
14:15.22				12	Gateshead	30	Jun
14:04.72	Dermot Donnelly		23.09.70	1	Antrim	6	Jul
14:05.2	Dave Robertson		4.08.73	2	Loughborough	1	Jun
14:05.91	Ian Hamilton		8.03.65	10	Oordegem, BEL	11	Aug
14:06.59	David Miles		16.11.65	15	Cork, IRE	22	Jun
14:07.8	Julian Moorhouse		13.11.71	3	Loughborough	1	Jun
14:09.4	Mark Hudspith		19.01.69	2	Jarrow	4	May
14:09.89	Richard Findlow		4.12.66	2	Sheffield	2	Jun
(30)							
14:10.70	Gerallt Owen		26.01.70	15	Philadelphia, USA	25	Apr
14:11.30	Carl Leonard		19.01.73	6	Philadelphia, USA	25	Apr
14:11.62	Paul Roden		18.04.65	2	Birmingham	6	Jul
14:11.64	Rob Birchall		14.06.70	3	Sheffield	2	Jun
14:12.75	Paul Taylor		9.01.66	1	Edinburgh	8	Jun
14:14.15	Richard Taylor		5.12.73	3	Bedford	27	May
14:14.80	Robert Quinn		10.12.65	1	Glasgow	12	May
14:14.81	Graeme Wight		3.06.65	2	Glasgow	12	May
14:15.0	Dale Laughlin		28.12.66	1	Hayes	3	Aug
14:15.8	Chris Robison		16.03.61	1	Portsmouth	2	Jul
(40)							
14:15.93	Steve Brooks		8.06.70	16	Kerkrade, HOL	17	May
14:16.13	Nick Hopkins		28.08.66	4	Loughborough	19	May
14:16.24	Matt O'Dowd	U23	13.04.76	2	Zoetermeer, HOL	7	Jul
14:16.25	Gary Staines		3.07.63	2	Kingston	17	Aug
14:16.34	Phil Mowbray		19.03.73	1	Sheffield	5	May
14:16.68	Dominic Bannister		1.04.68	5	Loughborough	19	May
14:17.1	Alaister Russell		17.06.68	2	Peterborough	4	May
14:17.3	Bill Foster		9.08.58	1	Watford	6	Jul
14:18.15	Paul Green		7.04.72	3	London (He)	31	Aug
14:18.17	Adrian Mussett		14.04.72	4	Bedford	27	May
(50)							
14:19.15	Dave Tune		29.10.70	5	Bedford	27	May
14:19.26	Jim Campbell		17.06.70	2	Antrim	6	Jul
14:19.9	Dave Lee		16.09.65	4	Loughborough	1	Jun
14:20.08 i	Andrew Wedlake		30.11.71	2	Syracuse, USA	18	Feb
14:20.1	Darrell Smith		10.04.67	2	Watford	6	Jul
14:20.6	Paul Larkins		19.05.63	1	Enfield	4	May
14:20.7	Martin Rees	V40	28.02.53	4	Watford	6	Jul
14:21	Stephen Green		28.07.70	2	Villeneuve d'Ascq, FRA	20	Jun
14:21.4	Mark Flint		19.02.63	1	Birmingham	18	Jun
14:21.78	Simon Cotton		26.07.67	2	Birmingham	2	Jun
(60)							
14:21.9	Rod Finch		5.08.67	1	Abingdon	24	Aug
14:22.9	Keith Anderson		10.08.57	1	Sheffield	11	May
14:22.9	Dave Swanston		30.11.61	1	Enfield	6	Jul
14:23.2	Mike Simpson		6.01.70	2	Enfield	4	May
14:23.42	Mark Steinle	U23	22.11.74	2	London (CP)	1	Jun
14:24 +e	Colin Moore		25.11.60	m	Villeneuve d'Ascq, FRA	20	Jun
14:25.05	Chris Nicolson		19.09.73	7	Loughborough	19	May
14:25.20	Nick Comerford		23.04.66	3	Liverpool	4	May
14:26.2	Daniel Leggate	U23	5.10.74	4	Watford	6	Jul
14:26.2	James Jackson		12.09.63	3	Portsmouth	21	Jul
(70)							
14:26.67	Greg Luke			4	Antrim	6	Jul

14:27.35	Nick McCaffrey		26.06.68	2	Birmingham	2 Jun
14:28.08	Sean Fenwick		20.07.70	3	Birmingham	2 Jun
14:29.7	Eamonn Martin		9.10.58	1	Basildon	18 May
14:29.92	John Kendall		23.09.69	3	London (CP)	1 Jun
14:31.00	Mark Benson		21.12.63	2	Sheffield	5 May
14:31.1	Andres Jones	U20	3.02.77	3	Street	6 May
14:31.6	Simon Bell		26.12.66	1	Jarrow	12 May
14:32.36	Stuart Bell		29.07.67	6	Sheffield	2 Jun
14:32.39	Nigel Stirk		13.03.72	4	Birmingham	2 Jun
	(80)					
14:32.6	Gareth Deacon		8.08.66	2	Loughborough	12 May
14:32.72	Michael Bulstridge		23.01.73	5	Birmingham	2 Jun
14:32.99	Nathan Vengdasalam		11.03.64	7	Sheffield	2 Jun
14:33.11	Adrian Callan		28.11.62	6	Glasgow	29 Jun
14:33.56	Simon Wilkinson	U20	27.08.77	6	Birmingham	2 Jun
14:33.8	Chris Buckley		26.07.61	4	Street	6 May
14:33.84	Steve Knight		17.10.63	7	Cardiff	25 May
14:34.31	Rob Fitzsimmons		16.08.64	4	Glasgow	12 May

Foreign

13:52.83	*John Downes*		*21.07.67*	*15*	*Portland, USA*	*12 May*
14:25.6	*Ian Harpur*		*24.04.67*	*2*	*Portsmouth*	*21 Jul*
14:28.8	*John Lisiewicz*		*18.07.62*	*1*	*Gateshead*	*22 May*
14:33.95	*Svein Risa*	*U23*	*7.03.74*	*3*	*Sheffield*	*5 May*

Additional Under 20 (1 - 2 above)

14:44.11	Allen Graffin		20.12.77	2	Bedford	27 Jul
14:53.87	Daniel Hyde		5.10.77	4	Bedford	27 Jul
14:54.77	Alex Oldfield		14.04.77	10	Birmingham	2 Jun
14:55.64	Sam Haughian		9.07.79	5	Bedford	27 Jul
15:01.48	Daniel Flint		15.06.77	6	Bedford	27 Jul
15:06.78	David Rose		26.06.78	1	Wishaw	13 Jul
15:10.54	Abdusalam Mohammed		20.03.79	7	Bedford	27 Jul

10000 METRES

27:59.72	Jon Brown		27.02.71	10	Atlanta, USA	29 Jul
	28:19.85			4h2	Atlanta, USA	26 Jul
	28:21.40			2	Birmingham	14 Jun
28:04.2	Ian Robinson		21.04.69	2	Walnut, USA	20 Apr
	28:46.06			5	Birmingham	14 Jun
28:20.80	Rob Denmark		23.11.68	1	Birmingham	14 Jun
28:24.39	Paul Evans		13.04.61	11h1	Atlanta, USA	26 Jul
	28:28.31			3	Birmingham	14 Jun
28:32.0	Andrew Pearson		14.09.71	17	Walnut, USA	20 Apr
28:37.87	Martin Jones		21.04.67	4	Koblenz, GER	16 May
28:44.09	Chris Sweeney		3.03.66	4	Birmingham	14 Jun
28:47.90	Dermot Donnelly		23.09.70	6	Birmingham	14 Jun
28:55.38	Steve Brooks		8.06.70	7	Birmingham	14 Jun
	13 performances to 29:00.0 by 9 athletes					
29:08.66	Ian Cornford		1.02.66	9	Birmingham	14 Jun
	(10)					
29:09.31	Mark Hudspith		19.01.69	10	Birmingham	14 Jun
29:10.40	Karl Keska		7.05.72	1	Westwood, USA	18 May
29:13.66	Paul Roden		18.04.65	11	Birmingham	14 Jun
29:14.34	Bill Foster		9.08.58	12	Birmingham	14 Jun
29:15.53	Colin Moore		25.11.60	13	Birmingham	14 Jun
29:18.74	Stephen Green		28.07.70	14	Birmingham	14 Jun
29:32.31	Mark Steinle	U23	22.11.74	15	Birmingham	14 Jun
29:40.4	Gary Staines		3.07.63	1	London (He)	31 Aug
29:48.47	Robert Quinn		10.12.65	16	Birmingham	14 Jun

29:49.91	Nick McCaffrey		26.06.68	17	Birmingham	14	Jun
(20)							
29:51.0	Tony O'Brien		14.11.70	1	Leeds (South)	8	Sep
29:51.2	Paul Green		7.04.72	2	Leeds (South)	8	Sep
29:54.12	Dale Rixon		8.07.66	1	Newport	1	Jun
29:56.52	Neil Wilkinson		12.03.69	2	Ayr	21	Jul
30:03.17	Graeme Croll		1.02.66	3	Ayr	21	Jul
30:05.49	Malcolm Campbell		3.01.71	18	Birmingham	14	Jun
30:06.01	Andres Jones	U20	3.02.77	4	Ayr	21	Jul
30:06.50	Charlie Thomson		17.06.65	5	Ayr	21	Jul
30:14.38	Chris Buckley		26.07.61	19	Birmingham	14	Jun
30:14.54	Carl Leonard		19.01.73	3	Knoxville, USA	11	Apr
(30)							
30:20.07	Stephen Harris		12.10.71	20	Birmingham	14	Jun
30:23.1	Simon Cotton		26.07.67	4	Bedford	26	May
30:23.1	Ian Grime		29.09.70	2	London (He)	31	Aug
30:23.37	Shaun Tobin		13.10.62	1	Newport	1	Jun
30:24.1	Matthew Clarkson		25.01.66	3	London (He)	31	Aug
30:24.2	Ali Eden			4	London (He)	31	Aug
30:24.93	Richard Findlow		4.12.66	21	Birmingham	14	Jun
30:35.54	Simon Wilkinson	U20	27.08.77	22	Birmingham	14	Jun
30:36.02	Brian Scally		9.05.66	6	Ayr	21	Jul
30:36.47	Alaister Russell		17.06.68	7	Ayr	21	Jul
(40)							
30:39.3	David Cameron		29.09.66	1	Glasgow	27	Aug
30:39.33	Eddie Stewart		15.12.56	8	Ayr	21	Jul
30:41.1	Andrew Little		1.01.64	2	Glasgow	27	Aug
30:44.8	Terry Wall		12.06.70	1	Barnsley	11	Aug
30:44.93	James Jackson		12.09.63	1	Enfield	4	Aug
30:49.41	Alan Puckrin		2.04.64	1	Edinburgh	19	May
30:50.29	Stuart Bell		29.07.67	23	Birmingham	14	Jun
30:52.56	Robert Holladay	U23	10.01.75	1	Sheffield	6	May
30:53.9	Ian Archbold		10.06.65	1	Jarrow	14	Aug
30:57.22	Alastair Douglas		20.12.60	10	Ayr	21	Jul
(50)							
31:03.32	Allen Graffin	U20	20.12.77	6	Bedford	26	May
31:06.6	Jeff Hornby		17.01.66	1	Leeds	19	Jun
31:06.83	Duncan Mason		8.12.68	3	Sheffield	1	Jun
31:08.2	Andy Coleman	U23	29.09.74	1	London (He)	28	Jul
31:09.7	Graham Lancaster			2	Jarrow	14	Aug

unconfirmed

29:16.47	Malcolm Campbell		3.01.71

Foreign

30:54.20	*Ian Harpur*		*24.04.67*	*4*	*Dublin (M), IRE*	*15*	*Jun*
30:59.0	*Amin Koikai*	*U23*	*5.01.74*	*1*	*Ilford*	*17*	*Sep*

10 KILOMETRES Road

28:07	Peter Whitehead		3.12.64	9	Atlanta, USA	4	Jul
28:33	Paul Evans		13.04.61	1	Peterborough	8	Apr
28:40				2	Perivale	8	Sep
28:38 A	Jon Brown		27.02.71	2	Boulder, USA	27	May
28:46 +				m	Tampa, USA	24	Feb
28:40	Paul Taylor		9.01.66	1	Cardiff	22	Sep
28:48				1	Peterborough	30	Jun
28:50	Richard Nerurkar		6.01.64	1	New Milton	31	Mar
28:51	Rob Denmark		23.11.68	3	Perivale	8	Sep
29:03					Prague, CZE	18	May
28:59	Martin Jones		21.04.67	1	Leyland	1	Sep

29:03	Glyn Tromans		17.03.69	2	Solihull	6	Oct
29:08	Chris Sweeney		3.03.66	1	St. Neots	26	May
29:10	Chris Robison		16.03.61	3	Solihull	6	Oct
	(10)						
29:11	Ian Cornford		1.02.66	1	Stafford	19	May
29:12	Mark Flint		19.02.63	1	Newport	10	Apr
29:12	Dermot Donnelly		23.09.70	4	Solihull	6	Oct
29:14	Dave Taylor		9.01.64	2	Stafford	19	May
29:16	Justin Chaston		4.11.68	5	San Antonio, USA	17	Mar
29:16	Dale Laughlin		28.12.66	1	Redditch	17	Aug
29:17	Tommy Murray		18.05.61	1	Troon	15	May
29:17	Andrew Pearson		14.09.71	3	Stafford	19	May
29:22	Mark Morgan		19.08.72	3	Cardiff	22	Sep
29:23	Mark Peters			2	Bath	9	Jun
	(20)						
29:23	Steve Brooks		8.06.70	5	Noordwijk, HOL	14	Jul
29:25	Phil Makepeace		15.03.64	3	Redditch	17	Aug
29:27	Chris Stephenson	U23	22.07.74	4	Cardiff	22	Sep
29:28	Glen Stewart		7.12.70	1	Strathclyde	6	Apr
29:28	Paul Davies-Hale		21.06.62	4	Redditch	17	Aug
29:28	Brian Rushworth		14.12.62	1	Newcastle	10	Nov
29:29	Richard Findlow		4.12.66	7	Solihull	6	Oct
29:30	Paul Roden		18.04.65	2	Peterborough	30	Jun
29:31	Robert Quinn		10.12.65	2	Strathclyde	6	Apr
29:31	Mike Simpson		6.01.70	2	St. Neots	26	May
	(30)						
29:33	Ian Hudspith		23.09.70	5	Stafford	19	May
29:34	Lyndon McKevitt			2	Staines	24	Mar
29:35	Graeme Croll		1.02.66	2	Helensburgh	23	May
29:35	Carl Thackery		14.10.62	5	Redditch	17	Aug
29:36	Stephen Harris		12.10.71	1	Chichester	4	Feb
29:36	David Ross		2.11.65	3	Strathclyde	6	Apr
29:36	Chris Parkes		17.04.64	1	Askern	22	May
29:37	Rob Birchall		14.06.70	2	Peterborough	8	Apr
29:38	Dave Tune		29.10.70	6	Redditch	17	Aug
29:43	Darren Hiscox			6	Cardiff	22	Sep
	(40)						
29:45	Brian Kirkwood	V40	20.09.52	1	Anstruther	22	Sep

short course

28:17	Ian Hudspith		23.09.70	9	Halluin, FRA	13	Oct
28:50	Mark Croasdale		10.01.60	16	Halluin, FRA	13	Oct
29:00	David Miles		16.11.65	19	Halluin, FRA	13	Oct

relay leg

27:49	Paul Taylor		9.01.66		Chiba, JAP	23	Nov
29:08	Ian Hudspith		23.09.70		Chiba, JAP	23	Nov
29:10	Jon Solly		28.06.63		Copenhagen, DEN	14	Apr

Foreign

29:26	*Siti Mohammed*		*21.05.62*	*4*	*Stafford*	*19*	*May*

short course

28:15	*Kassa Tadesse*	*U23*	*21.08.74*	*8*	*Halluin, FRA*	*13*	*Oct*

10 MILES Road

46:37	Paul Evans		13.04.61	5	Zaandam, HOL	22	Sep
46:57	Gary Staines		3.07.63	1	Portsmouth	6	Oct
47:04	Richard Nerurkar		6.01.64	2	Berne, SWZ	4	May
47:34	Glyn Tromans		17.03.69	4	Erewash	1	Sep
47:53	Peter Whitehead		3.12.64	4	Portsmouth	6	Oct
48:10	Ian Cornford		1.02.66	5	Portsmouth	6	Oct

48:14	Mark Flint		19.02.63	2	Leyland	18	Aug
48:26	Steve Jones	V40	4.08.55	11	Washington, USA	31	Mar
48:40	Dave Taylor		9.01.64	1	Sacramento, USA	15	Sep
48:45	Dale Laughlin		28.12.66	1	Bedford	26	Dec
(10)							
48:46	Martin Jones		21.04.67	3	Leyland	18	Aug
48:47	Stuart Bell		29.07.67	6	Portsmouth	6	Oct
48:51	Chris Robison		16.03.61	4	Leyland	18	Aug
48:51	Nick Jones			1	Llandudno	10	Nov
48:52	Dave Swanston		30.11.61	5	Leyland	18	Aug
49:00	Mick Hawkins		24.10.61	7	Portsmouth	6	Oct

downhill

| 47:54 | Allan Adams | | 11.09.72 | 1 | Motherwell | 14 | Apr |

HALF MARATHON

1:01:06	Richard Nerurkar		6.01.64	4	Vitry-sur-Seine, FRA	14	Apr
1:03:01					New Haven, USA	23	Jun
1:01:55	Paul Evans		13.04.61	2	South Shields	15	Sep
1:02:53	Ian Hudspith		23.09.70	6	Schevenigen, HOL	31	Mar
1:02:55	Mark Flint		19.02.63	1	Hastings	17	Mar
1:03:28	Gary Staines		3.07.63	4	South Shields	15	Sep
1:03:31					Reading	31	Mar
1:03:41	Justin Hobbs		12.03.69	1	Worcester	16	Mar
1:03:42	Steve Brace		7.07.61	1	Fleet	24	Mar
1:03:52				6	Setubal, POR	31	Mar
1:03:44	Dave Swanston		30.11.61	22	Palma, SPA	29	Sep
1:03:48	Mark Hudspith		19.01.69	2	Fleet	24	Mar
1:03:50	Bill Foster		9.08.58	3	Fleet	24	Mar
(10)							
1:03:50	Steve Brooks		8.06.70	1	Deurne, HOL	8	Sep
1:03:56	Brian Rushworth		14.12.62	4	Trosloop, HOL	13	Oct
1:03:57	Steve Knight		17.10.63	3	Worcester	16	Mar
1:03:57	Peter Fleming		5.01.61	14	Philadelphia, USA	22	Sep
1:04:00	Eamonn Martin		9.10.58	1	South Shields	15	Sep
1:04:04	Peter Whitehead		3.12.64	6	South Shields	15	Sep
1:04:09	Barry Royden		15.12.66	16	Schevenigen, HOL	31	Mar
1:04:14	Mark Peters			4	Worcester	16	Mar
1:04:16	Martin Cox			1	Bristol	12	May
1:04:17	Ian Cornford		1.02.66	1	Exeter	5	May
(20)							
1:04:31	Mark Steinle	U23	22.11.74	2	Hamburg, GER	15	Sep
1:04:42	Phil Makepeace		15.03.64	6	Glasgow	25	Aug
1:04:46	Tony O'Brien		14.11.70	1	Bolton	28	Jul
1:04:48	Dave Tune		29.10.70	2	Liverpool	2	Aug
1:04:50	Paul Roden		18.04.65	3	Liverpool	25	Aug
1:04:50	Dale Rixon		8.07.66	6	Trosloop, HOL	13	Oct
1:04:51	Graeme Croll		1.02.66	8	Glasgow	25	Aug
1:04:54	Mark Croasdale		10.01.60	10	South Shields	15	Sep
1:04:56	Darren Hiscox			11	South Shields	15	Sep

short course (49m)

| 1:03:32 | Jon Solly | | 28.06.63 | 12 | Milan, ITA | 30 | Mar |
| 1:03:50 | Martin McLoughlin | | 23.12.58 | 14 | Milan, ITA | 30 | Mar |

Foreign

1:04:25	*John Lisiewicz*		*18.07.62*	*2*	*Bristol*	*12*	*May*
1:04:27	*Siti Mohammed*		*21.05.62*	*1*	*Yate*	*14*	*Jul*
1:04:33	*Kassa Tadesse*	*U23*	*21.08.74*	*7*	*South Shields*	*15*	*Sep*

MARATHON

Time	Name		DOB	Pos	Location	Date	
2:08:52	Paul Evans		13.04.61	1	Chicago, USA	20	Oct
2:10:40				3	London	21	Apr
2:10:35	Steve Brace		7.07.61	2	Houston, USA	21	Jan
2:15:47				8	Belgrade, YUG	20	Apr
2:11:21	Eamonn Martin		9.10.58	4	Chicago, USA	20	Oct
2:11:25	Gary Staines		3.07.63	5	Chicago, USA	20	Oct
2:12:54				9	London	21	Apr
2:12:25	Jon Solly		28.06.63	2	Turin, ITA	12	May
2:13:39	Richard Nerurkar		6.01.64	5	Atlanta, USA	4	Aug
2:13:41	Dale Rixon		8.07.66	4	Puteaux, FRA	10	Nov
2:16:19	Mike O'Reilly		23.04.58	21	Tokyo, JAP	12	Feb
2:16:58	Peter Fleming		5.01.61	3	Duluth, USA	23	Jun
2:20:00				2	Columbus, USA	10	Nov
2:18:55	Mark Flint		19.02.63	32	Berlin, GER	29	Sep
(10)							
2:18:55	Bill Foster		9.08.58	19	Beijing, CHN	20	Oct
2:19:25	Mark Hudspith		19.01.69	18	London	21	Apr
2:19:36	Chris Penney		10.05.57	6	Seville, SPA	25	Feb
2:19:58	Stephen Green		28.07.70	5	Sacramento, USA	8	Dec
2:20:02	Chris Parkes		17.04.64	1	Sheffield	28	Apr
2:20:18	Steve Brooks		8.06.70	17	Eindhoven, HOL	13	Oct
	20 performances to 2:21:00 by 16 athletes						
2:21:36	Terry Mitchell		23.08.59	1	Belfast	6	May
2:21:37	Gregor Booth		31.08.62	2	Belfast	6	May
2:21:53	Shaun Tobin		13.10.62	21	Chicago, USA	20	Oct
2:22:13	John Ferrin		20.02.67	3	Belfast	6	May
(20)							
2:22:20	Mark Croasdale		10.01.60	6	Hamburg, GER	21	Apr
2:22:22	Alan Shepherd		28.04.69	46	Berlin, GER	29	Sep
2:22:28	Dave Mansbridge		4.06.64		Palma, SPA	15	Dec
2:22:37	Peter Whitehead		3.12.64	55	Atlanta, USA	4	Aug
2:22:40	Brian Rushworth		14.12.62	6	,.TAI	24	Nov
2:22:44	Sam Stevenson		20.12.63	26	London	21	Apr
2:22:58	Hugh Jones	V40	1.11.55	28	New York, USA	3	Nov
2:23:13	Peter Wilson		28.06.62	1	Abingdon	20	Oct
2:23:31	Ieuan Ellis		11.05.60	1	Leeds	14	Jul
2:23:32	Bashir Hussain		20.12.64	1	Manchester	13	Oct
(30)							
2:23:46	Dennis Walmsley			10	Lausanne, SWZ	13	Oct
2:23:59	Gary Bishop		3.08.63	29	London	21	Apr
2:24:11	Gary McIlroy		6.04.67	30	London	21	Apr
2:24:11	Jerry Hall		22.08.58	7	Dublin, IRE	28	Oct
2:24:14	Tony Duffy		26.06.56	31	London	21	Apr
2:24:32	Andrew Arrand		20.01.66	5	Gold Coast, AUS	21	Jul
2:25:28	Jon Hooper		22.07.64	2	Leeds	14	Jul
2:25:33	Tony Barden		15.10.60	34	London	21	Apr
2:25:39	Paul Froud		6.04.66	35	London	21	Apr
2:25:53	Scott Cohen		6.12.64	59	Boston, USA	16	Apr
(40)							
2:25:58	Steve Davies		4.02.58	28	Reims, FRA	20	Oct
2:26:16	Peter Smyth			4	Belfast	6	May
2:26:26	Mark Roberts		12.02.59	1	Stoke	16	Jun
2:26:59	Eddie Stewart		15.12.56		Prague, CZE	19	May
2:27:08	Robin Nash		9.02.59	66	Boston, USA	16	Apr
2:27:40	Peter Pleasants		29.07.62	38	London	21	Apr
2:27:49	P. Mangan			8	Dublin, IRE	28	Oct
2:28:02	Dave Hill	V45	31.12.50	39	London	21	Apr
2:28:05	Simon Bell		26.12.66	37	Rotterdam, HOL	28	Apr
2:28:17	Roy Smith			72	Boston, USA	16	Apr
(50)							

Time	Name	Cat	DOB	No	Location	Date
2:28:25	Fraser Clyne	V40	23.08.55	1	Greenock	15 Sep
2:28:30	John Duffy	V40	10.11.55	3	Malmo, SWE	Jul
2:28:32	Martin Ferguson		17.09.64	74	Boston, USA	16 Apr
2:28:54	Colin Deasy				Utrecht, HOL	27 May
2:29:05	Andy Holt		23.02.64	1	New Milton	8 Sep
2:29:05	James Jackson		12.09.63	2	Chiswick	22 Sep
2:29:16	John Weir		24.12.66	5	Belfast	6 May
2:29:26	Richard Sales		28.05.62	42	London	21 Apr
2:29:29	Craig Watters		18.07.67	2	Luton	1 Dec
2:29:34	Steve Lonnen		26.06.57	3	Chiswick	22 Sep
	(60)					
2:29:44	Kevin Vose		28.11.58	6	Belfast	6 May
2:29:44	Lee Kelly		11.06.62	4	Chiswick	22 Sep
2:29:52	Stephen Keywood		28.09.61	5	Chiswick	22 Sep
2:30:07	Simon Kinson		3.12.70	6	Chiswick	22 Sep
2:30:08	Ronnie James		14.12.64	7	Chiswick	22 Sep
2:30:11	Gary Eagle		28.12.60	45	London	21 Apr
2:30:38	Alan Ruben	V40		94	Boston, USA	16 Apr
2:30:43	Mark Gregory			3	Stoke	16 Jun
2:30:53	Stewart MacDonald			3	Manchester	13 Oct
2:30:58	Greg Dell		20.11.64	48	London	21 Apr
	(70)					
2:31:05	Simon Lund		22.12.65		Calvia, SPA	8 Dec
2:31:19	Mark Cursons		10.03.62	50	London	21 Apr
2:31:19	Paul Smith	V40	12.08.54	16	Amsterdam, HOL	3 Nov
2:31:26	Mike McGeoch	V40	15.08.55	57	London	21 Apr
2:31:29	David Laing		1.01.66	51	London	21 Apr
2:31:32	Simon Shiels			2	Nottingham	29 Sep
2:31:37	Brian Scally		9.05.66	3	Greenock	15 Sep
2:31:39	Paul Verity		22.12.56	53	London	21 Apr
2:31:41	Andy Wilton		14.12.60	54	London	21 Apr
2:31:47	Darren Hale		2.10.59	56	London	21 Apr
	(80)					
2:31:52	Maylo Donnelly	V40		8	Belfast	6 May
2:31:59	Geoff Robinson		20.06.59	57	London	21 Apr
2:32:08	Karl Wellstead		2.06.71	60	London	21 Apr
2:32:10	Reggie Hewitt			9	Belfast	6 May
2:32:16	Colin Moore		25.11.60	20	Sacramento, USA	8 Dec
2:32:17	Gary Hetherington		13.09.59	61	London	21 Apr
2:32:19	Derek Brown		23.01.60	63	London	21 Apr
2:32:19	Richie Bullen		6.10.60	17	Amsterdam, HOL	3 Nov
2:32:26	Simon Booth		10.05.68	64	London	21 Apr
2:32:31	David Thomson			1	Gosport	28 Apr
	(90)					
2:32:47	Mike Peters		1.10.60	66	London	21 Apr
2:32:52	Michael Miles	V40	11.04.53	3	Leeds	14 Jul
2:32:53	Bill Speake		24.01.71	67	London	21 Apr
2:32:58	Paul Rogers		24.03.65	132	Boston, USA	16 Apr
2:33:01	Shaun Milford		13.07.63	1	Paington	13 Oct
2:33:06	Dennis Smith	V45	26.01.49	68	London	21 Apr
2:33:10	John Redmond		15.10.57	69	London	21 Apr
2:33:11	Bernard Gaffney		8.06.61	70	London	21 Apr
2:33:12	Nick Lees		23.01.58	3	Nottingham	29 Sep
2:33:17	Jeff Martin			71	London	21 Apr
	(100)					

Foreign

Time	Name		DOB	No	Location	Date
2:19:22	Eddie Hyland		23.07.60	1	Karlsruhe, GER	22 Sep
2:23:52	Adri Hartveld		7.10.59		Naaldwijk, HOL	13 Apr
2:31:41	Michael Kazimierski		6.05.70	55	London	21 Apr

100 KILOMETRES (Road)

Time	Name	Cat	DOB	Pos	Venue	Date
6:56:13	Patrick Macke	V40	18.06.55		Saroma, JAP	23 Jun
7:35:37					Shimanto	20 Oct
7:02:00	Steve Moore	V45	17.12.47		Moscow,RUS	4 May
7:17:16				1	Edinburgh	21 Jul
7:28:14					Cleder, FRA	25 Aug
7:07:49	Willie Sichel	V40	1.10.53		Torhout, BEL	21 Jun
7:19:11					Moscow,RUS	4 May
7:31:46					Cleder, FRA	25 Aug
7:18:56	Martin Eccles		16.01.57		Cleder, FRA	25 Aug
7:38:08	Walter Hill			1	Greenwich	14 Apr
7:38:15	Don Ritchie	V50	6.07.44	2	Edinburgh	21 Jul
8:11:20					Cleder, FRA	25 Aug
7:58:55	James Zarei	V50	12.01.44	2	Greenwich	14 Apr
8:01:38	Simon Pride			3	Edinburgh	21 Jul
8:05:48	Shane Downes			4	Edinburgh	21 Jul
8:18:59	Brian Harney			5	Edinburgh	21 Jul

(10)

24 HOURS (Track)

Distance	Name	Cat	DOB	Pos	Venue	Date
220.490 km	Alden Barlow			1	Doncaster	25 May
219.689 km	Richard Brown	V45	18.11.46	1	Schiedam, HOL	18 May
217.675 km	Martin Eccles		16.01.57	20	Courcon, FRA	21 Sep
213.648 km	Jim Fletcher			2	Doncaster	25 May
207.360 km	Robert Brown			1	Hull	13 Jul
205.691 km	Geoff Oliver			3	Doncaster	25 May
202.549 km	Willie Sichel	V40	1.10.53	1	Tooting	12 Oct

1500 METRES STEEPLECHASE - Under 17

Time	Name	DOB	Pos	Venue	Date
4:22.81	Iain Murdoch	10.07.80	1	Birmingham	18 Aug
4:24.11	Simon Lees	19.11.79	1	Birmingham	20 Apr
4:24.33	Andrew Murphy	14.09.79	1	Sheffield	13 Jul
4:25.5	Tom Kingsnorth	15.10.79	2	Stoke	20 Jul
4:25.6	Adam Costello	12.09.79	1	Rotherham	23 Jun
4:27.03	Michael Henry	9.10.79	2	Birmingham	18 Aug
4:29.1	Jaron McKay	17.09.79	1	Dublin, IRE	22 Jun
4:29.90	Daniel Hewitt	13.11.79	3	Sheffield	13 Jul
4:29.9	Simon Wray	19.03.80	1	Telford	8 Jun
4:31.5	Gary Blackman	24.09.80	1	Wolverhampton	2 Jun

(10)

Time	Name	DOB	Pos	Venue	Date
4:31.9	Matt Lemon	6.02.80	1	Hoo	8 Jun
4:32.04	Keith Grant	17.03.80	4	Sheffield	13 Jul
4:33.3	Ross Gillespie		1	Antrim	17 Jun
4:34.79	Mark Smallwood	6.09.79	4	Birmingham	18 Aug
4:36.1	Chris Thompson	17.04.81	1	Windsor	21 Jul
4:36.7	Paul Gronow	14.09.79	1	Cwmbran	2 Jun
4:37.19	Danny Gray	23.10.80	1	Birmingham	8 Sep
4:37.6	Glen Davison	8.09.79	2	Middlesbrough	15 Jun
4:37.6	Kieron Farrelly	14.10.80	1	Walton	16 Jun
4:37.93	Niall Cameron	19.12.79	3h2	Birmingham	17 Aug

(20)

Time	Name	DOB	Pos	Venue	Date
4:38.00	Phil Eaves	28.02.80	3h1	Birmingham	17 Aug

2000 METRES STEEPLECHASE

Time	Name	Cat	DOB	Pos	Venue	Date
5:38.6	Spencer Duval		5.01.70	1	Loughborough	5 Jun
5:40.9	Carl Warren		28.09.69	2	Loughborough	5 Jun
5:47.1				1	Stoke	12 May
5:42.20	Spencer Newport		5.10.66	1	Luton	6 May
5:44.47	Stuart Stokes	U23	15.12.76	1	Cudworth	3 Aug

5:44.53	Mike Jubb		20.06.70	2	Barnsley	3 Aug
5:45.4	Ray Plant		13.05.68	3	Loughborough	5 Jun
5:46.03	Andy Coleman	U23	29.09.74	2	Luton	6 May
5:47.1	Dave Lee		16.09.65	4	Loughborough	5 Jun
5:48.08	Rob Berry		29.07.69	3	Barnsley	3 Aug
5:50.84	Lee Hurst		29.07.72	3	Luton	6 May
(10)						
5:51.7	Sean Fenwick		20.07.70	5	Loughborough	5 Jun
5:54.39	Pat Miller		21.02.67	4	Cudworth	3 Aug
5:55.1	Paul Morby	U20	15.01.79	1	Solihull	30 Jun
5:56.0	Danny Duke		23.12.68		Stellenbosch, RSA	18 Mar
5:56.2	Robert Brown	U20	3.03.78	1	Jarrow	12 May
5:56.9	Simon Wurr	U20	7.01.77	2	Solihull	30 Jun
5:57.93	Simon Bell		26.12.66	3	Luton	6 May
5:58.03	Stuart Bailey	U20	6.08.78	2	Sheffield	13 Jul
5:58.83	David Mitchinson	U20	4.09.78	3	Sheffield	13 Jul
5:59.0	Colin Palmer		27.07.67	1	Aldershot	26 Jun
(20)						
5:59.4	Ciaran McGuire	U23	1.07.74	1	Coventry	7 Jul
5:59.5	Andrew Hennessy	U20	24.08.77	1	Oxford	26 May
5:59.5	Phil Cook		7.05.69	1	Colwyn Bay	26 Aug
5:59.56	Joe Collins	U20	20.01.78	4	Sheffield	13 Jul
5:59.8	Mike Peters		1.10.60	2	Aldershot	26 Jun
5:59.9	Paul Martin	U20	10.07.78	1	Hoo	8 Jun

Additional Under 20 (1 - 8 above)

6:02.5	Delroy Simon		27.11.78	1	London (He)	8 Jun
6:02.6	Ben Whitby		6.01.77	1	Derby	15 Sep
(10)						
6:05.2	Gavin Maley		19.05.78	1	Thurrock	11 May
6:05.39	Tim Davis		25.01.78	1	London (He)	7 Jul
6:07.1	Matthew Amos		20.11.78	3	Solihull	30 Jun

3000 METRES STEEPLECHASE

8:26.33	Robert Hough		3.06.72	4	Hechtel, BEL	6 Jul
				2	Aarhus, DEN	20 Jun
	8:29.83					
	8:43.30			5	Birmingham	16 Jun
	8:49.49			3h1	Birmingham	14 Jun
8:28.32	Justin Chaston		4.11.68	5h2	Atlanta, USA	29 Jul
	8:28.50			9s2	Atlanta, USA	31 Jul
	8:29.19			1	Birmingham	16 Jun
	8:29.64			4	Portland, USA	12 May
	8:30.33			15	Brussels, BEL	23 Aug
	8:33.59			3	Madrid, SPA	2 Jun
	8:35.74			2	Istanbul, TUR	19 May
	8:36.4			5	Walnut, USA	21 Apr
	8:45.19			2h2	Birmingham	14 Jun
	8:47.6			1	London (He)	31 Aug
	8:49.2			1	Kingston	17 Aug
8:28.93	Keith Cullen		13.06.72	12	Stockholm, SWE	8 Jul
	8:30.69			6	Bratislava, SVK	29 May
	8:30.80			2	Birmingham	16 Jun
	8:31.26			6h3	Atlanta, USA	29 Jul
	8:46.74			11s1	Atlanta, USA	31 Jul
	8:47.88			1h1	Birmingham	14 Jun
8:36.71	Spencer Duval		5.01.70	3	Birmingham	16 Jun
	8:46.76			10h1	Atlanta, USA	29 Jul
	8:49.67			5h2	Birmingham	14 Jun
8:41.54	Mick Hawkins		24.10.61	4	Birmingham	16 Jun
	8:45.12			1h2	Birmingham	14 Jun

8:43.21	Kevin Nash	U20	6.02.77	1	London (CP)	2	Jun
8:44.26	Matt O'Dowd	U23	13.04.76	6	Birmingham	16	Jun
8:49.34				4h2	Birmingham	14	Jun
8:46.51	Spencer Newport		5.10.66	7	Birmingham	16	Jun
8:46.56				2	London (CP)	2	Jun
8:48.34	Lee Hurst		29.07.72	2h1	Birmingham	14	Jun
8:48.60	Dave Lee		16.09.65	2	Zofingen, SWZ	27	May
	(10)						
8:48.99	Carl Warren		28.09.69	3h2	Birmingham	14	Jun
8:49.03	Jason Humm		11.01.71	3	London (CP)	2	Jun
	35 performances to 8:50.0 by 12 athletes						
8:50.14	Adrian Green		30.05.68	4h1	Birmingham	14	Jun
8:50.37	Mike Jubb		20.06.70	6h2	Birmingham	14	Jun
8:50.40	Andrew Morgan-Lee		1.03.69	4	London (CP)	2	Jun
8:51.34	Graeme Croll		1.02.66	1	Edinburgh	16	Jun
8:51.52	Darren Preston	U23	19.12.74	7h2	Birmingham	14	Jun
8:52.64	Ray Plant		13.05.68	8h1	Birmingham	14	Jun
8:53.39	Simon Bell		26.12.66	9h1	Birmingham	14	Jun
8:54.1	Brian Montgomery	U23	19.07.74	4	Chapel Hill, USA	11	May
	(20)						
8:54.8	Chris Stephenson	U23	22.07.74	1	London (He)	9	Jun
8:54.91	Tom Buckner		16.04.63	10h1	Birmingham	14	Jun
8:56.92	Phil Cook		7.05.69	11h1	Birmingham	14	Jun
8:57.47	Pat Miller		21.02.67	9h2	Birmingham	14	Jun
8:58.7	Alan Crossan		6.01.72	2	London (He)	9	Jun
8:59.09	Ben Whitby	U20	6.01.77	1	Bedford	27	Jul
9:00.03	Tom Hanlon		20.05.67	12h1	Birmingham	14	Jun
9:01.8	Stuart Stokes	U23	15.12.76	1	Wakefield	11	Aug
9:02.77	Charlie Low	U23	9.10.74	13h1	Birmingham	14	Jun
9:03.10	Justin Reid		26.09.69	10h2	Birmingham	14	Jun
	(30)						
9:03.15	Hugh Brasher		28.09.64	6	London (CP)	2	Jun
9:04.8	Danny Duke		23.12.68	1	Salisbury	12	May
9:05.2	Patrick Davoren		13.03.72	1	London (WL)	17	Aug
9:05.85	Steve Cairns		3.11.67	1	Edinburgh	16	Jun
9:06.12	Donald Naylor		5.09.71	1	Sheffield	6	May
9:06.24	Martin Yelling		7.02.72	1	London (He)	1	Sep
9:06.66	Tim Hyde		22.02.72	11h2	Birmingham	14	Jun
9:06.7	Rob Berry		29.07.69	1	Wakefield	17	Aug
9:06.9	Darius Burrows	U23	8.08.75	1	Stoke	28	Jul
9:07.4	Graham Sunners		26.03.73	1	Portsmouth	21	Jul
	(40)						
9:07.69	Darren Mead		4.10.68	2	Birmingham	6	Jul
9:08.0	Mark Hirsch		31.03.63	2	Kingston	17	Aug
9:08.72	Andy Coleman	U23	29.09.74	5	Sheffield	25	Aug
9:09.06	Andy Eynon		1.09.62	4	Cardiff	25	May
9:09.1	Colin Palmer		27.07.67	1	Portsmouth	2	Jul
9:10.02	Dave Farrell		29.06.64	14h1	Birmingham	14	Jun
9:10.4	Ciaran McGuire	U23	1.07.74	1	London (He)	28	Jul
9:11.02	John Steel		27.02.63	2	Edinburgh	16	Jun
9:12.3	Roger Hackney		2.09.57	2	Portsmouth	2	Jul
9:12.82	Ben Reese	U23	29.03.76	1	Oxford, USA	18	May
	(50)						
9:13.0	Andy Beevers		3.05.73	1	Middlesbrough	20	Jul
9:14.7	Ali Eden			4	Watford	6	Jul
9:15.1	Kevin Usher		3.11.65	5	Watford	6	Jul
9:15.6	Eddie Broome		3.09.72	1	Bolton	14	Sep
9:15.78	Mark McDowell	U23	10.07.74	6	Dublin, IRE	15	Jun
9:17.5	Martin Roscoe		19.09.64	1	Blackpool	12	May
9:17.5	Steve O'Gara		3.12.69	2	Bolton	14	Sep
9:17.58	Jeff Pyrah		6.07.72	8	Sheffield	25	Aug

9:17.62	Chris Elliott	U23	29.05.75	4	Sheffield	6 May
9:17.9	Mike Hoey		29.04.69	1	London (TB)	3 Aug
(60)						
9:18.08	Simon Wurr	U20	7.01.77	2	Birmingham	2 Jun
9:18.97	Mark Dalkins		9.09.71	2	Newport	8 Jun
9:19.05	Stephen Norris		21.06.68	2	Antrim	7 Jul
9:19.37	Jon Pavis		4.10.66	4	Birmingham	6 Jul
9:19.55	Bashir Hussain		20.12.64	1	Cerritos, USA	18 May
9:20.0	Stuart Bailey	U20	6.08.78	2	Jarrow	4 May
9:20.0	Andrew Hennessy	U20	24.08.77	1	Exeter	23 Jun
9:20.2	Neil Wilkinson		12.03.69	1	Stretford	9 Jun
9:20.31	Iain Robertson	U23	23.06.75	1rB	Birmingham	6 Jul
9:20.5	William Burns		2		Blackpool	12 May
(70)						
9:21.6	Jason Lendon	U23	17.03.75	2	London (TB)	3 Aug
9:21.79	Ken Stirrat		1.03.70	4	Blackpool	16 Jun
9:21.9	Wayne Aylesbury		24.03.64	3	Jarrow	4 May
9:22.2	Simon Wilson		8.03.66	3	Watford	17 Aug
9:23.3	Dave Heath		22.05.65	4	Crawley	28 Jul
9:23.57	Craig Siddons		4.06.73	4	Sheffield	2 Jun
9:23.8	Andy Fooks	U23	26.04.75	1	Yeovil	28 Jul
9:24.1	Michael Hutchinson		5.10.65	2	Liverpool	9 Jun
9:24.3	Julian Emery			4	Bath	19 Jun
9:24.72	James Austin		9.08.65	3	Edinburgh	16 Jun
(80)						
9:25.0	Dean Coventon		3.11.70	6	Peterborough	4 May
9:25.9	Martin Amor		22.09.68	1	Liverpool	28 Jul
9:25.9	Joe Collins	U20	20.01.78	3	Cannock	7 Sep
9:26.6	Martin Ferguson		17.09.64	6	Enfield	6 Jul
9:29.2	Dave Baxter	U20	16.01.79	5	London (He)	31 Aug
9:29.4	Eddie Tonner		3.02.73	3	Glasgow	29 Jun
9:29.5	Donald Lennon-Jones		9.05.68	1	Thurrock	11 May

Additional Under 20 (1 - 7 above)

9:30.68	David Mitchinson		4.09.78	8h1	London (CP)	1 Jun
9:31.46	Paul Morby		15.01.79	2	Cannock	23 Jun
9:32.5	Robert Brown		3.03.78	9	Bedford	26 May
(10)						
9:41.49	Jamie Loxam		7.07.77	6	Bedford	27 Jul
9:43.8	Matthew Amos		20.11.78	1	Corby	12 May

Foreign

9:11.7	*John Mutai*			*1*	*Birmingham*	*10 Aug*
9:12.6	*Marc Poulin*			*2*	*Portsmouth*	*21 Jul*
9:16.0	*Svein Risa*	*U23*	*7.03.74*	*2*	*Bath*	*19 Jun*

60 METRES HURDLES - Indoor

7.51	Colin Jackson	18.02.67	1	Maebashi, JAP	12 Feb
7.57	Tony Jarrett	13.08.68	3	Stuttgart, GER	4 Feb
	7.62		1	Birmingham	10 Feb
	7.68		1h2	Stuttgart, GER	4 Feb
7.72	Neil Owen	18.10.73	2	Glasgow	24 Feb
	7.79		3	Vienna, AUT	17 Feb
	7.81		1	Birmingham	3 Feb
	7.86		3h1	Vienna, AUT	17 Feb
	7.87		2	Birmingham	27 Jan
	7.89		1	Birmingham	6 Jan
	7.89		7	Birmingham	10 Feb
	7.96		1h2	Birmingham	3 Feb

7.88		Andy Tulloch		1.04.67	3	Birmingham	3	Feb
		7.90			4	Birmingham	27	Jan
		7.90			4	Glasgow	24	Feb
		7.94			2h1	Birmingham	3	Feb
7.95		Brian Taylor		13.08.70	2	Birmingham	6	Jan
		17 performances to 8.00 by 5 athletes						
8.08		Ross Baillie	U20	26.09.77	2	Lievin, FRA	2	Mar
8.13		Hugh Teape		26.12.63	3h2	Birmingham	3	Feb
8.15		Jamie Quarry		15.11.72	1	Glasgow	17	Mar
8.16		Simon McAree	U23	28.12.75	3h1	Birmingham	3	Feb
8.22		Matthew Clements	U20	17.09.77	1h2	Birmingham	17	Feb
(10)								
8.23		James Archampong	U23	14.03.76	2	Glasgow	17	Mar
8.26		Mark Lambeth		3.09.72	4h1	Birmingham	3	Feb
8.28		Ererton Harrison		8.04.66	5h1	Birmingham	3	Feb
8.31		Paul Gripton	U23	9.11.76	1rB	Birmingham	3	Feb
8.32		Barry Thomas		28.04.72	2H	Valencia, SPA	28	Jan
8.34		Alex Kruger		18.11.63	H	Stockholm, SWE	10	Mar
8.35		Rafer Joseph		21.07.68	2H	Valencia, SPA	28	Jan
8.40		Andrew David		9.09.69	3rB	Birmingham	3	Feb
8.44		Andrew Carter	U17	18.10.79	4rB	Birmingham	3	Feb

Hand Timing

8.2		Mark Lambeth		(8.26)	1	London (Ha)	13	Jan
8.2		Matthew Clements	U20	(8.22)	1r2	London (CP)	10	Feb
8.3		Andrew David		(8.40)	1	London (CP)	6	Jan
8.4		William Gilles		15.02.73		London (CP)	21	Jan
8.4		Kirk Harries	U23	7.08.74	2	London (CP)	7	Dec

Foreign

8.3		*Pascal Renaud*		*20.04.70*	*2*	*London (Ha)*	*13*	*Jan*

75 METRES HURDLES - Under 13 (2'3")

12.57	A. Rees			Colwyn Bay	9	Sep
12.6	Christopher Bodys	29.12.83	1	Dumfries	18	Aug

80 METRES HURDLES - Under 15 (2'9")

11.10	1.8	Seb Bastow	11.10.81	1	Sheffield	13	Jul
11.3		John Marsden	23.10.81	1	Aberdare	28	Jul
		11.48	0.7		2	Birmingham	17	Aug
11.47	1.8	Jonathon Crawshaw	28.09.81	2	Sheffield	13	Jul
11.5	1.4	Ken McKeown	6.03.82	1	Pitreavie	19	Jun
		11.55	0.8		1	Birmingham	7	Sep
11.54	0.7	Phillip Walsh	26.10.81	3	Birmingham	17	Aug
11.54	1.8	Chris Jenkins	2.03.82	1P	Birmingham	21	Sep
11.68	0.2	Stephen Padmore	29.11.81	1h2	Sheffield	12	Jul
11.70	0.2	Darren Adams	4.02.82	2h2	Sheffield	12	Jul
11.77	0.2	Ian Ward	3.04.82	3h2	Sheffield	12	Jul
11.8		Nathan Palmer		1	Cwmbran	23	Jun
(10)							
11.86	1.8	Dominic Saben	27.02.82	5	Sheffield	13	Jul
11.9		Dominic Girdler	6.03.82	1	Cannock	31	Aug
		11.99	-0.2		2h2	Birmingham	17	Aug
12.00	-0.2	Alex Golding	3.12.81	3	Birmingham	8	Sep
12.0		Matthew Bradley	21.09.81	1	York	8	Jun
12.02	0.7	Graeme Lammie	3.10.81	6	Birmingham	17	Aug
12.03	0.8	Nange Ursell	1.10.81	1P	Birmingham	21	Sep
12.10	1.3	Faried Dkadik	21.12.81	3h1	Sheffield	12	Jul
12.1		Aidan Turnbull	1.09.81	2	Jarrow	11	May
12.1		M. Karim		3	Kingston	8	Jun

Time	Wind	Name	DOB	Pos	Venue	Day	Month
12.1		Matthew Horsham	13.10.81	1h1	Yeovil	8	Jun
(20)							
12.1		Oliver Price	10.12.81	1	London (He)	9	Jun
12.1		Martin Taylor	31.01.82	1	Glasgow	12	Jun
12.1		Ryan Gostick	12.02.82	1	Andover	30	Jun
12.1		Lolimar Pagkatipunan	17.11.82	1	London (Elt)	21	Jul
12.1		Christopher Fuller	2.02.82		Bournemouth		
12.11	0.8	David Brackstone	13.03.82	1h3	Sheffield	12	Jul
12.15	1.8	Matthew Barclay	28.01.82	1P	Birmingham	21	Sep
12.17	1.3	Aaron Musker	23.03.82	4h1	Sheffield	12	Jul

100 METRES HURDLES - Under 17 (3'0")

Time	Wind	Name	DOB	Pos	Venue	Day	Month
13.07	1.6	David O'Leary	3.08.80	1	Cudworth	3	Aug
13.22 w	2.7	Tyrone Carr	30.07.80	2	Sheffield	13	Jul
13.5				1	Basildon	8	Jun
13.52	1.5			1h1	Sheffield	12	Jul
13.33 w	2.7	Dan Brewer	10.08.80	3	Sheffield	13	Jul
13.34	1.9			2	Birmingham	17	Aug
13.4		Osagai Omenai	8.02.81	1	Southampton	15	Jun
13.49 w	2.3			3h3	Sheffield	12	Jul
13.63 w	2.7			4	Sheffield	13	Jul
13.91	0.4			1	Portsmouth	12	May
13.44	1.9	Robert Hollinger	11.10.80	3	Birmingham	17	Aug
13.44 w	2.3	Robert Newton	10.05.81	2h3	Sheffield	12	Jul
13.6	-1.1			1	Solihull	29	Jun
13.71	1.9			5	Birmingham	17	Aug
13.46	1.9	Chris Low	24.04.80	4	Birmingham	17	Aug
13.65 w	2.7	Patrick Brown	2.09.79	5	Sheffield	13	Jul
13.79	1.5			2h1	Sheffield	12	Jul
13.68	1.1	Chris Baillie	21.04.81	3h1	Birmingham	17	Aug
13.7		Steve Surety	18.02.80	1	Barking	1	Sep
(10)							
13.73 w	2.7	Marc Wareham	9.08.80	6	Sheffield	13	Jul
13.77	1.9			6	Birmingham	17	Aug
13.8		Jason McDade	3.04.80	1	Ipswich	16	Jun
14.14	0.6			2O	Birmingham	21	Sep
13.8		Shaun Robson	21.06.80	1	Brecon	1	Sep
14.14				2	Carmarthen	30	Jun
13.90 w	2.2	John Monds	24.03.80	3h2	Sheffield	12	Jul
14.2				1	Wrexham	19	May
13.9		Paul Campbell	29.01.80	2	Middlesbrough	15	Jun
13.9		Leon McRae	3.11.80	1O	Carn Brea	22	Jun
13.9		David Sargeant	23.01.80	1	Great Yarmouth	28	Jul
13.9 w	4.3	Kevin Knox	26.05.80	2	Stoke	22	Jun
13.91 w	2.2	Andrew Pearcy	5.04.80	4h2	Sheffield	12	Jul
14.15	-1.0			4	Cudworth	30	Jun
13.94 w	2.3	Sam Stephenson	15.05.80	4h3	Sheffield	12	Jul
14.17	0.0			3	Birmingham	8	Sep
(20)							
14.0		Michael Sleet	6.06.80	2	Hoo	8	Jun
14.12 w	2.3			6h3	Sheffield	12	Jul
14.0		Luke Gittins		1	Cwmbran	23	Jun
14.0		Colin Roberts	20.01.81	1	Cambridge	15	Sep
14.07	1.5			4h1	Sheffield	12	Jul
14.0 w	2.7	Paul Armstrong	20.10.79	2	Pitreavie	15	Jun
14.1	2.0			1h2	Pitreavie	15	Jun
14.13 w	2.3			4h2	Birmingham	17	Aug
14.03 w	2.3	Finlay Wright	7.02.81	5h3	Sheffield	12	Jul
14.2				1	Bracknell	9	Jun

14.07 w 2.2	Kevin Drury	30.09.79	5h2	Sheffield	12	Jul
14.12			1	Carmarthen	30	Jun
14.1	Neil Hewson	4.09.80	1	Hull	19	May
14.1 1.0	Lee Tindall	19.02.80	1	Portsmouth	8	Jun
14.13 1.5			5h1	Sheffield	12	Jul
14.1	Richard Gawthorpe	28.01.81	1	Sheffield	19	Jun
14.1 1.6	Ben Roberts	15.01.80	2	Swansea	6	Jul
14.11			1	Colwyn Bay	26	Aug
(30)						
14.1 w	Rhys Williams		1	Cardiff	8	May
14.16 w 2.3	Austen Smith	26.09.79	7h3	Sheffield	12	Jul
14.2	Gary Hall	25.07.80	O	Horsham	28	May
14.2	Jody Murfitt	3.12.79	1=	Norwich	9	Jun
14.2	Benjamin Seiden	21.02.80	2	Southampton	15	Jun
14.2 0.8	Michael Strain	11.09.79	2h2	Pitreavie	19	Jun
14.2	Chris Herring	3.03.81	1	Chester-Le-Street	23	Jun
14.2	Scott Porter	12.12.79	1	Carlisle	14	Jul
14.2	Paul Timba	21.03.80	1	Windsor	28	Jul

110 METRES HURDLES - Under 20 (3'3")

14.11 w 2.5	Tony Gill	19.09.77	1	Sheffield	13	Jul
14.78 -1.6			1	London (He)	10	Aug
14.18 w 2.5	Ben Warmington	20.03.79	2	Sheffield	13	Jul
14.86 -1.6			3	London (He)	10	Aug
14.29 w 2.5	Steven Scott	5.06.79	3	Sheffield	13	Jul
14.69 1.8			2h2	Sheffield	12	Jul
14.37 w 2.5	Richard Churchill	29.09.77	4	Sheffield	13	Jul
14.60 1.8			1h2	Sheffield	12	Jul
14.46 w 2.5	Nick Dowsett	24.11.78	5	Sheffield	13	Jul
15.36			D	Birmingham	22	Sep
14.53 w 2.1	Damien Greaves	19.09.77	2	London (He)	7	Jul
14.61 1.0			1h2	London (He)	7	Jul
14.68 w 2.9	Scott Exley	9.02.78	3h1	Sheffield	12	Jul
14.70 w 6.8	Adam Tibbets	14.12.78	2	Stoke	22	Jun
14.72 w 2.8	Stephen Edwards	13.06.77	1	Carmarthen	16	Jul
15.08 -0.7			1	Carmarthen	30	Jun
14.80 1.6	Duncan Malins	12.06.78	1	Crawley	12	May
(10)						
14.80 w 2.1	Richard Sear	21.08.79	3	London (He)	7	Jul
14.95 1.8			5h2	Sheffield	12	Jul
14.81 w 6.8	Charles Robertson-Adams	5.12.77	3rB	Stoke	22	Jun
14.85 w 2.5	Chris Hargrave	27.02.79	7	Sheffield	13	Jul
14.87 1.8			4h2	Sheffield	12	Jul
14.90 w 2.8	Kevin MacLennan	5.12.78	2	Carmarthen	16	Jul
14.98 w 6.8	Josef Bailey	2.12.77	3rB	Stoke	22	Jun
15.20 1.8			7h2	Sheffield	12	Jul
15.00 w 2.9	Roland Eva	6.09.78	5h1	Sheffield	12	Jul
15.27 -1.8			4	London (CP)	30	Jun
15.07 w 2.9	Dean Leslie	9.01.78	6h1	Sheffield	12	Jul
15.21 1.6			2	Crawley	12	May
15.11 -1.0	Fyn Corcoran	17.03.78	2D	Birmingham	22	Sep
15.12 -1.0	Mark Sweeney	26.02.77	1D	Worcester	25	Aug
15.15 w 2.1	Mathias George	24.09.77	5	London (He)	7	Jul
15.25 1.8			8h2	Sheffield	12	Jul
(20)						
15.16 w 2.8	Matthew Elias	25.04.79	3	Carmarthen	16	Jul
15.23 w 2.9	Tim Dalton	18.01.79	7h1	Sheffield	12	Jul
15.46 -1.8			5	London (CP)	30	Jun
15.29 w 2.1	Ben Gritz	21.11.77	6	London (He)	7	Jul
15.37 0.5	Ian Cawley	21.11.78	1	Portsmouth	12	May

14.92	-1.0	Mark Bushell	U23	22.10.76	1D	Birmingham	22	Sep

Hand Timing

14.3		Steven Scott	(14.69)	1	London (TB)	16	Jun
14.3 w		Leo Barker	26.12.78	1	Corby	18	May
		14.4		1D	Norwich	23	Jun
14.5		Ben Warmington	(14.86)	1	Middlesbrough	15	Jun
14.5	-2.1	Adam Tibbets	(14.70w)	1	Solihull	29	Jun
14.6		Tony Gill	(14.78)	1	Cleckheaton	8	Jun
14.9		Roland Eva	(15.27)	1	Kings Lynn	15	Jun
14.9 w	3.4	Liam Collins	23.10.78	4	Cudworth	29	Jun
		15.2		1	Blackpool	25	Aug
15.0		Nick Dowsett	(15.36)	1	Basildon	8	Jun
15.0	1.2	Kevin MacLennan	(14.90w)	1	Pitreavie	15	Jun
15.0		Charles Robertson-Adams	(14.81w)	1	Derby	15	Sep
15.0 w	3.4	Rob Collins	17.09.77	5	Cudworth	29	Jun
15.1		Mathias George	(15.25)	1rB	London (TB)	16	Jun
15.1		Dean Leslie	(15.21)	2rB	London (TB)	16	Jun
15.1		Fyn Corcoran	(15.11)	1D	Carn Brea	23	Jun
15.1		Scott Exley	(14.68w)	2D	Carn Brea	23	Jun
15.1		Tim Dalton	(15.46)	2	London (He)	28	Jun
15.3		Garry Turner	21.12.78	1	Derby	14	Apr
15.3		Ben Gritz	(15.29w)	2	Watford	12	Jun
15.4		Paul Crossley	30.03.79	1	Luton	16	Jun
15.4		Gary McCraken	23.01.78	1	Jarrow	16	Jun
15.5		L. Cheung	24.10.77	2	Basildon	8	Jun
15.5		Peter Carr	10.09.77	2D	Carn Brea	23	Jun
15.5	1.0	James Hillier	3.04.78	3	Swansea	6	Jul

110 METRES HURDLES

13.13	-0.1	Colin Jackson	18.02.67	1	Birmingham	15	Jun
13.13	0.2			2	Lausanne, SWZ	3	Jul
13.17	0.5			2s1	Atlanta, USA	29	Jul
13.19	0.6			4	Atlanta, USA	29	Jul
13.22	0.0			1	Brisbane, AUS	14	Mar
13.24	-0.5			1	Melbourne, AUS	29	Feb
13.24	0.8			1h1	Birmingham	15	Jun
13.24	0.2			2	Brussels, BEL	23	Aug
13.27	1.1			2	Bratislava, SVK	29	May
13.30	-0.6			1	Cape Town, RSA	12	Apr
13.30	1.4			1h1	Bratislava, SVK	29	May
13.33	0.5			4	Rome, ITA	5	Jun
13.33	1.4			1q3	Atlanta, USA	28	Jul
13.36	-0.1			1h4	Atlanta, USA	28	Jul
13.36	1.8			3=	Sheffield	25	Aug
13.37	1.1			2	Stockholm, SWE	8	Jul
13.38 A	0.0			1	Johannesburg, RSA	14	Apr
13.39	-2.7			1	Adelaide, AUS	26	Jan
13.40	0.0			3	Nuremberg, GER	7	Jun
13.40	0.2			6	Zurich, SWZ	14	Aug
13.43	0.5			3	Gateshead	19	Aug
13.48	-0.7			3	London (CP)	11	Aug
13.49 A	-2.4			3	Sestriere, ITA	7	Aug
13.63	-0.3			2	Madrid, SPA	2	Jun
13.75	-2.0			1h1	Sydney, AUS	9	Mar
13.93	-0.8			7	Monaco, MON	10	Aug

Mark	Wind	Name / Date	Pos	Venue	Date
13.24	1.1	Tony Jarrett 13.08.68	1	Bratislava, SVK	29 May
13.25	1.8		2	Sheffield	25 Aug
13.27	1.0		1h1	Ljubljana, SLO	26 May
13.32	-0.4		1	Ljubljana, SLO	26 May
13.32	1.0		1h2	Bratislava, SVK	29 May
13.32	-0.7		1	London (CP)	11 Aug
13.33	-0.6		2	Cape Town, RSA	12 Apr
13.33	0.5		3	Gateshead	19 Aug
13.35	0.2		2	Berlin, GER	30 Aug
13.36 A	-0.3		1	Pietersburg, RSA	3 Apr
13.38	-0.5		1rB	Zurich, SWZ	14 Aug
13.40	-0.4		1h2	Birmingham	15 Jun
13.41	-0.1		2	Birmingham	15 Jun
13.44 A	-1.4		1	Pretoria, RSA	3 Feb
13.45 i			1	Tampere, FIN	12 Feb
13.47	0.2		1h6	Atlanta, USA	28 Jul
13.48	1.9		1	Helsinki, FIN	25 Jun
13.51 A	0.5		2	Pretoria, RSA	8 Apr
13.58	-0.6		4	London (CP)	12 Jul
13.63 A	-0.1		1	Roodepoort, RSA	26 Jan
13.86 A	-2.4		5	Sestriere, ITA	7 Aug
13.92 A			1r2	Roodepoort, RSA	26 Jan
13.56	0.2	Andy Tulloch 1.04.67	3h2	Atlanta, USA	28 Jul
13.57	1.8		5	Sheffield	25 Aug
13.64	1.6		1h2	Ljubljana, SLO	26 May
13.64	2.0		1	Tampere, FIN	20 Aug
13.68	1.1		5	Bratislava, SVK	29 May
13.68	0.1		6q4	Atlanta, USA	28 Jul
13.69	-0.4		3	Ljubljana, SLO	26 May
13.69	-0.7		6	London (CP)	11 Aug
13.70	-0.1		3	Birmingham	15 Jun
13.70	0.0		1rB	Stockholm, SWE	8 Jul
13.73	1.9		4	Helsinki, FIN	25 Jun
13.74	0.4		1h3	Birmingham	15 Jun
13.85	1.0		3h2	Bratislava, SVK	29 May
13.85	-0.4		2	Lahti, FIN	18 Aug
13.87	-0.6		6	London (CP)	12 Jul
13.89			3	Budapest, HUN	20 Jun
13.61 A	0.0	Paul Gray 25.05.69	5	Johannesburg, RSA	14 Apr
13.70	-0.1		4	Birmingham	15 Jun
13.72	1.4		4h1	Bratislava, SVK	29 May
13.75	1.1		6	Bratislava, SVK	29 May
13.77	0.0		6	Nuremberg, GER	7 Jun
13.78	-0.5		3	Melbourne, AUS	29 Feb
13.79	0.2		7	Lausanne, SWZ	3 Jul
13.80	-1.6		2	Sydney, AUS	9 Mar
13.81	1.1		2rB	Stockholm, SWE	8 Jul
13.82	-0.3		1	Bedford	18 May
13.82	-0.4		2	Lucerne, SWZ	25 Jun
13.85	0.0		3	Brisbane, AUS	14 Mar
13.86	1.8		7	Sheffield	25 Aug
13.87	-0.7		7	London (CP)	11 Aug
13.90	-2.0		2h2	Sydney, AUS	9 Mar
13.90	0.4		2h3	Birmingham	15 Jun
13.96	-0.6		6	Cape Town, RSA	12 Apr
13.96	-0.6		8	London (CP)	12 Jul
13.62	0.6	Neil Owen 18.10.73	4	Tallinn, EST	9 Jun
13.68	0.3		4r2	Tallinn, EST	9 Jun
13.72	-0.1		5	Birmingham	15 Jun
13.75			2	Fullerton, USA	25 Apr

(Owen)		13.83 i			4	Tampere, FIN	12 Feb
		13.87	1.0		5h1	Ljubljana, SLO	26 May
		13.90	-0.6		7	London (CP)	12 Jul
		13.91	-0.4		6	Ljubljana, SLO	26 May
		13.96	-0.4		2h2	Birmingham	15 Jun
		13.97	1.8		8	Sheffield	25 Aug
		14.00	1.0		1	London (He)	31 Aug
13.90	0.8	Ken Campbell		30.09.72	2h1	Birmingham	15 Jun
		13.93	1.0		1h	Lidingo, SWE	4 Jun

95 performances to 14.00 by 6 athletes including 2 indoors (!)

14.01	1.8	Ross Baillie	U20	26.09.77	4	Sydney, AUS	25 Aug
14.03	1.6	Brian Taylor		13.08.70	1	Loughborough	19 May
14.04	1.8	Damien Greaves	U20	19.09.77	5	Sydney, AUS	25 Aug
14.13	0.3	Mark Stern		22.05.72	3	Cork, IRE	22 Jun
	(10)						
14.19	1.1	James Archampong	U23	14.03.76	1	Bedford	26 May
14.34	0.7	Greg Dunson		2.12.63	2	Kunzelsau, GER	7 Sep
14.44	0.4	Martin Nicholson		9.12.70	4h3	Birmingham	15 Jun
14.51	1.1	Adrian Caines	U23	13.11.74	1rB	Kunzelsau, GER	7 Sep
14.52	-0.2	Simon McAree	U23	28.12.75	3	Sheffield	5 May
14.52	-0.4	Chris Rawlinson		19.05.72	2	Cudworth	3 Aug
14.69	0.7	Anthony Southward		31.01.71	2D	Bedford	26 May
14.73	0.8	Hugh Teape		26.12.63	3h1	Birmingham	15 Jun
14.74		Colin Bovell		9.03.72	1	Gateshead	1 Sep
14.78	-0.4	Alex Kruger		18.11.63	5h2	Birmingham	15 Jun
	(20)						
14.85	-1.7	Ererton Harrison		8.04.66	1h2	London (CP)	2 Jun
14.86	-1.0	Matt Douglas	U23	26.11.76	1D	Worcester	25 Aug
14.88	0.8	Neal Petley		21.05.68	5h1	Birmingham	15 Jun
14.88		Liam Collins	U20	23.10.78	2	Gateshead	31 Aug
14.88		Richard Churchill	U20	29.09.77	3	Gateshead	31 Aug
14.90	-0.4	Tony Gill	U20	19.09.77	6h2	Birmingham	15 Jun
14.92		Martyn Hendry	U23	10.04.75	3	Glasgow	29 Jun
14.92	1.3	Ben Warmington	U20	20.03.79	3	Bedford	28 Jul
14.96	0.7	Barry Thomas		28.04.72	3D	Bedford	26 May
15.01	-0.1	Dean Macey	U20	12.12.77	1D2	Sydney, AUS	22 Aug
	(30)						
15.02	1.0	Paul Hibbert		31.03.65	4	London (He)	31 Aug
15.08	1.0	Kevin Lumsdon	U23	3.03.74	5	Birmingham	6 Jul
15.09		Billy Jewers		27.09.62	1D	Aldershot	14 Jun
15.10		Andrew David		9.09.69	2h1	London (CP)	2 Jun
15.10	0.1	Simon Shirley		3.08.66	3D	Lage, GER	16 Jun
15.11		Mensah Elliott	U23	29.08.76	4	Zoetermeer, HOL	6 Jul
15.13		Robert Mason	U23	13.09.75	3	Birmingham	1 Jun
15.15	0.7	Mark Bushell	U23	22.10.76	2D	Narbonne, FRA	28 Jul
15.16	0.8	Richard Hunter		12.01.71	7h1	Birmingham	15 Jun
15.18	-1.3	Paul Gripton	U23	9.11.76	7	Birmingham	20 Jul
	(40)						
15.18	1.0	Ayo Falola		29.07.68	5	London (He)	31 Aug
15.19	0.9	Sebastian Rosato		19.11.72	2h1	Sheffield	6 May
15.20	1.6	Andrew Bargh	U23	21.08.76	2	Edinburgh	8 Jun
15.20	1.0	Dalton Grant		8.04.66	6	London (He)	31 Aug
15.21		Dominic Bradley	U23	22.12.76	3h2	Sheffield	5 May
15.22	0.7	Rafer Joseph		21.07.68	4D	Bedford	26 May
15.22	1.3	Richard Sear	U20	21.08.79	8	Bedford	28 Jul
15.25	1.4	Rob Laing		30.07.66	4r2	Birmingham	6 Jul
15.27	1.0	Adrian Carter		7.02.68	7	London (He)	31 Aug
15.29		Matthew Johnson	U23	2.05.74	4h2	Sheffield	5 May
	(50)						
15.31	1.1	Kevin Furlong		19.05.70	8	Bedford	26 May
15.32	1.7	Leo Barker	U20	26.12.78	3D	Narbonne, FRA	28 Jul

15.34	-1.8	Jamie Quarry		15.11.72	1	Edinburgh	16	Jun
15.37	-0.6	William Gilles		15.02.73	1D	Bedford	26	May
15.38	-1.7	David Barnetson		1.07.71	1	Edinburgh	16	Jun
15.38	1.0	Dave Savage		13.11.72	8	London (He)	31	Aug
15.39	1.6	Nathan Hart		1.07.73	4	Edinburgh	8	Jun
15.41	1.6	Matthew Clements	U20	17.09.77	6	Loughborough	19	May
15.43	-0.6	Mark Perman		6.01.68	2D	Bedford	26	May
15.46	0.3	David Brooking		22.10.68	2	Luton	6	May
	(60)							
15.47	-0.5	Ciaran Doherty	U23	14.01.75	1D	Antrim	1	Sep
15.48	1.6	Steve Leader		24.11.66	5	Edinburgh	8	Jun
15.50	1.6	Steve Freeman		8.09.67	7	Loughborough	19	May
15.54	-2.3	David Kane		1.11.70	4rB	London (He)	9	Jun
15.56	-0.5	Tom Leeson		18.09.63	2D	Antrim	1	Sep
15.58	-1.7	Anthony Bliss		7.03.70	2h	London (CP)	2	Jun
15.63	-1.7	Barry Marsden		11.06.64	3h	London (CP)	2	Jun
15.67		Gavin Streather		14.04.71	7	Birmingham	1	Jun
15.67	1.6	Gary McCraken	U20	23.01.78	6	Edinburgh	8	Jun
15.69	-0.9	Paul Crossley	U20	30.03.79	3h2	Bedford	28	Jul
	(70)							

Wind Assisted

13.14	2.1	Jackson		(13.13)	1	Perth, AUS	28	Jan
	13.24	2.9			1	Gateshead	30	Jun
	13.26	4.3			1	Cardiff	25	May
13.25	2.9	Jarrett		(13.24)	2	Gateshead	30	Jun
	13.50	2.1			1h1	Riga, LAT	2	Jun
13.62	4.3	Gray		(13.87)	2	Cardiff	25	May
	13.63	2.7			2	Perth, AUS	28	Jan
	13.63	2.9			4	Gateshead	30	Jun
	13.84	4.5			2	Liverpool	4	May
13.65	2.1	Owen		(13.62)	3h1	Riga, LAT	2	Jun
	13.73	4.5			1	Liverpool	4	May
	13.89	2.9			5	Gateshead	30	Jun
13.82	2.1	Tulloch		(13.56)	4h1	Riga, LAT	2	Jun

13 performances to 14.00 by 5 athletes

14.14	4.3	James Archampong	U23	(14.19)	3	Cardiff	25	May
14.79	4.5	Ererton Harrison		(14.85)	5	Liverpool	4	May
14.81	2.1	Chris Hargrave	U20	(15.4)	1	London (He)	1	Sep
14.88	2.1	Mark Perman		(15.43)	2	London (He)	1	Sep
14.93	4.9	Adam Tibbets	U20	14.12.78	3rB	Loughborough	19	May
14.95	4.9	Dave Sweetman			4rB	Loughborough	19	May
14.96	4.5	Mark Lambeth		(15.0)	6	Liverpool	4	May
15.20	4.9	Perry Batchelor	U23	11.12.75	7rB	Loughborough	19	May
15.22	2.1	Mark Sweeney	U20	(15.2)	3	London (He)	1	Sep
15.26	2.1	Clarence Allen		(14.9)	4	London (He)	1	Sep
15.34	3.0	David Kane		(15.54)	4rB	Liverpool	4	May
15.44	4.5	Gareth Hughes		22.10.73	7	Liverpool	4	May
15.48	2.5	Stephen Edwards	U20	13.06.77	4h3	Bedford	28	Jul
15.55	2.6	Gary Gallagher		7.06.71	3	Antrim	7	Jul
15.66	4.0	Mike Coker		16.01.57	1rB	Edinburgh	8	Jun

Hand Timing

13.0 w	2.3	Tony Jarrett		(13.24)	1	Riga, LAT	2	Jun
13.5 w	2.3	Neil Owen		(13.62)	3	Riga, LAT	2	Jun
13.5 w	2.3	Andy Tulloch		(13.56)	4	Riga, LAT	2	Jun

3 performances to 14.0 by 3 athletes

14.1 w	2.2	James Archampong	U23	(14.19)	1	Watford	6	Jul
	14.3				1	Newport	1	Jun
14.4	1.8	Simon McAree	U23	(14.52)	1	Loughborough	5	Jun

14.5		Jamie Quarry		(15.34)	2	Loughborough	27 Apr
14.5 w	3.8	Martyn Hendry	U23	(14.92)	1	Glasgow	4 Aug
14.9	1.4				2	Peterborough	4 May
14.6 w	4.5	Mensah Elliott	U23	(15.11)	1	Abingdon	24 Aug
15.0					1	Kingston	20 Apr
14.7		Matthew Clements	U20	(15.41)	1	Bedford	7 Aug
14.7 w	4.5	Kirk Harries	U23	7.08.74	2	Abingdon	24 Aug
14.9					1	Hayes	3 Aug
14.7 w	4.5	Martin Holgate		2.11.65	3	Abingdon	24 Aug
14.8	1.4	Andy Gill		19.02.70	1	Peterborough	4 May
14.8		Phil Brilus		29.12.68	1	Southampton	18 May
14.8		Tim Tomkinson		31.10.68	2	Portsmouth	2 Jul
14.8 w	4.5	Richard Sear	U20	(15.22)	4	Abingdon	24 Aug
14.9		Ben Warmington	U20	(14.92)	1	Jarrow	11 May
14.9		Mike Robbins	U23	14.03.76	1	Sheffield	8 Jun
14.9		Clarence Allen		(15.26w)	1	London (WP)	12 Jun
14.9		Mark Perman		(15.43)	1	Barking	17 Aug
14.9 w	2.9	Mark Sweeney	U20	(15.22w)	1	Cannock	7 Sep
15.2					2	Brierley Hill	10 Aug
14.9 w	4.5	Kevin Lumsdon	U23	(15.08)	1	Leeds (South)	8 Sep
15.0		Mark Lambeth		(14.96w)	2	Burcht, BEL	1 Apr
15.0	2.0	David Barnetson		(15.38)	1	Aberdeen	28 Apr
15.0		Dominic Bradley	U23	(15.21)	1	Crewe	11 May
15.0		Andrew David		(15.10)	2	London (WP)	12 Jun
15.0		Roger Hunter	U23	10.03.76	1	Wakefield	17 Aug
15.0 w	4.5	Andrew Bargh	U23	(15.20)	5	Abingdon	24 Aug
15.1		Sebastian Rosato		(15.19)	1	Woodford	21 Apr
15.1		Kevin Furlong		(15.31)	1	Douglas, IOM	21 Jul
15.1		Ayo Falola		(15.18)	2rB	Stoke	17 Aug
15.1 w	2.2	Dave Savage		(15.38)	1	Cudworth	23 Jun
15.2		Mathias George	U20	24.09.77	2	Southampton	18 May
15.2		Rafer Joseph		(15.22)	1	Carn Brea	18 May
15.2		Paul Hourihan	U23	7.11.76	2D	Middlesbrough	14 Jul
15.2		Rob Laing		(15.25)	1	Liverpool	20 Jul
15.2	-1.3	Sean Saxon		11.12.71	2	Telford	17 Aug
15.2		Nathan Hart		(15.39)	3	Watford	17 Aug
15.2		David Vidgen	U23	27.09.74	1	Abingdon	17 Aug
15.3	-0.8	Chris Dorgu		11.12.69	3	Enfield	4 May
15.3		Gary Myles		3.02.63	3	Cannock	4 May
15.3		David Brooking		(15.46)	1	Exeter	22 Jun
15.3		Ciaran Doherty	U23	(15.47)	1rB	Enfield	6 Jul
15.3		Des Wilkinson		7.01.63	2	Portsmouth	13 Jul
15.3		Gavin Sunshine	U23	19.02.74	2	Worthing	17 Aug
15.3 w	4.5	Gareth Hughes		(15.44w)	2	Leeds (South)	8 Sep
15.4		Jon Wilkinson		17.02.62	1	Oldham	26 May
15.4		Chris Hargrave	U20	(14.81w)	1	Croydon	22 Jun
15.4	1.4	Livio Salvador-Aylott		18.07.73	2rB	Watford	6 Jul
15.4		Paul Crossley	U20	(15.69)	1	Luton	7 Jul
15.4		Roland Eva	U20	6.09.78	2	Luton	7 Jul
15.4		Nigel Hayman			1	Bournemouth	13 Jul
15.4		Barry Marsden		(15.63)	1	Yeovil	17 Aug
15.4		Alexis Sharp		31.10.72	4rB	Stoke	17 Aug
15.4 w	2.2	Terry Fidler		13.10.71	4	Watford	6 Jul
15.6	-2.2				1	Luton	23 Jun
15.4 w	4.5	Anthony Bliss		(15.58)	8	Abingdon	24 Aug
15.5					1	Basildon	18 May

15.5		David Kane		(15.54)	2	Kingston	20 Apr
15.5		Gary Smith		20.02.71	1	Norwich	4 May
15.5		Peter Crampton		4.06.69	1	Scunthorpe	6 May
15.5		Mark Chapman	U23	28.12.76	1	Jarrow	11 May
15.5		Frank Chapman		17.01.70	2	Cosford	18 Jun
15.5		Robert Fanning	U20	31.10.78	1	Kingston	22 Jun
15.5	1.4	John Franklin		1.03.66	3rB	Watford	6 Jul
15.5		Greg Richards	V40	25.04.56	D	Middlesbrough	14 Jul
15.5 w	2.9	William Wyllie		12.07.73	4	Cannock	7 Sep
15.6		Stephen Booth		21.10.71	3	Kingston	20 Apr
15.6		Paul Field		24.06.67	1	Telford	27 Apr
15.6		Howard Moscrop		16.12.57	1	Portsmouth	4 May
15.6		Martin Swingler		11.05.63	1rB	Norwich	4 May
15.6		Gary McCraken	U20	(15.67)	2	Jarrow	12 May
15.6		Andrew Haines		15.10.72	1	High Wycombe	18 May
15.6		James Hillier	U20	3.04.78	2	Newport	1 Jun
15.6		Phil Harries		7.04.66	1	Wakefield	6 Jul
15.6		Matthew Hill	U20	15.12.77	1	Lincoln	20 Jul
15.6 w	2.2	Gavin Streather		(15.67)	5	Watford	6 Jul

Foreign
15.1		*Pascal Renaud*		*20.04.70*	*3rB*	*Stoke*	*17 Aug*

400 METRES HURDLES

48.79	Jon Ridgeon		14.02.67	2rB	Zurich, SWZ	14 Aug
	49.04			3	London (CP)	11 Aug
	49.16			1	Birmingham	16 Jun
	49.25			4	London (CP)	12 Jul
	49.31			1h5	Atlanta, USA	29 Jul
	49.43			7s1	Atlanta, USA	31 Jul
	49.45			3	Rieti, ITA	1 Sep
	49.54			5	Malmo, SWE	27 Jun
	49.54			2	Gateshead	19 Aug
	49.55			5	Helsinki, FIN	25 Jun
	49.59			6	Stockholm, SWE	8 Jul
	49.64			3	Gateshead	30 Jun
	49.69			2	Sheffield	25 Aug
	49.83			1s2	Birmingham	15 Jun
	49.83			3	Rovereto, ITA	28 Aug
	49.84			2	Madrid, SPA	1 Jun
	49.87			1	Cardiff	25 May
	50.02			3	Hobart, AUS	25 Feb
	50.07			2	Istanbul, TUR	18 May
	50.12			5	Bratislava, SVK	29 May
	50.13			3	Melbourne, AUS	29 Feb
	50.14			1	Irvine, USA	4 May
	50.39			3	Reduit, MAU	21 Sep
	50.49			2	Melbourne, AUS	17 Feb
	50.55			1h1	Melbourne, AUS	16 Feb
	50.78			1h2	Hobart, AUS	25 Feb
	50.98			6	Walnut, USA	21 Apr
49.78	Peter Crampton		4.06.69	6h1	Atlanta, USA	29 Jul
	49.79			2	Birmingham	16 Jun
	49.93			2	Cardiff	25 May
	50.14			1	Bedford	27 May
	50.16			6	Gateshead	30 Jun
	50.35			1s1	Birmingham	15 Jun
	50.49			8	London (CP)	12 Jul
	50.69			1	Sheffield	11 May

50.00	Gary Cadogan		8.10.66	4	London (CP)	11	Aug
50.01				6	Helsinki, FIN	25	Jun
50.14				5	Gateshead	30	Jun
50.17				2	Ljubljana, SLO	26	May
50.20				4	Budapest, HUN	20	Jun
50.32				7	London (CP)	12	Jul
50.46				4	Gateshead	19	Aug
50.05	Lawrence Lynch		1.11.67	2s2	Birmingham	15	Jun
50.39				2	Bedford	27	May
50.40				1	London (CP)	2	Jun
50.75				1h1	London (CP)	1	Jun
50.75				5	Birmingham	16	Jun
50.16	Paul Thompson		22.03.72	1h1	Tempe, USA	17	May
51.00				1	Tempe, USA	18	May
50.18	Gary Jennings		21.02.72	6	London (CP)	12	Jul
50.41				6h7	Atlanta, USA	29	Jul
50.46				3	Birmingham	16	Jun
50.54				2s1	Birmingham	15	Jun
50.63				1	Nivelles, BEL	17	Aug
50.98				6	Sheffield	25	Aug
50.36	Chris Rawlinson		19.05.72	3	Tallinn, EST	9	Jun
50.88				1	Sheffield	2	Jun
50.97				4s2	Birmingham	15	Jun
50.52	Paul Hibbert		31.03.65	7	Gateshead	30	Jun
50.61				3s1	Birmingham	15	Jun
50.67				4	Birmingham	16	Jun
50.86				1	London (He)	9	Jun
50.85	Noel Levy	U23	22.06.75	3s2	Birmingham	15	Jun
50.97	Dave Savage		13.11.72	4s1	Birmingham	15	Jun
	64 performances to 51.00 by 10 athletes						
51.18	Barry Middleton	U23	10.03.75	6s2	Birmingham	15	Jun
51.20	Eddie Betts		18.02.71	5s1	Birmingham	15	Jun
51.47	Matt Douglas	U23	26.11.76	2	London (CP)	2	Jun
51.47	Anthony Borsumato		13.12.73	2	Birmingham	20	Jul
51.68	Greg Dunson		2.12.63	3	Kingston	17	Aug
51.95	Mark Bishop		12.02.67	4	London (CP)	2	Jun
52.01	Gary Telfer		10.01.65	3	Liverpool	4	May
52.2	Tony Williams		1.05.72	1h1	Sheffield	4	May
53.20				1	Sheffield	5	May
52.21	Douglas Thom		13.04.68	2	Belfast	22	Jun
52.26	Charles Robertson-Adams	U20	5.12.77	4h2	Birmingham	15	Jun
	(20)						
52.33	Tim Gwynne		20.01.71	5h2	Birmingham	15	Jun
52.38	Mark Rowlands	U20	18.04.78	1	Bedford	28	Jul
52.4	Andrew Bargh	U23	21.08.76	1	Bath	19	Jun
52.63				6	London (CP)	2	Jun
52.6	David Barnetson		1.07.71	1	Watford	17	Aug
53.24				1	Edinburgh	16	Jun
52.71	Phil Harries		7.04.66	2	Loughborough	19	May
52.8	Marvin Gray		18.12.71	1	Newport	1	Jun
52.82				3	Belfast	22	Jun
52.86	Carl Foster	U23	24.10.75	3	Sheffield	12	May
52.87	Ian Neely	U23	29.12.74	7	Dublin, IRE	9	Jun
53.0	Paul Beaumont		27.03.63	1	Aldershot	5	Jun
53.01	Lee Murphy	U20	11.03.77	1	London (CP)	30	Jun
	(30)						
53.07	Matt Lethbridge	U20	22.01.77	2	London (CP)	30	Jun
53.12	Jeremy Bridger	U23	23.09.75	5h1	Birmingham	15	Jun
53.26	James Hillier	U20	3.04.78	4	Bedford	28	Jul
53.31	Richard McDonald	U17	11.01.80	5	Bedford	28	Jul

53.4	Glenn Gray		21.04.68	2	Portsmouth	21	Jul
53.70				2rB	Birmingham	6	Jul
53.6	Adam Hartley		27.02.69	2	Enfield	4	May
53.71				5h4	Birmingham	15	Jun
53.6	Craig White		4.04.71	1	Cudworth	23	Jul
53.64				1rB	Kingston	17	Aug
53.6	Berian Davies		22.04.73	2	Watford	6	Jul
55.85				3h2	Newport	1	Jun
53.67	Mark Green		28.06.71	4h2	London (CP)	1	Jun
53.67	Andrew Judge	U23	24.05.75	1	London (He)	1	Sep
	(40)						
53.7	Richard Holt		28.11.71	4	Watford	6	Jul
54.29				3h1	London (CP)	1	Jun
53.7	Howard Moscrop		16.12.57	1	Swindon	13	Jul
53.71	David Gifford		9.03.73	3h3	Bedford	27	May
53.73	Simon Clifford	U23	22.03.75	3	Sheffield	5	May
53.86	John Bell		10.09.73	6	Sheffield	2	Jun
54.1	Robert Hough		3.06.72	1	Sheffield	22	Jun
54.12	Dave Griffin		5.12.63	5	London (He)	9	Jun
54.2	Andy Gill		19.02.70	1	Hull	14	Apr
54.22				3h2	Sheffield	2	Jun
54.2	John McIlwham		29.02.72	1	Blackpool	9	Jun
54.2	Steve Freeman		8.09.67	1	Cannock	23	Jun
54.52				4rB	Bedford	18	May
	(50)						
54.3	Dean Park	U20	23.09.77	3h1	Bedford	27	Jul
55.33				5	London (CP)	30	Jun
54.33	Matthew Elias	U20	25.04.79	4	Kingston	17	Aug
54.4	Anthony Pamah		11.11.63	3	London (CP)	18	Aug
54.55				4	London (He)	28	Jul
54.42	Fyn Corcoran	U20	17.03.78	2	Sheffield	13	Jul
54.5	Mark Purser		18.04.72	1	Croydon	12	May
54.65				h	London (CP)	1	Jun
54.5	Kevin Furlong		19.05.70	2	Douglas, IOM	6	Jul
54.5	Martin Holgate		2.11.65	3rB	Stoke	17	Aug
54.54	Mark Anderson	U20	5.11.77	2h1	Bedford	27	Jul
54.58	Russell Quelch	U20	9.09.78	3	Sheffield	13	Jul
54.6	Trystan Bevan	U23	22.08.75	2	Bristol	23	Jun
	(60)						
54.7	Andy Webster		11.11.66	1	Leeds	4	May
54.7	Andrew Kennard		2.01.66	1	Crawley	22	Jun
54.72	Steve Kneller		9.11.71	3rB	Kingston	17	Aug
54.75	Danny Heywood		27.05.71	2rB	Liverpool	4	May
54.79	David Goodger	U23	19.09.75	5h1	Bedford	27	May
54.8	Peter Bablister			1	Luton	23	Jun
54.90	Martin Steele		30.09.62	4	Sheffield	11	May
54.9	Neal Petley		21.05.68	2	Sheffield	22	Jun
55.06	Ian Wells		18.02.62	4rB	Kingston	17	Aug
55.1	Robert Lewis	U20	2.09.78	2	Luton	23	Jun
55.27				4	Sheffield	13	Jul
	(70)						
55.1	Paul Crossley	U20	30.03.79	3	Luton	23	Jun
55.18				4h4	Bedford	27	Jul
55.1	Jon Parker	U23	1.05.76	2	Cambridge	26	Jun
55.12	Neil Owen		18.10.73	4rB	Birmingham	6	Jul
55.12	Scott Chisholm	U20	20.10.77	2	London (He)	1	Sep
55.15	Keith Newton		12.12.68	h	London (CP)	1	Jun
55.2	Steve Lamb	U23	10.10.75	3	Loughborough	5	Jun
55.3	Glen Howe	U20	20.10.78	1	Jarrow	8	Jun
56.91				5h1	Sheffield	12	Jul
55.3	Terry Price		26.07.57	2	Kingston	22	Jun

55.32	David Keoghan	U20	9.10.78	3h3	Bedford	27	Jul
55.4	Gavin Streather		14.04.71	1	Woodford	27	Apr
55.50				4h1	Birmingham	2	Jun
(80)							
55.4	Jon Goodwin	U23	22.09.76	4h1	Sheffield	4	May
55.4	Andrew Hicks	U20	30.07.79	1	Oxford	9	Jun
55.62				4h2	London (CP)	29	Jun
55.43	Derek Paisley		1.12.73	4h3	Sheffield	4	May
55.44	Jon Heggie	U17	8.12.79	5h4	Bedford	27	Jul
55.5	Darren Gallagher		7.06.71	1rB	Peterborough	4	May
55.87				3	Antrim	7	Jul
55.5	Harvey Cossell	U23	1.12.74	1	Bromley	4	May
55.5	Paul Field		24.06.67	4	Portsmouth	4	May
55.77				1	London (Col)	3	Jul
55.5	Tim Lang		8.12.73	2	Sheffield	8	Jun
55.98				3	Cudworth	3	Aug
55.6	David Powell	U20	11.09.78	1	York	8	Jun
56.09				4h1	Sheffield	12	Jul
55.6	Mark Chapman	U23	28.12.76	2	Cosford	18	Jun
(90)							
55.6	Andrew Smith	U20	26.03.78	1	Middlesbrough	6	Jul
55.6	Richard Scott		14.09.73	1	Worthing	17	Aug
55.70	Duncan Harbour		17.10.66	4	Watford	17	Aug
55.7	Terry Mitchell			3	Croydon	12	May
55.7	John Squirrell	U23	16.12.75	1	London (BP)	15	May
55.72				6	Kingston	17	Aug
55.8	Mark Davidson		15.11.68	1	Aberdeen	6	Jun
55.85	Stefan Laffley	U20	10.09.77	6	Sheffield	13	Jul
55.9	S. Capel			1	High Wycombe	18	May
55.9	Jason Davenhill		3.10.69	1	Exeter	22	Jun
55.9	Darren Scott		7.03.69	3	Sheffield	22	Jun
(100)							
55.92	Colin Philip	U20	8.06.79	3	Carmarthen	16	Jul
55.98	Brian Steel		30.09.70	1	Edinburgh	12	May
56.0	Otis Griffiths		4.02.70	2	Cannock	7	Sep
56.0	Paul Williams			1	Cannock	7	Sep

Additional Under 20 (1 - 22 above)

56.2	Kerrin Young	U17	2.09.79	3	Antrim	25	Jun
56.2	Carl McMullen	U17	9.11.79	1	Stretford	17	Aug
56.50				1	Cudworth	30	Jun
56.3	S. Catherley			1	Gateshead	16	Jun
56.7	Michael Mason		16.06.77	1	Kingston	8	Jun
56.8	Duncan Howarth		20.02.79	1	Kings Lynn	11	May
56.91				3h1	London (CP)	29	Jun
56.8	Philip Carney		22.12.77	2	York	15	Jun

doubtful

54.1	M. Endersby			1	Basingstoke	3	Aug

disqualified

55.5	Duncan Harbour		17.10.66	(1)	Bournemouth	3	Aug

unconfirmed

56.2	Alastair Newmarch	U20	28.11.78			28	Jul

Foreign

53.65	*Nigel Keogh*		*18.07.67*	*3h2*	*London (CP)*	*1*	*Jun*
54.05	*Remi Edu*	*U20*	*14.12.78*	*3*	*London (CP)*	*30*	*Jun*

400 METRES HURDLES - Under 17

52.81	Richard McDonald	11.01.80	1	Pitreavie	10	Aug
52.81			1	Birmingham	18	Aug
53.8	Carl McMullen	9.11.79	2	Stoke	20	Jul
54.17			2	Birmingham	18	Aug
54.2	Jon Heggie	8.12.79	3	Stoke	20	Jul
54.44			1	Sheffield	13	Jul
54.8	Kerrin Young	2.09.79	4	Stoke	20	Jul
55.31			3	Pitreavie	10	Aug
55.32	Paul Armstrong	20.10.79	2	Edinburgh	12	May
56.0	Austin Ferns	12.01.81	1	London (WP)	2	Jun
56.55			4	Sheffield	13	Jul
56.3	Carl Daly	8.09.79	1	Basildon	8	Jun
56.46			3	Sheffield	13	Jul
56.31	Patrick Brown	2.09.79	4	Birmingham	18	Aug
56.50	Chris Woods	27.01.80	2h2	Birmingham	18	Aug
56.8	Neil Jones	22.10.79	3	Jarrow	23	Jun
(10)						
57.1	Chris Herring	3.03.81	1	Middlesbrough	8	Jun
57.3	Shaun Robson	21.06.80	7	Stoke	20	Jul
57.55			2	Carmarthen	30	Jun
57.39	Tony Seston	21.12.80	5	Sheffield	13	Jul
57.47	Kevin Drury	30.09.79	1	Carmarthen	30	Jun
57.6	Rhys Williams		3	London (WP)	15	Sep
57.7	James Chatt	11.02.80	2	London (Elt)	21	Jul
58.06			3h1	Birmingham	18	Aug
57.7	Jon Cuff	30.03.80	1	Worcester	22	Sep
58.0	Danny Haydon	22.11.79	1	Croydon	2	Jun
58.0	Robert Newton	10.05.81	1	Derby	21	Jul
58.09	Trevor Agard	12.03.80	4h1	Sheffield	12	Jul
(20)						
58.2	Kevin Allinson	5.03.80	1	Middlesbrough	5	May
58.35			5h1	Sheffield	12	Jul
58.44	Gary Stevenson	12.09.79	1	Glasgow	12	May
58.5	Gavin Lamb	23.09.79	1	Cleckheaton	8	Jun
58.5	Stephen Holmes	17.10.80	1	Bromley	21	Jul
58.52	Martin Cooper	6.09.79	2h2	London (CP)	29	Jun

HIGH JUMP

2.36 i	Steve Smith	29.03.73	1	Birmingham	10	Feb
2.35			3	Atlanta, USA	28	Jul
2.31			1	Birmingham	16	Jun
2.30 i			2	Birmingham	27	Jan
2.30 i			3	Stockholm, SWE	25	Feb
2.30			1	Hengelo, HOL	27	May
2.28 i			4	Balingen, GER	11	Feb
2.28			1	Gateshead	30	Jun
2.28			2	Lausanne, SWZ	3	Jul
2.28			4	London (CP)	12	Jul
2.28			Q	Atlanta, USA	26	Jul
2.27 i			5	Spala, POL	16	Feb
2.26 i			3	Lievin, FRA	18	Feb
2.26 i			2	Glasgow	24	Feb
2.26			5	Stockholm, SWE	8	Jul
2.25			5	Oslo, NOR	5	Jul
2.25			4=	Sheffield	25	Aug
2.24 i			2	Stuttgart, GER	4	Feb
2.20 i			9	Wuppertal, GER	2	Feb
2.20			4=	Seville, SPA	6	Jun
2.20			5	London (CP)	11	Aug

2.34 i	Dalton Grant		8.04.66	1	Birmingham	27	Jan
	2.33 i			2	Weinhelm, GER	1	Feb
	2.33			4	Eberstadt, GER	18	Aug
	2.31			2=	London (CP)	12	Jul
	2.30 i			2	Wuppertal, GER	2	Feb
	2.30			4	Nice, FRA	10	Jul
	2.30			2	Gateshead	19	Aug
	2.28			3	Rome, ITA	5	Jun
	2.28			3	Gateshead	30	Jun
	2.27			3	Madrid, SPA	1	Jun
	2.27			2	Birmingham	16	Jun
	2.26 i			1	Glasgow	24	Feb
	2.26			19Q	Atlanta, USA	26	Jul
	2.25			3	Rio de Janeiro, BRA	5	May
	2.25			4	Paris, FRA	28	Jun
	2.25			2	London (CP)	11	Aug
	2.25			4=	Sheffield	25	Aug
	2.24			1	Khania, GRE	8	Jun
	2.24			3	Duisburg, GER	12	Jun
	2.20			10	Lausanne, SWZ	3	Jul
	2.20			9	Zurich, SWZ	14	Aug
	2.20			7	Milan, ITA	7	Sep
2.26	James Brierley	U20	31.07.77	1	Nembro, ITA	3	Aug
	2.21			1	Bedford	28	Jul
	2.20 i			2	Birmingham	28	Jan
2.23 i	Brendan Reilly		23.12.72	1	Birmingham	28	Jan
2.21	Ben Challenger	U20	7.03.78	2=	Sydney, AUS	24	Aug
	2.20			1	Birmingham	20	Jul
2.20	Colin Bent		12.04.70	3	Birmingham	16	Jun
	2.20			7	Sheffield	25	Aug

51 performances to 2.20 by 6 athletes including 15 indoors

2.19 i	Mike Robbins	U23	14.03.76	1	Birmingham	3	Feb
	2.06			1	Lincoln	20	Jul
2.15 i	Rob Brocklebank	U23	12.10.76	1	Sheffield	20	Jan
	2.15			5	Birmingham	16	Jun
2.15 i	Andrew Lynch	U23	28.06.74	3	Birmingham	28	Jan
2.15	Geoff Parsons		14.08.64	6=	Pretoria, RSA	3	Feb
(10)							
2.15 i	Darren Joseph	U20	10.04.78	1	Birmingham	18	Feb
	2.10			7	Birmingham	16	Jun
2.15	Ian Holliday		9.12.73	1	Sheffield	2	Jun
2.15	Danny Graham	U20	3.08.79	1	Stoke	22	Jun
2.15	Richard Aspden	U23	15.10.76	1	Oordegem, BEL	10	Aug
2.14	Stuart Ohrland	U23	6.09.75	1	Abingdon	24	Aug
2.13 i	Colin McMaster	U20	15.01.80	1	Glasgow	1	Dec
	2.07	U17		1	Stoke	20	Jul
2.11 i	Stuart Smith	U23	2.08.76	2	Birmingham	7	Jan
2.11 i	Alex Kruger		18.11.63	1H	Stockholm, SWE	9	Mar
2.11	Damon Rutland	U23	10.07.75	1	Zoetermeer, HOL	7	Jul
2.10 i	Dean Macey	U20	12.12.77	1P	London (CP)	21	Jan
	2.05			2	Newport	8	Jun
(20)							
2.10 i	Mark Latham	U23	13.01.76	1	Glasgow	17	Mar
	2.06			2	Stoke	17	Aug
2.10	David Barnetson		1.07.71	1	Glasgow	29	Jun
2.10	Martin Lloyd	U17	18.06.80	1	London (Elt)	28	Sep
2.09	Paul Dovell	U20	5.05.77	5	Bedford	28	Jul
2.08	Tony Gilhooly	U23	26.03.76	1	Enfield	6	Jul
2.08	John Wallace		9.10.68	1	Cudworth	11	Aug
2.07	David Franks	U20	27.04.78	3	Sheffield	12	Jul
2.07	Daniel Slessor	U20	5.10.78	1	Grimsby	25	Aug

2.06	Matt Perry	U20	15.02.78	1	Newport	16	Jun
2.06	Paul Burraway		30.11.68	1	Stoke	17	Aug
(30)							
2.05 i	Ian Massey	U23	9.09.76	2	Sheffield	20	Jan
2.05				3	Sheffield	2	Jun
2.05 i	Tom Vanhinsbergh	U20	28.12.78	5	Birmingham	18	Feb
2.05				1	Crawley	12	May
2.05 i	Daniel Turner	U20	27.11.78	6	Birmingham	18	Feb
2.05				1	London (CP)	29	Jun
2.05	Darren Otter	U23	6.03.74	1	Sheffield	5	May
2.05	David Nolan	U23	16.05.75	3	Cardiff	25	May
2.05	Steve Ritchie		12.08.71	2	Coatbridge	23	Jun
2.05	Nathan Hart		1.07.73	1	Watford	17	Aug
2.05	Lee Spike	U17	20.02.80	1	Kirkby	15	Sep
2.04	Barry Thomas		28.04.72	6D	Lage, GER	15	Jun
2.03 i	Richard Laws	U23	8.10.75	8	Birmingham	3	Feb
2.00				1	Jarrow	17	Aug
(40)							
2.03	Tony Kuiper	U17	25.10.79	1	Liverpool	12	May
2.03	Duncan McInnes	U20	1.05.78	1	Pitreavie	15	Jun
2.03	James Howlett	U20	18.02.79	1	Peterborough	13	Jul
2.03 i	Stuart Livingstone	U20	29.08.79	1	Glasgow	15	Dec
2.00				2	Pitreavie	15	Jun
2.02	Billy Jewers		27.09.62	1	Portsmouth	13	Jul
2.01	Simon Shirley		3.08.66	10D	Lage, GER	15	Jun
2.01	Robert Toms	U17	7.08.80	1	Bromley	21	Jul
2.01	Ken McKeown	U15	6.03.82	1	Pitreavie	10	Aug
2.00 i	Dafydd Edwards	U23	19.09.74	5=	Birmingham	7	Jan
2.00 i	James Hind	U20	24.05.77	7	Birmingham	7	Jan
1.98				7	Sheffield	12	Jul
(50)							
2.00 i	Richard Stevens	U23	17.07.76	1	London (CP)	25	Feb
2.00				1	London (TB)	28	Apr
2.00	Craig Guite	U20	19.08.77	1	Rotherham	21	Apr
2.00	Gavin Neblett	U17	27.12.79	1	London (WF)	21	Apr
2.00	Ian Gidley		13.11.70	6	Liverpool	4	May
2.00	Andrew Weston		4.12.73	5	Sheffield	5	May
2.00	Rory Birbeck		24.09.73	2	Blackpool	12	May
2.00	Gavin Fisher	U20	18.11.77	1	Ipswich	12	May
2.00	James Leaver	U23	15.09.75	1	Bournemouth	12	May
2.00	Ian Murray-Tait	U17	31.01.80	1	Antrim	15	May
2.00	Warren Caswell		17.06.63	1	Walton	29	May
(60)							
2.00	Jason McDade	U17	3.04.80	1	Harrow	2	Jun
2.00	Marlon Huggins		11.02.71	4	London (CP)	2	Jun
2.00	Richard Sear	U20	21.08.79	1	Oxford	9	Jun
2.00	Edward Willers	U17	18.09.79	1	London (He)	28	Jun
2.00	Andrew Palmer	U20	13.04.77	3	London (CP)	29	Jun
2.00	Andrew Parker	U23	27.05.74	1	Scunthorpe	6	Jul
2.00	Mark Smith	U23	14.09.74	1	London (Elt)	3	Aug
2.00	Andrew Penk	U20	19.09.78	4	London (He)	10	Aug
2.00	Andrew Binns	U20	12.03.79	1	Wakefield	11	Aug
2.00	John Hopper		5.12.68	1	Luton	17	Aug
(70)							
2.00	Samson Oni	U17	25.06.81	2	Birmingham	18	Aug
2.00	James Hilston	U20	25.02.79	1	London (BP)	21	Aug
1.98	Ben Davies	U17	24.08.81	1	Brierley Hill	5	May
1.98	Neil Lucas	U20	2.10.78	2	Pitreavie	6	May
1.98	Stephen Rogers		1.09.71	2D	Bedford	25	May
1.98	Anthony Southward		31.01.71	1D	Bedford	25	May
1.98	Jon Roberts	U20	28.09.77	1	York	8	Jun

1.98	Mike Wright	U20	15.09.77	2	York	8	Jun
1.98	Andrew Cresswell	U17	4.04.80	1	Worcester	8	Jun
1.98	Wayne Gray	U17	7.11.80	1O	Hemel Hempstead	23	Jun
(80)							
1.98	Mark Roach		11.04.65	1	Barking	23	Jun
1.97 i	Scott Kenny	U17	20.02.80	2	Birmingham	18	Feb
1.91				Q	Birmingham	18	Aug
1.97	Stephen Wren	U23		1	Leamington	9	Jun
1.97	M. Flower			1	London (WF)	13	Jul
1.96 i	Rafer Joseph		21.07.68	7H	Valencia, SPA	27	Jan
1.96	Gary Graham	U23		2	Carlisle	28	Apr
1.96	Mark Ovens			1	Swindon	13	Jul
1.96	Darren Slater	U17		1	Peterborough	21	Jul
1.96	Andrew Judge	U23	24.05.75	1	Cheltenham	4	Aug
1.96	Mark Beer	U17	28.02.80	1	Derby	17	Aug
(90)							
1.96	Steve Bonnett	U20	13.07.78	1D	Birmingham	21	Sep

Foreign

2.25	*Mark Mandy*		*19.11.72*	*4=*	*Sheffield*	*25*	*Aug*
2.16 i	*Tyron Peacock*	*U23*	*16.12.76*	*3*	*Birmingham*	*3*	*Feb*
2.15				*1*	*London (He)*	*9*	*Jun*
2.05	*Pierre Faber*		*9.01.72*	*2*	*Sheffield*	*5*	*May*
2.00	*Olu Robincocker*	*U23*	*27.11.75*	*1*	*Stretford*	*4*	*May*

Additional Under 17 (1 - 17 above)

1.95	Paul Martin		7.09.79	1	Jarrow	5	May
1.95	Chris Petts		22.01.80	1	London (WP)	2	Jun
1.95	David Warren		5.12.79	1	Carlisle	8	Jun
(20)							
1.95	Darren Wright		7.09.79	1	Crewe	8	Jun
1.95	Neil Kelly		21.03.80	1O	Telford	23	Jun
1.95	Neil Dixon		16.09.80	2	Bebington	21	Jul
1.94	Sean Rutter		26.09.80	1	Gateshead	8	Jun
1.94	Kevin McKinson		6.09.80	1	London (Elt)	21	Jul
1.94	Ian Wilson		7.10.79	Q	Birmingham	18	Aug
1.93	Gareth Dyball		16.03.81	2	Peterborough	21	Jul
1.91	Andy Chaddock		13.03.80	2	Derby	8	Jun
1.91	Giles Henderson		9.03.80	1	St. Ives	8	Jun
1.91	Paul Mellor		31.05.80	Q	Sheffield	12	Jul
(30)							
1.91	Mark Elliott		12.08.80	Q	Birmingham	18	Aug
1.91	Carl Wallace		10.02.81	Q	Birmingham	18	Aug
1.91	Jamie Russell	U15	1.10.81	1P	Birmingham	21	Sep
1.90	Lewis Erdman		29.11.79	1P	London (BP)	3	May
1.90	John Monds		24.03.80	2	Blackburn	5	May
1.90	Jamie Dalton		20.09.79	1	Haverfordwest	18	May
1.90	Simon Bannister		16.04.81	1	Norwich	8	Jun
1.90	David Brining		27.02.80	2	Rotherham	23	Jun
1.90	Steven Miller		2.11.80	1	London (Nh)	21	Jul

Additional Under 15 (1 - 2 above)

1.85	Bomeme Barikor		22.05.82	1	Bromley	21	Jul
1.85	Chris Jenkins		2.03.82	1	Bebington	21	Jul
1.85	Dominic Girdler		6.03.82	1	Cannock	31	Aug
1.83	Dan Plank		27.04.82	1	Sheffield	13	Jul
1.83	Chris Harries		17.06.82	1	Carmarthen	21	Jul
1.82	Ben Smith		12.06.82	1	Watford	8	Jun
1.82	Matt Paice		19.06.83	1	Windsor	21	Jul
1.81	Tim Greenwood		22.11.82	2	Sheffield	13	Jul
(10)							
1.80	David Mayo		26.04.82	1	York	15	Jun

1.80	James Alix	24.12.81	1	Stoke	22	Jun
1.80	Ben Baldwin	16.09.81	1	Yeovil	21	Jul
1.80	Kim Harland	21.02.82	1	Carmarthen	8	Aug
1.80	Sean De Bourcier	4.01.82	1	Guernsey	7	Sep
1.78	Darren Locke	16.10.81	1	Gateshead	8	Jun
1.78	Jon Liddle	13.09.81	1	Exeter	15	Jun
1.77	Daniel O'Donnell	9.01.82	2P	Telford	23	Jun
1.76	Ben Rochford	28.10.81	1	Horsham	23	Jun

Under 13

1.65	P. Collins		1	Bath	17	Jul
1.65	David Smithan	7.11.83	2	Carmarthen	21	Jul
1.65	Peter Durham		1	Scunthorpe	27	Jul
1.60	Iain Ramsay	10.10.83	1	Wishaw	14	Jul
1.58	S. Opoku		1	Kingston	28	Jul
1.56	Ian Fenn	3.12.83	1	Crawley	6	Jun
1.55	N. Rutter		1	Enfield	15	Jul
1.55	A. Rees			Brecon	1	Sep
1.55	Colin Bailey	15.11.83		Blackburn	8	Sep
1.55	Andrew Kelly	26.09.83	1	Cambridge	15	Sep

POLE VAULT

5.71	Nick Buckfield		5.06.73	1	Birmingham	16	Jun
	5.30xo, 5.50o, 5.71xxo, 5.81xxx						
	5.65			3	Dijon, FRA	26	May
	5.61 i			1	Birmingham	3	Feb
	5.60			2	Nuremberg, GER	7	Jun
	5.60			5=	Karlskrona, SWE	28	Jun
	5.60			3	Gateshead	30	Jun
	5.55 i			Q	Stockholm, SWE	8	Mar
	5.55 i			7	Stockholm, SWE	9	Mar
	5.50 i			2	Birmingham	27	Jan
	5.50 i			2=	Birmingham	10	Feb
	5.50			1	Enfield	4	May
	5.50			2	Kerkrade, HOL	17	May
	5.50			1	Loughborough	19	May
	5.50			4	Madrid, SPA	2	Jun
	5.50			1	Budapest, HUN	20	Jun
	5.50			8	London (CP)	12	Jul
	5.50			3	Gateshead	19	Aug
	5.40 i			12=	Lievin, FRA	18	Feb
	5.40			20Q	Atlanta, USA	31	Jul
	5.40			6	Sheffield	25	Aug
	5.30 i			3	Glasgow	24	Feb
5.50	Paul Williamson	U23	16.06.74	1	Toulon, FRA	6	Jul
	5.45			1	London (He)	28	Jul
	5.45			1	Kingston	17	Aug
	5.40			2	Loughborough	19	May
	5.40			2	Tallinn, EST	9	Jun
	5.40			1	Sheffield	24	Jul
	5.40			4=	Sheffield	25	Aug
	5.35			1	Cork, IRE	22	Jun
	5.30			1	Telford	27	Apr
	5.30			1	Scunthorpe	11	May
	5.30			6=	Birmingham	16	Jun
	5.30			1	Woking	26	Jun
	5.30			1=	Stoke	28	Jun
	5.30			1	Cudworth	3	Aug
	5.30			9=	Linz, AUT	21	Aug

Mark	Name	Cat	DOB	Pos	Venue	Date	
5.50	Neil Winter	U23	21.03.74	9	London (CP)	12	Jul
5.40				2	Birmingham	16	Jun
5.40				1	Newport	10	Jul
5.40				24=Q	Atlanta, USA	31	Jul
5.30				3	Kingston	17	Aug
5.45	Mike Edwards		19.10.68	1	London (BP)	15	May
5.41				1	Portsmouth	11	May
5.40				1	San Angelo, USA	13	Apr
5.40				1	Hassleby, SWE	6	Jun
5.40				1	London (He)	9	Jun
5.36				2	Waco, USA	23	Mar
5.35				1	Liverpool	4	May
5.35				1	Lidingo, SWE	4	Jun
5.30				3	Birmingham	16	Jun
5.40 i	Matt Belsham		11.10.71	5=	Birmingham	10	Feb
5.35 i				2	Vienna, AUT	17	Feb
5.35				1	L'Aigle, FRA	28	Apr
5.30 i				2	Birmingham	3	Feb
5.30 i				4	Glasgow	24	Feb
5.30				1	Dormagen, GER	5	May
5.30				8	Birmingham	16	Jun
5.30				2	Kingston	17	Aug
5.30	Kevin Hughes		30.04.73	2	London (He)	9	Jun
5.30				5	Birmingham	16	Jun
5.30				1	Birmingham	6	Jul
5.30	Ian Tullett		15.08.69	4	Birmingham	16	Jun
5.30				5	Gateshead	30	Jun
5.30	Mike Barber		19.10.73	6=	Birmingham	16	Jun
5.30				1=	Stoke	28	Jun

66 performances to 5.30 by 8 athletes including 11 indoors

Mark	Name	Cat	DOB	Pos	Venue	Date	
5.21	Dean Mellor		25.11.71	1	Jarrow	4	May
5.20 i	Andy Ashurst		2.01.65	7	Birmingham	10	Feb
5.20				2	Sheffield	11	May
(10)							
5.20	Mark Hodgkinson		20.07.72	1	Stoke	24	Aug
5.15	Christian Linskey	U17	14.06.80	Q	Sydney, AUS	23	Aug
5.10	Mark Davis	U20	1.03.77	1	Corby	9	Jun
5.00	Neil Young	U20	20.02.77	1	Belfast	18	May
5.00	Ian Wilding	U23	3.03.75	2	Newport	1	Jun
5.00	Tim Thomas		18.11.73	1	Newport	8	Jun
5.00	Ben Flint	U20	16.09.78	2	Leeds	6	Jul
5.00	Mark Grant		17.05.71	3=	Birmingham	6	Jul
4.90	Barry Thomas		28.04.72	5=D	Lage, GER	16	Jun
4.90	Craig Guite	U20	19.08.77	3	Bedford	28	Jul
(20)							
4.90	Duncan Pearce		21.10.70	4	Peterborough	26	Aug
4.80 i	Egryn Jones		1.11.71	2	Birmingham	11	Feb
4.60				1	Cardiff	10	Mar
4.80 i	Bob Kingman		21.02.73	1	Birmingham	29	Feb
4.80				2	Telford	27	Apr
4.80	Mark Johnson		7.09.64	1	Grimsby	25	May
4.80	Matt Weaver		14.11.73	1	Barking	23	Jun
4.80	Paul Beswick		5.12.68	5	Peterborough	26	Aug
4.75	Robert Thickpenny	U23	17.07.76	1	Loughborough	22	Sep
4.70	David O'Neill	U23	19.01.76	2	Grimsby	25	May
4.70	Simon Shirley		3.08.66	12D	Gotzis, AUT	26	May
4.70	Dominic Shepherd	U23	11.12.76	2	Newport	8	Jun
(30)							
4.70	Steve McLennan	U20	17.11.78	1	London (CP)	29	Jun
4.70	Ian Noble	U20	2.04.77	3	Leeds	6	Jul
4.70	Warren Jousiffe	U20	27.05.77	2	Sheffield	13	Jul

4.65 i	Alex Kruger		18.11.63	10H	Stockholm, SWE	10 Mar
4.60 i	Robin Hill	U20	23.02.77	2	Wakefield	13 Jan
4.60				3	Sheffield	11 May
4.60	Matthew Buck	U23	5.04.74	1	Loughborough	27 Apr
4.60	Matthew Evans	U23	19.11.75	3	Jarrow	4 May
4.60	Glyn Price		12.09.65	4	Enfield	4 May
4.60	Brian Taylor		13.08.70	2D	Bedford	26 May
4.60	Dan Gilby		10.07.70	2	London (He)	28 Jul
(40)						
4.60	Rufus Cooper	U20	24.02.79	8	Peterborough	26 Aug
4.60	Andrew Penk	U20	19.09.78	1	Colwyn Bay	26 Aug
4.60	Doug Hamilton		19.05.61	1	Tweedbank	31 Aug
4.50	Iain Black		18.09.70	1	Edinburgh	16 Jun
4.50	Christian North	U23	2.02.74	1	Bath	19 Jun
4.50	Dave Gordon		20.03.68	6=	Watford	6 Jul
4.50	Leigh Walker	U20	17.08.77	5	Watford	6 Jul
4.50	Steve Leader		24.11.66	1D	Enfield	4 Aug
4.45	Richard Smith	U17	17.01.81	1	Birmingham	18 Aug
4.45	Tom Richards	U20	13.11.78	1	Exeter	24 Aug
(50)						
4.40 i	Gavin Card	U20	11.05.78	1	Gateshead	18 Jan
4.40	Eric Hollingsworth		6.12.62	D	Sydney, AUS	21 Jan
4.40 i	Stephen Rogers		1.09.71	2H	Birmingham	4 Feb
4.10				5D	Bedford	26 May
4.40 i	Peter Holt	U20	12.02.77	7	Birmingham	18 Feb
4.20				1	Scunthorpe	4 May
4.40 i	Stephen Smith	U17	13.02.80	2	Birmingham	18 Feb
4.30				2	Sheffield	12 Jul
4.40 i	Kevin Treen	U23	1.02.76	4	Glasgow	17 Mar
4.40				4	Sheffield	6 May
4.40	Brett Armstrong	U23	9.09.76	1	Rugby	28 Apr
4.40	Gary Jackson		28.04.68	1	Carlisle	28 Apr
4.40	Klemens Pollmeier		8.06.66	5	Sheffield	6 May
4.40	Terry Fidler		13.10.71	1	Crawley	11 May
(60)						
4.40	Rafer Joseph		21.07.68	3D	Bedford	26 May
4.40	Jamie Webb	U23	18.12.75	8	London (CP)	1 Jun
4.40	Mark Bushell	U23	22.10.76	1	Portsmouth	8 Jun
4.40	Anthony Southward		31.01.71	24=D	Lage, GER	16 Jun
4.40	Andy Buchanan		12.09.70	1	Aldershot	26 Jun
4.40	Darren Neport	U17	4.09.79	5	Watford	17 Aug
4.40	Livio Salvador-Aylott		18.07.73	1D	Antrim	1 Sep
4.30 i	Adam Davis		19.11.72	4	Bedford	17 Mar
4.30	Robert Bell	U20	17.12.77	1	Basildon	8 Jun
4.30	Alan Hardy		4.09.58	9	Newport	8 Jun
(70)						
4.30	James Palmer	U20	21.04.78	1	Abingdon	17 Aug
4.30	Mark Perman		6.01.68	1	London (He)	1 Sep
4.26	Douglas Graham	U20	1.01.77	1	Wishaw	13 Jul
4.25	Ian Parkinson	U20	12.02.79	1	High Wycombe	4 May
4.25	Scott Simpson	U20	21.07.79	2	Stoke	22 Jun
4.20 i	Dean Macey	U20	12.12.77	2	London (Ha)	13 Jan
4.20				15D	Sydney, AUS	22 Aug
4.20 i	Adam Pengilly	U20	14.10.77	1	Birmingham	11 Feb
4.10				2	Bath	17 May
4.20	Steve Gutteridge		5.07.71	1	Enfield	11 May
4.20	Nick Pritchard		5.12.72	1	Cwmbran	12 May
4.20	Garry Chiles		15.05.66	2	Barking	23 Jun
(80)						
4.20	Terry Gyorffy		28.01.65	3	Aldershot	26 Jun
4.20	Darren Beddows	U20	4.05.78	2	Swansea	6 Jul

4.20	Paul Howard		19.10.66	11	Watford	6	Jul
4.20	Alex Thomas	U17	31.12.79	3	Sheffield	12	Jul
4.20	Ian Gibb	U23	8.01.75	2	Aberdeen	28	Jul
4.20	Jon Yapp	U23	1.02.75	4	Stoke	28	Jul
4.20	Steve Gascoigne		20.12.66	1	Woking	17	Aug
4.20	Gavin Sunshine	U23	19.02.74	1	Worthing	17	Aug
4.15 i	Steve Francis	U20	31.01.79	17	Birmingham	7	Jan
4.15	Glyn Sutton	V50	3.05.45	1	Exeter	10	Aug
(90)							
4.15	Paul Harrison	U17	17.11.79	3	Birmingham	18	Aug
4.15	John Gullaksen	U17	24.02.80	2	Bolton	14	Sep
4.10	Richard Gammage		21.11.62	3	Woodford	21	Apr
4.10	Dean Robinson		25.06.70	1	Ashton-U-Lyne	28	Apr
4.10	Tony Matthews		17.12.62	7	Jarrow	4	May
4.10	Andrew Garner			2	Grantham	11	May
4.10	Chris Wills	U23	18.05.76	1	Worcester	9	Jun
4.10	Gareth Lease	U20	14.08.78	1	Exeter	15	Jun
4.10	William Gilles		15.02.73	1	Croydon	22	Jun
4.10	Brett Heath	U23	6.01.75	1	London (Elt)	22	Jun
(100)							
4.10	David McLeod		26.03.63	4	Glasgow	29	Jun
4.10	Phil Brilus		29.12.68	1	Hoo	13	Jul
4.10	David Ralson	U20	22.02.77	6D	Narbonne, FRA	28	Jul
4.10	Martyn Hole	U23	29.11.75	1	Southend	3	Aug
4.10	Phil Maton				Barking	17	Aug
4.10	C. Mills				Barking	17	Aug
4.10	Martin Densley	U17	1.05.81	3	Abingdon	24	Aug

Foreign

4.91 i	*Dylan McDermott*		*1.12.70*	*1*	*Nenagh, IRE*	*18*	*Feb*
4.70				*1*	*Kingston*	*15*	*May*
4.50	*Pierre Faber*		*9.01.72*	*D*	*Sheffield*	*28*	*Apr*
4.50	*Alan Burke*		*23.05.65*	*5*	*Newport*	*8*	*Jun*

Additional Under 17 (1 - 8 above)

4.00	Ashley Swain		3.10.80	5	Birmingham	18	Aug
4.00	Nick Waters		1.01.80	4	Great Yarmouth	31	Aug
(10)							
3.95	Adam Walker		16.11.79	8	Sheffield	12	Jul
3.90	Richard Baldock		22.04.80	1	Bedford	2	Jun
3.90	David Ingram		19.01.80	1	Crawley	8	Jun
3.90	Chris Boundy		25.12.79	1	Jarrow	12	Jun
3.90	Andrew Correy	U15	15.10.81	1	Birmingham	17	Aug
3.85	Steven Brown	U15	20.03.82	1	Bedford	2	Jun
3.80	Pat Campbell		10.03.80	1	Dublin, IRE	22	Jun
3.80	Paul Connelly		10.03.80	2	Cudworth	30	Jun
3.80	Charles Rule		22.05.80	3	Edinburgh	3	Jul
3.80	Paul Miles		14.09.80	1	Yeovil	21	Jul
(20)							
3.80	Mark Beharrell		10.01.81	1	Lincoln	28	Jul
3.80	Daniel Broadhead	U15	19.04.82	3	Birmingham	17	Aug
3.80	Jon Parry		13.04.80	8	Birmingham	18	Aug
3.80	Tom Abdy		3.05.81	9	Birmingham	18	Aug
3.70	R. Chapman			1	Birmingham	8	Jun
3.70	Kevin Howle			1	Stoke	24	Jul
3.70	Paul Thomas		1.10.80	2	Woking	1	Sep
3.60	David Raw		1.02.81	1	London (He)	28	Jun
3.60	Chris Type	U15	5.10.81	1	Carmarthen	21	Jul
3.60	Kevin Tufton		30.04.80	1	Peterborough	21	Jul
(30)							
3.60	James Phillips		6.08.80	2	Stoke	25	Aug

Additional Under 15 (1 - 4 above)

3.50	Anton Martinez		29.09.81	2	London (CP)	30	Jun
3.40	Graham Bowden		2.09.81	1	London (Elt)	21	Jul
3.35	Philip Wade		24.05.82	4	Sheffield	12	Jul
3.30	Danny Cunnane		12.04.83	1	Cannock	31	Aug
3.25	Stephen Day		10.02.82	5	Sheffield	12	Jul
3.15	Andrew MacDonald		19.05.83	6	Sheffield	12	Jul
	(10)						
3.10	Martin Waters		20.01.82	1	Hayes	2	Jun
3.10	David Sumner			1	Birmingham	8	Sep
3.00	Andy Lacey		29.03.82	2	Basildon	8	Jun
3.00	Daniel Randles		16.04.82	1	Gateshead	8	Jun
3.00	John Hutchinson		3.05.82	3	London (CP)	30	Jun
3.00	Neil Myatt		15.10.81	11	Sheffield	12	Jul
3.00	Philip Titmus		12.11.81	1	Yeovil	21	Jul
2.95	Cameron Johnston		22.10.82	3	London (He)	27	Jun
2.90	R. Peel			2	Leeds	21	Jul
2.90	C. Weedon			2	Birmingham	7	Sep

Under 13

2.20	Michael Parker	U13	29.10.83	4	Grimsby	29	Sep

LONG JUMP

7.97 w	3.8	Nathan Morgan	U20	30.06.78	1	Sheffield	13	Jul
		7.74	1.0		3	Sydney, AUS	22	Aug
		7.66 w	3.9		3	Nembro, ITA	3	Aug
		7.65	2.0		1	Bedford	28	Jul
		7.58	0.0		2	Tallinn, EST	9	Jun
		7.56			1	Loughborough	5	Jun
		7.51	1.7		*	Sheffield	13	Jul
		7.51	-0.3		Q	Sydney, AUS	21	Aug
7.86	1.5	Darren Ritchie	U23	14.02.75	1	Birmingham	15	Jun
		7.68 w			1	Edinburgh	11	May
		7.63 w	3.4		1	Glasgow	29	Jun
		7.51	0.5		1	Bedford	27	May
		7.48 i			1	Glasgow	21	Jan
7.79	0.2	Fred Salle		10.09.64	4	Istanbul, TUR	19	May
		7.68 w	3.5		1	Liverpool	5	May
		7.60	-1.4		5	Ljubljana, SLO	26	May
7.79 w	2.2	Steve Phillips		17.03.72	1	Birmingham	20	Jul
		7.75			1	London (FP)	30	Jun
		7.70	1.0		*	Birmingham	20	Jul
		7.69 i			1	Birmingham	6	Jan
		7.65 w	3.9		1	London (He)	9	Jun
		7.64 w	3.0		1	Birmingham	6	Jul
		7.63	1.3		1	Leamington	11	May
		7.61			1	Leamington	14	Apr
		7.60 w	3.9		1	Birmingham	1	Jun
		7.59	-0.5		1	Kingston	17	Aug
		7.59			1	Windsor	29	Sep
		7.57			1	Birmingham	10	Aug
		7.56 i			3	Birmingham	27	Jan
		7.55 i			1	Birmingham	11	Feb
		7.54			1	Welwyn	6	May
		7.54			2	Welwyn	26	Aug
		7.53			1	Sheffield	20	Apr
		7.53			1	Telford	14	Sep
		7.53 w	2.8		2	Liverpool	5	May
		7.52			1	Stoke	28	Jul
		7.50	-0.4		Q	Birmingham	14	Jun

Mark	Wind	Name	Cat	DOB	Pos	Venue	Date
(Phillips)		7.47 i			3	Glasgow	29 Feb
		7.47			1	Wrexham	4 Aug
		7.47			1	Sutton	22 Sep
		7.45			1	Crawley	7 Apr
		7.45 1.0			*	Birmingham	6 Jul
7.67	-0.3	Oni Onuorah		16.10.73	2	Birmingham	15 Jun
		7.62			5	Budapest, HUN	20 Jun
		7.52 i			2	Birmingham	6 Jan
7.60 i		Chris Davidson	U23	4.12.75	1	Birmingham	4 Feb
		7.57 i			5	Vienna, AUT	17 Feb
		7.54 0.9			1	Newport	8 Jun
		7.50			3	Hexham	14 Jul
7.57		Julian Flynn		3.07.72	1	Welwyn	26 Aug
		7.49			2	London (FP)	30 Jun
		7.49 1.3			1	Kunzelsau, GER	7 Sep
		7.48 w 2.5			2	Kingston	17 Aug
7.54	0.4	Stewart Faulkner		19.02.69	1	Luton	6 May
		7.50 -1.2			Q	Birmingham	14 Jun
		7.50 w 2.4			2	London (He)	9 Jun
		7.48			3	London (FP)	30 Jun
		7.47 -0.3			3	Birmingham	15 Jun
7.54 w	3.9	Barrington Williams	V40	11.09.55	2	Birmingham	1 Jun
		7.52 i			1	Birmingham	2 Mar
		7.42 0.6			*	Birmingham	1 Jun
7.51 w	3.3	Mark Bushell	U23	22.10.76	2	Sheffield	13 Jul
		7.22 0.4			1D	Narbonne, FRA	27 Jul
	(10)						
7.50 w	5.6	Steve Smith		29.03.73	3	Liverpool	4 May
7.48		Paul Johnson		8.03.68	1	Worcester	9 Jun
7.46 i		John King		13.02.63	3	Birmingham	3 Feb
		7.31 w 2.2			3	Bedford	27 May
		7.11 0.8			*	Bedford	27 May
7.46		John Shepherd		23.12.61	3	London (CP)	18 Aug

65 performances to 7.45 by 14 athletes including 10 indoors and 15 wind assisted

Mark	Wind	Name	Cat	DOB	Pos	Venue	Date
7.44 i		Carl Howard	U23	27.01.74	4	Birmingham	27 Jan
		7.31			1	Crawley	28 Jul
7.38 i		David Clerihew	U20	11.09.77	1	Lievin, FRA	2 Mar
		7.30 w 3.5			2	Glasgow	29 Jun
		7.29			1	Edinburgh	8 Jun
7.37		Femi Akinsanya		29.11.69	2	Watford	17 Aug
7.35 w	4.8	Simon Shirley		3.08.66	2D	Val De Reuil, FRA	29 Jun
		7.30 1.9			13D	Lage, GER	15 Jun
7.33 w	2.7	Barry Thomas		28.04.72	D	Val De Reuil, FRA	29 Jun
		7.13 2.0			2D	Bedford	26 May
7.32 w	3.2	Anthony Malcolm	U23	15.02.76	1	Newport	1 Jun
		7.16 i			2	Glasgow	17 Mar
		6.94 0.3			11Q	Birmingham	14 Jun
	(20)						
7.30		Gareth Devlin	U23	2.06.76	1	Londonderry	18 Aug
7.26 i		Andy Lewis		9.03.68	1	Glasgow	17 Mar
		7.17			1	Luton	23 Jun
7.26 w	3.2	Brian Taylor		13.08.70	1D	Bedford	25 May
		7.09 1.8			18D	Lage, GER	15 Jun
7.25		Essop Merrick	U23	24.05.74	1	Cambridge	17 Aug
7.24		Joe Sweeney		17.07.65	4	Watford	17 Aug
7.23 i		Alex Kruger		18.11.63	10H	Stockholm, SWE	9 Mar
7.23		Gary Smith		20.02.71	2	Croydon	22 Jun
7.23		Elphinston Hinds		15.07.60	1	Harrow	13 Jul
7.22		Gareth Davies		11.05.71	1	Oxford	18 May
7.22		Trevor Sinclair		6.08.61	2	Welwyn	13 Jul
	(30)						

7.21	0.3	John Munroe		6.01.69	2	London (CP)	1	Jun
7.20 i		Courtney Charles		13.11.68	7	Birmingham	4	Feb
		7.07	0.7		5	Kingston	17	Aug
7.18 i		Nigel Bourne		18.04.72	8	Birmingham	3	Feb
7.18 w		Kevin Hibbins	U17	7.11.80	1	Solihull	21	Jul
		6.74			1	Grantham	23	Jun
7.17 w		Mark Swales	U23	29.01.75	2	Harrow	13	Jul
7.15 w	2.2	Nick Dowsett	U20	24.11.78	2	London (He)	31	Aug
		6.87			4	Bedford	28	Jul
7.14		Manny Nsudoh		8.04.72	2	Luton	23	Jun
7.14		George Audu	U20	18.01.77	3	Bedford	28	Jul
7.14		Dean Macey	U20	12.12.77	1	Newport	4	Aug
7.13	1.3	Stuart Clarke	U23	16.10.75	3	London (CP)	1	Jun
	(40)							
7.13	1.8	William Gilles		15.02.73	5D	Narbonne, FRA	27	Jul
7.13 w		Stefan Rose	U23	7.04.75	5	Abingdon	24	Aug
7.12 w	2.9	Jan Irving	U20	4.03.77	1	Sheffield	1	Jun
7.11	-0.8	Mathias Ogbeta		19.06.68	4	London (He)	9	Jun
7.11		Matt Douglas	U23	26.11.76	1	Swindon	14	Aug
7.10 w	5.2	Andrew Thornton	U20	29.11.77	3	Sheffield	13	Jul
		6.86	1.9		*	Sheffield	13	Jul
7.08		Billy Jewers		27.09.62	1D	Aldershot	13	Jun
7.08		Alvin Walker		30.04.65	1	Portsmouth	3	Jul
7.07		Leo Barker	U20	26.12.78	1	Corby	18	May
7.07 w	4.3	Anthony Southward		31.01.71	3D	Bedford	25	May
		6.91	0.4		D	Lage, GER	15	Jun
	(50)							
7.06	-1.2	Brian Robinson	U17	3.09.80	3	Ljubljana, SLO	28	Sep
7.05 i		Jamie Quarry		15.11.72	3	Glasgow	17	Mar
		6.99	1.6		3	Newport	8	Jun
7.05	0.8	Stuart Wells	U20	26.07.79	1	London (CP)	30	Jun
7.05	0.6	Geoffrey Ojok	U20	19.05.79	6	Kingston	17	Aug
7.05 w	3.6	Ian Simpson		3.08.66	6	Liverpool	4	May
		6.98	0.4		3	Sheffield	2	Jun
7.04		Mark Lawrence		26.01.71	1	Nottingham	11	May
7.04		Denis Costello		3.12.61	1	London (BP)	18	May
7.04	1.5	Tendai Huntley	U23	12.09.76	5	London (CP)	1	Jun
7.04		Paul Ralph		16.12.67	4	Enfield	6	Jul
7.04 w	3.9	Andrew Roberts	U20	19.09.77	1	Leeds	8	Sep
	(60)							
7.03		Andy Wooding	U20	2.06.79	1	Colwyn Bay	7	Sep
7.02		Dan Dugard		21.06.65	1	Dartford	13	Jul
7.02		Robin Hynes	U20	22.04.77	1	Stretford	17	Aug
7.02	0.5	William Wyllie		12.07.73	1	Cannock	7	Sep
7.01		Alexis Sharp		31.10.72	1	Enfield	4	May
7.01 i		Steve Benton	U23	26.09.76	1	London (CP)	7	Dec
7.01 w		James Gilbert	U23	9.11.74	1	Liverpool	28	Jul
		6.87 i			3	Glasgow	21	Jan
		6.86			3	Edinburgh	11	May
6.99		John Royden			1	Bromley	28	Apr
6.97		Willie Stark	U20	11.03.77	1	Aberdeen	5	May
6.97 w		Chris Cotter		3.02.72	7	Liverpool	4	May
		6.92	0.8		6	London (CP)	1	Jun
	(70)							
6.96		H. Eoun			1	Watford	25	Sep
6.96		Brett Heath	U23	6.01.75	1D	Thurrock	28	Sep
6.95		Sam Nash		22.10.71	1	London (TB)	28	Apr
6.95		John Robert		17.01.69	1	Woodford	22	Jun
6.94		Stephen Rowbotham		6.03.68	2	Cudworth	23	Jun
6.94 w	2.9	Rafer Joseph		21.07.68	5D	Bedford	25	May
6.93		James Leaver	U23	15.09.75	6	Watford	17	Aug

6.92		Darren Joseph	U20	10.04.78	2	Telford	4 May
6.92		Toby Box		9.09.72	4	Sheffield	12 May
6.92 w		Ian Roberts		15.06.68	8	Liverpool	4 May
	(80)						
6.92 w	2.7	Mark Faulkner	U17	14.11.79	1	Sheffield	12 Jul
6.83	0.3				1	Stoke	20 Jul
6.90		Lee Edwards	U23	14.09.75	2	Newport	1 Jun
6.90		Stuart Finnie	U20	14.12.78	1	Antrim	8 Jun
6.90		S. Williams			1	Swindon	13 Jul
6.90		Andrew Cargill		25.10.69	1	Harrow	17 Jul

Foreign

8.16 w	8.0	*Carlos Castel-Branco*			1	*Lisbon, POR*	21 Apr
7.72					1	*London (TB)*	29 Jun
7.63	1.1	*Jonathon Kron*		16.02.73	4	*Ljubljana, SLO*	26 May
7.27		*Gary Munroe*		12.04.69	3	*Watford*	17 Aug
7.19		*Sebastian Maufrais*		18.01.70	1	*Sheffield*	11 May
7.07	0.8	*Olu Robincocker*	U23	27.11.75	2	*Sheffield*	2 Jun
6.93		*Ademola Oyediran*		27.11.59	1	*Bracknell*	23 Jun

Additional Under 20 (1 - 19 above)

6.89		Darren Hatton		21.03.79	1	Hoo	8 Jun
	(20)						
6.87 w	2.3	Peter Zdanowski		3.01.78	2	London (CP)	30 Jun
6.85		Phillip Pearce		3.04.79	1	Exeter	15 Jun
6.84		Nicky Gordon		7.01.77	4	Sheffield	12 May
6.83		Kevin Eaves		16.03.79	2	Kingston	8 Jun
6.81		Duncan Chau			2	Hoo	8 Jun

Additional Under 17 (1 - 3 above)

6.80		Alistair Gudgeon		26.10.79	1	Great Yarmouth	31 Aug
6.80		Alastair McInroy		21.06.80	1	Ayr	1 Sep
6.80 w	3.3	Rasheed Banda		18.03.80	2	Sheffield	12 Jul
6.59					1	London (He)	8 Jun
6.79		Wayne Hay		25.09.80	1	Windsor	28 Jul
6.76		Ian Kenny		12.10.79	1	Tullamore, IRE	Jul
6.74 w		Marc Mercer		27.10.79	1	Stoke	22 Jun
6.56 i					1	Birmingham	24 Feb
6.73 w	2.2	James Morris		2.12.79	5	Newport	1 Jun
6.68					1	Aberdare	12 May
	(10)						
6.64		Carl McMullen		9.11.79	1	Colwyn Bay	7 Sep
6.64 w	3.4	Adam Potter		12.04.80	4	Sheffield	12 Jul
6.61	1.0	Kirk King		18.09.80	6	Sheffield	12 Jul
6.61	0.9	Neil Bellamy		23.07.80	7	Sheffield	12 Jul
6.60		Syful Ahmed		25.10.79	1	Croydon	19 May
6.60	1.9	Chris Baillie		21.04.81	1	Pitreavie	10 Aug
6.59 i		Marc Newton		15.03.80	1P	Birmingham	3 Mar
6.59		Lewis Erdman		29.11.79		London (TB)	28 Apr
6.57		Jason McDade		3.04.80	1	Milton Keynes	4 Aug
6.56		Austin Ferns		12.01.81	1O	Walton	16 Jun
	(20)						
6.53		Jonathon Oparka		27.01.80	1	Dundee	10 Jun
6.49		Richard McDonald		11.01.80	1	Edinburgh	11 May
6.49	2.0	Richard Gawthorpe		28.01.81	8	Sheffield	12 Jul
6.48 w	2.5	Marko Stanojevic		1.10.79	9	Sheffield	12 Jul
6.47		Darren Wright		7.09.79	1	Worcester	24 Aug

Under 15

| 6.42 w | 2.5 | Gabriel Aboyo-Dana | | 20.11.81 | 1 | Birmingham | 8 Sep |
| 6.35 | 1.8 | Chris Jenkins | | 2.03.82 | 1 | Sheffield | 12 Jul |

6.30 w	2.2	David Mountford		23.06.82	2	Sheffield	12	Jul
5.99					1	Derby	21	Jul
6.18 w	2.4	Richard Danso			2	Birmingham	8	Sep
6.17					1	London (BP)	17	Aug
6.17		Tom Roe		25.06.82	1	Cambridge	15	Sep
6.16		Sebastian Coghlan		31.01.82	1	Exeter	15	Jun
6.16		Mark Awanah		23.09.82	1P	Birmingham	21	Sep
6.10		Dominic Girdler		6.03.82	1	Telford	14	Sep
6.09 w	2.9	Chris Tomlinson		15.09.81	2	Cudworth	29	Jun
5.91					1	Jarrow	12	May
6.07		Dwayne Grant		17.07.82	1	London (CP)	11	Mar
	(10)							
6.03		Peter Kiddell		2.09.81		Kingston	12	Apr
6.03		Tim Greenwood		22.11.82	1	Harrow	2	Jun
6.03		John Christmas		30.10.81	1	Welwyn	26	Aug
6.02		Matthew Barclay		28.01.82	4P	Birmingham	21	Sep
6.01	0.5	Oladipo Senbanjo		20.03.82	1	Birmingham	7	Sep
6.01 w		Martin Taylor		31.01.82	P	Bedford	25	May
5.97		Kieron Morgan		4.09.81	1	Croydon	8	Jun
5.97	1.5	Leon Burnett		12.09.81	4	Birmingham	8	Sep
5.95 i		Craig Thomas		28.09.81	1	Glasgow	23	Mar
5.94					1	Glasgow	11	May
5.94		Michael Gibson			2	Pitreavie	10	Aug
	(20)							
5.93		Tyrone Edger		29.03.82	1	Harrow	5	May
5.93	1.9	Andrew Roberts			5	Birmingham	8	Sep
5.93		Jamie Russell		1.10.81	5P	Birmingham	21	Sep

Overage

6.25 i		Dwayne Grant	U15	17.07.82	1	London (CP)	7	Dec
6.03 i		Nathan Palmer	U15		P	Glasgow	21	Dec

Under 13

5.20		J. Lau	U13			Cambridge	15	Sep
5.18		D. Whattley	U13		1	Enfield	15	Jul

TRIPLE JUMP

17.88	0.9	Jonathan Edwards		10.05.66	2	Atlanta, USA	27	Jul
		x - x - 17.15(-0.5) - 17.88 - x - x						
17.82	1.6				1	Helsinki, FIN	25	Jun
		16.78 - 17.82 - x - 15.25 - x - x						
17.79	-0.7				1	Zurich, SWZ	14	Aug
		17.17(-1.2) - 17.40(-2.2) - x - 17.15(-1.5) - p - 17.79						
17.79 w	3.3				1	Madrid, SPA	2	Jun
		x - x - 17.79w - p - x - p						
17.69	-0.5				1	Berlin, GER	30	Aug
		17.13(-0.4) - 15.82(0.5) - 17.26(-0.7) - 17.16(0.5) - 17.69 - p						
17.68	-1.6				1	Oslo, NOR	5	Jul
		17.22(-0.9) - 17.68 - p - 17.02(2.0) - x - 15.13(0.9)						
17.67 A	1.1				1	Sestriere, ITA	7	Aug
		17.11w(2.8) - 17.22w(4.2) - 17.26w(3.2) - x - 17.28(2.0) - 17.67						
17.59	1.3				1	Milan, ITA	7	Sep
		17.39(1.6) - 17.43(1.6) - p - x - x - 17.59						
17.59 w	3.7				1	Atlanta, USA	18	May
		17.03(0.3) - 17.59w - 17.45(1.4) - p - p - p						
17.55	0.0				1	Rome, ITA	5	Jun
		17.20 - 17.19 - x - x - x - 17.55						
17.52	1.4				1	London (CP)	12	Jul
		x - 17.29(0.8) - 15.21(0.8) - 17.52 - p - x						
17.50	0.0				1	Brussels, BEL	23	Aug
		17.00(0.7) - x - 17.18(-0.5) - 17.50 - p - p						

(Edwards)	17.45	1.4			*	Atlanta, USA	18 May
	17.38	-0.5			1	Gateshead	19 Aug
	x - 16.75(1.0) - p - 17.09(0.6) - p - 17.38						
	17.38	1.2			2	Tokyo, JAP	15 Sep
	17.29	0.3			1	Stockholm, SWE	8 Jul
	17.05(0.7) - 17.29 - 14.82(0.6) - p - p - x						
	17.02	1.0			1	Gateshead	30 Jun
	17.02 - x - p -16.90(0.9) - p - 14.31						
	16.96	0.0			Q	Atlanta, USA	27 Jul
	16.93(-0.6) - 16.96 - p						
	16.93	0.3			1	London (CP)	11 Aug
	16.93 - p - x - x - p - x						
	16.90	1.1			1	Sheffield	25 Aug
17.22 w 3.8	Francis Agyepong			16.06.65	1	Floro, NOR	25 May
	17.19 w 3.6				2	Riga, LAT	2 Jun
	17.18	0.4			2	Oslo, NOR	5 Jul
	17.12	0.9			1	Birmingham	15 Jun
	16.97 i				Q	Stockholm, SWE	9 Mar
	16.93 i				2	Stockholm, SWE	10 Mar
	16.92 i				1	Glasgow	24 Feb
	16.89	0.7			*	Riga, LAT	2 Jun
	16.77	1.2			2	London (CP)	12 Jul
	16.71	-1.4			13Q	Atlanta, USA	27 Jul
	16.67	0.8			2	Gateshead	30 Jun
	16.65 w 2.6				2	Sheffield	25 Aug
	16.63	-0.3			6	Brussels, BEL	23 Aug
	16.62	1.2			2	Gateshead	19 Aug
	16.59	1.1			5	Milan, ITA	7 Sep
	16.58	-0.2			3	London (CP)	11 Aug
	16.57	0.5			4	Helsinki, FIN	25 Jun
	16.57	1.5			3	Stockholm, SWE	8 Jul
	16.55 i				1	Birmingham	3 Feb
	16.55	0.0			6	Rome, ITA	5 Jun
	16.47 i				1	Vienna, AUT	17 Feb
	16.34	0.2			Q	Birmingham	14 Jun
	16.15 i				3	Birmingham	27 Jan
	16.12	1.2			2	Loughborough	19 May
16.58	1.0	Femi Akinsanya		29.11.69	2	Birmingham	15 Jun
	16.23	0.6			7	London (CP)	12 Jul
	16.23 w 3.3				1	Loughborough	19 May
	16.19				1	Peterborough	4 May
	16.17 w 2.2				7	Gateshead	30 Jun
	16.15	1.5			*	Gateshead	30 Jun
	16.05 i				4	Glasgow	24 Feb
16.53	1.6	Julian Golley		12.09.71	5	Riga, LAT	2 Jun
	16.45	0.5			Q	Birmingham	14 Jun
	16.44	1.7			4	Gateshead	30 Jun
	16.39	0.9			3	Birmingham	15 Jun
	16.25 w 2.6				6	London (CP)	12 Jul
	16.18	-0.7			1	Bedford	27 May
	16.09 wA				5	Sestriere, ITA	7 Aug
	16.05	0.6			*	London (CP)	12 Jul
	16.02				4	Loughborough	19 May
16.38	0.6	Tosi Fasinro		28.03.72	4	Birmingham	15 Jun
	16.05	0.2			Q	Birmingham	14 Jun
16.36	1.5	Onochie Achike	U23	31.01.75	5	Birmingham	15 Jun
	16.04	0.2			Q	Birmingham	14 Jun

64 performances to 16.00 by 6 athletes including 7 indoors and 9 wind assisted

15.90	0.3	John Herbert	20.04.62	Q	Birmingham	14 Jun
15.75	0.4	Joe Sweeney	17.07.65	1	Bracknell	12 May

15.74 w 3.7	James Peacock	U20	29.09.77	1	Sheffield	13	Jul
15.24				4	Nembro, ITA	3	Aug
15.67	Carl Howard	U23	27.01.74	3	Hexham	14	Jul
(10)							
15.67 w	Paul Ralph		16.12.67	1	Portsmouth	21	Jul
15.65				2	Enfield	6	Jul
15.63 0.6	Ezra Clarke	U23	9.12.74	1	Kingston	17	Aug
15.60 w 2.3	Keith Ible		9.11.68	1	Birmingham	6	Jul
15.24 1.1				*	Birmingham	6	Jul
15.53 w 5.9	Phillips Idowu	U20	30.12.78	2	Sheffield	13	Jul
15.12				1	London (TB)	16	Jun
15.45	Alvin Walker		30.04.65	1	Portsmouth	3	Jul
15.34	Michael McDonald		24.08.65	2	Peterborough	4	May
15.34 -1.1	Jonathan Wallace	U20	1.01.79	2	Ljubljana, SLO	28	Sep
15.26 1.3	Stuart Richmond		11.04.69	4	London (CP)	2	Jun
15.24	Derek Browne		28.09.66	1	Croydon	11	May
15.24 w 4.5	Courtney Charles		13.11.68	2	London (He)	9	Jun
15.17 0.6				3	London (He)	31	Aug
(20)							
15.19 w 2.7	Julian Flynn		3.07.72	2	London (He)	31	Aug
15.08				1	Stoke	28	Jul
15.14	James Leaver	U23	15.09.75	1	Barking	23	Jun
15.12	Dave Sanderson		6.05.71	1	Cudworth	23	Jun
15.12 1.2	Nicholas Thomas	U20	4.04.79	3	Sheffield	13	Jul
15.12	Paul Weston		6.10.67	1	Cheltenham	4	Aug
15.09 w	Jon Hilton	U23	11.01.74	1	Liverpool	28	Jul
14.96 -0.1				11Q	Birmingham	14	Jun
15.04 i	Marvin Bramble	U20	10.06.77	1	Birmingham	17	Feb
14.94				7	London (CP)	2	Jun
15.03	Vernon Samuels		15.10.64	1	Bath	12	May
15.00 -0.1	Rez Cameron		18.05.60	10Q	Birmingham	14	Jun
14.96 i	Adam Smith	U20	20.02.77	2	Birmingham	17	Feb
(30)							
14.96 -3.0	Neil McMenemy		6.04.67	1	Glasgow	29	Jun
14.94 w 3.5	Adrian Browne	U20	14.07.78	5	Sheffield	13	Jul
14.81				1	Bracknell	8	Jun
14.92	Michael Brown		6.05.62	3	London (CP)	18	Aug
14.89 w	Steve Ritchie		12.08.71	2	Liverpool	28	Jul
14.88 i	Charles Madeira-Cole	U20	29.11.77	4	Birmingham	17	Feb
14.80 1.7				3	Bedford	27	Jul
14.86	Ruddy Farquharson		26.03.61	2	Portsmouth	3	Jul
14.84 -0.8	Kori Stennett	U23	2.09.76	1	Birmingham	2	Jun
14.84	Junior Lewis		19.03.66	1	Welwyn	13	Jul
14.80 w 4.4	Michael Nesbeth	U20	1.03.79	6	Sheffield	13	Jul
14.79				1	Crawley	21	Apr
14.77	Sam Bobb	U23	29.08.75	1	Kingston	20	Apr
(40)							
14.76 0.6	Denis Costello		3.12.61	1	Cannock	7	Sep
14.72 1.6	Brian Robinson	U17	3.09.80	1	Sheffield	12	Jul
14.63 w 2.7	Leroy Knowles	U20	26.09.78	8	Sheffield	13	Jul
14.18				2	Luton	23	Jun
14.59 i	Matthew Randall		28.04.70	3	London (Ha)	27	Jan
14.56 1.9	Peter Francis	U17	28.08.80	2	Sheffield	12	Jul
14.55	Martin Rossiter		4.09.69	4	Peterborough	4	May
14.52	Khary Anderson	U20	29.11.77	2	Croydon	8	Jun
14.51	Arif Shah	U20	29.11.78	1	Leicester	8	Jun
14.48	Delroy Hulme		14.09.72	3	Stoke	17	Aug
14.38 1.2	Willie Stark	U20	11.03.77	2	Glasgow	29	Jun
(50)							
14.36 i	Julian Mason	U23	3.03.75	2	Glasgow	17	Mar
14.19 w 4.2				8	Loughborough	19	May
14.18				3	Sheffield	4	May

14.34		Jamie Quarry		15.11.72	2	Barking	23 Jun
14.32		Oluleke Ilo	U20	25.06.78	2	Kingston	8 Jun
14.32 w		Elphinston Hinds		15.07.60	1	Harrow	13 Jul
14.05					1	Worthing	22 Jun
14.29		Michael Keeton	U23	14.12.76	1	Corby	9 Jun
14.23 i		Dave McCalla			1	Birmingham	29 Feb
14.11					1	Woodford	21 Apr
14.22		Peter Wilkinson	U20	7.08.78	1	Middlesbrough	20 Jul
14.20		Christopher Spurling	U23	27.11.75	1	Leeds	8 Sep
14.18	1.0	Andy Lewis		9.03.68	4	Newport	8 Jun
14.18		Colin MacDonald		12.04.71	4	Edinburgh	8 Jun
(60)							
14.18	-0.4	Mark Lawrence		26.01.71	2	London (He)	1 Sep
14.17 w	4.7	Ben Hodson	U23	25.01.76	9	Loughborough	19 May
14.16		Wyn Morris		25.02.61	3	Croydon	22 Jun
14.13 w		Ian Rowe	U20	28.09.78	1	Portsmouth	12 May
14.04					6	Enfield	6 Jul
14.12 w		Charles Igbon	U20	20.04.79	3	Liverpool	28 Jul
14.06					3	Bracknell	8 Jun
14.11		Jamie French	U20	15.03.78	1	Cambridge	15 Sep
14.09		Shane Mott			1	Worthing	3 Aug
14.08		Jonathon Oparka	U17	27.01.80	1	Edinburgh	11 May
14.08		Joe Allison		16.09.59	1	Carn Brea	18 May
14.08		Syful Ahmed	U17	25.10.79	1	Croydon	19 May
(70)							
14.08		Mathias George	U20	24.09.77	4	Abingdon	24 Aug
14.07		Marc Grover	U20	25.02.78	2	Bracknell	8 Jun
14.06	1.3	Mathias Ogbeta		19.06.68	10	London (He)	9 Jun
14.03		Bunmi Fayomi	U20	13.07.79	1	Blackpool	8 Jun
14.01		Christopher Platt	U20	25.09.78	1	Leeds (South)	24 Aug
13.94		Richard McDonald	U17	11.01.80	1	Dundee	1 May
13.94		Simon Gee	U23	23.04.75	1	Leeds	8 Sep
13.93		John Donnelly	U17		1	Tullamore, IRE	1 Jun
13.92	-0.3	Albert Earle		10.01.58	5	Birmingham	2 Jun
13.92		Sam Nash		22.10.71	1	Yeovil	17 Aug
(80)							
13.90		Daniel Hutchinson	U17	25.12.79	1	Derby	8 Jun
13.90 w	3.1	Barry Woolley	U20	6.09.78	13	Sheffield	13 Jul

Foreign

16.25 w		Tayo Erogbogbo	U23	8.03.75	1	Sheffield	4 May
15.91	1.7					London (He)	9 Jun
15.65 w		Ademola Oyediran		27.11.59	2	Portsmouth	21 Jul
15.52					1	London (CP)	18 Aug
14.66		Olu Robincocker	U23	27.11.75	2	Cannock	7 Sep
14.38		Sebastian Maufrais		18.01.70	1	Hull	9 Jun

Additional Under 17 (1 - 7 above)

13.86	0.5	Simon Roper		20.09.79	4	Sheffield	12 Jul
13.83 w	3.8	Chris Tomlinson	U15	15.09.81	1	Sheffield	12 Jul
13.24	1.0				Q	Sheffield	12 Jul
13.66		David Millward		23.05.80	1	Liverpool	19 May
(10)							
13.60		Rasheed Banda		18.03.80	1	Crawley	5 May
13.60 w	3.4	Dean Taylor	U15	9.11.81	2	Sheffield	12 Jul
13.27	1.5				*	Sheffield	12 Jul
13.52	1.7	Tom Davies		25.05.80	7	Sheffield	12 Jul
13.49	0.8	Jonathon Miller		10.06.81	8	Sheffield	12 Jul
13.42		D. Street			1	Bradford	2 Jun
13.34 w	2.4	Rhys Williams			5	Stoke	20 Jul
13.27					1	Swansea	6 Jul
13.33		James Porter			1	Southampton	15 Jun

13.33		Carl McMullen		9.11.79	1	Leeds	21 Jul
13.31 w	2.2	Leon Burnett	U15	12.09.81	1	Birmingham	18 Aug
12.98					1	Birmingham	9 Jun
13.29	1.0	Chris Scarle			1	Birmingham	7 Sep
(20)							
13.28		John Donnery			6	Stoke	20 Jul
13.23	0.9	Alex Smith		2.11.79	5	Birmingham	8 Sep
13.21		Matthew Burley			1	Ipswich	23 Jun
13.18		Michael Strain		11.09.79	2	Wishaw	13 Jul

Additional Under 15 (1 - 3 above)

13.09	1.8	Nange Ursell	1.10.81	3	Sheffield	12 Jul
13.05 w	3.1	Oladipo Senbanjo	20.03.82	4	Sheffield	12 Jul
12.52	1.7			Q	Sheffield	12 Jul
12.98		Sebastian Coghlan	31.01.82	1	Yeovil	8 Jun
12.85	1.8	Malwyn Gordon	20.10.81	6	Sheffield	12 Jul
12.64 w	2.5	Tyrone Edger	29.03.82	7	Sheffield	12 Jul
12.58	2.0			Q	Sheffield	12 Jul
12.60 w	4.8	Peter Favell	16.03.82	2	Birmingham	18 Aug
12.48	1.5			*	Birmingham	18 Aug
12.52 w	4.8	Mark Awanah	23.09.82	3	Birmingham	18 Aug
(10)						
12.48 w	2.5	Damien Walters	6.04.82	Q	Sheffield	12 Jul
12.29	1.5			10	Sheffield	12 Jul
12.48 w	2.1	Iestin North	10.10.81	8	Sheffield	12 Jul
12.35	1.2			Q	Sheffield	12 Jul
12.48 w	3.0	Craig Elder	22.05.82	1	Wishaw	14 Jul
12.21	0.5			*	Birmingham	18 Aug
12.45		Peter Alexander	29.09.81	1	Hoo	8 Jun
12.44		Andrew White	1.05.82	1	Kingston	8 Jun
12.43 w	3.0	Craig Thomas	28.09.81	2	Wishaw	14 Jul
12.10				1	Pitreavie	23 Jun
12.34	-2.4	Dale Garland	13.10.81	8	Birmingham	17 Aug
12.25		Stephen Shalders		1	Swansea	6 Jul
12.14		Tom Jefferson		1	Bracknell	8 Jun
12.12		Olly Barkley	28.11.81	1	Carn Brea	8 Jun
(20)						
12.09		Richard Oparka	28.07.82	3	Wishaw	14 Jul
12.05		Jamie Russell	1.10.81	2	Barnsley	29 Jun
12.00		K. Otoo		2	Kingston	8 Jun

Under 13

10.45	Keith Stoddart	26.10.83	1	Pitreavie	21 Apr
10.23	Richard Hurren	24.09.83	4	Pitreavie	15 Jun
10.19	M. Goggins		1	Sandown, IOW	22 Sep
10.15	N. Sherbourne		1	Portsmouth	30 Jun

SHOT

19.67	Mark Proctor	15.01.63	1	London (TB)	2 Jun
19.15			1	Loughborough	1 Jun
19.13			1	Harrow	17 Jul
19.12 i			Q	Stockholm, SWE	8 Mar
18.92 i			2	Birmingham	27 Jan
18.70			1	London (WL)	21 Jul
18.64			1	London (WL)	26 May
18.53 i			12	Stockholm, SWE	8 Mar
18.45 i			1	Kings Lynn	21 Jan
18.18			1	Thurrock	3 Aug
18.09 i			1	Glasgow	24 Feb
18.02			5	London (CP)	12 Jul
17.98			1	Watford	15 May
17.91			3	Birmingham	15 Jun

19.62	Shaun Pickering		14.11.61	1	Stanford, USA	10	May
	19.32			1	Modesto, USA	11	May
	19.23			6	Madrid, SPA	1	Jun
	19.23			1	London (He)	9	Jun
	19.10 i			1	Birmingham	27	Jan
	19.10			1	Long Beach, USA	17	Feb
	19.07			1	Kingston	17	Aug
	18.86			1	Gateshead	19	Aug
	18.85			4	Walnut, USA	21	Apr
	18.83			3	Westwood, USA	11	Jul
	18.80			1	Eindhoven, HOL	8	Sep
	18.75			2	Salinas, USA	22	May
	18.63			2	Birmingham	15	Jun
	18.29			27Q	Atlanta, USA	26	Jul
	17.95			3	Stanford, USA	22	Mar
19.22	Matt Simson		28.05.70	1	Thurrock	26	Jun
	18.99			1	London (CP)	1	Jun
	18.95			3	Gateshead	30	Jun
	18.93			1	Cardiff	25	May
	18.84			1	Bournemouth	22	Jun
	18.82			1	Birmingham	15	Jun
	18.82			1	Bath	19	Jun
	18.58			4	London (CP)	12	Jul
	18.51			1	Lidingo, SWE	4	Jun
	18.20			1	London (BP)	18	May
18.85	Lee Newman		1.05.73	2	London (TB)	2	Jun
	18.56			2	London (CP)	1	Jun
	18.12			1	Playa de Las Americas,SPA	21	Apr
	18.11			1	London (CP)	11	May
	18.06			1	Luton	6	May
18.40	Steph Hayward	U23	30.07.74	1	Dublin, IRE	9	Jun
	18.20			1	Liverpool	28	Jul
	18.16			1	Glasgow	29	Jun
	18.07			3	Hexham	14	Jul
	17.92 i			2	Glasgow	24	Feb
	17.90			1	Bedford	26	May
	50 performances to 17.90 by 5 athletes including 7 indoors						
17.68 i	Simon Williams		17.10.67	1	Baton Rouge, USA	27	Jan
	15.78			2	Enfield	6	Jul
17.46	Mark Edwards	U23	2.12.74	1	Kunzelsau, GER	7	Sep
17.41	Jamie Cockburn		30.01.73	1	Thurrock	12	May
17.30	Carl Myerscough	U17	21.10.79	2	Nembro, ITA	3	Aug
17.21 i	Dave Callaway		4.09.63	1	Horsham	28	Jan
	16.72			1	Loughborough	19	May
	(10)						
17.02	Gary Sollitt		13.01.72	2	Bedford	18	May
16.77	Robert Russell	U23	5.08.74	6	Hexham	14	Jul
16.74	James Muirhead		26.01.71	1	Kirkby	15	Sep
16.65 i	Paul Reed		2.06.62	1	Gateshead	4	Feb
	16.10			1	Jarrow	11	May
16.44	Nigel Spratley		1.04.70	5	London (CP)	1	Jun
16.29 i	Emeka Udechuku	U20	10.07.79	3	Lievin, FRA	2	Mar
	16.20			4	Gateshead	19	Aug
16.17 i	Jim Mason		22.03.72	1	London (CP)	10	Feb
15.99	Steve Whyte		14.03.64	4	London (He)	9	Jun
15.97	Jason Mulcahy		26.05.73	2	Portsmouth	21	Jul
15.88	Antony Zaidman		18.03.62	1	Bromley	23	Jun
	(20)						
15.68	Steve Bergin		17.06.66	2	Jarrow	11	May
15.61	Bill Fuller	U23	19.10.76	1	London (TB)	29	Jun
15.54	Denzil McDonald		11.10.65	2	Watford	6	Jul

15.54	David Condon		11.04.72	1	Abingdon	17	Aug
15.51	Phil Adams		3.11.71	2	Loughborough	22	Sep
15.43	Matt Symonds		31.07.68	1	Abingdon	11	May
15.29	Simon Fricker	U23	14.07.75	1	High Wycombe	3	Aug
15.28	Scott Hayes		4.01.73	3	Braintree	1	Jun
15.28	Keith Ansell		30.03.62	2	Braintree	1	Sep
15.18	Carl Jennings		4.05.64	1	Hull	12	May
	(30)						
15.18	Matt Bundock	U23	18.11.76	2	London (WL)	21	Jul
15.10	John Nicholls		1.09.65	1	Bolton	20	Jul
15.04	Mark Davies		10.01.71	1	Tonbridge	3	Aug
15.02	Simon Armstrong		29.05.62	1	Bournemouth	11	May
14.96	John Painter ¶		12.06.58	1	Kings Lynn	11	May
14.95	Lee Wiltshire		26.07.62	2	Bournemouth	22	Jun
14.87	Morris Fox		30.04.63	1	Stoke	11	May
14.86 i	Andy Turner		29.08.63	3	Horsham	28	Jan
	14.72			2	Cardiff	25	May
14.80 i	Andrew Wain		2.06.65	2	Kings Lynn	1	Feb
	14.17			1	Bournemouth	13	Jul
14.78	Barry Nash		4.09.71	1	Milton Keynes	4	May
	(40)						
14.71	George Baker	U23	14.08.76	2	Abingdon	11	May
14.71	Glen Smith		21.05.72	1	Worcester	9	Jun
14.68 i	Alex Kruger		18.11.63	H	Stockholm, SWE	9	Mar
	14.54			2	Peterborough	4	May
14.67 i	Rafer Joseph		21.07.68	2H	Valencia, SPA	27	Jan
	14.27			1D	Bedford	25	May
14.64	Bruce Robb	U20	27.07.77	3	Bedford	27	Jul
14.62	Malcolm Fenton	V40	12.02.56	5	London (WL)		
14.60	Rob Smith		3.11.66	1	Coatbridge	23	Jun
14.49	Tony Soalla-Bell	U23	3.10.76	3	London (TB)	29	Jun
14.44	Eric Hollingsworth		6.12.62	D	Sydney, AUS	20	Jan
14.43 i	Francis Brebner		27.11.65	1	Glasgow	15	Dec
	(50)						
14.38	Craig Rogers	U23	14.02.76	1	Derby	23	Jun
14.35	Neville Thompson	V40	28.03.55	3	London (He)	28	Jul
14.34	Chris Symonds		15.11.70	2	Enfield	4	May
14.28	Greg Richards	V40	25.04.56	1	London (B Elms)	18	May
14.27	Neil Elliott		10.04.71	3	Glasgow	4	Aug
14.24	Robert Hewitt		6.07.67	1	Norwich	4	May
14.19	Mark Wiseman			2	Basingstoke	3	Aug
14.16	Simon Matthews		21.05.71	1	Lancaster	15	Jun
14.14	Colin Smith		11.09.57	1	Basingstoke	28	Apr
14.11	Paul Howard		19.10.66	6	London (He)	31	Aug
	(60)						
14.09	Martyn Fletcher		21.01.69	1	Telford	4	May
14.07	Gareth Gilbert		24.08.72	3	Stretford	4	Jun
14.06	Barry Thomas		28.04.72	D	Lage, GER	15	Jun
14.05	Rob Earle		15.09.60	3	Aachen, GER	8	Jun
14.05	Jeff Clare		21.03.65	9	London (He)	9	Jun
14.02	Guy Perryman		2.11.58	2	London (TB)	4	May
14.00	Liam McIntyre	U23	22.09.76	4	Glasgow	4	Aug
13.99	Bruce Shepherd		20.03.67	2	Elgin	20	Jul
13.96	Brian Taylor		13.08.70	2D	Bedford	26	May
13.95	Simon Shirley		3.08.66	D	Lage, GER	15	Jun
	(70)						
13.94	Ewart Hulse		21.01.62	2	Newport	1	Jun
13.93	Kevin Brown		10.09.64	10	London (He)	9	Jun
13.93	Mike Oliver	V40	23.03.53	1	Twickenham	8	Sep
13.92	Dave Locke		20.05.72	1	Ashton-U-Lyne	28	Apr
13.85	Gareth Cook		20.02.69	1	Kingston	4	May

13.82	Anthony Southward			31.01.71	4D	Bedford	25	May
13.82	Iain McMullan	U20		15.06.78	5	Belfast	22	Jun
13.82	Philip Davies			12.10.60	1	Bebington	21	Aug
13.81	Peter Beaton			5.04.72	5	Glasgow	4	Aug
13.77	Rory Birbeck			24.09.73	3	Cudworth	3	Aug
(80)								
13.75	Paul Williams	U20		21.09.77	1	Stafford	6	Jul
13.75	Mike Atkinson			6.03.58	2	Antrim	6	Jul
13.73	Brett Heath	U23		6.01.75	2	Cannock	7	Sep
13.71	James South	U23		4.01.75	10	Liverpool	4	May
13.69	Steve Thomas	V40		20.05.56	1	Ashton-U-Lyne	2	Jun
13.68	Adam Davis			19.11.72	1	Milton Keynes	23	Jun
13.63	Paul Stronach			18.05.68	1	Tamworth	28	Apr
13.63	Anthony Brannen			16.09.68	7	Watford	6	Jul
13.63	Graeme Stark			12.10.63	1	Telford	17	Aug
13.57	Daniel Brunt	U23		23.04.76	1	Derby	11	May
(90)								
13.55	Mark Enever	U23		15.03.74	4	London (TB)	4	May
13.52	Simon Keller	U23		10.11.76	1	Nottingham	12	May
13.51	Gary Herrington			31.03.61	2	Worcester	9	Jun
13.50	Simon James	U20		21.01.77	1	Stoke	28	Jul
13.49	Bryan Kelly			29.12.73	12	Liverpool	4	May
13.49	Paul Head			1.07.65	1	Birmingham	14	Jul
13.48	Mark Quigley	U23		6.11.74	1	Carlisle	14	Jul
13.46	John Thyer	U20		23.11.78	5	Bedford	27	Jul
13.44	Dean Macey	U20		12.12.77	1	Harrow	13	Jul
13.43	Nicholas Crimmen			15.07.65	1	Cudworth	17	Aug
(100)								
13.40	Jeremy Hames			17.11.70	2	Tamworth	28	Apr
13.39	Jamie Quarry			15.11.72	5	London (He)	28	Jul

downhill

14.80	Hamish Davidson	V40		25.05.54	1	Rothesay	24	Aug

Foreign

16.99	*Felix Hyde*	*U23*		*7.08.76*	*3*	*London (CP)*	*1*	*Jun*
15.19	*Pierre Faber*			*9.01.72*	*1*	*Hemel Hempstead*	*13*	*Jul*
15.12	*John Farrelly*			*4.12.67*	*1*	*Dublin (M), IRE*	*15*	*Jun*
15.01 i	*Pierre Charvet*			*23.08.73*	*8*	*Birmingham*	*4*	*Feb*
	14.33				*2*	*Stoke*	*28*	*Jul*
14.49	*John Menton*			*2.05.70*	*4*	*Dublin (M), IRE*	*15*	*Jun*
14.27	*Libor Krten*			*26.02.73*	*1*	*Bedford*	*4*	*May*
13.80	*David Horne*				*1*	*Glenurquhart*	*31*	*Aug*

Additional Under 20 (1 - 7 above)

13.33	Dave Irwin			18.12.78	5	Londonderry	18	Aug
13.16	James Bull			12.02.79	2	Barking	27	Jun
13.14	Simon Sephton			27.09.78	7	Bedford	27	Jul
(10)								
13.05	Steven Hale			20.04.77	5	Birmingham	2	Jun

SHOT - Under 20 - 6.25kg

17.30	Emeka Udechuku			10.07.79	1	Blackpool	25	Aug
15.56	Bruce Robb			27.07.77	1	Edinburgh	12	May
15.45	Iain McMullan			15.06.78	1	Antrim	25	May
15.23	Simon James			21.01.77	1	Sheffield	13	Jul
14.84	James Bull			12.02.79	1	Kings Lynn	16	Jun
14.71	Paul Williams			21.09.77	2	London (He)	10	Aug
14.69	John Thyer			23.11.78	1	Abingdon	4	Aug
14.41	Nick Barber			22.11.78	1	Sheffield	8	Jun
14.39	Simon Sephton			27.09.78	3	Sheffield	13	Jul

14.32 i	Tim King		10.12.77	1	Wakefield	13	Jan
13.97				1	Newport	4	Aug
(10)							
14.04	Scott Rider		22.09.77	1	Ipswich	4	Aug
13.98	Sudip Burman-Roy		15.01.78	2	London (He)	28	Jun
13.98	Andrew Rollins		20.03.78	1	Kirkby	15	Sep
13.87	Steven Hale		20.04.77	1	Worcester	12	May
13.83	Dave Irwin		18.12.78	2	Antrim	8	Jun
13.75	Iain Douglas		4.01.77	1	Annan	7	Jul
13.72	Ashley Cooper			2	Newport	4	Aug
13.56	Adrian Cluskey	U17	30.12.80	6	London (He)	10	Aug

SHOT - Under 17 - 5kg

21.20	Carl Myerscough		21.10.79	1	Blackpool	22	Sep
16.89	David Readle		10.02.80	1	Birmingham	18	Aug
16.44 i	Adrian Cluskey		30.12.80	1	London (CP)	7	Dec
15.51				1	London (CP)	30	Jun
15.22	Pete Waterman		12.09.79	1	London (He)	28	Jun
15.10 i	Graeme Allan		24.09.80	1	Birmingham	25	Feb
15.05				1	Inverness	14	Apr
15.03	Adrian Rawlings		21.11.80	1	Par	18	Aug
14.83	David Parker		28.02.80	1	Grimsby	21	Jul
14.70	Tony Quinn		14.01.81	1	Antrim	18	May
14.66	Andy Castle/Kemp		8.12.79	1	Street	12	May
14.58	Andrew Sheridan		1.11.79	4	Sheffield	12	Jul
(10)							
14.52	Jamie Hunt		29.11.79	1	Norwich	27	May
14.47	Martin Wilson		28.09.79	1	Ipswich	8	Jun
14.46	Lyndon Woodward		22.11.80	3	Birmingham	18	Aug
14.42	David Daniels		16.11.79	5	Sheffield	12	Jul
14.37 i	Andrew Waters		11.10.79	3	Birmingham	18	Feb
14.37	William Kirkpatrick		28.02.80	1	Antrim	25	May
14.26	Ryan Livingston			2	Antrim	25	May
14.10	Chris Marland		9.11.80	2	Wrexham	19	May
14.08	James Cottrell		19.12.80	3	Cudworth	30	Jun
14.07	Andy Frost		17.04.81	1	Sandown, IOW	23	May
(20)							
14.05	Warren Woad		16.03.80	1	Enfield	12	May
13.99 i	Craig Smith		1.03.81	2	Glasgow	29	Feb
13.98	Dean Knighton		16.03.80	1	Derby	8	Jun

light shot

15.76 i	Graeme Allan		24.09.80

SHOT - Under 15 - 4kg

15.00	Paul Archer		7.10.81	1	Wakefield	21	Aug
14.92	Felice Miele		24.11.81	1	Bedford	2	Jun
14.60	Liam Walsh		5.05.82	3	Pitreavie	10	Aug
14.51	Geoffrey Reid-Hughes		14.10.81	2	Birmingham	17	Aug
14.21	Mark Tinwell		18.11.81	1	Liverpool	25	Aug
14.20	Ben Davies		12.09.81	2	London (CP)	29	Jun
14.12	Paul Blackshaw		22.11.81	1	Stretford	8	Jun
14.03	Chris Wade		22.09.82	1	Cleckheaton	8	Jun
13.95	James Rumbold		4.11.81	1	Bournemouth	21	Apr
13.83	John Barnes		6.05.82	1	Tamworth	7	Sep
(10)							
13.76	Robert Morris		20.02.82	5	Birmingham	17	Aug
13.61	Daniel Batt		20.01.82	1	Southampton	15	Jun
13.59	Eddie Nicholls			3	Birmingham	8	Sep

13.55	Dylan Perryman		17.11.81	3	London (He)	7	Jul
13.30	Ashley Ali-nia		3.01.82	1	Worthing	27	May
13.23	Adam Major		2.11.81	1	Gordonstoun	13	Jun
13.23	Chris Jones			2	Swansea	6	Jul
13.10	Matthew Parkinson		21.12.81	1	Lincoln	1	Sep
13.04	Michael Riley		29.09.81	1	Blackpool	8	Jun
12.87	Mark Landon		9.11.81	1	Corby	8	Jun
	(20)						
12.86	Matthew Peleszok		17.10.81	1P	Birmingham	21	Sep

overage

16.10	Tony Quinn	U17	14.01.81	1	Pitreavie	10	Aug
13.62	Owen McCann	U17	15.07.81	1	Antrim	17	Aug

SHOT - Under 13 - 3.25kg

12.60	Carl Saggers			1	Enfield	26	Aug

DISCUS

62.40	Robert Weir		4.02.61	1	London (He)	31	Aug
				7	Salinas, USA	22	May
				15Q	Atlanta, USA	29	Jul
				1	Kingston	17	Aug
				5	Madrid, SPA	2	Jun
				1	Braintree	1	Sep
				1	Birmingham	6	Jul
				1	Birmingham	15	Jun
				3	Long Beach, USA	13	Jul
				7	Modesto, USA	11	May
				1	London (He)	9	Jun
				3	Stanford, USA	10	May
62.32	Glen Smith		21.05.72	1	Loughborough	1	Jun
				1	Birmingham	2	Jun
				1	Rugby	26	Jun
				1	Loughborough	19	May
				7	Halle, GER	11	May
				1	Hechtel, BEL	6	Jul
				1	Loughborough	15	May
				1	Bedford	27	May
				2	Kunzelsau, GER	7	Sep
				1	Gateshead	30	Jun
				1	Worcester	9	Jun
				1	Telford	4	May
58.66	Kevin Brown		10.09.64	2	Loughborough	1	Jun
				2	Loughborough	15	May
				1	Liverpool	4	May
				2	Birmingham	2	Jun
				13	Halle, GER	11	May
				2	Gateshead	30	Jun
				3	Birmingham	15	Jun
				4	Istanbul, TUR	19	May
				2	Birmingham	6	Jul
				1	Birmingham	20	Jul
				1	Loughborough	5	Jun
				2	Funchal, POR	25	May
58.04	Simon Williams		17.10.67	1	Glasgow	29	Jun
				2	Birmingham	15	Jun
				1	Enfield	24	Jul
				3	Gateshead	30	Jun
				1	Houston, USA	30	Mar
				1	London (He)	28	Jul
				1	Bromley	23	Jun
				1	London (CP)	1	Jun

56.66	Gary Herrington		31.03.61	4	Birmingham	15	Jun
55.74				1	London (Col)	3	Jul
56.46	Paul Reed		2.06.62	1	Jarrow	24	Apr
56.10	Perris Wilkins		12.11.68	1	Milton Keynes	23	Jun
55.68	Leith Marar		7.11.68	2	Enfield	24	Jul
55.58				2	London (He)	31	Aug
55.24				2	Kingston	17	Aug
	51 performances to 55.00 by 8 athletes						
54.74	Neville Thompson	V40	28.03.55	2	London (CP)	1	Jun
54.42	Lee Newman		1.05.73	1	London (CP)	11	May
(10)							
53.90	Peter Gordon	V45	2.07.51	1	Jarrow	1	Sep
53.76	Robert Russell	U23	5.08.74	1	Leeds (South)	8	Sep
53.38	Mark Proctor		15.01.63	3	Loughborough	1	Jun
53.22	Matt Symonds		31.07.68	3	London (CP)	1	Jun
52.20	Shaun Pickering		14.11.61	2	Westwood, USA	11	Jul
52.04	James Muirhead		26.01.71	2	Leeds (South)	8	Sep
52.00	Rafer Joseph		21.07.68	1	Bolton	Jul	
51.86	Steve Casey		26.02.66	4	London (He)	31	Aug
51.58	Denzil McDonald		11.10.65	1	Crawley	28	Jul
51.46	Scott Hayes		4.01.73	2	London (CP)	18	Aug
(20)							
51.04	Emeka Udechuku	U20	10.07.79	2	Nembro, ITA	3	Aug
50.60	Darrin Morris		28.07.67	5	Loughborough	1	Jun
50.60	Carl Myerscough	U17	21.10.79	1	Bedford	28	Jul
50.20	John Moreland		13.09.58	2	Belfast	22	Jun
49.84	Nick Woolcott		7.04.61	7	London (He)	31	Aug
49.72	Andrew Kruszewski		7.04.59	7	London (CP)	1	Jun
48.90	Jeff Clare		21.03.65	1	Stretford	12	May
48.66	Simon Fricker	U23	14.07.75	1	Exeter	25	Aug
48.56	Alexis Sharp		31.10.72	3	Crawley	28	Jul
48.54	Matt Simson		28.05.70	1	Thurrock	13	Jul
(30)							
48.04	James South	U23	4.01.75	6	Hexham	14	Jul
48.02	Michael Jemi-Alade		13.10.64	3	Edinburgh	8	Jun
47.76	Mark Davies		10.01.71	1	Luton	17	Aug
47.58	Ian Taylor		2.07.67	1	Telford	14	Sep
47.36	Bruce Robb	U20	27.07.77	1	Coatbridge	23	Jun
47.24	Eric Hollingsworth		6.12.62	3	Melbourne, AUS	11	Jan
47.18	Chris Symonds		15.11.70	3	Stoke	17	Aug
46.76	Steph Hayward	U23	30.07.74	1	Glasgow	4	Aug
46.58	Neil Sougrin		14.05.71	3	Peterborough	4	May
46.34	Stephen Ayre		20.10.67	3	Leeds	6	Jul
(40)							
46.26	Andy Turner		29.08.63	1	Crawley	23	Mar
46.24	Gareth Gilbert		24.08.72	3	Cardiff	25	May
46.14	Mark Edwards	U23	2.12.74	1	Loughborough	22	Sep
45.90	Scott Rider	U20	22.09.77	4	Bedford	28	Jul
45.88	Bryan Kelly		29.12.73	10	Liverpool	4	May
45.74	Steve Whyte		14.03.64	1	Luton	11	May
45.74	Gareth Cook		20.02.69	1	Braintree	18	May
45.50	Rory Birbeck		24.09.73	1	Pendle	9	Jun
45.50	Liam McIntyre	U23	22.09.76	2	Coatbridge	23	Jun
45.46	Alex Kruger		18.11.63	4	Enfield	6	Jul
(50)							
45.44	Greg Richards	V40	25.04.56	2D	Middlesbrough	14	Jul
45.08	Neil Griffin	V45	28.05.48	1	Sutton	9	Jun
44.32	Peter Russell		7.05.60	5	Dublin, IRE	9	Jun
44.32	Nicholas Crimmen		15.07.65	1	Bolton	14	Sep
44.26	Ben Walker	U20	8.06.78	2	Carn Brea	18	May
44.20	David Abernethy	V40	5.09.55	1	Exeter	10	Aug

44.16	Nigel Spratley		1.04.70	1	Milton Keynes	23	Jun
44.08	Rob Earle		15.09.60	2	Bolton	23	Jun
44.08	William Renshaw	V45	7.08.49	1	Lincoln	17	Aug
44.04	Paul Head		1.07.65	1	Birmingham	13	Jul
	(60)						
43.98	Neil Elliott		10.04.71	6	Peterborough	4	May
43.94	John Nicholls		1.09.65	1	Wrexham	27	Jul
43.84	Jeremy Hames		17.11.70	1	Tamworth	28	Apr
43.78	Alun Williams		22.06.62	1	Bristol	23	Jun
43.76	Morris Fox		30.04.63	5	Birmingham	2	Jun
43.74	Simon Armstrong		29.05.62	3	Bournemouth	11	May
43.40	M. Bloomfield	U23		1	Great Yarmouth	4	Aug
43.34	Mike Conerney		30.10.72	1	London (BP)	4	May
43.34	Mark Quigley	U23	6.11.74	7	Watford	17	Aug
43.32	Mark Wiseman			1	Portsmouth	2	Jul
	(70)						
43.22	Brett Heath	U23	6.01.75	1D	Thurrock	29	Sep
43.14	Mark Tout		24.01.61	3	Newport	8	Jun
43.10	Mike Small	V40	31.03.54	1	London (TB)	15	May
43.06	Geoff Tyler	V45	30.09.48	1	Colwyn Bay	7	Sep
43.02	Ian McMullan	U23	3.05.74	5	Antrim	3	Jul
42.96	John Painter ¶		12.06.58	1	Kings Lynn	11	May
42.92	Justin Bryan		16.08.69	1	Neath	28	Apr
42.92	Adam Tear	U23	12.08.75	1	Scunthorpe		May
42.80	Iain Park	U23	16.07.74	6	Edinburgh	8	Jun
42.60	Neal Hart		15.04.68	1	Tweedbank	23	Jun
	(80)						
42.60	Steven Hale	U20	20.04.77	5	Bedford	28	Jul
42.54	Pete Lowe		4.07.65	1	Cosford	18	Jun
42.48	Alan Rudkin	U20	5.11.78	1	Peterborough	26	Aug
42.42	Paul Howard		19.10.66	6	Newport	8	Jun
42.40	John Little	V40	14.04.53	1	Carlisle	12	May
42.30	Glen Townsend		23.04.64	1	Isle of Man	21	Jul
42.28	Bruce Shepherd		20.03.67	1	Aberdeen	29	Aug
42.22	Steve Angell		8.04.70	1	London (WL)	25	Aug
42.20	Bill Fuller	U23	19.10.76	3	Loughborough	5	Jun
42.10	Jamie Quarry		15.11.72	2	Loughborough	27	Apr
	(90)						
42.08	Barry Thomas		28.04.72	1D	Bedford	26	May
42.08	Peter Roberts		19.09.71	4	Stoke	28	Jul
42.04	Ivan Washington		18.11.56	1	Wakefield	11	Aug
41.94	Brian Taylor		13.08.70	2	Enfield	12	May
41.82	Hector Lawrence	U20	1.11.77	1	London (WF)	13	Jul
41.78	David Sweeney		9.02.62	3	Perivale	22	Jun
41.64	Bruce Taylor		4.11.72	2	Enfield	12	May
41.52	Gary Parsons			1	Harrow	13	Jul
41.50	Steven Lloyd	U23	20.03.74	1	Carlisle	31	Mar
41.32	Dean Macey	U20	12.12.77	D	Bonn, GER	5	May
	(100)						
41.32	Andrew Rollins	U20	20.03.78	4	Leeds (South)	8	Sep
41.30	Tim Creese			1	Lincoln	21	Apr
41.14	Jan Drzewiecki		29.11.57	1	Bromley	28	Apr
41.10	Richard Czernik		12.08.72	1	Worcester	12	May
41.08	Anthony Southward		31.01.71	3D	Bedford	26	May
41.08	Malcolm Fenton	V40	12.02.56	1	Cambridge		Jun
41.08	Noel Dixon		73	3	Cannock	7	Sep
41.02	Euan Davidson		8.12.73	1	Sutton	22	Sep
41.00	Neal Killen		10.04.59	1	Aldershot	26	Jun

Additional Under 20 (1 - 10 above)

| 40.22 | David Black | | 9.10.78 | 6 | Bedford | 28 | Jul |

51.24	John Menton		2.05.70	1	Cardiff	25 May
48.44	Garry Power		1.09.62	1	Woking	17 Aug
48.18	James Highland		2.06.65	1	Woking	18 Aug
46.58	Libor Krten		26.02.73	2	London (He)	18 May
44.98	Pierre Faber		9.01.72	1	Cambridge	26 Jun
44.48	Kengo Kubota		26.06.68	4	Glasgow	29 Jun
43.68	John Farrelly		4.12.67	4	Dublin (M), IRE	16 Jun
42.28	Pierre Charvet		23.08.73	3	Sheffield	4 May

DISCUS - Under 20 - 1.75kg

54.92	Emeka Udechuku		10.07.79	1	Blackpool	25 Aug
50.84	Scott Rider		22.09.77	1	Ipswich	4 Aug
48.26	Alan Rudkin		5.11.78	2	London (He)	10 Aug
47.72	Steven Hale		20.04.77	3	London (He)	10 Aug
46.96	Ben Walker		8.06.78	4	London (He)	10 Aug
46.96	Tom Hayman	U17	17.09.80	5	London (He)	10 Aug
46.94	Bruce Robb		27.07.77	1	Wishaw	13 Jul
46.40	Andrew Rollins		20.03.78	3	Sheffield	13 Jul
45.74	David Black		9.10.78	4	Sheffield	13 Jul
45.74	Luke Rosenberg	U17	29.06.80	2	Blackpool	25 Aug
(10)						
44.88	Alex Thompson		5.05.78	1	Yeovil	8 Jun
42.92	Steven Freestone		5.08.78	7	Sheffield	13 Jul
42.80	John Parkin		23.02.79	1	Colwyn Bay	6 Apr
42.40	Dean Macey		12.12.77	3	Gateshead	16 Jun
42.20	Iain McMullan		15.06.78	1	Tullamore, IRE	1 Jun
42.14	Joshua Pirt		21.08.78	2	Yeovil	8 Jun
41.74	George Skevis	U17	12.10.79	1	Woodford	4 Aug
41.46	Adam Richardson		13.04.78	1	Portsmouth	8 Jun
41.38	Charles Galloway		5.04.78	3	Yeovil	8 Jun
41.24	Ramin Mathieson		8.08.79	9	Sheffield	13 Jul
(20)						
41.14	John Thyer		23.11.78	1	Abingdon	4 Aug

DISCUS - Under 17 - 1.5kg

58.14	Carl Myerscough		21.10.79	1	Blackpool	12 May
51.30	Luke Rosenberg		29.06.80	1	Birmingham	8 Sep
47.84	Steve Stanford		9.12.79	1	Sheffield	12 Jul
47.18	Nathan Jones		10.03.80	1	Southampton	11 Jun
47.06	Tom Hayman		17.09.80	1	Stoke	20 Jul
46.40	Scot Thompson		10.08.81	1	Elgin	22 Sep
46.12	George Skevis		12.10.79	1	Crawley	26 Aug
45.90	Simon Williams		5.10.80	1	Bracknell	5 May
45.46	Anthony Allport		30.09.79	1	Coventry	2 Jun
44.22	Edward Coats		14.06.80	1O	Birmingham	22 Sep
(10)						
44.00	Andrew Waters		11.10.79	1	Oxford	9 Jun
43.60	Graeme Allan		24.09.80	2	Pitreavie	10 Aug
43.52	Martin Rowe		23.07.80	4	Sheffield	12 Jul
43.40	Adrian Cluskey		30.12.80	3	London (CP)	30 Jun
42.48	John Barnaby		8.10.79	6	Birmingham	18 Aug
42.46	William Kirkpatrick		28.02.80	1	Antrim	25 May
42.12	Ross Kidner		12.09.80	1	Milton Keynes	8 Jun
41.96	Scott Metcalfe		8.10.79	1	Corby	12 May
41.96	Mark Jones		15.03.80	1	Derby	12 May
41.80	James Provan		23.09.80	1	Welwyn	26 Aug
(20)						
41.64	Tony Quinn		14.01.81	2	Tullamore, IRE	1 Jun
41.04	David Parker		28.02.80	3	Cudworth	30 Jun
40.90	Eifion Robinson		12.05.80	1	Carmarthen	12 May

DISCUS - Under 15 - 1.25kg

45.88	Liam Walsh		5.05.82	1	Birmingham	17	Aug
44.46	Mark Tinwell		18.11.81	1	Birmingham	8	Sep
44.08	Felice Miele		24.11.81	1	London (CP)	29	Jun
43.42	James Rumbold		4.11.81	1	Sandown, IOW	22	Sep
42.18	Ben Davies		12.09.81	1		27	Apr
41.32	Geoffrey Reid-Hughes		14.10.81	2	Birmingham	17	Aug
40.82	John Barnes		6.05.82	3	Birmingham	17	Aug
40.44	Paul Archer		7.10.81	1	London (He)	27	Jun
39.88	Chris Orr		20.06.83	1	Carlisle	1	Sep
39.66	Eduard Morris		9.12.81	1	Bedford	8	Sep
	(10)						
39.22	R. Warren			1	Sutton	22	Sep
39.00	Adrian Hemery		6.08.82	1	Guildford	8	Sep
38.94	Paul Sprung		7.05.82	1	Liverpool	8	Jun
38.76	Ryan Dobie		20.01.82	1	Carlisle	8	Jun
38.64	Grant Murdoch		30.09.82	1	Basingstoke	10	Jul
38.48	Greig Urquhart		14.06.82	6	Birmingham	17	Aug
38.36	Alistair McKenzie		5.10.81	1	Woking	1	Sep
38.18	Peter Favell		16.03.82	4	Sheffield	12	Jul
38.12	Anthony Smith		11.01.83	1	Barking	1	Sep
38.00	James Taylor		22.06.83	1	Sheffield	8	Jun
	(20)						
37.88	Damien Fogg		5.03.82	1	Bebington	23	Jun
37.54	Russell Tyler			1	St. Albans	23	Jun
37.34	Robert Morris		20.02.82	2	Braintree	1	Sep
37.26	Philip Titmus		12.11.81	7	Sheffield	12	Jul
37.20	Christopher Hyndman		3.07.82	1	Jarrow	23	Jun

Overage

44.80	Tony Quinn	U17	14.01.81	1	Pitreavie	10	Aug

DISCUS - Under 13 - 1kg

38.50	Carl Saggers			1	Solihull	15	Sep
32.26	Kevin Quinn		23.12.83	1	Braintree	1	Sep

Overage

37.46	Philip Woods	U15		1	Antrim	25	May

HAMMER

75.10	David Smith	U23	2.11.74	1	Bedford	27	May
73.22				1	Hexham	14	Jul
72.58				1	Birmingham	16	Jun
71.44				2	Sheffield	25	Aug
71.30				1	Birmingham	6	Jul
71.26				2	London (He)	9	Jun
71.02				1	Rotherham	19	Jun
70.98				1	Cleckheaton	24	Aug
70.22				1	Luton	6	May
69.98				1	Kingston	17	Aug
69.52				1	Hull	14	Apr
69.32				32Q	Atlanta, USA	27	Jul
68.94				1	Grendon Hall	20	Oct
68.86				8	Halle, GER	11	May
68.80				5	Istanbul, TUR	18	May
68.76				2	London (He)	31	Aug
68.56				Q	Birmingham	15	Jun

73.66	Paul Head		1.07.65	1	Kingston	22	Jun
72.90				1B	Kingston	22	Jun
72.72				1B	Barking	27	Jun
72.60				1	Barking	27	Jun
72.44				1	Sheffield	25	Aug
71.86				1	Newport	8	Jun
71.48				2	Birmingham	16	Jun
71.02				1	London (He)	31	Aug
70.94				1	Enfield	4	May
70.78				2	Bedford	27	May
69.72				1	Watford	6	Jul
69.38				1	Crawley	28	Jul
69.28				1	Oordegem, BEL	10	Aug
69.08				1	Stoke	17	Aug
68.74				1	Glasgow	29	Jun
68.18				1	Birmingham	20	Jul
67.00				Q	Bedford	27	May
72.48	Mick Jones		23.07.63	1	Crawley	26	Jun
71.74				8	Madrid, SPA	2	Jun
71.66				1	London (He)	9	Jun
71.22				3	Birmingham	16	Jun
70.90				5	Halle, GER	11	May
69.98				Q	Birmingham	15	Jun
69.92				3	Bedford	27	May
69.62				2	Kingston	17	Aug
69.58				Q	Bedford	27	Aug
68.96				2	Luton	6	May
68.64				1	London (Col)	28	Apr
68.20				1	Loughborough	19	May
66.64				1	Liverpool	4	May
66.54				1	London (He)	28	Jul
68.62	Peter Vivian		5.11.70	3	Sydney, AUS	10	Mar
68.50				3	Perth, AUS	28	Jan
68.00				3	Brisbane, AUS	14	Mar
67.94				2	Adelaide, AUS	26	Jan
67.56				4	Birmingham	16	Jun
67.34	John Pearson		30.04.66	3	Sheffield	25	Aug
66.88	Shane Peacock		5.03.63	1	Hull	8	Apr
66.08	David Smith		21.06.62	1	Middlesbrough	1	Sep
	56 performances to 66.00 by 7 athletes						
64.00	Russell Devine		24.04.68	1	Melbourne, AUS	30	Nov
63.90	William Beauchamp		9.09.70	1	Harrow	17	Jul
63.54	Stephen Pearson		13.09.59	4	Birmingham	20	Jul
(10)							
63.08	Gareth Cook		20.02.69	5	London (Col)	28	Apr
62.68	Iain Park	U23	16.07.74	1	Enfield	6	Jul
62.24	Paul Barnard		27.07.72	3	Sheffield	1	Jun
62.20	Steve Minnikin		4.01.72	1	Sheffield	11	May
61.86	Rob Earle		15.09.60	2B	Barking	27	Jun
60.92	Craig Ellams		24.11.72	2	Stoke	28	Jul
60.82	Chris Howe		17.11.67	2	London (CP)	18	Aug
60.28	Robert Weir		4.02.61	6	London (He)	9	Jun
60.14	Malcolm Fenton	V40	12.02.56	3	Barking	27	Jun
59.68	Matt Spicer		18.05.71	1	Bath	19	Jun
(20)							
59.60	Shaun Pickering		14.11.61	8	Kingston	17	Aug
59.50	Anthony Swain	U23	17.01.75	3	Rotherham	19	Jun
59.42	Mike Floyd	U23	26.09.76	7	Birmingham	6	Jul
59.14	Wayne Clarke	U23	24.12.75	1	Peterborough	26	Aug
59.08	Graham Holder		16.01.72	4	London (CP)	18	Aug
58.60	Steve Whyte		14.03.64	1	Luton	12	May

58.48	Steve Sammut		3.05.67	1	Haslemere	13 Aug
58.38	Glen Kerr	U23	27.10.74	2b	London (Col)	28 Apr
58.24	Alan McNicholas	U23	10.12.74	1	Luton	17 Aug
58.12	Simon Bown	U23	21.11.74	1	Braintree	30 Jun
	(30)					
57.94	Matthew Bell	U20	2.06.78	2	Peterborough	26 Aug
57.48	Adrian Palmer		10.08.69	3	Belfast	22 Jun
57.14	Steve McEvoy		23.05.63	1	London (Col)	26 Jun
56.90	Gareth Jones		14.12.68	1	Cardiff	5 Jun
56.86	Andrew Benn	U20	2.09.77	2	Bromley	5 Jun
56.32	Mark Miller		10.11.71	2	Enfield	14 Apr
56.32	John Urquhart	U20	14.11.77	2	Bedford	27 Jul
56.22	Dave Allan		17.10.70	1	Glasgow	19 May
56.14	Maurice Hicks		1.01.70	1	Haslemere	16 May
55.88	Barrie Dickinson		17.09.67	3	Coventry	6 Jul
	(40)					
55.62	Steve Angell		8.04.70	2	London (WL)	25 Aug
55.46	David Nicholl		16.09.69	1	Cardiff	14 Apr
55.00	Russell Payne-Dwyer		11.09.60	1	Derby	23 Jun
54.14	Nigel Winchcombe		10.12.59	1	Grendon Hall	19 Aug
53.96	Dave Gisbey		2.05.60	1	Coatbridge	23 Jun
53.34	Eric Kerr		9.12.64	1	Portsmouth	13 Jul
53.32	Bill Fuller	U23	19.10.76	1	London (B Elms)	20 Jul
53.18	Bruce Shepherd		20.03.67	1	Inverness	13 Jul
53.04	Chris Walsh	U20	1.10.78	1	Middlesbrough	26 May
52.50	Rob Careless	U23	7.09.74	1	Telford	11 May
	(50)					
52.34	Stuart Spratley		18.07.72	12	London (He)	9 Jun
52.34	David Shenton	U20	20.10.77	6	Glasgow	29 Jun
52.24	Stuart Thurgood	U23	17.05.76	2	Loughborough	27 Apr
52.12	Nigel Spivey		18.10.58	1	Cambridge	24 Feb
51.76	Andy Turner		29.08.63	2	London (Nh)	13 Jun
51.68	Graham Middleton		17.09.60	2	Loughborough	22 Sep
51.64	Andy Charij			1	Basingstoke	3 Aug
51.46	Matt Hammond		26.09.68	1	Hull	9 Jun
51.38	Kevin Davies	U20	11.01.78	5	Bedford	27 Jul
51.10	Sean Jones		21.03.69	1	Portsmouth	2 Jul
	(60)					
50.96	Paul Dickenson	V45	4.12.49	1	London (Elt)	4 May
50.90	David Robinson	U20	12.01.78	2	Wakefield	17 Aug
50.84	Calum Bruce	U23	28.02.75	1	Pitreavie	5 May
50.72	Jason Dibble		15.02.71	3	Corby	9 Jun
50.64	Neil Curtis	U23	30.07.74	4	Coventry	6 Jul
50.56	Geoffrey Whaley		9.06.58	1	Carn Brea	4 Aug
50.54	A. Curran			2	Glasgow	4 Aug
50.08	Chris Mallon		4.08.72	4	Kingston	22 Jun
49.84	Mark Broughton		23.10.63	4	Loughborough	15 May
49.60	Ewart Hulse		21.01.62	4	Newport	1 Jun
	(70)					
49.58	Michael Madden		13.09.65	2	High Wycombe	3 Aug
49.54	Michael Reiss		17.06.63	1	Perivale	23 Jun
49.38	Eric Berry	V40	23.04.54	1	St. Ives	23 Jun
49.24	Andy Mitchell			2	Portsmouth	2 Jul
49.20	Mark Sheridan		17.06.70	1	Crawley	22 Jun
49.04	Barry Baptiste		17.07.67	3	Thurrock	3 Aug
49.00	Matt Simson		28.05.70	1	Bournemouth	22 Jun
48.90	Ross Kidner	U17	12.09.80	2	Windsor	29 Sep
48.88	Rafer Joseph		21.07.68	2	Hemel Hempstead	13 Jul
48.72	Barry Williams	V45	5.03.47	5	Wakefield	17 Aug
	(80)					
48.70	Douglas Aitchison		31.12.66	3	Glasgow	4 Aug

48.40	Douglas Read		15.04.67	2	Grendon Hall	19	Oct
48.34	Kenneth Smith		10.05.64	3	Cudworth	23	Jun
48.20	Keith Robinson	V40	9.02.52	2	Barking	23	Jun
47.94	Adam Devonshire	U20	2.03.79	1			
47.68	Ian McLaughlin	U20	4.01.77	7	Enfield	6	Jul
47.62	Chris Melluish	V50	15.07.44	8	Enfield	6	Jul
47.52	Alan Woods	V45	27.03.51	1	Bath	13	Jul
47.36	Peter Gordon	V45	2.07.51	1	Exeter	10	Aug
47.18	J. Kingwell			1	Welwyn	26	Aug
	(90)						
47.14	John Owen		28.10.64	6	Newport	8	Jun
47.14	Andrew Moore		9.08.68	4	Cudworth	23	Jun
47.12	Mark Roberson	U23	21.03.75	2	Bracknell	12	May
46.98	Robert Snow	U23	1.09.75	3	Haslemere		
46.96	Terry Lalley	V45	12.11.49	2	Bath	13	Jul
46.92	Simon Bowman		11.09.71	3	Kings Lynn	11	May
46.88	Tim Wurr	U20	1.03.79	8	Bedford	27	Jul
46.84	Brett Marsh	U23	20.01.76	4	Carn Brea	18	May
46.80	Damon Cripps		9.10.70	1	Neath	28	Apr
46.70	Martin Hayes	U20	31.08.79	1	Bury	6	Jul
	(100)						
46.28	Gary Herrington		31.03.61	2	Telford	4	May
46.26	Neil Bulman	U20	7.09.77	1	Carlisle	21	Apr
46.14	Chris O'Connell		17.01.59	2	Leeds	8	Sep
46.10	Neil Townsend		3.05.63	1	London (TB)	29	Jun

Foreign

65.30	*Phil Spivey*		*15.05.61*	*2*	*Crawley*	*26*	*Jun*
54.34	*Luigi Bellu*		*12.07.70*	*2*	*Bromley*	*23*	*Jun*
49.02	*Jiri Horak*	*U23*	*24.07.74*	*1*	*London (BP)*	*15*	*May*
47.36	*James Highland*		*2.06.65*	*1*	*Ipswich*	*3*	*Aug*

HAMMER - Under 20 - 6.25kg

61.76	John Urquhart		14.11.77	1	Middlesbrough	1	Sep
61.58	Andrew Benn		2.09.77	1	Bromley	5	Jun
59.48	Chris Walsh		1.10.78	1	Middlesbrough	15	Jun
59.14	Matthew Bell		2.06.78	1	Corby	5	Sep
55.62	David Shenton		20.10.77	1	Gateshead	8	Jun
55.40	David Robinson		12.01.78	3	London (He)	10	Aug
55.32	Kevin Davies		11.01.78	4	London (He)	10	Aug
54.56	Carl Gregory		17.08.77	2	London (Col)	28	Apr
54.22	Tim Wurr		1.03.79	5	London (He)	10	Aug
54.14	Tom Eden		16.05.79	1	Stretford	8	Jun
	(10)						
52.94	Andrew Grierson	U17	23.11.79	2	London (He)	25	Aug
52.58	Neil Bulman		7.09.77	1	Middlesbrough	27	May
52.38	Luke Rosenberg	U17	29.06.80	3	Gateshead	16	Jun
51.74	Adam Devonshire		2.03.79	1	Bedford	12	Jun
51.66	Ross Kidner	U17	12.09.80	5	Middlesbrough	1	Sep
51.62	Robin Walker		8.02.78	1	Bury	16	Jun
51.46	Ross Blight		28.05.77	6	London (He)	10	Aug
50.90	Martin Hayes		31.08.79	1	Colwyn Bay	7	Sep
50.54	Peter Fuller		30.04.78	1	Woking	14	Aug
50.12	Pete Waterman	U17	12.09.79	7	Middlesbrough	1	Sep
	(20)						
49.42	John Parkin		23.02.79	2	Blackpool	25	Aug
49.32	Nicholas Fogg		24.03.78	2	London (He)	7	Jul
48.72	Michael Sexton		26.05.79	1	Haslemere	27	May
47.24	Christopher Snook		6.06.79	4	Cleckheaton	24	Aug
46.46	Paul McNamara		3.10.78	5	Aldershot	4	Aug
46.18	Andy Frost	U17	17.04.81	1	Guildford	25	Aug

Unofficial Mark

52.74	Martin Hayes		31.08.79		Rugby	15	Jun

HAMMER - Under 17 - 5kg

62.98	Ross Kidner		12.09.80	1	Colchester	26	Aug
62.48	Andrew Grierson		23.11.79	1	London (Nh)	11	Aug
58.68	Andy Castle/Kemp		8.12.79	1	Exeter	15	Jun
58.16	Pete Waterman		12.09.79	1	Birmingham	8	Sep
56.52	Andy Frost		17.04.81	1	Aldershot	19	May
55.84	James Hawkins		14.12.79	3	Birmingham	17	Aug
55.30	Matthew Sutton	U15	8.09.81	3	Manchester	15	Sep
55.10	Graeme Allan		24.09.80	3	Stoke	20	Jul
53.74	James Punch		19.12.79	1	Corby	12	May
52.78	Jason Stone		15.10.80	1	Enfield	11	May
	(10)						
52.68	Chris Aherne		21.12.79	4	Stoke	20	Jul
52.64	John Barnes	U15	6.05.82	1	Cleckheaton	24	Aug
51.74	Christopher Adams		18.07.81	1	Birmingham	7	Sep
51.18	Gavin Minns		5.12.80	2	Cleckheaton	24	Aug
51.06	Ross Thompson	U15	7.12.81	3	Cleckheaton	24	Aug
51.06	David Little		28.02.81	4	Manchester	15	Sep
50.90	Thomas Cunnane		14.08.80	1	Jarrow	23	Jun
49.44	Gareth Driscoll		8.03.81	2	Braintree	1	Sep
49.34	James Ball		17.04.80	7	Sheffield	12	Jul
48.76	Kirk Capeling		27.02.80	4	Crawley	10	Aug
	(20)						
48.66	Nathan Bradfield			2	Windsor	21	Jul
48.38	Luke Rosenberg		29.06.80	2	Enfield	19	May
48.36	Neil Marshall		17.02.80	5	Middlesbrough	1	Sep
48.20	Brian Cooksley		5.04.80	1	Aberdare	31	Aug
48.18	Damien Howard	U15	23.11.81	5	Cleckheaton	24	Aug
48.12	David Jones		4.10.80	2	Stoke	22	Jun
48.08	Alan Kelsall		3.09.80	1	Basildon	8	Jun
47.98	Michael Bennett		22.11.80	1	Hoo	17	Jun
47.56	Paul Foster		20.10.79	1	Yate	26	May
47.04	Tom Harrington		27.10.79	2	Hoo	2	Jun

HAMMER - Under 15 - 4kg

65.42	Matthew Sutton		8.09.81	1	Windsor	29	Sep
61.32	John Barnes		6.05.82	1	Hull	8	Jun
58.88	Mark Landon		9.11.81	1	Corby	5	Sep
57.84	Damien Howard		23.11.81	3	Sheffield	13	Jul
57.56	Ross Thompson		7.12.81	2	Cleckheaton	24	Aug
55.78	Nick Williams		2.02.82	1	Stretford	25	Jun
52.64	Ashley Slater		23.09.81	1	Birmingham	8	Sep
49.72	Tim Whitehead		20.04.82	1	Woking	14	Aug
48.36	Adrian Hemery		6.08.82	2	Windsor	29	Sep
46.16	Adam Beauford		24.10.81	1	Exeter	15	Jun
	(10)						
44.10	Robert Watts		19.10.81	1	Yeovil	8	Jun
44.10	Oliver Hoad		1.10.81	2	London (He)	7	Jul
43.74	Michael McEvoy		26.04.82	3	London (He)	7	Jul
43.18	Matthew Grindle		3.01.82	1	Swansea	6	Jul
42.74	Ben Davies		12.09.81	2	Exeter	15	Jun
42.22	Eddie Nicholls			2	Birmingham	8	Sep
41.72	Mark Cawley		30.12.81	1	Leeds	21	Jul
40.90	Paul Archer		7.10.81	1	Bromley	21	Jul
40.38	Daniel Lewis			2	Birmingham	7	Sep
40.16	Alex Philips		29.09.81	12	Sheffield	13	Jul
	(20)						
40.08	Dafydd Mali			2	Swansea	6	Jul

JAVELIN

87.44	Steve Backley		12.02.69	2	Atlanta, USA	3	Aug
85.58				2	London (CP)	12	Jul
85.06				2	Gateshead	19	Aug
84.46				3	Tokyo, JAP	16	Sep
84.14				Q	Atlanta, USA	2	Aug
82.70				6	Zurich, SWZ	14	Aug
82.20				2	Sheffield	25	Aug
82.10				1	London (CP)	11	Aug
81.66				2	Gateshead	30	Jun
83.06	Nick Nieland		31.01.72	1	Birmingham	15	Jun
81.92				3	Sheffield	25	Aug
80.30				3	Gateshead	30	Jun
79.94				3	Halle, GER	11	May
79.70				4	London (CP)	11	Aug
77.22				6	Oslo, NOR	5	Jul
77.20				1	London (He)	31	Aug
76.52				2	Kingston	17	Aug
75.76				1	London (He)	9	Jun
75.74				25Q	Atlanta, USA	2	Aug
75.06				1	Liverpool	4	May
81.42	Mick Hill		22.10.64	2	Birmingham	15	Jun
80.60				4	Sheffield	25	Aug
80.48				Q	Atlanta, USA	2	Aug
80.26				3	London (CP)	11	Aug
80.14				4	Gateshead	19	Aug
79.24				5	Gateshead	30	Jun
78.76				2	Riga, LAT	2	Jun
78.58				12	Atlanta, USA	3	Aug
78.38				5	London (CP)	12	Jul
77.60				1	Leeds (South)	8	Sep
76.56				1	Sheffield	8	Jun
76.52				2	Ljubljana, SLO	26	May
81.06	Colin Mackenzie		30.06.63	1	Loughborough	19	May
78.74				3	Birmingham	15	Jun
77.42				4	Halle, GER	11	May
77.26				1	Ljubljana, SLO	26	May
75.40				1	La Spezia, ITA	21	Sep
75.20				7	London (CP)	11	Aug
75.16				8	Sheffield	25	Aug
78.54	Mark Roberson		13.03.67	1	Peterborough	26	Aug
77.80				2	Loughborough	19	May
77.60				1	Kingston	17	Aug
77.04				1	Stoke	28	Jul
76.76				1	Birmingham	20	Jul
76.26				1	Peterborough	14	Apr
75.52				6	London (CP)	11	Aug
77.84	Roald Bradstock		24.04.62	1	Northridge, USA	23	Mar
77.46				1	Tucson, USA	16	Mar
76.66 i	Stuart Faben	U23	28.02.75	3	Kajaani, FIN	3	Mar
73.70				1	St. Ives	1	May
	49 performances to 75.00 by 7 athletes including 1 indoors (!)						
74.60	Nigel Bevan		3.01.68	1	Belfast	22	Jun
72.76	Keith Beard		8.11.61	1	Amstelveen, HOL	18	Aug
70.38	Stefan Baldwin		26.04.70	1	Edinburgh	8	Jun
(10)							
69.90	Tony Smith		17.05.58	2	Birmingham	6	Jul
69.18	Gary Jenson		14.02.67	2	Peterborough	26	Aug
68.70	Robert Mullen		8.08.64	1	Portsmouth	2	Jul
68.26	David Parker	U17	28.02.80	3	Loughborough	19	May

67.14	Peter Yates		15.06.57	1	London (Elt)	4	May
66.78	Trevor Ratcliffe		9.03.64	1	London (CP)	2	Jun
66.68	Phil Parry		4.10.65	1	Harrow	13	Jul
66.62	Mark Francis	U20	23.09.77	1	Sheffield	13	Jul
66.48	Duncan MacDonald	U23	30.03.74	4	Loughborough	19	May
65.46	Dean Smahon		8.12.61	1	Antrim	3	Jul
	(20)						
64.52	Damien Crawford		22.08.68	1	Antrim	6	Jul
64.44	James Hurrion		11.11.73	2	Kunzelsau, GER	7	Sep
64.38	Steve Harrison		19.12.72	2	Sheffield	6	May
64.08	Stuart Loughran	U23	19.02.76	1	Colwyn Bay	26	Aug
64.02	Stewart McMillan		12.09.69	8	Birmingham	15	Jun
63.64	Richard Hooper		29.03.58	9	Birmingham	15	Jun
63.30	Dean Macey	U20	12.12.77	1D	Sydney, AUS	22	Aug
63.18	Simon Bennett		16.10.72	1	Bath	19	Jun
63.14	David Wilson		5.09.70	1	Ashton-U-Lyne	28	Apr
62.92	Simon Shirley		3.08.66	5D	Gotzis, AUT	26	May
	(30)						
62.88	Jason Oakes	U20	29.09.77	1	Jarrow	12	May
62.76	David Hanna	U23	13.12.75	4	Liverpool	4	May
62.76	Peter Johnson	U23	25.09.75	2	Sheffield	2	Jun
62.62	Paul Howard		19.10.66	2	Enfield	4	May
62.30	Chris Smith	U23	27.11.75	2	Liverpool	28	Jul
62.20	Richard Salt	U20	28.10.77	1	Lancaster	6	Jul
62.06	Damien McDaid	U20	17.07.78	1	Tullamore, IRE	4	Aug
62.06	Alistair Gidley		5.09.72	5	London (He)	31	Aug
61.96	Matt Atkins	U20	23.06.77	1	Sheffield	20	Apr
61.56	Matthew Bamford		19.09.58	2	Enfield	11	May
	(40)						
61.06	Mark Pinner		12.05.64	1	Cannock	14	Aug
60.92	Andrew Benn	U20	2.09.77	3	Luton	6	May
60.78	Stephen Rogers		1.09.71	1D	Bedford	26	May
60.72	Jon Clarke		20.11.67	4	Newport	8	Jun
60.58	Paul Morgan		5.07.65	1	Braintree	1	Jun
60.48	Andrew Yiannacou	U20	18.08.78	1	London (He)	8	Jun
60.40	Dean Johnson	U23	31.12.75	1	Sheffield	11	May
60.20	Barry Thomas		28.04.72	1D	Lisbon, POR	28	Apr
60.14	Simon Kearney	U23	28.07.74	1	London (WL)	17	Aug
60.06	Paul Cooper	U23	4.12.76	1	Braintree	30	Jun
	(50)						
59.94	Rob Laing		30.07.66	4	Kingston	17	Aug
59.76	David Pescod		15.04.73	2	York	6	Jul
59.30	Anthony Norman		5.07.63	1	Southend	3	Aug
59.28	David Brown		4.06.66	1	Luton	17	Aug
59.18	Pawlo Ostapowycz	V40	1.07.52	3	Sheffield (W)	22	Jun
59.10	Demetrio Barros		29.06.71	2	Stoke	17	Aug
59.06	David Sketchley	U23	25.02.76	1	Braintree	21	Apr
59.04	Tim Newenham		1.04.60	1	Kings Lynn	12	May
59.04	Dan Carter	U17	15.04.80	1	Colchester	26	Aug
58.98	Simon Carter	U23	5.03.75	1	Peterborough	4	May
	(60)						
58.94	Stuart Walker	U20	22.09.78	1	Scunthorpe	4	May
58.88	Ken Hayford		10.03.63	3	Edinburgh	8	Jun
58.80	Landley Darlington	U20	19.01.77	6	Loughborough	19	May
58.60	Fuat Fuat		20.09.71	1	Bromley	23	Jun
58.50	Robert Charlesworth	U20	25.03.79	1	Peterborough	14	Apr
58.44	Neil McLellan	U20	10.09.78	1	Watford	12	May
58.26	Stephen Melber	U20	26.02.79	1	Milton Keynes	8	Jun
58.12	Tim Kitney	U17	26.04.80	1	Ipswich	4	Aug
57.96	Kevin Murch		11.11.58	1	Solihull	7	Jul
57.78	Matt Allison		26.02.73	1	Sheffield	20	Apr
	(70)						

57.70	Tony Hatton		18.06.70	6	London (He)	9	Jun
57.64	Greg Hayward		28.01.64	1	Loughborough	1	Jun
57.58	John Trower	V40	6.02.56	3	Sheffield	8	Jun
57.48	Peter Fraser	U20	28.01.78	2	Aberdeen	28	Apr
57.48	Roger Killick	U23	20.11.76	1	Swansea	16	Jun
57.48	Jeremy Smyth	U20	11.08.78	1	Carmarthen	16	Jul
57.44	Steve Greening		15.02.68	2	Sheffield	4	Aug
57.42	Andy Clarke		10.08.70	2	Jarrow	4	May
57.42	Scott MacHardie		26.06.69	2	Bromley	23	Jun
57.38	Stephen Birse	U20	8.10.77	1	Aldershot	26	Jun
	(80)						
57.34	Jon Wilkinson		17.02.62	2	Sheffield	12	May
57.34	Mark Bishop		12.02.67	2	Cannock	7	Sep
57.32	Gregg Markham	U20	28.11.78	3	Sheffield	4	Aug
57.22	Sam Armstrong	U23	17.02.74	1	Greenock	28	Apr
57.14	Kevin Hill		17.06.73	4	Sheffield	8	Jun
57.06	Matthew Davies	U20	16.09.78	2	Carmarthen	16	Jul
57.02	Simon Achurch	U23	27.12.74	1	Bournemouth	3	Aug
56.92	Seth Kirkham	U23	9.09.75	1	Barking	23	Jun
56.66	Ben Jump		6.02.65	2	Glasgow	4	Aug
56.62	Stewart Maxwell		29.06.58	2	Coatbridge	23	Jun
	(90)						
56.58	Brent Starling	U23	19.05.76	2	Leeds	6	Jul
56.46	Alan Holloway		22.06.60	1	Yate	10	Aug
56.40	Mark Welch	U23	9.11.74	1	Aldershot	26	Jun
56.40	Gary Jones			1	Crawley	17	Jul
56.34	Ben Houghton	U17	6.08.80	4	Londonderry	18	Aug
56.26	Shane Lewis		22.08.72	2	Newport	1	Jun
56.24	Ken Taylor	V45	24.10.48	1	Stockport	17	Aug
56.10	Steve Thomas	U20	4.04.78	1	Colwyn Bay	26	Aug
56.10	Chris Thomas	U17	11.01.80	1	Colwyn Bay	26	Aug
55.98	Richard Atkinson	U23	9.10.74	3	Sheffield	12	May
	(100)						
55.88	Trevor Lloyd		1.08.66	1	London (TB)	3	Aug
55.84	James Apps	U17	29.04.80	2	Gateshead	16	Jun
55.68	Jamie Wilkinson	U23	21.04.74	1	Telford	Apr	
55.64	P. Poole			1	Cosford	18	Jun
55.62	Martin Troy	U23	13.07.76	2	Luton	17	Aug
55.60	Terry Gyorffy		28.01.65	2	Croydon	22	Jun
55.58	Sean Darlington		1.01.72	4	Sheffield	6	May
55.44	Alex Gibson	U20	3.11.77	1	Braintree	1	Sep
55.26	Matthew Lewis	U23	11.11.75	1	Loughborough	15	May
55.24	David Jones		6.10.69	4	Cannock	7	Sep
	(110)						
55.00	Wayne Powell		27.07.71	1	Leamington	10	Aug

Additional Under 20 (1 - 26 above)

54.94	Ian Burns		20.09.77	3	Gateshead	16	Jun
54.72	Damian Huntingford		11.06.77	3	Crawley	7	Apr
54.66	Keith Lavelle		13.05.77	1	Lancaster	7	Jul
54.50	Emeka Udechuku		10.07.79	2	London (CP)	18	Aug
	(30)						
54.10	Greg Magee		27.09.78	1	Tweedbank	31	Aug
53.86	Robert Lyon		23.03.77	8	Bedford	28	Jul
53.06	Tim Cattermole		17.08.77	1	Yeovil	8	Jun
53.02	Tim Phillips		13.01.79	2	Watford	8	Jun
53.02	Patrick Boundy		19.02.79	1	Crawley	17	Jul

Foreign

56.46	*Pierre Faber*		*9.01.72*	*3*	*Sheffield*	*6*	*May*
56.12	*James Highland*		*2.06.65*	*1*	*Ipswich*	*3*	*Aug*

JAVELIN - Under 17 - 700g

73.56	David Parker	28.02.80	1	Stoke	20 Jul
66.00	Dan Carter	15.04.80	1	Braintree	1 Sep
65.92	Tim Kitney	26.04.80	1	Pitreavie	10 Aug
63.26	Clifton Green	10.10.79	1O	Hoo	22 Sep
61.52	Ben Houghton	6.08.80	1	Tullamore, IRE	1 Jun
61.44	James Apps	29.04.80	1	Ipswich	23 Jun
60.94	Chris Thomas	11.01.80	1	Newport	10 Jul
59.34	Michael Allen	7.03.80	3	Stoke	20 Jul
59.10	Richard Brooks	3.07.80	1	Wrexham	21 Jul
57.98	Philips Olweny	14.02.81	1	High Wycombe	21 Jul
	(10)				
57.38	Philip Sharpe	6.03.81	1	Cudworth	3 Aug
55.96	Andrew Squire	30.09.79	6	Birmingham	17 Aug
55.70	Russell Oram	14.08.80	1	Guildford	8 Sep
55.54	Mark Smith	30.11.79	1	Wakefield	2 Jun
55.40	Mike Tarran	10.12.80	1	Yeovil	21 Jul
54.42	Matthew Tribble	17.10.79	1	Barking	1 Sep
54.32	Peter Watson	30.06.81	1O	Worcester	25 Aug
53.48	Tony Stanley-Clarke	10.10.80	1	Bracknell	8 Jun
53.22	Trevor Betts	9.10.79	1	Sandown, IOW	21 Jul
53.04	M. McCoy		1	Mansfield	13 Sep
	(20)				
52.94	Ashley Causer	25.09.79	1	Swindon	21 Jul
52.62	Shaun Groves	15.09.80	1	Cwmbran	12 May
52.62	Tony Rigby	22.02.80	9	Birmingham	17 Aug

JAVELIN - Under 15 - 600g

60.34	Richard Lainson	5.11.81	1	Birmingham	18 Aug
58.58	Rhys Williams	4.10.81	1	Pitreavie	10 Aug
56.32	Jonathan Lundman	7.12.81	1	London (CP)	29 Jun
53.74	Daniel Britton	25.09.81	3	Birmingham	18 Aug
53.32	Matthew Patience	22.12.81	1	London (He)	7 Jul
52.32	Alex Simpson	19.01.82	3	Sheffield	13 Jul
50.70	Keith Simpson	19.10.81	1	Inverness	8 Sep
49.86	James Roden	24.11.81	4	Birmingham	18 Aug
48.20	Christopher Leidy	6.12.81	2	Bournemouth	8 Jun
47.84	Martin Purdy	29.10.81	1	Hoo	8 Jun
	(10)				
47.76	Liam Walsh	5.05.82	2	Colwyn Bay	26 Aug
47.30	John Spencer		1	Jarrow	23 Jun
47.26	Alex Rowswell	18.03.82	1	Exeter	1 Sep
46.62	Mark Tinwell	18.11.81	1	Stretford	8 Jun
46.22	Owen Matthews	17.10.81	1	London (CP)	23 Jun
46.14	John King	6.10.81	1	Great Yarmouth	4 Aug
45.66	Paul Diamond	19.02.82	1	York	15 Jun
45.30	Chirag Patel	9.08.82	1	Basildon	27 May
44.96	D. Woodhouse	30.11.81	1	Colchester	7 Jul
44.50	Eric Workman		1	Aldershot	21 May
	(20)				
44.40	Joel Semple	19.09.81	2	Pitreavie	10 Aug
44.36	Chris Jenkins	2.03.82	1	Liverpool	11 May
44.34	Stuart Poole	29.09.81	7	Birmingham	18 Aug
44.22	Dylan Perryman	17.11.81	1	Bracknell	8 Jun
44.08	David Nicholls	5.09.81	1	Coventry	2 Jun

Unconfirmed

47.60	David Pilbury	13.05.82			

JAVELIN - Under 13 - 400g

39.18	Mike Groves		1	Cwmbran	12 May
38.88	Jon Whitefoot		1	Aberdare	28 Jul
37.86	M. Fidler		1	Carlisle	11 May
35.94	Colin Bailey	15.11.83	1	Wakefield	22 Sep

DECATHLON

7857 Simon Shirley   3.08.66   11   Lage, GER   16 Jun
11.19   7.30   13.95   2.01   50.38   15.10   40.22   4.70   60.98   4:30.90
     7614   19   Gotzis, AUT   26 May
11.25   7.19   14.34   1.91   49.89   15.41   40.86   4.70   62.92   4:57.68

7765 Barry Thomas   28.04.72   15   Lage, GER   16 Jun
11.37   6.91   14.06   2.04   50.20   15.23   39.86   4.90   58.42   4:30.99
     7701   1   Bedford   26 May
11.26   7.13   13.84   1.98   50.62   14.96   42.08   4.80   60.10   4:50.96
     7618   1   Lisbon, POR   28 Apr
11.32   7.01   13.94   1.96   50.00   15.2   39.66   4.73   60.20   4:40.09

7573 Brian Taylor   13.08.70   2   Bedford   26 May
10.68   7.26w   13.96   1.89   49.62   14.13   37.62   4.60   50.72   5:03.75

7480 Dean Macey   U20   12.12.77   2   Sydney, AUS   22 Aug
11.33   7.06   12.74   2.00   50.41   15.01   40.46   4.20   63.30   4:48.11
     7134   1   Bonn, GER   5 May
11.64   6.70   12.39   2.01   51.20   15.44   41.32   3.90   59.24   4:43.12

7425 Anthony Southward   31.01.71   25   Lage, GER   16 Jun
11.23   6.91   13.57   1.92   49.91   14.69   40.22   4.40   48.44   4:34.10
     7400 w   3   Bedford   26 May
11.27   7.07W   13.82   1.98   50.94   14.69   41.08   4.30   50.78   4:49.92
     7337   *   Bedford   26 May
     6.80w
     6815   2   Sheffield   28 Apr
11.50   6.58   12.81   1.91   51.6   15.13   37.22   4.00   51.76   5:00.48

7204 Eric Hollingsworth   6.12.62   1   Sydney, AUS   21 Jan
11.11   6.39   14.44   1.85   50.49   15.83   47.16   4.40   55.02   5:06.86

7174 Rafer Joseph   21.07.68   4   Bedford   26 May
11.29   6.94w   14.27   1.86   51.55   15.22   40.88   4.40   53.08   5:03.70
     6610   1   Antrim   1 Sep
11.99   6.06   14.19   1.91   54.32   16.35   43.86   4.20   54.26   5:09.62

7150 Stephen Rogers   1.09.71   5   Bedford   26 May
11.34   6.65w   12.75   1.98   50.72   15.82   39.08   4.10   60.78   4:49.97

6910 Billy Jewers   27.09.62   1   Aldershot   14 Jun
11.35   7.08   11.84   1.98   50.13   15.09   35.20   3.70   45.46   4:46.89

6839 Matt Douglas   U23   26.11.76   1   Worcester   25 Aug
11.29   7.01w   11.74   1.93   47.79   14.86   33.34   3.40   42.04   4:45.02

(10)

6834 Brett Heath   U23   6.01.75   1   Thurrock   29 Sep
12.0   6.96   13.51   1.85   52.2   15.7   43.22   4.10   48.68   4:42.8
     6622   2   Worcester   25 Aug
12.05   6.47   13.44   1.87   51.73   16.36   37.20   4.00   47.34   4:36.08
     6502   4   Middlesbrough   30 Jun
11.9   6.27   12.82   1.83   52.4   15.8   38.36   4.30   45.40   4:46.5
     6498   10   Narbonne, FRA   28 Jul
12.01   6.37   12.18   1.80   52.85   16.07   38.00   4.10   48.26   4:38.08

6829 Steve Leader   24.11.66   1   Enfield   4 Aug
11.63   6.54   12.35   1.85   52.40   15.94   38.10   4.50   47.98   4:35.87

6800 w William Gilles   15.02.73   6   Bedford   26 May
11.29   6.97W   10.49   1.86   50.87   15.37   34.30   3.80   50.44   4:34.62
     6790   *   Bedford   26 May
     6.93w
     6757   7   Narbonne, FRA   28 Jul
11.46   7.13   10.24   1.80   50.93   15.39   34.20   3.80   50.40   4:30.11

6798	Mark Bushell			U23	22.10.76	8	Narbonne, FRA	28 Jul
10.92	7.22	10.88	1.86	51.58	15.15	32.86	4.20	45.44	5:02.20
6455						7	Bedford	26 May
11.12	6.83w	11.59	1.86	52.33	15.51	34.76	4.00	40.46	5:17.78
6780	Roger Hunter			U23	10.03.76	3	Sheffield	28 Apr
11.57	6.42	11.62	1.88	51.3	15.61	37.64	4.00	52.88	4:37.99
6554						8	Narbonne, FRA	28 Jul
11.40	6.59	11.68	1.86	50.94	16.68	34.26	3.60	51.00	4:36.16
6764	Livio Salvador-Aylott				18.07.73	2	Enfield	4 Aug
11.24	6.61	11.45	1.85	50.66	16.06	32.62	4.30	51.58	4:44.84
6541						3	Antrim	1 Sep
11.47	6.26	11.10	1.73	50.13	15.96	33.82	4.40	52.02	4:56.38
6617	Leo Barker			U20	26.12.78	6	Narbonne, FRA	28 Jul
11.24	7.05	11.76	1.89	51.62	15.32	34.50	3.10	50.74	4:53.36
6577	Paul Hourihan			U23	7.11.76	2	Middlesbrough	30 Jun
11.6	6.84	11.08	1.95	52.6	15.2	33.80	3.60	48.46	4:36.2
6560	Greg Richards			V40	25.04.56	3	Enfield	4 Aug
11.88	6.78	13.01	1.88	54.94	16.03	44.38	4.00	47.78	5:10.26
6522						3	Middlesbrough	30 Jun
11.8	6.71	12.73	1.89	54.4	15.5	45.44	4.00	48.06	5:21.0
6559	Fyn Corcoran			U20	17.03.78	2	Antrim	1 Sep
11.56	6.52	12.97	1.82	50.62	15.77	34.38	3.30	50.32	4:38.85
(20)								
6541	Terry Gyorffy				28.01.65	2	Aldershot	14 Jun
11.54	6.71	12.54	1.86	52.88	16.20	34.96	3.80	52.38	4:55.35
6494	Par Esegbona				16.04.68	1	Blackpool	28 Jul
11.35	6.84	11.19	1.94	52.02	16.32	32.46	4.00	50.00	5:12.78
6484	Richard Czernik				12.08.72	2	Blackpool	28 Jul
11.16w	6.40w	12.39	1.85	51.05	16.36	37.30	3.40	50.80	5:00.46
6443	Terry Fidler				13.10.71	4	Enfield	4 Aug
11.78	6.48	11.70	1.73	52.81	15.73	34.56	4.40	49.04	4:55.63
6437	Adrian Ferrand				5.02.68	8	Bedford	26 May
11.58	6.26	12.38	1.95	53.17	15.82	36.66	3.80	42.98	4:53.26
6405	Mark Perman				6.01.68	2	Thurrock	29 Sep
11.9	6.68	11.67	1.82	51.7	15.2	39.68	4.20	44.52	5:21.1

41 performances to 6400 by 26 athletes

6371	Tom Leeson				18.09.63	5	Antrim	1 Sep
11.65	6.69	11.57	1.79	52.86	15.56	35.40	3.80	52.12	5:12.97
6364	Steve Garland				12.01.73	5	Enfield	4 Aug
11.62	6.27	10.81	1.88	51.13	16.59	32.80	3.70	48.68	4:36.09
6280	Rob Laing				30.07.66	3	Blackpool	28 Jul
11.76	6.75	12.28	1.79	53.78	15.94	36.02	3.80	55.52	5:34.34
6213	Matt Allison				26.02.73	1	Cudworth	15 Sep
11.6	6.12	11.79	1.64	51.9	16.1	40.38	3.40	57.46	4:56.5
(30)								
6205 w	Callum Orr				18.11.62	2	Ayr	21 Jul
11.21w	6.28W	11.40	1.80	51.45	16.50	32.84	3.70	37.40	4:43.38
6168						6	Antrim	1 Sep
11.54	5.89	11.51	1.85	50.74	16.71	33.90	3.70	36.52	4:35.45
6199	David Ralson			U20	22.02.77	1	Birmingham	2 Jun
11.60	6.21	11.88	1.77	52.23	16.74	33.22	3.90	49.78	4:59.32
6154	Martin Troy			U23	13.07.76	3	Aldershot	14 Jun
12.13	6.08	9.82	1.86	53.79	16.34	30.86	3.80	53.46	4:30.03
6143	Jon Wilkinson				17.02.62	4	Blackpool	28 Jul
12.15w	6.17w	11.85	1.79	54.78	16.44	37.76	3.90	51.96	4:59.46
6105 w	Ciaran Doherty			U23	14.01.75	4	Ayr	21 Jul
11.60	6.37W	11.58	1.95	54.11	15.66	31.96	3.00	53.82	5:19.30
6075						7	Antrim	1 Sep
11.73	5.96	11.36	1.88	53.13	15.47	36.20	3.00	46.68	5:06.47
5979	Brett Shea				17.04.71	4	Aldershot	14 Jun
11.79	6.54	10.31	1.74	52.82	17.09	31.96	3.90	45.36	4:56.41

5921	Michael Bull				6.06.70	6	Worcester		25 Aug
	11.53	6.45w	10.48	1.75	53.52	17.20	32.12	3.70	42.62	4:52.52
5906	David Powell		U20	11.09.78	3	Birmingham		2 Jun
	11.77	6.23	10.78	1.71	51.24	16.55	34.10	3.30	36.92	4:39.71
5887	Wayne Slater			25.04.73	8	Middlesbrough		30 Jun
	11.5	6.29	11.05	1.86	`53.8	16.3	34.72	3.60	45.96	5:30.8
5761	Dan Gilby			10.07.70	1	Hoo		22 Sep
	11.9	6.27	10.72	1.78	53.9	16.6	31.68	4.00	45.74	5:23.4

(40)

5758	Stuart Caudery			19.11.66	7	Enfield		4 Aug
	12.03	6.19	9.84	1.82	54.26	16.99	28.48	3.80	39.88	4:40.93
5755	Mark Sweeney		U20	26.02.77	4	Birmingham		2 Jun
	12.13	5.88	11.20	1.92	54.47	15.82	32.72	3.00	45.96	5:10.28
5750	Gurmukh Sahans		U20	8.10.78	5	Birmingham		2 Jun
	12.01	6.41	10.22	1.77	53.91	16.79	30.60	3.30	46.18	4:54.02
5741	Iain Black			18.09.70	5	Ayr		21 Jul
	12.14w	5.82w	9.50	1.86	55.00	18.19	30.36	4.40	43.18	4:46.83
5722	Paul Curran		U20	5.04.77	6	Birmingham		2 Jun
	12.05	6.23	9.53	1.86	52.69	17.36	29.04	2.70	43.96	4:22.56
5674	Geoff Ingram			31.01.68	2	Portsmouth		30 Jul
	11.4	6.53	9.70	1.67	53.5	16.6	29.30	3.40	44.44	5:02.1
5634	Brian Hughes			6.01.70	3	Thurrock		29 Sep
	12.4	6.46	9.50	1.76	55.3	16.4	34.22	3.90	47.70	5:23.8
5599	Lee Parkes		U23	23.12.76	2	Cudworth		15 Sep
	12.3	5.76	11.33	56.0	17.4	36.34	3.30	44.64	4:47.4
5535	Darren Dods		U23	26.12.74	5	Aldershot		14 Jun
	11.62	6.26	10.09	1.86	55.18	17.01	34.30	2.60	40.90	5:09.07
5506	Matthew Gillard		U23	11.07.75	2	Cudworth		15 Sep
	11.6	5.85	12.53	1.70	52.5	17.6	32.78	3.30	37.22	5:11.2

(50)

5498	Egryn Jones			1.11.71	1	Aberdare		4 Aug
	11.82	6.31	9.77	1.71	52.89	15.79	27.12	3.30	36.16	5:17.56
5445	Colin Hayton			22.07.59	2	Cudworth		15 Sep
	12.6	5.78	10.68	1.73	57.8	17.4	32.50	3.90	43.06	4:40.4
5430	Scott Walker		U20	9.09.77	7	Birmingham		2 Jun
	11.24	6.46	10.05	1.80	51.49	16.24	23.42	3.10	37.44	6:05.50
5338	Frank Chapman			17.01.70	3	Portsmouth (RN)		30 Jul
	11.6	5.72	10.78	1.70	53.1	15.8	23.42	2.90	41.40	5:06.9
5334	Paul Carroll		U20	25.01.78	8	Birmingham		2 Jun
	12.55	5.78	11.04	1.71	53.75	18.60	34.04	3.40	41.16	4:58.43
5314	Mark Roberts			1.09.69	1	Walton		16 Jun
	12.3	5.75	9.99	1.83	55.0	16.3	30.56	2.60	44.70	4:56.8
5269	David Hall			26.05.68	4	Portsmouth (RN)		30 Jul
	11.9	5.99	10.15	1.76	55.5	17.3	31.74	2.60	45.92	5:03.4
5231	Paul Attwood			13.12.69	5	Portsmouth (RN)		30 Jul
	11.6	6.32	10.05	1.67	52.2	17.4	28.34	2.30	42.30	5:01.8
5230	Keith Mainstone		U23	15.03.74	1	Worthing		15 Sep
	12.6	5.66	10.68	1.88	55.3	19.2	29.44	2.50	49.80	4:30.6
5214	Nicholas Walker			24.02.64	10	Middlesbrough		30 Jun
	12.0	5.95	10.02	1.61	53.6	17.4	33.84	3.40	36.12	5:14.2

(60)

5208	Paul Ralph			16.12.67	2	Hoo		22 Sep
	11.9	6.89	10.79	1.78	53.0	18.6	29.50	2.40	33.22	5:08.9
5200	Piers Sutton			25.06.70	8	Enfield		4 Aug
	12.38	5.94	10.40	1.67	54.73	17.92	31.74	2.70	36.28	4:36.36
5194	Simon White		U23	2.10.75	3	Hoo		22 Sep
	12.4	5.97	9.33	1.72	56.1	16.9	33.06	2.70	41.10	4:45.1
5192	Stuart Hammond			17.07.71	4	Thurrock		28 Sep
	12.2	5.58	10.32	1.70	56.4	16.7	28.12	3.30	51.94	5:23.3
5184	Steve Bonnett		U20	13.07.78	8	Blackpool		28 Jul
	12.30	6.16	8.57	1.94	55.00	19.14	24.56	3.00	34.10	4:32.40

5130   Ian Parker   U23   9.07.75   1   Lincoln   5 May
    12.6   5.71   9.95   1.78   55.0   18.4   32.56   2.60   45.42   4:43.3

5084   Paul Gilding   U23   2.10.75   2   Worthing   15 Sep
    12.1   6.54   9.10   1.97   56.9   16.4   24.44   2.40   34.78   5:18.2

5048   Ian Tomkins   23.03.68   3   Worthing   15 Sep
    12.6   6.03   10.96   1.79   54.6   18.4   26.28   2.60   37.74   4:43.2

5040   Eric Neilson   7.08.68   6   Portsmouth (RN)   30 Jul
    12.0   5.71   10.34   1.76   54.8   19.4   30.74   2.80   39.46   4:51.5

4997   Neil Fairlamb   U23   13.03.76   9   Blackpool   28 Jul
    11.94w   5.35   10.77   1.61   54.62   21.36   32.30   3.40   47.04   5:10.02

     (70)

4976   Stuart Ohrland   U23   6.09.75   5   Thurrock   29 Sep
    12.5   6.41   9.96   2.06   55.5   17.7   20.14   2.20   37.04   5:12.9

4966   Brendan McConville   U20   3.01.79   12   Antrim   1 Sep
    13.20   5.74   8.57   1.76   56.39   18.18   27.22   3.10   43.38   4:40.83

4949   Arron Bonning   U23   9.11.75   6   Thurrock   29 Sep
    12.6   6.29   9.79   1.73   58.1   18.3   26.26   3.70   44.90   5:35.5

4943   Stuart Richmond   11.04.69   4   Hoo   22 Sep
    11.7   6.56   7.98   1.84   55.0   17.6   20.90   2.60   31.62   5:04.2

4931   Mark Dobbie   U20   5.03.77   13   Antrim   1 Sep
    12.20   6.04   9.93   1.67   58.23   17.92   29.98   3.10   41.52   5:28.37

4906   Michael Cobham   U23   15.09.76   10   Blackpool   28 Jul
    11.70w   6.31w   8.54   1.73   55.96   18.96   28.62   2.80   43.32   5:42.42

Foreign
7581   *Pierre Faber*   *9.01.72*   *20*   *Gotzis, AUT*   *26 May*
    11.27   6.92   15.94   2.06   50.69   15.88   46.54   4.30   55.46   4:56.90

DECATHLON - Under 20 with Under 20 Implements

6762   Fyn Corcoran   17.03.78   2   Birmingham   22 Sep
    11.31   6.68   13.30   1.81   50.70   15.11   36.50   3.40   48.32   4:41.00

6592   Leo Barker   26.12.78   1   Norwich   23 Jun
    11.1   6.92   12.90   1.69   52.7   14.4   40.38   2.90   52.24   4:52.3

6068   Erik Toemen   1.07.78   3   Birmingham   22 Sep
    11.96   6.37w   10.18   1.87   54.19   16.30   30.58   3.90   44.06   4:43.24

6060   Gurmukh Sahans   8.10.78   4   Birmingham   22 Sep
    12.03   6.28w   10.36   1.72   53.32   16.01   39.24   3.30   48.24   4:43.65

5988   Mark Sweeney   26.02.77   1   Worcester   25 Aug
    12.24   5.82   11.93   1.87   54.92   15.12   38.08   3.20   48.32   5:08.36

5974   Nick Dowsett   24.11.78   5   Birmingham   22 Sep
    11.51   6.80   10.54   1.75   54.22   15.36   33.74   3.20   42.80   5:12.87

5942   Steve Bonnett   13.07.78   6   Birmingham   22 Sep
    12.19   6.25   10.00   1.96   52.86   16.69   30.26   3.40   36.02   4:25.09

5890   David Powell   11.09.78   1   York   23 Jun
    12.1   6.14   11.63   1.69   51.2   16.1   36.32   3.50   38.40   4:48.7

5884   Darren Hatton   21.03.79   1   Hoo   22 Sep
    12.0   6.59   10.93   1.86   54.9   16.6   35.56   3.00   51.36   4:59.8

5865   Adam Pengilly   14.10.77   1   Street/Yeovil   5 May
    11.6   6.09   11.70   1.69   54.4   16.7   34.80   3.60   46.64   4:53.8

     (10)

5865   Lee Black   26.11.78   7   Birmingham   22 Sep
    11.28   6.01w   8.42   1.78   50.18   16.78   25.88   3.40   38.94   4:28.73

5811   Paul Jones   11.04.78   1   Aberdare   4 Aug
    11.95   6.58   10.51   1.77   54.90   15.62w   29.14   3.60   46.32   5:20.83

5767   Scott Exley   9.02.78   2   Street/Yeovil   5 May
    11.5   6.04   11.23   1.78   52.3   15.5   34.88   2.80   34.26   4:53.0

5676   Clint Barrett   21.11.77   8   Birmingham   22 Sep
    12.12   5.99   10.40   1.69   53.36   16.39   33.16   2.70   47.32   4:36.72

5645   Paul Curran   5.04.77   1   Antrim   4 Aug
    12.2   6.25   10.52   1.90   53.8   16.8   29.66   2.60   42.78   4:30.9

5571	Ben Walker			8.06.78	2		Hemel Hempstead		23	Jun
	12.0	5.94w	13.20	1.71	53.0	16.5	42.08	2.80	39.20	5:28.9
5487	Steven Atkinson			12.04.79	10		Birmingham		22	Sep
	11.74	5.66	10.67	1.75	58.20	16.56	31.64	3.90	41.20	5:17.18
5485	Charles Madeira-Cole			29.11.77	2		Aberdare		4	Aug
	11.55	6.71	10.20	1.74	53.39	16.81w	25.42	3.00	38.32	5:17.62
5475	Paul Carroll			25.01.78	1		Telford		23	Jun
	12.1	6.10	12.78	1.78	53.7	20.2	36.28	3.40	37.22	4:51.8
5468	Mark Dobbie			5.03.77	1		Ayr		21	Jul
	12.16w	6.21	11.50	1.59	56.52	16.73	35.20	3.30	42.64	5:08.50

(20)

5347	Peter Carr			10.09.77	12		Birmingham		22	Sep
	12.00	5.78w	8.95	1.81	56.65	16.75	26.32	3.50	39.00	4:51.68
5303	Duncan Malins			12.06.78	1		Worthing		15	Sep
	12.0	6.62	9.61	1.67	54.5	15.5	28.98	2.60	43.42	5:26.7
5294	Philip Coad			11.10.78	13		Birmingham		22	Sep
	12.22	6.00	8.90	1.75	53.65	16.21	28.78	2.60	35.36	4:44.54
5263	Jonathan Holmes			13.11.78	14		Birmingham		22	Sep
	11.50	5.63	8.98	1.66	52.05	16.95	26.80	2.90	37.06	4:56.81
5180	Gavin Fisher			18.11.77	5		Norwich		23	Jun
	12.0	5.89	8.78	1.93	54.0	17.2	29.14	2.40	34.88	4:51.5
5150	Brendan McConville			3.01.79	2		Antrim		4	Aug
	13.0	5.71	9.77	1.84	55.6	17.2	30.54	3.00	42.38	4:51.9
5133	Owen Chaplin			2.12.77	1		Telford		15	Jun
	12.1	6.19	10.53	1.65	57.7	19.3	33.08	4.00	42.46	5:29.7
5083	Sam Allen			26.10.78	3		York		23	Jun
	12.4	5.34	10.52	1.75	53.1	17.8	28.08	2.70	45.36	4:57.1

Overage

7111 o	Mark Bushell		U23	22.10.76	1		Birmingham		22	Sep
	11.13	7.02	12.88	1.93	51.09	14.92	41.00	4.30	46.60	5:08.40
5483 o	David Bullock		U23	1.12.76	11		Birmingham		22	Sep
	11.96	6.15	9.46	1.66	52.21	17.78	30.58	2.90	40.46	4:33.63

OCTATHLON - Under 17

5158	Edward Coats			14.06.80	1		Worcester		25	Aug
	14.4	6.23w	49.04	51.98	1.72	38.90	12.41	4:43.60	(a)	
4951	Marc Newton			15.03.80	1		Telford		23	Jun
	15.2	6.15	40.20	53.3	1.86	29.64	13.17	4:26.9 (a)		
4847	Matthew Tribble			17.10.79	2		Birmingham		22	Sep
	14.97	6.06	52.56	53.46	1.68	36.44	10.78	4:51.45	(a)	
4813	Peter Watson			30.06.81	3		Birmingham		22	Sep
	15.44	6.11	43.66	52.97	1.77	36.14	11.95	4:55.19	(a)	
4781	Robert Hollinger			11.10.80	4		Birmingham		22	Sep
	13.94	5.78w	38.46	53.43	1.71	36.74	12.72	5:01.66	(a)	
4780	Jason McDade			3.04.80	1		Norwich		23	Jun
	13.9	6.29	37.56	55.0	1.91	30.88	12.99	5:15.7 (a)		
4650	Neil Kelly			21.03.80	5		Worcester		25	Aug
	15.0	5.92w	42.74	55.79	1.90	31.60	10.56	4:47.02	(a)	
4650	Darren Wright			7.09.79	5		Birmingham		22	Sep
	15.42	6.31	36.20	55.59	1.89	32.42	10.91	4:48.22	(a)	
4646	Sam Laskey			28.05.80	6		Birmingham		22	Sep
	16.22	5.89	41.82	56.02	1.83	38.56	11.82	4:52.22	(a)	
4639	Darel Russell			26.10.80	7		Birmingham		22	Sep
	14.36	6.22	34.98	53.59	1.74	34.16	10.19	4:53.81	(a)	

(10)

4621	Russell Oram			14.08.80	9		Birmingham		22	Sep
	16.68	5.95w	53.14	54.65	1.59	38.66	11.06	4:48.19	(a)	
4611	Edward Morris			3.03.80	10		Birmingham		22	Sep
	14.46	6.25	36.98	53.81	1.65	33.92	10.61	4:51.94	(a)	

4595	Clifton Green					10.10.79	1	Hoo	22 Sep
	12.1	11.67	5.82	53.3	27.02	1.48		63.26	4:45.6	(d)
4557	Anthony Sawyer					29.04.80	11	Birmingham	22 Sep
	16.05	5.92	33.82	52.41	1.68	37.16		11.76	4:50.20	(a)
4546	Gary Hall					25.07.80	12	Birmingham	22 Sep
	14.25	6.06	33.08	53.44	1.77	29.50		10.37	4:52.54	(a)
4495	Kevin Drury					30.09.79	2	Telford	23 Jun
	14.3	5.70	44.04	57.7	1.71	34.18		11.77	5:08.4	(a)
4479	Tom Payn					18.10.79	14	Birmingham	22 Sep
	16.34	5.91	39.42	52.24	1.68	27.18		9.09	4:15.92	(a)
4472	Neil Bellamy					23.07.80	15	Birmingham	22 Sep
	15.43	6.25	31.84	53.20	1.68	29.94		11.20	4:46.81	(a)
4469	Paul Timba					21.03.80	2	Enfield	4 Aug
	14.31	39.76	5.59	55.98	1.76	10.27		31.26	4:49.70	(b)
4448	David Parker					28.02.80	16	Birmingham	22 Sep
	15.63	5.53	63.96	59.51	1.53	40.90		13.45	5:47.36	(a)

(20)

4433	Leon McRae					3.11.80	2	Carn Brea	23 Jun
	13.9	5.72	27.84	52.9	1.83	27.66		9.03	4:41.3	(a)
4421	Gerard Plunkett					30.06.80	1	Cudworth	15 Sep
	15.9	5.44	9.87	57.0	32.36	1.72		44.66	4:43.3	(c)
4407	Scott Porter					12.12.79	18	Birmingham	22 Sep
	15.06	6.05	38.28	56.21	1.59	33.50		12.25	5:02.71	(a)
4386	Martin Cowan					16.11.80	19	Birmingham	22 Sep
	15.34	5.95	37.32	54.92	1.71	33.96		10.00	4:58.59	(a)
4376	Michael Allen					7.03.80	1	Antrim	1 Sep
	11.52	15.23	50.62	56.22	26.68	1.54		6.18	5:03.86	(e)
4372	Neil Gibbs					2.02.80	1	Street	5 May
	15.1	5.92	37.04	56.0	1.74	32.14		11.26	5:02.1	(a)
4309	Wayne Gray					7.11.80	4	Hemel Hempstead	23 Jun
	14.6	5.75	26.98	53.2	1.98	23.40		11.44	5:19.8	(a)
4280	Martin Lloyd					18.06.80	2	Hoo	22 Sep
	12.5	10.09	5.97	56.7	31.24	2.02		35.42	5:13.9	(d)
4274	John Heanley					25.09.80	20	Birmingham	22 Sep
	15.72	5.92	38.74	53.71	1.50	26.02		9.38	4:23.41	(a)
4253	Chris Low					24.04.80	9	Worcester	25 Aug
	13.6	6.22w	41.26	52.22	1.78	30.04		11.05	DNF	(a)

(30)

4249	Andrew East					25.07.81	4	York	23 Jun
	15.1	5.44	42.10	55.2	1.63	33.08		8.75	4:46.2	(a)
4207	Martin Rowe					23.07.80	1	Telford	15 Jun
	16.3	5.58	1.70	58.0	12.83	40.16		44.14	5:53.0	(f)
4204	Austin Ferns					12.01.81	1	Walton	16 Jun
	14.7	5.99	33.80	55.0	1.77	26.20		6.56	4:36.2	(a)

Order of Events
a) 100mH, LJ, JT, 400m, HJ, DT, SP, 1500m
b) 100mH, JT, LJ, 400m, HJ, SP, DT, 1500m
c) 100mH, LJ, SP, 400m, DT, HJ, JT, 1500m
d) 100m, SP, LJ, 400m, DT, HJ, JT, 1500m
e) SP, 100H, JT, 400m, DT, HJ, LJ, 1500m
f) 100mH, LJ, HJ, 400m, S, DT, JT, 1500m

PENTATHLON - Under 15

3014	Chris Jenkins				2.03.82	1	Birmingham	21 Sep
	11.54	11.03	6.15	1.76	2:16.81	(a)
2964	Jamie Russell				1.10.81	2	Birmingham	21 Sep
	12.78	9.10	5.93	1.91	2:09.21	(a)
2885	Matthew Peleszok				17.10.81	3	Birmingham	21 Sep
	13.19	12.86	5.60	1.61	2:05.78	(a)
2884	Dominic Girdler				6.03.82	4	Birmingham	21 Sep
	12.25	10.77	5.89	1.73	2:13.91	(a)

2874	Matthew Hendrickson				31.01.82	5	Birmingham	21	Sep
	12.64	11.81	5.89	1.64	2:11.27	(a)			
2840	Mark Awanah				23.09.82	6	Birmingham	21	Sep
	12.45	10.21	6.16	1.61	2:10.69	(a)			
2760	Gary Hunter				10.09.81	2	Blackpool	28	Jul
	5.71	12.20	9.66	1.66	2:11.78	(c)			
2754	James Anthony				30.03.82	1	Aberdare	3	Aug
	12.52	13.16	5.87	1.73	2:32.01	(a)			
2743	Matthew Barclay				28.01.82	7	Birmingham	21	Sep
	12.15	10.87	6.02	1.67	2:23.51	(a)			
2742	Nange Ursell				1.10.81	8	Birmingham	21	Sep
	12.03	9.30	5.50	1.61	2:07.46	(a)			
(10)									
2727	Roger Owens				26.10.81	1	Newport	27	Jun
	1.72	12.82	12.82	5.61	2:24.75	(b)			
2709	Ken McKeown				6.03.82	1	Pitreavie	8	Jun
	12.0	11.62	5.86	25.5	5:41.6	(d)			
2702	Tom Roe				25.06.82	9	Birmingham	21	Sep
	13.06	9.01	6.07	1.67	2:12.74	(a)			
2700	William Hodson				20.01.82	1	Norwich	23	Jun
	12.2	10.91	5.38	1.66	2:14.5	(a)			
2658	Daniel O'Donnell				9.01.82	3	Telford	23	Jun
	12.3	9.36	5.33	1.77	2:15.7	(a)			
2654	John Holtby				27.03.82	10	Birmingham	21	Sep
	12.68	12.24	5.31	1.55	2:14.65	(a)			
2643	Steve Foster				30.12.81	4	Telford	23	Jun
	12.3	12.48	5.53	1.53	2:19.4	(a)			
2611 w	Martin Taylor				31.01.82	2	Bedford	25	May
	12.19	10.17	6.01W	1.54	2:22.22	(a)			
	2562					*	Bedford	25	May
			5.78w						
2589	Gareth Parkin				5.12.81	11	Birmingham	21	Sep
	12.73	9.22	5.68	1.67	2:17.91	(a)			
2560	Paul Archer				7.10.81	1	Eltham	9	Jun
	13.7	13.77	4.91	1.66	2:19.5	(a)			
(20)									
2557	Andrew Johnson				10.09.81	1	Hemel Hempstead	23	Jun
	12.9	10.24	5.45	1.63	2:15.9	(a)			
2532	Oladipo Senbanjo				20.03.82	1	Mansfield	23	Jun
	12.4	9.26	5.96	1.65	2:26.1	(a)			
2531	Robert Shoreson				14.10.81	12	Birmingham	21	Sep
	12.70	9.60	5.18	1.61	2:13.42	(a)			
2517	Aidan Turnbull				1.09.81	2	York	23	Jun
	12.6	9.88	5.51	1.57	2:16.8	(a)			
2510	Kieron Morgan				4.09.81	2	Hemel Hempstead	23	Jun
	12.8	10.16	5.65w	1.51	2:16.0	(a)			

Order of Events

a)	80mH, SP, LJ, HJ, 800m
b)	HJ, 80mH, SP, LJ, 800m
c)	LJ, 80H, SP, HJ, 800m
d)	80mH, SP, LJ, 20, 800m

2000 Metres Walk - Track - Under 13

9:48.0	Lloyd Finch		26.10.83	3	Leicester	13	Jun
10:20.1	Paul Miles		28.04.84	1	Leicester	8	Jun
11:12.0	Thomas Pridmore		21.03.85	1	Brierley Hill	13	Oct
11:18.2	Luke Finch		21.09.85	2	Brierley Hill	13	Oct
11:20.0	Simeon Adams		1.07.84	2	Leicester	13	Feb
11:23.7	Paul Graham		17.02.86	3	Brierley Hill	13	Oct

Overage

9:32.1	Lloyd Finch		26.10.83	1	Brierley Hill	13	Oct

Road

9:16	Lloyd Finch		26.10.83	1	Dublin, IRE	28	Sep
10:01	Paul Miles		28.04.84	6	Dublin, IRE	28	Sep
10:05	Andrew Parker		10.12.83	1	Folkstone	4	May
10:27	Paul Graham		17.02.86	1	Tamworth	1	Dec
10:29	Luke Finch		21.09.85	2	Tamworth	1	Dec

3000 Metres Walk - Track

11:52.6	Steve Partington		17.09.65	1	Douglas, IOM	15	May
11:56.5				1	Douglas, IOM	21	Jul
12:01.7	Gary Witton		25.08.73	1	Crawley	11	May
12:10.0	Steve Hollier	U23	27.02.76	1	Rugby	18	Sep
12:11.5	Kevin Walmsley		6.09.67	2	Douglas, IOM	15	May
12:13.26	Andy Penn		31.03.67	1	Bedford	27	May
12:15.2	Steve Taylor		19.03.66	3	Douglas, IOM	15	May
12:16.10 i	Martin Young		11.07.72	1	Birmingham	11	Feb
12:26.61				3	Bedford	27	May
12:30.0				1	Loughborough	12	May
12:21.22	Richard Oldale		26.01.66	2	Bedford	27	May
12:27.1	Mark Easton		24.05.63	1	Woodford	10	Jul
12:30.0				1	Horsham	20	Mar
12:42.7	Jamie O'Rawe		3.02.73	1	Thurrock	12	May
(10)							
12:43.33 i	Stuart Monk	U20	23.03.79	1	Birmingham	18	Feb
13:49.5				3	Thurrock	12	May
12:53.14	Noel Carmody		24.12.56	2	London (CP)	2	Jun
12:54.0	Robert Mecham	U20	14.09.77	1	Horsham	16	Apr
12:58.0	Gareth Brown		10.05.68	1	Horsham	11	Jun
12:59.6	Jimmy Ball		17.02.63	1	Portsmouth	11	May
13:07.3	Brian Adams	V45	13.03.49	2	Loughborough	12	May
13:08.04	Andy O'Rawe		8.09.63	4	Abingdon	25	Aug
13:08.9	Ray Craggs		9.07.63	1	Birmingham	18	Jun
13:12.72 i	Bob Care	V45	8.04.47	1	Birmingham	3	Mar
13:32.42				1	Exeter	9	Aug
13:16.79	Derek Cross	V45	30.04.49	5	Bedford	27	May
(20)							
13:18.68	Karl Atton		14.09.71	6	Bedford	27	May
13:22.0	Matthew Hales	U17	6.10.79	1	Horsham	10	Sep
13:26.7	Allan King		3.12.56	3	Loughborough	12	May
13:29.8	Mabon Dane		19.07.71	2	London (BP)	13	Apr
13:29.8	Allan Callow	V50	4.09.45	4	Douglas, IOM	15	May
13:33.61 i	Scott Taylor	U20	28.07.78	2	Birmingham	11	Feb
13:46.1				4	Loughborough	12	May
13:39.62 i	Chris Smith		23.12.58	4	Birmingham	11	Feb
13:41.9	Jerry Everett		27.05.61	1	Woodford	12	Jun
13:46.3	Chris Hobbs	V40	2.04.55	8	Hoo	8	Sep
13:49.0	Darren Thorn		17.07.62	3	Rugby	18	Sep
(30)							

13:49.0	Dave Ratcliffe		17.11.60	4	Rugby	18	Sep
13:49.2	John Hall	V45	18.01.49	1	Bedford	14	Aug
13:50.50 i	Michael Kemp	U17	23.12.79	5	Birmingham	11	Feb
14:04.9				5	Loughborough	12	May

Additional Juniors

14:22.7	Nigel Whorlow	U17	26.11.80	2	London (BP)	14	Jul
14:52.32 i	Paul Spilane	U17	27.09.79	8	Birmingham	18	Feb
14:59.94	Robert Warren	U17	17.07.81	2	Crawley	11	May
15:02.62	Lloyd Finch	U13	26.10.83	1	Birmingham	21	Sep
15:05.1	Stephen Carridge	U15	31.12.81	5	Douglas, IOM	15	May
15:14.46	Dominic King	U15	30.05.83	3	Birmingham	21	Sep
15:27.0	Nathan Adams	U15	14.04.82	1	Enfield	31	Aug
15:27.34	Daniel King	U15	30.05.83	4	Birmingham	21	Sep

3000 Metres Walk - Road - Juniors

13:14	Michael Kemp	U17	23.12.79	1	Weymouth	17	Mar
13:25	Matthew Hales	U17	6.10.79	2	Weymouth	17	Mar
13:41	Thomas Taylor	U17	30.01.81	2	Dublin, IRE	28	Sep
13:56	Nigel Whorlow	U17	26.11.80	3	Dublin, IRE	28	Sep
14:32	Robert Warren	U17	17.07.81	4	Weymouth	17	Mar
14:35	Lloyd Finch	U15	26.10.83	1	Bradford	10	Nov
14:37	Stephen Carridge	U15	31.12.81	5	Dublin, IRE	28	Sep
14:52	Paul Spilane	U17	27.09.79	5	Weymouth	17	Mar
15:01	Nathan Adams	U15	14.04.82	1	Folkstone	4	May
15:02	Dominic King	U15	30.05.83	2	Folkstone	4	May
15:20	Daniel King	U15	30.05.83	1	Steyning	23	Jun
15:20	Chris Stanford	U15	9.02.82	6	Dublin, IRE	28	Sep
15:33	Paul Miles	U13	28.04.84	2	Solihull	16	Nov

5000 Metres Walk - Track - Juniors

21:58.57	Philip King	U23	25.11.74	5	Hexham	16	Jul
22:42.2	Michael Kemp	U20	23.12.79	4	Brierley Hill	13	Oct
22:57.7		U17		1	Enfield	31	Aug
22:47.37	David Keown	U23	18.07.74	6	Hexham	16	Jul
22:48.0	Matthew Hales	U20	6.10.79	1	Horsham	13	Nov
23:49.0		U17		1	Horsham	14	May
23:07.5	Scott Taylor	U20	28.07.78	6	Brierley Hill	13	Oct
23:56.6	Andrew Goudie	U20	4.10.78	2	Enfield	31	Aug
23:58.11	Thomas Taylor	U17	30.01.81	2	Birmingham	21	Sep
24:37.6	Nigel Whorlow	U17	26.11.80	4	Enfield	31	Aug

Road

22:20	Michael Kemp	U20	23.12.79	1	Bradford	10	Nov
22:22	Scott Taylor	U20	28.07.78	2	Bradford	10	Nov
22:29	Matthew Hales	U20	6.10.79	3	Bradford	10	Nov

10000 Metres Walk - Track

42:29.73	Steve Partington		17.09.65	1	Birmingham	15	Jun
43:20.2	Chris Cheeseman		11.12.58	1	Enfield	31	Aug
43:25.2	Jamie O'Rawe		3.02.73	1	Hornchurch	27	Mar
43:39.0	Martin Young		11.07.72	1	Rugby	18	May
44:15.75	Richard Oldale		26.01.66	3	Birmingham	15	Jun
45:23.5	Brian Adams	V45	13.03.49	1	Leicester	3	Dec
45:46.3	Steve Taylor		19.03.66	3	Enfield	31	Aug
45:47.8	Andy O'Rawe		8.09.63	2	Hornchurch	27	Mar
46:34.5	Stuart Monk	U20	23.03.79	3	Hornchurch	27	Mar
46:56.0	David Keown	U23	18.07.74	3	Rugby	18	May

(10)

47:07.0	Karl Atton		14.09.71	4	Rugby	18 May
47:23.42	Allan King		3.12.56	8	Birmingham	15 Jun
48:02.3	Mabon Dane		19.07.71	7	Enfield	31 Aug
48:06.96	Gary Witton		25.08.73	9	Birmingham	15 Jun
48:21.67	Colin Bradley	V40	2.02.56	1	Newport	1 Jun

Additional Juniors

48:47.9	Andrew Goudie	U20	4.10.78	5	Hornchurch	27 Mar
49:48.6	Matthew Hales	U17	6.10.79	7	Nembro, ITA	3 Aug
49:56.0	Michael Kemp	U17	23.12.79	8=	Rugby	18 May
49:56.0	Scott Taylor	U20	28.07.78	8=	Rugby	18 May

10000 Metres Walk - Road - Juniors

44:50	Michael Kemp	U20	23.12.79	1	Solihull	16 Nov
46:26	Stuart Monk	U20	23.03.79	4	Folkstone	4 May
47:04	Matthew Hales	U20	6.10.79	3	Bexley	7 Dec
47:24	Scott Taylor	U20	28.07.78	6	Tamworth	26 Oct
48:04	Andrew Goudie	U20	4.10.78	4	Bexley	7 Dec
51:15	Nigel Whorlow	U17	26.11.80	8	Solihull	16 Nov
52:14	Stephen Crane	U17	24.02.80	12	Coventry	3 Mar
53:15	Robert Warren	U17	17.07.81	15	Coventry	3 Mar

20 Kilometres Walk

1:23:58	Darrell Stone		2.02.68	1	Douglas, IOM	24 Feb
	1:24:30			15	Moscow,RUS	1 Jun
	1:25:38			41	Eisenhuttenstadt, GER	11 May
	1:26:44			1	Cardiff	21 Apr
1:25:40	Steve Partington		17.09.65	42	Eisenhuttenstadt, GER	11 May
	1:27:12			19	Moscow,RUS	1 Jun
	1:28:16			3	Douglas, IOM	24 Feb
	1:29:00			2	Cardiff	21 Apr
1:26:15	Chris Maddocks		28.03.57	2	Sligo, IRE	31 Mar
	1:28:27			4	Douglas, IOM	24 Feb
1:28:39	Andy Penn		31.03.67	21	Moscow,RUS	1 Jun
1:29:48	Martin Young		11.07.72	8	Sligo, IRE	31 Mar
1:29:50	Chris Cheeseman		11.12.58	6	Douglas, IOM	24 Feb
1:33:17	Richard Oldale		26.01.66	4	Cardiff	21 Apr
1:33:28	Kevin Walmsley		6.09.67	3	Dublin, IRE	28 Sep
1:34:05	Andy O'Rawe		8.09.63	4	Dublin, IRE	28 Sep
1:34:27	Steve Taylor		19.03.66	6	Cardiff	21 Apr
(10)						
1:35:25	Brian Adams	V45	13.03.49	1	Leicester	7 Dec
1:36:44	Jamie O'Rawe		3.02.73	2	Colchester	26 May
1:37:19	Noel Carmody		24.12.56	6	Dublin, IRE	28 Sep
1:37:20	Steve Hollier	U23	27.02.76	3	Sutton Coldfield	8 Jun
1:37:52	Jonathan Cocker		26.09.71	2	York	18 May
1:38:09	David Keown	U23	18.07.74	11	Douglas, IOM	24 Feb
1:38:16	Kevin Baker		12.12.57	4	Sutton Coldfield	8 Jun
1:38:41	Allan King		3.12.56	5	Sutton Coldfield	8 Jun
1:39:26	Les Morton		1.07.58	3	York	18 May
1:39:29	Mabon Dane		19.07.71	7	Dublin, IRE	28 Sep
(20)						
1:39:36	Allan Callow	V50	4.09.45	1	St. Johns, IOM	27 May

35 Kilometres Walk

2:56:03	Les Morton		1.07.58	21	Moscow,RUS	1 Jun
2:58:13	Gareth Brown		10.05.68	22	Moscow,RUS	1 Jun

50 Kilometres Walk

4:18:41	Chris Maddocks		28.03.57	34	Atlanta, USA	2	Aug
4:22:42	Chris Cheeseman		11.12.58	1	Horsham	7	Sep
4:24:01	Graham White		28.03.59	2	Horsham	7	Sep
4:27:04	Dennis Jackson	V50	29.06.45	3	Horsham	7	Sep
4:27:22	Gareth Brown		10.05.68	12	Podebrady, CZE	27	Apr
4:32:25	Steve Partington		17.09.65	4	Horsham	7	Sep
4:33:01 +	Kevin Walmsley		6.09.67	1m	Isle of Man	28	Apr
4:35:48	Karl Atton		14.09.71	5	Horsham	7	Sep
4:39:01	Allan King		3.12.56	6	Horsham	7	Sep
4:48:01	Chris Berwick	V50	1.05.46	7	Horsham	7	Sep
	(10)						
4:49:01	Jonathan Cocker		26.09.71	8	Horsham	7	Sep
4:52:00	Ed Shillabeer	V55	2.08.39	2	Schiedam, HOL	18	May
4:53:22	John Paddick	V50	31.08.43	1	Basildon	6	Apr
4:54:12	Mabon Dane		19.07.71	2	Basildon	6	Apr
4:55:16	Brian Adams	V45	13.03.49	9	Horsham	7	Sep
4:57:51	Sean Martindale		8.11.66	10	Horsham	7	Sep
4:59:35	Colin Bradley	V40	2.02.56	1	Burrator	5	May

100 Miles Walk

18:12:04	Richard Brown	V45	18.11.46	1	Colchester	4	Aug
20:37:46	Kevin Perry	V45	7.12.48	4	Colchester	4	Aug
20:47:07	Tony Collins	V50	1.10.42	6	Colchester	4	Aug

200 Kilometres Walk

23:44:23	Don Thompson	V60	20.01.33	14	Bazancourt, FRA	27	Apr
23:50:50	Bob Watts	V45	3.01.50	16	Bazancourt, FRA	27	Apr

4 x 100 METRES

38.67	National Team		3	Madrid, SPA	1	Jun
	(K Williams, D Braithwaite, J John, D Campbell)					
38.76	National Team		1	Ljubljana, SLO	26	May
	(K Williams, D Braithwaite, D Campbell, P White)					
39.45	National Team		6	Stockholm, SWE	8	Jul
	(A Jarrett, D Campbell, O Dako, I Mackie)					
39.98	National Junior Team	U20	3h1	Sydney, AUS	25	Aug
	(C Malcolm, J Henthorn, U Ugono, D Chambers)					
40.32	National Junior Team	U20	7	Sydney, AUS	25	Aug
	(C Malcolm, J Henthorn, U Ugono, D Chambers)					
40.47	Belgrave Harriers		4	Istanbul, TUR	18	May
	(L Paul, P Goedluck, H Korjie, J Fergus)					
40.48	Scotland		1	Belfast	22	Jun
	(R Baillie, K Campbell, D Walker, D Ritchie)					
40.49	Woodford Green AC		1	London (He)	31	Aug
	(M Smith, Josephus Thomas, Joslyn Thomas, A Falola)					
40.5	National Junior Team	U20	3	Nembro, ITA	3	Aug
	(C Malcolm, M Findlay, U Ugono, R Baillie)					
40.52	Thames Valley Harriers		1	London (He)	9	Jun
	(D Joyce, S McCourt, C Edmunds, S Turay)					
40.64	Haringey AC		2	London (He)	9	Jun
	(D Chambers, S Adepegba, M Adam, S Onuorah)					
40.71	Northern Ireland		2	Belfast	22	Jun
	(J McAdorey, I Craig, P Brizzell, M Allen)					
40.74	Wales		1	Cardiff	25	May
	(T Rutherford, D Turner, J Henthorn, C Jackson)					
40.75	Belgrave Harriers		3	London (He)	9	Jun
	(L Paul, P Goedluck, H Korjie, J Fergus)					

40.75	National Under 23 Team	2	Hexham	14	Jul
40.80	Sale	1	Liverpool	4	May
	(A Condon, T Box, O Dako, D Campbell)				
40.86	Midland Counties AA	1	Kunzelsau, GER	7	Sep
	(A Shah, C Henry, B Ghent, M Devonish)				
40.88	Shaftesbury Barnet Harriers	2	London (He)	31	Aug
	(*S Edu*, M McIntyre, R Edu, J Livingston)				
40.88	Belgrave Harriers	3	London (He)	31	Aug
	(M Dickson, P Goedluck, *H Korjie*, A Walcott)				
40.89	South of England AA	1	Birmingham	20	Jul

Additonal Club Teams (1 - 6 above)

41.19	Newham & Essex Beagles	4	London (He)	31	Aug
41.2	Cardiff	3	Kingston	17	Aug
41.49	Birchfield Harriers	5	London (He)	9	Jun
41.5	Team Solent	1	Watford	17	Aug
41.58	Coventry Godiva	1	London (He)	1	Sep
41.8	Windsor Slough & Eton	2	Crawley	28	Jul
42.0	Blackheath	3	Crawley	28	Jul
42.0	Notts	2	Brierley Hill	10	Aug
42.07	Wigan	1	Newport	8	Jun
42.1	Border	2	Liverpool	28	Jul
42.1	GEC Avionics	2	Watford	17	Aug
42.3	Brunel UC	1	Loughborough	27	Apr
42.3	Ballymena & Antrim	1	Antrim	27	Apr
42.3	Peterborough	2	Peterborough	4	May
42.3	Loughborough Students	1	Loughborough	15	May

Additional Under 20 Teams (1 - 3 above)

41.05	National Junior Team	1	Loughborough	19	May
41.23	National Junior 'B' team	2	Loughborough	19	May
41.61	Birchfield Harriers	1	Ljubljana, SLO	28	Sep
41.64	North of England AA	1	London (He)	10	Aug
41.70	South of England AA	2	London (He)	10	Aug
41.85	Bedfordshire Schools	1	Sheffield	13	Jul
41.90	London Schools	2	Sheffield	13	Jul

Additional Under 20 Club Teams (1 above)

42.7	Belgrave	1	Crawley	21	Apr
43.6	Millfield School	1	Oxford	11	May
43.6	Blackheath	2	Blackpool	25	Aug
43.7	Dulwich College	2	Oxford	11	May
43.8	Leeds City	1	Bolton	16	June
44.0	Haileybury College	1	London (He)	28	Jun
44.06	Ayr Seaforth	1	Ayr	21	Jul
44.2	Oundle School	3	Oxford	11	May
44.2	Luton United	1	Luton	16	Jun
44.2	Warrington	1	Derby	15	Sep

Under 17 Teams

42.0	England Schools	1	Stoke-on-Trent	20	Jul
42.31	West Midlands Schools	1	Sheffield	13	Jul
42.6	Scotland Schools	2	Stoke-on-Trent	20	Jul
42.77	Scotland	1	Pitreavie	10	Aug
43.14	Essex Schools	2	Sheffield	13	Jul
43.73	Leicestershire Schools	3	Sheffield	13	Jul
43.81	Blackheath Harriers	1	Birmingham	8	Sep
43.83	Staffordshire Schools	4	Sheffield	13	Jul
44.0	Ulster Schools	1	Dublin, IRE	22	Jun
44.26	Wiltshire Schools	1h2	Sheffield	13	Jul

Additional Under 17 Club Teams (1 above)

44.32	Birchfield Harriers		2	Birmingham	8 Sep
44.9	Belgrave		2	Bromley	21 Jul
44.9	Derby & County		1	Derby	21 Jul
45.2	Trent College		1h	London (He)	28 Jun
45.29	Gateshead		1	Birmingham	7 Sep
45.31	Birchfield Harriers	U15	1	Birmingham	8 Sep
45.4	Winchester College		2	London (He)	28 Jun
45.4	Dauntsey's School		3	London (He)	28 Jun
45.5	Windsor Slough & Eton		1	Hayes	2 Jun
45.7	Dudley & Stourbridge		1	Yate	2 Jun
45.7	High School of Glasgow		1	Pitreavie	8 Jun
45.7	Mandale	U15	1	Jarrow	23 Jul
45.7	Basildon		1	Havering	1 Sep

Additional Under 15 Teams (1 - 2 above)

44.66	West Midlands Schools	1	Sheffield	13 Jul
45.59	Cleveland Schools	2	Sheffield	13 Jul
45.60	Cardiff & Vale Schools	1	Swansea	6 Jul
45.87	Greater Manchester Schools	3	Sheffield	13 Jul

Additional Under 15 Club Teams (1 - 2 above)

46.1	Morpeth Harriers	2	Jarrow	23 Jul
46.67	Fife	1	Glasgow	29 Jun
46.8	Blackheath	1	Bromley	21 Jul
46.9	Belgrave	2	Bromley	21 Jul
47.09	Old Gaytonians	3	Birmingham	8 Sep
47.4	Gateshead	3	Jarrow	23 Jul
47.8	Sale	1	Bebington	21 Jul
47.8	Dartford	2	Bromley	15 Sep

Under 13 Club Teams

52.21	Blackheath	1	Birmingham	8 Sep
52.5	Bishop Stopford School	1	Enfield	15 Jul
52.63	Sale	2	Birmingham	8 Sep
53.0	Belgrave	1	London (CP)	23 Jun
53.2	Chelmsford	1	Colchester	18 Aug
53.6	Borough of Enfield	2	London (CP)	23 Jun
53.9	Shaftesbury Barnet Harriers	1	London (He)	21 Jul
54.1	Old Gaytonians	2	London (He)	21 Jul

4 x 200 METRES

1:24.87		National Team		2	Austin, USA	6 Apr
		(J John, T Box, D Ladejo, M Rosswess)				
1:25.05	i	England		1r2	Vienna, AUT	17 Feb
		(J Fergus, M Devonish, N Owen, A Condon)				
1:25.40	i	National Junior Team	U20	2	Lievin, FRA	2 Mar
		(D Chambers, I Horsbrough, R Baillie, J Henthorn)				
1:27.9		Belgrave	U20	1	London (TB)	31 Jul
		(J Hilston, R David, M Parper, M Dickson)				
1:28.42	i	Loughborough University		1	Birmingham	29 Feb
1:28.6		Belgrave	U20	1	London (TB)	21 Aug
1:29.61	i	Loughborough University		1	Glasgow	Mar
1:30.27	i	Brunel UC		2	Glasgow	Mar
1:30.5		Newham & Essex Beagles AC		1	Southampton	7 Jul

Note

1:28.73	National 'Mixed' Team	2	Gateshead	19 Aug
	(C Murphy, T Joseph, A Patrick, J Golding)			

Additional Club Teams (1 - 4 above)

1:31.3	Eton College	U20	1	Oxford	11	May
1:31.7	Dulwich College	U20	2	Oxford	11	May
1:31.8	Oxford University		1	Oxford	3	Mar
1:32.22 i	Staffordshire University		3	Glasgow		Mar
1:32.5	South London		2	London (BP)	15	May
1:32.6	Herne Hill		2	London (TB)	21	Aug

Additional Under 20 Teams (1 - 4 above)

1:31.98 i	England Schools	U17	1	Birmingham	25	Feb
1:34.27 i	Ayr Seaforth		1	Glasgow	23	Mar
1:34.7	Basildon		1	Colchester	26	Aug

Additional Under 17 Teams (1 above)

1:34.94 i	Scotland Schools		2	Birmingham	25	Feb
1:35.5	Ipswich		1	Colchester	26	Aug
1:35.94 i	Wales Schools		4	Birmingham	25	Feb
1:36.44 i	Perth Strathtay		1	Glasgow	23	Mar
1:36.9	Cannock & Stafford		1	Stafford	27	May
1:37.0 i	High School of Glasgow		1	Glasgow	18	Mar
1:37.3	Highgate School		1	Oxford	11	May
1:37.9	Fife	U15	1	Pitreavie	23	Jun
1:38.1	Millfield School		1h2	Oxford	11	May
1:38.1	Pitreavie		1	Pitreavie	23	Jun

Additional Under 15 Teams (1 above)

1:38.5	Notts	U15	1	Nottingham	4	Aug
1:39.38 i	West Midlands Schools		1	Birmingham	27	Feb
1:41.85 i	Perth Strathtay		1	Glasgow	23	Mar
1:42.2	Bedford Modern School		1	Oxford	11	May
1:42.93 i	Ayr Seaforth		2	Glasgow	23	Mar
1:43.2	Havering		1	Colchester	26	Aug
1:43.3	Highgate School		2	Oxford	11	May
1:43.7	Croydon		1	Croydon	14	Jul

Under 13 Teams

1:53.6	Chelmsford		1	Colchester	26	Aug

4 x 400 METRES

2:56.60	National Team		2	Atlanta, USA	3	Aug
	(I Thomas 44.92, J Baulch 44.19, M Richardson 43.62, R Black 43.87)					
2:59.85	National Team		1	Gateshead	19	Aug
	(J Baulch, M Hylton, M Richardson, R Black)					
3:01.36	National Team		1s1	Atlanta, USA	2	Aug
	(I Thomas, J Baulch, D Ladejo, M Richardson)					
3:01.79	National Team		1h1	Atlanta, USA	2	Aug
	(D Ladejo, J Baulch, M Hylton, M Richardson)					
3:03.38	National Team		1	Madrid, SPA	2	Jun
	(M Richardson, J Baulch, M Hylton, D Ladejo)					
3:06.66	National Under 23 Team		1	Hexham	14	Jul
	(C Henry, J Deacon, P Slythe, N Budden)					
3:06.76	National Junior Team	U20	3	Sydney, AUS	25	Aug
	(K Stewart, T Lerwill, M Rowlands, G Dearman)					
3:07.72 i	National Team		1	Glasgow	24	Feb
	(G Bullock, D Nolan, K Ulyatt, D Ladejo)					
3:08.36	National Junior Team	U20	2h1	Sydney, AUS	24	Aug
	(K Stewart, T Lerwill, M Rowlands, G Dearman)					
3:08.47 i	National Team		1	Birmingham	27	Jan
	(A Patrick, G Bullock, P Slythe, M Hylton)					

3:09.30	Belgrave Harriers	1	Istanbul, TUR	19 May
	(T Lerwill, J Ridgeon, C Rawlinson, D Nolan)			
3:09.78	Woodford Green AC	1	London (He)	31 Aug
	(C McCaw, P Amara, S Ciaravella, T O'Dell)			
3:10.42	Newham & Essex Beagles AC	2	London (He)	31 Aug
	(T Williams, P McBurney, A Francis, G Jennings)			
3:10.65	Thames Valley Harriers	3	London (He)	31 Aug
	(K Bentham, R Conteh, V Rose, E Williams)			
3:10.97	Shaftesbury Barnet Harriers	1	Kingston	17 Aug
	(M Stern, D McKenzie, G Dunson, *R Edu*)			
3:11.1	National Junior Team U20	2	Nembro, ITA	3 Aug
	(I Horsbrough, M Rowlands, K Stewart, G Dearman)			
3:11.23	Loughborough Students	1	Sheffield	6 May
3:11.4	Wigan & District H & AC	1	Jarrow	4 May
	(G Bullock, D Grindley, C Winrow, T Painter)			
3:11.69	Belgrave Harriers	1	Birmingham	6 Jul
	(T Lerwill, M Kloiber, L Samuel, D Nolan)			
3:11.9	Sale	1	Liverpool	28 Jul
	(C White, R Waters, J Gowon, D Savage)			

Additional National Teams
3:12.17	Wales	1	Cardiff	25 May
	(D Williams, P Harries, J Baulch, J Lloyd)			
3:12.96	Northern Ireland	1	Belfast	22 Jun
3:13.24	Scotland	3	Belfast	22 Jun
	(B Middleton, K Stewart, P Walker, I McGurk)			

Additional Club Teams (1 - 7 above)
3:12.01	Heriot Watt University	2	Sheffield	6 May
3:12.23	Birchfield Harriers	2	Birmingham	6 Jul
3:13.3	Windsor Slough & Eton	1	Watford	17 Aug
3:13.75	Cheltenham & Gloucester Univ	3	Sheffield	6 May
3:14.5	Morpeth	1	Sheffield	8 Jun
3:14.66	Cardiff	1	Liverpool	4 May
3:14.9	Team Solent	2	Watford	17 Aug
3:15.1	Brunel UC	2	Loughborough	27 Apr
3:15.4	Blackheath	2	Stoke-on-Trent	17 Aug
3:16.22	Swansea	2	Newport	8 Jun
3:16.7	City of Edinburgh AC	3	Enfield	6 Jul
3:16.8	Coventry Godiva	1	London (He)	28 Jul

Additional Under 20 Teams (1 - 3 above)
3:14.4	England Schools	U17 1	Stoke-on-Trent	20 Jul
	(R McNabb, J Heggie, C McMullen, D Naismith)			
3:14.5	Scotland Schools	U17 2	Stoke-on-Trent	20 Jul
	(C Carson, J Shenava, R McDonald, K Stewart)			
3:17.1	Belgrave Harriers	1	Woodford	4 Aug
3:17.73	National Junior Team	3	Loughborough	19 May
	(N Jennings, I Horsburgh, K Stewart, G Dearman)			
3:17.85	South of England AA	1	London (He)	10 Aug
3:18.42	Wales Schools	1	Carmarthen	16 Jul
3:18.83	North of England AA	2	London (He)	10 Aug
3:19.71	North East	1	Cudworth	3 Aug
3:19.78	Scotland Schools	2	Carmarthen	16 Jul
3:23.0	Middlesex AA	1	Crawley	10 Aug
3:23.33	Birchfield Harriers	4	Ljubljana, SLO	28 Sep

Additional Under 20 Club Teams (1 - 2 above)
3:23.8	Blackheath	2	Gateshead	16 Jun
3:25.1	Coventry Codiva	1	Derby	15 Sep

3:25.3	Luton United		1	Luton	16	Jun
3:25.8	Hillingdon		2	Luton	16	Jun
3:25.8	Borough of Hounslow		2	Derby	15	Sep
3:25.9	Wigan		1	Bury	16	Jun
3:27.1	Borough of Enfield		1	Enfield	25	Aug
3:28.1	Shaftesbury Barnet Harriers		3	Derby	15	Sep

Additional Under 17 Teams (1 - 2 above)

3:24.9	Wales Schools		3	Stoke-on-Trent	20	Jul
	(J Evans, L Farmer, R Phillips, M Bodden)					
3:27.8	Medway AC		1	Bromley	15	Sep
3:29.1	Derby & County AC		1	Derby	21	Jul
3:29.5	Mansfield H & AC		1	Coventry	2	Jun
3:30.58	Shaftesbury Barnet Harriers		1	Birmingham	7	Sep
3:30.6	Sussex AA		1	Crawley	10	Aug
3:30.92	Blackheath Harriers		1	Birmingham	8	Sep
3:31.0	Notts AC		2	Nottingham	23	Jun

Additional Under 17 Club Teams (1 - 6 above)

3:32.47	Liverpool Harriers		2	Birmingham	8	Sep
3:32.73	Sale		3	Birmingham	8	Sep
3:33.4	Perth Strathtay		1	Livingston	26	May
3:33.6	GEC Avionics		3	Bromley	15	Sep

Under 15 Teams

3:42.8	Blackheath		1	Bromley	15	Sep
3:43.1	Notts		1	Birmingham	7	Sep
3:45.4	Birchfield Harriers		1	Stafford	5	May
3:46.57	Old Gaytonians		2	Birmingham	8	Sep
3:46.7	Wirral		1	Rotherham	23	Jun
3:47.6	Shaftesbury Barnet Harriers		2	Birmingham	7	Sep
3:48.5	Haileybury College		1	London (He)	22	Jun
3:49.1	Mandale		2	Rotherham	23	Jun
3:49.6	Halesowen		1	Yeovil	21	Jul

Under 13 Teams

4:13.5	Blackheath		1	Bromley	15	Sep
4:30.4	GEC Avionics		2	Bromley	15	Sep

1600 METRES MEDLEY

3:36.0	Ministry of Defence		1	Bedford	14	Aug
3:36.0	Blackheath		1	Bromley	15	Sep
3:37.30	Metropolitan Police		1	Antrim	3	Jul
3:38.7	Dartford		2	Bromley	15	Sep
3:40.1	Lord Wandsworth College	U20	1	London (He)	22	Jun
3:41.0	Invicta East Kent		3	Bromley	15	Sep

Additional Under 20 Teams (1 above)

3:44.0	Highgate School	U16	1	London (He)	22	Jun
3:47.3	Cannock & Stafford	U17	1	Stafford	27	May
3:51.2	Lucozade Motherwell	U17	1	Wishaw	24	Aug
3:52.4	Haileybury College		2	London (He)	22	Jun
3:52.4	Harrow School		3	London (He)	22	Jun
3:52.4	Bedford School		4	London (He)	22	Jun
3:52.5	Southend High School	U16	2	London (He)	22	Jun

Additional Under 17 Teams (1 - 4 above)

3:56.0	Haileybury College	U15	1	London (He)	22	Jun
3:58.0	Bedford Modern School	U16	3	London (He)	22	Jun
3:58.8	Harriers College	U16	4	London (He)	22	Jun

Additional Under 15 Teams (1 above)

4:09.7	East Kilbride	1	Wishaw	24 Aug
4:10.9	Wellington	2	London (He)	22 Jun
4:11.0	Cannock & Stafford	1	Stafford	27 May
4:12.4	Bedford School	3	London (He)	22 Jun
4:12.9	Queen Elizabeth's Barnet	4	London (He)	22 Jun

Under 13 Teams

4:30.1	St Columb's College	1	Belfast	27 Jun
4:33.0	Queen Elizabeth's Barnet	1	London (He)	22 Jun

4 x 800 METRES

7:23.1	BMC National Squad		1	Watford	17 Jul
	(A Hart, A Knight, R Waters, J Mayo)				
7:41.3	Ron Allison's Squad		2	Watford	17 Jul
	(J Dupuy, J Mills, D McCormack, D Pamah)				
7:48.4	Ballymena & Antrim		1	Antrim	27 Apr
	(P McCormick, G Steele, D O'Loane, E King)				
7:48.9	Annadale Striders		2	Antrim	27 Apr
	(J Rodgers, M Wright, J Lyster, E O'Neill)				
7:49.0	Norfolk Olympiads		1	Havering	12 Sep
7:51.5	BMC U17 Squad	U17	1	Watford	17 Jul
	(M Curson, B Stopher, P Laslett, T Payn)				
7:52.2	Ken Leader's Squad		3	Watford	17 Jul
	(L Wells, C Simmons, S Hyams, L Mangleshot)				
7:55.6	Sparta		3	Antrim	27 Apr
	(M Farren, B Farren, G McGee, M McCausland)				
8:00.5	Crewe & Nantwich		1	Crewe	9 Jul
8:01.0	BMC East		4	Watford	17 Jul
	(W Davies, S Wilson, C Noon, P Farmer)				
8:01.0	Winchester College	U20	2	Watford	17 Jul
	(D Reid, T Powell-Jackson, M Best, E Matthews)				

Additional Under 20 Teams (1 - 2 above)

8:06.5	Millfield School	1	Oxford	11 May
8:08.1	Old Gaytonians	4	Watford	17 Jul

Additional Under 17 Teams (1 above)

8:16.4	Mansfield	1	Stafford	27 May
8:18.4	Wirral	2	Stafford	27 May

Under 15 Teams

9:06.2	Wirral	1	Crewe	9 Jul
9:12.9	Dr Challoner's School	1	Watford	17 Jul
9:13.8	Rotherham	1	Stafford	27 May

Under 13 Teams

10:34.0	Cannock & Stafford	1	Stafford	27 May

4 x 1500 METRES

15:32.6	BMC National Squad		1	Stretford	30 Apr
	(A Hart, C Murphy, L Cadwallader, N Caddy)				
16:03.2	BMC Junior Squad	U20	2	Stretford	30 Apr
	(T Mayo, A Oldfield, R Cartwright, A Jones)				
16:32.8	Oxford University		1	Oxford	3 Mar
16:37.2	Cambridge University		2	Oxford	3 Mar

X Northern Ireland age groups and therefore possibly including older athletes.

1996 LISTS - WOMEN

60 METRES - Indoors

7.33	Bev Kinch		14.01.64	1	Glasgow	24	Feb
	7.35			1h2	Stockholm, SWE	8	Mar
	7.36			4	Birmingham	10	Feb
	7.36			5s2	Stockholm, SWE	8	Mar
	7.39			1s1	Birmingham	3	Feb
	7.40			3	Vienna, AUT	17	Feb
	7.41			3	Birmingham	3	Feb
	7.42			1h4	Birmingham	3	Feb
	7.43			3h1	Vienna, AUT	17	Feb
	7.46			2	Birmingham	27	Jan
7.34	Marcia Richardson		10.02.72	1	Birmingham	3	Feb
	7.35			3	Birmingham	10	Feb
	7.39			1s2	Birmingham	3	Feb
	7.39			2	Glasgow	24	Feb
	7.43			1	Lievin, FRA	13	Jan
	7.43			1h1	Birmingham	3	Feb
	7.44			4	Birmingham	27	Jan
	7.49			1h1	Lievin, FRA	13	Jan
7.36	Geraldine McLeod		24.09.71	2	Birmingham	3	Feb
	7.44			2h2	Birmingham	3	Feb
	7.44			2s1	Birmingham	3	Feb
7.40	Danaa Callow		16.10.70	1	Birmingham	6	Jan
	7.42			1	Birmingham	27	Jan
	7.42			5	Birmingham	3	Feb
	7.43			1h2	Birmingham	3	Feb
	7.47			3s1	Birmingham	3	Feb
7.42	Stephanie Douglas		22.01.69	1h3	Birmingham	3	Feb
	7.43			3	Birmingham	27	Jan
	7.44			2s2	Birmingham	3	Feb
7.42	Sharon Williams		20.05.70	4	Birmingham	3	Feb
	7.46			3s2	Birmingham	3	Feb
	7.47			1h2	Glasgow	21	Jan
	7.50			2	Glasgow	21	Jan
7.47	Paula Thomas		3.12.64	7	Birmingham	10	Feb
7.49	Melanie Neef		26.05.70	1	Glasgow	21	Jan
7.49	Louise Fraser		10.10.70	2h3	Birmingham	3	Feb
7.50	Tatum Nelson	U20	17.12.78	1h1	Lievin, FRA	2	Mar
	37 performances to 7.50 by 10 athletes						
7.52	Gosha Rostek	U20	25.03.77	1r2	Lievin, FRA	2	Mar
7.59	Sarah Wilhelmy	U17	2.02.80	1	Birmingham	17	Feb
7.62	Tracy Joseph		29.11.69	3h3	Birmingham	3	Feb
7.62	Zoe Wilson	U23	28.08.76	1	Birmingham	24	Feb
7.63	Christine Bloomfield		12.02.68	1h2	Lievin, FRA	13	Jan
7.63	Sarah Claxton	U17	23.09.79	2	Birmingham	17	Feb
7.64	Dawn Rose	U20	25.01.79	1	Birmingham	24	Feb
7.67	Joice Maduaka		30.09.73	6rB	Birmingham	27	Jan
7.67	Ellena Ruddock	U23	23.02.76	2	Birmingham	24	Feb
7.69	Donna Fraser		7.11.72	8rB	Birmingham	27	Jan
	(20)						
7.69	Shani Anderson	U23	7.08.75	2h4	Birmingham	3	Feb
7.70	Ann Brooks		4.05.71	1h1	Birmingham	6	Jan
7.70	Libby Alder	U17	20.11.80	1	Birmingham	24	Feb
7.71	Sharon Tunaley		2.09.68	3	Birmingham	6	Jan
7.71	Lesley Owusu	U20	21.12.78	4	Birmingham	17	Feb
7.73	Paula Cohen		5.02.71	4	Birmingham	6	Jan
7.75	Elaine Sutcliffe		6.04.70	2	Sheffield	21	Jan
7.75	Sarah Oxley		3.07.73	1	Glasgow	16	Mar

7.76	Lorraine Robins		13.05.70	5B	Birmingham	3	Feb
7.77	Sarah Chesney		3.03.73	4h2	Birmingham	3	Feb
(30)							
7.77	Marcia Walker		27.05.70	5h2	Birmingham	3	Feb
7.77	Gael Davies	U20	5.02.79	2	Birmingham	24	Feb
7.78	Susan Williams	U20	2.06.77	4	Lievin, FRA	2	Mar
7.79	Gillian Hegney	U20	4.11.77	2	Glasgow	14	Jan

Additional Under 17 (1 - 3 above)

7.81	Kelly Thomas		9.01.81	4	Birmingham	17	Feb
7.82	Karen Scott		17.10.79	1	Glasgow	3	Feb
7.84	Kelli Bailey		8.09.79	2	Birmingham	28	Jan
7.85	Ayeesha Charles		4.09.79	3	Birmingham	28	Jan
7.92	Karlene Palmer		23.10.80	3h1	Birmingham	17	Feb
7.93	Carly Moody		9.06.80	4s1	Birmingham	17	Feb
7.95	Claire Jelley		27.11.79	3	Birmingham	11	Feb
(10)							
7.96	Emma Phillips		31.01.81	6s1	Birmingham	17	Feb
7.98	Rebecca White		5.06.80	4	Birmingham	28	Jan
7.99	Rachael Kay		8.09.80	1	Sheffield	21	Jan
7.99	Lisa Callan		10.10.80	1	Glasgow	29	Feb

Under 15

| 7.87 | Andrea Lang | | 6.03.82 | 2 | Birmingham | 25 | Feb |

Hand Timing

7.4	Kinch		(7.33i)	1	London (CP)	18	Dec
7.5				1h2	London (CP)	26	Jan
7.5				1r2	London (CP)	18	Dec
	3 performances to 7.5 by 1 athlete						
7.7	Sharon Tunaley		(7.71i)	2s1	Birmingham	6	Jan
7.7	Aattoma De Jesus	U23	23.08.74	3	London (CP)	13	Jan
7.7	Sarah Chesney		(7.77i)	3	London (CP)	20	Jan
7.7	Shelley-Anne Bowen	U20	12.05.79	1	London (CP)	20	Jan
7.7	Susan Williams	U20	(7.78i)	2	London (CP)	18	Dec

Under 17

| 7.8 | Lucy Atunumuo | | 4.11.80 | 2 | London (CP) | 18 | Dec |

Foreign

| *7.50* | *Elona Reinalda* | *U23* | *31.03.76* | *1rB* | *Birmingham* | *3* | *Feb* |
| *7.53* | *Evadne McKenzie* | *U23* | *19.05.75* | *4s1* | *Birmingham* | *3* | *Feb* |

75 METRES - Under 13

9.9		Sherie Pierre		15.05.84	1	Coventry	21	Jul
9.96 w	2.3	Joanne Wainwright		28.09.83	1	Birmingham	8	Sep
10.1					1	Stoke	21	Jul
10.0		Monique Parris		28.01.84	1	Thurrock	12	May
10.1		Hannah Wilhelmy		11.04.84	2	Thurrock	12	May
10.1		Marie Thornley			1	Mansfield	19	May
10.1		Heather Dudley		22.03.84	1	Telford	2	Jun
10.1		Ruth Brooke		2.09.83	1	Windsor	30	Jun
10.1		Charlene Payne		7.10.83	2	Windsor	30	Jun
10.1		Gemma Belcher		22.10.83	1	Brierley Hill	21	Jul
10.2		Gemma Bennett		4.01.84	3	Thurrock	12	May
(10)								
10.2		Kerry Everall			1	Yate	21	Jul
10.2		Sarah Biggs		16.12.83	2	Stoke	21	Jul

80 METRES - Under 13

10.6		Kimberley Mann		23.10.83	1	Scunthorpe	30	Jun
10.6		Joanne Wilkinson		9.02.84	2	Scunthorpe	30	Jun
10.6		C. Taylor			1	Jarrow	20	Jul
10.7		Joanne Wainwright		28.09.83	1	York	18	Aug
10.9		Gemma Belcher		22.10.83	1	Bracknell	30	Mar
11.0 w	2.9	Laura Bell		16.11.83	1	Portsmouth	29	Jun

100 METRES

11.39	-0.5	Simmone Jacobs		5.09.66	5h7	Atlanta, USA	26	Jul
	11.47	1.1			1s1	Birmingham	15	Jun
	11.47	-0.9			5q3	Atlanta, USA	26	Jul
	11.51	1.6			1	Loughborough	19	May
	11.51	0.3			7	Madrid, SPA	1	Jun
	11.56	0.2			1h3	Birmingham	14	Jun
	11.57	-1.1			2	Birmingham	15	Jun
	11.62	-0.2			6	London (CP)	12	Jul
11.42	0.2	Marcia Richardson		10.02.72	6h6	Atlanta, USA	26	Jul
	11.44	1.5			1	Gateshead	30	Jun
	11.47	1.0			3	Bratislava, SVK	29	May
	11.55	0.0			7q2	Atlanta, USA	26	Jul
	11.57	-0.2			4	London (CP)	12	Jul
	11.63	0.6			2s2	Birmingham	15	Jun
	11.65	0.9			3	Sheffield	25	Aug
11.46	2.0	Paula Thomas		3.12.64	1r2	Ljubljana, SLO	26	May
	11.51	1.2			1	Tallinn, EST	9	Jun
	11.53	1.1			2s1	Birmingham	15	Jun
	11.62	0.4			1	Bedford	18	May
	11.63 A	1.2			3	Pretoria, RSA	3	Feb
11.48	2.0	Geraldine McLeod		24.09.71	2r2	Ljubljana, SLO	26	May
	11.57 A	-0.1			2	Pretoria, RSA	8	Apr
	11.57	1.5			3	Gateshead	30	Jun
	11.59	0.9			2	Sheffield	25	Aug
	11.61 A	0.0			3	Johannesburg, RSA	14	Apr
	11.62	1.0			6	Bratislava, SVK	29	May
11.49	0.9	Sophia Smith	U23	8.12.74	1	Sheffield	25	Aug
	11.57	-0.5			1r1	Ljubljana, SLO	26	May
	11.62	1.5			5	Gateshead	30	Jun
	11.65	0.2			2h3	Birmingham	14	Jun
11.50	1.3	Bev Kinch		14.01.64	2	Lidingo, SWE	4	Jun
	11.52	1.5			2	Gateshead	30	Jun
	11.57	1.1			3s1	Birmingham	15	Jun
	11.59	0.0			5	Nuremberg, GER	7	Jun
	11.63	-0.4			4h2	Nuremberg, GER	7	Jun
	11.65	-0.1			2h4	Birmingham	14	Jun
11.52	1.0	Stephanie Douglas		22.01.69	5	Bratislava, SVK	29	May
	11.55	-1.1			1	Birmingham	15	Jun
	11.58	0.6			1s2	Birmingham	15	Jun
	11.61	-0.7			4h5	Atlanta, USA	26	Jul
	11.64	-0.1			1h4	Birmingham	14	Jun
	11.65	-0.3			1	Sheffield	2	Jun
11.54	1.8	Katharine Merry	U23	21.09.74	1h1	Bedford	27	May
11.60	1.5	Shani Anderson	U23	7.08.75	4	Gateshead	30	Jun

44 performances to 11.65 by 9 athletes

11.68	1.5	Aileen McGillivary		13.08.70	6	Gateshead	30	Jun
	(10)							
11.69 A	-0.1	Catherine Murphy	U23	21.09.75	3	Pretoria, RSA	8	Apr
	11.77	0.9			4	Sheffield	25	Aug
11.71	1.1	Christine Bloomfield		12.02.68	4s1	Birmingham	15	Jun
11.79	1.8	Tracy Joseph		29.11.69	2h1	Bedford	27	May

11.83	0.8	Gosha Rostek	U20	25.03.77	1h1	Katowice, POL	7	Jul
11.85	0.6	Joice Maduaka		30.09.73	5s2	Birmingham	15	Jun
11.86	1.2	Rebecca Drummond	U20	18.04.78	1h1	Bedford	27	Jul
11.87	1.6	Victoria Shipman	U20	31.03.77	3	Loughborough	19	May
11.89	0.9	Janine Whitlock		11.08.73	5	Sheffield	25	Aug
11.90	-0.6	Ellena Ruddock	U23	23.02.76	2rB	Loughborough	19	May
11.91	1.8	Donna Hoggarth		14.10.73	1h1	Sheffield	2	Jun
	(20)							
11.93	-0.3	Sue Rawlinson		13.10.70	2	Sheffield	2	Jun
11.94	-0.3	Danaa Callow		16.10.70	3=	Sheffield	2	Jun
11.95	-0.6	Ashia Hansen		5.12.71	4	Alfaz Del Pi, SPA	11	Apr
11.95	0.5	Shelley-Anne Bowen	U20	12.05.79	1h1	Sheffield	12	Jul
11.95	1.6	Emma Symonds	U20	5.06.77	1h2	Bedford	27	Jul
11.97	1.8	Ann Brooks		4.05.71	2h1	Sheffield	2	Jun
11.98	0.8	Debbie Mant	U23	11.10.75	3	Zoetermeer, HOL	7	Jul
11.98		Clova Court	V35	10.02.60	1rB	Biella, ITA	14	Sep
12.01	-0.6	Keeley Butler	U23	24.03.75	3rB	Loughborough	19	May
12.02		Zoe Wilson	U23	28.08.76	2	Birmingham	1	Jun
	(30)							
12.02	1.8	Vicki Jamison	U20	19.05.77	1	Antrim	6	Jul
12.03		Sinead Dudgeon	U23	9.07.76	1r2	Edinburgh	25	Aug
12.05	-0.4	Sharon Williams		20.05.70	1	Luton	6	May
12.05	1.6	Gillian Hegney	U20	4.11.77	2h2	Bedford	27	Jul
12.05	1.6	Emma Ania	U20	7.02.79	3h2	Bedford	27	Jul
12.06	1.1	Joanna Clark		11.02.73	7s1	Birmingham	15	Jun
12.06	1.4	Abiodun Oyepitan	U17	30.12.79	1	Birmingham	17	Aug
12.07	-0.6	Melanie Purkiss	U20	11.03.79	1rB	Bedford	27	Jul
12.08	-0.4	Donna Fraser		7.11.72	4	Luton	6	May
12.09	0.8	Jannette Niccolls	U23	7.09.76	4=	Zoetermeer, HOL	7	Jul
	(40)							
12.11	0.4	Paula Cohen		5.02.71	6	Bedford	18	May
12.11	0.9	Alison Davies	V35	6.04.61	6	Bedford	27	May
12.11	-0.8	Lesley Owusu	U20	21.12.78	2	London (CP)	30	Jun
12.11	1.2	Amanda Forrester	U20	29.09.78	2h1	Bedford	27	Jul
12.12	-0.3	Beccy Annan		13.03.70	5	Sheffield	2	Jun
12.12	-1.7	Sarah Wilhelmy	U17	2.02.80	1	London (CP)	30	Jun
12.13	0.5	Gael Davies	U20	5.02.79	2h1	Sheffield	12	Jul
12.13	1.0	Natalie Hynd	U20	30.01.78	2h3	Bedford	27	Jul
12.16	-0.6	Ena Waldo		29.06.63	6h2	Birmingham	14	Jun
12.16	0.5	Hannah Eatough	U20	14.08.79	3h1	Sheffield	12	Jul
	(50)							
12.17	1.4	Petrina Alleyne	U17	10.07.81	1s2	Sheffield	12	Jul
12.17	1.4	Kelli Bailey	U17	8.09.79	2	Birmingham	17	Aug
12.18	0.2	Sarah Oxley		3.07.73	4h3	Birmingham	14	Jun
12.18		Andrea Coore		23.04.69	2	Aldershot	26	Jun
12.18	2.0	Libby Alder	U17	20.11.80	2s1	Sheffield	12	Jul
12.18	2.0	Kelly Thomas	U17	9.01.81	3s1	Sheffield	12	Jul
12.18	1.4	Chantell Manning	U17	4.09.80	3	Birmingham	17	Aug
12.19		Evette Williams	U20	23.03.78	1	London (CP)	11	May
12.19	0.5	Emily Nicholls	U20	5.12.78	4h1	Sheffield	12	Jul
12.19	1.2	Denise Bolton	U20	1.02.77	3h1	Bedford	27	Jul
	(60)							
12.19	-3.3	Diane Allahgreen	U23	21.02.75	2	Cudworth	3	Aug
12.21	0.9	Claire Haslam		18.12.63	7	Bedford	27	May
12.21	1.5	Rachel Redmond	U15	7.12.81	1h2	Sheffield	12	Jul
12.21	1.6	Angharad James	U20	7.04.79	6h2	Bedford	27	Jul
12.22	-0.3	Jane Hale	U23	4.01.74	7	Sheffield	2	Jun
12.22	0.6	Louise Sharps	U20	9.07.77	1	Carmarthen	16	Jul
12.23	-1.7	Dawn Cousins		16.03.68	4s2	London (CP)	2	Jun
12.23	2.0	Sonya Green	U17	6.03.80	4s1	Sheffield	12	Jul
12.24	-0.4	Sarah Claxton	U17	23.09.79	7	Luton	6	May

Time	Wind	Name	Category	DOB	Pos	Venue	Date
12.24		Bianca Liston	U20	28.05.78	2	London (CP)	11 May
	(70)						
12.24	1.5	Clare Russell	U15	11.11.81	1h1	Sheffield	12 Jul
12.24	1.4	Andrea Hayles	U17	24.07.80	4	Birmingham	17 Aug
12.25	-1.7	Hayley Clements		17.09.68	5s2	London (CP)	2 Jun
12.25	-0.6	Dawn Rose	U20	25.01.79	8h2	Birmingham	14 Jun
12.25	1.6	Fiona Harrison	U15	30.11.81	1	Birmingham	17 Aug
12.25	1.4	Emma Phillips	U17	31.01.81	5	Birmingham	17 Aug
12.26	-0.1	Elaine Sutcliffe		6.04.70	4	Sheffield	11 May
12.26	-0.5	Sue Briggs		26.03.67	7	Birmingham	20 Jul
12.27		Michelle Jones	U23	6.01.75	3	London (CP)	11 May
12.29		Morag McGowan		22.08.69	4r2	Edinburgh	4 May

Additional Under 17 (1 - 11 above)

Time	Wind	Name	DOB	Pos	Venue	Date
12.33	2.0	Kate Denham	18.03.80	5s1	Sheffield	12 Jul
12.33	1.4	Lucy Atunumuo	4.11.80	6	Birmingham	17 Aug
12.34	1.4	Claudine Leger	17.05.80	5s2	Sheffield	12 Jul
12.35	-1.7	Dionne Howell	10.04.81	3	London (CP)	30 Jun
12.38		Elizabeth Lloyd	1.12.79	1	Wrexham	27 Jul
12.39	1.4	Natalie Gaynor	7.11.79	7	Birmingham	17 Aug
12.42		Susan Burnside	3.02.80	1	Edinburgh	5 Jun
12.46		Gail Evans	23.07.80	1	Swansea	6 Jul
12.50	0.8	Rachel Rogers	20.11.80	1	Portsmouth	11 May
	(20)					
12.50	1.4	Lisa Thomas	22.06.80	6s2	Sheffield	12 Jul
12.53	0.4	Denise Andrews	1.07.80	6h2	Sheffield	12 Jul
12.55	-0.2	Emily Freeman	24.11.80	5h1	Birmingham	17 Aug
12.56		Debbie Adams	7.03.80	2	Neath	28 Apr
12.57	0.6	Ruth Watson	29.11.79	3h2	London (He)	7 Jul
12.58	1.8	Rebecca White	5.06.80	1h1	Sheffield	2 Jun
12.59	0.7	Jenny Such	5.10.79	4h1	Sheffield	12 Jul
12.59	1.8	Rachael Kay	8.09.80	2	Birmingham	7 Sep

Wind Assisted

Time	Wind	Name	Category	(Legal)	Pos	Venue	Date
11.43	2.2	Jacobs		(11.39)	1	Fullerton, USA	25 Apr
11.48	2.2	Angela Thorp		7.12.72	2	Birmingham	7 Jul
11.45	2.2	Richardson		(11.42)	1	Richardson	7 Jul
		11.48	2.2		2	Helsinki, FIN	25 Jun
11.55	2.3	Douglas		(11.52)	1h2	Sheffield	2 Jun
		11.60	4.0		1	Cardiff	25 May
11.62	2.1	McLeod		(11.48)	1	London (He)	31 Aug
11.64	3.7	Aileen McGillivary		(11.68)	1	Edinburgh	2 Jun
		8 performances to 11.65 by 6 athletes					
11.66	4.0	Catherine Murphy	U23	(11.77)	2	Cardiff	25 May
11.68	4.3	Rebecca Drummond	U20	(11.86)	1	Sheffield	13 Jul
11.69	2.1	Christine Bloomfield		(11.71)	2	London (He)	31 Aug
11.84	2.2	Jannette Niccolls	U23	(12.09)	1h3	Sheffield	12 Jul
11.84	3.2	Kelly Thomas	U17	(12.18)	1	Sheffield	13 Jul
11.88	3.6	Janine Whitlock		(11.89)	1h3	Bedford	27 May
11.89	2.2	Zoe Wilson	U23	(12.02)	3	Birmingham	7 Jul
11.89	4.3	Shelley-Anne Bowen	U20	(11.95)	3	Sheffield	13 Jul
11.89	w?	Gillian Hegney	U20	(12.05)	1	Edinburgh	25 Aug
11.90	4.0	Donna Hoggarth		(11.91)	4	Cardiff	25 May
11.93	2.1	Natalie Hynd	U20	(12.13)	3	Bedford	27 Jul
11.94	2.1	Amanda Forrester	U20	(12.11)	4	Bedford	27 Jul
11.97	3.7	Alison Davies	V35	(12.11)	2h2	Bedford	27 May
11.97	2.2	Donna Fraser		(12.08)	5	Birmingham	7 Jul

11.97	2.1	Emma Ania	U20	(12.05)	7	Bedford	27	Jul
11.99	3.2	Kelli Bailey	U17	(12.17)	2	Sheffield	13	Jul
12.00	3.7	Dawn Flockhart		16.05.67	2	Edinburgh	2	Jun
12.03	2.3	Jane Hale	U23	(12.22)	3h2	Sheffield	2	Jun
12.04	2.9	Denise Bolton	U20	(12.19)	1rB	Birmingham	7	Jul
12.06	4.8	Rachel Redmond	U15	(12.21)	1s1	Sheffield	12	Jul
12.07	2.2	Dawn Rose	U20	(12.25)	3h3	Sheffield	12	Jul
12.08	3.7	Claire Haslam		(12.21)	3h2	Bedford	27	May
12.10	4.0	Helen Miles		2.03.67	5	Cardiff	25	May
12.13	3.2	Emma Phillips	U17	(12.25)	4	Sheffield	13	Jul
12.14	3.5	Katy Sketchley		9.07.73	3h2	Glasgow	29	Jun
12.14	3.5	Morag McGowan		(12.29)	4h2	Glasgow	29	Jun
12.14	3.2	Libby Alder	U17	(12.18)	5	Sheffield	13	Jul
12.16	2.6	Kate Denham	U17	(12.33)	1	London (He)	7	Jul
12.16	8.0	Fiona Harrison	U15	(12.25)	1s2	Street	24	Jul
12.21	2.6	Dionne Howell	U17	(12.35)	2	London (He)	7	Jul
12.21	4.8	Sophie Allen	U15	7.09.82	2s1	Sheffield	12	Jul
12.21	3.6	Rachel Smith	U17	5.11.80	4	Street	24	Jul
12.21	2.2	Karlene Palmer	U17	23.10.80	2	Birmingham	8	Sep
12.22	2.2	Sonya Green	U17	(12.23)	3	Birmingham	8	Sep
12.24	4.8	Stephanie Johnston	U15	9.10.81	3s1	Sheffield	12	Jul
12.24	2.2	Helen Roscoe	U17	4.12.79	4	Birmingham	8	Sep
12.26	2.4	Alison Thompson	U23	11.02.74	4h1	Glasgow	29	Jun
12.27	2.2	Maria Bolsover	U17	5.06.80	2h2	Cudworth	29	Jun
12.27	2.9	Christine Chambers		4.03.69	2rB	Birmingham	7	Jul
12.27	3.1	Melissa Anderson	U15	30.03.82	2	Sheffield	13	Jul

Additional Under 17

12.37	5.7	Emma Barnett		9.12.80	3s1	Street	24	Jul
12.38	2.6	Ruth Watson		(12.57)	5	London (He)	7	Jul
12.45	3.1	Tracy Martin		4.04.80	2	Stoke	22	Jun
12.47	3.3	Sara Todd		3.11.79	2h4	Cudworth	29	Jun
12.49	2.7	Emily Freeman		(12.55)	3s2	Cudworth	29	Jun
12.50	2.2	Denise Andrews		(12.53)	6	Birmingham	8	Sep
12.57	3.2	Katherine Livesey		15.12.79	1h1	Cudworth	29	Jun
12.58	3.3	Jane Taylor		18.02.80	3h4	Cudworth	29	Jun

Hand Timing

11.6 w	2.2	Smith	U23	(11.49)	3	Watford	5	May
11.5	1.6	Victoria Shipman	U20	(11.87)	2r1	Nembro, ITA	3	Aug
11.5 w	2.2	Katharine Merry	U23	(11.54)	1	Watford	5	May
11.5 w	2.2	Richardson		(11.42)	2	Watford	5	May
		11.5 w			1	Bracknell	11	May
11.5 w	2.9	Jacobs		(11.39)	1	London (He)	6	Jul
11.6	0.5	Catherine Murphy	U23	(11.77)	1	London (He)	28	Jul

7 performances to 11.6 by 6 athletes including 4 wind assisted

11.7 w		Sarah Claxton	U17	(12.24)	1	London (WP)	27	Apr
		12.1	0.0		2	Thurrock	11	May
11.8		Janine Whitlock		(11.89)	1	Bebington	19	Jun
11.8		Andrea Coore		(12.18)	1	Sheffield	4	Aug
11.8 w	4.1	Gosha Rostek	U20	(11.83)	1	Aberdeen	9	Jun
11.8 w	4.1	Dawn Flockhart		(12.00w)	2	Aberdeen	9	Jun
		12.1			1	Coatbridge	26	May
11.8 w		Melanie Purkiss	U20	(12.07)	1	Portsmouth	10	Aug
		12.0	1.7		4	Southampton	7	Jul
11.9		Danaa Callow		(11.94)	1	Blackpool	11	May
11.9	0.0	Sarah Wilhelmy	U17	(12.12)	1	Thurrock	11	May
11.9		Alison Davies	V35	(12.11)	1	Exeter	25	May

11.9	1.3	Zoe Wilson	U23	(12.02)	2	Loughborough	5 Jun
11.9		Melanie Neef		26.05.70	1	Pitreavie	18 Jun
11.9	2.0	Sue Rawlinson		(11.93)	2	Cudworth	23 Jun
11.9	1.5	Diane Allahgreen	U23	(12.19)	1	Liverpool	7 Jul
11.9		Gillian Hegney	U20	(12.05)	1	Coatbridge	4 Aug
11.9 w?		Joanna Clark		(12.06)	1	Welwyn	6 May
11.9 w?		Gael Davies	U20	(12.13)	1	Brierley Hill	26 May
12.0	0.8	Sharon Tunaley		2.09.68	1	Nottingham	11 May
12.0		Maria Bolsover	U17	(12.27w)	1	Mansfield	19 May
12.0	1.0	Jacqui Agyepong		5.01.69	2	London (He)	6 Jul
12.0		Jannette Niccolls	U23	(12.09)	1	Portsmouth	10 Aug
12.0		Amanda Forrester	U20	(12.11)	1	Cannock	18 Aug
12.0		Lesley Owusu	U20	(12.11)	1rB	Derby	18 Aug
12.0 w		Melanie Wilkins		18.01.73	2	Bracknell	12 May
12.1		Hayley Clements		(12.25)	1	Windsor	27 Apr
12.1	0.7	Sam Farquharson		15.12.69	1r2	Watford	5 May
12.1		Beccy Annan		(12.12)	2	Blackpool	11 May
12.1		Kim Goodwin		16.05.70	3	Blackpool	11 May
12.1		Kelli Bailey	U17	(12.17)	1	Telford	2 Jun
12.1		Helen Roscoe	U17	(12.24w)	2	Bebington	19 Jun
12.1		Kelly Thomas	U17	(12.18)	2	Croydon	22 Jun
12.1		Susan Williams	U20	2.06.77	1	London (B Elms)	17 Jul
12.1		Sarah Miles	U20	14.12.78	1	Braunton	20 Jul
12.1	1.6	Louise Sharps	U20	(12.22)	2	Kingston	17 Aug
12.1		Ellie Mardle	U20	27.07.78	1	Exeter	31 Aug
12.1	1.9	Sue Briggs		(12.26)	1	Leeds (South)	8 Sep
12.1 w	2.9	Paula Cohen		(12.11)	5r1	London (He)	6 Jul
12.1 w		Natalie Gaynor	U17	(12.39)	2	Portsmouth	10 Aug

Additional Under 17

12.2		Wendy Cox		1.09.79	1	Stoke	21 Jul
12.2 w		Sophie Williams		29.03.80	1	Bath	11 May
12.3		Ruth Watson		(12.57)	1	St. Ives	1 May
12.3	1.7	Jade Johnson		7.06.80	1s2	Croydon	11 May
12.3		Lindsay Impett		4.01.80	3	Exeter	25 May
12.3		Kate Denham		(12.33)	1	Andover	30 Jun
12.3		Claudine Leger		(12.34)	1	St. Ives	7 Jul
12.3 w		Victoria Williams		11.04.81	2	Bath	11 May
12.4		Sarah Nash		10.11.80	1	Leamington	21 Apr
12.4		Carly Moody		9.06.80	2	Braintree	21 Apr
12.4		Karlene Palmer		(12.21w)	2r2	Windsor	27 Apr
12.4		Naomi Hodge-Dallaway		1.06.81	1	London (Elt)	27 Apr
12.4		Laura Smith		16.11.80	1	Hull	7 May
12.4		Karen Scott		17.10.79	1	Coatbridge	26 May
12.4		Denise Andrews		(12.53)	1	Liverpool	2 Jun
12.4		Ayeesha Charles		4.09.79	1	Swindon	16 Jun
12.4		Amina Ceesay		19.11.79	1	Southampton	22 Jun
12.4		Judy Kotey		20.05.80	1	Bedford	7 Jul
12.4	0.9	Lisa Callan		10.10.80	5	Stoke	20 Jul
12.4		Susan Burnside		(12.42)	2	Coatbridge	4 Aug

Foreign

11.4 w	3.2	Evadne McKenzie	U23	19.05.75	1	Abingdon	24 Aug
		11.63 0.5			1	London (He)	1 Sep
11.70	0.4	Endurance Ojokolo	U23	29.09.75	3	Bedford	18 May
11.9		Elona Reinalda	U23	31.03.76	1	Burcht, BEL	28 Apr
		12.06 0.4			5	Bedford	18 May
12.1		Dion Graham	U20	27.09.78	1r2	Manchester	17 Aug
12.28	1.4	Jean Oyeyemi	U17	24.08.81	3s2	Sheffield	12 Jul

Additional Under 15 (1 - 6 above)

12.3		Johnston	(12.24w)	1	Middlesbrough	15	Jun
	12.39	1.5		2h1	Sheffield	12	Jul
12.3		Laura Watkins	1.01.82	1	Brierley Hill	21	Jul
	12.57	4.3		5	Stoke	22	Jun
12.39	1.5	Anderson	(12.27w)	2h2	Sheffield	12	Jul
12.39	1.7	Donna Maylor	20.05.82	1	Birmingham	8	Sep
12.40	1.5	Allen	(12.21w)	3h1	Sheffield	12	Jul
12.4		Erica Burfoot	28.12.81	1	Brierley Hill	21	Apr
	12.47			1	Swansea	6	Jul
12.4		Aimee Cutler	7.10.81	2	Telford	2	Jun
12.4	(10)	Sarah Zawada	9.04.82	1	Windsor	22	Jun
	12.42	-0.7		1	London (CP)	29	Jun
12.44	1.5	Charlene Shoneye	21.12.81	4h1	Sheffield	12	Jul
12.44 w	4.8	Elexi Walker	28.10.82	4s1	Sheffield	12	Jul
	12.56	1.4		1rB	Birmingham	8	Sep
12.44 w	4.8	Leonie Lightfoot	8.02.82	4=s1	Sheffield	12	Jul
12.47	2.0	Kimberley Canning	2.08.82	1	Edinburgh	2	Jun
12.5		Natalie Smellie	16.01.82	1	London (WF)	19	May
	12.56	-0.7		2	London (CP)	29	Jun
12.5		Michelle Nicholls	26.09.82	1	Windsor	30	Jun
12.5		Leah Tribe	3.09.81	2	Portsmouth	22	Jul
12.5		Lynsey Scott	28.01.82	1	Tweedbank	31	Aug
12.56	2.0	Wendy Thomson	28.06.82	2	Edinburgh	2	Jun
12.58	(20) 1.9	Stephanie Spinks	6.09.82	1h3	Sheffield	12	Jul

Under 13

12.7		Sherie Pierre	15.05.84	1	Kingston	10	Aug
12.8		Monique Parris	28.01.84	1	Ilford	7	Jul
13.0		Gemma Bennett	4.01.84	1	London (Col)	22	Jun
13.2		Marie Thornley		1	Oldham	26	May
13.2		Joanne Wainwright	28.09.83	1h1	Cleckheaton	8	Jun
13.2	0.5	Lyndsey Russell	11.09.83	1h2	Pitreavie	19	Jun
13.2		Michelle Johansen	1.02.84	1	Andover	30	Jun
13.2		Gemma Belcher	22.10.83	1	Deeside	27	Jul
13.2		Rebecca Geary	2.05.84	1	Bournemouth	25	Aug
13.2		Sarah Oldham	23.09.83	1	Tamworth	8	Sep

150 METRES

17.26	-0.3	Simmone Jacobs		5.09.66	4	London (CP)	11	Aug
17.61	-0.3	Catherine Murphy	U23	21.09.75	6	London (CP)	11	Aug
17.61	-0.3	Geraldine McLeod		24.09.71	7	London (CP)	11	Aug

Under 13

19.4		Vernicha James	6.06.84	1	Hoo	31	Aug
19.5		Sherie Pierre	15.05.84	1	Watford	2	Jun
19.7 w	4.8	Monique Parris	28.01.84	1	Southend	28	Apr
19.8		A. Clark		1	Stockport	21	Jul
20.0		Gemma Belcher	22.10.83	1	Brierley Hill	18	Aug
20.01	-2.2	Joanne Wainwright	28.09.83	1	Birmingham	8	Sep
20.1		Donna Chatting	30.10.83	1	Bracknell	30	Mar
20.1		Gemma Bennett	4.01.84	2	Southend	28	Apr
20.1		Charlene Payne	7.10.83	1	Windsor	30	Jun
20.2	(10)	Marie Thornley		1	Mansfield	19	May
20.2		Amy Spencer	19.09.85	1	Oldham	18	Aug
20.2		Adele Bevan	26.03.84				

very doubtful

19.8		Hazel Philp	21.10.83	1	Dundee	7	Jul

200 METRES

Time	Wind	Name	Cat	DOB	Pos	Place	Date	
22.88	1.6	Katharine Merry	U23	21.09.74	3	Madrid, SPA	2	Jun
23.14	1.0				2h4	Atlanta, USA	31	Jul
23.17	0.3				5q2	Atlanta, USA	31	Jul
23.29					2	Cork, IRE	22	Jun
23.30	-0.2				2	Birmingham	16	Jun
23.50	-0.5				1rB	Milan, ITA	19	May
23.62	-1.8				1s2	Birmingham	16	Jun
23.72	-0.6				1h1	Birmingham	15	Jun
22.95	1.5	Simmone Jacobs		5.09.66	1	Fullerton, USA	25	Apr
22.96	-0.4				6q3	Atlanta, USA	31	Jul
23.11	-0.2				1	Birmingham	16	Jun
23.22	-0.9				1	Long Beach, USA	20	Apr
23.29	-0.9				1s1	Birmingham	16	Jun
23.34	0.0				1	Ljubljana, SLO	26	May
23.36	0.1				5h5	Atlanta, USA	31	Jul
23.53	-1.2				1h2	Birmingham	15	Jun
23.41	0.1	Paula Thomas		3.12.64	1	Tallinn, EST	9	Jun
23.46	-0.2				3	Birmingham	16	Jun
23.71	-1.8				2s2	Birmingham	16	Jun
23.75	A -0.9				5	Pretoria, RSA	3	Feb
23.46 i		Catherine Murphy	U23	21.09.75	3	Birmingham	27	Jan
23.47	A -1.5				4	Pietersburg, RSA	3	Apr
23.52	A 0.1				1	Pretoria, RSA	8	Apr
23.52	-0.2				4	Birmingham	16	Jun
23.57	0.1				2	Tallinn, EST	9	Jun
23.63 i					1s1	Birmingham	4	Feb
23.67	-0.9				2s1	Birmingham	16	Jun
23.69 i					1	Birmingham	4	Feb
23.74	-0.4				1	Bedford	18	May
23.62 i		Melanie Neef		26.05.70	4	Birmingham	27	Jan
24.67	-1.5				1	Edinburgh	12	May
23.62	2.0	Donna Fraser		7.11.72	5	Fort-de-France, MRT	1	May
23.64	A 0.1	Geraldine McLeod		24.09.71	2	Pretoria, RSA	8	Apr
23.82 i					1rB	Birmingham	27	Jan
24.07					5	Cape Town, RSA	12	Apr
23.72	-0.2	Tracy Joseph		29.11.69	5	Birmingham	16	Jun
23.77	-1.8				3s2	Birmingham	16	Jun
23.73 i		Louise Fraser		10.10.70	2	Birmingham	4	Feb
23.75	-0.2	Jennifer Stoute		16.04.65	6	Birmingham	16	Jun
23.76	-0.9				3s1	Birmingham	16	Jun
		(10)						
23.80	1.5	Marcia Richardson		10.02.72	1	Birmingham	7	Jul
23.80	-0.6	Sophia Smith	U23	8.12.74	1	Cudworth	3	Aug

39 performances to 23.80 by 12 athletes including 5 indoors

Time	Wind	Name	Cat	DOB	Pos	Place	Date	
23.90	-0.2	Joice Maduaka		30.09.73	7	Birmingham	16	Jun
23.99	-0.6	Janine Whitlock		11.08.73	2	Cudworth	4	Aug
24.10 i		Sharon Williams		20.05.70	2h1	Birmingham	4	Feb
25.08	-0.6				5	Luton	6	May
24.11	-1.5	Sharon Tunaley		2.09.68	1	Birmingham	2	Jun
24.13	-1.2	Stephanie Douglas		22.01.69	1	Palafrugell, SPA	19	Jun
24.15	-0.2	Alison Davies	V35	6.04.61	8	Birmingham	16	Jun
24.17	-1.0	Christine Bloomfield		12.02.68	1	Birmingham	20	Jul
24.18	1.9	Sue Rawlinson		13.10.70	1rB	Loughborough	19	May
		(20)						
24.18	-1.1	Victoria Shipman	U20	31.03.77	3h6	Sydney, AUS	23	Aug
24.22 i		Clova Court	V35	10.02.60	3s2	Birmingham	4	Feb
24.25	1.0	Sarah Wilhelmy	U17	2.02.80	3	Bedford	28	Jul
24.35	-1.5	Ena Waldo		29.06.63	2	Birmingham	2	Jun
24.35	0.4	Bev Kinch		14.01.64	1h2	Oordegem, BEL	10	Aug

Time	Wind	Name	Cat	DOB	Pos	Venue	Date	
24.36	0.6	Louise Whitehead	U23	26.03.75	1	Sheffield	6	May
24.37	-0.2	Sinead Dudgeon	U23	9.07.76	1	Glasgow	29	Jun
24.39	-1.2	Shani Anderson	U23	7.08.75	3	Palafrugell, SPA	19	Jun
24.40	-0.5	Linda Staines		26.12.63	1	Stockholm, SWE	16	Jun
24.42	-0.2	Kerry Jury		19.11.68	1H	Narbonne, FRA	27	Jul
(30)								
24.43	1.3	Hayley Clements		17.09.68	3h1	London (CP)	2	Jun
24.43	0.9	Ellena Ruddock	U23	23.02.76	1	Kunzelsau, GER	7	Sep
24.44	-0.3	Denise Lewis		27.08.72	2H	Atlanta, USA	27	Jul
24.46	1.3	Stephanie Llewellyn		31.12.68	4h1	London (CP)	2	Jun
24.47 i		Lesley Owusu	U20	21.12.78	2rB	Birmingham	4	Feb
	24.48	2.0			1rB	Birmingham	7	Jul
24.49	0.8	Kim Goodwin		16.05.70	1h2	Sheffield	2	Jun
24.50		Sue Briggs		26.03.67	1h3	Sheffield	12	May
24.50	-0.4	Zoe Wilson	U23	28.08.76	7	Bedford	18	May
24.55		Dawn Flockhart		16.05.67	4	Edinburgh	4	May
24.61	0.5	Joanna Clark		11.02.73	3h2	London (CP)	2	Jun
(40)								
24.61	-0.2	Natalie Hynd	U20	30.01.78	2	Glasgow	29	Jun
24.67		Paula Cohen		5.02.71	2rB	Edinburgh	4	May
24.67	-0.2	Fiona Calder/Holliman		4.05.71	3	Glasgow	29	Jun
24.69	1.0	Debbie Mant	U23	11.10.75	1	Zoetermeer, HOL	7	Jul
24.72	-0.2	Emma Lindsay		11.04.71	4	Glasgow	29	Jun
24.74 i		Sarah Oxley		3.07.73	1	Birmingham	24	Feb
	24.88	1.5			5	Birmingham	7	Jul
24.76 i		Marcia Walker		27.05.70	3rB	Birmingham	4	Feb
	24.79	0.5			4h2	London (CP)	2	Jun
24.76 i		Allison Curbishley	U23	3.06.76	1s1	Glasgow	17	Mar
24.80	-1.9	Wendy Cox	U17	1.09.79	1	Cudworth	30	Jun
24.81	1.9	Gosha Rostek	U20	25.03.77	4h2	Bedford	28	Jul
(50)								
24.81	1.0	Susan Williams	U20	2.06.77	4	Bedford	28	Jul
24.82	1.0	Helen Roscoe	U17	4.12.79	5	Bedford	28	Jul
24.87	1.3	Claire Haslam		18.12.63	5h1	London (CP)	2	Jun
24.88	-1.8	Kelly Thomas	U17	9.01.81	2	London (CP)	29	Jun
24.89	1.7	Vikki Schofield		29.12.72	1H	Alhama, SPA	4	May
24.91	-1.1	Melanie Purkiss	U20	11.03.79	1	London (CP)	29	Jun
24.92		Angharad James	U20	7.04.79	1	Neath	28	Apr
24.92	-2.1	Louise Sharps	U20	9.07.77	2	London (He)	10	Aug
24.93	-0.8	Lee McConnell	U20	9.10.78	1	Wishaw	13	Jul
24.94	1.8	Dionne Howell	U17	10.04.81	1s2	Sheffield	13	Jul
(60)								
24.95	1.9	Keeley Butler	U23	24.03.75	3rB	Loughborough	19	May
24.96	0.6	Jane Hale	U23	4.01.74	2	Sheffield	6	May
24.97		Vicki Jamison	U20	19.05.77	1	Antrim	20	Apr
24.97	1.0	Ellie Mardle	U20	27.07.78	7	Bedford	28	Jul
25.01		Lisa Vannet	U23	8.11.74	4rB	Edinburgh	4	May
25.06	-0.4	Lucy Carter	U20	7.03.78	7	Bedford	18	May
25.07	1.8	Karlene Palmer	U17	23.10.80	2s2	Sheffield	13	Jul
25.07		Kimberley Canning	U15	2.08.82	1	Birmingham	18	Aug
25.08		Danaa Callow		16.10.70	5rB	Edinburgh	4	May
25.10	-1.7	Elaine Sutcliffe		6.04.70	4	Sheffield	12	May
(70)								
25.15	-0.2	Beccy Annan		13.03.70	3h1	Sheffield	2	Jun
25.16	0.8	Nicole Crosby	U23	23.10.76	3h2	Sheffield	2	Jun
25.16		Julie Forester		4.05.69	1	Wrexham	27	Jul
25.17	1.8	Tracy Martin	U17	4.04.80	3s2	Sheffield	13	Jul
25.19 i		Gael Davies	U20	5.02.79	1	Birmingham	24	Feb
25.20		Katherine Livesey	U17	15.12.79	1H	Blackpool	27	Jul
25.21	-0.8	Sharon Hollett	U20	26.12.78	3	Wishaw	13	Jul
25.22	-2.2	Sarah Zawada	U15	9.04.82	1	London (CP)	30	Jun

Time	Wind	Name	Cat	DoB	Pos	Venue	Date	
25.22		Erica Burfoot	U15	28.12.81	1	Swansea	6	Jul
25.23	1.6	Anne Hollman	U23	18.02.74	1H	Bedford	25	May
	(80)							
25.23	-1.3	Denise Bolton	U20	1.02.77	1H	Birmingham	1	Jun
25.24	0.8	Alison Thompson	U23	11.02.74	4h2	Sheffield	2	Jun
25.24	1.8	Emily Freeman	U17	24.11.80	4s2	Sheffield	13	Jul
25.25	-0.2	Juliana Palka	U20	9.05.77	5	Glasgow	29	Jun
25.27 i		Emma Symonds	U20	5.06.77	1h1	Birmingham	18	Feb
25.27	-1.5	Susan Burnside	U17	3.02.80	1	Wishaw	13	Jul
25.28		Bianca Liston	U20	28.05.78	1	London (CP)	12	May
25.28	1.4	Julie Howard		24.09.66	3h3	London (CP)	2	Jun

Additional Under 17 (1 - 10 above)

Time	Wind	Name	DoB	Pos	Venue	Date	
25.32	-1.5	Lisa Callan	10.10.80	2	Wishaw	13	Jul
25.32	-1.9	Ruth Watson	29.11.79	1h3	Birmingham	18	Aug
25.34	1.8	Rachel Rogers	20.11.80	5s2	Sheffield	13	Jul
25.42	-1.9	Emma Phillips	31.01.81	2	Cudworth	30	Jun
25.45	1.8	Natalie Gaynor	7.11.79	2h2	London (He)	7	Jul
25.48	-1.5	Karen Scott	17.10.79	3	Wishaw	13	Jul
25.50 i		Rachael Kay	8.09.80	2	Birmingham	25	Feb
25.50	-1.8	Eve Miller	1.12.79	5	London (CP)	29	Jun
25.53	-1.9	Maria Bolsover	5.06.80	3	Cudworth	30	Jun
25.54	-0.2	Rebecca White	5.06.80	4h1	Sheffield	2	Jun

Wind Assisted

Time	Wind	Name	Cat	(time)	Pos	Venue	Date	
23.36	3.1	Jacobs		(22.95)	3	Gateshead	30	Jun
		23.59	3.3		8	Sheffield	25	Aug
		23.64	2.4		1	Loughborough	19	May
23.57	3.5	Tracy Joseph		(23.72)	1H	Bedford	25	May
23.58	3.1	Murphy	U23	(23.52)	4	Gateshead	30	Jun
		23.60	2.3		1	London (He)	31	Aug
	6 performances to 23.80 by 3 athletes							
23.94	2.3	Clova Court	V35	(24.22i)	2	London (He)	31	Aug
23.96	4.0	Sarah Wilhelmy	U17	(24.25)	1	Sheffield	13	Jul
24.06	2.2	Denise Lewis		(24.44)	1H	Gotzis, AUT	25	May
24.08	2.3	Christine Bloomfield		(24.17)	3	London (He)	31	Aug
24.10	2.4	Sue Rawlinson		(24.18)	1	Sheffield	2	Jun
24.18	2.4	Louise Whitehead	U23	(24.36)	2	Sheffield	2	Jun
24.20	3.5	Kerry Jury		(24.42)	2H	Bedford	25	May
24.25	2.4	Kim Goodwin		(24.49)	3	Sheffield	2	Jun
24.30	3.4	Sinead Dudgeon	U23	(24.37)	1	Edinburgh	2	Jun
24.31	4.0	Helen Roscoe	U17	(24.82)	2	Sheffield	13	Jul
24.34	2.3	Vicki Jamison	U20	(24.97)	1	Antrim	6	Jul
24.38	4.0	Wendy Cox	U17	(24.80)	3	Sheffield	13	Jul
24.43	4.0	Dionne Howell	U17	(24.94)	4	Sheffield	13	Jul
24.51	3.9	Natalie Hynd	U20	(24.61)	1	Edinburgh	2	Jun
24.57	2.4	Paula Cohen		(24.67)	4	Sheffield	2	Jun
24.61	4.5	Melanie Purkiss	U20	(24.91)	2	Sheffield	13	Jul
24.62	4.5	Sarah Zawada	U15	(25.22)	1	Sheffield	13	Jul
24.66	4.5	Evette Williams	U20	23.03.78	3	Sheffield	13	Jul
24.67	3.4	Karlene Palmer	U17	(25.07)	1h2	Sheffield	12	Jul
24.69	4.5	Xanine Powell	U20	21.05.79	4	Sheffield	13	Jul
24.77	2.4	Beccy Annan		(25.15)	5	Sheffield	2	Jun
24.79	2.3	Lisa Vannet	U23	(25.01)	5	London (He)	31	Aug
24.83	4.5	Ellie Mardle	U20	(24.97)	5	Sheffield	13	Jul
24.87		Tracy Bishop	U20	1.05.79	1ro	Sheffield	13	Jul
24.87	2.3	Keeley Butler	U23	(24.95)	6	London (He)	31	Aug
24.90		Helen Pryer	U20	21.01.79	2ro	Sheffield	13	Jul

24.91	4.0	Emily Freeman	U17	(25.24)	6	Sheffield	13	Jul
24.97	2.2	Natalie Gaynor	U17	(25.45)	3h1	Sheffield	12	Jul
24.99	3.2	Nicole Crosby	U23	(25.16)	3h1	Sheffield	12	Jul
25.02	4.6	Rachel Redmond	U15	(25.39)	1	Stoke	22	Jun
25.02	5.1	Amanda Forrester	U20	29.09.78	1	Stoke	22	Jun
25.04	4.0	Tracy Martin	U17	(25.17)	7	Sheffield	13	Jul
25.06	2.2	Sonya Green	U17	6.03.80	3	Birmingham	8	Sep
25.07	3.5	Pauline Richards		30.06.68	5H	Bedford	25	May
25.07	3.4	Lindsay Fleet	U17	1.06.81	3h2	Sheffield	12	Jul
25.08	3.2	Joanne McDougall	U20	23.08.79	4h1	Sheffield	12	Jul
25.08	4.5	Laura Watkins	U15	1.01.82	2	Sheffield	13	Jul
25.09	3.9	Fiona Hutchison	U20	18.01.77	3	Edinburgh	2	Jun

Additional Under 17

25.14	4.1	Katherine Livesey		(25.20)	1H	Birmingham	21	Sep
25.26	3.4	Eve Miller		(25.50)	4h2	Sheffield	12	Jul
25.28	4.9	Rachel Rogers		(25.34)	2h4	Sheffield	12	Jul
25.29	2.2	Heather Brookes		17.07.81	4h1	Sheffield	12	Jul
25.30	2.2	Denise Andrews		1.07.80	4	Birmingham	8	Sep
25.32	2.2	Sarah Nash		10.11.80	5h1	Sheffield	12	Jul
25.37	2.2	Roseline Addo		7.06.80	6h1	Sheffield	12	Jul
25.42	4.9	Rebecca Martindale		31.12.80	3h4	Sheffield	12	Jul
25.57	4.4	Emily Parr		9.05.81	7s1	Sheffield	13	Jul

Hand Timing

23.4	1.5	Merry	U23	(22.88)	1	Leamington	11	May
23.6 w		Sophia Smith	U23	(23.80)	1	Derby	18	Aug
23.7 w		Marcia Richardson		(23.80)	2	Derby	18	Aug

3 performances to 23.7 by 3 athletes including 2 wind assisted

23.8 w		Clova Court	V35	(24.22i)	3	Derby	18	Aug
23.9		Louise Fraser		(23.73i)	1	Sheffield	12	Jun
23.9 w	7.2	Dawn Flockhart		(24.55)	1	Aberdeen	9	Jun
24.4					1	Aberdeen	28	Jul
24.0	1.4	Christine Bloomfield		(24.17)	1	Manchester	17	Aug
24.1		Sharon Tunaley		(24.11)	1	Nottingham	11	May
24.1		Alison Davies	V35	(24.15)	1	Exeter	25	May
24.2	1.3	Aileen McGillivary		13.08.70	2	London (He)	6	Jul
24.2		Lesley Owusu	U20	(24.48)	1rB	Derby	17	Aug
24.2	-0.6	Bev Kinch		(24.35)	1	Kingston	18	Aug
24.2 w		Louise Brunning		6.03.72	1	Loughborough	27	Apr
24.3		Joanna Clark		(24.61)	1	Windsor	22	Jun
24.3	1.4	Stephanie Llewellyn		(24.46)	2	Manchester	17	Aug
24.4 i		Allison Curbishley	U23	(24.76i)	1	Glasgow	17	Mar
24.4 w	7.2	Lee McConnell	U20	(24.93)	2	Aberdeen	9	Jun
24.4 w		Michelle Pierre		30.09.73	4	Derby	18	Aug
25.1					2	Hoo	10	Aug
24.5		Emma Symonds	U20	(25.27i)	2	Windsor	22	Jun
24.5		Ann Brooks		4.05.71	2	Rotherham	14	Jul
24.5		Vicki Jamison	U20	(24.97)	1	Antrim	20	Jul
24.5 w	7.2	Emma Lindsay		(24.72)	3	Aberdeen	9	Jun
24.6					1	Coatbridge	4	Aug
24.6		Lucy Carter	U20	(25.06)	1	Bournemouth	25	May
24.6		Sarah Zawada	U15	(25.22)	1	Portsmouth	8	Jun
24.6		Paula Cohen		(24.67)	2	Sheffield	12	Jun
24.6		Melanie Neef		(24.67)	1	Livingston	19	Jun
24.6		Marcia Walker		(24.79)	1	Harrow	17	Jul
24.7		Wendy Cox	U17	(24.80)	1	Pendle	5	May

24.7	-0.1	Alanna Rowbotham		11.01.70	1rB	Cardiff	5 May
24.7		Elaine Sutcliffe		(25.10)	1rB	Pendle	6 May
24.7		Ellie Mardle	U20	(24.97)	1	Exeter	26 Aug
24.7		Gosha Rostek	U20	(24.81)	1	Glasgow	15 Sep
24.7 w	2.6	Vicky Day		19.06.72	1	Thurrock	12 May
24.8					1	Woodford	27 Apr
24.7 w	2.4	Claire Haslam		(24.87)	2rB	London (He)	6 Jul
24.8					1	Hoo	20 Jul
24.7 w	2.4	Melanie Wilkins		18.01.73	2rB	London (He)	6 Jul
25.0					1	Bracknell	11 May
24.8		Sharon Williams		(25.08)	1	Southampton	27 Apr
24.8		Danaa Callow		(25.08)	1	Blackpool	11 May
24.8	1.5	Keeley Butler	U23	(24.95)	3	Leamington	11 May
24.8	0.4	Melanie Purkiss	U20	(24.91)	1	Barking	23 Jun
24.8		Kelly Holmes		19.04.70	1	Portsmouth	2 Jul
24.8		Helen Roscoe	U17	(24.82)	1	Carlisle	7 Jul
24.8		Sarah Oxley		(24.88)	2rB	Derby	18 Aug
24.8 w	3.9	Susan Williams	U20	(24.81)	1	Abingdon	25 Aug
24.9		Jackie White		12.01.71	1	Leamington	21 Apr
24.9		Tatum Nelson	U20	17.12.78	2	Hoo	25 May
24.9	0.3	Diane Allahgreen	U23	21.02.75	2	Liverpool	7 Jul
24.9		Jo Mahoney	U23	22.10.76	1	Cannock	18 Aug
24.9		Kimberley Canning	U15	(25.07)	1	Dumfries	15 Sep
24.9 w	2.2	Louise Sharps	U20	(24.92)	2	Carmarthen	16 Jul
25.0		Angela Hardman	U23	24.10.76	5	Sheffield	12 Jun
25.0		Tania Findlay		8.11.70	1	Bristol	16 Jun
25.0		Amanda Forrester	U20	(25.02w)		Stoke	22 Jun
25.0		Jocelyn Harwood	V35	21.11.57	2	Cannock	17 Aug
25.0 w		Rebecca White	U17	(25.54)	1	Grimsby	28 Apr
25.0 w	4.3	Catriona Slater	U20	27.01.77	1	Southend	28 Apr
25.1		Dawn Cousins		16.03.68	1	Norwich	27 Apr
25.1		Beccy Annan		(25.15)	2	Blackpool	11 May
25.1		Amanda Pritchard	U17	18.03.80	1	Cardiff	15 May
25.1		Lorraine Robins		13.05.70	2	Exeter	28 May
25.1		Rachel Redmond	U15	7.12.81	1	Jarrow	2 Jun
25.1		Sonya Green	U17	(25.06w)	2	Jarrow	2 Jun
25.1		Laura Watkins	U15	(25.08w)	1	Brierley Hill	21 Jul
25.1		Jannette Niccolls	U23	7.09.76	1	Portsmouth	10 Aug
25.1		Shelley-Anne Bowen	U20	12.05.79	2	Bracknell	10 Aug
25.1	1.2	Rachel King	U23	11.05.76	1rB	Kingston	18 Aug
25.1 w	2.2	Suzanne McGowan	U20	13.04.78	4	Carmarthen	16 Jul
25.1 w	2.2	Gael Davies	U20	(25.19i)	5	Carmarthen	16 Jul

Additional Under 17

25.2	Libby Alder		20.11.80	1	Cheltenham	8 Jun
25.3	Sarah Nash		(25.32w)	2	Leamington	21 Apr
25.3	Ruth Watson		(25.32)	1	Braintree	21 Apr
25.3	Eve Miller		(25.50)	2	Milton Keynes	23 Jun
25.4	Emma Phillips		(25.42)	3	Jarrow	2 Jun
25.4	Elizabeth Lloyd		1.12.79	1	Coventry	11 Aug
25.4	Lucy Atunumuo		4.11.80	1	Sutton	1 Sep
25.5	Kate Denham		18.03.80	1	Southampton	22 Jun
25.5	Judy Kotey		20.05.80	1	Bedford	7 Jul
25.5	Jennifer Meadows		17.04.81	2	Liverpool	21 Jul
25.5	Denise Andrews		(25.30w)	1	Derby	15 Sep

23.69	-1.1	*Elona Reinalda*	U23	31.03.76	1	*London (CP)*	2	*Jun*
24.05 w	4.5	*Dion Graham*	U20	27.09.78	1	*Sheffield*	13	*Jul*
	24.21	1.0			2	*Bedford*	28	*Jul*
24.11	1.8	*Evadne McKenzie*	U23	19.05.75	1	*London (He)*	1	*Sep*
24.64		*Endurance Ojokolo*	U23	29.09.75	1rB	*Edinburgh*	4	*May*

Additional Under 15 (1 - 5 above)

25.2		Leah Tribe	3.09.81	2	Windsor	22	Jun
	25.31 w 4.5			5	Sheffield	13	Jul
	25.39 1.9			1h1	Sheffield	12	Jul
25.24 w 4.5		Jenny McCarthy	22.02.82	3	Sheffield	13	Jul
	25.39 1.0			2h3	Sheffield	12	Jul
25.28 w 4.5		Charlene Barnes	25.05.82	4	Sheffield	13	Jul
25.39		Aimee Cutler	7.10.81	2	Cwmbran	29	Jun
	25.45			2	Swansea	6	Jul
25.39		Redmond	(25.1)	2	Birmingham	18	Aug
25.5 i		Fiona Harrison	30.11.81	2	Birmingham	18	Feb
	25.6			1rB	Sheffield	12	Jun
	(10)						
25.5 w	4.2	Natalie Smellie	16.01.82	1	Southend	28	Apr
	25.60 w 4.5			6	Sheffield	13	Jul
	25.74			3	Birmingham	18	Aug
25.6		Melissa Anderson	30.03.82	1	Middlesbrough	15	Jun
	25.78			1	Gateshead	31	Aug
25.7		Hanna Carroll	19.09.81	1	Liverpool	8	Jun
	25.73 w 4.5			7	Sheffield	13	Jul
25.76 w 2.1		Gaby Howell	25.01.82	4h2	Sheffield	12	Jul
25.77	-0.6	Elexi Walker	28.10.82	1	Birmingham	8	Sep
25.8	1.1	Wendy Thomson	28.06.82	1	Pitreavie	19	Jun
	26.06 w 2.3			2	Edinburgh	2	Jun
25.90 w 2.1		Danielle Clethro	13.03.82	5h2	Sheffield	12	Jul
25.92		Chevette Mais	22.09.82	1	London (CP)	12	May

Under 13

26.4	Vernicha James	6.06.84	1	London (Elt)	15	Jul
26.6	Gemma Tate	6.09.83	1	London (BP)	18	Aug
26.7	Sherie Pierre	15.05.84	1	Sutton	22	Jun
26.8	Monique Parris	28.01.84	1	Ilford	7	Jul
27.3	Adele Bevan	26.03.84		Worthing	27	May
27.4	Joanne Wainwright	28.09.83	1	Wakefield	22	Sep
27.4	Hannah Wilhelmy	11.04.84				
27.6	Gemma Bennett	4.01.84	1	London (Col)	22	Jun
27.60 1.6	Donna Chatting	30.10.83	1	Portsmouth	12	May
27.6	Alicia Bateson	6.11.83		London (TB)	28	Jul
(10)						
27.6	Jennifer Molloy	23.09.83	3	Harrow	7	Sep
27.61 2.0	Hazel Philp	21.10.83	1	Edinburgh	2	Jun

300 METRES

36.92	Phylis Smith		29.09.65	4	London (CP)	11	Aug
37.31	Donna Fraser		7.11.72	1	London (CP)	12	Jul
	37.32			5	London (CP)	11	Aug
37.47	Allison Curbishley	U23	3.06.76	6	London (CP)	11	Aug
37.72	Catherine Murphy	U23	21.09.75	2	London (CP)	12	Jul
37.92	Tracy Joseph		29.11.69	3	London (CP)	12	Jul
38.79 i	Louise Whitehead	U23	26.03.75	1	Birmingham	11	Feb
38.9	Dawn Flockhart		16.05.67	1	Aberdeen	7	Apr
39.25	Rebecca White	U17	5.06.80	1	Birmingham	17	Aug
39.3	Maria Bolsover	U17	5.06.80	1	Stoke	20	Jul
	39.32			1h4	Sheffield	12	Jul

LINFORD CHRISTIE. Is 1996 the end of the road for Britain's greatest sprinter?

IAN MACKIE. The young pretender for Linford's crown.

BLACK, BAULCH, LADEJO & THOMAS. Just some of the 400 metres crowd.

MARK RICHARDSON. Another athlete with aspirations in the 400 metres.

JOHN MAYOCK. Continues his steady progress in the middle distances.

PAUL EVANS. Ran a very fast marathon in Chicago.

RICHARD NERURKAR. Fifth in the Olympic marathon.

COLIN JACKSON. Another frustrating year but still highly ranked in the world.

JON RIDGEON. Magnificent comeback from injury.

STEVE SMITH. Bronze medal at the Olympics.

STEVE BACKLEY. Silver medal at the Olympics.

NICK BUCKFIELD. Raised the British Record and helped improve the overall standards of British vaulting.

CARL MYERSCOUGH. A 16-year old with a big future?

JONATHAN EDWARDS. Just missed Gold at the Olympics but is still the best triple jumper in the world.

KELLY HOLMES. Continues her position at the top of the 800 and 1500 metres.

PAULA RADCLIFFE. Beat Zola Budd's 5000 metre record.

DENISE LEWIS & ANGELA THORPE. Thorpe set a new British Record over the hurdles and Lewis won Bronze at the Olympics' multi-events.

TESSA SANDERSON. Showed how good a javelin thrower she is by making the Olympic team 3 years after retirement.

JANINE WHITLOCK. A series of British Records up to the magic 4 metres.

ASHIA HANSEN. Two British Records and an unlucky 4th at the Olympics.

39.34	Ruth Watson	U17	29.11.79	1h2	Sheffield	12	Jul
(10)							
39.61	Helen Roscoe	U17	4.12.79	1	Birmingham	8	Sep
39.64 i	Sally Evans	U23	14.05.75	2	Birmingham	11	Feb
39.9				1	Cheltenham	4	Aug
39.66	Lindsay Impett	U17	4.01.80	2h2	Sheffield	12	Jul
39.71	Karen Gear	U17	30.09.79	3	Birmingham	17	Aug
39.72	Susan Williams	U20	2.06.77	4	London (CP)	12	Jul
39.86	Carey Easton	U17	16.11.79	1	Wishaw	13	Jul

Additional Under 17 (1 - 7 above)

40.11	Amanda Pritchard		18.03.80	1	Swansea	6	Jul
40.13	Lucy Philp		27.12.79	4	Birmingham	17	Aug
40.17	Helen Lee		27.08.80	3h2	Sheffield	12	Jul
(10)							
40.20	Carmel Triggs		18.04.80	1	Street	24	Jul
40.24	Syreeta Williams		24.10.80	2	Birmingham	8	Sep
40.3	Sarah Wilhelmy		2.02.80	1	Thurrock	11	May
40.32	Claire Crosland		10.01.80	4h2	Sheffield	12	Jul
40.36	Jennifer Meadows		17.04.81	2	Birmingham	7	Sep
40.4	Ayeesha Charles		4.09.79	1	Abingdon	11	May
40.99				3h3	Birmingham	17	Aug
40.4	Sarah Johnson		20.07.80	1	Welwyn	16	Jun
40.96				3h1	Sheffield	12	Jul
40.51	Rebecca Lawford		27.04.80	5h2	Sheffield	12	Jul
40.56	Karlene Palmer		23.10.80	3	Birmingham	8	Sep
40.77	Vicky Edwards		7.02.80	6h2	Sheffield	12	Jul
(20)							
40.78	Lois Cresswell		12.01.81	1	Stoke	22	Jun
40.78	Lisa Whigham		14.08.80	3	Wishaw	13	Jul
40.78	Kamila Braithwaite		26.01.81	3h3	Birmingham	17	Aug
40.79	Lindsay Fleet		1.06.81	3	London (CP)	30	Jun
40.86	Lisa Wrigglesworth		11.05.80	3h4	Sheffield	12	Jul
40.88	Amina Ceesay		19.11.79	3h1	Birmingham	17	Aug
40.88	Rhian Cains		29.10.80	2h2	Birmingham	17	Aug
40.90	Abigail Naugher		26.02.80	2h1	Sheffield	12	Jul
41.00	Donna Porazinski		28.01.81	2	Swansea	6	Jul
41.0	Dominique Coldwell		6.09.79	1	York	15	Jun
(30)							
41.2	Rebecca Martindale		31.12.80	1	Carlisle	7	Jul
41.28	Hayley Zablockyj		10.04.81	6s2	Sheffield	13	Jul
41.3	Sarah Nash		10.11.80	1	Leamington	14	Apr
41.3	Yewande Ige		21.03.80	1	Croydon	11	May
41.3	Sonia Rice		8.01.81	2	Solihull	29	Jun

intermediate indoor times

38.1 +	Melanie Neef		26.05.70	1	Birmingham	4	Feb
38.4 +	Sally Gunnell		29.07.66	2	Birmingham	4	Feb
39.4 +	Lesley Owusu	U20	21.12.78		Birmingham	27	Jan
39.6 +	Stephanie Llewellyn		31.12.68		Birmingham	27	Jan

400 METRES

51.29	Phylis Smith		29.09.65	3h1	Atlanta, USA	26	Jul
51.56				2	Gateshead	19	Aug
51.74				1	Birmingham	16	Jun
51.74				3	Gateshead	30	Jun
52.0				1	Manchester	17	Aug
52.05				6	Berlin, GER	30	Aug
52.09				5	London (CP)	12	Jul
52.16				6q4	Atlanta, USA	27	Jul

(Smith)	52.36			1h3	Birmingham	15	Jun
	52.53			3	Sheffield	25	Aug
	52.76			1	L'Alfas Del Pi, SPA	11	Apr
	52.87			1	Edinburgh	4	May
51.45	Sally Gunnell		29.07.66	2	Gateshead	30	Jun
	52.96			1	Bedford	18	May
	53.07 i			2	Birmingham	4	Feb
	53.28 i			1	Glasgow	24	Feb
	53.87 i			6r2	Moscow,RUS	14	Feb
51.58	Donna Fraser		7.11.72	7q1	Atlanta, USA	27	Jul
	52.05			5	Gateshead	30	Jun
	52.37			7	Madrid, SPA	1	Jun
	52.78			3h6	Atlanta, USA	26	Jul
	52.88			4	Birmingham	16	Jun
	53.27			4	Rhede, GER	24	May
	53.27			5	Lucerne, SWZ	25	Jun
	53.39			1h2	Birmingham	15	Jun
	53.46			2	Basel, SWZ	27	May
	53.55			4	Azusa, USA	13	Apr
52.48	Georgina Oladapo		15.05.67	2	Birmingham	16	Jun
	53.22			1h1	Birmingham	15	Jun
	53.61			4	Gateshead	19	Aug
52.50 i	Melanie Neef		26.05.70	1	Birmingham	4	Feb
	53.23			7	Birmingham	16	Jun
	53.51			2h1	Birmingham	15	Jun
	53.65			6rB	Lucerne, SWZ	25	Jun
	53.81 i			1s1	Birmingham	3	Feb
	53.90			1	Belfast	22	Jun
	53.9			1	Pitreavie	18	Jun
52.71	Linda Staines		26.12.63	1h4	Birmingham	15	Jun
	52.92			5	Birmingham	16	Jun
	53.07			1	Stockholm, SWE	18	Jun
	53.41			2	Tallinn, EST	9	Jun
	53.44			1	London (CP)	2	Jun
	53.44			3	Lisbon, POR	21	Jun
	53.47			1	Birmingham	20	Jul
	53.57			1	Bedford	27	May
	53.95			4rB	Gateshead	30	Jun
	54.0			1	Crawley	28	Jul
52.76	Allison Curbishley	U23	3.06.76	3	Birmingham	16	Jun
	53.08			2	Bedford	18	May
	53.12			7	London (CP)	12	Jul
	53.19			2h4	Birmingham	15	Jun
	53.40			2	L'Alfas Del Pi, SPA	11	Apr
	53.43			7	Gateshead	30	Jun
	53.52 i			3	Birmingham	4	Feb
52.83	Lorraine Hanson		22.04.65	2	Cork, IRE	22	Jun
	52.99			2rB	Gateshead	30	Jun
	53.3			1	Derby	18	Aug
	53.48			1	Birmingham	1	Jun
	53.7			1	London (He)	31	Aug
53.22	Michelle Pierre		30.09.73	6	Birmingham	16	Jun
	53.44			2h2	Birmingham	15	Jun
	53.9			1	Croydon	12	May
53.52	Stephanie Llewellyn		31.12.68	1	Celle Ligure, ITA	17	Jul
	53.64			2	Bedford	27	May
	53.8			1	London (He)	6	Jul
	53.8			2	Manchester	17	Aug
	54.0			1	London (He)	28	Jul

(10)

53.78	Sharon Tunaley		2.09.68	3h2	Birmingham	15	Jun
54.00				8	Birmingham	16	Jun
53.79	Tracy Joseph		29.11.69	3B	Gateshead	30	Jun
53.8	Kelly Holmes		19.04.70	1	Portsmouth	2	Jul
53.86	Sue Rawlinson		13.10.70	3h1	Birmingham	15	Jun
	72 performances to 54.0 by 14 athletes including 6 indoors						
54.40	Sandra Leigh		26.02.66	3h4	Birmingham	15	Jun
54.53	Lesley Owusu	U20	21.12.78	1	Loughborough	19	May
54.54	Lisa Vannet	U23	8.11.74	5	Hexham	14	Jul
54.6	Emma Symonds	U20	5.06.77	2r2	Nembro, ITA	3	Aug
54.86				1	Bedford	28	Jul
54.65	Louise Fraser		10.10.70	3	Bedford	18	May
54.70	Dawn Flockhart		16.05.67	4h2	Birmingham	15	Jun
	(20)						
54.83	Helen Frost	U23	12.03.74	4h4	Birmingham	15	Jun
54.97	Kim Goodwin		16.05.70	1h1	Sheffield	1	Jun
54.99	Vicky Day		19.06.72	4	London (CP)	2	Jun
55.03	Vicki Jamison	U20	19.05.77	1	Glasgow	29	Jun
55.06	Alanna Rowbotham		11.01.70	4h1	Birmingham	15	Jun
55.2	Michelle Thomas		16.10.71	2	Watford	5	May
55.39				2	Birmingham	20	Jul
55.32	Pat Divine		21.10.67	1	Edinburgh	20	Apr
55.45	Sally Evans	U23	14.05.75	1	Sheffield	6	May
55.48	Sarah Stevenson		31.12.73	1r1	San Donato Milanese, ITA	19	May
55.49	Claire Raven		15.06.72	3	Birmingham	7	Jul
	(30)						
55.5	Julie Forester		4.05.69	1r2	London (He)	6	Jul
56.03				2	Cudworth	4	Aug
55.63	Emma Lindsay		11.04.71	3	Edinburgh	11	May
55.7	Tania Taylor	U23	7.10.76	1	Solihull	29	Jun
55.76				3	Birmingham	20	Jul
55.75	Gillian Cashell		5.04.64	2	Cardiff	25	May
55.79	Louretta Thorne	U20	6.05.77	1h1	Bedford	27	Jul
55.80	Amanda Pritchard	U17	18.03.80	1	Carmarthen	30	Jun
55.89 i	Louise Whitehead	U23	26.03.75	3h3	Birmingham	3	Feb
55.94	Sue Briggs		26.03.67	3	Edinburgh	4	May
55.98 i	Elaine Sutcliffe		6.04.70	3s1	Birmingham	3	Feb
57.28				8	Cork, IRE	22	Jun
56.0	Christine Amede		7.08.63	1r2	Derby	18	Aug
57.14 i				6s2	Birmingham	3	Feb
57.45				4h1	Bedford	27	May
	(40)						
56.09	Denise Facey		8.02.69	1	Sheffield	12	May
56.1	Carmen Collins/Michaelska		6.11.73	1	Perivale	22	Jun
56.17	Kathryn Bright	U23	27.03.76	3	Cardiff	25	May
56.18	Margaret Still		9.05.65	2	London (He)	1	Sep
56.2	Ena Waldo		29.06.63	1	Leamington	12	May
57.21				2h1	Birmingham	1	Jun
56.23	Hayley Clements		17.09.68	1	London (CP)	12	May
56.3	Kathy Thurston	U23	2.01.76	1r5	Stretford	25	Jun
56.86 i				4s1	Birmingham	3	Feb
56.3	Cathy Dawson		9.03.66	1	Horsham	18	Aug
56.32	Zoe Arnold	U23	10.11.76	2	Dublin, IRE	16	Jun
56.35	Katie Jones	U20	4.01.77	1	Cudworth	30	Jun
	(50)						
56.37	Katharine Eustace	U23	16.04.75	2	Sheffield	6	May
56.4	Lee McConnell	U20	9.10.78	4	London (He)	31	Aug
56.46	Nicole Bowring	U23	27.01.74	5	London (CP)	2	Jun
56.46	Stacey Jacques	U20	24.06.77	2h2	Bedford	27	Jul
56.48	Simone Harrison	U20	2.09.77	2	London (CP)	18	Aug
56.49	Sarah Roberts	U20	25.06.78	1	Swansea	6	Jul

Time	Name	Cat	DOB	Pos	Venue	Date
56.5	Hayley Parry		17.02.73	2	Loughborough	27 Apr
56.5	Dawn Gandy		28.07.65	2	London (He)	25 May
56.5	Tracey Duncan	U20	16.05.79	1	Gateshead	16 Jun
56.5	Susan Hendry	U23	30.06.76	1	Antrim	25 Jun
	(60)					
56.5	Lisa Harvey		9.04.68	1	Yate	11 Aug
56.5	Alison Mahindru		15.07.68	4	Manchester	17 Aug
56.54	Jennifer Meadows	U17	17.04.81	2	Venice, ITA	28 Sep
56.55	Juliana Palka	U20	9.05.77	3h2	Bedford	27 Jul
56.6	Debbie France		16.10.65	2	Sheffield	20 Apr
56.97				3h1	Sheffield	1 Jun
56.6	Anna Turner	U23	13.08.74	1	Wrexham	4 May
57.30				2	Newport	1 Jun
56.6	Kate Williams	U20	10.11.77	1	Leamington	25 Aug
56.67	Natalie Tait		24.08.72	4	Birmingham	7 Jul
56.7	Vicky Sterne		12.10.68	2	Leamington	12 May
56.7	Karen Gear	U17	30.09.79	2	Bath	19 Jun
	(70)					
56.7	Jeina Mitchell	U23	21.01.75	1	Croydon	20 Jul
56.71 i	Jo Sloane	U23	2.12.76	1	Glasgow	17 Mar
56.71	Elizabeth Williams	U20	2.06.77	1h3	Bedford	27 Jul
56.76	Claire-Marie Dillon		1.03.73	4rB	Loughborough	19 May
56.8	Zoe Crawford	U23	1.03.75	1	Scunthorpe	11 May
56.8	Julie Moore		5.12.73	2	Blackpool	12 May
56.86				4	Cudworth	4 Aug
56.8	Rachel Newcombe		25.02.67	1r6	Stretford	21 May
56.81	Tracy Ashcroft	U23	4.07.76	3	Cudworth	4 Aug
56.87	Lindsay Impett	U17	4.01.80	3	Luton	6 May
56.90	Christa Salt		17.06.64		Basel, SWZ	24 Aug
	(80)					
56.9	Caroline Wilkins	U23	28.08.75		Rugby	14 Jul
56.9	Ruth Watson	U17	29.11.79	1rB	Ipswich	4 Aug
56.97	Maureen Williams		22.06.69	3h1	London (CP)	1 Jun
56.98	Paula Fryer		14.07.69	2	Sheffield	12 May
57.1	Dyanna Clarke	V35	27.02.58	2	Portsmouth	20 Jul
57.1	Lucy Philp	U17	27.12.79	3	Coatbridge	4 Aug
57.16	Carey Easton	U17	16.11.79	2h1	Glasgow	29 Jun
57.19	Zoe Peatfield	U20	8.12.77	3	Cudworth	30 Jun
57.2 +	Jacqui Parker		15.10.66	1	Seville, SPA	6 Jun
57.2	Jenny Holden		21.09.73	2	Croydon	20 Jul
	(90)					
57.2	Veronica Boden	V35	23.12.58	2r2	Manchester	17 Aug
57.2	Claire Phillips	U20	2.04.78	1	Sutton	22 Sep
57.35				1	Bedford	7 Sep
57.3	Rebecca Wise/Adams		16.03.72	2	Sutton	22 Jun
57.39 i	Sarah Damm		12.09.70	2h1	Birmingham	6 Jan
57.4	Lucy Carter	U20	7.03.78	1	Luton	12 May
57.4	Suzanne Everson		23.03.72	2	Croydon	22 Jun
57.4	Kelly Woods	U23	28.05.75	5	London (He)	6 Jul
57.4	Leigh Ferrier/Reade		15.08.72	2	Telford	14 Sep
57.47	Lynne Robinson		21.06.69	1	Birmingham	21 Apr
57.48	Elaine Viney		20.12.71	3h3	London (CP)	1 Jun
	(100)					
57.49	Clare Hill	U23	14.12.76	2	Antrim	6 Jul
57.50 i	Rosie Thorner		7.08.67	3h1	Birmingham	6 Jan
57.50	Claire Haslam		18.12.63	2r2	Edinburgh	4 May
57.5	Anita Pace		18.10.67	2	Scunthorpe	11 May
57.5	Natalie Smethurst	U20	31.03.77	2	Gateshead	6 Jun
57.5	Rosalind Baker	U20	10.04.78	1	Crawley	12 Jun
57.5	Lisa Whigham	U17	14.08.80	2	Coatbridge	23 Jun

Additional Under 17 (1 - 8 above)

58.0	Lisa Wrigglesworth		11.05.80	1	Tweedbank	30	Jun
58.7	Helen Lee		27.08.80	3	Cudworth	23	Jun
(10)							
58.8	Rebecca White		5.06.80	1	Blackburn	17	Jul
59.0	Francesca Green		10.02.80	1rB	Oxford	25	May

Foreign

55.8	*Elona Reinalda*	*U23*	*31.03.76*	*2*	*Croydon*	*12*	*May*
55.9	*Orla Ryan*		*7.09.69*	*2*	*Crawley*	*28*	*Jul*
	56.17			*1*	*London (He)*	*1*	*Sep*
56.9	*Ronit Feigenbaum*		*3.11.63*	*1*	*Portsmouth*	*20*	*Jul*

600 METRES

1:28.40	Diane Modahl		17.06.66	1	Cardiff	25	May
1:28.62 +	Kelly Holmes		19.04.70	1	Birmingham	15	Jun
1:31.1	Gowry Retchakan	V35	21.06.60	1	Highgate	7	Aug
1:31.3	Rachel Jordan		29.01.72	2	Highgate	7	Aug
1:31.6	Cathy Dawson		9.03.66	3	Highgate	7	Aug
1:31.8 +	Michelle Faherty		10.08.68	1m	Manchester	30	Jul
1:32.81	Jeina Mitchell	U23	21.01.75	2	Cardiff	25	May
1:32.83 i+	Vickie Lawrence		9.06.73	m	Birmingham	27	Jan
1:33.60 i	Claire Raven		15.06.72	1	Birmingham	29	Feb
1:33.7	Dorothea Lee	U20	28.07.77	4	Highgate	7	Aug

Under 13

1:41.3	Holly O'Connor		9.12.83	1	Sutton	21	Jul
1:41.5	Adele Bevan		26.03.84	1	Crawley	12	May
1:42.4	Jemma Simpson		10.02.84	1	Carn Brea	7	Apr
1:42.6	Krista Cartlidge		8.12.83	1	Horsham	7	Jul
1:43.7	Laura Puddle		27.01.84	1	Bournemouth	21	Jul
1:43.7	Olivia Hines		19.10.83	1	London (TB)	28	Jul
1:43.7	Sarah Jasper		1.05.84	2	London (TB)	28	Jul
1:44.21	Hannah Cutler		25.01.84	1	Birmingham	8	Sep
1:44.8	Katherine Waugh			1	Hexham	21	Jul
1:44.94	Amy Spencer		19.09.85	1	Wrexham	3	Aug
(10)							
1:45.0	Jodie Palmer		23.10.83	1	London (PH)	3	Jul
1:45.1	Kim Searle		27.12.83	1	Jarrow	2	Jun
1:45.2	Meredith Hack		22.07.85	2	Bournemouth	21	Jul

800 METRES

1:57.84	Kelly Holmes		19.04.70	1	Birmingham	15	Jun
	1:58.20			2	Madrid, SPA	1	Jun
	1:58.49			3s1	Atlanta, USA	27	Jul
	1:58.53			1	Helsinki, FIN	25	Jun
	1:58.80			1h5	Atlanta, USA	26	Jul
	1:58.81			4	Atlanta, USA	29	Jul
	1:58.87			1	Ljubljana, SLO	26	May
	1:59.82			1	Gateshead	30	Jun
1:59.87	Diane Modahl		17.06.66	2	Birmingham	15	Jun
	2:00.69			8	Lausanne, SWZ	3	Jul
	2:00.80			1	Zagreb, CRO	21	Jun
	2:00.95			6	St. Denis, FRA	3	Jun
	2:00.97			4	Nice, FRA	10	Jul
	2:02.03			4	Bratislava, SVK	29	May
	2:03.67			3	Gateshead	30	Jun
	2:04.10			1	Blackburn	15	May
	2:04.23			9	Hengelo, HOL	27	May

2:02.12	Sonya Bowyer		18.09.72	1	Cardiff	25 May
	2:02.5			1	Loughborough	5 Jun
	2:02.85			4	Birmingham	15 Jun
	2:03.79			4	Lucerne, SWZ	26 Jun
	2:04.02			7	Sheffield	25 Aug
	2:04.1 mx			1	Stretford	6 Aug
	2:04.26			2	Loughborough	19 May
2:02.76	Natalie Tait		24.08.72	3	Birmingham	15 Jun
2:02.83	Lynn Gibson		6.07.69	4	London (CP)	12 Jul
	2:03.66			6	Sheffield	25 Aug
	2:04.3 mx			1	Watford	5 Jun
	2:04.5			1	Swindon	14 Aug
2:03.52	Vickie Lawrence		9.06.73	5	Birmingham	15 Jun
	2:04.8 mx			2	Stretford	20 Aug
	2:04.9 mx			1	Stretford	4 Jun
2:03.77	Hayley Parry		17.02.73	1	Loughborough	19 May
	2:03.86			2	Aarhus, DEN	20 Jun
	2:03.95			1	Sheffield	5 May
	2:04.15			3	Cardiff	25 May
	2:04.17			6	Birmingham	15 Jun
	2:04.51			1	Belfast	22 Jun
2:04.4 mx	Michelle Faherty		10.08.68	1	Stretford	20 Aug
	2:05.97			8	Sheffield	25 Aug
2:04.63	Vicky Sterne		12.10.68	2	Ljubljana, SLO	26 May
2:04.87	Jeina Mitchell	U23	21.01.75	1	London (CP)	2 Jun
(10)						
2:04.9 mx	Sue Parker		24.03.70	2	Stretford	4 Jun
	2:06.5			1r1	Manchester	30 Jul
	42 performances to 2:05.0 by 11 athletes					
2:05.5	Ann Griffiths		20.08.65	1	Stretford	30 Apr
	2:05.51 i+			m	Birmingham	10 Feb
2:05.91	Dianne Henaghan		6.08.65	1	Cudworth	4 Aug
2:06.02	Claire Raven		15.06.72	2h2	Birmingham	14 Jun
2:06.14 i	Phylis Smith		29.09.65	1	Birmingham	24 Feb
2:06.27 i	Angela Davies		21.10.70	3	Birmingham	27 Jan
	2:06.92			3	Oordegem, BEL	11 Aug
2:06.59	Ellen O'Hare	U20	4.02.78	2	Nembro, ITA	3 Aug
2:06.97	Christa Salt		17.06.64	4	Geneva, SWZ	15 Jun
2:07.1 mx	Sharon King		27.01.72	3	Stretford	20 Aug
	2:09.07			1h1	Sheffield	2 Jun
2:07.3	Shirley Griffiths		23.06.72	1	Jarrow	8 Jul
(20)						
2:07.31	Jacqui Parker		15.10.66	3h4	Birmingham	14 Jun
2:07.32	Amanda Pritchard	U17	18.03.80	2	Belfast	22 Jun
2:07.4 mx	Joanna Latimer		30.01.71	3	Stretford	4 Jun
	2:08.15			5	Dublin, IRE	9 Jun
2:07.50	Rachel Jordan		29.01.72	3h3	Birmingham	14 Jun
2:07.5	Dawn Gandy		28.07.65	2	Loughborough	18 May
2:07.5	Michelle Wilkinson		1.01.73	4r1	Manchester	30 Jul
2:07.5	Paula Fryer		14.07.69	1	Sheffield	4 Aug
2:07.6	Debbie Gunning		31.08.65	1	Harrow	7 Jul
2:07.61 i	Abigail Hunte		12.05.71	1	Boston, USA	27 Jan
	2:07.62			2h1	Birmingham	14 Jun
2:07.63	Lynne Robinson		21.06.69	1	Birmingham	21 Apr
(30)						
2:07.65	Wendy Lunn/Marshall		2.12.68	3h1	Birmingham	14 Jun
2:07.7	Tracy Ashcroft	U23	4.07.76	5r1	Manchester	30 Jul
2:08.2	Lisa Thompson		12.07.62	1	Horsham	18 Aug
2:08.21	Mary McClung		19.12.71	4h3	Birmingham	14 Jun
2:08.3 mx	Gowry Retchakan	V35	21.06.60	1r2	Harrow	1 Sep
	2:11.3			1r2	Woking	27 Apr

2:08.32	Teena Colebrook	V35	18.12.56	3h2	Birmingham	14	Jun
2:08.37	Lynne MacDougall		18.02.65	3	Belfast	22	Jun
2:08.92	Catherine Allsopp/Green		30.11.73	5h3	Birmingham	14	Jun
2:09.15	Gillian Cashell		5.04.64	1	Luton	6	May
2:09.17	Rachael Ogden	U20	23.07.79	3	Bedford	28	Jul
	(40)						
2:09.2	Julie Mitchell	U23	3.10.74	2	Bath	19	Jun
2:09.2	Debbie France		16.10.65	1	Cudworth	23	Jun
2:09.2	Alice Beecroft		25.05.73	2	Stretford	3	Sep
2:09.27	Heidi Hosking/Smith	U23	20.05.74	2h1	Sheffield	2	Jun
2:09.3	Philippa McCrea	U20	1.03.78	2	Jarrow	17	Jul
2:09.4	Karen McPherson		6.11.72	3	Stretford	3	Sep
2:09.48	Rachel Newcombe		25.02.67	5h2	Birmingham	14	Jun
2:09.49	Emma Davies	U20	9.10.78	5h5	Birmingham	14	Jun
2:09.5 mx	Kerry Smithson	U23	13.09.76	4	Stretford	4	Jun
	2:09.8			4	Stretford	30	Apr
2:09.5 mx	Helen Pattinson	U23	2.01.74	4	Stretford	16	Jul
	2:10.3			6	Stretford	30	Apr
	(50)						
2:09.59	Jillian Jones		23.12.69	7	Birmingham	20	Jul
2:09.6	Ann Terek		22.09.64		Dublin (M), IRE	21	Jul
2:09.6 mx	Sarah Bouchard	U23	23.10.74	3	Salford	10	Sep
	2:10.3			4	Stretford	3	Sep
2:09.63	Sarah Bentley		21.05.67	1	Sheffield	11	May
2:09.78	Lynn Taylor		5.08.67	6h2	Birmingham	14	Jun
2:09.82	Nicola Andrews		11.06.70	6h3	Birmingham	14	Jun
2:09.82	Sarah Bull	U23	4.06.75	5	Hexham	14	Jul
2:09.82	Dorothea Lee	U20	28.07.77	5	Bedford	28	Jul
2:09.9 mx?	Jenny Harnett	U23	11.03.76		Watford	26	Jun
	2:12.5			3	Southampton	27	Apr
2:10.1	Amanda Thorpe/Parkinson		21.07.71	3	Loughborough	18	May
	(60)						
2:10.42	Kathryn Waugh		20.02.73	5h2	Sheffield	2	Jun
2:10.47	Wendy Steele		7.01.66	1	Edinburgh	12	May
2:10.57	Rebecca Wise/Adams		16.03.72	5	London (CP)	2	Jun
2:10.6	Zoe Peatfield	U20	8.12.77	5	Stretford	3	Sep
2:10.7	Andrea Whitcombe		8.06.71	2	London (He)	25	May
2:10.8	Sarah Salmon	U23	9.09.74	4	Stretford	25	Jun
2:10.8	Christina Bourne		24.09.69	3	Southampton	7	Jul
2:10.9	Emma Ward	U15	2.01.82	1	Solihull	30	Jun
2:10.9 mx	Vicki Andrews		31.08.69	5	Stretford	6	Aug
	2:11.2			6	Stretford	3	Sep
2:11.04	Helen Daniel		24.10.63	1	London (CP)	11	May
	(70)						
2:11.1	Wendy Farrow		25.12.71	2	Derby	23	Jun
2:11.1	Susan Hendry	U23	30.06.76	3	Manchester	17	Aug
2:11.15 i	Rhonda MacPhee	U23	30.04.76	3	Birmingham	24	Feb
	2:11.6			5	Southampton	7	Jul
2:11.3	Jane Groves	U20	17.05.77	2	Stretford	21	May
2:11.3	Joanne Colleran		1.09.72	3	Stretford	21	May
2:11.3	Joanne Mersh	U23	19.10.74	4	London (He)	6	Jul
2:11.35	Julie McDevitt		15.03.73	2	Glasgow	12	May
2:11.4	Penny Thackray	U23	18.08.74	1	Bolton	14	Jul
2:11.4	Kelly Brownhill	U17	27.03.80	1rB	Manchester	30	Jul
2:11.5	Hayley Parkinson	U23	5.12.75	2r2	Manchester	17	Aug
	(80)						
2:11.60	Janet Holt	V35	10.10.56	3r2	Edinburgh	4	May
2:11.6	Nikki Daniels	U15	25.08.82	2	Solihull	30	Jun
2:11.65	Cathy Dawson		9.03.66	2h1	Bedford	26	May
2:11.8	Sarah Simmons	U23	12.01.75	3	Loughborough	27	Apr
2:11.87	Michelle Harries		4.01.72	4h1	London (CP)	1	Jun

263

2:11.9	Kathryn Bright	U23	27.03.76	1	Cardiff	7	Aug
2:11.99	Angela Coates/Bretherwick		2.04.67	3	Sheffield	11	May
2:12.0	Claire Entwistle	U23	9.12.76	7	Stretford	3	Sep
2:12.3	Pauline Quinn		2.08.70	1	Belfast	18	May
2:12.3	Elinor Doubell		27.09.71	7	London (He)	6	Jul
	(90)						
2:12.4	Sally Entwistle		27.09.73	3	Blackpool	12	May
2:12.4	Simone Hardy	U17	9.11.79	2	Stoke	20	Jul
2:12.4	Ceri Thomas		16.10.70	2	Cardiff	7	Aug
2:12.5	Laura McCabe	U17	24.01.80	1	Crewe	11	May
2:12.5	Maria Carville		8.12.73	2	Enfield	11	May
2:12.62	Susan Elam		22.07.63	3	London (CP)	11	May
2:12.62	Kirsty Baird		29.08.71	4	Glasgow	29	Jun
2:12.7	Claire Martin	U23	12.07.76		Cambridge	26	May
2:12.80	Karlene Tromans	U17	28.02.81	2	Street	25	Jul
2:12.88 i	Caroline Slimin		27.08.65	4	Birmingham	28	Jan
	2:12.97			3	London (He)	31	Aug
	(100)						
2:12.9	Jade Himsworth	U20	4.08.79	1	Grantham	12	May
2:12.95 i	Clare Hill	U23	14.12.76	3h2	Birmingham	3	Feb

Additional Under 17 (1 - 5 above)

2:13.2	Francesca Green		10.02.80	1	Hoo	8	Jun
2:13.2	Emily Hathaway		22.12.79	2	Solihull	29	Jun
2:13.21	Danielle McCarrick		30.11.79	4	Street	25	Jul
2:13.4	Sarah Mead		16.10.79	6	Southampton	7	Jul
2:13.4 mx	Alex Carter		1.04.80	5r7	Stretford	16	Jul
	(10)						
2:13.7	Wendy Davis		7.11.79	1	Dublin, IRE	22	Jun
2:13.8	Amber Gascoigne		5.09.79	2	Street	6	May
2:14.1	Camilla Waite		24.05.80	1	Swindon	8	Jun
2:14.1	Georgie Salmon		1.11.79	3	Cardiff	7	Aug
2:14.12	Carean Vernon		2.06.80	3	Sheffield	13	Jul
2:14.2	Karen Johns		18.08.80	4	Jarrow	17	Jul
2:14.3	Rebecca Evans		15.03.80	1	Cardiff	25	May
2:14.43	Sarah Littlewood		2.12.79	2h3	Sheffield	12	Jul
2:14.5	Tanya Brazier		14.11.80	1	Watford	8	Jun
2:14.7	Michelle Whalley		1.10.80	1	Liverpool	21	Jul
	(20)						
2:15.18	Joanna Ross		18.02.81	3h2	Birmingham	18	Aug
2:15.2 mx	Jessica Woolley		26.01.80	10	Southampton	7	Jul
	2:15.4			7	Loughborough	18	May
2:15.6	Kimberly Montador		23.06.81	5	Stoke	20	Jul
2:15.7	Hayley Griffin		20.07.80	3	Milton Keynes	22	Jun
2:16.0	Emma Alberts		22.11.79	2	Wakefield	28	Apr
2:16.3	Sharon Whitby		29.09.80	1	Bracknell	7	Sep
2:16.4	Jennifer Meadows		17.04.81	1	London (WF)	21	Apr
2:16.4	Tommy Kemp		5.03.80	1	Yeovil	28	Jul
2:16.6	Helen Robinson		25.02.81	2	Crewe	11	May
2:16.6	Elaine Leake		27.10.79	1	Scunthorpe	11	May
	(30)						
2:16.75	Charlotte Fearn		26.11.80	4	London (CP)	30	Jun
2:16.8	Caroline Walsh		29.04.80	1	Enfield	11	May

overage

2:15.68 i	Sarah Beattie	U20	30.11.79	3	Glasgow	15	Dec

Foreign

2:07.50	*Una English*		*14.08.70*	*1*	*Zurich, SWZ*	*2*	*Jun*

Additional Under 15 (1 - 2 above)

2:14.1	Carley Wilson		6.12.81	1	Gateshead	8	Jun
2:14.46	Iona McIntyre		14.03.83	1	Glasgow	15	Dec
2:15.49	Suzanne Hasler		7.04.82	2	Sheffield	13	Jul
2:15.81	Lisa Samuels		24.09.81	1	London (CP)	30	Jun
2:16.1	Jenny Mockler		28.08.82	1	Liverpool	25	Aug
2:16.28	Claire Taylor		24.10.82	3	Sheffield	13	Jul
2:16.3	Nicola Underwood		13.05.82	2	Middlesbrough	15	Jun
2:16.92	Amanda Child		28.11.81	2	London (CP)	30	Jun
(10)							
2:17.17	Catherine Riley		4.06.82	1h1	Sheffield	12	Jul
2:17.6	Emma Rutland		9.10.81	1	Blackburn	17	Jul
2:17.71	Natalie Holdsworth		24.12.81	3h3	Sheffield	12	Jul
2:17.9	Louise Aaron		19.04.82	1	Hull	7	Jul
2:18.3	Hannah Wood		17.11.81	1	Liverpool	21	Jul
2:18.85	Sophie Koehne		17.09.81	3	London (CP)	30	Jun
2:19.1	Nichola Coates		24.03.82	2	Jarrow	11	May
2:19.1	Julia Bleasdale		9.09.81	1	London (He)	7	Jun
2:19.1	Elizabeth Wheeler		31.10.81	2	Stoke	21	Jul
2:19.3	Claire Couper		29.04.82	2	Dundee	28	Apr
(20)							
2:19.4	Rachael Gibson		20.01.82	1	Grangemouth	24	Aug
2:19.5	Danielle Glover		26.07.82	1	Rugby	15	Jun
2:19.6	Isla Ross		26.12.81	1	Ayr	15	Jun

Under 13

2:20.6	Sarah Jasper		1.05.84	1	Kings Lynn	15	Jun
2:22.9	Jemma Simpson		10.02.84	1	Exeter	15	Jun
2:23.6	Adele Bevan		26.03.84	1	Crawley	28	May
2:25.04	Holly O'Connor		9.12.83	1	Wrexham	4	Aug
2:25.2	Nisha Desai		5.08.84	2	Middlesbrough	7	Jul
2:25.5	Jodie Palmer		23.10.83	2	Luton	7	Jul
2:26.4	Krista Cartlidge		8.12.83	M	Brighton	19	Jun
2:27.0	Katie Clark		30.09.83	1	Tweedbank	30	Jun
2:27.0	Laura Puddle		27.01.84	2	Birmingham	1	Jul
2:27.2	Lucy Robinson				London (He)	8	Jun
(10)							
2:27.6	Kim Searle		27.12.83	1	Grimsby	15	Jun
2:27.9	Sarah Bell		20.09.83	2	Watford	31	Jul

1000 METRES

2:39.80	Sonya Bowyer		18.09.72	5	London (CP)	11	Aug
2:40.07 i	Ann Griffiths		20.08.65	5	Birmingham	10	Feb
2:40.98	Jeina Mitchell	U23	21.01.75	8	London (CP)	11	Aug
2:47.53 i	Hayley Parry		17.02.73	1	Birmingham	29	Feb
2:47.86	Christa Salt		17.06.64		St Mard, BEL	19	Oct
2:48.74 i+	Angela Davies		21.10.70	1	Birmingham	4	Feb
2:48.8 i+	Shirley Griffiths		23.06.72	2	Birmingham	4	Feb

1500 METRES

4:01.13	Kelly Holmes		19.04.70	2	Oslo, NOR	5	Jul
	4:04.56			1	Rome, ITA	5	Jun
	4:05.88			1s2	Atlanta, USA	1	Aug
	4:07.36			2h3	Atlanta, USA	31	Jul
	4:07.46			11	Atlanta, USA	3	Aug
	4:08.14			1	Birmingham	16	Jun
	4:12.89			1	Port Elizabeth, RSA	8	Mar
4:08.42 +	Paula Radcliffe		17.12.73	7m	Zurich, SWZ	14	Aug
4:10.7 mx	Sonya Bowyer		18.09.72	1	Stretford	16	Jul
	4:17.4			3r1	Manchester	30	Jul

```
4:11.00    Alison Wyeth              26.05.64  12    Paris, FRA         28  Jun
           4:16.63                             5     Gateshead          30  Jun
4:11.57    Sue Parker               24.03.70   1     Stockholm, SWE     18  Jun
           4:11.96                             2     Funchal, POR       25  May
           4:12.75                             3     Cork, IRE          22  Jun
           4:13.02                             2     Birmingham         16  Jun
           4:16.21                             4     Gateshead          30  Jun
4:12.32    Lynn Gibson               6.07.69   2     Cork, IRE          22  Jun
           4:15.23                             3     Gateshead          19  Aug
           4:15.8                              1     Manchester         30  Jul
           4:16.31                             6     Birmingham         16  Jun
           4:16.4                              2     Manchester         15  May
4:13.40 i  Debbie Gunning           31.08.65   2     Birmingham         27  Jan
           4:17.02 i                           1     Glasgow             4  Feb
           4:17.4                              4r1   Manchester         30  Jul
4:13.52    Angela Davies            21.10.70   4     Cork, IRE          22  Jun
           4:14.66                             7     Madrid, SPA         2  Jun
           4:14.67                             4     Birmingham         16  Jun
           4:16.24 i                           1     Birmingham          4  Feb
           4:17.1                              2     Manchester         30  Jul
4:14.19    Michelle Faherty         10.08.68   3     Birmingham         16  Jun
           4:15.66                             5     Cork, IRE          22  Jun
4:15.68    Shirley Griffiths        23.06.72   5     Birmingham         16  Jun
           4:16.06                             6     Cork, IRE          22  Jun
       (10)
4:16.25 i  Ann Griffiths            20.08.65   3     Birmingham         27  Jan
           4:19.88                             1     Edinburgh           4  May
4:16.84    Helen Pattinson     U23   2.01.74   7     Birmingham         16  Jun
4:16.9     Hayley Parry             17.02.73  3r1    Manchester         15  May
           4:17.9                              5     Manchester         30  Jul
4:17.10    Lynne MacDougall         18.02.65   8     Birmingham         16  Jun
4:17.3 mx  Sonia McGeorge            2.11.64   1     Horsham             7  Jul
           4:19.40                             3     Loughborough       19  May
           40 performances to 4:18.0 by 15 athletes including 4 indoors
4:18.94    Amanda Thorpe/Parkinson  21.07.71  4h1    Birmingham         15  Jun
4:19.77    Vickie Lawrence           9.06.73   3     Barcelona, SPA     23  Jun
4:19.8     Jeina Mitchell      U23  21.01.75  6r1    Manchester         30  Jul
4:19.83    Sharon King              27.01.72  11     Birmingham         16  Jun
4:20.49    Liz Francis-Thomas       22.12.63   2     Sheffield          25  Aug
       (20)
4:20.6     Ann Terek                22.09.64  8r1    Manchester         30  Jul
4:21.14    Jo Davis/Pavey           20.09.73  4h2    Birmingham         15  Jun
4:21.3     Lynne Robinson           21.06.69   1     Watford             5  May
4:21.3     Caroline Pimblett   U23  28.01.75   1     Stretford          16  Jul
4:21.4     Wendy Farrow             25.12.71 10r1    Manchester         30  Jul
4:22.1     Jillian Jones            23.12.69   1     Swindon            14  Aug
4:22.3     Sarah Bentley            21.05.67   2     Watford             5  May
4:23.0     Penny Thackray      U23  18.08.74 11r1    Manchester         30  Jul
4:23.30    Christa Salt             17.06.64         Basel, SWZ          8  Jun
4:23.59    Sarah Bull          U23   4.06.75   6     Sheffield          25  Aug
       (30)
4:23.94    Jenny Harnett       U23  11.03.76  7h2    Birmingham         15  Jun
4:24.00    Sarah Salmon        U23   9.09.74  8h1    Birmingham         15  Jun
4:24.37 i  Caroline Slimin          27.08.65   5     Birmingham          4  Feb
           4:30.3                              1     Crawley            28  Jul
4:24.40    Rhonda MacPhee      U23  30.04.76  8h2    Birmingham         15  Jun
4:24.5     Teena Colebrook     V35  18.12.56         Irvine, USA        23  Mar
4:24.60    Janet Holt          V35  10.10.56   1     Malmo, SWE         28  Jul
4:25.0     Vicky Sterne             12.10.68   1     Watford            10  Jul
4:25.09    Lucy Field                1.05.71  9h2    Birmingham         15  Jun
4:25.29 i  Karen Hargrave           23.09.65   1     Bordeaux, FRA      13  Jan
4:25.3     Michelle Mann       U20   6.02.77   3     Stretford          16  Jul
```

4:25.47	Rhona Makepeace		7.08.62	2	Kunzelsau, GER	7	Sep
4:25.7	Julie Stacey		15.11.72	1	London (He)	28	Jul
4:25.80	Juliette Oldfield	U20	14.04.77	9h1	Birmingham	15	Jun
4:26.2	Lucy Elliott		9.03.66	2	Manchester	17	Aug
4:26.6	Elinor Doubell		27.09.71	3	Manchester	17	Aug
4:26.90	Liz Talbot	U23	5.12.74	10h1	Birmingham	15	Jun
4:27.08	Claire Martin	U23	12.07.76	3	Sheffield	6	May
4:27.1	Karen McPherson		6.11.72	1	Stretford	4	Jun
4:27.1	Andrea Whitcombe		8.06.71	2	London (He)	28	Jul
4:27.13	Pauline Quinn		2.08.70	7	Dublin, IRE	16	Jun
	(50)						
4:28.1	Ellen O'Hare	U20	4.02.78	3	Bath	19	Jun
4:28.1	Maria Carville		8.12.73	2	Bedford	7	Aug
4:28.42	Joanne Colleran		1.09.72	11h1	Birmingham	15	Jun
4:28.80	Julie Swann		15.07.62	4	Birmingham	2	Jun
4:28.90	Catherine Allsopp/Green		30.11.73	4	Sheffield	6	May
4:29.4	Julie Mitchell	U23	3.10.74	1	Crawley	17	Jul
4:29.56	Amanda Wright		14.07.68	5	Birmingham	2	Jun
4:29.57 i	Dorothea Lee	U20	28.07.77	3	Birmingham	17	Feb
4:29.69	Valerie Bothams	U23	19.03.75	4	Edinburgh	4	May
4:29.9	Dianne Henaghan		6.08.65	2	Jarrow	12	May
	(60)						
4:30.05	Michelle Lavercombe/Wannell		12.07.67	11h2	Birmingham	15	Jun
4:30.09	Ruth Carney/Mayo		12.10.68	9	Dublin, IRE	16	Jun
4:30.1	Adele Rankin		27.05.72	1	Stretford	11	May
4:30.2	Hayley Yelling	U23	3.01.74	1	Luton	23	Jun
4:30.3	Esther Evans		22.12.73	9	Stretford	16	Jul
4:30.5	Camilla Waite	U17	24.05.80	4	Bath	19	Jun
4:30.9	Debbie Sullivan		24.01.72	1	Colchester	26	Aug
4:31.16	Samantha Kennedy		13.04.71	14h1	Birmingham	15	Jun
4:31.2	Kathryn Waugh		20.02.73	1	Jarrow	8	Jul
4:31.3	Dawn James		4.01.67	2	Portsmouth	21	Jul
	(70)						
4:31.5	Amanda Tremble	U23	2.11.76	1	Cudworth	11	Aug
4:31.6	Sheila Fairweather	U20	24.11.77	2	Coatbridge	23	Jun
4:31.70	Jenny Mockler	U15	28.08.82	1	Cudworth	4	Aug
4:32.1	Karen Montador	U20	14.05.79	1	Pitreavie	26	Jun
4:32.1	Julie Mackay	U23	5.06.76	2	Watford	10	Jul
4:32.5	Anne Connolly	U20	18.02.78	11	Stretford	16	Jul
4:32.55 i	Sue Bevan	V35	15.12.59	4h2	Birmingham	4	Feb
4:32.7	Astrid Wingler		21.05.68	3	Stoke	28	Jul
4:32.9	Natalie Tait		24.08.72	3	Watford	5	May
4:33.0	Cathy Dawson		9.03.66	3	Watford	10	Jul
	(80)						
4:33.40	Jilly Ingman	U20	17.08.78	2	Sheffield	12	May
4:33.4	Hayley Parkinson	U23	5.12.75	4	London (He)	31	Aug
4:33.6	Louise Watson		13.12.71	3	Loughborough	27	Apr
4:33.80	Jane Groves	U20	17.05.77	7	Sheffield	6	May
4:33.8 mx	Vicki Andrews		31.08.69		Stretford	20	Aug

Foreign

4:11.33	*Una English*		*14.08.70*	*9*	*Nuremberg, GER*	*7*	*Jun*
4:15.3	*Nnenna Lynch*		*3.07.71*	*1r1*	*Manchester*	*15*	*May*
4:20.8	*Rebecca Spies*			*5r1*	*Manchester*	*15*	*May*
4:24.78	*Jill Bruce*		*25.07.73*	*3*	*Dublin, IRE*	*9*	*Jun*

Additional Under 17 (1 above)

4:34.49	Jodie Swallow		23.06.81	2	London (CP)	30	Jun
4:35.3	Georgie Salmon		1.11.79	5	Swindon	14	Aug
4:35.7	Tommy Kemp		5.03.80	6	Bath	19	Jun
4:36.0	Amanda Pritchard		18.03.80	7	Bath	19	Jun

4:37.3	Amber Gascoigne	5.09.79	2	Yeovil	8	Jun
4:37.31	Kate Grimshaw	26.10.79	2	Birmingham	17	Aug
4:37.8	Tanya Brazier	14.11.80	1	Crawley	27	Apr
4:40.14	Alex Carter	1.04.80	4	Sheffield	13	Jul
4:40.3	Sarah Beattie	30.11.79	1	Ayr	15	Jun
(10)						
4:40.5	Joanna Ross	18.02.81	4	Coatbridge	23	Jun
4:40.69	Jeanette Shorthall	9.09.80	3	Street	24	Jul
4:40.74 i	Emma Alberts	22.11.79	1	Birmingham	18	Feb
4:43.6			2	Jarrow	12	May
4:40.76	Hannah Norman	1.06.81	1	Wishaw	13	Jul
4:41.1	Caroline Walsh	29.04.80	1	Enfield	12	May
4:41.4	Jessica Woolley	26.01.80	7r2	Manchester	30	Jul
4:41.8	Helen Pearson	8.02.81	7	Stretford	25	Jun
4:41.82	Kelly Marsters	8.09.79	5	Sheffield	13	Jul
4:42.0	Donna Brown	1.05.81	1	Liverpool	21	Jul
4:42.5	Noeleen Murrin	22.12.79	3	Solihull	30	Jun
(20)						
4:43.0	Simone Hardy	9.11.79	1	Corby	12	May
4:43.6	Sarah Mead	16.10.79	10	Bath	19	Jun
4:43.7	Jackie Hogan	19.03.80	1	York	15	Jun
4:44.0	Carean Vernon	2.06.80	1	Walton	16	Jun
4:44.3	Lyndsay Robson	4.07.81	1	Middlesbrough	5	Jun
4:44.6	Jenni Hodgins	7.06.80	3	Exeter	25	Aug
4:44.7	Nicole Arkaah	2.03.80	11r2	Manchester	30	Jul

Additional Under 15 (1 above)

4:35.48	Emma Ward	2.01.82	1	Stoke	22	Jun
4:37.5	Carley Wilson	6.12.81	1	Jarrow	17	Jul
4:38.6	Nichola Coates	24.03.82	1	Gateshead	8	Jun
4:43.31	Sarah Jarvis	10.03.82	3	Birmingham	18	Aug
4:44.23	Louise Aaron	19.04.82	4	Sheffield	13	Jul
4:44.3	Emma Rutland	9.10.81	1	Blackpool	8	Jun
4:45.0	Lisa Williams	29.12.81	1	Watford	10	Jul
4:45.3	Nikki Daniels	25.08.82	1	Cannock	26	May
4:45.48	Iona McIntyre	14.03.83	1	Edinburgh	25	Aug
(10)						
4:45.74	Hattie Dean	2.02.82	7	Sheffield	13	Jul
4:46.5	Collette Fagan	16.06.82	2	Liverpool	2	Jun
4:47.60	Louise Whittaker	29.11.82	4h1	Sheffield	12	Jul
4:47.63	Julie Keene	2.04.82	5h1	Sheffield	12	Jul
4:47.63	Elizabeth Wheeler	31.10.81	4h2	Sheffield	12	Jul
4:48.37	Sophie Koehne	17.09.81	6h1	Sheffield	12	Jul
4:48.5	Gemma Viney	7.01.83	2	Crawley	12	Jun
4:48.75	Rachael Jablonski	6.12.81	7h1	Sheffield	12	Jul
4:49.47	Sarah Raven	22.11.82	2	London (CP)	30	Jun
4:49.62	Kirsty Doyle	20.08.82	4h1	Birmingham	18	Aug

Under 13

4:58.5	Zoe Jelbert	21.01.84	2	Exeter	15	Jun
5:02.0	Hannah Pardon	4.10.84	1	Ealing	22	'un
5:02.0	Lucy Thomas	2.11.84	1	Neath	4	Sep
5:02.6	Nisha Desai	5.08.84	1	Gateshead	3	Jul
5:03.6	Jodie Palmer	23.10.83	4	Kings Lynn	15	Jun
5:03.7	Jane Burns	7.02.84	5	Basildon	8	Jun
5:05.2	Holly O'Connor	9.12.83	1	Liverpool	12	May
5:05.4	Laura Gorin	9.11.83	1	Havering	31	Aug
5:05.5	Adele Bevan	26.03.84	1	Crawley	12	Jun
5:06.2	Vicki Turner	30.09.83	1	Bracknell	20	Jul
5:06.4	Sadie Crannis	8.10.83	1	London (TB)	28	Jul
5:07.7	Lucy Robinson			Thurrock	20	Jul
5:08.1	Olivia Hines	19.10.83	2	Sutton	31	Aug

1 MILE

Time	Name	Cat	DOB	Pos	Venue	Date
4:24.94	Paula Radcliffe		17.12.73	7	Zurich, SWZ	14 Aug
4:38.93	Lynn Gibson		6.07.69	1	London (He)	31 Aug
4:39.44	Michelle Faherty		10.08.68	2	London (He)	31 Aug
4:39.90	Sonya Bowyer		18.09.72	3	London (He)	31 Aug
4:40.93	Liz Francis-Thomas		22.12.63	5	London (He)	31 Aug
4:41.20	Jo Davis/Pavey		20.09.73	6	London (He)	31 Aug
4:44.60	Shirley Griffiths		23.06.72	1	Hong Kong, HK	3 Mar
4:44.79	Sarah Salmon	U23	9.09.74	8	London (He)	31 Aug
4:46.71	Sarah Bull	U23	4.06.75	9	London (He)	31 Aug
4:48.7	Dianne Henaghan		6.08.65	1	Hexham	1 Aug

2000 METRES

Time	Name	Cat	DOB	Pos	Venue	Date
5:49.0 +	Paula Radcliffe		17.12.73	m	Monaco, MON	10 Aug
6:05.43	Debbie Gunning		31.08.65	4	Lisbon, POR	21 Jun

3000 METRES

Time	Name	Cat	DOB	Pos	Venue	Date
8:37.07	Paula Radcliffe		17.12.73	3	Monaco, MON	10 Aug
8:51.3 +				5m	Cologne, GER	16 Aug
8:53.0 +				5m	London (CP)	12 Jul
8:56.25				1	Gateshead	19 Aug
8:57.5 +				4m	Brussels, BEL	23 Aug
9:04.4	Sarah Bentley		21.05.67	1	Cork, IRE	22 Jun
9:04.69 i	Sonia McGeorge		2.11.64	1	Birmingham	18 Feb
9:09.53				5	Madrid, SPA	2 Jun
9:05.45 i	Alison Wyeth		26.05.64	2	Glasgow	24 Feb
9:09.25				10	Nice, FRA	10 Jul

10 performances to 9:10.0 by 4 athletes including 2 indoors

Time	Name	Cat	DOB	Pos	Venue	Date
9:11.2 mx	Rhona Makepeace		7.08.62	1	Watford	31 Jul
9:15.1				7	Cork, IRE	22 Jun
9:11.68	Sue Parker		24.03.70	1	Edinburgh	4 May
9:19.4	Lucy Elliott		9.03.66	1	Manchester	17 Aug
9:19.6	Amanda Thorpe/Parkinson		21.07.71	8	Cork, IRE	22 Jun
9:21.2	Vikki McPherson		1.06.71	2	Manchester	17 Aug
9:22.2	Hayley Haining		6.03.72	4	Manchester	17 Aug
(10)						
9:23.5 mx	Penny Thackray	U23	18.08.74	1	Sheffield	24 Jul
9:48.16				8	Birmingham	17 Aug
9:25.41	Andrea Whitcombe		8.06.71	1	Birmingham	20 Jul
9:26.10	Mara Myers		13.08.73	1	London (CP)	2 Jun
9:26.12	Hayley Yelling	U23	3.01.74	2	London (CP)	2 Jun
9:26.46	Debbie Gunning		31.08.65	1	Birmingham	17 Aug
9:26.60	Wendy Ore		23.05.66	3	Dublin, IRE	9 Jun
9:26.6	Dianne Henaghan		6.08.65	1	Gateshead	7 Aug
9:26.75	Angela Davies		21.10.70	2	Birmingham	17 Aug
9:29.2	Louise Watson		13.12.71	10	Cork, IRE	22 Jun
9:29.40	Caroline Pimblett	U23	28.01.75	2	Edinburgh	4 May
(20)						
9:30.2	Angie Hulley		8.02.62	1	Leeds (South)	5 May
9:30.5 mx	Michelle Mann	U20	6.02.77	2	Stretford	25 Jun
9:43.23				1	Bedford	28 Jul
9:32.23 i	Karen Hargrave		23.09.65	2	Lievin, FRA	4 Feb
9:32.5	Amanda Tremble	U23	2.11.76	2	Gateshead	7 Aug
9:33.03	Catherine Berry	U23	8.10.75	4	Stanford, USA	10 May
9:33.9 mx	Wendy Farrow		25.12.71	3	Watford	5 Jun
9:52.1				1	Cannock	26 May
9:34.2	Jo Thompson	V35	30.10.58	1	Bath	11 May
9:35.64 i	Sarah Salmon	U23	9.09.74	1	Glasgow	17 Mar
9:40.87				2	Hexham	14 Jul

9:37.6	Tanya Povey	U20	13.04.79	2	Bath	19 Jun
9:37.68 i	Lynne Robinson		21.06.69	3	Birmingham	18 Feb
(30)						
9:37.9 mx	Helen Pattinson	U23	2.01.74	3	Stretford	25 Jun
9:39.1	Alison Barnes		6.11.69	1	Cardiff	5 May
9:39.8 mx	Astrid Wingler		21.05.68	1	Stretford	6 Aug
	9:59.0			3	Birmingham	7 Jul
9:40.52	Jillian Jones		23.12.69	4	Birmingham	17 Aug
9:40.92	Liz Francis-Thomas		22.12.63	6	Birmingham	17 Aug
9:41.8 mx	Sharon King		27.01.72	1	Loughborough	27 Apr
9:42.16	Ann Terek		22.09.64	4	Dublin, IRE	9 Jun
9:43.22	Debbie Sullivan		24.01.72	3	London (CP)	2 Jun
9:43.6	Ann MacPhail		3.05.70	5	London (He)	6 Jul
9:43.90	Katie Skorupska	U20	3.11.78	2	Bedford	28 Jul
(40)						
9:44.0 +	Amanda Wright		14.07.68	1k	Bedford	26 May
9:44.82	Catherine Dugdale	U23	29.11.74	7	Birmingham	17 Aug
9:44.91	Sheila Fairweather	U20	24.11.77	3	Bedford	28 Jul
9:45.4	Lucy Field		1.05.71	1	Solihull	29 Jun
9:45.5	Jo Davis/Pavey		20.09.73	1	Street	6 May
9:45.7 mx	Elaine Fee		22.07.70	2	Sheffield	24 Jun
9:46.1	Julie Swann		15.07.62	2	Street	6 May
9:46.25	Clare Pauzers		2.08.62	1	Aldershot	26 Jun
9:47.8	Zahara Hyde		12.01.63	1	Abingdon	24 Aug
9:47.9	Anna Kostilek		16.11.65	3	Street	6 May
(50)						
9:48.0	Meryl Whitley/Dodd		12.04.69	2	Leeds (South)	5 May
9:48.37	Michelle Lavercombe/Wannell		12.07.67	4	London (CP)	2 Jun
9:49.78	Dawn James		4.01.67	2	Aldershot	26 Jun
9:50.26	Sue Ridley		25.10.65	1	Edinburgh	4 May
9:50.91	Rachel Nicholson	U20	30.12.77	6	Edinburgh	4 May
9:51.1	Caroline Herbert		30.06.70	2	Abingdon	24 Aug
9:51.6 mx	Sharon Dixon		22.04.68	2	Loughborough	27 Apr
9:51.7	Joanne Holden		20.02.65	7	London (He)	6 Jul
9:51.85	Bev Hartigan		10.06.67	1	Birmingham	7 Jul
9:53.3	Pamela Morgan		16.04.65	2	Cardiff	5 May
(60)						
9:54.2	Ann Taswell		31.05.71	4	Street	6 May
9:54.87	Lisa Moody	U20	22.02.77	4	Bedford	28 Jul
9:55.2	Jodie Swallow	U17	23.06.81	1	Stoke	20 Jul
9:55.4	Ceri Thomas		16.10.70	5	Street	6 May
9:55.8 mx	Anne Connolly	U20	18.02.78	2	Stretford	30 Apr
9:56.17	Amy Waterlow	U20	29.07.78	1	Sheffield	13 Jul
9:56.9	Lisa Webb		9.10.65	1	Enfield	11 May
9:57.4	Rachel Jordan		29.01.72	1	Watford	5 May
9:57.5	Wendy Coombes/Williams		9.02.68	1	Salisbury	10 Aug
9:58.0	Liz Talbot	U23	5.12.74	1	Bournemouth	25 May
(70)						
9:58.4	Jenny Clague		6.08.73	1	Kingston	18 Aug
9:59.5	Alison Carr		30.08.66	2	Coatbridge	4 Aug
9:59.6	Sandra Green		30.10.67	2	Solihull	29 Jun

Foreign

9:01.6 mx	Una English		14.08.70		Melbourne, AUS	27 Mar
9:10.81	Teresa Duffy		6.07.69	1	Dublin, IRE	9 Jun
9:19.8 mx	Edwige Pitel		4.06.67	1	Watford	10 Jul
9:21.0	Berhane Dagne	U20	7.10.77	1	London (He)	6 Jul
9:34.2	Jill Bruce		25.07.73	1	Antrim	25 Jun
9:53.64	Hanna Smedstad	U23	30.03.76	5	London (CP)	1 Jun

Under 17 (1 above)

10:01.46	Kate Grimshaw	26.10.79	2	London (He)	10	Aug
10:03.4	Amber Gascoigne	5.09.79	1	Bath	15	May
10:05.1	Camilla Waite	24.05.80	3	Cheltenham	4	Aug
10:07.6	Caroline Walsh	29.04.80	1	Watford	12	Jun
10:09.05	Karen Fletcher	26.09.79	2	Bedford	28	Jul
10:10.3	Lyndsay Robson	4.07.81	1	Jarrow	8	Jun
10:12.1	Samantha Northey	18.04.80	2	Exeter	15	Jun
10:15.3	Clare Campbell	21.10.80	1	Horsham	22	Jun
10:16.87	Sarah Brew	9.01.81	1	Swansea	6	Jul
(10)						
10:18.4	Sue Crispey	8.01.81	1	Bedford	7	Sep
10:18.45	Georgie Salmon	1.11.79	1	Birmingham	2	Jun
10:19.1	Nicola Lilley	17.02.80	1	Southampton	27	Apr
10:22.36	Ceri Davies	19.08.80	7	Sheffield	12	Jul
10:23.42	Rebecca Everett	10.03.80	1	Birmingham	8	Sep
10:23.5	Jackie Hogan	19.03.80	2	Sheffield	20	Apr
10:24.4	Emma Satterly	25.04.80	1	Crawley	8	Jun
10:25.76	Leanne Appleton	3.03.81	10	Sheffield	12	Jul
10:26.4	Susan Partridge	4.01.80	5	Stoke	20	Jul
10:27.5	Louise Kelly	20.09.80	1	Middlesbrough	15	Jun
(20)						
10:27.8	Melissa Forster	30.03.80	2	Middlesbrough	15	Jun
10:30.3	Stacey Falk	9.06.80	3	Middlesbrough	15	Jun
10:30.4	Astra Hartney	7.01.80	1	Croydon	12	May
10:32.2	Katie Dennison	8.06.80	3	Sheffield	20	Apr
10:32.27	Noeleen Murrin	22.12.79	3	Birmingham	2	Jun
10:33.2	Jenny Cliff	9.05.81	1	Peterborough	15	Sep
10:33.21	Sarah Dugdale	16.05.80	1	Bedford	28	Jul
10:33.9	Lianne Harrison	17.06.80	2	Glasgow	25	Aug
10:34.00	Michelle Speller	3.02.80		Portsmouth	12	May
10:34.0	Jenni Hodgins	7.06.80	1	Exeter	7	Sep
(30)						
10:34.4	Claire Colmer	13.05.80	2	Hoo	8	Jun
10:34.4	Claire Gregory	30.12.79	4	Middlesbrough	15	Jun

5000 METRES

14:46.76	Paula Radcliffe	17.12.73	5	Cologne, GER	16	Aug
14:51.71			2	London (CP)	12	Jul
14:56.36			4	Milan, ITA	7	Sep
14:59.70			4	Brussels, BEL	23	Aug
15:09.50			2	Tokyo, JAP	16	Sep
15:13.11			5	Atlanta, USA	28	Jul
15:23.90			3h2	Atlanta, USA	26	Jul
15:28.46			1	Birmingham	16	Jun
15:29.04	Sonia McGeorge	2.11.64	13	Hengelo, HOL	27	May
15:48.33			2	Birmingham	16	Jun
16:01.92			13h3	Atlanta, USA	26	Jul
15:48.91	Alison Wyeth	26.05.64	3	Birmingham	16	Jun
16:09.36			9	London (CP)	12	Jul
16:18.96			19	Hengelo, HOL	27	May
16:24.74			15h1	Atlanta, USA	26	Jul
15:51.55	Jill Hunter	14.10.66	8	Sydney, AUS	10	Mar
15:55.80			9	Melbourne, AUS	29	Feb
15:53.84	Heather Heasman	27.09.63	8	Hechtel, BEL	6	Jul
16:00.85			1	Sheffield	2	Jun
15:56.15	Lucy Elliott	9.03.66	8	London (CP)	12	Jul
16:00.0	Andrea Whitcombe	8.06.71	1	Loughborough	19	May
16:03.40			4	Birmingham	16	Jun
16:05.36			11	Helsinki, FIN	25	Jun
16:04.12	Zahara Hyde	12.01.63	10	Portland, USA	12	May
16:07.09			5	Seattle, USA	6	Apr

271

16:06.2 mx	Vikki McPherson		1.06.71	1	Loughborough	1	Jun
16:11.6 mx				1	Wishaw	5	May
16:23.86	Sarah Bentley		21.05.67	5	Birmingham	16	Jun
(10)							
16:25.79	Wendy Ore		23.05.66	6	Birmingham	16	Jun
16:26.22	Penny Thackray	U23	18.08.74	1	Sheffield	5	May
16:26.62	Angie Hulley		8.02.62	2	Sheffield	2	Jun
16:28.32	Andrea Duke		6.07.73	3	Sheffield	2	Jun
16:29.69	Amanda Wright		14.07.68	1	Bedford	26	May
	33 performances to 16:30.0 by 15 athletes						
16:32.04	Hayley Yelling	U23	3.01.74	2	Sheffield	5	May
16:33.14	Louise Watson		13.12.71	2	Cape Town, RSA	13	Apr
16:35.36	Caroline Pimblett	U23	28.01.75	4	Sheffield	2	Jun
16:36.90	Sharon Dixon		22.04.68	3	Sheffield	5	May
16:41.67	Mara Myers		13.08.73	3	Oordegem, BEL	10	Aug
(20)							
16:41.9	Katie Skorupska	U20	3.11.78	1	Belfast	22	Jun
16:43.7	Angharad Mair	V35	30.03.61	2	Belfast	22	Jun
16:43.9	Angela Joiner		14.02.69	1	Kings Lynn	11	May
16:49.3	Amanda Tremble	U23	2.11.76	1	Jarrow	14	Aug
16:50.28	Meryl Whitley/Dodd		12.04.69	12	Birmingham	16	Jun
16:52.61	Alison Carr		30.08.66	1	Edinburgh	12	May
16:53.52	Pamela Morgan		16.04.65	6	Sheffield	2	Jun
16:55.3	Chaanah Fothergill		22.02.72	2	Stoke	28	Jul
16:56.20	Adele Rankin		27.05.72	4	Sheffield	5	May
16:56.9	Dawn James		4.01.67	1	Crawley	28	Jul
(30)							
16:59.3 mx	Elaine Fee		22.07.70	1	Street	6	May
17:14.40				13	Birmingham	16	Jun
17:00.6	Carol Holmes		13.12.63	1	Cannock	23	Jun
17:00.9	Rhona Makepeace		7.08.62	7	Loughborough	19	May
17:01.7	Ann MacPhail		3.05.70	2	Liverpool	28	Jul
17:06.1	Anna Kostilek		16.11.65	1	Swindon	14	Aug
17:06.44	Karen Rushton		10.07.67	2	Portsmouth	12	May
17:07.42	Caroline Herbert		30.06.70	1	London (CP)	18	Aug
17:09.01	Sue Ridley		25.10.65	1	Edinburgh	2	Jun
17:12.9	Dianne Henaghan		6.08.65	9	Loughborough	19	May
17:12.98	Alison Rose		27.09.67	2	Edinburgh	12	May
(40)							
17:14.5	Sonia Morley		1.03.66	1	Jarrow	5	Aug
17:17.4	Mandy Ayling		4.04.65	2	Watford	29	May
17:18.8	Jane Harrop	V35	25.07.60	1	Basingstoke	28	Apr
17:19.7	Jessica Turnbull	U23	4.07.75		Poiters, FRA	9	May
17:19.7	Lynn Maddison		17.08.67	4	Liverpool	28	Jul
17:23.3	Joanne Holden		20.02.65	1	London (He)	28	Jul
17:23.39	Lindsay Cairns		1.06.71	1	Glasgow	12	May
17:25.93	Vivienne Conneely	U23	4.01.76	7	Sheffield	5	May
17:27.9	Rita Quill		12.03.67	2	London (He)	28	Jul
17:28.0	Sally Eastall		5.01.63	1	Ipswich	11	May
(50)							
17:28.35	Marlene Gemmell		21.06.72	2	Edinburgh	2	Jun
17:30.2	Jill Cunningham		23.04.62	1	Derby	23	Jun
17:33.80	Catherine Mijovic	V35	11.04.61		San Donato Milanese, ITA	19	May

Foreign

15:53.47	*Teresa Duffy*		*6.07.69*	*14*	*St. Denis, FRA*	*3*	*Jun*
16:08.9	*Nnenna Lynch*		*3.07.71*	*2*	*Loughborough*	*19*	*May*
16:15.7	*Una English*		*14.08.70*	*13*	*Melbourne, AUS*	*29*	*Feb*
16:22.32	*Berhane Dagne*	*U20*	*7.10.77*	*1*	*London (He)*	*31*	*Aug*
17:07.8	*Jill Bruce*		*25.07.73*	*1*	*Antrim*	*20*	*Apr*
17:13.29	*Wendy Llewellyn*		*30.05.63*	*3*	*Bedford*	*26*	*May*
17:37.22	*Getenesh Tamirat*	*U20*	*11.07.77*	*2*	*Bedford*	*27*	*Jul*

10000 METRES

Time	Name	Cat	DOB	Pos	Venue	Date
33:17.74	Vikki McPherson		1.06.71	8	Koblenz, GER	16 May
	33:53.17			3	Birmingham	14 Jun
33:21.46	Louise Watson		13.12.71	1	Birmingham	14 Jun
	33:28.08			10	Koblenz, GER	16 May
	33:53.0			1	Loughborough	29 Jun
33:33.37	Angie Hulley		8.02.62	2	Birmingham	14 Jun
34:06.25	Amanda Wright		14.07.68	12	Koblenz, GER	16 May
34:11.76	Angharad Mair	V35	30.03.61	4	Birmingham	14 Jun
34:26.43	Sharon Dixon		22.04.68	1	Sheffield	6 May
34:28.13	Sally Goldsmith	V35	18.01.61	7	Pietrasanta, ITA	5 May
34:30.52	Jo Thompson	V35	30.10.58	5	Birmingham	14 Jun
34:37.5	Zahara Hyde		12.01.63	2	Loughborough	29 Jun
34:41.28	Mara Myers		13.08.73	2	Sheffield	6 May
	(10)					
34:44.89	Alison Rose		27.09.67	6	Birmingham	14 Jun
35:15.6	Caroline Herbert		30.06.70	1	Worthing	15 Sep
35:18.43	Julie Coleby	V40	5.11.55	7	Birmingham	14 Jun
35:26.82	Sue Ridley		25.10.65	1	Ayr	21 Jul
35:27.77	Lindsay Cairns		1.06.71	2	Ayr	21 Jul
35:54.43	Sally Lynch		6.11.64	8	Birmingham	14 Jun
36:30.3	Zina Marchant	V45	30.09.50	1	Exeter	9 Aug
36:45.3	Debbie Kilner		2.11.61	1	Aberdeen	2 May
37:43.3	Alison Fletcher	V35	8.06.61	1	Exeter	10 Aug

10 KILOMETRES ROAD

Time	Name	Cat	DOB	Pos	Venue	Date
31:41	Liz McColgan		24.05.64	1	Charleston, USA	30 Mar
	32:12			1	Arbroath	7 Jul
	32:12			1	Belfast	7 Sep
	32:30			1	Perth	1 Sep
	33:25			1	Raphoe	20 Oct
32:41	Jill Hunter		14.10.66	2	Melbourne, AUS	31 Mar
33:16	Yvonne Murray		4.10.64	1	Edinburgh	29 Sep
33:24	Amanda Wright		14.07.68	1	Telford	22 Dec
33:25	Heather Heasman		27.09.63	1	Eastleigh	17 Mar
33:25	Hayley Haining		6.03.72	1	Solihull	6 Oct
33:27	Karen Macleod	V35	24.04.58	1	Bourton	25 Feb
33:30	Sarah Bentley		21.05.67	1	Salford	5 Apr
33:30	Lucy Elliott		9.03.66	1	Perivale	8 Sep
33:44	Marian Sutton		7.10.63	3	Edinburgh	29 Sep
	(10)					
33:47	Wendy Ore		23.05.66	2	Cardiff	22 Sep
33:54	Zahara Hyde		12.01.63	1	Chichester	4 Feb
33:56	Jo Thompson	V35	30.10.58	1	Stafford	19 May
34:01	Caroline Herbert		30.06.70	1	Brighton	17 Nov
34:13	Loretta Sollars		29.10.63	1	Peterborough	8 Apr
34:15	Angie Hulley		8.02.62	2	Stafford	19 May
34:19	Mandy Ayling		4.04.65	1	Staines	24 Mar
34:19	Jane Palmer		7.10.66	1	Sheffield	1 Dec
34:24	Danielle Sanderson		26.10.62	4	Perivale	8 Sep
34:27	Penny Thackray	U23	18.08.74	1	Wakefield	14 Apr
	(20)					
34:34	Lynn Gibson		6.07.69	2	Eastleigh	17 Mar
34:35	Vikki McPherson		1.06.71	1	Grangemouth	15 Sep
34:36	Hayley Nash		30.05.63	1	Swansea	8 Sep
34:42	Andrea Duke		6.07.73	1	Bath	9 Jun
34:44	Gabby Collison		10.02.66	1	Totton	14 Apr
34:50	Zina Marchant	V45	30.09.50	2	Totton	14 Apr
34:52	Jane Shields	V35	23.08.60	1	Doncaster	27 Aug
34:54	Meryl Whitley/Dodd		12.04.69	1	Harrogate	28 Jul

273

34:55	Julie Briggs		13.03.69	2	Chichester	4 Feb
34:55	Angela Joiner		14.02.69	1	Croxton	5 May
	(30)					
34:55	Sue Dilnot		14.01.62	1	Poole	2 Jun
34:55	Carol Holmes		13.12.63	3	Cardiff	22 Sep
34:59	Wendy Farrow		25.12.71	1	Derby	17 Mar
35:00	Ruth Kingsborough		25.10.67	3	Chichester	4 Feb
35:00	Marlene Gemmell		21.06.72	1	Helensburgh	23 May
35:00	Trudi Thomson	V35	18.01.59	1	Frampton-on-Seven	8 Jul

intermediate time

33:00 +	Yvonne Murray		4.10.64	2m	South Shields	15 Sep

short course

32:46	Amanda Wright		14.07.68	1	Madrid, SPA	25 Feb
33:09	Sarah Bradbury		25.02.63	1	Seaford	19 Apr

relay leg

33:57	Suzanne Rigg		29.11.63		Copenhagen, DEN	13 Apr
33:59	Angie Hulley		8.02.62		Copenhagen, DEN	13 Apr

Foreign

33:35	*Cathy Shum*	*V35*	*30.05.61*	*2*	*Dublin, IRE*	*9 Jun*
33:54	*Teresa Duffy*		*6.07.69*	*1*	*Bangor*	*21 Sep*
34:23	*Berhane Dagne*	*U20*	*7.10.77*	*2*	*St. Neots*	*26 May*
34:39	*Jill Bruce*		*25.07.73*		*Lisburn*	*19 Jun*

10 MILES ROAD

52:53	Marian Sutton		7.10.63	2	Portsmouth	6 Oct
	55:24			1	Erewash	1 Sep
53:50	Yvonne Murray		4.10.64	4	Portsmouth	6 Oct
55:34	Karen Macleod	V35	24.04.58	1	Ballycotton, IRE	10 Mar
55:50	Hayley Nash		30.05.63	2	Erewash	1 Sep
55:52	Jo Thompson	V35	30.10.58	1	Woking	3 Mar
55:56	Danielle Sanderson		26.10.62	2	Woking	3 Mar
56:09	Carol Holmes		13.12.63	4	Erewash	1 Sep
56:19	Julie Coleby	V40	5.11.55	1	Thirsk	2 Jun
56:41	Zahara Hyde		12.01.63	4	Woking	3 Mar
56:43	Wendy Ore		23.05.66	5	Erewash	1 Sep
	(10)					
56:52	Angharad Mair		30.03.61	1	Rhondda	7 Jul
57:09	Caroline Herbert		30.06.70	1	Gosport	22 Sep
57:14	Sue Dilnot		14.01.62	1	Maidenhead	5 Apr
57:18	Loretta Sollars		29.10.63	6	Erewash	1 Sep
57:27	Lynn Harding	V35	10.08.61	1	Carlisle	16 Nov
57:35	Tracy Swindell		8.11.66	5	Woking	3 Mar
57:43	Carolyn Hunter-Rowe		25.01.64	1	Pocklington	1 Dec
57:44	Suzanne Rigg		29.11.63	1	Stockport	1 Dec
57:50	Susan Wightman	V35	24.10.60	6	Woking	3 Mar
57:51	Maria Bradley		2.01.63	5	Portsmouth	6 Oct
	(20)					
57:51	Melanie Bradley		12.03.63	5	Portsmouth	6 Oct
57:54	Lisa Hollick		1.01.70	2	Maidenhead	5 Apr
58:05	Trudi Thomson	V35	18.01.59	6	Portsmouth	6 Oct
58:45	Jane Harrop	V35	25.07.60	7	Woking	3 Mar
58:48	Dinah Cheverton		24.03.65	8	Woking	3 Mar
58:50	Sandra Branney	V40	30.04.54	2	Carlisle	16 Nov
58:56	Jackie Newton		28.08.64	2	Stockport	1 Dec

intermediate time

53:33 +	Liz McColgan		24.05.64	2m	South Shields	15 Sep

| 56:49 | Wendy Llewellyn | | 30.05.63 | 9 | Washington, USA | 31 | Mar |
| 56:56 | Cathy Shum | | 30.05.61 | 1 | Burton | 12 | May |

intermediate time

| 56:00 + | Wendy Llewellyn | | 30.05.63 | 1m | Tarves, FRA | 5 | Oct |

HALF MARATHON

1:10:04	Melanie Bradley		12.03.63	2	Fleet	24	Mar
1:10:28	Liz McColgan		24.05.64	1	South Shields	15	Sep
1:12:25	Yvonne Murray		4.10.64	5	South Shields	15	Sep
1:12:32	Suzanne Rigg		29.11.63	1	Wilmslow	31	Mar
1:13:04				1	Worcester	16	Mar
1:13:13	Sally Goldsmith	V35	18.01.61	1	Ferrara, ITA	18	Feb
1:13:50				1	Bologna, ITA	4	Feb
1:13:41	Marian Sutton		7.10.63	5	South Shields	15	Sep
1:14:22	Danielle Sanderson		26.10.62	2	Worcester	16	Mar
1:14:34	Trudi Thomson	V35	18.01.59	1	Helensburgh	21	Jul
1:14:46	Amanda Wright		14.07.68	4	Nice, FRA	31	Mar
1:15:02	Angharad Mair	V35	30.03.61	1	Reigate	16	Nov
(10)
1:15:05	Debbie Percival	V35	22.04.58	1	Hastings	17	Mar
1:15:28	Sue Dilnot		14.01.62	8	Vitry-sur-Seine, FRA	14	Apr
1:16:07	Sandra Branney	V40	30.04.54	1	Alloa	31	Mar
1:16:10	Hayley Nash		30.05.63	1	Bath	17	Mar
1:16:57	Tracy Swindell		8.11.66	4	Worcester	16	Mar
1:16:59	Paula Fudge	V40	30.03.52	1	Fleet	24	Mar
1:17:01	Hayley Haining		6.03.72	3	Glasgow	25	Aug
1:17:07	Bronwyn Cardy-Wise	V40	26.01.52	2	Helsby	21	Jan
1:17:11	Carol Holmes		13.12.63	3	Liverpool	25	Aug
1:17:12	Angela Allen		23.09.67	2	Bath	17	Mar
(20)
1:17:26	Carolyn Hunter-Rowe		25.01.64	3	Wilmslow	31	Mar
1:17:27	Zina Marchant	V45	30.09.50	1	Gloucester	28	Jul
1:17:28	Lisa Hollick		1.01.70	2	Gloucester	28	Feb
1:17:31	Jackie Newton		28.08.64	7	Trosloop, HOL	13	Oct
1:17:48	Julie Coleby	V40	5.11.55	1	Redcar	10	Mar
1:18:21	Zahara Hyde		12.01.63	1	Guernsey	8	Apr
1:18:38	Lindsay Cairns		1.06.71	6	Glasgow	25	Aug
1:18:43	Louise Cooper	U23	25.08.75	3	Helsby	21	Jan
1:18:49	Caroline Herbert		30.06.70	2	Hastings	17	Mar
1:18:57	Kate Burge			1	Stafford	24	Mar
(30)
1:19:08	Caroline Horne	V35	7.11.56	1	Reading	31	Mar
1:19:12	Shiela Allen	V35	1.09.57	2	Redcar	10	Mar
1:19:12	Karen Rushton		10.07.67	6	Worcester	16	Mar
1:19:19	Janice Moorekite	V35	1.05.57	1	Brighton	25	Feb
1:19:22	Clare Pauzers		2.08.62		Guernsey	8	Apr
1:19:23	Jan Rashleigh			1	Ashton-U-Lyne	26	May
1:19:45	Eleanor Threadgold			1	Londonderry	28	Sep
1:19:48	Joanne Holden		20.02.65	13	South Shields	15	Sep
1:19:49	Mel Ellis		16.04.64	14	South Shields	15	Sep
1:19:52	Diane Underwood	V40	20.12.52	1	Stratford	28	Apr
(40)
1:19:52	Angela Joiner		14.02.69	1	Norwich	9	Jun
1:19:53	Lynn Harding	V35	10.08.61	1	Peterlee	1	Sep

intermediate time

| 1:13:48 + | Liz McColgan | | 24.05.64 | 9m | Atlanta, USA | 28 | Jul |

Foreign

1:13:04	Cathy Shum	30.05.61	2	Wilmslow	31	Mar
1:13:17	Wendy Llewellyn	30.05.63	1	Tarves, FRA	5	Oct
1:15:32	Edwige Pitel	4.06.67	9	Vitry-sur-Seine, FRA	14	Apr

MARATHON

2:27:54	Liz McColgan		24.05.64	1	London	21	Apr
	2:30:50			3	Tokyo, JAP	17	Nov
	2:34:30			16	Atlanta, USA	28	Jul
2:30:41	Marian Sutton		7.10.63	1	Chicago, USA	20	Oct
2:33:50	Karen Macleod	V35	24.04.58	6	Houston, USA	21	Jan
	2:42:08			45	Atlanta, USA	28	Jul
2:34:11	Sally Goldsmith	V35	18.01.61	1	Vigarano Mainarda, ITA	3	Mar
2:38:47	Angharad Mair	V35	30.03.61	1	Reykjavik, ICE	18	Aug
2:38:52	Sally Eastall		5.01.63	12	Houston, USA	21	Jan
	2:38:59			14	London	21	Apr
2:39:46	Danielle Sanderson		26.10.62	15	London	21	Apr
	2:41:12			2	Dublin, IRE	28	Oct
2:44:39	Trudi Thomson	V35	18.01.59	5	Las Vegas, USA	11	Feb
2:44:48	Tracy Swindell		8.11.66	4	Dublin, IRE	28	Oct
2:45:12	Gillian Horovitz	V40	7.06.55	14	New York, USA	3	Nov
(10)							
2:45:42	Zina Marchant	V45	30.09.50	19	London	21	Apr
2:45:50	Debbie Noy		31.10.64	1	Gosport	28	Apr
2:46:19	Sandra Branney	V40	30.04.54	20	London	21	Apr
2:47:28	Jackie Newton		28.08.64	7	Dublin, IRE	28	Oct
2:48:05 +t	Carolyn Hunter-Rowe		25.01.64	1	Barry	3	Mar
	2:51:38			2	Manchester	13	Oct
2:48:49	Debbie Percival	V35	22.04.58	21	London	21	Apr
2:48:50	Janice Moorekite	V35	1.05.57	1	Manchester	13	Oct
2:51:26	Janette Picton		4.03.63	24	London	21	Apr
2:52:09	Suzanne Rigg		29.11.63	58	Atlanta, USA	28	Jul
2:53:25	R. Potter			3	Manchester	13	Oct
(20)							
2:53:57	Lesley Turner		1.08.66	1	Harrow	3	Nov
2:54:16	Lisa Hollick		1.01.70	27	London	21	Apr
2:55:02	Libby Jones		25.04.61	29	London	21	Apr
2:55:04	Avril Allen	V35	1.08.59	1	Nottingham	29	Sep
2:55:56	Meredith Blake		20.10.67	32	London	21	Apr
2:56:17	Kerry Wood			4	Manchester	13	Oct
2:56:47	Eleanor Robinson	V45	20.11.47	1	Greenock	15	Sep
2:56:57	Joanna Lodge		6.01.68	33	London	21	Apr
2:57:02	Sally Ellis	V35	17.05.58	5	Florence, ITA	1	Dec
2:57:08	Zoe Lowe		7.07.65	35	London	21	Apr
(30)							
2:57:56	Helen Grimshaw		2.08.62	1	Chiswick	22	Sep
2:58:08	L. Thomson			28	New York, USA	3	Nov
2:58:51	Jo Edwards		16.07.70	37	London	21	Apr
2:58:57	Barbara Stevens		2.05.56	1	Taunton	14	Apr
2:59:05	Nicola Swithenbank		10.12.63	38	London	21	Apr
2:59:33	Alice Hansen			39	London	21	Apr
2:59:35	Dawn James	V35	17.10.60	2	Chiswick	22	Sep
2:59:56	Kathryn Charnock		4.07.62	40	London	21	Apr
3:00:46	Z. Lewis			3	Chiswick	22	Sep
3:00:50	Anna Jeeves	V40	19.09.54	43	London	21	Apr
(40)							
3:01:15	Nicole Docker			2	Slough	1	Sep
3:01:26	Sue Morley	V35	11.10.57	45	London	21	Apr
3:01:31	Rachel Wilson	V40	13.03.56	2	Taunton	14	Apr
3:01:31	Caroline Hipkin		18.03.71	46	London	21	Apr
3:01:37	Alice Osbourne		27.02.67	47	London	21	Apr

3:02:36	K. Armstrong			4	Chiswick	22 Sep
3:02:53	Lynda Lee	V35	7.04.57	48	London	21 Apr
3:03:21	Melanie Bradley		12.03.63	49	London	21 Apr
3:04:36	Jill McGee			2	Sheffield	28 Apr
3:04:49	R. Teinila		1.01.73	3	Harrow	3 Nov
(50)						
3:04:57	Julia McGowan	V35	12.05.59	51	London	21 Apr
3:04:57	Anne-Marie Hughes		8.05.62	52	London	21 Apr
3:05:00	Caroline Jones	V35	29.03.60	3	Belfast	6 May
3:05:08	Elaine Flather		2.02.66	53	London	21 Apr
3:05:28	Frances Cooke	V35	8.12.56	55	London	21 Apr
3:05:30	Lesley Leggett	V35	3.04.58	56	London	21 Apr
3:05:45	Jane Bright	V45	24.03.50	57	London	21 Apr
3:05:56	Judith Burnett	V35	14.10.58	58	London	21 Apr
3:06:04	Kath Kaiser	V45	24.08.51	6	Manchester	13 Oct
3:06:06	Dorothy Smale	V35	26.05.60	59	London	21 Apr
(60)						
3:06:07	Sally Pitts	V35		1	Abingdon	20 Oct
3:06:20	Sarah Ing		10.11.63	60	London	21 Apr
3:06:23	Helene Diamantides			1	Fort William	28 Apr
3:06:36	Susan Cariss	V45	17.11.49	61	London	21 Apr
3:06:46	Patricia Trott		7.09.62	62	London	21 Apr
3:06:49	Phylis Flynn		15.06.62	5	Chiswick	22 Sep
3:06:51	Marilyn Clarke	V45	3.06.50	63	London	21 Apr
3:07:02	Lynne Quigley		19.02.69	64	London	21 Apr
3:07:05	Joanne Jenkins	V35	7.01.59	65	London	21 Apr
3:07:26	Tracy Owen		29.04.64	67	London	21 Apr
(70)						
3:07:36	P. Buckingham			2	Luton	1 Dec
3:07:45	Sue Ashley	V40	10.10.52	68	London	21 Apr
3:08:04	Susan Bolt			69	London	21 Apr
3:08:05	Jane Burthen		13.12.62	70	London	21 Apr
3:08:10	Andrea Dennison		22.04.63	71	London	21 Apr
3:08:25	Marilyn Gradden	V35	26.01.61	72	London	21 Apr
3:08:37	Annette Clark		4.05.61	73	London	21 Apr
3:08:41	Linda Way		17.09.64	74	London	21 Apr

Foreign
2:37:00	*Wendy Llewellyn*		*30.05.63*	*8*	*Rotterdam, HOL*	*28 Apr*
2:38:56	*Cathy Shum*	*V35*	*30.05.61*	*1*	*Dublin, IRE*	*28 Oct*
2:39:18	*Yvonne Danson*	*V35*	*22.05.59*	*36*	*Atlanta, USA*	*28 Jul*
2:53:54	*Sue Dolan*	*V35*		*2*	*Gosport*	*28 Apr*

100 KILOMETRES - Road

7:41:29	Carolyn Hunter-Rowe		25.01.64	1	Cleder, FRA	25 Aug
8:00:01	Eleanor Robinson	V45	20.11.47		Rognonas	28 Jan
8:13:00				1	Nantes, FRA	28 Sep
8:23:14					Cleder, FRA	25 Aug
8:27:36	Hilary Walker	V40	9.11.53	9	Nantes, FRA	28 Sep
8:45:56	Helene Diamantides				Cleder, FRA	25 Aug
8:53:53	Sylvia Watson	V45	29.09.47		Moscow,RUS	4 May
9:06:45	Kate Todd	V45	21.07.50		Edinburgh	21 Jul
9:36:50	Sharon Gayter				Moscow,RUS	4 May
9:46:26	Lesley Turner		1.08.66		Moscow,RUS	4 May

24 HOURS - Track

223.129 km	Eleanor Robinson	V45	20.11.47	3	Courcon,	22 Sep
207.156 km				1	Brno, SWZ	22 Feb
212.701 km	Sandra Brown	V45	1.04.49	4	Courcon,	22 Sep
190.846 km	Sharon Gayter				Courcon,	22 Sep

2000 METRES STEEPLECHASE

7:12.84	Stephanie Cook		7.02.72	1	Sheffield	4	May
7:23.90	Natasha Goddard		15.06.71	2	Sheffield	4	May
	(2' 6" Barriers ?)						

3000 METRES STEEPLECHASE (2' 6" Barriers)

11:46.8	Sally Dawson		1	Horsham	17	Aug

60 METRES HURDLES - Indoors

8.17	Jacqui Agyepong		5.01.69	1	Birmingham	3	Feb
8.22				1h2	Birmingham	3	Feb
8.20	Clova Court	V35	10.02.60	3	Glasgow	24	Feb
8.27				1	Birmingham	6	Jan
8.35				1	Birmingham	27	Jan
8.38				2h2	Birmingham	3	Feb
8.41				4	Birmingham	10	Feb
8.44				4	Birmingham	3	Feb
8.32	Diane Allahgreen	U23	21.02.75	2	Birmingham	6	Jan
8.38				2	Birmingham	27	Jan
8.32	Denise Lewis		27.08.72	1	Vienna, AUT	17	Feb
8.41				1h2	Vienna, AUT	17	Feb
8.32	Natasha Danvers	U20	19.09.77	1h2	Lievin, FRA	2	Mar
8.39				1	Birmingham	17	Feb
8.41				1r1	Lievin, FRA	2	Mar
8.37	Melanie Wilkins		18.01.73	3	Birmingham	3	Feb
8.43				5	Birmingham	10	Feb
8.44				4	Vienna, AUT	17	Feb
8.45				4	Glasgow	24	Feb
8.48				2h1	Birmingham	3	Feb
8.57				3	Birmingham	6	Jun
8.53	Jane Hale	U23	4.01.74	3h2	Birmingham	3	Feb
8.58				6	Birmingham	3	Feb
8.54	Vikki Schofield		29.12.72	2P	Valencia, SPA	28	Jan
8.57	Keri Maddox		4.07.72	5	Birmingham	3	Feb
8.58	Katy Sketchley		9.07.73	1	Glasgow	21	Jan
	26 performances to 8.60 by 10 athletes						
8.66	Denise Bolton	U20	1.02.77	1rB	Lievin, FRA	2	Mar
8.71	Rachael Kay	U17	8.09.80	1	Birmingham	17	Feb
8.74	Nicola Hall	U17	14.12.79	2	Birmingham	17	Feb
8.75	Lynne Fairweather	U17	15.01.80	3	Birmingham	17	Feb
8.76	Sarah Damm		12.09.70	3P	Valencia, SPA	28	Jan
8.81	Kerry Jury		19.11.68	1P	Birmingham	4	Feb
8.86	Julia Bennett		26.03.70	2P	Valencia, SPA	28	Jan
8.86	Katy Lestrange	U17	17.09.79	1h2	Birmingham	17	Feb
8.89	Pauline Richards		30.06.68	1	Glasgow	15	Dec
8.91	Sarah Akinbiyi	U17	23.08.81	3h3	Birmingham	17	Feb
	(20)						
8.93	Josephine Peet		4.12.71	1	Glasgow	17	Mar
8.95	Kate Forsyth	U20	5.06.79	1	Glasgow	3	Feb
8.95	Liz Fairs	U20	1.12.77	1	Birmingham	11	Feb
8.96	Julie Pratt	U20	20.03.79	3	Birmingham	17	Feb
8.97	Emma Anderson	U20	19.06.79	4	Birmingham	17	Feb
8.98	Katy Bartlett		6.05.73	4h1	Birmingham	3	Feb
8.99	Nicola Gautier	U20	21.03.78	P	Birmingham	4	Feb
8.99	Rachel King	U23	11.05.76	2	Glasgow	17	Mar

Hand Timing

8.9	Teresa Copeland		8.03.69	3	London (CP)	6	Jan
8.9	Orla Bermingham	U23	7.10.75	1	London (Ha)	13	Jan
8.9	Naomi Hodge-Dallaway	U17	1.06.81	1	Birmingham	25	Feb

9.0		Clare O'Sullivan	8.05.80	3	London (CP)	20 Jan
9.0		Sarina Mantle	19.01.81	1	London (CP)	7 Dec
9.11				2h4	Birmingham	17 Feb
9.04		Katherine Livesey	15.12.79	3	Sheffield	21 Jan
9.07		Cheryl Kennedy	10.02.80	6	Birmingham	17 Feb
	(20)					
9.07		Caroline Pearce	1.09.80	7	Birmingham	17 Feb
9.07		Leanda Adams	7.12.79	1	Birmingham	24 Feb
9.1		Sarah Claxton	23.09.79	1P	London (CP)	21 Jan
9.1		Mary Onianwa	20.01.81	1	London (CP)	24 Feb
9.17		Gillian Stewart	21.01.80	3	Glasgow	3 Feb
9.20		Eve Miller	1.12.79	4h4	Birmingham	17 Feb
9.2		Laura Eastman	23.12.80	h	Birmingham	24 Feb
9.26				2	Birmingham	24 Feb
9.22		Naomi Hodge-Dallaway	(8.9)	3h1	Birmingham	17 Feb
9.25		Anna Leyshon	19.01.80	3h2	Birmingham	17 Feb
9.26		Amy Bergiers	19.09.79	4h2	Birmingham	17 Feb

70 METRES HURDLES - Under 13

11.24	-0.4	Alana Watson	14.12.83	1	Birmingham	8 Sep
11.3		Jennifer Molloy	23.09.83	1	Bournemouth	25 Aug
11.6		Danielle Selley		1	Carmarthen	15 Jun
11.6		Hannah Coleman	26.09.83	1	Ipswich	18 Aug
11.6		Sarah Oldham	23.09.83	1	Tamworth	8 Sep
11.6		Holly Ferrier	13.07.84	1	Peterborough	29 Sep
11.7		Louise Cook	7.01.84	1	Ipswich	9 Jun
11.7		Melissa Rogers	2.09.83	2	London (TB)	28 Jul
11.72		Catriona Pennet	10.10.83	1	Edinburgh	25 Aug
11.77	-0.4	Amy Lloyd	20.11.83	2	Birmingham	8 Sep
	(10)					
11.78		Aileen Wilson	30.03.84	2	Edinburgh	25 Aug
11.8		Symone Belle	12.11.84	2	Ipswich	9 Jun
11.8		Alice Glenn	30.09.83	1	Brierley Hill	21 Jul
11.8		S. Mitchell		2	Brierley Hill	21 Jul
11.82	-0.4	Hannah Cutler	25.01.84	3	Birmingham	8 Sep

75 METRES HURDLES - Under 15

11.05 w 4.4		Helen Worsey	29.08.82	1	Sheffield	13 Jul
11.29	2.0			1h3	Sheffield	12 Jul
11.09 w 4.4		Luisa Giles	23.02.82	2	Sheffield	13 Jul
11.55	2.0			2h3	Sheffield	12 Jul
11.21 w 4.4		Sharon Davidge	15.09.81	3	Sheffield	13 Jul
11.44	1.5			2h1	Sheffield	12 Jul
11.43	1.5	Louise O'Callaghan	12.12.81	1h1	Sheffield	12 Jul
11.46 w 4.4		Felicity Breens	6.11.81	4	Sheffield	13 Jul
11.6				2	Leicester	8 Jun
11.62	0.6			1h2	Sheffield	12 Jul
11.49 w 4.4		Lisa Connolly	27.09.81	5	Sheffield	13 Jul
11.61	1.4			1	Birmingham	8 Sep
11.49 w 3.4		Lauren McLoughlin	8.09.82	2h1	Birmingham	17 Aug
11.5				2	Newport	10 Jul
11.64	0.4			2	Birmingham	17 Aug
11.50 w 4.4		Sara McGreavy	13.12.82	6	Sheffield	13 Jul
11.6				1	Brierley Hill	21 Jul
11.67	2.0			3h3	Sheffield	12 Jul
11.5		Stephanie Little	5.11.81	1	Newport	10 Jul
11.51 w 4.4		Hayley Smith	14.01.82	7	Sheffield	13 Jul
11.61				2	London (He)	7 Jul
	(10)					

11.69	1.4	Laura McShane	22.04.82	1p	Birmingham	27	Sep
11.7		Kirsty Roach	8.12.81	3	Leicester	8	Jun
11.7		Donna Chatfield	15.09.81	1	Southampton	15	Jun
11.7		Alyssa Fullelove	16.09.81	1	Coatbridge	4	Aug
		11.80	1.9		1	Edinburgh	2	Jun
11.7		Emily Young	31.07.83	1	Sandown, IOW	22	Sep
11.73	-1.3	Anne-Marie Massey	10.09.82	1h3	Cudworth	30	Jun
11.74	2.0	Zoe McKinnon	8.09.81	5h3	Sheffield	12	Jul
11.78	1.5	Rachel Webb	1.12.82	3h1	Sheffield	12	Jul
11.8		Grace Davidge	22.01.82	2	Southampton	15	Jun
11.8		Sarah Bullock	6.12.81	1	Middlesbrough	15	Jun
	(20)						
11.8		Charlotte Todd	7.12.81	2	Coatbridge	4	Aug
11.8		Gillian Leckie	1.09.81	3	Coatbridge	4	Aug

Under 13

12.0	Sarah Oldham	23.09.83	1	Worcester	22	Sep
12.5	Erica Hillan	1.02.84	1	York	15	Jun
12.6	Louise Cook	7.01.84	P	Norwich	14	May

80 METRES HURDLES - Under 17

11.25 w 3.2	Sarina Mantle	19.01.81	1	Sheffield	13	Jul
	11.62 0.5		1	Birmingham	17	Aug
11.27 w 3.2	Nicola Hall	14.12.79	2	Sheffield	13	Jul
	11.41 -1.8		1	London (CP)	30	Jun
11.39 w 3.2	Katy Lestrange	17.09.79	3	Sheffield	13	Jul
	11.47 1.3		1h3	Sheffield	12	Jul
11.4	Tamsin Stephens	2.08.80	1P	Dublin (M), IRE	28	Sep
11.44 w 3.2	Katherine Livesey	15.12.79	4	Sheffield	13	Jul
			1H	Blackpool	27	Jul
11.59 w 3.2	Naomi Hodge-Dallaway	1.06.81	5	Sheffield	13	Jul
	11.79 -0.1		2h4	Sheffield	12	Jul
11.6	Rachael Kay	8.09.80	1	Liverpool	2	Jun
	12.08 -0.3		1	Birmingham	7	Sep
11.6	Julie Davis	16.11.79	1	Dublin, IRE	22	Jun
	12.09		1	Tullamore, IRE	1	Jun
11.6 w	Sarah Claxton	23.09.79	1	London (WP)	27	Apr
	11.8 0.3		1	Thurrock	11	May
11.6 w 3.0	Sarah Porter	11.12.79	1	Croydon	11	May
	11.8		1	Sutton	20	Jul
	12.04		1rB	Bedford	7	Sep
	(10)					
11.62 w 2.5	Leanda Adams	7.12.79	2s2	Sheffield	12	Jul
	11.73 -0.1		1h4	Sheffield	12	Jul
11.65 0.9	Clare O'Sullivan	8.05.80	1h2	Sheffield	12	Jul
11.67 w 3.2	Lesley McGoldrick	12.09.79	7	Sheffield	13	Jul
	11.7		1	Wakefield	19	May
	12.07 0.2		2h1	Sheffield	12	Jul
11.72 w 3.5	Clare Turner	23.09.80	4s1	Sheffield	12	Jul
	11.82 0.9		3h2	Sheffield	12	Jul
11.79 w 2.5	Serena Bailey	2.01.81	6s2	Sheffield	12	Jul
	11.8		2	Basildon	8	Jun
	11.99 1.3		4h3	Sheffield	12	Jul
11.8	Emma Duck	9.02.81	1	Bournemouth	28	Jul
	11.93 0.9		3h2	Birmingham	17	Aug
11.85 0.5	Anna Leyshon	19.01.80	2	Birmingham	17	Aug
11.86 1.3	Amy Nuttell	6.02.80	3h3	Sheffield	12	Jul
11.89 0.9	Laura Eastman	23.12.80	4h2	Sheffield	12	Jul
11.9	Gemma Whitton	25.05.81	1	Livingston	22	May
(20)						

11.9		Victoria Williams		11.04.81	1	Yate	8	Jun
	12.02	1.3			5h3	Sheffield	12	Jul
11.9		Laura Haylock		20.02.80	1	St. Ives	8	Jun
	11.92 w	3.5			5s1	Sheffield	12	Jul
	11.93	-0.1			3h4	Sheffield	12	Jul
11.9		Amy Rutter		4.08.80	1	Carlisle	8	Jun
11.9		Cheryl Kennedy		10.02.80	1	Middlesbrough	15	Jun
11.9		Danielle Freeman		11.02.80	1	Leeds (South)	7	Jul
11.9		Sarah Nicolle		12.01.80	1	Brierley Hill	21	Jul
	12.02 w	3.2			3	Stoke	22	Jun
11.9		Sarah Lane		4.06.81	1	Brecon	1	Sep
	11.91	0.5			3	Birmingham	17	Aug
11.93	0.3	Eve Miller		1.12.79	1H	Enfield	3	Aug
12.0		Joanne Grant		17.12.79	2	Livingston	22	May
12.0		Laura Foster		22.07.81	1	Sheffield (W)	2	Jun
	(30)							
12.0		Sarah Akinbiyi		23.08.81	1	Croydon	8	Jun
	12.02	-1.8			4	London (CP)	30	Jun
12.0		Chloe Cozens		9.04.80	3H	Norwich	22	Jun
12.0		Sharon Crowle		6.09.80	2H	Carn Brea	22	Jun
12.0		Lucy Rann		5.09.80	1	Sandown, IOW	30	Jun
12.0		Amanda Williams		28.06.80	2	Kingston	27	Jul
12.0	-1.2	Gillian Stewart		21.01.80	2	Pitreavie	10	Aug
	12.02	-1.3			1H	Worcester	24	Aug
12.0		Amy Bergiers		19.09.79	2	Brecon	1	Sep

100 METRES HURDLES

12.80	0.7	Angela Thorp		7.12.72	5s1	Atlanta, USA	31	Jul
	12.93	1.7			2h4	Atlanta, USA	29	Jul
	12.99	-0.8			3q4	Atlanta, USA	29	Jul
	13.02	1.6			1	Loughborough	19	May
	13.04	-0.4			2	Gateshead	19	Aug
	13.09	-0.1			7h2	Zurich, SWZ	14	Aug
	13.13	1.1			3	London (CP)	11	Aug
	13.14	-1.7			5	London (CP)	12	Jul
	13.14	1.6			6	Sheffield	25	Aug
	13.26	-2.3			1	Birmingham	16	Jun
	13.28	1.7			1	Sheffield	12	May
	13.34	-2.2			1h1	Birmingham	16	Jun
13.18	-0.2	Denise Lewis		27.08.72	1H	Gotzis, AUT	25	May
	13.41	-2.3			3	Birmingham	16	Jun
	13.45	-1.2			1h2	Birmingham	16	Jun
	13.45	-1.6			2H3	Atlanta, USA	27	Jul
	13.52	1.1			6	London (CP)	11	Aug
	13.57	1.6			8	Sheffield	25	Aug
13.18	0.3	Jacqui Agyepong		5.01.69	2rB	Lausanne, SWZ	3	Jul
	13.24	-0.5			7h1	Atlanta, USA	29	Jul
	13.30	-0.4			4	Gateshead	19	Aug
	13.35	-1.7			6	London (CP)	12	Jul
	13.47	1.6			7	Sheffield	25	Aug
13.27	-2.3	Diane Allahgreen	U23	21.02.75	2	Birmingham	16	Jun
	13.28	0.6			3	Zagreb, CRO	21	Jun
	13.38	-2.2			2h1	Birmingham	16	Jun
	13.43	-0.1			3	Tallinn, EST	9	Jun
	13.44	0.8			1	Bedford	18	May
	13.48	-1.1			1	Sheffield	2	Jun
	13.50				2	Fullerton, USA	25	Apr
13.40	1.2	Sam Farquharson		15.12.69	6	Rhede, GER	24	May
	13.43	-0.4			5	Chemnitz, GER	19	May

13.41	1.3	Melanie Wilkins		18.01.73	1	Oordegem, BEL	10	Aug
		13.51	-2.3		4	Birmingham	16	Jun
		13.54	0.4		1	Celle Ligure, ITA	17	Jul
		13.59	-1.4		1	London (CP)	2	Jun
13.53	-0.4	Keri Maddox		4.07.72	1	Palafrugell, SPA	19	Jun
		13.57	1.3		1	Kunzelsau, GER	7	Sep
		13.58			1	Birmingham	1	Jun
		13.60	-2.3		5	Birmingham	16	Jun
13.59	1.6	Jane Hale	U23	4.01.74	2	Loughborough	19	May

41 performances to 13.60 by 8 athletes

13.65	-0.4	Clova Court	V35	10.02.60	2	Birmingham	20	Jul
13.74	1.9	Natasha Danvers	U20	19.09.77	1h2	Bedford	28	Jul
	(10)							
13.80		Michelle Campbell		24.02.69	2	Riverside, USA	24	May
13.86	-0.7	Katy Sketchley		9.07.73	2	Bedford	26	May
13.90	1.7	Vikki Schofield		29.12.72	3	Sheffield	12	May
13.95	1.9	Denise Bolton	U20	1.02.77	2h2	Bedford	28	Jul
14.04	1.8	Kerry Jury		19.11.68	1H	Narbonne, FRA	27	Jul
14.08	0.8	Julie Pratt	U20	20.03.79	3	Bedford	28	Jul
14.10	0.8	Liz Fairs	U20	1.12.77	4	Bedford	28	Jul
14.16	1.8	Pauline Richards		30.06.68	H	Narbonne, FRA	27	Jul
14.21	-0.3	Bethan Edwards		2.05.73	2	Cardiff	25	May
14.22	0.6	Tracy Joseph		29.11.69	1	Portsmouth	11	May
	(20)							
14.30	0.5	Anne Hollman	U23	18.02.74	1H	Bedford	25	May
14.34	0.2	Kate Forsyth	U20	5.06.79	3	Cudworth	30	Jun
14.35	-1.1	Kim Crowther-Price		19.01.66	3	Sheffield	2	Jun
14.39	0.6	Jocelyn Harwood	V35	21.11.57	1rB	Gateshead	31	Aug
14.40	-0.3	Rachel King	U23	11.05.76	3	Cardiff	25	May
14.41	1.4	Susan Jones	U20	8.06.78	1H	Sheffield	27	Apr
14.42	1.2	Rebecca Lewis	U20	31.12.77	H	Narbonne, FRA	27	Jul
14.46	-0.4	Bianca Liston	U20	28.05.78	5	Birmingham	20	Jul
14.49	0.4	Louise Batho	U23	27.11.76	2	Zoetermeer, HOL	7	Jul
14.51	0.2	Nicola Gautier	U20	21.03.78	3H	Narbonne, FRA	27	Jul
	(30)							
14.55	-0.7	Michala Gee	U23	8.12.75	4	Bedford	25	May
14.56		Non Evans		27.02.67	1	Neath	28	Apr
14.57		Teresa Copeland		8.03.69	2	Bedford	7	Sep
14.63	0.5	Kelly Sotherton	U23	13.11.76	3H	Bedford	25	May
14.63	0.5	Diana Bennett	U23	14.06.74	4H	Bedford	25	May
14.66	0.6	Joanne Suddes	U20	27.01.77	2	Gateshead	31	Aug
14.72	1.2	Emma Anderson	U20	19.06.79	3h1	Sheffield	12	Jul
14.74	0.5	Charmaine Johnson		4.06.63	6H	Bedford	25	May
14.76	1.2	Abigail Ashby	U20	23.11.77	4h1	Sheffield	12	Jul
14.77	1.2	Leanne Buxton	U20	27.05.78	1	Crawley	11	May
	(40)							
14.77	-0.7	Kay Reynolds		15.09.67	6	Bedford	26	May
14.78	0.7	Lorraine Brackstone	U20	15.02.78	4h1	Bedford	28	Jul
14.79	0.4	Samantha Male	U23	11.04.76	5	Zoetermeer, HOL	7	Jul
14.81	2.0	Lisa Williams	U20	11.04.78	5h2	Sheffield	12	Jul
14.82	1.9	Katy Lestrange	U17	17.09.79	6h2	Bedford	28	Jul
14.85	0.1	Julia Bennett		26.03.70	6H	Narbonne, FRA	27	Jul
14.87	1.2	Angie Nyhan	U20	13.04.78	4H	Narbonne, FRA	27	Jul
14.89	1.9	Claire Pearson	U20	23.09.78	7h2	Bedford	28	Jul
14.91	0.6	Clare Wise		22.08.69	2	Portsmouth	11	May
14.96	2.0	Clover Wynter-Pink	U20	29.11.77	6h2	Sheffield	12	Jul
	(50)							
14.98	-0.4	Clare Bushby	U23	7.09.76	2	Glasgow	29	Jun
14.98	-0.6	Tamsin Stephens	U17	2.08.80	2H	Antrim	31	Aug
15.01	-3.6	Sharon Price	U23	10.12.75	1	Birmingham	21	Apr
15.02	-1.1	Helen Blanchard		11.07.72	5	Sheffield	2	Jun

15.03	1.2	Kirsty Mayhead	U20	17.02.78	6h1	Sheffield	12	Jul
15.03	1.3	Clare Adams		20.10.72		Kunzelsau, GER	7	Sep
15.06	-0.4	Gillian Stewart	U17	21.01.80	3	Glasgow	29	Jun
15.13	-1.4	Alison McDonnell		28.06.72	6	London (CP)	1	Jun
15.14	-1.5	Sarah Damm		12.09.70	6r3	Milan, ITA	19	May
15.14	0.5	Rachel Stannard	U20	28.03.78	1	Carmarthen	16	Jul
	(60)							
15.14		Wendy Laing		29.12.62	1H	Blackpool	27	Jul
15.15	1.2	Debbie Woolgar		10.03.65	1	Crawley	11	May
15.15		Jackie Cooke	U23	20.06.76	4	Birmingham	1	Jun
15.18		Claire White		24.02.73	3h1	Bedford	26	May
15.19	-0.6	Julie Hollman	U20	16.02.77	3H	Antrim	31	Aug
15.21	0.5	Emma Lindsay		11.04.71	7H	Bedford	25	May
15.23		Jackie Jenner	U23	25.10.76	1	London (CP)	11	May
15.26	-0.4	Elaine Donald	U23	30.04.74	4	Glasgow	29	Jun

Wind Assisted

12.95	2.3	Thorp		(12.80)	1	Gateshead	30	Jun
		13.09	2.7		3	Madrid, SPA	2	Jun
13.13	2.3	Diane Allahgreen	U23	(13.27)	2	Gateshead	30	Jun
13.23	2.3	Melanie Wilkins		(13.41)	5	Gateshead	30	Jun
		13.40	3.2		2	Basel, SWZ	25	May
		13.50	3.0		1h1	Oordegem, BEL	10	Aug
13.38	2.5	Sam Farquharson		(13.40)	4h2	Chemnitz, GER	19	May
13.36	2.3	Agyepong		(13.18)	6	Gateshead	30	Jun
13.39	3.2	Keri Maddox		(13.53)	1	Basel, SWZ	25	May
		13.51	2.3		7	Gateshead	30	Jun

10 performances to 13.60 by 6 athletes

13.61	3.7	Michelle Campbell		(13.80)	3	Azusa, USA	13	Apr
13.72	2.2	Katy Sketchley		(13.86)	1	London (He)	1	Sep
13.79	3.4	Vikki Schofield		(13.90)	2H	Alhama, SPA	4	May
13.95	3.5	Kerry Jury		(14.04)	1H	Bedford	25	May
14.17	5.2	Sarah Damm		(15.14)	2H	Alhama, SPA	4	May
14.27	2.6	Kim Crowther-Price		(14.35)	4H	Bedford	25	May
14.30	2.7	Kate Forsyth	U20	(14.34)	4	Sheffield	13	Jul
14.38	2.7	Bianca Liston	U20	(14.46)	5	Sheffield	13	Jul
14.43	5.2	Julia Bennett		(14.85)	4H	Alhama, SPA	4	May
14.59	2.6	Emma Beales		7.12.71	6H	Bedford	25	May
14.66	2.7	Emma Anderson	U20	(14.72)	2	Stoke	22	Jun
14.67	2.2	Margaret Still		9.05.65	4	London (He)	1	Sep
15.00	2.5	Katie Jones	U20	4.01.77	4	Edinburgh	4	May
15.00	3.2	Belinda Samuels	U20	29.11.78	1rB	Birmingham	7	Jul
15.19	2.5	Katy Bartlett		6.05.73	5	Edinburgh	4	May
15.19	2.4	Jackie Tindal	U20	21.01.79	1H	Ayr	20	Jul

Hand Timing

13.3		Michelle Campbell		(13.80)	5r2	Walnut, USA	21	Apr
13.3 w	3.0	Clova Court	V35	(13.65)	1	London (He)	31	Aug
		(13.30 photo electric timing)						
		13.6	-1.5		2	La Spezia, ITA	21	Sep
13.3 w	3.0	Agyepong		(13.18)	2	London (He)	31	Aug
13.4	0.2	Thorp		(12.80)	1	Watford	6	May
13.5	1.8	Keri Maddox		(13.53)	1	Loughborough	5	Jun
13.5 w	2.3	Wilkins		(13.41)	1	London (He)	6	Jul

6 performances to 13.5 by 6 athletes including 3 wind assisted

13.7	2.3	Louise Fraser		10.10.70	2	London (He)	6	Jul
		13.8			1	Sheffield (W)	22	Jun
13.7 w	2.3	Denise Bolton	U20	(13.95)	2r2	Nembro, ITA	3	Aug
13.9 w	2.5	Kerry Jury		(14.04)	1	Leeds (South)	8	Sep
14.0 w	2.6	Bethan Edwards		(14.21)	1	Newport	1	Jun

14.0 w	2.6	Non Evans		(14.56)	2	Newport	1 Jun
14.0 w	3.0	Julie Pratt	U20	(14.08)	3	London (He)	31 Aug
14.0 w	2.5	Janine Whitlock		11.08.73	2	Leeds (South)	8 Sep
14.1		Anne Hollman	U23	(14.30)	1	Derby	23 Jun
14.1		Jocelyn Harwood	V35	(14.39)	1	Rotherham	10 Aug
14.1	1.7	Rachel King	U23	(14.40)	1	Kingston	18 Aug
14.1 w	3.6	Kay Reynolds		(14.77)	2	Abingdon	24 Aug
14.2					1	Bournemouth	25 May
14.2		Kim Crowther-Price		(14.35)	1H	Middlesbrough	29 Jun
14.3		Teresa Copeland		(14.57)	1	Hoo	20 Jul
14.3 w		Lorraine Brackstone	U20	(14.78)	1rB	Cannock	18 Aug
14.4 w	3.6	Samantha Male	U23	(14.79)	3	Abingdon	24 Aug
14.7	1.1				3	Croydon	11 May
14.4 w	2.8	Rebecca Lewis	U20	(14.42)	2	Blackpool	25 Aug
14.5		Lorna Silver	U23	10.01.74	1	Coatbridge	4 Aug
14.5 w	4.3	Gowry Retchakan	V35	21.06.60	3	Liverpool	6 Jul
14.7	1.7				4	Kingston	18 Aug
14.5 w	3.2	Katy Bartlett		(15.19w)	2rB	Manchester	17 Aug
14.7	0.1				2	London (He)	28 Jul
14.6		Emma Anderson	U20	(14.72)	1	Cannock	26 May
14.6		Clare Bushby	U23	(14.98)	1	Carlisle	14 Jul
14.6		Orla Bermingham	U23	7.10.75	3	Stoke	25 Jul
14.6 w	2.9	Katie Jones	U20	(15.00w)	1rB	London (He)	6 Jul
15.0					3	Gateshead	16 Jun
14.7		Margaret Still		(14.67w)	1rB	Pendle	6 May
14.7	1.1	Julia Bennett		(14.85)	2	Croydon	11 May
14.7	-1.5	Sharon Price	U23	(15.01)	1	Leamington	11 May
14.7		Cheryl Done		25.09.70	1	Portsmouth	2 Jul
14.7	0.1	Emma Beales		(14.59w)	3	London (He)	28 Jul
14.7		Sarah Claxton	U17	23.09.79	1	Cambridge	15 Sep
14.7		Alison McDonnell		(15.13)	1	Hemel Hempstead	15 Sep
14.7 w	3.0	Gillian Stewart	U17	(15.06)	5	London (He)	31 Aug
14.8		Kirsty Mayhead	U20	(15.03)	1rB	Southampton	27 Apr
14.8		Helen Blanchard		(15.02)	1rB	Cannock	26 May
14.8 w	3.3	Debbie Woolgar		(15.15)	2rB	Abingdon	24 Aug
14.9		Claire White		(15.18)	2	Rugby	28 Apr
14.9		Tracey Duncan	U20	16.05.79	1rB	Guildford	22 Jun
14.9		Clare Wise		(14.91)	1	Portsmouth	10 Aug
14.9		Elaine Donald	U23	(15.26)	2	Glasgow	25 Aug
14.9		Julie Hollman	U20	(15.19)	1	Peterborough	7 Sep
14.9 w	2.8	Allison English	U20	9.03.79	3	Blackpool	25 Aug
15.0		Paula Wilkin	U23	28.03.74	2	Hull	14 Apr
15.0		Stephanie Nicholson	U23	28.06.76	1	Bolton	16 Jun
15.0		Georgina Lee	U23	6.01.74	2	Carlisle	14 Jul
15.1		Rebecca Wiltshire		3.10.68	1	Barking	27 Apr
15.1		Michele Gillham	U23	8.10.74	2	Barking	27 Apr
15.1		Louise Schramm		18.12.71	2rB	Guildford	22 Jun
15.1	0.5	Jane Fuller	U23	21.04.76	2	Barking	23 Jun
15.1		Emma Green		25.01.64	3rB	Derby	17 Aug
15.1		Jackie Cooke	U23	(15.15)	2rB	Kingston	18 Aug
15.1 w	3.3	Wendy Laing		(15.14)	3rB	Liverpool	7 Jul

Additional Under 17

15.2		Yewande Ige		21.03.80	2	Norwich	27 Apr
15.2		Sarina Mantle		19.01.81	2	Enfield	10 Aug
15.2		Nicola Hall		14.12.79	2	Great Yarmouth	31 Aug
15.2		Eve Miller		1.12.79	2	Bournemouth	7 Sep
15.3		Clare O'Sullivan		8.05.80	2	Sutton	20 Jul

Foreign

14.5	1.1	Olive Burke	12.09.66	2rB	Derby	17	Aug
		14.81		1	Aldershot	26	Jun

300 METRES HURDLES - Under 17

43.08	Yewande Ige	21.03.80	1	Sheffield	13	Jul
43.2	Rachael Kay	8.09.80	1	Stretford	8	Jun
	45.61		1	Birmingham	7	Sep
43.80	Syreeta Williams	24.10.80	1	Birmingham	8	Sep
43.94	Laura Siddall	10.09.80	2	Sheffield	13	Jul
44.01	Sarah Akinbiyi	23.08.81	1	London (CP)	30	Jun
44.03	Tamsin Stephens	2.08.80	1	Pitreavie	10	Aug
44.07	Gemma Swetman	28.09.80	2	London (CP)	30	Jun
44.40	Lisa Whigham	14.08.80	2	Pitreavie	10	Aug
44.54	Lizz Mitchell	13.10.79	4	Sheffield	13	Jul
44.87	Nusrat Ceesay	18.03.81	1h2	Birmingham	18	Aug
	(10)					
44.97	Sara Todd	3.11.79	5	Sheffield	13	Jul
45.0	Carolynne Sutherland	4.09.80	2	Stoke	20	Jul
45.71	Julie Davis	16.11.79	2	Tullamore, IRE	1	Jun
45.78	Sarah Nicolle	12.01.80	2h3	Birmingham	18	Aug
45.9	Donna Porazinski	28.01.81	1	Brecon	1	Sep
46.0	Jo Hyslop	13.03.80	1	Solihull	30	Jun
46.0	Emma Reid	5.01.81	1	Dundee	7	Jul
46.01	Charlotte Randall	10.05.80	8	Sheffield	13	Jul
46.2	Sarah Porter	11.12.79	1	Kingston	27	Jul
46.3	Yvette Carlin	28.05.80	1	Leamington	11	May
	(20)					
46.3	Leanda Adams	7.12.79	2	Jarrow	2	Jun
46.39	Claire Gregory	12.01.80	5h2	Sheffield	12	Jul
46.39	Jennifer Farrow	16.10.79	3	Wishaw	13	Jul
46.4	Maria Bolsover	5.06.80	1	Mansfield	19	May
46.5	Lisa Thompson	25.04.81	2	Brecon	1	Sep
	46.57		1	Carmarthen	30	Jun
46.69	Heather Colquhoun	14.04.80	4	Wishaw	13	Jul
46.7	Carrie Hancox	8.08.80	2	Exeter	15	Jun
46.7	Natasha Davidson	8.09.79	3	Exeter	15	Jun
	46.83		5h1	Sheffield	12	Jul
46.7	Anna Leyshon	19.01.80	1	Aberdare	31	Aug
	46.85		2	Birmingham	7	Sep
46.75	Lucie Veitch	25.06.81	1	Cudworth	4	Aug
	(30)					
46.78	Serena Bailey	2.01.81	4	London (CP)	30	Jun
46.8	Laura Curtis	2.05.81	3	Jarrow	2	Jun
46.8	Maria Grantham	14.12.79	1	Middlesbrough	2	Jun
46.8	Sarah Stanley	22.05.81	1	Grantham	21	Jul

400 METRES HURDLES

54.65	Sally Gunnell	29.07.66	1	Birmingham	16	Jun
	55.29		2h2	Atlanta, USA	28	Jul
	55.35		1	Zagreb, CRO	21	Jun
	55.64		1h1	Birmingham	15	Jun
	55.84		3r2	Jena, GER	25	May
	56.03		3	Nuremberg, GER	7	Jun
	56.84		1	Madrid, SPA	1	Jun
56.43	Alyson Layzell	16.12.66	2	Birmingham	16	Jun
	57.39		1h2	Birmingham	15	Jun
	57.71		3	Dublin, IRE	9	Jun
	57.79		5	Lucerne, SWZ	25	Jun
	58.92		1	Newport	1	Jun

56.45	Louise Fraser		10.10.70	5	Birmingham	16	Jun
	56.67			2	Tallinn, EST	9	Jun
	56.87			1h3	Birmingham	15	Jun
	57.50			1	Luton	6	May
	57.53			2	Stockholm, SWE	18	Jun
	57.77			1h1	Sheffield	2	Jun
	57.85			1	Sheffield	2	Jun
	57.99			1	Loughborough	19	May
	58.10			1=	Bedford	27	May
	58.64			1	Edinburgh	4	May
	58.69			1h1	Bedford	27	May
56.61	Louise Brunning		6.03.72	4	Birmingham	16	Jun
	57.34			1	London (CP)	2	Jun
	57.67			2	Dublin, IRE	9	Jun
	57.83			2h2	Birmingham	15	Jun
	58.57			2	Loughborough	19	May
	58.99			2h1	London (CP)	1	Jun
57.03	Lorraine Hanson		22.04.65	2h3	Birmingham	15	Jun
	57.13			5	Birmingham	16	Jun
	58.24			1r2	Milan, ITA	19	May
	58.24			1rB	Nuremberg, GER	7	Jun
	58.92			4	Dublin, IRE	9	Jun
57.27	Vicki Jamison	U20	19.05.77	1	Bedford	28	Jul
	57.49			2h2	Sydney, AUS	22	Aug
	57.57			2	Sydney, AUS	23	Aug
	57.87			1	Belfast	22	Jun
	58.0			1r2	Nembro, ITA	3	Aug
	58.10			1=	Bedford	27	May
	58.41			2h4	Birmingham	15	Jun
57.78	Gowry Retchakan	V35	21.06.60	1h4	Birmingham	15	Jun
	57.85			6	Birmingham	16	Jun
	58.07			3	Ljubljana, SLO	26	May
	58.09			2	London (CP)	2	Jun
	58.34			1rB	Loughborough	19	May
	58.40			1h1	London (CP)	1	Jun
58.80	Sinead Dudgeon	U23	9.07.76	2h1	Birmingham	15	Jun
58.8	Allison Curbishley	U23	3.06.76	1	Sheffield	5	May
	59.47			3	Loughborough	19	May
58.85	Vyvyan Rhodes		5.05.73	3h1	Birmingham	15	Jun

50 performances to 59.0 by 10 athletes

59.39	Keri Maddox		4.07.72	1	Kunzelsau, GER	7	Sep
59.54	Sharon Allen		23.10.68	3h2	Birmingham	15	Jun
60.02	Margaret Still		9.05.65	1	Cudworth	4	Aug
60.21	Alanna Rowbotham		11.01.70	1h2	Sheffield	2	Jun
60.21	Kate Williams	U20	10.11.77	1	London (He)	10	Aug
60.28	Kathy Thurston	U23	2.01.76	4h2	Birmingham	15	Jun
60.28	Veronica Boden	V35	23.12.58	2	Cudworth	4	Aug
60.3	Tracey Duncan	U20	16.05.79	3	Manchester	17	Aug
	60.47			2	London (He)	10	Aug
60.31	Christine Amede		7.08.63	3	London (CP)	2	Jun
60.70	Jane Low	V35	26.08.60	1	Malmo, SWE	28	Jul
	(20)						
60.83	Clare Wise		22.08.69	4	London (CP)	2	Jun
60.87	Kate Norman	U23	1.01.76	5	London (CP)	2	Jun
60.9	Katy Bartlett		6.05.73	1	London (He)	28	Jul
	61.63			2	Edinburgh	4	May
61.0	Sara Elson		8.05.70	2	Hull	7	Jul
	62.98			2	Glasgow	29	Jun
61.1	Lorna Silver	U23	10.01.74	1	Dundee	28	Apr
	61.92			1	Edinburgh	12	May

61.19	Katie Jones	U20	4.01.77	2	Birmingham	20	Jul
61.45	Caroline Wilkins	U23	28.08.75	4h4	Birmingham	15	Jun
61.6	Alison Mahindru		15.07.68	1r2	Manchester	17	Aug
61.8	Jane Fuller	U23	21.04.76	2	London (He)	28	Jul
62.98				4h1	Sheffield	2	Jun
61.93	Pamela Johnstone	U20	16.03.79	1r2	Edinburgh	4	May

(30)

62.12	Cicely Hall	U20	12.10.78	2	Sheffield	13	Jul
62.2	Michele Gillham	U23	8.10.74	2	Barking	27	Apr
62.31				6h2	Birmingham	15	Jun
62.23	Julia Sykes	U23	27.05.75	5h3	Birmingham	15	Jun
62.28	Dextene McIntosh	U20	27.08.78	3	Sheffield	13	Jul
62.3	Jo Mahoney	U23	22.10.76	1	Cannock	18	Aug
63.35				5	Cudworth	4	Aug
62.6	Kim Crowther-Price		19.01.66	2	Derby	7	Jul
62.7	Alison McDonnell		28.06.72	2	London (He)	25	May
63.02				5h1	London (CP)	1	Jun
62.8	Suzanne Barrington		3.08.71	3	Derby	7	Jul
63.57				6	Birmingham	20	Jul
62.8	Clare Adams		20.10.72	2	Coventry	11	Aug
63.99				4	Kunzelsau, GER	7	Sep
62.9	Carol Dawkins	V35	8.12.60	2	Barking	23	Jun
63.55				2	Aldershot	26	Jun

(40)

62.9	Emma Lindsay		11.04.71	4	London (He)	6	Jul
62.97	Jo Sloane	U23	2.12.76	5	Birmingham	20	Jul
63.0	Anna Roze	U23	6.11.74	4	Sheffield	5	May
63.26				3rB	Loughborough	19	May
63.0	Anya Hutchinson	U20	16.07.77	4	Derby	7	Jul
63.11				4	London (He)	10	Aug
63.02	Rebecca Simpson	U20	22.12.77	4h2	Bedford	27	Jul
63.03	Leanne Buxton	U20	27.05.78	5h2	Bedford	27	Jul
63.14	Cathy Yarwood		17.06.69	6h2	Sheffield	2	Jun
63.2	Cathy Dawson		9.03.66	1	St. Ives	22	Jun
63.27	Anne Hollman	U23	18.02.74	4	Bedford	18	May
63.28	Joanne Oates	U20	21.02.78	6h2	Bedford	27	Jul

(50)

63.29	Elizabeth Waters	U20	19.02.77	5	London (He)	10	Aug
63.4	Josephine Peet		4.12.71	6	Sheffield	5	May
63.51				1	Birmingham	2	Jun
63.4	Isobel Donaldson		24.01.64	3	Portsmouth	21	Jul
63.86				4	London (He)	31	Aug
63.43	Sarah Damm		12.09.70	1	Birmingham	21	Apr
63.5	Jodi Hallett	U20	8.11.78	1	Leicester	26	May
63.98				2	Birmingham	2	Jun
63.5	Caroline Blackburn		6.08.71	2r2	Manchester	17	Aug
63.78				3h2	Sheffield	4	May
63.5	Elaine Donald	U23	30.04.74	1	Glasgow	25	Aug
64.88				2	Glasgow	12	May
63.80	Emma Tomkins	U20	31.01.78	3	London (CP)	30	Jun
63.85	Eleanor Chamberlain	U20	17.04.79	4	Sheffield	13	Jul
63.9	Jackie Cooke	U23	20.06.76	4	Liverpool	7	Jul
66.55				7	Birmingham	2	Jun

(60)

63.9	Julia Bennett		26.03.70	1	Abingdon	24	Aug
64.0	Jackie Cambridge		17.11.63	7	London (He)	6	Jul
64.96				6	Edinburgh	4	May
64.2	Wendy Laing		29.12.62	2	Liverpool	11	May
65.10				8h2	Sheffield	2	Jun
64.2	Dyanna Clarke	V35	27.02.58	1	Milton Keynes	23	Jun
64.2	Sandra Leigh		26.02.66	2	Peterborough	7	Sep

64.25	Teresa Copeland		8.03.69	1	Bedford	7	Sep
64.4	Niki Pocock	U20	9.05.79	1	Kingston	25	May
64.64				3h1	London (CP)	29	Jun
64.43	Joanna Cadman		1.06.68	5	Edinburgh	4	May
64.44	Tania Taylor	U23	7.10.76	3h3	Bedford	27	May
64.7	Louise Eden	U20	11.12.77	1	Stretford	11	May
(70)							
64.7	Caroline Heaney	U23	3.04.76	3	Enfield	12	May
64.7	Virginia Mitchell		29.01.63	2	Crawley	28	Jul
64.75	Carolyn Smith		6.10.61	2	Edinburgh	12	May
64.90	Linda Gabriel		27.07.64	5	London (He)	31	Aug
65.0	Kate Bullen		12.02.71	1r2	Watford	5	May
65.1	Sarah Griffiths	U20	24.04.78	1	Windsor	22	Jun
65.24				2	Bedford	7	Sep
65.2	Sarah Baigent		22.12.71	3	Windsor	22	Jun
65.2	Helen Nunn		15.09.71	3	Crawley	28	Jul
65.27	Sally Sagar	U20	28.03.77	2	Cudworth	29	Jun
65.3	Yewande Ige	U17	21.03.80	2	Norwich	27	Apr
(80)							
65.3	Georgina Lee	U23	6.01.74	4r2	Manchester	17	Aug
65.33	Judy Thomas		20.01.63	4	Birmingham	2	Jun
65.5	Kate Haywood	U23	23.12.74	2	Telford	27	Apr
65.53	Debbie Woolgar		10.03.65	1	Crawley	12	May
65.6	Rachel Mason	U20	10.06.77	1	Scunthorpe	12	May
65.6	Marie Griffiths		4.10.68	2r2	Derby	7	Jul
65.7	Linda Crocker	U20	2.04.79	2	St. Ives	22	Jun
65.7	Celia Brown	U20	22.01.77	3	Abingdon	24	Aug
65.8	Sara Johnson		10.07.70	2	Colwyn Bay	9	Jun
65.9	Sarah Burke		11.07.73	2	Bracknell	11	May
(90)							
65.97	Amanda Wilding	U20	3.05.79	2	Portsmouth	12	May
66.0	Katie Challoner	U20	18.09.78	1	Yate	11	Aug

HIGH JUMP

1.94	Debbie Marti		14.05.68	1	Tallinn, EST	9	Jun
1.94				1	Birmingham	15	Jun
1.92				1	Helsinki, FIN	25	Jun
1.90				1	Ljubljana, SLO	26	May
1.90				1	Gateshead	19	Aug
1.90				1	Sheffield	25	Aug
1.89 i				1	Birmingham	10	Feb
1.89 i				1	Glasgow	24	Feb
1.88				1	London (CP)	1	Jun
1.86				2	Croydon	12	May
1.86				1=	Bedford	18	May
1.86				3	Budapest, HUN	20	Jun
1.85 i				2	Birmingham	4	Feb
1.85				19=Q	Atlanta, USA	1	Aug
1.84 i				1	Glasgow	21	Jan
1.84				4	Salgotarjan, HUN	11	Sep
1.92	Lea Haggett		9.05.72	2	Birmingham	15	Jun
1.90				2	Hobart, AUS	25	Feb
1.90				16Q	Atlanta, USA	1	Aug
1.89				1	Perth, AUS	18	Feb
1.89				1	Croydon	12	May
1.88				1	Sydney, AUS	8	Mar
1.88				2	Brisbane, AUS	14	Mar
1.86				1=	Bedford	18	May
1.85				2	Gateshead	19	Aug
1.85				2	Sheffield	25	Aug
1.84				7	Madrid, SPA	2	Jun

1.89	Jo Jennings		20.09.69	3	Birmingham	15	Jun
	1.86			1	Manchester	17	Aug
	1.84			1	London (TB)	29	Jun
	1.84			2	Jona, SWZ	11	Aug
	1.84			5	Salgotarjan, HUN	11	Sep
1.88 i	Julia Bennett		26.03.70	1	Birmingham	7	Jan
	1.88			1H	Alhama, SPA	4	May
	1.85 i			3P	Stockholm, SWE	8	Mar
	1.84			2	Loughborough	19	May
	1.84			1H	Bedford	25	May
1.87	Susan Jones	U20	8.06.78	1	Sheffield	12	Jul
1.86 i	Michelle Dunkley	U20	26.01.78	3	Birmingham	27	Jan
	1.86 i			2	Birmingham	10	Feb
	1.86 i			4	Glasgow	24	Feb
	1.85 i			1	Birmingham	4	Feb
	1.85			2	Sheffield	12	Jul
	1.85			2	Bedford	28	Jul
	1.85			Q	Sydney, AUS	23	Aug
	1.85			1	Great Yarmouth	31	Aug
	1.84			1	Loughborough	19	May
1.85	Rachael Forrest	U20	25.12.77	1	Bedford	28	Jul
1.84	Denise Lewis		27.08.72	3	San Donato Milanese, ITA	19	May
	1.84			5H	Gotzis, AUT	25	May
1.84	Hazel Melvin		19.11.73	1	Coatbridge	4	Aug

51 performances to 1.84 by 9 athletes including 10 indoors

1.80 i	Kelly Thirkle		29.03.71	2=	Sheffield	21	Jan
	1.75			2	Edinburgh	4	May
	(10)						
1.80 i	Nicole Smallwood	U20	9.10.77	2	Birmingham	17	Feb
	1.78			4	Sheffield	12	Jul
1.80	Kerry Jury		19.11.68	1	Cudworth	23	Jun
1.80	Alison Evans		13.12.73	1	Bristol	14	Jul
1.79	Hayley Young	U17	26.09.79	1	Grantham	11	May
1.79	Chloe Cozens	U17	9.04.80	1	Sheffield	13	Jul
1.76 i	Diana Bennett	U23	14.06.74	2	Birmingham	4	Feb
	1.76			1	Kingston	10	Aug
1.76	Antonia Bemrose	U17·	3.09.79	2	Stoke	20	Jul
1.75 i	Lee McConnell	U20	9.10.78	2	Glasgow	14	Jan
	1.75			1	Carmarthen	16	Jul
1.75	Fiona McPhail		23.06.71	2	Watford	5	May
1.75	Julie Major		19.08.70	1	Thurrock	12	May
	(20)						
1.75	Sara Veevers	U23	26.04.74	5	Sheffield	2	Jun
1.75	Katherine Livesey	U17	15.12.79	1H	Birmingham	21	Sep
1.74 i	Vikki Schofield		29.12.72	5=P	Valencia, SPA	27	Jan
	1.73			4H	Alhama, SPA	4	May
1.74 i	Emma Lindsay		11.04.71	1P	Glasgow	18	Feb
	1.70			2	Coatbridge	4	Aug
1.73	Julie Crane	U23	26.09.76	1	New Haven, USA	6	Apr
1.73	Laura Freeman	U20	22.04.78	1	Coventry	14	Apr
1.73	Beth Orford	U17	25.03.81	3	Sheffield	13	Jul
1.73	Leone Dickinson	U23	5.11.75	1H	Cudworth	15	Sep
1.72	Rachel Harris	U15	15.02.82	1	Stoke	22	Jun
1.72	Sophie McQueen	U15	3.12.81	1	Sheffield	12	Jul
	(30)						
1.72	Jenny Brown	V35	21.05.59	1P	Malmo, SWE	25	Jul
1.71 i	Kerry Saunders	U20	28.03.77	1	Glasgow	17	Mar
	1.65			1	Derby	14	Apr
1.71	Jane Lilford		28.11.70	1	Birmingham (Spark)	21	Apr
1.71	Kelly Sotherton	U23	13.11.76	1	Portsmouth	11	May
1.71	Michelle Smith	U17	28.05.80	1	Tweedbank	30	Jun

1.71	Judith Payne	U17	7.07.80	1	Wakefield	14 Jul
1.71	Emma Beales		7.12.71	1	Enfield	10 Aug
1.70 i	Emma Kerr	U20	15.10.77	3	Glasgow	14 Jan
1.70				1	Wishaw	13 Jul
1.70 i	Jackie Vyfschaft		15.12.64	4	Glasgow	21 Jan
1.70				2	Belfast	22 Jun
1.70	Laura White	U17	5.09.79	1	Oldham	14 Apr
	(40)					
1.70	Teresa Andrews	U20	4.01.77	1	Sheffield	4 May
1.70	Bev Howarth	U23	4.09.76	3	Blackpool	12 May
1.70	Basilie Moffat	U20	8.04.78	7	Sheffield	2 Jun
1.70	Nicola Baker	U23	8.10.74	8	Sheffield	2 Jun
1.70	Jenny Reader	U20	23.12.77	1	Portsmouth	8 Jun
1.70	Michala Gee	U23	8.12.75	2	Cudworth	23 Jun
1.70	Louise Gittens	V35	9.03.60	1	Barking	23 Jun
1.70	Nicola Richens	U17	26.10.79	2	London (CP)	29 Jun
1.70	Julie Hynan	U17	23.05.80	2	Cudworth	30 Jun
1.70	Ayamba Akim		21.06.72	1	London (TB)	20 Jul
	(50)					
1.70	Lisa Bennington	U20	12.12.78	1	Grimsby	11 Aug
1.70	Shelley Bradley		24.11.72	1	Coventry	11 Aug
1.70	Gillian Black	U17	27.10.79	1	Edinburgh	25 Aug
1.68 i	Kelly Moreton	U17	18.09.79	1	Swansea	25 Feb
1.68				1H	Aberdare	3 Aug
1.68	Laura Bolton	U20	13.11.78	1	Croydon	8 Jun
1.68	Ione Fraser	U17	28.10.79	1	London (He)	8 Jun
1.68	Rebecca Weale	U20	7.02.78	1	Exeter	15 Jun
1.68	Justine Gordon	U17	10.05.80	1	London (BP)	22 Jun
1.68	Jennifer Farrell		8.04.65	2	Tweedbank	30 Jun
1.68	Denise Gayle	U17	11.09.79	1	Harrow	17 Jul
	(60)					
1.68	Sharon Woolrich	U23	1.05.76	2	Hoo	20 Jul
1.68	Sarah Johns	U17	24.10.80	1	Hoo	10 Aug
1.68	Fiona Lapka		17.12.66	2	Enfield	10 Aug
1.68	Julie Hollman	U20	16.02.77	1	Peterborough	26 Aug
1.68	Tracy Joseph		29.11.69	2H	Antrim	31 Aug
1.68	Sam Foster	U17	9.09.79	2	Hornchurch	1 Sep
1.68	Anna Biscoe	U17	13.09.79	1	Ilford	7 Sep
1.68	Nicola Gautier	U20	21.03.78	1H	Birmingham	21 Sep
1.67 i	Charmaine Johnson		4.06.63	3P	Birmingham	3 Feb
1.66				H	Val de Reuil, FRA	29 Jun
1.67 i	Claire Everett	U20	25.06.79	1P	Birmingham	4 Feb
1.66				8=	Sheffield	12 Jul
	(70)					
1.67	Jo Morris	U20	16.10.77	1H	Hemel Hempstead	22 Jun
1.67	Emily Jackson	U17	16.10.80	2	Leeds	25 Aug
1.66	Emily Tugwell	U20	26.05.78	1	Exeter	25 May
1.66	Alison James	U20	9.03.79	1	Cheltenham	8 Jun
1.66	Angela Martin	U17	26.11.80	1	Jarrow	16 Jun
1.66	Michelle Smith	U20	1.01.78	8=	Sheffield	12 Jul
1.66	Lesley Buchanan	U15	15.11.81	1	Wishaw	13 Jul
1.66	Danielle Freeman	U17	11.02.80	3H	Birmingham	21 Sep
1.66	Samantha Adamson	U15	27.03.82	1P	Birmingham	22 Sep
1.65 i	Sarah Claxton	U17	23.09.79	1P	London (CP)	21 Jan
	(80)					
1.65 i	Louise Gauld	U17	24.08.80	3	Glasgow	3 Feb
1.65 i	Jennifer Hills	U17	25.03.81	2	Birmingham	11 Feb
1.65 i	Kirsty Roger	U20	24.03.78	1P	Glasgow	18 Feb
1.65				2=	Wishaw	13 Jul
1.65	Rosalind Shuttleworth	U23	25.04.75	1	Crawley	7 Apr
1.65	Jackie Powell	U23	1.05.74	1	Tonbridge	8 Apr

1.65	Keira Stout	U17	6.03.80	1	Braintree	21 Apr
1.65	Helen Wanstall	U17	13.11.80	1	Kings Lynn	27 Apr
1.65	Debra Harvey	U23	13.11.75	1	Enfield	27 Apr
1.65	Lisa Brown	U23	16.03.76	5	Edinburgh	4 May
1.65	Emma Bryan			2	Bebington	5 May
	(90)					
1.65	Nadia Brewer	U17	14.04.80	1	London (CP)	11 May
1.65	Kay Reynolds		15.09.67	2	Bournemouth	25 May
1.65	Laura Curtis	U17	2.05.81	1	Hull	8 Jun
1.65	Dextene McIntosh	U20	27.08.78	1	Gateshead	16 Jun
1.65	Kelly Vine	U20	26.07.78	1	Bebington	16 Jun
1.65	Gillian Evans	V35	16.12.56	3	Cudworth	23 Jun
1.65	Louise Gentle	U20	4.09.78	1	Luton	23 Jun
1.65	Gillian Stewart	U17	21.01.80	1H	Ayr	20 Jul
1.65	Sarah Still	U23	24.09.75	1=	Ayr	20 Jul
1.65	Jenny Walker		28.01.69	3	Hoo	20 Jul
	(100)					
1.65	Claire Farquharson	U20	28.12.78	2	Braintree	20 Jul
1.65	Rachel Hems		10.12.69	4	London (He)	28 Jul
1.65	Hannah Wise	U23	8.10.74	2	Crawley	28 Jul
1.65	Laura Redmond	U17	19.04.81	1	Coatbridge	4 Aug
1.65	Carolyn May	U23	15.10.74	2	Portsmouth	10 Aug
1.65	Michele Marsella		10.01.68	3=	Derby	18 Aug
1.65 i	Pauline Richards		30.06.68	1	Glasgow	15 Dec

Foreign
1.85 i	*Dalia Mikneviciute*		5.09.70	2	*Birmingham*	7 Jan
1.85				1	*Cork, IRE*	22 Jun

Additional Under 17 (1 - 30 above)
1.64	Laura Rogers		26.06.80	2	Telford	21 Apr
1.64	Laura Smith		16.11.80	4	Jarrow	2 Jun
1.64	Victoria Bradshaw		10.12.80	1	Canvey Island	19 Jun
1.64	Yasmin Hussein		22.01.81	1	Coventry	21 Jul

Additional Under 15 (1 - 4 above)
1.64	Holly Clift		29.11.81	1	Windsor	15 Sep
1.63	Cathy Young		14.03.82	1	Grantham	8 Jun
1.63	Alex Hewett		10.09.82	1	St. Albans	7 Sep
1.61	Clare Quigg			1	Antrim	8 Jun
1.60	Jodie Hearne		17.09.81	1	Ilford	27 Apr
1.60	Rikki Saunders		20.02.82	2	Barking	27 Apr
	(10)					
1.60	Jennifer Glaysher		3.05.83	1	Blackpool	8 Jun
1.60	Laura O'Sullivan		30.04.82	2	Liverpool	8 Jun
1.60	Natalie Clark		4.09.82	2	Hull	8 Jun
1.60	C. Middleton			1	Swindon	8 Jun
1.60	Katie Thackeray		23.09.81	1	Windsor	22 Jun
1.60	Clare Banner		25.04.82	1	London (CP)	30 Jun
1.60	Danielle Parkinson		2.09.81	1	Blackburn	31 Aug
1.59	Donna Maylor		20.05.82	2	Birmingham	8 Sep

Under 13
1.58	Stephanie Higham		26.12.83	1	Carlisle	27 Jul
1.50	Symone Belle		12.11.84	2	Kings Lynn	27 May
1.50	I. Robertson			1	Birmingham	1 Jul
1.50	Sarah Henderson		27.09.83	1	Braintree	20 Jul
1.50	Carol Barber		1.09.83	1	Swindon	14 Aug
1.48	Ruth Brooke		2.09.83	1	Windsor	30 Jun
1.47	L. Corbett			1	Oldham	14 Jul
1.47	Susan Crawley		1.12.83	1	Tamworth	18 Aug

| 1.46 | Sasha Sheard | 27.09.83 | 1 | Windsor | 15 Sep |
| 1.46 | Nicola Britton | | 1 | Cambridge | 15 Sep |

overage

1.50 i	Susan Crawley	1.12.83	1	Coventry	8 Dec
1.46 i	Emma Nield	20.11.83	1	Glasgow	1 Dec
1.46 i	M. McKinley		2	Coventry	8 Dec

POLE VAULT

4.00	Janine Whitlock	11.08.73	1	Telford	14 Sep
	3.40(o) - 3.60(o) - 3.80(o) - 3.92(ox) - 4.00(o) - 4.10(xxx)				
	3.91		1	Lincoln	28 Jul
	3.91(o)				
	3.91 ts		1	Salgotarjan, HUN	11 Sep
	3.86 i		1	Birmingham	11 Dec
	3.85		1	Wrexham	3 Aug
	3.80 ts		1	Epsom	4 Jun
	3.80		1	London (CP)	18 Aug
	3.80		1	Stoke	24 Aug
	3.80		1	Peterborough	26 Aug
	3.80		1	London (He)	31 Aug
	3.80		1	Leeds (South)	8 Sep
	3.80		1	Grimsby	29 Sep
	3.75		1	Birmingham	20 Jul
	3.75		1	Stoke	14 Aug
	3.75		1	Manchester	17 Aug
	3.73		1	Cardiff	25 May
	3.70 i		2	Birmingham	4 Feb
	3.70		2	Birmingham	15 Jun
	3.70		8	Hechtel, BEL	6 Jul
	3.70 i		1	Birmingham	27 Nov
	3.60 i		2	Wakefield	13 Jan
	3.60 i		1	Birmingham	28 Jan
	3.60		3	Loughborough	19 May
	3.60		1	Carlisle	14 Jul
	3.60		1	Sheffield	24 Jul
	3.60		1	Wrexham	27 Jul
	3.60		1	Cudworth	4 Aug
	3.60		1	Bedford	6 Aug
	3.60		1	Sutton	22 Sep
	3.50 i		1	Glasgow	21 Jan
	3.50 i		6	Birmingham	10 Feb
	3.50		1	Crawley	23 Mar
	3.50		2	Bedford	18 May
3.90	Kate Staples	2.11.65	2	Ljubljana, SLO	26 May
	3.85 i		1	Glasgow	24 Feb
	3.85 i		11	Stockholm, SWE	8 Mar
	3.80		1	Birmingham	15 Jun
	3.80		1	Woking	26 Jun
	3.75		2	Riga, LAT	2 Jun
	3.75		1	Toulon, FRA	6 Jul
	3.70 i		3	Birmingham	27 Jan
	3.70 i		1	Birmingham	4 Feb
	3.70 i		5	Birmingham	10 Feb
	3.70		1	Loughborough	19 May
	3.60		1	Bedford	18 May
3.70 i	Linda Stanton	22.06.73	1	Wakefield	13 Jan
	3.70 i		3	Birmingham	4 Feb
	3.70 i		4	Birmingham	10 Feb
	3.70 i		4	Glasgow	24 Feb
	3.60 i		1	Birmingham	6 Jan

(Stanton)	3.60				2	Loughborough	19 May
	3.60				3	Riga, LAT	2 Jun
	3.60				6	Stockholm, SWE	8 Jul
	3.50 i				4	Birmingham	27 Jan
	3.50				3	Birmingham	15 Jun
3.70	Rhian Clarke	U20	19.04.77		1	London (He)	10 Aug
	3.70				3	Peterborough	26 Aug
	3.65 i				4	Lievin, FRA	2 Mar
	3.65				1	Newport	1 Jun
	3.65				2	Birmingham	20 Jul
	3.60				3	Nembro, ITA	3 Aug
	3.60				2	Manchester	17 Aug
	3.50 i				4	Birmingham	4 Feb
	3.50				4	Loughborough	19 May
	3.50				1	London (He)	6 Jul
	3.50				1	Bedford	27 Jul
3.70	Paula Wilson		20.11.69		2	Peterborough	26 Aug
	3.56				1	Cannock	14 Aug
3.55	Louise Schramm		18.12.71		1	Guildford	22 Jun
	3.50				2	Bedford	26 May
	3.50				4	Birmingham	15 Jun
	3.50				2	Woking	26 Jun
	3.50				1	Croydon	20 Jul
3.55	Emma Hornby		12.12.73		3	Wrexham	3 Aug
	3.50				1	Stoke	24 Jul
3.51 i	Clare Ridgley	U20	11.09.77		1	Birmingham	17 Feb
	3.50 i				1	Aldershot	28 Jan
	3.50				1	Luton	6 May
	3.50				1	Bedford	26 May
3.50	Fiona Harrison	U15	30.11.81		1	Stoke	24 Aug

82 performances to 3.50 by 9 athletes including 22 indoors

3.30 i	Claire Morrison/Adams		30.05.69		2	Birmingham	28 Jan
	3.30				6=	Birmingham	15 Jun
	(10)						
3.30	Katie Alexander	U23	28.04.74		1	Hoo	20 Jul
3.30	Stacey Dicker		19.12.73		1	Exeter	7 Sep
3.20	Larissa Lowe		19.08.69		6	Bedford	26 May
3.20	Samantha Stapleton		13.10.73		3	Manchester	17 Aug
3.20	Kimberly Rothman		6.09.64		5	Peterborough	26 Aug
3.20	Rebecca Roles	U17	14.12.79		1	Aberdare	31 Aug
3.15	Maria Newton		22.07.66		1	London (WF)	20 Jul
3.10 i	Sue Drummie		19.06.71		2	Aldershot	28 Jan
3.10	Fiona Peake	U20	31.05.77		1	Loughborough	27 Apr
3.10 ts	Katharine Horner	U20	6.01.78		3	Epsom	4 Jun
	(20)						
3.00	Becky Ridgley	U17	26.02.80		1	Portsmouth	11 May
3.00	Dawn-Alice Wright	U23	20.01.76		3	Woking	26 Jun
3.00	Kirsty Armstrong	U17	14.05.80		4	Bedford	27 Jul
3.00	Tracey Bloomfield	U17	13.09.79		3	Birmingham	17 Aug
3.00	Danielle Codd	U20	17.02.79		5	Manchester	17 Aug
3.00	Elizabeth Hughes	U20	9.06.77		1	Hoo	1 Sep
3.00 i	Alison Davies	V35	6.04.61		1	Horsham	22 Dec
2.95	Sarah Hartley	U17	4.05.81		1	Stoke	24 Aug
2.90 i	Julia Cockram		1.01.68		11	Birmingham	4 Feb
	2.85				1	Aldershot	20 Jul
2.90	Claudia Filce		11.11.72		6	Manchester	17 Aug
	(30)						
2.80	Elizabeth Beckingsale	U17	20.03.80		1	Norwich	8 Jun
2.80	Suzanne Woods	U23	29.12.76		1	Loughborough	22 Sep
2.70	Bonny Elms	U17	30.10.79		1	Cardiff	10 Mar
2.70	Rachel Foster	U23	1.09.76		2	Sheffield	12 May
2.70	Liz Tapper	U20	2.06.78		1	Loughborough	15 May

2.70	S. Lane	U20		6	Bedford	18	May
2.65 i	Alison Ronald		20.01.67	2	Glasgow	21	Jan
	2.60			1	Edinburgh	11	May
2.60 i	Joanna Whitfield	U20	5.01.78	5	Birmingham	17	Feb
2.60	Gissell Reddy	U17	25.09.79	3	Guildford	22	Jun
2.60	Natasha Whitehead			5	Woking	26	Jun
	(40)						
2.60	Lucy Webber		5.02.72	1	Enfield	10	Aug
2.55	Louise Simpson	U20	18.12.77	1	Cudworth	29	Jun
2.50 i	Lynsay Perides	U20	24.05.79	6	Birmingham	17	Feb
	2.40			1	Harrow	27	Apr
2.50	Barbara Bannon		25.04.70	2	Exeter	25	May
2.50	Samantha Joseph		11.09.70	2	Croydon	20	Jul
2.50	Helen Croskell		22.11.72	1	Welwyn	10	Aug
2.50	Carla Waygood	U17	29.11.79	1	Woking	31	Aug
2.45	Sophia Pugh	U20	24.04.78	2	Loughborough	1	Jun
2.45	Ruth Anness	U20	3.10.78	12	Bedford	27	Jul
2.45	Laura Patterson	U17	31.01.81	7	Birmingham	17	Aug
	(50)						
2.45	Jane Bailey		5.05.70	1	Middlesbrough	28	Aug
2.45	Janet Lyon		12.03.62	1	Aberdeen	21	Sep
2.40	Kerren Austin	U23	26.02.75	1	Luton	12	May
2.40	Debbie Singleton	V35	5.10.58	1	Walton	25	May
2.40	Elizabeth Day	U20	2.05.77	1	Cardiff	5	Jun
2.40	Kim Hobbs	U20	12.12.78	1	Grimsby	15	Jun
2.40	Kia Wnuk	U15	31.10.81	1	London (CP)	29	Jun
2.40	Teresa Copeland		8.03.69	1	Liverpool	7	Jul
2.40	Eirion Owen		30.07.63	1	Brecon	7	Jul
2.40	Sharon Beattie		26.11.72	1	Liverpool	11	Aug
	(60)						
2.40	Penny Hall	U20	13.01.77	1	Kingston	18	Aug
2.40	Amanda Brown	U23	11.05.75	2	Bedford	7	Sep
2.40	Karen Crooks	U23	15.01.75	1=	Exeter	7	Sep
2.40	Leanne Mellor	U23	17.03.76	2	Leeds (South)	8	Sep
2.40	Rachel Fox	U17	25.02.80	2	Grimsby	29	Sep
2.40 i	Kirsty Roger	U20	24.03.78	2=	Glasgow	15	Dec
2.40 i	Gillian Stewart	U17	21.01.80	2=	Glasgow	15	Dec
2.35	Kate Rowe	U20	13.09.78	1	Peterborough	15	Sep
2.32	Jenny Cunnane	V35	23.02.57	1	Ashton-U-Lyne	11	Aug
2.30 i	Kirsty Calcutt	U17	26.08.80	5	Birmingham	28	Jan
	(70)						
2.30	Bev Howarth	U23	4.09.76	4	Edinburgh	4	May
2.30	Sarah Beckingsale	U20		2	Cardiff	5	Jun
2.30	Sarah Ramminger	U23	1.10.75	2	Pitreavie	9	Jun
2.30	Daisy Nisbit	U15	10.07.83	1	London (He)	7	Jul
2.30	Lauren Storey	U13	22.09.83	1	Cleckheaton	5	Aug
2.30	Gill Hevingham	V40	24.06.54	1	Exeter	9	Aug
2.30	Amie Everitt	U20	1.11.78	7	Peterborough	26	Aug
2.30	Judi Stafford	V40	9.06.53	1	Lincoln	1	Sep
2.30	Monica Basu	U17	7.09.79	1	St. Albans	7	Sep
2.30 i	Noelle Bradshaw		18.12.63	1	London (CP)	7	Dec

Additional Under 15 (1 - 3 above)

2.25	Megan Freeth		1.02.82	1	Swansea	16	Sep
2.20	Donna Evol		28.08.83	2	Stoke	24	Aug
2.10	Caroline Nutt		7.06.83	1	Scunthorpe	30	Jun
2.10	Stephanie Cooper		16.09.82	2	London (He)	7	Jul
2.10	Jo-Anne Nightingale		3.05.83	3	Woking	1	Sep

uncertain circumstances

3.60	Allie Murray-Jessee		13.01.67	1	Las Cruces, USA	1	Jun

unconfirmed

2.70	Barbara Bannon		25.04.70	1	Crawley	27	Apr

LONG JUMP

6.66	0.6	Denise Lewis		27.08.72	4	Madrid, SPA	2	Jun
6.60	-1.3				3H	Gotzis, AUT	26	May
6.55	1.6				1	Birmingham	16	Jun
6.54	0.8				7	Linz, AUT	21	Aug
6.49 i					Q	Stockholm, SWE	9	Mar
6.48 i					1	Glasgow	24	Feb
6.45 i					1	Birmingham	27	Jan
6.42 i					8	Stockholm, SWE	10	Mar
6.39	-1.9				4	Milan, ITA	19	May
6.35					1	Watford	5	May
6.34 i					4	Vienna, AUT	17	Feb
6.33	0.7				24Q	Atlanta, USA	1	Aug
6.32	0.4				8=H	Atlanta, USA	28	Jul
6.23	1.2				2	London (He)	31	Aug
6.22					1	Derby	18	Aug
6.47 A	-2.7	Ashia Hansen		5.12.71	1	Roodepoort, RSA	26	Jan
6.11	-1.0				1	Alfaz Del Pi, SPA	11	Apr
6.47	0.9	Joanne Wise		15.03.71	1	London (He)	31	Aug
6.42	0.2				2	Birmingham	16	Jun
6.40	1.7				1	London (He)	28	Jul
6.39	1.7				1	Birmingham	20	Jul
6.38 w					1	Birmingham	7	Jul
6.35					1	Coventry	11	Aug
6.31					1	Stafford	12	Jun
6.27	0.1				1	Kunzelsau, GER	7	Sep
6.34 w	3.0	Sarah Claxton	U17	23.09.79	1	Sheffield	12	Jul
6.27 w	2.9				4	Mannheim, GER	15	Jun
6.24	0.0				*	Mannheim, GER	15	Jun
6.23	-0.3				1	Bedford	27	Jul
6.22	1.7				1	London (CP)	30	Jun
6.22					1	Cambridge	15	Sep
6.20	-0.5				1	Stoke	20	Jul
6.22		Debbie Marti		14.05.68	1	Bromley	10	Aug

33 performances to 6.20 by 5 athletes including 5 indoors and 3 wind assisted

6.14		Vikki Schofield		29.12.72	1	Cudworth	23	Jun
6.13		Liz Ghojefa		24.02.69	1	Kingston	25	May
6.13		Tracy Joseph		29.11.69	1	Bracknell	23	Jun
6.10		Ann Brooks		4.05.71	2	Watford	5	May
6.08		Jade Johnson	U17	7.06.80	1	London (TB)	28	Apr
	(10)							
6.08		Jackie White		12.01.71	1	Tamworth	28	Apr
6.05 w	2.3	Julia Bennett		26.03.70	2H	Alhama, SPA	5	May
6.01 i					2P	Valencia, SPA	28	Jan
5.96					2	Croydon	20	Jul
6.04		Diana Bennett	U23	14.06.74	1	Guildford	22	Jun
6.03	0.3	Andrea Coore		23.04.69	5	Birmingham	16	Jun
6.03 w	4.6	Rebecca Lewis	U20	31.12.77	1	Sheffield	13	Jul
5.71					1	Crewe	11	May
6.00		Caroline Black		19.05.72	1	Edinburgh	12	May
6.00	-0.2	Ruth Irving	U23	20.07.74	6	Birmingham	16	Jun
6.00 w	5.1	Debbie Harrison	U20	13.11.78	2	Sheffield	13	Jul
5.63	-0.3				4	Bedford	27	Jul
5.95 w	3.4	Danielle Freeman	U17	11.02.80	2	Sheffield	12	Jul
5.92	1.1				2	Bedford	27	Jul
5.94 w	3.6	Sarah Damm		12.09.70	4H	Alhama, SPA	5	May
5.88 i					1	Birmingham	24	Feb
5.80					2	Birmingham	1	Jun
	(20)							
5.91	1.7	Louise Eden	U20	11.12.77	1	Sheffield	1	Jun

5.89		Julie Hollman	U20	16.02.77	1	Loughborough	27	Apr
5.88	1.7	Tina Malcolm		8.09.67	10	Birmingham	16	Jun
5.86 w		Donna Maylor	U15	20.05.82	1	Sheffield	13	Jul
5.86 w	6.3	Kate Rogers	U20	13.02.79	4	Sheffield	13	Jul
5.60					1	Cleckheaton	8	Jun
5.85	1.6	Kim Hagger		2.12.61	4	London (He)	31	Aug
5.84		Caroline Warden		16.09.72	1	Nelson	28	Apr
5.83 w	3.3	Lea Haggett		9.05.72	2	Perth, AUS	3	Feb
5.83 w		Kelly Sotherton	U23	13.11.76	1	Manchester	17	Aug
5.72					2	London (He)	6	Jul
5.82	-0.5	Pauline Richards		30.06.68	1H	Bedford	26	May
	(30)							
5.82		Michelle Dunkley	U20	26.01.78	1	Great Yarmouth	31	Aug
5.81		Janine Whitlock		11.08.73	1	Sutton	22	Sep
5.80		Elizabeth Gibbens	U20	5.04.77	2	Loughborough	27	Apr
5.80		Emma Hughes	U17	15.09.80	1	Bedford	7	Jul
5.80 w	2.4	Kerry Jury		19.11.68	2H	Bedford	26	May
5.71	-2.0				*	Bedford	26	May
5.78 w	2.7	Fiona Harrison	U15	30.11.81	1	Birmingham	18	Aug
5.62	1.2				1	Cudworth	30	Jun
5.77		Denise Bolton	U20	1.02.77	1	London (WF)	21	Apr
5.77		Karen Skeggs		26.10.69	1	Hoo	10	Aug
5.76		Connie Henry		15.04.72	1	London (He)	25	May
5.75		Joanne Dear	U23	8.06.75	2	Crawley	28	Jul
	(40)							
5.74 w	2.2	Nicola Short		30.10.69	1	Newport	1	Jun
5.70					1	Cwmbran	11	May
5.72 i		Emma Lindsay		11.04.71	1P	Glasgow	18	Feb
5.49	-1.2				1	Bedford	25	May
5.72	1.6	Lynne Draper		10.05.67	3	London (CP)	2	Jun
5.71	1.8	Caroline Stead		14.09.71	5	Birmingham	20	Jul
5.71 w		Linda Davidson		29.05.70	2	Aberdeen	9	Jun
5.70		Evette Finikin		25.09.63	1	Hoo	20	Jul
5.70		Jayne McCoy/Green		17.03.72	2	Leeds (South)	8	Sep
5.69		Kim Crowther-Price		19.01.66	2	Cudworth	23	Jun
5.69		Angela Abrams		7.05.71	1	Aldershot	20	Jul
5.69		Gemma Holt		20.12.72	2	Hoo	10	Aug
	(50)							
5.69 w	3.1	Teresa Andrews	U20	4.01.77	2	Newport	1	Jun
5.68		Sarah Hanson		25.11.72	3	Birmingham	2	Jun
5.68		Catriona Slater	U20	27.01.77	1	Southampton	20	Jul
5.67		Pamela Anderson	U23	16.10.76	1	Sheffield	6	May
5.67	-0.2	Anne Hollman	U23	18.02.74	4H	Bedford	26	May
5.67		Rachel Kirby		18.05.69	3	Jona, SWZ	11	Aug
5.66		Kerensa Denham	U23	8.03.74	1	London (CP)	12	May
5.66		Lucy Atunumuo	U17	4.11.80	2	Croydon	8	Jun
5.64		Rachel Barron	U23	10.05.76	3	Cudworth	23	Jun
5.64		Laura Smith	U17	16.11.80	1	Cudworth	4	Aug
	(60)							
5.64		Ruth Williams		18.03.70	3	Cudworth	4	Aug
5.64 w	3.3	Kelly Williamson	U17	4.12.79	5	Sheffield	12	Jul
5.50					3	Stoke	28	Jul
5.63		Jane Taylor	U17	18.02.80	1	Rotherham	21	Apr
5.63	1.6	Michala Gee	U23	8.12.75	5	Bedford	26	May
5.62 w		Cherone Fearon	U17	4.03.80	1	Stoke	22	Jun
5.46					1	Bristol	14	Apr
5.61		Aimee Cutler	U15	7.10.81	1	Pitreavie	10	Aug
5.61		Sandra Cull	U23	10.12.75	1	Nelson	1	Sep
5.60	-1.5	Paula Thomas		3.12.64	3	Alfaz Del Pi, SPA	11	Apr
5.60		Sarah Ramminger	U23	1.10.75	1	Dundee	27	Apr
5.60		Josephine Peet		4.12.71	3	Sheffield	5	May

5.60		Catherine Burrows	U23	11.02.76	3	Sheffield	6 May
5.60		Leigh Hubbard	U20	30.09.77	1	Corby	8 Jun
5.60		Katherine Livesey	U17	15.12.79	1H	Telford	23 Jun
5.60		Tania Findlay		8.11.70	1	Bristol	14 Jul
5.60		Emma Beales		7.12.71	3	London (He)	28 Jul
5.59		Margaret Veldman	U23	7.06.74	1	Sheffield	20 Apr
5.59		Chloe Cozens	U17	9.04.80	1	Luton	11 May
5.59 w	2.2	Helen Armishaw	U17	4.10.80	6	Sheffield	12 Jul
5.57					2	Cudworth	4 Aug
5.58		Nadia Brewer	U17	14.04.80	1	Worthing	22 Jun
5.57 w	4.6	Belinda Samuels	U20	29.11.78	6	Sheffield	13 Jul
	(80)						
5.56		Yvette Carlin	U17	28.05.80	1	Rugby	15 Jun
5.56		Sarah Lane	U17	4.06.81	1	Cwmbran	3 Jul
5.56		Jackie Jenner	U23	25.10.76	1	Welwyn	10 Aug
5.56		Debbie Woolgar		10.03.65	1H	Worthing	15 Sep
5.56 w		Rachel Peacock	U15	18.05.82	2	Sheffield	13 Jul
5.31	1.7				1P	Birmingham	22 Sep
5.54 i		Charmaine Johnson		4.06.63	1P	London (CP)	21 Jan
5.54		Teresa Copeland		8.03.69	2	Kingston	18 Aug
5.53		Stephanie Nicholson	U23	28.06.76	4	Watford	5 May
5.53		Veronica Boden	V35	23.12.58	1	Sheffield	22 Jun
5.53		Hayley Warrilow	U17	10.04.80	1	Solihull	30 Jun
	(90)						
5.53		Sally Evans	U23	14.05.75	1	Loughborough	11 Aug
5.52		Rebecca White	U17	5.06.80	2	Sheffield	22 Jun
5.52		Sarah Still	U23	24.09.75	2	Aberdeen	28 Jul
5.52 w	2.7	Gemma Jones	U20	25.02.79	3	Newport	1 Jun
5.51		Maria Morganella	U17	2.10.79	1	Liverpool	11 Aug
5.50 i		Amelia Martin	U17	11.02.80	1	London (CP)	24 Feb
5.50		Leanne Milburn	U20	16.08.79	1	Carlisle	4 May
5.50		Lucy Butler	U15	18.11.81	1	Jarrow	2 Jun
5.50	1.4	Yinka Idowu		25.02.72	12	Birmingham	16 Jun
5.50		Bianca Liston	U20	28.05.78	1	Derby	15 Sep

Additional Under 17 (1 - 19 above)

5.49	-0.6	Vicky Reynolds		22.04.80	2	Cudworth	29 Jun
	(20)						
5.48		Dionne Howell		10.04.81	1	London (TB)	27 Apr
5.46		Lynsey Church		10.05.80	1	Coatbridge	4 Aug
5.45		Denise Gayle		11.09.79	1	Harlow	16 Jun
5.44		Jane Cuddy		28.05.81	1	Liverpool	8 Jun
5.44		Joanne Cozens		9.04.80	1	Bedford	12 Jun
5.44		Sarah Fettes		26.08.81	1	Ayr	15 Jun
5.43		Elizabeth Sherman		15.09.79	1P	Woking	18 Aug
5.43 w	3.5	Denise Andrews		1.07.80	1	Birmingham	8 Sep
5.42		Tolu Jegede		25.09.80	2	Basildon	8 Jun
5.41		Laura Yeardley		21.12.80	1	Sheffield	8 Jun
	(30)						
5.40		Libby Alder		20.11.80	1	Yate	27 May
5.40 w	4.8	Caroline Pearce		1.09.80	14	Sheffield	12 Jul

Additional Under 15 (1 - 5 above)

5.48 w		Kerry Powell		28.02.82	3	Sheffield	13 Jul
5.25					1	Exeter	15 Jun
5.46		Lynsey Scott		28.01.82	2	Pitreavie	10 Aug
5.46 w		Rebecca Bates		16.05.82	1	Stoke	22 Jun
5.26					2	Jarrow	2 Jun
5.46 w		Tina Thirwell		5.09.81	4	Sheffield	13 Jul
5.26					1	Stretford	8 Jun
5.42		Louise Denney		2.01.82	1	Ware	4 Aug

5.36 w	2.7	Nnenna Ezeogu	11.10.82	3	Birmingham	18	Aug
5.19				1	Ware	26	May
5.34 w		Fiona Holmes	12.12.82	5	Sheffield	13	Jul
5.28	1.9			Q	Sheffield	13	Jul
5.29 w		Joanne Owbridge	19.01.82	8	Sheffield	13	Jul
5.20				P	York	22	Jul
5.28 w		Michaela Paul	27.10.81	1	Woking	27	Apr
5.22				1	Enfield	13	Apr
5.28 w		Rachel Hogg	11.06.82	9	Sheffield	13	Jul
5.26 w		Mandy Crompton	25.03.82	3	Stoke	22	Jun
5.25	1.1	Kate Brewington	15.10.81	1	London (CP)	29	Jun
5.25		Kirsty Corbett	16.05.82	1	Watford	4	Aug
5.24		Rebecca Shiel	16.01.82	3	Jarrow	2	Jun
5.24 w	5.0	Vicky Hyland	27.10.81	1P	Bedford	26	May
5.00	1.9			*	Sheffield	13	Jul
(20)							
5.21 w		Elaine Smith	16.05.83	10	Sheffield	13	Jul

Under 13

5.15	Monique Parris	28.01.84	1	Ipswich	9	Jun
4.99	Michelle Johansen	1.02.84	1	Abingdon		
4.94	Rebecca Geary	2.05.84	1	Yeovil	9	Jun
4.89	Susan Pollard	2.12.83	1	Tamworth	30	Jun
4.82	Louise Cook	7.01.84	2	Ipswich	9	Jun
4.81	Lesley King	28.09.83	1	Perth	13	Jun
4.78	Donna Chatting	30.10.83	1	Southampton	20	Jul
4.74	Kimberley Mann	23.10.83	1	Tamworth	7	Sep
4.72	Sarah Ashdown	18.10.83	1	Bedford	7	Jul
4.71	Siobhan McVie	6.07.84	1	Wishaw	14	Jul
(10)						
4.71	Claire Muddiman	9.09.83	2	Tamworth	7	Sep
4.70	Joanne Wilkinson	9.02.84	1	Wakefield	19	May
4.68	Hannah Wilhelmy	11.04.84		Southend	25	May
4.68	Gemma Belcher	22.10.83	1	Telford	25	Jun

TRIPLE JUMP

14.78	1.6	Ashia Hansen	5.12.71	2	Sheffield	25	Aug
14.67	0.8			1	London (CP)	11	Aug
14.64 A	1.0			1	Pretoria, RSA	3	Feb
14.58 i				1	Birmingham	10	Feb
14.57 i				3	Lievin, FRA	18	Feb
14.57	1.2			1	Madrid, SPA	1	Jun
14.55	1.9			Q	Atlanta, USA	29	Jul
14.51	1.1			1	Gateshead	19	Aug
14.49	0.0			4	Atlanta, USA	31	Jul
14.32 i				Q	Stockholm, SWE	8	Mar
14.25	0.6			1	Birmingham	16	Jun
14.21	0.5			2	Bratislava, SVK	29	May
14.17	1.3			2	London (CP)	12	Jul
14.15 i				4	Stockholm, SWE	25	Feb
14.14	0.6			1	Gateshead	30	Jun
13.93	-1.2			5	Lausanne, SWZ	3	Jul
13.27				1	London (He)	6	Jul
14.04	1.6	Michelle Griffith	6.10.71	1	London (CP)	1	Jun
13.78	1.6			2	Birmingham	16	Jun
13.73	-0.5			5	London (CP)	11	Aug
13.73	0.7			3	Gateshead	19	Aug
13.70	0.9			18Q	Atlanta, USA	29	Jul
13.67	0.4			1	Ljubljana, SLO	26	May
13.60	1.6			4	Stockholm, SWE	8	Jul

(Griffith)	13.58	1.4				4	Gateshead	30 Jun
	13.58	0.2				4	London (CP)	12 Jul
	13.51 i					1	Glasgow	24 Feb
	13.51	0.8				6	Sheffield	25 Aug
	13.46 i					2	Birmingham	27 Jan
	13.43	1.9				7	Bratislava, SVK	29 May
	13.40					1	Enfield	11 May
	13.35 i					9	Birmingham	10 Feb
	13.35					1	Bedford	18 May
	13.29					1	Watford	5 May
	13.18 i					1	Birmingham	4 Feb
13.55	1.4	Connie Henry		15.04.72	6	London (CP)	11 Aug
	13.18	0.4				3	Birmingham	16 Jun
	13.07					2	Enfield	11 May
	13.06	0.8				6	Gateshead	30 Jun
13.28	1.3	Rachel Kirby		18.05.69	1	Basel, SWZ	25 May
	13.03 w	2.2				1	Jona, SWZ	11 Aug
13.03		Shani Anderson	U23	7.08.75	1	Sheffield	4 May

42 performances to 13.00 by 5 athletes including 8 indoors and 1 wind assisted

12.72	-0.2	Mary Agyepong		3.10.65	6	Birmingham	16 Jun
12.67	1.3	Caroline Stead		14.09.71	2	London (CP)	1 Jun
12.61 w		Karen Skeggs		26.10.69	1	Abingdon	24 Aug
	12.49 i					2	Lievin, FRA	13 Jan
	12.42					1	Bracknell	23 Jun
12.58 w	2.8	Katie Evans	U23	4.02.74	1	London (He)	31 Aug
	12.40					2	Birmingham	20 Jul
12.55	0.7	Pamela Anderson	U23	16.10.76	1	Glasgow	29 Jun
(10)								
12.51		Kerensa Denham	U23	8.03.74	1	London (CP)	11 May
12.46	1.3	Debbie Rowe		8.09.72	1	Birmingham	1 Jun
12.36 w	2.7	Elizabeth Gibbens	U20	5.04.77	1	London (CP)	30 Jun
	12.26 i					6	Lievin, FRA	2 Mar
	12.22	1.1				1	London (He)	10 Aug
12.27 w	3.5	Evette Finikin		25.09.63	2	London (He)	31 Aug
	12.10 i					2	London (CP)	6 Jan
	12.00					2	Manchester	17 Aug
12.21 w	2.3	Justina Cruickshank	U20	27.09.77	3	Loughborough	19 May
	12.18	-0.9				5	Bedford	26 May
12.20		Jodie Hurst	U20	21.06.77	1	Stoke	8 Jun
12.20 w		Rachel Atkinson		26.05.73	1	Liverpool	28 Jul
	11.66					2	Sheffield	11 May
12.15 i		Fiona Watt		29.01.73	2	Glasgow	21 Jan
	12.06 w					2	Edinburgh	2 Jun
	11.91	0.4				3	Glasgow	29 Jun
12.13 i		Margaret Still		9.05.65	1	Sheffield	21 Jan
	12.03	-1.1				1	Sheffield	2 Jun
12.11 i		Caroline Warden		16.09.72	2	Sheffield	21 Jan
	11.93	1.7				7	Bedford	26 May
(20)								
12.07 w	3.0	Jo Morris	U20	16.10.77	2	Sheffield	13 Jul
	11.85	1.2				2	London (CP)	30 Jun
12.06		Liz Ghojefa		24.02.69	1	Kingston	25 May
12.04		Lea Haggett		9.05.72	2	Perth, AUS	4 Feb
11.82	1.1	Julia Johnson	U17	21.09.79	1	London (CP)	30 Jun
11.79	0.4	Michelle Dunkley	U20	26.01.78	3	Kunzelsau, GER	7 Sep
11.76		Lucy Clements	U20	20.07.78	1	Birmingham	9 Jun
11.75		Liz Patrick	U20	29.08.77	1	Aldershot	20 Jul
11.74		Stephanie Aneto	U20	23.08.77	2	London (WF)	20 Jul
11.71		Hayley Warrilow	U17	10.04.80	1	Solihull	30 Jun
11.60 i		Lisa Brown	U23	16.03.76	3	Glasgow	21 Jan
(30)								

11.59	2.0	Tolu Jegede	U17	25.09.80	2	London (CP)	30	Jun
11.55 w	3.5	Helen Baker	U20	5.02.79	4	Sheffield	13	Jul
11.38					1	Exeter	8	Jun
11.50 i		Catherine Burrows	U23	11.02.76	1	Glasgow	16	Mar
11.38					1	Birmingham	24	Apr
11.49		Marcia Richardson		10.02.72	2	Derby	18	Aug
11.48		Dawn Jones		16.02.70	1	London (EL)	27	Apr
11.48		Emma Hughes	U17	15.09.80	1	Luton	10	Aug
11.44		Syreeta Williams	U17	24.10.80	1	Brierley Hill	4	Aug
11.43	-0.7	Jenny Brown	V35	21.05.59	4	Malmo, SWE	24	Jul
11.40 w	3.5	Fiona Hunter	U20	14.09.78	7	Bedford	28	Jul
11.34 i					3	Birmingham	18	Feb
11.23					1	Edinburgh	12	May
11.37		Joanne Stanley	U20	30.03.77	1	Jarrow	18	Aug
	(40)							
11.37 w		Jayne Ludlow	U20	7.01.79	2	Cardiff	25	May
11.30	1.0				*	Cardiff	25	May
11.37 w	2.2	Kelly Brow	U20	24.09.78	6	Sheffield	13	Jul
11.24					1	Cleckheaton	8	Jun
11.36		Jane Falconer	U23	20.09.74	3	Cambridge	27	Jun
11.36 w		Becky Ridgley	U17	26.02.80	1	Portsmouth	11	May
11.08					4	London (He)	25	May
11.35		Rebecca White	U17	5.06.80	1	Sheffield	22	Jun
11.35 w		Sarah Wellstead	U17	22.10.79	4	Birmingham	18	Aug
11.07					1	Woking	14	Aug
11.32		Joyce Adams	U17	25.03.80	1	Derby	15	Sep
11.31		Maurine Okwue	U20	13.05.78	1	Portsmouth	20	Jul
11.29		Faye Woodham	U20	1.12.77	2	Hoo	10	Aug
11.29 w		Michelle Johns	U17	12.03.80	6	Birmingham	18	Aug
11.01	1.7				*	Birmingham	18	Aug
	(50)							
11.28		Milly Clements	U20	20.05.77	2	Crawley	28	Jul
11.27		Louise Eden	U20	11.12.77	2	London (WF)	21	Apr
11.27		Ruth Irving	U23	20.07.74	3	Bebington	5	May
11.26		Kerry Saunders	U20	28.03.77	2	Brierley Hill	4	Aug
11.23 ?		Emily Tugwell	U20	26.05.78		,BEL	14	Sep
11.13					1	Exeter	25	Aug
11.21		Marcia Walker		27.05.70	3	Sutton	22	Jun
11.19	0.8	Katie Budd	U23	3.01.76	3	London (He)	28	Jul
11.18		Catherine Barnes	U20	28.09.77	1	Watford	10	Aug
11.18		Katie Jones	U20	4.01.77	4	Manchester	17	Aug
11.17		Gemma Robinson	U20	30.12.78	1	London (CP)	12	May
	(60)							
11.17	-1.7	Kelly Williamson	U17	4.12.79	1	Cudworth	30	Jun
11.15		Angela Williams	U17	13.05.81	1	Southampton	21	Apr
11.15		Andrea Hall	U20	28.01.77	1	Colchester	28	Apr
11.15	1.7	Christine Bloomfield		12.02.68	4	London (He)	31	Aug
11.13 i		Stacy McGivern	U23	14.12.76	2	London (CP)	27	Jan
11.12					2	Luton	10	Aug
11.13		Teresa Andrews	U20	4.01.77	6	Sheffield	4	May
11.13		Natasha Faulkner		8.07.73	1	Bedford	14	Aug
11.08		Joanne Scott	U23	31.12.76	1	Jarrow	12	May
11.07 i		Natalie Butler	U20	25.11.78	6	Birmingham	18	Feb
11.04					3	Windsor	27	Apr
11.06		Clare Soper		26.11.72	2	Bournemouth	25	May
	(70)							
11.05		Isobel Donaldson		24.01.64	1	Portsmouth	2	Jul
11.05		Helen Croskell		22.11.72	1	Welwyn	10	Aug
11.05		Claire Dalton	U17	21.09.80	1	Great Yarmouth	31	Aug
11.04		Natalie Wright		13.11.73	1	London (BP)	20	Jul
11.03		Jenny Todd	U20	23.10.78	4	London (WF)	21	Apr
11.02		Sarah Ramminger	U23	1.10.75	2	Coatbridge	26	May

| 11.52 | | *Dalia Mikneviciute* | | 5.09.70 | 2 | *Stoke* | 28 | *Jul* |

Additional Under 17 (1 - 13 above)

10.97		Louise Mathie	7.03.80	1	Crawley	11	May
10.97		Fay Womersley	11.11.80	1	Lincoln	1	Sep
10.96		Leanne Taylor	19.11.79	1	Lancaster	15	Jun
10.94		Hayley Young	26.09.79	1	Grantham	11	May
10.89 w		Joanne Cozens	9.04.80	9	Birmingham	18	Aug
10.78	1.8			9	Birmingham	18	Aug
10.81		Sam Foster	9.09.79	2	Basildon	16	Jun
10.80	1.9	Claire Gregory	12.01.80	10	Birmingham	18	Aug
(20)							
10.79		Claire Lomas	18.04.80	1	Wishaw	13	Jul
10.65		Caroline Doyle	3.10.79	1	Watford	8	Jun
10.64 w 2.9		Jessica Sample	3.01.80	4	London (CP)	30	Jun
10.64 w		Leona Canning	12.04.80	12	Birmingham	18	Aug
10.61				1	Glasgow	12	May
10.63		Lucy Connelly	7.11.80	2	Rotherham	14	Jul
10.62		Angela Hutt	5.07.81	1	Glasgow	25	Aug
10.61		Sally Ash	4.11.80	3	Great Yarmouth	31	Aug
10.61 w 2.1		Alice Twomey	18.07.81	5	London (CP)	30	Jun
10.51				1	Bracknell	12	May
10.59		Mary Devlin	14.09.79	2	Belfast	31	Jul
10.57		Mary Onianwa	20.01.81	1	Portsmouth	10	Aug
(30)							
10.53	0.4	Vicky Reynolds	22.04.80	4	Cudworth	30	Jun
10.52		Louise Gauld	24.08.80	2	Ayr	15	Jun
10.52		Natalie Taylor	2.01.80	2	Glasgow	25	Aug
10.50		Jenny McDonagh	23.04.81	1	Antrim	25	May
10.50		Sharon Crowle	6.09.80	1	Salisbury	10	Aug

SHOT

19.01	Judy Oakes	V35	14.02.58	3	Halle, GER	11	May
19.00				2	Madrid, SPA	2	Jun
18.76				1	Luton	6	May
18.72 i				4	Stockholm, SWE	9	Mar
18.70				1	Crawley	6	Jul
18.65				1	Birmingham	16	Jun
18.65				4	Cologne, GER	16	Aug
18.63 i				1	Birmingham	27	Jan
18.59 i				1	Glasgow	24	Feb
18.57 i				1	Birmingham	4	Feb
18.56				Q	Atlanta, USA	31	Jul
18.51				1	Playa de Las Americas,SPA	21	Apr
18.50				1	London (CP)	18	Aug
18.40 i				1	Vienna, AUT	17	Feb
18.34				11	Atlanta, USA	2	Aug
18.33 i				1	Horsham	28	Jan
18.28				2	Hengelo, HOL	27	May
18.20 i				1	London (CP)	25	Feb
18.11 i				1	London (CP)	6	Jan
17.96 i				1	London (CP)	10	Feb
17.50 i				1	London (CP)	7	Dec
16.81	Myrtle Augee		4.02.65	2	Birmingham	16	Jun
16.53				1	London (CP)	12	May
16.46				1	Croydon	22	Jun
16.22				1	Bromley	23	Jun
16.17				1	London (CP)	2	Jun
16.02				1	Bedford	27	May
15.86				1	London (He)	1	Sep
15.58				1	Portsmouth	21	Jul

15.80 i	Maggie Lynes		19.02.63	4	Birmingham	27	Jan
	15.58 i			2	Birmingham	4	Feb
	15.53 i			1	Horsham	13	Jan
	15.50 i			2	London (CP)	6	Jan
	13.89			2	Playa de Las Americas,SPA	21	Apr
	33 performances to 15.50 by 3 athletes including 14 indoors						
15.24	Sharon Andrews		4.07.67	1	Thurrock	12	May
14.76	Tracy Axten		20.07.63	1	Abingdon	24	Aug
14.67	Jo Duncan		27.12.66	1	Bedford	7	Sep
14.66	Alison Grey		12.05.73	4	Birmingham	16	Jun
14.60	Philippa Roles	U20	1.03.78	1	Neath	4	Sep
14.48	Debbie Callaway		15.07.64	1	Edinburgh	4	May
14.43	Emma Beales		7.12.71	1	Welwyn	8	Apr
	(10)						
14.42	Vickie Foster		1.04.71	2	London (CP)	18	Aug
14.36	Denise Lewis		27.08.72	6H	Gotzis, AUT	25	May
14.09 i	Natasha Smith	U20	6.06.77	1	Birmingham	18	Feb
	13.80			3	Zoetermeer, HOL	7	Jul
14.09	Charmaine Johnson		4.06.63	1	Bournemouth	22	Jun
14.03 i	Nicola Gautier	U20	21.03.78	1	Sheffield	22	Dec
	13.69			1	Cudworth	4	Aug
13.88	Jayne Berry		18.07.70	1	Cardiff	25	May
13.70	Christina Bennett	U20	27.02.78	4	Nembro, ITA	3	Aug
13.65	Lorraine Shaw		2.04.68	3	Edinburgh	4	May
13.62 i	Carol Bennett	U20	11.01.77	1	Wakefield	15	Dec
	13.19			2	Sheffield	13	Jul
13.49	Emma Merry	U23	2.07.74	2	Loughborough	15	May
	(20)						
13.46	Julie Dunkley	U17	11.09.79	2	Croydon	22	Jun
13.45	Eleanor Gatrell	U23	5.10.76	3	Portsmouth (RN)	21	Jul
13.45	Debbie Woolgar		10.03.65	1H	Worthing	14	Sep
13.31	Clova Court	V35	10.02.60	3	London (He)	31	Aug
13.21 i	Helen Wilding	U23	25.10.76	1	Wakefield	13	Jan
	13.06			4	Sheffield	13	Jul
13.19	Sharon Gibson		31.12.61	2	Cannock	18	Aug
13.10	Cathy-Ann Hill	U20	4.05.77	2	Abingdon	7	Sep
13.03	Anna-Lisa Howard	U20	18.04.78	1	Barking	23	Jun
12.99	Irene Duffin	V35	10.08.60	2	London (CP)	12	May
12.99	Jacqui McKernan		1.07.65	1	Loughborough	1	Jun
	(30)						
12.98 i	Sarah Damm		12.09.70	2P	Valencia, SPA	27	Jan
	12.04			2H	Bedford	25	May
12.91	Navdeep Dhaliwal	U20	30.11.77	1	Glasgow	20	Aug
12.86	Mary Anderson		2.09.67	1	Pitreavie	9	Jun
12.77	Gaynor Haskell	U23	11.08.76	4	Windsor	22	Jun
12.74	Pauline Richards		30.06.68	3H	Bedford	25	May
12.64	Angela Lambourn		9.04.66	1	Northampton	14	Jul
12.54	Jenny Kelly		20.06.70	6	London (He)	6	Jul
12.45	Tracy Shorts		4.11.72	2	Glasgow	11	May
12.43	Kim Crowther-Price		19.01.66	1	Rotherham	11	Aug
12.35	Vikki Shepherd	U17	26.01.80	1	Ashton-U-Lyne	11	Aug
	(40)						
12.34	Shelley Drew		8.08.73	7	Loughborough	19	May
12.24	Bronwin Carter	V45	25.04.51	1	Portsmouth	20	Jul
12.23	Gillian Burns		12.07.64	1	Derby	14	Sep
12.18	Fiona Hunter	U20	14.09.78	1	Dundee	28	Apr
12.14	Fay Champion		27.09.66	5	Birmingham	20	Jul
12.06	Catherine Garden	U20	4.09.78	2	Carmarthen	16	Jul
12.03	Donna Williams	U20	7.10.78	1	Stretford	11	May
12.03	Sara Allen		7.12.70	1	Stretford	11	May
12.02 i	Joanne Holloway	U23	10.05.76	3	London (CP)	7	Dec
	11.86			7	London (CP)	2	Jun

11.99	Julia Bennett		26.03.70	3H	Bedford	25	May
	(50)						
11.98	Helen Arnold	U20	5.10.78	3	Hoo	25	May
11.96	Alison Moffitt		6.10.69	1	Antrim	6	Jul
11.95	Angie Nyhan	U20	13.04.78	1	Leeds (South)	7	Jul
11.95	Karen Costello		21.10.68	5	London (He)	31	Aug
11.91	Clover Wynter-Pink	U20	29.11.77	3	Watford	5	May
11.91	Claire Burnett		17.10.72	6	London (CP)	2	Jun
11.91	Rebecca Lewis	U20	31.12.77	1H	Antrim	31	Aug
11.89	Irene Timmis		28.03.65	1	Southampton	7	Apr
11.87	Jackie Tindal	U20	21.01.79	1	Pitreavie	10	Aug
11.85	Jane Aucott		10.10.68	2	Coventry	11	Aug
	(60)						
11.85	Louise Batho	U23	27.11.76	3H	Antrim	31	Aug
11.83	Lesley Brannan	U23	13.09.76	4	Cardiff	25	May
11.81 i	Lynne Barnett	U23	12.08.74	2	Glasgow	21	Jan
	11.41			1	Pitreavie	25	Aug
11.80	Cheryl Done		25.09.70	1	Portsmouth	3	Jul
11.78	Julie McCorry	U17	7.11.79	2	Pitreavie	10	Aug
11.77	Sue Grant		10.05.69	2	Leeds (South)	8	Sep
11.74	Alison Dutch		25.05.65	1	Edinburgh	20	Apr
11.73	Natalie Kerr	U17	17.11.79	4	Kunzelsau, GER	7	Sep
11.72	Sharon Nash	U23	5.05.74	1	Sutton	20	Jul
11.66	Alyson Hourihan	V35	17.10.60	3	Loughborough	15	May
	(70)						
11.65	Evette Finikin		25.09.63	2	Kingston	10	Aug
11.63	Eleanor Garden	U23	20.11.76	3	Edinburgh	25	Aug
11.62	Lucy Rann	U17	5.09.80	1	Portsmouth	11	May
11.62	Karen Martin	U23	24.11.74	_	Stoke	28	Jul
11.61 i	Vikki Schofield		29.12.72		Birmingham	4	Feb
	11.57				Cudworth	23	Jun
11.61	Amy Wilson	U17	31.12.80		Luton	21	Apr
11.60	Esther Augee		1.01.64	3	Guildford	22	Jun
11.57	Lorraine Henry		16.09.67	1	Kings Lynn	11	May
11.57	Heather Seager		4.04.68	1	London (BP)	7	Sep
11.51	Diana Bennett	U23	14.06.74	1	Bedford	25	May
	(80)						
11.46	Noelle Bradshaw		18.12.63	2	Portsmouth	11	May
11.43	Sarah Henton		4.05.73	2	Cannock	26	May
11.43	Lyn Sprules	U23	11.09.75	1	Peterborough	7	Sep
11.42	Lorna Jackson	U23	9.01.74	7	London (He)	31	Aug
11.40	Amy Burton	U20	24.06.77	1	Nottingham	11	May
11.40	Michelle Woods	U17	2.08.80	1	Birmingham	7	Sep
11.37	Claire Everett	U20	25.06.79	1H	Birmingham	1	Jun
11.35	Leigh Dargan	U17	31.03.81	3	Sheffield	13	Jul
11.35	Caroline Monk	U23	7.09.75	1	Coventry	21	Aug
11.34	Karen Smith	U23	10.02.74	3	Pendle	5	May
	(90)						
11.34	Karen Ostersburg		23.09.65	3	Cannock	26	May
11.34	Claire Archer	U23	30.09.76	1	Jarrow	24	Aug
11.31	Joan MacPherson	U17	18.09.80	2	Basildon	16	Jun
11.30	Vanessa Duffy	V35		1	London (BP)	29	Apr
11.29	Wendy Dunsford	V35	22.03.60	2	Exeter	10	Aug
11.27 i	Tracy Page		3.02.72	1	Birmingham	29	Feb
11.26	Natasha Mighty		21.12.70	1	Bracknell	26	Aug
11.25	Kelly Sotherton	U23	13.11.76	9H	Bedford	25	May
11.25	Glenys Quailey		28.02.65	1	London (WF)	1	Jun
11.25	Kerry Jury		19.11.68	7H	Narbonne, FRA	27	Jul
	(100)						
11.23	Ann Gardner		11.10.68	2	Corby	12	May
11.23	Frances Reid-Hughes	U17	18.03.80	4	London (CP)	30	Jun
11.23	Teresa Andrews	U20	4.01.77	2	Newport	7	Jul
11.23	Karen Smith	U20	25.12.78	1H	Hoo	21	Sep

11.44	*Kelly Kane*		*U23*	*28.10.74*	*1*	*Blackburn*	*13 Jul*

Additional Under 17 (1 - 10 above)

11.13 i	Leslie Foord		13.01.81	1	London (CP)	7 Dec
11.10	Eva Massey		22.12.80	2	Dublin, IRE	22 Jun
10.92	Angharad Lloyd		11.09.80	3	Pitreavie	10 Aug
10.77	Rebecca Chamberlain		7.09.79	3	Croydon	20 Jul
10.76	Elaine Cank		5.12.79	1	Bristol	14 Jul
10.70	Tuvola Akiwumi		15.10.79	1	Croydon	11 May
10.58	Kelly Mellis		4.12.79	1	Birmingham (Spark)	21 Apr
10.53	Sadie Buckland		11.03.80	1	Braintree	28 Apr
10.50	Louise Coomer		5.10.80	1	Gateshead	6 Jul
10.49	Farah Louarradi		11.10.79	1	Braunton	20 Jul
	(20)					
10.48	Emma King		25.07.81	6	Birmingham	18 Aug
10.38	Gillian Stewart		21.01.80	1P	Pitreavie	8 Jun

SHOT - Under 15 - 3.25kg

12.96	April Kalu		31.03.82	1P	Telford	23 Jun
12.21	Elizabeth Bowyer		8.09.81	2	Sheffield	12 Jul
11.48	Rachel Harley		1.01.82	1	Birmingham	8 Sep
11.36	Lesley Ann Roy		3.01.82	1	Wishaw	14 Jul
11.29	Emma Morris		25.01.82	1	Burnley	18 Aug
10.99	Kim Cannon		27.07.82	1	Basildon	2 Jul
10.96	Katy Ndu		26.03.82	1	London (PB)	25 May
10.93	Fiona Isherwood		24.09.81	1	London (BP)	7 Sep
10.78 i	Joanne Street		30.12.82	1	Birmingham	27 Nov
10.74	Lucy Marshall		28.11.81	1	Loughborough	11 Aug
	(10)					
10.74 i	Claire Smithson		3.08.83	1	London (CP)	7 Dec
10.62				1	Brighton	7 Sep
10.69	Kate Morris		18.01.83	1	Kingston	27 May
10.64	Maria Coats		4.10.81	1	Exeter	7 Sep
10.60	Liz Edwards			1	Wrexham	4 Aug
10.17	Lisa Thompson		3.12.82	1	Elgin	22 Sep

unconfirmed

10.73	Chidi Nwanokwu		27.10.81

Under 13

10.03	Louise Finlay		2.10.83			Aug
9.02	Claire Stewart		14.10.83	3	Ayr	15 Jun

SHOT - Under 13 - 2.72kg

10.52	Faye Brennan		13.05.84	1	Horsham	18 Aug
10.33	Louise Finlay		2.10.83	1	Aberdare	12 May
10.15	Saffron Perryman		26.03.84	1	Windsor	15 Sep
9.46	Natalie Hayward		3.11.83	1	Tonbridge	2 Jul
9.34	Fay Roberts		2.11.83	1	Colchester	28 Jul
9.33	Ebony-Jewell Rainford-Brent		31.12.83	1	London (TB)	27 Jun
9.16	Sarah Tindwell		19.10.84	1	Stoke	21 Jul
9.13	Nicola Britton			1	Kings Lynn	18 Aug
9.11	Claire Stewart		14.10.83	1	Inverness	8 Sep

DISCUS

60.04	Jacqui McKernan		1.07.65	1	Loughborough	1 Jun
	58.88			20Q	Atlanta, USA	28 Jul
	58.08			1	Lidingo, SWE	4 Jun
	57.24			1	Antrim	6 Jul
	56.30			1	Belfast	22 Jun

(McKernan)	55.66			2	Dublin, IRE	9	Jun
	54.68			4	Gateshead	30	Jun
	54.12			1	Birmingham	15	Jun
	53.78			1	Antrim	27	Apr
	52.74			10	Linz, AUT	21	Aug
58.56	Debbie Callaway		15.07.64	1	Loughborough	19	May
	54.58			1	London (He)	31	Aug
	53.54			2	Bedford	27	May
	53.38			1	Braintree	1	Sep
	53.10			1	Edinburgh	4	May
	52.98			1	Luton	6	May
	52.84			1	Bromley	27	Apr
	52.74			1	Windsor	22	Jun
	52.68			2	Abingdon	24	Aug
	52.52			3	Birmingham	15	Jun
	52.12			1	Southampton	8	Sep
	52.06			5	Gateshead	30	Jun
57.34	Shelley Drew		8.08.73	1	Loughborough	5	Jun
	55.02			1	Sutton	22	Jun
	54.86			1	Birmingham	20	Jul
	54.70			1	Sheffield	5	May
	54.22			1	London (CP)	2	Jun
	53.92			2	Oordegem, BEL	11	Aug
	53.68			2	Birmingham	15	Jun
	53.14			13	Halle, GER	11	May
	53.02			3	Loughborough	19	May
	52.94			2	Loughborough	15	May
	52.88			1	Rugby	26	Jun
55.88	Tracy Axten		20.07.63	2	Loughborough	19	May
	55.38			1	Milton Keynes	22	Jun
	55.02			1	Abingdon	24	Aug
	54.20			1	Exeter	25	May
	54.14			1	Loughborough	15	May
	53.90			1	London (He)	3	Jul
	53.58			1	Bedford	27	May
	53.26			1	Liverpool	7	Jul
	53.02			1	Southampton	20	Jul
	52.90			2	London (CP)	2	Jun
	52.86			1	London (CP)	18	Aug
	52.64			4	Tallinn, EST	9	Jun
	52.28			2	Luton	6	May
52.34	Lorraine Shaw		2.04.68	2	Edinburgh	4	May
	52.00			1	Kunzelsau, GER	7	Sep
52.10	Sharon Andrews		4.07.67	1	Thurrock	11	May

49 performances to 52.00 by 6 athletes

51.32	Philippa Roles	U20	1.03.78	3	Belfast	22	Jun
51.24	Nicola Talbot		17.02.72	1	Birmingham	1	Jun
50.70	Emma Beales		7.12.71	2	Milton Keynes	22	Jun
49.74	Sarah Henton		4.05.73	2	London (He)	31	Aug
	(10)						
49.64	Emma Merry	U23	2.07.74	4	Loughborough	19	May
48.82	Alison Grey		12.05.73	7	Birmingham	15	Jun
48.76	Rachel Hopgood	U20	2.06.78	5	Bedford	27	May
48.24	Lauren Keightley	U20	2.08.79	1	Bedford	28	Jul
48.08	Donna Williams	U20	7.10.78	1	Sheffield	12	Jul
47.74	Rosanne Lister		9.05.69	1	Bromley	23	Jun
46.22	Susan Freebairn		22.08.65	1	Carlisle	14	Jul
45.52	Jayne Fisher		2.11.70	2	Cardiff	25	May
45.22	Vickie Foster		1.04.71	1	Exeter	25	Aug
44.52	Sarah Winckless		18.10.73	1	Cambridge	26	Jun
	(20)						

44.44	Natalie Kerr	U17	17.11.79	1	Birmingham	18	Aug
44.32	Myrtle Augee		4.02.65	2	London (He)	1	Sep
43.76	Jane Aucott		10.10.68	2	Coventry	11	Aug
43.56	Tasha Saint-Smith	U23	20.12.75	6	Loughborough	19	May
43.04	Tracy Shorts		4.11.72	3	Glasgow	11	May
43.00	Donna McEwan	U20	17.01.78	1	Leamington	11	May
43.00	Rebecca Hardy		11.11.68	1	London (BP)	7	Sep
42.66	Sarah Symonds		28.12.73	1	Rugby	28	Apr
42.66	Joanna Bradley	U20	23.08.79	1	London (CP)	29	Jun
42.62	Lynsey Herrington	U20	31.05.79	7	Bedford	27	May
(30)							
42.58	Claire Cameron	V35	3.10.58	2	Belfast	3	Jul
42.58	Susan Backhouse	U20	6.12.78	4	Sheffield	12	Jul
42.54	Eleanor Garden	U23	20.11.76	1	Aberdeen	9	Jun
42.44	Helen McCreadie	U23	10.05.75	4	Glasgow	11	May
42.26	Helen Wilding	U23	25.10.76	1	Bebington	21	Aug
41.70	Karen Smith	U23	10.02.74	1	Ashton-U-Lyne	11	Aug
41.66	Ayshea Everton		13.10.73	1	Leamington	11	Aug
41.48	Maggie Lynes		19.02.63	1	Playa de Las Americas,SPA	21	Apr
41.48	Jackie Wright	V40	8.10.53	2	Bracknell	7	Sep
41.46	Lorraine Henry		16.09.67	1	Kings Lynn	11	May
(40)							
41.12	Alyson Hourihan	V35	17.10.60	3	Loughborough	15	May
41.08	Jennifer Hewitt	U17	8.01.80	1	Eastbourne	20	Jul
40.98	Kelly Mellis	U17	4.12.79	1	Leamington	14	Jul
40.72	Amie Hill	U17	9.09.80	3	London (CP)	29	Jun
40.70	Grace Apiafi			10	Birmingham	15	Jun
40.62	Jenny Hope/Cooper		1.09.62	2	Birmingham	1	Jun
40.56	Fay Champion		27.09.66	1	Bristol	14	Jul
40.56	Catherine Garden	U20	4.09.78	5	Edinburgh	25	Aug
40.40	Irene Duffin	V35	10.08.60	1	Hoo	20	Jul
40.38	Christina Bennett	U20	27.02.78	1	London (He)	7	Jul
(50)							
40.24	Rebecca Roles	U17	14.12.79	1	Swansea	7	Apr
39.88	Joan MacPherson	U17	18.09.80	3	Sheffield	12	Jul
39.76	Navdeep Dhaliwal	U20	30.11.77	4	Bedford	28	Jul
39.56	Sara Allen		7.12.70	2	Sheffield	2	Jun
39.36	Emma Carpenter	U15	16.05.82	2	Exeter	25	Aug
39.32	Kate Semus		18.01.70	1	Harrow	17	Jul
39.04	Laura Wood	U20	31.10.78	6	Sheffield	12	Jul
38.84	Alex Hajipavlis	U17	3.10.80	1	Stoke	22	Jun
38.82	Suzanne Last		11.01.70	1	London (CP)	12	May
38.42	Alison Faben	U20	7.02.77	8	Sheffield	12	Jul
(60)							
38.28	Carly Burton	U17	14.10.80	2	Sutton	22	Jun
38.18	Amanda Sheppard		26.02.68	1	Salford	7	Jul
38.16	Debbie Woolgar		10.03.65	1	London (WP)	27	Apr
37.80	Frances Reid-Hughes	U17	18.03.80	1	Braintree	21	Apr
37.78	Leanne Garvie	U20	29.08.78	1	Tullamore, IRE	1	Jun
37.76	Elaine Cank	U17	5.12.79	1	Gateshead	16	Jun
37.76	Carol Bennett	U20	11.01.77	1	Sheffield	22	Jun
37.74	Heather Seager		4.04.68	2	London (BP)	7	Sep
37.62	Victoria Bateman		6.09.72	2	Bristol	23	Jun
37.52	Karen Ostersburg		23.09.65	5	Coventry	11	Aug
(70)							
37.28	Joanne John	U17	12.11.80	1	Perivale	25	May
37.12	Lyn Sprules	U23	11.09.75	1	Peterborough	7	Sep
37.06	Tammy Nicholls	U20	21.07.78	1	Basildon	8	Jun
37.04	Imogen Martin	U23	13.02.74	2	Southampton	20	Jul
37.04	Maria Hood	U17	20.12.79	3	Exeter	25	Aug
36.72	Claire Smithson	U15	3.08.83	1	Sutton	22	Sep

36.62	Sharon Nash	U23	5.05.74	1	Windsor	27	Apr
36.60	Catherine Lane	U23	18.11.76	1	Hemel Hempstead	20	Jul
36.60	Wendy Thomson	U23	24.06.75	1	London (WF)	20	Jul
36.58	Michelle Wallace		1.11.72	2	Bebington	5	May

Foreign

41.28	*Alana Wallace*		*28.07.65*	*1*	*Belfast*	*31*	*Jul*

Additional Under 17 (1 - 12 above)

35.90	Rachael Cox	27.06.80	2	Gateshead	16	Jun
35.28	Vicki Clark	23.09.80	5	Bromley	22	Jun
35.22	Vicky Williams	11.03.81	1	Tamworth	8	Sep
35.10	Sarah Strickleton	10.05.80	8	Sheffield	12	Jul
34.56	Eva Massey	22.12.80	1	Antrim	21	Jul
34.50	Anwen James	17.02.81	3	Leamington	25	Aug
34.34	Michelle Woods	2.08.80	1	Barking	1	Sep
34.24	Ann Anstey	14.11.80	1	Welwyn	8	Sep
	(20)					
34.00	Laura Eastwood	7.04.81	1	Colwyn Bay	7	Sep
33.98	Rebecca Smith	11.10.79	1	Derby	11	May
33.96	Hannah Corneby	22.01.81	2	Tamworth	8	Sep
33.84	Julie McCorry	7.11.79	3	Antrim	25	Jun
33.70	Sarah Stubbs	31.07.80	1	High Wycombe	11	May
33.14	Vicki Scott	21.09.80	1	Stockport	5	May
33.02	Katie Franklin	24.08.80	1	Kings Lynn	11	May

Additional Under 15 (1 - 2 above)

35.88	Emma Kirby	11.11.81	1	Bracknell	4	Aug
35.56	Lesley Ann Roy	3.01.82	1	Edinburgh	2	Jun
32.20	Natalie Jones	21.02.82	1	Ryde	22	Sep
32.04	Lucy Marshall	28.11.81	4	Sheffield	13	Jul
31.86	Jenny Duff	29.07.82	1	Coventry	10	Aug
31.78	Candie Lintern	5.02.82	1	Crawley	26	Aug
31.24	Emma Sheridan	24.02.82	1	Hoo	10	Aug
30.98	Chidi Nwanokwu	27.10.81	1	Kingston	17	Mar
	(10)					
30.48	Kate Morris	18.01.83	2	Hoo	10	Aug
30.32	Emma Bailey	21.06.82	1	Ipswich	9	Jun
30.20	Ebony Hancocks	17.03.82	1	Birmingham	8	Sep
30.04	Jemma Kelly	13.03.82	1	Carlisle	20	May
29.88	Joanne Street	30.12.82	1	Wrexham	4	Aug
29.88	Kelly Goodman	16.03.82	1	Peterborough	7	Sep
29.84	Kate Wilkinson	13.12.81	6	Sheffield	13	Jul
29.60	Rachel Harley	1.01.82	1	Leamington	12	May
29.48	Debbie Richards	20.10.82	1	Cardiff	2	Jun

Under 13

27.26	Sian Howe	11.04.84	1	Basildon	7	Sep

DISCUS - Under 13 - 0.75kg

31.46	Sian Howe	11.04.84	1	London (TB)	21	Sep
28.08	Claire Stewart	14.10.83	1	Elgin	22	Sep
26.26	Tanya Hunt	14.09.83	1	Bournemouth	25	Aug
24.72	Jennifer Wright	21.09.83	1	Sutton	31	Aug
24.08	Colette Doran	20.09.83	1	Wishaw	5	May
23.90	Candace Schofield	3.11.84	1	London (TB)	28	Jul
23.80	Jody Cockcroft	14.09.83	1	Portsmouth	29	Jun
23.70	Saffron Perryman	26.03.84	2	London (TB)	28	Jul
23.66	Louise Finlay	2.10.83				

HAMMER

61.34	Lorraine Shaw		2.04.68	1	Edinburgh	4	May
	60.58			1	London (Col)	28	Apr
	59.84			3	Halle, GER	11	May
	56.18			1	Manchester	17	Aug
	53.20			3	Diefflen, GER	30	Mar
59.54	Lyn Sprules	U23	11.09.75	1	Colchester	26	Aug
	59.18			2	Hexham	14	Jul
	58.74			1	Peterborough	7	Sep
	58.08			1	Windsor	29	Sep
	57.96			1	Liverpool	7	Jul
	57.88			1	Luton	23	Jun
	56.92			1	London (CP)	18	Aug
	56.82			1	London (CP)	1	Jun
	56.58			1	Birmingham	20	Jul
	56.36			1	Braintree	1	Sep
	55.64			1	Crawley	7	Apr
	55.48			1	Luton	6	May
	55.28			Q	Birmingham	14	Jun
	55.26			1	Cardiff	5	May
	54.70			1	Oordegem, BEL	10	Aug
	54.16			1	Birmingham	15	Jun
	53.66			1	Abingdon	24	Aug
	52.62			2	London (Col)	28	Apr
	52.04			1	Kingston	20	Apr
	51.78			9	Halle, GER	11	May
55.00	Ann Gardner		11.10.68	1	Peterborough	26	Aug
	54.66			1	Wolverhampton	11	Aug
	54.30			1	Cheltenham	4	Aug
	53.06			1	Telford	14	Sep
	51.58			2	Birmingham	15	Jun
	51.56			1	Corby	12	May
	51.32			1	Milton Keynes	23	Jun
	51.12			1	Great Yarmouth	31	Aug
	51.08			1	Corby	3	Sep
	51.02			1	Redditch	26	May
53.26	Sarah Moore		15.03.73	1	Cardiff	25	May
	52.90			1	Newport	1	Jun
	52.36			3	London (Col)	28	Apr
	52.02			1	Yate	11	Aug
	51.96			1	Middlesbrough	1	Sep
	51.84			1	Bebington	5	May
	51.68			Q	Birmingham	14	Jun
	51.46			1	Exeter	25	Aug
	51.14			1	Belfast	22	Jun
52.06	Diana Holden	U23	12.02.75	4	London (Col)	28	Apr
	51.52			3	Birmingham	15	Jun
	51.32			1	Bedford	18	May
	47 performances to 51.00 by 5 athletes						
50.72	Esther Augee		1.01.64	1	Hoo	25	May
50.62	Helen Arnold	U20	5.10.78	1	Bedford	27	Jul
50.32	Irene Duffin	V35	10.08.60	3	London (CP)	1	Jun
49.80	Samantha Burns-Salmond	U23	13.04.76	1	Scunthorpe	11	May
49.52	Rachael Beverley	U20	23.07.79	1B	London (Col)	28	Apr
	(10)						
48.98	Liz Pidgeon	U20	27.04.77	1	Florence, USA	21	Sep
48.90	Julie Kirkpatrick		14.07.72	1	Dublin (M), IRE	15	Jun
48.78	Suzanne Last		11.01.70	2	Cardiff	5	May
48.32	Helen McCreadie	U23	10.05.75	1	Aberdeen	9	Jun
48.20	Marina Semenova/Peacock		12.07.64	2	Scunthorpe	11	May

47.70	Angela Bonner		22.11.73	1	Cwmbran	11 May
47.68	Catherine Garden	U20	4.09.78	1	Wishaw	13 Jul
47.18	Jean Clark		5.10.68	2	London (He)	6 Jul
47.08	Lesley Brannan	U23	13.09.76	2	Cardiff	23 May
46.84	Sarah Harrison	U20	1.03.79	2	Hoo	20 Jul
	(20)					
46.36	Fiona Whitehead		31.05.70	1	Haslemere	13 Aug
46.32	Janet Smith		7.10.64	1	Kingston	12 Jun
46.06	Caroline Manning		5.03.73	1	Guildford	30 Jun
46.00	Diane Smith	V35	15.11.60	2	Cleckheaton	24 Aug
45.22	Lindsey Jones	U20	8.09.77	1	London (He)	1 Sep
45.00	Andrea Jenkins	U23	4.10.75	1	Bedford	7 Sep
44.90	Joanne Eley	U23	12.01.74	2	Cudworth	4 Aug
44.64	Debbie Callaway		15.07.64	1	Hoo	10 Aug
44.54	Julie Lavender	U23	9.11.75	1	Middlesbrough	7 Apr
44.30	Myrtle Augee		4.02.65	2	London (He)	1 Sep
	(30)					
43.90	Vickie Foster		1.04.71	1	Andover	7 Sep
43.78	Suzanne Roberts	U20	19.12.78	6	Bedford	27 Jul
43.52	Christina Bennett	U20	27.02.78	1	Kingston	10 Aug
43.34	Leanne Jones	U23	13.05.74	1	Cardiff	15 May
43.02	Claire Burnett		17.10.72	1	Kingston	25 May
42.86	Louise Kay	U20	1.12.77	7	Bedford	27 Jul
42.70	Karen Brown		31.08.68	3	Cudworth	4 Aug
42.66	Zoe Derham	U17	24.11.80	2	Exeter	25 Aug
42.66	Philippa Roles	U20	1.03.78	1	Aberdare	31 Aug
42.42	Tracy Shorts		4.11.72	3	Aberdeen	9 Jun
	(40)					
42.38	Sally Giles		6.04.62	1	Watford	22 Jun
42.32	Louise Campbell	U20	22.02.79	6	Dublin, IRE	9 Jun
41.66	Sheena Parry	U20	16.11.77	1	Wrexham	17 Aug
41.48	Imogen Martin	U23	13.02.74	1	Welwyn	7 Sep
41.30	Marcelle Edwards	U20	9.01.78	1	Gateshead	16 Jun
41.04	Carys Parry	U17	24.07.81	1	Aberdare	24 Aug
41.00	Jenny Cunnane	V35	23.02.57	5	Sheffield	1 Jun
40.74	Helen Wilding	U23	25.10.76	1	Cannock	23 Jun
40.56	Rachael Cox	U17	27.06.80	3	Birmingham	17 Aug
40.40	Lindsey Oliver	U20	12.03.78	1	Liverpool	20 Apr
	(50)					
40.36	Annette O'Conor		20.08.71	1	Bracknell	20 Jul
40.08	Vicki Clark	U17	23.09.80	1	Hoo	14 Jul
39.84	Rosaline Elueze		28.04.67	1	London (BP)	20 Jul
39.58	Marian Simpson	U20	2.11.77	1	Aberdeen	26 Sep
39.36	Rachel Stott	U23	3.09.74	1	Cambridge	21 Apr
39.32	Rachael Dunn	U20	4.03.79	2	Birmingham	1 Jun
38.44	Fay Champion		27.09.66	2	Bristol	14 Jul
38.32	Dee Groves	U20	21.12.77	1	Wrexham	4 May
38.30	Kim Thompson		5.01.73	6	Middlesbrough	1 Sep
37.98	Beatrice Simpson	V40	17.07.55	1	Dartford	12 Jul
	(60)					
37.96	Michelle Fields		15.05.73	4	Peterborough	26 Aug
37.86	Janine Favell	U17	7.12.79	1	Bolton	11 Aug
37.68	Claire Fawkes	U20	24.10.77	2	Thurrock	11 May
37.58	Linda Low		20.01.71	3	Edinburgh	2 Jun
37.56	Catherine Lane	U23	18.11.76	2	Abingdon	18 Aug
37.42	Natasha Smith	U20	6.06.77	1	Feltham	10 Aug
37.36	Sarah Symonds		28.12.73	1	Rugby	28 Apr
37.00	Rosanne Lister		9.05.69	2	Southampton	27 Apr
36.94	Llyn Perry	U20	21.02.79	1	Ipswich	4 Aug
36.90	Nicola Roberts		22.01.70	5	Cardiff	5 May
	(70)					

36.82	Wendy Dunsford	V35	22.03.60	1	Malmo, SWE	28	Jul
36.82	Elizabeth Whittle	U23	23.06.75	5	Derby	18	Aug
36.82	Jenny Earle	V35	28.11.58	1	Corby	20	Oct
36.60	Maria Phillips	V40	8.06.52	1	Woking	22	Jun
36.56	Kelly Shepherd	U23	15.12.75	2	Cannock	23	Jun
36.54	Laura Wood	U20	31.10.78	2	Gateshead	16	Jun
36.34	Susan Freebairn		22.08.65	5	Aberdeen	9	Jun
36.34	Janet Corlett		31.07.63	1	Leamington	11	Aug
36.24	Carice Allen	U20	25.09.77	2	Telford	16	Jun
35.92	Gemma Johnson	U20	21.07.78	3	Bebington	5	May
(80)							
35.90	Anna Town	U23	22.04.75	1	Thurrock	20	Jul
35.90	Julie Delesaux		22.04.69	1	Abingdon	7	Sep
35.70	Cheryl Cunnane	U20	8.02.77	2	Rotherham	21	Apr
35.68	Bethan Deverell	U23	23.08.76	1	Colwyn Bay	11	May
35.58	Karen Moody		20.07.67	2	Cannock	18	Aug
35.40	Jenny Clarke	V40	19.10.52	1	Peterborough	14	Apr
35.40	Lindsay Ross	U20	27.12.77	1	Glasgow	9	Jun
35.36	Angela Lambourn		9.04.66	1	Mansfield	21	Apr
35.32	Rebecca Hardy		11.11.68	2	Salisbury	10	Aug
35.28	Kelly Roberts	U23	24.01.76	1	Colwyn Bay	7	Sep
(90)							
35.16	Sarah Etherton	U20	19.10.78	3	London (CP)	2	Jun
35.16	Alison Faben	U20	7.02.77	2	Abingdon	7	Sep
35.06	Ross Alexander	V45	21.07.47	1	Exeter	23	Jun
35.04	Kirsty Holland	U20	23.10.78	1	Glasgow	17	Jul
34.86	Cath Kingsbury			3	Wrexham	17	Aug
34.72	Gemma Rolfe	U20	18.12.78	1	Nottingham	25	Jun
34.42	Tracey Bater			4	London (He)	28	Jul
34.20	Siobhan Hart	U23	15.06.75	2	Aldershot	20	Jul
34.20	Claire Cameron	V35	3.10.58	1	Exeter	10	Aug
34.02	Lesley Shrosbee	V45	24.11.46	1	London (Elt)	27	Apr

Additional Under 17 (1 - 5 above)

32.92	Joan MacPherson		18.09.80	1	Enfield	28	Apr
32.80	Jennifer Ayero		13.09.79	1	Bournemouth	7	Sep
32.62	Jacqui Findlayson		21.01.80	1	Elgin	20	Jul
32.02	Kim Marsh		8.07.81	5	Birmingham	17	Aug
31.98	Anna Swan		20.04.80	2	Bracknell	23	Jun
(10)							
31.94	Gillian Staerck		22.09.79	2	Guildford	25	Aug
31.52	Lorraine Hewitt		8.01.80	2	London (PH)	7	Sep
31.34	Maria Hood		20.12.79	3	Harrow	7	Sep
31.18	Vicki Scott		21.09.80	1	Colwyn Bay	7	Sep
30.88	Michelle Ryan		8.07.81	1	Portsmouth	11	May
30.88	Clare Pardo		9.08.81	2	Guildford	25	Aug
30.76	Kelly Mellis		4.12.79	1	London (Elt)	10	Aug

JAVELIN

64.06	Tessa Sanderson	V40	14.03.56	1	London (CP)	12	Jul
62.88				1	Birmingham	16	Jun
61.24				2	London (CP)	11	Aug
60.78				3	Gateshead	19	Aug
60.76				6	Stockholm, SWE	8	Jul
60.64				1	Bedford	18	May
60.60				1	Cardiff	25	May
59.66				5	Sheffield	25	Aug
58.86				14Q	Atlanta, USA	26	Jul
58.18				4	Madrid, SPA	2	Jun

60.12	Shelley Holroyd		17.05.73	2	Birmingham	16	Jun
57.60				2	Bedford	18	May
57.58				1	Colwyn Bay	6	Apr
57.26				1	Luton	6	May
56.72				2	Cardiff	25	May
55.76				1	London (He)	6	Jul
55.66				1	London (He)	31	Aug
54.72				27Q	Atlanta, USA	26	Jul
54.06				1	Stretford	11	May
53.98				5	London (CP)	12	Jul
52.38				1	Liverpool	20	Apr
58.20	Lorna Jackson	U23	9.01.74	3	Birmingham	16	Jun
55.68				1	Edinburgh	4	May
52.10				6	Sheffield	25	Aug
51.64				3	Ljubljana, SLO	26	May
51.52				7	Halle, GER	11	May
56.50	Denise Lewis		27.08.72	3	London (CP)	11	Aug
54.82				2H	Atlanta, USA	28	Jul
56.16	Sharon Gibson	V35	31.12.61	1	Bedford	27	May
56.10				4	Birmingham	16	Jun
54.60				6	Halle, GER	11	May
53.30				1	Stoke	28	Jul
53.08				1	Birmingham	1	Jun
52.22				1	Cannock	18	Aug
51.68				1	Birmingham	20	Jul
54.44	Mandy Liverton		1.09.72	1	Exeter	24	Sep
53.74	Karen Martin	U23	24.11.74	1	Derby	18	Aug
53.56				1	Portsmouth	3	Jul
51.52				6	London (CP)	11	Aug
51.48				2	Hexham	14	Jul
	40 performances to 51.00 by 7 athletes						
50.96	Karen Costello		21.10.68	1	Liverpool	28	Jul
50.80	Janine King		18.02.73	2	Edinburgh	4	May
49.10	Alison Moffitt		6.10.69	1	Dublin, IRE	16	Jun
	(10)						
49.00	Kelly Morgan	U17	17.06.80	1	London (WL)	27	Apr
48.34	Onyema Amadi		28.06.73	1	Newport	1	Jun
48.18	Lucy Stevenson		30.01.73	2	Sheffield	2	Jun
47.86	Noelle Bradshaw		18.12.63	1	Aldershot	26	Jun
47.76	Kirsty Morrison	U23	28.10.75	1	Bromley	23	Jun
47.68	Katherine Evans	U20	19.11.77	2	Birmingham	1	Jun
47.54	Katie Granger	U23	31.03.75	2	Exeter	24	Sep
47.32	Tammie Francis	U20	14.11.78	1	Croydon	20	Jul
47.04	Louise Smith	U20	11.07.77	1	London (CP)	30	Jun
45.90	Jenny Kemp	U17	18.02.80	5	Bedford	27	May
	(20)						
45.74	Sian Lax	U20	4.08.79	1	Telford	21	Apr
45.62	Tammy Carless	U20	10.01.77	1	Woodford	4	Aug
45.52	Jo Burton	U23	11.05.75	1	Bournemouth	11	May
45.48	Anna Bloxsome		17.04.73	1	Bracknell	23	Jun
45.46	Wendy Newman		31.08.71	3	Luton	6	May
45.32	Lucy Rann	U17	5.09.80	1	Crawley	26	Aug
45.26	Clova Court	V35	10.02.60	1	Watford	5	May
45.20	Paula Blank	U20	13.12.77	6	Bedford	27	May
45.04	Michelle Fields		15.05.73	3	Edinburgh	4	May
44.64	Linda Gray		23.03.71	1	Barking	23	Jun
	(30)						
44.24	Katrina Campbell		8.03.72	2	Dublin, IRE	16	Jun
43.78	Katie Amos	U20	13.11.78	1	Thurrock	20	Jul
43.76	Donna Loveland	U20	28.06.78	1	Ilford	7	Sep
43.64	Jenna Allen	U20	2.05.79	2	Loughborough	5	Jun
43.52	Emma Rich	U20	14.05.77	4	London (CP)	2	Jun

43.38	Nicky Cobb		2.11.71	1	Bracknell	12 May
43.24	Liz Pidgeon	U20	27.04.77		Wilmington, USA	9 Mar
43.20	Helen Potter	U23	25.06.74	5	Manchester	17 Aug
42.64	Joanne Walker	U20	2.03.78	1	Carmarthen	16 Jul
42.54	Emma Beales		7.12.71	1	London (He)	28 Jul
	(40)					
41.60	Sarah Simmans	U20	29.11.78	1	Oldham	7 Jul
41.56	Goldie Sayers	U15	16.07.82	1	Sheffield	12 Jul
41.52	Joanne Bruce	U20	26.10.78	1	Exeter	23 Jun
41.48	Jean Lintern	V45	13.03.51	1	London (Nh)	20 Jul
41.48	Nicola Gautier	U20	21.03.78	2H	Narbonne, FRA	28 Jul
41.32	Lynsey Ellis	U23	22.11.76	1	Wolverhampton	11 Aug
41.28	Louise Nutt	U17	6.09.79	1	Grantham	21 Jul
41.10	Christine Head	U17	18.12.79	1	Peterborough	26 Aug
41.02	Nicky Rolfe		19.08.69	2	Bracknell	11 May
40.98	Emma Lilley	U23	2.05.76	1	Leeds (South)	5 May
	(50)					
40.78	Amanda Brown	U23	11.05.75			27 May
40.50	Mari-Anne Daykin		16.02.73	1	Hoo	1 Sep
40.30	Rebecca Foster		14.04.71	1	London (He)	1 Sep
40.24	Esther Sneddon	U23	30.06.74	1	Dundee	27 Apr
40.22	Caroline Lloyd	U20	7.01.79	1	Liverpool	12 May
40.22	Michelle Kemp	U15	19.09.81	1	Bedford	7 Sep
39.94	Katy Watts	U17	25.03.81	2	Portsmouth	8 Jun
39.82	Rhian Hughes	U20	11.05.79	1	Swansea	6 Jul
39.78	Sara Fry		19.01.62	1	Loughborough	15 May
39.76	Hayley Martin	U23	25.05.76	1	Hoo	14 Jul
	(60)					
39.66	Siona Kelly	U23	19.04.74	7	London (He)	6 Jul
39.66	Isobel Donaldson		24.01.64	1H	Portsmouth	30 Jul
39.58	Lesley Lavers		6.08.68	1	London (He)	25 May
39.44	Joanna Parry	U20	5.03.78	2	Portsmouth	9 Jun
39.38	Lynn Hayhoe		20.03.63	7	Manchester	17 Aug
39.34	Vanessa Stennett			3	Exeter	27 Apr
39.26	Debbie Woolgar		10.03.65	1	London (WP)	27 Apr
39.26	Michelle Woods	U17	2.08.80	1	Coventry	21 Jul
39.20	Louise Batho	U23	27.11.76	2H	Birmingham	22 Sep
39.12	Chloe Cozens	U17	9.04.80	1H	Birmingham	22 Sep
	(70)					
39.10	Clare Lockwood	U17	7.10.79	3	Stoke	20 Jul
39.10	Mary Anderson		2.09.67	1	Livingston	24 Jul
39.00	Catherine Gunn		10.06.69	1	Newport	7 Jul
38.98	Nicola Lycett	U17	10.03.80	1	Cannock	1 May
38.92	Clover Wynter-Pink	U20	29.11.77	1H	Hemel Hempstead	23 Jun
38.92	Cheryl Done		25.09.70	2H	Portsmouth (RN)	30 Jul
38.92	Marie Pearson	U23	22.09.74	1	Sheffield	4 Aug
38.90	Sarah Damm		12.09.70	5H	Alhama, SPA	5 May
38.88	Kerry Jury		19.11.68	2H	Bedford	26 May
38.64	Julie Nightingale	U23	28.04.75	2	Crawley	12 May
	(80)					
38.62	Jennifer Ayero	U17	13.09.79	1	London (He)	8 Jun
38.60	Elizabeth Austin		22.02.72	1	Carlisle	7 Jul
38.46	Laurie Morrison		27.07.73	2	Perivale	25 May
38.42	Jessica Brooker	U17	6.01.81	1	Exeter	15 Jun
38.40	Katie Rowland		5.03.71	2	Birmingham	21 Apr
38.38	Lucy Cook	U23	11.09.75	1	Luton	23 Jun
38.32	Emily Kitney	U17	25.04.81	1	London (Elt)	28 Sep
38.28	Claire Archer	U23	30.09.76	1	Mandale	7 Apr
38.28	Linda Low		20.01.71	1	Inverness	12 May
38.26	Lydia Hanley	U17	2.02.81	2	Liverpool	12 May
	(80)					
38.16	Nicola Cox	U20	18.08.77	1	Rotherham	21 May

38.16	Diane Smith	V35	15.11.60	1	Ashton-U-Lyne	2	Jun
38.08	Angharad Richards	U23	9.12.76	4	Newport	1	Jun
38.06	Rachel Humphrey	U20	29.05.78	1	Southampton	20	Jul
38.04	Lynsay Munro	U20	1.02.77	2	Edinburgh	12	May
38.04	Diane Nuttall	U20	10.06.77	2	Ipswich	4	Aug
38.02	Emma Claydon	U17	1.06.80	2	Southend	16	Jun
38.00	Laura Harvey-Smith	U17	20.01.80	1	Great Yarmouth	28	Jul

Additional Under 17 (1 - 16 above)

37.68	Alison Neall	8.11.79	3	Norwich	27	Apr
37.02	Judy Kotey	20.05.80	1	St. Albans	16	Jun
36.88	Anyha Kerr	10.04.80	2	Bristol	23	Jun
36.72	Tracey Howard	11.02.81	2	Exeter	15	Jun
	(20)					
36.64	Carrie MacRae	2.09.80	1	Blackpool	12	May
36.60	Stacey Mohamed	22.01.80	1	Mandale	7	Apr
36.44	Danielle Freeman	11.02.80	1	Leeds (South)	7	Jul
35.82	Kate Pinner	21.12.79	1	Brierley Hill	4	Aug
35.66	Gillian Stewart	21.01.80	3	Pitreavie	10	Aug
35.34	Rehanne Skinner	13.11.79	1	York	15	Jun
35.34	Tara Holman	13.10.80	1	Watford	1	Jul
35.18	Yvette Greenhouse	21.10.80	2	Stoke	22	Jun

Additional Under 15 (1 - 2 above)

37.58	Amy Harvey	23.04.82	1	Kings Lynn	28	Jul
36.88	Rebecca Bailey	8.01.82	2	London (He)	7	Jul
36.14	Natasha Campbell	6.08.82	3	London (He)	7	Jul
36.02	Faye Bowring	22.10.81	1	Harrow	7	Sep
35.72	Melanie Vaggers	16.06.82	1	Birmingham	18	Aug
35.50	Melissa Ball	16.09.81	1	Worcester	22	Sep
35.42	Susan Theobald	4.03.83	1	Braintree	3	Jul
35.00	Samantha Lowe	23.02.82	1	Whitby Heath	8	Sep
	(10)					
34.96	Michelle Lonsdale	29.10.81	5	Sheffield	12	Jul
34.00	Nicola Smith	6.03.82	1	Aldershot	21	May
33.94	Carol Wallbanks	9.12.82	1	Carlisle	11	May
33.46	Katie Postoy	26.08.82	8	Sheffield	12	Jul
33.00	Lisa Kenney	17.02.83	1	Scunthorpe	12	May
32.52	Aimee Styles	1.05.82	1	Hemel Hempstead	1	May
32.46	Eve Russell	27.09.82	1	Harrow	27	Apr
32.28	Jemma Spellacy	27.11.82	1	Colchester	28	Jul

Under 13

30.20	Samantha Redd	16.02.84	2	Harrow	7	Sep
28.42	Tanya Hunt	14.09.83	1	Aldershot	7	Sep
25.90	Candace Schofield	3.11.84	1	Salisbury	10	Aug

JAVELIN - Under 13 - 400 gram

36.06	Samantha Redd	16.02.84	1	Horsham	1	Sep
31.50	Sarah Ashdown	18.10.83	1		29	Sep
30.40	Sarah Moss	17.11.83	1	Southampton	8	Sep
30.24	Colette Doran	20.09.83	1	Carlisle	24	Aug
29.28	Candace Schofield	3.11.84	1	Worthing	4	Aug
27.55	Sarah Ellis	27.10.83	1	Bournemouth	30	Jun
27.36	Francesca Ovidi	22.09.83	1	Sutton	31	Aug
26.76	S. Harris		1	Birmingham	1	Jul
26.58	Lindsey Welsh	29.11.83				
26.48	Tanya Hunt	14.09.83	1	Salisbury	7	Jul
	(10)					
26.42	G. Foulds		1	Kings Lynn	12	May
26.10	E. Gardner		2	Birmingham	1	Jul
25.96	Sian Howe	11.04.84	1	London (Elt)	9	Jun

HEPTATHLON

6645	Denise Lewis			27.08.72	2	Gotzis, AUT	26 May
	13.18	1.84	14.36	24.06w	6.60	47.86	2:16.84
	6489				3	Atlanta, USA	28 Jul
	13.45	1.77	13.92	24.44	6.32	54.82	2:17.41
5747 w	Julia Bennett			26.03.70	3	Alhama, SPA	5 May
	14.43W	1.88	11.98	25.53	6.05w	31.76	2:16.26
	5356				3	Bedford	26 May
	14.79w	1.84	11.99	25.78	5.55	32.72	2:26.55
	5251				9	Narbonne, FRA	28 Jul
	14.85	1.75	11.01	26.27	5.75	31.30	2:19.65
5703	Kerry Jury			19.11.68	1	Bedford	26 May
	13.95w	1.75	10.84	24.20w	5.80w	38.88	2:20.29
	5642				6	Narbonne, FRA	28 Jul
	14.04	1.75	11.25	24.42	5.71	35.80	2:17.99
	5434				24	Lage, GER	16 Jun
	14.26	1.72	11.02	24.43w	5.47	37.66	2:24.48
	5421				1	Antrim	1 Sep
	14.49	1.77	11.14	24.94	5.57	34.16	2:21.89
	5329				1	Sheffield	28 Apr
	14.45w	1.74	10.27	25.00w	5.61	33.70	2:21.98
5700	Vikki Schofield			29.12.72	5	Alhama, SPA	5 May
	13.79w	1.73	11.50	24.89	5.92w	34.84	2:15.78
	5362				28	Lage, GER	16 Jun
	14.22	1.63	11.14	25.13w	5.94	33.20	2:21.96
5618 w	Sarah Damm			12.09.70	6	Alhama, SPA	5 May
	14.17W	1.64	11.85	25.34	5.94w	38.90	2:14.70
5386	Pauline Richards			30.06.68	2	Bedford	26 May
	14.44	1.57	12.74	25.07w	5.82	36.22	2:22.63
	5217				10	Narbonne, FRA	28 Jul
	14.16	1.57	12.36	26.21	5.54	34.32	2:19.91
	5155 w				9	Alhama, SPA	5 May
	14.29W	1.61	12.45	25.33	5.64w	29.54	2:28.37
5339	Tracy Joseph			29.11.69	1	Enfield	4 Aug
	14.53	1.67	10.05	24.17	6.04	26.50	2:18.33
	5280				5	Bedford	26 May
	14.27w	1.63	10.37	23.57w	5.75	25.64	2:20.00
	5238				2	Lisbon, POR	28 Apr
	14.41	1.62	10.38	23.86	5.64	25.94	2:16.69
	5195				2	Antrim	1 Sep
	14.61	1.68	10.12	24.26	5.82	23.14	2:19.09
5332	Diana Bennett		U23	14.06.74	4	Bedford	26 May
	14.63	1.75	11.51	26.69	5.60	34.68	2:17.16
	5076				1	Bonn, GER	5 May
	14.94	1.68	11.12	27.30	5.76	30.78	2:18.94
5258	Anne Hollman		U23	18.02.74	6	Bedford	26 May
	14.30	1.63	10.16	25.23	5.67	37.50	2:23.53
5213	Nicola Gautier		U20	21.03.78	6	Narbonne, FRA	28 Jul
	14.51	1.57	12.64	25.83	5.34	41.48	2:26.40
	5208				1	Birmingham	22 Sep
	15.32	1.68	13.41	25.88	5.16	39.00	2:24.42
	5111				1	York	23 Jun
	14.9	1.63	12.58	25.8	5.17	38.88	2:23.9
	5080				1	Birmingham	2 Jun
	14.95	1.63	10.66	25.49	5.32	39.06	2:25.64
	5079				10	Sydney, AUS	24 Aug
	15.01	1.66	12.89	25.42	4.93	37.98	2:29.72

(10)

```
5114    Louise Batho           U23   27.11.76   2    Birmingham         22 Sep
        14.95     1.62    11.26    26.07          5.41     39.20      2:23.43
        5102                                      3    Antrim              1 Sep
        14.75     1.62    11.85    26.27          5.32     37.34      2:23.31
        5072                                      9    Narbonne, FRA      28  Jul
        14.68     1.60    11.59    25.97          5.31     38.34      2:26.47
        5020                                      1    Norwich            23 Jun
        14.7      1.58    11.71    25.9           5.39     38.18      2:27.0
5066    Charmaine Johnson            4.06.63     7    Val de Reuil, FRA  30 Jun
        15.08w    1.66    13.47    26.18w         5.16     37.00      2:31.37
5065    Kim Crowther-Price           19.01.66    1    Middlesbrough      30 Jun
        14.2      1.62    11.63    25.8           5.58     28.76      2:23.1
        5025                                      7    Bedford            26 May
        14.27w    1.57    11.72    25.70w         5.49     29.76      2:25.72
5047    Rebecca Lewis          U20   31.12.77    9    Narbonne, FRA      28  Jul
        14.42     1.54    10.95    25.43          5.59     34.18      2:26.41
        5030                                      2    Birmingham          2 Jun
        14.86     1.57    10.77    25.54          5.66     34.70      2:26.43
        5011                                      1    Telford            23 Jun
        14.6      1.56    11.46    25.6           5.70     36.20      2:31.9
        5007                                      4    Antrim              1 Sep
        14.82     1.56    11.19    25.70          5.38     35.78      2:24.12
        39 performances to 5000 by 14 athletes
4979    Emma Lindsay                 11.04.71    1    Ayr                21  Jul
        15.31w    1.65    11.17    25.23          5.42     29.92      2:24.86
4975    Julie Hollman          U20   16.02.77    5    Antrim              1 Sep
        15.19     1.68    10.31    26.03          5.61w    29.78      2:23.31
4930    Kelly Sotherton        U23   13.11.76    8    Bedford            26 May
        14.63     1.63    11.25    25.84          5.54     27.16      2:28.67
4875    Michala Gee            U23   8.12.75     1    Gateshead           2 Jun
        14.81     1.69    9.27     25.92          5.46     29.26      2:27.17
4833    Denise Bolton          U20   1.02.77     3    Birmingham          2 Jun
        14.35     1.54    9.29     25.23          5.59     25.86      2:24.38
4817    Debbie Woolgar               10.03.65    1    Worthing           15 Sep
        15.9      1.60    13.45    27.8           5.56     34.72      2:28.2
    (20)
4807    Clover Wynter-Pink     U20   29.11.77    2    Middlesbrough      30 Jun
        15.0      1.59    11.82    25.8           5.20     38.76      2:40.1
4805    Angie Nyhan            U20   13.04.78    4    Birmingham          2 Jun
        15.24     1.54    11.46    26.34          5.24     35.60      2:27.31
4767    Cheryl Done                  25.09.70    1    Portsmouth (RN)    30  Jul
        15.2      1.51    11.53    26.4           5.13     38.92      2:26.5
4759    Claire Everett         U20   25.06.79    5    Birmingham          2 Jun
        15.81     1.63    11.37    25.77          5.23     29.12      2:27.01
4672    Jenny Brown            V35   21.05.59    1    Hoo                22 Sep
        16.1      1.69    10.05    27.2           5.23     33.32      2:22.9
4664    Teresa Copeland              8.03.69     2    Hoo                22 Sep
        14.5      1.45    10.79    26.3           5.30     35.38      2:32.0
4626    Isobel Donaldson             24.01.64    2    Portsmouth         30  Jul
        15.7      1.48    8.37     26.7           5.36     39.66      2:18.5
4622    Jackie Tindal          U20   21.01.79    1    Ayr                21  Jul
        15.19w    1.56    11.35    26.30          4.93     32.46      2:32.30
4546    Wendy Laing                  29.12.62    1    Blackpool          28  Jul
        15.14     1.54    10.56    27.12          5.16     29.56      2:28.04
4499    Katie Budd             U23   3.01.76     2    Bonn, GER           5 May
        15.22     1.65    9.59     28.22          5.19     29.28      2:29.50
    (30)
4474    Abigail Ashby          U20   23.11.77    6    Birmingham          2 Jun
        15.26     1.60    10.02    27.28          5.07     30.94      2:34.44
4474    Sarah Still            U23   24.09.75    7    Antrim              1 Sep
        15.87     1.65    9.43     25.94          5.38     18.70      2:27.44
```

4466	Leanne Buxton		U20	27.05.78	3	Birmingham	22 Sep
	15.37	1.44	9.15	25.98	5.31	27.32	2:23.70
4370	Anne Carr		U23	1.05.76	2	Gateshead	2 Jun
	16.72	1.57	9.53	27.22	5.05	32.84	2:16.01
4344	Ruth Calvert		U23	22.10.75	2	Blackpool	28 Jul
	16.50	1.57	10.59	25.86	4.71	26.12	2:27.30
4308	Belinda Samuels		U20	29.11.78	5	Birmingham	22 Sep
	15.32	1.47	9.18	26.11	5.30	28.90	2:41.40
4297	Debbie Harrison		U20	13.11.78	6	Birmingham	22 Sep
	15.39	1.53	8.86	26.72	5.25w	27.86	2:37.93
4240	Julia Sykes		U23	27.05.75	1	Cudworth	15 Sep
	16.2	1.55	9.77	27.0	4.48	30.36	2:22.6
4239	Kirsty Roger		U20	24.03.78	9	Antrim	1 Sep
	15.78	1.59	9.19	27.76	5.09	24.10	2:29.60
4214	Kate Rogers		U20	13.02.79	2	York	23 Jun
	15.8	1.57	8.52	26.7	5.33	20.94	2:29.7
(40)							
4202	Leanne Milburn		U20	16.08.79	7	Birmingham	22 Sep
	16.99	1.47	7.56	25.31	5.30	31.12	2:33.87
4189	Fran Wilkins		U20	15.01.79	1	Worcester	25 Aug
	16.82	1.55	10.53	27.54	5.11	29.52	2:37.2
4163	Susan Jones		U20	8.06.78	5	Sheffield	28 Apr
	14.41	1.80	8.77	27.86w	5.14w	18.18	3:05.0
4078	Jo Morris		U20	16.10.77	3	Hemel Hempstead	23 Jun
	16.0	1.67	9.00	28.0	5.13	25.78	2:45.9
4069	Hannah Stares		U20	13.11.78	1	Carn Brea	23 Jun
	15.2	1.54	8.29	26.2	4.74	28.96	2:47.0
4047	Leone Dickinson		U23	5.11.75	3	Cudworth	15 Sep
	16.2	1.73	8.81	27.4	5.10	25.68	2:56.1
4035	Tamsin Stephens		U17	2.08.80	11	Antrim	1 Sep
	14.98	1.50	7.39	26.52	4.94	16.42	2:30.06
4026	Michelle Winter		U20	18.06.79	3	Telford	23 Jun
	16.0	1.53	7.31	28.2	5.30	27.50	2:32.5
4022	Jackie Vyfschaft			15.12.64	1	Antrim	1 Sep
	16.0	1.68	9.76	28.8	4.83	26.12	2:44.3
3948	Helen Baker		U20	5.02.79	2	Carn Brea	23 Jun
	15.5	1.54	7.81	26.6	4.97	24.42	2:46.4
(50)							
3918	Hazel Barker		V35	6.08.59	1	Sheffield	8 Sep
	16.94	1.55	10.33	27.69	4.63w	25.82	2:40.08
3900	Amanda Brown		U23	11.05.75	1	Walton	16 Jun
	16.3	1.44	8.47	27.1	4.70	33.44	2:41.0
3894	Kathryn Lane		U20	6.11.78	9	Birmingham	22 Sep
	16.32	1.47	7.69	27.21	5.05	21.88	2:32.66
3870	Suzanne Pearson		U20	31.08.77	3	Carn Brea	23 Jun
	16.5	1.43	7.79	26.0	4.89	20.40	2:28.5
3861	Laura Bolton		U20	22.01.79	10	Birmingham	22 Sep
	17.50	1.47	8.64	28.19	4.48	35.46	2:31.64
3854	Carmen Collins/Michaelska			6.11.73	3	Portsmouth (RN)	30 Jul
	19.0	1.42	7.90	25.9	4.55	30.62	2:18.4
3835	Esther Sneddon		U23	30.06.74	4	Ayr	21 Jul
	16.55w	1.53	9.43	30.25	4.43	37.62	2:42.69

HEPTATHLON - Under 17

4830 w	Katherine Livesey			15.12.79	1	Birmingham	22 Sep
	11.67	1.75	9.39	25.14W	5.32	24.08	2:30.07
4790					1	Blackpool	28 Jul
	11.66	1.68	9.24	25.20	5.44	25.08	2:29.58
4780	Danielle Freeman			11.02.80	1	York	23 Jun
	12.3	1.63	9.25	26.2	5.47	34.64	2:25.2

4746	Chloe Cozens			9.04.80	2	Birmingham		22 Sep			
	12.33	1.69	9.78	26.57w	5.18	39.12	2:35.50				
4460	Gillian Stewart			21.01.80	2	Worcester		25 Aug			
	12.02	1.63	10.01	26.9	5.10	35.50	2:47.00				
4318	Laura Redmond			19.04.81	2	Ayr		21 Jul			
	13.12	1.62	9.40	27.76	5.06	31.56	2:31.34				
4318	Yvette Carlin			28.05.80	4	Birmingham		22 Sep			
	12.42	1.48	8.73	26.74	5.41w	26.86	2:29.20				
4311 w	Joanne Cozens			9.04.80	5	Birmingham		22 Sep			
	12.56	1.57	8.56	25.65W	5.08	25.20	2:33.33				
	4167				3	Worcester		25 Aug			
	12.74	1.60	9.38	26.7	5.02	21.00	2:33.62				
4260	Hayley Young			26.09.79	2	Norwich		23 Jun			
	12.3	1.73	8.06	28.1	5.19	27.04	2:40.3				
4255	Eve Miller			1.12.79	1	Enfield		4 Aug			
	11.93	1.49	8.97	25.74	4.67	23.86	2:27.73				
4212	Christine Head			18.12.79	3	Norwich		23 Jun			
	12.8	1.52	9.40	27.4	4.95	38.02	2:42.4				
(10)											
4197 w	Victoria Williams			11.04.81	6	Birmingham		22 Sep			
	12.06	1.45	8.84	26.07W	5.13w	26.34	2:38.27				
	4071				1	Carn Brea		23 Jun			
	11.9	1.48	8.17	25.9	5.19	23.18	2:46.2				
4179	Amy Nuttell			6.02.80	4	Norwich		23 Jun			
	11.9	1.46	9.02	26.9	5.09	27.64	2:37.0				
4178 w	Laura Smith			16.11.80	7	Birmingham		22 Sep			
	12.87	1.57	6.58	25.70W	5.45w	24.44	2:37.91				
	3994				3	York		23 Jun			
	13.3	1.54	6.39	26.4	5.58	21.50	2:36.9				
4171	Syreeta Williams			24.10.80	8	Birmingham		22 Sep			
	12.38	1.33	9.36	25.95w	5.02	23.04	2:23.08				
4095	Laura Curtis			2.05.81	2	York		23 Jun			
	12.6	1.60	8.00	27.4	4.69	23.50	2:25.7				
4089	Kelly Moreton			18.09.79	1	Aberdare		4 Aug			
	12.51	1.68	7.28	27.22	4.97	19.66	2:33.88				
4070	Elizabeth Sherman			15.09.79	2	Enfield		4 Aug			
	12.42	1.55	8.45	27.95	4.93	28.20	2:37.47				
4050	Laura White			5.09.79	9	Birmingham		22 Sep			
	12.58	1.60	8.94	26.94	5.09	19.92	2:42.80				
4049	Maria Grantham			14.12.79	2	Telford		23 Jun			
	12.7	1.46	8.53	26.9	5.07	25.64	2:33.0				
4014	Catherine Ryan			4.02.80	3	Telford		23 Jun			
	13.3	1.61	8.72	27.8	5.02	24.40	2:36.3				
(20)											
4008 w	Dionne Howell			10.04.81	11	Birmingham		22 Sep			
	12.97	1.54	7.34	25.58W	5.14w	16.66	2:33.64				
3993	Gemma Swetman			28.09.80	1	Hemel Hempstead		23 Jun			
	12.7	1.51	7.51	26.9	5.14w	22.92	2:34.1				
3968	Donna Porazinski			28.01.81	2	Aberdare		4 Aug			
	12.39	1.50	6.66	26.00	4.96	15.28	2:26.37				
3968	Michelle Johns			12.03.80	12	Birmingham		22 Sep			
	13.08	1.48	8.30	27.63	4.95	22.28	2:25.79				
3945	Laura Siddall			10.09.80	4	York		23 Jun			
	12.4	1.51	6.86	26.6	4.83	24.44	2:35.2				
3911	Maria Morganella			2.10.79	4	Telford		23 Jun			
	14.6	1.40	8.23	26.2	5.31	27.60	2:34.4				
3880	Abigail Naugher			26.02.80	16	Birmingham		22 Sep			
	13.33	1.54	6.80	26.67w	4.37	24.18	2:25.46				
3834	Jo Hyslop			13.03.80	18	Birmingham		22 Sep			
	12.69	1.60	7.90	27.66	4.54	23.06	2:41.84				
3829	Judy Kotey			20.05.80	2	Hemel Hempstead		23 Jun			
	13.6	1.42	8.89	26.6	5.11	33.48	2:59.3				

PENTATHLON - Under 15

3005	April Kalu				31.03.82	1	Telford	23	Jun
	12.3	12.96	1.46	4.97	2:45.5				
2993	Fiona Harrison				30.11.81	1	Cudworth	15	Sep
	5.30	12.0	8.55	1.57	2:43.0				
2974	Tina Thirwell				5.09.81	2	Telford	23	Jun
	12.1	8.80	1.55	5.00	2:35.7				
2923	Samantha Adamson				27.03.82	1	Birmingham	22	Sep
	12.27	7.92	1.66	4.31	2:29.68				
2922	Sharon Davidge				15.09.81	2	Birmingham	22	Sep
	11.52	7.95	1.51	4.90	2:35.11				
2870	Cathy Young				14.03.82	4	Birmingham	22	Sep
	12.43	7.75	1.60	4.79	2:35.89				
2869	Lyndsey Clark				28.11.81	3	Telford	23	Jun
	11.9	7.69	1.46	4.72	2:26.3				
2819	Rebecca Shiel				16.01.82	1	York	23	Jun
	12.7	7.90	1.48	5.10	2:34.2				
2786	Sara McGreavy				13.12.82	6	Birmingham	22	Sep
	12.05	8.02	1.36	4.98	2:30.04				
2769	Laura McShane				22.04.82	7	Birmingham	22	Sep
	11.69	6.25	1.54	4.79	2:37.52				
(10)									
2760	Danielle Parkinson				2.09.81	8	Birmingham	22	Sep
	12.48	5.13	1.54	4.96	2:45.04				
2749	Melanie Vaggers				16.06.82	1	Carn Brea	23	Jun
	12.6	9.11	1.49	4.49	2:34.9				
2745	Helen Thieme				28.09.81	1	Birmingham	20	Apr
	12.55	9.10	1.53	4.58	2:41.43				
2743	Alex Hewett				10.09.82	9	Birmingham	22	Sep
	12.92	8.18	1.60	4.66	2:41.96				
2742	Vicky Young				14.03.82	10	Birmingham	22	Sep
	12.17	8.79	1.54	4.69	2:47.30				
2737	Suzie Furlonger				30.09.81	4	Telford	23	Jun
	12.8	7.39	1.52	4.80	2:34.4				
2713	Jodie Hearne				17.09.81	2	Norwich	23	Jun
	12.1	7.82	4.50	1.57	2:43.5				
2713	Alyssa Fullelove				16.09.81	1	Ayr	21	Jul
	11.97	9.10	1.40	4.53	2:36.70				
2260	Louise Cook				7.01.84	12	Norwich	23	Jun
	4.59	12.6	8.31	1.36	3:06.0				
2206	Melissa Rogers				2.09.83	2	Welwyn	18	Jul
	4.39	12.7	6.20	1.35	2:50.2	(20)			

PENTATHLON - Under 13

2335	Catriona Pennet				10.10.83	1	Ayr	21	Jul
	4.19	11.73	8.35	1.30	2:41.40				
2317	Krista Cartlidge				8.12.83	1	Worthing	15	Sep
	4.11	12.9	7.84	1.33	2:32.1				
2304	Heather Wood				2.07.84	1	Blackpool	28	Jul
	4.23	12.74	7.72	1.38	2:40.18				
2250	Danielle Selley					1	Aberdare	4	Aug
	4.62	11.65	6.51	1.33	2:51.88				
2172	Siobhan McVie				6.07.84	2	Ayr	21	Jul
	4.68	13.45	7.67	1.36	2:55.52				
2013	Claire Webber				13.12.83	3	Ayr	21	Jul
	3.92	13.43	5.90	1.27	2:34.69				
2011	Samantha Judd				22.10.83	2	Worthing	15	Sep
	12.3	3.86	8.09	1.27	2:55.1				
2002	Samantha Houlden				27.11.83	7	Lincoln	5	May
	14.1	6.96	4.34	13.3	2:59.3	(75mh)			

1996	Emma McElroy				16.09.83	1	Antrim	1	Sep
	3.94	13.42	5.92	1.25	2:34.37				
1956	Amy Lloyd				20.11.83	2	Blackpool	28	Jul
	4.22	12.32	6.99	1.23	2:57.80				

2000 METRES WALK - Track - Under 13

10:31.0	Kelly Mann		8.09.83	1	Birmingham	29	May
11:02.4	Laura Fryer		3.12.83	2	Enfield	31	Aug
11:04.9	Sophie Hales		30.03.85	1	Brierley Hill	13	Oct
11:17.0	Hayley Hutchings		14.11.83	3	Enfield	31	Aug
11:21.5	Laura Stepniak		24.01.85	4	Enfield	31	Aug
11:36.1	Jade Shipley		5.04.84	6	Enfield	31	Aug
11:54.7	Nicky Reynolds		24.06.85	3	Brierley Hill	13	Oct

Road
10:03	Kelly Mann		8.09.83	1	Steyning	23	Jun
10:38	Hayley Hutchings		14.11.83	4	Dublin, IRE	28	Sep
10:39	Laura Fryer		3.12.83	2	Steyning	23	Jun
10:42	Natalie Evans		15.11.83	5	Dublin, IRE	28	Sep
10:55	Laura Stepniak		24.01.85	1	Bradford	10	Nov
10:56	Sophie Hales		30.03.85	2	Bradford	10	Nov

2500 METRES WALK - Track - Under 15

12:42.43	Amy Hales		16.03.82	1	Birmingham	21	Sep
12:49.3	Louise Richmond		15.12.81	1	Solihull	29	Jun
12:53.3	Kelly Mann	U13	8.09.83	1	Leamington	11	May
12:53.80	Katie Ford		21.10.81	2	Birmingham	21	Sep
12:59.05	Natalie Watson		29.01.83	3	Birmingham	21	Sep
13:03.37	Vanessa Caines		17.04.83	4	Birmingham	21	Sep
13:11.62	Samantha Campbell			5	Birmingham	21	Sep
13:43.90	Jo Sealy		24.03.82	1	London (CP)	12	May
13:47.10	Nicola Phillips		23.04.83	9	Birmingham	21	Sep

Under 13
13:52.59	Laura Fryer		3.12.83	10	Birmingham	21	Sep
13:58.56	Natalie Evans		15.11.83	11	Birmingham	21	Sep

Road
13:17	Katie Ford		21.10.81	2	London (CP)	3	Feb
13:25	Jo Sealy		24.03.82	2	Bexley	9	Mar

3000 METRES WALK - Track

13:06.27	Vicky Lupton		17.04.72	1	Bedford	27	May
	13:16.53			1	Sheffield	11	May
13:16.23	Verity Snook		13.11.70	2	Bedford	27	May
14:04.72	Melanie Wright		5.04.64	3	Bedford	27	May
14:05.5	Catherine Charnock	U23	3.05.75	1	Carlisle	11	May
14:06.0	Karen Kneale		23.04.69	1	Douglas, IOM	21	Jul
14:15.0	Liz Corran	V40	23.09.55	2	Douglas, IOM	21	Jul
14:23.50	Sylvia Black	V35	16.04.58	1	Birmingham	20	Jul
14:37.29	Brenda Lupton	V40	5.10.52	2	Sheffield	11	May
14:39.24 i	Sarah Bennett	U17	27.07.80	7	Lievin, FRA	2	Mar
	14:56.10			1	Birmingham	21	Sep
14:46.10	Kath Horwill	U23	26.01.75	3	Birmingham	20	Jul
(10)							
14:55.0	Sharon Tonks		18.04.70	1	Worcester	11	May
14:59.9	Lisa Crump	U23	30.03.76	2	Brierley Hill	13	Oct
15:03.0	Claire Childs/Walker		8.10.72	2	Tamworth	11	Aug
15:04.7	Debbie Wallen	U20	28.05.79	2	Luton	6	May

319

15:06.1	Nina Howley	U20	22.01.78	4	Sheffield	11	May
15:06.2	Sandra Brown	V45	1.04.49	1	London (BP)	2	Sep
15:09.3	Nikki Huckerby	U20	27.02.78	3	Brierley Hill	13	Oct
15:11.44	Becky Tisshaw	U17	8.02.81	2	Birmingham	21	Sep
15:14.6	Amy Hales	U15	16.03.82	1	Enfield	31	Aug
15:16.4	Natalie Watson	U15	29.01.83	2	Enfield	31	Aug
(20)							
15:23.0	Lynne Bradley		21.05.67	2	Bedford	14	Aug
15:27.0	Sarah Brown		28.09.64	1	Horsham	17	Apr
15:34.83	Sally Warren	U20	29.01.78	3	London (He)	10	Aug
15:41.1	Cath Reader	V40	19.10.54	3	Luton	6	May
15:47.8	Fiona Rose		2.01.64	4	Luton	6	May
15:49.35	Sian Woodcock	U17	13.01.80	3	Birmingham	21	Sep
15:52.71 i	Ann Lewis	V45	29.12.47	2	Birmingham	2	Mar
15:55.0				1	Portsmouth	6	May
16:00.8	Cressida Van Doorn	U20	27.09.77	1	Walton	16	Jun
16:03.8	Katie Ford	U15	21.10.81	3	Enfield	31	Aug
16:09.0	Suzanne Ford-Dunn		25.04.73	2	Horsham	10	Jan
(30)							
16:13.1	Vanessa Caines	U15	17.04.83	4	Enfield	31	Aug
16:13.8	Kelly-Anne Parker-Smith	U17	10.02.81	1	London (BP)	14	Jul
16:19.07	Katherine Brook	U20	15.06.79	6	Sheffield	11	May
16:23.07 i	Clare Ellis	U20	27.04.78	5	Birmingham	18	Feb
16:23.8	Jo Sealy	U15	24.03.82	5	Enfield	31	Aug
16:27.1	Louise Richmond	U15	15.12.81	9	Brierley Hill	13	Oct
16:28.7	Lynne Newton	V45	19.05.47	2	Crawley	2	Jul
16:31.0	Liz Ford-Dunn		13.05.71	4	Horsham	10	Jan
16:33.6	Rebecca Pridmore	U15	19.12.82	1	Loughborough	12	May
16:35.3	Lisa Airey	U17	19.12.80	2	Solihull	29	Jun

Road - Junior

14:34	Sarah Bennett	U17	27.07.80	1	Dublin, IRE	28	Sep
14:39	Becky Tisshaw	U17	8.02.81	1	Dublin, IRE	28	Sep
14:44	Nikki Huckerby	U20	27.02.78	1	Dublin, IRE	28	Sep
14:47	Amy Hales	U15	16.03.82	1	Steyning	23	Jun
15:01	Sally Warren	U20	29.01.78	2	Dublin, IRE	28	Sep
15:26	Katie Ford	U15	21.10.81	3	Folkstone	4	May
15:36	Louise Richmond	U15	15.12.81	6	Dublin, IRE	28	Sep
15:58	Rebecca Pridmore	U15	19.12.82	2	Weymouth	17	Mar
15:42	Kelly Mann	U15	8.09.83	1	Tamworth	1	Dec
16:00	Rachel Reilly	U15	19.11.82	4	Steyning	23	Jun
16:02	Lisa Airey	U17	19.12.80	10	Dublin, IRE	28	Sep
16:03	Samantha Campbell	U15		6	Steyning	23	Jun
16:08	Jo Sealy	U15	24.03.82	7	Steyning	23	Jun
16:14	Tracey Robinson	U15	28.09.81	4	Weymouth	17	Mar
16:19	Nicola Phillips	U15	23.04.83	8	Steyning	23	Jun

5000 METRES WALK - Track

23:04.57	Vicky Lupton		17.04.72	1	Birmingham	15	Jun
23:19.0				1	Tamworth	11	Aug
24:14.7	Melanie Wright		5.04.64	1	Solihull	30	Jun
24:16.1	Verity Snook		13.11.70	1	Enfield	8	Aug
24:40.69	Karen Kneale		23.04.69	1	Cudworth	4	Aug
24:40.91	Liz Corran	V40	23.09.55	2	Cudworth	4	Aug
24:48.19	Nina Howley	U20	22.01.78	2	Bedford	28	Jul
25:00.22	Catherine Charnock	U23	3.05.75	3	Birmingham	15	Jun
25:26.55	Brenda Lupton	V40	5.10.52	2	Sheffield	1	Jun
25:46.52	Nikki Huckerby	U20	27.02.78	1	Birmingham	21	Sep
25:50.10	Sarah Bennett	U17	27.07.80	3	Bedford	28	Jul
(10)							

25:57.5	Lisa Crump	U23	30.03.76	2	Sheffield	4	Sep
26:06.47	Debbie Wallen	U20	28.05.79	7	Birmingham	15	Jun
26:09.16	Sally Warren	U20	29.01.78	2	Birmingham	21	Sep
26:09.6	Elaine Callanin	V35	13.09.60	2	Solihull	30	Jun
26:47.0	Amy Hales	U15	16.03.82	1	Horsham	15	Dec
26:54.4	Becky Tisshaw	U17	8.02.81	4	Enfield	31	Aug
26:57.01	Sian Woodcock	U17	13.01.80	5	Bedford	28	Jul
26:59.0	Clare Ellis	U20	27.04.78	2	Birmingham	29	May
27:02.29	Ann Lewis	V45	29.12.47	1	Exeter	10	Aug
27:03.88	Lynne Bradley		21.05.67	8	Birmingham	15	Jun
(20)							
27:41.97	Katherine Brook	U20	15.06.79	8	Bedford	28	Jul
27:55.35	Cressida Van Doorn	U20	27.09.77	4	Birmingham	21	Sep

Road

22:30	Vicky Lupton		17.04.72	1	Holmewood	13	Apr
	23:05			1	Bolton	6	Jul
	23:09 +			m	Atlanta, USA	29	Jul
	23:43			1	Sheffield	25	Feb
23:13	Lisa Langford		15.03.67	1	Sutton Coldfield	17	Feb
23:36	Verity Snook		13.11.70	1	London (CP)	3	Feb
	23:45 +			2=m	Douglas, IOM	24	Feb
	23:59			1	Bexley	7	Dec
23:45 +	Carolyn Partington		27.06.66	2=m	Douglas, IOM	24	Feb
23:58	Melanie Wright		5.04.64	2	Holmewood	13	Apr
24:12	Catherine Charnock	U23	3.05.75	1	Bradford	10	Nov
24:22	Karen Kneale		23.04.69	3	Bolton	6	Jul
24:26	Sylvia Black	V35	16.04.58	4	Bolton	6	Jul
24:32	Lisa Crump	U23	30.03.76	2	Bradford	10	Nov
24:44	Kath Horwill	U23	26.01.75	5	Bolton	6	Jul
(10)							
25:07	Becky Tisshaw	U17	8.02.81	2	Bexley	7	Dec
25:17	Claire Childs/Walker		8.10.72	1	Coventry	9	Jul
25:18	Debbie Wallen	U20	28.05.79	3	Folkstone	4	May
25:19	Liz Corran	V40	23.09.55	1	St. Johns, IOM	17	Mar
25:22	Nikki Huckerby	U20	27.02.78	16	Moscow, RUS	1	Jun
25:23	Brenda Lupton	V40	5.10.52	3	Holmewood	13	Apr
25:36	Sandra Brown	V45	1.04.49	2	London (CP)	3	Feb
26:03	Sharon Tonks		18.04.70	2	Tamworth	24	Feb
26:05	Sally Warren	U20	29.01.78	7	Holmewood	13	Apr
26:20	Lynne Bradley		21.05.67	4	Sheffield	25	Feb
(20)							
26:22	Katie Ford	U17	21.10.81	4	Bradford	10	Nov
26:29	Louise Richmond	U17	15.12.81	5	Bradford	10	Nov
26:33	Clare Ellis	U20	27.04.78	5	Folkstone	4	May
26:37	Lynsey Tozer	U23	6.12.75	9	Holmewood	13	Apr
26:46	Ann Lewis	V45	29.12.47	3	Bexley	9	Mar
27:04	Cressida Van Doorn	U20	27.09.77	3	Bexley	7	Dec
27:09	Katherine Brook	U20	15.06.79	7	Bradford	10	Nov
27:10	Suzanne Ford-Dunn		25.04.73	3	Bexley	10	Feb
27:19	Gill Watson		26.05.64	7	Sheffield	25	Feb
27:27	Lisa Airey	U17	19.12.80	4	Steyning	23	Jun
(30)							
27:28	Sarah Brown		28.09.64	1	Steyning	24	Feb

Foreign

23:23	*Perri Williams*		*2.06.66*	*1*	*Bexley*	*19*	*Oct*

10000 METRES WALK - Track

49:15.0	Vicky Lupton		17.04.72	1	Enfield	31	Aug
50:52.3	Kim Baird/Braznell	V40	28.02.56	2	Enfield	31	Aug
51:17.1	Liz Corran	V40	23.09.55	3	Enfield	31	Aug
52:43.3	Claire Childs/Walker		8.10.72	4	Enfield	31	Aug
53:38.3	Kath Horwill	U23	26.01.75	5	Enfield	31	Aug
54:24.2	Brenda Lupton	V40	5.10.52	6	Enfield	31	Aug
56:00.3	Lynne Bradley		21.05.67	7	Enfield	31	Aug
56:05.0	Lisa Crump	U23	30.03.76	1	Bradford	20	Jul
56:24.5	Cath Reader	V40	19.10.54	1	Hornchurch	27	Mar
56:26.3	Ann Lewis	V45	29.12.47	7	Enfield	31	Aug

10000 METRES WALK - Road

47:05	Vicky Lupton		17.04.72	33	Atlanta, USA	29	Jul
	47:19			12	Podebrady, TCH	27	Apr
	47:35			1	Coventry	3	Mar
	47:48			1	Cardiff	21	Apr
47:12	Verity Snook		13.11.70	27	Moscow, RUS	1	Jun
	47:54			13	Podebrady, TCH	27	Apr
	48:13			3	Douglas, IOM	24	Feb
	48:18			1	Bexley	9	Mar
48:00	Carolyn Partington		27.06.66	2	Douglas, IOM	24	Feb
48:27	Lisa Langford		15.03.67	2	Cardiff	21	Apr
48:47	Melanie Wright		5.04.64	2	Coventry	3	Mar
	49:15			31	Moscow, RUS	1	Jun
	49:51			17	Podebrady, TCH	27	Apr
49:37	Karen Kneale		23.04.69	1	St. Johns, IOM	26	May
50:45	Kim Baird/Braznell	V40	28.02.56	4	Cardiff	21	Apr
51:37	Liz Corran	V40	23.09.55	1	Douglas, IOM	11	Feb
52:12	Lisa Crump	U23	30.03.76	1	Sheffield	26	Nov
52:23	Nikki Huckerby	U20	27.02.78	1	Birmingham	14	Dec
	(10)						
52:34	Claire Childs/Walker		8.10.72	4	Dublin, IRE	28	Sep
52:42	Catherine Charnock	U23	3.05.75	2	Leicester	15	Sep
52:57	Brenda Lupton	V40	5.10.52	6	Cardiff	21	Apr
53:26	Kath Horwill	U23	26.01.75	7	Cardiff	21	Apr
53:54	Lynne Bradley		21.05.67	3	Sheffield	26	Nov
55:18	Sally Warren	U20	29.01.78	3	Weymouth	17	Mar
55:19	Debbie Wallen	U20	28.05.79	1	East Molesey	14	Jan
55:51	Sarah Bennett	U20	27.07.80	2	Birmingham	14	Dec
56:12	Ann Lewis	V45	29.12.47	2	East Molesey	14	Jan
57:26	Maureen Cox	V45	7.09.50	13	Cardiff	21	Apr

20 KILOMETRES WALK

1:43:57	Vicky Lupton		17.04.72	1	York	18	May
1:47:10	Liz Corran	V40	23.09.55	2	Brugge, BEL	29	Jun
1:48:46	Sandra Brown	V45	1.04.49	2	Horsham	7	Sep
1:52:39	Cath Reader	V40	19.10.54	5	Brugge, BEL	29	Jun
1:53:19	Brenda Lupton	V40	5.10.52	2	York	18	May
1:54:15	Verity Snook		13.11.70	3	Horsham	7	Sep
1:55:00	Lynne Bradley		21.05.67	5	Horsham	7	Sep
1:56:14	Ann Lewis	V45	29.12.47	9	Brugge, BEL	29	Jun

50 KILOMETRES WALK

5:43:14	Jeanette Bleach	V45	22.06.48	1	Burrator	5	May
5:53:16	Pam Ficken	V55	25.07.41	1	Basildon	9	Apr

100 MILES WALK

19:42:53	Sandra Brown	V45	1.04.49	1	Colchester	4	Aug

322

4 x 100 METRES

43.88	National Team		3h2	Atlanta, USA	2 Aug
	(A Thorp, M Richardson, S Jacobs, K Merry)				
43.93	National Team		8	Atlanta, USA	3 Aug
	(A Thorp, M Richardson, S Jacobs, K Merry)				
44.07	National Team		7	Madrid, SPA	1 Jun
	(S Smith, P Thomas, S Jacobs, C Murphy)				
44.99	National Under 23 Team		1	Hexham	14 Jul
	(D Allahgreen, C Murphy, S Smith, L Whitehead)				
45.49	National Junior Team	U20	3h2	Sydney, AUS	25 Aug
	(M Rostek, S Wilhelmy, S Williams, V Shipman)				
46.1	Shaftesbury Barnet Harriers		1	London (He)	6 Jul
	(C Ajunwa, C Murphy, C Haslam, J Agyepong)				
46.3	Shaftesbury Barnet Harriers		1	London (He)	28 Jul
46.31	North of England AA		1	Birmingham	20 Jul
	(J Whitlock)				
46.36	South East		1	Luton	6 May
	(A Davies, S Williams, E Reinalda, J Maduaka)				
46.38	Midland Counties		2	Birmingham	20 Jul
46.4	National Junior Team	U20	3	Nembro, ITA	3 Aug
	(M Rostek, S Wilhelmy, S Williams, V Shipman)				
46.41	South of England AA		3	Birmingham	20 Jul
46.5	Birchfield Harriers		1	Derby	17 Aug
46.55	Essex Ladies AC		1	Edinburgh	4 May
46.6	Windsor Slough & Eton AC		2	Derby	17 Aug
46.66	Trafford AC		2	Edinburgh	4 May
46.67	Scotland		1	Belfast	22 Jun
	(A McGillivary, S Dudgeon, D Flockhart, K Sketchley)				
46.7	Aldershot Farnham & D AC		1	Crawley	28 Jul
46.73	Yorkshire AA	U20	1	Cudworth	3 Aug
46.75	Birchfield Harriers		1	London (He)	31 Aug
	(S Oxley, C Court, D Lewis, G McLeod)				
46.80	Midland Counties		1	Kunzelsau, GER	7 Sep
	(E Ruddock, Z Wilson, V Shipman, R Drummond)				

Additional National Teams

47.17	Wales	1	Cardiff	25 May
	(H Miles, C Murphy, A James, H Paines)			
48.35	Northern Ireland	3	Belfast	22 Jun

Additional Club Teams (1 - 6 above)

46.9	Edinburgh Woollen Mill	1	Liverpool	28 Jul
47.5	Rotherham	1	Cudworth	23 Jun
47.6	City of Glasgow	1	Coatbridge	23 Jun
47.8	Brunel UC	1	Loughborough	27 Apr
47.8	Derby	1	Derby	23 Jun
47.95	Wigan	3	Birmingham	7 Jul
48.01	Coventry Godiva	4	London (He)	31 Aug
48.04	Loughborough Students	4	Loughborough	19 May
48.13	Team Solvent	1	London (He)	1 Sep
48.2	Basingstoke & Mid Hants	2	Crawley	28 Jul
48.3	Croydon	1	Luton	23 Jun
48.49	Wakefield	1	Sheffield	11 May
48.5	Ealing Southall & Middlesex	3	Crawley	28 Jul
48.7	Walton	1	Walton	25 May
48.7	Sale	5	Manchester	17 Aug

Additional Under 20 Teams (1 - 3 above)

46.9	England Schools	U17	1	Stoke	20 Jul
	(H Roscoe, K Bailey, S Claxton, K Thomas)				

46.93	National Junior 'B' Team		2	Loughborough	19 May
	(D Rose, S Williams, A James, T Nelson)				
46.93	National Junior Team		3	Loughborough	19 May
	(G Hegney, S Wilhelmy, M Rostek, S Claxton)				
47.42	London Schools		1	Sheffield	13 Jul
47.64	Essex Schools	U17	1	Sheffield	13 Jul
	(included S Claxton and S Wilhelmy)				
47.80	South of England AA		1	London (He)	10 Aug
47.84	Merseyside AA		2	Cudworth	3 Aug
47.87	Scotland	U17	2	Pitreavie	10 Aug
	(G Stewart, L Philp, S Burnside, K Scott)				

Additional National Teams

| 48.09 | Wales | | 2 | London (He) | 10 Aug |
| | (L Bryant, E Davies, R James, K Williams) | | | | |

Under 20 Club Teams

48.37	Wigan		3	Venice, ITA	28 Sep
48.8	Birchfield Harriers		1	Derby	15 Sep
48.9	Telford		1	Brierley Hill	4 Aug
49.1	Essex Ladies		1	Blackpool	25 Aug
49.11	Birchfield Harriers	U17	1	Birmingham	8 Sep
49.4	Liverpool Harrier	U17	1	Liverpool	2 Jun
49.4	Coventry Godiva	U17	2	Coventry	11 Aug
49.6	Trafford		2	London (WF)	21 Apr
49.6	Windsor Slough & Eton	U17	1	Coventry	20 Jul
49.7	Sale		3	Blackpool	25 Aug
49.9 X	LaganValley	U17	1	Antrim	27 Apr
49.9	Newham & Essex Beagles	U17	1	Stafford	27 May
49.9	Gateshead		1	Bolton	16 Jun

Additional Under 17 Teams (1 - 3 above)

48.08	West Yorkshire Schools		2	Sheffield	13 Jul
48.1	Wales Schools		2	Stoke	20 Jul
48.96	Surrey Schools		3	Sheffield	13 Jul
49.07	Hampshire Schools		2h1	Sheffield	13 Jul
49.11	Birchfield Harriers		1	Birmingham	8 Sep
49.14	Berkshire Schools		3h1	Sheffield	13 Jul

Additional Under 17 Club Teams (1 - 6 above)

50.1	Sale		1	Jarrow	2 Jun
50.1	Gateshead		1	Hull	7 Jul
50.1	Edinburgh Woollen Mill		1	Stoke	20 Jul
50.2	Dartford		3	Coventry	20 Jul

Under 15 Teams

49.26	West Midlands Schools		1h2	Sheffield	13 Jul
49.41	Scotland		2	Pitreavie	10 Aug
49.66	Greater Manchester Schools		2	Sheffield	13 Jul
49.7	City of Stoke		1	Stoke	20 Jul
49.73	Cheshire Schools		3	Sheffield	13 Jul
49.81	Buckinghamshire Schools		4	Sheffield	13 Jul
50.07	Gwent Schools		1	Swansea	6 Jul
50.08	Staffordshire Schools		5	Sheffield	13 Jul
50.21	Greater Manchester AA		1	Cudworth	3 Aug
50.22	Wales		3	Pitreavie	10 Aug

Additional Under 15 Club Teams (1 above)

50.35	Gateshead		1	Birmingham	7 Sep
50.5	Sale		1	Hull	7 Jul
50.6	Birchfield Harriers		1	Coventry	11 Aug

51.2	St George's School		1	Pitreavie	8	Jun
51.2	City of Glasgow		1	Aberdeen	9	Jun
51.3	Torfaen		1	Brierley Hill	20	Jul
51.43	Swansea		2	Birmingham	7	Sep
51.6	Derby		2	Cannock	26	May
51.6	Braintree & District		1	Watford	2	Jun
51.6	Blackheath		1	Bromley	15	Sep

Under 13 Teams

54.0	Dartford		1	Bromley	15	Sep
54.18	West District		1	Edinburgh	2	Jun
54.3	Reading		1	Neath	20	Jul
54.5	Lincolnshire AA		1			
55.0	Wolverhampton & Bilston		1	Brierley Hill	20	Jul

4 x 200 METRES

1:38.34 i	National Junior Team	U20	3	Lievin, FRA	2	Mar
	(V Shipman, L Owusu, S Wilhelmy, S Williams)					
1:41.62 i	England Schools	U17	1	Birmingham	25	Feb
1:42.69 i	Brunel UC		1	Birmingham	29	Feb
1:43.28 i	Loughborough University		2	Birmingham	29	Feb
1:44.23 i	Scotland Schools	U17	3	Birmingham	25	Feb
1:44.55 i	Wales Schools	U17	4	Birmingham	25	Feb
1:45.2	Walton		1	London (B)	17	Jul
1:46.1	Newham & Essex Beagles	U17	1	Stafford	27	May
1:46.8	Ashford		1	Bromley	15	Sep
1:46.9 i	Glasgow University		1	Glasgow	28	Feb

Additional Club Teams (1 - 6 above)

1:46.9	Dartford	U17	1	Bromley	15	Sep
1:47.3	Millfield School	U20	1	Oxford	11	May
1:47.73 i	Birmingham University		3	Birmingham	29	Feb
1:47.85 i	Ayr Seaforth	U17	1	Glasgow	23	Mar

Additional Under 17 Teams (1 - 5 above)

1:49.2	Invicta East Kent		2	Bromley	15	Sep
1:49.9	Cambridge Harriers		3	Bromley	15	Sep
1:50.0	Blackheath	U15	1	Bromley	15	Sep
1:50.12 i	Hamilton		1h1	Glasgow	23	Mar
1:50.4	Bromley Ladies	U15	2	Bromley	15	Sep
1:50.90 i	Victoria Park AAC		3	Glasgow	23	Mar
1:50.9	Medway		2	Hoo	11	Aug

Additional Under 15 Club Teams (1 - 2 above)

1:51.1	Royal Sutton Coldfield		1	Stafford	27	May
1:51.1	Derby Ladies (Derbyshire AA)		1	Tamworth	7	Sep
1:52.8	Havering Mayesbrook		1	Colchester	26	Aug
1:53.3	Braintree & District		2	Colchester	26	Aug
1:54.00 i	Victoria Park AAC		1h2	Glasgow	23	Mar
1:54.2	Cambridge Harriers		3	Bromley	15	Sep
1:54.8	Wolverhampton & Bilston		2	Stafford	27	May
1:54.8	Brighton & Hove		1	Horsham	9	Jun

Under 13 Teams

2:01.8	Crawley		1	Horsham	9	Jun
2:02.2	Loughton		1	Colchester	26	Aug
2:02.4	Horsham Blue Star		2	Horsham	9	Jun
2:02.5 X	Regent House School		1	Antrim	30	Jul
2:02.8	Worthing		3	Horsham	9	Jun

4 x 400 METRES

3:28.13	National Team		4h1	Atlanta, USA	2 Aug
	(P Smith, A Curbishley, D Fraser, G Oladapo)				
3:31.80	National Team		5	Madrid, SPA	2 Jun
	(D Fraser, A Curbishley, T Joseph, S Gunnell)				
3:37.47i	National Team		2	Birmingham	27 Jan
	(M Neef, D Fraser, L Owusu, A Curbishley)				
3:38.09i	National Team		2	Glasgow	24 Feb
	(D Fraser, L Owusu, E Sutcliffe, A Rowbotham)				
3:40.12	Northern Ireland		1	Belfast	22 Jun
	(Z Arnold, V Jamison, J Latimer, S Llewellyn)				
3:41.48	Birchfield Harriers		1	Milan, ITA	19 May
	(S Stevenson, V Sterne, D Lewis, L Hanson)				
3:41.8	Edinburgh Woollen Mill		1	London (He)	6 Jul
	(A Curbishley, D Flockhart, L Vannet, E Lindsay)				
3:42.21	Scotland		2	Belfast	22 Jun
	(S Dudgeon, L Vannet, M Neef, D Flockhart)				
3:42.84	Sale		1	Edinburgh	4 May
	(D Modahl)				
3:43.07	England		1	Loughborough	19 May
3:43.3	Shaftesbury Barnet Harriers		2	London (He)	6 Jul
	(A Ridley, A Forrester, M Walker, S Llewellyn)				
3:43.56	South of England AA		1	Birmingham	20 Jul
3:43.74	Loughborough Students		1	Sheffield	6 May
3:44.4	Birchfield Harriers		1	Watford	4 May
	(E Waldo, M Thomas, L Hanson, C Court)				
3:44.8	National Junior Team	U20	2	Nembro, ITA	3 Aug
	(E Symonds, A Pritchard, V Jamison, L Owusu)				
3:44.84	National Under 23 Team		3	Hexham	14 Jul
3:45.2	Shaftesbury Barnet Harriers		1	London (He)	28 Jul
	(C Murphy)				
3:45.2	Basingstoke & Mid Hants		1	Crawley	28 Jul
	(T Joseph, T Cornell, A Davies, L Staines)				
3:45.29	Wales		1	Cardiff	25 May
	(G Cashell, A Turner, H Parry, A Layzell)				
3:45.30	Edinburgh Woollen Mill		2	Edinburgh	4 May

Additional Club Teams (1 - 6 above)

3:46.02	Birmingham University		2	Sheffield	6 May
3:47.2	Essex Ladies		1	Manchester	17 Aug
3:49.5	City of Glasgow		1	Coatbridge	23 Jun
3:49.84	Trafford		3	Edinburgh	4 May
3:50.0	Aberdeen		1	Coatbridge	4 Aug
3:50.40	Wakefield		1	Leeds (S)	8 Sep
3:50.85	Team Solent		1	London (He)	1 Sep
3:50.9	Croydon		1	Croydon	22 Jun
3:52.5	Aldershot Farnham & District		2	Crawley	28 Jul
3:52.76	Wigan	U20	2	Venice, ITA	28 Sep
3:53.0	Windsor Slough & Eton		2	Watford	4 May
3:53.1	Coventry Godiva		2	London (He)	28 Jul
3:54.1	Hallamshire		3	Watford	4 May
3:54.5	Peterborough		1	Derby	23 Jun

Additional Under 20 Teams (1 - 2 above)

3:49.86	National Junior Team		3	Loughborough	19 May
	(P Johnson, V Jamison, E Symonds, L Thorne)				
3:51.92	South of England AA		1	London (He)	10 Aug
3:53.77	North of England AA		2	London (He)	10 Aug
	(L Newton, J Oates, R Ogden, S Jacques)				
3:57.44	Wales		3	London (He)	10 Aug

3:58.64	Midland Counties AA		4	London (He)	10 Aug
	(L Waters, S Ross, A Hutchinson, L Rice)				
3:58.7	Essex Ladies		1	Gateshead	16 Jun
4:01.05	Wales Schools		1	Carmarthen	16 Jul
4:01.6	Birchfield Harriers		1	Telford	16 Jun

Additional National Team

| 4:09.2 | Northern Ireland | | 2 | Londonderry | 18 Aug |

Additional Under 20 Club Teams (1 - 3 above)

4:03.7	Trafford		1	Newport	4 Aug
4:06.5	Medway		2	Derby	15 Sep
4:08.5	Bromley Ladies		1	Luton	16 Jun
4:08.5	Ipswich		1	Enfield	25 Aug

Under 17 Teams

4:16.2 X	Lagan Valley		1	Antrim	27 Apr
4:17.3	Hertford & Ware		2	Welwyn G C	6 May
4:19.8	Crawley		1	Horsham	9 Jun
4:23.0	Verlea		3	Welwyn G C	6 May

3 x 800 METRES

6:53.8 +	Shaftesbury Barnet / BMC East			Watford	17 Jul
	(L Webb, R Felton, J McKay)				
	First three legs of 4 x 800 Metres Relay				
6:55.0	Lisburn		1	Antrim	27 Apr
7:01.6	Ballymena & Antrim		2	Antrim	27 Apr
7:10.4	Achilles		1	Oxford	3 Mar
7:18.1	Crawley	U17	1	Horsham	9 Jun
7:19.0	Oxford University		2	Oxford	3 Mar
7:21.4	Basildon	U15	1	Thurrock	17 Jul
7:25.9	Chelmsford	U15	2	Thurrock	17 Jul
7:27.8	Royal Sutton Coldfield	U15	1	Stafford	27 May
7:27.8	Blackheath	U15	1	Bromley	15 Sep

Additional Under 17 Teams (1 above)

7:29.1	Bexley Borough		1	Bromley	15 Sep
7:31.97	City of Glasgow		1	Glasgow	29 Jun
7:33.0	Phoenix	U15	1	Horsham	9 Jun
7:33.0	Medway	U15	2	Bromley	15 Sep

Under 13 Teams

| 7:34.9 | Basildon | | 1 | Thurrock | 17 Jul |
| 7:48.3 | Havering Mayesbrook | | 2 | Thurrock | 17 Jul |

4 x 800 METRES

8:39.6	BMC National Junior Squad U20		1	Watford	17 Jul
	(R Ogden, E Davies, E O'Hare, D Lee)				
8:41.1	BMC National Squad		2	Watford	17 Jul
	(R Jordan, C Raven, C Goff, M Faherty)				
9:20.9	Gateshead		1	Jarrow	23 Jul
9:21.7	BMC East		3	Watford	17 Jul
	(L Webb, R Felton, J McKay, V Watts)				
9:22.0	Jarrow & Hebburn		2	Jarrow	23 Jul

4 x 1500 METRES

18:12.1	BMC National Squad		1	Stretford	30 Apr
	(J Swann, C Pimblett, A Thorpe, M Faherty)				
19:06.7	BMC Junior Squad	U20	2	Stretford	30 Apr
	(M Mann, J Oldfield, A Pritchard, C Goff)				

MENS INDEX

A BDY Thomas U17 3.05.81, Northampton :
PV - 3.80
ABERNETHY David J. V40 5.09.55, Barr & F :
DT - 44.20 (46.70-85)
ABOYO-DANA Gabriel U15 20.11.81, Belgrave :
100 - 11.3w/11.56, 200 - 23.50,
LJ - 6.42w/5.54
ACHIKE Onochie U23 31.01.75, Crawley :
200 - 21.6 (22.15-95),
TJ - 16.36 (16.67w/16.53-94)
ACHURCH Simon U23 27.12.74, Peterborough :
JT - 57.02 (60.16-95)
ADAM Marcus 28.02.68, Haringey :
100 - 10.55 (10.14w-90/10.23-91),
200 - 21.37 (20.10w-90/20.41-92)
ADAMS Allan 11.09.72, Victoria Park AAC :
10MR - 47:54dh
ADAMS Brian V45 13.03.49, Leics WC :
3kW - 13:07.3 (12:02.2-76),
10kW - 45:23.5 (42:40.0-75),
20kW - 1:35:25 (1:27:46-75),
50kW - 4:55:16 (4:15:22-78)
ADAMS Christopher U17 18.07.81, C of Stoke :
HTY - 51.74
ADAMS Darren U15 4.02.82, Belgrave :
80HB - 11.70
ADAMS Nathan U15 14.04.82, Sheffield RWC :
3kW - 15:27.0, 3kWR - 15:01
ADAMS Philip 3.11.71, Sale :
SP - 15.51 (15.58-92)
ADAMS Simeon U13 1.07.84, Sheffield RWC :
2kW - 11:20.0
ADAMS Tom U20 22.08.77, :
800 - 1:54.9
ADEPEGBA Sunny 6.06.71, Haringey :
200 - 21.52 (21.4w-95/21.5-90)
AFILAKA Carl 13.07.68, Oxford City/TRI :
100 - 10.5 (10.87-95)
AFILAKA Michael 16.11.71, N & EB/Staffs Un :
60 - 6.88i (6.80i-95),
100 - 10.60w/10.65 (10.46w/10.63-95),
200 - 21.6w/21.8/21.86
(21.09w-93/21.2-95/21.22-94)
AGARD Trevor U17 12.03.80, Hounslow :
400HY - 58.09
AGYEPONG Francis K. 16.06.65, Shaft Barnet :
TJ - 17.22w/17.18
(17.29wA/17.24w/17.18-95/15.85w-86)
AHERNE Christopher U17 21.12.79, Cardiff :
HTY - 52.68 (53.34-95)
AHMED Syful U17 25.10.79, Belgrave :
LJ - 6.60, TJ - 14.08
AIREY Martin 28.10.70, Brighton/E Anglia Un :
600 - 1:20.3, 800 - 1:50.2, 1500 - 3:48.0
AITCHISON Douglas 31.12.66, Perth :
HT - 48.70 (49.90-90)
AKINSANYA Oluwafemi 29.11.69, Peterbro :
LJ - 7.37, TJ - 16.58
AL-KOWARRI Ahmed U20 30.11.78, Aberdeen :
400 - 48.99
ALDWINKLE Matthew U23 23.08.74, Notts :
400 - 48.6/48.64 (48.5-94/48.57-95)
ALEXANDER Peter U15 29.09.81, Medway :
TJ - 12.45
ALEXANDER Tim U17 6.09.79, Medway :
800 - 1:57.73

ALFRED Ricky U20 20.12.77, Milton Keynes :
200 - 22.10
ALI-NIA Ashley U15 3.01.82, Worthing :
SPB - 13.30
ALIX James U15 24.12.81, Dudley & Stourb :
HJ - 1.80
ALLAN David Neil 17.10.70, Inverness :
HT - 56.22 (60.12-95)
ALLAN Graeme U17 24.09.80, Elgin :
SPY - 15.76ilht/15.10i/15.05, DTY - 43.60,
HTY - 55.10
ALLEN Clarence 1.04.64, Herne Hill :
110H - 14.9/15.26w (14.8-92/14.82-94)
ALLEN Mark 23.09.66, Border :
200 - 20.90
ALLEN Michael U17 7.03.80, Ballymena & A :
JTY - 59.34, OctY - 4376
ALLEN Sam U20 26.10.78, Rowntrees :
DecJ - 5083
ALLENBY Robert U17 15.10.79, Cleethorpes :
100 - 11.15w (11.3-95)
ALLINSON Kevin U17 5.03.80, Mandale :
400HY - 58.2/58.35
ALLISON Joseph 16.09.59, Newham & E B :
TJ - 14.08 (15.93w-86/15.86-85)
ALLISON Matthew 26.02.73, Leeds :
JT - 57.78, Dec - 6213 (6673-94)
ALLPORT Anthony U17 30.09.79, Birchfield :
DTY - 45.46
AMOR Martin 22.09.68, Copeland :
3kSt - 9:25.9 (9:11.1-92)
AMOS Guy 15.06.63, Norwich :
800 - 1:52.5 (1:51.3-94)
AMOS Matthew U20 20.11.78, Northampton :
2kSt - 6:07.1, 3kSt - 9:43.8
ANDERSON Keith 10.08.57, Bingley :
5k - 14:22.9 (14:09.00-94)
ANDERSON Khary U20 29.11.77, Southwark :
TJ - 14.52
ANDERSON Mark U20 5.11.77, City of Stoke :
400H - 54.54
ANGELL Steven 8.04.70, Old Gaytonians :
DT - 42.22, HT - 55.62 (58.36-95)
ANGUS Daniel U15 15.07.82, Mandale :
100 - 11.3/11.31w (11.89-95),
200 - 22.48w/22.65
ANSELL Keith 30.03.62, Braintree :
SP - 15.28
ANTHONY James U15 30.03.82, Neath :
PenB - 2754
ANTHONY Tristan U15 16.12.82, Verlea :
100 - 11.5/11.59, 200 - 22.63w/23.03
ANTINORI Glenn U17 5.04.80, Shaft Barnet :
800 - 1:57.41
ANTOINE Mark 20.10.69, Cambridge Harriers :
60 - 6.9i
APPS James U17 29.04.80, Blackheath :
JT - 55.84, JTY - 61.44
ARCHAMPONG James Quarshie U23
14.03.76, Swansea :
200 - 21.9, 60H - 8.23i (8.01i-94),
110H - 14.1w/14.14w/14.19 (14.18-94)
ARCHBOLD Ian 10.06.65, Morpeth :
10k - 30:53.9 (29:47.16-92)
ARCHER Clayton U23 29.05.76, Thames VH :
200 - 21.5/22.18 (21.54-95), 400 - 46.83

ARCHER Paul U15 7.10.81, Blackheath :
  SPB - 15.00, DTB - 40.44, HTB - 40.90,
  PenB - 2560
ARMSTRONG Brett U23 9.09.76, Rowheath :
  PV - 4.40 (4.60-95)
ARMSTRONG J. Simon 29.05.62, Bournem'th :
  SP - 15.02 (16.52-90), DT - 43.74 (50.22-92)
ARMSTRONG Paul U17 20.10.79, Pitreavie :
  100HY - 14.0w/14.1/14.13w/14.54,
  400HY - 55.32
ARMSTRONG Samuel U23 17.02.74, Nithsdale :
  JT - 57.22 (58.20-95)
ARNOLD Peter U15 29.06.82, Jarrow & H :
  400 - 52.8
ARRAND Andrew 20.01.66, :
  Mar - 2:24:32
ARRO Tony 31.10.72, Herne Hill/AUS :
  400 - 48.9
ASHE Richard U23 5.10.74, Hillingdon :
  800 - 1:49.38, 1500 - 3:41.2, 1M - 3:59.98
ASHURST Andrew John 2.01.65, Sale :
  PV - 5.20i/5.20 (5.45i-92/5.40-88/5.00-85)
ASPDEN Richard U23 15.10.76, Belgrave :
  HJ - 2.15 (2.16-95)
ATKINS Matthew U20 23.06.77, Derby & Co :
  JT - 61.96 (64.68-95)
ATKINSON Michael A. 6.03.58, Annadale Str :
  SP - 13.75 (16.35-81)
ATKINSON Richard U23 9.10.74, Wakefield :
  JT - 55.98 (67.22-93)
ATKINSON Steven U20 12.04.79, Middlesbro :
  DecJ - 5487
ATTON Karl R. 14.09.71, Leics WC :
  3kW - 13:18.68 (12:42.3-94),
  10kW - 47:07.0 (45:14.7-92), 50kW - 4:35:48
ATTWOOD Paul 13.12.69, Royal Navy :
  Dec - 5231
ATWELL Robert U15 17.10.81, Cheltenham :
  400 - 52.56
AUDU George U20 18.01.77, Thames Valley :
  LJ - 7.14
AUSTIN James 9.08.65, Clydesdale :
  3kSt - 9:24.72 (9:05.32-94)
AVIS Mark 22.10.71, Team Solent :
  100 - 10.7/10.97, 200 - 21.7w/21.8
AWANAH Mark U15 23.09.82, Lewisham :
  LJ - 6.16, TJ - 12.52w, PenB - 2840
AYLESBURY Wayne Paul 24.03.64, Leeds :
  3kSt - 9:21.9 (8:38.81-92)
AYRE Stephen C. 20.10.67, Morpeth :
  DT - 46.34 (48.56-95)

BABLISTER Peter, Southend :
  400H - 54.8
BACKLEY Stephen James 12.02.69, Camb H :
  JT - 87.44 (91.46-92)
BADDELEY Andrew U15 20.06.82, Wirral :
  1500 - 4:18.1
BAILEY Colin U13 15.11.83, Burnley :
  HJ - 1.55, JTC - 35.94
BAILEY Josef U20 2.12.77, City of Stoke :
  110HJ - 14.98w/15.20
BAILEY Matthew U17 16.02.81, Barnsley :
  800 - 1:57.49
BAILEY Stuart U20 6.08.78, Wigan :
  800 - 1:53.5, 2kSt - 5:58.03, 3kSt - 9:20.0
BAILLIE Christopher U17 21.04.81, Victoria P :
  100HY - 13.68, LJ - 6.60

BAILLIE Ross U20 26.09.77, Victoria Park :
  60 - 6.93i (6.89i-95), 100 - 10.54w/10.62,
  200 - 21.71i/21.80
    (21.6w-95/21.67i-94/21.7/21.75-95),
  60H - 8.08i (8.04i-95), 110H - 14.01
BAIRD Lawrence U20 14.12.77, Cleethorpes :
  400 - 48.08
BAKER George U23 14.08.76, Newham & EB:
  SP - 14.71
BAKER Kevin H. 12.12.57, Weymouth :
  20kW - 1:38:16
BAKER Peter 6.02.73, Portsmouth :
  1500 - 3:50.84 (3:49.5-93)
BALDOCK Richard U17 22.04.80, Bed & Co :
  PV - 3.90
BALDOCK Sean U23 3.12.76, Hastings :
  200 - 21.67, 400 - 46.80
BALDWIN Ben U15 16.09.81, Bristol :
  HJ - 1.80
BALDWIN Stefan M. 26.04.70, Peterborough :
  JT - 70.38 (72.92-93)
BALL James R. 17.02.63, Steyning :
  3kW - 12:59.6 (12:20.0-87)
BALL James U17 17.04.80, Bedford & County :
  HTY - 49.34
BALL Matthew U20 7.09.78, Hallamshire :
  200 - 21.7w/21.77w/22.01
BALOGUN Anthony 7.02.66, Woodford Green :
  800 - 1:52.62 (1:49.2-91)
BAMFORD Matthew 19.09.58, Hillingdon :
  JT - 61.56 (61.98-95)
BANDA Rasheed U17 18.03.80, Blackheath :
  LJ - 6.80w/6.59, TJ - 13.60
BANNISTER Dominic 1.04.68, Shaftesbury B :
  5k - 14:16.68 (14:08.85-95)
BANNISTER Hugh U20 26.08.78, Llanelli :
  400 - 49.48
BANNISTER Simon U17 16.04.81, Norwich :
  HJ - 1.90
BANNON Clayton U20 15.03.77, Hounslow :
  800 - 1:54.7
BAPTISTE Barry 17.07.67, Newham & E B :
  HT - 49.04 (57.34-90)
BARBER Michael W. 19.10.73, Birch/Staffs Un :
  PV - 5.30 (5.42-95)
BARBER Nick U20 22.11.78, Hallamshire :
  SPJ - 14.41
BARCLAY Matthew U15 28.01.82, Essex Sch :
  80HB - 12.15, LJ - 6.02, PenB - 2743
BARDEN Anthony J. 15.10.60, Basildon :
  Mar - 2:25:33 (2:24:21-95)
BARDEN Spencer Christian 31.03.73, GEC :
  1500 - 3:43.8, 1M - 4:02.1,
  3k - 7:58.4 (7:58.08-93), 5k - 13:52.34
BARGH Andrew U23 21.08.76, T Sol/Loughbro :
  110H - 15.0w/15.20, 400H - 52.4/52.63
BARIKOR Bomeme U15 22.05.82, Blackheath :
  HJ - 1.85
BARKER Leo U20 26.12.78, Diss :
  110HJ - 14.3w/14.4, 110H - 15.32, LJ - 7.07,
  Dec - 6617, DecJ - 6592
BARKLEY Olly U15 28.11.81, :
  TJ - 12.12
BARLOW Alden, Doncaster :
  24HrT - 220.490km (221.920km-95)
BARNABY John U17 8.10.79, Scarborough :
  DTY - 42.48

329

BARNARD Paul 27.07.72, City of Edinburgh/
  Birchfield/North East SH :
  HT - 62.24 (62.70-95)
BARNES John U15 6.05.82, Hull Springhead :
  SPB - 13.83, DTB - 40.82,
  HTY - 52.64, HTB - 61.32
BARNETSON David 1.07.71, City of Edinburgh :
  400 - 48.8, 110H - 15.0/15.38 (15.23-95),
  400H - 52.6/53.24, HJ - 2.10 (2.19-92)
BARRETT Clint U20 21.11.77, Braintree :
  DecJ - 5676
BARROS Demetrio 29.06.71, Hounslow :
  JT - 59.10 (66.92-93)
BARRY William U17 4.09.79, Chorley :
  800 - 1:56.5
BARTON Tim 3.10.70, Charnwood :
  100 - 10.7/10.82w/10.95 (10.7-95), 200 - 21.9
BASTOW Sebastian U15 11.10.81, Mandale :
  80HB - 11.10
BATCHELOR Perry U23 11.12.75, Cov G :
  110H - 15.20w (14.7w/14.81w/14.9/15.10-94)
BATEMAN Ian U15 6.02.82, Chester & Ellesm :
  800 - 2:04.6
BATES Stephen U15 5.11.81, Doncaster :
  1500 - 4:19.10
BATT Daniel U15 20.01.82, Hamps Sch :
  SPB - 13.61
BAULCH James Steven 3.05.73, Cardiff :
  200 - 20.97 (20.84-94), 300 - 32.25, 400 - 44.57
BAXTER Dave U20 16.01.79, Sale :
  3kSt - 9:29.2
BAXTER Geoffrey U17 9.12.79, GEC :
  800 - 1:56.8, 1500 - 4:03.75
BEARD Keith 8.11.61, Leiden :
  JT - 72.76 (76.10r-91/73.88-90)
BEARDSALL Simon 16.06.70, Dorking & M V :
  1500 - 3:50.6
BEASLEY Graham U20 24.10.77, Luton :
  100 - 10.7w/11.07 (10.7/10.93-94),
  200 - 21.20w/21.62 (21.34-95)
BEATON Peter 5.04.72, Pitreavie :
  SP - 13.81 (14.29-94)
BEATTIE Jim 22.07.73, Lochgelly :
  400 - 48.7 (47.73-95)
BEAUCHAMP William 9.09.70, Thames VH :
  HT - 63.90
BEAUFORD Adam U15 24.10.81, Yeovil Oly :
  HTB - 46.16
BEAUMONT Paul 27.03.63, Belgrave/Army :
  400H - 53.0 (51.23-89)
BEDDOWS Darren U20 4.05.78, Swansea :
  PV - 4.20
BEER Mark U17 28.02.80, Chesterfield :
  HJ - 1.96
BEERAJE Jason U20 10.05.77, Kingston & P :
  800 - 1:54.5,
BEEVERS Andrew 3.05.73, Leeds :
  3kSt - 9:13.0
BEHARRELL Mark U17 10.01.81, City of Hull :
  PV - 3.80
BELL John U15 2.04.82, Fife :
  100 - 11.5w/11.88
BELL John 10.09.73, Newham & EB/Loughbro :
  400H - 53.86 (53.70-92)
BELL Matthew U20 2.06.78, Corby :
  HT - 57.94, HTJ - 59.14
BELL Michael U20 23.11.77, Coventry Godiva :
  400 - 48.80 (48.51-95)

BELL Robert U20 17.12.77, Thurrock :
  PV - 4.30
BELL Simon 26.12.66, Lincoln Well/RAF :
  5k - 14:31.6, Mar - 2:28:05, 2kSt - 5:57.93,
  3kSt - 8:53.39
BELL Stuart 29.07.67, Chester Le Street :
  5k - 14:32.36 (14:23.1-95),
  10k - 30:50.29 (29:45.6-95), 10MR - 48:47
BELLAMY Neil U17 23.07.80, C of Plymouth :
  LJ - 6.61, OctY - 4472
BELLU Luigi 12.07.70, Enfield/ITA :
  HT - 54.34
BELSHAM Matthew 11.10.71, Sale :
  PV - 5.40i/5.35 (5.35-93)
BENJAMIN Timothy U15 2.05.82, Cardiff :
  100 - 11.33, 200 - 23.2/23.21
BENN Andrew U20 2.09.77, Blackheath/WLHS :
  HT - 56.86, HTJ - 61.58, JT - 60.92
BENNETT Christopher U17 18.10.80, Soton C :
  200 - 22.20w/22.55, 400 - 49.42
BENNETT Michael U17 22.11.80, Blackheath :
  HTY - 47.98
BENNETT Paul 9.08.71, Rotherham :
  800 - 1:52.26 (1:51.1-93)
BENNETT Simon 16.10.72, N Devon :
  JT - 66.58
BENSON Mark 21.12.63, Liverpool H :
  3k - 8:22.34i/9:15.0 (8:18.0-95), 5k - 14:31.00
BENT Colin 12.04.70, Shaftesbury B/RAF :
  HJ - 2.20
BENTHAM Kermitt E. 16.04.60, Thames VH :
  400 - 48.31 (46.57-87)
BENTHAM Nicolas Peter 7.12.70, Highgate :
  800 - 1:50.2 (1:49.4-92),
  1500 - 3:49.32 (3:48.9-93)
BENTON Steven U23 26.09.76, Thurrock :
  LJ - 7.01i
BERGIN Steven 17.06.66, Gateshead :
  SP - 15.68 (16.09-89)
BERRY Eric H. V40 23.04.54, Yeovil Oly :
  HT - 49.38 (62.00-74)
BERRY Robert 29.07.69, Liverpool Pembroke :
  3k - 8:22.7, 2kSt - 5:48.08, 3kSt - 9:06.7
BERWICK Christopher V50 1.05.46, Leics WC :
  50kW - 4:48:01 (4:23:22-86)
BEST Mark U17 9.09.79, Winchester :
  1500 - 4:06.9
BESWICK Paul A. 5.12.68, GEC :
  PV - 4.80 (4.80ns-94)
BETTS Edward G. 18.02.71, Thames Valley :
  400H - 51.20 (51.15-94)
BETTS Trevor U17 9.10.79, Isle of Wight :
  JTY - 53.22
BEVAN Nigel Charles 3.01.68, Belgrave :
  JT - 74.60 (81.70-92)
BEVAN Trystan 23.08.75, Swansea :
  400H - 54.6 (55.41-95)
BEYNON Daniel U15 23.01.82, Swansea :
  1500 - 4:19.72
BIGNALL Douglas U23 20.10.74, Haringey :
  100 - 10.6/10.62, 200 - 21.60
BILBY Andrew U17 20.02.80, Sutton & Dist :
  400 - 50.8/51.05
BINNS Andrew U20 12.03.79, Barrow & Furn :
  HJ - 2.00
BIRBECK Rory 24.09.73, Hyndburn :
  HJ - 2.00 (2.00-93), SP - 13.77 (13.88-94),
  DT - 45.50

BIRCHALL Robert 14.06.70, Peterborough :
  5k - 14:11.64, 10kR - 29:37 (29:33-94)
BIRD Justin Paul 3.05.71, Morpeth :
  200 - 21.9/22.06, 400 - 48.59 (47.68-94)
BIRSE Stephen U20 8.10.77, Middlesbro & C :
  JT - 57.38 (57.92-95)
BISHOP Gary 3.08.63, Croydon :
  Mar - 2:23:59*
BISHOP Mark Andrew Paul 12.02.67, Havering :
  400H - 51.95 (51.28-89), JT - 57.34 (63.48-90)
BLACK David James U20 9.10.78, Cann & S :
  DT - 40.22, DTJ - 45.74
BLACK Iain Russell 18.09.70, C of Edinburgh :
  PV - 4.50, Dec - 5741 (5943-91)
BLACK Lee U20 26.11.78, Corby :
  400 - 49.0/49.48 (49.47-95), DecJ - 5865
BLACK Roger Anthony 31.03.66, Team Sol :
  100 - 10.48 (10.4-87), 200 - 20.5w/20.56,
  300 - 32.26 (32.06+-91/32.08-86), 400 - 44.37
BLACKMAN Gary U17 24.09.80, Solihull & SH :
  1.5kSt - 4:31.5
BLACKSHAW Paul U15 22.11.81, Sale :
  SPB - 14.12
BLADE Martin 30.05.68, Team Solent :
  400 - 47.39
BLIGHT Ross U20 28.05.77, Cardiff :
  HTJ - 51.46 (54.18-94)
BLISS Anthony 7.03.70, Brighton :
  110H - 15.4w/15.5/15.58 (15.5-93)
BLOOMFIELD M. U23, Great Yarmouth :
  DT - 43.40
BOBB Samuel U23 29.08.75, Blackh/Brunel Un :
  TJ - 14.77
BODEN Sam U17 16.02.80, Cambridge & C :
  800 - 1:56.3, 1500 - 3:59.84, 3k - 8:41.4
BODYS Christopher U13 29.12.83, Cumnock :
  75HC - 12.6
BOLTON Richard U13 1.10.83, Wolves & B :
  200 - 24.7
BOLTON Thomas U13 24.11.83, Basingstoke :
  800 - 2:16.6
BONELLE Clive 2.04.71, East Cheshire :
  3k - 8:13.6
BONICH Daniel M. U20 22.11.78, Bexley :
  100 - 10.8/10.89
BONNETT Stephen U20 13.07.78, Scunthorpe :
  HJ - 1.96, Dec - 5184, DecJ - 5942
BONNING Arron U23 9.11.75, Havering :
  Dec - 4949
BOOTH Gregor 31.08.62, Stranraer :
  Mar - 2:21:37
BOOTH Simon 10.05.68, Keswick :
  Mar - 2:32:26
BOOTH Stephen R. 21.10.71, Oxford C/Ach :
  110H - 15.6 (14.97-95)
BOOTHROYD Jason 26.11.69, Sale/Mich Un :
  1500 - 3:45.73 (3:44.2-91),
  1M - 4:07.41i (4:06.73i-95)
BORSUMATO Anthony 13.12.73, City of Stoke/
  Staffs Univ : 400H - 51.47
BOUNDY Christohpher U17 25.12.79, Gate :
  PV - 3.90
BOUNDY Patrick U20 19.02.79, Hounslow :
  JT - 53.02
BOURNE Nigel 18.04.72, Queens Park :
  LJ - 7.18i (6.98-95)
BOVELL Colin 9.03.72, Newham & Essex B :
  110H - 14.74 (14.1/14.17-94)

BOWDEN Graham U15 2.09.81, Haringey :
  PV - 3.40
BOWDITCH Kristen Robert U23 14.01.75,
  City of Stoke : 1500 - 3:46.5,
  3k - 8:09.29 (8:04.66-95), 5k - 13:55.32
BOWEN Edward U23 3.02.76, Leamington :
  1500 - 3:50.06
BOWLING Luke U15 4.11.81, Cambridge & C :
  100 - 11.51
BOWMAN Simon 11.09.71, Diss :
  HT - 46.92 (50.34-95)
BOWN Simon Paul U23 21.11.74, Haringey :
  HT - 58.12 (58.28-95)
BOX Toby 9.09.72, Sale :
  100 - 10.48A/10.66w/10.80
    (10.07w-94/10.32-95),
  200 - 21.13A (20.72-94), LJ - 6.92
BOYLE Tim U20 4.07.78, Tipton :
  3k - 8:34.74
BRACE Steven 7.07.61, Bridgend :
  HMar - 1:03:42 (1:02:29-90), Mar - 2:10:35
BRACKSTONE David U15 13.03.82, C of Stoke :
  80HB - 12.11
BRADFIELD Nathan U17, Windsor S & E :
  HTY - 48.66
BRADLEY Colin V40 2.02.56, Trowbridge :
  10kW - 48:21.67 (46:00.3-87),
  50kW - 4:59:35 (4:33:42-87)
BRADLEY Darren U15 7.01.82, Darlington :
  1500 - 4:18.53
BRADLEY Dominic U23 22.12.76, Stockport :
  110H - 15.0/15.21
BRADLEY Matthew U15 21.09.81, :
  80HB - 12.0
BRADSTOCK Arne Roald 24.04.62, Enfield :
  JT - 77.84 (85.34-83)
BRAITHWAITE Darren 20.01.69, Haringey :
  60 - 6.63i (6.51i-95), 100 - 10.13 (10.12-95),
  150 - 15.24 (15.09w-95),
  200 - 20.60A/21.02 (20.47-95)
BRAMBLE Marvin U20 10.06.77, Blackheath :
  TJ - 15.04i/14.94 (15.25w-93/15.23-95)
BRANNEN Anthony 16.09.68, City of Stoke :
  SP - 13.63 (14.06-95)
BRASHER Hugh 28.09.64, Hounslow :
  3kSt - 9:03.15 (8:54.59-95)
BREBNER Francis 27.11.65, SGA (Prof) :
  SP - 14.43i
BREND Peter A. U20 2.02.77, Team Solent :
  400 - 48.8/49.34 (48.4/48.50-94)
BREWER Daniel U17 10.08.80, Blackheath :
  100HY - 13.33w/13.34,
BRIDGER Jeremy U23 23.09.75, Team Sol :
  400H - 53.12
BRIDGER Peter U15 6.09.81, Luton :
  800 - 2:04.78
BRIERLEY James U20 31.07.77, Telford :
  HJ - 2.26
BRIERLEY Timothy U15 3.12.81, Basingstoke :
  800 - 2:05.3
BRIFFETT Stephen U20 22.10.78, Highgate :
  800 - 1:54.97
BRILUS Philip S. 29.12.68, Harlow :
  110H - 14.8 (14.50-90), PV - 4.10 (4.30-91)
BRINING David U17 27.02.80, Leeds :
  HJ - 1.90
BRITTON Daniel U15 25.09.81, Bournemouth :
  JTB - 53.74

BRIZZELL Paul U23 3.10.76, Ballym & A/IRE :
200 - 21.20w/21.56 (21.50-95)
BROADHEAD Daniel U15 19.04.82, Rotherham :
PV - 3.80
BROCKLEBANK Robert J. U23 12.10.76,
Blackburn : HJ - 2.15i/2.15 (2.16-95)
BROOKING David 22.10.68, City of Plymouth :
110H - 15.3/15.46 (15.0-94/15.34-95)
BROOKS Richard U17 3.07.80, Southport :
JTY - 59.10
BROOKS Stephen 8.06.70, Bing/Iowa St Univ :
5k - 14:15.93 (13:52.54-94), 10k - 28:55.38,
10kR - 29:23, HMar - 1:03:50, Mar - 2:20:18
BROOM Kevin U15 20.11.81, Morpeth :
3k - 9:37.8
BROOME Edward 3.09.72, Blackpool/Oxf Un :
3kSt - 9:15.6 (9:14.9-95)
BROUGHTON Mark A. 23.10.63, Met. Police :
HT - 49.84 (54.28-93)
BROWN David 4.06.66, Thurrock :
JT - 59.28 (61.32-91)
BROWN Derek 23.01.60, Cheltenham :
Mar - 2:32:19
BROWN Gareth 21.07.67, City of Edinburgh :
800 - 1:50.38 (1:47.15-93)
BROWN Gareth J. 10.05.68, Steyning :
3kW - 12:58.0 (12:36.91-87), 35kW - 2:58:13,
50kW - 4:27:22
BROWN Jonathan M. 27.02.71, Sheffield :
3k - 7:55.9+e (7:51.72-93),
5k - 13:20.10 (13:19.78-93), 10k - 27:59.72
10kR - 28:38A (27:20dh-95/28:05-93),
BROWN Jotham U15 18.03.82, Blackheath :
100 - 11.04w/11.28, 200 - 22.80
BROWN Kevin 10.09.64, Haringey :
SP - 13.93 (14.66-95), DT - 58.66 (59.50-95)
BROWN Michael 6.05.62, Haringey :
TJ - 14.92 (16.15-89)
BROWN Patrick U17 2.09.79, Gateshead :
100HY - 13.65w/13.79, 400HY - 56.31
BROWN Paul U13 8.10.83, Charnwood :
800 - 2:14.3, 1500 - 4:39.7
BROWN Richard V50 18.11.46, Surrey WC :
24HrT - 219.689km, 18:12:04 (16:50:28-93)
BROWN Robert, :
24HrT - 207.360km
BROWN Robert U20 3.03.78, Elswick :
2kSt - 5:56.2, 3kSt - 9:32.5 (9:28.4-95)
BROWN Steven U15 20.03.82, Southend :
PV - 3.85
BROWN Stuart 22.11.72, Deeside :
HJ - 2.00
BROWNE Adrian Stephen U20 14.07.78,
Windsor S & E : TJ - 14.94w/14.81
BROWNE Curtis U23 11.09.75, Birchfield :
60 - 6.77i
BROWNE Derek 28.09.66, Belgrave :
TJ - 15.24 (15.95-93)
BRUCE Calum U23 28.02.75, Pitreavie :
HT - 50.84 (52.54-95)
BRUNT Daniel U23 23.04.76, Chesterfield :
SP - 14.07i/13.57
BRYAN Justin 16.08.69, Torfaen :
DT - 42.92
BRYAN Lee U15 24.11.81, Coventry Godiva :
100 - 11.5/11.90, 200 - 22.76w/22.90
BUCHANAN Andrew I. 12.09.70, AF&D :
PV - 4.40 (4.50-94)

BUCK Matthew U23 5.04.74, W Gr/Brunel Un :
PV - 4.60
BUCKFIELD Nicholas 5.06.73, Crawley :
200 - 21.53, 400 - 47.4, PV - 5.71
BUCKLEY Christopher T.P. 26.07.61, Westb :
5k - 14:33.8 (13:41.34-84),
10k - 30:14.38 (29:38.16-86)
BUCKNALL Martyn 2.11.70, City of Stoke :
400 - 48.55
BUCKNER Thomas Christopher 16.04.63, Havant :
3kSt - 8:54.91 (8:25.50-92)
BUDDEN Nicholas U23 17.11.75, Norwich :
200 - 21.10, 400 - 46.34
BULL Andrew 26.06.69, Sheffield :
100 - 10.6 (10.77w-92/10.93-88),
200 - 21.7 (21.3-95/21.61w-93/21.78-92)
BULL James U20 12.02.79, Ipswich :
SP - 13.16, SPJ - 14.84
BULL Michael P. 6.06.70, Notts :
Dec - 5921
BULLEN Richie 6.10.60, Les Croupiers :
Mar - 2:32:19 (2:25:58-86)
BULLOCK David U23 1.12.76, Here & W Sch :
DecJ - 5483o (5464-94)
BULLOCK David U23 18.12.74, Shaft Barnet :
800 - 1:50.9
BULLOCK Guy Ross U23 15.10.75, Wigan :
100 - 10.7w (10.8-95), 300 - 32.73, 400 - 45.76,
200 - 21.3 (21.25A-95/21.80w/21.82-93)
BULLOCK Simon U17 22.11.80, Hereford :
400 - 50.76
BULMAN Neil Andrew U20 7.09.77, Mand/NESH :
HT - 46.26, HTJ - 52.58
BULSTRIDGE Michael 23.01.73, Birchfield :
5k - 14:32.72
BUNDOCK Matthew U23 18.11.76, Blackheath :
SP - 15.18
BUNNEY Elliot John 11.12.66, C of Edinburgh :
100 - 10.99 (10.20-86)
BURGESS Paul William 10.11.70, Wigan :
800 - 1:51.6 (1:47.80-91),
1500 - 3:49.5 (3:46.83-89)
BURGIN Scott U17 2.04.80, Rotherham :
400 - 50.70
BURKE Alan P. 23.05.65, Hounslow/IRE :
PV - 4.50 (5.00-89)
BURKE John 18.05.70, London Irish/IRE :
3k - 8:22.0 (8:02.84-95)
BURKE Raymond Nicholas 11.11.69, S B :
60 - 6.85i (6.71i-92),
100 - 10.68w/10.95 (10.39-92)
BURLEY Darren U17 13.01.80, Blackheath :
100 - 10.7db/11.0/11.04, 200 - 21.50w/21.94
BURLEY Matthew U17, Medway :
TJ - 13.21
BURMAN-ROY Sudip U20 15.01.78, Blackh :
SPJ - 13.98 (14.15-95)
BURNETT Leon U15 12.09.81, Birchfield :
LJ - 5.97, TJ - 13.31w/12.98
BURNS Ian T. U20 20.09.77, Gateshead :
JT - 54.94
BURNS William, Preston :
3kSt - 9:20.5
BURRAWAY Paul 30.11.68, Hounslow :
HJ - 2.06 (2.10-93)
BURROWS Darius U23 8.08.75, Birchfield :
1500 - 3:46.1, 1M - 4:08.56, 3k - 7:58.7,
5k - 13:54.42, 3kSt - 9:06.9

332

BURT James U17, Eastbourne College :
100 - 11.0
BUSHELL Mark Anthony U23 22.10.76, T Sol :
110HJ - 14.92o (14.64w/14.95-94),
110H - 15.15 (14.7w/14.72w-95),
PV - 4.40, LJ - 7.51w/7.22 (7.25-95),
Dec - 6798 (6839-95), DecJ - 7110o

CADDY Neil U20 18.03.75, Newquay & P :
800 - 1:49.5, 1500 - 3:39.1, 1M - 3:55.84,
2k - 5:02.99, 3k - 7:58.14i/8:03.59
CADOGAN Gary A. 8.10.66, Haringey :
400 - 48.19i (46.37-87), 400H - 50.00 (49.07-94)
CADWALLADER Lee 17.01.69, Liverpool H :
800 - 1:48.37 (1:47.43-93),
1500 - 3:49.30 (3:43.39-95),
1M - 4:03.3 (4:02.00-94)
CAINES Adrian U23 13.11.74, Birchfield :
110H - 14.51
CAINES Daniel U20 15.05.79, R S Coldfield :
200 - 21.57
CAIRNS Steven 3.11.67, Scottish Borders :
3kSt - 9:05.85 (9:03.45-95)
CALDWELL Ben U15 3.03.82, Bolton :
400 - 52.3/52.52, 800 - 2:04.64
CALLAN Adrian 28.11.62, Shettleston :
5k - 14:33.11 (13:58.93-88)
CALLAWAY David J. 4.09.63, Haringey :
SP - 17.21i/16.72 (17.55-93)
CALLOW J. Allan V50 4.09.45, Manx H :
3kW - 13:29.8 (13:06.0-72),
20kW - 1:39:36 (1:34:14-73)
CALVERT Ewan 28.11.73, TVH/Clydesdale :
800 - 1:49.65 (1:49.06-95)
CAMERON David 29.09.66, Shettleston :
10k - 30:39.3 (30:36.35-92)
CAMERON Leon U13, Sale :
100 - 12.25w, 200 - 24.79
CAMERON Niall U17 19.12.79, Forres :
1.5kSt - 4:37.93
CAMERON Rezlimond 18.05.60, Thames VH :
TJ - 15.00 (16.32w-89/16.20-88)
CAMERON Trevor U23 25.11.76, Shaft Barnet :
100 - 10.91 (10.29w/10.5/10.54-94)
CAMPBELL Darren A. 12.09.73, Sale :
100 - 10.17, 150 - 15.44,
200 - 20.98 (20.55w/20.86-93)
CAMPBELL Ian 6.09.71, Har/Dundee HH :
800 - 1:51.35 (1:49.95-93),
1500 - 3:43.13i/3:50.52
(3:43.05i-94/3:43.64-93), 1M - 4:10.0
CAMPBELL James 17.06.70, Annadale Str :
5k - 14:19.26 (13:48.9-94)
CAMPBELL Kenneth William 30.09.72,
Thames Valley/Edinburgh SH : 60 - 6.88i,
100 - 10.88, 110H - 13.90 (13.86-94)
CAMPBELL Malcolm 3.01.71, Winchester :
3k - 8:16.90, 10k - 29:16.47un/30:05.49
CAMPBELL Patrick U17 10.03.80, N Down :
PV - 3.80
CAMPBELL Paul A. U17 29.01.80, Mandale :
100HY - 13.9
CAMPBELL Paul W. U17 26.03.80, Mandale :
200 - 22.76w/22.9/22.95, 400 - 50.42
CANNING Dale U20 12.06.78, Stockport :
800 - 1:52.6 (1:52.0-95)
CAPEL S., Swindon :
400H - 55.9

CAPELING Kirk U17 27.02.80, Paddock Wood :
HTY - 48.76
CARD Gavin U20 11.05.78, Morpeth :
PV - 4.40i (4.20-95)
CARE Robert V45 8.04.47, Rowheath :
3kW - 13:12.52i/13:32.42 (13:12.4-87)
CARELESS Robert U23 7.09.74, Telford :
HT - 52.50 (54.28-95)
CARGILL Andrew 25.10.69, Haringey :
LJ - 6.90
CARMODY Noel V40 24.12.56, Cambridge H :
3kW - 12:53.14 (12:26.49-91),
20kW - 1:37:19 (1:34:38-90)
CARNEY Philip U20 22.12.77, Wakefield :
400H - 56.8/58.99
CARR Peter U20 10.09.77, Penzance :
110HJ - 15.5, DecJ - 5347
CARR Tyrone U17 30.07.80, Newham & E B :
100HY - 13.22w/13.5/13.52
CARRIDGE Stephen U15 31.12.81, Manx H :
3kW - 15:05.1, 3kWR - 14:37
CARROLL Paul U20 25.01.78, Liverpool Pem :
Dec - 5334, DecJ - 5475 (5560-95)
CARSON Christopher U17 26.10.79, Loch'lly :
100 - 10.8w/11.0/11.04 (10.99w/11.0-95),
150 - 15.9dt, 200 - 21.76,
400 - 49.7 (48.79-95)
CARTER Adrian R. 7.02.68, Thames Valley :
110H - 15.27 (14.72w/14.75-90)
CARTER Andrew U17 18.10.79, Cannock & S :
60H - 8.44i
CARTER Daniel U17 15.04.80, Braintree :
JT - 59.04, JTY - 66.00
CARTER Simon U23 5.03.75, GEC/Read Un :
JT - 58.98 (61.54-93)
CARTER Thomas U15 20.08.82, Vale Royal :
1500 - 4:16.49
CARTWRIGHT N. U15, Coventry Godiva :
3k - 9:39.6
CARTWRIGHT Russell U20 13.10.77, Cov G :
800 - 1:52.6, 1500 - 3:48.4,
CARTWRIGHT Thomas U20 22.06.79, Cov G :
800 - 1:53.30
CASEY Stephen 26.02.66, Woodford Green :
DT - 51.86 (58.64-91)
CASTEL-BRANCO Carlos, Belgrave/ANO :
LJ - 8.16w/7.72
CASTLE Andrew U17 8.12.79, Yeo O see KEMP
CASTILLO Richard U15 3.12.81, :
400 - 53.41
CASWELL Warren 17.06.63, Woodford Green :
HJ - 2.00 (2.20i/2.18-90)
CATHERLEY S. U20, Sale :
400H - 56.3
CATTERMOLE Tim U20 17.08.77, Som Sch :
JT - 53.06 (55.48-95)
CAUDERY Stuart 19.11.66, Cornwall AC :
Dec - 5758 (5785-91)
CAUSER Ashley U17 25.09.79, Rowheath :
JTY - 52.94
CAWLEY Ian U20 21.11.78, Bournemouth :
110HJ - 15.37
CAWLEY Mark U15 30.12.81, Mandale :
HTB - 41.72
CHADDOCK Andrew U17 13.03.80, Stockport :
HJ - 1.91
CHALLENGER Ben U20 7.03.78, Charnwood :
HJ - 2.21

CHAMBERS Dwain Anthony U20 5.04.78, Har :
  60 - 6.68i, 100 - 10.42 (10.41-95),
  200 - 21.38 (21.37-95)
CHAMPION Michael U23 3.01.75, Blackheath :
  200 - 21.81w/22.13 (21.4w/21.65w-94/21.69-95)
CHAPLIN Owen U20 2.12.77, Telford :
  DecJ - 5133 (5563-95)
CHAPMAN Frank 17.01.70, RAF :
  110H - 15.5, Dec - 5338
CHAPMAN Ken 13.04.67, :
  3k - 8:23.6
CHAPMAN Mark U23 28.12.76, Basildon :
  110H - 15.5, 400H - 55.6 (56.95-95)
CHAPMAN R. U17, West Midland Sch :
  PV - 3.70
CHARIJ Andrij, Basingstoke & MH :
  HT - 51.64 (52.72-93)
CHARLES Courtney 13.11.68, Thames Valley :
  LJ - 7.20i/7.07 (7.54-94),
  TJ - 15.24w/15.17 (16.38w/16.09-90)
CHARLESWORTH Robert U20 25.03.79,
  Peterborough : JT - 58.50
CHARVET Pierre 23.08.73, Birch/Birm U/FRA :
  SP - 15.01i/14.33, DT - 42.28
CHARVILLE Michael U15 7.05.82, Mandale :
  400 - 52.53
CHASTON Justin 4.11.68, Belgrave :
  1500 - 3:50.95 (3:46.58-95),
  5k - 13:55.86 (13:51.86-95),
  10kR - 29:16, 3kSt - 8:28.32 (8:23.90-94)
CHATT James U17 11.02.80, Dartford :
  100 - 10.9w/11.08, 200 - 22.08w/22.1/22.26,
  400 - 50.0, 400HY - 57.7/58.06
CHAU Duncan U20, Invicta :
  LJ - 6.81
CHEESEMAN Christopher 11.12.58,
  Surrey WC/Crawley/Thames H & H :
  10kW - 43:20.2 (43:05.11-93),
  20kW - 1:29:50 (1:29:11-94), 50kW - 4:22:42
CHEUNG L. U20 24.10.77, :
  110HJ - 15.5
CHILES Garry 15.05.66, Norwich :
  PV - 4.20 (4.35-94)
CHIN Darren U17 20.06.81, Hounslow :
  100 - 11.12w/11.27
CHISHOLM Scott U20 20.10.77, Pitreavie :
  400H - 55.12 (54.98-95)
CHRISTIE Linford 2.04.60, Thames Valley :
  60 - 6.59i (6.43+-91/6.47i-95),
  100 - 10.00w/10.0/10.03 (9.87-93),
  150 - 15.08 (14.74w-95/14.97-94),
  200 - 20.25w/20.29 (20.09-88)
CHRISTMAS John U15 30.10.81, Hert & W :
  LJ - 6.03
CHURCHILL Richard Stephen U20 29.09.77,
  Stainforth : 110HJ - 14.37w/14.60, 110H - 14.88
CIARAVELLA Simon 24.11.73, Woodford Gr :
  200 - 22.0/22.16 (21.87-93), 400 - 47.49 (47.33-93)
CLARE Jeffrey M. 21.03.65, Sale :
  SP - 14.05 (15.76-87), DT - 48.90 (55.60-88)
CLARK Dean 20.12.73, Hillingdon :
  800 - 1:50.6
CLARKE Andrew 10.08.70, Wigan :
  JT - 57.42 (61.14-95)
CLARKE Jonathan 20.11.67, Swansea :
  JT - 60.72 (68.74-86)
CLARKE S. Ezra U23 9.12.74, Shaftesbury B :
  TJ - 15.63

CLARKE Stuart U23 16.10.75, Bournemouth :
  LJ - 7.13
CLARKE Wayne A. R. U23 24.12.75,
  Peterborough/Eastern R HS : HT - 59.14
CLARKSON Matthew J.S. 25.01.66, Birchfield :
  10k - 30:24.1
CLEGG Andrew 8.09.73, Liverpool H :
  100 - 10.8 (10.80w-94/10.8-93/10.97-94)
CLEMENTS Matthew U20 17.09.77, Haringey :
  60H - 8.2i/8.22i, 110H - 14.7/15.41
CLERIHEW David U20 11.09.77, C of Edin :
  LJ - 7.38i/7.30w/7.29
CLIFFORD Simon U23 22.03.75, T Solent :
  400H - 53.73
CLUSKEY Adrian U17 30.12.80, Blackheath :
  SPJ - 13.56, SPY - 16.44i/15.51,
  DTY - 43.40
CLYNE Fraser J. V40 23.08.55, Aberdeen :
  Mar - 2:28:25 (2:11:50-84)
COAD Philip U20 11.10.78, :
  DecJ - 5294
COATS Edward U17 14.06.80, Guildford & G :
  DTY - 44.22, OctY - 5158
COBHAM Michael U23 15.09.76, Southport :
  Dec - 4906
COCKBURN James P. 30.01.73, Haringey :
  SP - 17.41
COCKER Jonathan 26.09.71, York :
  20kW - 1:37:52, 50kW - 4:49:01 (4:33:01-95)
COGHLAN Sebastian U15 31.01.82, Taunton :
  LJ - 6.16, TJ - 12.98
COHEN Scott 6.12.64, Leslie Deans RC :
  Mar - 2:25:53 (2:20:17-95)
COKER Michael G. 16.01.57, Team Solent :
  110H - 15.66w (15.21-88)
COKER Raymond 28.07.73, Sale :
  100 - 10.51, 200 - 21.19
COLEMAN Andy U23 29.09.74, Enfield :
  10k - 31:08.2, 2kSt - 5:46.03, 3kSt - 9:08.72
COLLIN Robert John 27.07.61, Peterborough :
  200 - 22.0 (21.4/21.58w-88/21.77-89)
COLLINS Joseph U20 20.01.78, Norwich :
  2kSt - 5:59.56, 3kSt - 9:25.9
COLLINS Liam U20 23.10.78, Gateshead :
  110HJ - 14.9w/15.2 (15.2-95), 110H - 14.88
COLLINS P. U13, City of Bath :
  HJ - 1.65
COLLINS Robert U20 17.09.77, Gateshead :
  110HJ - 15.0w (16.22-95)
COLLINS Tony V50 1.10.42, Birchfield :
  100MW - 20:47:07 (20:13:28-92)
COMBE Michael U20 24.12.78, Scottish Bord :
  800 - 1:53.60 (1:52.5-95), 1500 - 3:54.57
COMERFORD Nick 23.04.66, Cardiff :
  1500 - 3:42.20, 1M - 4:07.48, 5k - 14:25.20
CONDON Allyn U23 24.08.74, Sale :
  100 - 10.33w/10.36, 150 - 15.86,
  200 - 20.64w/20.84
CONDON David 11.04.72, Southend :
  SP - 15.54 (16.41-94)
CONERNEY Michael 30.10.72, Braint/Camb U :
  DT - 43.34 (44.28-93)
CONNELLY Paul U17 10.03.80, Barnsley :
  PV - 3.80
COOK Austin James Gareth 20.02.69,
  Sutton & D/WLHS : SP - 13.85 (14.59-90),
  DT - 45.74 (49.20-90),
  HT - 63.08 (67.32-91)

COOK Philip 7.05.69, Cardiff :
1M - 4:09.4, 2kSt - 5:59.5 (5:47.8-90),
3kSt - 8:56.92 (8:55.6-93)
COOKSLEY Brian U17 5.04.80, Cardiff :
HTY - 48.20
COOPER Ashley U20, Birchfield :
SPJ - 13.72
COOPER Martin U17 6.09.79, Havering :
400HY - 58.52
COOPER Paul U23 4.12.76, Woodford Green :
JT - 60.06 (65.34-95)
COOPER Rufus U20 24.02.79, Hounslow :
PV - 4.60
COPPIN Glen U15 16.01.83, Barking & Dag :
800 - 2:03.5, 1500 - 4:17.6, 3k - 9:18.7
CORCORAN Fyn U20 17.03.78, Cornwall AC :
110HJ - 15.1/15.11, 400H - 54.42,
Dec - 6559, DecJ - 6762
CORNFORD Ian James 1.02.66, Shaft Barnet :
10k - 29:08.66, 10kR - 29:11, 10MR - 48:10,
HMar - 1:04:17 (1:03:11-91)
CORR Kevin U20 17.04.79, Jarrow & Heb :
800 - 1:55.0
CORREY Andrew U15 15.10.81, City of Stoke :
PV - 3.90
COSSELL Harvey U23 1.12.74, Invicta :
400H - 55.5
COSTELLO Adam U17 12.09.79, Elswick :
1.5kSt - 4:25.6
COSTELLO Denis M. 3.12.61, Norwich : ·
LJ - 7.04 (7.68w-88/7.62-85),
TJ - 14.76 (15.66-83)
COTTER Christopher 3.02.72, Shaftesbury B :
LJ - 6.97w/6.92 (7.67w/7.47-93)
COTTON Simon 26.07.67, Tipton :
3k - 8:23.9, 5k - 14:21.78, 10k - 30:23.1
COTTRELL James U17 19.12.80, Derby & Co :
SPY - 14.08
COVENTON Dean 3.11.70, Enfield :
3kSt - 9:25.0 (9:11.6-95)
COWAN Lloyd 8.07.62, Shaftesbury Barnet :
200 - 21.8 (21.3w-93/21.48w/21.7-86/21.71-93)
COWAN Martin U17 16.11.80, Frome :
OctY - 4386
COX Elliott U17 7.01.80, Crawley :
400 - 50.9/51.08
COX Martin, City of Bath :
HMar - 1:04:16
CRAGGS Ian U23 6.10.76, Gateshead :
200 - 22.0w (22.12w-94/22.34-95)
CRAGGS Ray 9.07.63, RAF :
3kW - 13:08.9
CRAIG Ian 20.08.69, Border :
100 - 10.49w/10.70 (10.4wdb-93/10.67-95),
200 - 21.22w/21.7 (21.86-95)
CRAMPTON Peter 4.06.69, Spenborough :
110H - 15.5 (15.2-93), 400H - 49.78 (49.26-94)
CRANE Stephen U17 24.02.80, Surrey WC :
10kWR - 52:14
CRAWFORD Damien 22.08.68, L Irish/Sparta :
JT - 64.52 (70.34-91)
CRAWSHAW Jonathon U15 28.09.81, Craw :
80HB - 11.47
CREABY Christian U20 11.10.78, Leeds :
400 - 49.4/50.35
CREESE Tim, Holbeach :
DT - 41.30

CRESSWELL Andrew U17 4.04.80, Birchfield :
HJ - 1.98
CRIMMEN Nicholas 15.07.65, Spenborough :
SP - 13.43, DT - 44.32 (46.00-86)
CRIPPS Damon 9.10.70, Worcester :
HT - 46.80 (50.76-95)
CRITCHLEY Kim 15.07.73, Rown/Oklah St Un :
1500 - 3:45.17, 1M - 4:06.14i (4:00.15-95)
CRITCHLEY Martin U23 9.11.74, N S Poly :
100 - 10.90
CROASDALE Mark 10.01.60, Lancaster & M :
10kR - 28:50sh (29:44-95),
HMar - 1:04:54 (1:03:47-93),
Mar - 2:22:20 (2:17:45-93)
CROLL Graeme 1.02.66, Cambuslang :
10k - 30:03.17 (29:50.69-95),
10kR - 29:35, HMar - 1:04:51,
3kSt - 8:51.34 (8:40.49-95)
CROSS Derek V45 30.04.49, Verlea :
3kW - 13:16.79 (13:03.01-94)
CROSSAN Alan 6.01.72, Haringey :
3kSt - 8:58.7
CROSSLEY Paul U20 30.03.79, Luton :
110HJ - 15.4, 110H - 15.4/15.69,
400H - 55.1/55.18
CROTHERS Graham U15, Lisburn :
100 - 11.3w/12.1
CRUMP James U15 8.09.81, Vauxhall :
400 - 52.77
CUDDY Grant U20 6.01.77, Sale :
800 - 1:50.0, 1500 - 3:47.4
CUFF John U17 30.03.80, Stroud :
400HY   7.7 (58.25-95)
CULLEN Keith John 13.06.72, Chelmsford :
3k - 7:53.97, 5k - 13:27.00,
3kSt - 8:28.93 (8:26.05-95)
CUNNANE Danny U15 12.04.83, Wakefield :
PV - 3.30
CUNNANE Thomas U17 14.08.80, Wakefield :
HTY - 50.90
CURRAN A., Kilmarnock :
HT - 50.54
CURRAN Paul U20 5.04.77, North Down :
Dec - 5722, DecJ - 5645
CURSONS Mark D. 10.03.62, Old Gaytonians :
Mar - 2:31:19 (2:27:37-94)
CURTIS Neil U23 30.07.74, Corby :
HT - 50.64 (55.62-94)
CURTIS Paul U17 29.05.80, Medway :
400 - 49.5/50.06
CZERNIK Richard 12.08.72, Dudley & Stour :
DT - 41.10, Dec - 6484

D AKO Owusu 23.05.73, Sale :
60 - 6.83i, 100 - 10.30w/10.35,
150 - 15.50, 200 - 20.58 (20.57-95)
DALKINS Mark 9.09.71, City of Stoke :
3kSt - 9:18.97 - 95
DALTON Jamie U17 20.09.79, Preseli :
HJ - 1.90
DALTON Timothy U20 18.01.79, Old Gayt :
110HJ - 15.1/15.23w/15.46
DALY Carl U17 8.09.79, Newham & Essex B :
400HY - 56.3/56.46
DALY Shane 21.03.73, Leeds/Clydesdale/IRE :
800 - 1:51.2 (1:50.4-93)
DALY Steven U17 29.12.79, Elan Valley :
100 - 10.89, 200 - 22.15

DANE Mabon 19.07.71, Colchester H :
3kW - 13:29.8, 10kW - 48:02.3,
20kW - 1:39:29, 50kW - 4:54:12
DANIELS David U17 16.11.79, Enfield :
SPY - 14.42
DANIELS Leon U23 1.11.75, Solihull & S H :
100 - 10.95 (10.78w-94)
DANSO Evans 29.11.72, Thames Valley :
100 - 10.8/10.92 (10.6w-95/10.79-91)
DANSO Richard U15, Belgrave :
LJ - 6.18w/6.17
DARBY Brian 14.10.72, Coventry G/Loughbro :
400 - 47.97 (47.64-92)
DARLINGTON Landley Sean U20 19.01.77,
Peterbro/Loughbro : JT - 58.80 (60.06-95)
DAVENHILL Jason C.M. 3.10.69, Exeter/RAF :
400H - 55.9 (52.65-93)
DAVID Andrew 9.09.69, Cambridge Harriers :
60H - 8.3i/8.40i (8.29i-95),
110H - 15.0/15.10 (14.83-95)
DAVID Richard U20 15.08.77, Belgrave :
100 - 10.98, 400 - 48.7/48.85
DAVIDSON Christopher U23 4.12.75, N & E B :
100 - 10.79, 200 - 21.67, LJ - 7.60i/7.54
DAVIDSON Euan 8.12.73, Guildford & G :
DT - 41.02 (41.34-95)
DAVIDSON Hamish V40 25.05.54, SGA (Prof) :
SP - 14.80dh (17.44-78)
DAVIDSON Mark 15.11.68, TVH/Aberdeen :
200 - 22.06i (21.07w/21.6-89/21.90i/22.11-90),
400H - 55.8 (50.79-89)
DAVIES Ben U17 24.08.81, City of Bath :
HJ - 1.98
DAVIES Benjamin John U15 12.09.81, Sher Sch :
SPB - 14.20, DTB - 42.18, HTB - 42.74
DAVIES Berian Rhys 22.04.73, Swansea :
400H - 53.6/55.85
DAVIES Gareth M. 11.05.71, Cardiff :
LJ - 7.22 (7.62-94)
DAVIES Kevin U20 11.01.78, Shaftesbury B :
HT - 51.38, HTJ - 55.32
DAVIES Mark Howard 10.01.71, Tonbridge :
SP - 15.04 (15.56-92), DT - 47.76 (53.06-92)
DAVIES Matthew 23.07.71, Woodford Green :
800 - 1:49.9, 1500 - 3:44.2
DAVIES Matthew U20 16.09.78, Swansea :
JT - 57.06
DAVIES Philip 12.10.60, Wirral :
SP - 13.82 (14.41-87)
DAVIES Stephen 4.02.58, Tipton :
Mar - 2:25:58 (2:22:55-90)
DAVIES Tom U17 25.05.80, Thames Valley :
TJ - 13.52
DAVIES-HALE Paul 21.06.62, Cannock & St :
2M - 8:59.0 (8:26.09-88),
10kR - 29:28 (28:17-85)
DAVIS Adam Gareth 19.11.72, Corby :
PV - 4.30i (4.70-92), SP - 13.68
DAVIS Jonathon U20 5.03.78, Lagan Valley :
100 - 10.96
DAVIS Luke U17 1.01.80, Tipton :
100 - 10.44w/10.7/10.71, 200 - 21.7/22.13
DAVIS Mark U20 1.03.77, Corby :
PV - 5.10
DAVIS Richard U20 3.05.78, Bedford & Co :
100 - 10.75w/10.81
DAVIS Timothy U20 25.01.78, Invicta :
2kSt - 6:05.39 (6:02.78-95)

DAVISON Glen U17 8.09.79, Houghton-le-Sp :
1.5kSt - 4:37.6
DAVOILE Ryan James U20 29.09.78, Cov G :
800 - 1:53.25 (1:52.64-95)
DAVOREN Patrick 13.03.72, Brighton :
800 - 1:52.0, 1500 - 3:48.0,
1M - 4:08.59 (4:04.6-95), 3kSt - 9:05.2
DAWSON Nicholas U20 11.05.78, Hastings :
200 - 21.79w/22.02
DAY Stephen U15 10.02.82, Shaftesbury B :
PV - 3.25
DE BOURCIER Sean U15 4.01.82, Jersey :
HJ - 1.80
DEACON David William 19.03.65, Morpeth :
100 - 10.7 (10.62-95),
200 - 21.9 (21.19w-94/21.24-93)
DEACON Gareth 8.08.66, Coventry Godiva :
5k - 14:32.6
DEACON Jared Mark U23 15.10.75, Morpeth :
100 - 10.93 (10.8-95), 200 - 21.14,
300 - 32.78, 400 - 46.02
DEARMAN Geoffrey U20 4.08.77, Hounslow :
400 - 47.0/47.40 (47.02-95)
DEASY Colin, Coventry Godiva :
Mar - 2:28:54
DELL Gregory J. 20.11.64, Vale of Aylesbury :
Mar - 2:30:58 (2:28:12-94)
DENMARK Robert N. 23.11.68, Basildon :
1500 - 3:40.9+e (3:37.99-95),
1M - 3:55.39 (3:55.38-90),
2k - 5:04.11, 3k - 7:45.45 (7:39.55-93),
5k - 13:31.36 (13:10.24-92),
10k - 28:20.80 (28:03.34-94),
10kR - 28:51 (28:36-92)
DENSLEY Martin Richard U17 1.05.81,
Ealing,S & M : PV - 4.10
DERHAM James U15 8.02.82, GEC :
400 - 52.52
DESAI Ketan Kumar U15 1.12.82, Morpeth :
800 - 2:04.30
DEVINE J. Russell 24.04.68, Inverness :
HT - 64.00 (65.36-94)
DEVLIN Gareth U23 2.06.76, Loughborough :
LJ - 7.30
DEVONISH Marlon U23 1.06.76, Coventry G :
60 - 6.84i, 100 - 10.41, 200 - 20.86
DEVONSHIRE Adam U20 2.03.79, Bed & Co :
HT - 47.94, HTJ - 51.74
DIAMOND Paul U15 19.02.82, Notts :
JTB - 45.66
DIBBLE Jason 15.02.71, Cannock & Stafford :
HT - 50.72
DICKENSON Derek Paul V45 4.12.49, Dac & T :
HT - 50.96 (73.20-76)
DICKINSON Barrie 17.09.67, Coventry G :
HT - 55.88
DICKSON Marlon U20 17.11.78, Belgrave :
100 - 10.62w/10.65, 200 - 21.6/21.70
DIXON Matthew U20 26.12.78, Wigan :
800 - 1:53.1, 1500 - 3:51.38
DIXON Neil U17 16.09.80, Gateshead :
HJ - 1.95
DIXON Noel   73, Southend :
DT - 41.08 (42.58-94)
DJAN Geoffrey U15 21.07.82, Derby & Co :
400 - 52.5/52.64
DKADIK Faried U15 21.12.81, Swindon :
80HB - 12.10

DOBBIE Mark U20 5.03.77, Aberdeen :
  Dec - 4931 (5165w-95), DecJ - 5468 (5632-95)
DOBBS Robert U15 19.04.82, :
  400 - 53.95
DOBIE Ryan U15 20.01.82, Cumbrian Sch :
  DTB - 38.76
DODS Darren U23 26.12.74, Army :
  Dec - 5535
DOHERTY Ciaran U23 14.01.75, Border :
  110H - 15.3/15.47 (15.16-94),
  Dec - 6105w/6075
DONALDSON Alasdair U20 21.06.77, Pitr :
  400 - 49.4 (48.7-95/50.32-93),
  800 - 1:49.9, 1500 - 3:53.01i/3:55.29
DONKIN Bradley 6.12.71, Barton :
  800 - 1:48.25
DONNELLY Dermot 23.09.70, Annadale Str :
  3k - 8:18.7 (8:00.58-93),
  5k - 14:04.72 (13:47.0-94),
  10k - 28:47.90, 10kR - 29:12
DONNELLY John U17, :
  TJ - 13.93
DONNELLY Maylo V40, North Belfast :
  Mar - 2:31:52
DONNERY John U17, :
  TJ - 13.28
DONOVAN Daniel 8.10.70, Team Solent :
  200 - 21.9/22.18i (21.9/21.94-95),
  400 - 48.8 (47.8/47.87-94)
DORGU Christopher 11.12.69, Hounslow :
  110H - 15.3 (14.6-95/14.71-94)
DORSET Scott 10.04.69, Newham & Essex B :
  200 - 21.89i/21.9/22.12 (21.4/21.88-89)
DOUGLAS Alastair M. 20.12.60, Vict P/W & B :
  10k - 30:57.22 (29:29.39-88)
DOUGLAS Iain U20 4.01.77, Nithsdale/Bord :
  SPJ - 13.75 (13.91-95)
DOUGLAS James 4.04.71, Notts :
  200 - 22.0w
DOUGLAS Matthew U23 26.11.76, Milton K :
  400 - 47.79, 110H - 14.86, 400H - 51.47,
  LJ - 7.11, Dec - 6839
DOUGLAS Robin U15 20.12.81, Epsom & E :
  1500 - 4:21.6
DOVELL Paul U20 5.05.77, Dorchester :
  HJ - 2.09
DOWNES John 21.07.67, Salford/IRE :
  5k - 13:52.83 (13:29.91-94)
DOWNES Shane, :
  100kR - 8:05:48 (6:55:12-95)
DOWNIE Kieron U17 19.11.79, Newham & EB :
  200 - 22.20w/22.49
DOWSETT Nicholas J.E. U20 24.11.78, W Gr :
  110HJ - 14.46w/15.0/15.36,
  LJ - 7.15w/6.87, DecJ - 5974
DRAPER Anthony U23 23.04.74, Blackheath :
  400 - 48.9, 800 - 1:51.5 (1:50.78-94)
DRISCOLL Gareth U17 8.03.81, West Norfolk :
  HTY - 49.44
DRURY Kevin U17 30.09.79, Oswestry :
  100HY - 14.07w/14.12 (14.0/14.10-95),
  400HY - 57.47, OctY - 4495
DRZEWIECKI Jan 29:11.57, Bracknell :
  DT - 41.14 (44.40-91)
DUFFY Anthony V40 26.06.56, Trafford :
  Mar - 2:24:14 (2:17:09-89)
DUFFY John V40 10.11.55, Greenock Glen :
  Mar - 2:28:30 (2:18:44-87)

DUGARD Daniel 21.06.65, Ilford :
  LJ - 7.02 (7.15-89)
DUKE Adam 5.10.73, Thames VH/Loughbro :
  800 - 1:49.3 (1:48.8-92), 1500 - 3:42.5
DUKE Daniel James Maxwell 23.12.68, Bris :
  2kSt - 5:56.0 (5:45.07-88),
  3kSt - 9:04.8 (8:49.53-88)
DUKE Thomas U15 16.10.81, Retford :
  800 - 2:05.5
DULLFORCE Jason Mark 6.08.70, Enfield :
  1500 - 3:49.4 (3:37.88-92)
DUNNE Nicholas U17 12.02.80, Dudley & St :
  1500 - 4:06.9
DUNSON J. Gregory 2.12.63, RAF/Shaft B :
  110H - 14.34 (14.23w-89/14.29-86),
  400H - 51.68 (50.88-92)
DUPUY Jason 31.01.71, Bexley :
  600 - 1:19.4, 800 - 1:50.91
DURHAM Peter U13, Cleethorpes :
  HJ - 1.65
DUVAL Spencer Gavin 5.01.70, Cannock & St :
  2kSt - 5:38.6 (5:33.09-92),
  3kSt - 8:36.71 (8:24.64-95)
DYBALL Gareth U17 16.03.81, Woodford Gr :
  HJ - 1.93

E AGLE Gary 28.12.60, Bristol :
  Mar - 2:30:11 (2:29:22-94)
EARLE Albert St.Clair 10.01.58, Wolves & B :
  TJ - 13.92 (15.14-79)
EARLE Robert B. 15.09.60, Haringey :
  SP - 14.05 (14.87i-93/14.80-86),
  DT - 44.08 (59.00-85), HT - 61.86 (62.60-95)
EAST Andrew U17 25.07.81, Humberside Sch :
  OctY - 4249
EAST Michael John U20 20.01.78, Portsm :
  800 - 1:52.57, 1500 - 3:50.48
EASTON Mark Jonathan 24.05.63, Surrey WC :
  3kW - 12:27.1 (11:24.4-89)
EATON Shaun U13, Belgrave :
  100 - 12.5
EAVES Kevin U20 16.03.79, Croydon :
  LJ - 6.83
EAVES Philip U17 28.02.80, Halesowen :
  1.5kSt - 4:38.00
ECCLES Martin 16.01.57, Orkney Islands :
  100kR - 7:18:56, 24HrT 217.675km
EDEN Ali, Woodford Green :
  10k - 30:24.2, 3kSt - 9:14.7
EDEN Tom U20 16.05.79, Trafford :
  HTJ - 54.14
EDGER Tyrone U15 29.03.82, Highgate :
  LJ - 5.93, TJ - 12.64w/12.58
EDMUNDS Cypren 20.06.70, Thames Valley :
  60 - 6.89i, 100 - 10.6w/10.65w/10.74
  (10.59w-95/10.7-94/10.74-95),
  150 - 16.31, 200 - 21.00
EDU Remi U20 14.12.78, Shaftesbury B/NIG :
  400 - 47.76, 400H - 54.05
EDU Seni U23 4.03.74, Shaftesbury Barnet :
  60 - 6.91i, 200 - 21.53,
  100 - 10.76w/10.8/10.85 (10.8-93)
EDWARDS Dafydd U23 19.09.74, Cardiff :
  HJ - 2.00i (2.10i-94/2.05-91)
EDWARDS Jonathan David 10.05.66, Gate :
  100 - 10.48, TJ - 17.88 (18.43w/18.29-95)
EDWARDS Lee U23 14.09.75, Cardiff :
  LJ - 6.90 (6.99-95)

337

EDWARDS Mark Simon U23 2.12.74,
Charnwood/Loughborough Studnts :
SP - 17.46, DT - 46.14
EDWARDS Michael 19.10.68, Belgrave :
PV - 5.45 (5.52-93)
EDWARDS Noel 16.12.72, Leamington :
800 - 1:50.86
EDWARDS Stephen U20 13.06.77, Carm :
110HJ - 14.72w/15.08 (14.8-94),
110H - 15.48w (15.83-95)
EGAN James Nicholas U23 12.11.75, Skyrac :
100 - 10.74/10.76w (10.64w-95)
ELDER Craig U15 22.05.82, Whitemoss :
TJ - 12.48w/12.21
ELIAS Matthew U20 25.04.79, Cardiff :
110HJ - 15.16w/15.96, 400H - 54.33
ELLAMS Craig 24.11.72, City of Stoke :
HT - 60.92
ELLIOTT Christopher John U23 29.05.75,
Portsmouth/Northumblerland Un :
3kSt - 9:17.62 (8:59.57-94)
ELLIOTT Mark U17 12.08.80, Avonside :
HJ - 1.93i/1.91
ELLIOTT Mensah U23 29.08.76, Blackheath :
110H - 14.6w/15.0/15.11
ELLIOTT Neil 10.04.71, C of Edinburgh/Helen :
SP - 14.27 (14.42-95), DT - 43.98 (44.94-94)
ELLIS Ieuan T. 11.05.60, Elswick :
Mar - 2:23:31 (2:13:21-86)
ELLIS Joel U17 2.09.79, Sparkhill :
1500 - 4:07.5 (4:07.5-95)
ELLIS-SMITH James 11.09.72, Reigate/
Oklahoma St U : 800 - 1:52.1, 1500 - 3:46.14
EMERY Julian, Westbury :
3kSt - 9:24.3
ENDERSBY M., West Norfolk :
400H - 54.1db
ENEVER Mark S. U23 15.03.74, Thurrock :
SP - 13.55
ENGLISH Desmond 6.06.67, Havering/IRE :
800 - 1:48.8 (1:48.4-91), 1500 - 3:41.13
EOUN H., :
LJ - 6.96
ERDMAN Lewis U17 29.11.79, Herne Hill :
HJ - 1.90, LJ - 6.59,
EROGBOGBO Temitayo Faruq U23 8.03.75,
Birchfield/Loughborough Studnts/NIG :
TJ - 16.25w/15.91 (16.32-95)
ERSKINE Craig U13 26.09.83, Lochgelly :
400 - 56.5
ESEGBONA Unuakpor H. 16.04.68, C of Stoke :
Dec - 6494
EVA Roland U20 6.09.78, Huntingdon :
110HJ - 14.9/15.00w/15.27, 110H - 15.4
EVANS Aaron U15 15.02.82, Blackheath :
200 - 22.75w/23.07, 400 - 50.88
EVANS Matthew U23 19.11.75, Telf/Staffs Un :
PV - 4.60
EVANS Paul William 13.04.61, Belgrave :
3k - 7:55.29, 5k - 13:47.40 (13:25.38-95),
10k - 28:24.39 (27:47.79-93),
10kR - 28:33 (28:13-95), 10MR - 46:37,
HMar - 1:01:55 (1:00:09sh-95), Mar - 2:08:52
EVERETT Jerry 27.05.61, Colchester H :
3kW - 13:41.9
EXLEY Scott U20 9.02.78, Yeovil Olympiads :
110HJ - 14.68w/15.1, DecJ - 5767

EYNON Andrew 1.09.62, Swansea :
3kSt - 9:09.06 (9:08.9-95)
EYRE Simon Peter U17 30.10.80, Crawley :
800 - 1:55.9

F ABEN Stuart U20 28.02.75, Haringey :
JT - 76.66i/73.70 (74.24-95)
FABER Pierre 9.01.72, Dac & Tring/RSA :
HJ - 2.06, PV - 4.50, SP - 15.94, DT - 46.54,
JT - 56.46 (60.58-95), Dec - 7581
FAIRBANK Gary U13 7.03.84, Isle of Wight :
3k - 10:15.0
FAIRBROTHER Simon 28.03.68, Haringey :
800 - 1:51.14 (1:47.7-92),
1500 - 3:42.86 (3:38.64-92)
FAIRCLOUGH Lee 23.06.70, Team Solent :
100 - 10.8/10.84w/10.89
(10.7-93/10.78w/10.89-95),
200 - 21.6w/21.85 (21.5-93), 400 - 47.2/47.61
FAIRLAMB Neil U23 13.03.76, City of Stoke :
Dec - 4997
FALKNER Ryan U17 20.11.79, Oadby & Wig :
3k - 8:55.0
FALOLA Ayo 29.07.68, Woodford Green :
100 - 10.66 (10.3w/10.50-95),
200 - 21.31 (20.93w-95/21.15-91),
400 - 48.62, 110H - 15.1/15.18 (14.89-95)
FANNING Robert U20 31.10.78, Milton K :
110H - 15.5
FARMER Jonathan U17 23.09.80, Burton :
100 - 10.97w
FARMER Lea U17 22.01.80, Torfaen :
400 - 50.5/50.60
FARQUHARSON Ruddy A. 26.03.61, Tel/RAF :
TJ - 14.86 (15.59w/15.57-85)
FARRELL David W. 29.06.64, Border :
3kSt - 9:10.02 (9:02.37-93)
FARRELL Kevin U20 31.10.77, Havering :
100 - 10.98 (10.96-95), 200 - 21.51w/21.63
FARRELLY John 4.12.67, London Irish/IRE :
SP - 15.12, DT - 43.68 (47.52-89)
FARRELLY Kieron U17 14.10.80, Blackheath :
1.5kSt - 4:37.6
FARROW Kevin U23 8.09.75, Derby & Co :
1500 - 3:48.44, 1M - 4:09.78i,
3k - 8:21.37i (8:28.25-93)
FARRUGIA Emmanuel U15 19.07.82, Morn :
400 - 52.2/52.45
FARRUGIA Michael U15 19.07.82, Blackheath :
200 - 23.51w/23.6/23.68
FASINRO Ibrahim 'Tosi' 28.03.72, Haringey :
TJ - 16.38 (17.30w/17.21-93)
FAULKNER Mark Peter U17 14.11.79, T Sol :
LJ - 6.92w/6.83
FAULKNER Stewart 19.02.69, Birchfield :
LJ - 7.54 (8.15-90)
FAVELL Peter U15 16.03.82, Chesterfield :
TJ - 12.60w/12.48, DTB - 38.18,
FAYOMI Bunmi U20 13.07.79, Blackburn :
TJ - 14.03
FENN Ian U13 3.12.83, Worthing :
HJ - 1.56
FENTON Malcolm L. V40 12.02.56, N & E B :
SP - 14.62, DT - 41.08 (47.40-79),
HT - 60.14 (62.42-82)
FENWICK Sean 20.07.70, Tipton :
5k - 14:28.08, 2kSt - 5:51.7

FERGUS Jason R. 11.10.73, Belgrave :
  60 - 6.70i (6.68i-95),
  100 - 10.52 (10.34w-94/10.4-93/10.44-92),
  200 - 21.4w/21.49i/22.53 (21.33-92)
FERGUSON Graham U17 18.01.80, Cambus :
  1500 - 4:07.3, 3k - 8:42.4
FERGUSON Martin M. 17.09.64, C of Edinb :
  Mar - 2:28:32 (2:26:45-95),
  3kSt - 9:26.6 (9:17.0-95)
FERNS Austin U17 12.01.81, Hercules Wimb :
  400HY - 56.0/56.55, LJ - 6.56, OctY - 4204
FERRAND Adrian J. 5.02.68, Newham & E B :
  Dec - 6437 (6726-93)
FERRIN John 20.02.67, North Belfast :
  Mar - 2:22:13 (2:18:40-95)
FIDLER M. U13, Copeland :
  JTC - 37.86
FIDLER Terrence R. 13.10.71, Crawley :
  110H - 15.4w/15.6 (15.1w-91/15.20-94),
  PV - 4.40 (4.50-91), Dec - 6443 (6683-91)
FIELD Paul C. 24.06.67, Met. Police :
  110H - 15.6 (14.61w-94/14.8-95/14.89-94),
  400H - 55.5/55.77 (55.5-93)
FINCH Lloyd U13 26.10.83, Leics WC :
  2kW - 9:32.1o/9:48.0, 2KWR - 9:16,
  3kW - 15:02.62, 3kWR - 14:35o
FINCH Luke U13 21.09.85, Leics WC :
  2kW - 11:18.2, 2KWR - 10:29
FINCH Rodney 5.08.67, Soton City/Army :
  800 - 1:50.8, 1500 - 3:42.0 (3:37.97-93),
  2k - 5:06.95, 5k - 14:21.9 (14:03.27-93)
  3k - 7:58.63i/8:15.04 (7:53.99i-94/7:59.33-93),
FINDLAY Mark U20 20.03.78, Blackheath :
  60 - 6.90i, 100 - 10.60w/10.69 (10.55w-95),
  200 - 21.17w/21.29
FINDLOW Richard David 4.12.66, Bradford :
  3k - 8:11.59 (7:59.09-90),
  5k - 14:09.89 (13:44.58-92),
  10k - 30:24.93 (29:32.67-95),
  10kR - 29:29 (29:19-92)
FINNIE Stuart U20 14.12.78, Lisburn :
  LJ - 6.90 (6.99w-95)
FIRTH Simon U17 20.10.79, Halifax :
  1500 - 4:06.81
FISHER Gavin U20 18.11.77, West Suffolk :
  HJ - 2.00, DecJ - 5180
FITTALL Ross U17 4.09.79, Dursley :
  800 - 1:56.74, 1500 - 3:59.31
FITZSIMMONS Robert Gerald 16.08.64, Kilb :
  5k - 14:34.31 (14:17.62-93)
FLAHERTY Stephen U17 16.10.79, Ipswich :
  200 - 22.54w/22.68, 400 - 51.02,
FLANAGAN Matt U15 10.07.82, Tonbridge :
  1500 - 4:20.40, 3k - 9:22.38
FLEMING Keith 26.06.65, Windsor S & E :
  100 - 10.8
FLEMING Peter Ross 5.01.61, L Deans RC :
  HMar - 1:03:57 (1:02:52-93),
  Mar - 2:16:58 (2:13:33-93)
FLETCHER Jim, :
  24HrT - 213.648km
FLETCHER Martyn 21.01.69, Birchfield :
  SP - 14.09 (16.48-92)
FLINT Benjamin U20 16.09.78, Rotherham :
  PV - 5.00
FLINT Daniel U20 15.06.77, Gateshead :
  5k - 15:01.48

FLINT Mark A. 19.02.63, Telford/RAF :
  5k - 14:21.4 (13:54.5-90),
  10kR - 29:12 (28:38-94),
  10MR - 48:14 (47:16-93),
  HMar - 1:02:55 (1:01:56-93),
  Mar - 2:18:55 (2:12:07-94)
FLOWER M., Waveney :
  HJ - 1.97
FLOYD Michael U23 26.09.76, Sale/NWHS :
  HT - 59.42
FLYNN Alex U15 2.08.82, Bicester RR :
  3k - 9:39.65
FLYNN Julian T. 3.07.72, Birchfield :
  LJ - 7.57, TJ - 15.19w/15.08 (15.32-93)
FOGG Damien U15 5.03.82, Wirral :
  DTB - 37.88
FOGG Nicholas U20 24.03.78, Shaftesbury B :
  HTJ - 49.32
FOOKS Andrew U23 26.04.75, Wells :
  3kSt - 9:23.8 (8:56.83-95)
FORBES Brian U23 6.09.74, Mid Ulster :
  400 - 48.4/48.49
FORD Antony U15 26.05.83, Blackpool :
  1500 - 4:14.5
FORDER Martin John 7.08.70, GEC :
  800 - 1:51.4 (1:48.51-92), 1500 - 3:42.1
FOSTER Carl U23 24.10.75, Hallamshire :
  400H - 52.86
FOSTER Paul U17 20.10.79, Yate :
  HTY - 47.56
FOSTER Steve U15 30.12.81, G. Manch Sch :
  100 - 11.48w/11.62, PenB - 2643
FOSTER William R.G. 9.08.58, Blackheath :
  5k - 14:17.3 (13:59.29-88),
  10k - 29:14.34, HMar - 1:03:50,
  Mar - 2:18:55 (2:15:49-95)
FOX Morris 30.04.63, City of Stoke :
  SP - 14.87 (14.95-95), DT - 43.76 (46.40-95)
FRANCIS Alex U23 15.07.74, Newham & E B :
  100 - 10.7, 200 - 21.6 (22.05w-95/22.11-94),
  400 - 47.15
FRANCIS Mark U20 23.09.77, Sutton & Dist :
  100 - 10.8, JT - 66.62
FRANCIS Peter U17 28.08.80, Blackheath :
  TJ - 14.56
FRANCIS Steven U20 31.01.79, Newport :
  PV - 4.15i (4.40-95)
FRANKLIN John 1.03.66, Woodford Green :
  110H - 15.5 (15.1w-90/15.13-91/15.2-95)
FRANKS David U20 27.04.78, Wigan :
  HJ - 2.07 (2.07-95)
FRASER Peter U20 28.01.78, Aberdeen :
  JT - 57.48
FREARY Paul 3.04.68, Bolton :
  1500 - 3:46.7 (3:43.3-91), 5k - 13:55.34
FREEMAN Stephen 8.09.67, Liverpool Pem :
  110H - 15.50,
  400H - 54.2/54.52 (52.8/52.89-92)
FREESTONE Steven U20 5.08.78, Charn :
  DTJ - 42.92
FRENCH Jamie U20 15.03.78, Holbeach :
  TJ - 14.11
FRICKER Simon David U23 14.07.75, T Solent :
  SP - 15.29, DT - 48.66
FROST Andrew U17 17.04.81, Isle of Wight :
  SPY - 14.07, HTJ - 46.18, HTY - 56.52
FROST Steven U15 12.12.81, Thurrock :
  1500 - 4:20.79

FROUD Paul M. 6.04.66, Brighton :
Mar - 2:25:39 (2:22:18-94)
FUAT Fuat 20.09.71, Enfield :
JT - 58.60 (58.60-95)
FUGALLO Alexander 28.01.70, Shaftesbury B :
200 - 21.60 (21.20w-89/21.2/21.26-90)
FULFORD Andrew U15 23.06.82, Swindon RR :
400 - 52.8, 800 - 1:59.3
FULLER Christopher U15 2.02.82, Havant :
80HB - 12.1
FULLER Peter U20 30.04.78, Epsom & Ewell :
HTJ - 50.54
FULLER William U23 19.10.76, Epsom & E :
SP - 15.61 (15.64-95), DT - 42.20,
HT - 53.32 (53.66-95)
FURLONG Kevin 19.05.70, Manx H :
110H - 15.1/15.31 (15.1/15.26-95), 400H - 54.5

G AFFNEY Bernard P. 8.06.61, Massey F :
Mar - 2:33:11 (2:27:11-92)
GAJJAR Kieran U23 25.09.76, Wakefield :
200 - 21.9 (22.03w/22.06-94), 400 - 49.0
GALLAGHER Darren 7.06.71, Annad Str/GEC :
400H - 55.5/55.87 (54.0-94/54.23-93)
GALLAGHER Gary 7.06.71, GEC/Staffs Univ :
110H - 15.55w (15.0-94/15.20w-93/15.33-94)
GALLOWAY Charles U20 5.04.78, Som Sch :
DTJ - 41.38
GAMMAGE Richard D. 21.11.62, RAF :
PV - 4.10 (5.00-84)
GANLEY Thomas U15 6.04.82, Invicta :
1500 - 4:21.9, 3k - 9:30.65
GARDENER Jason U23 18.09.75, C of Bath :
60 - 6.55i, 100 - 10.41w/10.5 (10.25-94)
GARDENER Neil U15 7.09.81, Derby & Co :
800 - 2:04.9, 1500 - 4:14.12
GARDNER Anthony U17 19.09.80, Cann & St :
200 - 22.44w/22.8 (24.57-95)
GARDNER Paul 5.08.69, Telford/RAF :
1500 - 3:44.9, 1M - 4:06.0
GARLAND Dale U15 13.10.81, Guernsey :
TJ - 12.34
GARLAND Stephen 12.01.73, Liverpool Pem :
Dec - 6364
GARNER Andrew, Lincoln Well :
PV - 4.10
GARRETT Lee U20 2.09.78, BH Mansfield :
1500 - 3:54.3
GASCOIGNE Stephen 20.12.66, Blackheath :
PV - 4.20 (4.70-88)
GAWTHORPE Richard U17 28.01.81, Derby :
100HY - 14.1, LJ - 6.49
GEE Simon U23 23.04.75, Liverpool H :
TJ - 13.94 (14.60-94)
GEORGE Mathias U20 24.09.77, Belgrave :
110HJ - 15.1/15.5w/15.25,
110H - 15.2/15.88w, TJ - 14.08
GETTINBY Gareth U20, North Down :
100 - 10.8/10.99w
GHENT Brendon U23 7.09.76, Coventry G :
60 - 6.93i, 100 - 10.6/10.63, 200 - 21.2w/21.28
GIBB Bruce U15 10.10.81, Perth :
200 - 23.55
GIBB Ian U23 8.01.75, Harmeny :
PV - 4.20
GIBBS Neil U17 2.02.80, Yeovil Olympiads :
OctY - 4372

GIBSON Alex U20 3.11.77, Brentwood :
JT - 55.44
GIBSON Michael U15, :
LJ - 5.94
GIDLEY Alistair 5.09.72, Old Gaytonians :
JT - 62.06 (62.88-93)
GIDLEY Ian 13.11.70, Sale :
HJ - 2.00 (2.05-93)
GIFFORD David 9.03.73, Cannock & Stafford :
400H - 53.71 (53.34-94)
GILBERT Gareth 24.08.72, Cardiff/Liv Univ :
SP - 14.07, DT - 46.24 (46.34-95)
GILBERT James U23 9.11.74, C of Edinburgh :
LJ - 7.01w/6.87i/6.86
GILBERT Richard U17 29.06.80, Scarbro :
1500 - 4:06.49
GILBY Clive Roger 24.02.66, Cambridge H :
800 - 1:49.09 (1:47.33-95)
GILBY Daniel P. 10.07.70, Cambridge H :
PV - 4.60 (5.00-91), Dec - 5761 (5961-95)
GILDING Paul U23 2.10.75, Brighton :
HJ - 1.97, Dec - 5084
GILHOOLY Tony U23 26.03.76, Cambus/ESH :
HJ - 2.08
GILL Andrew Robert 19.02.70, GEC :
110H - 14.8 (14.41w-89/14.91-91),
400H - 54.2/54.22 (52.78-91)
GILL Anthony U20 19.09.77, Bingley :
110HJ - 14.11w/14.6/14.78, 110H - 14.90
GILL Anthony U13, Mandale :
400 - 56.5
GILLARD Matthew U23 11.07.75, Wakefield :
Dec - 5506 (5817-95)
GILLES William 15.02.73, Croydon :
60H - 8.4i, 110H - 15.37, PV - 4.10,
LJ - 7.13, Dec - 6800w/6790
GILLESPIE Ian 18.05.70, Birchfield :
1500 - 3:41.1 (3:40.72-93),
1M - 4:01.1 (3:58.64-93),
3k - 7:53.49, 5k - 13:40.68
GILLESPIE Ross U17, Lagan Valley :
1.5kSt - 4:33.3
GIRAUD Martin U20 16.11.77, Hercules Wimb :
60 - 6.87i (6.76i-95),
100 - 10.75w/10.78 (10.6w-95/10.7-94)
GIRDLER Dominic U15 6.03.82, Leics Cor :
80HB - 11.9/11.99, HJ - 1.85,
LJ - 6.10, Dec - 6800w/6790
GIRVAN Richard U23 26.07.76, Annadale Str :
800 - 1:51.4 (1:49.95-95)
GISBEY David Edward 2.05.60, C of Edinburgh :
HT - 53.96 (55.70-95)
GITTINS Luke U17, Cardiff :
100HY - 14.0
GLENTON Bradford 2.11.69, Soton City :
1500 - 3:49.40 (3:44.09-92)
GOEDLUCK Philip Adrian Troy 10.09.67, Bel :
100 - 10.67 (10.3w/10.43w-95/10.48-94),
200 - 21.6/22.09 (20.73w-95/20.79-94)
GOGGINS M. U13, Ryde :
TJ - 10.19
GOLDING Alexander U15 3.12.81, Mandale :
100 - 11.5w/11.52, 200 - 23.07w/23.20,
80HB - 12.00
GOLDING Julian U23 17.02.75, Blackheath :
100 - 10.47A/10.5/10.53 (10.30-95),
150 - 15.83 (15.38w-95),
200 - 20.69w/20.76 (20.69w/20.7/20.75-95)

GOLLEY Julian Quintin Patrick 12.09.71, TVH :
TJ - 16.53 (17.06-94)
GOODGER David U23 19.09.75, Newport :
400H - 54.79 (53.8/54.09-95)
GOODWIN Jon U23 22.09.76, C of Plymouth :
400H - 55.4 (54.97-95)
GORDON David 20.03.68, N & EB/Loughbro :
PV - 4.50 (4.75-94/4.85Aun-93)
GORDON Dominic U17 7.01.81, Bristol :
100 - 11.16w/11.3/11.42
GORDON Malwyn U15 20.10.81, :
TJ - 12.85
GORDON Nicholas U20 7.01.77, Bourne :
LJ - 6.84 (7.18w/7.07-93)
GORDON Peter V45 2.07.51, Gateshead :
DT - 53.90 (61.62-91), HT - 47.36 (63.20-82)
GOSNALL Toby 21.04.71, Birchfield :
800 - 1:52.1
GOSTICK Ryan U15 12.02.82, Oxford City :
80HB - 12.1/12.45
GOUDIE Andrew U20 4.10.78, Bexley :
5kW - 23:56.6, 10kW - 48:47.9,
10kWR - 48:04
GOUDIE William U17 16.12.80, Wirral :
1500 - 4:03.9
GOWAN Joseph 18.11.67, Sale :
400 - 49.04 (48.25-92)
GRAFFIN Allen Gordon U20 20.12.77, Tonb :
800 - 1:54.6, 1500 - 3:51.6, 3k - 8:24.22,
5k - 14:44.11 (14:16.8-95), 10k - 31:03.32
GRAFFIN Andrew Neill U20 20.12.77, Tonb :
800 - 1:52.6, 1500 - 3:47.8, 3k - 8:33.07
GRAHAM Daniel U20 3.08.79, Liverpool H :
HJ - 2.15
GRAHAM Douglas U20 1.01.77, C of Edinburgh :
PV - 4.26
GRAHAM Gary U23, Gateshead :
HJ - 1.96
GRAHAM Grant 27.12.72, Clydesdale :
800 - 1:49.2, 1500 - 3:49.3 (3:43.2-95),
1M - 4:09.65 (4:02.8-95)
GRAHAM Paul U13 17.02.86, Belgrave :
2kW - 11:23.7, 2KWR - 10:27
GRANT Dalton 8.04.66, Haringey :
110H - 15.20,
HJ - 2.34i/2.33 (2.37i-94/2.36-91)
GRANT Dwayne U15 17.07.82, Blackheath :
LJ - 6.25io/6.07
GRANT Keith U17 17.03.80, Pendle :
1.5kSt - 4:32.04 (4:29.38-95)
GRANT Mark 17.05.71, Thames Valley :
PV - 5.00 (5.10-95)
GRAY Daniel U17 23.10.80, Sale :
1.5kSt - 4:37.19
GRAY Glenn 21.04.68, Thames Valley :
400H - 53.4/53.70
GRAY Marvin 18.12.71, Cardiff :
400 - 48.38dq/48.63, 400H - 52.8/52.82
GRAY Paul 25.05.69, Cardiff :
110H - 13.61A/13.70/13.87 (13.53-94)
GRAY Wayne U17 7.11.80, Blackheath :
100 - 10.88w/11.07, HJ - 1.98, OctY - 4309
GREAVES Damien David U20 19.09.77, N & EB :
60 - 6.9i, 100 - 10.56w/10.79,
110HJ - 14.53w/14.61 (14.0/14.40-95),
110H - 14.04
GREEN Adrian David 30.05.68, Woodford Gr :
3kSt - 8:50.14

GREEN Ben U23 30.03.76, Haslemere :
100 - 10.97, 200 - 22.02
GREEN Clifton Paul U17 10.10.79, Medway :
JTY - 63.26 (64.18-95), OctY - 4595
GREEN Mark 28.06.71, Hounslow :
400H - 53.67 (53.1-95)
GREEN Paul 7.04.72, Sale :
3k - 8:10.0, 5k - 14:18.15, 10k - 29:51.2
GREEN Stephen Harold 18.02.71, Sale :
1k - 2:23.7 (2:21.95-94),
1500 - 3:42.01 (3:39.19-94),
3k - 8:06.9 (8:03.82i/8:05.45-95)
GREEN Stephen 28.07.70, Bingley :
5k - 14:21 (14:17.2-94), 10k - 29:18.74,
Mar - 2:19:58
GREENING Stephen 15.02.68, Birchfield :
JT - 57.44 (63.24-91)
GREENWOOD Tim U15 22.11.82, Oxford City :
HJ - 1.81, LJ - 6.03
GREGORY Carl U20 17.08.77, Hounslow :
HTJ - 54.56
GREGORY Mark, Silverdale :
Mar - 2:30:43
GRIERSON Andrew U17 23.11.79, Reading :
HTJ - 52.94, HTY - 62.48
GRIFFIN David 5.12.63, Cardiff :
400H - 54.12 (52.07-95)
GRIFFIN Mark U23 16.02.75, Walt/London Un :
800 - 1:49.32 (1:49.27-94), 1500 - 3:43.5
GRIFFIN Neil V45 28.05.48, Windsor S & E :
DT - 45.08 (51.66-80)
GRIFFITH Mark U15 25.11.81, Enfield :
1500 - 4:15.5, 3k - 9:18.33
GRIFFITHS Otis 4.02.70, Havering :
400 - 49.0 (48.6-94), 400H - 56.0
GRIME Ian 29.09.70, Newham & Essex B :
800 - 1:49.3 (1:49.10-94), 1500 - 3:40.1,
3k - 7:55.4, 10k - 30:23.1
GRINDLE Matthew U15 3.01.82, Cardiff :
HTB - 43.18
GRINDLEY David 29.10.72, Wigan :
200 - 21.39 (20.89w-93),
300 - 33.79 (32.35+/32.45-93),
400 - 45.66 (44.47-92)
GRINNELL Luke U20 21.03.79, Bristol :
100 - 10.9 (10.96w/11.07-95)
GRIPTON Paul U23 9.11.76, Bromsgrove & R :
60H - 8.31i, 110H - 15.18 (15.1-94/15.13-95)
GRITZ Ben U20 21.11.77, Old Gaytonians :
110HJ - 15.29w/15.3/15.70 (15.2-95)
GRONOW Paul U17 14.09.79, Cardiff :
3k - 8:51.6, 1.5kSt - 4:36.7
GROVER Marc U20 25.02.78, Windsor S & E :
TJ - 14.07
GROVES Mike U13, Torfaen :
JTC - 39.18
GROVES Shaun U17 15.09.80, Torfaen :
JTY - 52.62
GUDGEON Alistair U17 26.10.79, Peterbro :
LJ - 6.80 (6.83w-95)
GUEGAN Michael Gerald 19.09.66, T Solent :
800 - 1:50.26 (1:47.90-92)
GUEST James U23 29.07.74, Thurr/London Un :
800 - 1:52.4, 1500 - 3:45.50
GUITE Craig U20 19.08.77, Rotherham :
HJ - 2.00, PV - 4.90
GULLAKSEN John U17 24.02.80, City of Hull :
PV - 4.15

GURR David 20.06.70, GEC :
  200 - 21.86w
GUTTERIDGE Steven T. 5.07.71, Highgate :
  PV - 4.20 (4.80-93)
GWYNNE Timothy J. 20.01.71, Birchfield :
  400H - 52.33 (51.08-94)
GYORFFY Terry 28.01.65, Basingstoke & MH :
  PV - 4.20 (4.20-95), JT - 55.60 (57.04-95),
  Dec - 6541 (6648-95)

HACKNEY Roger Graham 2.09.57,
  AF&D/RAF : 3kSt - 9:12.3 (8:18.91-88)
HAINES Andrew 15.10.72, Swindon :
  110H - 15.6/15.72 (15.1-92/15.13w/15.17-91)
HALE Darren 2.10.59, Sheffield :
  Mar - 2:31:47
HALE Steven U20 20.04.77, Rowheath :
  SP - 13.05, SPJ - 13.87, DT - 42.60,
  DTJ - 47.72
HALES Matthew U17 6.10.79, Steyning :
  3kW - 13:22.0, 3kWR - 13:25,
  5kW - 22:48.0o/23:49.0, 5kWR - 22:29o,
  10kW - 49:48.6, 10kWR - 47:04o
HALL David 26.05.68, Army :
  Dec - 5269
HALL Dominic 21.02.71, Highgate :
  800 - 1:50.70
HALL Gary U17 25.07.80, Sutton & District :
  100HY - 14.2/14.34, OctY - 4546
HALL Jeremy P. 22.08.58, Swansea :
  Mar - 2:24:11 (2:18:51-90)
HALL John D. V45 18.01.49, Belgrave :
  3kW - 13:49.2 (12:53.28-82)
HAMBLIN Imran U15 26.06.82, Blackheath :
  800 - 2:05.04
HAMER Nigel U23 1.01.76, Derby & Co :
  400 - 49.0
HAMES Jeremy E. 17.11.70, Charnwood :
  SP - 13.40 (13.95-94), DT - 43.84 (43.86-95)
HAMILTON Douglas W. 19.05.61, ESH :
  PV - 4.60 (4.75-87)
HAMILTON Ian 8.03.65, Medway :
  5k - 14:05.91
HAMMOND Matthew 26.09.68, Scunthorpe :
  HT - 51.46
HAMMOND Stuart 17.07.71, Tower Hamlets :
  Dec - 5192
HAND James U17 11.06.80, C of Edinburgh :
  800 - 1:56.7
HANLON Thomas 20.05.67, LD RC/Border :
  3k - 8:06.09i (7:51.31-92),
  3kSt - 9:00.03 (8:12.58-91)
HANNA David U23 13.12.75, Cardiff :
  JT - 62.76 (63.22-95)
HARBOUR Duncan 17.10.66, Peterborough :
  400H - 55.5/55.70 (53.4/53.68-93)
HARDY Alan P. 4.09.58, Blackheath :
  PV - 4.30 (4.50-92)
HARGRAVE Christopher U20 27.02.79, Beds :
  110HJ - 14.85w/14.87, 110H - 14.81w/15.4
HARLAND Ben U17 2.09.79, Carmarthen :
  100 - 11.20, 200 - 22.60
HARLAND Kim U15 21.02.82, Carmarthen :
  HJ - 1.80
HARNEY Brian, Rotherham :
  100kR - 8:18:59
HARPER Ben U20 9.11.78, Braintree :
  400 - 49.0/49.12

HARPUR Ian 24.04.67, London Irish/IRE :
  3k - 8:15.7, 5k - 14:25.6,
  10k - 30:54.20 (29:49.63-94)
HARRIES Christopher U15 17.06.82, Carm :
  HJ - 1.83
HARRIES Kirk U23 7.08.74, Hillingdon :
  60H - 8.4i (8.3i-94), 110H - 14.7w/14.9 (14.76-95)
HARRIES Philip James Charles 7.04.66,
  Derby & Co/Loughborough Studnts :
  110H - 15.6 (14.8-88/15.35-90),
  400H - 52.71 (50.01-88)
HARRINGTON Thomas U17 27.10.79, SB :
  HTY - 47.04
HARRIS Aaron U17 19.07.80, Blackheath :
  100 - 10.86w/10.98
HARRIS Chris, Woking :
  400 - 48.8
HARRIS Stephen 12.10.71, Crawley :
  10k - 30:20.07, 10kR - 29:36
HARRISON Ererton W. 8.04.66, Thames VH :
  60H - 8.28i (8.10i-89),
  110H - 14.79w/14.85 (14.11-91)
HARRISON Paul U17 17.11.79, Southend :
  PV - 4.15
HARRISON Sean U15 25.01.82, Liv H/Sutton :
  200 - 23.62w/23.92, 400 - 53.1
HARRISON Stephen 19.12.72, Blackh/Leeds P :
  JT - 64.38 (75.32-95)
HART Andrew 13.09.69, Coventry Godiva :
  800 - 1:46.57, 1k - 2:18.78, 1500 - 3:42.0,
  1M - 4:02.3 (4:01.8-95)
HART Nathan 1.07.73, Windsor S & E :
  110H - 15.2/15.39, HJ - 2.05 (2.10-93)
HART Neal 15.04.68, Scottish Borders :
  DT - 42.60
HARTLEY Adam 27.02.69, Leeds :
  400H - 53.6/53.71 (53.15-94)
HARTVELD Adri 7.10.59, City of Stoke/HOL :
  Mar - 2:23:52 (2:15:32-86)
HASSAN Eshref U17 7.12.79, Belgrave :
  400 - 50.6/50.81
HATTON Anthony 18.06.70, Har/Loughbro :
  JT - 57.70 (71.86-93)
HATTON Darren U20 21.03.79, Medway :
  LJ - 6.89, DecJ - 5884
HAUGHIAN Samuel U20 9.07.79, Hounslow :
  3k - 8:29.7, 5k - 14:55.64
HAWKINS Christopher Michael 24.10.61, Bing :
  10MR - 49:00, 3kSt - 8:41.54 (8:36.55-95)
HAWKINS James U17 14.12.79, Medway :
  HTY - 55.84 (59.80-95)
HAY Wayne U17 25.09.80, Reading :
  LJ - 6.79
HAYDON Daniel U17 22.11.79, Walton :
  400HY - 58.0/59.62
HAYES Kevin 10.11.70, Nuneaton :
  1500 - 3:48.95
HAYES Martin U20 31.08.79, Chesterfield :
  HT - 46.70, HTJ - 52.74un/50.90
HAYES Scott 4.01.73, Thames Valley :
  SP - 15.28 (15.98i/15.62-95),
  DT - 51.46 (52.26-95)
HAYFORD Kenneth N. 10.03.63, Camb H :
  JT - 58.88 (69.90-87)
HAYMAN Nigel, Bournemouth :
  110H - 15.4
HAYMAN Thomas U17 17.09.80, BH Mansfield :
  DTJ - 46.96, DTY - 47.06

HAYTON Colin 22.07.59, Leeds :
Dec - 5445 (6253-88)
HAYWARD Gregory 28.01.64, Peterbro/RAF :
JT - 57.64 (61.96-90)
HAYWARD Stephan U23 30.07.74, Sale/S Bord :
SP - 18.40, DT - 46.76 (47.76-94)
HEAD Paul 1.07.65, Newham & Essex B :
SP - 13.49 (14.33-92), DT - 44.04 (44.12-89),
HT - 73.66 (74.02-90)
HEALY Graham 27.04.70, Havering :
100 - 10.8 (10.85w-91),
200 - 21.4w/21.6 (21.6-91/22.11-90),
400 - 47.9/47.94i/48.36 (47.47-91)
HEALY Philip 1.10.70, Ballydrain/Border :
800 - 1:50.42, 1500 - 3:40.95, 1M - 4:01.2
HEANLEY John U17 25.09.80, Windsor S & E :
800 - 1:58.0, OctY - 4274
HEATH Brett U23 6.01.75, Havering :
PV - 4.30, LJ - 6.96,
SP - 13.73, DT - 43.22, Dec - 6834
HEATH David J. 22.05.65, Blackheath :
1500 - 3:42.56 (3:41.0-89), 3kSt - 9:23.3
HEDMAN Graham U20 6.02.79, Braintree :
400 - 48.52
HEGGIE Jonathan U17 8.12.79, Hallamshire :
400H - 55.44, 400HY - 54.2/54.44
HEGGIE Simon U23 12.01.76, Morpeth :
400 - 47.90
HEMERY Adrian U15 6.08.82, Windsor S & E :
DTB - 39.00, HTB - 48.36
HENDERSON Giles U17 9.03.80, :
HJ - 1.91
HENDERSON James Alistair 28.03.69, C of E:
60 - 6.91i (6.66i-87),
100 - 10.85w/10.91 (10.21-87)
HENDRICKSON Matthew U15 31.01.82,
Beds Sch : PenB - 2874
HENDRY Martyn U23 10.04.75, C of Edinburgh :
110H - 14.5w/14.9/14.92
HENNESSY Andrew U20 24.08.77, Wells :
800 - 1:53.6, 1500 - 3:52.1,
2kSt - 5:59.5, 3kSt - 9:20.0
HENRY Corri U23 9.12.76, Notts :
100 - 10.5w/10.8 (11.00w-94/11.01-95),
200 - 20.8w/21.34, 400 - 46.50
HENRY Michael U17 9.10.79, Isle of Wight :
1.5kSt - 4:27.03
HENSHAW Matthew U20 16.05.78, Stockport :
100 - 10.98w
HENTHORN James U20 20.02.77, Carm :
100 - 10.38w/10.45 (10.41-95),
200 - 21.41i/21.46 (21.12-95)
HEPPEL Neil U17 17.09.79, Brentwood :
3k - 8:54.11
HERBERT John A.A. 20.04.62, Haringey :
TJ - 15.90 (17.41-85)
HERBERT Scott U23 12.02.74, Milton Keynes :
60 - 6.91i, 100 - 10.8/10.89 (10.6w-93),
200 - 21.20
HERRING Christopher U17 3.03.81, Hartlep :
100HY - 14.2, 400HY - 57.1/59.54
HERRINGTON Gary 31.03.61, Rugby :
SP - 13.51 (13.96-88), DT - 56.66,
HT - 46.28 (48.34-88)
HETHERINGTON Gary 13.09.59, Durham :
Mar - 2:32:17
HEWITT Daniel U17 13.11.79, Lincoln Well :
1.5kSt - 4:29.90

HEWITT Reggie, North Belfast :
Mar - 2:32:10
HEWITT Robert 6.07.67, Norwich :
SP - 14.24
HEWSON Neil U17 4.09.80, Bolton :
400 - 51.0/51.10, 100HY - 14.1
HEYWOOD Danny 27.05.71, Cardiff :
400H - 54.75 (53.9/54.53-95)
HIBBERD Matthew J. 23.06.73, Thames VH :
800 - 1:52.6 (1:49.2-92), 1k - 2:23.3 (2:22.7-95)
HIBBERT Paul N. 31.03.65, Birchfield :
400 - 47.38, 110H - 15.02, 400H - 50.52
HIBBINS Kevin U17 7.11.80, Grantham :
100 - 11.11.63, LJ - 7.18w/6.74 (6.74-95)
HICKS Andrew U20 30.07.79, Banbury :
400H - 55.4/55.62
HICKS Maurice 1.01.70, Hounslow/Junc 10 :
HT - 56.14
HIGHLAND James 2.06.65, Diss/AUS :
DT - 48.18 (53.56-86), HT - 47.36,
JT - 56.12 (73.96-87)
HILL David V45 31.12.50, Thames H & H :
Mar - 2:28:02 (2:16:36-84)
HILL Kevin 17.06.73, Wigan :
JT - 57.14 (66.60-94)
HILL Matthew U20 15.12.77, Stainforth :
400 - 49.60, 110H - 15.6
HILL Michael Christopher 22.10.64, Leeds :
JT - 81.42 (86.94-93)
HILL Robin U20 23.02.77, Sheffield :
PV - 4.60i/4.60 (4.60-95)
HILL Walter, Crawley :
100kR - 7:38:08
HILLIER James U20 3.04.78, Newport :
110HJ - 15.5/15.51 (15.4-95),
110H - 15.6, 400H - 53.26
HILSTON James U20 25.02.79, Belgrave :
400 - 48.60 (48.35-95), HJ - 2.00
HILTON Jonathan U23 11.01.74, Sale :
TJ - 15.09w/14.96 (15.06-94)
HIND James U20 24.05.77, Leamington :
HJ - 2.00i/1.98
HINDS Elphinston 15.07.60, Thames Valley :
LJ - 7.23 (7.38-82),
TJ - 14.32w/14.05 (15.20w-85/14.82-91)
HIRSCH Mark 31.03.63, Birchfield :
3kSt - 9:08.0
HISCOX Darren, Bridgend :
10kR - 29:43, HMar - 1:04:56
HOAD Oliver U15 1.10.81, Cambridge H :
HTB - 44.10
HOBBS Christopher V40 2.04.55, Medway :
3kW - 13:46.3 (12:57.0-88)
HOBBS Justin 12.03.69, Cardiff :
HMar - 1:03:41
HOCK Stuart U17 5.05.80, Wigan :
100 - 11.14w/11.2/11.45,
200 - 22.7 (23.49-95/23.65w-94)
HODGKINSON Mark R. 20.07.72, Birchfield :
PV - 5.20
HODGSON Gary U15 21.03.82, Telford :
1500 - 4:20.13
HODSON Ben U23 25.01.76, Old Gaytonians :
TJ - 14.17w/13.88 (14.27-95)
HODSON William U15 20.01.82, Norfolk Sch :
PenB - 2700
HOEY Michael 29.04.69, Bournemouth :
3kSt - 9:17.9 (9:06.6-95)

343

HOGBIN P. U13, Dorchester :
1500 - 4:38.1
HOLDER Graham P. 16.01.72, Bexley :
HT - 59.08
HOLE Martyn U23 29.11.75, Thurrock :
PV - 4.10
HOLGATE Martin C. 2.11.65, Woodford Gr :
110H - 14.7w, 400H - 54.5 (54.2/54.51-95)
HOLLADAY Robert U23 10.01.75, Roth/Loughbro :
10k - 30:52.56
HOLLIDAY Ian 9.12.73, Shaftesbury Barnet :
HJ - 2.15
HOLLIER Steve U23 27.02.76, Wolves & B :
3kW - 12:10.0, 20kW - 1:37:20
HOLLIMAN Brian 12.08.72, Irvine :
400 - 48.5/49.27
HOLLINGER Robert U17 11.10.80, Rotherham :
100HY - 13.44, OctY - 4781
HOLLINGSWORTH Eric M. 6.12.62, Old Gayt :
PV - 4.40 (4.80-93), SP - 14.44 (15.27-93),
DT - 47.24 (50.12-92), Dec - 7204 (7748-93)
HOLLINGSWORTH Ivan U23 20.05.75,
Gate/Northumblerland Un : 1500 - 3:48.32
HOLLOWAY Alan J. 22.06.60, Charn/Loughbro :
JT - 56.46 (67.62-89)
HOLME Oliver U15 10.11.81, Surrey Sch :
800 - 2:04.84
HOLMES Jonathan U20 13.11.78, Darlington :
DecJ - 5263
HOLMES Stephen U17 17.10.80, Blackheath :
400HY - 58.5/59.88
HOLT Andrew 23.02.64, Verlea :
Mar - 2:29:05 (2:24:26-93)
HOLT Peter U20 12.02.77, Spenborough :
PV - 4.40i/4.20 (4.30-93)
HOLT Richard 28.11.71, Blackheath/Sheff Un :
400H - 53.7/54.29 (52.11-95)
HOLTBY John U15 27.03.82, City of Hull :
PenB - 2654
HOOPER Jonathan 22.07.64, Bridgend :
Mar - 2:25:28 (2:18:40-89)
HOOPER Richard J.G. 29.03.58, Birchfield :
JT - 63.64 (70.10-89)
HOOTON Robin 5.05.73, C of Edinb/Bris Un :
800 - 1:47.7, 1k - 2:19.61, 1M - 4:08.51
HOPKINS Nicholas J. 28.08.66, Reigate :
3k - 8:07.00i/8:15.79 (7:59.66-90),
5k - 14:16.13 (14:05.08-95)
HOPPER John 5.12.68, Luton :
HJ - 2.00 (2.15i-90/2.11-88)
HOQUE Nizamul U20 19.09.78, Blackheath :
100 - 10.8w, 200 - 22.0 (22.79-95),
400 - 48.53
*HORAK Jiri U23 24.07.74, Hercules Wim/CS :
HT - 49.02 (52.22-95)*
HORNBY Jeff 17.01.66, Spenborough :
10k - 31:06.6 (29:53.9-91)
*HORNE P. David, SGA (Prof)/USA :
SP - 13.80*
HORSBURGH Ian Joseph U20 10.01.78,
Scottish Bord/Edinburgh SH : 100 - 10.90w,
200 - 21.80i/21.90, 400 - 47.8/48.24
HORSHAM Matthew U15 13.10.81, Wells :
80HB - 12.1
HOUGH Matthew U17 1.06.80, Sale :
200 - 22.70w/22.8/23.12

HOUGH Robert S.D. 3.06.72, Sheffield :
800 - 1:49.8, 1k - 2:23.4,
1500 - 3:41.3, 1M - 4:00.42,
3k - 7:52.9, 3kSt - 8:26.33, 400H - 54.1
HOUGHTON Ben U17 6.08.80, Bally & A :
JT - 56.34, JTY - 61.52
HOURIHAN Paul U23 7.11.76, Liverpool H :
110H - 15.2, Dec - 6577
HOUSTON Ross U17 5.12.79, Central :
1500 - 4:05.42
HOWARD Carl U23 27.01.74, N & EB/Brun U :
LJ - 7.44i/7.31 (7.76-93), TJ - 15.67 (15.97-95)
HOWARD Damien U15 23.11.81, W Norfolk :
HTY - 48.18, HTB - 57.84
HOWARD Paul 19.10.66, Woodford Green :
PV - 4.20 (4.40-90), SP - 14.11,
DT - 42.42 (43.06-90), JT - 62.62 (65.10-91)
HOWARTH Duncan U20 20.02.79, Norwich :
400H - 56.8/56.91
HOWE Christopher W. 17.11.67, Woodford Gr/
Loughborough : HT - 60.82 (63.74-90)
HOWE Glen U20 20.10.78, Gateshead :
400H - 55.3/56.91
HOWLE Kevin U17, City of Stoke :
PV - 3.70
HOWLETT James U20 18.02.79, Peterbro :
HJ - 2.03
HUDSPITH Ian 23.09.70, Morpeth :
5k - 13:54.6, HMar - 1:02:53,
10kR - 28:17sh/29:08RL/29:33 (29:17-92)
HUDSPITH Mark E. 19.01.69, Morpeth :
5k - 14:09.4 (13:51.73-91),
10k - 29:09.31 (29:02.38-92),
HMar - 1:04:48 (1:02:50dh?-95),
Mar - 2:19:25 (2:11:58-95)
HUGGINS Mark 20.12.68, Leeds :
400 - 48.1
HUGGINS Marlon A. 11.02.71, Thames VH :
HJ - 2.00 (2.12i-89/2.11-94)
HUGHES Andy 10.07.67, RAF/Shaftesbury B :
100 - 10.8 (10.59db-95)
HUGHES Brian C. 6.01.70, Birchfield :
Dec - 5634 (6098-93)
HUGHES Gareth 22.10.73, Liverpool H :
110H - 15.3w/15.44w (15.2-93/15.31-94)
HUGHES Kevin M. 30.04.73, Haringey :
PV - 5.30 (5.50i/5.30-95)
HULME Delroy 14.09.72, City of Stoke :
TJ - 14.48 (15.50w-91/15.26-90)
HULSE G.Ewart W. 21.01.62, Colwyn Bay :
SP - 13.94 (14.09-93), HT - 49.60 (54.62-91)
HUMM Jason Alex 11.01.71, Cambridge H :
3kSt - 8:49.03
HUNT Jamie U17 29.11.79, Norwich :
SPY - 14.52 (15.02-95)
HUNTER Gary U15 10.09.81, West (I.O.M.) :
200 - 23.46w/23.68, 400 - 52.6,
800 - 2:04.7, PenB - 2760
HUNTER Richard 12.01.71, Belgrave :
110H - 15.16 (14.79w-89/14.8/14.99-95)
HUNTER Roger U23 10.03.76, Skyrac :
110H - 15.0 (15.33w-95), Dec - 6780 (6925-95)
HUNTINGFORD Damian U20 11.06.77, GEC :
JT - 54.72 (59.18-94)
HUNTLEY Tendai U23 12.09.76, Blackheath :
200 - 21.9/22.17, LJ - 7.04 (7.16w/7.11-95)
HURREN Richard U13 24.09.83, Falkirk :
TJ - 10.23

HURRION James 11.11.73, Cov G/Ox Un :
JT - 64.44 (70.16r/68.84-91)
HURST Craig 30.12.70, City of Stoke :
100 - 10.8 (10.7w-89/10.75w/10.8/10.91-92),
200 - 21.9 (21.7-94/21.72w/21.81-92)
HURST Lee 29.07.72, Altrincham :
2kSt - 5:50.84, 3kSt - 8:48.34
HUSSAIN Bashir 20.12.64, Stockport :
Mar - 2:23:32, 3kSt - 9:19.55 (9:18.8-87)
HUTCHINSON Daniel U17 25.12.79, Bourne :
TJ - 13.90
HUTCHINSON John U15 3.05.82, St Albans :
PV - 3.00
HUTCHINSON Michael Innes 5.10.65, Traff :
3kSt - 9:24.1 (8:50.61-92)
HUTCHISON David 18.08.70, Harmeny :
200 - 22.0
HUXTABLE Sean 27.10.70, Dudley & Stourb :
100 - 10.7w/10.78
HYDE Daniel U20 5.10.77, Torbay :
3k - 8:26.4, 5k - 14:53.87
HYDE Felix U23 7.08.76, Old Gayt/GHA :
SP - 16.99 (17.38-95)
HYDE Timothy 22.02.72, Windsor S & E :
3k - 8:23.8 (8:22.1-95), 3kSt - 9:06.66
HYLAND Eamonn 23.07.60, Redhill/IRE :
Mar - 2:19:22 (2:17:58-92)
HYLTON Mark U23 24.09.76, Windsor S & E :
100 - 10.84 (10.8-95/11.02un-93),
200 - 21.2/21.88i+ (21.09-95),
300 - 32.76, 400 - 45.57
HYNDMAN Christopher U15 3.07.82, Middlesbro :
DTB - 37.20
HYNES Robin U20 22.04.77, Wirral :
LJ - 7.02

IBLE Keith 9.11.68, Shaftesbury Barnet :
TJ - 15.60w/15.24 (15.36-95)
IDDON Christopher U15 8.10.82, Bolton :
1500 - 4:18.2
IDOWU Phillips U20 30.12.78, Belgrave :
TJ - 15.53w/15.12
IFILL Rowland A. U23 11.11.75, V of Aylesbury :
400 - 48.8/49.31
IGBON Charles U20 20.04.79, Belgrave :
TJ - 14.12w/14.06
ILLIDGE Sam U20 4.02.77, Lincoln Well :
800 - 1:54.1
ILO Oluleke U20 25.06.78, Belgrave :
TJ - 14.32
INGRAM David U17 19.01.80, Brighton :
PV - 3.90
INGRAM Geoff 31.01.68, RAF :
Dec - 5674 (5841-94)
IROCHE Lance U20 22.06.78, Devon Sch :
100 - 10.84w/11.01
IRVING Andrew U15 30.09.81, Halifax :
200 - 23.27w/23.3/24.30
IRVING Christopher U15 30.09.81, Halifax :
100 - 11.5
IRVING Jan U20 4.03.77, Wirral :
LJ - 7.12w (7.13w-95/7.02-94)
IRWIN Chris U15 3.11.82, :
100 - 11.58
IRWIN David U20 18.12.78, Annadale Str :
SP - 13.33, SPJ - 13.83
ISLES Tiernan U17 7.01.80, Luton :
800 - 1:57.8

JACK Donley 7.11.66, Thames Valley :
200 - 21.4/21.84
JACKSON Colin Ray 18.02.67, Brecon :
60H - 7.51i (7.30i-94),
110H - 13.13 (12.8w-90/12.91-93)
JACKSON Darren U20 21.10.78, Enfield :
200 - 22.0 (23.42-95)
JACKSON Dennis V50 29.06.45, York :
50kW - 4:27:04 (4:03:08-86/4:13:00-83)
JACKSON Gary 28.04.68, Birchfield :
PV - 4.40 (4.90-86)
JACKSON James 12.09.63, AF&D :
5k - 14:26.2, 10k - 30:44.93, Mar - 2:29:05
JAMES Ronnie 14.12.64, Cornwall AC :
Mar - 2:30:08 (2:26:35-95)
JAMES S. U15, Halesowen :
3k - 9:37.5
JAMES Simon U20 21.01.77, Telford :
SP - 13.50, SPJ - 15.23
JAMIESON Paul 21.06.73, Liverpool Pem :
200 - 21.90 (21.7-95)
JARRETT Anthony Alexander 13.08.68, Har :
100 - 10.41A (10.45-94), 60H - 7.57i (7.42i-95),
110H - 13.0w/13.24 (13.00-93)
JEFFERIES Robert U17 4.10.79, Derby & Co :
800 - 1:56.8
JEFFERSON Tom U15, :
TJ - 12.14
JEMI-ALADE Michael 13.10.64, C of Edinburgh :
DT - 48.02 (52.38-87)
JENKINS Christopher U15 2.03.82, Liv H :
80HB - 11.54, HJ - 1.85, LJ - 6.35,
JTB - 44.36, PenB - 3014
JENNINGS Carl F. 4.05.64, Birchfield :
SP - 15.18 (17.47-87)
JENNINGS Gary 21.02.72, N & EB/Loughbro :
400 - 47.7/48.61 (46.95-95),
400H - 50.18 (49.82-95)
JENNINGS Neil U20 18.09.77, Mandale :
400 - 48.40
JENSON Gary 14.02.67, :
JT - 69.18 (79.54r-91/78.54-89)
JEWERS William S. 27.09.62, Basingstoke :
110H - 15.09 (14.8-86), HJ - 2.02 (2.14-86),
LJ - 7.08 (7.26-86), Dec - 6910 (7136-89)
JOHN Jason 17.10.71, Birchfield :
60 - 6.59i, 200 - 20.87 (20.51w-93/20.86-95),
100 - 10.25w/10.30 (10.08w/10.23-94)
ROBERT John 17.01.69, Bracknell :
LJ - 6.95
JOHNSON Andrew U15 10.09.81, Herts & W :
PenB - 2557
JOHNSON Dean U23 31.12.75, Sheffield :
JT - 60.40 (60.50-93)
JOHNSON Mark 7.09.64, Haringey :
PV - 4.80 (5.26-91)
JOHNSON Matthew U23 2.05.74, Herts & W/
Birmingham Univ. : 110H - 15.29
JOHNSON Paul 8.03.68, Birchfield :
LJ - 7.48 (7.94i/7.93i-89/7.87w-88/7.85-89)
JOHNSON Peter U23 25.09.75, Liverpool H :
JT - 62.76
JOHNSTON Anthony 23.08.68, RAF/Irvine :
800 - 1:48.4, 1500 - 3:45.6, 1M - 4:03.6
JOHNSTON Cameron U15 22.10.82, Croydon :
PV - 2.95
JONES Andres U20 3.02.77, Cardiff :
3k - 8:26.66, 5k - 14:31.1, 10k - 30:06.01

JONES Chris U15, Cardiff :
SPB - 13.23
JONES David U17 4.10.80, Liverpool H :
HTY - 48.12
JONES David 6.10.69, Trafford :
JT - 55.24 (63.04-90)
JONES Egryn 1.11.71, Cardiff :
PV - 4.80i/4.60 (4.90-95), Dec - 5498
JONES Gareth 14.12.68, Cardiff :
HT - 56.90 (59.40-94)
JONES Gary, Verlea :
JT - 56.40
JONES Marc D. 7.07.66, Epsom & Ewell :
100 - 10.7w
JONES Mark U17 15.03.80, Chesterfield :
DTY - 41.96
JONES Martin John 21.04.67, Horwich :
3k - 8:09.0, 5k - 14:04+e/14:15.22 (13:55.3-93),
10k - 28:37.87 (28:33.18-94),
10kR - 28:59 (28:24-94),
10MR - 48:46 (48:36-92)
JONES Matthew U17 15.09.79, Crewe & N :
1500 - 4:03.21
JONES Michael 23.07.63, Shaft B/WLHS :
HT - 72.48
JONES Nathan U17 10.03.80, Ryde :
DTY - 47.18
JONES Neil U17 22.10.79, Warrington :
200 - 22.73, 400HY - 56.8
JONES Nick, Tipton :
10MR - 48:51
JONES Paul U20 11.04.78, Colwyn Bay :
DecJ - 5811
JONES Robin Evans Hugh V40 1.11.55,
Ranelagh : Mar - 2:22:58 (2:09:24-82)
JONES Sean 21.03.69, Thames Valley/Army :
HT - 51.10 (54.88-92)
JONES Stephen H. V40 4.08.55, Newport :
10MR - 48:26 (46:20un-79/46:49-89)
JOSEPH Darren U20 10.04.78, Solihull & S H :
HJ - 2.15i/2.10, LJ - 6.92
JOSEPH Rafer E.L. 21.07.68, Dacorum & Tr :
60H - 8.35i (8.24i-94),
110H - 15.2/15.22 (14.7/15.03w/15.06-94),
HJ - 1.96i (1.98-91), PV - 4.40 (4.81-94),
LJ - 6,94w, SP - 14.67i/14.27 (14.68i-94),
DT - 52.00, HT - 48.88, Dec - 7174 (7663-94)
JOUSIFFE Warren U20 27.05.77, Hounslow :
PV - 4.70
JOYCE Colin U15 21.10.81, Braintree :
400 - 52.8, 800 - 1:59.64
JOYCE Daniel U23 9.09.74, Thames Valley :
60 - 6.8i/6.84i (6.8i-95), 200 - 21.49.
100 - 10.47 (10.33w-95/10.47-93)
JUBB Michael 20.06.70, Derby & Co :
2kSt - 5:44.53, 3kSt - 8:50.37
JUDGE Andrew U23 24.05.75, Cov G/Loughbro :
400H - 53.67, HJ - 1.96
JUMP Ben Anderson 6.02.65, Aberdeen :
JT - 56.66 (57.70-92)

K ABISWA Samuel 28.10.66, Windsor S&E :
200 - 22.02 (21.7/21.82-93),
400 - 48.3/48.59 (47.5-94/48.05-95)
KANE David 1.11.70, Thames Valley :
110H - 15.34w/15.5/15.54
KARIM M. U15, :
80HB - 12.1

KAZIMIERSKI Michael 6.05.70, Belgrave/POL :
Mar - 2:31:41
KEARNEY Simon U23 28.07.74, Worthing :
JT - 60.14
KEATING Tyrone U15 25.02.82, Braintree :
100 - 11.48, 200 - 22.91
KEETON Michael U23 14.12.76, Notts :
TJ - 14.29
KEITH Andrew 25.12.71, Hereford :
1500 - 3:41.4 (3:39.06-93),
3k - 8:01.8 (7:49.83i-94/7:54.37-95),
5k - 14:00.58 (13:48.13-95)
KELLER Simon U23 10.11.76, Newark :
SP - 13.52 (14.40-95)
KELLY Andrew J. U13 26.09.83, Norwich :
HJ - 1.55
KELLY Bryan 29.12.73, Liverpool H :
SP - 13.49 (15.75-93), DT - 45.88 (46.86-93)
KELLY Lee 11.06.62, Army :
Mar - 2:29:44
KELLY Neil U17 21.03.80, Western (I.O.M.) :
HJ - 1.95, OctY - 4650
KELLY Perry 1.10.69, Haringey :
100 - 10.80
KELLY Sean 8.11.72, Rowntrees :
800 - 1:52.2 (1:49.9-95)
KELSALL Alan U17 3.09.80, Newham & EB :
HTY - 48.08
KEMP Andrew U17 8.12.79, Yeovil Oly
(nee CASTLE) : SPY - 14.66, HTY - 58.68
KEMP Michael U17 23.12.79, Leics WC :
3kW - 13:50.50i/14:04.9,
3kWR - 13:14, 5kW - 22:42.2o/22:57.7,
5kWR - 22:20o, 10kW - 49:56.0,
10kWR - 44:50o
KENDALL John 23.09.69, AF&D :
5k - 14:29.92 (14:16.45-93)
KENNARD Andrew 2.01.66, Walton :
400H - 54.7 (53.1-95/53.58-90)
KENNY Ian U17 12.10.79, :
LJ - 6.76
KENNY Scott U17 20.02.80, Shettleston :
HJ - 1.97i/1.91 (1.94-95)
KENT David U13 15.12.83, Oadby & Wigston :
800 - 2:15.5, 1500 - 4:34.8, 3k - 10:08.9
KENTISH Neil U20 30.09.77, Northampton :
400 - 49.4/49.56
KEOGH Nigel 18.07.67, Blackheath/IRE :
400H - 53.65 (52.89-91)
KEOGHAN David U20 9.10.78, Bolton :
400H - 55.32
KEOWN David U23 18.07.74, Roadhogs :
5kW - 22:47.37 (22:47.0-93),
10kW - 46:56.0, 20kW - 1:38:09
KERR Eric 9.12.64, Luton :
HT - 53.34 (54.58-95)
KERR Glen U23 27.10.74, Bedford & County :
HT - 58.38
KERR Hugh U23 4.01.76, Haringey/Ayr S :
400 - 48.91 (47.69i/47.75-95)
KESKA Karl 7.05.72, Birchfield/Oregon Univ. :
1500 - 3:42.71, 3k - 8:03.94,
5k - 13:56.06, 10k - 29:10.40
KEYWOOD Stephen J. 28.09.61, Tonbridge :
Mar - 2:29:52 (2:28:50-93)
KIDDELL Peter U15 2.09.81, Belgrave :
LJ - 6.03

346

KIDNER Ross David U17 12.09.80, TVH/WLHS :
DTY - 42.12, HT - 48.90,
HTJ - 51.66, HTY - 62.98
KILLEN Neal A. 10.04.59, Aldershot S/Rown :
DT - 41.00 (44.10-95)
KILLICK Roger U23 20.11.76, Banbury :
JT - 57.48
KILSHAW Jay U17 19.10.79, Thurrock :
200 - 22.6, 400 - 49.67
KING Allan V40 3.12.56, Roadhogs :
3kW - 13:26.7 (12:08.8-85),
10kW - 47:23.42 (43:37.9-80),
20kW - 1:38:41 (1:28:30-85),
50kW - 4:39:01 (4:13:25-83)
KING Daniel U15 30.05.83, Colchester H :
3kW - 15:27.34, 3kWR - 15:20
KING Dominic U15 30.05.83, Colchester H :
3kW - 15:14.46, 3kWR - 15:02
KING Edward U23 26.11.75, B & A/Sale :
400 - 48.27, 800 - 1:48.5
KING John Stewart 13.02.63, Haringey :
LJ - 7.46i/7.31w/7.11 (7.94w-86/7.91-87)
KING John U15 6.10.81, Great Yarmouth :
JTB - 46.14,
KING Kirk U17 18.09.80, Blackheath :
LJ - 6.61
KING Philip U23 25.11.74, Coventry RWC :
5kW - 21:58.57 (20:05.7-95)
KING Richard U15 5.04.82, Holmfirth :
1500 - 4:13.59
KING Shane U23 8.02.74, Kendal :
200 - 22.0, 400 - 48.80
KING Timothy John U20 10.12.77, Peterbro :
SPJ - 14.32i/13.97
KINGMAN Robert 21.02.73, N & EB/RAF :
PV - 4.80i/4.80 (5.02-94)
KINGSNORTH Tom U17 15.10.79, C of Bath :
1.5kSt - 4:25.5
KINGWELL J., Verlea :
HT - 47.18
KINSON Simon 3.12.70, Leamington :
Mar - 2:30:07 (2:25:17-95)
KIRK Neil U20 14.09.78, GEC :
800 - 1:52.04
KIRKHAM Seth U23 9.09.75, Old Gaytonians :
JT - 56.92 (59.76-95)
KIRKPATRICK William U17 28.02.80, Lagan V :
SPY - 14.37, DTY - 42.46
KIRKWOOD Brian V40 20.09.52, Leslie D RC :
10kR - 29:45
KITNEY Timothy J. U17 26.04.80, Medway :
JT - 58.12, JTY - 65.92
KLOIBER Matthew 22.11.71, Belgrave :
800 - 1:51.25 (1:50.8-95)
KNELLER Steven 9.11.71, Birchfield :
400H - 54.72
KNIGHT Andrew G. 26.10.68, Cambridge H :
600 - 1:18.5, 800 - 1:48.7 (1:48.38-94)
KNIGHT Andrew 11.11.73, Luton/Loughbro :
100 - 10.8 (10.6w?-95/10.7-93/10.72-95),
200 - 22.05w/22.66 (21.4-93/21.62-94)
KNIGHT Steve 17.10.63, Cardiff :
5k - 14:33.84 (14:20.45-94), HMar - 1:03:57
KNIGHTON Dean U17 16.03.80, Derby & Co :
SPY - 13.98
KNOWLES Leroy U20 26.09.78, Beds & Co :
TJ - 14.63w/14.18

KNOWLES Richard U23 12.11.75, Sol & S H :
200 - 21.8, 400 - 46.83
KNOX Kevin U17 26.05.80, City of Stoke :
100HY - 13.9w
KOIKAI Amin U23 5.01.74, Ilford/KEN :
10k - 30:59.0 (30:11.0-94)
KORJIE Haroun 17.02.72, Belgrave/SLE :
100 - 10.3/10.70 (10.46-94),
200 - 21.1/21.57 (21.31-94)
KRON Jonathon 16.02.73, Windsor S & E/IRE :
LJ - 7.63 (7.78-95)
KRTEN Libor 26.02.73, Hercules Wimb/CZE :
SP - 14.27 (14.43-95), DT - 46.58
KRUGER Alexander Eaton 18.11.63, Border :
60H - 8.34i (8.32i-93), 110H - 14.78 (14.76-95),
HJ - 2.11i (2.20-88), DT - 45.46,
PV - 4.65i (4.90i/4.90-95),
LJ - 7.23i (7.57w-89/7.45-94),
SP - 14.68i/14.54 (14.79i-95/14.76-94)
KRUSZEWSKI Andrew P. 7.04.59, Camb H :
DT - 49.72 (51.26-92)
KUBOTA Kengo 26.06.68, C of E/StrathU/JAP :
DT - 44.48 (44.74-94)
KUIPER Anthony U17 25.10.79, Liverpool Pem :
HJ - 2.03

L ACEY Andy U15 29.03.82, :
PV - 3.00
LADEJO Du'aine 14.02.71, Belgrave :
200 - 21.31w/21.41i+ (20.96-93),
300 - 32.75A (32.73-94), 400 - 44.66
LAFFLEY Stefan U20 10.09.77, Sale :
400H - 55.85
LAING David 1.01.66, Ipswich Joggers :
Mar - 2:31:29
LAING Robert H. 30.07.66, Liverpool H :
110H - 15.2/15.25
(14.7w/14.8/14.82w-91/14.90-92),
JT - 59.94 (67.48-87), Dec - 6280 (7076-89)
LAINSON Richard U15 5.11.81, Isle of Wight :
JTB - 60.34
LALLEY Terry V45 12.11.49, Cardiff :
HT - 46.96 (49.18-90)
LAMB Gavin U17 23.09.79, Pudsey & Bram :
400HY - 58.5/61.10
LAMB Steven U23 10.10.75, City of Stoke :
400H - 55.2 (53.55-94)
LAMBERT Christopher U17 6.04.81, Belgrave :
100 - 11.15w/11.5 (12.71-95), 200 - 22.67
LAMBETH Mark 3.09.72, Haringey :
60H - 8.2i/8.26i (7.83i-95),
110H - 14.96w/15.0 (14.02-95)
LAMING Robert U15 26.06.82, Medway :
1500 - 4:14.0
LAMMIE Graeme U15 3.10.81, Perth :
80HB - 12.02 (12.0-95)
LANCASTER Graham, Sunderland :
10k - 31:09.7
LANDON Mark U15 9.11.81, Corby :
SPB - 12.87, HTB - 58.88
LANG Tim 8.12.73, Wigan :
400H - 55.5/55.98
LARKINS Paul Stephen 19.05.63, N & E B :
1500 - 3:45.9 (3:35.94-87),
5k - 14:20.6 (13:53.0-91)
LASHORE Akinola 28.03.73, Blackheath :
60 - 6.9i, 100 - 10.6w/10.75, 200 - 21.58

LASKEY Sam U17 28.05.80, Exeter :
OctY - 4646
LASLETT Paul U17 12.05.80, AF&D :
800 - 1:55.1, 1500 - 4:05.3
LATHAM Mark U23 13.01.76, C of S/Staffs U :
HJ - 2.10i/2.06 (2.11-94)
LAU J. U13, Chelmsford :
LJ - 5.20
LAUGHLIN Dale 28.12.66, Chelmsford :
5k - 14:15.0 (13:43.29-91),
10kR - 29:16 (28:55-93), 10MR - 48:45
LAVELLE Keith U20 13.05.77, Liverpool H :
JT - 54.66
LAWRENCE Hector U20 1.11.77, Haringey :
DT - 41.82 (42.74-95)
LAWRENCE Mark 26.01.71, Leeds/Notts Univ :
LJ - 7.04 (7.33-93), TJ - 14.18 (14.52-93)
LAWS Oliver U17 18.03.80, Wenlock O :
1500 - 4:04.6, 3k - 8:40.1
LAWS Richard U23 8.10.75, Morpeth :
HJ - 2.03i/2.00 (2.10-95)
LAWTON Christopher 6.01.73, Team Solent :
400 - 49.0
LEADER Steven 24.11.66, Enfield :
110H - 15.48 (15.2-89/15.46-94),
PV - 4.50 (4.90-90), Dec - 6829 (7078-94)
LEAMAN Ian U20 14.10.78, Exeter :
200 - 21.87w/22.10
LEASE Gareth U20 14.08.78, Bristol :
PV - 4.10
LEAVER James U23 15.09.75, Team Solent :
HJ - 2.00 (2.11-95), LJ - 6.93, TJ - 15.14
LEDGERWOOD Daniel U15 24.03.83, AF&D :
3k - 9:38.3
LEE David James 16.09.65, Blackheath :
3k - 8:14.4 (8:09.94-88),
5k - 14:19.9 (14:11.77-90),
2kSt - 5:47.1 (5:38.0-95),
3kSt - 8:48.60 (8:31.22-92)
LEES Nicholas 23.01.58, Long Eaton :
Mar - 2:33:12 (2:16:38-83)
LEES Simon U17 19.11.79, Solihull & S H :
800 - 1:53.4, 1500 - 3:58.6, 1.5kSt - 4:24.11
LEESON Thomas J. 18.09.63, Aberdeen :
110H - 15.56 (14.5-87/14.53w/14.75-85),
Dec - 6371 (7643w/7565-85)
LEGGATE Daniel U23 5.10.74, Old Gayt :
5k - 14:26.2
LEIDY Christopher U15 6.12.81, Dorset Sch :
JTB - 48.20
LEIGH Anthony 27.12.65, City of Stoke :
100 - 10.85w/10.92 (10.79w/10.8-91),
200 - 21.8/21.96 (21.8-93)
LEMON Matthew U17 6.02.80, GEC :
1.5kSt - 4:31.9
LENDON Jason U23 17.03.75, Havering :
3kSt - 9:21.6
LENNON-JONES Donald 9.05.68, N & E B :
3kSt - 9:29.5 (9:06.4-89)
LEONARD Carl 19.01.73, Swansea :
1500 - 3:47.22 (3:45.07-95),
5k - 14:11.30 (14:09.12-95),10k - 30:14.54
LERWILL Thomas U20 17.05.77, Belgrave :
400 - 47.9 (47.57-95), 800 - 1:47.27
LESLIE Dean U20 9.01.78, Crawley :
110HJ - 15.07w/15.1/15.21
LETHBRIDGE Matthew U20 22.01.77, Crawley :
400H - 53.07

LEVY Jason 30.05.70, RAF :
400 - 48.4/49.47 (48.95i-92)
LEVY Myrone U17 12.02.81, Birchfield :
100 - 11.18, 200 - 22.47
LEVY Noel U23 22.06.75, Belgrave :
400 - 48.00 (47.8-92/47.82-93),
400H - 50.85 (50.70-94)
LEWIS Andrew 9.03.68, Hounslow :
LJ - 7.26i/7.17 (7.53/7.39-94), TJ - 14.18
LEWIS Benjamin U17 6.03.81, Birchfield :
100 - 10.75w/10.99, 200 - 21.55w/21.66
LEWIS Daniel U15, Shaftesbury Barnet :
HTB - 40.38
LEWIS Junior 19.03.66, Verlea :
TJ - 14.84
LEWIS Matthew U23 11.11.75, Sale :
JT - 55.26
LEWIS Philip E. 12.01.70, Tonb/Edinb Un :
200 - 21.8w (21.70w-95/21.8-91/22.15-95),
400 - 49.0 (47.8-95)
LEWIS Robert U20 2.09.78, Bedford & Co :
400H - 55.1/55.27
LEWIS Robert 2.10.67, Tonbridge :
100 - 10.8 (10.5w/10.53w/10.6/10.64-90),
200 - 21.8w (21.8-90/22.14-91)
LEWIS Shane 22.08.72, Swansea :
JT - 56.26 (69.68-94)
LEWIS-FRANCIS Mark U15 4.09.82, Birch :
100 - 11.31w/11.37
LIDDLE Jonathan U15 13.09.81, Wells :
HJ - 1.78
LILL Andrew Richard 9.08.71, Newham & E B :
800 - 1:47.83 (1:46.37-92)
LINSKEY Christian U17 14.06.80, Barnsley :
PV - 5.15
LISIEWICZ John 18.07.62, Morpeth/AUS :
5k - 14:28.8 (14:01.24-94), HMar - 1:04:25
LITTLE Andrew 1.01.64, Shettleston :
10k - 30:41.1
LITTLE David U17 28.02.81, Border :
HTY - 51.06
LITTLE John V40 14.04.53, Border :
DT - 42.40 (43.70-95)
LIVESEY Christopher U17 8.08.80, Preston :
3k - 8:55.9
¶LIVINGSTON Jason Christopher 17.03.71,
Shaftesbury Barnet : 100 - 10.42 (10.09-92),
200 - 21.76 (21.01-92)
LIVINGSTON Ryan U17, Campbell College :
SPY - 14.26
LIVINGSTONE Stuart U20 29.08.79, C of E :
HJ - 2.03i/2.00
LLOYD Joseph 9.04.73, Swansea :
400 - 47.76
LLOYD Martin U17 18.06.80, Bexley :
HJ - 2.10, OctY - 4280
LLOYD Steven J. U23 20.03.74, Border :
DT - 41.50 (43.94-94)
LLOYD Trevor 1.08.66, Telford/RAF :
JT - 55.88 (60.22-87)
LOBO Jason 18.09.69, Blackburn :
800 - 1:48.8 (1:47.7-89),
1500 - 3:49.2 (3:44.14-93),
3k - 8:12.88i (8:24.2-86)
LOCKE Darren U15 16.10.81, :
HJ - 1.78
LOCKE Dave 20.05.72, Tipton :
SP - 13.92

348

LOCKER David Alan U23 28.03.75, C of Stoke :
  800 - 1:49.72i/1:51.1,
  1500 - 3:47.8, 1M - 4:07.76i
LONG Nicholas U20 1.02.79, Liverpool H :
  100 - 10.83w (11.00-95)
LONNEN Steve 26.06.57, Army :
  Mar - 2:29:34
LONSDALE Ian 8.09.71, Peterborough :
  100 - 10.7/10.79w/10.88
      (10.5w-92/10.61w-91/10.74-90),
  200 - 21.90w (21.7-91)
LOUGH Gareth 6.07.70, Anna Str/Loughbro :
  800 - 1:48.3 (1:48.03-95),
  1500 - 3:37.35 (3:34.76-95),
  1M - 4:00.0 (3:55.91-95),
  2k - 5:02.98, 3k - 7:54.12 (7:49.45-95)
LOUGHRAN Stuart U23 19.02.76, Swansea :
  JT - 64.08
LOVE Julian U20 21.06.78, :
  200 - 22.0
LOW Charles U23 9.10.74, Newquay & Par :
  3kSt - 9:02.77
LOW Chris U17 24.04.80, Arbroath :
  100HY - 13.46, OctY - 4253 (4712-95)
LOWE Peter 4.07.65, Sheffield :
  DT - 42.54
LOWTHIAN Ian U17 10.10.80, Liverpool H :
  400 - 50.69 (50.65-95)
LOXAM Jamie U20 7.07.77, Stockport :
  3kSt - 9:41.49
LUCAS Neil U20 2.10.78, Lisburn :
  HJ - 1.98
LUKE Greg, North Belfast :
  5k - 14:26.67
LUMSDON Kevin U23 3.03.74, Sale :
  110H - 14.9w/15.08 (14.20-94)
LUND Simon N. 22.12.65, Wigan Phoenix :
  Mar - 2:31:05 (2:27:39-94)
LUNDMAN·Jonathan U15 7.12.81, Braintree :
  JTB - 56.32
LUSTGARTEN Anders U23 9.02.74, Ox C/Ox U :
  200 - 21.7, 400 - 46.93
LYNCH Andrew U23 28.06.74, Thames Valley :
  HJ - 2.15i (2.18-95)
LYNCH Lawrence 1.11.67, Haringey :
  400 - 49.00i (47.02-93), 400H - 50.05
LYNCH Richard A. 14.07.64, North London :
  800 - 1:51.6 (1:48.0-89)
LYON Robert U20 23.03.77, Kilmarnock :
  JT - 53.86

MACDONALD Alexander U17 12.04.80,
  Shet : 800 - 1:56.9, 1500 - 3:59.9
MACDONALD Andrew U15 19.05.83, Barn:
  PV - 3.15
MACDONALD Colin 12.04.71, C of Edinburgh :
  TJ - 14.18 (14.20w-95)
MACDONALD Duncan J. U23 30.03.74, TVH :
  JT - 66.48
MACDONALD Stewart, Bingley :
  Mar - 2:30:53
MACEY Dean U20 12.12.77, Old Gaytonians :
  110H - 15.01, HJ - 2.10i/2.05 (2.13-95),
  PV - 4.20i/4.20, LJ - 7.14, SP - 13.44,
  DT - 41.32, DTJ - 42.40, JT - 63.30,
  Dec - 7480
MACFADYEN John 1.08.72, C of E/Strath Un :
  800 - 1:51.96 (1:50.46-92)

MACHARDIE Scott 26.06.69, Cambridge H :
  JT - 57.42 (65.68-92)
MACKE Patrick V40 18.06.55, Grantham :
  100kR - 6:56:13 (6:52:39-89)
MACKENZIE Colin T. 30.06.63, N& EB :
  JT - 81.06 (82.60r-91/82.38-93)
MACKIE Ian U23 27.02.75, Pitreavie :
  60 - 6.74i, 100 - 10.17, 150 - 15.23,
  200 - 21.58 (20.91-94)
MACLENNAN Kevin U20 5.12.78, Black Isle :
  110HJ - 14.90w/15.0
MADAR Abdi U15 25.11.81, Blackheath :
  1500 - 4:21.9
MADDEN Michael J. 13.09.65, Newquay & P :
  HT - 49.58 (55.92-93)
MADDOCKS Christopher Lloyd 28.03.57,
  Plymouth City W :
  20kW - 1:26:15 (1:22:12-92),
  50kW - 4:18:41 (3:51:37-90)
MADEIRA-COLE Charles U20 29.11.77, Carm :
  TJ - 14.88i/14.80, DecJ - 5485
MAGEE Greg U20 27.09.78, Scottish Borders :
  JT - 54.10
MAINSTONE Keith U23 15.03.74, Horsham BS :
  Dec - 5230
MAITLAND Peter 21.01.73, Newham & E B :
  60 - 6.78i (6.75i-95), 200 - 21.45i (20.96-94)
MAJOR Adam U15 2.11.81, :
  SPB - 13.23
MAKEPEACE Philip A. 15.03.64, Leics Cor :
  10kR - 29:25 (29:12-92),
  HMar - 1:04:42 (1:04:28-92)
MALCOLM Anthony U23 15.02.76, Salisbury :
  LJ - 7.32w/7.16i/6.94 (7.21-95)
MALCOLM Christian U20 3.06.79, Cardiff :
  60 - 6.9i (6.95i-95), 100 - 10.5/10.60,
  200 - 21.27
MALEY Gavin U20 19.05.78, Havering :
  2kSt - 6:05.2
MALI Dafydd U15, Eryri Sch :
  HTB - 40.08
MALINS Duncan U20 12.06.78, Crawley :
  110HJ - 14.80, DecJ - 5303
MALLON Chris 4.08.72, Richmond & Twick :
  HT - 50.08
MALLOWS Andrew U15 18.01.82, Notts :
  1500 - 4:20.1, 3k - 9:36.6
MANDY Mark 19.11.72, Cannock & Staff/IRE :
  HJ - 2.25 (2.25-95)
MANGAN P., Duncairn :
  Mar - 2:27:49
MANGLESHOT Lawrence Philip 28.05.63,
  Woodford Gr : 1500 - 3:49.5 (3:43.74-89)
MANSBRIDGE David C. 4.06.64, Telford :
  Mar - 2:22:28 (2:22:23-94)
MARAR Leith 7.11.68, Belgrave :
  DT - 55.68
MARGIOTTA Stuart 19.11.69, GEC :
  800 - 1:49.4, 1500 - 3:42.37,
  1M - 4:03.2, 3k - 8:14.7 (8:09.30-91)
MARK Alastair U15 8.12.81, Northampton :
  100 - 11.53w/11.62,
MARK Kevin U23 15.09.76, Ealing,S & Mx :
  100 - 10.7 (10.38w-93/10.60-94)
MARKHAM Gregory U20 28.11.78, Scun :
  JT - 57.32
MARLAND Chris U17 9.11.80, Deeside :
  SPY - 14.10

349

MARSDEN Barry 11.06.64, Wycombe :
110H - 15.4/15.63
MARSDEN John U15 23.10.81, Barry :
80HB - 11.3/11.48
MARSH Brett U23 20.01.76, Newquay & Par :
HT - 46.84
MARSHALL Neil U17 17.02.80, Sale :
HTY - 48.36
MARTIN Adam U15 12.10.81, Sale :
400 - 52.4/53.27
MARTIN Eamonn Thomas 9.10.58, Basildon :
5k - 14:29.7 (13:17.84-89),
HMar - 1:04:00 (1:02:52-93),
Mar - 2:11:21 (2:10:50-93)
MARTIN Jeffrey, Army/Bristol :
Mar - 2:33:17 (2:24:18-92)
MARTIN Paul U17 7.09.79, Hallamshire :
HJ - 1.95
MARTIN Paul U20 10.07.78, Tonbridge :
2kSt - 5:59.9
MARTINDALE Sean 8.11.66, York :
50kW - 4:57:51 (4:12:00-93)
MARTINEZ Anton U15 29.09.81, Cambridge H :
PV - 3.50
MASON Duncan 8.12.68, Salford :
10k - 31:06.83
MASON James Ryder 22.03.72, Belgrave :
SP - 16.17i (16.74-95)
MASON Julian U23 3.03.75, Skyrac :
TJ - 14.36i/14.19w/14.18
MASON Michael U20 16.06.77, Sutton & Dist :
400H - 56.7/57.18
MASON Robert U23 13.09.75, City of Stoke :
110H - 15.13
MASSEY Ian U23 9.09.76, Liverpool H :
HJ - 2.05i/2.05 (2.05-95)
MATE Anthony U23 15.12.74, Gateshead :
800 - 1:49.7, 1500 - 3:44.79 (3:44.63-95),
1M - 4:06.0
MATE Brett U23 15.12.74, Gateshead :
800 - 1:51.8
MATHIESON Ramin U20 8.08.79, Bristol :-
DTJ - 41.24
MATHIESON Simon U20 20.01.79, Bristol :
400 - 49.1/49.81 (49.49-95)
MATON Phil, Basingstoke & MH :
PV - 4.10
MATTHEWS Anthony D. 17.12.62, Leeds :
PV - 4.10 (4.60-90)
MATTHEWS Edward U20 17.09.77, Winch :
800 - 1:54.39
MATTHEWS Lawrence 11.08.65, Salf/Ox Un :
3k - 8:21.93i (8:02.8-90)
MATTHEWS Owen U15 17.10.81, Luton :
JTB - 46.22
MATTHEWS Simon 21.05.71, Kendal :
SP - 14.16 (15.17i-95/14.81-94)
MAUFRAIS Sebastian 18.01.70, Bingley/FRA :
LJ - 7.19, TJ - 14.38
MAXWELL Stewart 29.06.58, Wirral/RAF :
JT - 56.62 (63.70-86)
MAYNARD Darrell 21.08.61, Belgrave/Army :
400 - 48.2 (48.2-88/48.79-93),
800 - 1:50.85 (1:49.5a-88)
MAYO David U15 26.04.82, Hull Springhead :
HJ - 1.80

MAYO James U23 24.02.75, Cannock & Staff :
800 - 1:48.2, 1k - 2:22.18, 1500 - 3:44.0,
1M - 4:05.4
MAYO Thomas U20 2.05.77, C & S/Loughbro :
800 - 1:54.1, 1500 - 3:43.4
MAYOCK John Paul 26.10.70, C & Stafford :
1k - 2:18.48, 1500 - 3:33.38, 1M - 3:50.32,
2k - 5:00.91
MCADOREY John U23 16.09.74, B & A/IRE :
60 - 6.87i,
100 - 10.71w/10.8/10.89 (10.7w/10.85-91),
200 - 21.93 (21.82-94)
MCAREE Simon U23 28.12.75, N & E B :
60H - 8.16i,
110H - 14.4/14.52 (14.43-94)
MCBRIDE Allan U17 31.12.79, Inverclyde :
100 - 10.9w/11.2/11.21, 200 - 22.34
MCBURNEY Paul 14.03.72, Newham & E B :
100 - 10.8 (10.7dt-90/10.7w-94/10.91-92),
200 - 21.5 (20.81-94),
400 - 48.0/48.08 (46.49-94)
MCCAFFREY Nick Philip 26.06.68, OWLS :
3k - 8:23.0, 5k - 14:27.35, 10k - 29:49.91
MCCALLA Dave, Coventry Godiva/RAF :
TJ - 14.23i/14.11 (14.40-95)
MCCANN Owen U17 15.07.81, Annadale Str :
SPB - 13.62o
MCCAW Charles 21.01.72, Woodford Gr/OxUn :
800 - 1:52.2
MCCONVILLE Brendan U20 3.01.79, N Down :
Dec - 4966, DecJ - 5150
MCCORMACK Danny U23 22.03.75, Vauxhall :
1500 - 3:50.4, 3k - 8:23.5
MCCOURT Steven 6.05.71, Thames Valley :
150 - 16.35, 200 - 21.70 (21.03w-94/21.28-95)
MCCOY Bryan U23 31.12.75, Ballymena & A :
400 - 48.68 (48.68-94)
MCCOY M. U17, Doncaster :
JTY - 53.04
MCCRAKEN Gary U20 23.01.78, Border :
110HJ - 15.4, 110H - 15.6/15.67
MCDADE Jason U17 3.04.80, Ipswich :
100HY - 13.8/14.14, HJ - 2.00,
LJ - 6.57, OctY - 4780
MCDAID Damien U20 17.07.78, Cuchulainn :
JT - 62.06
MCDERMOTT Dylan 1.12.70, Epsom & E/IRE :
PV - 4.91i (4.85-90)
MCDONALD Wayne/Ali 5.10.70, Haringey :
400 - 47.19A/47.83 (45.88-91)
MCDONALD Denzil 11.10.65, Newham & E B :
SP - 15.54 (16.10-94), DT - 51.58 (55.04-95)
MCDONALD Michael John 24.08.65,
Ballymena & Antrim/Border/Queen's Univ :
TJ - 15.34 (15.78-94)
MCDONALD Richard U17 11.01.80, Perth :
400 - 49.3/49.59, 800 - 1:56.23,
400H - 53.31, 400HY - 52.81,
LJ - 6.49, TJ - 13.94 (13.95w-95)
MCDOWELL Mark U23 10.07.74, Dromore :
3kSt - 9:15.78 (9:13.65-92)
MCEVOY Michael U15 26.04.82, Thames VH :
HTB - 43.74
MCEVOY Stephen 23.05.63, Met. Police :
HT - 57.14
MCGEOCH Michael I. V40 15.08.55, L Croup :
Mar - 2:31:26 (2:17:58-83)

MCGOAY Ian 13.10.69, Ealing,Southall & Mx :
100 - 10.7, 200 - 21.7w/21.8/22.16
MCGUIRE Ciaran U23 1.07.74, Coventry G :
2kSt - 5:59.4, 3kSt - 9:10.4
MCGURK Iain 17.10.71, Kirkintillock :
400 - 47.65
MCHARDY Stephen U23 8.01.76, Birchfield :
400 - 47.43
MCILROY Brian U15, Liverpool H :
400 - 53.8/53.94
MCILROY Gary 6.04.67, Epsom & Ewell :
Mar - 2:24:11
MCILWHAM John 29.02.72, Blackpool :
400H - 54.2 (53.89-94)
MCINDOE Aaron U15 19.05.82, Ayr Seaforth :
800 - 2:00.51io/2:01.8, 1500 - 4:19.4
MCINNES Duncan U20 1.05.78, East Kilbride :
HJ - 2.03
MCINROY Alastair U17 21.06.80, Irvine :
LJ - 6.80
MCINTYRE Liam U23 22.09.76, C of E :
SP - 14.00 (14.16-95), DT - 45.50
MCINTYRE Mark 14.10.70, Shaftesbury Barn :
100 - 10.76 (10.3w-95/10.60-91)
MCKAY Jaron U17 17.09.79, :
1.5kSt - 4:29.1
MCKAY Kevin John 9.02.69, Sale :
800 - 1:48.5 (1:45.35-92),
1k - 2:21.04 (2:17.63-89),
1500 - 3:37.90 (3:35.94-92)
MCKENNA Kevin U15 3.01.82, East Kilbride :
1500 - 4:21.9, 3k - 9:35.63
MCKENZIE Alistair U15 5.10.81, Croydon :
DTB - 38.36
MCKENZIE David Colin 3.09.70, Shaft Barnet :
100 - 10.7w/10.89,
200 - 21.23A (21.3w-95/21.5-94/21.54-90),
300 - 32.89, 400 - 46.28 (45.47-94)
MCKEOWN Kenneth U15 6.03.82, Ayr S :
80HB - 11.5/11.55, HJ - 2.01, PenB - 2709
MCKEVITT Lyndon, Wirral :
10kR - 29:34
MCKINLAY Warren U15 4.10.81, Braintree :
800 - 2:05.27, 1500 - 4:19.1
MCKINSON Kevin U17 6.09.80, Cambridge H :
HJ - 1.94
MCLAUGHLIN Ian U20 4.01.77, W S&E/WLHS :
HT - 47.68 (51.50-93)
MCLEAN Colin U17 7.06.80, Cuchulainn :
800 - 1:56.37, 1500 - 3:58.6
MCLELLAN Neil U20 10.09.78, Steve & N H:
JT - 58.44
MCLENNAN Stephen U20 17.11.78, Hounslow :
PV - 4.70
MCLEOD David 26.03.63, Morpeth :
PV - 4.10 (4.60-93)
MCLEOD Sinclair U17 12.12.80, Haringey :
200 - 22.4/22.91w/23.57
MCLOUGHLIN Martin 23.12.58, Liverpool Pem:
HMar - 1:03:50sh (1:02:45-94)
MCMASTER Colin U17 15.01.80, Law & Dist :
HJ - 2.13io/2.07
MCMENEMY Neil 6.04.67, N & E B/Central :
TJ - 14.96 (15.13-94)
MCMILLAN Stewart 12.09.69, C of E/Pitr :
JT - 64.02
MCMULLAN Iain U20 15.06.78, Lisburn :
SP - 13.82, SPJ - 15.45, DTJ - 42.20

MCMULLAN Ian U23 3.05.74, Met. Police :
DT - 43.02 (47.10-91)
MCMULLEN Carl U17 9.11.79, Warrington :
400 - 49.8/50.42, 400H - 56.2/56.50,
400HY - 53.8/54.17, LJ - 6.64, TJ - 13.33
MCNABB Richard John U17 22.02.80, Roth :
200 - 22.3, 400 - 48.7/48.71 (48.34-95),
MCNAMARA Paul U20 3.10.78, Luton :
HTJ - 46.46
MCNICHOLAS Alan U23 10.12.74, Bed & Co :
HT - 58.24
MCRAE Leon U17 3.11.80, City of Bath :
100 - 11.1, 100HY - 13.9/14.28, OctY - 4433
MEAD Darren 4.10.68, Belgrave :
3kSt - 9:07.69 (8:37.68-93)
MECHAM Robert U20 14.09.77, Steyning :
3kW - 12:54.0
MELBER Stephen U20 26.02.79, Milton K :
JT - 58.26
MELLOR Dean 25.11.71, Rotherham :
PV - 5.21 (5.30-95)
MELLOR Paul U17 31.05.80, Trafford :
HJ - 1.91
MELLUISH Christopher J. V50 15.07.44,
Cambridge H : HT - 47.62 (62.10-74)
MENLOVE M. U17, Ilford :
400 - 50.5
MENTON John 2.05.70, London Irish/IRE :
SP - 14.49 (14.76-95), DT - 51.24 (52.96-93)
MERCER Marc U17 27.10.79, Hereford :
LJ - 6.74w/6.56i/6.42
MERRICK Essop U23 24.05.74, Team Solent :
LJ - 7.25
METCALFE Scott U17 8.10.79, Northampton :
DTY - 41.96
MIDDLETON Barry U23 10.03.75,
Aberdeen/Heriot Watt :
100 - 10.91w, 200 - 21.8 (22.18w/22.40-95),
400 - 48.3/48.89 (48.84i-95), 400H - 51.18
MIDDLETON Graham 17.09.60, Cannock & S :
HT - 51.68 (55.20-86)
MIELE Felice U15 24.11.81, Haringey :
SPB - 14.92, DTB - 44.08,
MILES David 16.11.65, Gateshead :
3k - 8:15.2 (8:02.03-94),
5k - 14:06.59 (13:46.66-94),
10kR - 29:00sh (29:43-94)
MILES Mark Thomas U20 24.03.77, S & S H :
1500 - 3:48.3 (3:48.1-95),
3k - 8:27.32i (8:45.48-93)
MILES Michael V40 11.04.53, :
Mar - 2:32:52 (2:24:55-92)
MILES Paul U17 14.09.80, Birchfield :
PV - 3.80
MILES Paul U13 28.04.84, Leics WC :
2kW - 10:20.1, 2KWR - 10:01, 3kWR - 15:33
MILFORD Shaun 13.07.63, Newquay & Par :
Mar - 2:33:01 (2:26:48-92)
MILLARD Chris 19.07.66, Swansea :
200 - 21.9/22.77 (22.34-95)
MILLER Jonathon U17 10.06.81, Birchfield :
TJ - 13.49
MILLER Mark 10.11.71, Enfield :
HT - 56.32 (56.84-95)
MILLER Patrick 21.02.67, Barrow & Furness :
2kSt - 5:54.39 (5:46.5-92), 3kSt - 8:57.47
MILLER Steven U17 2.11.80, Newham & E B :
HJ - 1.90

MILLS C., Winchester :
PV - 4.10
MILLS Joseph 9.07.72, Chelmsford :
800 - 1:52.4 (1:51.30-94),
1500 - 3:46.1 (3:45.7-94)
MILLWARD David U17 23.05.80, Sale :
TJ - 13.66
MINNIKIN Steve 4.01.72, Doncaster :
HT - 62.20
MINNS Gavin U17 5.12.80, Holbeach :
HTY - 51.18
MITCHELL Andrew U23 30.07.76, Kilb/Border :
400 - 48.9/49.48 (48.96-95)
MITCHELL Andy, Royal Navy :
HT - 49.24 (50.32-93)
MITCHELL Ian U23 10.03.76, Skyrac :
1500 - 3:50.7 (3:47.3-95)
MITCHELL Terrence 23.08.59, Fife :
Mar - 2:21:36 (2:17:56-92)
MITCHELL Terry, Woking :
400H - 55.7
MITCHELL Wayne U23 25.12.74, Sale :
100 - 10.8 (10.7/10.88-95)
MITCHINSON David U20 4.09.78, Swindon :
2kSt - 5:58.83, 3kSt - 9:30.68
MOHAMMED Abdusalam U20 20.03.79, Houns :
3k - 8:39.39, 5k - 15:10.54
MOHAMMED Siti 21.05.62, Thames VH/MAR :
10kR - 29:26, HMar - 1:04:27
MOLE Adam U23 31.08.75, North'ton/ Brunel U :
400 - 48.2 (47.84-93), 800 - 1:51.43
MONDS John U17 24.03.80, Wigan :
100HY - 13.90w/14.2, HJ - 1.90
MONEY Daniel U23 7.10.76, Sale :
60 - 6.86i, 100 - 10.5w/10.57 (10.48w-95),
200 - 21.0w/21.28 (21.21-95)
MONK Stuart U20 23.03.79, Loughton :
3kW - 12:43.33i/13:49.5 (12:52.9-95),
10kW - 46:34.5, 10kWR - 46:26 (46:11-95)
MONTGOMERY Brian U23 19.07.74, :
3kSt - 8:54.1
MOONEY John U17 23.10.79, Morpeth :
1500 - 4:03.55
MOORE Andrew 9.08.68, Rotherham :
HT - 47.14 (49.78-92)
MOORE Colin 25.11.60, Bingley :
5k - 14:24+e (13:33.95-90),
10k - 29:15.53 (28:13.13-90),
Mar - 2:32:16 (2:13:34-94)
MOORE Daniel U15 8.11.81, Blackheath :
3k - 9:35.9
MOORE Stephen R. V45 17.12.47, Herts & W :
100kR - 7:02:00
MOORHOUSE Julian 13.11.71, Leeds :
1500 - 3:45.4, 3k - 8:10.1 (8:04.9-95),
5k - 14:07.8
MORBY Paul James U20 15.01.79, S & S H :
800 - 1:54.5, 1500 - 3:50.5, 2kSt - 5:55.1,
3kSt - 9:31.46
MORELAND John R. 13.09.58, Rugby :
DT - 50.20 (51.76-95)
MORGAN Derek N. 4.04.69, Bristol :
100 - 10.7/11.62 (10.6-93/10.77-89),
MORGAN Kieron U15 4.09.81, Lewisham :
LJ - 5.97, PenB - 2510
MORGAN Mark 19.08.72, Cardiff :
10kR - 29:22

MORGAN Nathan U20 30.06.78, Leics Cor :
LJ - 7.97w/7.74
MORGAN Paul 5.07.65, H&W :
JT - 60.58 (70.12-87)
MORGAN-LEE Andrew 1.03.69, Woodford Gr :
3k - 8:21.40, 3kSt - 8:50.40
MORLEY Roger U20 20.09.77, Lincoln Well :
800 - 1:55.0 (1:52.59-95)
MORRELL Anthony 3.05.62, Morpeth :
800 - 1:47.94 (1:44.59-88)
MORRIS Carl U17 5.05.80, Wells :
1500 - 4:07.36
MORRIS Darrin L. 28.07.67, Belgrave/Pitr :
DT - 50.60 (58.58-91)
MORRIS Eduard U15 9.12.81, Northampton :
DTB - 39.66
MORRIS Edward U17 3.03.80, Stourport :
OctY - 4611
MORRIS James U17 2.12.79, Swansea :
LJ - 6.73w/6.68
MORRIS Michael U23 16.07.74, North S Poly :
800 - 1:52.5,
MORRIS Robert U15 20.02.82, Hertford & W :
SPB - 13.76, DTB - 37.34
MORRIS Wyn 25.02.61, Shaftesbury Barnet :
TJ - 14.16 (15.28w-85/15.19-89)
MORRISON Clive 19.09.65, Coventry Godiva :
200 - 21.98i (21.8-92/22.00w-86/22.15-93)
MORTON Leslie 1.07.58, Sheffield RWC :
20kW - 1:39:26 (1:26:31sh-93/1:27:16-89),
35kW - 2:56:03 (2:37:27-91)
MOSCROP Howard W. 16.12.57, Swindon :
110H - 15.6 (14.6w/14.8-81/15.35-93),
400H - 53.7 (51.4-84/52.66-93)
MOSES Alistair U20 5.07.78, Reigate :
1500 - 3:51.30
MOSLEY Stephen J. 10.01.66, Cardiff :
800 - 1:51.6, 1500 - 3:47.4 (3:47.1-94),
1M - 4:08.7 (4:06.9-93)
MOSS Christopher U20 17.06.79, Blackheath :
400 - 49.2, 800 - 1:50.62
MOSS Jonathan U20 24.09.78, Sale :
200 - 22.18
MOTT Shane, Worthing :
TJ - 14.09
MOULTON David U15 7.09.81, Blackheath :
400 - 51.9/51.92, 800 - 2:02.5
MOUNTFORD David U15 23.06.82, C of Stoke :
LJ - 6.30w/5.99
MOWBRAY Philip 19.03.73, Edin Un/C of E :
1500 - 3:45.7 (3:41.63-94),
5k - 14:16.34 (14:08.08-95)
MUIRHEAD James Cameron 26.01.71,
Liv H/Loughbro : SP - 16.74, DT - 52.04
MULCAHY Jason 26.05.73, Blackheath :
SP - 15.97 (15.98-93)
MULLEN Robert 8.08.64, Army :
JT - 68.70
MUNROE Gary 12.04.69, N & E B/RAF/CAN :
LJ - 7.27
MUNROE John 6.01.69, Thames Valley/RAF :
LJ - 7.21 (7.65i/7.64-95)
MURCH Kevin 11.11.58, Rugby :
JT - 57.96 (69.02-89)
MURDOCH Grant U15 30.09.82, Basingstoke :
100 - 11.56w/11.57, DTB - 38.64
MURDOCH Iain U17 10.07.80, Avonside :
800 - 1:57.6, 1500 - 3:59.9, 1.5kSt - 4:22.81

MURFITT Jody U17 3.12.79, West Norfolk :
100HY - 14.2 (14.2/15.52-95)
MURPHY Andrew U17 14.09.79, Shaft Barnet :
1500 - 4:06.1, 1.5kSt - 4:24.33
MURPHY Ciaran 2.09.71, Sale :
1500 - 3:47.2 (3:43.42-95),
1M - 4:08.74 (3:58.68-95)
MURPHY Denis U15 22.09.81, Ealing,S & Mx :
800 - 2:03.79
MURPHY Lee U20 11.03.77, Reading :
400 - 48.63, 400H - 53.01
MURRAY Alan 2.05.67, Kilmarnock :
400 - 48.82 (48.1-93/48.34-87)
MURRAY Thomas 18.05.61, Spango Valley :
10kR - 29:17
MURRAY-TAIT Ian U17 31.01.80, B & Antrim :
HJ - 2.00 (1.90-95)
MUSKER Aaron U15 23.03.82, C of Plymouth :
80HB - 12.17
MUSSETT Adrian 14.04.72, Chelmsford :
5k - 14:18.17
MUTAI John, Bromsgrove & R/KEN :
3kSt - 9:11.7
MYATT Neil U15 15.10.81, Telford :
PV - 3.00
MYERSCOUGH Carl Andrew U17 21.10.79,
Blackpool : SP - 17.30, SPY - 21.20,
DT - 50.60, DTY - 58.14
MYLES Gary 3.02.63, Cannock & Stafford :
110H - 15.3/15.75 (14.55-83)

N AISMITH David U17 15.12.79,
Derby & Co : 400 - 48.05
NASH Barry 4.09.71, Milton Keynes :
SP - 14.78 (14.99-95)
NASH Kevin U20 6.02.77, AF&D :
3kSt - 8:43.21
NASH Robin 9.02.59, Westbury :
Mar - 2:27:08 (2:14:52-94)
NASH Sam 22.10.71, Queens Park :
LJ - 6.95, TJ - 13.92 (14.20-93)
NAYLOR Donald 5.09.71, Swansea/Camb Un :
3kSt - 9:06.12
NEBLETT Gavin U17 27.12.79, Blackheath :
HJ - 2.00
NEELY Ian U23 29.12.74, East Kilbride :
400H - 52.87
NEILSON Eric 7.08.68, Royal Navy :
Dec - 5040
NEPORT Darren U17 4.09.79, Enfield :
PV - 4.40
NERURKAR Richard David 6.01.64, Bingley :
10kR - 28:50 (28:25-94),
10MR - 47:04 (46:02-93),
HMar - 1:01:06, Mar - 2:13:39 (2:10:03-93)
NESBETH Michael U20 1.03.79, Croydon :
TJ - 14.80w/14.79
NEWENHAM Timothy O. 1.04.60, Norwich/
Loughborough : JT - 59.04 (70.30-89)
NEWMAN Lee Jon 1.05.73, Belgrave :
SP - 18.85, DT - 54.42 (58.34-94)
NEWMARCH Alastair U20 28.11.78, Linc W :
400H - 56.2un
NEWPORT Spencer John 5.10.66, Blackheath :
3k - 8:00.3, 5k - 13:49.74,
2kSt - 5:42.20 (5:37.74-90),
3kSt - 8:46.51 (8:40.87-92)

NEWTON Keith 12.12.68, Woodford Green :
400H - 55.15 (54.33-95)
NEWTON Marc D. U17 15.03.80, Tamworth :
400 - 50.80, LJ - 6.59i/6.15 (6.56-95),
OctY - 4951 (5144-95)
NEWTON Robert U17 10.05.81, BH Mansfield :
100HY - 13.44w/13.6/13.71, 400HY - 58.0
NICHOLL David 16.09.69, Border :
HT - 55.46
NICHOLLS David U15 5.09.81, Cannock & St :
JTB - 44.08
NICHOLLS Eddie U15, Liverpool H :
SPB - 13.59, HTB - 42.22
NICHOLLS John S. 1.09.65, Sale :
SP - 15.10 (15.48-95), DT - 43.94 (44.56-88)
NICHOLSON Martin 9.12.70, Birchfield :
110H - 14.44 (13.8/14.14-94)
NICOLSON Christian 19.09.73, T Sol/Edin U :
1M - 4:08.4, 3k - 8:23.18i (8:05.0-95),
5k - 14:25.05
NIELAND Nicholas 31.01.72, Shaft B/Bris U :
JT - 83.06
NIXON Robert U17 20.09.79, Colchester & T :
400 - 50.60, 800 - 1:57.9
NOBLE Ian U20 2.04.77, Leeds :
PV - 4.70
NOLAN David 25.07.69, Belgrave/Army :
100 - 10.8, 200 - 21.5 (21.16-95),
300 - 32.90, 400 - 46.20
NOLAN David U23 16.05.75, Swan/Sheff U :
HJ - 2.05 (2.06-94)
NORMAN Andrew U15 27.01.82, Newton Abb :
200 - 23.42w
NORMAN Anthony 5.07.63, Woking :
JT - 59.30 (68.72-87)
NORRIS Stephen 21.06.68, Salisbury :
3kSt - 9:19.05
NORTH Christian I.R. U23 2.02.74, Bristol :
PV - 4.50 (4.90-92)
NORTH Iestin U15 10.10.81, :
TJ - 12.48w/12.35
NSUDOH Immanuel 8.04.72, Croydon :
LJ - 7.14
NUNES Marlon U15 7.12.81, Birchfield :
400 - 53.6/53.96
NUTTALL John Barry 11.01.67, Preston :
1500 - 3:42.55 (3:40.6-90),
2k - 5:05.3+/5:06.33,
3k - 7:36.40, 5k - 13:17.48 (13:16.70-95)

O 'BRIEN Anthony 14.11.70, Liverpool H :
10k - 29:51.0, HMar - 1:04:46
O'CONNELL Christopher A. 17.01.59, Leeds :
HT - 46.14 (52.98-87)
O'DELL Timothy 29.05.70, Woodford Green :
100 - 10.7/10.75 (10.7-95),
200 - 21.5w/21.58 (21.31-95),
300 - 33.50, 400 - 46.40 (46.34-95)
O'DONNELL Daniel U15 9.01.82, Sale :
HJ - 1.77, PenB - 2658
O'DONOVAN David 26.10.72, Shaftesbury B :
3k - 8:24.5 (8:24.5-90)
O'DOWD Matthew U23 13.04.76, Swindon :
1500 - 3:47.6, 3k - 8:15.5, 5k - 14:16.24,
3kSt - 8:44.26
O'GARA Stephen 3.12.69, Wallsend :
1500 - 3:48.1, 1M - 4:06.9, 3k - 8:16.5,
3kSt - 9:17.5

O'LEARY David U17 3.08.80, Liverpool H :
100HY - 13.07
O'NEILL David U23 19.01.76, Peterborough :
PV - 4.70
O'RAWE Andy 8.09.63, Southend :
3kW - 13:08.04 (12:52.8-94),
10kW - 45:47.8, 20kW - 1:34:05
O'RAWE Jamie 3.02.73, Southend :
3kW - 12:42.7 (12:21.8-95),
10kW - 43:25.2, 20kW - 1:36:44 (1:34:52-95)
O'REILLY Michael 23.04.58, Highgate :
Mar - 2:16:19 (2:10:39-93)
OAKES Jason U20 29.09.77, Gateshead :
JT - 62.88
OCTAVE Philip U20 12.06.78, Hillingdon :
400 - 48.6/51.39
OGBETA Mathias 19.06.68, Sale :
LJ - 7.11 (7.26-95), TJ - 14.06 (15.66-95)
OGUNYEMI Akeem U23 4.06.74, Haringey :
100 - 10.7/10.99
OHRLAND Stuart U23 6.09.75, Chelm/Loughbro :
HJ - 2.14 (2.17-94), Dec - 4976
OJEX Bola 14.06.71, Birchfield :
60 - 6.9i, 100 - 10.8
OJOK Geoffrey U20 19.05.79, Belgrave :
LJ - 7.05
OKOTIE Mclean 31.07.69, Thames Valley :
60 - 6.90i, 100 - 10.5/10.60 (10.5/10.60-94),
200 - 21.9w
OLD Alan U17 1.12.79, Gateshead :
1500 - 4:03.38, 3k - 8:55.13
OLD Christopher U20 3.12.77, Houghton-l-Sp :
1500 - 3:52.0, 3k - 8:26.8
OLDALE Richard 26.01.66, Sheffield RWC :
3kW - 12:21.22, 10kW - 44:15.75,
20kW - 1:33:17 (1:34:21.6t-95)
OLDFIELD Alex U20 14.04.77, Kettering :
5k - 14:54.77
OLIVER Geoff, :
24HrT - 205.691km (222.720-94)
OLIVER Michael J. V40 23.03.53, Brighton :
SP - 13.93 (15.67-91)
OLUWA Bode U23 15.11.76, Herne Hill/NIG:
100 - 10.77w/10.8/10.86 (10.7-95)
OLWENY Philips U17 14.02.81,
Ealing,Southall & Mx : JTY - 57.98
OMENAI Osagai U17 8.02.81, Winchester :
100HY - 13.4/13.49w/13.91
OMONUA Samson U23 16.06.76, Haringey :
60 - 6.90i, 100 - 10.5/10.59,
ONI Samson U17 25.06.81, Belgrave :
HJ - 2.00
ONUORAH Onochie C. 16.10.73, Shaft Barn :
60 - 6.85i, 100 - 10.5/10.51,
LJ - 7.67 (7.81w-95)
OPARKA Jonathon U17 27.01.80, Dundee HH :
LJ - 6.53, TJ - 14.08
OPARKA Richard U15 28.07.82, Tayside :
TJ - 12.09
OPOKU S. U13, Belgrave :
HJ - 1.58
ORAM Russell U17 14.08.80, Basingstoke :
JTY - 55.70, OctY - 4621
ORR Callum J. 18.11.62, City of Edinburgh :
Dec - 6205w/6168 (6695-88)
ORR Christopher U15 20.06.83, Carlisle :
DTB - 39.88

OSBOURN Michael, Gosforth :
800 - 1:52.7
OSTAPOWYCZ Pawlo H. V40 1.07.52, Traff :
JT - 59.18 (60.38-93)
OTOO K. U15, :
TJ - 12.00
OTTER Darren U23 6.03.74, Donc/Sheff Univ :
HJ - 2.05 (2.07-93)
OVENS Mark, Swindon :
HJ - 1.96
OWEN Gerallt 26.01.70, Swansea :
5k - 14:10.70
OWEN John N. 28.10.64, Swansea :
HT - 47.14 (52.96-95)
OWEN Neil 18.10.73, Belgrave :
60H - 7.72i (7.86i-94), 400H - 55.12,
110H - 13.5w/13.62 (13.60-95)
OWEN Sion U20 6.03.79, Crewe & Nantwich :
800 - 1:54.41
OWENS Roger U15 26.10.81, Preseli :
PenB - 2727
OXLEY John U15 7.03.82, Newport :
400 - 53.61
OYEDIRAN Ademola 27.11.59, Herne H/NIG :
LJ - 6.93 (7.26w-95/7.13-86),
TJ - 15.65w/15.52 (15.91i/15.78-84)

P ACKER Julian U17 2.09.79, Exeter :
400 - 50.73
PADDICK John V50 31.08.43, :
50kW - 4:53:22 (4:24:13-80)
PADMORE Stephen U15 29.11.81, :
80HB - 11.68
PAGE Chris U17 13.11.80, City of Bath :
400 - 49.84
PAGKATIPUNAN Lolimar U15 17.11.82, Har :
80HB - 12.1
PAICE Matthew U15 19.06.83, Windsor S & E :
HJ - 1.82
¶PAINTER John J. T. 12.06.58, Norwich :
SP - 14.96 (16.32i/16.09-89),
DT - 42.96 (50.36-88)
PAINTER Trevor 10.08.71, Wigan :
400 - 48.70 (47.79A-95/48.04-94)
PAISLEY Derek 1.12.73, Pitreavie/Edin Univ :
400H - 55.43 (52.83-94)
PALMER Adam U13 21.04.84, Peterborough :
PV - 2.20
PALMER Adrian M. 10.08.69, Cardiff :
HT - 57.48 (62.56-94)
PALMER Andrew U20 13.04.77, Soton City :
HJ - 2.00 (2.00-95)
PALMER Colin 27.07.67, Medway/Army :
2kSt - 5:59.0, 3kSt - 9:09.1
PALMER James U20 21.04.78, Norwich :
PV - 4.30
PALMER Nathan U15, Cardiff :
80HB - 11.8, LJ - 6.03io/5.74
PAMAH Anthony 11.11.63, Cambridge H :
400H - 54.4/54.55 (54.2-91/54.30-93)
PAMAH David 27.11.64, Belgrave :
800 - 1:51.2 (1:50.44-93)
PARK Dean U20 23.09.77, Newham & E B :
400H - 54.3/55.33 (55.16-95)
PARK Iain U23 16.07.74, GEC/Falkirk/NESH :
DT - 42.80, HT - 62.68
PARKER Andrew U23 27.05.74, Lincoln Well :
HJ - 2.00 (2.00-92)

PARKER Andrew U13 10.12.83, Wolves & B :
2KWR - 10:05
PARKER David U17 28.02.80, Shaftesbury B :
SPY - 14.83, DTY - 41.04, JT - 68.26,
JTY - 73.56, OctY - 4448
PARKER Ian U23 9.07.75, Lincoln Well :
Dec - 5130
PARKER James U17 28.10.79, Somerset Sch :
800 - 1:57.60
PARKER Jonathon U23 1.05.76, Birchfield :
400H - 55.1 (53.80-95)
PARKER Jonathon S. U15 27.02.82, Oadby & W :
3k - 9:32.68
PARKER Michael U13 29.10.83, City of Hull :
PV - 2.20
PARKES Christopher A. 17.04.64, Rotherham :
10kR - 29:36, Mar - 2:20:02 (2:17:54-88)
PARKES Lee U23 23.12.76, Rotherham :
Dec - 5599
PARKIN Gareth U15 5.12.81, Burnley :
PenB - 2589
PARKIN John U20 23.02.79, Sale :
DTJ - 42.80, HTJ - 49.42
PARKINSON Ian Philip U20 12.02.79, Wyc :
PV - 4.25
PARKINSON Matthew U15 21.12.81, Holb :
SPB - 13.10
PARPER Michael U20 20.05.78, Belgrave :
400 - 48.54
PARRY Jonathan U17 13.04.80, Swansea :
PV - 3.80
PARRY Philip John 4.10.65, Old Gaytonians :
JT - 66.68 (70.00-94)
PARSONS Gary, Cambridge & Colr'dge :
DT - 41.52 (42.08-93)
PARSONS Geoffrey Peter 14.08.64, Tamw :
HJ - 2.15 (2.31-94)
PARTINGTON Stephen W. 17.09.65, Manx H :
3kW - 11:52.6/11:56.5 (11:33.4-95),
10kW - 42:29.73 (41:14.61-95),
20kW - 1:25:40 (1:24:09sh-94/1:24:18-90),
50kW - 4:32:25 (4:48:51+-93)
PASSEY Adrian 2.09.64, Bromsgrove & R :
2M - 8:49.79, 5k - 13:53.44 (13:22.73-95)
PATEL Chirag U15 9.08.82, Thurrock :
JTB - 45.30
PATIENCE Matthew U15 22.12.81, Winch :
JTB - 53.32
PATRICK Adrian Leroy John 15.06.73, WS & E :
60 - 6.70i, 100 - 10.3/10.38,
200 - 20.9/20.93w/21.02 (20.62w-95),
300 - 32.89, 400 - 46.06 (45.63-95)
PAUL Lenox 25.05.58, Belgrave/Army :
100 - 10.8 (10.25w-91/10.32-93)
PAVIS Jon 4.10.66, Sale :
3kSt - 9:19.37 (9:04.78-90)
PAYN Tom U17 18.10.79, Colchester & T :
800 - 1:56.7, OctY - 4479
PAYNE Stephen U20 30.01.78, Andover :
400 - 49.3/49.50
PAYNE-DWYER Russell H. 11.09.60, Birch :
HT - 55.00 (56.62-86)
PEACOCK James U20 29.09.77, Thurrock :
TJ - 15.74w/15.24
PEACOCK Shane 5.03.63, Birchfield :
HT - 66.88 (71.60-90)
PEACOCK Tyron U23 16.12.76, Liv H/RSA :
HJ - 2.16i/2.15

PEARCE Duncan James 21.10.70, Sale :
PV - 4.90
PEARCE Phillip U20 3.04.79, :
LJ - 6.85
PEARCY Andrew U17 5.04.80, Rowntrees :
100HY - 13.91w/14.15
PEARSON Andrew 14.09.71, Longwood :
2M - 8:58.0, 10k - 28:32.0,
10kR - 29:17 (28:21-95)
PEARSON John T. 30.04.66, Charn/WLHS :
HT - 67.34
PEARSON Stephen G. 13.09.59, Sale/NWHS :
HT - 63.54 (65.24-94)
PEEL R. U15, Morpeth :
PV - 2.90
PELESZOK Matthew Jon U15 17.10.81, Shrews :
400 - 52.5, 800 - 2:01.2 (2:04.96-95),
SPB - 12.86, PenB - 2885
PENGILLY Adam U20 14.10.77, Charnwood :
PV - 4.20i/4.10, DecJ - 5865
PENK Andrew U20 19.09.78, Cardiff :
HJ - 2.00 (2.05-95), PV - 4.60
PENN Andrew S. 31.03.67, Coventry RWC :
3kW - 12:13.26 (11:39.54-91),
20kW - 1:28:39 (1:23:34-92)
PENNEY Christopher J. 10.05.57, Stourport :
Mar - 2:19:36 (2:17:45-92)
PENNEY Ross U13 28.06.85, C of Plymouth :
3k - 10:23.5
PERIGO Phillip U20 25.09.78, Stainforth :
100 - 10.55w/10.60,
200 - 21.23w/21.51 (21.5-95)
PERMAN Mark R. 6.01.68, Havering :
110H - 14.88w/14.9/15.43 (15.24-92),
PV - 4.30 (4.30-93), Dec - 6405 (6606-93)
PERRY Kevin V45 7.12.48, Southend :
100MW - 20:37:46
PERRY Matthew Robin U20 15.02.78, Cardiff :
HJ - 2.06
PERRYMAN Dylan U15 17.11.81, Reading :
SPB - 13.55, JTB - 44.22
PERRYMAN Guy St.D.M. 2.11.58, Reading :
SP - 14.02 (16.58-89)
PESCOD David 15.04.73, Sunderland :
JT - 59.76
PETERS Mark, Bingley :
10kR - 29:23 (29:12-95), HMar - 1:04:14
PETERS Mike 1.10.60, Havant :
Mar - 2:32:47, 2kSt - 5:59.8
PETLEY Neal Stewart 21.05.68, Warrington :
110H - 14.88, 400H - 54.9
PETTS Chris U17 22.01.80, Ashford :
HJ - 1.95
PHILIP Colin U20 8.06.79, Edinburgh SH :
400H - 55.92
PHILIPS Alex U15 29.09.81, Bedford & Co :
HTB - 40.16
PHILLIPS James U17 6.08.80, Telford :
PV - 3.60
PHILLIPS Steven 17.03.72, Birchfield :
LJ - 7.79w/7.75 (7.91-91)
PHILLIPS Tim U20 13.01.79, Verlea :
JT - 53.02
PHILLS Mark 26.07.64, Old Gaytonians :
60 - 6.90i, 200 - 21.59 (21.29-93),
100 - 10.69 (10.5w-95/10.55-91)

PICKERING Shaun Desforges 14.11.61, Har :
SP - 19.62, DT - 52.20 (54.38-89),
HT - 59.60 (68.64-84)
PILBURY David U15 13.05.82, Medway :
JTB - 47.60un
PINNER Mark 12.05.64, Sale :
JT - 61.06 (65.74-93)
PIRT Joshua U20 21.08.78, Somerset Sch :
DTJ - 42.14
PLANK Daniel U15 27.04.82, Birchfield :
HJ - 1.83,
PLANT Raymond 13.05.68, Tipton :
3k - 8:23.4, 2kSt - 5:45.4, 3kSt - 8:52.64
PLASKETT Simon U20 9.04.79, Wycombe :
400 - 49.50
PLATT Christopher U20 25.09.78, Bolton :
TJ - 14.01
PLEASANTS Peter 29.07.62, Barnsley :
Mar - 2:27:40 (2:24:07-95)
PLUMMER Daniel U17 4.01.81, Blackheath :
100 - 10.67w/10.9/11.02, 200 - 22.61
PLUNKETT Gerard U17 30.06.80, Hallam :
OctY - 4421
POLLARD Mark U15 25.02.82, Inverclyde :
1500 - 4:18.0
POLLMEIER Klemens 8.06.66, Bath Un/Bris :
PV - 4.40 (4.55unc-95)
PONTING Mark U20 28.04.77, Cardiff :
400 - 48.84 (47.94-94)
POOLE P., RAF :
JT - 55.64
POOLE Scott U20 31.03.78, Lagan Valley :
800 - 1:54.36
POOLE Stuart U15 29.09.81, Cannock & Staff :
JTB - 44.34
POORE Stuart 30.12.72, Team Solent :
1500 - 3:43.0, 1M - 4:03.12,
3k - 8:12.81 (8:07.6un-93)
PORTER James U17, Team Solent :
TJ - 13.33
PORTER Scott U17 12.12.79, :
100HY - 14.2/14.61, OctY - 4407
POTTER Adam U17 12.04.80, City of Bath :
LJ - 6.64w/6.05
POULIN Marc, Oxford Univ/CAN :
3kSt - 9:12.6
POVEY Solomon U17 8.02.80, Bournemouth :
100 - 10.98w/11.04,
POWELL Dalton 20.08.63, Belgrave :
100 - 10.7/10.87 (10.7-91),
200 - 21.88 (21.1db/21.24w/21.26-92)
POWELL David U20 11.09.78, Richmond & Z :
400H - 55.6/56.09, Dec - 5906,
DecJ - 5890
POWELL Wayne 27.07.71, Stroud :
JT - 55.00 (59.36-93)
POWER Garry 1.09.62, Herne Hill/IRE :
DT - 48.44 (48.98-86)
PRESTON Darren U23 19.12.74, Enf/Brunel U :
3kSt - 8:51.52
PRICE Glyn A. 12.09.65, Swansea :
PV - 4.60 (4.80-90)
PRICE Oliver U15 10.12.81, Shaftesbury B :
80HB - 12.1/12.33
PRICE Sean Myrion 4.01.63, Swansea :
800 - 1:52.0 (1:49.67-86)
PRICE Terence P. 26.07.57, N & EB/R Navy :
400H - 55.3 (52.39-93)

PRIDE Simon, Keith :
100kR - 8:01:38
PRIDMORE Thomas U13 21.03.85, Leics WC :
2kW - 11:12.0
PRIOR Carl U15 20.01.82, Deeside :
3k - 9:39.9
PRITCHARD Nicholas 5.12.72, Cardiff :
PV - 4.20 (4.60-95)
PROCTOR Mark A. 15.01.63, N & EB/RAF :
SP - 19.67, DT - 53.38 (54.28-93)
PROUDLOVE Michael 26.01.70, City of Stoke :
1500 - 3:48.1 (3:45.0-91)
PROVAN James U17 23.09.80, Verlea :
DTY - 41.80
PUCKRIN Alan 2.04.64, Inverclyde :
10k - 30:49.41 (29:32.29-94)
PUNCH James U17 19.12.79, Corby :
HTY - 53.74 (55.92-95)
PURDY Martin U15 29.10.81, Sevenoaks :
JTB - 47.84
PURSER Mark 18.04.72, Croydon :
400H - 54.5/54.65 (52.26-93)
PURVES Grant 6.04.73, City of Edinburgh :
800 - 1:50.5 (1:49.75-95)
PUSEY M. U20, :
100 - 10.99w
PYRAH Jeff 6.07.72, Hallamshire :
3kSt - 9:17.58

QUARRY James S. 15.11.72,
Old Gaytonians/Brunel Univ/Falkirk :
60H - 8.15i (8.1i/8.15i-94),
110H - 14.5/15.34 (14.10-94),
LJ - 7.05i/6.99 (7.40w-95/7.19-91),
TJ - 14.34, SP - 13.39 (13.93-95),
DT - 42.10 (43.18)
QUELCH Russell U20 9.09.78, AF&D :
400H - 54.58
QUIGLEY Mark U23 6.11.74, Copeland :
SP - 13.48 (13.77-93), DT - 43.34 (45.92-93)
QUINN Anthony U17 14.01.81, Annadale Str :
SPY - 14.70, SPB - 16.10o (14.92-95),
DTY - 41.64, DTB - 44.80o (44.96-95)
QUINN Kevin U13 23.12.83, Chelmsford :
DTC - 32.26
QUINN Robert 10.12.65, Kilbarchan :
5k - 14:14.80 (14:00.91-95),
10k - 29:48.47 (29:14.23-95), 10kR - 29:31

RALPH Paul 16.12.67, GEC :
LJ - 7.04 (7.20w/7.19-95),
TJ - 15.67w/15.65 (15.72w/15.67-95),
Dec - 5208
RALSON David U20 22.02.77, Oxford City :
PV - 4.10, Dec - 6199
RAMSAY Iain U13 10.10.83, Inverness :
HJ - 1.60
RANDALL Matthew 28.04.70, Hastings :
TJ - 14.59i (15.37-95)
RANDLES Daniel U15 16.04.82, Morpeth :
PV - 3.00
RANGER Tom U20 20.11.77, Peterborough :
800 - 1:53.47
RANKIN Stuart 26.06.70, Army/Falkirk :
3k - 8:21.43
RATCLIFFE David 17.11.60, Coventry RWC :
3kW - 13:49.0 (13:30.0-86)

RATCLIFFE Trevor 9.03.64, Dacorum & Tring :
   JT - 66.78
RAW David U17 1.02.81, Gateshead :
   PV - 3.60
RAWLINGS Adrian U17 21.11.80, Newq & Par :
   SPY - 15.03,
RAWLINSON Christopher 19.05.72, Belgrave :
   400 - 48.85, 110H - 14.52, 400H - 50.36
RAWLINSON Paul U15 17.10.81, Wirral :
   400 - 51.84
RAYNER Andrew U15 16.01.82, Blackheath :
   1500 - 4:21.9
READ Douglas 15.04.67, Milton Keynes :
   HT - 48.40 (55.54-88)
READ Graeme U17 24.10.79, Morpeth :
   200 - 22.44w/22.9
READ Tony U15 14.10.81, East Grinstead :
   1500 - 4:21.0
READLE David U17 10.02.80, Liverpool Pem :
   SPY - 16.89
REDMOND John 15.10.57, City of Hull :
   Mar - 2:33:10 (2:27:50-94)
REED Paul 2.06.62, Morpeth :
   SP 16.65i/16.10 (17.04-88), DT - 56.46
REES A. U13, Brecon :
   75HC - 12.57, HJ - 1.55
REES Martin V40 28.02.53, Swansea :
   5k - 14:20.7
REES-JONES Steve U23 24.12.74, Brighton :
   800 - 1:50.71
REESE Ben U23 29.03.76, Wirral/East Mich U:
   1500 - 3:47.4a, 1M - 4:04.83i,
   3kSt - 9:12.82 (9:09.24-94)
REGIS John Paul Lyndon 13.10.66, Belgrave :
   60 - 6.78i (6.71i-91),
   100 - 10.39A (10.07w-90/10.15-93),
   200 - 20.33A (19.87A-94/19.94-93),
   300 - 32.51 (31.67-92)
REID Iain U20 20.07.77, Cambuslang :
   3k - 8:37.82
REID Justin 26.09.69, Gateshead :
   3kSt - 9:03.10 (8:55.61-92)
REID-HUGHES Geoffrey U15 14.10.81, Tun W :
   SPB - 14.51, DTB - 41.32
REILLY Brendan Anthony John 23.12.72, Bel :
   HJ - 2.23i (2.32i-94/2.31-92)
REISS Michael 17.06.63, Highgate :
   HT - 49.54 (50.60-94)
RENAUD Pascal 20.04.70, Crawley/FRA :
   60H - 8.3i (8.3i/8.38i-94),
   110H - 15.1 (14.58-92)
RENFREE Andrew U23 18.05.75, Newq & Par :
   800 - 1:51.7, 1500 - 3:46.3, 1M - 4:05.9
RENSHAW William V45 7.08.49, Rotherham :
   DT - 44.08 (45.16-80)
REY Michael 19.07.68, Windsor S & E :
   100 - 10.6/10.86w/10.91 (10.58-89),
   200 - 21.40 (21.2w-91/21.23-90)
RICHARDS Gregory Roy V40 25.04.56, N Lond :
   110H - 15.5 (14.80w-85/14.94-87),
   SP - 14.28 (15.24-94), DT - 45.44 (50.66-91),
   Dec - 6560 (7740-87)
RICHARDS Henry U17 15.05.81, Charnwood :
   100 - 11.1/11.22w/11.33, 200 - 22.6/23.23
RICHARDS Matthew U20 11.10.77, Newport :
   400 - 49.45
RICHARDS Thomas U20 13.11.78, Oxford C :
   PV - 4.45

RICHARDSON Adam U20 13.04.78, T Solent :
   DTJ - 41.46
RICHARDSON James U17 14.12.79, Bed & Co :
   800 - 1:56.5
RICHARDSON Mark Austin 26.07.72, WS & E :
   200 - 20.6w/20.85, 300 - 32.14, 400 - 44.52
RICHMOND Stuart Anthony 11.04.69, GEC :
   TJ - 15.26, Dec - 4943
RIDER Scott U20 22.09.77, Enfield :
   SPJ - 14.04, DT - 45.90, DTJ - 50.84
RIDGEON Jonathan Peter 14.02.67, Belgrave :
   200 - 21.9 (20.9-92/21.08-87),
   400 - 47.7 (46.75-92), 400H - 48.79 (48.73-92)
RIGBY Tony U17 22.02.80, Bedford & County :
   JTY - 52.62
RILEY Michael U15 29.09.81, Lancashire Sch :
   SPB - 13.04
RISA Svein U23 7.03.74, Bristol/Bristol Univ. :
   5k - 14:33.95, 3kSt - 9:16.0
RITCHIE Darren U23 14.02.75, Sale/Sc Bord :
   100 - 10.8w, LJ - 7.86
RITCHIE Don V50 6.07.44, Moray RR :
   100kR - 7:38:15 (6:51:14-89)
RITCHIE Stephen 12.08.71, Pitreavie :
   HJ - 2.05 (2.18-89), TJ - 14.89w
RIXON Dale 8.07.66, Bridgend :
   10k - 29:54.12, HMar - 1:04:50 (1:04:19-94),
   Mar - 2:13:41
ROACH Mark 11.04.65, Old Gaytonians :
   HJ - 1.98 (2.10-85)
ROACHE Desmond U23 5.01.76, Clydesdale :
   800 - 1:50.4 (1:49.18-95),
   1500 - 3:45.2 (3:44.98-95),
   1M - 4:05.87, 3k - 8:17.3i (8:29.1-95)
ROBB Bruce U20 27.07.77, Pitreavie :
   SP - 14.64 (15.03-95),
   SPJ - 15.56 (16.18-95),
   DT - 47.36, DTJ - 46.94 (48.86-95)
ROBB Curtis 7.06.72, Liv H/Sheffield Univ :
   800 - 1:45.73 (1:44.92-93),
   1500 - 3:38.95 (3:38.56-93)
ROBBINS Michael U23 14.03.76, Rotherham :
   110H - 14.9 (14.98-94),
   HJ - 2.19i/2.06 (2.17-95)
ROBERSON Mark W. U23 21.03.75, Milton K :
   HT - 47.12 (47.88-94)
ROBERSON Mark 13.03.67, Haringey :
   JT - 78.54 (80.92-88)
ROBERTS Andrew U20 19.09.77, Wigan :
   LJ - 7.04w/6.76 (7.03-95)
ROBERTS Andrew U17 8.03.80, Gateshead :
   100 - 11.1
ROBERTS Andrew U15, Old Gaytonians :
   LJ - 5.93
ROBERTS Ben U17 15.01.80, Colwyn Bay :
   100HY - 14.1/14.11
ROBERTS Colin U17 20.01.81, Norwich :
   100HY - 14.0/14.07
ROBERTS Ian 15.06.68, Cardiff :
   LJ - 6.92w (7.19w-92/7.10-95)
ROBERTS Johnathan U20 28.09.77, Leeds :
   HJ - 1.98
ROBERTS Mark 1.09.69, Kingston & Poly :
   Dec - 5314
ROBERTS Mark S. 12.02.59, Potteries Mar :
   Mar - 2:26:26 (2:19:19-92)
ROBERTS Peter 19.09.71, Swansea :
   DT - 42.08 (44.52-90)

ROBERTSON David James 4.08.73, Tonb :
800 - 1:52.08, 1500 - 3:43.9 (3:40.90-92),
5k - 14:05.2
ROBERTSON Iain U23 23.06.75, Birchfield :
3kSt - 9:20.31
ROBERTSON-ADAMS Charles U20 5.12.77,
Telford : 110HJ - 14.81w/15.0 (15.61-95),
400H - 52.26
ROBINCOCKER Olubunmi U23 27.11.75,
Trafford/Fife/SLE : HJ - 2.00 (2.00-93),
LJ - 7.07 (7.14-95), TJ - 14.66 (14.94-95)
ROBINSON Brian U17 3.09.80, Birchfield :
LJ - 7.06, TJ - 14.72
ROBINSON David U20 12.01.78, Gate/NESH :
HT - 50.90, HTJ - 55.40
ROBINSON Dean 25.06.70, Tipton :
PV - 4.10 (4.30-90)
ROBINSON Eifion U17 12.05.80, Carmarthen :
DTY - 40.90
ROBINSON Geoff 20.06.59, Chester L Street :
Mar - 2:31:59
ROBINSON Ian 21.04.69, Preston/Iowa St Un :
3k - 8:08.4 (8:01.12i-92/8:04.3-94),
10k - 28:04.2
ROBINSON Keith V40 9.02.52, Havering :
HT - 48.20 (53.38-81)
ROBISON Christopher 16.03.61, Shettleston :
2M - 8:59.0 (8:41.20-86),
5k - 14:15.8 (13:54.66-84),
10kR - 29:10, 10MR - 48:51 (48:27-91)
ROBSON Philip U20 7.02.77, Reading :
200 - 21.64w/21.94
ROBSON Shaun U17 21.06.80, Newport :
100HY - 13.8/14.14, 400H - 57.3/57.55
ROCHFORD Ben U15 28.10.81, Herc Wimb :
HJ - 1.76
RODEN James U15 24.11.81, Chorley :
JTB - 49.86
RODEN Paul Anthony 18.04.65, Sale :
3k - 8:12.8 (8:01.3-86),
5k - 14:11.62 (13:52.4-86),
10k - 29:13.66 (29:03.07-92),
10kR - 29:30 (29:14-92),
HMar - 1:04:50 (1:03:19-93)
RODGERS John, Annadale Striders :
800 - 1:52.6
ROE Thomas U15 25.06.82, Norwich :
LJ - 6.17, PenB - 2702
ROGERS Craig U23 14.02.76, Birchfield :
SP - 14.38
ROGERS Paul A. 24.03.65, Tipton :
Mar - 2:32:58 (2:29:48-94)
ROGERS Stephen A. 1.09.71, Liverpool Pem :
HJ - 1.98, PV - 4.40i/4.10 (4.60-95),
JT - 60.78, Dec - 7150 (7295-95)
ROHLEDER Richard U15 28.02.82, Haringey :
800 - 2:03.59
ROHLEDER William U15 28.02.82, Haringey :
800 - 2:05.26,
ROLLINS Andrew U20 20.03.78, Wigan :
SPJ - 13.98, DT - 41.32, DTJ - 46.40
ROPER Simon U17 20.09.79, Derby & Co :
TJ - 13.86
ROSATO Sebastian 19.11.72, GEC/Camb Un :
110H - 15.1/15.19
(14.79w-95/14.8db-93/14.8-94/14.97-95)
ROSCOE Martin Peter 19.09.64, Leeds :
3kSt - 9:17.5 (8:53.2-89)

ROSE Andrew U15 17.08.82, Braintree :
100 - 11.11w/11.33, 200 - 23.6
ROSE David U20 26.06.78, Border :
3k - 8:37.8, 5k - 15:06.78
ROSE Stefan U23 7.04.75, Team Solent :
LJ - 7.13w/6.78 (7.18-94)
ROSE Vincent 21.08.71, Thames Valley :
400 - 48.17 (47.29-94)
ROSEN Alexander 30.09.71, Haringey :
800 - 1:51.5 (1:50.89-92), 1500 - 3:49.8
ROSENBERG Luke U17 29.06.80, Old Gayt :
DTJ - 45.74, DTY - 51.30,
HTJ - 52.38, HTY - 48.38
ROSS David 2.11.65, Scottish Borders :
10kR - 29:36
ROSSITER Martin R. 4.09.69, Peterborough/
Reading University : TJ - 14.55 (14.76-95)
ROSSWESS Michael 11.06.65, Birchfield :
60 - 6.67i (6.54i-94),
100 - 10.32w/10.38 (10.07w-94/10.15-91),
200 - 21.25 (20.48w-90/20.51-88)
ROWBOTHAM Stephen 6.03.68, Rotherham :
LJ - 6.94 (7.12-94)
ROWE Ian U20 28.09.78, Team Solent :
TJ - 14.13w/14.04
ROWE Martin U17 23.07.80, Wenlock O :
DTY - 43.52, OctY - 4207
ROWEN Daniel U17 30.12.79, Solihull & S H :
1500 - 4:06.2
ROWLANDS Mark Stuart U20 18.04.78, Swan :
400 - 48.75, 400H - 52.38
ROWSWELL Alex U15 18.03.82, Yeovil Oly :
JTB - 47.26
ROYDEN Barry Mark 15.12.66, Medway :
HMar - 1:04:09 (1:02:25-94)
ROYDEN John, Bracknell :
LJ - 6.99
RUBEN Alan V40, :
Mar - 2:30:38
RUBENIS Richard 10.11.73, Telford :
60 - 6.90i (6.90i-95),
100 - 10.8 (10.5w/10.7/10.77-94),
200 - 22.0 (21.54w-95/21.6-94),
400 - 48.6 (47.4/47.76-94)
RUDKIN Alan U20 5.11.78, Peterborough :
DT - 42.48, DTJ - 48.26
RULE Charles U17 22.05.80, City of Edinb :
PV - 3.80
RUMBOLD James U15 4.11.81, Bournemouth :
SPB - 13.95, DTB - 43.42,
RUMBOLT Courtney Orville 26.07.69, S B :
60 - 6.8i/6.83i (6.77i-89),
100 - 10.6w (10.37w-88/10.48-90)
RUSH Martin Gavin 25.12.64, Bideford :
3k - 8:22.4
RUSHWORTH Brian 14.12.62, Sunderland :
10kR - 29:28 (29:04-88),
HMar - 1:03:56 (1:03:35-90), Mar - 2:22:40
RUSSELL Alaister 17.06.68, Bord/Law & Dist :
3k - 8:21.9 (8:19.79-93), 5k - 14:17.1,
10k - 30:36.47 (29:52.16-95)
RUSSELL Darel U17 26.10.80, Woodford Gr :
OctY - 4639
RUSSELL Jamie U15 1.10.81, Rotherham :
800 - 2:04.27, HJ - 1.91, LJ - 5.93,
TJ - 12.05, PenB - 2964
RUSSELL Matthew U17 20.01.81, Havering :
100 - 10.8w/11.04, 200 - 21.89w/22.20

RUSSELL Peter 7.05.60, RUC :
DT - 44.32
RUSSELL Robert U23 5.08.74, Sale :
SP - 16.77, DT - 53.76
RUTHERFORD Tremayne 19.06.72, Cardiff :
60 - 6.79i (6.74i-95), 200 - 21.50 (21.20-93),
100 - 10.47w/10.5/10.66 (10.4w?/10.44-94)
RUTLAND Damon U23 10.07.75, Newq & Par :
HJ - 2.11 (2.13-95)
RUTTER N. U13, East Grinstead :
HJ - 1.55
RUTTER Sean U17 26.09.80, Gateshead :
HJ - 1.94

S ABEN Dominic U15 27.02.82, Sutton & D :
80HB - 11.86
SAGGERS Carl U13, Enfield :
SPC - 12.60, DTC - 38.50
SAHANS Gurmukh U20 8.10.78, Hounslow :
Dec - 5750, DecJ - 6060
SALAMI Raymond U23 11.04.75, Herne Hill :
60 - 6.84i, 100 - 10.6/10.78, 200 - 21.5
SALES Richard 28.05.62, Norwich :
Mar - 2:29:26
SALLE Frederick Ebong 10.09.64, Belgrave :
LJ - 7.79 (7.58-83)
SALT Jonathan U17 14.12.79, Coventry G :
800 - 1:57.4
SALT Richard U20 28.10.77, Lancaster & M :
JT - 62.20
SALVADOR-AYLOTT Livio 18.07.73, O Gayt :
200 - 21.8, 110H - 15.4 (15.1-93/15.76-94),
PV - 4.40 (4.50-94), Dec - 6764 (7024-94)
SAMMUT Steven 3.05.67, Team Solent :
HT - 58.48
SAMPSON Paul U20 12.07.77, Wakefield :
100 - 10.48w/10.71, 200 - 21.9/21.98
SAMUEL Lewis John Derek 12.02.66, Bel :
200 - 21.34 (21.1w?-91), 400 - 48.29 (46.53-90)
SAMUEL Rohan 30.01.66, Old Gaytonians :
100 - 10.8/10.99
(10.5w-89/10.58w-92/10.6/10.73-89)
SAMUELS Vernon George 15.10.64, Bristol :
TJ - 15.03 (16.82w-89/16.75-88)
SANDERSON David 6.05.71, Sale :
TJ - 15.12 (15.72w-93/15.29-92)
SANDY George 22.04.71, Hercules Wimb :
400 - 47.86
SARGEANT David U17 23.01.80, Chelmsford :
100HY - 13.9
SAVAGE David 13.11.72, Sale :
400 - 47.12, 110H - 15.1w/15.38 (15.34-95),
400H - 50.97
SAWYER Anthony J. U17 29.04.80, Wycombe :
OctY - 4557
SAXON Sean 11.12.71, Telford :
110H - 15.2
SCALLY Brian 9.05.66, Shettleston :
10k - 30:36.02, Mar - 2:31:37
SCANLAN Kevin U13 24.03.84, Woodford Gr :
800 - 2:17.0, 3k - 10:20.9
SCANLON Robert U23 13.04.74, Cov G/Loughbro :
800 - 1:51.4, 1500 - 3:41.3, 3k - 8:08.6
SCARLE Chris U17, City of Stoke :
TJ - 13.29
SCOTT Darren 7.03.69, Liverpool H :
100 - 10.6w (10.70w/10.74-95), 400H - 55.9,
200 - 21.3w/21.5/21.59i/21.71w (21.3/21.35-95)

SCOTT Duncan U15 5.02.82, Elswick :
3k - 9:39.5
SCOTT Richard 14.09.73, Exeter :
400H - 55.6 (53.7/53.98-95)
SCOTT Steven U20 5.06.79, Belgrave :
110HJ - 14.29w/14.3/14.69
SCOTT-BOYLE Oladipo U23 17.06.74, Herc W :
200 - 21.8, 400 - 48.99dq (49.1-95)
SEAR Richard U20 21.08.79, Oxford City :
110HJ - 14.80w/14.95, 110H - 14.8w/15.22,
HJ - 2.00
SEIDEN Benjamin U17 21.02.80, :
100HY - 14.2
SEMPLE Joel U15 19.09.81, Lagan Valley :
100 - 11.5w, JTB - 44.40
SENBANJO Oladipo U15 20.03.82, Notts :
LJ - 6.01, TJ - 13.05w/12.52, PenB - 2532
SEPHTON Simon U20 27.09.78, Rotherham :
SP - 13.14, SPJ - 14.39
SESAY Mark Gavin 13.12.72, Leeds/Un Alabm :
400 - 47.5un/48.1 (47.7-95),
800 - 1:49.34i/1:49.4 (1:48.30-90)
SESTON Tony U17 21.12.80, Ipswich :
400HY - 57.39
SEXTON Michael U20 26.05.79, Haslemere :
HTJ - 48.72
SHAH Arif U20 29.11.78, Coventry Godiva :
100 - 10.8/11.36, TJ - 14.51
SHALDERS Stephen U15, :
TJ - 12.25
SHARP Alexis 31.10.72, Blackheath :
110H - 15.4 (15.68-91), LJ - 7.01 (7.04-91),
DT - 48.56
SHARP Stephen U23 31.12.75, Hillingdon :
800 - 1:52.7, 1500 - 3:48.7
SHARPE Philip U17 6.03.81, Lancaster & M :
JTY - 57.38
SHAW Mark 6.01.65, Newport :
3k - 8:24.8
SHEA Brett 17.04.71, Andover :
Dec - 5979
SHENAVA John U17 5.02.81, Falkirk :
400 - 50.8 (52.79-95)
SHENTON David U20 20.10.77, Gate/NESH :
HT - 52.34, HTJ - 55.62
SHEPHERD Alan 28.04.69, Morpeth :
Mar - 2:22:22
SHEPHERD Bruce David 20.03.67, A'deen/Elg :
SP - 13.99 (14.50-93), DT - 42.28 (42.76-91),
HT - 53.18
SHEPHERD Dominic U23 11.12.76, C of Stoke :
PV - 4.70 (4.90-94)
SHEPHERD John S. 23.12.61, Enfield :
LJ - 7.46 (7.89w-86/7.66-88)
SHERBAN John Ian 30.07.64, Shaf B/Falk :
5k - 13:58.50 (13:39.43-91)
SHERBOURNE N. U13, AF&D :
TJ - 10.15
SHERIDAN Andrew U17 1.11.79, Blackheath :
SPY - 14.58
SHERIDAN Mark D. 17.06.70, Crawley :
HT - 49.20 (56.02-91)
SHEVYN Michael 12.12.71, Birchfield :
800 - 1:50.70
SHIELS Simon, Wrexham :
Mar - 2:31:32
SHILLABEER Edmund H. V55 2.08.39,
Ply City W : 50kW - 4:52:00 (4:28:06-86)

359

SHIPP James U20 10.11.77, Great Yarmouth :
400 - 48.9/48.96 (48.44-95)
SHIRLEY Simon 3.08.66, Belgrave :
110H - 15.10 (14.7/14.82-94),
HJ - 2.01 (2.09-85), PV - 4.70 (4.70-88),
LJ - 7.35w/7.30 (7.56w-88/7.55-86),
SP - 13.95 (14.59-95), JT - 62.92 (65.00-93),
Dec - 7857 (8036AUS-88/7980-94)
SHORESON Robert U15 14.10.81, Derbs Sch :
PenB - 2531
SICHEL William V40 1.10.53, Orkney Islands :
100kR - 7:07:49, 24HrT - 202.549km
SIDDONS Craig 4.06.73, Sheffield :
3kSt - 9:23.57
SILVA Andre U17 18.11.80, Cardiff :
100 - 10.6wdb/11.41 (11.29-95)
SIMON Delroy U20 27.11.78, Old Gaytonians :
2kSt - 6:02.5
SIMPSON Alexander U15 19.01.82, GEC :
JTB - 52.32
SIMPSON Ian Simon Fraser 3.08.66, Sale :
LJ - 7.05w/6.98 (8.04w/7.98-89)
SIMPSON Jonathan U15 27.05.82, C of Edinb :
400 - 53.5/54.51
SIMPSON Keith U15 19.10.81, Aberdeen :
JTB - 50.70
SIMPSON Michael 6.01.70, Hounslow :
5k - 14:23.2 (14:19.6-94), 10kR - 29:31
SIMPSON Scott U20 21.07.79, Oxford City :
PV - 4.25
SIMSON Matthew 28.05.70, Thurrock :
SP - 19.22 (19.49-94), DT - 48.54, HT - 49.00
SINCLAIR Trevor 6.08.61, Bedford Harriers :
LJ - 7.22 (7.56w/7.50i/7.47-84)
SINGLETON David U17 21.10.79, Swindon :
400 - 51.01
SKEETE John U20 8.09.78, Blackheath :
200 - 22.0 (21.78-95/22.26w-94)
SKELTON Matthew 8.11.72, Tonbridge :
1500 - 3:41.8, 1M - 4:05.0,
3k - 7:58.82i (8:18.7-91)
SKETCHLEY David U23 25.02.76, T Solent :
JT - 59.06 (59.84-95)
SKEVIS George U17 12.10.79, Crawley :
DTJ - 41.74, DTY - 46.12 (47.10-95)
SKINNER Michael U17 21.11.79, Blackheath :
1500 - 4:03.64
SKORNIA Robert U13 19.03.84, Devonia AC :
3k - 10:03.3
SLATER Ashley U15 23.09.81, Cannock & St :
HTB - 52.64
SLATER Darren U17, Bedford & County :
HJ - 1.96
SLATER Wayne A. 25.04.73, Woodford Gr :
Dec - 5887
SLEET Michael U17 6.06.80, Invicta :
100HY - 14.0/14.12w/14.37
SLESSOR Daniel U20 5.10.78, Border :
HJ - 2.07
SLYTHE Paul J. U23 5.09.74, GEC :
100 - 10.58w/10.7/10.73, 200 - 21.22,
300 - 32.73, 400 - 46.52
SMAHON Dean Carey 8.12.61, Lisburn/RUC :
JT - 65.46 (67.60-94)
SMALL Michael V40 31.03.54, Belgrave :
DT - 43.10 (44.14-88)
SMALLWOOD Mark U17 6.09.79, Bexley :
1.5kSt - 4:34.79

SMITH Adam U20 20.02.77, Annadale Str :
TJ - 14.96i (14.82-95)
SMITH Alex U17 2.11.79, Mandale :
TJ - 13.23
SMITH Andrew U20 26.03.78, Mandale :
400 - 49.5/49.58, 400H - 55.6/57.26
SMITH Anthony U15 11.01.83, Thurrock :
DTB - 38.12
SMITH Austen U17 26.09.79, Stroud :
100HY - 14.16w (14.0/14.70-95)
SMITH Ben U15 12.06.82, Shaftesbury B :
HJ - 1.82
SMITH Brendan U20 20.07.77, Sale :
800 - 1:51.8, 1k - 2:25.4,
1500 - 3:45.6, 3k - 8:19.7
SMITH C. Anthony 17.05.58, Shaftesbury B :
JT - 69.90 (69.94-91)
SMITH Christopher James U23 27.11.75,
C of Edinburgh/Arbr : JT - 62.30
SMITH Christopher J. 23.12.58, Leics WC :
3kW - 13:39.62i (12:05.0-87)
SMITH Colin P. 11.09.57, Portsmouth :
SP - 14.14 (15.54-89)
SMITH Craig U17 1.03.81, City of Edinburgh :
SPY - 13.99i/13.36
SMITH Darrell Luke 10.04.67, Blackheath :
3k - 8:13.5 (8:00.02i-91/8:04.5-95),
5k - 14:20.1 (13:58.62-92)
SMITH David 21.06.62, North East SH :
HT - 66.08 (77.30-85)
SMITH David U23 2.11.74, Belgrave/ERHS :
HT - 75.10
SMITH David U15 5.10.81, Middlesbro & C :
200 - 23.04w/23.16
SMITH Dennis P. V45 26.01.49, :
Mar - 2:33:06 (2:27:32-95)
SMITH Gary 20.02.71, Shaftesbury Barnet :
110H - 15.5 (14.87w/15.00-91),
LJ - 7.23 (7.35-93)
SMITH Glen E. 21.05.72, Solihull & S Heath :
SP - 14.71, DT - 62.32
SMITH Kenneth M. 10.05.64, Rowheath :
HT - 48.34 (56.28-85)
SMITH Mark U17 30.11.79, Wakefield :
JTY - 55.54
SMITH Mark U23 14.09.74, Old Gaytonians :
HJ - 2.00 (2.07-91)
SMITH Mark Richard 18.11.71, Woodford Gr :
100 - 10.8 (10.4w-90/10.55-95),
200 - 21.9/22.19 (20.85w/20.87-90),
400 - 47.8 (46.44A/46.60-95)
SMITH Matthew U23 26.12.74, Old Gayt :
1500 - 3:49.2 (3:48.8-95), 3k - 8:22.52i (9:35.6-89)
SMITH Neil U15, Old Gaytonians :
400 - 53.29
SMITH Paul W. V40 12.08.54, Brecon/Les Cr :
Mar - 2:31:19 (2:21:24-91)
SMITH Richard William U17 17.01.81, Peterbro :
PV - 4.45
SMITH Robert Mark 3.11.66, Edinburgh SH :
SP - 14.60 (15.14i-90/15.06-91)
SMITH Roy, Blackheath :
Mar - 2:28:17
SMITH Stephen U17 13.02.80, Peterborough :
PV - 4.40i/4.30
SMITH Steven 29.03.73, Liverpool H :
HJ - 2.36i/2.35 (2.38i-94/2.37-92),
LJ - 7.50w (7.65w-93/7.51-92)

SMITH Stuart U23 2.08.76, Coventry Godiva :
HJ - 2.11i (2.11-94)
SMITHAN David U13 7.11.83, Swansea :
HJ - 1.65
SMYTH Jeremy U20 11.08.78, Stromness :
JT - 57.48
SMYTH Peter, North Belfast :
Mar - 2:26:16
SNOOK Christopher U20 6.06.79, Mandale :
HTJ - 47.24
SNOW Robert U23 1.09.75, Guild& G/Junc 10 :
HT - 46.98
SOALLA-BELL Anthony U23 3.10.76, Herne H :
SP - 14.49
SOLLITT Gary 13.01.72, Team Solent :
SP - 17.02
SOLLY Jonathon 28.06.63, Bingley :
10kR - 29:10RL (28:03-86),
HMar - 1:03:32sh (1:02:57-90),
Mar - 2:12:25 (2:12:07-90)
SOUGRIN Neil 14.05.71, Enfield :
DT - 46.58 (47.82-94)
SOUTH James U23 4.01.75, Shaftesbury B :
SP - 13.71 (14.00-95), DT - 48.04 (48.32-94)
SOUTHWARD Anthony 31.01.71, Stockport :
110H - 14.69, HJ - 1.98, PV - 4.40,
LJ - 7.07w/6.91, SP - 13.82,
DT - 41.08, Dec - 7425
SPAWFORTH Darren 1.08.69, Wakefield :
800 - 1:50.4 (1:49.6-91),
1500 - 3:40.82 (3:40.48-92),
3k - 8:20.6 (8:03.4-92)
SPEAIGHT Neil U20 9.09.78, Huntingdon :
800 - 1:54.73
SPEAKE William J. 24.01.71, Bilderston B :
Mar - 2:32:53 (2:26:49-94)
SPENCER Alex U13, Liverpool Pembroke :
800 - 2:13.4
SPENCER John U15, Wakefield :
JTB - 47.30
SPICER Matthew William 18.05.71, Bristol :
HT - 59.68
SPIKE Lee U17 20.02.80, Liverpool H :
HJ - 2.05
SPILANE Paul U17 27.09.79, Leics WC :
3kW - 14:52.32i (15:48.0-95),
3kWR - 14:52
SPIVEY Nigel 18.10.58, Camb & C/Camb Un :
HT - 52.12 (58.12-89)
SPIVEY Philip 15.05.61, Belgrave/AUS :
HT - 65.30 (70.94-86)
SPRATLEY Nigel 1.04.70, Reading :
SP - 16.44 (17.96-94), DT - 44.16 (47.14-94)
SPRATLEY Stuart J. 18.07.72, Shaftesbury B :
HT - 52.34 (60.96-92)
SPRUNG Paul U15 7.05.82, Liverpool H :
DTB - 38.94
SPURLING Christopher U23 27.11.75, Sale :
TJ - 14.20
SQUIRE Andrew U17 30.09.79, Cannock & S :
JTY - 55.96
SQUIRRELL John U23 16.12.75, Belgrave :
400H - 55.7/55.72
ST.GEORGE Dominic M.T. U17 12.10.79, Eton :
800 - 1:56.1

STAINES Gary Martin 3.07.63, Belgrave :
3k - 8:13.21 (7:41.79-90),
5k - 14:16.25 (13:14.28-90),
10k - 29:40.4 (27:48.73-91),
10MR - 46:57 (46:11-93),
HMar - 1:03:28, Mar - 2:11:25
STAMP Terence 18.02.70, Newham & E B :
60 - 6.76i 100 - 10.5/10.64 (10.47-95)
STANFORD Chris U15 9.02.82, Belgrave :
3kWR - 15:20
STANFORD Steven U17 9.12.79, Liverpool H :
DTY - 47.84
STANLEY David U20 16.01.79, Basingstoke :
800 - 1:52.15
STANLEY-CLARKE Antony U17 10.10.80, Bel :
JTY - 53.48
STANOJEVIC Marko U17 1.10.79, :
LJ - 6.48w/6.38
STARK Graeme 12.10.63, Rotherham :
SP - 13.63 (14.88i-94/14.70-85)
STARK William U20 11.03.77, Aberdeen :
LJ - 6.97 (7.07w/7.06-95),
TJ - 14.38 (14.55-95)
STARLING Brent U23 19.05.76, Rotherham :
JT - 56.58
STARLING James Mark 13.08.67, Woodford Gr :
1500 - 3:50.86 (3:44.77-91)
STEEL Brian 30.09.70, City of Edinburgh :
400H - 55.98
STEEL John A. 27.02.63, City of Edinburgh :
3kSt - 9:11.02 (8:54.86-88)
STEEL Peter 11.12.73, Stroud :
1500 - 3:49.3
STEELE Martin Douglas 30.09.62, Longwood :
400 - 49.0 (47.4-90/48.65-93),
800 - 1:51.21i (1:43.84-93), 400H - 54.90
STEINLE Mark U23 22.11.74, Blackheath :
1500 - 3:51.0, 3k - 8:17.5 (8:10.1-95),
5k - 14:23.42 (14:03.82-94),
10k - 29:32.31 (29:07.33-95), HMar - 1:04:31
STENNETT Kori U23 2.09.76, Cheltenham :
TJ - 14.84 (15.02-94)
STEPHENSON Christian U23 22.07.74, Card :
1M - 4:04.9, 5k - 13:50.04,
10kR - 29:27, 3kSt - 8:54.8
STEPHENSON Sam U17 15.05.80, Belgrave :
100HY - 13.94w/14.17
STERN Mark 22.05.72, Shaftesbury Barnet :
100 - 10.90 (10.68w-93/10.8-90),
200 - 21.7 (21.62w-93/21.7-91),
110H - 14.13 (14.11w-93)
STEVENS Daniel U20 1.08.77, Bexley :
800 - 1:52.89
STEVENS Richard U23 17.07.76, Herne Hill :
HJ - 2.00i/2.00 (2.03-93)
STEVENSON Gary U17 12.09.79, Kilbarchan :
400 - 50.7/51.62, 400HY - 58.44 (57.3-95)
STEVENSON Samuel 20.12.63, Telford :
Mar - 2:22:44
STEWART Eddie V40 15.12.56, Cambuslang :
10k - 30:39.33 (30:22.0-93),
Mar - 2:26:59 (2:23:40-95)
STEWART Glen 7.12.70, City of Edinburgh :
800 - 1:49.2, 1500 - 3:38.66,
1M - 3:59.56, 2k - 5:05.97, 10kR - 29:28
STEWART Jonathan U17 15.06.80, Halifax :
1500 - 4:02.3, 3k - 8:43.9

361

STEWART Kris U17 11.04.80, Scottish Bord :
  100 - 10.8/11.04, 200 - 21.72,
  400 - 47.6/47.86
STICKINGS Nigel 1.04.71, GEC :
  100 - 10.91 (10.4w-92/10.56w/10.60-93),
  200 - 21.3 (20.84w-93/21.0-92/21.14-93)
STILL Matthew U17 1.12.79, Basingstoke :
  200 - 22.7/23.02 (22.6/22.88-95),
  400 - 49.25
STIRK Nigel 13.03.72, Leics Cor :
  5k - 14:32.39 (14:21.76-93)
STIRRAT Kenneth A. 1.03.70, Falkirk :
  3kSt - 9:21.79 (8:49.26-94)
STODDART Keith U13 26.10.83, C of Edinb :
  TJ - 10.45
STOKES Stuart U23 15.12.76, Bolton :
  2kSt - 5:44.47, 3kSt - 9:01.8
STONE Darrell Richard 2.02.68, Steyning :
  20kW - 1:23:58 (1:23:27sh-93)
STONE Jason James U17 15.10.80, Houns :
  HTY - 52.78
STONE Kairnil U23 21.10.76, Torbay :
  1500 - 3:50.38
STOPHER Brian U17 8.04.80, AF&D :
  800 - 1:56.13, 1500 - 4:04.52
STRAIN Michael U17 11.09.79, Victoria Park :
  200 - 22.7 (25.16w-95),
  100HY - 14.2/14.40, TJ - 13.18
STRANG David Maxwell 13.12.68, Haringey :
  800 - 1:45.81,
  1k - 2:24.73A (2:18.31i-93/2:21.7A-87),
  1500 - 3:49.09A (3:36.53-94)
STREATHER Gavin Blair 14.04.71,
  Woodford Green/Loughborough Studnts :
  110H - 15.6w/15.67 (15.1/15.15-94),
  400H - 55.4/55.50 (53.18-91)
STREET D. U17, Liverpool Pembroke :
  TJ - 13.42
STRONACH Paul A.G. 18.05.68, Severn :
  SP - 13.63 (13.96-89)
STUCKEY Andy 24.04.72, Rowheath :
  800 - 1:51.73
SUMNER David U15, Blackheath :
  PV - 3.10
SUNNERS Graham 26.03.73, Liv Pem/RAF :
  3kSt - 9:07.4
SUNSHINE Gavin S. U23 19.02.74, N & E B :
  110H - 15.3 (14.94-93), PV - 4.20 (4.70-92)
SURETY Steven U17 18.02.80, Basildon :
  200 - 22.6w, 100HY - 13.7
SUTTON Glyn V50 3.05.45, Newport :
  PV - 4.15 (4.40-90)
SUTTON Matthew U15 8.09.81, Wolves & B :
  HTY - 55.30, HTB - 65.42
SUTTON Piers 25.06.70, Southampton City :
  Dec - 5200
SWAIN Anthony Michael U23 17.01.75,
  Wakefield/ERHS : HT - 59.50
SWAIN Ashley U17 3.10.80, Team Solent :
  PV - 4.00
SWALES Mark U23 29.01.75, Old Gaytonians :
  LJ - 7.17w (7.00-94)
SWANSTON David 30.11.61, Border :
  5k - 14:22.9 (14:10.98-90),
  10MR - 48:52 (48:08-90),
  HMar - 1:03:44 (1:02:40-92)
SWANWICK Adam U15 4.01.82, Birchfield :
  3k - 9:36.80

SWEENEY Christopher 3.03.66, Tipton :
  5k - 13:43.49, 10k - 28:44.09, 10kR - 29:08
SWEENEY Conor U15 28.12.81, Annadale Str :
  800 - 2:02.7, 1500 - 4:11.40
SWEENEY David 9.02.62, Sparta/Herne Hill :
  DT - 41.78 (47.22-94)
SWEENEY Joseph L. 17.07.65, W S & E :
  LJ - 7.24 (7.41-87), TJ - 15.75 (16.26-91)
SWEENEY Mark U20 26.02.77, Notts :
  110HJ - 15.12, 110H - 14.9w/15.2/15.22w,
  Dec - 5755, DecJ - 5988
SWEETMAN David, Charnwood :
  110H - 14.95w
SWIFT-SMITH Justin U23 28.08.74, SB :
  800 - 1:48.9, 1500 - 3:47.7 (3:45.40-93),
  1M - 4:09.8
SWINGLER Martin 11.05.63, Airedale :
  110H - 15.6 (15.2w-88/15.34-87)
SYMONDS Christopher M. 15.11.70,
  Hounslow/W London IHE :
  SP - 14.34 (15.37-91), DT - 47.18 (50.46-92)
SYMONDS Matthew John 31.07.68, TVH :
  SP - 15.43 (15.59-94), DT - 53.22 (54.36-95)
SYNNERMANN Per 13.12.71, Loughbro :
  1500 - 3:51.7

TADESSE Kassa U23 21.08.74, Bel/ETH :
  10kR - 28:15sh (29:05-94),
  HMar - 1:04:33 (1:03:54-94)
TARRAN Michael U17 10.12.80, Cheltenham :
  JTY - 55.40
TATHAM Alan U23 29.04.76, Derby & Co/
  Loughbro : 3k - 8:22.46i
TAYLOR Brian P.J.P. 13.08.70, Old Gayt :
  60 - 6.91i (6.78i-93), 60H - 7.95i (7.81i-95),
  100 - 10.64w/10.68 (10.35-93),
  110H - 14.03 (13.7db/13.9-93),
  PV - 4.60 (5.00-91), LJ - 7.26w/7.09 (7.37-93),
  SP - 13.96 (14.63-93), DT - 41.94 (42.38-94),
  Dec - 7573 (7787-93)
TAYLOR Bruce 4.11.72, Old Gaytonians :
  DT - 41.64
TAYLOR David 9.01.64, Blackheath :
  10kR - 29:14 (29:11-95), 10MR - 48:40
TAYLOR Dean U15 9.11.81, :
  TJ - 13.60w/13.27
TAYLOR Greg U20 1.08.77, Cannock & St :
  800 - 1:53.1
TAYLOR Ian J. 2.07.67, Telford :
  DT - 47.58 (49.44-93)
TAYLOR James U15 22.06.83, Hallamshire :
  DTB - 38.00
TAYLOR Kenneth V45 24.10.48, Blackburn :
  JT - 56.24 (64.98-86)
TAYLOR Martin U15 31.01.82, Victoria Park :
  80HB - 12.1, LJ - 6.01w/5.72,
  PenB - 2611w/2562
TAYLOR Paul Thomas 9.01.66, Border :
  5k - 14:12.75 (13:45.31-89),
  10kR - 27:49RL/28:40 (28:32-94)
TAYLOR Richard 5.12.73, Coventry Godiva :
  5k - 14:14.15
TAYLOR Scott U20 28.07.78, Leics WC :
  3kW - 13:33.61i/13:46.1, 5kW - 23:07.5,
  5kWR - 22:22, 10kW - 49:56.0,
  10kWR - 47:24

362

TAYLOR Steve 19.03.66, Manx H :
3kW - 12:15.2, 10kW - 45:46.3 (44:38.2-92),
20kW - 1:34:27 (1:28:46-92)
TAYLOR Thomas U17 30.01.81, Leics WC :
3kWR - 13:41, 5kW - 23:58.11
TEAPE Hugh D. 26.12.63, Enfield :
60H - 8.13i (7.69i-92),
110H - 14.73 (13.44-92)
TEAR Adam U23 12.08.75, Grimsby :
DT - 42.92
TELFER Gary 10.01.65, Thames Valley :
400H - 52.01 (51.29-95)
THACKERY Carl Edward 14.10.62, Hallam :
10kR - 29:35 (28:22-86)
THICKPENNY Robert U23 17.07.76, Peterbro :
PV - 4.75
THIE James U20 27.06.78, Westbury :
1500 - 3:54.94, 3k - 8:34.17
THOM Douglas 13.04.68, B & A/Sc Bord/Bord :
400 - 48.61, 400H - 52.21
THOMAS Alexander U17 31.12.79, Rowheath :
PV - 4.20
THOMAS Andrew U20 15.05.79, Liverpool H :
800 - 1:50.61
THOMAS Barry V.S. 28.04.72, Sheffield :
60H - 8.32i, 110H - 14.96 (14.62w-95/14.81-92),
HJ - 2.04 (2.05-92), PV - 4.90 (5.00-92),
LJ - 7.33w/7.13 (7.44-92),
SP - 14.06, DT - 42.08, JT - 60.20 (60.30-95),
Dec - 7765 (7766-95)
THOMAS Chris U17 11.01.80, Torfaen :
JT - 56.10, JTY - 60.94
THOMAS Craig U15 28.09.81, Airdrie :
LJ - 5.95i/5.94, TJ - 12.43w/12.10
THOMAS Iwan U23 5.01.74, Newham & E B :
200 - 21.2/21.30+/21.41A,
300 - 32.52, 400 - 44.66A/44.69
THOMAS Jonathan U15, Bridgend :
100 - 11.61
THOMAS Josephus 11.07.71, Wood Gr/SLE :
60 - 6.74i (6.71i-94),
100 - 10.2/10.33w/10.43,
200 - 20.6/21.13 (20.93A-95)
THOMAS Joslyn 11.07.71, Woodford Gr/SLE :
100 - 10.59w (10.4w/10.54-94),
200 - 21.6/22.15 (21.2/21.29-94)
THOMAS Mark 1.06.72, Sheffield :
200 - 21.8
THOMAS Nicholas U20 4.04.79, Blackheath :
TJ - 15.12
THOMAS Paul U17 1.10.80, Southampton C :
PV - 3.70
THOMAS Stephen U20 4.04.78, Swansea :
JT - 56.10
THOMAS Steve V40 20.05.56, Barrow & F :
SP - 13.69 (15.19-84)
THOMAS Timothy 18.11.73, Swansea :
PV - 5.00 (5.20ns/5.10-94)
THOMPSON Alexander U20 5.05.78, Wells :
DTJ - 44.88
THOMPSON Chris U17 17.04.81, AF&D :
3k - 8:58.79, 1.5kSt - 4:36.1
THOMPSON Don V60 20.01.33, Folkestone :
200kW - 23:44:23
THOMPSON Gavin U17 9.04.80, Crawley :
1500 - 4:02.37, 3k - 8:52.7
THOMPSON Jason 16.11.71, Dartford :
400 - 49.0, 600 - 1:19.8, 800 - 1:50.1

THOMPSON Neville L. V40 28.03.55, SB :
SP - 14.35 (15.26i-88/15.15-87),
DT - 54.74 (55.68-93),
THOMPSON Paul 22.03.72, Birch/Idaho Univ :
400H - 50.16
THOMPSON Ross U15 7.12.81, Gateshead :
HTY - 51.06, HTB - 57.56
THOMPSON Scot U17 10.08.81, Nairn :
DTY - 46.40
THOMPSON Stephen U15 5.12.82, Tunb W :
3k - 9:26.89
THOMSON Charles 17.06.65, Cambuslang :
10k - 30:06.50
THOMSON David, Portsmouth :
Mar - 2:32:31
THOMSON Matthew U15 20.09.81, Weston :
800 - 2:04.3, 1500 - 4:15.69, 3k - 9:17.77
THORN Darren M.M. 17.07.62, Cov RWC :
3kW - 13:49.0 (12:15.0-89)
THORNTON Andrew U20 29.11.77, Elswick :
LJ - 7.10w/6.86
THORNTON David 27.07.73, Hynd/Loughbro :
800 - 1:51.9 (1:51.0-95)
THURGOOD Stuart U23 17.05.76, Loughbro/
Newham & Essex B : HT - 52.24 (52.56-95)
THYER John U20 23.11.78, City of Plymouth :
SP - 13.46, SPJ - 14.69, DTJ - 41.14
TIBBETS Adam U20 14.12.78, Dudley & Stour :
200 - 22.14w (23.9-95),
110HJ - 14.5/14.70w, 110H - 14.93w
TIETZ Michael U20 14.09.77, Birchfield :
100 - 10.57, 200 - 21.7/21.75
TIMBA Paul U17 21.03.80, Windsor S & E :
100HY - 14.2, OctY - 4469
TINDALL Lee U17 19.02.80, Portsmouth :
100HY - 14.1/14.13
TINWELL Mark U15 18.11.81, Sale/NWHS :
SPB - 14.21, DTB - 44.46,
JTB - 46.62 (47.78-95)
TIPTON Carl U20 4.02.77, Bridgnorth :
800 - 1:54.98
TITMUS Philip U15 12.11.81, Cheltenham :
PV - 3.00, DTB - 37.26,
TOBIN Shaun 13.10.62, Swansea :
10k - 30:23.37, Mar - 2:21:53
TODD Raymond U15 7.03.82, Fife :
400 - 53.9
TOEMEN Erik U20 1.07.78, Notts :
DecJ - 6068
TOMKINS Ian 23.03.68, Haywards Heath :
Dec - 5048
TOMKINSON Tim 31.10.68, Sale/Army :
110H - 14.8 (14.5-92/14.74w-93/15.00-94)
TOMLINSON Christopher U15 15.09.81, Mand :
LJ - 6.09w/5.91, TJ - 13.83w/13.24
TOMS Robert U17 7.08.80, Reading :
HJ - 2.01
TONNER Edward 3.02.73, Kilmarnock :
3kSt - 9:29.4 (9:24.2-94)
TONNER James U23 3.06.75, Kilmarnock :
800 - 1:52.34, 1500 - 3:50.6
TOPLISS Stephen U20 17.07.78, Peterbro :
100 - 10.8/10.90, 200 - 21.8/22.13
TOUT Mark J. 24.01.61, Hounslow :
DT - 43.14 (44.94-90)
TOWNSEND Glen 23.04.64, Western (I.O.M.) :
DT - 42.30 (44.24-90)

TOWNSEND Neil 3.05.63, Herne Hill :
HT - 46.10 (47.34-95)
TREACY Brian Francis 29.07.71, Anna Str :
1500 - 3:40.47 (3:38.93-94), 3k - 7:55.83
TREEN Kevin U23 1.02.76, Birchfield :
PV - 4.40i/4.40 (4.50i-94/4.40-93)
TRIBBLE Matthew U17 17.10.79, Bed & Co:
JTY - 54.42, OctY - 4847
TROMANS Glyn 17.03.69, Coventry Godiva :
10kR - 29:03, 10MR - 47:34
TROWER John V40 6.02.56, Telford :
JT - 57.58 (63.82-89)
TROY Martin U23 13.07.76, Luton :
JT - 55.62, Dec - 6154
TUCKER Stephen 30.12.62, Shettleston :
100 - 10.7w/10.8
(10.6w-88/10.70w-94/10.8/10.82-92),
200 - 22.0 (21.5w-87/21.7/21.97w-94/22.07-92)
TUFTON Kevin U17 30.04.80, Havering :
PV - 3.60
TULBA-MORRISON Phillip William 20.09.73,
Basingstoke : 800 - 1:50.0, 1500 - 3:46.0
TULLETT Ian Roger 15.08.69, Belgrave :
PV - 5.30 (5.30i/5.30-92)
TULLOCH Andrew George 1.04.67, Belgrave :
60H - 7.88i (7.76i-93),
110H - 13.5w/13.56 (13.52-94)
TUNE David 29.10.70, Rotherham :
5k - 14:19.15 (14:09.49-94),
10kR - 29:38, HMar - 1:04:48
TURNBULL Aidan U15 1.09.81, Houghton-le-Sp :
80HB - 12.1, PenB - 2517
TURNER Andrew 29.08.63, Crawley :
SP - 14.86i/14.72 (14.74-94),
DT - 46.26 (47.40-95), HT - 51.76
TURNER Daniel U20 27.11.78, Havant :
HJ - 2.05i/2.05
TURNER Douglas 2.12.66, Cardiff :
60 - 6.74i, 100 - 10.26w (10.58-95),
150 - 15.34, 200 - 20.43
TURNER Garry U20 21.12.78, Notts :
110HJ - 15.3
TYLER Geoffrey A. V45 30.09.48, Sale :
DT - 43.06 (55.42-80)
TYLER Russell U15, St Albans :
DTB - 37.54
TYPE Chris U15 5.10.81, Cardiff :
PV - 3.60

UDECHUKU Emeka U17 10.07.79, Blackh :
SP - 16.29i/16.20, SPJ - 17.30,
DT - 51.04, DTJ - 54.92, JT - 54.50
UGONO Uvie U20 8.03.78, Herne Hill :
60 - 6.9i (6.98i-95), 100 - 10.46w/10.55,
200 - 21.29
ULYATT Kent 10.04.72, Norwich :
200 - 21.3 (21.46-95),
400 - 47.04i/47.4 (46.31-95)
URQUHART Greig U15 14.06.82, Helensb :
DTB - 38.48
URQUHART Ronald John U20 14.11.77, Shett :
HT - 56.32, HTJ - 61.76
URSELL Nangeloum U15 1.10.81, Lewisham :
80HB - 12.03, TJ - 13.09, PenB - 2742
USHER Kevin 3.11.65, Hounslow :
3kSt - 9:15.1 (9:03.3-90)

VANHINSBERGH Tom U17 28.12.78, Craw :
HJ - 2.05i/2.05 (2.06-95)
VAUX-HARVEY Matthew U23 30.03.76, Stour :
3k - 8:22.07
VENESS Luke 5.12.73, Brighton :
800 - 1:50.3, 1500 - 3:46.6 (3:47.4un-94)
VENGDASALAM Natham 11.03.64, Liv Pem :
5k - 14:32.99
VERITY Paul V40 22.12.56, :
Mar - 2:31:39
VIDAL Nigel 18.11.72, Thames Valley :
60 - 6.9i
VIDGEN David U23 27.09.74, Oxford City :
110H - 15.2 (15.1/15.31-95)
VIVIAN Peter J.P. 5.11.70, Thames VH/WLHS :
HT - 68.62 (71.28-95)
VOSE Kevin J. 28.11.58, St Helens :
Mar - 2:29:44 (2:23:56-91)

WADDINGTON Anthony U23 30.06.75, Read :
100 - 10.8,
200 - 21.9/22.20 (21.8-95/22.10w-94)
WADE Christopher U15 22.09.82, Halifax :
SPB - 14.03
WADE Philip U15 24.05.82, City of Bath :
PV - 3.35
WAIN Andrew 2.06.65, Nene VH/Camb Un :
SP - 14.80i/14.17 (14.52-95)
WALCOTT Andrew U23 11.01.75, Belgrave :
100 - 10.88 (10.60w/10.64-95), 200 - 21.15
WALCOTT Mark 24.11.73, Birchfield :
100 - 10.7w/10.95 (10.6w-92/10.67-94),
200 - 21.74 (21.5/21.60-93)
WALKER Adam U17 16.11.79, Crawley :
PV - 3.95
WALKER Alvin 30.04.65, Mandale/Army :
LJ - 7.08 (7.36-94), TJ - 15.45
WALKER Ben T. U20 8.06.78, Dacorum & Tr :
DT - 44.26, DTJ - 46.96, DecJ - 5571
WALKER Darren U23 21.03.75, Crewe & N :
200 - 22.02w (21.4w-92/21.5/21.56w/21.59-93)
WALKER Douglas 28.07.73, N & EB/C of E :
100 - 10.51w (10.69-91),
200 - 20.67 (20.53w-95),
300 - 33.15, 400 - 46.95
WALKER Leigh U20 17.08.77, Craw/Loughbro :
PV - 4.50
WALKER Nicholas O. 24.02.64, Severn :
Dec - 5214 (5510-92)
WALKER Paul 2.12.73, Liverpool H/City of E :
400 - 48.2/48.21, 800 - 1:48.94 (1:47.53-93)
WALKER Robin U20 8.02.78, Scunthorpe :
HTJ - 51.62
WALKER Scott U20 9.09.77, Warrington :
Dec - 5430
WALKER Stuart U20 22.09.78, Derby & Co :
JT - 58.94
WALL Darren U17 6.04.80, Team Solent :
200 - 22.42w/22.51
WALL Terry 12.06.70, Morpeth :
3k - 8:19.4, 10k - 30:44.8 (30:37.7-95)
WALLACE Carl U17 10.02.81, Cannock & St :
HJ - 1.91
WALLACE John 9.10.68, Morpeth :
HJ - 2.08 (2.16-90)
WALLACE Jonathan U20 1.01.79, Birchfield :
TJ - 15.34

WALLING Andrew 3.04.73, Sale :
  800 - 1:50.9 (1:50.6-95), 1500 - 3:50.4
WALMSLEY Dennis, Bourton RR :
  Mar - 2:23:46 (2:21:19-95)
WALMSLEY Kevin 6.09.67, Manx H :
  3kW - 12:11.5, 20kW - 1:33:28, 50kW - 4:33:01+
WALPOLE Aidan, Salford :
  3k - 8:22.2
WALSH Christopher U20 1.10.78, Mand/NESH :
  HT - 53.04, HTJ - 59.48
WALSH James U15 22.09.81, Rowheath :
  3k - 9:36.90
WALSH Liam U15 5.05.82, Deeside :
  SPB - 14.60, DTB - 45.88,
  JTB - 47.76 (50.42-95)
WALSH Phillip U15 26.10.81, Isle of Wight :
  80HB - 11.54
WALSH Robert U17, :
  100 - 11.1wdb
WALTERS Damien U15 6.04.82, :
  TJ - 12.48w/12.29
WARD Ian U15 3.04.82, Chester Le Street :
  80HB - 11.77
WARD James U20 28.07.77, Mansfield :
  100 - 10.9, 200 - 22.0
WARD Richard J. S. U15 5.05.82, Sutton & D :
  1500 - 4:12.2, 3k - 9:13.60
WAREHAM Marc U17 9.08.80, Medway :
  100HY - 13.73w/13.77
WARISO Solomon Christopher 11.11.66, Har :
  60 - 6.88i (6.72i-94),
  100 - 10.65w/10.79 (10.3-95/10.33-94),
  200 - 20.64 (20.50-95)
WARMINGTON Ben U20 20.03.79, N Shields P:
  110HJ - 14.18w/14.5/14.86, 110H - 14.9/14.92
WARREN Carl 28.09.69, Cannock & Stafford :
  1500 - 3:48.0 (3:47.72-95),
  2kSt - 5:40.9 (5:37.9-95),
  3kSt - 8:48.99 (8:40.74-95)
WARREN David U17 5.12.79, Barrow & Furn:
  HJ - 1.95
WARREN R. U15, Walton :
  DTB - 39.22
WARREN Robert U17 17.07.81, Steyning :
  3kW - 14:59.94, 3kWR - 14:32, 10kWR - 53:15
WASHINGTON Ivan V40 18.11.56, Sheffield :
  DT - 42.04 (46.06-88)
WASSELL Michael, Solihull & S Heath :
  1500 - 3:48.9
WATERMAN Peter U17 12.09.79, Belgrave :
  SPY - 15.22 (15.89-95), HTJ - 50.12, HTY - 58.16
WATERS Andrew U17 11.10.79, Oxford City :
  SPY - 14.37i/13.24, DTY - 44.00
WATERS Martin U15 20.01.82, Isle of Wight :
  PV - 3.10
WATERS Nicholas U17 1.01.80, Enfield :
  PV - 4.00
WATERS Rupert 3.01.72, Sale/Manchester U :
  800 - 1:47.9, 1k - 2:23.66, 1500 - 3:46.8
WATKINS Ben U20 12.11.78, Norwich :
  200 - 22.04w/22.23
WATSON Garth 20.04.73, East Cheshire :
  800 - 1:51.32 (1:50.2-95),
  1k - 2:25.3, 1500 - 3:50.89i/3:51.8
WATSON James 4.10.67, City of Edinburgh :
  100 - 10.8w/10.97w (10.88w/10.95-91), 200 - 21.9
WATSON Peter U17 30.06.81, Oxford City :
  JTY - 54.32, OctY - 4813

WATTERS Craig 18.07.67, :
  Mar - 2:29:29
WATTS Robert V45 3.01.50, London Vid :
  200kW - 23:50:50
WATTS Robert U15 19.10.81, Somerset Sch :
  HTB - 44.10
WEAVER Matthew 14.11.73, Old Gayt/Oxf Un :
  PV - 4.80 (4.90-94)
WEBB Jamie U23 18.12.75, Belgrave :
  PV - 4.50
WEBSTER Andrew 11.11.66, Sale :
  400H - 54.7 (54.8-88)
WEDLAKE Andrew 30.11.71, Bournem'th/Prov Un :
  3k - 8:05.72i (8:05.06i-94/8:17.9-92),
  5k - 14:20.08i (14:11.37-94)
WEEDON C. U15, Shaftesbury Barnet :
  PV - 2.90
WEIR John 24.12.66, North Belfast :
  Mar - 2:29:16
WEIR Robert B. 4.02.61, Birchfield :
  DT - 62.40 (63.56-95), HT - 60.28 (75.08-82)
WELCH Mark U23 9.11.74, Army/Kettering :
  JT - 56.40 (58.94-92)
WELLS Ian 18.02.62, Belgrave :
  400H - 55.06 (53.3-91/53.34-95)
WELLS Louis U20 6.02.78, Enfield :
  800 - 1:52.57
WELLS Stuart U20 26.07.79, Havering :
  LJ - 7.05
WELLSTEAD Karl 2.06.71, Basingstoke & MH :
  Mar - 2:32:08
WELSH Graeme U23 8.10.75, Border :
  100 - 10.8 (10.7-95/10.94w-93/10.99-95),
  200 - 21.70
WEST Terence 19.11.68, Morpeth :
  800 - 1:47.70,
  1500 - 3:43.51i/3:49.75 (3:43.39i-94/3:47.1-92)
WESTON Andrew D. 4.12.73, Read/Loughbro :
  HJ - 2.00 (2.11-92)
WESTON Paul 6.10.67, Bristol :
  TJ - 15.12 (15.46-92)
WHALEY Geoffrey 9.06.58, City of Plymouth :
  HT - 50.56 (62.16-80)
WHALLEY Robert 11.02.68, C of Stoke/Staffs U :
  1500 - 3:40.7, 1M - 4:06.9 (4:02.1-92),
  3k - 7:52.6, 5k - 13:51.99
WHATTLEY D. U13, St Bernadettes :
  LJ - 5.18
WHITBY Benedict U20 6.01.77, Hounslow :
  1500 - 3:53.93, 2kSt - 6:02.6 (5:59.67-95),
  3kSt - 8:59.09
WHITE Adrian Paul U23 1.09.74,
  Thames VH/Loughboro : 60 - 6.76i,
  100 - 10.4/10.42 (10.40-95), 200 - 20.79
WHITE Andrew U15 1.05.82, :
  TJ - 12.44
WHITE Craig Elliot 4.04.71, Sale :
  400H - 53.6/53.64 (52.20-94)
WHITE Edward 16.11.73, Sale/Man Univ :
  200 - 21.63 (21.12-95)
WHITE Graham 28.03.59, Brighton :
  50kW - 4:24:01 (4:14:59-95)
WHITE Simon U23 2.10.75, Blackheath :
  Dec - 5194
WHITE Steffan 21.12.72, Coventry Godiva :
  800 - 1:51.7, 1500 - 3:41.1 (3:41.02-94),
  1M - 4:01.53 (4:00.61-94),
  3k - 8:03.20 (8:01.90i-94)

365

WHITEFOOT Jon U13, Neath :
JTC - 38.88
WHITEHEAD Peter Kenneth 3.12.64, Skyrac :
10kR - 28:07 (28:23-95),
10MR - 47:53 (47:51-93),
HMar - 1:04:04 (1:02:33-95),
Mar - 2:22:37 (2:12:23-95)
WHITEHEAD Timmon U15 20.04.82, Guild & G :
HTB - 49.72
WHITEMAN Anthony 13.11.71, GEC/WLIHE :
800 - 1:47.8, 1k - 2:18.8i, 1500 - 3:34.47,
1M - 3:54.87, 3k - 7:57.59i,
WHORLOW Nigel U17 26.11.80, Belgrave :
3kW - 14:22.7, 3kWR - 13:56, 5kW - 24:37.6,
10kWR - 51:15
WHYTE Stephen A. 14.03.64, Thames Valley :
SP - 15.99 (17.78-89), DT - 45.74 (50.40-94),
HT - 58.60 (67.82-89)
WIGHT Graeme 3.06.65, Shettleston :
5k - 14:14.81
WILD Jonathan 30.08.73, Sale/OklahSt Un :
800 - 1:50.22 (1:49.39-95), 1k - 2:24.71i,
1500 - 3:41.48 (3:41.40-95), 5k - 13:45.1,
3k - 7:53.10i/8:07.4 (7:55.16-95)
WILDE Ryan U15 25.12.81, :
400 - 53.69
WILDING Ian U23 3.03.75, C of S/Loughbro :
PV - 5.00 (5.00ex-94)
WILKINS Perris 12.11.68, Banbury :
DT - 56.10
WILKINSON Desmond F. 7.01.63, Luton :
110H - 15.3 (14.3-86/14.35w-84/14.49-86)
WILKINSON James Gareth U23 21.04.74, Tel :
JT - 55.68 (58.60-92)
WILKINSON Jonathon 17.02.62, Spenbro :
110H - 15.4, JT - 57.34 (62.34-95),
Dec - 6143 (6259-94)
WILKINSON Neil 12.03.69, Cambuslang/Man U :
3k - 8:24.7, 10k - 29:56.52, 3kSt - 9:20.2
WILKINSON Peter U20 7.08.78, Middlesbro :
TJ - 14.22
WILKINSON Simon U20 27.08.77, Dudley & St :
5k - 14:33.56, 10k - 30:35.54,
WILL Nigel Simon 18.10.67, Enfield :
200 - 22.0 (20.7w-90/20.91-89),
WILLERS Edward U17 18.09.79, Braintree :
HJ - 2.00 (2.00-95)
WILLETTS Thomas U17 26.09.79, Sparkhill :
100 - 10.93w/11.05
WILLIAMS Alun 22.06.62, Torfaen/RAF :
DT - 43.78
WILLIAMS Andrew U15 9.03.82, Birchfield :
100 - 11.47w/11.60, 200 - 23.41
WILLIAMS Anthony Richard 1.05.72, N & EB :
400H - 52.2/53.20 (50.31-95)
WILLIAMS Barrington Chester V40 11.09.55,
Birchfield : 60 - 6.92i (6.65i-88),
100 - 10.69w (10.27w/10.34-88),
LJ - 7.54w/7.52i/7.42 (8.05i/8.01-89)
WILLIAMS Barry V45 5.03.47, Trafford :
HT - 48.72 (73.86-76)
WILLIAMS David U23 22.12.75, Bath Univ. :
400 - 48.43
WILLIAMS Edward 1.10.70, Thames Valley :
400 - 47.86 (46.84-94), 800 - 1:49.41
WILLIAMS Kevin 15.12.71, Cardiff :
60 - 6.67i, 100 - 10.35,
200 - 21.98i (21.47w-94/21.70-95)

WILLIAMS Nicholas U15 2.02.82, Trafford :
HTB - 55.78
WILLIAMS Paul U20 21.09.77, Charnwood :
SP - 13.75, SPJ - 14.71
WILLIAMS Paul, Trafford :
400H - 56.0
WILLIAMS Rhys U17, Bicester RR :
100HY - 14.1w (14.9-95), 400HY - 57.6,
TJ - 13.34w/13.27
WILLIAMS Rhys U15 4.10.81, Swansea :
JTB - 58.58
WILLIAMS Richard U15 22.10.81, S Barnet :
3k - 9:37.3
WILLIAMS S., Yeovil Olympiads :
LJ - 6.90
WILLIAMS Simon David U17 5.10.80, Basingst :
DTY - 45.90
WILLIAMS Simon Alexander 17.10.67, Enfield :
SP - 17.68i/15.78 (19.44i-89/19.17-91),
DT - 58.04 (68.68-87)
WILLIAMS Terry 15.11.68, Shaftesbury B :
100 - 10.45 (10.17w/10.23-94),
200 - 21.12 (20.50-94)
WILLIAMSON Paul U23 16.06.74, TVH/Staffs U :
PV - 5.50
WILLS Chris U23 18.05.76, Birchfield :
PV - 4.10 (4.40-93)
WILSON Alloy U17 25.01.80, Blackheath :
400 - 48.71
WILSON David 7.09.68, Annadale Striders :
1500 - 3:50.0 (3:41.28-94)
WILSON David 5.09.70, Tipton :
JT - 63.14 (64.86-88)
WILSON Graeme U20 11.06.78, Border :
100 - 10.98, 200 - 22.13
WILSON Ian U17 7.10.79, Coventry Godiva :
HJ - 1.94 (1.95-95)
WILSON Martin U17 28.09.79, Norwich :
SPY - 14.47
WILSON Paul 12.11.69, Un West Cape :
3k - 8:12.9, 5k - 13:56.04
WILSON Peter 28.06.62, White Horse :
Mar - 2:23:13
WILSON Simon 8.03.66, Team Solent :
3kSt - 9:22.2 (9:06.6-89)
WILSON Vincent 1.04.73, Jarrow & Hebburn :
800 - 1:50.4 (1:49.47-94),
1500 - 3:43.38, 1M - 4:04.5
WILTON Andrew 14.12.60, Tipton :
Mar - 2:31:41 (2:27:27-93)
WILTSHIRE Lee 26.07.62, Portsmouth :
SP - 14.95 (17.41-94)
WINCHCOMBE Nigel C. 10.12.59, Lincoln W :
HT - 54.14 (59.18-88)
WINROW Craig Nicholas 22.12.71, Wigan :
400 - 49.0 (48.0-90/48.38A-92/48.56-91),
800 - 1:45.69, 1k - 2:20.64 (2:20.46-93)
WINTER Neil Stephen U23 21.03.74, S B :
PV - 5.50 (5.60-95)
WISE P. U13, Portsmouth :
100 - 12.3
WISEMAN Mark, Army/Basingstoke & MH :
SP - 14.19 (14.66-94), DT - 43.32 (48.84-95)
WITCHALLS Bruno U23 22.03.75,
Dorking & Mole V/Loughbro : 1k - 2:25.3i
WITTON Gary 25.08.73, Brighton :
3kW - 12:01.7,
10kW - 48:06.96 (44:38.57-95)

WOAD Warren U17 16.03.80, Old Gaytonians :
  SPY - 14.05 (14.08-95)
WODU Ejike U23 15.12.74, Blackheath :
  100 - 10.7 (10.38w/10.55-93)
WOODHOUSE D. U15 30.11.81, Brentwood :
  JTB - 44.96
WOODHOUSE Mark U23 1.11.75, Norwich/
  Loughbro : 60 - 6.91i,
  100 - 10.6/10.67w/10.70
  (10.4w?-95/10.61w-93/10.68-95),
  200 - 21.3w/21.51w/21.59
WOODING Andrew U20 2.06.79, Colwyn Bay :
  LJ - 7.03
WOODS Alan P. V45 27.03.51, Birchfield :
  HT - 47.52 (57.24-78)
WOODS Christopher U17 27.01.80, Walton :
  400HY - 56.50
WOODS Philip U15, Mid Ulster :
  DTC - 37.46o
WOODWARD Lyndon U17 22.11.80, Cann & S :
  SPY - 14.46,
WOOLCOTT Nicholas D. 7.04.61, Haringey :
  DT - 49.84 (55.34-88)
WOOLLEY Barry U20 6.09.78, Burton :
  TJ - 13.90w/13.63
WORKMAN Eric U15, AF&D :
  JTB - 44.50
WRAY Simon U17 19.03.80, Oswestry :
  1.5kSt - 4:29.9
WREN Stephen U23, Cheltenham :
  HJ - 1.97
WRIGHT Darren U17 7.09.79, Wrexham :
  HJ - 1.95, LJ - 6.47, OctY - 4650
WRIGHT Finlay U17 7.02.81, Eton :
  100HY - 14.03w/14.2/14.36
WRIGHT Michael U20 15.09.77, Scarborough :
  HJ - 1.98 (2.00-94)
WRIGHT Simon U15 27.09.81, Hereford :
  200 - 23.70
WURR Simon U20 7.01.77, Leam/Durham Un :
  3k - 8:37.1, 2kSt - 5:56.9, 3kSt - 9:18.08
WURR Timothy U20 1.03.79, Leamington :
  HT - 46.88, HTJ - 54.22

WYLLIE William 12.07.73, Trafford :
  110H - 15.5w (14.91-92),
  LJ - 7.02 (7.33w-92/7.11-94)

Y AMBASU Aiah 10.11.73, Thames Valley :
  100 - 10.7
YAPP Jonathan U23 1.02.75, Telford :
  PV - 4.20 (4.50-94)
YATES Matthew Stewart 4.02.69, Belgrave :
  800 - 1:50.0 (1:45.05-92),
  1k - 2:20.97i (2:16.34-90),
  1500 - 3:42.60 (3:34.00-91),
YATES Peter Derek 15.06.57, Dacorum & Tr :
  JT - 67.14 (85.28-83)
YELLING Martin 7.02.72, Bedford & County :
  1500 - 3:47.6 (3:46.92-95),
  3k - 8:07.0, 3kSt - 9:06.24
YIANNACOU Andrew U20 18.08.78, Enfield :
  JT - 60.48
YOUNG Andrew U20 20.06.77, Victoria Park H/
  Loughbro : 800 - 1:50.25
YOUNG Colin U17 11.12.79, BH Mansfield :
  400 - 50.0 (52.13-95), 800 - 1:56.55
YOUNG Kerrin U17 2.09.79, North Down :
  400H - 56.2/58.05, 400HY - 54.8/55.31
YOUNG Martin 11.07.72, Roadhogs :
  3kW - 12:16.10i/12:26.61 (3:28.72-87),
  10kW - 43:39.0, 20kW - 1:29:48 (1:30:28.6t-95)
YOUNG Neil U20 20.02.77, Shaftesbury Barnet :
  PV - 5.00
YUSUF Yacin U20 20.12.77, Croydon :
  800 - 1:53.33, 1500 - 3:53.39 (3:53.0-95)

Z AIDMAN Antony Adam 18.03.62, Enf :
  SP - 15.88 (17.87i-83/17.22-81)
ZAREI James V50 12.01.44, Croydon :
  100kR - 7:58:55 (7:18:18-89)
ZAWADSKI Adam U23 19.12.74,
  Newquay & Par/Loughborough Studnts :
  800 - 1:52.7, 1500 - 3:45.7, 1M - 4:04.50
ZDANOWSKI Peter U20 3.01.78, Wycombe :
  LJ - 6.87w (6.70-95)

With the change of age group descriptions it is obvious that changes must be made to the names of the events. Whilst this is easy to organanize in the main lists, it is much more difficult with the index where a concise code is required. I have, therefore, decided to keep the previous descriptions of the events. This should not cause any confusion since the age group of each athlete is clearly shown in the new form eg U15 but some examples will clarify this.

A **J** after an event is used to designate an Under 20 event
eg 110HJ - 110 metres hurdles with 3'3" hurdles

A **Y** or an **I** is an Under 17 event (men and women)
eg 100HY - 100 metres hurdles with 3' 0" hurdles HeptI - Heptathlon with Under 17 implements

A **B** or a **G** is an Under 15 event (men and women)
eg JTB - 600 gram Javelin SPG - 3.25kg Shot

A **C** or an **M** is an Under 13 event (men and women)
eg SPC - 3.25kg Shot SPM - 2.72kg Shot

WOMENS INDEX

AARON Louise U15 19.04.82, Hull Spr :
  800 - 2:17.9, 1500 - 4:44.23
ABRAMS Angela 7.05.71, Belgrave :
  LJ - 5.69 (5.70-90)
ADAMS Claire 30.05.69, Bris (nee MORRISON) :
  PV - 3.30i/3.30 (3.40i/3.30-95)
ADAMS Clare 20.10.72, R Sutton Coldfield :
  100H - 15.03, 400H - 62.8/63.99
ADAMS Debbie U17 7.03.80, Newport :
  100 - 12.56
ADAMS Joyce U17 25.03.80, Birchfield :
  TJ - 11.32
ADAMS Leanda U17 7.12.79, City of Stoke :
  60H - 9.07i, 80HI - 11.62w/11.73, 300H - 46.3
ADAMS Rebecca 16.03.72, Bright (nee WISE) :
  400 - 57.3, 800 - 2:10.57
ADAMSON Samantha U15 27.03.82, Hert & W :
  HJ - 1.66, PenG - 2923
ADDO Roseline U17 7.06.80, Newbury :
  200 - 25.37w/25.60
AGYEPONG Jacqueline 5.01.69, Shaft Barnet :
  100 - 12.0 (11.7-94/11.72w-88/11.81-93),
  60H - 8.17i (8.01i-95), 100H - 13.18 (12.90-95)
AGYEPONG Mary Andray 3.10.65, Shaft B :
  TJ - 12.72 (13.56-92)
AIREY Lisa U17 19.12.80, Solihull & S Heath :
  3kW - 16:35.3 (16:33.0-95),
  3kWR - 16:02, 5kWR - 27:27
AKIM Ayamba 21.06.72, Herne Hill :
  HJ - 1.70
AKINBIYI Sarah U17 23.08.81, Tower Haml :
  60H - 8.91i, 80HI - 12.0/12.02, 300H - 44.01
AKIWUMI Tuvola U17 15.10.79, Hercules W :
  SP - 10.70 (11.09-95)
ALBERTS Emma U17 22.11.79, Gateshead :
  800 - 2:16.0 (2:14.64-94),
  1500 - 4:40.74i/4:43.6 (4:36.4-94)
ALDER Elizabeth U17 20.11.80, Severn :
  60 - 7.70i, 100 - 12.14w/12.18 (12.09-95),
  200 - 25.2 (25.63w-94), LJ - 5.40
ALEXANDER Katie U23 28.04.74, Shaft B :
  PV - 3.30
ALEXANDER Ross V45 21.07.47, Bournem'th :
  HT - 35.06
ALLAHGREEN Diane U23 21.02.75, Liv H :
  100 - 11.9/12.19 (11.7-94/11.78w/11.88-93),
  200 - 24.9 (24.39w-93/24.81-94),
  60H - 8.32i, 100H - 13.13w/13.27 (13.25-94)
ALLEN Angela 23.09.67, Keyham Plodders :
  HMar - 1:17:12
ALLEN Avril E. V35 1.08.59, Kimberley Str :
  Mar - 2:55:04
ALLEN Carice U20 25.09.77, Telford :
  HT - 36.24 (39.80-95)
ALLEN Jenna U20 2.05.79, Charnwood :
  JT - 43.64
ALLEN Sara 7.12.70, Sale :
  SP - 12.03 (12.65-95), DT - 39.56 (42.90-95)
ALLEN Sharon 23.10.68, Essex L :
  400H - 59.54 (58.98-90)
ALLEN Sheila V35 1.09.57, Houghton-le-Spr :
  HMar - 1:19:12
ALLEN Sophie U15 7.09.82, Ipswich :
  100 - 12.21w/12.40
ALLEYNE Petrina U17 10.07.81, Reading :
  100 - 12.17

ALLSOPP Catherine 30.11.73, Kettering :
  (see GREEN)
AMADI Onyema 28.06.73, Cardiff :
  JT - 48.34 (49.04-94)
AMEDE Christine F. 7.08.63, Windsor S & E :
  400 - 56.0/57.14i/57.45 (55.35-90), 400H - 60.31
AMOS Katie U20 13.11.78, Thurrock :
  JT - 43.78 (44.56-95)
ANDERSON Emma U20 19.06.79, Stoke :
  60H - 8.97i, 100H - 14.6/14.66w/14.72
ANDERSON Mary Caroline 2.09.67, City of E :
  SP - 12.86 (15.48-85), JT - 39.10 (49.08-87)
ANDERSON Melissa U15 30.03.82, Cram :
  100 - 12.27w/12.39, 200 - 25.6/25.78
ANDERSON Pamela U23 16.10.76, City of G :
  LJ - 5.67 (5.74-94), TJ - 12.55
ANDERSON Shani U23 7.08.75, Shaft Barnet :
  60 - 7.69i, 100 - 11.60, 200 - 24.39, TJ - 13.03
ANDREWS Denise U17 1.07.80, Birchfield :
  100 - 12.4/12.50w/12.53,
  200 - 25.30w/25.5, LJ - 5.43w/4.75
ANDREWS Nicola 11.06.70, Shaftesbury B :
  800 - 2:09.82
ANDREWS Sharon Nivan 4.07.67, Essex L :
  SP - 15.24 (15.80-93), DT - 52.10 (56.24-94)
ANDREWS Teresa U20 4.01.77, Preseli :
  HJ - 1.70 (1.79-94), LJ - 5.69w/5.21 (5.61-95),
  TJ - 11.13, SP - 11.23
ANDREWS Vicki 31.08.69, Wolves & B :
  800 - 2:10.9mx/2:11.2 (2:09.4-95),
  1500 - 4:33.8mx
ANETO Stephanie U20 23.08.77, Essex L :
  TJ - 11.74
ANIA Emma Candece U20 7.02.79, Shaft B :
  100 - 11.97w/12.05
ANNAN Charlotte Rebecca 13.03.70, Bury :
  100 - 12.1/12.12 (12.1/12.21w-92),
  200 - 24.77w/25.1/25.15 (25.0-89)
ANNESS Ruth U20 3.10.78, West Suffolk :
  PV - 2.45
ANSTEY Ann U17 14.11.80, Verlea :
  DT - 34.24
APIAFI Grace, :
  DT - 40.70
APPLETON Leanne U17 3.03.81, Bristol :
  3k - 10:25.76
ARCHER Claire U23 30.09.76, Mandale :
  SP - 11.34, JT - 38.28 (39.02-95)
ARKAAH Nicole U17 2.03.80, Trafford :
  1500 - 4:44.7
ARMISHAW Helen U17 4.10.80, Sale :
  LJ - 5.59w/5.57
ARMSTRONG K., :
  Mar - 3:02:36
ARMSTRONG Kirsty U17 14.05.80, Woking :
  PV - 3.00
ARNOLD Helen U20 5.10.78, Portsmouth :
  SP - 11.98 (12.16-94), HT - 50.62
ARNOLD Zoe U23 10.11.76, Lagan Valley :
  400 - 56.32
ASH Sally U17 4.11.80, Norwich :
  TJ - 10.61
ASHBY Abigail U20 23.11.77, Rowntrees :
  100H - 14.76, Hep - 4474 (4466-95)
ASHCROFT Tracy U23 4.07.76, Jarrow & H :
  400 - 56.81, 800 - 2:07.7

368

ASHDOWN Sarah U13 18.10.83, Beds & Co :
LJ - 4.72, JTM - 31.50
ASHLEY Susan E. V40 10.10.52, Epsom & E :
Mar - 3:07:45 (2:57:49-90)
ATKINSON Rachel 26.05.73, Sale/Leeds Univ :
TJ - 12.20w/11.66 (11.82-94)
ATUNUMUO Lucy U17 4.11.80, Hercules Wim :
60 - 7.8i, 100 - 12.33, 200 - 25.4, LJ - 5.66
AUCOTT Jane Christine 10.10.68, Cov G :
SP - 11.85 (12.99i-86/12.89-93),
DT - 43.76 (55.52-90)
AUGEE Esther 1.01.64, Essex L :
SP - 11.60 (11.73-94), HT - 50.72 (56.76-93)
AUGEE Myrtle Sharon Mary 4.02.65, Bromley :
SP - 16.81 (19.03-90), DT - 44.32 (49.44-95),
HT - 44.30 (46.64-95)
AUSTIN Elizabeth 22.02.72, Warrington :
JT - 38.60 (40.70-91)
AUSTIN Kerren U23 26.02.75, Bedford & Co :
PV - 2.40 (2.50-93)
AXTEN Tracy 20.07.63, Hounslow :
SP - 14.76 (14.90-95), DT - 55.88
AYERO Jennifer U17 13.09.79, Ealing,S & Mx :
HT - 32.80, JT - 38.62
AYLING Amanda 4.04.65, Parkside :
5k - 17:17.4, 10kR - 34:19

B ACKHOUSE Susan U17 6.12.78, Leeds :
DT - 42.58
BAIGENT Sarah 22.12.71, Reading :
400H - 65.2 (62.5-90/62.92-94)
BAILEY Emma U15 21.06.82, Braintree :
DT - 30.32
BAILEY Jane 5.05.70, Middlesbro & C :
PV - 2.45
BAILEY Kelli U17 8.09.79, Telford :
60 - 7.84i, 100 - 11.99w/12.1/12.17
BAILEY Rebecca U15 8.01.82, Cornwall AC :
JT - 36.88
BAILEY Serena U17 2.01.81, Essex L :
80HI - 11.79w/11.8/11.99, 300H - 46.78
BAIRD Kim V40 28.02.56, Dudley & Stourbr :
(see BRAZNELL)
BAIRD Kirsty 29.08.71, City of Glasgow :
800 - 2:12.62
BAKER Helen U20 5.02.79, Exeter :
TJ - 11.55w/11.38, Hep - 3948
BAKER Nicola U23 8.10.74, Gateshead :
HJ - 1.70 (1.77-95)
BAKER Rosalind U20 10.04.78, Crawley :
400 - 57.5/57.51
BALL Melissa U15 16.09.81, Gloucester L :
JT - 35.50
BANNER Clare U15 25.04.82, Guildford & G :
HJ - 1.60,
BANNON Barbara 25.04.70, Cornwall AC :
PV - 2.70un/2.50 (2.60-95)
BARBER Carol U13 1.09.83, Swindon :
HJ - 1.50
BARKER Hazel A. V35 6.08.59, Leeds :
Hep - 3918 (4190-87)
BARNES Alison 6.11.69, Bournemouth :
3k - 9:39.1 (9:09.1-92)
BARNES Catherine U20 28.09.77, Winch :
TJ - 11.18 (11.49-95)
BARNES Charlene U15 25.05.82, R Sutton C :
200 - 25.28w/26.49

BARNETT Emma U17 9.12.80, Sale :
100 - 12.37w/13.2 (12.9-95)
BARNETT Lynne U23 12.08.74, Perth :
SP - 11.81i/11.41 (12.83-93)
BARRINGTON Suzanne 3.08.71, Camb Univ/
City of Stoke : 400H - 62.8/63.57
BARRON Rachel U23 10.05.76, Wolves & B :
LJ - 5.64
BARTLETT Katherine 6.05.73, Shaftesbury B :
60H - 8.98i, 400H - 60.9/61.63 (61.54-94),
100H - 14.5w/14.7/15.19w (14.54-94)
BASU Monica U17 7.09.79, St Albans :
PV - 2.30,
BATEMAN Victoria 6.09.72, City of Stoke :
DT - 37.62 (40.42-91)
BATER Tracey, Team Solent :
HT - 34.42
BATES Rebecca U15 16.05.82, City of Stoke :
LJ - 5.46w/5.26
BATESON Alicia U13 6.11.83, Wycombe :
200 - 27.6
BATHO Louise U23 27.11.76, Thurrock :
100H - 14.49, SP - 11.85 (11.88-94),
JT - 39.20, Hep - 5114
BEALES Emma Jay 7.12.71, Milton Keynes :
100H - 14.59w/14.7 (14.31-95),
HJ - 1.71 (1.76-92), SP - 14.43 (14.53-92),
LJ - 5.60 (6.20w?/5.99-92),
DT - 50.70 (54.68-95), JT - 42.54
BEATTIE Sarah U17 30.11.79, Perth :
800 - 2:15.68io, 1500 - 4:40.3
BEATTIE Sharon 26.11.72, Border :
PV - 2.40
BECKINGSALE Elizabeth U17 20.03.80, Norw :
PV - 2.80
BECKINGSALE Sarah U20, Cardiff :
PV - 2.30
BEECROFT Alice 25.05.73, Wakefield :
800 - 2:09.2
BELCHER Gemma U13 22.10.83, Wolves & B :
75 - 10.1, 80 - 10.9, 100 - 13.2, 150 - 20.0
BELL Laura U13 16.11.83, Hamps Sch :
80 - 11.0w
BELL Sarah U13 20.09.83, Parkside :
800 - 2:27.9
BELLE Symone U13 12.11.84, Tower Haml :
70HM - 11.8, HJ - 1.50
BEMROSE Antonia Marie U17 3.09.79, AF&D :
HJ - 1.76
BENNETT Carol U20 11.01.77, Hull Spring :
SP - 13.62i/13.19, DT - 37.76
BENNETT Christina Jayne U20 27.02.78, E & E :
SP - 13.70, DT - 40.38, HT - 43.52
BENNETT Diana Faye U23 14.06.74, E & E :
100H - 14.63 (14.47-94), HJ - 1.76i/1.76,
LJ - 6.04, SP - 11.51, Hep - 5332
BENNETT Gemma U13 4.01.84, Loughton :
75 - 10.2, 100 - 13.0, 150 - 20.1, 200 - 27.6
BENNETT Julia Margaret 26.03.70, E & E :
60H - 8.86i,
100H - 14.43w/14.7/14.85 (14.74-95),
400H - 63.9 (62.2-94/62.81-95),
HJ - 1.88i/1.88 (1.92i-90/1.89-94),
LJ - 6.05w/6.01i/5.96 (6.12-94),
SP - 11.99, Hep - 5747w/5356 (5496-95)
BENNETT Sarah U17 27.07.80, Birchfield :
3kW - 14:39.24i/14:56.10, 3kWR - 14:34,
5kW - 25:50.10, 10kWR - 55:51o

369

BENNINGTON Lisa U20 12.12.78, Grimsby :
   HJ - 1.70,
BENTLEY Sarah 21.05.67, Birchfield :
   800 - 2:09.63 (2:08.2-95), 1500 - 4:22.3,
   3k - 9:04.4 (9:10.9mx-95),
   5k - 16:23.86 (15:53.86-95), 10kR - 33:30
BERGIERS Amy U17 19.09.79, Carmarthen :
   60H - 9.26i, 80HI - 12.0/12.25 (12.19w-95)
BERMINGHAM Orla U23 7.10.75, Essex L :
   60H - 8.9i (8.54i-95),
   100H - 14.6 (13.8w-95/13.87w-94/13.93-95)
BERRY Catherine U23 8.10.75, Kingston & P :
   3k - 9:33.03 (9:25.86-94)
BERRY Jayne N. 18.07.70, Cardiff :
   SP - 13.88 (15.09-93)
BEVAN Adele U13 26.03.84, Crawley :
   150 - 20.2, 200 - 27.3, 600 - 1:41.5,
   800 - 2:23.6, 1500 - 5:05.5
BEVAN Susan F. V35 15.12.59, Essex L :
   1500 - 4:32.55i (4:19.-86)
BEVERLEY Rachael U20 23.07.79, Mandale :
   HT - 49.52
BIGGS Sarah U13 16.12.83, Peterborough :
   75 - 10.2,
BISCOE Anna U17 13.09.79, Southend :
   HJ - 1.68 (1.70-95)
BISHOP Tracy U20 1.05.79, Parkside :
   200 - 24.87w/25.38 (24.92-95)
BLACK Caroline E. 19.05.72, Edinburgh WM :
   LJ - 6.00 (6.03w-91/6.00-92)
BLACK Gillian U17 27.10.79, City of Glasgow :
   HJ - 1.70
BLACK Sylvia V35 16.04.58, Birchfield :
   3kW - 14:23.50 (13:42.10-90),
   5kWR - 24:26 (23:13-93)
BLACKBURN Caroline 6.08.71, Essex L :
   400H - 63.5/63.78
BLAKE Meredith 20.10.67, Serpentine :
   Mar - 2:55:56
BLANCHARD Helen 11.07.72, City of Stoke :
   100H - 14.8/15.02 (14.7-94)
BLANK Paula U20 13.12.77, Verlea :
   JT - 45.20
BLEACH Jeanette V45 22.06.48, Steyning :
   50kW - 5:43:14
BLEASDALE Julia U15 9.09.81, Hillingdon :
   800 - 2:19.1
BLOOMFIELD Christine 12.02.68, Essex L :
   60 - 7.63i, 100 - 11.69w/11.71 (11.59-93),
   200 - 24.0/24.08w/24.17 (23.70-93),
   TJ - 11.15 (11.47-94)
BLOOMFIELD Tracey U17 13.09.79, Guild & G :
   PV - 3.00
BLOXSOME Anna 17.04.73, Cheltenham :
   JT - 45.48 (48.60-91)
BODEN Veronica V. V35 23.12.58, Trafford :
   400 - 57.2/57.61 (55.1-87/55.50-94),
   400H - 60.28 (58.8-87/59.53-78),
   LJ - 5.53 (5.89w-77/5.78-78)
BOLSOVER Maria Teresa U17 5.06.80, Hallam :
   100 - 12.0/12.27w (12.47-94),
   200 - 25.53 (24.58w-94/24.80-95),
   300 - 39.3/39.32 (38.95-95),
   300H - 46.4 (44.7-95)
BOLT Susan, South West RR :
   Mar - 3:08:04 (3:07:32-92)

BOLTON Denise U20 1.02.77, Wigan :
   100 - 12.04w/12.19, 60H - 8.66i,
   200 - 25.23 (25.00-94/25.15w-95),
   100H - 13.7w/13.95, LJ - 5.77 (5.81-93)
BOLTON Laura U20 13.11.78, Thames Valley :
   HJ - 1.68,
BOLTON Laura U20 22.01.79, Newquay & P :
   Hep - 3861
BONNER Angela 22.11.73, Cardiff :
   HT - 47.70
BOTHAMS Valerie U23 19.03.75, City of Glas :
   1500 - 4:29.69 (4:28.2-95)
BOUCHARD Sarah U23 23.10.74, Trafford :
   800 - 2:09.6mx/2:10.3 (2:08.94-93)
BOURNE Christina 24.09.69, Team Solent :
   800 - 2:10.8
BOWEN Shelley-Anne U20 12.05.79, Reading :
   60 - 7.7i (7.83i-95), 100 - 11.89w/11.95,
   200 - 25.1/25.51 (25.1/25.29-95)
BOWRING Faye U15 22.10.81, Bournemouth :
   JT - 36.02
BOWRING Nicole U23 27.01.74, Tonbridge :
   400 - 56.46
BOWYER Elizabeth U15 8.09.81, Wirral :
   SPG - 12.21
BOWYER Sonya 18.09.72, Sale/Loughbro :
   800 - 2:02.12 (2:01.67-95), 1k - 2:39.80,
   1500 - 4:10.7mx/4:17.4, 1M - 4:39.90
BRACKSTONE Lorraine U20 15.02.78, Stoke :
   100H - 14.3w/14.78
BRADBURY Sarah 25.02.63, AF&D :
   10kR - 33:09sh (34:15-95)
BRADLEY Joanna U20 23.08.79, Ashford :
   DT - 42.66
BRADLEY Lynne 21.05.67, Sheffield RWC :
   3kW - 15:23.0, 5kW - 27:03.88,
   5kWR - 26:20, 10kW - 56:00.3,
   10kWR - 53:54, 20kW - 1:55:00
BRADLEY Maria 2.01.63, Overton :
   10MR - 57:51
BRADLEY Melanie 12.03.63, Army/AF&D :
   10MR - 57:51, HMar - 1:10:04,
   Mar - 3:03:21 (2:52:22-92)
BRADLEY Shelley 24.11.72, Trafford :
   HJ - 1.70 (1.75-89)
BRADSHAW Noelle E. 18.12.63, Portsm Fare :
   PV - 2.30i, SP - 11.46 (12.26-95),
   JT - 47.86 (52.40-93)
BRADSHAW Victoria U17 10.12.80, Ipswich :
   HJ - 1.64
BRAITHWAITE Kamila U17 26.01.81, Croy :
   300 - 40.78
BRANNAN Lesley U23 13.09.76, Wrexham :
   SP - 11.83 (12.10-95), HT - 47.08
BRANNEY Sandra V40 30.04.54, City of Glas :
   10MR - 58:50 (54:05dh-91/55:26-89),
   HMar - 1:16:07 (1:12:22-86),
   Mar - 2:46:19 (2:35:03-89)
BRAZIER Tanya U17 14.11.80, Steve & N H :
   800 - 2:14.5, 1500 - 4:37.8
BRAZNELL Kim V40 28.02.56, Dudley & Stour
   (nee BAIRD) : 10kW - 50:52.3,
   10kWR - 50:45 (49:39-95)
BREENS Felicity J. U15 6.11.81, Leics Cor :
   75HG - 11.46w/11.6/11.62
BRENNAN Faye U13 13.05.84, Worthing :
   SPM - 10.52

370

BRETHERWICK Angela 2.04.67, Bingley
(nee COATES) : 800 - 2:11.99 (2:06.9-88)
BREW Sarah U17 9.01.81, Preseli :
3k - 10:16.87
BREWER Nadia U17 14.04.80, Blackheath :
HJ - 1.65 (1.66-94), LJ - 5.58
BREWINGTON Kate U15 15.10.81, Havering :
LJ - 5.25
BRIGGS Julie 13.03.69, Crawley :
10kR - 34:55
BRIGGS Susan 26.03.67, Trafford :
100 - 12.1/12.26
(11.6w-85/11.8-88/11.82w-89/12.00-93),
200 - 24.50 (24.02i-92/24.1/24.17w-89/24.18-94),
400 - 55.94
BRIGHT Jane V45 24.03.50, Maidstone :
Mar - 3:05:45 (3:02:36-95)
BRIGHT Kathryn U23 27.03.76, Newport :
400 - 56.17, 800 - 2:11.9 (2:10.80-93)
BRITTON Nicola U13, West Norfolk :
HJ - 1.46, SPM - 9.13
BROOK Katherine U20 15.06.79, Bingley :
3kW - 16:19.07, 5kW - 27:41.97,
5kWR - 27:09
BROOKE Ruth U13 2.09.83, Reading :
75 - 10.1, HJ - 1.48
BROOKER Jessica U17 6.01.81, Exeter :
JT - 38.42
BROOKES Heather U17 17.07.81, Buxton :
200 - 25.29w/26.04
BROOKS Ann 4.05.71, City of Hull :
60 - 7.70i (7.69i-95),
100 - 11.97 (11.8w-94/11.91-95),
200 - 24.5, LJ - 6.10 (6.38w-94/6.16-95)
BROW Kelly U20 24.09.78, Bingley :
TJ - 11.37w/11.24
BROWN Amanda U23 11.05.75, Stamford & D :
PV - 2.40, JT - 40.78 (43.50-95), Hep - 3900
BROWN Celia U20 22.01.77, Chelmsford :
400H - 65.7/66.25 (63.67-94)
BROWN Donna U17 1.05.81, Cannock & Staff :
1500 - 4:42.0,
BROWN Jennifer A. V35 21.05.59, Ashford :
HJ - 1.72 (1.73-89), TJ - 11.43,
Hep - 4672 (4803w-89/4757-90)
BROWN Karen Louise 31.08.68, Sale :
HT - 42.70 (47.10-93)
BROWN Lisa U23 16.03.76, Edinburgh WM :
HJ - 1.65 (1.81-95),
TJ - 11.60i (11.96w/11.91-95)
BROWN Sandra V45 1.04.49, Surrey WC :
24HrT - 212.701km (199.278km-95),
3kW - 15:06.2, 5kWR - 25:36 (25:02-92),
20kW - 1:48:46 (1:48:29-91),
100MW - 19:42:53 (18:50:29-92)
BROWN Sarah A. 28.09.64, Steyning :
3kW - 15:27.0 (13:48.0-87),
5kWR - 27:28 (23:57-87)
BROWNHILL Kelly U17 27.03.80, Trafford :
800 - 2:11.4,
BRUCE Jill 25.07.73, Dromore/IRE :
1500 - 4:24.78 (4:20.18-95),
3k - 9:34.2 (9:22.6-95), 5k - 17:07.8,
10kR - 34:39 (33:59-95)
BRUCE Joanne U20 26.10.78, Woking :
JT - 41.52
BRUNNING Louise 6.03.72, Sutt & D/Loughbro :
200 - 24.2w (24.7-95), 400H - 56.61

BRYAN Emma, Notts :
HJ - 1.65
BUCHANAN Lesley U15 15.11.81, East Kilb :
HJ - 1.66,
BUCKINGHAM P., Guernsey :
Mar - 3:07:36
BUCKLAND Sadie U17 11.03.80, Braintree :
SP - 10.53
BUDD Katie J. U23 3.01.76, Shaftesbury B :
TJ - 11.19, Hep - 4499 (4620-95)
BULL Sarah U23 4.06.75, Derby LAC :
800 - 2:09.82, 1500 - 4:23.59, 1M - 4:46.71
BULLEN Kate 12.02.71, Birchfield :
400H - 65.0 (64.11-95)
BULLOCK Sarah U15 6.12.81, Middlesbro & C :
75HG - 11.8/11.83
BURFOOT Erica U15 28.12.81, Cardiff :
100 - 12.4/12.47, 200 - 25.22
BURGE Kate, Staffs H :
HMar - 1:18:57
BURKE Olive C. 12.09.66, Croydon/IRE :
100H - 14.5/14.81 (14.50-95)
BURKE Sarah 11.07.73, Bracknell :
400H - 65.9 (62.52-93)
BURNETT Claire 17.10.72, City of Plymouth :
SP - 11.91 (12.35-95), HT - 43.02
BURNETT Judith A. V35 14.10.58, C of Bath :
Mar - 3:05:56 (2:51:21dh-94/2:51:33-91)
BURNS Gillian 12.07.64, Wirral :
SP - 12.23 (12.96-90)
BURNS Jane U13 7.02.84, Basildon :
1500 - 5:03.7
BURNS-SALMOND Samantha U23 13.04.76,
Trafford : HT - 49.80
BURNSIDE Susan U17 3.02.80, Edinburgh WM :
100 - 12.4/12.42, 200 - 25.27
BURROWS Catherine U23 11.02.76, Wigan :
LJ - 5.60,
TJ - 11.50i/11.38 (11.79w/11.72i/11.69-95)
BURTHEN Jane 13.12.62, Warrington :
Mar - 3:08:05
BURTON Amy U20 24.06.77, Notts :
SP - 11.40
BURTON Carly U17 14.10.80, Ashford :
DT - 38.28
BURTON Joanna U23 11.05.75, Dorchester :
JT - 45.52 (52.14-94)
BUSHBY Clare U23 7.09.76, Sale :
100H - 14.6/14.98 (14.3w/14.37w/14.58-95)
BUTLER Keeley U23 24.03.75, Coventry G/
Loughbro : 100 - 12.01,
200 - 24.8/24.87w/24.95 (24.4w/24.45-93)
BUTLER Lucy U15 18.11.81, Gateshead :
LJ - 5.50
BUTLER Natalie U20 25.11.78, Windsor S & E :
TJ - 11.07i/11.04
BUXTON Leanne U20 27.05.78, Brighton :
100H - 14.77, 400H - 63.03, Hep - 4466

CADMAN Joanna 1.06.68, Edinburgh WM :
400H - 64.43 (60.7/61.06-93)
CAINES Vanessa U15 17.04.83, Steyning :
2.5kW - 13:03.37, 3kW - 16:13.1
CAINS Rhian U17 29.10.80, Telford :
300 - 40.88
CAIRNS Lindsay 1.06.71, Kilmarnock :
5k - 17:23.39, 10k - 35:27.77,
HMar - 1:18:38

371

CALCUTT Kirsty U17 26.08.80, Wells :
PV - 2.30i
CALDER Fiona 4.05.71, City of Glasgow :
(see HOLLIMAN)
CALLAN Lisa U17 10.10.80, City of Glasgow :
60 - 7.99i, 100 - 12.4 (12.47w/12.93-95),
200 - 25.32
CALLANIN Elaine V35 13.09.60, Solihull & SH :
5kW - 26:09.6 (24:09.66-95)
CALLAWAY Deborah A. 15.07.64, AF&D :
SP - 14.48 (14.88-93), DT - 58.56, HT - 44.64
CALLOW Danaa L. 16.10.70, Sale :
60 - 7.40i, 100 - 11.9/11.94 (11.58w/11.60-94),
200 - 24.8/25.08 (24.2-94/24.86-92)
CALVERT Ruth U23 22.10.75, Bingley :
Hep - 4344 (4068-93)
CAMBRIDGE Jacqueline 17.11.63, Sale :
400H - 64.0/64.96 (59.88-91)
CAMERON Claire V35 3.10.58, C of Glasgow :
DT - 42.58 (46.34-85), HT - 34.20
CAMPBELL Clare U17 21.10.80, Steve & NH :
3k - 10:15.3
CAMPBELL Katrina 8.03.72, Lisburn :
JT - 44.24 (45.02-95)
CAMPBELL Louise U20 22.02.79, Lagan V :
HT - 42.32
CAMPBELL Michelle 24.02.69, Essex L :
100H - 13.3/13.61w/13.80 (13.08w-95/13.26-90)
CAMPBELL Natasha U15 6.08.82, Medway :
JT - 36.14
CAMPBELL Samantha U15, Dartford :
2.5kW - 13:11.62, 3kWR - 16:03
CANK Elaine U17 5.12.79, Telford :
SP - 10.76, DT - 37.76
CANNING Kimberley U15 2.08.82, Law & Dist :
100 - 12.47, 200 - 24.9/25.07
CANNING Leona U17 12.04.80, Garscube :
TJ - 10.64w/10.61
CANNON Kim U15 27.07.82, Basildon :
SPG - 10.99
CARDY-WISE Bronwyn G. V40 26.01.52,
Broms & R : HMar. - 1:17:07 (1:14:06-86)
CARISS Susan V45 17.11.49, Bingley :
Mar - 3:06:36
CARLESS Tammy U20 10.01.77, Braintree :
JT - 45.62
CARLIN Yvette U17 28.05.80, Rugby :
300H - 46.3, LJ - 5.56, Hepl - 4318
CARNEY Ruth 12.10.68, Lisburn :
(see MAYO)
CARPENTER Emma U15 16.05.82, Exeter :
DT - 39.36
CARR Alison 30.08.66, Dundee HH :
3k - 9:59.5, 5k - 16:52.61
CARR Anne U23 1.05.76, City of Stoke :
Hep - 4370 (4526-95)
CARROLL Hanna U15 19.09.81, Liverpool H :
200 - 25.7/25.73w/26.36
CARTER Alexandra U17 1.04.80, Vale Royal :
800 - 2:13.4mx, 1500 - 4:40.14
CARTER Bronwin A. V45 25.04.51, Portsm F :
SP - 12.24 (13.89-84)
CARTER Lucy U20 7.03.78, Bedford & Co :
200 - 24.6/25.06 (24.4/24.55-95), 400 - 57.4
CARTLIDGE Krista U13 8.12.83, Brighton :
600 - 1:42.6, 800 - 2:26.4, PenM - 2317
CARVILLE Maria 8.12.73, Hillingdon :
800 - 2:12.5 (2:08.73-95), 1500 - 4:28.1

CASHELL Gillian 5.04.64, Team Solent :
400 - 55.75 (54.35-94), 800 - 2:09.15
CEESAY Amina U17 19.11.79, Newham & EB :
100 - 12.4, 300 - 40.88
CEESAY Nusrat U17 18.03.81, Newham & EB :
300H - 44.87
CHALLONER Katie U20 18.09.78, Telford :
400H - 66.0
CHAMBERLAIN Eleanor U20 17.04.79, Birch :
400H - 63.85
CHAMBERLAIN Rebecca U17 7.09.79,
Bournemouth : SP - 10.77 (11.20-95)
CHAMBERS Christine A. 4.03.69, Derby LAC :
100 - 12.27w (11.68w-92/11.75w-88)
CHAMPION Fay 27.09.66, Yate :
SP - 12.14 (13.30-95),
DT - 40.56 (44.64-95), HT - 38.44
CHARLES Ayeesha U17 4.09.79, Oxford City :
60 - 7.85i (7.73i-94), 300 - 40.4/40.99,
100 - 12.4 (12.2-94/12.44-95)
CHARNOCK Catherine U23 3.05.75, Barr & F :
3kW - 14:05.5 (14:28.25-95),
5kW - 25:00.22, 5kWR - 24:12, 10kWR - 52:42
CHARNOCK Kathryn 4.07.62, Wigan Phoenix :
Mar - 2:59:56
CHATFIELD Donna U15 15.09.81, Guild & G :
75HG - 11.7/11.88
CHATTING Donna U13 30.10.83, Soton City :
150 - 20.1, 200 - 27.60, LJ - 4.78
CHESNEY Sarah 3.03.73, Essex L :
60 - 7.7i/7.77i (7.65i-94)
CHEVERTON Dinah 24.03.65, Newport :
10MR - 58:48
CHILD Amanda U15 28.11.81, Milton Keynes :
800 - 2:16.92
CHILDS Claire 8.10.72, Coventry RWC :
(see WALKER)
CHURCH Lynsey U17 10.05.80, Victoria Pk .
LJ - 5.46
CLAGUE Jennifer 6.08.73, Liverpool H :
3k - 9:58.4 (9:21.54-93)
CLARK A. U13, Hallamshire :
150 - 19.8
CLARK Annette V35 4.05.61, S London :
Mar - 3:08:37
CLARK Jean 5.10.68, Edinburgh WM :
HT - 47.18 (50.12-95)
CLARK Joanna 11.02.73, AF&D :
100 - 11.9w?/12.06, 200 - 24.3/24.61
CLARK Katie U13 30.09.83, Copeland :
800 - 2:27.0
CLARK Lyndsey U15 28.11.81, Pendle :
PenG - 2869
CLARK Natalie U15 4.09.82, Hull Springhead :
HJ - 1.60
CLARK Vicki U17 23.09.80, Invicta :
DT - 35.28, HT - 40.08
CLARKE Dyanna V35 27.02.58, Thames VH :
400 - 57.1 (52.98-79), 400H - 64.2 (62.9-94)
CLARKE Jenny V40 19.10.52, Peterborough :
HT - 35.40 (36.08-94)
CLARKE Marilyn V45 3.06.50, Wimbledon :
Mar - 3:06:51
CLARKE Rhian U20 19.04.77, Essex L :
PV - 3.70

CLAXTON Sarah U17 23.09.79, Colchester & T :
  60 - 7.63i, 60H - 9.1i (8.88i-95),
  100 - 11.7w/12.1/12.24
      (11.88w-94/12.0-95/12.19-94),
  80HI - 11.6w/11.8 (11.5/11.57-95),
  100H - 14.7, HJ - 1.65i (1.65-95),
  LJ - 6.34w/6.24
CLAYDON Emma Jayne U17 1.06.80, Med :
  JT - 38.02 (39.78-95)
CLEMENTS Hayley D. 17.09.68, Dartford :
  100 - 12.1/12.25 (11.77-85),
  200 - 24.43 (23.4w-85/23.8/23.90-86),
  400 - 56.23 (54.62-94)
CLEMENTS Lucy U20 20.07.78, Solihull & SH :
  TJ - 11.76
CLEMENTS Melinda U20 20.05.77, W S & E :
  TJ - 11.28
CLETHRO Danielle-Louise U15 13.03.82, Roth :
  200 - 25.90w/26.64
CLIFF Jennifer U17 9.05.81, Peterborough :
  3k - 10:33.2
CLIFT Holly U15 29.11.81, Basingstoke & MH :
  HJ - 1.64
COATES Angela 2.04.67, Bingley :
  (see BRETHERWICK)
COATES Nichola U15 24.03.82, Cramlington :
  800 - 2:19.1 (2:18.1-95),
  1500 - 4:38.6 (4:37.7-95)
COATS Maria U15 4.10.81, Guildford & G :
  SPG - 10.64
COBB Nicola 2.11.71, Windsor S & E :
  JT - 43.38
COCKCROFT Jody U13 14.09.83, Hamps Sch :
  DTM - 23.80
COCKRAM Julia 1.01.68, Belgrave :
  PV - 2.90i/2.85 (2.90i-95)
CODD Danielle U20 17.02.79, Trafford :
  PV - 3.00
COHEN Paula 5.02.71, Trafford :
  60 - 7.73i, 200 - 24.57w/24.6/24.67 (23.64-92),
  100 - 12.1w/12.11 (11.6-94/11.63-93)
COLDWELL Dominique U17 6.09.79, Hull Ach :
  300 - 41.0/41.97
COLEBROOK Christine 'Teena' V40 18.12.56,
  Peterbro : 800 - 2:08.32 (2:01.65-84),
  1500 - 4:24.5 (4:07.69-90)
COLEBY Julie V40 5.11.55, Durham :
  10k - 35:18.43, 10MR - 56:19 (55:57-82),
  HMar - 1:17:48
COLEMAN Hannah U13 26.09.83, Ipswich :
  70HM - 11.6
COLLERAN Joanne 1.09.72, Liverpool H :
  800 - 2:11.3 (2:11.3mx-95),
  1500 - 4:28.42 (4:32.0mx-95)
COLLINS Carmen 6.11.73, Ealing,S & M/Army :
  (see MICHAELSKA)
COLLISON Gabrielle 10.02.66, Belgrave :
  10kR - 34:44 (34:32-95)
COLMER Claire U17 13.05.80, Bexley :
  3k - 10:34.4
COLQUHOUN Heather U17 14.04.80, Vict Pk:
  300H - 46.69
CONNEELY Vivienne U23 4.01.76, Neath :
  5k - 17:25.93
CONNELLY Lucy U17 7.11.80, City of Hull :
  TJ - 10.63
CONNOLLY Anne U20 18.02.78, Skyrac :
  1500 - 4:32.5, 3k - 9:55.8mx/10:08.57

CONNOLLY Lisa U15 27.09.81, Liverpool H :
  75HG - 11.49w/11.61
COOK Louise U13 7.01.84, West Norfolk :
  70HM - 11.7, 75HG - 12.6,
  LJ - 4.82, PenG - 2260
COOK Lucy U23 11.09.75, Croydon :
  JT - 38.38 (45.58-94)
COOK Stephanie 7.02.72, Oxford Univ :
  2kSt - 7:12.84
COOKE Frances V40 8.12.56, Thorney :
  Mar - 3:05:28 (3:04:41-94)
COOKE Jacqueline U23 20.06.76, Rotherham :
  100H - 15.1/15.15 (14.9-95/14.96w-93/15.14-94),
  400H - 63.9/66.55 (65.15-95)
COOMBES Wendy Jane 9.02.68, Salisbury :
  (see WILLIAMS)
COOMER Louise U17 5.10.80, :
  SP - 10.50
COOPER Jennifer 1.09.62, Wolves & B
  (nee HOPE) : DT - 40.62 (43.94-90)
COOPER Louise J. U23 25.08.75, Rossendale :
  HMar - 1:18:43
COOPER Stephanie U15 16.09.82, Peterbro :
  PV - 2.10
COORE Andrea 23.04.69, Essex L :
  100 - 11.8/12.18 (12.17-89),
  LJ - 6.03 (6.26w/6.14-89)
COPELAND Teresa Jayne 8.03.69, Ashford :
  60H - 8.9i (8.88i-91),
  100H - 14.3/14.57 (14.03-93),
  400H - 64.25 (61.92-93), PV - 2.40,
  LJ - 5.54 (5.96-90), Hep - 4664 (5050-90)
CORBETT Kirsty U15 16.05.82, Ilford :
  LJ - 5.25
CORBETT L. U13, Leigh :
  HJ - 1.47
CORLETT Janet 31.07.63, Leamington :
  HT - 36.34
CORNEBY Hannah U17 22.01.81, Cann & St :
  DT - 33.96
CORRAN Elizabeth V40 23.09.55, Manx H :
  3kW - 14:15.0 (14:11.1-95), 5kW - 24:40.91,
  5kWR - 25:19 (24:51-95),
  10kW - 51:17.1 (51:03.0-95),
  10kWR - 51:37 (51:34-95), 20kW - 1:47:10
COSTELLO Karen 21.10.68, C of G/Heriot W :
  SP - 11.95 (12.64-94), JT - 50.96 (54.50-94)
COUPER Claire U15 29.04.82, Falkirk :
  800 - 2:19.3,
COURT Clova V35 10.02.60, Birchfield :
  100 - 11.98
      (11.5w-90/11.55w-95/11.6-87/11.69-95),
  200 - 23.8w/23.94w/24.22i (23.57-90),
  60H - 8.20i (8.12i-94),
  100H - 13.3w/13.6/13.65 (13.04-94),
  SP - 13.31 (14.23-93), JT - 45.26 (55.30-91)
COUSINS Dawn 16.03.68, Basildon :
  100 - 12.23 (11.9-89/12.00-90),
  200 - 25.1 (24.1-89/24.40w-95/24.49-91)
COX Maureen V45 7.09.50, Manx H :
  10kWR - 57:26 (56:08-95)
COX Nicola U20 18.08.77, Rotherham :
  JT - 38.16 (39.64-94)
COX Rachael U17 27.06.80, Birchfield :
  DT - 35.90, HT - 40.56
COX Wendy U17 1.09.79, Gateshead :
  100 - 12.2 (12.44w/12.56-95),
  200 - 24.38w/24.7/24.80 (24.66-95)

COZENS Chloe U17 9.04.80, Bedford & Co :
80HI - 12.0/12.29, HJ - 1.79, LJ - 5.59,
JT - 39.12, Hepl - 4746
COZENS Joanne U17 9.04.80, Bedford & Co :
LJ - 5.44, TJ - 10.89w/10.78,
Hepl - 4311w/4167
CRANE Julie U23 26.09.76, Notts :
HJ - 1.73 (1.81-94)
CRANNIS Sadie U13 8.10.83, Swindon :
1500 - 5:06.4
CRAWFORD Zoe U23 1.03.75, City of Hull :
400 - 56.8
CRAWLEY Susan U13 1.12.83, Solihull & S H :
HJ - 1.50io/1.47
CRESSWELL Lois U17 12.01.81, R Sutton C :
300 - 40.78
CRISPEY Susan U17 8.01.81, Bedford & Co :
3k - 10:18.4
CROCKER Linda U20 2.04.79, Huntingdon :
400H - 65.7/67.57
CROMPTON Mandy U15 25.03.82, Radcliffe :
LJ - 5.26w/5.09
CROOKS Karen U23 15.01.75, Thurrock :
PV - 2.40
CROSBY Nicole U23 23.10.76, Bingley :
200 - 24.99w/25.16
CROSKELL Helen 22.11.72, Tonbridge :
PV - 2.50, TJ - 11.05
CROSLAND Claire U17 10.01.80, Skyrac :
300 - 40.32
CROWLE Sharon L. U17 6.09.80, Newq & P :
80HI - 12.0/12.22, TJ - 10.50
CROWTHER-PRICE Kimberley 19.01.66,
Middlesbro & C :
100H - 14.2/14.27w/14.35 (14.22w-94/14.30-86),
400H - 62.6 (64.72-90),
LJ - 5.69 (5.95w/5.79-88),
SP - 12.43, Hep - 5065 (5297-86)
CRUICKSHANK Justina U20 27.09.77, Traff :
TJ - 12.21w/12.18
CRUMP Lisa U23 30.03.76, Sheffield RWC :
3kW - 14:59.9, 5kW - 25:57.5, 5kWR - 24:32,
10kW - 56:05.0, 10kWR - 52:12
CUDDY Jane U17 28.05.81, Liverpool H :
LJ - 5.44,
CULL Sandra U23 10.12.75, Wirral :
LJ - 5.61 (5.79-94)
CUNNANE Cheryl U20 8.02.77, Wakefield :
HT - 35.70 (43.52-95)
CUNNANE Jennifer V35 23.02.57, Wakefield :
PV - 2.32, HT - 41.00 (41.90-95)
CUNNINGHAM Jill 23.04.62, Derby LAC :
5k - 17:30.2
CURBISHLEY Allison U23 3.06.76, Edin WM :
200 - 24.4i/24.76i, 300 - 37.47,
400 - 52.76, 400H - 58.8
CURTIS Laura U17 2.05.81, Hull Springhead :
300H - 46.8, HJ - 1.65, Hepl - 4095
CUTLER Aimee Louise U15 7.10.81, Torfaen :
100 - 12.4/12.78, 200 - 25.39w/25.45,
LJ - 5.61
CUTLER Hannah U13 25.01.84, Birchfield :
600 - 1:44.21, 70HM - 11.82

D AGNE Berhane U20 7.10.77, Ex L/ETH :
3k - 9:21.0,
5k - 16:22.32 (16:17.5mx-95),
10kR - 34:23

DALTON Claire U17 21.09.80, Norwich :
TJ - 11.05
DAMM Sarah 12.09.70, Birchfield :
400 - 57.39i (56.4-95), 60H - 8.76i,
100H - 14.17w/15.14 (14.78-95),
400H - 63.43 (61.1-95),
LJ - 5.94w (5.89-95),
SP - 12.98i/12.04 (12.44-95),
JT - 38.90 (39.36-95), Hep - 5618w (5392-95)
DANIEL Helen J. 24.10.63, Cambridge H :
800 - 2:11.04 (2:01.86-87)
DANIELS Nikki U15 25.08.82, City of Stoke :
800 - 2:11.6, 1500 - 4:45.3
DANSON Yvonne V35 22.05.59, Formby/SIN :
Mar - 2:39:18 (2:30:53-95)
DANVERS Natasha U20 19.09.77, Croydon :
60H - 8.32i, 100H - 13.74 (13.45-95)
DARGAN Leigh U17 31.03.81, Hastings :
SP - 11.35
DAVIDGE Grace U15 22.01.82, Basing & MH :
75HG - 11.8/11.93
DAVIDGE Sharon U15 15.09.81, Exeter :
75HG - 11.21w/11.44, PenG - 2922
DAVIDSON Linda 29.05.70, City of Glasgow :
LJ - 5.71w (5.95-92)
DAVIDSON Natasha U17 8.09.79, C of Plym :
300H - 46.7/46.83
DAVIES Alison V35 6.04.61, Woking :
100 - 11.9/11.97w/12.11
    (11.77w-95/11.9-93/11.93-94),
200 - 24.1/24.15 (23.87-93), PV - 3.00i
DAVIES Angela 21.10.70, Basingstoke & MH/
Loughborough Studnts :
800 - 2:06.27i/2:06.92 (2:03.67-94),
1k - 2:48.74i+ (2:44.15-92),
1500 - 4:13.52 (4:09.29-94),
3k - 9:26.75 (9:14.1-94)
DAVIES Ceri U17 19.08.80, Telford :
3k - 10:22.36
DAVIES Emma U20 9.10.78, Andover :
800 - 2:09.49
DAVIES Gael U20 5.02.79, Gloucester L :
60 - 7.77i, 100 - 11.9w?/12.13,
200 - 25.1w/25.19i/25.6/25.61 (25.3-95)
DAVIS Joanne 20.09.73, Bristol :
(see PAVEY)
DAVIS Julie U17 16.11.79, Lagan Valley :
80HI - 11.6/12.09, 300H - 45.71
DAVIS Wendy U17 7.11.79, Lagan Valley :
800 - 2:13.7
DAWKINS Carol A. V35 8.12.60, Team Solent :
400H - 62.9/63.55 (58.28-85)
DAWSON Catherine 9.03.66, Highgate :
400 - 56.3 (54.77-92), 600 - 1:31.6,
800 - 2:11.65 (2:03.17-94), 1500 - 4:33.0,
400H - 63.2 (59.46-93)
DAWSON Sally, Herne Hill :
3KSTW - 11:46.8
DAY Elizabeth U20 2.05.77, Cardiff :
PV - 2.40
DAY Victoria 19.06.72, Essex L :
200 - 24.7w/24.8 (24.45w/24.6-95),
400 - 54.99 (54.08-95)
DAYKIN Mari-Anne L. 16.02.73, Tonbridge :
JT - 40.50 (46.08-93)
DE JESUS Aattoma U23 23.08.74, :
60 - 7.7i

374

DEAN Harriet U15 2.02.82, Radley :
1500 - 4:45.74
DEAR Joanne M. U23 8.06.75, Windsor S & E :
LJ - 5.75 (6.33-93)
DELESAUX Julie 22.04.69, Blackheath :
HT - 35.90
DENHAM Kate U17 18.03.80, Soton City :
100 - 12.16w/12.3/12.33 (12.2-95),
200 - 25.5/26.07 (24.69-95)
DENHAM Kerensa U23 8.03.74, Blackheath :
LJ - 5.66 (5.89-94), TJ - 12.51
DENNEY Louise U15 2.01.82, Bedford & Co :
LJ - 5.42
DENNISON Andrea M. 22.04.63, Bradford :
Mar - 3:08:10 (3:06:19-94)
DENNISON Katie U17 8.06.80, City of Hull :
3k - 10:32.2
DERHAM Zoe U17 24.11.80, Yate :
HT - 42.66
DESAI Nisha U13 5.08.84, Morpeth :
800 - 2:25.2, 1500 - 5:02.6
DEVERELL Bethan U23 23.08.76, Wrexham :
HT - 35.68
DEVLIN Mary U17 14.09.79, Ballinascreen :
TJ - 10.59
DHALIWAL Navdeep U20 30.11.77, C of E :
SP - 12.91, DT - 39.76 (40.08-94)
DIAMANTIDES Helene, :
Mar - 3:06:23, 100kR - 8:45:56
DICKER Stacey 19.12.73, Shaftesbury Barnet :
PV - 3.30
DICKINSON Leone U23 5.11.75, Bingley :
HJ - 1.73 (1.75-94), Hep - 4047 (4026-94)
DILLON Claire-Marie 1.03.73, BH Mansfield :
400 - 56.76
DILNOT Susan Mary 14.01.62, Soton City :
10kR - 34:55 (33:18-87),
10MR - 57:14 (55:27-93),
HMar - 1:15:28 (1:12:41sh-89/1:14:43-94)
DIVINE Patricia 21.10.67, Edinburgh WM :
400 - 55.32 (54.64-90)
DIXON Sharon Jane 22.04.68, Parkside :
3k - 9:51.6mx (9:21.90-93),
5k - 16:36.90 (16:24.83-91), 10k - 34:26.43
DOCKER Nicole, :
Mar - 3:01:15
DODD Meryl 12.04.69, Bingley (nee WHITELY) :
3k - 9:48.0, 5k - 16:50.28, 10kR - 34:54
DOLAN Sue V35, Imperial/IRE :
Mar - 2:53:54
DONALD Elaine U23 30.04.74, Victoria Park :
100H - 14.9/15.26,
400H - 63.5/64.88 (63.5-94/64.04-95)
DONALDSON Isobel 24.01.64, AF&D/WRAF :
400H - 63.4/63.86 (62.9-93),
TJ - 11.05 (11.20-94), JT - 39.66 (42.78-85),
Hep - 4626 (5038-93)
DONE Cheryl 25.09.70, West (I.O.M.)/WRAF :
100H - 14.7, SP - 11.80,
JT - 38.92, Hep - 4767 (4670-92)
DORAN Colette U13 20.09.83, Carlisle :
DTM - 24.08, JTM - 30.24
DOUBELL Elinor 27.09.71, AF&D :
800 - 2:12.3 (2:11.9-90), 1500 - 4:26.6
DOUGLAS L. Stephanie 22.01.69, Sale :
60 - 7.42i (7.21i-95), 100 - 11.52 (11.27-91),
200 - 24.13 (23.17-94)

DOYLE Caroline U17 3.10.79, St Albans :
TJ - 10.65
DOYLE Kirsty U15 20.08.82, Barry :
1500 - 4:49.62
DRAPER Lynne 10.05.67, Horsham BS :
LJ - 5.72 (5.87-95)
DREW Shelley Jean 8.08.73, Sutton & Dist/
Birm Univ. : SP - 12.34, DT - 57.34
DRUMMIE Susan 19.06.71, Hounslow :
PV - 3.10i (3.10i/3.00-95)
DRUMMOND Rebecca Louise U20 18.04.78,
Stoke : 100 - 11.68w/11.86 (11.50w-94/11.59-95)
DUCK Emma U17 9.02.81, Southampton City :
80HI - 11.8/11.93
DUDGEON Sinead U23 9.07.76, Edin WM :
100 - 12.03 (11.8-94/11.88w-93/11.93-95),
200 - 24.30w/24.37
(23.9w-94/24.17w-95/24.22-94), 400H - 58.80
DUDLEY Heather U13 22.03.84, Wolves & B :
75 - 10.1
DUFF Jennifer U15 29.07.82, Coventry G :
DT - 31.86
DUFFIN Irene M. V35 10.08.60, Shaft Barnet :
SP - 12.99 (14.44-90),
DT - 40.40 (44.90-87), HT - 50.32
DUFFY Teresa 6.07.69, Essex L/IRE :
3k - 9:10.81, 5k - 15:53.47, 10kR - 33:54
DUFFY Vanessa V35, Met. Police :
SP - 11.30 (11.51-94)
DUGDALE Catherine U23 29.11.74, Cardiff :
3k - 9:44.82
DUGDALE Sarah U17 16.05.80, Skipton :
3k - 10:33.21
DUKE Andrea 6.07.73, Mandale :
5k - 16:28.32, 10kR - 34:42 (34:17-95)
DUNCAN Joanne 27.12.66, Essex L :
SP - 14.67
DUNCAN Tracey U20 16.05.79, Essex L :
400 - 56.5, 100H - 14.9, 400H - 60.3/60.47
DUNKLEY Julie U17 11.09.79, Dartford :
SP - 13.46
DUNKLEY Michelle U20 26.01.78, Kettering :
HJ - 1.86i/1.85 (1.87-95), LJ - 5.82, TJ - 11.79
DUNN Rachael U20 4.03.79, Gloucester L :
HT - 39.32
DUNSFORD Wendy J. V35 22.03.60, Park :
SP - 11.29 (13.55-88), HT - 36.82
DUTCH Alison 25.05.65, Edinburgh WM :
SP - 11.74 (12.48-91)

EARLE Jenny V35 28.11.58, BH Mansfield :
HT - 36.82
EASTALL Sally R. 5.01.63, St Edmunds P :
5k - 17:28.0,
Mar - 2:38:52 (2:29:29-91)
EASTMAN Laura U17 23.12.80, Bridgnorth :
60H - 9.2i/9.26i, 80HI - 11.89
EASTON Carey U17 16.11.79, Hamilton :
300 - 39.86, 400 - 57.16
EASTWOOD Laura U17 7.04.81, Deeside :
DT - 34.00
EATOUGH Hannah U20 14.08.79, Blackburn :
100 - 12.16
EDEN Louise U20 11.12.77, Trafford :
400H - 64.7, LJ - 5.91 (5.97w/5.94-95),
TJ - 11.27 (11.62-95)
EDWARDS Bethan 2.05.73, Cardiff :
100H - 14.0w/14.21 (13.57-92)

EDWARDS Elizabeth U15, Wrexham :
SPG - 10.60
EDWARDS Jo 16.07.70, Oxford Univ :
Mar - 2:58:51
EDWARDS Marcelle U20 9.01.78, Essex L :
HT - 41.30
EDWARDS Vicky U17 7.02.80, City of Bath :
300 - 40.77
ELAM Susan 22.07.67, Dartford :
800 - 2:12.62 (2:11.0-92)
ELEY Joanne U23 12.01.74, Derby LAC :
HT - 44.90
ELLIOTT Lucy 9.03.66, Shaftesbury Barnet :
1500 - 4:26.2 (4:18.54-91), 3k - 9:19.4,
5k - 15:56.15, 10kR - 33:30
ELLIS Clare U20 27.04.78, Solihull & S Heath :
3kW - 16:23.07i (15:20.86-93),
5kW - 26:59.0 (26:19.78-94),
5kWR - 26:33 (25:38-95)
ELLIS Lynsey U23 22.11.76, Wolves & B :
JT - 41.32
ELLIS Melanie 16.04.64, Shaftesbury Barnet :
HMar - 1:19:49,
ELLIS Sally V35 17.05.58, Birchfield :
Mar - 2:57:02 (2:33:24-89)
ELLIS Sarah U13 27.10.83, Havant :
JTM - 27.55
ELMS Bonny U17 30.10.79, Newport :
PV - 2.70
ELSON Sara Jo-Anne 8.05.70, Gateshead :
400H - 61.0/62.98 (58.19-92)
ELUEZE Rosaline 28.04.67, Barnet :
HT - 39.84
ENGLISH Allison U20 9.03.79, Hull Spring :
100H - 14.9w/15.4/15.46
ENGLISH Una Marie Clare 14.08.70,IRE :
800 - 2:07.50 (2:03.5-92), 1500 - 4:11.33,
3k - 9:01.6mx (9:10.0-92), 5k - 16:15.7
ENTWISTLE Claire U23 9.12.76, Wigan :
800 - 2:12.0 (2:11.2-95)
ENTWISTLE Sally 27.09.73, Rossendale :
800 - 2:12.4 (2:11.51-94)
ETHERTON Sarah U20 19.10.78, Dartford :
HT - 35.16
EUSTACE Katharine U23 16.04.75, Bristol :
400 - 56.37 (55.33-93)
EVANS Alison C. 13.12.73, Solihull & S H :
HJ - 1.80
EVANS Esther 22.12.73, City of Glasgow :
1500 - 4:30.3 (4:28.62i-94)
EVANS Gail U17 23.07.80, Carmarthen :
100 - 12.46
EVANS Gillian V40 16.12.56, Hull Achilles :
HJ - 1.65 (1.91-83)
EVANS Katherine V. U23 4.02.74, Birchfield :
TJ - 12.58w/12.40
EVANS Katherine U20 19.11.77, Coventry G :
JT - 47.68
EVANS Natalie U13 15.11.83, Wolves & B :
2KWR - 10:42, 2.5kW - 13:58.56
EVANS Non 27.02.67, Swansea :
100H - 14.0w/14.56 (14.2/14.28-95)
EVANS Rebecca U17 15.03.80, Bridgend :
800 - 2:14.3
EVANS Sally U23 14.05.75, Tipton :
300 - 39.64i/39.9, 400 - 55.45, LJ - 5.53
EVERALL Kerry U13, Yate :
75 - 10.2

EVERETT Claire U20 25.06.79, Norwich :
HJ - 1.67i/1.66 (1.74i-94/1.71-93),
SP - 11.37, Hep - 4759
EVERETT Rebecca U17 10.03.80, Birchfield :
3k - 10:23.42
EVERITT Amie U20 1.11.78, Huntingdon :
PV - 2.30
EVERSON Suzanne 23.03.72, Dartford :
400 - 57.4
EVERTON Ayshea 13.10.73, Leamington :
DT - 41.66 (45.18-92)
EVOL Donna U15 28.08.83, Reading :
PV - 2.20
EZEOGU Nnenna U15 11.10.82, N& E B :
LJ - 5.36w/5.19

FABEN Alison U20 7.02.77, Hunt :
DT - 38.42 (39.30-95), HT - 35.16
FACEY Denise 8.02.69, Hallamshire :
400 - 56.09 (55.30-92)
FAGAN Collette U15 16.06.82, C of Glasgow :
1500 - 4:46.5
FAHERTY Michelle M. 10.08.68, Skyrac :
600 - 1:31.8+,
800 - 2:04.4mx/2:05.97 (2:05.3-95),
1500 - 4:14.19, 1M - 4:39.44 (4:38.64-95)
FAIRS Elizabeth U20 1.12.77, Hallamshire :
60H - 8.95i, 100H - 14.10
FAIRWEATHER Lynne U17 15.01.80, Lassw :
60H - 8.75i
FAIRWEATHER Sheila U20 24.11.77, C of G :
1500 - 4:31.6 (4:28.67-95), 3k - 9:44.91
FALCONER Jane Olivia U23 20.09.74, Ex L/
Camb Un : TJ - 11.36 (12.37w/12.10-93)
FALK Stacey U17 9.06.80, Gateshead :
3k - 10:30.3 (10:29.79-95)
FARQUHARSON Claire U20 28.12.78, Horsh :
HJ - 1.65 (1.70-95)
FARQUHARSON Samantha 15.12.69, Croy :
100 - 12.1 (11.78-94),
100H - 13.38w/13.40 (12.9mf/13.08-94)
FARRELL Jennifer 8.04.65, Border :
HJ - 1.68 (1.86-86)
FARROW Jennifer U17 16.10.79, Fife :
300H - 46.39
FARROW Wendy 25.12.71, Derby LAC :
800 - 2:11.1 (2:11.1-92), 1500 - 4:21.4,
3k - 9:33.9mx/9:52.1 (9:31.91-94),
10kR - 34:59
FAULKNER Natasha 8.07.73, Weymouth :
TJ - 11.13
FAVELL Janine U17 7.12.79, Chesterfield :
HT - 37.86
FAWKES Claire U20 24.10.77, Braintree :
HT - 37.68
FEARN Charlotte U17 26.11.80, Shaft Barnet :
800 - 2:16.75
FEARON Cherone U17 4.03.80, Bristol :
LJ - 5.62w/5.46
FEE Elaine 22.07.70, Birchfield :
3k - 9:45.7mx, 5k - 16:59.3mx/17:14.40
FEIGENBAUM Ronit 3.11.63, Highgate/ISR :
400 - 56.9 (56.8/57.11-95)
FERRIER Holly U13 13.07.84, Stamford & D :
70HM - 11.6
FERRIER Leigh 15.08.72, Sale :
(see READE)

376

FETTES Sarah U17 26.08.81, C of Glasgow :
  LJ - 5.44
FICKEN Pam V55 25.07.41, Surrey WC :
  50kW - 5:53:16
FIELD Lucy 1.05.71, Bristol :
  1500 - 4:25.09, 3k - 9:45.4
FIELDS Michelle 15.05.73, Peterborough :
  HT - 37.96, JT - 45.04 (50.48-93)
FILCE Claudia Dawn 11.11.72, AF&D :
  PV - 2.90 (3.00-95)
FINDLAY Tania 8.11.70, Yate :
  200 - 25.0/25.58 (25.0-95), LJ - 5.60
FINDLAYSON Jacqui U17 21.01.80, Invern :
  HT - 32.62 (32.64-95)
FINIKIN Evette 25.09.63, Shaftesbury Barnet :
  LJ - 5.70 (6.29w/6.25i/6.14-89),
  TJ - 12.27w/12.10i/12.00 (13.46-91),
  SP - 11.65 (12.05-87)
FINLAY Louise U13 2.10.83, Rhondda :
  SPG - 10.03, SPM - 10.33, DTM - 23.66
FISHER Jayne 2.11.70, Swansea :
  DT - 45.52
FLATHER Elaine F. 2.02.66, Southampton RR :
  Mar - 3:05:08 (2:47:11-95)
FLEET Lindsay U17 1.06.81, Bromley :
  200 - 25.07w/25.68 (25.05w/25.26-95),
  300 - 40.79
FLETCHER Alison K. V35 8.06.61, Camb H :
  10k - 37:43.3 (35:18.59-93)
FLETCHER Karen 26.09.79, Kirk Hallam :
  3k - 10:09.05
FLOCKHART Dawn 16.05.67, Edinburgh WM :
  100 - 11.8w/12.00w/12.1 (11.7w-84/11.80-85),
  200 - 23.9w/24.4/24.55 (23.71-84),
  300 - 38.9, 400 - 54.70 (54.4-95)
FLYNN Phylis 15.06.62, :
  Mar - 3:06:49
FOORD Leslie U17 13.01.81, Andover :
  SP - 11.13i
FORD Katie U15 21.10.81, Sheffield RWC :
  2.5kW - 12:53.80, 2.5kWR - 13:17,
  3kW - 16:03.8, 3kWR - 15:26, 5kWR - 26:22o
FORD-DUNN Elizabeth 13.05.71, Steyning :
  3kW - 16:31.0 (16:10.0-95)
FORD-DUNN Suzanne 25.04.73, Steyning :
  3kW - 16:09.0 (15:38.0-95),
  5kWR - 27:10 (26:43-95)
FORESTER Julie 4.05.69, Shaftesbury Barn :
  200 - 25.16, 400 - 55.5/56.03 (55.78-94)
FORREST Rachael U20 25.12.77, Birchfield :
  HJ - 1.85 (1.87-96)
FORRESTER Amanda U20 29.09.78, C of S :
  100 - 11.94w/12.0/12.11,
  200 - 25.0/25.02w (25.0/25.16-95)
FORSTER Melissa U17 30.03.80, Morpeth :
  3k - 10:27.8
FORSYTH Kate U20 5.06.79, North Shields P :
  60H - 8.95i (8.87i-94), 100H - 14.30w/14.34
FOSTER Laura U17 22.07.81, Halifax :
  80HI - 12.0/12.46
FOSTER Rachel U23 1.09.76, Barnsley :
  PV - 2.70 (2.70-95)
FOSTER Rebecca 14.04.71, Wakefield :
  JT - 40.30 (43.26-89)
FOSTER Samantha U17 9.09.79, Basildon :
  HJ - 1.68 (1.72-95), TJ - 10.81
FOSTER Vickie 1.04.71, Salisbury :
  SP - 14.42, DT - 45.22 (48.62-93), HT - 43.90

FOTHERGILL Chaanah 22.02.72, Hallamshire/
  Cambridge Univ : 5k - 16:55.3
FOULDS G. U13, Diss :
  JTM - 26.42
FOX Rachel U17 25.02.80, Barnsley :
  PV - 2.40
FRANCE Deborah 16.10.65, Hull Achilles :
  400 - 56.6/56.97, 800 - 2:09.2 (2:06.9-90)
FRANCIS Tammie U20 14.11.78, Bournem'th :
  JT - 47.32
FRANCIS-THOMAS Elizabeth 22.12.63, Card :
  1500 - 4:20.49, 1M - 4:40.93, 3k - 9:40.92
FRANKLIN Katie U17 24.08.80, Norwich :
  DT - 33.02
FRASER Donna Karen 7.11.72, Croydon :
  60 - 7.69i (7.69i-93),
  100 - 11.97w/12.08 (11.77w-91/11.88-93),
  200 - 23.62 (23.44w/23.47-95),
  300 - 37.31, 400 - 51.58
FRASER Ione U17 28.10.79, Thames Valley :
  HJ - 1.68
FRASER Louise 10.10.70, Trafford :
  60 - 7.49i,
  200 - 23.73i/23.9 (23.4-95/23.41w/24.13-91),
  400 - 54.65 (53.55-92),
  100H - 13.7w/13.8 (13.36-91),
  400H - 56.45 (56.26-92)
FREEBAIRN Susan 22.08.65, C of Glasgow :
  DT - 46.22 (46.70-94), HT - 36.34 (37.30-95)
FREEMAN Danielle U17 11.02.80, Leeds :
  80HI - 11.9/12.25, HJ - 1.66,
  LJ - 5.95w/5.92, JT - 36.44, Hepl - 4780
FREEMAN Emily U17 24.11.80, Spenborough :
  100 - 12.49w/12.55, 200 - 24.91w/25.24
FREEMAN Laura U20 22.04.78, Coventry G :
  HJ - 1.73
FREETH Megan U15 1.02.82, Swansea :
  PV - 2.25,
FROST Helen U23 12.03.74, Birchfield :
  400 - 54.83 (54.32-92)
FRY Sara 19.01.62, Met. Police/Lincoln Well :
  JT - 39.78 (47.70-78)
FRYER Laura U13 3.12.83, Belgrave :
  2kW - 11:02.4, 2KWR - 10:39,
  2.5kW - 13:52.59
FRYER Paula Tracy 14.07.69, Sale :
  400 - 56.98 (54.7-92/55.34-94),
  800 - 2:07.5 (1:59.76-91)
FUDGE Paula V40 30.03.52, Hounslow :
  HMar - 1:16:59 (1:11:37-88)
FULLELOVE Alyssa U15 16.09.81, Kilb :
  75HG - 11.7/11.80, PenG - 2713
FULLER Jane K. U23 21.04.76, Parkside :
  100H - 15.1 (14.9-95), 400H - 61.8/62.98
FURLONGER Susan U15 30.09.81, Oswestry :
  PenG - 2737

G ABRIEL Linda 27.07.64, Coventry G :
    400H - 64.90 (63.46-94)
GANDY Dawn Suzanne 28.07.65, T Solent :
  400 - 56.5 (53.8/53.98-87),
  800 - 2:07.5 (2:01.87-88)
GARDEN Catherine U20 4.09.78, Pitreavie :
  SP - 12.06, DT - 40.56 (42.72-94),
  HT - 47.68
GARDEN Eleanor U23 20.11.76, Pitreavie :
  SP - 11.63 (11.69-95), DT - 42.54

GARDNER Ann 11.10.68, Corby :
  SP - 11.23 (12.84-87), HT - 55.00
GARDNER E. U13, :
  JTM - 26.10
GARVIE Leanne U20 29.08.78, :
  DT - 37.78
GASCOIGNE Amber U17 5.09.79, Wells :
  800 - 2:13.8, 1500 - 4:37.3, 3k - 10:03.4
GATRELL Eleanor U23 5.10.76, Woking :
  SP - 13.45
GAULD Louise U17 24.08.80, C of Edinburgh :
  HJ - 1.65i/1.60, TJ - 10.52
GAUTIER Nicola U20 21.03.78, Hallamshire :
  60H - 8.99i, 100H - 14.51, HJ - 1.68,
  SP - 14.03i/13.69, JT - 41.48, Hep - 5213
GAYLE Denise U17 11.09.79, Barnet :
  HJ - 1.68, LJ - 5.45
GAYNOR Natalie U17 7.11.79, Sutton & Dist :
  100 - 12.1w/12.39, 200 - 24.97w/25.45
GAYTER Sharon, Mandale :
  100kR - 9:36:50 (8:12:03-95),
  24HrT - 190.846km (204.674-94)
GEAR Karen U17 30.09.79, N Devon :
  300 - 39.71, 400 - 56.7/57.56
GEARY Rebecca S. U13 2.05.84, Yeovil Oly :
  100 - 13.2, LJ - 4.94
GEE Michala U23 8.12.75, Rotherham :
  100H - 14.55 (15.08w?-93), HJ - 1.70,
  LJ - 5.63, Hep - 4875 (4625-94)
GEMMELL Marlene 21.06.72, Strathkelvin :
  5k - 17:28.35, 10kR - 35:00
GENTLE Louise U20 4.09.78, Bedford & Co :
  HJ - 1.65 (1.70-95)
GHOJEFA Elizabeth 24.02.69, Epsom & E :
  LJ - 6.13 (6.32w-94/6.27-95),
  TJ - 12.06 (12.64-93)
GIBBENS Elizabeth U20 5.04.77, Bromley :
  LJ - 5.80, TJ - 12.36w/12.26i/12.22 (12.42-95)
GIBSON Lynn M. 6.07.69, Oxford City :
  800 - 2:02.83 (2:02.34-92),
  1500 - 4:12.32 (4:05.75-94),
  1M - 4:38.93 (4:31.17-94), 10kR - 34:34
GIBSON Rachael U15 20.01.82, Harmeny :
  800 - 2:19.4
GIBSON Sharon Angela V35 31.12.61, Notts :
  SP - 13.19 (13.50-82), JT - 56.16 (62.32-87)
GILES Luisa U15 23.02.82, City of Stoke :
  75HG - 11.09w/11.55
GILES Sally 6.04.62, Serpentine :
  HT - 42.38
GILLHAM Michele U23 8.10.74, Tonbridge :
  100H - 15.1 (15.0-92/15.10-93),
  400H - 62.2/62.31
GITTENS Louise A. V35 9.03.60, Soton City :
  HJ - 1.70 (1.94-80)
GLAYSHER Jennifer U15 3.05.83, Preston :
  HJ - 1.60
GLENN Alice U13 30.09.83, Leamington :
  70HM - 11.8
GLOVER Danielle U15 26.07.82, North'ton :
  800 - 2:19.5
GODDARD Natasha 15.06.71, :
  2kSt - 7:23.90
GOLDSMITH Sally V35 18.01.61, EdinWM :
  10k - 34:28.13, HMar - 1:13:13,
  Mar - 2:34:11
GOODMAN Kelly U15 16.03.82, Peterbro :
  DT - 29.88

GOODWIN Kim 16.05.70, City of Hull :
  100 - 12.1, 200 - 24.25w/24.49,
  400 - 54.97 (54.64-95)
GORDON Justine U17 10.05.80, Andover :
  HJ - 1.68
GORIN Laura U13 9.11.83, Thurrock :
  1500 - 5:05.4
GRADDEN Marilyn J. V35 26.01.61, E & E :
  Mar - 3:08:25 (2:55:59-95)
GRAHAM Dion Dainti-Ann U20 27.09.78, Ex L/
  JAM : 100 - 12.1, 200 - 24.05w/24.21
GRANGER Katie U23 31.03.75, Exeter :
  JT - 47.54 (50.32-93)
GRANT Joanne U17 17.12.79, Motherwell :
  80HI - 12.0/12.30 (12.29w-95)
GRANT Sue 10.05.69, Wakefield :
  SP - 11.77
GRANTHAM Maria U17 14.12.79, East Ches :
  300H - 46.8 (49.33-95), Hepl - 4049
GRAY Linda 23.03.71, Lincoln Well :
  JT - 44.64 (45.68-94)
GREEN Catherine 30.11.73, Kettering
  (nee ALLSOPP) : 800 - 2:08.92 (2:07.6-94),
  1500 - 4:28.90 (4:26.71-95)
GREEN Emma 25.01.64, Hallamshire :
  100H - 15.1 (14.2/14.29w-87/14.58-91)
GREEN Francesca U17 10.02.80, Bromley :
  400 - 59.0, 800 - 2:13.2
GREEN Jayne 17.03.72, Wirral (nee MCCOY):
  LJ - 5.70 (6.24w-90/6.14-91)
GREEN Sandra 30.10.67, Wolves & B :
  3k - 9:59.6
GREEN Sonya U17 6.03.80, Sale :
  100 - 12.22w/12.23,
  200 - 25.06w/25.1/26.07
GREENHOUSE Yvette U17 21.10.80, :
  JT - 35.18
GREGORY Claire U17 12.01.80, Hallamshire :
  300H - 46.39, TJ - 10.80
GREGORY Claire U17 30.12.79, Teesdale :
  3k - 10:34.4
GREY Alison Helen 12.05.73, C of Glasgow :
  SP - 14.66 (15.85i/15.69-94),
  DT - 48.82 (52.52-94)
GRIFFIN Hayley U17 20.07.80, Milton Keynes :
  800 - 2:15.7,
GRIFFITH Michelle Amanda 6.10.71, W S & E :
  TJ - 14.04 (14.08-94)
GRIFFITHS Ann Margaret 20.08.65, Sale :
  800 - 2:05.5/2:05.51+ (1:59.81-94),
  1k - 2:40.07i (2:39.29-90),
  1500 - 4:16.25i/4:19.88 (4:07.59-92)
GRIFFITHS Marie 4.10.68, Cannock & Staff :
  400H - 65.6 (64.2-93)
GRIFFITHS Sarah B. U20 24.04.78, W S & E :
  400H - 65.1/65.24 (64.3-95)
GRIFFITHS Shirley 23.06.72, Cramlington :
  800 - 2:07.3, 1k - 2:48.8i+,
  1500 - 4:15.68, 1M - 4:44.60
GRIMSHAW Helen 2.08.62, Hounslow :
  Mar - 2:57:56
GRIMSHAW Kate U17 26.10.79, North S Poly :
  1500 - 4:37.31, 3k - 10:01.46
GROVES Dee U20 21.12.77, Torfaen :
  HT - 38.32
GROVES Jane U20 17.05.77, Vale Park :
  800 - 2:11.3 (2:10.80-95),
  1500 - 4:33.80

GUNN Catherine 10.06.69, Torfaen :
    JT - 39.00 (43.56-87)
GUNNELL Sally Jane Janet 29.07.66, Ex L :
    300 - 38.4i+ (36.44-93),
    400 - 51.45 (51.04-94),
    400H - 54.65 (52.74-93)
GUNNING Deborah 31.08.65, Andover :
    800 - 2:07.6 (2:05.65-93),
    1500 - 4:13.40i/4:17.4 (4:12.69-90),
    2k - 6:05.43 (5:45.15-93),
    3k - 9:26.46 (9:12.12-94)

HACK Meredith U13 22.07.85, Bournem'th :
    600 - 1:45.2
HAGGER Kim V35 2.12.61, Essex L :
    LJ - 5.85 (6.70-86)
HAGGETT Lea M. 9.05.72, Croydon :
    HJ - 1.92, LJ - 5.83w (5.81-95),
    TJ - 12.04 (12.45-95)
HAINING Hayley 6.03.72, City of Glasgow :
    3k - 9:22.2 (9:12.28-91),
    10kR - 33:25, HMar - 1:17:01
HAJIPAVLIS Alexandra U17 3.10.80, Rowh :
    DT - 38.84 (39.38-95)
HALE Jane U23 4.01.74, Sale :
    100 - 12.03w/12.22, 200 - 24.96,
    60H - 8.53i, 100H - 13.59
HALES Amy U15 16.03.82, Steyning :
    2.5kW - 12:42.43, 3kW - 15:14.6,
    3kWR - 14:47, 5kW - 26:47.0,
HALES Sophie U13 30.03.85, Steyning :
    2kW - 11:04.9, 2KWR - 10:56
HALL Andrea U20 28.01.77, Bedford & Co :
    TJ - 11.15
HALL Cicely U20 12.10.78, Norwich :
    400H - 62.12
HALL Nicola U17 14.12.79, Ipswich :
    60H - 8.74i, 80HI - 11.27w/11.41 (11.40-95),
    100H - 15.2
HALL Penny U20 13.01.77, Cardiff :
    PV - 2.40
HALLETT Jodi U20 8.11.78, Bristol :
    400H - 63.5/63.98
HANCOCKS Ebony U15 17.03.82, Birchfield :
    DT - 30.20
HANCOX Carrie U17 8.08.80, Swindon :
    300H - 46.7/48.19 (46.39-95)
HANLEY Lydia U17 2.02.81, Liverpool H :
    JT - 38.26
HANSEN Alice, Parkside :
    Mar - 2:59:33
HANSEN Ashia 5.12.71, Shaftesbury Barnet :
    100 - 11.95 (11.7-95/11.81w-94),
    LJ - 6.47A/6.11 (6.27-94), TJ - 14.78
HANSON Lorraine I. 22.04.65, Birchfield :
    400 - 52.83 (50.93-91),
    400H - 57.03 (56.70-89)
HANSON Sarah 25.11.72, Birchfield :
    LJ - 5.68 (5.79-95)
HARDING Lynn V35 10.08.61, Houghton-le-Sp :
    10MR - 57:27 (56:03-89),
    HMar - 1:19:53 (1:13:09-89)
HARDMAN Angela U23 24.10.76, Barnsley :
    200 - 25.0/25.60
HARDY Rebecca J. 11.11.68, Highgate :
    DT - 43.00 (44.54-95), HT - 35.32
HARDY Simone U17 9.11.79, Kettering :
    800 - 2:12.4, 1500 - 4:43.0

HARGRAVE Karen 23.09.65, :
    1500 - 4:25.29i (4:09.46-89),
    3k - 9:32.23i (8:48.72-90)
HARLEY Rachel U15 1.01.82, Birchfield :
    SPG - 11.48, DT - 29.60
HARNETT Jennifer U23 11.03.76, Medway :
    800 - 2:09.9mx?/2:12.5 (2:10.8-95),
    1500 - 4:23.94
HARRIES Michelle 4.01.72, Essex L :
    800 - 2:11.87 (2:05.88-91)
HARRIS Rachel U15 15.02.82, Liverpool H :
    HJ - 1.72,
HARRIS S. U13, :
    JTM - 26.76
HARRISON Deborah U20 13.11.78, R S C :
    LJ - 6.00w/5.63, Hep - 4297
HARRISON Fiona Jane U15 30.11.81, Barn :
    100 - 12.16w/12.25, 200 - 25.5i/25.6,
    PV - 3.50, LJ - 5.78w/5.62, PenG - 2993
HARRISON Lianne U17 17.06.80, C of E :
    3k - 10:33.9
HARRISON Sarah U20 1.03.79, Shaft Barnet :
    HT - 46.84
HARRISON Simone U20 2.09.77, Croydon :
    400 - 56.48
HARROP Jane V35 25.07.60, Havant :
    5k - 17:18.8 (17:06.6-95), 10MR - 58:45
HART Siobhan U23 15.06.75, Guildford & G :
    HT - 34.20 (36.06-94)
HARTIGAN Beverley Marie 10.06.67, Birch :
    3k - 9:51.85 (9:03.88i-90/9:10.4-92)
HARTLEY Sarah U17 4.05.81, Spenborough :
    PV - 2.95
HARTNEY Astra U17 7.01.80, Woking :
    3k - 10:30.4
HARVEY Amy U15 23.04.82, Braintree :
    JT - 37.58
HARVEY Debra Jayne U23 13.11.75,
    Soton City : HJ - 1.65 (1.73-94)
HARVEY Lisa 9.04.68, Westbury :
    400 - 56.5/58.05
HARVEY-SMITH Laura U17 20.01.80, Brain :
    JT - 38.00
HARWOOD Jocelyn A. V35 21.11.57, M & C :
    200 - 25.0 (24.5/24.84-93),
    100H - 14.1/14.39 (13.79-89)
HASKELL Gaynor U23 11.08.76, AF&D :
    SP - 12.77
HASLAM Claire M. 18.12.63, Shaft Barnet :
    100 - 12.08w/12.21 (12.0-91/12.10-92),
    200 - 24.7w/24.8/24.87 (24.4-91/24.79-92),
    400 - 57.50 (56.63-95)
HASLER Suzanne U15 7.04.82, R Sutton C :
    800 - 2:15.49
HATHAWAY Emily U17 22.12.79, R Sutton C :
    800 - 2:13.2
HAYHOE Lynn M. 20.03.63, Shaft Barnet :
    JT - 39.38 (55.70-92)
HAYLES Andrea U17 24.07.80, Cambridge H :
    100 - 12.24
HAYLOCK Laura U17 20.02.80, Camb & C :
    80HI - 11.9/11.92w/11.93
HAYWARD Natalie U13 3.11.83, Tonbridge :
    SPM - 9.46
HAYWOOD Katherine U23 23.12.74, Stourprt :
    400H - 65.5 (63.72-93)
HEAD Christine U17 18.12.79, Norwich :
    JT - 41.10, HepI - 4212

HEANEY Caroline U23 3.04.76, Ealing,S & Mx.:
  400H - 64.7
HEARNE Jodie U15 17.09.81, Ilford :
  HJ - 1.60, PenG - 2713
HEASMAN Heather 27.09.63, Horwich :
  5k - 15:53.84, 10kR - 33:25 (32:31-94)
HEGNEY Gillian U20 4.11.77, C of Glasgow :
  60 - 7.79i (7.72i-94),
  100 - 11.89w?/11.9/12.05 (11.87w-95)
HEMS Rachel J. 10.12.69, Coventry Godiva :
  HJ - 1.65 (1.76-85)
HENAGHAN Dianne 6.08.65, Morpeth :
  800 - 2:05.91, 1500 - 4:29.9,
  1M - 4:48.7, 3k - 9:26.6, 5k - 17:12.9
HENDERSON Sarah U13 27.09.83, Woking :
  HJ - 1.50
HENDRY Susan U23 30.06.76, C of Glasgow :
  400 - 56.5 (55.96-94), 800 - 2:11.1
HENRY Corinne 15.04.72, Shaftesbury B :
  LJ - 5.76 (6.12w?/6.05-91), TJ - 13.55
HENRY Lorraine 16.09.67, Shaftesbury B :
  SP - 11.57 (13.09-88), DT - 41.46 (43.88-90)
HENTON Sarah 4.05.73, Birch/Birm Univ. :
  SP - 11.43, DT - 49.74
HERBERT Caroline 30.06.70, Arena :
  3k - 9:51.1, 5k - 17:07.42,
  10k - 35:15.6, 10kR - 34:01,
  10MR - 57:09, HMar - 1:18:49
HERRINGTON Lynsey U20 31.05.79, AF&D :
  DT - 42.62 (41.86dh-95)
HEVINGHAM Gill V40 24.06.54, N Devon :
  PV - 2.30
HEWETT Alexandra U15 10.09.82, Hillingdon :
  HJ - 1.63, PenG - 2743
HEWITT Jennifer U17 8.01.80, Medway :
  DT - 41.08
HEWITT Lorraine U17 8.01.80, Medway :
  HT - 31.52
HIGHAM Stephanie U13 26.12.83, Carlisle :
  HJ - 1.58
HILL Amie U17 9.09.80, Oxford City :
  DT - 40.72
HILL Cathy-Ann U20 4.05.77, Team Solent :
  SP - 13.10
HILL Clare U23 14.12.76, Sparta :
  400 - 57.49 (56.17-95), 800 - 2:12.95i/2:16.41
HILLAN Erica U13 1.02.84, Hull Springhead :
  75HG - 12.5
HILLS Jennifer U17 25.03.81, Yeovil Oly :
  HJ - 1.65i/1.58 (1.63-95)
HIMSWORTH Jade U20 4.08.79, Holbeach :
  800 - 2:12.9 (2:12.57-94)
HINES Olivia U13 19.10.83, Hercules Wimb :
  600 - 1:43.7, 1500 - 5:08.1
HIPKIN Caroline W. 18.03.71, Ryston :
  Mar - 3:01:31
HOBBS Kim U20 12.12.78, Hull Achilles :
  PV - 2.40
HODGE-DALLAWAY Naomi U17 1.06.81,
  Tower Hamlets : 100 - 12.4,
  60H - 8.9i/9.22i (9.22i-95), 80HI - 11.59w/11.79
HODGINS Jenni U17 7.06.80, Exeter :
  1500 - 4:44.6, 3k - 10:34.0
HOGAN Jackie U17 19.03.80, Scarborough :
  1500 - 4:43.7 (4:40.4-95),
  3k - 10:23.5 (10:11.9-95)
HOGG Rachel U15 11.06.82, Copeland :
  LJ - 5.28w/5.05

HOGGARTH Donna 14.10.73, Preston :
  100 - 11.90w/11.91 (11.55w/11.61-92)
HOLDEN Diana U23 12.02.75, Hounslow :
  HT - 52.06 (54.42-95)
HOLDEN Genevieve 21.09.73, Oxford City :
  400 - 57.2 (55.86-91)
HOLDEN Joanne 20.02.65, Shaftesbury Barn :
  3k - 9:51.7 (9:37.95-94),
  5k - 17:23.3 (16:37.16-95), HMar - 1:19:48
HOLDSWORTH Natalie U15 24.12.81, Holm :
  800 - 2:17.71
HOLLAND Kirsty U20 23.10.78, Giffnock :
  HT - 35.04
HOLLETT Sharon U20 26.12.78, Victoria Pk :
  200 - 25.21
HOLLICK Lisa 1.01.70, Shaftesbury Barnet :
  10MR - 57:54, HMar - 1:17:28, Mar - 2:54:16
HOLLIMAN Fiona 4.05.71, City of Glasgow
  (nee CALDER) : 200 - 24.67 (24.63-95)
HOLLMAN Anne Marie U23 18.02.74, Peterbro :
  200 - 25.23, 100H - 14.1/14.30,
  400H - 63.27 (61.56-93), LJ - 5.67,
  Hep - 5258 (5187w-93)
HOLLMAN Julie U20 16.02.77, Peterborough :
  100H - 14.9/15.19 (15.01w-94/15.08-95),
  HJ - 1.68 (1.70-93), LJ - 5.89 (5.99-94),
  Hep - 4975 (4878-94)
HOLLOWAY Joanne U23 10.05.76, W S & E :
  SP - 12.02i/11.86
HOLMAN Tara U17 13.10.80, Verlea :
  JT - 35.34
HOLMES Carol 13.12.63, Notts :
  5k - 17:00.6, 10kR - 34:55 (34:08-95),
  10MR - 56:09, HMar - 1:17:11 (1:15:16-95)
HOLMES Fiona U15 12.12.82, Kendal :
  LJ - 5.34w/5.28
HOLMES Kelly 19.04.70, Ealing,S & Mx/Army :
  200 - 24.8 (25.29-95), 400 - 53.8 (54.51-95),
  600 - 1:28.62+ (1:26.0+-95),
  800 - 1:57.84 (1:56.21-95), 1500 - 4:01.13
HOLROYD Shelley 17.05.73, Essex L :
  JT - 60.12
HOLT Gemma 20.12.72, AF&D :
  LJ - 5.69 (5.86w/5.81-91)
HOLT Janet M. V40 10.10.56, Trafford :
  800 - 2:11.60 (2:05.9-89),
  1500 - 4:24.60 (4:16.9-89)
HOOD Maria U17 20.12.79, Bournemouth :
  DT - 37.04, HT - 31.34
HOPE Jennifer 1.09.62, Wolves & B :
  (see COOPER)
HOPGOOD Rachel U20 2.06.78, Hallamshire :
  DT - 48.76
HORNBY Emma 12.12.73, Birchfield :
  PV - 3.55
HORNE Caroline A. V40 7.11.56, Crawley :
  HMar - 1:19:08 (1:13:43-84)
HORNER Katharine U20 6.01.78, Dorking :
  PV - 3.10ts (3.00-95)
HOROVITZ Gillian P. V40 7.06.55, AF&D :
  Mar - 2:45:12 (2:36:52-92)
HORWILL Katherine U23 26.01.75, Dudley & S :
  3kW - 14:46.10 (14:41.0-93), 5kWR - 24:44,
  10kW - 53:38.3 (52:48.5-92),
  10kWR - 53:26 (51:20-95)
HOSKING Heidi U23 20.05.74, Liverpool Pem :
  (see SMITH)

HOULDEN Samantha U13 27.11.83, Linc Sch :
PenM - 2002
HOURIHAN Alyson J. V35 17.10.60, Cardiff :
SP - 11.66 (12.41-92), DT - 41.12 (43.58-92)
HOWARD Anna-Lisa U20 18.04.78, Norwich :
SP - 13.03
HOWARD Julie 24.09.66, City of Plymouth :
200 - 25.28
(24.2w?-93/24.37w-95/24.4-93/24.72-95)
HOWARD Tracey U17 11.02.81, Bournem'th :
JT - 36.72
HOWARTH Beverley U23 4.09.76, Sale :
HJ - 1.70 (1.73-93), PV - 2.30 (2.30-94)
HOWE Sian U13 11.04.84, Ashford :
DT - 27.26, DTM - 31.46, JTM - 25.96
HOWELL Dionne U17 10.04.81, Herne Hill :
100 - 12.21w/12.35 (12.2w-95),
200 - 24.43w/24.94, LJ - 5.48, Hepl - 4008w
HOWELL Gaby U15 25.01.82, Brighton :
200 - 25.76w/26.15,
HOWLEY Nina U20 22.01.78, Sheffield RWC :
3kW - 15:06.1, 5kW - 24:48.19
HUBBARD Leigh M. U20 30.09.77, Banbury :
LJ - 5.60 (5.61-95)
HUCKERBY Nikki U20 27.02.78, Birchfield :
3kW - 15:09.3, 3kWR - 14:44,
5kW - 25:46.52, 5kWR - 25:22, 10kWR - 52:23
HUGHES Anne-Marie 8.05.62, Shettleston :
Mar - 3:04:57 (3:03:39-95)
HUGHES Elizabeth U20 9.06.77, Bromley :
PV - 3.00
HUGHES Emma L. U17 15.09.80, Luton :
LJ - 5.80, TJ - 11.48
HUGHES Rhian U20 11.05.79, Colwyn Bay :
JT - 39.82
HULLEY Angela J. 8.02.62, Leeds :
3k - 9:30.2 (9:17.05-90),
5k - 16:26.62 (15:41.11-90),
10k - 33:33.37 (32:42.84-89),
10kR - 33:59RL/34:15 (33:21-94)
HUMPHREY Rachel U20 29.05.78, Luton :
JT - 38.06
HUNT Tanya U13 14.09.83, Salisbury :
DTM - 26.26, JT - 28.42, JTM - 26.48 (30.16-95)
HUNTE Abigail 12.05.71, Shaftesbury Barnet :
800 - 2:07.61i/2:07.62 (2:02.47-95)
HUNTER Fiona U20 14.09.78, Dundee HH :
TJ - 11.40w/11.34i/11.23 (11.81db-95),
SP - 12.18
HUNTER Jill 14.10.66, Valli :
5k - 15:51.55 (15:09.98-92),
10kR - 32:41 (31:42-89)
HUNTER-ROWE Carolyn 25.01.64, Pud & B :
10MR - 57:43, HMar - 1:17:26,
Mar - 2:48:05+t/2:51:38 (2:40:28-94),
100kR - 7:41:29 (7:27:19-93)
HURST Jodie U20 21.06.77, City of Stoke :
TJ - 12.20
HUSSEIN Yasmin U17 22.01.81, Shaft Barnet :
HJ - 1.64
HUTCHINGS Hayley U13 14.11.83, Steyning :
2kW - 11:17.0, 2KWR - 10:38
HUTCHINSON Anya U20 16.07.77, Notts :
400H - 63.0/63.11
HUTCHISON Fiona U20 18.01.77, C of Glas :
200 - 25.09w (24.3w/24.69-94)
HUTT Angela U17 5.07.81, Perth :
TJ - 10.62

HYDE Zahara 12.01.63, Havant :
3k - 9:47.8 (9:05.49-91), 5k - 16:04.12,
10k - 34:37.5 (33:23.25-94),
10kR - 33:54 (33:46-95),
10MR - 56:41 (56:11-94), HMar - 1:18:21
HYLAND Victoria U15 27.10.81, Sale :
LJ - 5.24w/5.00
HYNAN Julie U17 23.05.80, Liverpool H :
HJ - 1.70 (1.70-95)
HYND Natalie U20 30.01.78, Pitreavie :
100 - 11.93w/12.13 (12.00-95),
200 - 24.51w/24.61
HYSLOP Joanne U17 13.03.80, Coventry G :
300H - 46.0/47.09, Hepl - 3834

IDOWU Oluyinka 25.02.72, Essex L :
LJ - 5.50 (6.73-93)
IGE Yewande U17 21.03.80, Sutton & District :
300 - 41.3, 100H - 15.2/15.98,
300H - 43.08, 400H - 65.3
IMPETT Lindsay U17 4.01.80, Wimborne :
100 - 12.3 (12.2-95), 300 - 39.66, 400 - 56.87
ING Sarah 10.11.63, Swindon :
Mar - 3:06:20
INGMAN Jilly U20 17.08.78, Barnsley :
1500 - 4:33.40
IRVING Ruth U23 20.07.74, Wirral/Camb Un :
LJ - 6.00 (6.28-94), TJ - 11.27 (11.98-95)
ISHERWOOD Fiona U15 24.09.81, ColchH :
SPG - 10.93

JABLONSKI Rachael U15 6.12.81, Tip :
1500 - 4:48.75
JACKSON Emily U17 16.10.80, Gateshead :
HJ - 1.67
JACKSON Lorna U23 9.01.74, Edinburgh WM :
SP - 11.42 (12.38-95), JT - 58.20
JACOBS Kim Simmone Geraldine 5.09.66, SB :
100 - 11.39 (11.26w-84/11.31-88),
150 - 17.26, 200 - 22.95
JACQUES Stacey U20 24.06.77, Hallamshire :
400 - 56.46 (55.68-94)
JAMES Alison U20 9.03.79, Cheltenham :
HJ - 1.66 (1.70-95)
JAMES Angharad U20 7.04.79, Swansea :
100 - 12.21, 200 - 24.92
JAMES Anwen U17 17.02.81, Swansea :
DT - 34.50,
JAMES Dawn 4.01.67, AF&D :
1500 - 4:31.3, 3k - 9:49.78, 5k - 16:56.9
JAMES Dawn V35 17.10.60, Stowmarket :
Mar - 2:59:35
JAMES Vernicha U13 6.06.84, Cambridge H :
150 - 19.4, 200 - 26.4
JAMISON Victoria U20 19.05.77, Lagan Val :
100 - 12.02, 200 - 24.34w/24.5/24.97,
400 - 55.03, 400H - 57.27
JARVIS Sarah U15 10.03.82, Wycombe :
1500 - 4:43.31
JASPER Sarah U13 1.05.84, Huntingdon :
600 - 1:43.7, 800 - 2:20.6
JEEVES Anna V40 19.09.54, Shaft Barnet :
Mar - 3:00:50
JEGEDE Tolu U17 25.09.80, Newham & E B :
LJ - 5.42, TJ - 11.59
JELBERT Zoe U13 21.01.84, Newquay & Par :
1500 - 4:58.5

JELLEY Claire U17 27.11.79, Derby LAC :
60 - 7.95i (7.83i-95)
JENKINS Andrea U23 4.10.75, Bedford & Co :
HT - 45.00
JENKINS Joanne V35 7.01.59, Canterbury H :
Mar - 3:07:05
JENNER Jackie U23 25.10.76, Tonbridge :
100H - 15.23 (14.84w/15.0/15.12-95),
LJ - 5.56
JENNINGS Joanne 20.09.69, Essex L :
HJ - 1.89 (1.94i-93/1.90-88)
JOHANSEN Michelle U13 1.02.84, Oxford C :
100 - 13.2, LJ - 4.99
JOHN Joanne E. U17 12.11.80, Ealing,S & Mx :
DT - 37.28
JOHNS Karen U17 18.08.80, Shildon :
800 - 2:14.2 (2:11.19-94)
JOHNS Michelle U17 12.03.80, Invicta :
TJ - 11.29w/11.01, Hepl - 3968
JOHNS Sarah U17 24.10.80, Southend :
HJ - 1.68
JOHNSON Charmaine R. 4.06.63, W S & E :
100H - 14.74 (14.36-94),
HJ - 1.67i/1.66 (1.72-89),
LJ - 5.54i/5.16 (6.00w-90/5.92-92),
SP - 14.09 (14.29-93), Hep - 5066 (5495-92)
JOHNSON Gemma Lynne U20 21.07.78, Notts :
HT - 35.92
JOHNSON Jade U17 7.06.80, Herne Hill :
100 - 12.3 (12.2w/12.62-95),
LJ - 6.08 (6.24w/6.13-95)
JOHNSON Julia U17 21.09.79, Invicta :
TJ - 11.82
JOHNSON Sara 10.07.70, Carmarthen :
400H - 65.8 (65.10-95)
JOHNSON Sarah J. U17 20.07.80, Bed & Co :
300 - 40.4/40.96
JOHNSTON Stephanie U15 9.10.81, Barr & F :
100 - 12.24w/12.3/12.39
JOHNSTONE Pamela U20 16.03.79, Edin WM :
400H - 61.93
JOINER Angela 14.02.69, Charnwood :
5k - 16:43.9, 10kR - 34:55, HMar - 1:19:52
JONES Caroline V35 29.03.60, Carmarthen :
Mar - 3:05:00 (2:58:45-91)
JONES Dawn 16.02.70, Harlow :
TJ - 11.48
JONES Elizabeth V35 25.04.61, Hailsham :
Mar - 2:55:02 (2:54:03-95)
JONES Gemma U20 25.02.79, Torfaen :
LJ - 5.52w/5.28 (5.47-95)
JONES Jillian 23.12.69, Southampton City :
800 - 2:09.59 (2:04.97-93),
1500 - 4:22.1 (4:16.0-93), 3k - 9:40.52
JONES Katie U20 4.01.77, Trafford :
400 - 56.35, 100H - 14.6w/15.00w/15.0,
400H - 61.19, TJ - 11.18
JONES Leanne U23 13.05.74, Rhondda :
HT - 43.34
JONES Lindsey U20 8.09.77, Wakefield :
HT - 45.22
JONES Michelle U23 6.01.75, Dartford :
100 - 12.27 (12.1w-90)
JONES Natalie U15 21.02.82, Ryde :
DT - 32.20
JONES Susan Eva U20 8.06.78, Wigan :
100H - 14.41 (14.3w/14.4-94),
HJ - 1.87, Hep - 4163 (4142-95)

JORDAN Rachel 29.01.72, Birchfield :
600 - 1:31.3, 800 - 2:07.50, 3k - 9:57.4
JOSEPH Samantha 11.09.70, Windsor S & E :
PV - 2.50
JOSEPH Tracy Carol 29.11.69, Basing & MH :
60 - 7.62i (7.42i-89), 100 - 11.79,
200 - 23.57w/23.72, 300 - 37.92 (37.48-93),
400 - 53.79 (53.23-91), 100H - 14.22,
HJ - 1.68, LJ - 6.13, Hep - 5339
JUDD Samantha U13 22.10.83, Brighton :
PenM - 2011
JURY Kerry 19.11.68, Wakefield :
200 - 24.20w/24.42, 60H - 8.81i,
100H - 13.9w/13.95w/14.04, HJ - 1.80,
LJ - 5.80w/5.71, SP - 11.25 (11.28-92),
JT - 38.88, Hep - 5703

KAISER Kath M. V45 24.08.51, Valli :
Mar - 3:06:04 (2:55:03-94)
KALU April U15 31.03.82, Sale :
SPG - 12.96, PenG - 3005
KANE Kelly U23 28.10.74, Blackpool/IRE :
SP - 11.44 (13.70-93)
KAY Louise U20 1.12.77, Bolton :
HT - 42.86
KAY Rachael U17 8.09.80, Wigan :
60 - 7.99i, 100 - 12.59 (12.1-95),
200 - 25.50i (24.44-95), 60H - 8.71i,
80HI - 11.6/12.08, 300H - 43.2/45.61
KEENE Julie U15 2.04.82, Sale :
1500 - 4:47.63
KEIGHTLEY Lauren U20 2.08.79, Bracknell :
DT - 48.24 (47.56dh-95)
KELLY Jemma U15 13.03.82, Barrow & Furn :
DT - 30.04
KELLY Jennifer A. 20.06.70, Peterborough :
SP - 12.54 (14.88i-90/14.73-91)
KELLY Louise U17 20.09.80, Barrow & Furn :
3k - 10:27.5
KELLY Siona U23 19.04.74, Sale :
JT - 39.66 (43.46-94)
KEMP Jennifer U17 18.02.80, Liverpool Pem :
JT - 45.90
KEMP Michelle U15 19.09.81, Sutton & Dist :
JT - 40.22
KEMP Thomasin U17 5.03.80, Yeovil Oly :
800 - 2:16.4, 1500 - 4:35.7 (4:32.37-95)
KENNEDY Cheryl U17 10.02.80, Jarrow & H :
60H - 9.07i, 80HI - 11.9/12.27 (12.19-95)
KENNEDY Samantha 13.04.71, Solihull & S H :
1500 - 4:31.16
KENNEY Lisa U15 17.02.83, Hull Springhead :
JT - 33.00
KERR Anyha U17 10.04.80, Bristol :
JT - 36.88,
KERR Emma U20 15.10.77, Ayr Seaforth :
HJ - 1.70i/1.70 (1.70-95)
KERR Natalie V.S. U17 17.11.79, R Sutton C :
SP - 11.73, DT - 44.44
KILNER Debbie V35 2.11.61, Aberdeen :
10k - 36:45.3 (36:22.7-95)
KINCH Beverly 14.01.64, Hounslow :
60 - 7.33i (7.13i-86), 200 - 24.2/24.35 (23.57-93),
100 - 11.50 (11.1w-87/11.13w-83/11.2-84/11.29-90)
KING Emma U17 25.07.81, Guernsey :
SP - 10.48
KING Janine 18.02.73, Trafford :
JT - 50.80

382

KING Lesley U13 28.09.83, :
LJ - 4.81
KING Rachel U23 11.05.76, Cardiff :
200 - 25.1, 60H - 8.99i (8.90i-95),
100H - 14.1/14.40 (13.99w/14.03-95)
KING Sharon Marie 27.01.72, Sale :
800 - 2:07.1mx/2:09.07 (2:08.27-95),
1500 - 4:19.83, 3k - 9:41.8mx (9:43.36i-94)
KINGSBOROUGH Ruth 25.10.67, Overton :
10kR - 35:00
KINGSBURY Cath, Rhondda :
HT - 34.86
KIRBY Emma U15 11.11.81, Bracknell :
DT - 35.88
KIRBY Rachel 18.05.69, Blackheath :
LJ - 5.67 (6.02-94), TJ - 13.28 (13.64-94)
KIRKPATRICK Julie 14.07.72, Birchfield :
HT - 48.90
KITNEY Emily U17 25.04.81, Medway :
JT - 38.32
KNEALE Karen 23.04.69, Manx H :
3kW - 14:06.0 (14:05.1-95), 5kW - 24:40.69,
5kWR - 24:22 (24:21-95), 10kWR - 49:37
KOEHNE Sophie U15 17.09.81, Shaft Barnet :
800 - 2:18.85, 1500 - 4:48.37
KOSTILEK Anna 16.11.65, Westbrook :
3k - 9:47.9 (9:35.97-90), 5k - 17:06.1
KOTEY Judy U17 20.05.80, St Albans :
100 - 12.4, 200 - 25.5, JT - 37.02, Hepl - 3829

L AING Wendy J. 29.12.62, Liv H :
100H - 15.1w/15.14
(14.14w-93/14.2-81/14.35-86),
400H - 64.2/65.10 (59.8-86/61.77-93),
Hep - 4546 (5351-93)
LAMBOURN Angela J. 9.04.66, Northampton :
SP - 12.64 (13.75-91), HT - 35.36 (36.92-92)
LANE Catherine U23 18.11.76, Dacorum & Tr :
DT - 36.60 (38.60-95), HT - 37.56
LANE Kathryn U20 6.11.78, Bromsgrove & R :
Hep - 3894
LANE S. U20, Shaftesbury Barnet :
PV - 2.70
LANE Sarah U17 4.06.81, Torfaen :
80HI - 11.9/11.91, LJ - 5.56
LANG Andrea U15 6.03.82, Ayr Seaforth :
60 - 7.87i
LANGFORD Lisa Martine 15.03.67, W & B :
5kWR - 23:13 (22:01-89),
10kWR - 48:27 (45:42-87)
LAPKA Fiona 17.12.66, Exeter :
HJ - 1.68 (1.74-84)
LAST Suzanne F. 11.01.70, Medway :
DT - 38.82, HT - 48.78
LATIMER Joanna M. 30.01.71, Sale/Oxford U :
800 - 2:07.4mx/2:08.15 (2:03.27-94)
LAVENDER Julie U23 9.11.75, Sunderland :
HT - 44.54 (51.62-94)
LAVERCOMBE Michelle 12.07.67, Exeter :
(see WANNELL)
LAVERS Lesley 6.08.68, Parkside :
JT - 39.58 (40.18-90)
LAWFORD Rebecca U17 27.04.80, Sale :
300 - 40.51
LAWRENCE Victoria 9.06.73, Blackpool :
600 - 1:32.83i+, 800 - 2:03.52, 1500 - 4:19.77

LAX Sian U20 4.08.79, Telford :
JT - 45.74
LAYZELL Alyson 16.12.66, Cheltenham :
400H - 56.43
LEAKE Elaine U17 27.10.79, City of Hull :
800 - 2:16.6,
LECKIE Gillian U15 1.09.81, Perth :
75HG - 11.8/11.88
LEE Dorothea U20 28.07.77, Yeovil Oly/Ox U :
600 - 1:33.7, 800 - 2:09.82 (2:06.67-94),
1500 - 4:29.57i
LEE Georgina U23 6.01.74, Sale :
100H - 15.0, 400H - 65.3
LEE Helen U17 27.08.80, Rotherham :
300 - 40.17, 400 - 58.7
LEE Lynda V35 7.04.57, Leeds :
Mar - 3:02:53
LEGER Claudine U17 17.05.80, Havering :
100 - 12.3/12.34 (12.2-95)
LEGGETT Lesley V35 3.04.58, Herne Hill :
Mar - 3:05:30
LEIGH Sandra C. 26.02.66, Stevenage & NH :
400 - 54.40 (52.75-91), 400H - 64.2 (61.8-93)
LESTRANGE Katy U17 17.09.79, Warrington :
60H - 8.86i, 80HI - 11.39w/11.47, 100H - 14.82
LEWIS Ann V45 29.12.47, AF&D :
3kW - 15:52.71i/15:55.0, 5kW - 27:02.29,
5kWR - 26:46, 10kW - 56:26.3,
10kWR - 56:12, 20kW - 1:56:14
LEWIS Denise 27.08.72, Birchfield :
200 - 24.06w/24.44, 60H - 8.32i,
100H - 13.18, HJ - 1.84,
LJ - 6.66 (6.67-95), SP - 14.36,
JT - 56.50, Hep - 6645
LEWIS Rebecca U20 31.12.77, Sale :
100H - 14.4w/14.42,
LJ - 6.03w/5.71 (5.73-94),
SP - 11.91 (11.96-95), Hep - 5047
LEWIS Z., :
Mar - 3:00:46
LEYSHON Anna U17 19.01.80, Swansea :
60H - 9.25i (9.14i-95),
80HI - 11.85 (11.8-95), 300H - 46.7/46.85
LIGHTFOOT Leonie U15 8.02.82, C of Stoke :
100 - 12.44w/12.63
LILFORD Jane 28.11.70, Banbury :
HJ - 1.71 (1.78-89)
LILLEY Emma U23 2.05.76, Bingley :
JT - 40.98 (44.08-95)
LILLEY Nicola U17 17.02.80, Medway :
3k - 10:19.1 (10:16.38-95)
LINDSAY Emma 11.04.71, Edin WM/Lisburn :
200 - 24.5w/24.6/24.72 (24.18-94),
400 - 55.63, 100H - 15.21 (14.96-94),
400H - 62.9 (64.39-91),
HJ - 1.74i/1.70 (1.75-88),
LJ - 5.72i/5.49 (5.90i-93/5.89w-94/5.72-91),
Hep - 4979 (5353-94)
LINTERN Candie U15 5.02.82, Crawley :
DT - 31.78
LINTERN Jean V45 13.03.51, Crawley :
JT - 41.48 (51.04-76)
LISTER Rosanne 9.05.69, Medway :
DT - 47.74 (53.66-91),
HT - 37.00 (37.74-95)
LISTON Bianca U20 28.05.78, Bromley :
100 - 12.24, 200 - 25.28,
100H - 14.38w/14.46, LJ - 5.50 (5.70-95)

LITTLE Stephanie U15 5.11.81, Newport :
 75HG - 11.5/11.87
LITTLEWOOD Sarah J. U17 2.12.79, Bingley :
 800 - 2:14.43
LIVERTON Amanda Jayne 1.09.72, Exeter :
 JT - 54.44 (57.84-90)
LIVESEY Katherine U17 15.12.79, Blackpool :
 100 - 12.57w (12.4w-95), 200 - 25.14w/25.20,
 60H - 9.04i (8.93i-95), 80HI - 11.44w/11.66,
 HJ - 1.75, LJ - 5.60, Hepl - 4830w/4790
LLEWELLYN Stephanie 31.12.68, Shaft Barn :
 200 - 24.3/24.46 (24.2/24.38-95), 300 - 39.6i+,
 400 - 53.52 (52.4/52.54-95)
LLEWELLYN Wendy 30.05.63, Serpentine/NZ :
 5k - 17:13.29 (16:28.18-94),
 10MR - 56:00+/56:49, HMar - 1:13:17,
 Mar - 2:37:00/2:42:06 (2:40:35-95)
LLOYD Amy U13 20.11.83, Wakefield :
 70HM - 11.77, PenM - 1956
LLOYD Angharad U17 11.09.80, Carmarthen :
 SP - 10.92
LLOYD Caroline U20 7.01.79, Liverpool H :
 JT - 40.22
LLOYD Elizabeth U17 1.12.79, Cannock & St :
 100 - 12.38, 200 - 25.4/26.02
LOCKWOOD Clare U17 7.10.79, Colwyn Bay :
 JT - 39.10
LODGE Joanna 6.01.68, Hounslow :
 Mar - 2:56:57
LOMAS Claire U17 18.04.80, Perth :
 TJ - 10.79
LONSDALE Michelle U15 29.10.81, Wakefield :
 JT - 34.96
LOUARRADI Farah U17 11.10.79, C of Bath :
 SP - 10.49
LOVELAND Donna U20 28.06.78, Southend :
 JT - 43.76
LOW Jane Kathryn V35 26.08.60, C of Glas :
 400H - 60.70 (58.43-94)
LOW Linda 20.01.71, Aberdeen :
 HT - 37.58 (41.32-94), JT - 38.28 (41.08-93)
LOWE Larissa 19.08.69, Reading :
 PV - 3.20
LOWE Samantha U15 23.02.82, Bury :
 JT - 35.00
LOWE Zoe A. 7.07.65, St Albans :
 Mar - 2:57:08 (2:49:28-95)
LUDLOW Jayne U20 7.01.79, Cardiff :
 TJ - 11.37w/11.30 (12.14-94)
LUNN Wendy 2.12.68, Reading :
 (see MARSHALL)
LUPTON Brenda V40 5.10.52, Sheffield RWC :
 3kW - 14:37.29, 5kW - 25:26.55 (24:18.6-84),
 5kWR - 25:23 (24:05-82),
 10kW - 54:24.2 (50:10.2-84),
 10kWR - 52:57 (50:22-83),
 20kW - 1:53:19 (1:48:00-83)
LUPTON Victoria Anne 17.04.72, Sheff RWC :
 3kW - 13:06.27 (12:59.3-95),
 5kW - 23:04.57 (21:52.4-95),
 5kWR - 22:30 (21:36-92),
 10kW - 49:15.0 (45:18.8-95),
 10kWR - 47:05 (45:28sh-93/45:48-94),
 20kW - 1:43:57 (1:42:47-95)
LYCETT Nicola U17 10.03.80, Newcastle :
 JT - 38.98
LYNCH Nnenna 3.07.71, Oxford Univ/USA :
 1500 - 4:15.3 (4:12.44-95), 5k - 16:08.9

LYNCH Sally A. 6.11.64, Newport :
 10k - 35:54.43 (34:24.21-91)
LYNES Margaret Tracey 19.02.63, Essex L :
 SP - 15.80i/13.89 (16.57-94),
 DT - 41.48 (44.76-93)
LYON Janet 12.03.62, Aberdeen :
 PV - 2.45

MACDOUGALL Lynne 18.02.65, C of Glas :
 800 - 2:08.37 (2:01.11-84),
 1500 - 4:17.10 (4:05.96-84)
MACKAY Julie Karen U23 5.06.76, Shaft B :
 1500 - 4:32.1 (4:28.6-93)
MACLEOD Karen M. A. V35 24.04.58, C of E :
 10kR - 33:27, Mar - 2:33:50 (2:33:16-94),
 10MR - 55:34 (53:42dh-93/54:34-92)
MACPHAIL Ann 3.05.70, City of Glasgow :
 3k - 9:43.6, 5k - 17:01.7
MACPHEE Rhonda U23 30.04.76, GEC :
 800 - 2:11.15i/2:11.6 (2:10.0-95),
 1500 - 4:24.40
MACPHERSON Joan U17 18.09.80, Basing & MH :
 SP - 11.31, DT - 39.88, HT - 32.92
MACRAE Carrie U17 2.09.80, Blackpool :
 JT - 36.64
MADDISON Lynn 17.08.67, Trafford :
 5k - 17:19.7
MADDOX Keri 4.07.72, Cannock & S/Staffs U :
 60H - 8.57i (8.47i-92), 400H - 59.39,
 100H - 13.39w/13.5/13.53 (13.20w/13.24-93)
MADUAKA Joice 30.09.73, Bromley :
 60 - 7.67i (7.59i-92),
 100 - 11.85 (11.74w/11.81-95),
 200 - 23.90 (23.81-95)
MAHINDRU Alison 15.07.68, City of Glasgow :
 400 - 56.5/58.46 (56.1-95),
 400H - 61.6 (60.7/60.95-95)
MAHONEY Joanne U23 22.10.76, Wirral :
 200 - 24.9, 400H - 62.3/63.35 (60.73-95)
MAIR Angharad V35 30.03.61, Newport :
 5k - 16:43.7, 10k - 34:11.76, 10MR - 56:52,
 HMar - 1:15:02, Mar - 2:38:47
MAIS Chevette U15 22.09.82, GEC :
 200 - 25.92
MAJOR Julie 19.08.70, Shaftesbury Barnet :
 HJ - 1.75 (1.85-94)
MAKEPEACE Rhona 7.08.62, Charnwood :
 1500 - 4:25.47 (4:14.2-91), 5k - 17:00.9,
 3k - 9:11.2mx/9:15.1 (9:03.51-92)
MALCOLM Tina J. 8.09.67, Essex L :
 LJ - 5.88 (6.19-87)
MALE Samantha U23 11.04.76, AF&D :
 100H - 14.4w/14.7/14.79 (14.64w-95)
MANN Kelly U13 8.09.83, Solihull & S Heath :
 2kW - 10:31.0 (10:09.0-95), 2KWR - 10:03,
 2.5kW - 12:53.3, 3kWR - 15:42o
MANN Kimberley U13 23.10.83, Barnsley :
 80 - 10.6, LJ - 4.74
MANN Michelle Louise U20 6.02.77, Preston :
 1500 - 4:25.3 (4:24.7mx-95),
 3k - 9:30.5mx/9:43.23 (9:38.0mx-95)
MANNING Caroline Louise 5.03.73, Woking :
 HT - 46.06 (47.06-95)
MANNING Chantell U17 4.09.80, Essex L :
 100 - 12.18
MANT Deborah U23 11.10.75, AF&D :
 100 - 11.98 (11.7w?/11.75w/11.88-93),
 200 - 24.69 (23.96w/24.08-93)

MANTLE Sarina Leah U17 19.01.81, N & E B :
   60H - 9.0i/9.11i, 80HI - 11.25w/11.62,
   100H - 15.2
MARCHANT Zina D. V45 30.09.50, C of Bath :
   10k - 36:30.3 (35:52.1-90),
   10kR - 34:50 (34:28-90),
   HMar - 1:17:27 (1:13:38-90),
   Mar - 2:45:42 (2:39:26-91)
MARDLE Eleanor U20 27.07.78, Exeter :
   100 - 12.1, 200 - 24.7/24.83w/24.97
MARSELLA Michele Dawn 10.01.68, Cov G :
   HJ - 1.65 (1.86-87)
MARSH Kim U17 8.07.81, Newquay & Par :
   HT - 32.02
MARSHALL Lucy U15 28.11.81, Charnwood :
   SPG - 10.74, DT - 32.04
MARSHALL Wendy 2.12.68, Reading
   (nee LUNN) : 800 - 2:07.65
MARSTERS Kelly U17 8.09.79, Ryston :
   1500 - 4:41.82
MARTI Debora Jane 14.05.68, Bromley :
   HJ - 1.94 (1.94i-91),
   LJ - 6.22 (6.22w-85/6.19-92)
MARTIN Amelia U17 11.02.80, Blackheath :
   LJ - 5.50i/4.99
MARTIN Angela U17 26.11.80, Border :
   HJ - 1.66
MARTIN Claire U23 12.07.76, Newport :
   800 - 2:12.7, 1500 - 4:27.08
MARTIN Hayley U23 25.05.76, Camb H/Ox U :
   JT - 39.76 (43.06-95)
MARTIN Imogen Dee U23 13.02.74, Luton :
   DT - 37.04 (39.40-93), HT - 41.48 (42.48-95)
MARTIN Karen Lesley U23 24.11.74,
   Derby LAC/WRAF : SP - 11.62 (11.98-94),
   JT - 53.74 (55.72-92)
MARTIN Tracy U17 4.04.80, Coventry Godiva :
   100 - 12.45w/12.6/12.73 (12.6/12.64-95),
   200 - 25.04w/25.17
MARTINDALE Rebecca U17 31.12.80, Border :
   200 - 25.42w/25.7/25.81, 300 - 41.2
MASON Rachel U20 10.06.77, Hull Achilles :
   400H - 65.6/66.61
MASSEY Anne-Marie U15 10.09.82, Liv.H :
   75HG - 11.73
MASSEY Eva U17 22.12.80, North Down :
   SP - 11.10, DT - 34.56
MATHIE Louise U17 7.03.80, Crawley :
   TJ - 10.97
MAY Carolyn U23 15.10.74, Guildford & G :
   HJ - 1.65 (1.76-91)
MAYHEAD Kirsty U20 17.02.78, Epsom & E :
   100H - 14.8/15.03
MAYLOR Donna U15 20.05.82, Birchfield :
   100 - 12.39 (12.3-95), HJ - 1.59,
   LJ - 5.86w/4.89 (5.21-95)
MAYO Ruth 12.10.68, Lisburn (nee CARNEY):
   1500 - 4:30.09 (4:30.08-95)
MCCABE Laura U17 24.01.80, Vale Royal :
   800 - 2:12.5
MCCARRICK Danielle U17 30.11.79, Manx :
   800 - 2:13.21
MCCARTHY Jenny U15 22.02.82, Warrington :
   200 - 25.24w/25.39
MCCLUNG Mary 19.12.71, Edinburgh WM :
   800 - 2:08.21 (2:05.64-95)

MCCOLGAN Elizabeth 24.05.64, Dundee HH :
   10kR - 31:41 (30:38-89),
   10MR - 53:33+ (52:14-92),
   HMar - 1:10:28/1:13:48+ (1:07:11-92),
   Mar - 2:27:54 (2:27:32-91)
MCCONNELL Lee U20 9.10.78, C of Glasgow :
   200 - 24.4w/24.93 (24.0w/24.89w/24.9-94),
   400 - 56.4, HJ - 1.75i/1.75 (1.78-94)
MCCORRY Julie U17 7.11.79, Ballymena & A :
   SP - 11.78, DT - 33.84
MCCOY Jayne 17.03.72, Wirral :
   (see GREEN)
MCCREA Philippa U20 1.03.78, Gateshead :
   800 - 2:09.3,
MCCREADIE Helen U23 10.05.75, Edin WM :
   DT - 42.44 (43.58-94), HT - 48.32
MCDEVITT Julie 15.03.73, City of Glasgow :
   800 - 2:11.35,
MCDONAGH Jenny U17 23.04.81, Lagan Val:
   TJ - 10.50
MCDONNELL Alison 28.06.72, Parkside :
   100H - 14.7/15.13, 400H - 62.7/63.02
MCDOUGALL Joanne U20 23.08.79, Southp't :
   200 - 25.08w/25.63 (25.3-95)
MCELROY Emma U13 16.09.83, Bally & A :
   PenM - 1996
MCEWAN Donna U20 17.01.78, Leamington :
   DT - 43.00
MCGEE Jill, Lancaster & Morcambe :
   Mar - 3:04:36
MCGEORGE Sonia Marian 2.11.64, Brighton/
   Loughborough Studnts : 5k - 15:29.04,
   1500 - 4:17.3mx/4:19.40 (4:10.75-90),
   3k - 9:04.69i/9:09.53 (8:51.33-90)
MCGILLIVARY Aileen 13.08.70, Edinburgh WM :
   100 - 11.64w/11.68 (11.43w-93/11.54-92),
   200 - 24.2 (23.29-93)
MCGIVERN Stacy U23 14.12.76, Peterbro :
   TJ - 11.13i/11.12 (11.64-95)
MCGOLDRICK Lesley U17 12.09.79, Gate :
   80HI - 11.67w/11.7/12.07 (11.71-95)
MCGOWAN Julia H. V35 12.05.59, Brighton :
   Mar - 3:04:57 (2:36:31-86)
MCGOWAN Morag 22.08.69, City of Glasgow :
   100 - 12.14w/12.29 (11.78w/11.97-93)
MCGOWAN Suzanne U20 13.04.78, Mothw :
   200 - 25.1w/26.25 (24.79w-95/24.9/24.99-93)
MCGREAVY Sara U15 13.12.82, Leamington :
   75HG - 11.50w/11.6/11.67, PenG - 2786
MCINTOSH Dextene U20 27.08.78, Essex L :
   400H - 62.28, HJ - 1.65 (1.68-94)
MCINTYRE Iona U15 14.03.83, Edinburgh WM :
   800 - 2:14.46, 1500 - 4:45.48
MCKENZIE Evadne U23 19.05.75, E,S&M/JAM :
   60 - 7.53i, 100 - 11.4w/11.63, 200 - 24.11
MCKERNAN Jacqueline Lena 1.07.65, Lisburn/
   Loughbro : SP - 12.99 (13.31i-91/13.20-92),
   DT - 60.04 (60.72-93)
MCKINLEY M. U13, Preseli :
   HJ - 1.46io/1.45
MCKINNON Zoe U15 8.09.81, Horsham BS :
   75HG - 11.74,
MCLEOD Geraldine Ann 24.09.71, Birchfield :
   60 - 7.36i, 100 - 11.48 (11.2-94/11.46w-93),
   150 - 17.61,
   200 - 23.64A/23.82i/24.07 (23.4-93/23.47-94)
MCLOUGHLIN Lauren U15 8.09.82, Newport :
   75HG - 11.49w/11.5/11.64

MCPHAIL Fiona 23.06.71, Wigan/WRAF :
  HJ - 1.75 (1.75-95)
MCPHERSON Karen 6.11.72, Trafford :
  800 - 2:09.4 (2:06.3-91), 1500 - 4:27.1 (4:25.1-91)
MCPHERSON Vikki 1.06.71, C of G/Glas Un:
  3k - 9:21.2 (9:10.1-92), 5k - 16:06.2mx,
  10k - 33:17.74 (32:32.42-93),
  10kR - 34:35 (33:05-92)
MCQUEEN Sophie U15 3.12.81, Cleethorpes :
  HJ - 1.72
MCSHANE Laura U15 22.04.82, Hallamshire :
  75HG - 11.69, PenG - 2769
MCVIE Siobhan U13 6.07.84, Ayr Seaforth :
  LJ - 4.71, PenM - 2172
MEAD Sarah U17 16.10.79, Torfaen :
  800 - 2:13.4, 1500 - 4:43.6
MEADOWS Jennifer U17 17.04.81, Wigan :
  200 - 25.5 (25.3-95/25.52-94), 300 - 40.36,
  400 - 56.54, 800 - 2:16.4 (2:14.88-95)
MELLIS Kelly U17 4.12.79, Banbury :
  SP - 10.58, DT - 40.98 (41.96-95), HT - 30.76
MELLOR Leanne U23 17.03.76, Rotherham :
  PV - 2.40 (3.10-94)
MELVIN Hazel 19.11.73, City of Glasgow :
  HJ - 1.84
MERRY Emma Louise U23 2.07.74, Cov G :
  SP - 13.49 (13.62-93), DT - 49.64 (52.58-93)
MERRY Katharine U23 21.09.74, Birchfield :
  100 - 11.5w/11.54 (11.27w/11.34-94),
  200 - 22.88 (22.85-94)
MERSH Joanne U23 19.10.74, Essex L :
  800 - 2:11.3
MICHAELSKA Carmen 6.11.73, Ealing,
  Southall & Mx/Army (nee COLLINS) :
  400 - 56.1 (57.71-89), Hep - 3854
MIDDLETON C. U15, Wilts Sch :
  HJ - 1.60
MIGHTY A. D. Natasha 21.12.70, Radley :
  SP - 11.26 (11.46-92)
MIJOVIC Catherine H. V35 11.04.61, Birch :
  5k - 17:33.80 (16:47.18-95)
MIKNEVICIUTE Dalia 5.09.70, Essex L/LIT :
  HJ - 1.85i/1.85, TJ - 11.52
MILBURN Leanne U20 16.08.79, Copeland :
  LJ - 5.50, Hep - 4202
MILES Helen Louise 2.03.67, Cardiff :
  100 - 12.10w (11.4/11.41w/11.50-88)
MILES Sarah U20 14.12.78, Newbury :
  100 - 12.1/12.31w/12.51 (12.10w-93)
MILLER Eve U17 1.12.79, Hertford & Ware :
  200 - 25.26w/25.3/25.50, 60H - 9.20i,
  80HI - 11.93, 100H - 15.2, Hepl - 4255
MITCHELL Elizabeth U17 13.10.79, Essex L :
  300H - 44.54
MITCHELL Jeina Sophia U23 21.01.75, Croy :
  400 - 56.7, 600 - 1:32.81, 800 - 2:04.87,
  1k - 2:40.98, 1500 - 4:19.8 (4:19.09-92)
MITCHELL Julie U23 3.10.74, Brighton :
  800 - 2:09.2, 1500 - 4:29.4
MITCHELL S. U13, Bromsgrove & R :
  70HM - 11.8
MITCHELL Virginia 29.01.63, Woking :
  400H - 64.7 (64.05-95)
MOCKLER Jennifer U15 28.08.82, Liv H :
  800 - 2:16.1, 1500 - 4:31.70
MODAHL Diane Dolores 17.06.66, Sale :
  600 - 1:28.40 (1:26.18-87),
  800 - 1:59.87 (1:58.65-90)

MOFFAT Basilie U20 8.04.78, Bingley :
  HJ - 1.70
MOFFITT Alison J. 6.10.69, North Down :
  SP - 11.96, JT - 49.10
MOHAMED Stacey U17 22.01.80, Jarrow & H :
  JT - 36.60
MOLLOY Jennifer U13 23.09.83, Bournem'th :
  200 - 27.6, 70HM - 11.3
MONK Caroline U23 7.09.75, Halesowen :
  SP - 11.35
MONTADOR Karen U20 14.05.79, Central :
  1500 - 4:32.1 (4:35.4mx-95)
MONTADOR Kimberly U17 23.06.81, Central :
  800 - 2:15.6
MOODY Carly U17 9.06.80, Braintree :
  60 - 7.93i, 100 - 12.4/12.69 (12.4-95)
MOODY Karen 20.07.67, Cannock & Stafford :
  HT - 35.58
MOODY Lisa U20 22.02.77, City of Glasgow :
  3k - 9:54.87
MOORE Julie 5.12.73, Manx/Loughbro :
  400 - 56.8/56.86 (55.07-95)
MOORE Sarah Louise 15.03.73, Bristol :
  HT - 53.26
MOOREKITE Janice D. V35 1.05.57, Invicta :
  HMar - 1:19:19 (1:17:07-94),
  Mar - 2:48:50 (2:48:06-95)
MORETON Kelly U17 18.09.79, Newport :
  HJ - 1.68i/1.68 (1.71-95), Hepl - 4089
MORGAN Kelly U17 17.06.80, Salisbury :
  JT - 49.00
MORGAN Pamela 16.04.65, Liverpool H :
  3k - 9:53.3, 5k - 16:53.52
MORGANELLA Maria U17 2.10.79, Border :
  LJ - 5.51, Hepl - 3911
MORLEY Sonia 1.03.66, Jarrow & Hebburn :
  5k - 17:14.5
MORLEY Suzanne V35 11.10.57, Brighton :
  Mar - 3:01:26
MORRIS Emma U15 25.01.82, Burnley :
  SPG - 11.29
MORRIS Joanna U20 16.10.77, Newbury :
  HJ - 1.67 (1.67-93), TJ - 12.07w/11.85,
  Hep - 4078 (4209-95)
MORRIS Kate U15 18.01.83, Dartford :
  SPG - 10.69, DT - 30.48
MORRISON Claire 30.05.69, Bristol :
  (see ADAMS)
MORRISON Kirsty U23 28.10.75, Medway :
  JT - 47.76 (59.36-93)
MORRISON Laurie 27.07.73, E,S & Mx/Army :
  JT - 38.46 (39.40-95)
MOSS Sarah U13 17.11.83, Hamps Sch :
  JTM - 30.40
MUDDIMAN Claire U13 9.09.83, Chesterfield :
  LJ - 4.71
MUNRO Lynsay U20 1.02.77, Edinburgh WM :
  JT - 38.04 (41.92-95)
MURPHY Catherine Ann U23 21.09.75, S B :
  100 - 11.6/11.66w/11.69A/11.77 (11.63w-94),
  150 - 17.61, 300 - 37.72,
  200 - 23.46i/23.47A/23.52 (23.40-95)
MURRAY Yvonne Carole Grace 4.10.64, Moth :
  10kR - 33:00+/33:16 (33:01-84),
  10MR - 53:50 (54:49un-84), HMar - 1:12:25
MURRAY-JESSEE Alison 13.01.67, : :
  PV - 3.60S (3.00un-95)

386

MURRIN Noeleen U17 22.12.79, Sol & S H :
  1500 - 4:42.5, 3k - 10:32.27
MYERS Mara 13.08.73, Parkside :
  3k - 9:26.10, 5k - 16:41.67, 10k - 34:41.28

N ASH Hayley L. 30.05.63, Newport :
  10kR - 34:36 (33:10-89),
  10MR - 55:50 (55:32-94),
  HMar - 1:16:10 (1:13:16-94)
NASH Sarah U17 10.11.80, Leamington :
  100 - 12.4 (13.38-95),
  200 - 25.3/25.32w/26.16, 300 - 41.3
NASH Sharon U23 5.05.74, GEC :
  SP - 11.72 (12.67-93), DT - 36.62 (44.32-93)
NAUGHER Abigail U17 26.02.80, Sunderland :
  300 - 40.90, Hepl - 3880
NDU Katy U15 26.03.82, Herts Sch :
  SPG - 10.96
NEALL Alison U17 8.11.79, Croydon :
  JT - 37.68 (37.86-94)
NEEF Melanie 26.05.70, City of Glasgow :
  60 - 7.49i (7.36i-95),
  100 - 11.9/12.33 (11.6w-95/11.69w-88/11.70-95),
  200 - 23.62i/24.6/24.67 (23.35-95),
  300 - 38.1i+ (37.33-94),
  400 - 52.50i/53.23 (51.18-95)
NELSON Tatum U20 17.12.78, GEC :
  60 - 7.50i (7.55i-94),
  200 - 24.9 (24.35w/24.51-93)
NEWCOMBE Rachel 25.02.67, Liverpool H :
  400 - 56.8 (55.19-92), 800 - 2:09.48
NEWMAN Wendy 31.08.71, Essex L :
  JT - 45.46
NEWTON Jackie 28.08.64, Stockport :
  10MR - 58:56 (58:31-95),
  HMar - 1:17:31, Mar - 2:47:28
NEWTON Lynne V45 19.05.47, Portsmouth :
  3kW - 16:28.7
NEWTON Maria Angela 22.07.66, Ashford :
  PV - 3.15
NICCOLLS Jannette U23 7.09.76, Herc Wimb :
  100 - 11.84w/12.0/12.09 (12.07-95),
  200 - 25.1 (24.8/24.96w-95/25.51-92)
NICHOLLS Emily U20 5.12.78, Westbury :
  100 - 12.19
NICHOLLS Michelle U15 26.09.82, W S & E :
  100 - 12.5/12.95
NICHOLLS Tamara U20 21.07.78, Basildon :
  DT - 37.06 (38.86-94)
NICHOLSON Rachel U20 30.12.77, Shaft B :
  3k - 9:50.91
NICHOLSON Stephanie U23 28.06.76, C of H :
  100H - 15.0 (14.96w-94/15.10-95), LJ - 5.53
NICOLLE Sarah U17 12.01.80, Telford :
  80HI - 11.9/12.02w/12.10, 300H - 45.78
NIELD Emma U13 20.11.83, Lanark & L T C :
  HJ - 1.46io/1.45
NIGHTINGALE Jo-Anne U15 3.05.83, Wyc :
  PV - 2.10
NIGHTINGALE Julie U23 28.04.75, Eastb GS :
  JT - 38.64 (42.80-95)
NISBIT Daisy U15 10.07.83, Ashford :
  PV - 2.30
NORMAN Hannah U17 1.06.81, Pitreavie :
  1500 - 4:40.76
NORMAN Katrina U23 1.01.76, Walton :
  400H - 60.87 (60.15-95)

NORTHEY Samantha U17 18.04.80, Belgrave :
  3k - 10:12.1
NOY Deborah 31.10.64, Havant :
  Mar - 2:45:50 (2:35:18-91)
NUNN Helen 15.09.71, Ashford :
  400H - 65.2
NUTT Caroline U15 7.06.83, Scunthorpe :
  PV - 2.10
NUTT Louise U17 6.09.79, Norwich :
  JT - 41.28
NUTTALL Diane U20 10.06.77, Braintree :
  JT - 38.04 (39.24-95)
NUTTELL Amy U17 6.02.80, Holbeach :
  80HI - 11.86, Hepl - 4179
NWANOKWU Chidinma U15 27.10.81, Herne H :
  SPG - 10.73un/9.49 (9.61-95),
  DT - 30.98/25.42
NYHAN Angela U20 13.04.78, Rowntrees :
  100H - 14.87, SP - 11.95, Hep - 4805 (4523-95)

O 'CALLAGHAN Louise U15 12.12.81,
  Cambridge Harriers : 75HG - 11.43
O'CONNOR Holly U13 9.12.83, St Helens :
  600 - 1:41.3, 800 - 2:25.04, 1500 - 5:05.2
O'CONOR Annette 20.08.71, Bracknell :
  HT - 40.36 (42.32-90)
O'HARE Ellen U20 4.02.78, Cirencester :
  800 - 2:06.59, 1500 - 4:28.1 (4:28.1-95)
O'SULLIVAN Clare U17 8.05.80, Sutton & D :
  60H - 9.0i, 80HI - 11.65, 100H - 15.3
O'SULLIVAN Laura U15 30.04.82, Liv H :
  HJ - 1.60
OAKES Judith Miriam V35 14.02.58, Croydon :
  SP - 19.01 (19.36-88)
OATES Joanne U20 21.02.78, Bingley :
  400H - 63.28
OGDEN Rachael U20 23.07.79, Rowntrees :
  800 - 2:09.17 (2:08.78-95)
OJOKOLO Endurance U23 29.09.75, Ex L/NIG :
  100 - 11.70, 200 - 24.64
OKWUE Maurine U20 13.05.78, Thames VH :
  TJ - 11.31
OLADAPO Georgina 15.05.67, Hounslow :
  400 - 52.48
OLDFIELD Juliette U20 14.04.77, Birchfield :
  1500 - 4:25.80
OLDHAM Sarah U13 23.09.83, Dudley & St :
  100 - 13.2, 70HM - 11.6, 75HG - 12.0
OLIVER Lindsey U20 12.03.78, Liverpool H :
  HT - 40.40
ONIANWA Mary U17 20.01.81, Herc Wimb :
  60H - 9.1i, TJ - 10.57
ORE Wendy E. 23.05.66, Cardiff :
  3k - 9:26.60 (9:14.72-94), 5k - 16:25.79,
  10kR - 33:47 (33:15-94),
  10MR - 56:43 (55:10-94)
ORFORD Beth U17 25.03.81, Coventry G :
  HJ - 1.73
OSBOURNE Alice 27.02.67, Canterbury H :
  Mar - 3:01:37
OSTERSBURG Karen 23.09.65, Birchfield :
  SP - 11.34 (11.84-93), DT - 37.52 (38.74-93)
OVIDI Francesca U13 22.09.83, Bracknell :
  JTM - 27.36
OWBRIDGE Joanne U15 19.01.82, Hull Spr :
  LJ - 5.29w/5.20
OWEN Eirion 30.07.63, Brecon :
  PV - 2.40

OWEN Tracy A. 29.04.64, Arena :
Mar - 3:07:26 (3:03:32-94)
OWUSU Lesley U20 21.12.78, Windsor S & E :
60 - 7.71i, 100 - 12.0/12.11 (12.10-93),
200 - 24.2/24.47i/24.48 (24.34w/24.41-95),
300 - 39.4i+ (38.21-95), 400 - 54.53
OXLEY Sarah E. 3.07.73, Birchfield :
60 - 7.75i (7.68i-94), 100 - 12.18 (12.04-94),
200 - 24.74i/24.8/24.88
(24.13w-94/24.38i-95/24.6/24.65-94)
OYEPITAN Abiodun U17 30.12.79, Braintree :
100 - 12.06
OYEYEMI Jean U17 24.08.81, Shaft B/NIG :
100 - 12.28 (11.86w-94/12.18-95)

P ACE Anita 18.10.67, Hull Achilles :
400 - 57.5 (57.3-95)
PAGE Tracy 3.02.72, Braintree :
SP - 11.27i (12.59-88)
PALKA Juliana U20 9.05.77, City of Glasgow :
200 - 25.25, 400 - 56.55
PALMER Jane 7.10.66, Sheffield :
10kR - 34:19
PALMER Jodie U13 23.10.83, West Norfolk :
600 - 1:45.0, 800 - 2:25.5, 1500 - 5:03.6
PALMER Karlene J. U17 23.10.80, Reading :
60 - 7.92i (7.83i-95),
100 - 12.21w/12.4/12.62 (12.2/12.43-95),
200 - 24.67w/25.07 (24.84-95), 300 - 40.56
PARDO Clare U17 9.08.81, Guildford & G :
HT - 30.88
PARDON Hannah U13 4.10.84, Luton :
1500 - 5:02.0
PARKER Jacqueline T. 15.10.66, T Solent :
400 - 57.2+ (54.07-89),
800 - 2:07.31 (2:03.78i-93/2:04.8mx/2:06.44-95)
PARKER Susan 24.03.70, Sale :
800 - 2:04.9mx/2:06.5 (2:05.50-93),
1500 - 4:11.57, 3k - 9:11.68 (9:06.2-92)
PARKER-SMITH Kelly-Anne U17 10.02.81, Bel :
3kW - 16:13.8
PARKINSON Amanda 21.07.71, Hyndburn
(nee THORPE) : 800 - 2:10.1 (2:09.5-94),
1500 - 4:18.94 (4:12.9mx-95),
3k - 9:19.6 (9:17.4mx-94)
PARKINSON Danielle U15 2.09.81, Rochdale :
HJ - 1.60 (1.60-95), PenG - 2760
PARKINSON Hayley U23 5.12.75, Edin WM :
800 - 2:11.5, 1500 - 4:33.4 (4:33.1-94)
PARR Emily U17 9.05.81, Norwich :
200 - 25.57w/26.17
PARRIS Monique U13 28.01.84, Ilford :
75 - 10.0, 100 - 12.8, 150 - 19.7w,
200 - 26.8, LJ - 5.15
PARRY Carys U17 24.07.81, Rhondda :
HT - 41.04
PARRY Hayley 17.02.73, Swansea :
400 - 56.5, 800 - 2:03.77,
1k - 2:47.53i, 1500 - 4:16.9
PARRY Joanna U20 5.03.78, Soton City :
JT - 39.44
PARRY Sheena U20 16.11.77, Rhondda :
HT - 41.66 (42.66-95)
PARTINGTON Carolyn 27.06.66, Manx :
5kWR - 23:45+ (23:04-94),
10kWR - 48:00 (46:26-95)
PARTRIDGE Susan U17 4.01.80, East Kilb :
3k - 10:26.4
PATRICK Elizabeth U20 29.08.77, Kingst & P :
TJ - 11.75

PATTERSON Laura U17 31.01.81, Wycombe :
PV - 2.45
PATTINSON Helen U23 2.01.74, Preston :
800 - 2:09.5mx/2:10.3, 1500 - 4:16.84
PAUL Michaela U15 27.10.81, Ealing,S & Mx :
LJ - 5.28w/5.22
PAUZERS Clare 2.08.62, Herne HI/Lond RR :
3k - 9:46.25, HMar - 1:19:22
PAVEY Joanne 20.09.73, Bristol (nee DAVIS) :
1500 - 4:21.14, 1M - 4:41.20, 3k - 9:45.5
PAYNE Charlene U13 7.10.83, Windsor S & E :
75 - 10.1, 150 - 20.1
PAYNE Judith U17 7.07.80, Wakefield :
HJ - 1.71
PEACOCK Marina 12.07.64, Birchfield
(nee SEMENOVA) : HT - 48.20
PEACOCK Rachel U15 18.05.82, Wimborne :
LJ - 5.56w/5.31
PEAKE Fiona U20 31.05.77, Woking :
PV - 3.10
PEARCE Caroline U17 1.09.80, Huntingdon :
60H - 9.07i, LJ - 5.40w/5.37 (5.47-95)
PEARSON Claire U20 23.09.78, Leics Cor :
100H - 14.89
PEARSON Helen U17 8.02.81, Cornwall AC :
1500 - 4:41.8
PEARSON Marie U23 22.09.74, Barnsley :
JT - 38.92
PEARSON Suzanne U20 31.08.77, Som Sch :
Hep - 3870
PEATFIELD Zoe U20 8.12.77, Stockport :
400 - 57.19, 800 - 2:10.6
PEET Josephine 4.12.71, Bristol :
60H - 8.93i (8.76i-93), 400H - 63.4/63.51,
LJ - 5.60 (5.74w?-93/5.64-88)
PENNET Catriona U13 10.10.83, Aberdeen :
70HM - 11.72 (11.70w-95), PenM - 2335
PERCIVAL Deborah J. V35 22.04.58, Cant H :
HMar - 1:15:05, Mar - 2:48:49
PERIDES Lynsay U20 24.05.79, Beds & Co:
PV - 2.50i/2.40 (2.60-95)
PERRY Llyn U20 21.02.79, Braintree :
HT - 36.94
PERRYMAN Saffron U13 26.03.84, Reading :
SPM - 10.15, DTM - 23.70
PHILLIPS Claire U20 2.04.78, Sutton :
400 - 57.2/57.35
PHILLIPS Emma U17 31.01.81, Wakefield :
60 - 7.96i, 100 - 12.13w/12.25,
200 - 25.4/25.42
PHILLIPS Maria V40 8.06.52, Queens Park :
HT - 36.60
PHILLIPS Nicola U15 23.04.83, Dartford :
2.5kW - 13:47.10, 3kWR - 16:19
PHILP Hazel U13 21.10.83, Arbroath :
150 - 19.8dt, 200 - 27.61
PHILP Lucy U17 27.12.79, Edinburgh WM :
300 - 40.13, 400 - 57.1
PICTON Janette 4.03.63, Burnham :
Mar - 2:51:26
PIDGEON Elizabeth U20 27.04.77, Essex L :
HT - 48.98, JT - 43.24
PIERRE Michelle 30.09.73, Croydon :
200 - 24.4w/25.1 (24.8-95/25.25-90), 400 - 53.22
PIERRE Sherie U13 15.05.84, ShaftBarnet :
75 - 9.9, 100 - 12.7, 150 - 19.5, 200 - 26.7
PIMBLETT Caroline U23 28.01.75, Sale :
1500 - 4:21.3, 3k - 9:29.40, 5k - 16:35.36
PINNER Kate U17 21.12.79, City of Stoke :
JT - 35.82

PITEL Edwige 4.06.67, Shaftesbury B/FRA :
3k - 9:19.8mx (9:31.05-95), HMar - 1:15:32
PITTS Sally V35, :
Mar - 3:06:07
POCOCK Nicola U20 9.05.79, AF&D :
400H - 64.4/64.64
POLLARD Susan U13 2.12.83, Solihull & S H :
LJ - 4.89
PORAZINSKI Donna-Marie U17 28.01.81, Newp:
300 - 41.00, 300H - 45.9, Hepl - 3968
PORTER Sarah U17 11.12.79, Sutton & Dist :
80HI - 11.6w/11.8/12.04, 300H - 46.2
POSTOY Katie U15 26.08.82, Basildon :
JT - 33.46
POTTER Helen U23 25.06.74, Trafford :
JT - 43.20 (45.06-93)
POTTER R., Belle Vue :
Mar - 2:53:25
POVEY Tanya U20 13.04.79, South West RR :
3k - 9:37.6
POWELL Jacqueline U23 1.05.74, Paddock W:
HJ - 1.65 (1.74-90)
POWELL Kerry U15 28.02.82, Wilts Sch :
LJ - 5.48w/5.25
POWELL Xanine U20 21.05.79, Cambridge H :
200 - 24.69w/25.64
PRATT Julie U20 20.03.79, Essex L :
60H - 8.96i (8.82i-95),
100H - 14.0w/14.08
PRICE Sharon U23 10.12.75, R Sutton C:
100H - 14.7/15.01 (14.4w-95/14.43w-93/14.61-95)
PRIDMORE Rebecca U15 19.12.82, Leics WC :
3kW - 16:33.6, 3kWR - 15:58 (15:51o-95)
PRITCHARD Amanda U17 18.03.80, Cardiff :
200 - 25.1 (26.82-94), 300 - 40.11,
400 - 55.80, 800 - 2:07.32, 1500 - 4:36.0
PRYER Helen U20 21.01.79, Windsor S & E :
200 - 24.90w/25.5/25.52 (25.01-95)
PUDDLE Laura U13 27.01.84, Hounslow :
600 - 1:43.7, 800 - 2:27.0
PUGH Sophia U20 24.04.78, Charnwood :
PV - 2.45
PURKISS Melanie U20 11.03.79, T Solent :
100 - 11.8w/12.0/12.07,
200 - 24.61w/24.8/24.91 (24.53-95)

QUAILEY Glenys 28.02.65, Beds & Co :
SP - 11.25
QUIGG Clare U15, Ballymena & Antrim :
HJ - 1.61
QUIGLEY Lynne 19.02.69, Red Rose :
Mar - 3:07:02 (2:56:42-95)
QUILL Rita 12.03.67, Milton Keynes :
5k - 17:27.9
QUINN Pauline 2.08.70, Ballymena & Antrim :
800 - 2:12.3 (2:11.8-95), 1500 - 4:27.13

RADCLIFFE Paula J. 17.12.73, Beds & Co :
1500 - 4:08.42+ (4:06.84-95),
1M - 4:24.94, 2k - 5:49.0+ (5:39.20-93),
3k - 8:37.07, 5k - 14:46.76
RAINFORD-BRENT Ebony-Jewell U13
31.12.83, London Sch : SPM - 9.33
RAMMINGER Sarah Jane U23 1.10.75, Arb :
PV - 2.30, LJ - 5.60 (5.81-94),
TJ - 11.02 (11.47w/11.23-94)
RANDALL Charlotte U17 10.05.80, C of Plym :
300H - 46.01
RANKIN Adele 27.05.72, Oldham & Royton :
1500 - 4:30.1 (4:26.4-90), 5k - 16:56.20

RANN Lucy U17 5.09.80, Isle of Wight :
80HI - 12.0/12.95, SP - 11.62, JT - 45.32
RASHLEIGH Jan V35, Bolton :
HMar - 1:19:23 (1:19:06-94)
RAVEN Claire Heather 15.06.72, Cov Godiva/
Loughbro : 400 - 55.49 (53.99-92),
600 - 1:33.60i (1:30.3-89), 800 - 2:06.02
RAVEN Sarah U15 22.11.82, Southend :
1500 - 4:49.47
RAWLINSON Susan 13.10.70, Roth/Leeds P :
100 - 11.9/11.93 (11.8/11.89-94),
200 - 24.10w/24.18 (23.5/23.80w/24.13-94),
400 - 53.86 (53.4/53.69-95)
READE Leigh 15.08.72, Sale (nee FERRIER) :
400 - 57.4 (54.76-94)
READER Catherine V40 19.10.54, Colch H :
3kW - 15:41.1 (15:07.1-91),
10kW - 56:24.5 (52:43.3-92),
20kW - 1:52:39 (1:48:22-92)
READER Jennifer U20 23.12.77, Soton City :
HJ - 1.70
REDD Samantha U13 16.02.84, Brighton :
JT - 30.20, JTM - 36.06
REDDY Gissell U17 25.09.79, Essex L :
PV - 2.60
REDMOND Laura A. U17 19.04.81, C of Edin :
HJ - 1.65, Hepl - 4318
REDMOND Rachel U15 7.12.81, City of Stoke :
100 - 12.06w/12.21,
200 - 25.02w/25.1/25.39 (25.39-95)
REID Emma U17 5.01.81, Lochgelly :
300H - 46.0/47.40
REID-HUGHES Frances U17 18.03.80, Tonb :
SP - 11.23 (11.26-95), DT - 37.80
REILLY Rachel U15 19.11.82, Wolves & B :
3kWR - 16:00
REINALDA Elona U23 31.03.76, Essex L/AUS :
60 - 7.50i, 100 - 11.9/12.06 (11.90-95),
200 - 23.69, 400 - 55.8
RETCHAKAN Gowry P. V35 21.06.60, Thurr :
600 - 1:31.1, 400H - 57.78 (54.63-92),
800 - 2:08.3mx/2:11.3 (2:07.37i-93),
100H - 14.5w/14.7 (14.0-92/14.52w-89)
REYNOLDS Kay 15.09.67, Radley :
HJ - 1.65, 100H - 14.1w/14.2/14.77
(14.1w/14.2-87/14.68w-90/14.77-87)
REYNOLDS Nicky U13 24.06.85, Birchfield :
2kW - 11:54.7
REYNOLDS Victoria U17 22.04.80, Blackpool :
LJ - 5.49 (5.58w-95), TJ - 10.53 (11.05w-95)
RHODES Vyvyan Anne 5.05.73, Hallamshire :
400H - 58.85 (58.02-92)
RICE Sonia U17 8.01.81, Coventry Godiva :
300 - 41.3/42.07
RICH Emma U20 14.05.77, Yeovil Olympiads :
JT - 43.52
RICHARDS Angharad U23 9.12.76, Guild & G :
JT - 38.08 (46.20-93)
RICHARDS Debbie U15 20.10.82, Bristol :
DT - 29.48
RICHARDS Pauline 30.06.68, Birch/C of E :
200 - 25.07w/25.33 (24.76-93), 60H - 8.89i,
100H - 14.16, HJ - 1.65i, LJ - 5.82 (5.93-95),
SP - 12.74 (13.18-95), Hep - 5386 (5420-94)
RICHARDSON Marcia M. 10.02.72, W S & E :
60 - 7.34i, 100 - 11.42 (11.39w-94),
200 - 23.7w/23.80 (23.4-93/23.53-95),
TJ - 11.49 (11.83-93)
RICHENS Nicola U17 26.10.79, Oxford City :
HJ - 1.70

389

RICHMOND Louise U15 15.12.81, Sol & S H :
2.5kW - 12:49.3, 3kW - 16:27.1,
3kWR - 15:36, 5kWR - 26:29o
RIDGLEY Becky U17 26.02.80, Team Solent :
PV - 3.00, TJ - 11.36w/11.08
RIDGLEY Clare Louise U20 11.09.77, T Sol :
PV - 3.51i/3.50
RIDLEY Susan 25.10.65, Edinburgh WM :
3k - 9:50.26 (9:27.94-93),
5k - 17:09.01 (16:51.80-94), 10k - 35:26.82
RIGG Suzanne 29.11.63, Warrington :
10kR - 33:57RL (32:35-92),
10MR - 57:44 (53:42-93),
HMar - 1:12:32 (1:12:07-93),
Mar - 2:52:09 (2:34:21-95)
RILEY Catherine U15 4.06.82, Lancs Sch :
800 - 2:17.17
ROACH Kirsty U15 8.12.81, Leics Cor :
75HG - 11.7/12.12
ROBERTS Fay U13 2.11.83, Norwich :
SPM - 9.34
ROBERTS Kelly U23 24.01.76, Wrexham :
HT - 35.28
ROBERTS Nicola 22.01.70, Liverpool H :
HT - 36.90
ROBERTS Sarah U20 25.06.78, Forr of Dean :
400 - 56.49,
ROBERTS Suzanne U20 19.12.78, Bingley :
HT - 43.78
ROBERTSON I. U13, Cheshire Sch :
HJ - 1.50
ROBINS Lorraine A. 13.05.70, Hounslow :
60 - 7.76i (7.5i-93/7.52i-94),
200 - 25.1 (24.7-94)
ROBINSON Eleanor M. V45 20.11.47, Border :
Mar - 2:56:47 (2:45:12-90),
100kR - 8:00:01 (7:48:33-89),
24HrT - 223.129km (213.504km-95)
ROBINSON Gemma U20 30.12.78, Dartford :
TJ - 11.17
ROBINSON Helen U17 25.02.81, Vale Royal :
800 - 2:16.6
ROBINSON Lucy U13, Enfield :
800 - 2:27.2, 1500 - 5:07.7
ROBINSON Lynne Elizabeth 21.06.69, Cov G :
400 - 57.47 (54.6/54.69-86),
800 - 2:07.63 (2:02.0-89),
1500 - 4:21.3 (4:10.32-94),
3k - 9:37.68i (9:55.9-93)
ROBINSON Tracey U15 28.09.81, Leics WC :
3kWR - 16:14
ROBSON Lyndsay U17 4.07.81, Shildon :
1500 - 4:44.3, 3k - 10:10.3
ROGER Kirsty U20 24.03.78, Inverness :
HJ - 1.65i/1.65 (1.65i-95),
PV - 2.40i, Hep - 4239
ROGERS Kate U20 13.02.79, Skyrac :
LJ - 5.86w/5.60, Hep - 4214
ROGERS Laura U17 26.06.80, Telford :
HJ - 1.64
ROGERS Melissa A. U13 2.09.83, Dac & T :
70HM - 11.7, PenG - 2206
ROGERS Rachel U17 20.11.80, Soton City :
100 - 12.50, 200 - 25.28w/25.34
ROLES Philippa U20 1.03.78, Swansea :
SP - 14.60, DT - 51.32, HT - 42.66
ROLES Rebecca U17 14.12.79, Swansea :
PV - 3.20, DT - 40.24
ROLFE Gemma U20 18.12.78, Windsor S & E :
HT - 34.72 (39.84-95)

ROLFE Nicola 19.08.69, Newbury :
JT - 41.02 (42.82-95)
RONALD Alison 20.01.67, Edinburgh WM :
PV - 2.65i/2.60 (2.75-95)
ROSCOE Helen U17 4.12.79, Liverpool H :
100 - 12.1/12.24w (12.34-95), 300 - 39.61,
200 - 24.31w/24.8/24.82 (24.49-95)
ROSE Alison 27.09.67, Edinburgh WM :
5k - 17:12.98 (16:41.51-93),
10k - 34:44.89 (33:57.86-94)
ROSE Dawn U20 25.01.79, Leamington :
60 - 7.64i (7.63i-95),
100 - 12.07w/12.25 (11.93w/12.2-94/12.25-95)
ROSE Fiona A. 2.01.64, Cambridge Harriers :
3kW - 15:47.8 (14:51.3-92)
ROSS Isla U15 26.12.81, Black Isle :
800 - 2:19.6
ROSS Joanna U17 18.02.81, Victoria Park :
800 - 2:15.18, 1500 - 4:40.5
ROSS Lindsay U20 27.12.77, Nithsdale :
HT - 35.40
ROSTEK Malgorzata U20 25.03.77, C of Glas :
60 - 7.52i (7.69i-94), 100 - 11.8w/11.83,
200 - 24.7/24.81
ROTHMAN Kimberly 6.09.64, :
PV - 3.20
ROWBOTHAM Alanna Jane 11.01.70, Roth :
200 - 24.7 (24.28-94), 400 - 55.06 (54.49-94),
400H - 60.21 (60.0-95)
ROWE Deborah 8.09.72, Coventry Godiva :
TJ - 12.46
ROWE Kate U20 13.09.78, Peterborough :
PV - 2.35
ROWLAND Katie 5.03.71, Birchfield :
JT - 38.40 (48.66-93)
ROY Lesley Ann U15 3.01.82, Pitreavie :
SPG - 11.36, DT - 35.56
ROZE Anna U23 6.11.74, Shaftesbury Barnet :
400H - 63.0/63.26 (61.31-95)
RUDDOCK Ellena U23 23.02.76, Rugby :
60 - 7.67i, 100 - 11.90 (11.70-95),
200 - 24.43
RUSHTON Karen 10.07.67, Soton & E'lgh :
5k - 17:06.44, HMar - 1:19:12
RUSSELL Clare U15 11.11.81, Oldham & R :
100 - 12.24,
RUSSELL Eve U15 27.09.82, C of Plymouth :
JT - 32.46
RUSSELL Lyndsey U13 11.09.83, Fife :
100 - 13.2
RUTLAND Emma U15 9.10.81, Blackpool :
800 - 2:17.6, 1500 - 4:44.3
RUTTER Amy U17 4.08.80, Border :
80HI - 11.9/12.25
RYAN Catherine U17 4.02.80, Shrewsbury :
HepI - 4014 (4068-95)
RYAN Michelle U17 8.07.81, Jersey :
HT - 30.88
RYAN Orla 7.09.69, Ealing,Southall & Mx/IRE :
400 - 55.9/56.17

S AGAR Sally U20 28.03.77, Rotherham :
400H - 65.27 (65.2-95)
SAINT-SMITH Tasha U23 20.12.75, Enfield :
DT - 43.56 (44.68-94)
SALMON Georgina U17 1.11.79, Bristol :
800 - 2:14.1, 1500 - 4:35.3, 3k - 10:18.45
SALMON Sarah U23 9.09.74, Newquay & Par :
800 - 2:10.8, 1500 - 4:24.00,
1M - 4:44.79, 3k - 9:35.64i/9:40.87

SALT Christa 17.06.64, Basel :
  400 - 56.90, 800 - 2:06.97,
  1k - 2:47.86 (2:47.22-95), 1500 - 4:23.30
SAMPLE Jessica U17 3.01.80, St Albans :
  TJ - 10.64w/10.41
SAMUELS Belinda U20 29.11.78, Birchfield :
  100H - 15.00w/15.32,
  LJ - 5.57w/5.30 (5.57w/5.55-94), Hep - 4308
SAMUELS Lisa U15 24.09.81, Steven & NH :
  800 - 2:15.81
SANDERSON Danielle 26.10.62, Watford :
  10kR - 34:24 (33:57-93),
  10MR - 55:56 (55:42-94),
  HMar - 1:14:22 (1:13:11-94),
  Mar - 2:39:46 (2:36:29-94)
SANDERSON Theresa Ione V40 14.03.56,
  Hounslow : JT - 64.06 (73.58-83)
SATTERLY Emma U17 25.04.80, Phoenix :
  3k - 10:24.4
SAUNDERS Kerry U20 28.03.77, Derby LAC :
  HJ - 1.71i/1.65 (1.70-94), TJ - 11.26 (11.30-95)
SAUNDERS Rikki U15 20.02.82, Herts & W :
  HJ - 1.60,
SAYERS Goldie U15 16.07.82, Peterborough :
  JT - 41.56
SCHOFIELD Candace U13 3.11.84, Worthing :
  DTM - 23.90, JT - 25.90, JTM - 29.28
SCHOFIELD Victoria 29.12.72, Rotherham :
  200 - 24.89, 60H - 8.54i, 100H - 13.79w/13.90,
  HJ - 1.74i/1.73 (1.78-95), LJ - 6.14 (6.28-95),
  SP - 11.61i/11.57 (11.84-94), Hep - 5700
SCHRAMM Louise 18.12.71, Epsom & Ewell :
  100H - 15.1 (14.74-92), PV - 3.55
SCOTT Joanne U23 31.12.76, Darlington :
  TJ - 11.08 (11.40-94)
SCOTT Karen U17 17.10.79, Ayr Seaforth :
  60 - 7.82i, 200 - 25.48,
  100 - 12.4/12.62w/12.90 (12.19w/12.52-95)
SCOTT Lynsey U15 28.01.82, Scottish Bord :
  100 - 12.5, LJ - 5.46
SCOTT Victoria U17 21.09.80, Liverpool H :
  DT - 33.14, HT - 31.18
SEAGER Heather 4.04.68, Yeovil Olympiads :
  SP - 11.57 (11.72-94), DT - 37.74 (38.72-92)
SEALY Joanne U15 24.03.82, Dartford :
  2.5kW - 13:43.90, 2.5kWR - 13:25,
  3kW - 16:23.8, 3kWR - 16:08
SEARLE Kim U13 27.12.83, Hull Springhead :
  600 - 1:45.1, 800 - 2:27.6
SELLEY Danielle U13, Preseli :
  70HM - 11.6, PenM - 2250
SEMENOVA Marina 12.07.64, Birchfield :
  (see PEACOCK)
SEMUS Kate 18.01.70, Parkside :
  DT - 39.32
SHARPS Louise U20 9.07.77, Swansea :
  100 - 12.1/12.22 (12.16-94), 200 - 24.9w/24.92
SHAW Lorraine A. 2.04.68, Sale :
  SP - 13.65 (14.21-94), DT - 52.34 (55.04-94),
  HT - 61.34 (64.90-95)
SHEARD Sasha U13 27.09.83, Windsor S & E :
  HJ - 1.46
SHEPHERD Kelly U23 15.12.75, Charnwood :
  HT - 36.56
SHEPHERD Victoria U17 26.01.80, Wakefield :
  SP - 12.35
SHEPPARD Amanda 26.02.68, Halifax :
  DT - 38.18 (37.68-95)
SHERIDAN Emma U15 24.02.82, Essex L :
  DT - 31.24

SHERMAN Elizabeth U17 15.09.79, Thurrock :
  LJ - 5.43, Hepl - 4070
SHIEL Rebecca U15 16.01.82, Gateshead :
  LJ - 5.24, PenG - 2819
SHIELDS Jane Elizabeth V35 23.08.60, Sheff :
  10kR - 34:52 (32:38-85)
SHIPLEY Jade U13 5.04.84, Solihull & S H :
  2kW - 11:36.1
SHIPMAN Vic... ...U20 31.03.77, Derby LAC :
  100 - 11.5/11..87, 200 - 24.18 (24.08-95)
SHONEYE Charlene U15 21.12.81, S London :
  100 - 12.44
SHORT Nicola 30.10.69, Torfaen :
  LJ - 5.74w/5.70 (5.82-88)
SHORTHALL Jeanette U17 9.09.80, Liv H :
  1500 - 4:40.69,
SHORTS Tracy 4.11.72, Edinburgh WM :
  SP - 12.45 (12.55-95), DT - 43.04, HT - 42.42
SHROSBEE Lesley V50 24.11.46, Harlow :
  HT - 34.02
SHUM Cathy V35 30.05.61, Cannock & St/IRE :
  10kR - 33:35 (33:21-95), 10MR - 56:56 (55:49-95),
  HMar - 1:13:04 (1:12:48-94),
  Mar - 2:38:56 (2:38:14-93)
SHUTTLEWORTH Rosalind U23 25.04.75, Lew :
  HJ - 1.65 (1.70i-93/1.69-92)
SIDDALL Laura U17 10.09.80, Barnsley :
  300H - 43.94, Hepl - 3945
SILVER Lorna U23 10.01.74, Dundee HH :
  100H - 14.5 (14.3w-95/14.59-94),
  400H - 61.1/61.92 (59.9/60.58-94)
SIMMANS Sarah U20 29.11.78, Oldham & R :
  JT - 41.60
SIMMONS Sarah U23 12.01.75, Hounslow :
  800 - 2:11.8 (2:11.8-93),
SIMPSON Beatrice V40 17.07.55, Bromley :
  HT - 37.98
SIMPSON Jemma U13 10.02.84, Newq & Par :
  600 - 1:42.4, 800 - 2:22.9
SIMPSON Louise U20 18.12.77, City of Hull :
  PV - 2.55
SIMPSON Marian U20 2.11.77, Aberdeen :
  HT - 39.58
SIMPSON Rebecca U20 22.12.77, Guild & G :
  400H - 63.02
SINGLETON Debbie V35 5.10.58, Walton :
  PV - 2.40
SKEGGS Karen 26.10.69, Ashford :
  LJ - 5.77 (6.29w/6.09-89),
  TJ - 12.61w/12.49i/12.42 (12.93w/12.89-92)
SKETCHLEY Katy 9.07.73, Team Solent :
  100 - 12.14w, 60H - 8.58i,
  100H - 13.72w/13.86
SKINNER Rehanne U17 13.11.79, Scarb :
  JT - 35.34 (35.60-95)
SKORUPSKA Katie U20 3.11.78, Fife :
  3k - 9:43.90, 5k - 16:41.9
SLATER Catriona U20 27.01.77, Chelmsford :
  200 - 25.0w (25.44-93), LJ - 5.68 (5.70-95)
SLIMIN Caroline 27.08.65, Basingstoke & MH :
  800 - 2:12.88i/2:12.97 (2:08.6-94),
  1500 - 4:24.37i/4:30.3 (4:18.61-94),
SLOANE Joanne U23 2.12.76, Coventry G :
  400 - 56.71i/58.54 (54.59-95), 400H - 62.97
SMALE Dorothy V35 26.05.60, Hounslow :
  Mar - 3:06:06
SMALLWOOD Nicole U20 9.10.77, Hales :
  HJ - 1.80i/1.78
SMEDSTAD Hanna U23 30.03.76, Padd W/FIN :
  3k - 9:53.64

SMELLIE Natalie U15 16.01.82, Essex L :
100 - 12.5/12.56, 200 - 25.5w/25.60w/25.74
SMETHURST Natalie U20 31.03.77, Wigan :
400 - 57.5/58.11
SMITH Carolyn V35 6.10.61, Dundee HH :
400H - 64.75 (62.95-94)
SMITH Diane V35 15.11.60, Hull Spartan :
HT - 46.00, JT - 38.16
SMITH Elaine U15 16.05.83, Middlesbro & C :
LJ - 5.21w/4.92
SMITH Hayley U15 14.01.82, West Norfolk :
75HG - 11.51w/11.61
SMITH Heidi U23 20.05.74, Liv Pem
(nee HOSKING) : 800 - 2:09.27
SMITH Janet 7.10.64, Windsor S & E :
HT - 46.32 (46.88-94)
SMITH Karen U23 10.02.74, Sale :
SP - 11.34 (12.16-94), DT - 41.70 (46.64-93)
SMITH Karen U20 25.12.78, Medway :
SP - 11.23
SMITH Laura U17 16.11.80, Hull Springhead :
100 - 12.4, HJ - 1.64,
LJ - 5.64, Hepl - 4178w/3994
SMITH Louise U20 11.07.77, Ipswich :
JT - 47.04
SMITH Michelle Louise U20 1.01.78, T Solent :
HJ - 1.66 (1.70-94)
SMITH Michelle U17 28.05.80, Scottish Bord :
HJ - 1.71
SMITH Natasha U20 6.06.77, Hounslow :
SP - 14.09i/13.80, HT - 37.42
SMITH Nicola U15 6.03.82, AF&D :
JT - 34.00
SMITH Phylis 29.09.65, Sale :
300 - 36.92, 400 - 51.29 (50.40-92),
800 - 2:06.14i (2:08.5-94)
SMITH Rachel U17 5.11.80, Trafford :
100 - 12.21w/12.6
SMITH Rebecca U17 11.10.79, Derby LAC :
DT - 33.98
SMITH Sophia U23 8.12.74, Hallamshire :
100 - 11.49, 200 - 23.6w/23.80 (23.57-93)
SMITHSON Claire U15 3.08.83, Brighton :
SPG - 10.74i/10.62, DT - 36.72
SMITHSON Kerry U23 13.09.76, Hyndburn :
800 - 2:09.5mx/2:09.8
SNEDDON Esther U23 30.06.74, Central :
JT - 40.24, Hep - 3835 (4290w-94/4243-95)
SNOOK Verity A. 13.11.70, AF&D :
3kW - 13:16.23, 5kW - 24:16.1 (23:22.52-94),
5kWR - 23:36 (22:45+-94),
10kWR - 47:12 (46:06-94), 20kW - 1:54:15
SOLLARS Loretta 29.10.63, Leeds :
10kR - 34:13, 10MR - 57:18
SOPER Clare 26.11.72, Ashford :
TJ - 11.06
SOTHERTON Kelly Jade U23 13.11.76,
Peterbro : 100H - 14.63 (14.54w-95),
HJ - 1.71, LJ - 5.83w/5.72 (5.84-95),
SP - 11.25, Hep - 4930 (4961-95)
SPELLACY Jemma U15 27.11.82, Castle Pt :
JT - 32.28
SPELLER Michelle U17 3.02.80, Havering :
3k - 10:34.00
SPENCER Amy U13 19.09.85, Wigan :
150 - 20.2, 600 - 1:44.94
SPIES Rebecca, Oxford Univ/USA :
1500 - 4:20.8
SPINKS Stephanie U15 6.09.82, West Norfolk :
100 - 12.58

SPRULES Lyn U23 11.09.75, Hounslow :
SP - 11.43 (11.44-95),
DT - 37.12 (40.72-93), HT - 59.54
STACEY Julie 15.11.72, Bromley :
1500 - 4:25.7 (4:21.70-91)
STAERCK Gillian U17 22.09.79, Guild & G :
HT - 31.94
STAFFORD Judi V40 9.06.53, Lincoln Well :
PV - 2.30
STAINES Linda 26.12.63, Basingstoke & MH :
200 - 24.40 (23.1/23.51-89),
400 - 52.71 (50.98-91)
STANLEY Joanne U20 30.03.77, Elswick :
TJ - 11.37
STANLEY Sarah U17 22.05.81, Notts :
300H - 46.8
STANNARD Rachel U20 28.03.78, Newport :
100H - 15.14
STANTON Linda Mary 22.06.73, Rotherham :
PV - 3.70i/3.60 (3.72-95)
STAPLES Katharine 2.11.65, Essex L :
PV - 3.90
STAPLETON Samantha 13.10.73, Sale :
PV - 3.20 (3.20-94)
STARES Hannah U20 13.11.78, Yate :
Hep - 4069
STEAD Caroline 14.09.71, Parkside :
LJ - 5.71 (5.71-95), TJ - 12.67
STEELE Wendy E. 7.01.66, Edinburgh WM :
800 - 2:10.47 (2:10.2-95)
STENNETT Vanessa, Walton :
JT - 39.34
STEPHENS Tamsin U17 2.08.80, Lagan Val :
80HI - 11.4, 100H - 14.98,
300H - 44.03, Hep - 4035
STEPNIAK Laura U13 24.01.85, Sheff RWC :
2kW - 11:21.5, 2KWR - 10:55
STERNE Victoria 12.10.68, Birchfield :
400 - 56.7, 800 - 2:04.63, 1500 - 4:25.0
STEVENS Barbara V40 2.05.56, Redhill :
Mar - 2:58:57
STEVENSON Lucy 30.01.73, Sale :
JT - 48.18 (52.00-92)
STEVENSON Sarah Anne Louise 31.12.73,
Birch : 400 - 55.48
STEWART Claire U13 14.10.83, Elgin :
SPG - 9.02, SPM - 9.11, DTM - 28.08
STEWART Gillian U17 21.01.80, City of Glas :
60H - 9.17i (9.10i-95),
80HI - 12.0/12.02 (11.89w/11.96-95),
100H - 14.7w/15.06, HJ - 1.65, PV - 2.40i,
SP - 10.38, JT - 35.66, Hepl - 4460
STILL Margaret 9.05.65, Wakefield :
400 - 56.18, 100H - 14.67w/14.7 (14.7/15.26-90),
400H - 60.02 (58.44-88), TJ - 12.13i/12.03
STILL Sarah U23 24.09.75, Aberdeen :
HJ - 1.65 (1.65-94), LJ - 5.52 (5.74-94),
Hep - 4474 (4643-94)
STOREY Lauren U13 22.09.83, Spenborough :
PV - 2.30
STOTT Rachel U23 3.09.74, Cambridge Univ :
HT - 39.36
STOUT Keira U17 6.03.80, Braintree :
HJ - 1.65 (1.67-94)
STOUTE Jennifer Elaine 16.04.65, Essex L :
200 - 23.75 (22.73-92)
STREET Joanne U15 30.12.82, Tamworth :
SPG - 10.78i/10.07, DT - 29.88
STRICKLETON Sarah U17 10.05.80, Wigan :
DT - 35.10 (35.46-95)

STUBBS Sarah J. U17 31.07.80, Wycombe :
DT - 33.70
STYLES Aimee U15 1.05.82, Dacorum & Tr :
JT - 32.52
SUCH Jennifer U17 5.10.79, Chesterfield :
100 - 12.59 (12.50-95)
SUDDES Joanne U20 27.01.77, North S Poly :
100H - 14.66 (14.64w-95)
SULLIVAN Deborah 24.01.72, Havering :
1500 - 4:30.9 (4:30.8-89), 3k - 9:43.22
SUTCLIFFE Elaine 6.04.70, Wakefield :
60 - 7.75i (7.74i-95),
100 - 12.26 (11.8/11.94w/12.03-90),
200 - 24.7/25.10 (24.3-95/24.48-94),
400 - 55.98i/57.28 (54.35-95)
SUTHERLAND Carolynne U17 4.09.80, EWM :
300H - 45.0
SUTTON Marian 7.10.63, Westbury :
10kR - 33:44 (32:55-94),
10MR - 52:53/55:24 (54:17-93),
HMar - 1:13:41 (1:11:42-93), Mar - 2:30:41
SWALLOW Jodie U17 23.06.81, Brentwood :
1500 - 4:34.49, 3k - 9:55.2
SWAN Anna U17 20.04.80, Havant :
HT - 31.98
SWANN Julie 15.07.62, Wolverhampton & B :
1500 - 4:28.80 (4:26.07i-94/4:27.0-93),
3k - 9:46.1
SWETMAN Gemma U17 28.09.80, Brighton :
300H - 44.07, Hepl - 3993
SWINDELL Tracy 8.11.66, Thurrock :
10MR - 57:35, HMar - 1:16:57, Mar - 2:44:48
SWITHENBANK Nicola 10.12.63, Redhill :
Mar - 2:59:05
SYKES Julia U23 27.05.75, Hallamshire :
400H - 62.23 (61.68-94), Hep - 4240
SYMONDS Emma U20 5.06.77, Norwich :
100 - 11.95, 400 - 54.6/54.86,
200 - 24.5/25.27i (24.74w/24.97-95)
SYMONDS Sarah Louise 28.12.73, Radley :
DT - 42.66 (47.50-90), HT - 37.36 (40.58-95)

TAIT Natalie J. 24.08.72, Windsor S & E :
400 - 56.5, 800 - 2:02.76 (2:02.69-95),
1500 - 4:32.9 (4:17.9-95)
TALBOT Elizabeth U23 5.12.74, Beds & Co :
1500 - 4:26.90 (4:19.09-95),
3k - 9:58.0 (9:29.8-95)
TALBOT Nicola 17.02.72, Telford :
DT - 51.24 (54.24-93)
TAMIRAT Getenesh U20 11.07.77, Ex L/ETH :
5k - 17:37.22 (17:08.9mx-95)
TAPPER Elizabeth U20 2.06.78, Charnwood :
PV - 2.70
TASWELL Ann 31.05.71, Wells :
3k - 9:54.2 (9:54.1-95)
TATE Gemma U13 6.09.83, Dartford :
200 - 26.6
TAYLOR C. U13, Morpeth :
80 - 10.6
TAYLOR Claire U15 24.10.82, North S P :
800 - 2:16.28,
TAYLOR Jane U17 18.02.80, City of Hull :
100 - 12.58w/12.7 (12.86-95), LJ - 5.63
TAYLOR Leanne U17 19.11.79, Lancs & Morc :
TJ - 10.96
TAYLOR Lynn Caroline 5.08.67, Woking :
800 - 2:09.78 (2:06.5-93)
TAYLOR Natalie U17 2.01.80, Girvan :
TJ - 10.52 (10.76-95)

TAYLOR Tania U23 7.10.76, Birchfield :
400 - 55.7/55.76, 400H - 64.44
TEINILA R. 1.01.73, Serpentine :
Mar - 3:04:49
TEREK Ann 22.09.64, Lisburn :
800 - 2:09.6, 1500 - 4:20.6,
3k - 9:42.16 (9:28.39-95)
THACKERAY Katie U15 23.09.81, W S & E :
HJ - 1.60
THACKRAY Penny U23 18.08.74, Spen :
800 - 2:11.4, 1500 - 4:23.0,
3k - 9:23.5mx/9:48.16 (9:35.76-94),
5k - 16:26.22, 10kR - 34:27
THEOBALD Susan U15 4.03.83, Braintree :
JT - 35.42
THIEME Helen U15 28.09.81, Notts :
PenG - 2745 (2755-95)
THIRKLE Kelly Michelle 29.03.71, Sale :
HJ - 1.80i/1.75 (1.88i-92/1.85-91)
THIRWELL Tina M. U15 5.09.81, Sale :
LJ - 5.46w/5.26, PenG - 2974
THOMAS Ceri 16.10.70, Cardiff :
800 - 2:12.4, 3k - 9:55.4
THOMAS Judy P. 20.01.63, Birchfield :
400H - 65.33 (63.99-93)
THOMAS Kelly U17 9.01.81, Dartford :
60 - 7.81i, 100 - 11.84w/12.1/12.18,
200 - 24.88
THOMAS Lisa U17 22.06.80, Shaftesbury B :
100 - 12.50 (12.24w-94/12.40-95)
THOMAS Lucy A. U13 2.11.84, Neath :
1500 - 5:02.0
THOMAS Michelle 16.10.71, Birchfield :
400 - 55.2/55.39 (54.01-92)
THOMAS Paula 3.12.64, Trafford :
60 - 7.47i (7.23i-87),
100 - 11.46 (11.13w-88/11.15-94),
200 - 23.41 (22.69-94),
LJ - 5.60 (6.07w-88/6.04-95)
THOMPSON Alison Kate U23 11.02.74, Sale :
100 - 12.26w (11.8w?-93/11.86db/11.88-94),
200 - 25.24 (24.3w/24.48w-93/24.58-92)
THOMPSON Joanne V35 30.10.58, C of Bath :
3k - 9:34.2 (9:15.54-93),
10k - 34:30.52 (33:56.04-94),
10kR - 33:56 (33:10-93),
10MR - 55:52 (55:20-94)
THOMPSON Kimberley 5.01.73, Gateshead :
HT - 38.30 (44.46-94)
THOMPSON Lisa 12.07.62, Bromley :
800 - 2:08.2 (2:04.85-90)
THOMPSON Lisa U17 25.04.81, Colwyn Bay :
300H - 46.5/46.57
THOMPSON Lisa U15 3.12.82, Nairn :
SPG - 10.17
THOMSON L., :
Mar - 2:58:08
THOMSON Trudi V35 18.01.59, Pitreavie :
10kR - 35:00 (34:59-95), 10MR - 58:05,
HMar - 1:14:34, Mar - 2:44:39 (2:38:23-95)
THOMSON Wendy U23 24.06.75, Essex L :
DT - 36.60 (38.24-93)
THOMSON Wendy U15 28.06.82, C of Glas :
100 - 12.56, 200 - 25.8/26.06w/26.66
THORNE Louretta U20 6.05.77, Wycombe :
400 - 55.79 (54.27-94)
THORNER Rosie 7.08.67, Bristol :
400 - 57.50i (55.86-95)
THORNLEY Marie U13, Oldham & Royton :
75 - 10.1, 100 - 13.2, 150 - 20.2

THORP Angela Caroline 7.12.72, Wigan :
100 - 11.48w (12.02-94), 100H - 12.80
THORPE Amanda 21.07.71, Hyndburn :
(see PARKINSON)
THREADGOLD Eleanor, Bray :
HMar - 1:19:45
THURSTON Kathy U23 2.01.76, Trafford :
400 - 56.3/56.86i (57.50-95), 400H - 60.28
TIMMIS Irene 28.03.65, Southampton City :
SP - 11.89
TINDAL Jacqueline U20 21.01.79, Edin WM :
100H - 15.19w/15.41, SP - 11.87, Hep - 4622
TINDWELL Sarah U13 19.10.84, Sale :
SPM - 9.16
TISSHAW Rebecca U17 8.02.81, Dartford :
3kW - 15:11.44, 3kWR - 14:39,
5kW - 26:54.4, 5kWR - 25:07
TODD Charlotte U15 7.12.81, Edinburgh WM :
75HG - 11.8 (12.35w-95)
TODD Jennifer U20 23.10.78, Sale :
TJ - 11.03
TODD Kate V45 21.07.50, Kilmarnock :
100kR - 9:06:45
TODD Sarah L. U17 3.11.79, Jarrow & Hebb :
100 - 12.47w/12.5/12.85 (12.61-94),
300H - 44.97
TOMKINS Emma U20 31.01.78, Croydon :
400H - 63.80
TONKS Sharon J. 18.04.70, Bromsgrove & R :
3kW - 14:55.0 (14:38.5-95),
5kWR - 26:03 (25:04-95)
TOWN Anna U23 22.04.75, Verlea :
HT - 35.90 (36.48-94)
TOZER Lynsey U23 6.12.75, Birchfield :
5kWR - 26:37 (25:35-92)
TREMBLE Amanda U23 2.11.76, North S P :
1500 - 4:31.5 (4:22.70-95),
3k - 9:32.5 (9:27.5-95), 5k - 16:49.3
TRIBE Leah U15 3.09.81, Portsmouth :
100 - 12.5/12.72, 200 - 25.2/25.31w/25.39
TRIGGS Carmel U17 18.04.80, Elan Valley :
300 - 40.20
TROMANS Karlene U17 28.02.81, Birchfield :
800 - 2:12.80
TROTT Patricia 7.09.62, :
Mar - 3:06:46
TUGWELL Emily U20 26.05.78, Cornwall AC :
HJ - 1.66, TJ - 11.23?/11.13
TUNALEY Sharon 2.09.68, Notts :
60 - 7.7i/7.71i, 400 - 53.78 (53.58-95),
100 - 12.0 (11.5w-85/11.53w-86/11.6-87/11.80-85),
200 - 24.1/24.11 (23.6-95/23.94w-88)
TURNBULL Jessica U23 4.07.75, Bury :
5k - 17:19.7 (16:57.5-95)
TURNER Anna U23 13.08.74, Cardiff :
400 - 56.6/57.30
TURNER Clare U17 23.09.80, Dartford :
80HI - 11.72w/11.82
TURNER Lesley 1.08.66, Rowheath :
Mar - 2:53:57 (2:41:09-93), 100kR - 9:46:26
TURNER Vicki U13 30.09.83, Bracknell :
1500 - 5:06.2
TWOMEY Alice U17 18.07.81, Newbury :
TJ - 10.61w/10.51

UNDERWOOD Diane R. V40 20.12.52, Cent :
HMar - 1:19:52 (1:16:33-90)
UNDERWOOD Nicola U15 13.05.82, Carl/Asp :
800 - 2:16.3

VAGGERS Melanie U15 16.06.82, C of Ply :
JT - 35.72, PenG - 2749
VAN DOORN Cressida U20 27.09.77, Sut & D :
3kW - 16:00.8, 5kW - 27:55.35, 5kWR - 27:04
VANNET Lisa U23 8.11.74, Edinburgh WM :
200 - 24.79w/25.01 (24.93-95), 400 - 54.54
VEEVERS Sara U23 26.04.74, Pendle :
HJ - 1.75
VEITCH Lucie U17 25.06.81, North Shields P :
300H - 46.75
VELDMAN Margaret U23 7.06.74, Altrincham :
LJ - 5.59
VERNON Carean U17 2.06.80, Herc Wimb :
800 - 2:14.12, 1500 - 4:44.0 (4:43.91-94)
VINE Kelly U20 26.07.78, Spenborough :
HJ - 1.65
VINEY Elaine 20.12.71, Peterborough :
400 - 57.48 (56.25-95)
VINEY Gemma U15 7.01.83, Blackheath :
1500 - 4:48.5 (4:54.8-95)
VYFSCHAFT Jackie 15.12.64, B & A :
HJ - 1.70i/1.70 (1.72i/1.71-82), Hep - 4022

WAINWRIGHT Joanne L. U13 28.09.83,
Wake : 75 - 9.96w/10.1, 80 - 10.7,
100 - 13.2, 150 - 20.01, 200 - 27.4
WAITE Camilla U17 24.05.80, Andover :
800 - 2:14.1, 1500 - 4:30.5, 3k - 10:05.1
WALDO V. Ena 29.06.63, Birchfield :
100 - 12.16 (11.55w/11.6/11.72-88),
200 - 24.35 (23.60w-88/23.8-87/23.82-88),
400 - 56.2/57.21 (55.1/55.20-88)
WALKER Claire 8.10.72, Cov RWC (nee CHILDS) :
3kW - 15:03.0 (14:45.8-94), 5kWR - 25:17,
10kW - 52:43.3, 10kWR - 52:34
WALKER Elexi U15 28.10.82, Birchfield :
100 - 12.44w/12.56, 200 - 25.77
WALKER Hilary C. V40 9.11.53, Serpentine :
100kR - 8:27:36 (7:50:01-93)
WALKER Jennifer 28.01.69, Shaftesbury B:
HJ - 1.65 (1.76-88)
WALKER Joanne U20 2.03.78, Kilmarnock :
JT - 42.64 (47.14-95)
WALKER Marcia 27.05.70, Shaftesbury Barn :
60 - 7.77i, TJ - 11.21 (11.54-95),
200 - 24.6/24.76i/24.79 (24.36w-93/24.4-94)
WALLACE Alana 28.07.65, B & A/IRE :
DT - 41.28
WALLACE Michelle 1.11.72, Notts :
DT - 36.58 (41.50-93)
WALLBANKS Carol U15 9.12.82, Workington :
JT - 33.94
WALLEN Debbie U20 28.05.79, AF&D :
3kW - 15:04.7, 5kW - 26:06.47,
5kWR - 25:18, 10kWR - 55:19
WALSH Caroline U17 29.04.80, Shaft Barnet :
800 - 2:16.8, 1500 - 4:41.1, 3k - 10:07.6
WANNELL Michelle 12.07.67, Exeter (nee
LAVERCOMBE) : 1500 - 4:30.05 (4:26.52-88),
3k - 9:48.37 (9:45.6-87)
WANSTALL Helen U17 13.11.80, Invicta :
HJ - 1.65 (1.65-95)
WARD Emma U15 2.01.82, City of Stoke :
800 - 2:10.9, 1500 - 4:35.48
WARDEN Caroline 16.09.72, Preston :
LJ - 5.84 (6.03w/5.85-93),
TJ - 12.11i/11.93 (12.31-94)
WARREN Sally U20 29.01.78, Steyning :
3kW - 15:34.83, 3kWR - 15:01,
5kW - 26:09.16, 5kWR - 26:05, 10kWR - 55:18

394

WARRILOW Hayley U17 10.04.80, C of Stoke :
  LJ - 5.53, TJ - 11.71
WATERLOW Amy U20 29.07.78, Sale :
  3k - 9:56.17
WATERS Elizabeth U20 19.02.77, Kettering :
  400H - 63.29
WATKINS Laura U15 1.01.82, Telford :
  100 - 12.3/12.57w/12.64 200 - 25.08w/25.1
WATSON Alana U13 14.12.83, Dartford :
  70HM - 11.24
WATSON Gillian 26.05.64, Sheffield RWC :
  5kWR - 27:19 (25:33-93)
WATSON Louise Carole 13.12.71, GEC/Loughbro :
  1500 - 4:33.6 (4:22.9-89),
  3k - 9:29.2 (9:16.45-92),
  5k - 16:33.14 (15:57.06-95), 10k - 33:21.46
WATSON Natalie U15 29.01.83, Solihull & SH :
  2.5kW - 12:59.05, 3kW - 15:16.4
WATSON Ruth U17 29.11.79, Peterborough :
  100 - 12.3/12.38w/12.57 (12.3-95),
  200 - 25.3/25.32 (24.9/24.99w/25.11-95),
  300 - 39.34, 400 - 56.9
WATSON Sylvia A. V45 29.09.47, Valley Str :
  100kR - 8:53:53 (8:13:00-93)
WATT Fiona 29.01.73, City of Glasgow :
  TJ - 12.15i/12.06w/11.91 (12.15i-95)
WATTS Katy U17 25.03.81, Basing & MH :
  JT - 39.94
WAUGH Katherine U13, North Shields Poly :
  600 - 1:44.8
WAUGH Kathryn 20.02.73, Liverpool H :
  800 - 2:10.42, 1500 - 4:31.2
WAY Linda 17.09.64, :
  Mar - 3:08:41
WAYGOOD Carla U17 29.11.79, Bournem'th :
  PV - 2.50
WEALE Rebecca U20 7.02.78, Yeovil Oly:
  HJ - 1.68
WEBB Lisa J. 9.10.65, Shaftesbury Barnet :
  3k - 9:56.9 (9:11.45-88)
WEBB Rachel U15 1.12.82, Bedford & County :
  75HG - 11.78
WEBBER Claire U13 13.12.83, Arbroath :
  PenM - 2013
WEBBER Lucy 5.02.72, Exeter :
  PV - 2.60
WELLSTEAD Sarah U17 22.10.79, Sut & D :
  TJ - 11.35w/11.07
WELSH Lindsey U13 29.11.83, Yeovil Oly :
  JTM - 26.58
WHALLEY Michelle U17 1.10.80, Wigan :
  800 - 2:14.7
WHEELER Elizabeth U15 31.10.81, Derby LAC :
  800 - 2:19.1, 1500 - 4:47.63
WHIGHAM Lisa U17 14.08.80, Victoria Park :
  300 - 40.78, 400 - 57.5, 300H - 44.40
WHITBY Sharon U17 29.09.80, Crawley :
  800 - 2:16.3
WHITCOMBE Andrea 8.06.71, Parkside :
  800 - 2:10.7, 1500 - 4:27.1 (4:14.56-90),
  3k - 9:25.41 (8:58.59-91), 5k - 16:00.0
WHITE Claire 24.02.73, Rugby :
  100H - 14.9/15.18 (14.6/15.11w-95)
WHITE Jacqueline 12.01.71, Tamworth :
  200 - 24.9 (24.97-94), LJ - 6.08 (6.11w-95)
WHITE Laura U17 5.09.79, Hyndburn :
  HJ - 1.70 (1.72-95), Hepl - 4050 (4069-95)

WHITE Rebecca U17 5.06.80, Blackburn :
  60 - 7.98i, 100 - 12.58 (12.2/12.39w/12.48-95),
  200 - 25.0w/25.54 (25.0/25.41w/25.42-95),
  300 - 39.25, 400 - 58.8 (58.6-95),
  LJ - 5.52, TJ - 11.35 (11.36-95)
WHITEHEAD Fiona 31.05.70, Croy/WLIHE :
  HT - 46.36 (52.84-93)
WHITEHEAD Louise U23 26.03.75, Liv Pem :
  200 - 24.18w/24.36 (24.1-93), 300 - 38.79i,
  400 - 55.89i (54.92-95)
WHITEHEAD Natasha, :
  PV - 2.60
WHITLEY Meryl 12.04.69, Bingley :
  (see DODD)
WHITFIELD Joanna U20 5.01.78, Bristol :
  PV - 2.60i (2.70i/2.70-95)
WHITLOCK Janine 11.08.73, Trafford :
  100 - 11.8/11.88w/11.89, 200 - 23.99,
  100H - 14.0w (14.1/14.47-95),
  PV - 4.00, LJ - 5.81
WHITTAKER Louise U15 29.11.82, Sale :
  1500 - 4:47.60
WHITTLE Elizabeth U23 23.06.75, Wigan :
  HT - 36.82 (37.96-94)
WHITTON Gemma U17 25.05.81, Motherwell :
  80HI - 11.9/12.32
WIGHTMAN Susan Julia V35 24.10.60, Card :
  10MR - 57:50 (53:25un/55:36-88)
WILDING Amanda J. U20 3.05.79, Soton City :
  400H - 65.97
WILDING Helen U23 25.10.76, Wirral :
  SP - 13.21i/13.06 (13.88-95),
  DT - 42.26 (42.90-95), HT - 40.74
WILHELMY Hannah U13 11.04.84, Southend :
  75 - 10.1, 200 - 27.4
WILHELMY Sarah U17 2.02.80, Southend :
  60 - 7.59i (7.54i-95),
  100 - 11.9/12.12 (11.83"-95),
  200 - 23.96w/24.25 (24.19-95), 300 - 40.3
WILKIN Paula U23 28.03.74, City of Hull :
  100H - 15.0 (14.3/14.43w-95/15.33-94)
WILKINS Caroline U23 28.08.75, Cardiff :
  400 - 56.9, 400H - 61.45
WILKINS Frances U20 15.01.79, Birchfield :
  Hep - 4189
WILKINS Melanie 18.01.73, AF&D :
  100 - 12.0w, 200 - 24.7w/25.0 (24.47w/24.7-94),
  60H - 8.37i, 100H - 13.23w/13.41 (13.1/13.34-95)
WILKINSON Joanne U13 9.02.84, Hull Spring :
  80 - 10.6, LJ - 4.70
WILKINSON Kate U15 13.12.81, Blackpool :
  DT - 29.84
WILKINSON Michelle 1.01.73, Sale :
  800 - 2:07.5 (2:06.3-90)
WILLIAMS Amanda U17 28.06.80, Bracknell :
  80HI - 12.0
WILLIAMS Angela U17 13.05.81, Dartford :
  TJ - 11.15
WILLIAMS Donna Maria U20 7.10.78, Sale :
  SP - 12.03 (12.34-95), DT - 48.08
WILLIAMS Elizabeth U20 2.06.77, Walton :
  400 - 56.71 (55.47-95)
WILLIAMS Evette U20 23.03.78, Dartford :
  100 - 12.19 (12.0-95),
  200 - 24.66w (23.95w/24.04-95)
WILLIAMS Kathryn U20 10.11.77, Swansea :
  400 - 56.6 (57.85-95), 400H - 60.21
WILLIAMS Lisa S. U20 11.04.78, Telford :
  100H - 14.81

395

WILLIAMS Lisa U15 29.12.81, Chelmsford :
  1500 - 4:45.0
WILLIAMS Maureen 22.06.69, Thames Valley :
  400 - 56.97 (56.7-95)
WILLIAMS Perri 2.06.66, London Irish/IRE :
  5kWR - 23:23 (23:19-95)
WILLIAMS Ruth E. 18.03.70, Darlington :
  LJ - 5.64 (5.76i/5.65-92)
WILLIAMS Sharon 20.05.70, Team Solent :
  60 - 7.42i, 100 - 12.05 (11.53-95),
  200 - 24.10i/24.8/25.08 (23.80w/23.9/23.91-95)
WILLIAMS Sophie Ann U17 29.03.80, C of Bath :
  100 - 12.2w/12.63 (12.4-95)
WILLIAMS Susan U20 2.06.77, Walton :
  60 - 7.7i/7.78i, 300 - 39.72,
  100 - 12.1 (12.0w-94/12.1-95/12.39-93),
  200 - 24.8w/24.81 (24.11w-94/24.2-95/24.27-94)
WILLIAMS Syreeta U17 24.10.80, Birchfield :
  300 - 40.24, 300H - 43.80, TJ - 11.44, Hepl - 4171
WILLIAMS Vicky U17 11.03.81, Cannock & St :
  DT - 35.22
WILLIAMS Victoria U17 11.04.81, Clevedon :
  100 - 12.3w (13.04w/13.2/13.77-95),
  80HI - 11.9/12.02, Hepl - 4197w/4071
WILLIAMS Wendy Jane 9.02.68, Salisbury
  (nee COOMBES): 3k - 9:57.5 (9:38.5-92)
WILLIAMSON Kelly Louise U17 4.12.79, Der :
  LJ - 5.64w/5.50 (5.66w-94/5.58i-95), TJ - 11.17
WILSON Aileen U13 30.03.84, EWM/Rutland :
  70HM - 11.78
WILSON Amy U17 31.12.80, Ipswich :
  SP - 11.61
WILSON Carley U15 6.12.81, Morpeth :
  800 - 2:14.1, 1500 - 4:37.5
WILSON Paula 20.11.69, Birchfield :
  PV - 3.70
WILSON Rachel V40 13.03.56, Bristol :
  Mar - 3:01:31
WILSON Zoe U23 28.08.76, Coventry Godiva :
  60 - 7.62i, 100 - 11.89w/11.9/12.02, 200 - 24.50
WILTSHIRE Rebecca S.C. 3.10.68, Hounslow :
  100H - 15.1 (14.41w/14.5/14.55-88)
WINCKLESS Sarah Katherine 18.10.73, E & E/
  Cambridge Univ : DT - 44.52 (53.16-94)
WINGLER Astrid 21.05.68, Hallamshire :
  1500 - 4:32.7, 3k - 9:39.8mx/9:59.0
WINTER Michelle U20 18.06.79, Wigan :
  Hep - 4026 (3871-95)
WISE Clare L. 22.08.69, AF&D :
  100H - 14.9/14.91 (14.9-94), 400H - 60.83
WISE Hannah U23 8.10.74, Woking :
  HJ - 1.65 (1.68-92)
WISE Joanne 15.03.71, Coventry Godiva :
  LJ - 6.47 (6.69w-88/6.57-92)
WISE Rebecca 16.03.72, Brighton :
  (see ADAMS)
WNUK Kia U15 31.10.81, Croydon :
  PV - 2.40
WOMERSLEY Fay U17 11.11.80, Holbeach :
  TJ - 10.97
WOOD Hannah U15 17.11.81, Solihull & S H :
  800 - 2:18.3
WOOD Heather U13 2.07.84, West (I.O.M.) :
  PenM - 2304
WOOD Kerry, Manchester YMCA :
  Mar - 2:56:17
WOOD Laura U20 31.10.78, Trafford :
  DT - 39.04, HT - 36.54
WOODCOCK Sian U17 13.01.80, Bingley :
  3kW - 15:49.35, 5kW - 26:57.01

WOODHAM Faye U20 1.12.77, Medway :
  TJ - 11.29
WOODS Kelly U23 28.05.75, Peterborough :
  400 - 57.4 (56.14-95)
WOODS Michelle U17 2.08.80, Basildon :
  SP - 11.40, DT - 34.34 (37.74-95), JT - 39.26
WOODS Suzanne U23 29.12.76, Basildon/
  Loughbro: PV - 2.80
WOOLGAR Deborah 10.03.65, Worthing :
  100H - 14.8w/15.15 (14.3w/14.38-89),
  400H - 65.53 (63.6-93), LJ - 5.56 (5.81-86),
  SP - 13.45 (14.18-89), DT - 38.16 (40.92-91),
  JT - 39.26 (41.08-89),
  Hep - 4817 (5434w-90/5380-89)
WOOLLEY Jessica U17 26.01.80, Bristol :
  800 - 2:15.2mx/2:15.4, 1500 - 4:41.4
WOOLRICH Sharon U23 1.05.76, Portsm F :
  HJ - 1.68 (1.70-94)
WORSEY Helen U15 29.08.82, Oadby & W :
  75HG - 11.05w/11.29
WRIGGLESWORTH Lisa U17 11.05.80,
  Scot Bord : 300 - 40.86, 400 - 58.0
WRIGHT Amanda 14.07.68, Shaftesbury B :
  1500 - 4:29.56 (4:27.5-94),
  3k - 9:44.0+ (9:06.7-92),
  5k - 16:29.69 (16:04.51-92),
  10k - 34:06.25 (33:26.79-92),
  10kR - 32:46sh/33:24, HMar - 1:14:46
WRIGHT Dawn-Alice U23 20.01.76, Cov G :
  PV - 3.00 (3.10-94)
WRIGHT Jackie V40 8.10.53, Bracknell :
  DT - 41.48 (49.58-75)
WRIGHT Jennifer U13 21.09.83, Bracknell :
  DTM - 24.72
WRIGHT Melanie 5.04.64, Nuneaton :
  3kW - 14:04.72 (13:49.0-93),
  5kW - 24:14.7 (23:47.0-94),
  5kWR - 23:58/24:13 (23:24-95),
  10kWR - 48:47 (47:40sh-93/48:18-92)
WRIGHT Natalie 13.11.73, Richmond & T :
  TJ - 11.04
WYETH Alison 26.05.64, Parkside :
  1500 - 4:11.00 (4:03.17-93),
  3k - 9:05.45i/9:09.25 (8:38.42-93),
  5k - 15:48.91 (15:00.37-95)
WYNTER-PINK Clover U20 29.11.77, Croy :
  100H - 14.96 (14.5w/14.81-95), SP - 11.91,
  JT - 38.92 (44.20-93), Hep - 4807 (5143-95)

YARWOOD Cathy 17.06.69, Bolton :
  400H - 63.14 (63.0-95)
YEARDLEY Laura U17 21.12.80, Hallamshire :
  LJ - 5.41
YELLING Hayley U23 3.01.74, Hounslow :
  1500 - 4:30.2, 3k - 9:26.12, 5k - 16:32.04
YOUNG Catherine U15 14.03.82, Stam & D :
  HJ - 1.63, PenG - 2870
YOUNG Emily U15 31.07.83, Isle of Wight :
  75HG - 11.7
YOUNG Hayley U17 26.09.79, Stamford & D :
  HJ - 1.79, TJ - 10.94 (11.06-95),
  Hepl - 4260 (4272-95)
YOUNG Vicky U15 14.03.82, Stamford & D :
  PenG - 2742

ZABLOCKYJ Hayley U17 10.04.81, Linc W :
  300 - 41.28
ZAWADA Sarah U15 9.04.82, AF&D :
  100 - 12.4/12.42 (12.25-95),
  200 - 24.6/24.62w/25.22 (24.94-95)

TSB JUNIOR RANKINGS 1996

Men Under 20

1.	James Brierley	Shrops	(HJ)	1122
2.	Tom Lerwill	Essex	(800)	1106
3.	Dwain Chambers	Mx	(100)	1092
4.	Ross Baillie	Scot West	(110H)	1092
5.	Damien Greaves	Essex	(110H)	1087
6.	Kevin Nash	Surrey	(3KST)	1083
7.	Corri Henry	Notts	(400)	1083
8.	Jamie Henthorn	Dyfed	(100)	1083
9.	Ben Challenger	Leics	(HJ)	1078
10.	Nathan Morgan	Leics	(LJ)	1076
11.	Tom Mayo	West Mid	(1500)	1074
12.	Sean Baldock	Sussex	(400)	1065
13.	Dean Macey	Essex	(DEC)	1060
14.	Tony Gill	W. Yorks	(110HJ)	1058
15.	Uvie Ugono	London	(100)	1052
16.	Ben Warmington	Northumb	(110HJ)	1048
17.	Brendan Smith	Gtr Man.	(1500)	1047
18.	Michael Tietz	Derbs	(100)	1046
19.	Geoff Dearman	Mx	(400)	1045
20.	Charles Robertson-Adams	Shrops	(400H)	1044
21.	Christian Malcolm	Gwent	(200)	1041
22.	Mark Rowlands	W. Glam	(400H)	1039
23.	Mark Findlay	Essex	(200)	1038
24.	Emeka Udechuku	London	(DTJ)	1038
25.	Phillip Perigo	S. Yorks	(100)	1037
26.	Alasdair Donaldson	Scot	(800)	1034
27.	Steven Scott	London	(110HJ)	1033
28.	Grant Cuddy	Gtr Man.	(800)	1031
29.	Danny Graham	Mersey	(HJ)	1026
30.	Mark Davis	Northants	(PV)	1024
31.	Andy Young	Scot West	(800)	1024
32.	Marlon Dickson	London	(100)	1022
33.	Richard Churchill	S. Yorks	(110HJ)	1021
34.	Andrew Graffin	Kent	(1500)	1020
35.	Ben Whitby	Mx	(3KST)	1020
36.	Andrew Thomas	Mersey	(800)	1015
37.	Chris Moss	Kent	(800)	1015
38.	Mark Miles	Warks	(1500)	1014
39.	Lee Murphy	Kent	(400H)	1013
40.	Russell Cartwright	Leics	(1500)	1013
41.	Matt Lethbridge	Sussex	(400H)	1011
42.	Mark Bushell	Hants	(DECJ)	1011
43.	Nick Dowsett	Essex	(110HJ)	1009
44.	Paul Sampson	W. Yorks	(100)	1005
45.	James Hillier	Gwent	(400H)	1004
46.	James Peacock	Essex	(TJ)	1003
47.	Leo Barker	Northants	(110HJ)	1002
48.	Neil Young	NI	(PV)	1001
49.	Ben Flint	S. Yorks	(PV)	1001
50.	Daniel Caines	Warks	(200)	999

Women Under 20

1.	Vicki Jamison	NI	(400H)	1115
2.	Susan Jones	Gtr Man.	(HJ)	1091
3.	Michelle Dunkley	Northants	(HJ)	1072
4.	Rachael Forrest	Shrops	(HJ)	1072
5.	Natasha Danvers	Kent	(100H)	1069
6.	Rhian Clarke	Suffolk	(PV)	1066
7.	Victoria Shipman	Derbs	(100)	1055
8.	Lesley Owusu	Berks	(400)	1047
9.	Michelle Mann	Lancs	(3K)	1047
10.	Denise Bolton	Gtr Man.	(100H)	1044
11.	Emma Symonds	Norfolk	(400)	1040
12.	Gosha Rostek	Scot West	(100)	1039
13.	Ellen O'Hare	Gloucs	(800)	1038
14.	Kate Williams	Mid Glam	(400H)	1037
15.	Rebecca Drummond	Staffs	(100)	1033
16.	Tracey Duncan	Mx	(400H)	1031
17.	Julie Pratt	Essex	(100H)	1028
18.	Tanya Povey	Devon	(3K)	1026
19.	Liz Fairs	Derbs	(100H)	1026
20.	Philippa Roles	W. Glam	(DT)	1018
21.	Shelley-Anne Bowen	Berks	(100)	1017
22.	Nicola Gautier	S. Yorks	(HEP)	1017
23.	Clare Ridgley	Hants	(PV)	1013
24.	Katie Jones	Gtr Man.	(400H)	1012
25.	Juliette Oldfield	Nothants	(1500)	1007
26.	Katie Skorupska	Scot East	(3K)	1007
27.	Louretta Thorne	Bucks	(400)	1006
28.	Natalie Hynd	Scot East	(200)	1005
29.	Nicole Smallwood	West Mid	(HJ)	1005
30.	Sheila Fairweather	Scot West	(3K)	1004
31.	Louise Batho	Essex	(HEP)	1003
32.	Emma Ania	Mx	(100)	1000
33.	Gillian Hegney	Scot West	(100)	1000
34.	Kate Forsyth	Northumb	(100H)	998
35.	Jannette Niccolls	London	(100)	998
36.	Melanie Purkiss	Hants	(100)	996
37.	Rachael Ogden	Somerset	(800)	995
38.	Pamela Johnstone	Scot East	(400H)	993
39.	Rebecca Lewis	Ches	(HEP)	993
40.	Philippa McCrea	Cumbria	(800)	992
41.	Emma Davies	Hants	(800)	989
42.	Amanda Forrester	Staffs	(100)	989
43.	Susan Williams	Surrey	(200)	989
44.	Rachel Hopgood	N. Yorks	(DT)	988
45.	Cicely Hall	Norfolk	(400H)	988
46.	Rachel Nicholson	Herts	(3K)	987
47.	Lucy Carter	Beds	(200)	987
48.	Gael Davies	Gloucs	(100)	986
49.	Dextene McIntosh	Essex	(400H)	984
50.	Bianca Liston	Kent	(100H)	984

TSB JUNIOR RANKINGS 1996

Men Under 17

1. Carl Myerscough	Lancs	(SPY)	1232
2. David Parker	N. Yorks	(JTY)	1053
3. Christian Linskey	S. Yorks	(PV)	1035
4. Richard McDonald	Scot East	(400HY)	1021
5. Luke Davis	West Mid	(100)	1016
6. Kris Stewart	Scot East	(400)	1009
7. David Naismith	Derbs	(400)	991
8. David O'Leary	Mersey	(100HY)	990
9. Ben Lewis	West Mid	(200)	987
10. Ross Kidner	Bucks	(HTY)	985
11. Martin Lloyd	Kent	(HJ)	983
12. David Readle	Mersey	(SPY)	980
13. Andrew Grierson	Berks	(HTY)	978
14. Carl McMullen	Ches	(400HY)	977
15. Edward Coats	Surrey	(OCTY)	977
16. Luke Rosenberg	Herts	(DTY)	975
17. Chris Carson	Scot East	(200)	973
18. Jon Heggie	Derbs	(400HY)	961
19. Colin McMaster	Scot West	(HJ)	957
20. Richard McNabb	S. Yorks	(400)	953
21. Alloy Wilson	Essex	(400)	953
22. Steven Daly	Mersey	(100)	952
23. Dan Carter	Essex	(JTY)	952
24. Tim Kitney	Bucks	(JTY)	951
25. Daniel Plummer	Essex	(100)	949
26. Darren Burley	London	(200)	948
27. Dan Brewer	London	(100HY)	945
28. Simon Lees	West Mid	(800)	942
29. Tyrone Carr	Essex	(100HY)	942
30. Lee Spike	Mersey	(HJ)	940
31. Marc Newton	Staffs	(OCTY)	939
32. Iain Murdoch	Scot West	(1.5KST)	939
33. Kerrin Young	NI	(400HY)	938
34. Robert Hollinger	S. Yorks	(100HY)	929
35. Andrew Murphy	Herts	(1.5KST)	927
36. Andy Castle/Kemp	Somerset	(HTY)	926
37. Aaron Harris	London	(100)	926
38. Chris Low	Scot East	(100HY)	925
39. Brian Robinson	West Mid	(LJ)	925
40. Paul Armstrong	Scot East	(400HY)	924
41. Tony Kuiper	Mersey	(HJ)	922
42. Matthew Still	Hants	(400)	922
43. Matthew Tribble	Beds	(OCTY)	920
44. Pete Waterman	Kent	(HTY)	919
45. Tom Kingsnorth	Avon	(1.5KST)	918
46. Adam Costello	Northumb	(1.5KST)	917
47. Steve Stanford	Mersey	(DTY)	916
48. Clifton Green	Kent	(JTY)	916
49. Matthew Russell	Essex	(200)	914
50. Peter Watson	Ox	(OCTY)	914

Women Under 17

1. Sarah Claxton	Essex	(LJ)	1043
2. Sarah Wilhelmy	Essex	(200)	1033
3. Amanda Pritchard	Card	(800)	1026
4. Katherine Livesey	Lancs	(HEPI)	1023
5. Hayley Young	Lincs	(HJ)	1015
6. Danielle Freeman	W. Yorks	(HEPI)	1015
7. Chloe Cozens	Beds	(HJ)	1015
8. Nicola Hall	Suffolk	(80HI)	1014
9. Sarina Mantle	Essex	(80HI)	1014
10. Jade Johnson	London	(LJ)	1012
11. Rebecca White	Lancs	(300)	1006
12. Helen Roscoe	Ches	(200)	1005
13. Katy Lestrange	Ches	(80HI)	1004
14. Maria Bolsover	S. Yorks	(300)	1003
15. Ruth Watson	Cambs	(300)	1002
16. Yewande Ige	Surrey	(300H)	1001
17. Abiodun Oyepitan	Mx	(100)	998
18. Wendy Cox	Durham	(200)	992
19. Rachael Kay	Gtr Man.	(300H)	988
20. Lindsay Impett	Dorset	(300)	988
21. Dionne Howell	London	(200)	988
22. Antonia Bemrose	Hants	(HJ)	986
23. Karen Gear	Devon	(300)	986
24. Kelly Thomas	Kent	(200)	984
25. Kelly Morgan	Wilts	(JT)	982
26. Jennifer Meadows	Gtr Man.	(400)	982
27. Carey Easton	Scot West	(300)	980
28. Petrina Alleyne	Berks	(100)	979
29. Kelli Bailey	Shrops	(100)	979
30. Libby Alder	Gloucs	(100)	977
31. Chantell Manning	London	(100)	977
32. Tamsin Stephens	NI	(80HI)	977
33. Clare O'Sullivan	Surrey	(80HI)	976
34. Jodie Swallow	Essex	(3K)	975
35. Syreeta Williams	West Mid	(300H)	975
36. Karlene Palmer	Berks	(200)	974
37. Camilla Waite	Wilts	(1500)	973
38. Laura Siddall	W. Yorks	(300H)	970
39. Gillian Stewart	Scot East	(HEPI)	970
40. Sonya Green	Cumbria	(100)	969
41. Lucy Philp	Scot East	(300)	968
42. Sarah Akinbiyi	London	(300H)	967
43. Andrea Hayles	London	(100)	967
44. Helen Lee	Notts	(300)	966
45. Gemma Swetman	Sussex	(300H)	965
46. Carmel Triggs	Mersey	(300)	965
47. Emma Phillips	W. Yorks	(100)	965
48. Leanda Adams	Staffs	(80HI)	963
49. Tracy Martin	West Mid	(200)	962
50. Claire Crosland	W. Yorks	(300)	960

TSB JUNIOR RANKINGS 1996

Men Under 15

1.	Matthew Sutton	Staffs	(HTB)	938
2.	Ken McKeown	Scot West	(HJ)	905
3.	John Barnes	Humber	(HTB)	883
4.	Richard Lainson	Hants	(JTB)	877
5.	Daniel Angus	Cleve	(200)	855
6.	Rhys Williams	Dyfed	(JTB)	854
7.	Mark Landon	Northants	(HTB)	851
8.	Joe Brown	London	(100)	843
9.	Seb Bastow	Cleve	(80HB)	842
10.	Damien Howard	Norfolk	(HTB)	837
11.	Ross Thompson	Durham	(HTB)	833
12.	Aaron Evans	Kent	(400)	832
13.	Tim Benjamin	S. Glam	(100)	829
14.	Andrew Rose	Essex	(100)	829
15.	Tristan Anthony	Herts	(200)	826
16.	Jonathan Lundman	Essex	(JTB)	824
17.	Lee Bryan	Warks	(200)	823
18.	Liam Walsh	Clwyd	(DTB)	823
19.	Tyrone Keating	Essex	(200)	822
20.	Jamie Russell	S. Yorks	(HJ)	820
21.	Mark Lewis-Francis	West Mid	(100)	819
22.	Nick Williams	Ches	(HTB)	810
23.	Chris Tomlinson	Cleve	(TJ)	806
24.	Mark Tinwell	Gtr Man.	(DTB)	799
25.	Chris Jenkins	Mersey	(PENB)	799
26.	Andrew Fulford	Wilts	(800)	797
27.	Felice Miele	Mx	(DTB)	792
28.	David Smith	Cleve	(200)	791
29.	Colin Joyce	Essex	(800)	789
30.	Daniel Britton	Dorset	(JTB)	789
31.	Alex Golding	Cleve	(200)	786
32.	Matthew Patience	Hants	(JTB)	784
33.	Dean Taylor	Beds	(TJ)	784
34.	Luke Bowling	Cambs	(100)	782
35.	Paul Rawlinson	Mersey	(400)	782
36.	Jonathon Crawshaw	Surrey	(80HB)	781
37.	James Rumbold	Dorset	(DTB)	781
38.	John Marsden	S. Glam	(80HB)	779
39.	David Moulton	Surrey	(400)	778
40.	Dale Garland	Hants	(400HY)	772
41.	Dominic Girdler	Leics	(PENB)	771
42.	Matthew Peleszok	Shrops	(PENB)	771
43.	Alex Simpson	Kent	(JTB)	770
44.	Gabriel Aboyo-Dana	London	(100)	769
45.	Bomeme Barikor	London	(HJ)	769
46.	Phillip Walsh	Hants	(80HB)	769
47.	Ashley Slater	Staffs	(HTB)	768
48.	Matthew Hendrickson	Beds	(PENB)	768
49.	Grant Murdoch	Hants	(100)	766
50.	Chris Irwin	Gtr Man.	(100)	764

Women Under 15

1.	Fiona Harrison	S. Yorks	(PV)	1013
2.	Sarah Zawada	Hants	(200)	987
3.	Helen Worsey	Leics	(75HG)	984
4.	Luisa Giles	Staffs	(75HG)	976
5.	Rachel Redmond	Staffs	(100)	972
6.	Kimberley Canning	Scot West	(200)	970
7.	Clare Russell	Gtr Man.	(100)	967
8.	Emma Ward	Staffs	(800)	966
9.	Jenny Mockler	Mersey	(1500)	964
10.	Erica Burfoot	S. Glam	(200)	958
11.	Nikki Daniels	Staffs	(800)	955
12.	Louise O'Callaghan	London	(75HG)	952
13.	Sharon Davidge	Devon	(75HG)	952
14.	Laura Watkins	Shrops	(200)	949
15.	Rachel Harris	Mersey	(HJ)	948
16.	Sophie McQueen	Humber	(HJ)	948
17.	Jenny McCarthy	Ches	(200)	945
18.	Leah Tribe	Hants	(200)	945
19.	Aimee Cutler	Gwent	(200)	941
20.	Stephanie Johnston	Cumbria	(100)	941
21.	Melissa Anderson	Northumb	(100)	941
22.	Donna Maylor	West Mid	(100)	941
23.	Sophie Allen	Suffolk	(100)	940
24.	Charlene Shoneye	Surrey	(100)	933
25.	Carley Wilson	Northumb	(1500)	923
26.	Charlene Barnes	West Mid	(200)	920
27.	Natalie Smellie	Essex	(200)	919
28.	Elexi Walker	West Mid	(200)	917
29.	Hayley Smith	Norfolk	(75HG)	916
30.	Lisa Connolly	Ches	(75HG)	916
31.	Nichola Coates	Northumb	(1500)	915
32.	Felicity Breens	Leics	(75HG)	915
33.	Wendy Thomson	Scot East	(100)	913
34.	Lauren McLoughlin	Gwent	(75HG)	911
35.	Stephanie Spinks	Norfolk	(100)	909
36.	Iona McIntyre	Scot East	(800)	909
37.	Chevette Mais	Kent	(200)	906
38.	Sara McGreavy	Warks	(75HG)	905
39.	Andrea Lang	Scot West	(100)	904
40.	Hanna Carroll	Mersey	(200)	904
41.	April Kalu	Gtr Man.	(SPG)	902
42.	Gaby Howell	Sussex	(200)	902
43.	Leonie Lightfoot	Ches	(100)	901
44.	Laura McShane	S. Yorks	(75HG)	901
45.	Lucy Butler	Northumb	(LJ)	900
46.	Goldie Sayers	Cambs	(JT)	896
47.	Alex Cooke	Herts	(200)	895
48.	Stefanie Oates	Derbs	(100)	894
49.	Jordannah Fryers	Gtr Man.	(100)	894
50.	Rachel Harris	Here &W	(100)	894

AMENDMENTS TO BRITISH ATHLETICS 1996

From Arnold Black, members of NUTS and readers

MEN

400:	Under 13 - delete Alexander 57.4, time was 67.4.
	Delete Stephenson 59.8, not Under 13.
800:	Brown 1:54.62 - on 2 Jul not 1 Jun.
1500:	add to U17 - 4:06.0 Michael Combe 24.12.78 (1) Dumfries 2 Jul.
3000:	Puckrin 8:12.0i - 2nd not 3rd.
10000:	add 31:18.1 David Cameron (Shettleston) 29.09.66 (1) Carlisle 30 Apr;
	amend Reid 30:37.0 - 16 Sep not 12 Sep.
10k Road:	add 29:26 Peter Fleming 5.01.61 (6) Washington, USA 30 Apr;
	amend Murray 29:34 - 16 Sep not 10 Sep.
Marathon:	note Stewart 2:34:40 - dob 15.12.56.
3000SC:	Downie 9:23.2 - 23 Apr not 23 May;
	add to U20 - 9:42.0 Gary McCafferty (London Irish) 17.07.76 (1) Tonbridge 5 Aug.
80mH:	Cowie 11.8 - Gregor Cowie, dob 3.09.80.
400mH:	Under 17 - Amend Menzies 57.2, 1st not 2nd.
HJ:	Robb 2.00 - correct dob to 24.04.76;
	add to U15 - 1.76 Barry Millar (Spango Valley) 1.04.81 (2) Greenock 25 Jun.
LJ:	Quarry 7.40w - note legal 7.18/ -0.2 (D) Fukuoka, JAP 1 Sep;
	add 6.87 Mel Fowler 7.07.66 (3) Coatbridge 23 Apr;
	add to U15 5.81 Graeme Allan 24.09.80 (1) Elgin 7 May.
SP:	add 13.42i Andreas Olsson SWE (Glas. Cal. Univ) 29.04.73 (2) Glasgow 11 Mar.
HT:	Shepherd 49.16 on 21 May not 20 May.
JT:	Delete 58.20 Kevin Shepherd (was 53.20).

WOMEN

100:	Flockhart 12.27 was +2.3.
600:	add 1:32.84 Mary McClung (1) Edinburgh 5 Nov.
10k Road:	add 34:05 Karen Hargrave (1) Lucon, FRA 19 Mar.
LJ:	Anderson 5.62w - note 5.51 was +1.2.
JT:	add to U15 31.26 Louise Telford (Lochgelly) 7.01.82 (1) Grangemouth 26 Mar.
Relays:	Girls U13 4 x 200m - add 1:58.0 City of Plymouth (1) Reading 3 Sep.

Late Additions to 1996 Lists

As usual, amendments continue to come to light and this group of men's changes were found after the men's lists were sent to the printer. The index should contain these amendments.

100:	10.96w 2.5 Darren Scott 7.03.69 3h2 Sheffield 2 Jun;
	Under 20 - 10.9 James Ward 28.07.77 (1) Sheffield 12 Jun.
110H:	15.2 Paul Hourihan date 30 Jun.
HJ:	2.00m Stuart Brown 22.11.72 (1) Wrexham 4 May;
	add 2.06 Pierre Faber D Gotzis, AUT 25 May (remove 2.05m);
	add 1.97 Paul Gilding D Worthing 14 Sep;
	add 1.93i Mark Elliott (1) Glasgow 14 Dec.
PV:	4.50m Jamie Webb Southend 6 Jul (remove 4.40m);
	4.30m Brett Heath Middlesbrough 30 Jun;
	2.20m U13 Adam Palmer (2) Peterborough 15 Sep.
SP:	add 15.94 Pierre Faber (25) Gotzis, AUT 25 May (remove 15.19m);
	add 14.07i Daniel Brunt (2) Sheffield 22 Dec.
DT:	add 46.54 Pierre Faber (26) Gotzis, AUT 25 May (remove 44.98m).
JT:	66.58 Simon Bennett (1) Exeter 8 Sep (remove 63.18);
	Delete 55.58 Sean Darlington (Landley).
DEC:	6205w Callum Orr - 100m 11.21 not windy.